Anonymous

Post Office Directory

Salzwasser

Anonymous

Post Office Directory

1. Auflage | ISBN: 978-3-84604-864-1

Erscheinungsort: Frankfurt, Deutschland

Erscheinungsjahr: 2020

Salzwasser Verlag GmbH

Reprint of the original, first published in 1870.

POST OFFICE DIRECTORY.

LIST OF POST OFFICES

IN

THE UNITED STATES

ARRANGED ALPHABETICALLY AND GIVING THE SALARIES
OF THE POSTMASTERS.

ALSO

AN APPENDIX

CONTAINING THE NAMES OF POST OFFICES ARRANGED BY STATES AND COUNTIES,

WITH

MONEY-ORDER OFFICES,

AND

OTHER POSTAL INFORMATION

REVISED AND CORRECTED BY THE POST OFFICE DEPARTMENT,
TO SEPTEMBER 1, 1870.

WASHINGTON.
GOVERNMENT PRINTING OFFICE.
1870.

OFFICERS OF THE DEPARTMENT.

POSTMASTER GENERAL.
JOHN A. J. CRESWELL, of Maryland.

CHIEF CLERK POST OFFICE DEPARTMENT.
E. L. CHILDS, of New Hampshire.

APPOINTMENT OFFICE.
FIRST ASSISTANT POSTMASTER GENERAL.
JAMES W. MARSHALL, of New Jersey.

CHIEF CLERK.
JAMES H. MARR, of Maryland.

CONTRACT OFFICE.
SECOND ASSISTANT POSTMASTER GENERAL.
GILES A. SMITH, of Illinois.

CHIEF CLERK.
JOHN L. FRENCH, of Ohio.

FINANCE OFFICE.
THIRD ASSISTANT POSTMASTER GENERAL.
WILLIAM H. H. TERRELL, of Indiana.

CHIEF CLERK.
WILLIAM M. IRELAND, of Pennsylvania

CHIEF OF DIVISION, DEAD-LETTER OFFICE.
CHARLES LYMAN, of Vermont.

SUPERINTENDENT OF THE MONEY-ORDER OFFICE.
C. F. MACDONALD, of Massachusetts.

SUPERINTENDENT OF THE OFFICE OF FOREIGN MAILS.
JOSEPH H. BLACKFAN, of New Jersey.

SUPERINTENDENT OF RAILWAY MAIL SERVICE.
GEORGE B. ARMSTRONG, of Illinois.

SUPERINTENDENT OF BLANK AGENCY.
N. A. GRAY, of Ohio

TOPOGRAPHER.
WALTER L. NICHOLSON, of District of Columbia.

SUPERINTENDENT OF POST OFFICE BUILDING AND DISBURSING CLERK.
FRANK A. MACARTNEY, of Pennsylvania.

AUDITOR OF THE TREASURY FOR THE POST OFFICE DEPARTMENT.
JACOB J. MARTIN, of Alabama.

CHIEF CLERK.
J. M. McGREW, of Ohio.

ORGANIZATION OF THE DEPARTMENT.

The direction and management of the Post Office Department are assigned by the Constitution and laws to the Postmaster General. That its business may be the more conveniently arranged and prepared for its final action, it is distributed among several bureaus, as follows: The Appointment Office, in charge of the First Assistant Postmaster General; the Contract Office, including the Inspection Division, in charge of the Second Assistant Postmaster General; the Finance Office, in charge of the Third Assistant Postmaster General; and the Money-order Office, and the office of Foreign Mails, each in charge of its superintendent.

APPOINTMENT OFFICE.—The First Assistant Postmaster General: To this office is assigned all business which relates to the establishment and discontinuance of post offices, changes of sites and names, appointment and removal of postmasters, route and local agents, and the giving of instructions to postmasters; also, the readjustment of postmasters' salaries, once in two years, under the act approved 1st July, 1864, and in special cases, as much oftener as may be deemed necessary. All applications for allowances, in post offices of the first and second classes, for rent, fuel, lights, and clerks, and all applications for allowances at separating offices, are examined in this office, and submitted to the Postmaster General for his decision. Postmarking and rating stamps, letter balances, blanks, wrapping paper, and twine are also furnished from this office.

CONTRACT OFFICE.—The Second Assistant Postmaster General: To this office is assigned the business of arranging the mail service of the United States, and placing the same under contract, embracing all correspondence and proceedings respecting the frequency of trips, mode of conveyance, and times of departures and arrivals on all the routes; the course of the mails between the different sections of the country, the points of mail distribution, and the regulations for the government of the domestic mail service of the United States. It prepares the advertisements for mail proposals, receives the bids, and has charge of the annual and occasional mail lettings, and the adjustment and execution of the contracts. All applications for the establishment or alteration of mail arrangements, and for mail messengers, should be sent to this office. All claims should be submitted to it for transportation service not under contract. From this office all postmasters at the ends of routes receive the statement of mail arrangements prescribed for the respective routes, and to it application should be made for mail bags, locks, and keys. It reports weekly to the Auditor all contracts executed, and all orders affecting the accounts for mail transportation; prepares the statistical exhibits of the mail service, and the reports to Congress of the mail lettings, giving a statement of each bid; also, of the contracts made, the new service originated, the curtailments ordered, and the additional allowances granted within the year.

[INSPECTION DIVISION.]—This division, formerly a distinct office, is now merged in and made part of the Contract Office. To this division is assigned the duty of receiving and examining the registers of the arrivals and departures of the mails, certificates of the service of route agents, and reports of mail failures; noting the delinquencies of contractors, and preparing cases thereon for the action of the Postmaster General; furnishing blanks for mail registers, reports of mail failures, and other duties which may be necessary to secure a faithful and exact performance of all mail contracts and service.

All cases of mail depredation, or violation of law by private expresses, or by the forging or illegal use of postage stamps, are under the supervision of this office, and should be reported to it.

All communications respecting lost money, lost letters, mail depredations, or other violations of law, should be directed "Contract Office, Inspection Division, Post Office Department."

All registers of the arrivals and departures of the mails, certificates of the service of route agents, and clerks in railway post offices, reports of mail failures, applications for blank registers, and reports of failures, and all complaints against contractors for irregular or imperfect service, should be directed "Contract Office, Inspection Division, Post Office Department."

[TOPOGRAPHICAL DIVISION.]—The Topographical Division of the department, attached to the Contract Office, consisting of the Topographer of the department and assistants, is charged with the preparation of the post-route maps and diagrams, and with the keeping up of the geographical information requisite for the various branches of the postal service.

Communications for this division (including contributions of maps and diagrams, which, for their general utility, are earnestly requested) should be directed "Second Assistant Postmaster General, Topographer, Post Office Department."

FINANCE OFFICE.—The Third Assistant Postmaster General: To this office is assigned the issuing of warrants and drafts in payment of balances reported by the Auditor to be due to mail contractors and other persons, and the superintendence of the rendition by postmasters of their quarterly returns of postages. It has charge of the DEAD-LETTER OFFICE, and of the issuing of postage stamps and stamped envelopes for the prepayment of postage.

To the Third Assistant Postmaster General postmasters at draft offices should direct their letters reporting quarterly the net proceeds of their offices, and those at depositing offices their certificates of deposit; to him should also be directed the weekly and monthly returns of the depositaries of the department, as well as all applications and receipts for postage stamps and stamped envelopes, and for dead letters.

MONEY-ORDER OFFICE.—To this office is assigned the general supervision and control of the postal money-order system throughout the United States.

OFFICE OF FOREIGN MAILS.—To this office is assigned the supervision of the ocean mail-steamship lines, and foreign postal arrangements.

TO THE AUDITOR FOR THE POST OFFICE DEPARTMENT postmasters should address their quarterly accounts and all correspondence in relation thereto.

POST ROADS.

Post roads, by law, are—1. Those roads of the country which are declared post roads by various acts of Congress. 2. All waters on which steamboats regularly pass from port to port. 3. The navigable canals of the several States for the time during which the mail may be carried thereon. 4. All railroads and plank roads in the United States. 5. Those roads on which the Postmaster General causes the mail to be carried from the nearest post offices, on legally declared post roads, to court-houses not otherwise provided with the mail. 6. All roads to special offices. 7. And such as are established by the Postmaster General as post routes under the tenth section of the act of March 3, 1851, in cities and towns where the postmasters are appointed by the President of the United States.

The general authority to establish post roads is not vested in the Postmaster General, nor can he extend or lengthen those already established. He can only place mail service on such roads as have been declared post roads by act of Congress, and for the expense of which appropriation has been made.

MAIL CONTRACTS.

The Union is divided into four Mail Contract Sections. A letting for one of these sections occurs every year, and contracts are made at such lettings for four consecutive years, commencing on the first day of July.

The sections and their current contract terms are—

1. Maine, New Hampshire, Vermont, Massachusetts, Rhode Island, Connecticut, and New York; current term to end 30th June, 1873.

2. New Jersey, Pennsylvania, Delaware, Maryland, (including District of Columbia,) and Ohio; current term to end 30th June, 1872.

3. West Virginia, Virginia, North Carolina, South Carolina, Georgia, Florida, Alabama, Mississippi, Louisiana, Texas, Arkansas, and Indian Territory; current term to end 30th June, 1871.

4. Tennessee, Kentucky, Missouri, Iowa, Illinois, Indiana, Michigan, Wisconsin, Minnesota, Dakota, Nebraska, Kansas, Colorado, New Mexico, Arizona, Utah, Montana, Idaho, Washington, Oregon, California, Nevada, Alaska, and Wyoming; current term to end 30th June, 1874.

LIST OF POST OFFICES IN THE UNITED STATES.

ABBREVIATION OF NAMES OF STATES AND TERRITORIES.

Ala .... Alabama.
Alaska ... Alaska Ter.
Ariz .. ... Arizona Ter.
Ark...... Arkansas.
Cal ...... California.
Colo ..... Colorado Ter.
Conn .... Connecticut.
Dak ..... Dakota Ter.
Del ...... Delaware.
D. C...... Dist. of Columbia.
Fla ...... Florida.
Ga........ Georgia.
Idaho.... Idaho Ter.
Ill .... Illinois.
Ind ...... Indiana.
Ind. T.... Indian Ter.
Iowa .. ... Iowa.

Kans.... Kansas.
Ky...... Kentucky.
La ...... Louisiana.
Me...... Maine.
Md...... Maryland.
Mass .... Massachusetts.
Mich .... Michigan.
Minn.... Minnesota.
Miss .. ... Mississippi.
Mo...... Missouri.
Mont.... Montana Ter.
Nebr .... Nebraska.
Nev ..... Nevada.
N. H .... New Hampshire.
N. J ..... New Jersey.
N. Mex.. New Mexico Ter.
N. Y..... New York.

N. C..... North Carolina.
Ohio .... Ohio.
Oreg .... Oregon.
Pa ...... Pennsylvania.
R. I..... Rhode Island.
S. C..... South Carolina.
Tenn.... Tennessee.
Tex ..... Texas.
Utah..... Utah Ter.
Vt ...... Vermont.
Va ...... Virginia.
Wash ... Washington Ter.
W. Va... West Virginia.
Wis ..... Wisconsin.
Wyo.... Wyoming Ter.

EXPLANATIONS.

The name of the office is given first, then the county, and last the State or Territory.
Offices having a (*) affixed, denote money-order offices.
Those printed in SMALL CAPITAL letters designate the capitals of the States and Territories.
Those printed in *italics*, with a small *c. h.* in parentheses, indicate the county seats.
Those printed in *italics*, with a large *C. H.*, form a part of the name of the office, and also indicate the county seats.

LIST

OF

POST OFFICES IN THE UNITED STATES,

(ARRANGED ALPHABETICALLY,)

WITH THE SALARIES OF THE POSTMASTERS.

ACC		ADA	
AARONSBURGH, Centre, Pa	$120	Accord, Ulster, N. Y	$140
Aaron's Run, Montgomery, Ky	16	Accotink, Fairfax, Va	73
Abbeville, (c. h.,) Henry, Ala	180	Ackermanville, Northampton, Pa	35
Abbeville, (c. h.,) Wilcox, Ga	10	Ackerville, Washington, Wis	41
Abbeville, (c. h.,) Vermillion, La	100	Ackley,* Hardin, Iowa	1,000
Abbeville, Lafayette, Miss	50	Acme, Grand Traverse, Mich	26
Abbeville C. H., Abbeville, S. C	630	Acomb, McLennan, Tex	12
Abbeyville, Medina, Ohio	12	Acorn Hill, Frederick, Va	9
Abbot, Piscataquis, Me	34	Acra, Greene, N. Y	110
Abbottsburgh, Bladen, N. C	24	Acton, Marion, Ind	170
Abbott's Creek, Davidson, N. C	27	Acton, York, Me	44
Abbottstown, Adams, Pa	67	Acton, Middlesex, Mass	180
Abbot Village, Piscataquis, Me	70	Acton, Hood, Texas	12
Abb's Valley, Tazewell, Va	7	Acushnet, Bristol, Mass	210
Abbyville, Mecklenburgh, Va	25	Acworth, Cobb, Ga	280
Aberdeen, Ohio, Ind	24	Acworth, Sullivan, N. H	140
Aberdeen, Harford, Md	240	Ada, Kent, Mich	320
Aberdeen,* (c. h.,) Monroe, Miss	650	Ada, Choctaw, Miss	12
Aberdeen, Brown, Ohio	170	Ada, Ray, Mo	72
Aberdeen, Smith, Texas	12	Ada,* Hardin, Ohio	640
Aberdeen Junction, Monroe, Miss	12	Ada, Sheboygan, Wis	13
Aberfoil, Bullock, Ala	6	Adair, McDonough, Ill	37
Abernathy, Perry, Mo	16	Adairsville, Bartow, Ga	230
Abilene, (c. h.,) Dickinson, Kans	350	Adairville, Logan, Ky	130
Abingdon,* Knox, Ill	900	Adaline, Marshall, W. Va	1
Abingdon, Jefferson, Iowa	95	Adams, Wilcox, Ga	6
Abingdon, Harford, Md	91	Adams, Adams, Ill	82
Abingdon,* Washington, Va	1,100	Adams, Decatur, Ind	120
Abington, Windham, Conn	130	Adams, Berkshire, Mass	1,100
Abington, Wayne, Ind	40	Adams, Mower, Minn	100
Abington, Plymouth, Mass	550	Adams, Jefferson, N. Y	1,100
Abington, Montgomery, Pa	81	Adams, Seneca, Ohio	20
Abiqui, Rio Arriba, N. Mex	12	Adams, Armstrong, Pa	41
Aboite, Allen, Ind	12	Adams, Walworth, Wis	16
Absecom,* Atlantic, N. J	330	Adams' Basin, Monroe, N. Y	130
Abscota, Calhoun, Mich	25	Adamsburgh, Jefferson, Ark	10
Academia, Juniata, Pa	160	Adamsburgh, Westmoreland, Pa	53
Academy, Ontario, N. Y	25	Adams Centre, Jefferson, N. Y	350
Academy, Pocahontas, W. Va	48	Adams Centre, Adams, Wis	12
Acasto, Clarke, Mo	22	Adams' Mills, Pulaski, Ky	24
Accident, Alleghany, Md	41	Adams' Mills, Muskingum, Ohio	58
Accokeek, Prince George's, Md	12	Adams Peak, Pottawatomie, Kans	12
Accokeek, Stafford, Va	15	Adams' Ridge, Defiance, Ohio	8
Accomack C. H., Accomack, Va	130	Adams' Run, Colleton, S. C	74

* Money-order office.

AIK

Adams' Station, Albany, N. Y	$12
Adams' Station, Robertson, Tenn	10
Adamstown, Frederick, Md	180
Adamstown, Lancaster, Pa	50
Adamsville, Bradley, Ark	10
Adamsville, Kent, Del	16
Adamsville, Franklin, Mass	22
Adamsville, Cass, Mich	110
Adamsville, Washington, N. Y	39
Adamsville, Muskingum, Ohio	140
Adamsville, Crawford, Pa	100
Adamsville, Newport, R. I	82
Adamsville, McNairy, Tenn	41
Adamsville, Beaver, Utah	10
Adamsville, Harrison, W. Va	16
Adario, Richland, Ohio	31
Addams' Tavern, Berks, Pa	2
Addison, Du Page, Ill	140
Addison, Humboldt, Iowa	9
Addison, Lenawee, Mich	170
Addison, Steuben, N. Y	1,200
Addison, Gallia, Ohio	30
Addison, Somerset, Pa	260
Addison, Addison, Vt	52
Addison, Washington, Wis	33
Addison Hill, Steuben, N. Y	76
Addison Point, Washington, Me	190
Adel, (c. h.,) Dallas, Iowa	580
Adelante, Napa, Cal	12
Adelescat, Union, Dak	15
Adeline, Ogle, Ill	96
Adell, Sheboygan, Wis	53
Adelphi, Polk, Iowa	13
Adelphi, Ross, Ohio	140
Adena, Jefferson, Ohio	26
Adkins' Mills, Wayne, W. Va	12
Adrian, Hancock, Ill	12
Adrian, (c. h.,) Lenawee, Mich	2,800
Adrian, Steuben, N. Y	57
Adrian, Seneca, Ohio	120
Adrian, Armstrong, Pa	12
Adriance, Dutchess, N. Y	77
Advance, Indiana, Pa	12
Adyeville, Perry, Ind	15
Aeriel, Marion, S. C	12
Aetna, Newaygo, Mich	12
Afton, Scott, Ind	12
Afton, (c. h.,) Union, Iowa	820
Afton, Washington, Minn	130
Afton, Chenango, N. Y	290
Afton, Clermont, Ohio	46
Afton, Nelson, Va	120
Afton, Rock, Wis	68
Agatha, Vinton, Ohio	89
Agawam, Hampden, Mass	120
Agency City,* Wapello, Iowa	350
Agnew's Mills, Venango, Pa	41
Agricola, Mahaska, Iowa	17
Agricultural College, Prince George's, Md	12
Agricultural College, Centre, Pa	140
Ahnapee, Kewaunee, Wis	140
Ai, Fulton, Ohio	48
Aid, Lawrence, Ohio	25
Aiden Lair, Essex, N. Y	12
Aiken, Barnwell, S. C	1,100

ALB

Aiken, Bell, Tex	$12
Ainsworth, Washington, Iowa	240
Ainsworth Station, Cook, Ill	54
Airey's, Dorchester, Md	11
Air Hill, Montgomery, Ohio	20
Air Line, Hart, Ga	25
Air Mount, Yalabusha, Miss	16
Airy Dale, Huntingdon, Pa	16
Aken, Richland, Wis	11
Akersville, Fulton, Pa	8
Akin, Franklin, Ill	9
Akron, Peoria, Ill	21
Akron, Fulton, Ind	83
Akron, Tuscola, Mich	17
Akron, Harrison, Mo	12
Akron, Erie, N. Y	350
Akron, (c. h.,) Summit, Ohio	2,600
Akron, Lancaster, Pa	80
Alabama, Genesee, N. Y	120
Alabama, Houston, Tex	26
Alabama, Polk, Wis	12
Alabaster, Iosco, Mich	36
Alafia, Hillsborough, Fla	12
Alameda, Alameda, Cal	99
Alamo, Contra Costa, Cal	33
Alamo, Montgomery, Ind	59
Alamo, Kalamazoo, Mich	18
Alanthus Grove, Gentry, Mo	5
Alanthus Hill, Hancock, Tenn	12
Alaska, Morgan, Ind	25
Alaska, Kent, Mich	180
Alaska, Kewaunee, Wis	12
Alba, Fillmore, Minn	10
Alba, Jasper, Mo	10
Alba, Bradford, Pa	110
Albanville, Monroe, Wis	18
Albany, (c. h.,) Dougherty, Ga	1,700
Albany, Whitesides, Ill	330
Albany, Delaware, Ind	39
Albany, Davis, Iowa	14
Albany, Nemaha, Kans	97
Albany, (c. h.,) Clinton, Ky	60
Albany, Oxford, Me	48
Albany, (c. h.,) Gentry, Mo	280
ALBANY,* (c. h.,) Albany, N. Y	4,000
Albany, Tuscarawas, Ohio	15
Albany, (c. h.,) Linn, Oreg	600
Albany, Berks, Pa	12
Albany, Henry, Tenn	12
Albany, Orleans, Vt	140
Albany, Green, Wis	370
Albany Centre, Orleans, Vt	12
Albemarle, Assumption, La	12
Albemarle, (c. h.,) Stanly, N. C	81
Albert Lea, (c. h.,) Freeborn, Minn	760
Alberton, Howard, Md	90
Alberton's, Duplin, N. C	12
Albia, (c. h.,) Monroe, Iowa	1,200
Albion, Mendocino, Cal	25
Albion, (c. h.,) Edwards, Ill	330
Albion, (c. h.,) Noble, Ind	340
Albion, Marshall, Iowa	240
Albion, Kennebec, Me	91
Albion, Calhoun, Mich	2,200
Albion, Wright, Minn	11
Albion, (c. h.,) Orleans, N. Y	2,500

ALI   ALM

Albion, Ashland, Ohio	$36	Alkire's Mills, Lewis, W. Va	$10
Albion,* Erie, Pa	290	Allamakee, Allamakee, Iowa	13
Albion, Providence, R. I	78	Allamuchy, Warren, N. J	140
Albion, Dane, Wis	200	Allandale, Banks, Ga	4
Albrightsville, Carbon, Pa	14	Allard's Corners, Orange, N. J	25
Albuquerque, (c. h.,) Bernalillo, N.		Allatoona, Bartow, Ga	68
Mex	970	Allbright, Preston, W. Va	13
Alburgh, Grand Isle, Vt	170	*Allegan,* (c. h.,) Allegan, Mich	1,900
Alburgh Centre, Grand Isle, Vt	76	Allegany, Cattaraugus, N. Y	460
Alburgh Springs, Grand Isle, Vt	180	Alleghany, Sierra, Cal	88
Alburtis, Lehigh, Pa	160	Alleghany Spring, Montgomery, Va.	210
Alcona, Alcona, Mich	25	Alleghany Station, Alleghany, Va.	12
Alcony, Miami, Ohio	12	Allegheny,* Allegheny, Pa	3,100
Alden, McHenry, Ill	110	Allegheny Bridge, McKean, Pa	51
Alden, Hardin, Iowa	260	Allemance, Guilford, N. C	6
Alden, Freeborn, Minn	16	Alleman's, Clearfield, Pa	12
Alden, Erie, N. Y	290	Allen, Miami, Ind	52
Alden, Polk, Wis	12	Allen, Lyon, Kans	15
Alden Centre, Erie, N. Y	12	Allen, Hillsdale, Mich	300
Alden's Corners, Dane, Wis	27	Allen, Allegany, N. Y	12
Aldenville, Wayne, Pa	72	Allen, Cumberland, Pa	110
Alder Brook, Franklin, N. Y	10	Allen Centre, Allegany, N. Y	18
Alder Creek, Oneida, N. Y	93	Allendale, Wabash, Ill	24
Alderley, Dodge, Wis	110	Allendale, Green, Ky	30
Aldie, Loudoun, Va	160	Allendale, Ottawa, Mich	17
Aledo, (c. h.,) Mercer, Ill	860	Allendale, Worth, Mo	77
Aleman, Socorro, N. Mex	12	Allendale, Bergen, N. J	12
Aleppo, Greene, Pa	12	Allendale, Barnwell, S. C	65
Alert, Decatur, Ind	12	Allenport, Washington, Pa	38
Alert, Butler, Ohio	12	Allen's, Richmond, Ga	10
Alexander, Morgan, Ill	120	Allen's, Eaton, Mich	12
Alexander, Washington, Me	77	Allen's, Miami, Ohio	48
Alexander, Genesee, N. Y	210	Allen's Creek, Amherst, Va	120
Alexandria, Merced, Cal	12	Allen's Factory, Marion, Ala	10
Alexandria, Madison, Ind	200	Allen's Fork, Jackson, W. Va	5
Alexandria, Campbell, Ky	130	Allen's Fresh, Charles, Md	42
Alexandria, (c. h.,) Rapides, La	950	Allen's Grove, Scott, Iowa	31
Alexandria, (c. h.,) Douglas, Minn	420	Allen's Grove, Walworth, Wis	160
Alexandria, Clarke, Mo	330	Allen's Hill, Ontario, N. Y	200
Alexandria, Grafton, N. H	98	Allen Springs, Allen, Ky	12
Alexandria, Jefferson, N. Y	220	Allen's Springs, Pope, Ill	14
Alexandria, Licking, Ohio	200	Allen's Station, Steuben, N. Y	13
Alexandria, Huntingdon, Pa	320	Allen's Store, Prentiss, Miss	5
Alexandria, De Kalb, Tenn	130	Allenstown, Merrimack, N. H	24
Alexandria, (c. h.,) Alexandria, Va.	2,700	Allensville, Todd, Ky	150
Alfonte, Madison, Ind	27	Allensville, Person, N. C	6
Alford, Berkshire, Mass	80	Allensville, Vinton, Ohio	44
Alfordsville, Daviess, Ind	71	Allensville, Mifflin, Pa	94
Alfred, (c. h.,) York, Me	540	Allenton, Wilcox, Ala	67
Alfred, Allegany, N. Y	160	Allenton, St. Louis, Mo	61
Alfred, Meigs, Ohio	35	Allenton, Washington, R. I	70
Alfred Centre,* Allegany, N. Y	420	Allentown, Monmouth, N. J	300
Algansee, Branch, Mich	10	*Allentown,* (c. h.,) Lehigh, Pa	2,600
Algiers, Orleans, La	270	Allenville, Cape Girardeau, Mo	12
Algodon, Ionia, Mich	10	Alleyton, Colorado, Tex	100
Algodones, Santa Aña, N. Mex	12	Alliance,* Stark, Ohio	2,300
Algona, (c. h.,) Kossuth, Iowa	550	Allis Hollow, Bradford, Pa	13
Algonac, St. Clair, Mich	250	Allison, Dubuque, Iowa	31
Algonquin, McHenry, Ill	140	Alloa, Columbia, Wis	34
Algonquin, Carroll, Ohio	17	Allowaystown, Salem, N. J	170
Alhambra, Madison, Ill	58	Allston, Middlesex, Mass	310
Alhambra, Trempealeau, Wis	8	Alma, Marion, Ill	100
Alice, Oceana, Mich	17	Alma, Whitley, Ind	12
Alice, Cedar, Mo	12	*Alma,* (c. h.,) Wabaunsee, Kans	120
Aliceton, Boyle, Ky	34	Alma, Gratiot, Mich	400
Alida, Davis, Kans	10	Alma, Allegany, N. Y	15

* Money-order office.

ALT

AMI

Alma, Ross, Ohio	$12
Alma, Rusk, Tex	10
Alma, Weber, Utah	12
Alma, Page, Va	31
Alma, (c. h.,) Buffalo, Wis	390
Alma City, Waseca, Minn	65
Almeda, Newton, Mo	18
Almena, Van Buren, Mich	34
Almira, Benzie, Mich	37
Almond, Randolph, Ala	17
Almond, Allegany, N. Y	430
Almond, Portage, Wis	92
Almont, Lapeer, Mich	770
Almoral, Delaware, Iowa	18
Alna, Lincoln, Me	73
Alonzaville, Shenandoah, Va	12
Alpena,* (c. h.,) Alpena, Mich	1,000
Alpha, Scott, Ind	50
Alpha, Clinton, Ky	12
Alpha, Grundy, Mo	41
Alpha, Greene, Ohio	80
Alpharetta, (c. h.,) Milton, Ga	67
Alpine, Talladega, Ala	120
Alpine, Clark, Ark	16
Alpine, Chattooga, Ga	12
Alpine, Fayette, Ind	12
Alpine, Wapello, Iowa	28
Alpine, Kent, Mich	30
Alpine, Schuyler, N. Y	92
Alpine, York, Pa	12
Alpine City, Utah, Utah	27
Alpine Depot, Morgan, W. Va	21
Alps, Rensselaer, N. Y	16
Alquina, Fayette, Ind	10
Alsace, Berks, Pa	8
Alstead, Cheshire, N. H	280
Alstead Centre, Cheshire, N. H	23
Altamont, Shelby, Iowa	12
Altamont, Alleghany, Md	63
Altamont, (c. h.,) Grundy, Tenn	63
Alta Vista, Daviess, Mo	190
Alta Vista, Russell, Va	6
Altay, Schuyler, N. Y	96
Altenburgh, Perry, Mo	100
Altha, Stoddard, Mo	12
Alto, Howard, Ind	19
Alto, Kent, Mich	8
Alto, Franklin, Tenn	22
Alto, Cherokee, Tex	41
Alton,* Madison, Ill	2,700
Alton, Crawford, Ind	89
Alton, Penobscot, Me	30
Alton, Kent, Mich	21
Alton, (c. h.,) Oregon, Mo	29
Alton, Belknap, N. H	270
Alton, Wayne, N. Y	120
Alton, Franklin, Ohio	73
Alton, McKean, Pa	100
Altona,* Knox, Ill	990
Altona, Marshall, Ky	12
Altona, Bates, Mo	59
Altona, Clinton, N. Y	50
Alton Bay, Belknap, N. H	12
Alton Junction, Madison, Ill	38
Altoona, Polk, Iowa	140
Altoona, Wilson, Kans	12

Altoona,* Blair, Pa	$2,800
Alum Bank, Bedford, Pa	55
Alum Creek, Delaware, Ohio	13
Alum Creek, Bastrop, Tex	15
Alum Rock, Clarion, Pa	9
Alum Springs, Rockbridge, Va	22
Alva, Aroostook, Me	55
Alvarado, Alameda, Cal	70
Alvarado, Stenben, Ind	12
Alvarado, Johnson, Tex	15
Alverson, Ingham, Mich	13
Alvira, Union, Pa	20
Alviso, Santa Clara, Cal	45
Alvon, Greenbrier, W. Va	12
Amador City, Amador, Cal	76
Amadore, Sanilac, Mich	12
Amagansett, Suffolk, N. Y	96
Amanda, Fairfield, Ohio	240
Amandaville, Hart, Ga	4
Amandaville, Cumberland, Ky	14
Amazonia, Andrew, Mo	77
Amber, Mason, Mich	12
Amber, Martin, Minn	5
Amber, Onondaga, N. Y	39
Amberson's Valley, Franklin, Pa	25
Amboy,* Lee, Ill	1,400
Amboy, Miami, Ind	63
Amboy, Jasper, Iowa	12
Amboy, Hillsdale, Mich	22
Amboy, Ashtabula, Ohio	84
Amboy Centre, Oswego, N. Y	41
Ambrose, Indiana, Pa	12
Amelia, Clermont, Ohio	180
Amelia, C. H., Amelia, Va	310
Amenia, Dutchess, N. Y	760
Amenia Union, Dutchess, N. Y	150
America, Wabash, Ind	24
America City, Nemaha, Kans	68
American Fork, Utah, Utah	130
American Ranch, Shasta, Cal	20
Americus,* (c. h.,) Sumter, Ga	2,000
Americus, Tippecanoe, Ind	36
Americus, Lyon, Kans	170
Americus, (c. h.,) Jackson, Miss	15
Americus, Montgomery, Mo	12
Ames, Story, Iowa	780
Ames, Montgomery, N. Y	85
Amesbury, Essex, Mass	1,400
Amesville, Athens, Ohio	260
Amherst, Hancock, Me	24
Amherst,* Hampshire, Mass	2,300
Amherst, Fillmore, Minn	12
Amherst, (c. h.,) Hillsborough, N. H	420
Amherst, Lorain, Ohio	80
Amherst, Portage, Wis	95
Amherst C. H., Amherst, Va	250
Amish, Johnson, Iowa	27
Amissville, Rappahannock, Va	78
Amite City, (c. h.,) Tangipahoa, La	440
Amity, Clark, Ark	24
Amity, Livingston, Ill	16
Amity, Johnson, Ind	50
Amity, Scott, Iowa	54
Amity, Aroostook, Me	19
Amity, Orange, N. Y	38
Amity, Yam Hill, Oreg	61

* Money-order o e.

Amity, Washington, Pa	$40	Angola, Erie, N. Y	$310
Amity Hill, Iredell, N. C	16	Angola, Clermont, Ohio	9
Amityville, Suffolk, N. Y	170	Anita, Cass, Iowa	78
Amo, Hendricks, Ind	150	Anna,* Union, Ill	620
Amoskeag, Hillsborough, N. H	32	Anna, Shelby, Ohio	150
Amsden, Montcalm, Mich	22	Annapolis, Crawford, Ill	29
Amsterdam, Cass, Ind	20	Annapolis, Parke, Ind	140
Amsterdam,* Montgomery, N. Y	2,200	ANNAPOLIS,* (c. h.,) Anne Arundel, Md	2,400
Amsterdam, Jefferson, Ohio	80	Annapolis, Jefferson, Ohio	42
Amsterdam, Botetourt, Va	100	Annapolis Junction, Anne Arundel, Md	240
Anacostia, Washington, D. C	80		
Anaheim, Los Angeles, Cal	220	Ann Arbor,* (c. h.,) Washtenaw, Mich	3,500
Anahuac, Chambers, Tex	12		
Analomink, Monroe, Pa	51	Annâton, Grant, Wis	49
Anamosa,* (c. h.,) Jones, Iowa	990	Annawan, Henry, Ill	430
Anandale, Dutchess, N. Y	200	Annieville, Clay, Iowa	12
Anandale, Butler, Pa	16	Annin Creek, McKean, Pa	11
Anawauk, Le Sueur, Minn	8	Annisquam, Essex, Mass	160
Anchorage, Buffalo, Wis	23	Annville,* Lebanon, Pa	430
Ancona, Livingston, Ill	89	Anoka, Cass, Ind	14
Ancora, Camden, N. J	12	Anoka,* (c. h.,) Anoka, Minn	650
Ancram, Columbia, N. Y	120	Anson, Somerset, Me	73
Ancram Centre, Columbia, N. Y	12	Ansonia, New Haven, Conn	1,400
Ancram Lead Mines, Columbia, N. Y	22	Ansonia, Darke, Ohio	88
Andalusia, Sanford, Ala	28	Ansonville, Anson, N. C	31
Andalusia, Rock Island, Ill	200	Ansonville, Clearfield, Pa	140
Andalusia, Bucks, Pa	170	Antelope, Yolo, Cal	10
Anderson, Mendocino, Cal	24	Antelope, Charles Mix, Dak	12
Anderson,* (c. h.,) Madison, Ind	1,200	Antelope, Marion, Kans	12
Anderson, Pope, Minn	16	Antelope, Jefferson, Nebr	12
Anderson, Alcorn, Miss	12	Antes Fort, Lycoming, Pa	110
Andèrson, Clinton, Mo	31	Antestown, Blair, Pa	140
Anderson, Ross, Ohio	48	Anthony, Delaware, Ind	7
Anderson, (c. h.,) Grimes, Tex	320	Anthony, Hunterdon, N. J	16
Anderson, Burnett, Wis	10	Anthony, Kent, R. I	200
Anderson, C. H.,* Anderson, S. C	730	Anthony House, Nevada, Cal	12
Andersonburgh, Perry, Pa	65	Antioch, Pickens, Ala	6
Anderson's Mills, Butler, Pa	19	Antioch,* Contra Costa, Cal	560
Anderson's Mills, Pickens, S. C	12	Antioch, Troup, Ga	230
Anderson's Store, Caswell, N. C	12	Antioch, Lake, Ill	110
Andersonville, Pickens, Ala	12	Antioch, Huntingdon, Ind	270
Andersonville, Sumter, Ga	76	Antioch, Washington, Ky	24
Andersonville, Franklin, Ind	70	Antioch, Alcorn, Miss	20
Andes, Delaware, N. Y	360	Antioch, Robeson, N. C	12
Andover, Tolland, Conn	190	Antioch, Monroe, Ohio	59
Andover, Henry, Ill	540	Antioch, York, S. C	6
Andover, Oxford, Me	230	Antioch, Gibson, Tenn	12
Andover,* Essex, Mass	2,300	Antioch, Lavaca, Tex	15
Andover, Merrimack, N. H	210	Antoine, Clark, Ark	62
Andover, Sussex, N. J	200	Antreville, Abbeville, S. C	18
Andover,* Allegany, N. Y	520	Antrim, Watonwan, Minn	15
Andover, Ashtabula, Ohio	170	Antrim, Hillsborough, N. H	320
Andover, Windsor, Vt	52	Antrim, Guernsey, Ohio	90
Andrew, (c. h.,) Jackson, Iowa	510	Antrim City, Antrim, Mich	76
Andrew Chapel, Madison, Tenn	16	Antwerp, Jefferson. N. Y	570
Andrew Johnson, Martin, Minn	15	Antwerp,* Paulding, Ohio	290
Andrews, Morrow, Ohio	37	Apache Pass, Pima, Ariz	12
Andrews, Spottsylvania, Va	90	Apalachicola, (c. h.,) Franklin, Fla	370
Andrusville, Franklin, N. Y	100	Apalachin, Tioga, N. Y	130
Andy, Monongalia, W. Va	4	Aplington, Butler, Iowa	200
Angelica, (c. h.,) Allegany, N. Y	860	Apollo, Armstrong, Pa	330
Angelica, Shawanaw, Wis	28	Apopka, Orange, Fla	12
Angel's Camp, Calaveras, Cal	160	Appanoose, Hancock, Ill	37
Angerona, Jackson, W. Va	15	Appanoose, Franklin, Kans	12
Angola, Sussex, Del	12	Apperson's, Charles City, Va	12
Angola,* (c. h.,) Steuben, Ind	480		

* Money-order office.

Applebachsville, Bucks, Pa........	$58	Argentine, Genesee, Mich..........	$59
Apple Creek, Wayne, Ohio.........	190	Argo, Jefferson, Ala	12
Applegate, Jackson, Oreg	24	Argo, Carroll, Ill.................	28
Apple Grove, Marion, Ala	12	Argo, Lucas, Iowa	8
Apple Grove, Meigs, Ohio..........	23	Argo, Winona, Minn	25
Apple Grove, York, Pa	25	Argo, Crawford, Mo...............	6
Apple Grove, Louisa, Va	12	Argos, Marshall, Ind ....:......	230
Apple River, Jo. Daviess, Ill	360	Argus, Crenshaw, Ala............	12
Appleton, Bourbon, Kans	67	Argusville, Schoharie, N. Y	91
Appleton, Knox, Me...............	100	Argyle, Winnebago, Ill...........	37
Appleton, Cape Girardeau, Mo.....	110	Argyle, Penobscot, Me...........	19
Appleton, Licking, Ohio...........	54	Argyle, Washington, N. Y......	430
Appleton, Lawrence, Tenn	7	Argyle, La Fayette, Wis..........	180
Appleton, (c. h.,) Outagamie, Wis..	2,200	Arica, DeKalb, Mo	12
Applewood, Caroline, Va....	15	Ariel, Wayne, Pa.......	30
Appling, (c. h.,) Columbia, Ga.....	20	Arington, Atchison, Kans.	12
Appomattox, C. H., Appomattox, Va.	22	Arion, Cloud, Kans...............	12
Aptos, Santa Cruz, Cal	12	Arizona, Burt, Nebr.............	39
Apulia, Onondaga, N. Y	85	Arizona City,* Yuma, Ariz....... ..	360
Aquasco, Prince George's, Md.....	86	Arizonia, Claiborne, La...........	12
Aquashicola, Carbon, Pa	21	Arkabutla, De Soto, Miss....	12
Aquilla, Franklin, Ga.............	12	Arkada, Mason, Wash...........	3
Aquone, Macon, N. C	12	*Arkadelphia,* (c. h.,) Clark, Ark....	480
Arabia, Lawrence, Ohio	44	Arkansas City, Cowley, Kans.....	12
Arago,* Richardson, Nebr	260	Arkansas Post, Arkansas, Ark.....	21
Aransas, Bee, Texas..............	12	Arkansaw, Pepin, Wis	14
Ararat, Susquehanna, Pa	41	Arkdale, Adams, Wis.............	59
Ararat, Patrick, Va	5	Arkport, Steuben, N. Y.......	460
Arba, Randolph, Ind......	45	Arkwright Summit, Chautauqua,	
Arbela, Scotland, Mo	25	N. Y............................	15
Arbor Hill, Adair, Iowa	28	Arland, Jackson, Mich............	32
Arbor Hill, Augusta, Va	27	Arlington,* Bureau, Ill....	400
Arbor Vitae, Bullock, Ala.........	17	Arlington, Middlesex, Mass.	760
Arbuckle, Mason, W. Va...........	92	Arlington, Van Buren, Mich......	22
Arcade,* Wyoming, N. Y	370	Arlington, Sibley, Minn...........	12
Arcadia, Morgan, Ill.............	56	Arlington, Phelps, Mo............	740
Arcadia, Hamilton, Ind...........	150	Arlington, Hancock, Ohio........	38
Arcadia, Crawford, Kans	76	Arlington, Wayne, Pa...........	12
Arcadia, Bienville, La	18	Arlington, Bennington, Vt........	350
Arcadia, Wayne, N. Y	210	Arlington, Alexandria, Va.......	38
Arcadia, Davidson, N. C	10	Armada, Macomb, Mich..........	370
Arcadia, Hancock, Ohio	110	Armagh, Indiana, Pa.......	160
Arcadia, Washington, R. I..... ...	38	Armenia, Juneau, Wis...........	14
Arcadia, Sullivan, Tenn	36	Armiesburgh, Parke, Ind.........	27
Arcadia, Trempealeau, Wis	90	Armington, Tazewell, Ill.........	50
Arcana, Grant, Ind	12	Armonk, Westchester, N. Y....,. .	99
Arcanum, Darke, Ohio	240	Armstrong, Vanderburgh, Ind.....	7
Arcata, Humboldt, Cal	180	Armstrong's Corners, Fond du Lac,	
Archbald, Luzerne, Pa......	290	Wis............................	11
Archbold, Fulton, Ohio...........	240	Armstrong's Grove, Emmett, Iowa.	10
Archer, Alachua, Fla	33	Armstrong's Mills, Belmont, Ohio.	20
Archer, Harrison, Ohio	12	Armuchee, Floyd, Ga.......	12
Archerville, Campbell, Tenn.......	12	Arnaudville, St. Landry, La......	15
Arch Spring, Blair, Pa	54	Arnettsville, Monongalia, W. Va..	34
Arcola,* Douglas, Ill	720	Arney, Owen, Ind...............	68
Arcola, Allen, Ind...............	62	Arneytown, Burlington, N. J......	5
Arcola, Monona, Iowa............	12	Arnheim, Brown, Ohio...........	32
Arcola, St. Helena, La............	74	*Arno,* (c. h.,) Douglas, Mo.`..........	25
Arcola, Bergen, N. J.............	12	Arnoldsburgh, Calhoun, W. Va.....	12
Arcola, Loudoun, Va......	61	Arnold's Mills, Pickens, S. C......	4
Arena, Iowa, Wis.................	270	Arnold's Store, Anne Arundel, Md..	8
Arenac, Bay, Mich...............	180	Arnold's Store, Bedford, Tenn.....	12
Arendahl, Fillmore, Minn.........	120	Arnoldsville, Buchanan, Mo.......	21
Arendtsville, Adams, Pa..........	86	Arnoldton, Campbell, Va..........	18
Arenzville, Cass, Ill	130	Arnot, Tioga, Pa...............	200
*Argenta, Lander, Nev	12		

Aroma, Kankakee, Ill	$68	Ashport, Lauderdale, Tenn	$12
Aroma, Dickinson, Kans	13	Ash Ridge, Massac, Ill	8
Arrington, Nelson, Va	160	Ash Ridge, Brown, Ohio	20
Arrow Rock, Saline, Mo	560	Ashtabula,* Ashtabula, Ohio	2.000
Arroyo, Elk, Pa	25	Ashton, Lee, Ill	530
Arroyo Grande, San Luis Obispo, Cal	12	Ashton, Clarke, Mo	23
		Ashton, Providence, R. I	220
Artesia, Lowndes, Miss	190	Ashton, Dane, Wis	74
Arthursburgh, Dutchess, N. Y	75	Ashuelot, Cheshire, N. H	180
Arvonia, Osage, Kans	12	Ashville, (c. h.,) St. Clair, Ala	96
Asbury, La Salle, Ill	100	Ashwood, Tensas, La	25
Asbury, Warren, N. J	150	Askeaton, Brown, Wis	12
Ascension, Sullivan, Ind	80	Askew, Phillips, Ark	19
Ascutneyville, Windsor, Vt	140	Aspen Hill, Giles, Tenn	51
Ashaway, Washington, R. I	280	Aspen Well, Charlotte, Va	17
Ashborough, Clay, Ind	19	Asper, Livingston, Mo	12
Ashborough, (c. h.,) Randolph, N. C.	260	Aspin Grove, Rockingham, N. C	12
Ashburn, Pike, Mo	2	Aspinwall, Nemaha, Nebr	240
Ashburnham, Worcester, Mass	670	Aspinwall, Bradford, Pa	27
Ashburnham Depot, Worcester, Mass	470	Assabet, Middlesex, Mass	410
		Assamoosick, Southampton, Va	12
Ashby, Middlesex, Mass	240	Assumption, Christian, Ill	420
Ashbysburgh, Hopkins, Ky	4	Assumption, (c. h.,) Assumption, La	60
Ashby's Mills, Montgomery, Ind	46	Assyria, Barry, Mich	22
Ash Creek, Oktibbeha, Miss	12	Astoria, Fulton, Ill	200
Ashepoo, Colleton, S. C	12	Astoria, Wright, Mo	16
Asherville, Mitchell, Kan	12	Astoria, Queens, N. Y	840
Asheville,* (c. h.) Buncombe, N. C.	900	Astoria,* (c. h.,) Clatsop, Oreg	530
Ashfield, Franklin, Mass	340	Asylum, Bradford, Pa	29
Ash Flat, Lawrence, Ark	8	Atalissa, Muscatine, Iowa	230
Ashford, Windham, Conn	120	Atalla, Etowah, Ala	12
Ashford, Cattaraugus, N. Y	72	Atchison,* (c. h.,) Atchison, Kans	3,200
Ashford, Fond du Lac, Wis	19	Atchison, Washington, Pa	14
Ash Grove, Iroquois, Ill	51	Atco, Camden, N. J	160
Ash Grove Tippecanoe, Ind	14	Athalia, Lawrence, Ohio	44
Ash Grove, Greene, Mo	100	Athens,* (c. h.,) Limestone, Ala	540
Ashippen, Watonwan, Minn	12	Athens,* Clarke, Ga	2,500
Ashippun, Dodge, Wis	21	Athens, Menard, Ill	220
Ashkum, Iroquois, Ill	78	Athens, Fayette, Ky	39
Ashland, (c. h.,) Clay, Ala	12	Athens, Claiborne, La	18
Ashland, Cass, Ill	140	Athens, Somerset, Me	220
Ashland, Henry, Ind	57	Athens, Calhoun, Mich	120
Ashland, Wapello, Iowa	61	Athens, Monroe, Miss	12
Ashland, Boyd, Ky	460	Athens, Clarke, Mo	110
Ashland, Aroostook, Me	79	Athens, Richardson, Nebr	26
Ashland, Middlesex, Mass	490	Athens, Greene, N. Y	240
Ashland, Newaygo, Mich	28	Athens,* (c. h.,) Athens, Ohio	1,200
Ashland, Dodge, Minn	12	Athens, Bradford, Pa	740
Ashland, Boone, Mo	130	Athens, McMinn, Tenn	520
Ashland, (c. h.,) Saunders, Nebr	350	Athens, (c. h.,) Henderson, Tex	44
Ashland, Grafton, N. H	530	Athens, Windham, Vt	37
Ashland, Greene, N. Y	99	Athensville, Greene, Ill	40
Ashland,* (c. h.,) Ashland, Ohio	1,700	Athlone, Monroe, Mich	61
Ashland,* Schuylkill, Pa	2,100	Athol, Worcester, Mass	610
Ashland, Hanover, Va	340	Athol, Warren, N. Y	24
Ashland City, (c.h.,) Cheatham, Tenn	20	Athol. Jackson, Wis	12
Ashland Mills, Jackson, Oreg	120	Athol Depot, Worcester, Mass	1,100
Ashley,* Washington, Ill	910	Atkinson, Henry, Ill	380
Ashley, Kent, Mich	24	Atkinson, Piscataquis, Me	55
Ashley, Pike, Mo	230	Atkinson, Rockingham, N. H	65
Ashley, Delaware, Ohio	240	Atkinson Depot, Rockingham, N. H.	110
Ashley Falls, Berkshire, Mass	150	Atkinson's Mills, Mifflin, Pa	14
Ashley Mills, Pulaski, Ark	12	Atkinsonville, Owen, Ind	12
Ashleyville, Hampden, Mass	25	Atlanta, Columbia, Ark	12
Ashlick, Randolph, W. Va	1	Atlanta, San Joaquin, Cal	18
Ashmore, Coles, Ill	180	ATLANTA,* (c. h.,) Fulton, Ga	4,000

* Money-order office.

Atlanta, Alturas, Idaho	$49	Augusta, Butler, Kans	$62
Atlanta,* Logan, Ill	1,000	Augusta, Bracken, Ky	440
Atlanta, Buchanan, Iowa	3	AUGUSTA,* (c. h.,) Kennebec	3,000
Atlanta, Winn, La	12	Augusta, Kalamazoo, Mich	450
Atlanta, Macon, Mo	140	Augusta, (c. h.,) Perry, Miss	16
Atlanta, Pickaway, Ohio	25	Augusta, St. Charles, Mo	110
Atlantic,* Cass, Iowa	1,100	Augusta, Oneida, N. Y	80
Atlantic City,* Atlantic, N. J	1,400	Augusta, Carroll, Ohio	160
Atlantic City, Sweet Water, Wyo	12	Augusta, Northumberland, Pa	21
Atlanticville, Suffolk, N. Y	19	Augusta, Houston, Tex	14
Atlas, Pike, Ill	19	Augusta, Eau Claire, Wis	430
Atlas, Genesee, Mich	82	Augusta Station, Marion, Ind	63
Atlas, Belmont, Ohio	28	Auman's Hill, Montgomery, N. C	15
Atlee's Station, Hanover, Va	12	Aumsville, Marion, Oreg	25
Atoka, Choctaw Nation, Ind. T	12	Auraria, Lumpkin, Ga	21
Atoy, Cherokee, Tex	12	Aurelia, Cherokee, Iowa	12
Attanam, Yakima, Wash	12	Aurelius, Ingham, Mich	60
Attica,* Fountain, Ind	1,200	Aurelius, Cayuga, N. Y	62
Attica, Marion, Iowa	84	Auriesville, Montgomery, N. Y	26
Attica, Saunders, Nebr	12	Aurora, Etowah, Ala	10
Attica, Wyoming, N. Y	1,100	Aurora,* Kane, Ill	3,800
Attica,* Seneca, Ohio	250	Aurora,* Dearborn, Ind	1,600
Attica, Green, Wis	54	Aurora, Keokuk, Iowa	10
Attila, Williamson, Ill	14	Aurora, Marshall, Ky	16
Attleborough, Bristol, Mass	1,000	Aurora, Hancock, Me	30
Attleborough, Bucks, Pa	300	Aurora, Steele, Minn	12
Attlebury, Dutchess, N. Y	28	Aurora, Wright, Mo	12
Atwater, Kandiyohi, Minn	12	Aurora,* (c. h.,) Esmeralda, Nev	500
Atwater, Portage, Ohio	210	Aurora, Cayuga, N. Y	690
Atwater Centre, Portage, Ohio	12	Aurora, Portage, Ohio	210
Atwood, Kosciusko, Ind	130	Aurora, Washington, Wis	25
Atwood, Antrim, Mich	12	Aurorahville, Waushara, Wis	*94
Atwood, Armstrong, Pa	13	Aurora Mills, Marion, Oreg	*45
Aubrey, Johnson, Kans	72	Au Sable, Iosco, Mich	360
Auburn,* Lee, Ala	500	Au Sable Forks, Essex, N. Y	370
Auburn, Arkansas, Ark	20	Austen, Preston, W. Va	25
Auburn,* (c. h.,) Placer, Cal	410	Austerlitz, Kent, Mich	65
Auburn, Gwinnett, Ga	12	Austerlitz, Columbia, N. Y	54
Auburn, Sangamon, Ill	340	Austin, Prairie, Ark	150
Auburn,* (c. h.,) De Kalb, Ind	450	Austin, Cook, Ill	40
Auburn, Mahaska, Iowa	8	Austin, Scott, Ind	140
Auburn, Shawnee, Kans	100	Austin, Oakland, Mich	20
Auburn,* Logan, Ky	330	Austin,* (c. h.,) Mower, Minn	1,900
Auburn,* (c. h.,) Androscoggin, Me.	2,000	Austin, (c. h.,) Tunica, Miss	39
Auburn, Worcester, Mass	100	Austin, Cass, Mo	230
Auburn, Lincoln, Mo	92	Austin,* (c. h.,) Lander, Nev	2,000
Auburn, Rockingham, N. H	110	Austin, Wilson, Tenn	25
Auburn, Salem, N. J	30	AUSTIN,* (c. h.,) Travis, Texas	3,100
Auburn,* (c. h.,) Cayuga, N. Y	4,000	Austinburgh, Ashtabula, Ohio	290
Auburn, Wake, N. C	15	Austin's Mills, Hawkins, Tenn	20
Auburn, Geauga, Ohio	130	Austinville, Bradford, Pa	57
Auburn, Baker, Oreg	110	Australia, Bolivar, Miss	16
Auburn, Schuylkill, Pa	130	Autaugaville, Autauga, Ala	24
Auburn, Cannon, Tenn	12	Ava, Jackson, Ill	20
Auburn Centre, Susquehanna, Pa	44	Ava, Oneida, N. Y	50
Auburn Dale, Middlesex, Mass	470	Ava, Noble, Ohio	23
Auburn Four Corners, Susquehanna, Pa	58	Ava, Buchanan, Va	12
		Avalanche, Vernon, Wis	20
Audenried, Carbon, Pa	420	Averill's Station, Midland, Mich	160
Aughwick Mills, Huntingdon, Pa	24	Avery, Jo Daviess, Ill	13
Auglaize, Van Wert, Ohio	13	Avery, Berrien, Mich	100
Au Gres, Bay, Mich	18	Averysborough, Harnett, N. C	9
Augusta, (c. h.,) Woodruff, Ark	320	Avery's Creek, Buncombe, N. C	6
Augusta,* (c. h.,) Richmond, Ga	4,000	Avilla, Noble, Ind	120
Augusta, Hancock, Ill	470	Avilla, Jasper, Mo	120
Augusta, Des Moines, Iowa	82	Aviston, Clinton, Ill	110

BAI   BAL

Avoca, Lawrence, Ala	$10	Bailey's Harbor, Door, Wis	$72
Avoca, Lawrence, Ind	12	Bailey's Mill, Leon, Fla	140
Avoca, Pottawattomie, Iowa	12	Bailey's Mills, Belmont, Ohio	12
Avoca, Jefferson, Mo	31	Bailey's Store, Shelby, Ky	12
Avoca, Cass, Nebr	5	Baileyville, Ogle, Ill	170
Avoca, Steuben, N. Y	360	Baileyville, Washington, Me	9
Avola, Iowa, Wis	340	*Bainbridge,* (c. h.,) Decatur, Ga	1,100
Avola, Vernon, Mo	8	Bainbridge, Williamson, Ill	16
Avon, Hartford, Conn	130	Bainbridge, Putnam, Ind	310
Avon, Fulton, Ill	440	Bainbridge, Christian, Ky	35
Avon, Polk, Iowa	19	Bainbridge, Berrien, Mich	49
Avon, Coffey, Kans	18	Bainbridge, Clinton, Mo	12
Avon, Franklin, Me	41	Bainbridge, Chenango, N. Y	640
Avon, St. Genevieve, Mo	6	Bainbridge,* Ross, Ohio	330
Avon, Livingston, N. Y	880	Bainbridge, Lancaster, Pa	210
Avon, Lorain, Ohio	140	Bairdstown, Oglethorpe, Ga	110
Avon, Lebanon, Pa	39	Bairdstown, Sullivan, Mo	15
Avon Centre, Rock, Wis	19	Baiting Hollow, Suffolk, N. Y	58
Avondale, Chester, Pa	310	Baker, Jefferson, Iowa	12
Avondale, Polk, Wis	17	Baker, St. Clair, Mo	12
Avonia, Erie, Pa	12	*Baker City,* (c. h.,) Baker, Oreg	320
Avon Lake, Lorain, Ohio	20	Baker's Basin, Mercer, N. J	20
Aydelott, Benton, Ind	6	Bakersfield, Kern, Cal	30
Ayer's Hill, Potter, Pa	5	Bakersfield, Franklin, Vt	210
Ayer's Point, Washington, Ill	74	Baker's Gap, Johnson, Tenn	12
Ayer's Village, Essex, Mass	12	Baker's Grove, Barton, Mo	8
Ayersville, Putnam, Mo	12	Baker's Run, Hardy, W. Va	120
Ayersville, Stokes, N. C	8	Bakerstown, Allegheny, Pa	85
Ayersville, Defiance, Ohio	16	Bakersville, Litchfield, Conn	62
Aylett's, King William, Va	150	Bakersville, Washington, Md	35
Ayr, Goodhue, Minn	13	*Bakersville,* (c. h.,) Mitchell, N. C	5
Azalia, Bartholomew, Ind	23	Bakersville, Coshocton, Ohio	59
Aztalan, Jefferson, Wis	59	Bakersville, Somerset, Pa	23
		Balaka, Randolph, Ind	14
B.		Balbec, Jay, Ind	40
		Balcony Falls, Rockbridge, Va	60
BABCOCK HILL, Oneida, N. Y	18	Bald Creek, Yancey, N. C	6
Babylon, Hampshire, Mass	21	Bald Eagle, York, Pa	8
Babylon, Suffolk, N. Y	480	Bald Hill, Clearfield, Pa	7
Bacchus, Hopkins, Tex	12	Bald Knob, Taney, Mo	12
Bachelor's Hall, Pittsylvania, Va	24	Bald Knob, Boone, W. Va	6
Bachelor's Retreat, Oconee, S. C	21	Bald Mount, Luzerne, Pa	39
Bach Grove, Wright, Iowa	16	Bald Mountain, Gilpin, Colo	730
Bachman, Montgomery, Ohio	30	Baldwin, St. Mary's, La	12
Bachman's Mills, Carroll, Md	10	Baldwin, Butler, Pa	33
Back Creek Valley, Frederick, Va	37	Baldwin City,* Douglas, Kans	400
Backville, Brown, Minn	7	Baldwin's Mills, Jackson, Mich	88
Bacon, Coshocton, Ohio	20	Baldwin's Mills, Waupacca, Wis	12
Bacon Creek, Hart, Ky	110	Baldwinsville, Edgar, Ill	12
Bacon Hill, Saratoga, N. Y	49	Baldwinsville, Worcester, Mass	250
Baden, Keokuk, Iowa	71	Baldwinsville, Onondaga, N. Y	1,200
Baden, St. Louis, Mo	130	Baldwyn, Lee, Miss	250
Baden, Gage, Nebr	12	Ballard's Falls, Washington, Kans	12
Baden, Beaver, Pa	94	Ballard Vale, Essex, Mass	240
Baden Baden, Bond, Ill	21	Ballardsville, Boone, W. Va	11
Badger, Portage, Wis	29	Ball Camp, Knox, Tenn	14
Badger Hill, Tama, Iowa	25	Ballena, San Diego, Cal	12
Badito, (c. h.,) Huerfano, Colo	32	Ball Play, Etowah, Ala	12
Bad River, Gratiot, Mich	40	Ball-Play, Monroe, Tenn	12
Bagdad, Shelby, Ky	140	Ball's Pond, Fairfield, Conn	21
Bagdad, Smith, Tenn	9	*Ballston,* (c. h.,) Saratoga, N. Y	1,800
Bagdad, Williamson, Tex	25	Ballston Centre, Saratoga, N. Y	30
Baggettsville, Robertson, Tenn	12	Ballstown, Ripley, Ind	20
Bahala, Copiah, Miss	24	Ballsville, Powhatan, Va	53
Bailey Hollow, Luzerne, Pa	100	Ballwin, St. Louis, Mo	35
Bailey's Creek, Osage, Mo	8	Ballyclough, Dubuque, Iowa	7

* Money-order office.

BAR   BAR

Balm, Blount, Ala.	$12	Barkhamsted, Litchfield, Conn	$71
Balm, Mercer, Pa	55	Barlow, Washington, Ohio	110
Balmoral, Otter Tail, Minn	12	Bar Mills, York, Me	119
Baltic, New London, Conn	560	Barnard, Linn, Kans	12
Baltimore,* Baltimore, Md	4,000	Barnard, Piscataquis, Me	14
Baltimore, Barry, Mich	38	Barnard, Charlevoix, Mich	21
Baltimore, Fairfield, Ohio	150	Barnard, Windsor, Vt	160
Bamberg, Barnwell, S. C	320	Barnard's, Armstrong, Pa	18
Bamberg, Sheboygan, Wis	8	Barnardsville, Roane, Tenn	10
Bancroft, Aroostook, Me	21	Barnegat, Ocean, N. J	130
Bancroft, Berkshire, Mass	49	Barnerville, Schoharie, N. Y	56
Bancroft, Freeborn, Minn	18	Barnes, Richland, Ohio	16
Bancroft, Daviess, Mo	92	Barnes' Corners, Lewis, N. Y	60
Bandera, (c. h.,) Bandera, Tex	42	Barnes' Cross Roads, Dale, Ala	13
Bangall, Dutchess, N. Y	170	Barnes' Store, Tishemingo, Miss	13
Bangor, Butte, Cal	26	Barneston, Chester, Pa	23
Bangor, Marshall, Iowa	120	Barnesville, Pike, Ga	460
Bangor, Morgan, Ky	12	Barnesville, Bourbon, Kans	58
Bangor, (c. h.,) Penobscot, Me	4,000	Barnesville, Montgomery, Md	44
Bangor, Van Buren, Mich	100	Barnesville, Clinton, Mo	33
Bangor, Franklin, N. Y	120	Barnesville,* Belmont, Ohio	1,000
Bangor, Northampton, Pa	12	Barnesville, Schuylkill, Pa	53
Bangor, La Crosse, Wis	330	Barnesville, Charlotte, Va	160
Bank Lick, Kenton, Ky	12	Barnet, Caledonia, Vt	340
Banks, Faribault, Minn	46	Barnhart's Mills, Butler, Pa	69
Bankston, Saline, Ill	13	Barnsborough, Gloucester, N. J	36
Bankston, Dubuque, Iowa	3	*Barnstable, (c. h.,)* Barnstable, Mass.	680
Bankston, Choctaw, Miss	39	Barnstead, Belknap, N. H	56
Banksville, Fairfield, Conn	28	Barnum, Adams, Wis	31
Banksville, Banks, Ga	11	Barnumton, Camden, Mo	9
Bannack City, (c. h.,) Beaver Head, Mont.	340	Barnwell, Barnwell, S. C	320
Banner, Jackson, Kans	4	Barracksville, Marion, W. Va	71
Banner, Calhoun, Miss	15	Barre, Worcester, Mass	1,000
Banner, Fond du Lac, Wis	24	Barre, Washington, Vt	550
Bannerville, Snyder, Pa	44	Barre Centre, Orleans, N. Y	97
Banquete, Nueces, Tex	8	Barre Forge, Huntingdon, Pa	68
Banta, San Joaquin, Cal	12	Barre Mills, La Crosse, Wis	62
Bantam, Clermont, Ohio	82	Barren, Harrison, Ind	19
Bantam Falls, Litchfield, Conn	180	Barren Creek Springs, Wicomico, Md.	49
Baptistown, Hunterdon, N. J	49	Barren Hill, Montgomery, Pa	56
Baptist Valley, Tazewell, Va	12	Barren Plain, Robertson, Tenn	17
Baraboo, (c. h.,) Sauk, Wis	1,500	Barren Springs, Fentress, Tenn	12
Baraga, Houghton, Mich	23	Barre Plains, Worcester, Mass	29
Barber, Faribault, Minn	75	Barret's Station, St. Louis, Mo	19
Barber's Mills, Wells, Ind	15	Barrett, Marshall, Kans	45
Barbersville, Jefferson, Ind	16	Barrettsville, Hampshire, W. Va	14
Barbour's Mills, Lycoming, Pa	30	Barreville, McHenry, Ill	79
Barboursville, (c. h.,) Knox, Ky	200	Barrington, Strafford, N. H	72
Barbourville, Delaware, N. Y	27	Barrington, Yates, N. Y	39
Barclay, Black Hawk, Iowa	13	Barrington, Bristol, R. I	25
Barclay, Bradford, Pa	250	Barrington Centre, Bristol, R. I	94
Bardolph, McDonough, Ill	240	Barrington Station, Cook, Ill	410
Bardstown, (c. h.,) Nelson, Ky	960	Barrittsville, Dawson, Ga	12
Bardstown Junction, Bullitt, Ky	24	*Barron, (c. h.,)* Barron, Wis	12
Bardwell's Ferry, Franklin, Mass	17	Barr's Store, Macoupin, Ill	25
Bareville, Lancaster, Pa	64	Barry, Pike, Ill	570
Barfield, Mississippi, Ark	45	Barry, Frederick, Md	87
Bargaintown, Atlantic, N. J	30	Barry, Clay, Mo	130
Bargersville, Johnson, Ind	20	Barry, Cuyahoga, Ohio	8
Barhamsville, New Kent, Va	42	Barry, Schuylkill, Pa	19
Baring, Washington, Me	110	Barrytown, Dutchess, N. Y	320
Bark Camp Mills, Whitley, Ky	3	Barryville, Delaware, Iowa	20
Barkersville, Saratoga, N. Y	42	Barryville, Barry, Mich	14
Barkesdale, Halifax, Va	17	Barryville, Sullivan, N. Y	110
Barkeyville, Venango, Pa	12	Barryville, Stark, Ohio	25
		Bart, Lancaster, Pa	94

* Money-order office.

BAT

Bartholomew, Drew, Ark	$8
Bartlett, Fremont, Iowa	60
Bartlett, Carroll, N. H	27
Bartlett, Washington, Ohio	120
Bartlett, Shelby, Tenn	130
Barton, Colbert, Ala	68
Barton, Alleghany, Md	360
Barton. Newaygo, Mich	7
Barton, Barton, Mo	12
Barton, Tioga, N. Y	130
Barton, Anderson, Tex	4
Barton,* Orleans, Vt	460
Barton, Washington, Wis	170
Bartonia, Randolph, Ind	28
Barton Landing, Orleans, Vt	260
Bartonsville, Monroe, Pa	27
Bartonsville, Windham, Vt	110
Bartow, Jefferson, Ga	120
Bartramville, Lawrence, Ohio	8
Bartville, Lancaster, Pa	20
Basco, Hancock, Ill	66
Bascom, Seneca, Ohio	23
Base Lake, Washtenaw, Mich	47
Base Line, Crawford, Kans	12
Basham's Gap, Morgan, Ala	29
Bashan, Meigs, Ohio	14
Basil, Fairfield, Ohio	110
Basin Spring, Williamson, Tenn	7
Basking Ridge, Somerset, N. J	210
Basnettsville, Marion, W. Va	16
Bassett's Mill, El Paso, Colo	26
Bassett's Station, Kenosha, Wis	65
Bass Lake, Faribault, Minn	26
Bass Station, Jackson, Ala	12
Bass Wood, Richland, Wis	18
Bastinville, Hickman, Tenn	8
Bastrop, (c. h.,) Morehouse, La	400
Bastrop, (c. h.,) Bastrop, Tex	800
Bastross, Lycoming, Pa	12
Batavia, Solano, Cal	12
Batavia,* Kane, Ill	1,600
Batavia, Branch, Mich	14
Batavia,* (c. h.,) Genesee, N. Y	2,500
Batavia, (c. h.,) Clermont, Ohio	400
Batchellerville, Saratoga, N. Y	92
Batchelor's Rest, Pendleton, Ky	12
Bateham, Sullivan, Ind	4
Bates, Sangamon, Ill	39
Bates, Osceola, Mich	12
Batesville,* (c. h.,) Independence, Ark	580
Batesville, Ripley, Ind	170
Batesville, Panola, Miss	120
Batesville, Noble, Ohio	120
Batesville, Spartanburgh, S. C	10
Batesville, Albemarle, Va	12
Bath, Placer, Cal	71
Bath, Mason, Ill	420
Bath,* (c. h.,) Sagadahoc, Me	2,600
Bath, Clinton, Mich	64
Bath, Grafton, N. H	300
Bath,* (c. h.,) Steuben, N. Y	2,200
Bath, Beaufort, N. C	5
Bath, Summit, Ohio	41
Bath, Northampton, Pa	280
Bath, Edgefield, S. C	51

BEA

Bath, C. H., Bath, Va	$220
Bath Alum, Bath, Va	66
Baton Rouge,* (c. h.,) East Baton Rouge, La	2,100
Batten's Mills, Gilmer, W. Va	12
Battenville, Washington, N. Y	24
Battleborough, Edgecombe, N. C	310
Battle Creek, Tehama, Cal	12
Battle Creek,* Calhoun, Mich	3,500
Battle Creek, Madison, Nebr	12
Battle Creek Mines, Marion, Tenn	12
Battle Ground, Tippecanoe, Ind	260
Battle Mountain, Humboldt, Nev	12
Baughman, Wayne, Ohio	68
Baugh's Station, Logan, Ky	6
Baumstown, Berks, Pa	25
Bavington, Washington, Pa	40
Baxter Springs,* Cherokee, Kans	990
Bay, Gasconade, Mo	80
Bayard, Columbiana, Ohio	94
Bayborough, Horry, S. C	12
Bay City, Pope, Ill	53
Bay City,* (c. h.,) Bay, Mich	3,000
Bay City, Pierce, Wis	52
Bayfield, (c. h.,) Bayfield, Wis	90
Bay Hill, Walworth, Wis	9
Bay Hundred, Talbot, Md	20
Bay Minette, Baldwin, Ala	12
Baynesville, Westmoreland, Va	16
Bayonne, Hudson, N. J	50
Bayou Barbary, Livingston, La	10
Bayou Boeuf, St. Landry, La	10
Bayou Chicot, St. Landry, La	18
Bayou Goula, Iberville, La	50
Bayou Tunica, West Feliciana, La	61
Bay Port, Hernando, Fla	4
Bay Ridge, Kings, N. Y	32
Bay River, Craven, N. C	25
Bay Settlement, Brown, Wis	12
Bay Shore, Suffolk, N. Y	280
Bay Side, Queens, N. Y	10
Bay Springs, Prentiss, Miss	22
Bay View, Cecil, Md	74
Bay View, Essex, Mass	12
Bay View, Northampton, Va	26
Bayview, Milwaukee, Wis	12
Bayville, Ocean, N. J	12
Bazaar, Chase, Kans	16
Bazetta, Trumbull, Ohio	300
Beach Haven, Luzerne, Pa	120
Beach Pond, Wayne, Pa	75
Beach Ridge, Niagara, N. Y	23
Beacon, Ogle, Ill	12
Beacon, Mahaska, Iowa	170
Beacon Falls, New Haven, Conn	230
Bealeton, Fauquier, Va	74
Beall's Mills, Gilmer, W. Va	12
Beallsville, Montgomery, Md	66
Beallsville, Monroe, Ohio	110
Beallsville, Washington, Pa	140
Beamsville, Darke, Ohio	11
Bean Blossom, Brown, Ind	30
Bean's Corners, Franklin, Me	55
Bean's Station, Grainger, Tenn	110
Beantown, Charles, Md	35
Bear, Richland, Wis	15

* Money-order office.

BEA   BEE

Bear Branch, Ohio, Ind	$21	Beaver Head Rock, Madison, Mont.	$12
Bear Branch, Richmond, N. C	10	Beaver Kill, Sullivan, N. Y	15
Bear Canyon, Douglas, Colo	15*	Beaver Meadows, Carbon, Pa	230
Bear Creek, Henry, Ga	24	Beaver Pond, Lexington, S. C	3
Bear Creek, Jay, Ind	29	Beaver Ridge, Knox, Tenn	5
Bear Creek, Hinds, Miss	12	Beaver Run, Sussex, N. J	12
Bear Creek, Cedar, Mo	12	Beaver Springs, Snyder, Pa	64
Bear Creek, Luzerne, Pa	30	Beaverton, Sanford, Ala	5
Bear Creek, Waupaca, Wis	19	Beavertown, Snyder, Pa	50
Beard's Station, Oldham, Ky	72	Beaver Valley, St. Clair, Ala	8
Beardstown, (c. h.,) Cass, Ill	1,000	Beaver Valley, New Castle, Del	62
Beardstown, Perry, Tenn	19	Beaver Valley, Columbia, Pa	34
Bear Gap, Northumberland, Pa	18	Beaverville, Iroquis, Ill	8
Bear Grove, Guthrie, Iowa	45	Bechtelsville, Berks, Pa	22
Bear Lake, Manistee, Mich	65	Beckersville, Berks, Pa	17
Bear Lake, Warren, Pa	100	Becket, Berkshire, Mass	380
Bear Lake Mills, Van Buren, Mich.	20	Becket Centre, Berkshire, Mass	24
Bear River, Emmett, Mich	10	Beckett's Store, Pickaway, Ohio	53
Bearsville, Ulster, N. Y	35	Beckleysville, Baltimore, Md	21
Beartown, Deer Lodge, Mont	12	Beck's Creek, Shelby, Ill	9
Beartown, Lancaster, Pa	24	Beck's Grove, Brown, Ind	12
Bear Valley, Mariposa, Cal	110	Beck's Mills, Washington, Ind	4
Bear Valley, Wabashaw, Minn	33	Beck's Mills, Holmes, Ohio	12
Bear Valley, Richland, Wis	32	Beck's Mills, Washington, Pa	21
Bear Wallow, Henderson, N. C	19	Beckville, Panola, Tex	12
Beasley's Fork, Adams, Ohio	7	Beckwith, Plumas, Cal	12
Beatrice, (c. h.,) Gage, Nebr	620	Beddington, Washington, Me	6
Beattie's Ford, Lincoln, N. C	38	Bedford, Pike, Ill	28
Beatty,* Westmoreland, Pa	310	*Bedford,* (c. h.,) Lawrence, Ind	840
Beattyville, Lee, Ky	49	*Bedford,* (c. h.,) Taylor, Iowa	420
Beatyestown, Warren, N. J	48	*Bedford,* (c. h.,) Trimble, Ky	140
Beaty's Mills, Marion, W. Va	8	Bedford, Middlesex, Mass	220
Beauford, Blue Earth, Minn	8	Bedford, Calhoun, Mich	110
Beaufort, Franklin, Mo	40	Bedford, Livingston, Mo	58
Beaufort, (c. h.,) Carteret, N. C	700	Bedford, Hillsborough, N. H	71
Beaufort, (c. h.,) Beaufort, S. C	1,000	*Bedford,* (c. h.,) Westchester, N. Y	190
Beaumont, (c. h.,) Jefferson, Tex	120	Bedford, Cuyahoga, Ohio	400
Beaver, Winona, Minn	68	*Bedford,* (c. h.,*) Bedford, Pa	1,200
Beaver, Douglas, Mo	4	Bedford, Bedford, Tenn	12
Beaver, Pike, Ohio	23	Bedford Springs, Bedford, Pa	27
Beaver, Clackamas, Oreg	12	Bedford Station, Westchester, N. Y.	210
Beaver, (c. h.,) Beaver, Pa	720	Bedias, Grimes, Tex	10
Beaver, Anderson, Tex	12	Bedminster, Bucks, Pa	8
Beaver, (c. h.,) Beaver, Utah	180	Bed Rock, Klamath, Cal	12
Beaver, Thurston, Wash	3	Beebe Plain, Orleans, Vt	160
Beaver Bay, (c. h.,) Lake, Minn	50	Bee Branch, Van Buren, Ark	5
Beaver Brook, Sullivan, N. Y	8	Bee Caves, Travis, Tex	12
Beaver Centre, Crawford, Pa	40	Beech, Licking, Ohio	14
Beaver City, Newton, Ind	16	Beech Creek, Ashley, Ark	12
Beaver Creek, Dale, Ala	16	Beech Creek, Clinton, Pa	210
Beaver Creek, Pueblo, Colo	16	Beecher, Will, Ill	12
Beaver Creek, Bond, Ill	83	Beech Fork, Washington, Ky	18
Beaver Creek, Washington, Md	19	Beech Grove, Rush, Ind	120
Beaver Creek, Gratiot, Mich	15	Beech Grove, Coffee, Tenn	20
Beaver Creek, Jefferson, Tenn	12	Beech Hill, Mason, W. Va	12
Beaver Crossing, Seward, Nebr	38	Beechland, Washington, Ky	12
Beaver Dam, Kosciusko, Ind	18	Beech Spring, Lee, Va	29
Beaver Dam, Ohio, Ky	8	Beech Wood, Sullivan, N. Y	10
Beaver Dam, Union, N. C	5	Beech Wood, Cameron, Pa	160
Beaver Dam, Allen, Ohio	61	Beech Wood, Sheboygan, Wis	24
Beaver Dam,* Dodge, Wis	1,600	Beech Woods, Newton, Ark	12
Beaver Dam Depot, Hanover, Va.	65	Beechy Mire, Union, Ind	27
Beaver Dams, Schuyler, N. Y	23	Bee Creek, Pike, Ill	16
Beaver Falls, (c. h.,) Renville, Minn.	99	Bee Creek, Bledsoe, Tenn	12
Beaver Falls, Lewis, N. Y	12	Beekman, Dutchess, N. Y	81
Beaver Falls, Beaver, Pa	950	Beekmantown, Clinton, N. Y	25

* Money-order office.

BEL

Beeler's Station, Marshall, W. Va	$10	Belle Prairie, Hamilton, Ill	$31
Bee Lick, Lincoln, Ky	12	Belle Prairie, Morrison, Minn	23
Beemerville, Sussex, N. J	25	Belle River, St. Clair, Mich	38
Bee Ridge, Knox, Mo	39	Belle Union, Putnam, Ind	12
Beers, Allegheny, Pa	18	Belle Vale, West Baton Rouge, La	12
Beersheba Springs, Grundy, Tenn	12	Belle Valley, Erie, Pa	16
Beesley's Point, Cape May, N. J	81	Belle Vernon, Wyandot, Ohio	38
Bee Spring, Edmonson, Ky	7	Belle Vernon, Fayette, Pa	230
Beetown, Grant, Wis	130	Belleview, Calhoun, Ill	30
Beetrace, Appanoose, Iowa	21	Belleview, Iron, Mo	10
Beeville, (c. h.,) Bee, Tex	8	Belleview, Davidson, Tenn	41
Belair, Richmond, Ga	74	Belleview, Rusk, Tex	24
Bel Air, (c. h.,) Harford, Md	470	Belleville, Conecuh, Ala	17
Belair, Lancaster, S. C	12	*Belleville,* (c. h.,) St. Clair, Ill	2,300
Belbend, Luzerne, Pa	53	Belleville, Hendricks, Ind	81
Belcher, Washington, N. Y	34	Belleville, Republic, Kans	12
Belchertown, Hampshire, Mass	850	Belleville, Wayne, Mich	180
Belden, Wabash, Ind	38	Belleville, Fillmore, Minn	9
Belden, Broome, N. Y	12	Belleville, Essex, N. J	380
Beldenville, Pierce, Wis	11	Belleville, Jefferson, N. Y	320
Belew Creek Mills, Forsyth, N. C	12	Belleville,* Richland, Ohio	490
Belew's Creek, Jefferson, Mo	16	Belleville, Mifflin, Pa	120
Belfast, Lee, Iowa	15	Belleville, Wood, W. Va	81
Belfast, (c. h.,) Waldo, Me	2,300	Belleville, Dane, Wis	110
Belfast, Baltimore, Md	7	Bellevoir, Chatham, N. C	4
Belfast, Allegany, N. Y	280	Bellevue, Dallas, Ala	39
Belfast, Clermont, Ohio	19	Bellevue,* Jackson, Iowa	570
Belfast, Northampton, Pa	54	*Bellevue,* (c. h.,) Bossier, La	100
Belfast Mills, Russell, Va	12	Bellevue,* Eaton, Mich	410
Belgium, Ozaukee, Wis	59	*Bellevue,* (c. h.,) Sarpy, Nebr	200
Belgrade, Kennebec, Me	210	Bellevue,* Huron, Ohio	1,100
Belgrade, Washington, Mo	12	Bellevue, Yam Hill, Oreg	21
Belgrade Mills, Kennebec, Me	78	Bellevue, Washington, Utah	20
Belinda, Lucas, Iowa	10	Bellevue, Bedford, Va	45
Belington, Barbour, W. Va	53	Bell Factory, Madison, Ala	44
Belknap, Armstrong, Pa	15	Bellfair Mills, Stafford, Va	12
Bell, Highland, Ohio	12	Bellingham, Norfolk, Mass	72
Bell Air, Crawford, Ill	40	Bellmore, Parke, Ind	65
Bell Air, Cooper, Mo	40	Bellona, Yates, N. Y	170
Bell Air, Hardin, Tenn	12	Bellota, San Joaquin, Cal	12
Bellaire,* Belmont, Ohio	1,400	Bellows Falls,* Windham, Vt	1,200
Bellasylva, Wyoming, Pa	13	Bell Plain, Marshall, Ill	53
Bellbrook, Greene, Ohio	110	Bellport, Suffolk, N. Y	220
Bellbuckle, Bedford, Tenn	85	Bell's Cross-Roads, Louisa, Va	10
Bell Center, Crawford, Wis	60	Bell's Depot, Haywood, Tenn	370
Belle Air, Johnson, Iowa	28	Bell's Landing, Monroe, Ala	12
Belle Centre, Logan, Ohio	220	Bell's Mills, Jefferson, Pa	20
Belle Creek, Goodhue, Minn	30	Bell's Store, Columbia, Ark	14
Belle Creek, Washington, Nebr	12	Bell's Valley, Rockbridge, Va	12
Bellefontaine, Choctaw, Miss	44	Bellton, Marshall, W. Va	70
Bellefontaine, St. Louis, Mo	40	Belltown, Monroe, Tenn	6
Bellfontaine, (c. h.,) Logan, Ohio	2,100	Bellvale, Orange, N. Y	92
Bellefonte, Jackson, Ala	80	Bellview, Lebanon, Pa	12
Bellefonte, (c. h.,) Centre, Pa	1,900	Bellville, Hamilton, Fla	7
Belle Fountain, Mahaska, Iowa	73	*Bellville,* (c. h.,) Austin, Tex	180
Bellefountain, Columbia, Wis	16	Bellwood, Wilson, Tenn	12
Belle Grove, Greenwood, Kans	12	Belmond, Wright, Iowa	130
Belle Haven, Accomack, Va	68	Belmont, Crawford, Ark	9
Belle Isle, Onondaga, N. Y	130	Belmont, San Mateo, Cal	16
Bellemont, Warren, Iowa	12	Belmont, Woodson, Kans	15
Bellemonte, Lancaster, Pa	69	Belmont, Bullitt, Ky	100
Belle Plain, Cumberland, N. J	23	Belmont, Waldo, Me	37
Belle Plaine,* Benton, Iowa	910	Belmont, Middlesex, Mass	230
Belle Plaine,* Scott, Minn	250	Belmont, Kent, Mich	12
Belle Plaine, Shawanaw, Wis	70	Belmont, Mississippi, Mo	12
Belle Point, Delaware, Ohio	16	*Belmont,* (c. h.,) Nye, Nev	520

* Money-order office.

BEN | BER

Belmont, Belknap, N. H	$180	Bennington Furnace. Blair, Pa	$48
Belmont, (*c. h.*,) Allegany, N. Y	580	Benona, Oceana, Mich	93
Belmont, Belmont, Ohio	140	Bensalem, Bucks, Pa	12
Belmont, Gonzales, Tex	120	Benson, Franklin, Ky	12
Belmont, La Fayette, Wis	170	Benson, Chippewa, Minn	12
Belmore, Putnam, Ohio	86	Benson, Hamilton, N. Y	14
Beloit, Mitchell, Kans	12	Benson, Rutland, Vt	260
Beloit, Mahoning, Ohio	150	Benson Centre, Hamilton, N. Y	15
Beloit,* Rock, Wis	2,800	Benson Grove, Winnebago, Iowa	3
Belpassi, Marion, Oreg	93	Benson Landing, Rutland, Vt	48
Belpre, Washington, Ohio	280	Ben's Run, Tyler, W. Va	11
Belton, Anderson, S. C	68	Bent Branch, Pike, Ky	12
Belton, (*c. h.*,) Bell, Tex	400	Bent Creek, Appomattox, Va	13
Beltsville, Prince George's, Md	200	Bentivoglio, Albemarle, Va	75
Belvidere,* (*c. h.*,) Boone, Ill	2,300	Bentley's Springs, Baltimore, Md	67
Belvidere, Monona, Iowa	12	Bentleyville, Washington, Pa	70
Belvidere,* (*c. h.*,) Warren, N. J	1,000	Bently, Hancock, Ill	120
Belvidere, Allegany, N. Y	190	Bently Creek, Bradford, Pa	51
Belvidere, Perquimons, N. C	36	Bent Mountain, Roanoke, Va	12
Belvidere, Lamoille, Vt	23	Benton, Lowndes, Ala	180
Belvidere Corners, Lamoille, Vt	2	*Benton*, (*c. h.*,) Saline, Ark	87
Belvoir, Douglas, Kans	12	Benton, Mono, Cal	31
Belvoir, Vernon, Mo	12	Benton, Columbia, Fla	12
Bem, Green, Wis	25	*Benton*, (*c. h.*,) Franklin, Ill	350
Bement,* Piatt, Ill	610	Benton, Elkhart, Ind	69
Bemus Heights, Saratoga, N. Y	75	Benton Mills, Iowa	23
Bemus Point, Chautauqua, N. Y	110	*Benton*, (*c. h.*,) Marshall, Ky	70
Benaja, Rockingham, N. C	12	Benton, Bossier, La	12
Benbow, Marion, Mo	39	Benton, Kennebec, Me	85
Bendersville, Adams, Pa	160	Benton, Washtenaw, Mich	8
Benela, Calhoun, Miss	27	Benton, Carver, Minn	36
Benevola, Washington, Md	33	Benton, Yazoo, Miss	100
Benezett, Elk, Pa	57	Benton, Scott, Mo	30
Benford's Store, Somerset, Pa	28	Benton, Saunders, Nebr	14
Ben Franklin, Lamar, Tex	8	Benton, Grafton, N. H	43
Bengal, Clinton, Mich	5	Benton, Holmes, Ohio	65
Benham's Store, Ripley, Ind	15	Benton, Columbia, Pa	49
Benicia,* Solano, Cal	950	*Benton*, (*c. h.*,) Polk, Tenn	89
Benjamin, Lewis, Mo	12	Benton, La Fayette, Wis	86
Ben Lomond, Sevier, Ark	79	Benton Centre, Benton, Iowa	12
Bennet's Corners, Madison, N. Y	48	Benton Centre, Yates, N. Y	110
Bennett, Allegheny, Pa	72	Benton City, Audrian, Mo	12
Bennett's Bayou, Fulton, Ark	5	Benton Harbor,* Berrien, Mich	1,200
Bennettsburgh, Schuyler, N. Y	38	Benton Ridge, Hancock, Ohio	40
Bennett's Corners, Medina, Ohio	27	Benton's Ferry, Livingston, La	10
Bennett's Creek, Steuben, N. Y	17	Benton's Ferry, Marion, W. Va	69
Bennett's Landing, Tunica, Miss	12	Benton's Port, Van Buren, Iowa	300
Bennett's Mills, Ocean, N. J	18	*Bentonville*, (*c. h.*,) Benton, Ark	290
Bennett's River, Fulton, Ark	5	Bentonville, Fayette, Ind	77
Bennett's Station, Sumter, Ala	12	Bentonville, Adams, Ohio	72
Bennett's Switch, Miami, Ind	49	Bentonville, Warren, Va	12
Bennettstown, Christian, Ky	24	Bent's Fort, Bent, Colo	40
Bennettsville, Etowah, Ala	12	Benvenue, Dauphin, Pa	53
Bennettsville, Clarke, Ind	25	Benville, Jennings, Ind	23
Bennettsville, Chenango, N. Y	58	Benwood, Marshall, W. Va	140
Bennettsville, (*c. h.*,) Marlborough, S. C	800	*Benzonia*, (*c. h.*,) Benzie, Mich	190
Bennington, Edwards, Ill	12	Beowawe, Lander, Nev	12
Bennington, Switzerland, Ind	55	Berdan, Greene, Ill	57
Bennington, Ottawa, Kans	21	Berea, Franklin, Kans	22
Bennington, Shiawassee, Mich	84	Berea, Madison, Ky	110
Bennington, Hillsborough, N. H	170	Berea,* Cuyahoga, Ohio	1,200
Bennington, Wyoming, N. Y	46	Bergen, McLeod, Minn	6
Bennington, Morrow, Ohio	84	Bergen, Hudson, N. J	730
Bennington,* (*c. h.*,) Bennington, Vt	1,900	Bergen,* Genesee, N. Y	500
Bennington Centre, Bennington, Vt	230	Bergen Point, Hudson, N. J	250
		Berger, Franklin, Mo	120

* Money-order office.

BER | BEV

Berger's Store, Pittsylvania, Va....	$20	Bertrand, Berrien, Mich..........	$39
Bergholtz, Niagara, N. Y..........	50	Bertrandville, La Fayette, La......	12
Berkeley Springs, (c. h.,) Morgan, W.		Berville, St. Clair, Mich..........	24
Va.............................	360	Berwick, Warren, Ill.............	110
Berkey, Lucas, Ohio	11	Berwick, York, Me................	12
Berkley, Madison, Ala.............	11	Berwick, Seneca, Ohio...........	98
Berkley, Bristol, Mass............	30	Berwick, Columbia, Pa...........	650
Berkley's, Somerset, Pa	12	Berzelia, Columbia, Ga..........	85
Berkshire, Berkshire, Mass	82	Beta, Fulton, Ohio	4
Berkshire, Tioga, N. Y...........	140	Bethalto, Madison, Ill...........	230
Berkshire, Delaware, Ohio........	51	Bethania, Forsyth, N. C	38
Berkshire, Franklin, Vt	79	Bethany, New Haven, Conn	22
Berlin, Hartford, Conn	320	Bethany, Jefferson, Ga	36
Berlin, Sangamon, Ill	170	Bethany, Parke, Ind	14
Berlin, Clinton, Ind.............	20	*Bethany*,* (c. h.,) Harrison, Mo......	430
Berlin, Hardin, Iowa............	25	Bethany, Genesee, N. Y..........	49
Berlin, Bracken, Ky.............	37	Bethany, Butler, Ohio..........	100
Berlin, Worcester, Md...........	390	Bethany, Wayne, Pa	83
Berlin,* Worcester, Mass.........	81	Bethany, York, S. C	2
Berlin, Ottawa, Mich...........	260	Bethany,* Brooke, W. Va.........	420
Berlin, Steele, Minn...........	37	Bethel, Fairfield, Conn	710
Berlin, Camden, N. J...........	100	Bethel, Morgan, Ill.............	74
Berlin, Rensselaer, N. Y	220	Bethel, Wayne, Ind	26
Berlin, Holmes, Ohio...........	79	Bethel, Fayette, Iowa...........	33
Berlin, Somerset, Pa	300	Bethel, Marion, Kans...........	12
Berlin, Marshall, Tenn	13	Bethel, Bath, Ky...............	90
Berlin, Washington, Tex	57	Bethel,* Oxford, Me.............	730
Berlin, Washington, Vt	58	Bethel, Branch, Mich	16
Berlin, Southampton, Va	29	Bethel, Anoka, Minn	13
Berlin,* Green Lake, Wis........	1,700	Bethel, Shelby, Mo.............	90
Berlin Centre, Mahoning, Ohio	63	Bethel, Sullivan, N. Y	100
Berlin Centre, Wayne, Pa	14	Bethel, Clermont, Ohio..........	210
Berlin Cross Roads, Jackson, Ohio..	150	Bethel, Polk, Oreg	30
Berlin Falls, Coos, N. H..........	220	Bethel, Berks, Pa	65
Berlin Heights, Erie, Ohio........	290	Bethel, Giles, Tenn	12
Berlin Station, Erie, Ohio.........	75	Bethel, Anderson, Tex..........	6
Berlinsville, Northampton, Pa	18	Bethel, Windsor, Vt	580
Berlinville, Erie, Ohio..........	44	Bethel Corners, Cayuga, N. Y....	22
Bermudian, Adams, Pa...........	23	Bethel Springs, McNairy, Tenn	120
Bernadotte, Fulton, Ill	71	Bethesda, Belmont, Ohio	48
Bernalillo, Bernalillo, N. Mex	20	Bethesda, Lancaster, Pa..........	21
Bernard, Brunswick, N. C	12	Bethesda, Williamson, Tenn......	15
Bernard Station, Wharton, Tex....	12	Bethlehem, Litchfield, Conn.......	130
Bernardston, Franklin, Mass	510	Bethlehem, Clarke, Ind	31
Berne, Camden, Ga.............	12	Bethlehem, Wayne, Iowa.........	46
Berne, Dodge, Minn.............	10	Bethlehem, Henry, Ky	12
Berne, Albany, N. Y............	96	Bethlehem, Caroline, Md	28
Berne, Noble, Ohio.............	65	Bethlehem, Grafton, N. H........	300
Bernhard's Bay, Oswego, N. Y......	92	Bethlehem, Hunterdon, N. J	67
Bernville, Berks, Pa.............	170	Bethlehem,* Northampton, Pa	2,200
Berrien Centre, Berrien, Mich.....	17	Bethlehem, Clarendon, S. C	5
Berrien Springs,*(c. h.,) Berrien, Mich	540	Bethlehem Centre, Albany, N. Y ...	7
Berros Creek, San Luis Obispo, Cal.	12	Bethpage, McDonald, Mo..........	10
Berry, Sangamon, Ill	12	Betsey Lake, Grand Traverse, Mich.	16
Berry Hill, Rockingham, N. C......	12	Bettsville, Seneca, Ohio	45
Berrysburgh, Dauphin, Pa.........	160	*Beulah*, (c. h.) Bolivar, Miss........	12
Berry's Lick, Butler, Ky	14	Beulah, Johnson, N. C...........	5
Berry's Mill, Franklin, Me.........	59	Beulahville, King William, Va	12
Berry's Station, Harrison, Ky......	90	Bevans, Sussex, N. J	7
Berrysville, Highland, Ohio	68	Beverly, Adams, Ill	78
Berryton, Cass, Ill	16	Beverly, Christian, Ky	12
Berryvale, Siskiyou, Cal	12	Beverly, Essex, Mass.............	1,600
Berryville, Carroll, Ark	24	Beverly, Macon, Mo.............	12
Berryville, Wayne, Ky...........	21	Beverly, Burlington, N. J.........	570
Berryville, (c. h.,) Clarke, Va	540	Beverly,* Washington, Ohio.......	410
Bertram, Linn, Iowa.............	25	*Beverly*, (c. h.,) Randolph, W. Va....	120

* Money-order office.

Beverly Farms, Essex, Mass	$230	Big Prairie, Wayne, Ohio	$84
Beverly Station, Platte, Mo	12	*Big Rapids,* (*c. h.,*) Mecosta, Mich.	960
Bevier, Macon, Mo	170	Big Reedy, Edmonson, Ky	12
Bevis Tavern, Hamilton, Ohio	33	Big Renox, Cumberland, Ky	5
Bewleyville, Breckinridge, Ky	130	Big River, Pierce, Wis	12
Bible Grove, Clay, Ill	24	Big River Mills, St. Francois, Mo	31
Bible Grove, Scotland, Mo	13	Big Rock, Kane, Ill	47
Bickley's Mills, Russell, Va	6	Big Rock, Scott, Iowa	42
Bicknell, Knox, Ind	23	Big Rock, Harlan, Ky	2
Biddeford,* York, Me	2,500	Big Run, Athens, Ohio	83
Biddeford Pool, York, Me	70	Big Run, Jefferson, Pa	61
Bidwell's Bar, Butte, Cal	34	Big Sandy, Benton, Tenn	44
Biehle, Perry, Mo	21	Big Savanna, Dawson, Ga	21
Big Bar, Trinity, Cal	13	Big Sioux, Union, Dak	12
Big Beaver, Oakland, Mich	71	Big Skin Creek, Lewis, W. Va	20
Big Bend, Polk, Ark	5	Big Spring, Shelby, Ill	23
Big Bend, Avoyelles, La	25	Big Spring, Breckinridge, Ky	110
Big Bend, Venango, Pa	23	Big Spring, Ottawa, Mich	19
Big Bend, Calhoun, W. Va	12	Big Spring, Fillmore, Minn	31
Big Bend, Waukesha, Wis	39	Big Spring, Montgomery, Mo	20
Big Brook, Oneida, N. Y	3	Big Spring, Jackson, N. C	12
Big Buffalo, Harrison, W. Va	2	Big Spring, Cumberland, Pa	46
Big Cane, St. Landry, La	78	Big Spring, Meigs, Tenn	13
Big Clear Creek, Greenbrier, W. Va.	8	Big Spring, Adams, Wis	46
Big Clifty, Grayson, Ky	37	Big Spring Depot, Montgomery, Va.	65
Big Coon, Jackson, Ala	12	Big Springs, Douglas, Kans	65
Big Cove Tannery, Fulton, Pa	40	Big Springs, Chickasaw, Miss	12
Big Creek, Geneva, Ala	22	Big Springs, Logan, Ohio	30
Big Creek, Greene, Ark	30	Big Stone Gap, Wise, Va	7
Big Creek, Forsyth, Ga	40	Big Sycamore, Clay, W. Va	4
Big Creek, Mecosta, Mich	29	Big Thompson, Larimer, Colo	58
Big Creek, Texas, Mo	16	Big Timber, Riley, Kans	13
Big Creek, Steuben, N. Y	12	Big Tree, Greene, Pa	12
Big Creek, Edgefield, S. C	4	Big Tree Corners, Erie, N. Y	21
Big Creek, Cocke, Tenn	12	Big Trees, Calaveras, Cal	12
Big Creek, Monroe, Wis	28	Big Woods, Wright, Minn	48
Big Dry Creek, Fresno, Cal	12	Bijou Basin, El Paso, Colo	9
Bigelow, Holt, Mo	12	Billerica, Middlesex, Mass	330
Big Falls, Alamance, N. C	17	Billings, Dutchess, N. Y	12
Big Flats, Chemung, N. Y	230	Billingsly, Washington, Ark	19
Big Flats, Adams, Wis	12	Billingsville, Union, Ind	38
Big Foot Prairie, McHenry, Ill	52	Biloxi, Harrison, Miss	250
Big Fork, Polk, Ark	8	Bingamon, Marion, W. Va	12
Big Grove, Pottawattomie, Iowa	45	Bingham, Somerset, Me	170
Biggsville, Henderson, Ill	400	Bingham, Monroe, Ohio	12
Big Hill, Labette, Kans	45	Bingham Canyon, Salt Lake, Utah	12
Big Hill, Madison, Ky	17	Bingham Centre, Potter, Pa	4
Big Hollow, Greene, N. Y	9	Bingham's Mills, Tioga, N. Y	12
Big Indian, Cass, Ind	12	Binghamton, Solano, Cal	99
Big Island, Bedford, Va	130	*Binghamton,* (*c. h.,*) Broome, N. Y.	3,400
Big Labette, Neosho, Kans	12	Binghamton, Ontagamie, Wis	31
Big Lake, Sherburne, Minn	66	Binkley's Bridge, Lancaster, Pa	14
Bigler, Adams, Pa	29	Birchardville, Susquehanna, Pa	9
Big Lick, Stanly, N. C	5	Birch Cooley, Renville, Minn	21
Big Lick,* Roanoke, Va	360	Birch Lick, Jackson, Ky	12
Big Meadows, Plumas, Cal	12	Birch River, Nicholas, W. Va	12
Big Mound, Lee, Iowa	35	Birch Run, Saginaw, Mich	89
Big Muddy, Franklin, Ill	19	Birch Run Ville, Chester, Pa	12
Big Neck, Adams, Ill	23	Birch Tree, Shannon, Mo	12
Big Oak Flat, Tuolumne, Cal	96	Birch Wood, Hamilton, Tenn	42
Big Patch, Grant, Wis	45	Bird Hill, Carroll, Md	11
Big Pine, Inyo, Cal	12	Birdsall, Allegany, N. Y	3
Big Plain, Madison, Ohio	30	Birdsborough, Berks, Pa	380
Big Pond, Sanford, Ala	12	Bird's Bridge, Will, Ill	12
Big Pond, Bradford, Pa	12	Birdseye, Dubois, Ind	3
Big Prairie, Newaygo, Mich	12	Bird's Run, Guernsey, Ohio	20

* Money-order office.

BLA BLA

Birdston, Navarro, Tex.	$8	Black Oak Point, Hickory, Mo.	$16
Birdsville, Livingston, Ky.	33	Black Oak Ridge, Daviess, Ind.	33
Birk's City, Daviess, Ky.	13	Black Point, Marin, Cal.	15
Birmingham, Schuyler, Ill.	27	Black River, Jefferson, N. Y.	100
Birmingham, Miami, Ind.	12	Black River, Lorain, Ohio	59
Birmingham,* Van Buren, Iowa.	320	Black River, King, Wash.	12
Birmingham, Marshall, Ky.	100	Black River Chapel, New Hanover,	
Birmingham, Oakland, Mich.	550	N. C.	6
Birmingham, Burlington, N. J.	10	*Black River Falls,** (c. h.,) Jackson,	
Birmingham, Erie, Ohio.	240	Wis	1,200
Birmingham, Huntingdon, Pa.	200	Black Rock, Fairfield, Conn.	90
Biscayne, (c. h.,) Dade, Fla.	3	Black Rock, Baltimore, Md.	7
Bishop Creek, Mono, Cal.	81	Black Rock, Grant, W. Va.	14
Bishop Hill, Henry, Ill.	370	Blacks and Whites, Nottoway, Va.	290
Bishop's Head, Dorchester, Md.	15	Blacksburgh, Montgomery, Va.	250
Bishop's Station, Mason, Ill.	12	Black's Gap, Franklin, Pa.	12
Bishop's Store, Pulaski, Ga.	12	*Blackshear,** (c. h.,) Pierce, Ga.	12
Bishop Street, Jefferson, N. Y.	12	Black's Mills, Monmouth, N. J.	79
Bishopville, Worcester, Md.	12	Black Springs, Montgomery, Ark.	12
Bishopville, Morgan, Ohio.	25	Black Stocks, Chester, S. C.	98
Bishopville, Sumter, S. C.	89	Blackstone, Livingston, Ill.	12
Bismarck, Wabaunsee, Kans.	12	Blackstone, Worcester, Mass.	880
Bismarck, St. Francois, Mo.	77	Blacksville, Monongalia, W. Va.	38
Bismarck, Cuming, Nebr.	12	Black Swamp, Sandusky, Ohio.	22
Bissell's, Geauga, Ohio.	78	Black's Wells, Choctaw, Miss.	8
Bitter Creek, Carbon, Wyo.	12	*Blackville,* (c. h.,) Barnwell, S. C.	380
Biven's Grove, Marshall, Iowa.	10	Black Walnut, Ogle, Ill.	24
Black Ash, Crawford, Pa.	12	Black Walnut, Palo Alto, Iowa.	11
Black Bear, Klamath, Cal.	12	Black Walnut, Wyoming, Pa.	13
Blackberry, Kane, Ill.	12	Black Walnut, Halifax, Va.	69
Blackberry Ridge, Oceana, Mich.	24	Black Water, Morgan, Ky.	12
Blackberry Station, Kane, Ill.	430	Blackwater, Sussex, Del.	33
Black Bird, New Castle, Del.	37	Blackwell's Station, St. Francois,	
Black Brook, Clinton, N. Y.	130	Mo.	40
Black Brook, Polk, Wis.	12	Blackwoodtown, Camden, N. J.	140
Black Creek, Allegany, N. Y.	160	Bladenborough, Bladen, N. C.	15
Black Creek, Wilson, N. C.	44	Bladensburgh, Wapello, Iowa.	12
Black Creek, Holmes, Ohio.	34	Bladensburgh, Prince George's, Md.	170
Black Creek, Luzerne, Pa.	8	Bladensburgh, Knox, Ohio.	64
Black Diamond, Contra Costa, Cal.	12	Bladon Springs, Choctaw, Ala.	86
Black Earth, Dane, Wis	540	Blain, Perry, Pa.	120
Blackfish, Crittenden, Ark.	12	Blaine, Lawrence, Ky.	7
Blackfoot City, Deer Lodge, Mont.	340	Blain's Cross Roads, Grainger, Tenn	24
Black Fork, Tucker, W. Va.	4	Blair, Randolph, Ill.	34
Black Hawk, Carroll, Miss.	71	Blair, Barry, Mich.	14
Black Hawk, Beaver, Pa.	25	*Blair,* (c. h.,) Washington, Nebr.	510
Black Hawk, Sauk, Wis.	58	Blair, Hancock, W. Va.	9
Black Hawk Mills, Posey, Ind.	24	Blairsburgh, Hamilton, Iowa.	23
Black Hawk Point, Gilpin, Colo.	1,600	Blairstown,* Benton, Iowa.	870
Black Horse, Harford, Md.	43	Blairstown, Warren, N. J.	430
Black Horse, Chester, Pa.	52	*Blairsville,* (c. h.,) Union, Ga.	99
Blackinton, Berkshire, Mass.	240	Blairsville, Williamson, Ill.	5
Black Jack, Scott, Ark.	10	Blairsville, Posey, Ind.	30
Black Jack, Douglas, Kans.	92	Blairsville,* Indiana, Pa.	840
Black Jack, Hocking, Ohio.	18	Blairsville, York, S. C.	4
Black Jack, Robertson, Tenn.	19	Blakeley, Scott, Minn.	67
Black Jack Grove, Hopkins, Tex.	6	Blakeley, Kitsap, Wash.	10
Black Jack Springs, Fayette, Tex.	16	*Blakely,* (c. h.,) Early, Ga.	190
Black Lake, Muskegon, Mich.	50	Blakely, Stokes, N. C.	4
Blackleysville, Wayne, Ohio.	20	Blakesburgh, Wapello, Iowa.	180
Black Lick, Franklin, Ohio.	72	Blake's Ferry, Randolph, Ala.	10
Black Lick Station, Indiana, Pa.	85	Blakeville, Black Hawk, Iowa.	10
Blackman's Mills, Sampson, N. C.	3	Blakeville, Cheshire, N. H.	63
Black Mingo, Williamsburgh, S. C.	73	Blanchard, Piscataquis, Me.	23
Black Oak, Caldwell, Mo.	22	Blanchard, Centre, Pa.	12
Black Oak, Hopkins, Tex.	10	Blanchardville, La Fayette, Wis.	58

* Money-order office.

BLO

Blanchester, Clinton, Ohio........	$330
Blanco, (c. h.,) Blanco, Tex..........	47
Bland C. H., Bland, Va	10
Blandinsville,* McDonough, Ill....	390
Blandon, Berks, Pa...............	83
Blandville, (c. h.,) Ballard, Ky......	140
Blanford, Hampden, Mass.........	130
Blanket Hill, Armstrong, Pa......	7
Blauveltville, Rockland, N. Y......	71
Blawenburgh, Somerset, N. J......	67
Bleakwood, Newton, Tex...........	12
Bledsoe, Crittenden, Ark..........	12
Bleecker, Fulton, N. Y............	100
Blendon, Ottawa, Mich.............	62
Bliss, Miller, Mo.................	12
Blissfield, Lenawee, Mich.........	420
Bliven's Mills, McHenry, Ill.......	40
Blockville, Chautauqua, N. Y.....	22
Blodget Mills, Cortland, N. Y.....	73
Blodgett, Scott, Mo...............	12
Bloody Run, Bedford, Pa..........	380
Bloom, Cook, Ill..................	140
Bloom, Wood, Ohio................	38
Bloom Centre, Logan, Ohio........	38
Bloomer, Sebastian, Ark..........	7
Bloomer Centre, Montcalm, Mich..	20
Bloomery, Hampshire, W. Va......	25
Bloomfield, Sonoma, Cal..........	160
Bloomfield, Hartford, Conn.......	170
Bloomfield, Edgar, Ill............	100
Bloomfield,* (c. h.,) Greene, Ind.....	290
Bloomfield,* (c. h.,) Davis, Iowa....	900
Bloomfield, Nelson, Ky...........	75
Bloomfield, (c. h.,) Stoddard, Mo....	250
Bloomfield,* Essex, N. J..........	810
Bloomfield, Morrow, Ohio.........	39
Bloomfield, Crawford, Pa.........	28
Bloomfield, Essex, Vt............	6
Bloomfield, Loudoun, Va.........	39
Bloomfield, Walworth, Wis.......	140
Bloomingburgh, Sullivan, N. Y....	180
Bloomingburgh, Fayette, Ohio....	150
Bloomingdale, Du Page, Ill........	180
Bloomingdale, Parke, Ind.........	140
Bloomingdale, Van Buren, Mich...	72
Bloomingdale, Passaic, N. J.......	100
Bloomingdale, Essex, N. Y........	110
Bloomingdale, Jefferson, Ohio....	87
Bloomingdale, Luzerne, Pa........	12
Bloomingdale, Vernon, Wis.......	80
Blooming Grove, Franklin, Ind....	59
Blooming Grove, Linn, Kans......	220
Blooming Grove, Waseca, Minn....	26
Blooming Grove, Orange, N. Y....	340
Blooming Grove, Dane, Wis.......	21
Bloomingport, Randolph, Ind.....	33
Blooming Prairie, Steele, Minn....	12
Blooming Rose, Phelps, Mo.......	9
Bloomingsburgh, Fulton, Ind.....	20
Bloomington, Benton, Ark	12
Bloomington,* (c. h.,) McLean, Ill...	4,000
Bloomington,* (c. h.,) Monroe, Ind..	1,500
Bloomington, Alleghany, Md......	200
Bloomington, Hennepin, Minn.....	36
Bloomington, Macon, Mo.........	55
Bloomington, Clinton, Ohio......	68

BLU

Bloomington, Clearfield, Pa.......	$12
Bloomington, Tipton, Tenn........	31
Bloomington, Rich, Utah..........	12
Bloomington, Grant, Wis.........	290
Bloomington Ferry, Hennepin, Minn	39
Blooming Valley, Crawford, Pa....	110
Bloomingville, Erie, Ohio.........	14
Bloomsburgh,* (c. h.,) Columbia, Pa.	1,600
Bloomsburgh, Halifax, Va.........	24
Bloomsbury, Hunterdon, N. J.....	170
Bloomsdale, St. Genevieve, Mo.....	12
Bloom Switch, Scioto, Ohio.......	12
Bloomville, Delaware, N. Y........	85
Bloomville, Seneca, Ohio..........	110
Bloserville, Cumberland, Pa.......	22
Blossburgh,* Tioga, Pa............	600
Blossom Hill, Princess Anne, Va...	4
Blossom Prairie, Lamar, Tex......	12
Blossvale, Oneida, N. Y...........	41
Blount's Ferry, Columbia, Fla.....	10
Blount Springs, Blount, Ala.......	40
Blountsville, (c. h.,) Blount, Ala.....	35
Blountsville, Henry, Ind..........	72
Blountsville, (c. h.,) Sullivan, Tenn.	130
Blowing Rock, Watauga, N. C.....	12
Blue Ball, Butler, Ohio...........	31
Blue Ball, Lancaster, Pa..........	33
Blue Bell, Montgomery, Pa........	54
Blue Canyon, Placer, Cal.........	31
Blue Creek, Franklin, Ind........	11
Blue Creek, Adams, Ohio.........	23
Blue Eagle, Clay, Mo.............	12
Blue Earth City,* (c. h.,) Faribault, Minn	610
Blue Eye, Stone, Mo.............	12
Blue Grass, Vermilion, Ill.........	79
Blue Grass, Fulton, Ind..........	15
Blue Grass, Scott, Iowa..........	130
Blue Hill, Hancock, Me...........	280
Blue Hill Falls, Hancock, Me......	45
Blue Island, Cook, Ill............	440
Blue Island, (c. h.,) Saline, Nebr...	12
Blue Knob, Blair, Pa.............	12
Blue Lake, Muskegon, Mich.......	7
Blue Lick, Franklin, Ala..........	12
Blue Lick, Clarke, Ind...........	24
Blue Lick, Allen, Ohio...........	13
Blue Lick Springs, Nicholas, Ky...	73
Blue Mill, Jackson, Mo...........	20
Blue Mound, Livingston, Mo......	12
Blue Mound, Dane, Wis...........	20
Blue Mounds, Linn, Kans.........	4
Blue Mountain, Calhoun, Ala......	66
Blue Mountain, Izard, Ark........	21
Blue Mountain, Northampton, Pa..	25
Blue Point, Poweshiek, Iowa......	4
Blue Point, Suffolk, N. Y.........	120
Blue Pond, Cherokee, Ala.........	5
Blue Rapids, Marshall, Kans......	12
Blue Ridge, Shelby, Ind..........	24
Blue Ridge, Harrison, Mo........	23
Blue Ridge, Henderson, N. C......	28
Blue Ridge, Botetourt, Va........	66
Blue River, Grant, Wis...........	75
Blue Rock, Muskingum, Ohio......	57

* Money-order office.

BOL | BOO

Blue Rock, Chester, Pa	$91	Bolivar, Tuscarawas, Ohio	$170
Blue Spring, Gordon, Ga	12	Bolivar, Westmoreland, Pa	89
Blue Springs, Volusia, Fla	8	Bolivar,* (c. h.,) Hardeman, Tenn	450
Blue Springs, Jackson, Mo	24	Bolling's Landing, Buckingham, Va.	12
Blue Springs, Gage, Nebr	6	Bolster's Mills, Cumberland, Me	63
Blue Stone, Tazewell, Va	22	Bolton, Tolland, Conn	59
Blue Sulphur Springs, Greenbrier, W. Va	33	Bolton, Worcester, Mass	150
		Bolton, Harrison, Mo	12
Blue Valley, York, Nebr	12	Bolton, Warren, N. Y	99
Blue Wing, Granville, N. C	13	Bolton, Brunswick, N. C	12
Bluff, Fayette, Tex	61	Bolton, Chittenden, Vt	17
Bluff City, Livingston, Mo	8	Bolton's Depot, Hinds, Miss	340
Bluff Creek, Johnson, Ind	17	Boltonville, Cobb, Ga	15
Bluff Dale, Greene, Ill	12	Boltonville, Iowa, Iowa	12
Bluff Point, Jay, Ind	30	Boltonville, Orange, Vt	56
Bluff Point, Yates, N. Y	23	Boltonville, Washington, Wis	69
Bluff Point, Hickman, Tenn	12	Bolt's Fork, Boyd, Ky	6
Bluff Spring, Clay, Ala	13	Boman's Bluff, Henderson, N. C	1
Bluff Spring, Talbot, Ga	10	Bombay, Franklin, N. Y	78
Bluff Springs, Escambia, Fla	12	Bon Accord, Johnston, Iowa	19
Bluffton, Yell, Ark	12	Bonaparte,* Van Buren, Iowa	410
Bluffton,* (c. h.,) Wells, Ind	560	Bon Aqua, Hickman, Tenn	6
Bluffton, Winneshiek, Iowa	47	Bonbrook, Franklin, Va	23
Bluffton, Muskegon, Mich	77	Bonchea, St. Croix, Wis	17
Bluffton, Montgomery, Mo	59	Bond's Station, Shelby, Tenn	12
Bluffton,* Allen, Ohio	230	Bond's Village, Hampden, Mass	140
Bluffton, Beaufort, S. C	57	Bonduel, Shawanaw, Wis	42
Blumfield, Saginaw, Mich	19	Bondville, Bennington, Vt	88
Blumfield Junction, Saginaw, Mich.	38	Bone Camp, Madison, N. C	4
Blytheville, Jasper, Mo	29	Bone Cave, Van Buren, Tenn	7
Boalsburgh, Centre, Pa	120	Bone Creek, Ritchie, W. Va	12
Boardman, Mahoning, Ohio	42	Bone Gap, Edwards, Ill	32
Boardman, St. Croix, Wis	24	Bonfil's Station, St. Louis, Mo	16
Boar's Head, Rockingham, N. H	12	Bonham, (c. h.,) Fannin, Tex	590
Boatland, Fentress, Tenn	10	Bonhomme, (c. h.,) Bonhomme, Dak.	22
Boaz, Graves, Ky	12	Bonhomme, St. Louis, Mo	4
Boaz, Richland, Wis	16	Bonn, Washington, Ohio	33
Bodenham, Giles, Tenn	15	Bonneau's Depot, Charleston, S. C.	120
Bodinesville, Lycoming, Pa	29	Bonner, Jackson, La	16
Body Camp, Bedford, Va	7	Bonnet Carre, St. John Baptist, La.	20
Boerne (c. h.,) Kendall, Tex	71	Bonnie Brook, Butler, Pa	11
Boeuf Creek, Franklin, Mo	17	Bonny Eagle, Cumberland, Me	45
Boggstown, Shelby, Ind	71	Bono, Douglas, Ill	12
Boggsville, Roane, W. Va	3	Bono, Lawrence, Ind	10
Boggy Depot, Choctaw N., Ind. T.	20	Bono, Washington, Nebr	7
Bogue, Columbus, N. C	20	Bonsack's Roanoke, Va	220
Bogue Chitto, Lincoln, Miss	38	Bontear, St. Francois, Mo	12
Bohemia, La Crosse, Wis	50	Bonus, Boone, Ill	24
Bohon, Mercer, Ky	17	Bonwell, Edgar, Ill	23
Boiling Springs, Cumberland, Pa	87	Booker's Mills, Tyler, W. Va	12
Boilston, Henderson, N. C	12	Boone, Boone, Ark	12
Bois Brule, Perry, Mo	12	Boone, Dallas, Iowa	59
Bois D'Arc, Greene, Mo	12	Boone, (c. h.,) Watauga, N. C	26
Boise City,* (c. h.,) Ada, Idaho	1,800	Boone Furnace, Carter, Ky	12
Boistfort, Lewis, Wash	11	Boonesborough,* (c. h.,) Boone, Iowa.	1,200
Boke's Creek, Union, Ohio	28	Boone's Mill, Franklin, Va	24
Bolckow, Andrew, Mo	12	Booneville, Scott, Ark	13
Bold Spring, Franklin, Ga	19	Booneville, Pueblo, Colo	150
Boles, Scott, Ark	12	Booneville, (c. h.,) Owsley, Ky	110
Boles, Franklin, Mo	77	Booneville, (c. h.,) Prentiss, Miss	250
Bolinas, Marin, Cal	48	Booneville, Yadkin, N. C	9
Bolington, Loudoun, Va	22	Booneville, Clinton, Pa	12
Bolivar, Frederick, Md	28	Booneville, Lincoln, Tenn	12
Bolivar, Bolivar, Miss	68	Boon Grove, Porter, Ind	14
Bolivar,* (c. h.,) Polk, Mo	280	Boon Hill, Johnston, N. C	36
Bolivar, Allegany, N. Y	120	Boonsborough, Washington, Ark	220

Boonsborough, Washington, Md...	$320	Bowensburgh, Hancock, Ill........	$290
Boon's Creek, Washington, Tenn..	10	Bowen's Corners, Oswego, N. Y	15
Boon Spring, Clinton, Iowa	7	Bowen's Mills, Barry, Mich........	35
Boonton,* Morris, N. J.............	880	Bowen's Prairie, Jones, Iowa	29
Boonville, (*c. h.,*) Warrick, Ind	290	Bowenville, Carroll, Ga....	23
Boonville, (*c. h.,*) Cooper, Mo..... ..	2,000	Bowenville, Fauquier, Va........ ...	140
Boonville,* Oneida, N. Y...........	1,100	Bower, Clearfield, Pa...............	36
Boot, Richland, Ill.................	12	Bower Hill, Washington, Pa	17
Booth Bay, Lincoln, Me............	310	Bower's City, Carroll, Mo	12
Boothby Hill, Harford, Md........	12	Bower's Mills, Lawrence, Mo	14
Booth Corner, Delaware, Pa.......	17	Bower's Station, Berks, Pa	46
Boothsville, Marion, W. Va.......	84	Bowerston, Harrison, Ohio	100
Bordentown,* Burlington, N. J....	1,900	Bowersville, Hart, Ga.............	5
Border Plains, Webster, Iowa......	40	Bowersville, Greene, Ohio....... ..	87
Bordley, Union, Ky...............	11	Bowerville, Jefferson, Nebr........	12
Bordoville, Franklin, Vt...........	26	Bowling Brook, St. Genevieve, Mo.	12
Borodino, Onondaga, N. Y........	69	Bowling Green, Fayette, Ill.......	3
Boscawen, Merrimack, N. H.......	210	*Bowling Green,* (*c. h.,*) Clay, Ind ...	330
Boscobel, Westchester, N. Y.......	58	*Bowling Green,* (*c. h.,*) Warren, Ky.	2,000
Boscobel,* Grant, Wis.............	1,000	*Bowling Green,* (*c. h.,*) Pike, Mo	300
Bosqueville, McLennan, Tex	12	Bowling Green,* Wood, Ohio......	450
Bossardsville, Monroe, Pa..........	25	*Bowling Green,* (*c. h.,*) Caroline, Va..	240
Bostick, Jefferson, Ga.............	40	Bowlusville, Clark, Ohio..........	60
Bostick's Mills, Richmond, N. C....	19	*Bowman's Creek, Wyoming, Pa...	31
Boston, Thomas, Ga................	180	Bowman's Mills, Rockingham, Va..	48
Boston, Wayne, Ind...............	46	Bowmansville, Erie, N. Y.........	84
Boston, Nelson, Ky	30	Bowmansville, Lancaster, Pa......	27
BOSTON,* (*c. h.,*) Suffolk, Mass...	4,000	Bowne, Kent, Mich...............	41
Boston, Erie, N. Y.................	130	Boxborough, Middlesex, Mass. ...	36
Boston, Allegheny, Pa.............	09	Boxford, Essex, Mass......	120
Boston, (*c. h.,*) Bowie, Tex........	160	Boxford, DeKalb, Mo.............	12
Boston, Culpeper, Va..............	22	Boxley, Hamilton, Ind............	100
Boston Corner, Columbia, N. Y.....	120	Box Spring, Talbot, Ga............	25
Boston Mills, Linn, Oreg.........	12	Boxville, Union, Ky..............	10
Boston Station, Pendleton, Ky.....	110	Boyd, Dallas, Mo.................	5
Boston Store, Montgomery, Ind....	29	Boyd Lake, Piscataquis, Me.......	12
Bostwick Lake, Kent, Mich........	21	Boyd's Corner, Putnam, N. Y......	16
Boswell, Mahoning, Ohio..........	17	Boyd's Landing, Hardin, Tenn....	12
Boswell's, Fluvanna, Va...........	150	Boyd's Mill, Wise, Tex...........	12
Botany, Shelby, Iowa.............	20	Boyd's Mills, Coshocton, Ohio.....	26
Botavia, Jefferson, Iowa...........	230	Boyd's Station, Harrison, Ky......	140
Botetourt Springs, Roanoke, Va....	100	Boyd's Switch, Jackson, Ala......	12
Botland, Nelson, Ky	12	Boydston's Mills, Kosciusko, Ind...	21
Bouckville, Madison, N. Y........	150	Boydsville, Graves, Ky...........	38
Boulder, (*c. h.,*) Boulder, Colo	220	*Boydton,* (*c. h.,*) Mecklenburgh, Va..	300
Boulder Valley, Jefferson, Mont....	100	Boyer River, Crawford, Iowa......	47
Boundary, Jay, Ind....	26	Boyerstown, Berks, Pa............	230
Boundbrook, Somerset, N. J.... ...	510	Boykin's Depot, Southampton, Va..	130
Bounty Land, Oconee, S. C	12	Boylan's Grove, Butler, Iowa.....	66
Bourbon, Marshall, Ind............	400	Boyler's Mill, Morgan, Mo........	18
Bourbon, Crawford, Mo............	33	Boyleston, Henry, Iowa...........	12
Bourbonnais Grove, Kankakee, Ill .	87	Boylston, Worcester, Mass.........	53
Bourneville, Ross, Ohio......... ...	120	Boylston Centre, Worcester, Mass..	69
Boutonville, Westchester, N. Y.....	19	Boylston Centre, Oswego, N. Y....	12
Boutte, St. Charles, La............	140	Boyne, Charlevoix, Mich.........	12
Bovina, Tama, Iowa	14	Boynton, Tazewell, Ill............	36
Bovina, Warren, Miss.............	28	*Bozeman,* (*c. h.,*) Gallatin, Mont....	590
Bovina, Delaware, N. Y............	27	Bozrah, New London, Conn.......	110
Bovina Valley, Delaware, N. Y.....	51	Bozrahville, New London, Conn....	140
Bovine, Gibson, Ind...............	10	Braceville, Grundy, Ill...........	230
Bow, Merrimack, N. H.............	12	Braceville, Trumbull, Ohio........	86
Bowdoin, Sagadahoc, Me..........	15	Bracken, Huntingdon, Ind........	12
Bowdoin Centre, Sagadahoc, Me ...	36	Brackney, Susquehanna, Pa.......	28
Bowdoinham, Sagadahoc, Me	510	Braddock's Field, Allegheny, Pa...	320
Bowdon, Carroll, Ga..............	85	Braddyville, Page, Iowa...........	95
Bowen, Grenada, Miss.............	12	Braden's Knobs, Bledsoe, Tenn....	13

* Money-order office

BRA   BRE

Braden Station, Fayette, Tenn....	$12	Brandonville, Preston, W. Va......	$89
Bradenville, Westmoreland, Pa....	62	Brandt, Miami, Ohio............	57
Bradford, Stark, Ill..............	150	Brandtwood, Starke, Ind........	16
Bradford, Harrison, Ind..........	20	Brandy Camp, Elk, Pa..........	12
Bradford, Chickasaw, Iowa........	236	Brandy Station, Culpeper, Va.....	64
Bradford, Bracken, Ky...........	24	Brandywine, Prince George's, Md..	41
Bradford, Penobscot, Me	120	Brandywine Manor, Chester, Pa...	62
Bradford, Essex, Mass.........'....	380	Brandywine Summit, Delaware, Pa.	64
Bradford, Merrimack, N. H....	340	Branford, New Haven, Conn......	830
Bradford, Steuben, N. Y......	120	Branson, San Diego, Cal.........	12
Bradford, Miami, Ohio......	12	Brant, Erie, N. Y...............	93
Bradford, McKean, Pa	250	Brant, Calumet, Wis...........	19
Bradford, * Orange, Vt...........	1,000	Brantford, Sherburne, Minn......	16
Bradford Centre, Orange, Vt	17	Brantingham, Lewis, N. Y........	12
Bradford Springs, Sumter, S. C....	12	Brashear, St. Mary's, La.........	84
Bradfordsville, Marion, Ky	45	Brasher Falls, St. Lawrence, N. Y.	300
Bradley, Bradley, Ark............	16	Brasher Iron Works, St. Lawrence,	
Bradley, Jackson, Ill.............	18	N. Y..........................	56
Bradley, Allegan, Mich..........	90	Brassfield, Wake, N. C..........	12
Bradleyville, Taney, Mo..........	1	Bratsberg, Fillmore, Minn........	120
Bradrickville, Lawrence, Ohio	12	Brattleborough,* Windham, Vt...	2,300
Bradshaw, Giles, Tenn	12	Bratton, Nemaha, Nebr..........	12
Bradtville, Grant, Wis	19	Bratton's Mills, Robertson, Ky....	8
Brady, Kalamazoo, Mich....	300	Braxton C. H., Braxton, W. Va....	62
Brady, Indiana, Pa..............	190	Bray's Mills, Bartholomew, Ind....	10
Brady's, Richland, Wis..........	11	Brazil,* Clay, Ind................	1,000
Brady's Bend, Armstrong, Pa..... ..	560	Brazito, Cole, Mo...............	20
Brady's Mill, Alleghany, Md.......	71	Brazos Santiago, Cameron, Texas..	120
Bradyville, Adams, Ohio....	20	Brazoria, (c. h.,) Brazoria, Texas..	180
Bradyville, Cannon, Tenn	12	Breakabeen, Schoharie, N. Y......	80
Brafford's Store, Knox, Ky........	12	Breakneck, Butler, Pa...........	78
Braggs, Lowndes, Ala...........	12	Breathedsville, Washington, Md..	89
Braggville, Middlesex, Mass	58	Breaux Bridge, St. Martin's, La...	64
Braidwood, Will, Ill....	220	Breckinridge, (c. h.,) Summit, Colo..	40
Brainard's, Warren, N. J.........	110	Breckinridge, Caldwell, Mo.......	·290
Brainerd, Rensselaer, N. Y........	110	Breckinridge, Vernon, Wis........	21
Braintree, Norfolk, Mass.........	170	Breckville, Madison, Wis.........	12
Braintree, Orange, Vt	83	Breeding's, Adair, Ky...........	16
Braman's Corners, Schenectady,		Breedsville, Van Buren, Mich.....	190
N. Y...........................	39	Breese, Greene, Ill..............	56
Bramlette, Gallatin, Ky	28	Breesport, Chemung, N. Y........	120
Branch, Paulding, Ga	12	Breinigsville, Lehigh, Pa.........	63
Branch, Manitowoc, Wis	10	Bremen, Randolph, Ill...........	42
Branch Dale, Schuylkill, Pa.......	110	Bremen, Marshall, Ind...........	160
Branch Junction, Westmoreland, Pa	59	Bremen, Muhlenburgh, Ky.......	43
Branchport, Yates, N. Y	200	Bremen, Fairfield, Ohio..........	220
Branch Shore, Monmouth, N. J.....	270	Bremo Bluff, Fluvanna, Va........	82
Branch's Store, Duplin, N. C	12	Bremond, Robertson, Texas.......	310
Branchville, St. Clair, Ala.........	13	Brenford, Kent, Del..............	22
Branchville, Drew, Ark	51	Brenham,* (c. h.,) Washington, Tex.	2,800
Branchville, Prince George's, Md ..	20	Brentsville, (c. h.,) Prince William,	
Branchville, Sussex, N. J.......	250	Va................................	40
Branchville, Orangeburgh, S. C	130	Brentwood, Rockingham, N. H....	66
Branchville, Southampton, Va.....	38	Brentwood, Suffolk, N. Y.........	77
Brandenburgh, (c. h.,) Meade, Ky....	96	Brentwood, Williamson, Tenn.....	90
Brandon, DeKalb, Ala............	12	Bretzville, Dubois, Ind...........	11
Brandon, Buchanan, Iowa.........	51	Brevard, (c. h.,) Transylvania, N. C.	20
Brandon, Oakland, Mich......	20	Brewer, Penobscot, Me...........	420
Brandon, Douglas, Minn......	12	Brewer's Mills, Marshall, Ky......	26
Brandon,* (c. h.,) Rankin, Miss	610	Brewersville, Jennings, Ind.......	38
Brandon, Knox, Ohio............	50	Brewerton, Onondaga, N. Y.......	170
Brandon,* Rutland, Vt...........	1,400	Brewerton, Laurens, S. C.........	4
Brandon, Prince George, Va.......	100	Brewer Village, Penobscot, Me....	180
Brandon, Fond du Lac, Wis	370	Brewerville, Randolph, Ill........	12
Brandon Church, Prince George, Va.	14	Brewster, Barnstable, Mass.......	230
Brandonville, Schuylkill, Pa	37	Brewster's Station, Putnam, N. Y..	980

* Money-order office.

BRI

BRO

Brewton, Escambia, Ala............	$12
Brick Church, Guilford, N. C......	3
Brick Church, Giles, Tenn.........	46
Brickerville, Lancaster, Pa........	32
Brickland, Lunenburgh, Va.........	13
Brick Meeting House, Cecil, Md...	150
Brick Mill, Blount, Tenn..........	12
Bricksburgh, Ocean, N. J..........	690
Bricksville, Cuyahoga, Ohio.......	140
Brickton, Cook, Ill...............	10
Brickville, Merced, Cal...........	12
Bridgeborough, Burlington, N. J..	60
Bridge Creek, Carroll, Mo........	12
Bridge Creek, Wasco, Oreg........	12
Bridgehampton, Suffolk, N. Y.....	370
Bridgeport, Jackson, Ala..........	140
Bridgeport, (c. h.,) Mono, Cal......	10
Bridgeport,* Fairfield, Conn......	4,000
Bridgeport, Lawrence, Ill.........	340
Bridgeport, Marion, Ind..........	120
Bridgeport, Jackson, Iowa........	12
Bridgeport, Franklin, Ky.........	60
Bridgeport, Frederick, Md........	13
Bridgeport, Warren, Mo..........	12
Bridgeport, Gloucester, N. J......	130
Bridgeport, Madison, N. Y.......	61
Bridgeport, Belmont, Ohio........	870
Bridgeport, Polk, Oreg...........	22
Bridgeport, Montgomery, Pa.....	220
Bridgeport, Cocke, Tenn.........	12
Bridgeport, Harrison, W. Va......	160
Bridgeport, Crawford, Wis........	66
Bridgeport Centre, Saginaw, Mich.	110
Bridger Station, Uintah, Wyo.....	12
Bridgeton, Parke, Ind............	30
Bridgeton,* Cumberland, Me......	630
Bridgeton, Newaygo, Mich........	49
Bridgeton, St. Louis, Mo.........	110
Bridgeton,* (c. h.,) Cumberland, N.J.	2,000
Bridgetown, Caroline, Md........	8
Bridge Valley, Bucks, Pa.........	43
Bridgeville, Pickens, Ala.........	88
Bridgeville, Sussex, Del..........	350
Bridgeville, Gratiot, Mich........	53
Bridgeville, Warren, N. J........	91
Bridgeville, Sullivan, N. Y.......	45
Bridgeville, Muskingum, Ohio....	31
Bridgewater, Litchfield, Conn.....	200
Bridgewater, Aroostook, Me......	99
Bridgewater,* Plymouth, Mass....	1,100
Bridgewater, Grafton, N. H......	52
Bridgewater, Oneida, N. Y.......	180
Bridgewater, Burke, N. C........	25
Bridgewater, Williams, Ohio......	18
Bridgewater, Bucks, Pa..........	91
Bridgewater, Windsor, Vt........	220
Bridgewater, Rockingham, Va....	330
Bridle Creek, Grayson, Va........	10
Bridport, Addison, Vt...........	230
Briensburgh, Marshall, Ky........	12
Brier Creek, Columbia, Pa........	12
Brierfield, Bibb, Ala.............	200
Brier Hill, St. Lawrence, N. Y....	91
Briggsville, Luzerne, Pa..........	23
Briggsville, Marquette, Wis.......	67
BrighamCity,(c. h.,) Box Elder, Utah.	400
Bright, Dearborn, Indiana........	$18
Brighton, Sacramento, Cal........	71
Brighton, Macoupin, Ill...........	940
Brighton, La Grange, Ind........	15
Brighton,* Washington, Iowa.....	290
Brighton, Somerset, Maine........	36
Brighton, Montgomery, Md.......	55
Brighton,* Middlesex, Mass......	1,000
Brighton, Livingston, Mich.......	330
Brighton, Polk, Mo..............	18
Brighton, Monroe, N. Y.........	230
Brighton, Lorain, Ohio..........	44
Brighton, Beaufort, S. C........	14
Brighton, Kenosha, Wis.........	14
Brighton Station, Lincoln, Tenn...	8
Bright Star, Hopkins, Tex.......	210
Brightwood, Washington, D. C	25
Brillion, Calumet, Wis...........	13
Brimfield,* Peoria, Ill	340
Brimfield, Noble, Ind	200
Brimfield, Hampden, Mass.......	360
Brimfield, Portage, Ohio	44
Brindletown, Burke, N. C	10
Brinkerton, Clarion, Pa	19
Brinkley, Monroe, Ark	12
Brinkleyville, Halifax, N. C	12
Brinley's Station, Preble, Ohio.....	54
Brinsonville, Burke, Ga	12
Brinton, Champaign, Ohio	12
Brinton, Allegheny, Pa..........	12
Briscoe, Sullivan, N. Y	12
Briscoe Run, Wood, W. Va	11
Bristersburgh, Fauquier, Va.....	21
Bristoe Station, Prince William, Va.	64
Bristol,* Hartford, Conn	1,400
Bristol, (c. h.,) Liberty, Fla	20
Bristol, Kendall, Ill............	170
Bristol, Elkhart, Ind............	570
Bristol, Worth, Iowa............	74
Bristol, Lincoln, Me	140
Bristol, Anne Arundel, Md.......	100
Bristol,* Grafton, N. H	690
Bristol, Ontario, N. Y	110
Bristol, Morgan, Ohio	22
Bristol,* Bucks, Pa.............	1,800
Bristol,* (c. h.,) Bristol, R. I......	1,500
Bristol,* Sullivan, Tenn.........	910
Bristol, Addison, Vt	460
Bristol, Kenosha, Wis..........	140
Bristol Centre, Ontario, N. Y	81
Bristol Station, Kendall, Ill	210
Bristolville, Trumbull, Ohio......	120
Bristoria, Greene, Pa...........	12
Bristow Station, Warren, Ky	120
British Hollow, Grant, Wis......	83
Brittain, Rutherford, N. C.......	7
Brittain's, Pulaski, Mo	12
Britton, Woodruff, Ark.........	12
Britton's Neck, Marion, S. C	19
Britt's Landing, Perry, Tenn	37
Broadalbin, Fulton, N. Y	340
Broad Axe, Montgomery, Pa......	20
Broad Brook, Hartford, Conn.....	250
Broad Creek, Queen Anne, Md.....	83
Broad Creek Neck, Talbot, Md.....	10
Broad Ford, Fayette, Pa	160

* Money-order office.

BRO   BRO

Broadford, Smyth, Va	$19	Brooklyn, Anne Arundel, Md	$18
Broadhead, Rockcastle, Ky	12	Brooklyn,* Jackson, Mich	380
Broad Mountain, Schuylkill, Pa	41	Brooklyn, Hennepin, Minn	29
Broad Ripple, Marion, Ind	13	Brooklyn, Harrison, Mo	35
Broad Run, Frederick, Md	14	*Brooklyn,* (c. h.,) Kings, N. Y	4,000
Broad Run Station, Fauquier, Va	74	Brooklyn, Cuyahoga, Ohio	140
Broad Shoals, Polk, Tenn	5	Brooklyn, Susquehanna, Pa	170
Broad Top, Huntingdon, Pa	140	Brooklyn, Halifax, Va	16
Broadway, Warren, N. J	75	Brooklyn, Green, Wis	140
Broadway, Union, Ohio	100	Brooklyn Village, Cuyahoga, Ohio.	120
Broadway Depot, Rockingham, Va.	110	Brook Neal, Campbell, Va	29
Broadwell, Logan, Ill	99	Brooks, Waldo, Me	180
Broadwell, Harrison, Ky	17	Brooks' Grove, Livingston, N. Y	46
Brock, Darke, Ohio	7	Brookside, Osceola, Mich	16
Brockett's Bridge, Fulton, N. Y	150	Brookside, Morris, N. J	89
Brockport,* Monroe, N. Y	1,900	Brookston, White, Ind	360
Brocktown, Pike, Ark	4	Brooks' Vale, New Haven, Conn	35
Brockway, St. Clair, Mich	110	Brooksville, Blount, Ala	12
Brockway, Stearns, Minn	10	Brooksville, Hancock, Me	53
Brockway Centre, St. Clair, Mich	88	Brooksville, Addison, Vt	96
Brockway's Mills, Piscataquis, Me	20	Brook Vale, Prince William, Va	12
Brockwayville, Jefferson, Pa	200	Brookville, Ogle, Ill	60
Brocton, Chautauqua, N. Y	410	*Brookville,* (c. h.,) Franklin, Ind	760
Brodbecks, York, Pa	9	Brookville, Jefferson, Iowa	30
Brodhead, Allegheny, Pa	25	Brookville, Saline, Kans	12
Brodhead,* Green, Wis	810	*Brookville,* (c. h.,) Bracken, Ky	110
Brodheadsville, Monroe, Pa	44	Brookville, Montgomery, Md	150
Brodie's Landing, Decatur, Tenn	12	Brookville, Noxubee, Miss	320
Broken Arrow, St. Clair, Ala	11	Brookville, Granville, N. C	7
Brokenburgh, Spottsylvania, Va	17	Brookville, Montgomery, Ohio	53
Broken Straw, Chautauqua, N. Y	63	*Brookville,* (c. h.,) Jefferson, Pa	1,000
Broken Sword, Crawford, Ohio	43	Brookville, St. Croix, Wis	150
Bronson, Levy, Fla	12	Broomall, Delaware, Pa	12
Bronson's Prairie, Branch, Mich	540	Broome Centre, Schoharie, N. Y	28´
Bronxville, Westchester, N. Y	190	Broomtown, Cherokee, Ala	7
Brook, Newton, Ind	47	Brosley, Cass, Mo	12
Brookdale, Susquehanna, Pa	39	Brotherton, St. Louis, Mo	8
Brookeland, Sabine, Tex	5	Brothertown, Calumet, Wis	49
Brookfield, Fairfield, Conn	300	Brotzmanville, Warren, N. J	1
Brookfield, Shelby, Ind	51	Brower, Berks, Pa	31
Brookfield, Clinton, Iowa	49	Brower's Mills, Randolph, N. C	11
Brookfield, Worcester, Mass	610	Browne Hill, Wythe, Va	39
Brookfield, Eaton, Mich	21	Brownfield, Oxford, Me	200
Brookfield,* Linn, Mo	1,400	Brownhelm, Lorain, Ohio	88
Brookfield, Carroll, N. H	23	Brown Hill, Crawford, Pa	9
Brookfield, Madison, N. Y	250	Browning, Schuyler, Ill	25
Brookfield, Trumbull, Ohio	200	Browning, Carroll, Iowa	12
Brookfield, Tioga, Pa	14	Browningsville, Bracken, Ky	12
Brookfield, Orange, Vt	180	Brownington, Butler, Pa	24
Brookfield Centre, Fairfield, Conn	100	Brownington, Orleans, Vt	75
Brookfield Centre, Waukesha, Wis.	65	Brownsborough, Madison, Ala	91
Brookhaven, (c. h.,) Lincoln, Miss	940	Brownsborough, Oldham, Ky	52
Brookland, Potter, Pa	42	Brownsborough, Washington, Tenn.	24
Brooklandville, Baltimore, Md	24	Brownsborough, Henderson, Texas.	12
Brooklin, Hancock, Me	130	Brownsburgh, Hendricks, Ind	150
Brookline, Jackson, La	16	Brownsburgh, Bucks, Pa	58
Brookline, Norfolk, Mass	1,900	Brownsburgh, Rockbridge, Va	180
Brookline, Hillsborough, N. H	130	Brown's Corners, Huntington, Ind.	12
Brooklyn, Conecuh, Ala	38	Brown's Cove, Albemarle, Va	8
Brooklyn, Alameda, Cal	280	Brown's Creek, Harrison, W. Va	17
Brooklyn, (c. h.,) Windham, Conn	590	Brownsdale, Butler, Pa	15
Brooklyn, Schuyler, Ill	44	Brown's Mills, Davis, Iowa	12
Brooklyn, Morgan, Ind	88	Brown's Mills, Muskegon, Mich	12
Brooklyn,* Poweshiek, Iowa	500	Brown's Mills, Burlington, N. J	6
Brooklyn, Linn, Kans	22	Brown's Mills, Washington, Ohio	31
Brooklyn, Butler, Ky	12	Brown's Mills, Franklin, Pa	54

* Money-order office.

BRU · BUC

Brownsport Furnace, Decatur, Tenn	$12	Brush Valley, Indiana, Pa........	$85
Brown's Station, Preble, Ohio.....	12	Brushville, Waushara, Wis.......	12
Brown's Store, Northumberland, Va	12	Brushy Creek, Anderson, S. C.....	6
Brownstown, Fayette, Ill.........	12	Brushy Fork, Douglas, Ill........	23
Brownstown, (c. h.,) Jackson, Ind .	360	Brushy Prairie, La Grange, Ind...	22
Brownstown, Wayne, Mich...... .	210	Brushy Run, Pendleton, W. Va...	12
Brown's Valley, Yuba, Cal........	160	Brussels, Door, Wis...........	12
Brown's Valley, Montgomery, Ind.	29	Bruynswick, Ulster, N. Y........	34
Brownsville, Yuba, Cal..........	20	*Bryan,* (c. h.,) Williams, Ohio	1,500
Brownsville, Paulding, Ga........	12	*Bryan,* (c. h.,) Brazos, Tex.........	2,000
Brownsville, Union, Ind.........	110	Bryan, Uintah, Wyo...........	380
Brownsville, (c. h.,) Edmonson, Ky..	24	Bryansville, York, Pa...........	20
Brownsville, Piscataquis, Me......	170	Bryant, Fulton, Ill...........	97
Brownsville, Washington, Md.....	57	Bryantown, Charles, Md........	90
Brownsville, Cass, Mich.........	74	Bryantsburgh, Jefferson, Ind.....	16
Brownsville, Houston, Minn.... ..	340	Bryant's Creek, Monroe, Ind	16
Brownsville, Saline, Mo.........	320	Bryant's Pond, Oxford, Me........	160
Brownsville, Granville, N. C......	5	Bryantsville, Lawrence, Ind.......	· 16
Brownsville, Licking, Ohio	140	Bryantsville, Garrard, Ky.........	160
Brownsville, Linn, Oreg...... ...	150	Bucatunna, Wayne, Miss.........	65
Brownsville,* Fayette, Pa...... ...	1,200	*Buchanan,* (c. h.,) Haralson, Ga....	25
Brownsville, Marlborough, S. C...	10	Buchanan, Lawrence, Ky........	21
Brownsville, (c.h.,) Haywood, Tenn	1,400	Buchanan,* Berrien, Mich........	1,200
Brownsville, (c.h.,) Cameron, Tex..	3,000	Buchanan, Bollinger, Mo....	30
Brownsville, Windsor, Vt........	180	Buchanan, Granville, N. C.......	10
Browntown, Bradford, Pa........	17	Buchanan, Perry, Ohio...........	20
Brownville, Mitchell, Iowa.......	31	Buchanan, Allegheny, Pa.........	1,800
Brownville, (c. h.,) Nemaha, Nebr..	1,300	Buchanan, Botetourt, Va........	190
Brownville, Jefferson, N. Y........	280	Buck, Lancaster, Pa............	40
Brownwood, (c. h.,) Brown, Tex....	12	Buck Branch, Jasper, Mo.......	12
Bruceport, Chehalis, Wash........	39	Buck Creek, Bremer, Iowa......	66
Bruce's Lake, Fulton, Ind........	23	Buck Creek, Richland, Wis..... ..	12
Bruceton Mills, Preston, W. Va...	72	Buck Eye, Yolo, Cal............	75
Bruceville, Bullock, Ala......	7	Buckeye, Garrard, Ky....	12
Bruceville, La Salle, Ill..........	7	Buckeye Cottage, Perry, Ohio.....	24
Bruceville, Knox, Ind...........	130	Buckeye Cove, Pocahontas, W. Va.	11
Bruceville, Carroll, Md......	22	Buckeystown, Frederick, Md......	180
Bruin, Carter, Ky......	12	Buckfield, Oxford, Me....	360
Bruin, Butler, Pa...............	40	*Buckannon,* (c. h.,) Upshur, W. Va .	320
Bruington, King and Queen, Va...	22	Buck Head, Morgan, Ga.........	32
Bruin's Cross Roads, Parke, Ind...	33	Buck Head, Fairfield, S. C.......	12
Brumfield Station, Boyle, Ky......	10	Buck Hollow, Franklin, Vt........	16
Brumfieldville, Berks, Pa.........	36	Buck Horn, Independence, Ark ...	18
Brumley, Miller, Mo.............	17	Buck Horn, Brown, Ill..........	19
Brunersburgh, Defiance, Ohio.....	28	Buck Horn, Mahaska, Iowa.......	13
Brunnerville, Lancaster, Pa.......	36	Buck Horn, Ohio, Ky............	23
Brunot, Wayne, Mo.............	23	Buckhorn, Bienville, La.........	9
Brunswick, (c. h.,) Glynn, Ga......	440	Buckhorn, Winston, Miss.........	8
Brunswick, Peoria, Ill......	16	Buckhorn, Columbia, Pa.........	79
Brunswick, Lake, Ind...........	43	Buck Horn, Pendleton, W. Va....	5
Brunswick,* Cumberland, Me.....	2,200	Buckhorn, Adams, Wis......	12
Brunswick, (c. h.,) Kanebec, Minn..	33	Buckingham, Hartford, Conn.... .	56
Brunswick,* Chariton, Mo........	1,200	Buckingham,* Tama, Iowa........	210
Brunswick, Medina, Ohio........	130	Buckingham, Bucks, Pa.........	190
Brunswick, Essex, Vt............	4	*Buckingham C.H.,* Buckingham, Va.	160
Brush Creek, Perry, Ala.........	6	Buckinn, Madison, Ill...........	12
Brush Creek, Butte, Cal.........	35	Buckland, Hartford, Conn.......	100
Brush Creek, Fayette, Iowa.......	98	Buckland, Franklin, Mass.........	94
Brush Creek, Laclede, Mo.......	75	Buckland, Gates, N. C...........	12
Brush Creek, Muskingum, Ohio...	12	Buckland, Prince William, Va....	55
Brush Creek, Beaver, Pa......	15	Buckley, Iroquois, Ill...........	400
Brushey, Choctaw N., Ind. T......	12	Buckley, Highland, Ohio.... ...	8
Brushland, Delaware, N. Y........	19	Bucklin,* Linn, Mo............	440
Brush Prairie, McLeod, Minn......	16	Buckluxy, Choctaw N., Ind. T....	12
Brush Run, Washington, Pa.......	45	Buckmanville, Bucks, Pa........	39
Brush's Mills, Franklin, N. Y......	230	Buck Mountain, Carbon, Pa.......	160

* Money-order office.

Buckner's Station, Oldham, Ky...	$39	Buffalo Shoals, Wayne, W. Va	$7
Buckner's Station, Louisa, Va.....	12	Buffalo Valley, Putnam, Tenn......	12
Buck's, Columbiana, Ohio	38	Buffaloville, Spencer, Ind..........	19
Buck Shoal, Halifax, Va	12	Buford, Macoupin, Ill	15
Buckskin, Park, Colo	50	Buford, Ohio, Ky	28
Buckskin, Gibson, Ind ....·.....	15	Buford, Highland, Ohio	49
Buck's Mills, Hancock, Me.........	12	Buford's, Bedford, Va	120
Bucksport,* Hancock, Me	1,100	Buford's Station, Giles, Tenn	69
Bucksport Centre, Hancock, Me....	35	Buhlsville, Gentry, Mo	12
Buck's Ranch, Plumas, Cal	12	Bula, Goochland, Va	6
Buckstown, Somerset, Pa...........	42	Bulger, Washington, Pa............	37
Bucksville, Bucks, Pa	48	Bullard's, Twiggs, Ga	12
Bucksville, Horry, S. C	12	Bullard's Bar, Yuba, Cal...........	37
Buckton, Warren, Va	12	Bull Creek, Georgetown, S. C	12
Buck Valley, Fulton, Pa...........	16	Bull Creek, Wood, W. Va..........	68
Bucyrus, (c. h.,) Crawford, Ohio....	2,100	Bulliona, Alpine, Cal	55
Buda, Bureau, Ill	540	Bullitsville, Boone, Ky............	22
Budd's Creek, St. Mary's, Md	16	Bullock, Crenshaw, Ala	10
Budd's Lake, Morris, N. J	85	Bullock Creek, York, S. C	10
Budd Town, Burlington, N. J	12	Bull Run, Knox, Tenn.............	33
Buddville, Centre, Pa	30	Bull's Gap, Hawkins, Tenn	140
Buel, Sanilac, Mich	10	Bull's Head, Dutchess, N. Y	24
Buel, Montgomery, N. Y	37	Bull's Mills, Christian, Mo.........	4
Buena, Van Wert, Ohio...........	10	Bulltown, Braxton, W. Va..........	17
Buena Vista, Amador, Cal	12	Bullville, Orange, N. Y	96
Buena Vista, (c. h.,) Marion, Ga	160	Bumpass, Louisa, Va..............	78
Buena Vista, Stephenson, Ill.......	94	Bunceton, Cooper, Mo	200
Buena Vista, Clinton, Iowa.......	13	Buncomb, Brown, Kans	12
Buena Vista, Prince George's, Md..	20	Buncombe, Pettis, Mo.............	10
Buena Vista, Saginaw, Mich.......	12	Bunker Hill, Macoupin, Ill........	860
Buena Vista, Chickasaw, Miss	92	Bunker Hill, Miami, Ind..........	110
Buena Vista, Steuben, N. Y	14	Bunker Hill, Lyon, Kans	12
Buena Vista, Duplin, N. C	12	Bunker Hill, Ingham, Mich.......	18
Buena Vista, Tuscarawas, Ohio	20	Bunker Hill, Giles, Tenn	10
Buena Vista, Polk, Oregon	12	Bunker Hill, Bedford, Va	4
Buena Vista, Allegheny, Pa........	92	Bunker's Hill, Grant, Wis	12
Buena Vista, Greenville, S. C	12	Bunner's, Marion, W. Va	12
Buena Vista, Carroll, Tenn	8	Bunn's Bluff, Orange, Tex.........	10
Buena Vista, Shelby, Texas........	8	Buras, Plaquemines, La	110
Buena Vista, Portage, Wis	22	Burbank, Monongalia, Minn.......	18
Buffalo, Sangamon, Ill	100	Burbank, Wayne, Ohio.............	170
Buffalo, Scott, Iowa...............	99	Burbois, Gasconade, Mo	47
Buffalo, Wilson, Kans.............	30	Burch's, Kent, Mich...............	50
Buffalo, La Rue, Ky...............	54	Burdett, Bates, Mo................	12
Buffalo, (c. h.,) Wright, Minn.......	26	Burdett, Schuyler, N. Y...........	260
Buffalo, (c. h.,) Dallas, Mo........	130	Burdickville, Leelenaw, Mich......	48
*Buffalo,** (c. h.,) Erie, N. Y..........	4,000	Bureau Junction, Bureau, Ill	84
Buffalo, Guernsey, Ohio	16	Burem's Store, Hawkins, Tenn....	12
Buffalo, Washington, Pa..........	24	Burford's Landing, Wilcox, Ala....	12
Buffalo, Humphreys, Tenn.........	12	Burfordville, Cape Girardeau, Mo ..	12
Buffalo, Putnam, W. Va	140	Burgaw Depot, New Hanover, N. C.	23
Buffalo, Buffalo, Wis.............	53	Burgess, Clinton, Iowa	49
Buffalo Bluff, Putnam, Fla	12	Burgess, Dinwiddie, Va...........	5
Buffalo Cross Roads, Union, Pa.....	36	Burget's Corner, Clinton, Ind......	16
Buffalo Ford, Randolph, N. C	3	Burgettstown, Washington, Pa	220
Buffalo Forge, Rockbridge, Va.....	21	Burgh Hill, Trumbull, Ohio	190
Buffalo Fork, Kossuth, Iowa.......	15	Burk, Benton, Iowa	16
Buffalo Grove, Buchanan, Iowa....	23	Burke, Franklin, N. Y	51
Buffalo Mills, Bedford, Pa	6	Burke, Caledonia, Vt.............	45
Buffalo Mills, Rockbridge, Va......	23	Burke's Garden, Tazewell, Va......	69
Buffalo Paper Mill, Cleveland, N. C.	6	Burke's Mills, Augusta, Ga	51
Buffalo Plains, Erie, N. Y	16	*Burkesville,* (c. h.,) Cumberland, Ky.	260
Buffalo Pond, Washington, Va.....	130	Burkesville, Nottaway, Va.........	190
Buffalo Prairie, Rock Island, Ill ...	19	Burkettsville, Frederick, Md	170
Buffalo Ridge, Washington, Tenn..	7	Burkeville, Newton, Tex..........	31
Buffalo Run, Centre, Pa...........	21	Burk's Station, Fairfax, Va........	12

* Money-order office.

BUR

Burksville, Monroe, Ill	$31
Burleson, Franklin, Ala	10
*Burlingame,** (c. h.,) Osage, Kans	1,300
Burlingham, Sullivan, N. Y	18
Burlingham, Meigs, Ohio	24
Burlington,* Boulder, Colo	390
Burlington, Hartford, Conn	66
Burlington, Kane, Ill	69
Burlington, Carroll, Ind	76
*Burlington,** (c. h.,) Des Moines, Iowa	3,400
*Burlington,** (c. h.,) Coffey, Kans	430
Burlington, (c. h.,) Boone, Ky	86
Burlington, East Baton Rouge, La.	7
Burlington, Penobscot, Me	55
Burlington, Middlesex, Mass	44
Burlington, Calhoun, Mich	80
Burlington, Boone, Mo	49
Burlington,* Burlington, N. J	2,200
Burlington, Otsego, N. Y	51
Burlington, Lawrence, Ohio	91
Burlington, Bradford, Pa	130
Burlington, (c. h.,) Chittenden, Vt.	3,100
Burlington, Mineral, W. Va	85
Burlington,* Racine, Wis	880
Burlington Flats, Otsego, N. Y	150
Burnersville, Barbour, W. Va	34
Burnet, (c. h.,) Burnet, Tex	63
Burnett, Santa Clara, Cal	10
Burnett, Vigo, Ind	12
Burnett, Dodge, Wis	16
Burnett's Creek, White, Ind	160
Burnett Station, Dodge, Wis	200
Burnettsville, Somerset, Md	81
Burney's Mills, Randolph, N. C	12
Burnhamsville, Todd, Minn	12
Burnham Village, Waldo, Me	120
Burning Springs,* Wirt, W. Va	350
Burnip's Corners, Allegan, Mich	40
Burns, Henry, Ill	28
Burns, Shiawassee, Mich	14
Burns, Allegany, N. Y	79
Burns, La Crosse, Wis	47
Burnside, Hartford, Conn	190
Burnside, Hancock, Ill	250
Burnside, Clinton, Ind	12
Burnside, Lapeer, Mich	84
Burnside, Orange, N. Y	12
Burnside, Clearfield, Pa	64
Burnside, Buffalo, Wis	27
Burns' Mills, Bedford, Pa	12
Burns' Station, Dickson, Tenn	67
Burnsville, Dallas, Ala	12
Burnsville, Bartholomew, Ind	29
Burnsville, Tishemingo, Miss	150
Burnsville, (c. h.,) Yancey, N. C	44
Burnt Cabins, Fulton, Pa	83
Burnt Chimney, Rutherford, N. C	15
Burnt Corn, Monroe, Ala	12
Burnt Hills, Saratoga, N. Y	110
Burnt Ordinary, James City, Va	56
Burnt Prairie, White, Ill	92
Burnt Ranch, Trinity, Cal	12
Burntville, Brunswick, Va	9
Burr, Vernon, Wis	12
Burrageville, Worcester, Mass	54
Burrell, Westmoreland, Pa	53

BUT

Burrillville, Providence, R. I	$160
Burritt, Winnebago, Ill	4
Burr Oak, Winneshiek, Iowa	130
Burr Oak,* St. Joseph, Mich	650
Burr Oak, Harrison, Mo	12
Burr Oak, Otoe, Nebr	12
Burr Oak, La Crosse, Wis	40
Burrows, Carroll, Ind	60
Burr's Mills, Jefferson, N. Y	8
Burrsville, Caroline, Md	25
Burrville, Litchfield, Conn	110
Bursonville, Bucks, Pa	12
Burton, Adams, Ill	72
Burton, Geauga, Ohio	270
Burton, Washington, Tex	12
Burton, Wetzel, W. Va	74
Burtonsville, Montgomery, N. Y	87
Burtville, Potter, Pa	12
Burwood, San Joaquin, Cal	14
Busaco, Miami, Ind	28
Bushberg, Jefferson, Mo	12
Bush Hill, Randolph, N. C	65
Bushkill, Pike, Pa	92
Bush Kiln Centre, Northampton, Pa	18
Bushnell,* McDonough, Ill	1,100
Bushnell Centre, Montcalm, Mich	21
Bushnell's Basin, Monroe, N. Y	17
Bushnellsville, Greene, N. Y	20
Bush's Store, Laurel, Ky	7
Bushville, Sullivan, N. Y	18
Bushy Fork, Person, N. C	5
Businessburgh, Belmont, Ohio	16
Buskirk's Bridge, Washington, N. Y	120
Busseron, Knox, Ind	19
Busseyville, Jefferson, Wis	44
Busti, Howard, Iowa	45
Busti, Chautauqua, N. Y	180
Butler, (c. h.,) Choctaw, Ala	94
Butler, (c. h.,) Taylor, Ga	280
Butler, Montgomery, Ill	390
Butler, De Kalb, Ind	460
Butler, Keokuk, Iowa	20
Butler, Washington, Kans	12
Butler, Pendleton, Ky	110
Butler, Baltimore, Md	24
Butler, Branch, Mich	21
*Butler,** (c. h.,) Bates, Mo	1,200
Butler, Johnson, Nebr	7
Butler, Richland, Ohio	150
*Butler,** (c. h.,) Butler, Pa	1,000
Butler, Johnson, Tenn	4
Butler, Freestone, Tex	20
Butler, Milwaukee, Wis	42
Butler Centre, (c. h.,) Butler, Iowa	88
Butler's Landing, Jackson, Tenn	23
Butler Springs, Butler, Ala	12
Butlersville, Allen, Ky	7
Butlerville, Jennings, Ind	180
Butlerville, Tama, Iowa	82
Butlerville, Warren, Ohio	53
Butte City, Deer Lodge, Mont	120
Butte Creek, Clackamas, Oreg	10
Butte des Morts, Winnebago, Wis	55
Butternuts, Otsego, N. Y	510
Butternut Valley, Blue Earth, Minn	24
Butte Valley, Butte, Cal	35

* Money-order office.

CAI | CAL

Butte Valley, Huerfano, Colo	$12
Butteville, Marion, Oreg	55
Battsville, Grundy, Mo	12
Butztown, Northampton, Pa	21
Buxton, Clinton, Ill	14
Buxton, York, Me	38
Buxton Centre, York, Me	110
Buyerstown, Lancaster, Pa	44
Byersville, Livingston, N. Y	13
Byfield, Essex, Mass	98
Byhalia, Marshall, Miss	75
Byhalia, Union, Ohio	6
Byington, Pike, Ohio	21
Bynumville, Chariton, Mo	17
Byram, Hinds, Miss	16
Byrd's Springs, Jefferson, Ark	12
Byrne, Putnam, Tenn	9
Byrneville, Harrison, Ind	11
Byromville, Dooly, Ga	20
Byron, Houston, Ga	57
Byron, Ogle, Ill	210
Byron, Woodson, Kans	12
Byron, Oxford, Me	8
Byron, Shiawassee, Mich	270
Byron, Olmsted, Minn	150
Byron, Osage, Mo	13
Byron, Genesee, N. Y	180
Byron, Greene, Ohio	21
Byron, Fond du Lac, Wis	38
Byron Centre, Kent, Mich	47

C.

CABELL, C. H., Cabell, W. Va	130
Caberey, Kankakee, Ill	14
Cabin Creek, Lewis, Ky	22
Cabinet, Montgomery, Pa	160
Cabin Hill, Delaware, N. Y	21
Cabin Point, Surry, Va	57
Cable, Champaign, Ohio	77
Cable City, Deer Lodge, Mont	12
Cabot, Washington, Vt	320
Cacapon Depot, Morgan, W. Va	35
Cacey's Station, Fulton, Ky	20
Cache Creek, Yolo, Cal	49
Cadaretta, Choctaw, Miss	17
Caddo Grove, Johnson, Tex	12
Cade's Cove, Blount, Tenn	3
Cadet, Washington, Mo	28
Cadiz, Henry, Ind	99
Cadiz,* (c. h.,) Trigg, Ky	450
Cadiz, Cattarangus, N. Y	57
Cadiz,* (c. h.,) Harrison, Ohio	1,000
Cadiz, Green, Wis	28
Cadosia Valley, Delaware, N. Y	37
Cadron, Conway, Ark	3
Cadwallader, Tuscarawas, Ohio	65
Cady, Macomb, Mich	33
Cady's Falls, Lamoille, Vt	63
Cady's Tunnel, Bath, Va	120
Cadyville, Clinton, N. Y	62
Cageville, Haywood, Tenn	16
Cahaba, Dallas, Ala	150
Cahoka, Clarke, Mo	77
Cahto, Mendocino, Cal	180
Cainesville, Harrison, Mo	99

Cain's, Gwinnett, Ga	$18
Cain's, Lancaster, Pa	84
Cain's Store, Pulaski, Ky	7
Cainsville, Wilson, Tenn	15
Cainville, Rock, Wis	24
Ca Ira, Cumberland, Va	49
Cairo, Thomas, Ga	130
Cairo,* (c. h.,) Alexander, Ill	3,600
Cairo, Putnam, Ind	23
Cairo, Louisa, Iowa	66
Cairo, Henderson, Ky	35
Cairo, Randolph, Mo	55
Cairo, Greene, N. Y	250
Cairo, Stark, Ohio	11
Cairo, Ritchie, W. Va	180
Calahaln, Davie, N. C	9
Calais,* Washington, Me	2,400
Calais, Monroe, Ohio	71
Calais, Washington, Vt	60
Calamine, La Fayette, Wis	72
Calcutta, Columbiana, Ohio	53
Caldwell, Appanoose, Iowa	16
Caldwell, Essex, N. J	200
Caldwell, (c. h.,) Warren, N. Y	720
Caldwell, Orange, N. C	12
Caldwell,* (c. h.,) Noble, Ohio	220
Caldwell, (c. h.,) Burleson, Tex	40
Caldwell Prairie, Racine, Wis	43
Caldwell's Store, Leon, Tex	20
Caleb's Valley, Stewart, Tenn	12
Caledonia, (c. h.,) Pulaski, Ill	43
Caledonia, Ringgold, Iowa	32
Caledonia, Kent, Mich	40
Caledonia,* (c. h.,) Houston, Minn	190
Caledonia, Lowndes, Miss	24
Caledonia, Washington, Mo	190
Caledonia, Livingston, N. Y	330
Caledonia, Marion, Ohio	220
Caledonia, Elk, Pa	69
Caledonia, Rusk, Tex	12
Caledonia, Goochland, Va	12
Caledonia Centre, Racine, Wis	39
Caledonia Station, Boone, Ill	170
Caledonia Station, Kent, Mich	12
Calera, Shelby, Ala	12
Caler's Hill, Jackson, N. C	12
Calf Creek, Searcy, Ark	12
Calhoun, Lowndes, Ala	21
Calhoun, Columbia, Ark	24
Calhoun, (c. h.,) Gordon, Ga	550
Calhoun, Richland, Ill	100
Calhoun, Harrison, Iowa	18
Calhoun, (c. h.,) McLean, Ky	180
Calhoun, Madison, Miss	16
Calhoun, Henry, Mo	270
Calhoun, Transylvania, N. C	18
Calhoun, Barbour, W. Va	17
Calhoun's Mills, Abbeville, S. C	13
Calico, Johnson, Ark	12
California, Campbell, Ky	58
California, Branch, Mich	56
California,* (c. h.,) Moniteau, Mo	920
California, Hamilton, Ohio	170
California, Washington, Pa	140
Calistoga, Napa, Cal	26
Calla, Pawnee, Nebr	12

CAM

Callaghan's, Alleghany, Va	$58
Callahan, Nassau, Fla	15
Callahan's Ranch, Siskiyou, Cal	13
Callanan's Corners, Albany, N.Y	12
Calland's, Pittsylvania, Va	13
Callao, La Porte, Ind	25
Callao, Macon, Mo	170
Callaway, Josh Bell, Ky	4
Callensburgh, Clarion, Pa	140
Callicoon, Sullivan, N.Y	84
Callicoon Depot, Sullivan, N.Y	170
Calliope, (c. h.,) Sioux, Iowa	12
Calloway, Upshur, Tex	20
Calmar,* Winnishiek, Iowa	580
Calmus, Clinton, Iowa	210
Caln, Chester, Pa	57
Calno, Warren, N.J	4
Caloma, Marion, Iowa	40
Calumet, Cook, Ill	120
Calumet, Houghton, Mich	1,400
Calumet Village, Fond du Lac, Wis.	82
Calvary, Decatur, Ga	12
Calvary, Morgan, Ohio	12
Calvary, Fond du Lac, Wis	12
Calvert,* Robertson, Tex	2,000
Calverton, Suffolk, N.Y	32
Calverton Mills, Baltimore, Md	20
Calvert's, St. Francis, Ark	12
Calvin, Cass, Mich	10
Calvin, Huntingdon, Pa	13
Calvin's Corners, Crawford, Pa	12
Calvy, Franklin, Mo	14
Camac, Warren, Ga	12
Camackville, Lee, Iowa	12
Camanche, Calaveras, Cal	47
Camanche, Clinton, Iowa	270
Camargo, Douglas, Ill	200
Camargo, Lancaster, Pa	18
Camas Valley, Douglas, Oreg	12
Camba, Jackson, Ohio	54
Cambra, Luzerne, Pa	62
Cambria, San Luis Obispo, Cal	39
Cambria, Wayne, Iowa	13
Cambria, Niagara, N.Y	75
Cambria, Cambria, Pa	12
Cambria,* Columbia, Wis	560
Cambria Mills, Hillsdale, Mich	140
Cambridge, Dallas, Ala	12
Cambridge, (c. h.,) Henry, Ill	640
Cambridge, Story, Iowa	110
Cambridge, Somerset, Me	56
Cambridge, (c. h.,) Dorchester, Md.	610
Cambridge,* Middlesex, Mass	2,200
Cambridge, Lenawee, Mich	26
Cambridge, Isanti, Minn	32
Cambridge, Saline, Mo	180
Cambridge,* Washington, N.Y	1,000
Cambridge, (c. h.,) Guernsey, Ohio	1,100
Cambridge, Lancaster, Pa	44
Cambridge, Lamoille, Vt	240
Cambridge, Dane, Wis	240
Cambridgeborough, Crawford, Pa	240
Cambridge City,* Wayne, Ind	1,200
Cambridgeport,* Middlesex, Mass	2,200
Cambridgeport, Windham, Vt	140
Camden, (c. h.,) Wilcox, Ala	630

CAM

Camden, (c. h.,) Ouachita, Ark	$1,200
Camden, Kent, Del	400
Camden, Schuyler, Ill	10
Camden, Carroll, Ind	200
Camden,* Knox, Me	940
Camden, Hillsdale, Mich	200
Camden, Madison, Miss	12
Camden, Ray, Mo	200
Camden, Seward, Nebr	83
Camden, (c. h.,) Camden, N.J	2,500
Camden, Oneida, N.Y	1,300
Camden, Preble, Ohio	340
Camden, (c. h.,) Kershaw, S.C	750
Camden, (c. h.,) Benton, Tenn	230
Camden C. H., Camden, N.C	23
Camden Mills, Rock Island, Ill	250
Camden Point, Platte, Mo	60
Cameron, Scriven, Ga	12
Cameron, Warren, Ill	180
Cameron,* Clinton, Mo	930
Cameron, Steuben, N.Y	100
Cameron, New Hanover, N.C	23
Cameron, Monroe, Ohio	24
Cameron, Cameron, Pa	200
Cameron, (c. h.,) Milam, Tex	300
Cameron, Marshall, W.Va	290
Cameron Mills, Steuben, N.Y	67
Camilla, (c. h.,) Mitchell, Ga	140
Camillus, Onondaga, N.Y	280
Campbell, Coles, Ill	56
Campbell, Ionia, Mich	40
Campbell C. H., Campbell, Va	82
Campbell Hall, Orange, N.Y	12
Campbell's Bridge, Marion, S.C	17
Campbellsburgh, Washington, Ind.	140
Campbellsburgh, Henry, Ky	120
Campbell's Mills, Windham, Conn	6
Campbell's Station, Knox, Tenn	29
Campbellstown, Preble, Ohio	34
Campbellsville, (c. h.,) Taylor, Ky	240
Campbellsville, Giles, Tenn	19
Campbellton, Jackson, Fla	24
Campbellton, (c. h.,) Campbell, Ga	53
Campbellton, Franklin, Mo	10
Campbelltown, Steuben, N.Y	250
Campbelltown, Lebanon, Pa	110
Campbellville, Sullivan, Pa	7
Camp Call, Cleveland, N.C	6
Camp Creek, Lancaster, Nebr	18
Camp Creek, Greene, Tenn	12
Camp Elkwater, Randolph, W.Va.	1
Campello, Plymouth, Mass	360
Camp Grant, Humboldt, Cal	16
Camp Grove, Stark, Ill	92
Camp Halleck, Elko, Nev	130
Camp Hill, Cumberland, Pa	120
Camp Izard, Marion, Fla	6
Camp McDermitt, Humboldt, Nev.	100
Camp Melvin, Bexar, Tex	12
Campobello, Spartanburgh, S.C	94
Campo Seco, Calaveras, Cal	96
Camp Point,* Adams, Ill	510
Camp Ridge, Williamsburgh, S.C	8
Camp Run, Crawford, Ohio	11
Camp Stanton, De Kalb, Ala	12
Camp Stockton, Presidio, Tex	400

* Money-order office.

CAN CAP

Campti, Natchitoches, La.........	$14	*Cannelton,* (*c. h.,*) Perry, Ind	$610
Campton, Coweta, Ga..............	12	Cannelton, Kanawha, W. Va......	40
Campton, Kane, Ill	64	Cannon City, Rice, Minn	48
Campton, Delaware, Iowa.........	13	Cannon River Falls, Goodhue, Minn	340
Campton, (*c. h.,*) Wolfe, Ky	12	Cannonsburgh, Boyd, Ky..........	7
Campton, Grafton, N. H	80	Cannonsburgh, Kent, Mich......	74
Campton Village, Grafton, N. H....	270	Cannonsburgh, Hancock, Ohio.....	42
Camptonville,* Yuba, Cal	240	Cannonsburgh,* Washington, Pa..	750
Camptown, Bradford, Pa...........	130	Cannon's Mill, Columbiana, Ohio..	20
Campville, Litchfield, Conn	29	Cannon's Station, Fairfield, Conn..	12
Campville, Tioga, N. Y	74	Cannon's Store, Sevier, Tenn	10
Camp Watson, Grant, Oreg........	12	Cannonsville, Delaware, N. Y......	180
Can, Huron, Mich.................	12	Canoe, Winnishiek, Iowa........	19
Cana, Jennings, Ind	12	Canoe Camp, Tioga, Pa.........	12
Canaan, Litchfield, Conn.........	420	Canoe Creek, Blair, Pa...........	45
Canaan, Jefferson, Ind...........	20	Canoe Ridge, Jefferson, Pa	26
Canaan, Somerset, Me	240	Canoe Station, Escambia, Ala	12
Canaan, Gasconade, Mo	21	Canoga, Seneca, N. Y.............	110
Canaan, Grafton, N. H...........	220	Canoochee, Emanuel, Ga	21
Canaan, Columbia, N. Y..........	55	Canoper, Adams, Ind.............	10
Canaan, Wayne, Ohio.............	76	Canterbury, Windham, Conn......	130
Canaan, Wayne, Pa...............	72	Canterbury, Kent, Del............	130
Canaan, Essex, Vt	80	Canterbury, Merrimack, N. H......	120
Canaan Centre, Columbia, N. Y....	73	Canton, Lawrence, Ark..........	5
Canaan Four Corners, Columbia,		Canton, Hartford, Conn.........	47
N. Y...........................	310	*Canton,* (*c. h.,*) Lincoln, Dak.......	120
Canaan Valley, Litchfield, Conn..	29	*Canton,* (*c. h.,*) Cherokee, Ga.......	79
Canaanville, Athens, Ohio.........	48	Canton,* Fulton, Ill	2,400
Canada Road, Somerset, Me	12	Canton, Washington, Ind.........	75
Canadensis, Monroe, Pa	100	Canton, Jackson, Iowa............	46
Canadice, Ontario, N. Y	53	Canton, Trigg, Ky	92
Canajoharie, Montgomery, N. Y....	1,300	Canton, Oxford, Me..............	230
Canal, Warrick, Ind	31	Canton,* Norfolk, Mass..........	1,200
Canal, Venango, Pa..............	19	Canton, Wayne, Mich.............	58
Canal Dover, Tuscarawas, Ohio....	430	*Canton,* (*c. h.,*) Madison, Miss......	2,000
Canal Fulton, Stark, Ohio.........	390	Canton,* Lewis, Mo	1,000
Canal Lewisville, Coshocton, Ohio.	28	Canton, Stanton, Nebr...........	14
Canal Winchester,* Franklin, Ohio.	240	Canton, Salem, N. J.............	22
Canandaigua, Lenawee, Mich.....	120	*Canton,* (*c. h.,*) St. Lawrence, N. Y.	1,600
Canandaigua, (*c. h.,*) Ontario, N. Y.	2,700	*Canton,* (*c. h.,*) Stark, Ohio........	2,600
Canarsie, Kings, N. Y............	32	Canton, Bradford, Pa...........	570
Canaseraga, Allegany, N. Y........	330	*Canton,* (*c. h.,*) Van Zandt, Tex.....	58
Canastota, Madison, N. Y..........	1,200	Canton, Marion, W. Va...........	10
Candia, Rockingham, N. H........	150	Canton Centre, Hartford, Conn....	98
Candia Village, Rockingham, N. H.	110	Canton Point, Oxford, Me........	43
Candor, Tioga, N. Y..............	690	Cantrelle, St. James, La..........	54
Candor, Washington, Pa	58	Cantrell's x Roads, McMinn, Tenn.	17
Caneadea, Allegany, N. Y........	170	Canville, Neosho, Kans..........	36
Cane Creek, Conway, Ark........	17	Cany Hollow, Lee, Va..........	12
Cane Creek, Walker, Ga..........	12	*Canyon City,* (*c. h.,*) Fremont, Colo.	160
Cane Creek, Butler, Mo..........	16	*Canyon City,* (*c. h.,*) Grant, Oreg...	630
Cane Creek, Chatham, N. C........	12	Canyon Ferry, Meagher, Mont....	32
Cane Hill, Cedar, Mo............	10	Capac, St. Clair, Mich............	110
Cane Ridge, Claiborne, La........	12	Cap Au Gris, Lincoln, Mo	35
Cane Spring Depot, Bullitt, Ky....	31	Capay, Yolo, Cal	20
Cane Valley, Adair, Ky..........	22	Cape Elizabeth Depot, Cumberland,	
Caney, Ouachita, Ark...........	39	Me...........................	66
Caney, Howard, Kans...........	12	Cape Girardeau,* Cape Girardeau,	
Caney, Ozark, Mo..............	12	Mo...........................	1,400
Caney, Matagorda, Tex..........	63	Capell's Mills, Richmond, N. C	12
Caney Branch, Green, Tenn.......	23	Cape May,* Cape May, N. J	2,000
Caney Spring, Marshall, Tenn	25	*Cape May C. H.,* Cape May, N. J...	250
Caneyville, Grayson, Ky..........	16	Cape Neddick, York, Me	120
Canfield, Fillmore, Minn.........	6	Cape Porpoise, York, Me.........	80
Canfield, (*c. h.,*) Mahoning, Ohio..	570	Caperville, Northampton, Va......	40
Canisteo, Steuben, N. Y..........	410	Cape Vincent,* Jefferson, N. Y.....	860

* Money-order office.

3 P O

CAR

Capioma, Nemaha, Kans	$43	Carpenteria, Santa Barbara, Cal	$12
Capistrano, Los Angeles, Cal	7	Carpenter's Eddy, Delaware, N. Y.	12
Caplinger's Mills, Cedar, Mo	12	Carpenter's Store, Clinton, Mo	10
Capon Bridge, Hampshire, W. Va.	72	Carpentersville, Kane, Ill	200
Capon Springs, Hampshire, W. Va.	25	Carpentersville, Putnam, Ind	71
Cappelu, St. Charles, Mo	12	Carpentersville, Warren, N. J	38
Capper's Spring, Frederick, Va	5	Carpenterville, Shannon, Mo	12
Capp's Creek, Newton, Mo	24	Carriage Point, Chickasaw N., Ind.	
Capron, Boone, Ill	240	Ter	12
Captina, Belmont, Ohio	18	Carrick, Allegheny, Pa	29
Carbon, Webster, Iowa	12	Carrick's Ford, Tucker, W. Va	12
Carbon, Carbon, Pa	30	Carritunk, Somerset, Me	21
Carbon, Carbon, Wyo	12	Carrizo, (c, h.,) Zapata, Tex	12
Carbon Cliff, Rock Island, Ill	83	Carroll, Carroll, Ind	34
Carbondale,* Jackson, Ill	1,400	Carroll, Penobscot, Me	55
Carbondale, Osage, Kans	12	Carroll, Baltimore, Md	37
Carbondale,* Luzerne, Pa	1,200	Carroll, Coos, N. H	11
Carbon Hill, Johnson, Mo	12	Carroll, Fairfield, Ohio	130
Carbonvale, Kanawha, W. Va	41	Carroll, Clinton, Pa	7
Cardiff, Mitchell, Iowa	8	Carroll, Madison, Tenn	12
Cardiff, Onondaga, N. Y	81	Carroll City, Carroll, Iowa	440
Cardington,* Morrow, Ohio	980	Carrollton, (c. h.,) Pickens, Ala	110
Cardville, Washington, Pa	12	Carrollton, (c. h.,) Carroll, Ark	50
Carey,* Wyandot, Ohio	560	Carrollton, (c. h.,) Carroll, Ga	200
Caribou, Aroostook, Me	100	Carrollton,* (c. h.,) Greene, Ill	1,300
Carimona, Fillmore, Minn	52	Carrollton, Hancock, Ind	36
Carl, Adams, Iowa	16	Carrollton, (c. h.,) Carroll, Iowa	65
Carleton, Muskegon, Mich	12	Carrolton,* (c. h.,) Carroll, Ky	520
Carlin, Lander, Nev	230	Carrollton, (c. h.,) Jefferson, La	120
Carlinville,* (c. h.,) Macoupin, Ill	220	Carrollton, Carroll, Md	19
Carlisle,* Sullivan, Ind	290	Carrollton, Saginaw, Mich	130
Carlisle, Warren, Iowa	69	Carrollton, Fillmore, Minn	10
Carlisle, (c. h.,) Nicholas, Ky	440	Carrollton, (c. h.,) Carroll, Miss	360
Carlisle, Middlesex, Mass	55	Carrollton,* (c. h.,) Carroll, Mo	1,500
Carlisle, Eaton, Mich	15	Carrollton, Cattaraugus, N. Y	12
Carlisle, Schoharie, N. Y	77	Carrollton,* (c. h.,) Carroll, Ohio	460
Carlisle,* (c. h.,) Cumberland, Pa.	2,500	Carrollton, Upshur, Tex	6
Carlisle Springs, Cumberland, Pa.	28	Carrollton Station, Montgomery,	
Carlisle Station, Warren, Ohio	140	Ohio	70
Carlstadt, Bergen, N. J	130	Carrolltown, Cambria, Pa	200
Carlton, Orleans, N. Y	110	Carr's, Lewis, Ky	30
Carlton, Kewaunee, Wis	34	Carrsville, Livingston, Ky	86
Carlton's Store, King and Queen,		Carrsville, Isle of Wight, Va	67
Va	10	Carrville, Washington, Tenn	12
Carlyle,* (c. h.,) Clinton, Ill	630	Carryall, Paulding, Ohio	13
Carlyle, Allen, Kans	87	Carson, Jefferson, Ark	12
Carmel, Hamilton, Ind	160	Carson, Huerfano, Colo	12
Carmel, Penobscot, Me	150	Carson, Brown, Kans	42
Carmel,* (c. h.,) Putnam, N. Y	490	Carson, Huron, Ohio	8
Carmel, Highland, Ohio	13	Carson City, Montcalm, Mich	48
Carmi,* (c. h.,) White, Ill	380	CARSON CITY,* (c. h.,) Ormsby, Nev.	1,600
Carmichael's, Greene, Pa	180	Carson's Landing, Bolivar, Miss	18
Carnero, Saguache, Colo	12	Carter, Uintah, Wyo	60
Carnesville, (c. h.,) Franklin, Ga	62	Carter Camp, Potter, Pa	19
Carney, Wyoming, Pa	12	Carter Hill, Erie, Pa	9
Caro,* (c. h.,) Tuscola, Mich	420	Carter's Bridge, Albemarle, Va	21
Carolina, Marion, S. C	12	Cartersburgh, Hendricks, Ind	37
Carolina, Falls, Tex	12	Cartersburgh, Pittsylvania, Va	12
Carolina Mills, Washington, R. I.	150	Carter's Creek Station, Maury,	
Carolina Seminary, Greene, N. C.	10	Tenn	12
Caroline, Jefferson, Nebr	12	Carter's Depot, Carter, Tenn	56
Caroline, Tompkins, N. Y	37	Carter's Furnace, Carter, Tenn	12
Caroline Centre, Tompkins, N. Y.	41	Carter's Mills, Moore, N. C	15
Caroline Depot, Tompkins, N. Y.	58	Carter's Mills, Patrick, Va	12
Carondelet, St. Louis, Mo	690	Carter's Store, Randolph, Ala	12
Carpenter, Lycoming, Pa	12	Cartersville,* (c. h.,)Bartow, Ga	1,200

* Money-order office.

CAS — CAT

Cartersville, Tishemingo, Miss.....	$46	Cassity's Mills, Rowan, Ky	$4
Cartersville Parker, Tex	22	*Cassopolis,* (c. h.,) Cass, Mich	820
Cartersville, Cumberland, Va	150	Cass Station, Bartow, Ga..........	99
Carthage, Tuscaloosa, Ala.........	15	Casstown, Miami, Ohio...........	99
Carthage, (c. h.,) Hancock, Ill	1,200	Cassville, Bartow, Ga	79
Carthage, Rush, Ind	180	Cassville, Howard, Ind..........	31
Carthage, Campbell, Ky.........	15	*Cassville,* (c. h.,) Barry, Mo.........	98
Carthage, (c. h.,) Leake, Miss	150	Cassville, Ocean, N. J	25
Carthage, (c. h.,) Jasper, Mo.......	1,400	Cassville, Oneida, N. Y..	210
Carthage, Jefferson, N. Y	1,000	Cassville, Harrison, Ohio.........	35
Carthage, (c. h.,) Moore, N. C......	80	Cassville, Huntingdon, Pa.........	150
Carthage, Hamilton, Ohio.........	220	Cassville, Monongalia, W. Va......	36
Carthage, (c. h.,) Smith, Tenn	230	Cassville, Grant, Wis.............	260
Carthage, (c. h.,) Panola, Tex	130	Castalia, Winneshiek, Iowa	160
Carthage Landing, Dutchess, N. Y..	150	Castalia, Nash, N. C.............	18
Carthagena, Mercer, Ohio	47	Castalia, Erie, Ohio..............	150
Caruthersville, Pemiscot, Mo	10	Castalian Springs, Sumner, Tenn ..	81
Carver, Plymouth, Mass	14	Castana, Monona, Iowa...........	57
Carver,* Carver, Minn	490	Castania Grove, Lincoln, N. C	9
Carver's Harbor, Knox, Me	260	Castile, Wyoming, N. Y	640
Carversville, Bucks, Pa.....	150	Castine, Hancock, Me.............	550
Carverton, Luzerne, Pa	3	Castine, Darke, Ohio.............	33
Cary, Wake, N. C.....	18	Castle, Randolph, Ind............	12
Cary Station, McHenry, Ill	94	Castle, Andrew, Mo	12
Carysville, Champaign, Ohio	30	Castleberry, Conecuh, Ala.......	12
Caryville, Norfolk, Mass	75	Castle Craig, Campbell, Va.......	37
Caryville, Campbell, Tenn.........	12	Castle Creek, Broome, N. Y.......	67
Casady's Corner, Boone, Iowa	54	Castle Fin, York, Pa.............	46
Casanova, Fauquier, Va......	46	Castle Garden, Blue Earth, Minn ..	5
Casa, Perry, Ark .....-.......	12	Castle Grove, Jones, Iowa........	12
Cascade,* Dubuque, Iowa........	880	Castle Hayne, New Hanover, N. C..	12
Cascade, Kent, Mich	60	Castle Hill, Aroostook, Me........	30
Cascade, Olmsted, Minn............	14	Castleman's Ferry, Clarke, Va....	16
Cascade, Pittsylvania, Va.........	35	Castle Rock, Dakota, Minn........	43
Cascade, Sheboygan, Wis.........	140	Castle Rock, Osage, Mo..........	24
Cascades, (c. h.,) Skamania, Wash ..	22	Castle Rock, Cowlitz, Wash.	18
Cascade Valley, Broome, N. Y......	14	Castle Rock, Grant, Wis....	75
Casco, Cumberland, Me	78	Castleton, Stark, Ill.............	12
Casco, St. Clair, Mich	17	Castleton, Marion, Ind..........	55
Casco, Kewaunee, Wis	21	Castleton, Rensselaer, N. Y....	380
Case, Laclede, Mo...............	10	Castleton,* Rutland, Vt..........	780
Caseville, Huron, Mich............	37	Castleton, Culpeper, Va..........	17
Casey, Clark, Ill........	160	Castleville, Buchanan, Iowa	8
Casey, Adair, Iowa.............	230	Castor, Bollinger, Mo...	12
Casey Creek, Adair, Ky..........	15	Castroville, Monterey, Cal.......	520
Caseyville, St. Clair, Ill.....	130	*Castroville,* (c. h.,) Medina, Tex...	87
Caseyville, Union, Ky..........	270	Caswell, La Fayette, Miss..	12
Cash Creek, Lake, Colo....	12	Catalpa Grove, Greene, Ky	12
Casher's Valley, Jackson, N. C.....	9	Catalpa Grove, Marshall, Tenn	12
Cashtown, Adams, Pa............	69	Cataract, Owen, Ind	20
Caskaid, Putnam, Ohio...........	11	Cataract, Monroe, Wis...........	76
Casky's Station, Christian, Ky.....	47	Catasauqua, Lehigh, Pa............	1,500
Casnovia, Kent, Mich	140	Catatonk, Tioga, N. Y..........	98
Cass, Franklin, Ark............	5	Cataula, Harris, Ga............	26
Cass, Du Page, Ill............	27	Catawba, Pendleton, Ky...........	32
Cass, Hillsdale, Mich............	21	Catawba, Clark, Ohio............	69
Cass, Venango, Pa	57	Catawba, Roanoke, Va............	16
Cassadaga, Chautauqua, N. Y......	100	Catawba Island, Ottawa, Ohio....	21
Cassandra, Walker, Ga...........	12	Catawba Station, Catawba, N. C...	170
Cass Bridge, Saginaw, Mich	9	Catawissa, Franklin, Mo....... ...	120
Cass City, Tuscola, Mich	65	Catawissa, Columbia, Pa.........	500
Casscoe, Arkansas, Ark...........	12	Cat Creek, Lowndes, Ga..........	12
Cassel, Wright, Minn.............	14	Catfish, Edgar, Ill..............	12
Cassella, Lake, Ind	12	Catfish, Clarion, Pa.............	12
Cassell Prairie, Sauk, Wis........	10	Catfish, Marion, S. C............	12
Casselman, Somerset, Pa.......	12	Catharine, Schuyler, N. Y	120

* Money-order office.

CED   CEN

Catharine Lake, Onslow, N. C	$7	Cedar Dale, Sanilac, Mich	$13
Cathey's Creek, Transylvania, N. C.	2	Cedar Falls,* Black Hawk, Iowa	2,200
Cathlamet, (c. h.,) Wahkiakum, Wash	12	Cedar Falls, Dunn, Wis	59
Catlett, Fauquier, Va	150	Cedar Fork, Menomonee, Mich	24
Catlettsburgh,* Boyd, Ky	500	Cedar Fork, Union, Tenn	12
Catlin, Vermilion, Ill	180	Cedar Fork, Caroline, Va	23
Catlin, Parke, Ind	65	Cedar Grove, Jefferson, Ala	5
Cato, Crawford, Kans	150	Cedar Grove, Walker, Ga	56
Cato, Montcalm, Mich	43	Cedar Grove, Franklin, Ind	58
Cato, Rankin, Miss	30	Cedar Grove, Orange, N. C	10
Cato, Cayuga, N. Y	130	Cedar Grove, Kaufman, Tex	24
Cato, Manitowoc, Wis	24	Cedar Grove, Sheboygan, Wis	96
Catocton Furnace, Frederick, Md	55	Cedar Grove Mills, Rockbridge, Va.	28
Caton, Steuben, N. Y	69	Cedar Hill, Jefferson, Mo	12
Catonsville, Baltimore, Md	300	Cedar Hill, Albany, N. Y	31
Catskill,* (c. h.,) Greene, N. Y.	2,200	Cedar Hill, Anson, N. C	36
Catskill Station, Columbia, N. Y.	44	Cedar Hill, Fairfield, Ohio	23
Cat Spring, Austin, Tex	67	Cedar Hill, Robertson, Tenn	74
Cattaraugus, Cattaraugus, N. Y.	210	Cedar Hill, Dallas, Tex	58
Caudle Mills, Anson, N. C	12	Cedar Junction, Missoula, Mont	12
Caughdenoy, Oswego, N. Y	' 43	Cedar Keys, Levy, Fla	10
Cave, Franklin, Ill	23	Cedar Lake, Lake, Ind	35
Cave, White, Tenn	32	Cedar Lake, Scott, Minn	6
Cave City, Barren, Ky	200	Cedar Lake, Atlantic, N. J	12
Cave Creek, Newton, Ark	8	Cedar Lake, Herkimer, N. Y	51
Cave in Rock, Hardin, Ill	45	Cedar Lake, Waushara, Wis	52
Cavendish, Windsor, Vt	400	Cedar Lane, Greene, Tenn	12
Cave Pump, Camden, Mo	8	Cedar Mills, Renville, Minn	12
Caverna, Hart, Ky	230	Cedar Mills, Adams, Ohio	12
Cave Spring, Floyd, Ga	310	Cedar Mountain, Transylvania, N. C	15
Cave Spring, Carter, Tenn	16	Cedar Plains, Morgan, Ala	6
Cave Spring, Roanoke, Va	10	Cedar Point, Chase, Kans	12
Cave Spring Station, Logan, Ky	12	Cedar Point, Page, Va	15
Cavetown, Washington, Md	35	Cedar Rapids,* Linn, Iowa	2,500
Cavettsville, Westmoreland, Pa	35	Cedar Rock, Franklin, N. C	12
Cawker City, Mitchell, Kans	12	Cedar Run, Grand Traverse, Mich.	12
Cayo Largo, Monroe, Fla	12	Cedar Run, Lycoming, Pa	34
Cayuga, Livingston, Ill	110	Cedar Springs, Cherokee, Ala	12
Cayuga, Cayuga, N. Y	220	Cedar Springs, Kent, Mich	370
Cayuse, Umatilla, Oreg	12	Cedar Springs, Clinton, Pa	53
Cayuta, Schuyler, N. Y	49	Cedartown, (c. h.,) Polk, Ga	160
Cayutaville, Schuyler, N. Y	12	Cedar Tree, Hernando, Fla	3
Cazenovia,* Madison, N. Y	1,500	Cedar Vale, Howard, Kans	12
Cazenovia, Richland, Wis	79	Cedar Valley, Black Hawk, Iowa.	32
Cecil, Paulding, Ohio	140	Cedar Valley, Wayne, Ohio	24
Cecilton, Cecil, Md	360	Cedar Valley, Utah, Utah	13
Cedar, Fayette, Tex	19	Cedarville, Siskiyou, Cal	12
Cedar Bluff, Cherokee, Ala	170	Cedarville, Stephenson, Ill	140
Cedar Bluff, Johnson, Ill	20	Cedarville, Allen, Ind	28
Cedar Bluff, Cedar, Iowa	40	Cedarville, Martin, Minn	7
Cedar Bluff, Tazewell, Va	8	Cedarville, Dade, Mo	12
Cedar Bluffs, Saunders, Nebr	78	Cedarville, Cumberland, N. J	84
Cedarburgh, Ozaukee, Wis	240	Cedarville, Herkimer, N. Y	110
Cedar Bush, Davidson, N. C	1	Cedarville, Greene, Ohio	400
Cedar Chapel, Hardeman, Tenn	10	Cedarville, Chehalis, Wash	6
Cedar City, Callaway, Mo	120	Cedron, Clermont, Ohio	14
Cedar City, Iron, Utah	200	Celestine, Dubois, Ind	12
Cedar Creek, Dorchester, Md	4	Celina, Perry, Ind	12
Cedar Creek, Barry, Mich	19	Celina,* (c. h.,) Mercer, Ohio	400
Cedar Creek, Ocean, N. J	74	Celina, Jackson, Tenn	39
Cedar Creek, Cumberland, N. C	12	Cementville, Clarke, Ind	12
Cedar Creek, Greene, Tenn	13	Centenary, Buckingham, Va	6
Cedar Creek, Bastrop, Tex	11	Center, Shelby, Tex	61
Cedar Creek, Frederick, Va	5	Center, Monongalia, W. Va	3
Cedar Creek, Washington, Wis	73	Center, Rock, Wis	44
Cedar Creek Landing, Perry, Tenn.	12	Center Mills, Montgomery, Va	12

* Money-order office.

CEN

Centerville, (c. h.,) Appanoose, Iowa	$640
Centerville, Davis, Utah	34
Central, St. Louis, Mo	110
Central, Columbia, Pa	8
Central Bridge, Schoharie, N. Y	170
Central City, (c. h.,) Gilpin, Colo	4,000
Central City, Marion, Ill	88
Central City, Linn, Iowa	80
Central City, Anderson, Kans	16
Central City, Putnam, Mo	16
Central City, Grant, N. Mex	12
Central College, Franklin, Ohio	83
Central Falls, Providence, R. I	1,100
Central House, Butte, Cal	29
Centralia,* Marion, Ill	2,200
Centralia, Nemaha, Kans	220
Centralia, Boone, Mo	290
Centralia, Columbia, Pa	250
Centralia, Wood, Wis	230
Central Institute, Coosa, Ala	15
Central Lake, Antrim, Mich	15
Central Park, Queens, N. Y	110
Central Plains, Fluvanna, Va	51
Central Point, Caroline, Va	37
Central Square, Oswego, N. Y	200
Central Station, Doddridge, W. Va.	86
Central Village, Windham, Conn	240
Central Village, Bristol, Mass	39
Centre, (c. h.,) Cherokee, Ala	72
Centre, Schuyler, Ill	10
Centre, Howard, Ind	60
Centre, Page, Iowa	27
Centre, Metcalfe, Ky	21
Centre, Eaton, Mich	17
Centre, Texas, Mo	4
Centre, Guilford, N. C	27
Centre, Montgomery, Ohio	74
Centre, Perry, Pa	58
Centre Barnstead, Belknap, N. H	96
Centre Belpre, Washington, Ohio	46
Centre Bend, Morgan, Ohio	8
Centre Berlin, Rensselaer, N. Y	14
Centre Bridge, Bucks, Pa	60
Centre Brook, Middlesex, Conn	190
Centre Brunswick, Rensselaer, N. Y	36
Centreburgh, Knox, Ohio	70
Centre Cambridge, Washington, N.Y	61
Centre Chanisteo, Steuben, N. Y	21
Centre Conway, Carroll, N. H	44
Centre Creek, Martin, Minn	16
Centre Creek, Jasper, Mo	140
Centre Cross, Essex, Va	12
Centredale, Providence, R. I	75
Centre Effingham, Carroll, N. H	120
Centrefield, Oldham, Ky	8
Centrefield, Highland, Ohio	28
Centre Groton, New London, Conn	30
Centre Grove, Person, N. C	4
Centre Hall, Centre, Pa	150
Centre Harbor, Belknap, N. H	420
Centre Hill, White, Ark	17
Centre Hill, Hartford, Conn	69
Centre Hill, Centre, Pa	71
Centre Lebanon, York, Me	19
Centre Lincolnville, Waldo, Me	34
Centre Lisle, Broome, N. Y	130

Centre Lovell, Oxford, Me	$63
Centre Mills, Centre, Pa	69
Centre Montville, Waldo, Me	20
Centre Moreland, Wyoming, Pa	41
Centre Moriches, Suffolk, N. Y	170
Centre Ossipee, Carroll, N. H	100
Centre Point, Sevier, Ark	71
Centre Point, Knox, Ill	17
Centre Point, Clay, Ind	100
Centre Point, Linn, Iowa	220
Centre Point, Monroe, Ky	13
Centreport, Suffolk, N. Y	73
Centreport, Berks, Pa	24
Centre Road Station, Crawford, Pa	160
Centre Rutland, Rutland, Vt	640
Centre Sandwich, Carroll, N. H	290
Centre Sidney, Kennebec, Me	40
Centre Square, Switzerland, Ind	34
Centre Square, Montgomery, Pa	37
Centre Star, Lauderdale, Ala	12
Centre Strafford, Strafford, N. H	35
Centreton, Morgan, Ind	79
Centreton, Salem, N. J	37
Centreton, Huron, Ohio	140
Centre Town, Cole, Mo	80
Centretown, Mercer, Pa	27
Centre Valley, Hendricks, Ind	50
Centre Valley, Cass, Nebr	6
Centre Valley, Otsego, N. Y	18
Centre Valley, Lehigh, Pa	92
Centre View, Johnson, Mo	140
Centre View, Monroe, Ohio	20
Centre Village, Charlton, Ga	21
Centre Village, Broome, N. Y	100
Centre Village, Delaware, Ohio	40
Centreville, (c. h.,) Bibb, Ala	30
Centreville, Montgomery, Ark	12
Centreville, Alameda, Cal	200
Centreville, Lake, Colo	12
Centreville, New Castle, Del	100
Centreville, Boise, Idaho	38
Centreville, Piatt, Ill	12
Centreville, (c. h.,) Wayne, Ind	590
Centreville, Linn, Kans	18
Centreville, Bourbon, Ky	62
Centreville, St. Mary's, La	140
Centreville, (c. h.,) Queen Anne, Md.	550
Centreville, Barnstable, Mass	180
Centreville, (c. h.,) St. Joseph, Mich.	690
Centreville, Anoka, Minn	23
Centreville, Amite, Miss	12
Centreville, (c. h.,) Reynolds, Mo	16
Centreville, Lancaster, Nebr	14
Centreville, Hunterdon, N. J	36
Centreville, Allegany, N. Y	100
Centreville, Montgomery, Ohio	96
Centreville, Washington, Oreg	18
Centreville, Crawford, Pa	200
Centreville, Kent, R. I	360
Centreville, (c. h.,) Hickman, Tenn	72
Centreville, (c. h.,) Leon, Tex	80
Centreville, Fairfax, Va	58
Centreville Station, St. Clair, Ill	62
Centre White Creek, Washington, N. Y	44
Centropolis, Franklin, Kans	71

* Money-order office.

CHA   CHA

Ceralvo, Ohio, Ky	$16	Chapel Hill, Perry, Ohio	$26
Ceredo, Wayne, W. Va	57	Chapel Hill, Marshall, Tenn	89
Ceres, Clayton, Iowa	52	Chapel Hill, Washington, Tex	250
Ceres, Allegany, N. Y	140	Chapel Hill, Fluvanna, Va	59
Ceresco, Calhoun, Mich	190	Chapin, Morgan, Ill	110
Ceresco, Lyon, Minn	12	Chapin, Franklin, Iowa	19
Ceresco, Saunders, Nebr	12	Chapinville, Ontario, N. Y	41
Cerro Gordo, Inyo, Cal	12	Chapinville, Crawford, Pa	7
Cerro Gordo, (c. h.,) Holmes, Fla	6	Chaplin, Windham, Conn	93
Cerro Gordo,* Piatt, Ill	880	Chaplin, Nelson, Ky	29
Cerro Gordo, Randolph, Ind	24	Chapman, Merrick. Nebr	12
Cerro Gordo, Columbus, N. C	24	Chapman, Snyder, Pa	27
Cerro Gordo, Hardin, Tenn	12	Chapman Quarries, Northampton,	
Cerulean Springs, Trigg, Ky	12	Pa	88
Cessford, Cedar, Iowa	10	Chapman's Creek, Dickinson, Kans.	72
Ceylon, Greene, Pa	12	Chapmanville, Logan, W. Va	4
Chadd's Ford, Delaware, Pa	240	Chappaqua, Westchester, N. Y	230
Chadwick's Mills, Oneida, N. Y	58	Chappell's Bridge, Newberry, S. C.	5
Chagrin Falls,* Cuyahoga, Ohio	660	Chaptico, St. Mary's, Md	91
Chain Lake Centre, Martin, Minn	43	Chardon,* (c. h.,) Geauga, Ohio	600
Chain of Rocks, Lincoln, Mo	12	Chariton,* (c. h.,) Lucas, Iowa	1,500
Chalk Bluff, Marion, Ala	15	Charlemont, Franklin, Mass	300
Chalk Level, St. Clair, Mo	18	Charlemont, Bedford, Va	11
Chalk Level, Harnett, N. C	2	Charles City,* (c. h.,) Floyd, Iowa	1,500
Chalk Level, Pittsylvania, Va	44	Charles City C. H., Charles City, Va.	12
Chalk Spring, Santa Rosa, Fla	12	Charles River Village, Norfolk, Mass	53
Chalmers, White, Ind	54	Charleston, Franklin, Ark	20
Chalybeate, Johnson, Mo	12	Charleston, Yola, Cal	3
Chalybeate Springs, Meriwether,		Charleston,* (c. h.,) Coles, Ill	2,200
Ga	6	Charleston, Lee, Iowa	73
Chalybes, Litchfield, Conn	100	Charleston, Penobscot, Me	11
Chamberlain, Allen, Ind	10	Charleston, (c. h.,) Tallahatchee, Miss	250
Chambers C. H.,* Chambers, Ala	410	Charleston, (c. h.,) Mississippi, Mo	320
Chambersburgh, Pike, Ill	37	Charleston, Montgomery, N. Y	35
Chambersburgh, Orange, Ind	30	Charleston, Tioga, Pa	25
Chambersburgh, Clarke, Mo	16	Charleston,* (c. h.,) Charleston, S. C.	4,000
Chambersburgh, Montgomery, Ohio	12	Charleston, Bradley, Tenn	240
Chambersburgh,* (c. h.,) Franklin, Pa	2,400	Charleston, Hopkins, Tex	12
Chambers Creek, Ellis, Texas	24	Charleston Four Corners, Montgom-	
Chambers' Valley, Carroll, Va	14	ery, N. Y	100
Chambersville, Calhoun, Ark	24	Charlestown,* (c. h.,) Clarke, Ind	630
Chambersville, New Castle, Del	9	Charlestown, Cecil, Md	81
Chambersville, Indiana, Pa	41	Charlestown,* Middlesex, Mass	2,300
Chamblissburgh, Bedford, Va	13	Charlestown,* Sullivan, N. H	770
Chamois, Osage, Mo	190	Charlestown, Portage, Ohio	64
Champagnolle, Union, Ark	12	Charlestown, Luzerne, Pa	25
Champaign,* Champaign, Ill	2,300	Charlestown, Washington, R. I	16
Champion, Jefferson, N. Y	65	Charlestown,* Jefferson, W. Va	920
Champlain, Clinton, N. Y	930	Charlestown, Calumet, Wis	42
Champlin, Hennepin, Minn	49	Charlesville, Bedford, Pa	16
Chanceford, York, Pa	59	Charlevoix, (c. h.,) Charlevoix, Mich.	160
Chandaller, Keokuk, Iowa	16	Charlie Hope, Brunswick, Va	34
Chandler's Valley, Warren, Pa	55	Charloe, Paulding, Ohio	28
Chandlersville, Muskingum, Ohio	98	Charlotte, Clinton, Iowa	56
Chandlerville, Cass, Ill	280	Charlotte, Washington, Me	38
Chaneysville, Bedford, Pa	15	Charlotte,* (c. h.,) Eaton, Mich	1,600
Changewater, Warren, N. J	49	Charlotte, Monroe, N. Y	220
Channahatchee, Elmore, Ala	6	Charlotte,* (c. h.,) Mecklenburgh,	
Channahon, Will, Ill	170	N. C	2,500
Chantilly, Lincoln, Mo	12	Charlotte, (c. h.,) Dickson, Tenn	100
Chautilly, Fairfax, Va	36	Charlotte, Chittenden, Vt	170
Chapel, Howell, Mo	12	Charlotte C. H., Charlotte, Va	360
Chapel Hill, Campbell, Ga	6	Charlotteburgh, Passaic, N. J	12
Chapel Hill, La Fayette, Mo	75	Charlotte Centre, Chautauqua, N.Y.	20
Chapel Hill, Monmouth, N. J	31	Charlotte Hall, St. Mary's, Md	140
Chapel Hill,* Orange, N. C	520	Charlottesville, Hancock, Ind	120

* Money-order office.

CHE CHE

Charlottesville,* (c. h.,) Albemarle, Va	$2,400
Charlotteville, Schoharie, N. Y	150
Charlton, Worcester, Mass	120
Charlton, Saratoga, N. Y	190
Charlton City, Worcester, Mass	89
Charlton Depot, Worcester, Mass	220
Chartiers, Allegheny, Pa	16
Chase, Johnson, Iowa	13
Chaseburgh, Vernon, Wis	53
Chase's Mills, St. Lawrence, N. Y	12
Chase's Mills, Tioga, Pa	12
Chaseville, Otsego, N. Y	82
Chaska, (c. h.,) Carver, Minn	230
Chatata, Bradley, Tenn	60
Chatawa, Pike, Miss	230
Chateaugay, Franklin, N. Y	700
Chateaugay Lake, Franklin, N. Y	31
Chatfield,* Fillmore, Minn	760
Chatfield, Crawford, Ohio	54
Chatfield, Navarro, Tex	8
Chatham, Sangamon, Ill	270
Chatham, Buchanan, Iowa	48
Chatham, Barnstable, Mass	510
Chatham, Wright, Minn	23
Chatham, Morris, N. J	220
Chatham, Columbia, N. Y	160
Chatham, Licking, Ohio	38
Chatham, Chester, Pa	130
Chatham Centre, Columbia, N. Y	100
Chatham Centre, Medina, Ohio	160
Chatham Hill, Smyth, Va	51
Chatham Port, Barnstable, Mass	80
Chatham Run, Clinton, Pa	66
Chatham Valley, Tioga, Pa	13
Chatham Village, Columbia, N. Y	860
Chatsworth,* Livingston, Ill	1,100
Chattahoochee, Gadsden, Fla	77
Chattan, Adams, Ill	46
Chattanooga,* Hamilton, Tenn	2,600
Chatterton, King George, Va	38
Chattoogaville, Chattooga, Ga	6
Chaumont, Jefferson, N. Y	270
Chauncey, Tippecanoe, Ind	39
Chauncey, Athens, Ohio	55
Chazy, Clinton, N. Y	120
Cheat Mountain, Randolph, W. Va	12
Chebanse, Iroquois, Ill	520
Chebeague Island, Cumberland, Me	38
Cheboygan, (c. h.,) Cheboygan, Mich	120
Checo, Cherokee, Kans	12
Cheektowaga, Erie, N. Y	42
Cheesland, Angelina, Tex	5
Chehalis Point, Chehalis, Wash	15
Chellis, Woodson, Kans	9
Chelmsford, Middlesex, Mass	170
Chelsea, Tama, Iowa	160
Chelsea, Butler, Kans	12
Chelsea,* Suffolk, Mass	2,700
Chelsea, Washtenaw, Mich	660
Chelsea, Delaware, Pa	18
Chelsea*, (c. h.,) Orange, Vt	870
Cheltenham, St. Louis, Mo	23
Cheltenham, Montgomery, Pa	140
Chemung, McHenry, Ill	95

Chemung, Chemung, N. Y	$210
Chemung Centre, Chemung, N. Y	12
Chenango, Lawrence, Pa	8
Chenango, Brazoria, Tex	12
Chenango Forks, Broome, N. Y	200
Cheneyville, Rapides, La	45
Chengwatana, (c. h.,) Pine, Minn	40
Chenoa,* McLean, Ill	1,100
Chepachet, Providence, R. I	160
Chepstow, Washington, Kans	12
Chepultepec, Blount, Ala	2
Chequist, Davis, Iowa	20
Cheraw,* Chesterfield, S. C	800
Cherino, Nacogdoches, Tex	15
Cherokee, Colbert, Ala	130
Cherokee, Butte, Cal	56
Cherokee, (c. h.,) Cherokee, Iowa	35
Cherokee, Crawford, Kans	12
Cherokee, Lawrence, Ky	12
Cherokee, San Saba, Tex	12
Cherokee Mills, Cherokee, Ga	12
Cherokee Mound, Cherokee, Kans	12
Cherry Box, Shelby, Mo	23
Cherry Camp, Harrison, W. Va	160
Cherry Creek, Arapahoe, Colo	12
Cherry Creek, Woodson, Kans	12
Cherry Creek, Pontotoc, Miss	22
Cherry Creek, Chautauqua, N. Y	120
Cherryfield, Transylvania, N. C	5
Cherry Flats, Tioga, Pa	35
Cherry Fork, Adams, Ohio	92
Cherry Grove, Saline, Ark	10
Cherry Grove, Fillmore, Minn	26
Cherry Grove, Schuyler, Mo	48
Cherry Grove, Platte, Nebr	12
Cherry Grove, Hamilton, Ohio	61
Cherry Grove, Washington, Tenn	4
Cherry Grove, Rockingham, Va	21
Cherry Hill, Cecil, Md	93
Cherry Hill, Erie, Pa	48
Cherry Lane, Alleghany, N. C	4
Cherry Lane, King William, Va	12
Cherry Point City, Edgar, Ill	15
Cherry Ridge, Wayne, Pa	31
Cherry Run Depot, Morgan, W. Va	41
Cherry Spring, Gillespie, Tex	6
Cherrystone, Northampton, Va	140
Cherry Tree, Venango, Pa	65
Cherry Valley,* Winnebago, Ill	460
Cherry Valley, Worcester, Mass	220
Cherry Valley, Otsego, N. Y	630
Cherry Valley, Ashtabula, Ohio	92
Cherry Valley, Washington, Pa	20
Cherryville, Montgomery, Kans	12
Cherryville, Crawford, Mo	24
Cherryville, Hunterdon, N. J	19
Cherryville, Gaston, N. C	74
Cherryville, Northampton, Pa	70
Chesaning, Saginaw, Mich	350
Chesapeake, Lawrence, Mo	34
Chesapeake City,* Cecil, Md	540
Cheshire,* New Haven, Conn	580
Cheshire, Berkshire, Mass	410
Cheshire, Allegan, Mich	8
Cheshire, Ontario, N. Y	67
Cheshire, Gallia, Ohio	150

* Money-order office.

CHI

Chesnut Bluffs, Dyer, Tenn	$16
Chesnut Creek, (c. h.,) Baker, Ala	3
Chesnut Fork, Bedford, Va	8
Chesnut Grove, Shelby, Ky	4
Chesnut Grove, Lycoming, Pa	7
Chesnut Grove, Chester, S. C	35
Chesnut Hill, Washington, Ind	23
Chesnut Hill, Middlesex, Mass	12
Chesnut Level, Lancaster, Pa	83
Chesnut Mound, Smith, Tenn	8
Chesnut Ridge, St. Genevieve, Mo	12
Chesnut Ridge, Dutchess, N. Y	20
Chesnut Ridge, Yadkin, N. C	3
Chest, Clearfield, Pa	23
Chester, Jefferson, Ala	5
Chester, Desha, Ark	12
Chester, Middlesex, Conn	440
Chester,* (c. h.,) Randolph, Ill	630
Chester, Wayne, Ind	14
Chester, Howard, Iowa	14
Chester, Jefferson, Kans	12
Chester, Penobscot, Me	10
Chester, Hampden, Mass	300
Chester, Eaton, Mich	12
Chester, Olmsted, Minn	10
Chester, Rockingham, N. H	270
Chester, Morris, N. J	310
Chester, Orange, N. Y	580
Chester, Meigs, Ohio	50
Chester,* Delaware, Pa	2,400
Chester,* Windsor, Vt	560
Chester, Chesterfield, Va	65
Chester C. H.,* Chester, S. C	1,100
Chester Centre, Hampden, Mass	35
Chester Cross Roads, Geauga, Ohio	110
Chesterfield, New London, Conn	43
Chesterfield, Macoupin, Ill	150
Chesterfield, Madison, Ind	77
Chesterfield, Hampshire, Mass	88
Chesterfield, Cheshire, N. H	86
Chesterfield C. H., Chesterfield, S. C	20
Chesterfield C. H., Chesterfield, Va	12
Chesterfield Factory, Cheshire, N. H	110
Chester Hill,* Morgan, Ohio	200
Chester Springs, Chester, Pa	220
Chester Station, Dodge, Wis	29
Chesterton, Porter, Ind	250
Chestertown,* (c. h.,) Kent, Md	780
Chestertown, Warren, N. Y	320
Chester Valley, Chester, Pa	77
Chesterville, Franklin, Me	72
Chesterville, Kent, Md	200
Chesterville, Pontotoc, Miss	14
Chesterville, Morrow, Ohio	240
Chesterville, Chester, Pa	32
Chest Springs, Cambria, Pa	95
Chetco, Curry, Oreg	19
Chetopah,* Labette, Kans	610
Cheviot, Hamilton, Ohio	92
Chewalla, McNairy, Tenn	12
Chew's Landing, Camden, N. J	16
Chewsville, Washington, Md	29
CHEYENNE CITY,* (c. h.,) Laramie, Wyo	2,800
Cheyney, Delaware, Pa	99
Chicago,* (c. h.,) Cook, Ill	4,000

CHI

Chicago, Marion, Ky	$75
Chicago, Douglas, Nebr	100
Chichester, Merrimack, N. H	62
Chickamauga, Hamilton, Tenn	5
Chickamauga Station, Hamilton, Tenn	8
Chickaming, Berrien, Mich	31
Chickasabogue, Mobile, Ala	12
Chickasaw, Franklin, Ala	12
Chickasaw,* (c. h.,) Chickasaw, Iowa	120
Chicken Creek, Juab, Utah	49
Chickies, Lancaster, Pa	160
Chick's Springs, Greenville, S. C	6
Chico,* Butte, Cal	730
Chicopee,* Hampden, Mass	2,000
Chicopee Falls,* Hampden, Mass	1,200
Chicora, Chicot, Ark	12
Chikalah, Yell, Ark	12
Childersburgh, Talladega, Ala	230
Childress' Store, Montgomery, Va	12
Childsville, Mitchell, N. C	4
Chilesburgh, Fayette, Ky	69
Chilesburgh, Caroline, Va	12
Chilhowee, Blount, Tenn	12
Chilhowie, Johnson, Mo	12
Chili, Calaveras, Cal	25
Chili, Hancock, Ill	47
Chili, Miami, Ind	88
Chili, Monroe, N. Y	44
Chili, Coshocton, Ohio	37
Chillicothe,* Peoria, Ill	820
Chillicothe, Wapello, Iowa	78
Chillicothe,* (c. h.,) Livingston, Mo	2,100
Chillicothe,* (c. h.,) Ross, Ohio	2,400
Chillisquaque, Northumberland, Pa	50
Chilmark, Dukes, Mass	87
Chilo, Clermont, Ohio	48
Chilton,* (c. h.,) Calumet, Wis	290
Chiltonville, Plymouth, Mass	100
Chimney Point, Addison, Vt	19
Chimney Rock, Rutherford, N. C	10
China, Kennebec, Me	200
China, St. Clair, Mich	33
China Grove, Pike, Ala	8
China Grove, Pike, Miss	14
China Grove, Rowan, N. C	51
China Grove, Williamsburgh, S. C	16
Chincoteague, Accomack, Va	29
Chincoteague Island, Accomack, Va	9
Chinese Camp, Tuolumne, Cal	210
Chinkapin Hill, Sangamon, Ill	12
Chinkapin Roof, Jackson, Ky	12
Chinook, Pacific, Wash	12
Chipman's Point, Addison, Vt	24
Chipmonk Cooley, Vernon, Wis	12
Chippenhook Springs, Rutland, Vt	12
Chippewa, New Castle, Del	22
Chippewa, Wayne, Ohio	140
Chippewa City, (c. h.,) Chippewa, Minn	10
Chippewa City, Chippewa, Wis	100
Chippewa Falls,* (c. h.,) Chippewa, Wis	1,300
Chippewa Lake, Mecosta, Mich	12
Chisago City, (c. h.,) Chisago, Minn	90
Chisago Lake, Chisago, Minn	170

* Money-order office.

CIR   CLA

Chismville, Scott, Ark	$6	Circleville,* (c. h.,) Pickaway, Ohio.	$2,000
Chittenango, Madison, N. Y	840	Circleville, Williamson, Tex	19
Chittenango Falls, Madison, N. Y	21	Circleville, Loudoun, Va	22
Chittenango Station, Madison, N. Y	12	Cisco, Placer, Cal	12
Chittenden, Rutland, Vt	34	Cistern, Fayette, Tex	12
Choconut, Susquehanna, Pa	18	Citico, Monroe, Tenn	8
Choconut Centre, Broome, N. Y	13	Citronelle, Mobile, Ala	40
Chocoville, Sebastian, Ark	12	City, Dutchess, N. Y	80
Choctaw Agency, Choctaw N., Ind. T	15	City Island, Westchester, N. Y	57
Choctaw Agency, Oktibbeha, Miss	96	City Point, Platte, Mo	86
Choctaw Bluff, Clarke, Ala	12	City Point, Prince George, Va	100
Choctaw Corner, Clarke, Ala	32	Civer, Fulton, Ill	37
Choteau Creek, Bonhomme, Dak	12	Civil Bend, Daviess, Mo	25
Christiana, New Castle, Del	130	Claiborne, Monroe, Ala	74
Christiana, Dakota, Minn	63	Claiborne, Jasper, Miss	20
Christiana, Lancaster, Pa	310	Claire Springs, Cedar, Mo	29
Christiana, Williamson, Tenn	10	Clairville, Sonoma, Cal	28
Christiana, Dane, Wis	44	Clanton, Madison, Iowa	7
Christiansburgh, Wapello, Iowa	10	'laquato, (c. h.,) Lewis, Wash	20
Christiansburgh, Shelby, Ky	140	Clara, Potter, Pa	10
Christiansburgh, Champaign, Ohio	85	Claremont, Richland, Ill	100
Christiansburgh,* (c. h.,) Montgomery, Va	750	Claremont, Dodge, Minn	70
		Claremont,* Sullivan, N. H	2,000
Christiansville, Mecklenburgh, Va	39	Claremont, Allegheny, Va	12
Christy's Prairie, Clay, Ind	16	Claremont Wharf, Surry, Va	12
Chrome, Chester, Pa	12	Clarence,* Cedar, Iowa	670
Chrome Hill, Harford, Md	21	Clarence, Calhoun, Mich	11
Chronicle, Catawba, N. C	4	Clarence, Shelby, Mo	420
Chuckatuck, Nansemond, Va	92	Clarence, Erie, N. Y	160
Chula Depot, Amelia, Va	210	Clarence Centre, Erie, N. Y	120
Chulafinnee, Cleburne, Ala	55	Clarenceville, Queens, N. Y	12
Chulahoma, Marshall, Miss	57	Clarendon, (c. h.,) Monroe, Ark	420
Chulasky, Northumberland, Pa	16	Clarendon, Orleans, N. Y	190
Chunkey's Station, Newton, Miss	30	Clarendon, Rutland, Vt	53
Church Creek, Dorchester, Md	99	Clarendon Centre, Calhoun, Mich	10
Church Grove, Knox, Tenn	3	Clarendon Springs, Rutland, Vt	180
Church Hill, Christian, Ky	12	Claridon, Geauga, Ohio	88
Church Hill, Queen Anne, Md	190	Clarinda,* (c. h.,) Page, Iowa	760
Church Hill, Jefferson, Miss	14	Clarington, Monroe, Ohio	260
Church Hill, Trumbull, Ohio	12	Clarington, Forest, Pa	20
Churchill, Ottawa, Kans	21	Clarion, (c. h.,) Wright, Iowa	120
Churchland, Norfolk, Va	10	Clarion,* (c. h.,) Clarion, Pa	730
Church's Corners, Hillsdale, Mich	12	Clark, Mercer, Pa	270
Churchtown, Columbia, N. Y	14	Clark Centre, Clark, Ill	20
Churchtown, Lancaster, Pa	63	Clarke, Wilson, Kans	11
Church View, Middlesex, Va	15	Clarke City, Clarke, Mo	12
Churchville, Harford, Md	190	Clarke Station, Lake, Ind	12
Churchville, Monroe, N. Y	340	Clarkestown, Lycoming, Pa	13
Churchville, Augusta, Va	150	Clarkesville, (c. h.,) Habersham, Ga.	130
Churubusco, Whitley, Ind	53	Clark's, Coshocton, Ohio	96
Churubusco, Clinton, N. Y	94	Clarksborough, Gloucester, N. J	150
Cicero, Hamilton, Ind	180	Clarksborough, St. Lawrence, N. Y	12
Cicero, Madison, Mont	12	Clarksburgh, Decatur, Ind	99
Cicero, Onondaga, N. Y	210	Clarksburgh, Montgomery, Md	78
Cicero, Defiance, Ohio	29	Clarksburgh, Marquette, Mich	230
Cimarron, Mora, N. Mex	100	Clarksburgh, Moniteau, Mo	120
Cincinnati, Washington, Ark	40	Clarksburgh, Monmouth, N. J	45
Cincinnati, Appanoose, Iowa	86	Clarksburgh, Erie, N. Y	19
Cincinnati, Pawnee, Nebr	12	Clarksburgh, Ross, Ohio	71
Cincinnati,* (c. h.,) Hamilton, Ohio	4,000	Clarksburgh, Indiana, Pa	56
Cincinnatus, Cortland, N. Y	300	Clarksburgh, Carroll, Tenn	25
Cinnaminson, Burlington, N. J	120	Clarksburgh,* (c. h.,) Harrison, W. Va	1,200
Circle, Vermilion, Ill	12	Clark's Corner, Ashtabula, Ohio	12
Circleville, Tazewell, Ill	7	Clark's Creek, Grant, Ky	12
Circleville, Jackson, Kans	38	Clark's Factory, Delaware, N. Y	47
Circleville, Orange, N. Y	23	Clark's Falls, New London, Conn	37

* Money-order office.

Clarksfield, Huron, Ohio	$160	Claysville, Mineral, W. Va	$12
Clark's Fork, Cooper, Mo	28	*Clayton, (c. h.,)* Barbour, Ala	300
Clark's Fork, York, S. C	6	Clayton, Hempstead, Ark	12
Clark's Green, Luzerne, Pa	92	Clayton, Contra Costa, Cal	40
Clark's Grove, Freeborn, Minn	47	Clayton, Kent, Del	290
Clark's Hill, Tippecanoe, Ind	100	*Clayton, (c. h.,)* Rabun, Ga	47
Clark's Mills, Oneida, N. Y	88	Clayton,* Adams, Ill	590
Clark's Mills, Moore, N. C	12	Clayton, Hendricks, Ind	190
Clark's Mills, Manitowoc, Wis	73	Clayton, Clayton, Iowa	120
Clarkson, Monroe, N. Y	180	Clayton, Harford, Md	46
Clarkson, Columbiana, Ohio	19	Clayton, Lenawee, Mich	300
Clark's Prairie, Daviess, Ind	56	Clayton, Faribault, Minn	45
Clarkston, Oakland, Mich	270	Clayton, Gloucester, N. J	480
Clarkstown, (c. h.,) Rockland, N. Y	96	Clayton, Jefferson, N. Y	490
Clarksville, (c. h.,) Johnson, Ark	800	Clayton, Johnston, N. C	90
Clarksville, El Dorado, Cal	40	Clayton, Montgomery, Ohio	75
Clarksville, Hamilton, Ind	12	Clayton, Berks, Pa	42
Clarksville, Butler, Iowa	310	Claytona, Noble, Ohio	8
Clarksville, Howard, Md	96	Clayton Centre, Jefferson, N. Y	67
Clarksville, Pike, Mo	710	Claytonville, Brown, Kans	14
Clarksville, Merrick, Nebr	12	Claytonville, Transylvania, N. C	4
Clarksville, Coos, N. H	8	Clay Village, Shelby, Ky	84
Clarksville, Hunterdon, N. J	320	Clayville, Oneida, N. Y	650
Clarksville, Albany, N. Y	59	Clear Branch, Washington, Tenn	1
Clarksville, Clinton, Ohio	270	Clear Branch, Washington, Va	15
Clarksville, Greene, Pa	61	Clear Creek, Marion, Ark	12
Clarksville, (c. h.,) Montgomery, Tenn	2,700	Clear Creek, Monroe, Ind	12
		Clear Creek, Alamakee, Iowa	10
Clarksville, (c. h.,) Red River, Tex	430	Clear Creek, Nemaha, Kans	18
Clarksville, Mecklenburgh, Va	220	Clear Creek, Chautauqua, N. Y	33
Clarkton, Dunklin, Mo	12	Clear Creek, Mecklenburgh, N. C	4
Clarno, Green, Wis	12	Clear Creek, Fairfield, Ohio	54
Claryville, Sullivan, N. Y	12	Clear Creek, Clackamas, Oreg	14
Claussville, Lehigh, Pa	11	Clear Creek, Greene, Tenn	5
Claverack, Columbia, N. Y	640	Clear Creek, Raleigh, W. Va	12
Clay, Washington, Iowa	25	Clear Creek Falls, Winston, Ala	10
Clay, Webster, Ky	8	Clear Creek Landing, Alexander, Ill	20
Clay, Clarke, Mo	12	*Clearfield,* (c. h.,) Clearfield, Pa	1,300
Clay, Onondaga, N. Y	89	Clearfield Bridge, Clearfield, Pa	18
Clay, Jackson, Ohio	84	Clear Lake, Steuben, Ind	12
Clay C. H., Clay, W. Va	10	Clear Lake, Cerro Gordo, Iowa	240
Clay Bank, Oceana, Mich	12	Clear Lake, Sherburne, Minn	16
Clay Bank, Middlesex, N. J	12	Clear Port, Fairfield, Ohio	23
Clay Banks, Door, Wis	16	Clear Spring, Clark, Ark	12
Clay Brook, Madison, Tenn	12	Clear Spring, Graves, Ky	5
Clayburgh, Clinton, N. Y	36	Clear Spring, Washington, Md	310
Clay Centre, (c. h.,) Clay, Kans	97	Clear Spring, York, Pa	40
Clay City, Clay, Ill	300	Clear Spring, Grainger, Tenn	2
Clayford, Jones, Iowa	22	Clearville, Bedford, Pa	36
Clay Hill, Marengo, Ala	4	Clear Water, Antrim, Mich	18
Clay Hill, Lincoln, Ga	12	Clear Water, Wright, Minn	280
Clay Hill, Wexford, Mich	12	Clear Water Harbor, Hillsborough, Fla	6
Clay Hill, Titus, Tex	12		
Clay Lick, Licking, Ohio	66	Cleaveland, Oswego, N. Y	380
Clay Lick, Franklin, Pa	42	*Cleaveland,* (c. h.,) Bradley, Tenn	1,200
Clay Mills, Jones, Iowa	13	Cleburne, Johnson, Tex	250
Claymont, New Castle, Del	350	Cleek's Mills, Bath, Va	11
Claypool, Warren, Ky	4	Clemansville, Winnebago, Wis	23
Clay's Grove, Lee, Iowa	65	Clement, Clinton, Ill	220
Clay's Prairie, Edgar, Ill	12	Clementsville, Jackson, Tenn	12
Claysville, Marshall, Ala	5	Clendenin, Kanawha, W. Va	16
Claysville, Washington, Ind	13	Cleona, Brown, Ind	8
Claysville, Harrison, Ky	25	Cleopatra, Mercer, Mo	24
Claysville, Boone, Mo	44	Clermont, Marion, Ind	110
Claysville, Guernsey, Ohio	74	Clermont,* Fayette, Iowa	460
Claysville, Washington, Pa	200	Clermont, Columbia, N. Y	74

Clermont Mills, Harford, Md	$38	Clinton, Laurens, S. C	$75
Clermontville, McKean, Pa	4	Clinton, (c. h.,) Anderson, Tenn	160
Cleveland, (c. h.,) White, Ga	58	Clinton, (c. h.,) De Witt, Tex	210
Cleveland, Henry, Ill	12	Clinton, Ohio, W. Va	24
Cleveland, Hancock, Ind	78	Clinton,* Rock, Wis	750
Cleveland, Fayette, Ky	24	Clinton Corners, Dutchess, N. Y	38
Cleveland, Le Sueur, Minn	84	Clinton Corners, Wyoming, Pa	8
Cleveland,* (c. h.,) Cuyahoga, Ohio	4,000	Clintondale, Ulster, N. Y	55
Cleves, Hamilton, Ohio	170	Clinton Falls, Steele, Minn	33
Clifford, Bartholomew, Ind	62	Clinton Furnace, Monongalia, W.Va	12
Clifford, Lapeer, Mich	6	Clinton Hollow, Dutchess, N. Y	23
Clifford, Susquehanna, Pa	82	Clinton Lock, Parke, Ind	12
Clifton, Wilcox, Ala	58	Clinton Mills, Clinton, N. Y	64
Clifton, Iroquois, Ill	420	Clinton Point, Dutchess, N. Y	24
Clifton, Union, Ind	22	Clinton Station, Hunterdon, N. J	160
Clifton, Louisa, Iowa	170	Clinton Station, Clinton, Ohio	16
Clifton, Washington, Kans	12	Clinton Valley, Clinton, Ohio	18
Clifton, Penobscot, Me	29	Clintonville, Kane, Ill	190
Clifton, Schuyler, Mo	18	Clintonville, Bourbon, Ky	40
Clifton, Nemaha, Nebr	4	Clintonville, Cedar, Mo	39
Clifton, Passaic, N. J	12	Clintonville, Clinton, N. Y	250
Clifton, Colfax, N. Mex	12	Clintonville, Franklin, Ohio	24
Clifton, Monroe, N. Y	72	Clintonville, Venango, Pa	89
Clifton, Greene, Ohio	130	Clintonville, Greenbrier, W. Va	27
Clifton, Luzerne, Pa	40	Clintonville, Waupacca, Wis	47
Clifton, Wayne, Tenn	69	Clio, Barbour, Ala	12
Clifton, Bosque, Tex	8	Clio, Wayne, Ind	10
Clifton, Cache, Utah	12	Clio, Pulaski, Ky	20
Clifton, Mason, W. Va	48	Clio, Genesee, Mich	390
Clifton, Monroe, Wis	8	Clio, Marlborough, S. C	20
Clifton Dale, Essex, Mass	78	Cliola, Adams, Ill	12
Clifton Forge, Alleghany, Va	74	Clipper Gap, Placer, Cal	23
Clifton Hill, Randolph, Mo	69	Clipper Mills, Butte, Cal	71
Clifton Mills, Breckinridge, Ky	24	Clipper Mills, Gallia, Ohio	12
Clifton Mills, Pierce, Wis	12	Clitherall, Otter Tail, Minn	10
Clifton Park, Saratoga, N. Y	130	Clockville, Madison, N. Y	240
Clifton Springs,* Ontario, N. Y	980	Clokey, Washington, Pa	33
Clifton Station, Fairfax, Va	67	Clonmell, Lancaster, Pa	22
Clifty, Madison, Ark	10	Clopton, Dale, Ala	12
Clifty, Decatur, Ind	97	Closter, Bergen, N. J	190
Clifty, Todd, Ky	4	Clouser's Mills, Montgomery, Ind	5
Clifty, Fayette, W. Va	12	Cloutarf, Dane, Wis	10
Clifty Dale, Maries, Mo	9	Cloutierville, Natchitoches, La	20
Climax Prairie, Kalamazoo, Mich	150	Clove, Sussex, N. J	13
Cline's Mills, Augusta, Va	12	Clove, Dutchess, N. Y	11
Clinton, Greene, Ala	110	Clove Branch Junction, Dutchess, N. Y	12
Clinton, (c. h.,) Van Buren, Ark	20	Clover Bend, (c. h.,) Lawrence, Ark.	12
Clinton, Middlesex, Conn	630	Clover Bottom, Jackson, Ky	6
Clinton, (c. h.,) Jones, Ga	80	Clover Bottom, Franklin, Mo	12
Clinton,* (c. h.,) De Witt, Ill	1,100	Clover Creek, Blair, Pa	58
Clinton, Vermillion, Ind	190	Cloverdale, Sonoma, Cal	90
Clinton,* Clinton, Iowa	3,100	Cloverdale, Dade, Ga	12
Clinton, Douglas, Kans	150	Cloverdale, Putnam, Ind	190
Clinton, (c. h.,) Hickman, Ky	120	Cloverdale, Benton, Mo	8
Clinton,* (c. h.,) East Feliciana, La.	710	Cloverdale, Botetourt, Va	210
Clinton, Kennebec, Me	210	Clover Dale, Doddridge, W. Va	12
Clinton,* Worcester, Mass	2,000	Clover Depot, Halifax, Va	170
Clinton, Lenawee, Mich	640	Clover Green, Spottsylvania, Va	13
Clinton, Hinds, Miss	290	Clover Hill, Hunterdon, N. J	44
Clinton,* (c. h.,) Henry, Mo	1,300	Clover Hill, Blount, Tenn	12
Clinton, (c. h.,) Stanton, Nebr	9	Cloverland, Clay, Ind	62
Clinton, Hunterdon, N. J	630	Clover Orchard, Alamance, N. C	5
Clinton, Oneida, N. Y	2,200	Cloverport, Breckinridge, Ky	310
Clinton, (c. h.,) Sampson, N. C	180	Clovesville, Delaware, N. Y	23
Clinton, Summit, Ohio	180	Cloyd's Creek, Blount, Tenn	12
Clinton, Allegheny, Pa	84		

* Money-order office.

COD | COL

Clyde, Jasper, Iowa	$46	Coelk, Livingston, La	$12
Clyde, Cloud, Kans.	110	Coe Ridge, Cuyahoga, Ohio	35
Clyde, Wayne, N. Y	1,600	Coesse, Whitley, Ind	120
Clyde,* Sandusky, Ohio	1,200	Coeymans, Albany, N. Y	260
Clyde Mills, St. Clair, Mich	16	Coeymans Hollow, Albany, N Y	86
Clyman, Dodge, Wis	41	Coffadeliah, Neshoba, Miss	6
Clymer, Chautauqua, N. Y	250	Coffee, Clay, Ind	15
Clymore, Labette, Kans.	12	Coffee Landing, Hardin, Tenn	12
Coal Bank, Thurston, Wash	6	Coffee Run, Huntingdon, Pa	32
Coal Bluff, Washington, Pa.	60	Coffeeville, (c. h.,) Yalabusha, Miss..	200
Coalburgh, Trumbull, Ohio	170	Coffeeville, Upshur, Tex	60
Coalburgh, Kanawha, W. Va	73	Coffeysburgh, Daviess, Mo	12
Coal Centre, Linn, Kans	12	Coffeyville, Montgomery, Kans	12
Coal City, Venango, Pa	27	Coffin's Summit, Dutchess, N. Y	12
Coal Creek, Boulder, Colo	8	Cogan House, Lycoming, Pa	11
Coal Creek, Keokuk, Iowa	69	Cogan Station, Lycoming, Pa	120
Coal Creek, Ottawa, Kans	12	Cog Hill, McMinn, Tenn	11
Coal Creek, Campbell, Tenn	12	Cohansey, Cumberland, N. J	12
Coal Dale, Perry, Ohio	20	Cohasset, Norfolk, Mass	440
Coal Grove, Lawrence, Ohio	44	Cohoctah, Livingston, Mich	7
Coalmont, Huntington, Pa	66	Cohocton, Steuben, N. Y	340
Coal River Marshes, Raleigh, W.Va.	5	Cohoes,* Albany, N. Y	2,600
Coal Run, Pike, Ky	10	Coila, Washington, N. Y	110
Coal Run, Washington, Ohio	56	Coinjock, Currituck, N. C	5
Coalsmouth, Kanawha, W. Va	120	Coitsville, Mahoning, Ohio	24
Coalton, Monroe, Iowa	14	Cokesbury, Abbeville, S. C	150
Coalton, Boyd, Ky	110	Colaparchee, Monroe, Ga	71
Coal Valley, Rock Island, Ill	200	Colburn, Tippecanoe, Iud	50
Coal Valley, Allegheny, Pa	84	Colchester,* New London, Conn	824
Coalville, Livingston, Ill	26	Colchester, McDonough, Ill	300
Coalville, (c. h.,) Summit, Utah	91	Colchester, Delaware, N. Y	16
Coalville, Lincoln, W. Va	12	Colchester, Chittenden, Vt	120
Coast Fork, Lane, Oreg	12	Cold Brook, Herkimer, N. Y	72
Coast Range, Colusa, Cal	14	Coldbrook Springs, Worce ster,	
Coatesville, Hendricks, Ind	84	Mass	100
Coatesville, Chester, Pa	1,300	Cold Creek, Bradford, Pa	12
Coatopa, Sumter, Ala	16	Colden, Erie, N. Y	100
Coatsburgh, Adams, Ill	98	Coldenham, Orange, N. Y	200
Coatsville, Schuyler, Mo	12	Cold Neck, Cooper, Mo	16
Cobalt, Middlesex, Conn	130	Cold Spring, El Dorado, Cal	13
Cobb, Randolph, Ill	31	Cold Spring, Fairfield, Conn	74
Cobb, Iowa, Wis	20	Cold Spring, Shelby, Ill	30
Cobb River, Waseca, Minn	13	Cold Spring, Campbell, Ky	77
Cobb's Creek, Matthews, Va	12	Cold Spring, Berkshire, Mass	26
Cobham, Warren, Pa	37	Cold Spring, Cape May, N. J	160
Cobham, Albermarle, Va	170	Cold Spring,* Putnam, N. Y	1,200
Cobleskill, Schoharie, N. Y	870	Cold Spring, Wayne, Pa	14
Cob Moo Sa, Oceana, Mich	10	Cold Spring, Bledsoe, Tenn	12
Coburgh, Monmouth, N. J	10	Cold Spring, Polk, Tex	100
Coburn's Corners, De Kalb, Ind..	23	Cold Spring, Jefferson, Wis	22
Coburn's Store, Union, N. C	12	Cold Spring City, Stearns, Minn	83
Cocalico, Lancaster, Pa	13	Cold Spring Harbor, Suffolk, N. Y	150
Cochecton, Sullivan. N. Y	290	Cold Springs, Edgefield, S. C	6
Cochecton Centre, Sullivan, N. Y.	65	Cold Stream, Hampshire, W. Va	6
Cochessett, Plymouth, Mass	85	Cold Water, Cross, Ark	25
Cochituate, Middlesex, Mass	91	Coldwater, Franklin, Iowa	10
Cochran, Pulaski, Ga	12	Coldwater, Callaway, Ky	11
Cochran's Mills, Armstrong, Pa	47	Cold Water,* (c. h.,) Branch, Mich..	2,600
Cochransville, Chester, Pa	230	Coldwater, De Soto, Miss	80
Cochranton, Marion, Ohio	23	Cold Water, Wayne, Mo	42
Cochranton, Crawford, Pa	330	Cold Water, Monroe, N. Y	19
Cockeysville,* Baltimore, Md	300	Cold Water, Mercer, Ohio	45
Cocolamus, Juniata, Pa	32	Cold Water, Doddridge, W. Va	12
Coddle Creek, Cabarrus, N. C	8	Cold Well, White, Ark	10
Codorus, York, Pa	53	Cold Well, Union, S. C	12
Cody's Mills, Kent, Mich	79	Coldwell's Store, Anderson, Ky	2

* Money-order office.

COL   COL

Office	$
Colebrook, Litchfield, Conn	$140
Colebrook, Coos, N. H	460
Colebrook, Ashtabula, Ohio	73
Colebrook, Lebanon, Pa	12
Colebrookdale, Berks, Pa	50
Colebrook River, Litchfield, Conn	88
Cole Camp, Benton, Mo	89
Cole Creek, Fountain, Ind	17
Colegrove, McKean, Pa	25
Colegrove's Point, Sutter, Cal	12
Coleman's Depot, Randolph, Ga	12
Colemansville, Harrison, Ky	17
Colemanville, Lancaster, Pa	34
Colerain, Franklin, Mass	100
Colerain, Bertie, N. C	89
Colerain, Belmont, Ohio	75
Colerain, Lancaster, Pa	28
Colerain Forge, Huntingdon, Pa	40
Colesburgh, Delaware, Iowa	260
Colesburgh, Potter, Pa	28
Cole's Corners, De Kalb, Ind	10
Cole's Creek, Columbia, Pa	14
Cole's Ferry, Charlotte, Va	44
Colesville, Montgomery, Md	15
Colesville, Sussex, N. J	45
Colesville, Broome, N. Y	12
Colesville, Stokes, N. C	6
Coleta, Clay, Ala	5
Coleta, Whitesides, Ill	110
Coleville, Mono, Cal	22
Coleville, Bossier, La	12
Colfax, Placer, Cal	220
Colfax, Fremont, Colo	12
Colfax, Warren, Ill	16
Colfax, Clinton, Ind	130
Colfax, Jasper, Iowa	200
Colfax, (c. h.,) Grant, La	12
Colfax, Mason, Mich	21
Colfax, Sullivan, Mo	6
Colfax, Guilford, N. C	12
Colfax, Fairfield, Ohio	12
Colfax, Huntingdon, Pa	13
Colfax, Van Zandt, Tex	12
Colfax, Dunn, Wis	12
Collamer, Whitley, Ind	44
Collamer, Onondaga, N. Y	170
Collamer, Cuyahoga, Ohio	140
Collamer, Chester, Pa	40
College Corner, Jay, Ind	54
College Corner, Butler, Ohio	210
College Grove, Williamson, Tenn	74
College Hill, Middlesex, Mass	130
College Hill, Hamilton, Ohio	610
College Mound, Macon, Mo	80
College Point, Queens, N. Y	270
College Springs, Page, Iowa	200
Collegeville, Saline, Ark	12
Collegeville, San Joaquin, Cal	12
Collegeville, Montgomery, Pa	300
Collettsville, Caldwell, N. C	8
Colley, Sullivan, Pa	16
Collier's Mill, Ocean, N. J	10
Collierstown, Rockbridge, Va	44
Colliersville, Otsego, N. Y	140
Colliersville, Shelby, Tenn	280
Collington, Prince George's, Md	130

Office	$
Collingwood, Onondaga, N. Y	$21
Collingwood, Fairfax, Va	12
Collins, Erie, N. Y	100
Collinsburgh, Bossier, La	61
Collins Centre, Erie, N. Y	120
Collins Depot, Hampden, Mass	95
Collinsville, Etowah, Ala	14
Collinsville,* Hartford, Conn	730
Collinsville,* Madison, Ill	580
Collinsville, Lewis, N. Y	56
Collinsville, Butler, Ohio	78
Collinsville, Frederick, Va	5
Collinwood, Meeker, Minn	12
Collomsville, Lycoming, Pa	50
Colman, St. Louis, Mo	12
Colmar, McDonough, Ill	40
Colo, Story, Iowa	190
Cologne, Mason, W. Va	69
Coloma, Cherokee, Ala	10
Coloma, El Dorado, Cal	100
Coloma, Parke, Ind	12
Coloma, Woodson, Kans	20
Coloma, Berrien, Mich	120
Coloma, Carroll, Mo	98
Coloma, Waushara, Wis	44
Colon, St. Joseph, Mich	290
Colona Station, Henry, Ill	150
Colony, Knox, Mo	24
Colora, Cecil, Md	130
Colorado City, (c. h.,) El Paso, Colo	200
Colosse, Oswego, N. Y	74
Colquit, (c. h.,) Miller, Ga	25
Coltharp's, Houston, Tex	8
Colton, St. Lawrence, N. Y	270
Colton, Henry, Ohio	70
Colt's Neck, Monmouth, N. J	100
Columbia, Henry, Ala	25
Columbia,* Tuolumne, Cal	540
Columbia, Tolland, Conn	98
Columbia, Monroe, Ill	230
Columbia, Fayette, Ind	48
Columbia, Marion, Iowa	50
Columbia, (c. h.,) Adair, Ky	280
Columbia, (c. h.,) Caldwell, La	120
Columbia, Washington, Me	190
Columbia, Jackson, Mich	28
Columbia, (c. h.,) Marion, Miss	14
Columbia, (c. h.,) Boone, Mo	1,400
Columbia, Coos, N. H	19
Columbia, Warren, N. J	33
Columbia, Herkimer, N. Y	23
Columbia, (c. h.,) Tyrrel, N. C	12
Columbia, Hamilton, Ohio	140
Columbia,* Lancaster, Pa	2,300
COLUMBIA,* (c. h.,) Richland, S. C	3,000
Columbia,* (c. h.,) Maury, Tenn	1,400
Columbia, Brazoria, Tex	210
Columbia, Fluvanna, Va	270
Columbia Centre, Licking, Ohio	67
Columbia City,* (c. h.,) Whitley, Ind	940
Columbia X Roads, Bradford, Pa	78
Columbia Farm, Venango, Pa	270
Columbia Furnace, Shenandoah, Va	33
Columbiana, (c. h.,) Shelby, Ala	300
Columbiana, Columbiana, Ohio	520
Columbian Grove, Lunenburgh, Va	12

* Money-order office.

CON

Columbia Station, Lorain, Ohio....	$70
Columbiaville, Lapeer, Mich	52
Columbus, Hempstead, Ark	25
Columbus, Madison, Fla....	12
Columbus, (c. h.,) Muscogee, Ga....	3,600
Columbus, Adams, Ill.............	110
Columbus, (c. h.,) Bartholomew, Ind	1,800
Columbus, (c. h.,) Cherokee, Kans..	73
Columbus,* Hickman, Ky	610
Columbus, St. Clair, Mich........	67
Columbus, (c. h.,) Lowndes, Miss ..	2,200
Columbus, Johnson, Mo...........	93
Columbus, (c. h.,) Platte, Nebr	600
Columbus, Esmeralda, Nev........	12
Columbus, Burlington, N. J.......	230
Columbus, Chenango, N.Y	95
Columbus, (c. h.,) Polk, N.C	45
COLUMBUS,* (c. h.,) Franklin, Ohio.	4,000
Columbus, Warren, Pa............	430
Columbus, (c. h.,) Colorado, Tex...	980
Columbus,* Columbia, Wis........	1,300
Columbus City,* Louisa, Iowa.....	350
Columbus Grove,* Putnam, Ohio..	570
Colusa, (c. h.,) Colusa, Cal....... ..	700
Comanche, Comanche, Tex........	12
Comann's Well, Sussex, Va........	12
Comettsburgh, Beaver, Pa	6
Comfort, Kerr, Tex......	99
Comly, Montour, Pa	12
Commack, Suffolk, N.Y..........	84
Commerce, Oakland, Mich	150
Commerce, Tunica, Miss	12
Commerce, (c. h.,) Scott, Mo......	170
Commerce, Wilson, Tenn..........	8
Commerce Mills, Polk, Iowa.......	12
Commiskey, Jennings, Ind....	12
Communia, Clayton, Iowa.........	23
Como, Whitesides, Ill	99
Como, Henry, Tenn	30
Como Depot, Panola, Miss.........	34
Comorn, King George, Va.........	120
Company's Shops, Alamance, N. C..	330
Competine, Wapello, Iowa....	18
Competition, Laclede, Mo	16
Compton, Los Angeles, Cal........	12
Comstock, Wapello, Iowa	24
Comstock, Kalamazoo, Mich.......	63
Comstock's Landing, Washington, N.Y...................	140
Conaway, Tyler, W.Va	3
Conception, Nodaway, Mo.........	12
Concord, Lawrence, Ala	9
Concord, Sussex, Del....	90
Concord, Gadsden, Fla	12
Concord, Pike, Ga..............	12
Concord, Morgan, Ill............	120
Concord, Hancock, Iowa.........	12
Concord, Lewis, Ky....	85
Concord, Somerset, Me..........	5
Concord, (c. h.,) Middlesex, Mass ..	1,000
Concord, Jackson, Mich..........	220
Concord, Dodge, Minn...........	84
Concord, Calhoun, Miss..........	8
Concord, Callaway, Mo..........	92
CONCORD,* (c. h.,) Merrimack, N.H.	3,000
Concord, (c. h.,) Cabarrus, N.C ...	540

CON

Concord, Lake, Ohio	$58
Concord, Franklin, Pa...........	56
Concord, Knox, Tenn	150
Concord, Hardin, Tex	17
Concord, Essex, Vt..............	45
Concord, Jefferson, Wis	61
Concord Church, Mercer, W. Va....	24
Concord Depot, Campbell, Va.....	150
Concordia, (c. h.,) Cloud, Kans......	12
Concordia, La Fayette, Mo	130
Concord Station, Erie, Pa........	130
Concordville, Delaware, Pa.......	210
Concrete, De Witt, Tex..........	200
Condit, Delaware, Ohio	22
Conejos, (c. h.,) Conejos, Colo	59
Conemaugh, Cambria, Pa	130
Conerly's, Pike, Miss............	8
Conestoga, Lancaster, Pa........	40
Conesus, Livingston, N.Y........	20
Conesus Centre, Livingston, N.Y..	180
Conesville, Muscatine, Iowa	12
Conesville, Schoharie, N.Y	34
Conewango, Cattaraugus, N.Y....	35
Confederate × Roads, Muskingum, Ohio	12
Confidence, Wayne, Iowa..........	44
Congress, Wayne, Ohio...........	64
Congruity, Westmoreland, Pa.....	38
Conklin Centre, Broome, N.Y.....	45
Conklingville, Saratoga, N.Y......	90
Conklin Station, Broome, N.Y....	12
Conlogue, Edgar, Ill	53
Conlogue, Jackson, Ind..........	21
Conneaut,* Ashtabula, Ohio......	1,100
Conneautville,* Crawford, Pa	700
Connecticut Lake, Coos, N.H.....	260
Connellsville, Fayette, Pa........	860
Conner's Creek, Wayne, Mich......	16
Conner's Mills, Cooper, Mo	12
Connersville, (c. h.,) Fayette, Ind ..	1,600
Connersville, Harrison, Ky	9
Connor's Mills, Floyd, Va.........	12
Connor's Station, Wyandotte, Kans.	16
Connotton, Harrison, Ohio.......	79
Conn's Creek, Shelby, Ind........	170
Conococheague, Washington, Md ..	28
Conover, Miami, Ohio...........	89
Conowingo, Cecil, Md	24
Conquest, Cayuga, N.Y	100
Conrad's Store, Rockingham, Va...	12
Conshohocken, Montgomery, Pa ...	770
Constableville, Lewis, N.Y.......	390
Constance, Boone, Ky...........	12
Constantia, Oswego, N.Y.........	170
Constantia, Delaware, Ohio	58
Constantia Centre, Oswego, N.Y...	14
Constantine, St. Joseph, Mich	1,000
Constitution, Washington, Ohio ...	80
Constitution, York, Pa	25
Consville, Henry, Mo...........	110
Content, Colorado, Tex..........	72
Contoocook Village, Merrimack, N.H.	250
Contreras, Butler, Ohio..........	24
Convent, (c. h.,) St. James, La......	370
Convis Centre, Calhoun, Mich.....	25

* Money-order office.

COP   COR

Office	Amount	Office	Amount
Conway, Aroostook, Me	$26	Copenhagen, Caldwell, La	$15
Conway, Franklin, Mass	540	Copenhagen, Lewis, N. Y	570
Conway, Livingston, Mich	12	Copenhagen, Caldwell, N. C	6
Conway, Leake, Miss	19	Copi, Johnson, Iowa	18
Conway, Carroll, N. H	170	Copley, Summit, Ohio	110
Conwayborough, (c. h.,) Horry, S. C	2	Copopa, Lorain, Ohio	32
Conway's Landing, Mendocino, Cal.	12	Copperas Hill, Orange, Vt	60
Conyers, Newton, Ga	150	Copper Creek, Rock Island, Ill	6
Conyersville, Henry, Tenn	18	Copper Falls Mine, Keweenaw, Mich	420
Conyngham, Luzerne, Pa	95	Copper Harbor, Keweenaw, Mich	140
Cooch's Bridge, New Castle, Del	12	Copper Hill, Hunterdon, N. J	52
Coody's Bluff, Cherokee N., Ind. T.	12	Copper Hill, Floyd, Va	10
Cookerly, Vigo, Ind	10	Copper Mines, Clay, Ala	15
Cooksburgh, Albany, N. Y	59	Copperopolis, Calaveras, Cal	330
Cooksburgh, Forest, Pa	12	Copper Vale, Lassen, Cal	7
Cook's Corners, Franklin, N. Y	17	Copper Valley, Floyd, Va	5
Cook's Ford, Jefferson, Kans	18	Coquille, Coos, Oreg	12
Cook's Mills, Coles, Ill	12	Coral, McHenry, Ill	25
Cook's Station, Newaygo, Mich	12	Coral, Montcalm, Mich	23
Cookstown, Burlington, N. J	43	Coral City, Trempealeau, Wis	100
Cook's Valley, Wabashaw, Minn	30	Coral Hill, Barren, Ky	22
Cook's Valley, Chippewa, Wis	12	Coral Hill, Elko, Nev	12
Cooksville, Howard, Md	28	Coralville, Johnson, Iowa	12
Cooksville, Rock, Wis	52	Coram, Suffolk, N. Y	31
Cookville, (c. h.,) Putnam, Tenn	99	Corbandale, Montgomery, Tenn	71
Cool Bank, Pike, Ill	12	Corbettsville, Broome, N. Y	51
Coolbaugh's, Monroe, Pa	24	Corcoran, Hennepin, Minn	12
Cooleysville, Steele, Minn	12	Cordaville, Worcester, Mass	210
Cool Spring, Ohio, Ky	6	Cordelia, Solano, Cal	12
Cool Spring, Iredell, N. C	23	Cordova, Rock Island, Ill	390
Cool Spring, Jefferson, Pa	12	Cordova, Grant, Ky	10
Coolville, Athens, Ohio	160	Cordova, Talbot, Md	12
Cool Well, Amherst, Va	43	Cordova, Le Sueur, Minn	63
Coomer, Niagara, N. Y	31	Corfu,* Genesee, N. Y	290
Coon Creek, Anoka, Minn	12	Corinna, Penobscot, Me	240
Coon Creek, Barton, Mo	21	Corinna, Wright, Minn	8
Coonewar, Lee, Miss	37	Corinna Centre, Penobscot, Me	31
Coon Island, Washington, Pa	21	Corinne, Box Elder, Utah	1,200
Coon Prairie, Vernon, Wis	190	Corinth, Williamson, Ill	26
Coon Rapids, Carroll, Iowa	10	Corinth, Grant, Ky	63
Coon's Corners, Crawford, Pa	18	Corinth, Penobscot, Me	31
Coon Valley, Vernon, Wis	110	Corinth,* (c. h.,) Alcorn, Miss	2,300
Cooper, Washington, Me	13	Corinth, Saratoga, N. Y	170
Cooper, Kalamazoo, Mich	100	Corinth, Orange, Vt	110
Cooperdale, Cambria, Pa	12	Cork, Hillsborough, Fla	20
Coopers, Franklin, Va	4	Cork, Ashtabula, Ohio	20
Coopersburgh, Lehigh, Pa	180	Cornelia, Johnson, Mo	88
Cooper's Gap, Rutherford, N. C	2	Cornersville, Dorchester, Md	33
Cooper's Hill, Osage, Mo	37	Cornersville, Giles, Tenn	290
Cooper's Mills, Lincoln, Me	110	Corn Grove, Calhoun, Ala	17
Cooper's Plains, Steuben, N. Y	130	Corning, Adams, Iowa	400
Cooperstown, Brown, Ill	27	Corning, Nemaha, Kans	12
Cooperstown,* (c. h.,) Otsego, N. Y	2,000	Corning, Holt, Mo	12
Cooperstown, Venango, Pa	170	Corning,* (c. h.,) Steuben, N. Y	2,400
Cooperstown, Manitowoc, Wis	53	Cornish, York, Me	230
Coopersville, Wapello, Iowa	16	Cornish, Sibley, Minn	12
Coopersville, Ottawa, Mich	290	Cornish Flat, Sullivan, N. H	210
Coopersville, Clinton, N. Y	37	Cornishville, Mercer, Ky	37
Coopertown, Robertson, Tenn	19	Cornplanter, Warren, Pa	20
Coos, Coos, N. H	290	Cornsville, Scott, Va	9
Coosa, Floyd, Ga	20	Cornton, Windham, Vt	72
Coosawhatchie, Beaufort, S. C	12	Cornville, La Salle, Ill	12
Coote's Store, Rockingham, Va	51	Cornville, Somerset, Me	25
Copake, Columbia, N. Y	190	Cornwall, Litchfield, Conn	170
Copake Iron Works, Columbia, N. Y	170	Cornwall, Madison, Mo	12
Copeland, Telfair, Ga	3	Cornwall, Orange, N. Y	430

* Money-order office.

COT   COV

Cornwall, Lebanon, Pa	$140	Cottonville, Jackson, Iowa	$45
Cornwall, Addison, Vt	90	Cottonwood, Tehama, Cal	32
Cornwall Bridge, Litchfield, Conn	180	Cottonwood, Gallatin, Ill	12
Cornwall Hollow, Litchfield, Conn	21	Cottonwood, Brown, Minn	7
Cornwallis, Ritchie, W. Va	50	*Cottonwood Falls,* (c. h.,) Chase, Kans	180
Cornwall Landing, Orange, N. Y	420	Cottonwood Grove, Bond, Ill	40
Cornwallville, Greene, N. Y	11	Cottonwood Point, Pemiscot, Mo	44
Corona, Coffey, Kans	12	Cottonwood Springs,* Lincoln, Nebr	520
Corpus Christi, (c. h.,) Nueces, Tex	1,400	Cotuit Port, Barnstable, Mass	320
Correctionville, Woodbury, Iowa	60	Couchville, Davidson, Tenn	8
Corrieville, Wabash, Ill	12	*Coudersport,* (c. h.,) Potter, Pa	460
Corriganville, Alleghany, Md	12	Coultersville, Randolph, Ill	140
Corry, Erie, Pa	2,800	Coultersville, Butler, Pa	82
Corsica, Morrow, Ohio	84	Council Bend, Crittenden, Ark	12
Corsica, Jefferson, Pa	110	*Council Bluffs,* (c. h.,) Pottawattomie, Iowa	3,400
Corsicana, Barry, Mo	49		
Corsicana, (c. h.,) Navarro, Tex	310	*Council Grove,* (c. h.,) Morris, Kans	450
Cortland, Jackson, Ind	15	Council Hill, Jo Daviess, Ill	50
Cortland Centre, Kent, Mich	76	Council Hill, Clayton, Iowa	43
Cortland Village, (c. h.,) Cortland, N. Y	2,200	Council Hill Station, Jo Daviess, Ill	84
		Counover,* Winneshiek, Iowa	220
Corunna, De Kalb, Ind	150	Countsville, Lexington, S. C	12
Corunna, (c. h.,) Shiawassee, Mich	860	County Line, Campbell, Ga	12
Corvallis, (c. h.,) Benton, Oreg	600	County Line, Tippecanoe, Ind	12
Corydon, (c. h.,) Harrison, Ind	340	County Line, Eaton, Mich	18
Corydon, (c. h.,) Wayne, Iowa	800	County Line, Niagara, N. Y	45
Corydon, Warren, Pa	190	County Line, Davie, N. C	18
Corymbo, La Porte, Ind	12	County Line, Lincoln, Tenn	12
Coshocton, (c. h.,) Coshocton, Ohio	1,800	County Line X Roads, Charlotte, Va	10
Cosmos, Renville, Minn	12	Coupville, Island, Wash	110
Cosmosa, Sedgwick, Kans	12	Courter, Miami, Ind	12
Costigon, Bath, Ky	12	Courtland, Lawrence, Ala	430
Costilla, Costilla, Colo	32	Courtland, Nicollet, Minn	24
Cosumne, Sacramento, Cal	35	Courtland Station, De Kalb, Ill	260
Cote Gelee, La Fayette, La	12	Courtney, Grimes, Tex	55
Cote Sans Dessein, Callaway, Mo	16	Coushatta Chute, Natchitoches, La	12
Cotile, Rapides, La	40	Cove, Polk, Ark	12
Cotile Landing, Rapides, La	12	Cove, Union, Oreg	39
Cottage, Hardin, Iowa	49	Covo City, Whitfield, Ga	12
Cottage, Cattaraugus, N. Y	38	Cove Creek, Etowah, Ala	5
Cottage, Huntingdon, Pa	34	Cove Creek, Tazewell, Va	12
Cottage Grove, Klamath, Cal	4	Cove Creek, Wayne, W. Va	12
Cottage Grove, Douglas, Ill	31	Cove Dale, Hamilton, Ohio	20
Cottage Grove, Union, Ind	53	*Coveland,* (c. h.,) Island, Wash	12
Cottage Grove, Washington, Minn	150	Covell, McLean, Ill	12
Cottage Grove, Lane, Oreg	55	Covelo, Mendocino, Cal	12
Cottage Grove, Dane, Wis	48	Coventry, Tolland, Conn	130
Cottage Hill, Dubuque, Iowa	25	Coventry, Chenango, N. Y	180
Cottage Hill, Muskingum, Ohio	23	Coventry, Kent, R. I	180
Cottage Home, Lincoln, N. C	10	Coventry, Orleans, Vt	210
Cottage Inn, La Fayette, Wis	20	Coventry Centre, Kent, R. I	55
Cottage Mills, Chattahoochee, Ga	6	Coventry Depot, Tolland, Conn	80
Cottageville, Jackson, W. Va	56	Coventryville, Chenango, N. Y	100
Cottle's Mills, Covington, Ala	12	Covo Point, Calvert, Md	12
Cottleville, St. Charles, Mo	79	Covert, Van Buren, Mich	12
Cotton Gin, Freestone, Tex	100	Covert, Seneca, N. Y	81
Cotton Gin Port, Monroe, Miss	15	Cove Station, Huntingdon, Pa	66
Cotton Grove, Henry, Iowa	12	Coveton, Barbour, W. Va	6
Cotton Hill, Sangamon, Ill	16	Coveville, Saratoga, N. Y	17
Cotton Hill, Fayette, W. Va	6	*Covington,* (c. h.,) Newton, Ga	720
Cotton Plant, Woodruff, Ark	27	*Covington,* (c. h.,) Fountain, Ind	780
Cotton Plant, Marion, Fla	12	*Covington,* (c. h.,) Kenton, Ky	3,300
Cotton Plant, Tippah, Miss	23	*Covington,* (c. h.,) St. Tammany, La	110
Cotton Plant, Lamar, Tex	12	Covington, Dakota, Nebr	12
Cotton Valley, Greene, N. C	12	Covington, Wyoming, N. Y	29
Cottonville, Marshall, Ala	6	Covington, Richmond, N. C	9

* Money-order office.

CRA   CRO

Covington, Miami, Ohio	$380	Crawford, Oglethorpe, Ga	$150
Covington, Tioga, Pa	260	Crawford, Gallatin, Ill	6
Covington, (c. h.,) Tipton, Tenn	210	Crawford, Crawford, Iowa	12
Covington, Hill, Tex	10	Crawford, Washington, Me	9
Covington, (c. h.,) Alleghany, Va	360	Crawford, Isabella, Mich	10
Covode, Indiana, Pa	59	Crawford House, Coos, N. H	12
Cowan, Delaware, Ind	12	Crawford's Fork, Cass, Mo	33
Cowan, Union, Pa	30	Crawfordsville, Crittenden, Ark	12
Cowan, Franklin, Tenn	140	*Crawfordsville,* (c. h.,) Montgomery,	
Cowanesque Valley, Tioga, Pa	33	Ind	2,000
Cowan's Ford, Mecklenburgh, N. C.	12	Crawfordsville, Washington, Iowa	160
Cowansville, Armstrong, Pa	50	Crawfordsville, Crawford, Kans	240
Cowikee, Barbour, Ala	14	Crawfordsville, Linn, Oreg	12
Cowle's Station, Macon, Ala	12	*Crawfordville,* (c. h.,) Wakulla, Fla	33
Cowlesville, Wyoming, N. Y	110	*Crawfordville,* (c. h.,) Taliaferro, Ga	250
Cowlitz, Lewis, Wash	35	Crawfordville, Lowndes, Miss	370
Cowpasture Bridge, Alleghany, Va.	12	Creagerstown, Frederick, Md	35
Cow Run, Washington, Ohio	12	Cream Ridge, Livingston, Mo	12
Cow Skin, Douglas, Mo	4	Creek Agency, Creek Nation, Ind. T.	14
Coxsackie, Greene, N. Y	1,100	Creek Centre, Warren, N. Y	58
Cox's Creek, Clayton, Iowa	48	Creek Locks, Ulster, N. Y	75
Cox's Creek, Nelson, Ky	12	Creekside, Indiana, Pa	12
Cox's Mills, Wayne, Ind	8	Creelsborough, Russell, Ky	34
Cox's Mills, Gilmer, W. Va	13	Creighton, Guernsey, Ohio	19
Coyleville, Butler, Pa	47	Cremona, Neosho, Kans	12
Coytee, Blount, Tenn	12	Crescent, Saratoga, N. Y	150
Coyville, Wilson, Kans	72	*Crescent City,* (c. h.,) Del Norte, Cal	200
Crab Orchard, Williamson, Ill	59	Crescent City, Iroquois, Ill	65
Crab Orchard, Lincoln, Ky	400	Crescent City, Pottawattamie, Iowa	28
Crab Orchard, Ray, Mo	45	Crescent Hill, Bates, Mo	160
Crab Orchard, Johnson, Nebr	23	Crescent Mills, Plumas, Cal	12
Crab Tree, Haywood, N. C	8	Cresco,* Howard, Iowa	1,100
Crab Tree, Westmoreland, Pa	31	Cresskill, Bergen, N. J	59
Cracow, Huron, Mich	12	Cresson, Cambria, Pa	360
Craftsbury, Orleans, Vt	94	Cressona, Schuylkill, Pa	330
Craggie Hope, Cheatham, Tenn	12	Crestline,* Crawford, Ohio	1,300
Craig, Switzerland, Ind	14	Creston,* Ogle, Ill	610
Craig, Holt, Mo	36	Creston, Union, Iowa	12
Craighead, Mecklenburgh, N. C	12	Creswell, St. Clair, Ill	12
Craig's Mills, Washington, Va	10	Creswell, Jefferson, Ind	12
Craigsville, Orange, N. Y	28	Creswell, Keokuk, Iowa	12
Craigsville, Gaston, N. C	5	Creswell, Labette, Kans	12
Craigsville, Armstrong, Pa	12	Creswell, Antrim, Mich	12
Craigsville, Lancaster, S. C	8	Creswell, Cortland, N. Y	12
Craigsville, Augusta, Va	94	Creswell, Jefferson, Ohio	12
Crain's Creek, Moore, N. C	24	Creswell, Lancaster, Pa	29
Cram's Corner, Carroll, N. H	18	Creswell, Houston, Tex	12
Cranberry, Allen, Ohio	12	Crete, Will, Ill	210
Cranberry, Venango, Pa	89	Crete, Saline, Nebr	12
Cranberry Creek, Fulton, N. Y	26	Crete, Indiana, Pa	10
Cranberry Forge, Mitchell, N. C	6	Creve Coeur, St. Louis, Mo	16
Cranberry Isles, Hancock, Me	51	Cribb's, Westmoreland, Pa	12
Cranberry Plains, Carroll, Va	38	Cridersville, Auglaize, Ohio	66
Cranberry Prairie, Mercer, Ohio	11	Crigler's Mills, Ralls, Mo	12
Cranbury, Middlesex, N. J	410	Criglersville, Madison, Va	27
Crandall, Lorain, Ohio	28	Crisfield, Somerset, Md	120
Crandell's Corners, Washington,		Crisp's Cross Roads, Harrison, Ind.	8
N. Y	43	Crittenden, Franklin, Ill	16
Cranesville, Montgomery, N. Y	38	Crittenden, Cass, Ind	7
Cranesville, Preston, W. Va	2	Crittenden, Grant, Ky	120
Crantord, Union, N. J	140	Crittenden, Daviess, Mo	12
Cranston Print Works, Providence,		Crittenden, Erie, N. Y	82
R. I	250	Crittenden Springs, Crittenden, Ky	6
Crapo, Osceola, Mich	12	*Crockett,* (c. h.,) Houston, Tex	340
Crary's Mills, St. Lawrence, N. Y	110	Crockett's Bluff, Arkansas, Ark	21
Crawford, Russell, Ala	63	Croftsville, Tazewell, Va	12

* Money-order office.

CRO

Croghan, Lewis, N. Y	$66
Cromwell, Middlesex, Conn	650
Cromwell, Noble, Ind	13
Cromwell, Union, Iowa	32
Cromwell, Ohio, Ky	44
Crook, Boone, W. Va	88
Crooked Creek, Steuben, Ind	72
Crooked Creek, Stokes, N. C	10
Crooked Creek, Tioga, Pa	57
Crooked Fork, Morgan, Tenn	8
Crooked Hill, Montgomery, Pa	14
Crooked Tree, Noble, Ohio	16
Crooksville, Perry, Ohio	17
Croom, Prince George's, Md	63
Cropper's Depot, Shelby, Ky	12
Cropsey, Gage, Nebr	12
Cropseyville, Rensselaer, N. Y	40
Cropwell, St. Clair, Ala	24
Crosbyville, Chester, S. C	5
Cross, Ringgold, Iowa	20
Cross, Lyon, Kans	12
Cross Anchor, Spartanburgh, S. C	27
Cross Anchor, Greene, Tenn	12
Cross Creek Village, Washington, Pa	110
Cross Cut, Lawrence, Pa	90
Cross Fork, Clinton, Pa	16
Cross Hill, Kennebec, Me	44
Cross Hollow, Benton, Ark	12
Crossing, La Porte, Ind	190
Crossingville, Crawford, Pa	66
Cross Keys, De Kalb, Ga	56
Cross Keys, Camden, N. J	22
Cross Keys, Union, S. C	33
Cross Keys, Rockingham, Va	43
Cross Kill Mills, Berks, Pa	46
Crossland, Callaway, Ky	12
Cross Plains, Calhoun, Ala	12
Cross Plains, Ripley, Ind	18
Cross Plains, Metcalfe, Ky	12
Cross Plains, Robertson, Tenn	100
Cross Plains, Dane, Wis	190
Cross River, Westchester, N. Y	72
Cross Roads, Charles, Md	15
Cross Roads, Madison, Ohio	110
Cross Roads, York, Pa	40
Cross Timbers, Hickory, Mo	12
Cross Timbers, Ellis, Tex	12
Crossville, De Kalb, Ala	12
Crossville, Gates, N. C	12
Crossville, (c. h.,) Cumberland, Tenn	130
Crosswicks, Burlington, N. J	230
Crothersville, Jackson, Ind	220
Croton, Lee, Iowa	69
Croton,* Newaygo, Mich	180
Croton, Hunterdon, N. J	6
Croton, Delaware, N. Y	120
Croton, Licking, Ohio	150
Croton Falls, Westchester, N. Y	400
Croton Landing, Westchester, N. Y	260
Crouse's Store, Dutchess, N. Y	12
Crow Creek, ——, Dak	12
Crowder's Mountain, Gaston, N. C	7
Crowley, Greene, Ark	12
Crown City, Gallia, Ohio	12
Crown Point,* (c. h.,) Lake, Ind	580

CUM

Crown Point, Essex, N. Y	$170
Crown Point Centre, Essex, N. Y	210
Crownsville, Anne Arundel, Md	63
Crow River, Meeker, Minn	14
Crow's Landing, Stanislaus, Cal	12
Crow's Mills, Greene, Pa	6
Crowville, Warrick, Ind	12
Crow Wing, (c. h.,) Crow Wing, Minn	100
Croxton, Jefferson, Ohio	10
Croyden, Sullivan, N. H	83
Croyden, Morgan, Utah	75
Croyden Flat, Sullivan, N. H	23
Cruger, Woodford, Ill	76
Crum Creek, Fulton, N. Y	25
Crum Elbow, Dutchess, N. Y	22
Crumley's, Henry, Ga	12
Crumpton, Queen Anne, Md	140
Crnso, Seneca, N. Y	10
Crystal, Tama, Iowa	57
Crystal, Montcalm, Mich	64
Crystal Hill, Montgomery, Ark	8
Crystal Lake, McHenry, Ill	250
Crystal Lake, Hancock, Iowa	12
Crystal Lake, Waupaca, Wis	25
Crystal Spring, Yates, N. Y	75
Crystal Springs,* Copiah, Miss	480
Cuba, Fulton, Ill	160
Cuba, Owen, Ind	15
Cuba, Republic, Kans	12
Cuba, Crawford, Mo	200
Cuba,* Allegany, N. Y	1,300
Cuba, Rutherford, N. C	12
Cuba, Clinton, Ohio	34
Cuba, Ouachita, La	12
Cuba, Shelby, Tenn	13
Cuba Landing, Humphreys, Tenn	12
Cuba Station, Sumter, Ala	50
Cub Creek, Jefferson, Nebr	12
Cub Hill, Baltimore, Md	21
Cub Prairie, Jefferson, Ill	12
Cucamonga, San Bernardino, Cal	12
Cuckoo, Louisa, Va	43
Cuddebackville, Orange, N. Y	73
Cuffey's Cove, Mendocino, Cal	12
Cnivre, Lincoln, Mo	8
Culdrum, Morrison, Minn	17
Cullen, Herkimer, N. Y	35
Culleoka, Maury, Tenn	190
Culloden, Monroe, Ga	63
Culpeper,* (c. h.) Culpeper, Va	1,100
Culver's Station, Tippecanoe, Ind	83
Culverton, Hancock, Ga	140
Cumberland, Marion, Ind	97
Cumberland, Cumberland, Me	160
Cumberland,* (c. h.) Allegany, Md	2,200
Cumberland, Choctaw, Miss	12
Cumberland, Guernsey, Ohio	220
Cumberland C. H., Cumberland, Va	17
Cumberland Centre, Cumberland, Me	89
Cumberland City, Clinton, Ky	28
Cumberland City, Stewart, Tenn	51
Cumberland Furnace, Dixon, Tenn	20
Cumberland Gap, Claiborne, Tenn	50
Cumberland Hill, Providence, R. I	52

* Money-order office.

Cumberland Iron Works, Stewart, Tenn	$16	**D.**	
Cumberland Valley, Bedford, Pa...	46	Dacada, Sheboygan, Wis...........	$47
Cuming City, Washington, Nebr..	200	Dacusville, Pickens, S. C...........	10
Cumming, (c. h.) Forsyth, Ga......	160	*Dadeville, (c. h.,)* Tallapoosa, Ala ..	290
Cummingsville, Goliad, Tex........	12	Dadeville, Dade, Mo...............	75
Cummington, Hampshire, Mass....	220	Dagger's Springs, Botetourt, Va...	12
Cummington West Village, Hampshire, Mass...................	150	Daggett's Mills, Tioga, Pa.........	26
		Dagsborough, Sussex, Del.........	46
Cummin's Creek, Ellis, Tex.......	11	*Dahlonega, (c. h.,)* Lumpkin, Ga....	170
Cumminsville, Hamilton, Ohio....	350	Dahlonega, Wapello, Iowa.........	53
Cumru, Berks, Pa	7	Daileyville, Karnes, Tex...........	12
Cunningham, Clarion, Pa..........	220	Daingerfield, Titus, Tex...........	190
Cunningham's Mills, Ritchie,W.Va.	2	Dairy, Washington, Iowa..........	7
Cunningham's Station, Floyd, Ga..	12	Dairyland, Ulster, N. Y..........	12
Cunningham's Store, Person, N. C.	12	Dakota, Stephenson, Ill...........	120
Cupola, Chester, Pa...............	12	*Dakota,* (c. h.,) Dakota, Nebr......	320
Curdsville, Daviess, Ky...........	29	Dakota, Waushara, Wis...........	41
Curdsville, Buckingham, Va	75	*Dakotah, (c. h.,)* Humboldt, Iowa..	180
Curllsville, Clarion, Pa...........	150	Dalby, Allamakee, Iowa..........	44
Curl's Wharf, Henrico, Va........	12	Dale, Spencer, Ind...............	83
Curran, Sangamon, Ill	62	Dale, Campbell, Ky..............	19
Currant Creek, Fremont, Colo....	12	Dale, Wyoming, N. Y...........	28
Carriersville, Moore, N. C........	5	Dale, Berks, Pa.................	31
Currie's Store, Caddo, La.........	12	Dale City, Guthrie, Iowa.........	35
Currituck C. H., Currituck, N. C....	29	Daleville, Dale, Ala.............	10
Currobee, Habersham, Ga.........	12	Daleville, Delaware, Ind........	82
Curry's Run, Harrison, Ky........	22	Daleville, Lauderdale, Miss......	46
Curryville, Pike, Mo.............	12	Daleville, Luzerne, Pa..........	53
Curtin, Dauphin, Pa..............	32	Dalhoff, St. Charles, Mo........	20
Curtis' Corner, Androscoggin, Me..	44	Dallam's Creek, Logan, Ky......	4
Curtis' Mills, Alamance, N. C.....	6	*Dallas, (c. h.,)* Polk, Ark	39
Curtisville, Tipton, Ind..........	46	*Dallas, (c. h.,)* Paulding, Ga	84
Curtisville, Berkshire, Mass.......	78	Dallas, Marion, Iowa	19
Curveton, Cass, Ind..............	34	Dallas, Pulaski, Ky.............	18
Curwinsville, Clearfield, Pa.......	430	**Dallas, Clinton, Mich**	100
Cush, Clearfield, Pa..............	6	Dallas, Webster, Mo.............	23
Cushing, Tuscaloosa, Ala..........	12	*Dallas, (c. h.,)* Gaston, N. C......	89
Cushing, Knox, Me	29	Dallas, Highland, Ohio..........	58
Cushing, Polk, Wis	12	*Dallas,* (c. h.,) Polk, Oreg.......	180
Cusseta, Chambers, Ala..........	130	Dallas, Luzerne, Pa.............	63
Cusseta, (c. h.) Chattahoochee, **Ga.**	96	Dallas, Hamilton, Tenn..........	12
Custar, Wood, Ohio..............	160	*Dallas,* (c. h.,) Dallas, Tex......	700
Custard's, Crawford, Pa..........	26	Dallas, Marshall, W. Va........	93
Cutchogue, Suffolk, N. Y.........	280	Dallasburgh, Warren, Ohio......	110
Cutband, Red River, Tex	8	Dallas Centre, Dallas, Iowa......	12
Cuthbert, (c. h.) Randolph, Ga	660	Dallas City,* Hancock, Ill.......	380
Cutler, Washington, Me..........	98	Dallastown, York, Pa...........	49
Cutler, Washington, Ohio........	46	Dallies, Surry, Va.............	58
Cuttingsville, Clackamas, Oreg ...	12	Dalmanutha, Guthrie, Iowa......	42
Cuttingsville, Rutland, Vt........	160	Dalmatia, Northumberland, Pa....	95
Cut Off, Drew, Ark..............	42	Dalson, Clark, Ill..............	18
Cuyahoga Falls, Summit, Ohio....	970	*Dalton,* (c. h.,) Whitfield, Ga......	1,100
Cuyler, Cortland, N. Y..........	81	Dalton, Wayne, Ind............	39
Cuylerville, Livingston, N. Y.....	79	Dalton, Berkshire, Mass.........	360
Cylon, St. Croix, Wis...........	120	Dalton, Chariton, Mo...........	12
Cynthiana, Posey, Ind...........	79	Dalton, Coos, N. H............	83
Cynthiana, (c. h.,) Harrison, Ky....	1,100	Dalton, Bladen, N. C...........	16
Cynthiana, Pike, Ohio...........	42	Dalton,* Wayne, Ohio	270
Cypre-mort, St. Mary's, La.........	12	Dalton's Corners, Wayne, Mich....	12
Cypress, Monroe, Ark...........	20	Damariscotta Mills, Lincoln, Me...	84
Cypress, Perry, Tenn............	10	Damascoville, Columbiana, Ohio...	130
Cypress, Kenosha, Wis..........	20	Damascus, Stephenson, Ill........	17
Cypress Creek, Desha, Ark	16	Damascus, Montgomery, Md......	20
Cypress Creek, Johnson, Ill	7	Damascus, Scott, Miss..........	17
Cypress Top, Harris, Tex	15	Damascus, Clackamas, Oreg......	12
Cyruston, Lincoln, Tenn..........	11	**Damascus, Wayne, Pa**............	130

* Money-order office.

DAR

DAY

Dames' Quarter, Somerset, Md	$14	Darksville, Randolph, Mo	$24
Damiansville, Clinton, Ill	16	Darlington, Montgomery, Ind	130
Dana, Worcester, Mass	110	Darlington, St. Helena, La	20
Danborough, Bucks, Pa	50	Darlington, Harford, Md	250
Danburgh, Wilkes, Ga	22	Darlington, Richland, Ohio	31
Danbury, (c. h.,) Fairfield, Conn	2,600	Darlington, Beaver, Pa	160
Danbury, Grafton, N. H	150	*Darlington,* (c. h.,) La Fayette, Wis	1,200
Danbury, (c. h.,) Stokes, N. C	10	*Darlington C. H.,* Darlington, S. C.	650
Danby, Du Page, Ill	130	Darlington Heights, Prince Edward, Va	3
Danby, Ionia, Mich	20	Darnestown, Montgomery, Md	120
Danby, Tompkins, N. Y	170	Darnstadt, St. Clair, Ill	54
Danby, Rutland, Vt	260	Darrtown, Butler, Ohio	120
Danby Four Corners, Rutland, Vt	70	*Dartford,* (c. h.,) Green Lake, Wis	230
Dancyville, Haywood, Tenn	160	Dartmouth, Bristol, Mass	120
Dandridge, (c. h.,) Jefferson, Tenn	240	Darwin, Clark, Ill	29
Dane, Dane, Wis	48	Darwin, Meeker, Minn	10
Danforth, Johnson, Iowa	23	Darysaw, Jefferson, Ark	12
Danforth Station, Iroquois, Ill	120	Dassel, Meeker, Minn	12
Daniel's Landing, Bladen, N. C	12	Dauphin, Dauphin, Pa	260
Danielsville, (c. h.,) Madison, Ga	120	Dauphine, Osage, Mo	80
Danielsville, Northampton, Pa	91	*Davenport,* (c. h.,) Scott, Iowa	4,000
Danielsville, Dickson, Tenn	12	Davenport, Delaware, N. Y	120
Dannemora, Clinton, N. Y	310	Davenport Centre, Delaware, N.Y.	110
Dansville, Ingham, Mich	326	Davidsburgh, York, Pa	12
Dansville, Livingston, N. Y	2,200	Davidson, Montgomery, Ohio	12
Danube, Herkimer, N. Y	12	Davidson, Sullivan, Pa	8
Danvers, McLean, Ill	220	Davidson College, Mecklenburgh, N. C	70
Danvers, Essex, Mass	1,000	Davidson's Ferry, Fayette, Pa	37
Danvers Centre, Essex, Mass	210	Davidson's River, Transylvania, N. C	26
Danversport, Essex, Mass	230	Davidsonville, Anne Arundel, Md	180
Danville, Morgan, Ala	80	Davidsville, Somerset, Pa	53
Danville, (c. h.,) Yell, Ark	87	*Davis,* Stephenson, Ill	370
Danville, Contra Costa, Cal	110	Davisborough, Washington, Ga	160
Danville, (c. h.,) Vermilion, Ill	2,000	Davisburgh, Oakland, Mich	210
Danville, (c. h.,) Hendricks, Ind	660	Davis City, Decatur, Iowa	12
Danville, Des Moines, Iowa	210	Davis Corners, Adams, Wis	25
Danville, (c. h.,) Boyle, Ky	2,000	Davis Mill, Alleghany, Md	12
Danville, Androscoggin, Me	140	Davis' Mills, Bedford, Va	21
Danville, Alcorn, Miss	11	Davison, Genesee, Mich	47
Danville, (c. h.,) Montgomery, Mo	240	Davistown, Greene, Pa	21
Danville, Rockingham, N. H	36	Davisville, Yolo, Cal	310
Danville, Warren, N. J	36	Davisville, Sanilac, Mich	100
Danville, Knox, Ohio	72	Davisville, Bucks, Pa	85
Danville, (c. h.,) Montour, Pa	2,400	Davisville, Washington, R. I	78
Danville, Benton, Tenn	120	Davisville, Wood, W. Va	35
Danville, Montgomery, Tex	36	Dawkin's Mills, Jackson, Ohio	18
Danville, Caledonia, Vt	290	Dawn, Livingston, Mo	250
Danville, Pittsylvania, Va	1,600	Dawn, Darke, Ohio	65
Danville, Dodge, Wis	94	*Dawson,* (c. h.,) Terrell, Ga	650
Darby, Delaware, Pa	310	Dawson, Sangamon, Ill	67
Darby Creek, Madison, Ohio	200	Dawson's Mill, Richardson, Nebr	49
Darbyville, Pickaway, Ohio	67	Dawson's Station, Fayette, Pa	100
Darcey's Store, Montgomery, Md	46	*Dawsonville,* (c. h.,) Dawson, Ga	84
Dardanelle,* Yell, Ark	800	Dawsonville, Montgomery, Md	59
Daretown, Salem, N. J	160	Dawsonville, Greene, Va	21
Darien, Fairfield, Conn	140	Day, Saratoga, N. Y	35
Darien, (c. h.,) MacIntosh, Ga	430	Day Book, Yancey, N. C	5
Darien, Clark, Ill	22	Day's Store, Greene, Pa	33
Darien, Kossuth, Iowa	12	Daysville, Ogle, Ill	50
Darien, Genesee, N. Y	88	Daysville, Todd, Ky	25
Darien, Walworth, Wis	280	Daysville, Oswego, N. Y	49
Darien Centre, Genesee, N. Y	110	Daysville, Loudoun, Va	12
Darien Depot, Fairfield, Conn	320	Dayton, Marengo, Ala	170
Dark Corner, Campbell, Ga	10		
Darke, Darke, Ohio	14		
Darkesville, Berkeley, W. Va	56		

* Money-order office.

DED ·   DEL

Dayton, La Salle, Ill	$75	Deedsville, Miami, Ind	$12
Dayton, Tippecanoe, Ind	140	Deem, Owen, Ind	18
Dayton, Bourbon, Kans	21	Deep Creek, Clay, Kans	12
Dayton, Campbell, Ky	12	Deep Creek, Anson, N. C	12
Dayton, York, Me	12	Deep Creek, Chesterfield, S. C	12
Dayton, Howard, Md	6	Deep Creek, Norfolk, Va	43
Dayton, Berrien, Mich	150	Deep Cut, McHenry, Ill	25
Dayton, Hennepin, Minn	81	Deep Cut, Auglaize, Ohio	39
Dayton, Cass, Mo	12	Deep Ford, Dent, Mo	11
Dayton, (c. h.,) Lyon, Nev	300	Deep River, Middlesex, Conn	650
Dayton, Middlesex, N. J	78	Deep River, Lake, Ind	30
Dayton, Cattaraugus, N. Y	45	Deep River, Poweshick, Iowa	160
Dayton, Wake, N. C	7	Deep River, Guilford, N. C	13
Dayton,* (c. h.,) Montgomery, Ohio.	4,000	Deer Creek, Tazewell, Ill	42
Dayton, Yam Hill, Oreg	160	Deer Creek, Carroll, Ind	32
Dayton, Armstrong, Pa	170	Deer Creek, Carter, Ky	12
Dayton, Rockingham, Va	41	Deer Creek, Livingston, Mich	16
Dayton, Green, Wis	97	Deer Creek, Pickaway, Ohio	8
Dayton City, De Kalb, Mo	12	Deerfield, Lake, Ill	41
Daytonville, Labette, Kans	12	Deerfield, Randolph, Ind	12
Dayville, Grant, Oreg	7	Deerfield, Chickasaw, Iowa	21
Dead River, Somerset, Me	37	Deerfield, Franklin, Mass	380
Deakyneville, New Castle, Del	37	Deerfield, Lenawee, Mich	180
Deal, Monmouth, N. J	66	Deerfield, Steele, Minn	12
Deal's Island, Somerset, Md	67	Deerfield, Vernon, Mo	12
Dean Lake, Wright, Minn	4	Deerfield, Rockingham, N. H	90
Dean's Corners, Lake, Ill	35	Deerfield, Oneida, N. Y	81
Dean's Corners, Saratoga, N. Y	41	Deerfield, Portage, Ohio	130
Deansville, Oneida, N. Y	130	Deerfield, Augusta, Va	31
Deansville, Dane, Wis	51	Deerfield, Dane, Wis	55
Dearbornville, Wayne, Mich	240	Deerfield Centre, Rockingham, N. H	140
Deardorff's Mills, Tuscarawas, Ohio.	7	Deerfield Prairie, De Kalb, Ill	19
Deatonsville, Amelia, Va	38	Deerfield Street, Cumberland, N. J	62
Deatsville, Nelson, Ky	44	Deerfield Village, Warren, Ohio	93
Deavertown, Morgan, Ohio	80	Deering, Hillsborough, N. H	37
Debello, Vernon, Wis	9	Deer Isle, Hancock, Me	190
Deblois, Washington, Me	7	Deer Lick, Williams, Ohio	37
De Bruce, Sullivan, N. Y	15	Deer Lick, Mason, W. Va	5
Decapolis, Madison, Va	12	Deer Lodge City,* (c. h.,) Deer Lodge,	
Decatur,* Morgan, Ala	740	Mont	460
Decatur, (c. h.,) De Kalb, Ga	130	Deer Park, Washington, Ala	27
Decatur,* (c. h.,) Macon, Ill	3,000	Deer Park, La Salle, Ill	52
Decatur,* (c. h.,) Adams, Ind	360	Deer Park, Alleghany, Md	150
Decatur, Decatur, Iowa	120	Deer Park, Suffolk, N. Y	150
Decatur, Van Buren, Mich	1,100	Deer Plain, Calhoun, Ill	30
Decatur, Newton, Miss	12	Deer Ridge, Lewis, Mo	43
Decatur,* Burt, Nebr	300	Deer River, Lewis, N. Y	77
Decatur, Otsego, N. Y	25	Deersville, Harrison, Ohio	120
Decatur, Brown, Ohio	100	Deer Valley, Park, Colo	12
Decatur, Mifflin, Pa	10	Deer Walk, Wood, W. Va	12
Decatur, (c. h.,) Meigs, Tenn	87	Defiance,* (c. h.,) Defiance, Ohio	1,300
Decatur, (c. h.,) Wise, Tex	71	Defreestville, Rensselaer, N. Y	12
Decaturville, Camden, Mo	11	De Golier, McKean, Pa	29
Decaturville, Washington, Ohio	8	De Graff, Logan, Ohio	360
Decaturville, Decatur, Tenn	80	Deisher's Mill, Botetourt, Va	5
Decherd, Franklin, Tenn	290	De Kalb,* (c. h.,) Kemper, Miss	48
Deckard, Crawford, Pa	24	De Kalb, Buchanan, Mo	82
Decker's Point, Indiana, Pa	34	De Kalb, St. Lawrence, N. Y	80
Decker's Station, Knox, Ind	47	De Kalb, Crawford, Ohio	20
Deckertown, Sussex, N. J	460	De Kalb, Bowie, Tex	17
Deckerville, Sanilac, Mich	8	De Kalb Centre,* De Kalb, Ill	940
Decorah,* (c. h.,) Winneshiek, Iowa.	1,800	De Kalb Junction, St. Lawrence,	
Decoria, Blue Earth, Minn	3	N. Y	150
Decosta, Atlantic, N. J	36	Dekorra, Columbia, Wis	24
Dedham, Hancock, Me	74	Delafield, Waukesha, Wis	250
Dedham,* (c. h.,) Norfolk, Mass	1,400	Delanco, Burlington, N. J	85

* Money-order office.

Delano, Wright, Minn	$12	Denmark, Madison, Tenn	$130
Delano, Schuylkill, Pa	110	Denmark, Brown, Wis	75
Delanti, Hardin, Iowa	85	Dennard's Bluff, Monroe, Ala	12
De La Palma, Brown, Ohio	12	Denning, Ulster, N. Y	7
De Lassus, St. Francois, Mo	12	Denning's, Carroll, Md	12
Delavan,* Tazewell, Ill	930	Dennis, Appanoose, Iowa	12
Delavan,* Walworth, Wis	1,200	Dennis, Barnstable, Mass	170
Delaware, Yell, Ark	12	Dennison, Clark, Ill	12
Delaware, Ripley, Ind	24	Dennison, Ottawa, Mich	39
Delaware, Delaware, Iowa	150	Dennison, Tuscarawas, Ohio	12
Delaware,* (c. h.,) Delaware, Ohio	2,700	Dennis Port, Barnstable, Mass	300
Delaware, Pike, Pa	20	Dennisville, Cape May, N. J	170
Delaware City, Summit, Colo	22	Denny, Warren, Ill	20
Delaware City,* New Castle, Del	610	Dennysville, Washington, Me	190
Delaware City, Leavenworth, Kans	17	Dent, Hamilton, Ohio	53
Delaware Grove, Mercer, Pa..▲.	64	Dent, Greene, Pa	5
Delaware Station, Warren, N. J	140	Denton,* (c. h.,) Caroline, Md	260
Delaware Water Gap, Monroe, Pa	300	Denton, Wayne, Mich	96
Delhi, Jersey, Ill	100	Denton, (c. h.,) Denton, Tex	130
Delhi, (c. h.,) Delaware, Iowa	150	Dent's Run, Elk, Pa	180
Delhi, Richland, La	44	DENVER,* (c. h.,) Arapahoe, Colo	4,000
Delhi,* (c. h.,) Delaware, N. Y	1,200	Denver, Hancock, Ill	110
Delhi, Hamilton, Ohio	57	Denver, Miami, Ind	28
Delight, Greene, Pa	12	Denver, Bremer, Iowa	51
De Lisle, Darke, Ohio	28	Denver, Newaygo, Mich	37
Dell Delight, Benton, Mo	7	Denverton, Solano, Cal	50
Dellona, Sauk, Wis	36	Denville, Morris, N. J	110
Dell Prairie, Adams, Wis	19	Depauville, Jefferson, N. Y	110
Dellville, Perry, Pa	15	De Pere,* Brown, Wis	770
Delmar, Sussex, Del	25	De Peyster, St. Lawrence, N. Y	61
Delmont, Anderson, Kans	12	Deposit, Jefferson, Ky	17
De Loche's Landing, Natchitoches, La	12	Deposit,* Broome, N. Y	970
		De Pue, Bureau, Ill	36
Delphi,* (c. h.,) Carroll, Ind	1,300	Deputy, Jefferson, Ind	12
Delphi, Onondaga, N. Y	95	Derby,* New Haven, Conn	2,500
Delphos, Ottawa, Kans	20	Derby, Perry, Ind	45
Delphos,* Van Wert, Ohio	740	Derby, Orleans, Vt	330
Delpsburgh, Northampton, Pa	120	Derby Line,* Orleans, Vt	870
Del Rey, Iroquois, Ill	52	Derinda, Jo Daviess, Ill	48
Delroy, Wayne, Mich	12	De Roche, Clark, Ark	5
Delta, Randolph, Ala	3	Derry, Rockingham, N. H	380
Delta, McLean, Ill	22	Derry Church, Dauphin, Pa	35
Delta, Parke, Ind	5	Derry Depot, Rockingham, N. H	170
Delta, (c. h.,) Madison, La	72	Derry Station Westmoreland, Pa	74
Delta, Eaton, Mich	26	De Ruyter, Madison, N. Y	510
Delta, Oneida, N. Y	110	Des Arc, Prairie, Ark	280
Delta,* Fulton, Ohio	450	Deschutes, Wasco, Oreg	12
Delta, York, Pa	52	Deselm, Kankakee, Ill	15
Delta Mills, Walla Walla, Wash	90	Deseret, Millard, Utah	6
Delton, Sauk, Wis	150	DES MOINES,* (c. h.,) Polk, Iowa	4,000
Deming, Hamilton, Ind	44	De Soto, Jackson, Ill	240
Democracy, Knox, Ohio	53	De Soto,* Dallas, Iowa	350
Democrat, Walker, Ala	6	De Soto, Johnson, Kansas	150
Democrat, Buncombe, N. C	12	De Soto, Clark, Miss	180
Demopolis,* (c. h.,) Marengo, Ala	1,200	De Soto, Jefferson, Mo	220
Demos, Belmont, Ohio	38	De Soto, Washington, Nebr	50
De Mossville, Pendleton, Ky	87	De Soto, Vernon, Wis	220
Dempseytown, Venango, Pa	82	De Soto Front, De Soto, Miss	12
Denison, (c. h.,) Crawford, Iowa	440	Desotoville, Choctaw, Ala	58
Denison, Herkimer, N. Y	21	Des Peres, St. Louis, Mo	25
Denmark, Perry, Ill	32	Des Plaines, Cook, Ill	110
Denmark,* Lee, Iowa	360	Detour, Chippewa, Mich	12
Denmark, Oxford, Me	140	Detroit, Sanford, Ala	10
Denmark, Tuscola, Mich	17	Detroit, Pike, Ill	78
Denmark, Lewis, N. Y	60	Detroit, Dickinson, Kans	240
Denmark, Ashtabula, Ohio	14	Detroit, Somerset, Me	130

* Money-order office.

DIO | DOO

Detroit,° (c. h.,) Wayne, Mich	$4,000	Dirigo, Kennebec, Me	$45
Devall's Bluff,° (c. h.,) Prairie, Ark.	460	Dirt Town, Chattooga, Ga	45
De View, Woodruff, Ark	47	Disco, Macomb, Mich	89
Dewart, Northumberland, Pa	140	Dismal, Sampson, N. C	12
De Witt, (c. h.,) Arkansas, Ark	120	Disputanta, Prince George, Va	12
De Witt, De Witt, Ill	80	Ditney Hill, Dubois, Ind	10
De Witt,° (c. h.,) Clinton, Iowa	1,300	Dittmer's Store, Jefferson, Mo	12
De Witt, Clinton, Mich	340	Dividing Creek, Cumberland, N. J.	47
De Witt, Carroll, Mo	250	Dividing Ridge, Pendleton, Ky	12
De Witt, Cuming, Nebr	19	Dividing Ridge, Somerset, Pa	4
De Witt, Onondaga, N. Y	57	Dix, Jefferson, Ill	37
De Wittville, Chautauqua, N. Y	87	Dixfield, Oxford, Me	230
Dexter, Perry, Ind	12	Dixfield Centre, Oxford, Me	42
Dexter,° Dallas, Iowa	310	Dix Hills, Suffolk, N. Y	48
Dexter, Cowley, Kans	12	Dixmont, Penobscot, Me	89
Dexter,° Penobscot, Me	1,100	Dixmont, Allegheny, Pa	180
Dexter, Washtenaw, Mich	810	Dixmont Centre, Penobscot, Me	24
Dexter, Jefferson, N. Y	210	Dixon, Solano, Cal	12
Dexter, Meigs, Ohio	5	Dixon, Dawson, Ga	29
D'Hanis, Medina, Tex	6	*Dixon,*° (c. h.,) Lee, Ill	2,600
Dialton, Clark, Ohio	28	Dixon, Scott, Iowa	39
Diamond, Venango, Pa	12	*Dixon,* (c. h.,) Webster, Ky	89
Diamond Bluff, Pierce, Wis	59	Dixon, Pulaski, Mo	12
Diamond City, (c. h.,) Meagher, Mont.	350	Dixon, Van Wert, Ohio	35
Diamond Cross, Randolph, Ill	12	Dixon, Wyoming, Pa	15
Diamond Grove, Jasper, Mo	12	Dixon's Springs, Smith, Tenn	68
Diamond Hill, Anson, N. C	12	Dixonville, Indiana, Pa	12
Diamond Hill, Providence, R. I	72	Doaksville, Choctaw, Ind. T	14
Diamond Lake, Lake, Ill	76	Dobb's Ferry, Westchester, N. Y	420
Diamond Mountain, White Pine, Nev	12	*Dobson,* (c. h.,) Surry, N. C	30
		Doctor Town, Wayne, Ga	37
Diamond Spring, El Dorado, Cal	93	Doddsville, Schuyler, Ill	40
Diamond Springs, Morris, Kans	19	Dodge, Guthrie, Iowa	7
Diana, Lewis, N. Y	16	Dodge Centre, Dodge, Minn	160
Diana Mills, Buckingham, Va	12	Dodge City, Steele, Minn	8
Dias Creek, Cape May, N. J	39	Dodge's Corners, Waukesha, Wis	31
Dickensonville, Russell, Va	8	Dodgeville, Des Moines, Iowa	99
Dickersonville, Niagara, N. Y	14	*Dodgeville,*° (c. h.,) Iowa, Wis	770
Dickeysville, Grant, Wis	19	Dodsonville, Jackson, Ala	11
Dickeyville, Aroostook, Me	12	Dodsonville, Highland, Ohio	23
Dickinson, Franklin, N. J	14	Doe Run, Chester, Pa	93
Dickinson, Cumberland, Pa	120	Dog Creek, Putnam, Ohio	62
Dickinson, Centre, Franklin, N. Y	94	Doko, Fairfield, S. C	37
Dickinson's, Franklin, Va	8	Dolington, Bucks, Pa	34
Dickson, Colbert, Ala	90	Dolingville, Jefferson, Pa	12
Dickson, Dickson, Tenn	150	Dolten's Station, Cook, Ill	59
Dicksonburgh, Crawford, Pa	52	Dona Ana, Dona Ana, N. Mex	12
Dido, Choctaw, Miss	8	Donald, Washington, Kans	12
Diehlstadt, Scott, Mo	12	Donaldson, Schuylkill, Pa	77
Dificult, Smith, Tenn	16	*Donaldsonville,* (c. h.,) Ascension, La.	510
Dighton, Bristol, Mass	290	Donally's Mills, Perry, Pa	45
Dille's Bottom, Belmont, Ohio	20	Donation, Huntingdon, Pa	26
Dillingersville, Lehigh, Pa	18	Doncaster, Charles, Md	22
Dillon, Tazewell, Ill	37	Donegal, Westmoreland, Pa	49
Dillon, Phelps, Mo	23	Donelson, Davidson, Tenn	71
Dillon's Run, Hampshire, W. Va	3	Donersville, Burnett, Wis	12
Dillsborough, Dearborn, Ind	160	Dongola, Union, Ill	370
Dillsburgh, York, Pa	120	Doniphan, Doniphan, Kans	230
Dilworthtown, Chester, Pa	46	*Doniphan,* (c. h.,) Ripley, Mo	94
Dimock, Susquehanna, Pa	84	Don Juan, Perry, Ind	6
Dimon, Leavenworth, Kans	24	Donley, Washington, Pa	12
Dingman's Ferry, Pike, Pa	86	Donnaldsville, Abbeville, S. C	93
Dinsmore, Shelby, Ohio	30	Donnellson, Montgomery, Ill	46
Dinsmore, Washington, Pa	37	Donnelsville, Clark, Ohio	69
Dinwiddie C. H., Dinwiddie, Va	28	Doolittle's Mills, Perry, Ind	12
Diona, Coles, Ill	12	Door Creek, Dane, Wis	97

° Money-order office.

Door Village, La Porte, Ind	$64	Dover, Dutchess, N. Y	$480
Dora, Pike, Ark	12	Dover, Craven, N. C	14
Dora, Wabash, Ind	47	Dover, Cuyahoga, Ohio	68
Dora, Labette, Kans	12	Dover, York, Pa	57
Doran, Mitchell, Iowa	19	*Dover, (c. h.,) Stewart, Tenn*	180
Doraville, Broome, N. Y	7	Dover, Windham, Vt	52
Dorcheat, Columbia, Ark	12	Dover, Iowa, Wis	13
Dorchester, Macoupin, Ill	95	Dover Centre, Olmsted, Minn	74
Dorchester, Allamakee, Iowa	100	Dover Furnace, Dutchess, N. Y	14
Dorchester, Norfolk, Mass	250	*Dover Hill, (c. h.,)* Martin, Ind	110
Dorchester, Grafton, N. H	32	Dover Mines, Goochland, Va	59
Dorlan's Mills, Chester, Pa	12	Dover South Mills, Piscataquis, Me	22
Dormansville, Albany, N. Y	19	Dove's Creek, Elbert, Ga	6
Dornsife, Northumberland, Pa	12	Dove's Depot, Darlington, S. C	150
Dorr, Allegan, Mich	12	Dow, Cass, Ind	12
Dorrance, Luzerne, Pa	18	Dowagiac,* Cass, Mich	1,700
Dorret's Run, Hardin, Ky	7	Dowdallville, Peoria, Ill	13
Dorrville, Washington, R. I	36	Dowd's Landing, Coahoma, Miss	12
Dorset, De Kalb, Ill	32	Downer's Grove, Du Page, Ill	190
Dorset, Ashtabula, Ohio	25	Downey, Cedar, Iowa	150
Dorset, Bennington, Vt	200	Downey's Spring, Randolph, Ark	12
Dorset, Monroe, Wis	13	Down Hill, Crawford, Ind	6
Dorsey, Madison, Ill	34	*Downieville,* (c. h.,) Sierra, Cal	800
Dorseyville, Allegheny, Pa	11	Downing's Mills, Strafford, N. H	92
Doty's Corner, Steuben, N. Y	11	Downingsville, Grant, Ky	18
Dotyville, Fond du Lac, Wis	57	Downington, Meigs, Ohio	46
Double Bridge, Lunenburgh, Va	2	Downingtown, Chester, Pa	800
Double Bridges, Lauderdale, Tenn.	12	Downsville, Union, La	13
Double Horn, Burnet, Tex	32	Downsville, Washington, Md	23
Double Pipe Creek, Carroll, Md	45	Downsville, Delaware, N. Y	140
Double Shoal, Cleveland, N. C	6	Downsville, Dunn, Wis	83
Double Springs, Benton, Ark	12	Doyle, Marion, Kans	7
Double Springs, Oktibbeha, Miss	58	Doylesburgh, Franklin, Pa	18
Double Wells, Warren, Ga	380	Doyle's Mills, Juniata, Pa	12
Doud Station, Van Buren, Iowa	110	Doylesport, Barton, Mo	12
Dougherty's Station, Alameda, Cal.	45	*Doylestown,* (c. h.,) Bucks, Pa	1,400
Douglas, Coffee, Ga	12	Doylestown, Columbia, Wis	130
Douglas, Knox, Ill	100	Dracut, Middlesex, Mass	49
Douglas, Jackson, La	8	Drady's, Wayne, Ga	20
Douglas, Allegan, Mich	110	Drake, Gasconade, Mo	23
Douglas, Gentry, Mo	13	Drake's Branch, Charlotte, Va	86
Douglas, Rockingham, N. C	12	Drake's Creek, Madison, Ark	12
Douglas Centre, Clay, Iowa	12	Drake's Mills, Crawford, Pa	37
Douglas Centre, Marquette, Wis	27	Drakestown, Morris, N. J	20
Donglas City, Trinity, Cal	39	Drakesville, Davis, Iowa	170
Douglass, Worcester, Mass	66	Drakesville, Morris, N. J	110
Douglass, Fayette, Iowa	82	Dranesville, Fairfax, Va	16
Douglass, Butler, Kans	83	Draper, Salt Lake, Utah	39
Douglass, Montgomery, Pa	16	Drapersville, Mecklenburgh, Va	12
Douglass, Nacogdoches, Tex	20	Dravosburgh, Allegheny, Pa	100
Douglassville, Berks, Pa	310	Draw Bridge, Sussex, Del	59
Douglassville, Davis, Tex	24	Draw Bridge, Dorchester, Md	13
Dousman, Waukesha, Wis	28	Drayton Plains, Oakland, Mich	58
Dover, (c. h.,) Pope, Ark	24	Drehersville, Schuylkill, Pa	29
Dover, Merced, Cal	12	Dresbach, Winona, Minn	23
DOVER,* (c. h.,) Kent, Del	1,200	Dresden, Lincoln, Me	24
Dover, Bureau, Ill	310	Dresden, Pettis, Mo	290
Dover, Boone, Ind	31	Dresden, Yates, N. Y	240
Dover, Lee, Iowa	69	Dresden,* Muskingum, Ohio	680
Dover, Shawnee, Kans	11	*Dresden, (c. h.,)* Weakley, Tenn	510
Dover, Mason, Ky	130	Dresden, Navarro, Tex	110
Dover, (c. h.,) Piscataquis, Me	330	Dresden Mills, Lincoln, Me	94
Dover, Norfolk, Mass	72	Dresselville, Le Sueur, Minn	20
Dover, La Fayette, Mo	250	Dresserville, Cayuga, N. Y	30
Dover, (c. h.,) Strafford, N. H	2,900	Drewersburgh, Franklin, Ind	27
Dover,* Morris, N. J	1,300	Drewryville, Southampton, Va	12

* Money-order office.

DUG | DUN

Drewsville, Cheshire, N. H	$86	Dugger's Ferry, Carter, Tenn	$6
Dreyspring, Montgomery, Ala.	12	Dug Hill, Carroll, Md	17
Driftwood, Cameron, Pa	760	Dug Spur, Carroll, Va	12
Drum's, Luzerne, Pa	68	Dugway, Oswego, N. Y	43
Drury, Rock Island, Ill	3	Dukedom, Weakley, Tenn	43
Dry Branch, Franklin, Mo	12	Dulaney's Valley, Baltimore, Md	16
Dry Brook, Ulster, N. Y	7	Du Luth, (c. h.,) St. Louis, Minn	1,000
Dry Cove, Jackson, Ala	12	Dumas, Tippah, Miss	6
Dry Creek, Lawrence, Ala	68	Dumas Ferry, Anson, N. C	12
Dry Creek, Linn, Iowa	31	Dumfries, Prince William, Va	58
Dry Creek, Crawford, Mo	20	Dummerston, Windham, Vt	120
Dryden, Tama, Iowa	33	Dumontville, Fairfield, Ohio	28
Dryden, Lapeer, Mich	130	Dunbar, Washington, Ohio	20
Dryden, Sibley, Minn	9	Dunbar, Fayette, Pa	140
Dryden, Jefferson, Nebr	12	Dunbarton, Merrimack, N. H	83
Dryden, Tompkins, N. Y	500	Dunbarton, Adams, Ohio	30
Dry Fork, Barren, Ky	7	Dunbarton, Barnwell, S. C	19
Dry Grove, Hinds, Miss	98	Duncan, Monroe, Ark	12
Dry Hill, Lauderdale, Tenn	24	Duncan, Stark, Ill	12
Dry Mills, Cumberland, Me	20	Duncan, Mercer, Ky	21
Dry Ponds, Catawba, N. C	9	Duncan, Allegheny, Pa	130
Dry Ridge, Grant, Ky	67	Duncan Creek, Vernon, Mo	12
Dry Ridge, Hamilton, Ohio	24	Duncannon, Perry, Pa	610
Dry Run, Scott, Ky	12	Duncanon, Stephenson, Ill	11
Dry Run, Prentiss, Miss	5	Duncan's Creek, Rutherford, N. C	5
Dry Run, Franklin, Pa	73	Duncan's Falls, Muskingum, Ohio	98
Drytown, Amador, Cal	100	Duncan's Mills, Sonoma, Cal	75
Dryville, Berks, Pa	14	Duncan's Mills, Fulton, Ill	38
Dry Wood, Vernon, Mo	6	Duncan's Mills, Scott, Va	5
Duane, Franklin, N. Y	8	Duncan's Retreat, Kane, Utah	9
Duanesburgh, Schenectady, N. Y	100	Duncansville, Blair, Pa	140
Dublin, Fayette, Ala	12	Duncombe, Webster, Iowa	12
Dublin, (c. h.,) Laurens, Ga	90	Dundaff, Susquehanna, Pa	129
Dublin,* Wayne, Ind	670	Dundarrach, Robeson, N. C	12
Dublin, Graves, Ky	7	Dundas, Richland, Ill	23
Dublin, Harford, Md	140	Dundas, Rice, Minn	200
Dublin, Cheshire, N. H	160	Dundas, Pulaski, Mo	18
Dublin, Franklin, Ohio	120	Dundas, Vinton, Ohio	69
Dublin, Bucks, Pa	83	Dundas, Calumet, Wis	11
Dublin, Pulaski, Va	480	Dundee, Kane, Ill	400
Dublin Mills, Fulton, Pa	17	Dundee, Monroe, Mich	200
Dubois, Pulaski, Ga	12	Dundee, Franklin, Mo	68
Dubois, Washington, Ill	160	Dundee, Yates, N. Y	830
Dubuque,* (c. h.,) Dubuque, Iowa	4,000	Dundee, Tuscarawas, Ohio	47
Duchateau, Door, Wis	9	Dundee, Fond du Lac, Wis	14
Duck Creek, Walker, Ga	6	Dun Ellen, Middlesex, N. J	12
Duck Creek, Warren, Ill	58	Dungannon, Columbiana, Ohio	36
Duckers, Woodford, Ky	120	Dun Glen, Humboldt, Nev	120
Duck Hill, Carroll, Miss	28	Dunham, Washington, Ohio	14
Duck Pond, Cumberland, Me	12	Dunkard, Greene, Pa	18
Duck Port, Madison, La	12	Dunkinsville, Adams, Ohio	21
Duck River, Hickman, Tenn	12	Dunkirk, Jay, Ind	140
Ducktown,* Polk, Tenn	250	Dunkirk, Calvert, Md	72
Dudley, Edgar, Ill	140	Dunkirk,* Chautauqua, N. Y	2,600
Dudley, Wapello, Iowa	12	Dunkirk, Hardin, Ohio	270
Dudley, Worcester, Mass	200	Dunkirk, Dane, Wis	20
Dudley, Wayne, N. C	90	Dunkle's Store, Lawrence, Mo	21
Dudley, Huntingdon, Pa	280	Dunlap, Harrison, Iowa	180
Dudleytown, Jackson, Ind	43	Dunlap, Hamilton, Ohio	32
Dodleyville, Bond, Ill	30	Dunlap, (c. h.,) Sequatchie, Tenn	37
Duelin, Benton, Minn	12	Dunlapsville, Union, Ind	49
Due West, Abbeville, S. C	150	Dunleith, Jo Daviess, Ill	420
Duff, Dubois, Ind	5	Dunleith, Wayne, W. Va	12
Duffield, Charles, Md	24	Dunlevy, Warren, Ohio	19
Duffield's, Jefferson, W. Va	180	Dunmore, Luzerne, Pa	510
Dugansville, Mercer, Ky	3	Dunmore, Pocahontas, W. Va	60

* Money-order office.

DYE

Dunn, Moultrie, Ill	$1
Dunnings, Luzerne, Pa	150
Dunningsville, Washington, Pa	41
Dunnington, Hickman, Tenn	12
Dunningville, Allegan, Mich	12
Dunn's Rock, Transylvania, N. C	9
Dunn's Store, Caroline, Va	10
Dunnsville, Albany, N. Y	20
Dunnsville, Essex, Va	100
Dunnville, Dunn, Wis	17
Dunreith, Henry, Ind	170
Dunsfort, Washington, Pa	12
Dunstable, Middlesex, Mass	83
Dunton, Cook, Ill	270
Dupage, Will, Ill	20
Du Plain, Clinton, Mich	77
Duplainville, Waukesha, Wis	29
Dupont, Jefferson, Ind	200
Dupont, Putnam, Ohio	12
Dupont, Waupaca, Wis	84
Dupree's Old Store, Charlotte, Va	19
Duquoin,* Perry, Ill	1,300
Durand, (c. h.,) Pepin, Wis	360
Durand Station,° Winnebago, Ill	400
Durant's Neck, Perquimons, N. C	12
Durango, Dubuque, Iowa	11
Durant,* Cedar, Iowa	360
Durant, Holmes, Miss	330
Durbin's Corners, Williams, Ohio	36
Durell, Bradford, Pa	12
Durgen's Creek, Lewis, Mo	8
Durham, Middlesex, Conn	200
Durham, Hancock, Ill	11
Durham, Androscoggin, Me	92
Durham, Strafford, N. H	170
Durham, Greene, N. Y	220
Durham, Bucks, Pa	59
Durham Centre, Middlesex, Conn	65
Durham Hill, Waukesha, Wis	13
Durham's, Orange, N. C	180
Durhamville, Oneida, N. Y	320
Durhamville, Lauderdale, Tenn	46
Durlach, Lancaster, Pa	72
Duroc, Benton, Mo	12
Dushore,* Sullivan, Pa	280
Dustin, De Kalb, Ill	14
Dutch Creek, Washington, Iowa	86
Dutche's Creek, Yell, Ark	12
Dutch Flat,* Placer, Cal	760
Dutch Hill, St. Clair, Ill	8
Dutch Hill, Crawford, Pa	8
Dutch Neck, Mercer, N. J	46
Dutchtown, Cape Girardeau, Mo	12
Dutchville, Granville, N. C	9
Dutzow, Warren, Mo	12
Duxbury, Plymouth, Mass	450
Dwaar's Kill, Ulster, N. Y	29
Dwight,* Livingston, Ill	1,200
Dyberry, Wayne, Pa	29
Dyckesville, Kewaunee, Wis	48
Dyeusburgh, Crittenden, Ky	72
Dye, Martin, Ind	12
Dyer, Lake, Ind	82
Dyer Brook, Aroostook, Me	4
Dyersburgh, (c. h.,) Dyer, Tenn	260
Dyer's Station, Gibson, Tenn	85

EAR

Dyersville,* Dubuque, Iowa	$500
Dykeman's, Putnam, N. Y	26
Dyson's, Guernsey, Ohio	39
Dyson's Mill, Edgefield, S. C	9
Dysortville, McDowell, N. C	16

E.

Eagle, Bremer, Iowa	6
Eagle, Clinton, Mich	11
Eagle, Harrison, Mo	220
Eagle, Cass, Nebr	12
Eagle, Wyoming, N. Y	12
Eagle, Warren, Pa	8
Eagle, Waukesha, Wis	290
Eagle Bridge, Rensselaer, N. Y	81
Eagle City, Sibley, Minn	12
Eagle Corners, Richland, Wis	12
Eagle Creek, Bradley, Ark	25
Eagle Creek, Lyon, Kans	12
Eagle Creek, Clackamas, Oreg	16
Eagle Foundry, Huntingdon, Pa	13
Eagle Furnace, Roane, Tenn	10
Eagle Grove, Hart, Ga	5
Eagle Grove, Wright, Iowa	54
Eagle Harbor, Keweenaw, Mich	200
Eagle Harbor, Orleans, N. Y	169
Eagle Hill, Owen, Ky	10
Eagle Iron Works, Wythe, Va	12
Eagle Lake, Will, Ill	29
Eagle Lake, Colorado, Tex	36
Eagle Landing, Pulaski, Ark	12
Eagle Mills, Fayette, Ala	12
Eagle Mills, Rensselaer, N. Y	49
Eagle Mills, Iredell, N. C	18
Eagle Mills, Vinton, Ohio	27
Eagle Pass, (c. h.,) Maverick, Tex	340
Eagle Point, Ogle, Ill	38
Eagle Point, Berks, Pa	8
Eagle River, (c. h.,) Keweenaw, Mich.	280
Eagle Rock, Oneida, Idaho	12
Eagle Rock, Wake, N. C	17
Eagle Rock, Venango, Pa	32
Englesfield, Clay, Ind	8
Eagle's Mere, Sullivan, Pa	6
Eagle Springs, Jefferson, Ind	12
Eagle Springs, Coryell, Tex	12
Eagle Station, Carroll, Ky	12
Eagle Tannery, Wayne, Tenn	12
Eagletown, Hamilton, Ind	23
Eagle Village, Wyoming, N. Y	91
Eagleville, Siskiyou, Cal	34
Eagleville, Tolland, Conn	100
Eagleville, Ashtabula, Ohio	75
Eagleville, Montgomery, Pa	27
Eagleville, Rutherford, Tenn	16
Eakle's Mills, Washington, Md	43
Earle, Lucas, Iowa	12
Earle's, Muhlenburgh, Ky	13
Earlesville, Spartanburgh, S. C	12
Earley, Elk, Pa	12
Earleysville, Albemarle, Va	45
Earlham, Madison, Iowa	150
Earlobion, Obion, Tenn	12
Earlville,* La Salle, Ill	910

* Money-order office.

Earlville, Delaware, Iowa	$470
Earlville, Madison, N. Y	310
Earlville, Portage, Ohio	59
Earlville, Berks, Pa	27
Early Grove, Marshall, Miss	26
Earpsborough, Johnston, N.C	10
Eartmon, Pulaski, Ga	12
East Abington, Plymouth, Mass	520
Easta Boga, Talladega, Ala	12
East Acworth, Sullivan, N. H	14
East Albany, Orleans, Vt	41
East Alburgh, Grand Isle, Vt	120
Eastaloe, Pickens, S. C	5
East Alton, Belknap, N. H	12
East Amherst, Erie, N. Y	34
East Andover, Merrimack, N. H	160
East Arcade, Wyoming, N. Y	20
East Arlington, Bennington, Vt	150
East Ashford, Cattaraugus, N. Y	49
East Auburn, Androscoggin, Me	39
East Aurora, Erie, N. Y	230
East Avon, Livingston, N. Y	200
East Baldwin, Cumberland, Me	59
East Bangor, Penobscot, Me	21
East Barnard, Windsor, Vt	130
East Beekmantown, Clinton, N. Y	65
East Bend, Ford, Ill	12
East Bend, Yadkin, N. C	21
East Benton, Kennebec, Me	28
East Benton, Luzerne, Pa	13
East Berkshire, Tioga, N. Y	1
East Berkshire, Franklin, Vt	140
East Berlin, Hartford, Conn	260
East Berlin, Adams, Pa	110
East Berne, Albany, N. Y	38
East Bethany, Genesee, N. Y	100
East Bethel, Windsor, Vt	100
East Bethlehem, Washington, Pa	120
East Blackstone, Worcester, Mass	92
East Bloomfield, Ontario, N. Y	490
East Boston, Madison, N. Y	57
East Bowdoinham, Sagadahoc, Me	48
East Boyleston, Oswego, N. Y	12
East Bradford, Penobscot, Me	20
East Branch, Delaware, N. Y	13
East Brewster, Barnstable, Mass	94
East Bridgewater, Plymouth, Mass	470
East Bridgewater, Susquehanna, Pa	25
East Brimfield, Hampden, Mass	66
East Brook, Lawrence, Pa	53
East Brookfield, Worcester, Mass	280
East Brookfield, Orange, Vt	72
East Bucksport, Hancock, Me	10
East Burke, Caledonia, Vt	210
East Burlington, Kane, Ill	12
East Cabot, Washington, Vt	26
East Calais, Washington, Vt	91
East Cambridge, Middlesex, Mass	1,900
East Cambridge, Lamoille, Vt	12
East Canaan, Litchfield, Conn	200
East Canaan, Grafton, N. H	416
East Canton, Bradford, Pa	50
East Carmel, Columbiana, Ohio	12
East Carlton, Orleans, N. Y	120
East Castle Rock, Dakota, Minn	33
East Chain Lakes, Martin, Minn	19

East Charlemont, Franklin, Mass	$52
East Charleston, Tioga, Pa	17
East Charleston, Orleans, Vt	54
East Chatham, Columbia, N. Y	310
East Chatham, Tioga, Pa	12
East Chester, Westchester, N. Y	410
East Clarence, Erie, N. Y	34
East Clarendon, Rutland, Vt	51
East Claridon, Geauga, Ohio	68
East Clarksfield, Huron, Ohio	19
East Clarkson, Monroe, N. Y	33
East Cleveland, Cuyahoga, Ohio	390
East Cobleskill, Schoharie, N. Y	30
East Concord, Merrimack, N. H	89
East Concord, Erie, N. Y	25
East Constable, Franklin, N. Y	120
East Corinth, Penobscot, Me	270
East Corinth, Orange, Vt	190
East Cornwall, Litchfield, Conn	18
East Coventry, Chester, Pa	12
East Coventry, Orleans, Vt	48
East Craftsbury, Orleans, Vt	63
East Creek, Cape May, N. J	31
East Creek, Herkimer, N. Y	80
East Dayton, Tuscola, Mich	29
East Deering, Hillsborough, N. H	34
East De Kalb, St. Lawrence, N. Y	45
East Delavan, Walworth, Wis	12
East Dennis, Barnstable, Mass	200
East Derry, Rockingham, N. H	12
East Dickinson, Franklin, N. Y	49
East Dimock, Susquehanna, Pa	10
East Dixfield, Oxford, Me	98
East Dixmont, Penobscot, Me	40
East Dorset, Bennington, Vt	270
East Douglass, Worcester, Mass	460
East Dover, Piscataquis, Me	14
East Dover, Windham, Vt	47
East Durham, Greene, N. Y	98
East Eddington, Penobscot, Me	67
East Eden, Hancock, Me	200
East Eden, Erie, N.Y	18
East Elba, Genesee, N. Y	39
East Elma, Erie, N. Y	19
East Elmore, Lamoille, Vt	13
East Enterprise, Switzerland, Ind	66
Eastern, Franklin, Ill	2
East Evans, Erie, N. Y	30
East Exeter, Penobscot, Me	40
East Fairfield, Columbiana, Ohio	150
East Fairfield, Franklin, Vt	64
East Falmouth, Barnstable, Mass	100
East Finley, Washington, Pa	28
East Fishkill, Dutchess, N. Y	64
East Florence, Oneida, N. Y	56
Eastford, Windham, Conn	130
East Fork, Montgomery, Ill	20
East Fork, Metcalfe, Ky	9
East Foxborough, Norfolk, Mass	71
East Franklin, Franklin, Vt	120
East Freedom, Blair, Pa	86
East Freetown, Bristol, Mass	33
East Fryeburgh, Oxford, Me	16
East Gaines, Orleans, N. Y	50
East Gainesville, Wyoming, N. Y	160
East Gallatin, Gallatin, Mont	12

EAS   EAS

East Galway, Saratoga, N. Y	$22	East Laport, Jackson, N. C	$13
East Genoa, Cayuga, N. Y	35	East Lebanon, Grafton, N. H	77
East Georgia, Franklin, Vt	59	East Lee, Berkshire, Mass	100
East German, Chenango, N. Y	65	East Lempster, Sullivan, N. H	48
East Germantown, Wayne, Ind	180	East Leon, Cattaraugus, N. Y	30
East Gibson, Manitowoc, Wis	13	East Leroy, Calhoun, Mich	17
East Gilead, Branch, Mich	57	East Lewistown, Mahoning, Ohio	66
East Glastenbury, Hartford, Conn	43	East Lexington, Middlesex, Mass	90
East Glenville, Schenectady, N. Y	23	East Liberty, Logan, Ohio	30
East Gloucester, Essex, Mass	370	East Liberty, Fayette, Pa	55
East Granby, Hartford, Conn	110	East Limington, York, Me	34
East Granger, Allegany, N. Y	6	East Lincoln, Penobscot, Me	40
East Granville, Hampden, Mass	47	East Line, Saratoga, N. Y	54
East Granville, Addison, Vt	30	East Litchfield, Litchfield, Conn	61
East Greenbush, Rensselaer, N. Y	78	East Livermore, Androscoggin, Me.	84
East Greene, Chenango, N. Y	79	East Liverpool,* Columbiana, Ohio.	720
East Greene, Erie, Pa	19	East Long Meadow, Hampden, Mass	130
East Greensborough, Orleans, Vt	36	East Lowell, Penobscot, Me	38
East Greenville, Stark, Ohio	28	East Lyme, New London, Conn	150
East Greenwich, Washington, N. Y.	85	East McDonough, Chenango, N. Y.	8
East Greenwich,* (c. h.,) Kent, R. I.	1,000	East Machias, Washington, Me	470
East Greenwood, Muskingum, Ohio	20	East Madison, Somerset, Me	97
East Grove, Chemung, N. Y	4	East Madison, Carroll, N. H	29
East Groveland, Livingston, N. Y	70	East Maine, Broome, N. Y	9
East Guilford, Chenango, N. Y	91	Eastman, Crawford, Wis	44
East Haddam, Middlesex, Conn	660	Eastmansville, Ottawa, Mich	170
Eastham, Barnstable, Mass	76	East Marion, Suffolk, N. Y	69
East Hamburgh, Erie, N. Y	150	East Marshfield, Plymouth, Mass	130
East Hamilton, Madison, N.Y	75	East Masonville, Delaware, N. Y	57
East Hampden, Penobscot, Me	90	East Mauch Chunk, Carbon, Pa	12
East Hampstead, Rockingham, N.H.	12	East Medway, Norfolk, Mass	180
East Hampton, Middlesex, Conn	440	East Melrose, Monroe, Iowa	120
East Hampton,* Hampshire, Mass.	2,000	East Meredith, Delaware, N. Y	12
East Hampton, Suffolk, N. Y	410	East Meriden, Steele, Minn	4
East Hanover, Lebanon, Pa	40	East Middleborough, Plymouth,	
East Hardwick, Caledonia, Vt	210	Mass	25
East Harpswell, Cumberland, Me	75	East Middlebury, Addison, Vt	110
East Hartford, Hartford, Conn	280	East Milan, Monroe, Mich	12
East Harwich, Barnstable, Mass	46	East Monmouth, Kennebec, Me	25
East Haven, New Haven, Conn	56	East Monroe, Highland, Ohio	80
East Haven, Essex, Vt	25	East Montpelier, Washington, Vt	74
East Haverhill, Essex, Mass	59	East Montville, Waldo, Me	14
East Haverhill, Grafton, N. H	120	East Moriches, Suffolk, N. Y	98
East Hebron, Oxford, Me	62	East Moultonborough, Carroll, N. H	12
East Hebron, Potter, Pa	28	East Nassau, Rensselaer, N. Y	41
East Hempfield, Lancaster, Pa	55	East New Market, Dorchester, Md.	140
East Hickory, Forest, Pa	58	East Newport, Penobscot, Me	35
East Highgate, Franklin, Vt	110	East New Portland, Somerset, Me	27
East Holden, Penobscot, Me	50	East New Sharon, Franklin, Me	52
East Holliston, Middlesex, Mass	76	East New Vineyard, Franklin, Me	6
East Homer, Cortland, N. Y	38	East New York, Kings, N. Y	1,000
East Homer, Potter, Pa	12	East Nichols, Tioga, N. Y	11
East Houndsfield, Jefferson, N. Y	27	East Nodoway, Adams, Iowa	13
East Hubbardton, Rutland, Vt	14	East Northfield, Cook, Ill	18
East Hutchinson, McLeod, Minn	12	East Northport, Waldo, Me	31
East Jaffrey, Cheshire, N. H	270	East Northwood, Rockingham, N.H.	110
East Java, Wyoming, N. Y	39	East North Yarmouth, Cumberland,	
East Jewett, Greene, N. Y	9	Me	51
East Kendall, Orleans, N. Y	54	East Norwalk, Huron, Ohio	58
East Kent, Litchfield, Conn	13	East Norwich, Queens, N. Y	100
East Killingly, Windham, Conn	130	East Oasis, Waushara, Wis	15
East Kingston, Rockingham, N. H.	91	Easton, Fairfield, Conn	55
East Knox, Waldo, Me	87	Easton, Leavenworth, Kans	81
East Lamoine, Hancock, Me	36	Easton, Aroostook, Me	29
East Landaff, Grafton, N. H	10	Easton,* (c. h.,) Talbot, Md	1,100
East Lansing, Tompkins, N. Y	18	Easton, Bristol, Mass	180

* Money-order office.

EAS EAS

Easton, Ionia, Mich	$26	East Rush, Susquehanna, Pa	$6
Easton, Buchanan, Mo	160	East Rush Creek, Perry, Ohio	93
Easton, Washington, N. Y	110	East Rushford, Allegany, N. Y	19
Easton, Wayne, Ohio	45	East Saginaw,* Saginaw, Mich	3,300
Easton, (c. h.,) Northampton, Pa	3,800	East Saint Louis,* St. Clair, Ill	830
Easton, Monongalia, W. Va	23	East Salamanca, Cattaraugus, N. Y.	12
Easton, Adams, Wis	42	East Salem, Washington, N. Y	33
East Orange, Essex, N. J	180	East Salem, Juniata, Pa	36
East Orange, Schuyler, N. Y	12	East Salisbury, Essex, Mass	70
East Orange, Delaware, Ohio	12	East Sandwich, Barnstable, Mass.	22
East Orange, Orange, Vt	57	East Sangerville, Piscataquis, Me.	15
East Orangeville, Wyoming, N. Y.	12	East Sandy, Venango, Pa	19
East Orleans, Barnstable, Mass	110	East Sandy Creek,* Oswego, N. Y.	400
East Orrington, Penobscot, Me	36	East Schodack, Rensselaer, N. Y.	15
East Otis, Berkshire, Mass	20	East Schuyler, Herkimer, N. Y	48
East Otisfield, Cumberland, Me	67	East Scott, Cortland, N. Y	8
East Otto, Cattaraugus, N. Y	170	East Setauket, Suffolk, N. Y	130
East Palermo, Waldo, Me	40	East Sharon, Norfolk, Mass	7
East Palermo, Oswego, N. Y	20	East Sharon, Potter, Pa	20
East Palestine, Columbiana, Ohio.	320	East Sharpsburgh, Blair, Pa	18
East Palmyra, Wayne, N. Y	91	East Sheffield, Berkshire, Mass	72
East Parsonfield, York, Me	69	East Shelburne, Franklin, Mass	10
East Paw Paw, De Kalb, Ill	100	East Shelby, Orleans, N. Y	43
East Pembroke, Plymouth, Mass	64	East Sheldon, Franklin, Vt	22
East Pembroke, Merrimack, N. H.	12	East Smithfield, Bradford, Pa	270
East Pembroke, Genesee, N. Y	150	East Somerville, Middlesex, Mass.	540
East Penfield, Monroe, N. Y	59	East Springfield, Sullivan, N. H	11
East Pepperell, Middlesex, Mass.	280	East Springfield, Otsego, N. Y	120
East Peru, Oxford, Me	18	East Springfield, Jefferson, Ohio	100
East Pharsalia, Chenango, N. Y	57	East Springfield, Erie, Pa	200
East Pike, Wyoming, N. Y	120	East Springhill, Bradford, Pa	24
East Pitcairn, St. Lawrence, N. Y.	15	East Stoneham, Oxford, Me	39
East Pittston, Kennebec, Me	82	East Stoughton, Norfolk, Mass	290
East Plainfield, Sullivan, N. H	45	East Stroudsburgh, Monroe, Pa	140
East Plymouth, Ashtabula, Ohio	16	East Sullivan, Hancock, Me	69
East Poestenkill, Rensselaer, N. Y.	20	East Sullivan, Cheshire, N. H	49
East Point, Fulton, Ga	7	East Sumner, Oxford, Me	85
East Poland, Androscoggin, Me	71	East Sycamore, Hamilton, Ohio	30
Eastport, Fremont, Iowa	92	East Taunton, Bristol, Mass	230
Eastport,* Washington, Me	2,200	East Tawas, Iosco, Mich	290
Eastport, Tishemingo, Miss	40	East Templeton, Worcester, Mass.	340
East Porter, Niagara, N. Y	15	East Thetford, Orange, Vt	61
East Portland, Multnomah, Oreg.	12	East Thompson, Windham, Conn	10
East Poultney, Rutland, Vt	180	East Thorndike, Waldo, Me	12
East Prairieville, Rice, Minn	27	East Tilton, Belknap, N. H	99
East Princeton, Worcester, Mass.	79	East Toledo, Lucas, Ohio	460
East Providence, Providence, R. I.	69	East Townsend, Huron, Ohio	120
East Putnam, Windham, Conn	93	East Traverse Bay, Grand Traverse,	
East Randolph, Norfolk, Mass	280	Mich	16
East Randolph, Cattaraugus, N. Y.	350	East Troupsburgh, Steuben, N. Y.	9
East Randolph, Orange, Vt	140	East Troy, Bradford, Pa	20
East Raymond, Cumberland, Me	46	East Troy,* Walworth, Wis	340
East Readfield, Kennebec, Me	16	East Troy Lake, Walworth, Wis	28
East Richford, Franklin, Vt	21	East Trumbull, Ashtabula, Ohio	51
East Richland, Belmont, Ohio	73	East Turner, Androscoggin, Me	47
East Ridge, Clearfield, Pa	3	East Union, Wayne, Ohio	26
East Ringgold, Pickaway, Ohio	23	East Unity, Sullivan, N. H	12
East River, New Haven, Conn	180	East Varick, Seneca, N. Y	39
East Rochester, Strafford, N. H	150	East Vassalborough, Kennebec, Me.	190
East Rochester, Columbiana, Ohio.	110	East Venice, Cayuga, N. Y	40
East Rockaway, Queens, N. Y	12	*Eastville,* (c. h.,) Northampton, Va.	250
East Rockport, Cuyahoga, Ohio	92	East Vincent, Chester, Pa	280
East Rodman, Jefferson, N. Y	18	East Virgil, Cortland, N. Y	12
East Roxbury, Washington, Vt	23	East Wakefield, Carroll, N. H	26
East Rumford, Oxford, Me	16	East Wales, Androscoggin, Me	7
East Rupert, Bennington, Vt	69	East Wallingford, Rutland, Vt	240

* Money-order office.

EDD | EDI

East Walpole, Norfolk, Mass	$120	Eddyville, Armstrong, Pa	$29
East Wareham, Plymouth, Mass	160	Eden, Lincoln, Dak	37
East Warren, Washington, Vt	50	Eden, Effingham, Ga	57
East Washington, Sullivan, N. H	120	Eden, Iroquois, Ill	12
East Waterborough, York, Me	28	Eden, Hancock, Ind	22
East Waterford, Juniata, Pa	110	Eden, Fayette, Iowa	28
East Watertown, Jefferson, N. Y	12	Eden, Atchison, Kans	13
East Weare, Hillsborough, N. H	73	Eden, Hancock, Me	24
East Westmoreland, Cheshire, N. H	59	Eden, Ingham, Mich	47
East Weymouth, Norfolk, Mass	440	Eden, Faribault, Minn	12
East Whately, Franklin, Mass	120	Eden, Erie, N. Y	110
East Wheatland, Will, Ill	24	Eden, Randolph, N. C	33
East Wilson, Niagara, N. Y	19	Eden, McKean, Pa	4
East Wilton, Franklin, Me	250	Eden, Laurens, S. C	12
East Windham, Cumberland, Me	14	Eden, Lamoille, Vt	36
East Windham, Greene, N. Y	14	Eden, Fond du Lac, Wis	8
East Windsor, Hartford, Conn	37	Edenburgh, Shenandoah, Va	140
East Windsor, Berkshire, Mass	48	Eden Mills, La Grange, Ind	9
East Windsor Hill, Hartford, Conn	170	Eden Mills, Lamoille, Vt	41
East Winthrop, Kennebec, Me	56	Eden Prairie, Hennepin, Minn	77
East Woburn, Middlesex, Mass	75	Eden's Ridge, Sullivan, Tenn	12
East Woodhull, Steuben, N. Y	12	Edenton, Madison, Ky	9
East Woodstock, Windham, Conn	150	Edenton, St. Lawrence, N. Y	14
East Worcester, Otsego, N. Y	180	*Edenton,* (c. h.,) Chowan, N. C	660
East Wrightstown, Brown, Wis	20	Edenton, Clermont, Ohio	36
Eaton, Crawford, Ill	18	Eden Valley, Erie, N. Y	24
Eaton, Delaware, Ind	54	Edenville, Marshall, Iowa	35
Eaton, Madison, N. Y	400	Edenville, Midland, Mich	67
Eaton, (c. h.,) Preble, Ohio	970	Edenville, Orange, N. Y	24
Eaton, Wyoming, Pa	29	Edenville, Erie, Pa	3
Eaton, Manitowoc, Wis	79	Edes Falls, Cumberland, Me	45
Eaton Centre, Carroll, N. H	47	Edesville, Kent, Md	62
Eaton Rapids, Eaton, Mich	790	*Edgard,* (c. h.,) St. John Baptist, La.	110
Eatonton, (c. h.,) Putnam, Ga	630	Edgar Springs, Phelps, Mo	13
Eatontown, Monmouth, N. J	300	*Edgartown,* (c. h.,) Dukes, Mass	730
Eatonville, Herkimer, N. Y	30	Edgecomb, Lincoln, Me	60
Eau Claire, Berrien, Mich	55	*Edgefield C. H.,* Edgefield, S. C	200
Eau Claire, Butler, Pa	34	Edgefield Junction, Davidson, Tenn	110
Eau Claire, (c. h.,) Eau Claire, Wis.	1,800	Edge Hill, Reynolds, Mo	12
Eau Galle, Dunn, Wis	87	Edge Hill, King George, Va	72
Eau Pleine, Portage, Wis	47	Edgemont, Delaware, Pa	50
Ebenezer, Greene, Mo	23	Edgerton, El Paso, Colo	12
Ebenezer, Erie, N. Y	110	Edgerton, Kent, Mich	12
Ebenezer, Preble, Ohio	20	Edgerton,* Williams, Ohio	510
Ebenezer, Indiana, Pa	35	Edgerton, Rock, Wis	340
Ebensburgh, (c. h.,) Cambria, Pa	950	Edgewood, Effingham, Ill	150
Eberly's Mill, Cumberland, Pa	42	Edgewood, Harford, Md	110
Echo, Armstrong, Pa	23	Edgeworth, Sullivan, Tenn	13
Echo, Macon, Tenn	12	Edgwood, Siskiyou, Cal	12
Echo, Live Oak, Tex	10	Edgwood, Bucks, Pa	70
Echo City, Summit, Utah	12	*Edina,* (c. h.,) Knox, Mo	460
Eckley, Carroll, Ohio	8	Edinborough, Montgomery, N. C	4
Eckley, Luzerne, Pa	370	Edinborough, Erie, Pa	630
Eckmansville, Adams, Ohio	92	Edinburgh, Christian, Ill	55
Ecleto, Karnes, Tex	10	Edinburgh,* Johnson, Ind	920
Economy, Wayne, Ind	91	Edinburgh, Jones, Iowa	7
Economy, Macon, Mo	23	Edinburgh, Hillsdale, Mich	4
Economy, Beaver, Pa	67	Edinburgh, Leake, Miss	17
Ecorse, Wayne, Mich	65	Edinburgh, Grundy, Mo	81
Eddington, Penobscot, Me	65	Edinburgh, Mercer, N. J	10
Eddington, Bucks, Pa	140	Edinburgh, Saratoga, N. Y	52
Eddytown, Yates, N. Y	130	Edinburgh, Portage, Ohio	150
Eddyville, Pope, Ill	8	Edinburgh, Lawrence, Pa	100
Eddyville,* Wapello, Iowa	1,000	*Edinburgh,* (c. h.,) Hidalgo, Tex	26
Eddyville, (c. h.,) Lyon, Ky	210	Edington, Rock Island, Ill	120
Eddyville, Cattaraugus, N. Y	36	Edisto Island, Colleton, S. C	110

* Money-order office.

Edith, Shenandoah, Va.	$9
Edmeston, Otsego, N. Y	110
Edmonton,* (*c. h.,*) Metcalfe, Ky.	88
Edna, Cass, Iowa	15
Edneyville, Henderson, N. C.	5
Edom, Rockingham, Va.	19
Edon, Williams, Ohio	59
Edray, Pocahontas, W. Va.	21
Edsallville, Bradford, Pa.	14
Edwards, Jefferson, Ky	9
Edwards, St. Lawrence, N. Y	150
Edwards, Sheboygan, Wis.	40
Edwardsburgh, Cass, Mich	240
Edwards' Depot, Hinds, Miss	190
Edwardsport, Knox, Ind	110
Edwards' Station, Peoria, Ill	33
Edwardsville, (*c. h.,*) Cleburne, Ala.	28
Edwardsville,* (*c. h.,*) Madison, Ill.	1,000
Edwardsville, Floyd, Ind	24
Edwardsville, Wyandotte, Kans	110
Edwardsville, St. Lawrence, N. Y	32
Edwardsville, Warren, Ohio	27
Edwina, Monroe, Ohio	4
Eel River, Humboldt, Cal	57
Eel River, Allen, Ind	23
Effingham,* (*c. h.,*) Effingham, Ill	1,000
Effingham, Atchison, Kans	12
Effingham, Carroll, N. H	20
Effingham Falls, Carroll, N. H	74
Effingham Station, Marion, S. C	72
Effort, Monroe, Pa	16
Efird's Mills, Stanly, N. C	1
Egan Canyon, Lander, Nev	25
Eggertsville, Erie, N. Y	36
Egg Harbor, Door, Wis	17
Egg Harbor City,* Atlantic, N. J.	470
Eggleston's Springs, Giles, Va.	13
Egg's Point, Washington, Miss	120
Eglantine, Van Buren, Ark	12
Egypt, Effingham, Ga.	30
Egypt, Chickasaw, Miss	71
Egypt, Monroe, N. Y	210
Egypt, Wharton, Tex	16
Egypt, Monroe, W. Va	10
Egypt Depot, Chatham, N. C	100
Egypt Mills, Cape Girardeau, Mo	8
Egypt Mills, Pike, Pa	12
Ehrenberg, Yuma, Ariz	12
Eighteen Mile, Pickens, S. C.	8
Eight Mile Creek, Harrison, Tex.	11
Eight Mile Grove, Cass, Nebr.	12
Eighty-Eight, Barren, Ky	12
Eitzen, Houston, Minn	34
Ekonk, Windham, Conn	13
Ela, Lake, Ill.	15
Elam, Delaware, Pa	43
Elamsville, Patrick, Va	1
Elba, (*c. h.,*) Coffee, Ala.	22
Elba, Gallatin, Ill	12
Elba, Winona, Minn	37
Elba, Genesee, N. Y	180
Elbaville, Davie, N. C.	12
Elberfeld, Warrick, Ind	10
Elberton, (*c. h.,*) Elbert, Ga	170
Elbinsville, Bedford, Pa	9
Elbow Spring, Barren, Ky	12

Elbridge, Edgar, Ill.	$22
Elbridge, Onondaga, N. Y	270
El Dara, Pike, Ill	83
Eldena, Lee, Ill.	52
Elder's Ridge, Indiana, Pa	80
Elderton, Armstrong, Pa	130
Eldora,* (*c. h.,*) Hardin, Iowa	870
El Dorado, (*c. h.,*) Union, Ark	210
El Dorado, El Dorado, Cal	87
El Dorado, Saline, Ill	56
El Dorado, Fayette, Iowa	61
El Dorado, (*c. h.,*) Butler, Kans	140
El Dorado, Clarke, Mo	150
El Dorado, Colfax, Nebr	12
El Dorado, Preble, Ohio.	66
El Dorado, Baker, Oreg	12
El Dorado, Blair, Pa	31
El Dorado, Culpeper, Va.	6
El Dorado, Fond du Lac, Wis	22
El Dorado Mills, Fond du Lac, Wis.	53
Eldred, Saunders, Nebr	12
Eldred, Wayne, Pa.	15
Eldredgeville, Ford, Ill	12
Eldredsville, Sullivan, Pa	32
Eldridge, Walker, Ala	9
Eleroy, Stephenson, Ill.	80
Eleven Mile, Potter, Pa	12
Elgin, Jackson, Ark.	44
Elgin,* Kane, Ill	2,500
Elgin, Fayette, Iowa	73
Elgin, Genesee, Mich	12
Elgin, Wabashaw, Minn	55
Elgin, Cattarangus, N. Y	25
Elida, Winnebago, Ill	70
Elida, Allen, Ohio	88
Elimsport, Lycoming, Pa	53
Elisabeth, Marshall, Kans.	12
Eliza, Mercer, Ill	1
Eliza, Houston, Tex.	8
Elizabeth, Jo Daviess, Ill	270
Elizabeth, Harrison, Ind	85
Elizabeth,* (*c. h.,*) Union, N. J	3,800
Elizabeth, Allegheny, Pa.	400
Elizabeth City,* (*c. h.,*) Pasquotank, N. C.	480
Elizabeth Furnace, Augusta, Va.	43
Elizabeth Port, Union, N. J	1,300
Elizabethton, (*c. h.,*) Carter, Tenn.	100
Elizabethtown, (*c. h.,*) Hardin, Ill	130
Elizabethtown, Bartholomew, Ind	190
Elizabethtown, Anderson, Kans	13
Elizabethtown,* (*c. h.,*) Hardin, Ky.	1,000
Elizabethtown, (*c. h.,*) Colfax, N. Mex.	600
Elizabethtown,* (*c. h.,*) Essex, N. Y.	370
Elizabethtown, (*c. h.,*) Bladen, N. C.	76
Elizabethtown, Lancaster, Pa	380
Elizabethville, Pendleton, Ky	4
Elizabethville, Dauphin, Pa.	95
Elizaville, Boone, Ind.	46
Elizaville, Fleming, Ky	160
Elizaville, Columbia, N. Y	21
Elk, Decatur, Iowa	13
Elk, Saginaw, Mich	16
Elk, Pocahontas, W. Va	6
Elk, Manitowoc, Wis	5
Elkader,* (*c. h.,*) Clayton, Iowa	730

* Money-order office.

ELL　　　　　　　　　　　　ELM

Elk City, Montgomery, Kans	$12	Ellengowan, Baltimore, Md	$82
Elk City, Barbour, W. Va	12	Ellenorah, Gentry, Mo	24
Elk Creek, Spencer, Ky	49	*Ellensberg, (c. h.,)* Curry, Oreg	38
Elk Creek, Texas, Mo	12	Ellenton, Palo Alto, Iowa	12
Elk Creek, Otsego, N. Y	12	Ellenville,* Ulster, N. Y	1,300
Elk Creek, Erie, Pa	68	Ellerslie, Harris, Ga	10
Elk Creek, Grayson, Va	20	Ellerslie, Alleghany, Md	12
Elk Creek, Trempealeau, Wis	25	Ellery, Chautauqua, N. Y	72
Elk Cross Roads, Ashe, N. C	8	Ellicott, Erie, N. Y	24
Elk Dale, Chester, Pa	59	*Ellicott City,* (c. h.,) Howard, Md	1,100
Elk Falls, (c. h.,) Howard, Kans	12	*Ellicottsville,** (c. h.,) Cattaraugus,	
Elk Grove, Sacramento, Cal	41	N. Y	860
Elk Grove, Cook, Ill	16	*Ellijay,* (c. h.,) Gilmer, Ga	59
Elk Grove, La Fayette, Wis	37	Ellington, Tolland, Conn	220
Elkhart,* Elkhart, Ind	2,400	*Ellington,* (c. h.,) Hancock, Iowa	33
Elkhart, Polk, Iowa	55	Ellington, Tuscola, Mich	59
Elkhart City,* Logan, Ill	510	Ellington, Dodge, Minn	8
Elk Hill Mills, Goochland, Va	12	Ellington, Chautauqua, N. Y	280
Elkhorn, Washington, Ill	150	Ellingwood's Corner, Waldo, Me	27
Elk Horn, Shelby, Iowa	12	Elliot, York, Me	25
Elkhorn, Lincoln, Kans	18	Elliota, Fillmore, Minn	110
Elk Horn, Lawrence, Mo	12	Elliot Depot, York, Me	20
Elk Horn, Polk, Oreg	12	Elliott, San Joaquin, Cal	10
Elk Horn, (c. h.,) Walworth, Wis	960	Elliott, Grenada, Miss	20
Elkhorn City, Douglas, Nebr	40	Elliottsburgh, Perry, Pa	55
Elk Horn Grove, Carroll, Ill	51	Elliott's Cross Roads, Morgan, Ohio	16
Elkin, Surry, N. C	41	Elliott's Mill, Panola, Miss	17
Elkinsville, Brown, Ind	4	Elliottstown, Effingham, Ill	33
Elk Lake, Susquehanna, Pa	24	Elliottsville, Monroe, Mo	12
Elkland, Tuscola, Mich	16	El lis, San Joaquin, Cal	12
Elkland, Webster, Mo	12	El'is, Ellis, Kans	12
Elkland, Tioga, Pa	230	Ellis, Portage, Wis	12
Elk Lick, Somerset, Pa	140	Ellisburgh, Jefferson, N. Y	100
Elk Mills, McDonald, Mo	15	Ellisburgh, Potter, Pa	25
Elk Mills, Chester, Pa	12	Ellisdale, Ocean, N. J	99
Elko, (c. h.,) Elko, Nev	890	Ellis Grove, Randolph, Ill	38
Elk Point, (c. h.,) Union, Dak	230	Ellison, Warren, Ill	51
Elkport, Clayton, Iowa	87	Elliston, Grant, Ky	12
Elk Rapids, (c. h.,) Antrim, Mich	130	Ellistown, Lee, Miss	9
Elk Ridge Landing, Howard, Md	86	Ellisville, Columbia, Fla	24
Elk River, Clinton, Iowa	28	Ellisville, Fulton, Ill	110
Elk River Station, Sherburne, Minn	210	*Ellisville,* (c. h.,) Jones, Miss	10
Elk Run, Tioga, Pa	13	Ellisville, St. Louis, Mo	20
Elk Run, Fauquier, Va	5	Ellisville, Kewaunee, Wis	10
Elk Shoals, Iredell, N. C	7	Ellittsville, Monroe, Ind	190
Elk Spring, Warren, Ky	1	Ellsworth, Johnson, Ark	12
Elkton, Crawford, Ill	14	Ellsworth, Litchfield, Conn	61
Elkton, (c. h.,) Todd, Ky	430	Ellsworth, Vigo, Ind	24
*Elkton,** (c. h.,) Cecil, Md	1,400	Ellsworth, Madison, Iowa	18
Elkton, Hickory, Mo	67	*Ellsworth,** (c. h.,) Ellsworth, Kans	1,000
Elkton, Columbiana, Ohio	32	*Ellsworth,** (c. h.,) Hancock, Me	1,400
Elkton, Giles, Tenn	74	Ellsworth, Nye, Nev	41
Elkview, Chester, Pa	80	Ellsworth, Grafton, N. H	16
Elkville, Jackson, Ill	69	Ellsworth, St. Lawrence, N. Y	62
Elkville, Wilkes, N. C	12	Ellsworth, Mahoning, Ohio	83
Ella, Pepin, Wis	12	*Ellsworth,* (c. h.,) Pierce, Wis	160
Ellaville, (c. h.,) Schley, Ga	38	Ellwood, Hopkins, Ky	6
Elleard, St. Louis, Mo	66	Ellwood, Schuylkill, Pa	25
Ellejoy, Blount, Tenn	10	Elm, Wayne, Mich	26
Ellenborough, Ritchie, W. Va	140	Elm, Linn, Mo	12
Ellenborough, Grant, Wis	28	Elm, Fayette, Pa	86
Ellenburgh, Clinton, N. Y	140	Elma, Erie, N. Y	51
Ellenburgh Centre, Clinton, N. Y	190	Elma, Chehalis, Wash	11
Ellenburgh Depot, Clinton, N. Y	79	Elm Bluff, Dallas, Ala	5
Ellendale, Sussex, Del	68	Elmendaro, Lyon, Kans	8
Ellendale Forge, Dauphin, Pa	20	Elmer, Salem, N. J	150

* Money-order office.

ELY   ENF

Elm Flat, Chautauqua, N. Y	$16	*Elyton,* (*c. h.,*) Jefferson, Ala	$100
Elm Grove, Adams, Ill	10	Emanuel, Bonhomme, Dak	7
Elm Grove, Franklin, Mass	16	Emaus, Lehigh, Pa	140
Elm Grove, Holt, Mo	55	Emaus, Bedford, Va	12
Elm Grove, Jefferson, Nebr	12	Embarrass, Waupaca, Wis	52
Elm Grove, Ohio, W. Va	66	Embden, Somerset, Me	7
Elm Grove, Waukesha, Wis	35	Embreeville, Chester, Pa	37
Elm Hall, Gratiot, Mich	97	Embryville, Washington, Tenn	12
Elm Hill, Montgomery, Ky	12	Emerald, Adams, Ohio	12
Elmhurst, Du Page, Ill	240	Emerald, Anderson, Kans	12
Elmington, Nelson, Va	26	Emerald Grove, Rock, Wis	110
Elmira, Stark, Ill	72	Emerson, Mills, Iowa	12
Elmira, Eaton, Mich	6	Emerson, Marion, Mo	25
Elmira, * (*c. h.,*) Chemung, N. Y	3,600	Emerson, Otoe, Nebr	16
Elmira, Fulton, Ohio	56	Emery, Fulton, Ohio	12
Elmore, Peoria, Ill	70	Emery, Monroe, Wis	50
Elmore, Faribault, Minn	10	Emery's Mills, York, Me	30
Elmore, Richardson, Nebr	18	Emigrant Gap, Placer, Cal	10
Elmore, Ottawa, Ohio	650	Emigsville, York, Pa	38
Elmore, Lamoille, Vt	83	Emilie, Bucks, Pa	49
Elmore, Fond du Lac, Wis	12	Eminence, Logan, Ill	12
Elm Point, Bond, Ill	37	Eminence, Morgan, Ind	45
Elmsford, Westchester, N. Y	18	Eminence, Henry, Ky	640
Elm Springs, Washington, Ark	44	*Eminence,* (*c. h.,*) Shannon, Mo	27
Elm Springs, Butler, Iowa	40	Eminence, Schoharie, N. Y	24
Elm Store, Randolph, Ark	20	Emison Station, Knox, Ind	12
Elm Tree, Weakley, Tenn	8	Emlenton, Venango, Pa	280
Elm Wood, Carroll, Ark	12	Emma, Butler, Ala	12
Elmwood,* Peoria, Ill	400	Emma, White, Ill	20
Elm Wood, Saline, Mo	130	Emmaville, Fulton, Pa	17
Elmwood, Cass, Nebr	44	Emmett, Lake, Ill	12
Elo, Winnebago, Wis	45	Emmett, Emmett, Iowa	13
Elon, Allamakee, Iowa	30	Emmett, St. Clair, Mich	12
Elora, Lincoln, Tenn	13	Emmett, Paulding, Ohio	15
El Paso, Conway, Ark	28	Emmettsburgh, Deer Lodge, Mont.	12
El Paso, El Paso, Colo	12	Emmettsville, Ada, Idaho	12
El Paso,* Woodford, Ill	1,600	*Emmittsburg,* (*c. h.,*) Palo Alto, Iowa	17
El Paso, (*c. h.,*) El Paso, Tex	80	Emmittsburgh,* Frederick, Md	860
El Paso, Pierce, Wis	62	Emmonsburgh, Herkimer, N. Y	64
Elrod, Ripley, Ind	44	Emmorton, Harford, Md	95
Elroy, Juneau, Wis	46	Emmorton, Richmond, Va	12
Elsah, Jersey, Ill	80	Emory, Washington, Va	340
El Sauz, Hidalgo, Tex	12	Empire, Wright, Iowa	12
Elsie, Clinton, Mich	250	Empire, Leelenaw, Mich	68
Elsinor, McLean, Ill	12	Empire, Fond du Lac, Wis	27
Elsinore, Allen, Kans	22	Empire City, Clear Creek, Colo	55
Elston, Labette, Kans	12	Empire City, Dakota, Minn	20
Elston Station, Cole, Mo	72	Empire City, Ormsby, Nev	140
Eltham, Westmoreland, Va	12	*Empire City,* (*c. h.,*) Coos, Oreg	180
Elton, Cattaraugus, N. Y	24	Empire Iron Works, Trigg, Ky	16
Elton, Walworth, Wis	22	Empire Junction, Columbia, Wis	17
Elvaston, Hancock, Ill	160	Empire Prairie, Andrew, Mo	58
Elvira, Johnson, Ill	14	*Emporia,* * (*c. h.,*) Lyon, Kans	1,600
Elvira, Clinton, Iowa	41	*Emporium,* * (*c. h.,*) Cameron, Pa	890
Elwell, Bradford, Pa	8	Emuckfaw, Tallapoosa, Ala	4
Elwin, Macon, Ill	70	Enders, Dauphin, Pa	22
Elwood, Will, Ill	220	Endor, Will, Ill	12
Elwood, Madison, Ind	200	Enfield, Hartford, Conn	290
Elwood, Doniphan, Kans	140	Enfield, White, Ill	83
Elwood, Steele, Minn	6	Enfield, Penobscot, Me	92
Elwood, Atlantic, N. J	270	Enfield, Hampshire, Mass	350
Elwood, Suffolk, N. Y	12	Enfield, Grafton, N. H	430
Ely, Warrick, Ind	200	Enfield, Tompkins, N. Y	12
Elyria, * (*c. h.,*) Lorain, Ohio	1,800	Enfield, Halifax, N. C	420
Elysburgh, Northumberland, Pa	46	Enfield, King William, Va	11
Elysian, Le Sueur, Minn	72	Enfield Centre, Grafton, N. H	230

* Money-order office.

ERI　　　　　　　EUH

Enfield Centre, Tompkins, N. Y....	$39	Erin, Washington, Kans......	$16
Engleman's Mills, Dade, Mo.......	25	Erin, Calhoun, Miss............	9
Englewood, Cook, Ill...............	25	Erin, Chemung, N. Y............	6
Englewood, Bergen, N. J..........	580	Erin, Stewart, Tenn........	12
English, Crawford, Ind............	10	Erin, St. Croix, Wis............	41
English Centre, Lycoming, Pa.....	68	Erin Shades, Henrico, Va.	6
English Lake, Stark, Ind..........	32	Errol, Coos, N. H.....	37
English Prairie, McHenry, Ill......	15	Ervin, Howard, Ind.............	37
English's Creek, Atlantic, N. J....	52	Erving, Franklin, Mass..........	200
English Settlement, Marion, Iowa.	15	Erwin Centre, Steuben, N. Y......	35
Englishtown, Monmouth, N. J.....	180	Erwinna, Bucks, Pa.............	76
Englishville, Kent, Mich..........	22	Erwinsville, Cleveland, N. C......	5
Ennisville, Huntingdon, Pa........	37	Escatawpa, Washington, Ala	12
Enoch, Noble, Ohio......	19	Escoheag, Kent, R. I............	12
Enochsburgh, Franklin, Ind.......	50	Esconawba,* (c. h.,) Delta, Mich....	790
Enola, Iredell, N. C..............	10	Eskridge, Wabaunsee, Kans.......	12
Enon, Bullock, Ala...............	45	Esofia, Vernon, Wis.............	12
Enon, Perry, Miss................	7	Esopus, Ulster, N. Y......	210
Enon, Clark, Ohio............	150	Esparanza, St. John's, Fla	12
Enon College, Sumner, Tenn	26	Esperance, Schoharie, N. Y....	300
Enon Valley, Lawrence, Pa........	380	Espy, Columbia, Pa.............	240
Enoree, Spartanburgh, S. C........	6	Espyville, Crawford, Pa	84
Enosburgh, Franklin, Vt..........	100	Essex,* Middlesex, Conn.........	720
Enosburgh Falls,* Franklin, Vt....	150	Essex, Essex, Mass...............	250
Ensley, Newaygo, Mich...........	10	Essex, Clinton, Mich............	12
Enterline, Dauphin, Pa............	21	Essex,* Essex, N. Y......	420
Enterprise, Lee, Ga................	12	Essex, Chittenden. Vt...........	210
Enterprise, Wayne, Ill............	20	Essex Junction, Chittenden, Vt....	250
Enterprise, Spencer, Ind......	58	Esteina, Saunders, Nebr..........	12
Enterprise, Black Hawk, Iowa.....	19	Estella, Ringgold, Iowa..........	9
Enterprise, Winona, Minn........	69	Estell Flats, Carter, Ky.........	12
Enterprise, (c. h.,) Clark, Miss......	770	Estelville, Atlantic, N. J..........	25
Enterprise, McDonald, Mo:......	19	Estherville, (c. h.,) Emmett, Iowa...	150
Enterprise, Hocking, Ohio.........	12	Estill's Fork, Jackson, Ala	8
Enterprise, Lancaster, Pa.........	260	Estill Springs, Franklin, Tenn.....	55
Enterprise, Morgan, Utah....	19	Estillville, (c. h.,) Scott, Va........	100
Enterprise, Vernon, Wis	14	Ethel, Mercer, Ill...............	11
Enterprise Landing, Charleston, S.C.	12	Etlah, Franklin, Mo..............	24
Enterprize, Volusia, Fla...........	92	Etna, Coles, Ill......	67
Eola, Polk, Oreg.................	42	Etna, Penobscot, Me........	48
Ephraim, San Pete, Utah.........	500	Etna, Fillmore, Minn...........	48
Ephraim, Door, Wis......	90	Etna, Scotland, Mo.........	89
Ephratah, Fulton, N. Y..........	72	Etna, Tompkins, N. Y...........	150
Ephratah, Lancaster, Pa..........	310	Etna, Licking, Ohio.............	89
Epping, Rockingham, N. H........	310	Etna, Allegheny, Pa............	180
Epsom, Daviess, Ind..............	12	Etna, Smith, Tex...............	12
Epsom, Merrimack, N. H.........	120	Etna, La Fayette, Wis...........	70
Epworth, Dubuque, Iowa.	370	Etna Centre, Penobscot, Me.......	20
Equality, Coosa, Ala.............	10	Etna Green, Kosciusko, Ind......	120
Equality, Gallatin, Ill.............	140	Etna Mills, Siskiyou, Cal.........	24
Equality, Saline, Nebr......	12	Etna Mills, King William, Va.....	12
Equality, Anderson, S. C..........	14	Etters, York, Pa................	230
Equinunk, Wayne, Pa	170	Ettie, Tama, Iowa..............	12
Erastus, Banks, Ga...............	9	Ettieville, Gentry, Mo...........	12
Erata, Jones, Miss................	2	Ettrick, Trempealeau, Wis........	21
Ercildoun, Chester, Pa......	100	Euclid, Onondaga, N. Y..........	86
Erfurt, Jefferson, Wis............	57	Euclid, Cuyahoga, Ohio..........	69
Erie, Whitesides, Ill	120	Eudora, Douglas, Kans...........	250
Erie, Lawrence, Pa...............	16	Eufaula,* Barbour, Ala..........	2,000
Erie,* (c. h.,) Neosho, Kans........	500	Eugene, Knox, Ill...............	42
Erie, Monroe, Mich...............	170	Eugene, Vermillion, Ind..........	170
Erie, McDonald, Mo.............	8	Eugene, Ringgold, Iowa..........	6
Erie,* (c. h.,) Erie, Pa.............	3,100	Eugene, Shawnee, Kans..........	400
Erie, Roane, Tenn............	18	Eugene City, Carroll, Mo.........	12
Erieville, Madison, N. Y.........	80	Eugene City,* (c. h.,) Lane, Oreg...	610
Erin, Meriwether, Ga......	10	Euharley, Bartow, Ga............	76

* Money-order office.

EXC | FAI

Eulalia, Potter, Pa	$8	Excelsior Mills, Jo Daviess, Ill	$36
Eulia, Macon, Tenn	12	Exchange, Montour, Pa	16
Eunice, Chicot, Ark	13	Exeter, Scott, Ill	140
Euphemia, Preble, Ohio	49	Exeter, Penobscot, Me	130
Eureka,* (c. h.,) Humboldt, Cal	610	Exeter, Monroe, Mich	8
Eureka, Woodford, Ill	930	Exeter,* (c. h.,) Rockingham, N. H.	1,700
Eureka,* (c. h.,) Greenwood, Kans	230	Exeter, Otsego, N. Y	50
Eureka, Clinton, Mich	75	Exeter, Luzerne, Pa	14
Eureka, St. Louis, Mo	61	Exeter, Washington, R. I	27
Eureka, Lander, Nev	12	Exeter, Green, Wis	13
Eureka, Sullivan, N. Y	24	Exeter Mills, Penobscot, Me	20
Eureka, Gallia, Ohio	94	Exeter Station, Berks, Pa	66
Eureka, Winnebago, Wis	330	Exira, (c. h.,) Audubon, Iowa	150
Eustis, Franklin, Me	12	Exonville, Wabaunsee, Kans	12
Eutaw,* (c. h.,) Greene, Ala	840	Experiment Mills, Monroe, Pa	75
Eutaw, Limestone, Tex	17	Express Ranch, Baker, Oreg	25
Eva, Barry, Mo	13	Exton, Chester, Pa	70
Evans, (c. h.,) Weld, Colo	130	Eyer's Grove, Columbia, Pa	10
Evans, Erie, N. Y	73	Eyota, Olmsted, Minn	530
Evansburgh, Coshocton, Ohio	60		
Evansburgh, Crawford, Pa	120	**F**	
Evans' Landing, Harrison, Ind	12		
Evans' Mills, Jefferson, N. Y	390	FABER'S MILLS, Nelson, Va	65
Evansport, Defiance, Ohio	54	Fabius, Onondaga, N. Y	240
Evanston,* Cook, Ill	1,600	Fabius, Hardy, W. Va	11
Evanston, Uintah, Wyo	12	Fackler, Etowah, Ala	12
Evansville, Washington, Ark	52	Factory Point, Bennington, Vt	430
Evansville, Randolph, Ill	80	Factory Village, Franklin, Mass	12
Evansville,* (c. h.,) Vanderburgh, Ind	4,000	Factoryville, Cass, Nebr	56
		Factoryville, Tioga, N. Y	150
Evansville, Douglas, Minn	65	Factoryville, Wyoming, Pa	280
Evansville, Columbia, Pa	25	Fagleysville, Montgomery, Pa	25
Evansville, Preston, W. Va	80	Fairbank, Buchanan, Iowa	150
Evansville,* Rock, Wis	790	Fair Bluff, Columbus, N. C	62
Evanswood, Waupaca, Wis	12	Fairburn, Campbell, Ga	110
Evart, Osceola, Mich	12	Fairbury,* Livingston, Ill	1,500
Eveland Grove, Mahaska, Iowa	15	Fairbury, (c. h.,) Jefferson, Nebr	59
Eveline, Buchanan, Mo	19	Fairchild, Eau Claire, Wis	12
Eve Mills, Monroe, Tenn	22	Fair Dale, Oswego, N. Y	36
Evendale, Juniata, Pa	45	Fairdale, Susquehanna, Pa	65
Evening Shades, (c. h.,) Sharp, Ark	27	Fair Dealing, Marshall, Ky	12
Everett, Cass, Mo	70	Fairfax, Linn, Iowa	260
Evergreen, (c. h.,) Conecuh, Ala	340	Fairfax, Highland, Ohio	23
Ever Green, Washington, Ark	5	Fairfax, Franklin, Vt	360
Evergreen, Santa Clara, Cal	12	Fairfax C. H., Fairfax, Va	250
Evergreen, Tama, Iowa	22	Fairfield, (c. h.,) Fairfield, Conn	470
Evergreen, Avoyelles, La	110	Fairfield,* (c. h.,) Wayne, Ill	380
Evergreen, Appomattox, Va	48	Fairfield, Franklin, Ind	150
Everittstown, Hunterdon, N. J	54	Fairfield,* (c. h.,) Jefferson, Iowa	1,500
Everton, Fayette, Ind	63	Fairfield, Nelson, Ky	110
Ewald, Faribault, Minn	12	Fairfield, Somerset, Me	45
Ewan's Mills, Gloucester, N. J	8	Fairfield, St. Mary's, Md	63
Ewing, Franklin, Ill	20	Fairfield, Lenawee, Mich	150
Ewing, Jackson, Ind	78	Fairfield, Benton, Mo	44
Ewing, Hocking, Ohio	21	Fairfield, Herkimer, N. Y	310
Ewing's Corner, Hancock, Ohio	12	Fairfield, Hyde, N. C	20
Ewing's Mills, Allegheny, Pa	38	Fairfield, Greene, Ohio	150
Ewing's Neck, Cumberland, N. J	23	Fairfield, Marion, Oreg	12
Ewington, Gallia, Ohio	50	Fairfield, Adams, Pa	110
Ewingville, Mercer, N. J	36	Fairfield, Bedford, Tenn	10
Excello, Macon, Mo	12	Fairfield, (c. h.,) Freestone, Tex	180
Excelsior, Pueblo, Colo	19	Fairfield, Utah, Utah	14
Excelsior, Hennepin, Minn	170	Fairfield, Franklin, Vt	146
Excelsior, Morgan, Mo	25	Fairfield, Rockbridge, Va	71
Excelsior, Northumberland, Pa	12	Fairfield, Rock, Wis	22
Excelsior, Richland, Wis	35	Fairfield Centre, De Kalb, Ind	27

* Money-order office.

FAI   FAR

Office	$
Fairfield Centre, Lycoming, Pa....	$9
Fairfield Corners, Somerset, Me...	47
Fair Garden, Sevier, Tenn.........	6
Fair Grove, Greene, Mo...........	66
Fair Grove, Tuscola, Mich........	14
Fair Grove, Davidson, N. C.......	5
Fair Haven, New Haven, Conn....	1,300
Fair Haven, Carroll, Ill..........	24
Fairhaven, Bristol, Mass.........	990
Fair Haven, St. Clair, Mich.......	45
Fair Haven, Stearns, Minn........	76
Fair Haven, Cayuga, N. Y........	86
Fair Haven, Preble, Ohio.........	130
Fair Haven,* Rutland, Vt........	1,000
Fair Hill, Cecil, Md.............	65
Fair Hill, Rockingham, Va.......	47
Fair Hill, Marshall, W. Va.......	6
Fairland, Shelby, Ind............	210
Fairlee, Kent, Md...............	35
Fairlee, Orange, Vt.............	140
Fairmont, (c. h.,) Martin, Minn....	140
Fairmont, Clarke, Mo...........	130
Fairmont,* (c. h.,) Marion, W. Va..	680
Fair Mount, Gordon, Ga.........	59
Fairmount,* Vermilion, Ill........	350
Fairmount, Grant, Ind..........	130
Fairmount, Leavenworth, Kans...	67
Fairmount, Jefferson, Ky........	51
Fairmount, Somerset, Md........	12
Fair Mount, Hunterdon, N. J.....	23
Fair Mount, Onondaga, N. Y.....	31
Fairmount Springs, Luzerne, Pa....	27
Fair Oaks, San Mateo, Cal.......	6
Fair Play, Randolph, Ala........	12
Fair Play, El Dorado, Cal........	12
Fair Play, (c. h.,) Park, Colo.......	540
Fair Play, Washington, Md.......	43
Fair Play, Polk, Mo............	28
Fair Play, Jefferson, Ohio.......	28
Fair Play, Oconee, S. C.........	26
Fair Play, Grant, Wis..........	98
Fair Point, Goodhue, Minn.......	23
Fairport, Muscatine, Iowa.......	16
Fairport, De Kalb, Mo..........	12
Fairport, Monroe, N. Y.........	1,800
Fairport, Granville, N. C.......	5
Fairton, Cumberland, N. J......	96
Fairview, Walker, Ala..........	12
Fairview, Dallas, Ark...........	12
Fairview, Lincoln, Dak.........	12
Fairview, Fulton, Ill...........	300
Fairview, Randolph, Ind.........	32
Fairview, Jones, Iowa.........	60
Fairview, Brown, Kans.........	14
Fairview, Christian, Ky........	96
Fairview, Concordia, La........	15
Fairview, Washington, Md.......	16
Fairview, Mason, Mich.........	18
Fairview, Fillmore, Minn.......	14
Fairview, St. Louis, Mo........	13
Fairview, Bergen, N. J.........	84
Fairview, Cattaraugus, N. Y.....	24
Fairview, Buncombe, N. C......	150
Fairview, Guernsey, Ohio......	180
Fairview,* Erie, Pa............	350
Fairview, Greenville, S. C.......	18

Office	$
Fairview, Anderson, Tenn.........	$12
Fair View, Wilson, Tex..........	12
Fair View, San Pete, Utah......	39
Fairview, (c. h.,) Hancock, W. Va...	110
Fairview, Grant, Wis..........	58
Fairview Village, Montgomery, Pa.	44
Fairville, Saline, Mo...........	12
Fairville, Wayne, N. Y.........	68
Fairville, Chester, Pa..........	59
Fair Water, Fond du Lac, Wis	95
Fair Weather, Adams, Ill.......	41
Faison's Depot, Duplin, N. C	11
Falcon, Columbia, Ark.........	82
Falkland, Pitt, N. C...........	65
Fallassburgh, Kent, Mich....	20
Fall Brook, Tioga, Pa.........	460
Fall City, Dunn, Wis.........	14
Fall Creek, Marion, Ind.......	10
Fall Creek, Bedford, Tenn.......	12
Fallen Timber, Cambria, Pa......	41
Falling Creek, Lenoir, N. C......	12
Falling Spring, Greenbrier, W. Va.	12
Falling Springs, Douglas, Mo.....	12
Falling Waters, Berkeley, W. Va..	51
Fallowfield, Crawford, Pa......	55
Fall River,* Bristol, Mass........	3,400
Fall River, Columbia, Wis....	210
Falls, Wyoming, Pa........	85
Falls Branch, Washington, Tenn...	20
Fallsburgh, Sullivan, N. Y.......	43
Fallsburgh, Licking, Ohio.......	15
Falls Church, Fairfax, Va.........	130
Falls City,* (c. h.,) Richardson, Nebr.	300
Fallsington, Bucks, Pa.........	60
Falls Mill, Sullivan, N. Y.......	12
Falls Mills, Lincoln, W. Va.......	5
Falls of Blaine, Lawrence, Ky......	3
Falls of Rough, Grayson, Ky......	16
Fallston, Harford, Md	150
Falls Village,* Litchfield, Conn....	530
Falmouth, Rush, Ind..........	38
Falmouth, (c. h.,) Pendleton, Ky....	330
Falmouth, Cumberland, Me......	140
Falmouth, Barnstable, Mass......	420
Falmouth, Lancaster, Pa........	49
Falmouth, Stafford, Va.........	110
Falun, Saline, Kans...........	12
Fame, Greenwood, Kans........	12
Fancy Creek, Richland, Wis......	23
Fancy Farm, Graves, Ky........	46
Fancy Gap, Carroll, Va........	5
Fancy Grove, Bedford, Va.......	13
Fancy Hill, Iredell, N. C.......	4
Fancy Hill, Rockbridge, Va.......	75
Fanlight, Wetzel, W. Va........	12
Fannettsburgh, Franklin, Pa......	86
Fannin, Rankin, Miss.........	16
Farabee's Station, Washington, Ind.	14
Faribault,* (c. h.,) Rice, Minn.......	2,300
Farina, Fayette, Ill...........	260
Farley, Dubuque, Iowa........	270
Farley, Platte, Mo............	65
Farlington, Crawford, Kans......	12
Farlinville, Linn, Kans........	87
Farmdale, Franklin, Ky........	250
Farmer, Defiance, Ohio.........	93

* Money-order office.

Farmer City, De Witt, Ill	$530	Farmwell, Loudoun, Va	$180
Farmers, Rowan, Ky	11	Farnham, Erie, N. Y	52
Farmers, Sanilac, Mich	12	Farnham, Richmond, Va	12
Farmersburgh, Clayton, Iowa	47	Farnham × Roads, Richmond, Va	12
Farmers' Creek, Jackson, Iowa	12	Farnumsville, Worcester, Mass	110
Farmers' Creek, Lapeer, Mich	33	Farrandsville, Clinton, Pa	53
Farmers' Grove, Fillmore, Minn	12	Farribaville, Sevier, Ark	12
Farmers' Grove, Southampton, Va.	11	Fassett, Bradford, Pa	35
Farmers' Grove, Green, Wis	44	Fatama, Wilcox, Ala	12
Farmers' Institute, Tippecanoe, Ind.	32	Faunsdale, Marengo, Ala	12
Farmers' Mills, Putnam, N. Y	19	Fauquier White Sulphur Springs,	
Farmers' Retreat, Dearborn, Ind	40	Fauquier, Va	41
Farmers' Station, Owen, Ind	12	Fawn Grove, York, Pa	44
Farmers' Station, Clinton, Ohio	60	Fawn River, St. Joseph, Mich	16
Farmers' Valley, Hamilton, Nebr	12	Faxon, Sibley, Minn	54
Farmers' Valley, McKean, Pa	44	Fayette, Greene, Ill	52
Farmers' Valley, Monroe, Wis	4	Fayette,* Fayette, Iowa	580
Farmersville, Lowndes, Ala	12	Fayette, Kennebec, Me	85
Farmersville, Tulare, Cal	24	Fayette,* (c. h.,) Jefferson, Miss	470
Farmersville, Posey, Ind	22	Fayette,* (c. h.,) Howard, Mo	580
Farmersville, Mahaska, Iowa	10	Fayette, Seneca, N. Y	110
Farmersville, (c. h.,) Union, La	360	Fayette, Allegheny, Pa	6
Farmersville, Livingston, Mo	67	Fayette, La Fayette, Wis	53
Farmersville, Cattaraugus, N. Y	70	Fayette C. H., Fayette, Ala	67
Farmersville, Montgomery, Ohio	65	Fayette City, Fayette, Pa	160
Farmersville, Lancaster, Pa	33	Fayette Ridge, Kennebec, Me	14
Farmersville, Collin, Tex	30	Fayette Springs, Fayette, Pa	17
Farmersville, Dodge, Wis	48	Fayetteville,* (c. h.,) Washington,	
Farmer Village, Seneca, N. Y	390	Ark	750
Farm Hill, Olmsted, Minn	24	Fayetteville, (c. h.,) Fayette, Ga	26
Farmingdale, Monmouth, N. J	230	Fayetteville, St. Clair, Ill	54
Farmingdale, Queens, N. Y	180	Fayetteville, Lawrence, Ind	18
Farmington, Washington, Ark	19	Fayetteville, Clay, Kans	12
Farmington, San Joaquin, Cal	79	Fayetteville, Johnson, Mo	80
Farmington, Hartford, Conn	470	Fayetteville, Onondaga, N. Y	800
Farmington, Kent, Del	120	Fayetteville, (c. h.,) Cumberland,	
Farmington,* Fulton, Ill	890	N. C	1,700
Farmington,* Van Buren, Iowa	410	Fayetteville, Brown, Ohio	110
Farmington, Atchison, Kans	12	Fayetteville, Franklin, Pa	190
Farmington, Graves, Ky	33	Fayetteville,* (c. h.,) Lincoln, Tenn	660
Farmington,* (c. h.,) Franklin, Me	1,300	Fayetteville, Fayette, Tex	98
Farmington, Cecil, Md	20	Fayetteville, (c. h.,) Windham, Vt	200
Farmington, Oakland, Mich	300	Fayetteville, (c. h.,) Fayette, W. Va	73
Farmington,* Dakota, Minn	450	Fayville, Worcester, Mass	130
Farmington, (c. h.,) St. Francois, Mo.	260	Fearing, Washington, Ohio	20
Farmington, Strafford, N. H	550	Fearn's Springs, Winston, Miss	15
Farmington, Ontario, N. Y	93	Feasterville, Bucks, Pa	66
Farmington, Davie, N. C	58	Feasterville, Fairfield, S. C	12
Farmington, Trumbull, Ohio	110	Federal Hill, Hartford, Md	12
Farmington, Fayette, Pa	86	Federal Point, Putnam, Fla	12
Farmington, Marshall, Tenn	41	Federalsburgh, Carroll, Md	240
Farmington, Grayson, Tex	66	Federalton, Athens, Ohio	10
Farmington, (c. h.,) Davis, Utah	61	Feeding Hills, Hampden, Mass	150
Farmington, Marion, W. Va	89	Feed Spring, Harrison, Ohio	10
Farmington, Jefferson, Wis	41	Feesburgh, Brown, Ohio	55
Farmington Centre, Tioga, Pa	13	Felchville, Windsor, Vt	220
Farmington Centre, Polk, Wis	39	Felicity,* Clermont, Ohio	250
Farmington Falls, Franklin, Me	110	Fellowship, Burlington, N. J	50
Farmington Hill, Tioga, Pa	19	Fellowsville, Preston, W. Va	38
Farmland, Randolph, Ind	250	Felton, Kent, Del	300
Farm Ridge, La Salle, Ill	75	Felts, Ingham, Mich	10
Farm's Village, Hartford, Conn	25	Felt's Mills, Jefferson, N. Y	86
Farmsville, Woolford, Ill	16	Femme Osage, St. Charles, Mo	73
Farmville, Pitt, N. C	55	Fenner, Madison, N. Y	30
Farmville, Henderson, Tenn	12	Fennimore, Grant, Wis	100
Farmville,* Prince Edward, Va	1,000	Fenns, Shelby, Ind	12

*Money-order office.

FIN

Fenn's Bridge, Jefferson, Ga.	$12
Fenn's Mills, Allegan, Mich.	55
Fenton, Whitesides, Ill	12
Fenton, St. Louis, Mo	25
Fenton, Wood, Ohio	10
Fentonville,* Genesee, Mich	1,000
Fentonville, Chautauqua, N. Y	29
Fentriss, Guilford, N. C	10
Ferdinaud, Mercer, Ill	9
Ferdinand, Dubois, Ind	120
Fergus Falls, Otter Tail, Minn	12
Ferguson, St. Louis, Mo	12
Ferguson's Corners, Yates N. Y	12
Ferguson's Station, Logan, Ky	66
Fergusonville, Delaware, N. Y	110
Fernandez de Taos, (c. h.,) Tex., N. Mex	47
Fernandina,* (c. h.,) Nassau, Fla	1,000
Fern Creek, Jefferson, Ky	12
Ferndale, Humboldt, Cal	53
Fern Leaf, Mason, Ky	30
Fern Valley, Palo Alto, Iowa	8
Ferris, Hancock, Ill	12
Ferris, Montcalm, Mich	12
Ferrisburgh, Addison, Vt	90
Ferrona, Clinton, N. Y	12
Ferry, Mahaska, Iowa	12
Ferry Point, Norfolk, Va	23
Ferrysburgh, Ottawa, Mich	160
Ferry Village, Cumberland, Me	12
Ferryville, St. Clair, Ala	12
Ferryville, Crawford, Wis	10
Fertigs, Venango, Pa	18
Fertile, Worth, Iowa	12
Fertility, Lancaster, Pa	7
Festina, Winneshiek, Iowa	61
Fetherolffsville, Berks, Pa	16
Fetterman, Taylor, W. Va	120
Fiatt, Fulton, Ill	16
Fiddletown, Amador, Cal	120
Fidelity, Jersey, Ill	70
Fidelity, Jasper, Mo	27
Fidelity, Miami, Ohio	12
Field Bend, Pike, Pa	22
Fieldon, Jersey, Ill	70
Fieldsborough, New Castle, Del	10
Fife's, Goochland, Va	15
Fifteen Mile Grove, Tama, Iowa	38
Fig Grove, Coosa, Ala	12
Filer City, Manistee, Mich	12
Fillmore, Montgomery, Ill	20
Fillmore, Putnam, Ind	120
Fillmore, Dubuque, Iowa	9
Fillmore, Barry, Mich	63
Fillmore, Fillmore, Minn	81
Fillmore, Andrew, Mo	160
Fillmore, Monmouth, N. J	61
Fillmore, Allegany, N. Y	100
Fillmore, Washington, Ohio	18'
Fillmore, Centre, Pa	37
Fillmore, Sequatchie, Tenn	2
Fillmore, Randolph, W. Va	3
Fillmore, Washington, Wis	70
Fillmore City, (c. h.,) Millard, Utah	140
Fincastle, Brown, Ohio	41
Fincastle, Campbell, Tenn	23

FIV

Fincastle, Henderson, Tex	$12
Fincastle,* (c. h.,) Botetourt, Va	390
Findley,* (c. h.,) Hancock, Ohio	1,800
Findley's Lake, Chautauqua, N. Y	35
Findley's Mills, Jackson, Ind	5
Fine, St. Lawrence, N. Y	46
Fine Creek Mills, Powhatan, Va	39
Finksburgh, Carroll, Md	65
Fink's Creek, Lewis, W. Va	12
Finley Station, Cumberland, N. J	14
Finleyville, Washington, Pa	75
Finney's Creek, Saline, Mo	12
Fir Cap, Sierra, Cal	12
Firebaugh, Fresno, Cal	20
Fire Island, Suffolk, N. Y	12
Fireplace, Suffolk, N. Y	53
Fire Prairie, Jackson, Mo	12
First Broad, Rutherford, N. C	5
First Fork, Cameron, Pa	13
Fish Creek, Steuben, Ind	13
Fish Creek, Jefferson, Mont	12
Fish Creek, Oneida, N. Y	12
Fish Creek, Door, Wis	56
Fish Dam, Wake, N. C	6
Fish Dam, Union, S. C	12
Fisher, Clarion, Pa	20
Fisherman's Bay, Sonoma, Cal	71
Fisher's, Ontario, N. Y	69
Fishersburgh, Madison, Ind	25
Fisher's Ferry, Northumberland, Pa	68
Fisher's Landing, Decatur, Tenn	12
Fisher's Point, Jackson, W. Va	9
Fishersville,* Merrimack, N. H	900
Fishersville, Augusta, Va	160
Fisherville, Jefferson, Ky	63
Fisherville, Dauphin, Pa	32
Fish Haven, Rich, Utah	8
Fish Hook, Pike, Ill	24
Fishing Creek, Dorchester, Md	8
Fishing Creek, Cape May, N. J	10
Fishing Creek, Columbia, Pa	12
Fishkill, Dutchess, N. Y	680
Fishkill on the Hudson, Dutchess, N. Y	1,200
Fishkill Plains, Dutchess, N. Y	40
Fish Lake, Elkhart, Ind	5
Fish Pond, Tallapoosa, Ala	10
Fish Springs, Inyo, Cal	12
Fiskedale, Worcester, Mass	270
Fiskeville, Providence, R. I	72
Fisk's Corners, Winnebago, Wis	10
Fitchburgh,* Worcester, Mass	3,000
Fitchburgh, Ingham, Mich	50
Fitchburgh, Dane, Wis	55
Fitchville, Huron, Ohio	98
Fithian, Vermilion, Ill	12
Fitts Hill, Franklin, Ill	23
Fitz Henry, Ogle, Ill	24
Fitz Henry, Westmoreland, Pa	49
Fitzpatrick's, Bullock, Ala	12
Fitzwatertown, Montgomery, Pa	42
Fitzwilliam, Cheshire, N. H	340
Fitzwilliam Depot, Cheshire, N. H	190
Five Corners, Miami, Ind	12
Five Corners, Cayuga, N. Y	120
Five Lakes, Lapeer, Mich	12

* Money-order office.

FLI   FLU

Five Mile, Hale, Ala	$5	Flint, Steuben, Ind	$59
Five Mile, Brown, Ohio	20	Flint, Mahaska, Iowa	25
Five Mile, Pickens, S. C	4	Flint,* (c. h.,) Genesee, Mich	2,600
Five Mile House, Milwaukee, Wis	12	Flint, Franklin, Ohio	12
Five Points, Gloucester, N. J	17	Flint Creek, Ontario, N. Y	24
Five Points, Pickaway, Ohio	23	Flint Factory, Madison, Ala	12
Flackville, St. Lawrence, N. Y	28	Flint Hill, St. Charles, Mo	24
Flagg Spring, Campbell, Ky	12	Flint Hill, Rappahannock, Va	44
Flaggtown, Somerset, N. J	68	Flint Island, Meade, Ky	83
Flag Pond, Washington, Tenn	12	Flint Ridge, Lancaster, S. C	12
Flag Springs, Andrew, Mo	12	Flint River, Morgan, Ala	12
Flagstaff, Somerset, Me	40	Flint's Mills, Washington, Ohio	23
Flag Station, Ogle, Ill	67	Flint Stone, Alleghany, Md	70
Flanders, Morris, N. J	140	Flintville, Lincoln, Tenn	19
Flanders, Suffolk, N. Y	12	Flintville, Brown, Wis	12
Flat, Pike, Ohio	40	Flinty Branch, Yancey, N. C	14
Flat Branches, Forsyth, N. C	12	Flippin, Monroe, Ky	8
Flatbrook, Columbia, N. Y	25	Flippo's, Caroline, Va	16
Flatbrookville, Sussex, N. J	28	Flora, Clay, Ill	610
Flatbush, Kings, N. Y	270	Flora Dale, Adams, Pa	31
Flat Creek, Barry, Mo	18	Floraville, St. Clair, Ill	27
Flat Creek, Montgomery, N. Y	21	Florence, (c. h.,) Lauderdale, Ala	930
Flat Creek, Bedford, Tenn	13	Florence, Pima, Ariz	12
Flat Fork, Anson, N. C	2	Florence, Drew, Ark	12
Flat Fork, Roane, W. Va	2	Florence, Stewart, Ga	12
Flat Gap, Jefferson, Tenn	10	Florence, Pike, Ill	68
Flatlands, Kings, N. Y	53	Florence, Switzerland, Ind	120
Flat Lick, Knox, Ky	22	Florence, Benton, Iowa	360
Flatonia, Fayette, Tex	12	Florence, Boone, Ky	170
Flat River, St. Francois, Mo	12	Florence, Howard, Md	12
Flat River, Orange, N. C	7	Florence, Hampshire, Mass	680
Flat Rock, Talladega, Ala	5	Florence, St. Joseph, Mich	32
Flat Rock, Crawford, Ill	9	Florence, Morgan, Mo	34
Flat Rock, Shelby, Ind	62	Florence, Douglas, Nebr	100
Flat Rock, Neosho, Kans	12	Florence, Burlington, N. J	30
Flat Rock, Bourbon, Ky	14	Florence, Oneida, N. Y	160
Flat Rock, Henderson, N. C	44	Florence, Erie, Ohio	77
Flat Rock, Seneca, Ohio	84	Florence, Washington, Pa	95
Flat Rock, Kershaw, S. C	14	Florence, Darlington, S. C	360
Flat Rock, Lewis, Tenn	6	Florence, Williamson, Tex	48
Flat Rock, Mason, W. Va	12	Florence City, Idaho, Idaho	24
Flat Shoal, Surry, N. C	7	Florence Station, Stephenson, Ill	42
Flat Shoals, Meriwether, Ga	12	Florence Station, McCracken, Ky	23
Flat Top, Mercer, W. Va	12	Florence Station, Rutherford, Tenn	12
Flatwoods, Fayette, Pa	84	Florid, Putnam, Ill	56
Flat Woods, Braxton, W. Va	15	Florida, Madison, Ind	42
Fleetville, Luzerne, Pa	43	Florida, Berkshire, Mass	21
Fleetwood, Berks, Pa	150	Florida, Monroe, Mo	68
Fleming, Liberty, Ga	56	Florida, Orange, N. Y	370
Fleming, Livingston, Mich	20	Florida, Henry, Ohio	94
Fleming, Cayuga, N. Y	120	Florin, Sacramento, Cal	20
Fleming, Washington, Ohio	42	Floris, Davis, Iowa	47
Fleming, Centre, Pa	200	Florisant, St. Louis, Mo	160
Flemingsburgh,* (c. h.,) Fleming, Ky	640	Flourtown, Montgomery, Pa	12
Flemingsville, Tioga, N. Y	23	Flower Creek, Pendleton, Ky	33
Flemington, Marion, Fla	28	Flower Creek, Oceana, Mich	21
Flemington,* (c. h.,) Hunterdon, N. J	1,200	Flowerfield, St. Joseph, Mich	160
Flemington, Columbus, N. C	12	Flowerville, White, Ind	16
Flemington, Clinton, Pa	130	Floyd, Floyd, Iowa	220
Flemington, Taylor, W. Va	110	Floyd, Oneida, N. Y	18
Flemingville, Linn, Iowa	8	Floyd C. H., Floyd, Va	160
Flemming's Ranch, Weld, Colo	8	Floyd's Creek, Adair, Mo	4
Fletcher, Miami, Ohio	100	Floyd's Knobs, Floyd, Ind	35
Fletcher, Franklin, Vt	77	Flukes, Botetourt, Va	45
Flint, Cherokee N., Ind. T	5	Flushing, Genesee, Mich	440
Flint, Pike, Ill	35	Flushing,* Queens, N. Y	1,600

* Money-order office.

FOR   FOR

Office	$	Office	$
Flushing, Belmont, Ohio	$130	Forest House, Potter, Pa	$12
Fluvanna, Chautauqua, N. Y	54	Forest Lake, Washington, Minn	12
Fly Creek, Cherokee, Kans	12	Forest Lake, Susquehanna, Pa	25
Fly Creek, Otsego, N Y	160	Forest Lake Centre, Susquehanna,	
Fly Mountain, Ulster, N. Y	180	Pa	25
Flynn's Lick, Jackson, Tenn	12	Forest Mound, Wabashaw, Minn	26
Fogelsville, Lehigh, Pa	68	Forest Oak, Montgomery, Md	43
Folk's Station, Harrison, Ohio	12	Foreston, Ogle, Ill	740
Folkville, Morgan, Ala	12	Foreston, Howard, Iowa	26
Folsom City,* Sacramento, Cal	360	Forest Port, Oneida, N. Y	240
Folsomdale, Wyoming, N. Y	50	Forest Station, Clayton, Ga	12
Folsomville, Warrick, Ind	21	Forestville, Hartford, Conn	360
Fonda,* (c. h.,) Montgomery, N. Y	980	Forestville, Madison, Ind	13
Fond du Lac, St. Louis, Minn	10	Forestville, Delaware, Iowa	61
Fond du Lac,* (c. h.,) Fond du Lac,		Forestville, Prince George's, Md	94
Wis	3,800	Forestville, Sanilac, Mich	70
Fouta Flora, Burke, N. C	12	Forestville, Fillmore, Minn	59
Fontanelle,* (c. h.,) Adair, Iowa	320	Forestville, Chautauqua, N. Y	610
Fontanelle, Washington, Nebr	150	Forestville, Wake, N. C	270
Fontania, Miami, Kans	12	Forestville, Marion, S. C	5
Fontenoy, Brown, Wis	12	Forestville, Shenandoah, Va	16
Foote, Iowa, Iowa	17	Forestville, Door, Wis	20
Footville, Yadkin, N. C	12	Forge Village, Middlesex, Mass	97
Footville, Rock, Wis	140	Fork, Mecosta, Mich	12
Forbestown, Butte, Cal	82	Forked River, Ocean, N. J	12
Ford, Geauga, Ohio	27	Forkland, Nottoway, Va	19
Fordham, Westchester, N. Y	550	Fork Meeting House, Baltimore, Md	40
Ford's Creek, Catahoula, La	5	Fork Mountain, Mitchell, N. C	2
Ford's Depot, Dinwiddie, Va	54	Forkner's Hill, Webster, Mo	78
Ford's Ferry, Crittenden, Ky	24	Forks, Columbia, Pa	23
Ford's Store, Hart, Ga	4	Forksburgh, Marion, W. Va	4
Fordsville, Ohio, Ky	22	Forks of Capon, Hampshire, W. Va	12
Fordsville, Marion, Miss	1	Forks of Elkhorn, Franklin, Ky	25
Fordtown, Sullivan, Tenn	8	Forks of Pigeon, Haywood, N. C	11
Fordyce, Greene, Pa	16	Forks of Salmon, Klamath, Cal	12
Forest, Livingston, Ill	390	Forkston, Wyoming, Pa	25
Forest, Scott, Miss	150	Forksville, Ouachita, La	12
Forest, Clinton, N. Y	46	Forksville, Sullivan, Pa	51
Forest,* Hardin, Ohio	280	Forksville, Mecklenburgh, Va	10
Forest, Clearfield, Pa	12	Forktown, Wicomico, Md	94
Forest, Richland, Wis	39	Fork Union, Fluvanna, Va	50
Forest Bay, Huron, Mich	8	Forrester, Sanilac, Mich	140
Forestburgh, Sullivan, N. Y	43	Forsyth,* (c. h.,) Monroe, Ga	770
Forest City, St. Francis, Ark	12	Forsyth, (c. h.,) Taney, Mo	12
Forest City, Sierra, Cal	80	Forsythe, Macon, Ill	79
Forest City, Mason, Ill	96	Fort Abercrombie, Shyenne, Dak	710
Forest City, (c. h.,) Winnebago, Iowa	160	Fort Adams, Wilkinson, Miss	30
Forest City, Muskegon, Mich	20	Fort Ancient, Warren, Ohio	69
Forest City,* Meeker, Minn	170	Fort Ann, Washington, N. Y	520
Forest City,* Holt, Mo	340	Fort Arbuckle, Chickasaw N., Ind.	
Forest City, Sarpy, Nebr	100	T	670
Forest Dale, Lawrence, Ohio	12	Fort Atkinson, Winneshiek, Iowa	120
Forest Dale, Rutland, Vt	93	Fort Atkinson,* Jefferson, Wis	1,300
Forest Depot, Bedford, Va	17	Fort Benton, (c. h.,) Choteau, Mont	380
Forest Grove, Gloucester, N. J	94	Fort Bidwell, Siskiyou, Cal	12
Forest Grove, Washington, Oreg	190	Fort Blackimore, Scott, Va	6
Forest Hill,* Placer, Cal	190	Fort,Branch,* Gibson, Ind	320
Forest Hill, Decatur, Ind	71	Fort Bridger,* (c. h.,) Uintah, Wyo	350
Forest Hill, Lyon, Kans	23	Fort Browder, Barbour, Ala	20
Forest Hill, Harford, Md	77	Fort Buffington, Cherokee, Ga	6
Forest Hill, Gratiot, Mich	51	Fort Calhoun, Washington, Nebr	170
Forest Hill, Union, Pa	36	Fort Clark,* Kinney, Tex	30
Forest Hill, Monroe, W. Va	20	Fort Collins, Larimer, Colo	12
Forest Home, Amador, Cal	80	Fort Colville, (c. h.,) Stevens, Wash	130
Forest Home, Poweshiek, Iowa	16	Fort Concho, Bexar, Tex	520
Forest Home, Franklin, Kans	33	Fort Covington, Franklin, N. Y	410

* Money-order office.

FOR

Fort Covington Centre, Franklin, N. Y	$12
Fort Craig, Socorro, N. Mex	290
Fort Cummings, Grant, N. Mex	150
Fort Dade, Hernando, Fla	4
Fort Davis, Presidio, Tex	260
Fort Deposit, Lowndes, Ala	160
Fort Dodge, * (c. h.,) Webster, Iowa	2,100
Fort Edward,* Washington, N. Y	1,600
Fort Fairfield,* Aroostook, Me	160
Fort Fred Steele, Carbon, Wyo	12
Fort Gaines, (c. h.,) Clay, Ga	400
Fort Garland, Costilla, Colo	110
Fort Gay, Wayne, W. Va	24
Fort George, Duval, Fla	12
Fort Gibson, Cherokee N., Ind. T	440
Fort Gratiot, St. Clair, Mich	12
Fort Griffin, Shackelford, Tex	190
Fort Halleck, Carbon, Wyo	12
Fort Hamilton,* Kings, N. Y	750
Fort Hampton, Limestone, Ala	69
Fort Harker, Ellsworth, Kans	680
Fort Henry, Randolph, Mo	23
Fort Hill, Lake, Ill	19
Fort Howard, Brown, Wis	1,000
Fort Hunter, Montgomery, N. Y	83
Fort Jennings, Putnam, Ohio	24
Fort Jesup, Sabine, La	12
Fort Jones, Siskiyou, Cal	240
Fort Kearney,* Kearney, Nebr	360
Fort Kent, Aroostook, Me	26
Fort Lamar, Madison, Ga	20
Fort Laramie, Laramie, Wyo	460
Fort Larned, Pawnee, Kans	140
Fort Leavenworth, Leavenworth, Kans	1,000
Fort Lee, Bergen, N. J	99
Fort Lemhi, Lemhi, Idaho	12
Fort Lincoln, Bourbon, Kans	120
Fort Littleton, Fulton, Pa	47
Fort Lupton, Weld, Colo	12
Fort Lyon, (c. h.,) Bent, Colo	470
Fort Lyon, Benton, Mo	99
Fort McKavett, Menard, Tex	390
Fort Madison, * (c. h.,) Lee, Iowa	2,000
Fort Mill, York, S. C	69
Fort Miller, Washington, N. Y	130
Fort Mitchell, Russell, Ala	12
Fort Montgomery, Orange, N. Y	130
Fort Motte, Orangeburgh, S. C	72
Fort Payne, De Kalb, Ala	12
Fort Pike, Orleans, La	41
Fort Plain, Warren, Iowa	68
Fort Plain,* Montgomery, N. Y	1,500
Fort Quitman, El Paso, Tex	150
Fort Randall, (c. h.,) Todd, Dak	450
Fort Recovery, Mercer, Ohio	•.210
Fort Ridgely,* Nicollet, Minn	81
Fort Riley, Davis, Kans	370
Fort Ripley, Morrison, Minn	100
Fort Ritner, Lawrence, Ind	55
Forts, Dallas, Ala	20
Fort Scott, * (c. h.,) Bourbon, Kans	2,600
Fort Selden, Dona Ana, N. Mex	340
Fort Seneca, Seneca, Ohio	13
Fort Shaw, Lewis and Clarke, Mont	110

FOU

Fort Sill, Choctaw N., Ind. T	$800
Fort Simcoe, Klikitat, Wash	12
Fort Smith,* Sebastian, Ark	2,400
Fort Snelling, Hennepin, Minn	130
Fort's Station, Robertson, Tenn	50
Fort Stanton, Socorro, N. Mex	150
Fort Stephens, Kemper, Miss	14
Fort Sully, Buffalo, Dak	580
Fortsville, Saratoga, N. Y	41
Fort Taylor, Hernando, Fla	5
Fort Tongass, ——, Alaska	12
Fort Totten, ——, Dak	52
Fort Union, Mora, N. Mex	1,700
Fort Valley, Houston, Ga	790
Fortville, Hancock, Ind	190
Fort Wadsworth, Deuel, Dak	12
Fort Wallace, Wallace, Kans	430
Fort Washington, Prince George's, Md	150
Fort Washita, Chickasaw N., Ind. T.	51
Fort Wayne, * (c. h.,) Allen, Ind	4,000
Fort Willopa, Chehalis, Wash	10
Fort Worth, (c. h.,) Tarrant, Tex	560
Fort Wrangel, ——, Alaska	12
Forty Fort, Luzerne, Pa	• 4
Foster, Bracken, Ky	100
Foster, Providence, R. I	52
Foster, Fond du Lac, Wis	47
Fosterburgh, Madison, Ill	44
Foster Centre, Providence, R. I	27
Fosterdale, Sullivan, N. Y	28
Foster's, Tuscaloosa, Ala	20
Foster's Crossings, Warren, Ohio	160
Foster's Cross Roads, Bledsoe, Tenn.	7
Foster's Mills, Armstrong, Pa	63
Foster's Ridge, Perry, Ind	10
Fosterville, Cayuga, N. Y	37
Fosterville, Rutherford, Tenn	76
Fosterville, Anderson, Tex	12
Fostoria,* Seneca, Ohio	850
Fostoria, Blair, Pa	43
Foundryville, Columbia, Pa	10
Fountain, El Paso, Colo	19
Fountain, Fountain, Ind	21
Fountain Bluff, Jackson, Ill	12
Fountain City,* Buffalo, Wis	310
Fountain Creek, Stephenson, Ill	12
Fountain Creek, Maury, Tenn	20
Fountaindale, Winnebago, Ill	12
Fountain Dale, Adams, Pa	26
Fountain Green, Hancock, Ill	150
Fountain Green, Harford, Md	20
Fountain Green, San Pete, Utah	61
Fountain Head, Sumner, Tenn	45
Fountain Hill, Ashley, Ark	10
Fountain Inn, Greenville, S. C	9
Fountain Run, Monroe, Ky	34
Fountain Spring, Wood, W. Va	10
Fountaintown, Shelby, Ind	64
Fourche á Renault, Washington, Mo	12
Four Corners, Huron, Ohio	74
Four Mile, Butler, Kans	12
Four Mile, Dunklin, Mo	21
Four Mile Branch, Monroe, Tenn	10
Four Mile Prairie, Perry, Ill	12
Fourth Crossing, Calaveras, Cal	20

* Money-order office.

FRA   FRE

Four Towns, Oakland, Mich	$21	Franklin, Decatur, Iowa	$39
Foust's Mills, Randolph, N. C	10	Franklin,* (c. h.,) Simpson, Ky	740
Fowler, Adams, Ill	120	Franklin, (c. h.,) St. Mary's, La	750
Fowler, St. Lawrence, N. Y	41	Franklin, Hancock, Me	160
Fowler, Trumbull, Ohio	120	Franklin,* Norfolk, Mass	900
Fowler's, Brooke, W. Va	37	Franklin, Oakland, Mich	120
Fowler's Knob, Nicholas, W. Va	12	Franklin, Renville, Minn	11
Fowler's Landing, Humphreys, Tenn	16	Franklin, Howard, Mo	130
Fowler's Mills, Geauga, Ohio	42	Franklin,* Merrimack, N. H	1,300
Fowlersville, Rice, Minn	3	Franklin, Essex, N. J	160
Fowlersville, Columbia, Pa	29	Franklin, Delaware, N. Y	750
Fowlerville, Livingston, Mich	160	Franklin, (c. h.,) Macon, N. C	100
Fowlerville, Livingston, N. Y	280	Franklin,* Warren, Ohio	570
Fowling Creek, Caroline, Md	25	Franklin, Lane, Oreg	19
Fox, Wells, Ind	24	Franklin,* (c. h.,) Venango, Pa	2,800
Fox, Ray, Mo	16	Franklin,* (c. h.,) Williamson, Tenn	870
Foxborough,* Norfolk, Mass	1,100	Franklin, Cache, Utah	40
Foxburgh, Clarion, Pa	84	Franklin, Franklin, Vt	240
Fox Creek, St. Louis, Mo	19	Franklin, Pierce, Wash	4
Foxcroft,* Piscataquis, Me	440	Franklin, (c. h.,) Pendleton, W. Va	160
Fox Lake, Lake, Ill	35	Franklin, Sheboygan, Wis	12
Fox Lake,* Dodge, Wis	850	Franklin Centre, Lee, Iowa	97
Fox River, Kenosha, Wis	14	Franklin City, Norfolk, Mass	46
Foxville, Frederick, Md	12	Franklin College, Davidson, Tenn	44
Framingham, Middlesex, Mass	1,000	Franklin Corners, Erie, Pa	33
Frampton, Lawrence, Ohio	16	Franklin Crossing, Rock Island, Ill	12
Francesville, Pulaski, Ind	160	Franklindale, Bradford, Pa	41
Francisco, Gibson, Ind	55	Franklin Depot, Southampton, Va	390
Francisco, Stokes, N. C	10	Franklin Falls, Franklin, N. Y	48
Franciscoville, Jackson, Mich	78	Franklin Furnace, Sussex, N. J	160
Francis Creek, Manitowoc, Wis	45	Franklin Furnace, Scioto, Ohio	92
Francistown, Hillsborough, N. H	300	Franklin Grove,* Lee, Ill	640
Franconia, Chisago, Minn	55	Franklin Grove, Page, Iowa	22
Franconia, Grafton, N. H	190	Franklin Iron Works, Oneida, N. Y	14
Franconia, Montgomery, Pa	3	Franklin Mills, Des Moines, Iowa	28
Frank, Seneca, Ohio	12	Franklin's X Roads, Hardin, Ky	14
Frankenlust, Saginaw, Mich	17	Franklin Springs, Franklin, Ga	6
Frankenmuth, Saginaw, Mich	49	Franklin Square, Columbiana, Ohio	86
Frankford, Sussex, Del	81	Franklin Station, Coshocton, Ohio	67
Frankford, Mower, Minn	46	Franklinton, Henry, Ky	22
Frankford, Pike, Mo	200	Franklinton, (c. h.,) Washington, La	23
Frankford, Greenbrier, W. Va	52	Franklinton, Schoharie, N. Y	62
Frankfort, Franklin, Ala	69	Franklinton, Franklin, N. C	330
Frankfort, Franklin, Ill	25	Franklintown, York, Pa	20
Frankfort,* (c. h.,) Clinton, Ind	490	Franklinville, Carroll, Md	18
Frankfort, Montgomery, Iowa	12	Franklinville, Gloucester, N. J	130
Frankfort, Marshall, Kans	320	Franklinville, Cattaraugus, N. Y	280
FRANKFORT,* (c. h.,) Franklin, Ky	2,400	Franklinville, Randolph, N. C	51
Frankfort, Waldo, Me	190	Franklinville, Huntingdon, Pa	48
Frankfort, Benzie, Mich	160	Frank Pierce, Johnson, Iowa	13
Frankfort, L'Eau qui Court, Nebr	13	Frankstown, Blair, Pa	63
Frankfort, Herkimer, N. Y	540	Frankton, Madison, Ind	140
Frankfort, Ross, Ohio	210	Franktown, (c. h.,) Douglas, Colo	50
Frankfort, Mineral, W. Va	56	Franktown, Washoe, Nev	25
Frankfort, Pepin, Wis	53	Franktown, Northampton, Va	68
Frankfort Hill, Herkimer, N. Y	15	Frankville, Winneshiek, Iowa	160
Frankfort Springs, Beaver, Pa	130	Frankville, Alleghany, Md	11
Frankfort Station, Will, Ill	240	Frankville, Howell, Mo	12
Frank Hill, Winona, Minn	24	Frankville, Clark, Wis	16
Franklin, Henry, Ala	3	Fransonia, Richland, Ill	14
Franklin, Fulton, Ark	75	Fraser, Macomb, Mich	66
Franklin, Sacramento, Cal	25	Frazer, Chester, Pa	100
Franklin, New London, Conn	49	Frazeysburgh, Muskingum, Ohio	260
Franklin, (c. h.,) Heard, Ga	38	Frazier's Bottom, Putnam, W. Va	11
Franklin, Morgan, Ill	120	Frederica, Kent, Del	330
Franklin,* (c. h.,) Johnson, Ind	1,200	Frederica, Glynn, Ga	32

* Money-order office.

Frederica, Bremer, Iowa	$15	Freeman's Landing, Hancock, W.	
Frederick,* (c. h.,) Frederick, Md	2,500	Va	$58
Frederick, Mahoning, Ohio	5	Freemansville, Cherokee, Ga	18
Frederick, Montgomery, Pa	43	Freemanton, Effingham, Ill	20
Fredericksburgh, Washington, Ind	47	Freeo, Ouachita, Ark	31
Fredericksburgh, Chickasaw, Iowa	190	Freeport, Sacramento, Cal	18
Fredericksburgh, Osage, Mo	11	Freeport,* (c. h.,) Stephenson, Ill	3,200
Fredericksburgh, Wayne, Ohio	250	Freeport, Shelby, Ind	16
Fredericksburgh, Lebanon, Pa	82	Freeport, Winneshiek, Iowa	67
Fredericksburgh, (c. h.,) Gillespie,		Freeport, Cumberland, Me	420
Tex	470	Freeport, Queens, N. Y	83
Fredericksburgh,* Spottsylvania,		Freeport, Harrison, Ohio	93
Va	2,000	Freeport,* Armstrong, Pa	700
Frederick's Hall, Louisa, Va	170	Freeport, Cowlitz, Wash	44
Fredericksville, Schuyler, Ill	92	Freeshade, Middlesex, Va	10
Fredericksville, Berks, Pa	3	Free Soil, Fillmore, Minn	12
Fredericktown, Coffey, Kans	4	Freestone, Sonoma, Cal	37
Fredericktown, Washington, Ky	24	Freestone, Scioto, Ohio	120
Fredericktown,* (c. h.,) Madison, Mo	370	Freetown, Jackson, Ind	24
Fredericktown,* Knox, Ohio	750	Freetown, Bristol, Mass	210
Fredericktown, Washington, Pa	65	Freetown Corners, Cortland, N. Y	52
Fredie, Butler, Mo	12	Free Union, Albemarle, Va	29
Fredon, Sussex, N. J	14	Freeville, Tompkins, N. Y	23
Fredonia, Chambers, Ala	37	Freistadt, Ozaukee, Wis	31
Fredonia, Williamson, Ill	20	Frelsburgh, Colorado, Tex	110
Fredonia, Crawford, Ind	17	Fremont, Steuben, Ind	230
Fredonia, Louisa, Iowa	91	Fremont, Mahaska, Iowa	99
Fredonia, (c. h.,) Wilson, Kans	12	Fremont, Lyon, Kans	12
Fredonia, Caldwell, Ky	33	Fremont, Shiawassee, Mich	26
Fredonia, Washtenaw, Mich	42	Fremont, Freeborn, Minn	13
Fredonia, Licking, Ohio	68	Fremont,* (c. h.,) Dodge, Nebr	1,000
Fredonia, Mercer, Pa	12	Fremont, Rockingham, N. H	59
Fredonia,* Chautauqua, N. Y	1,700	Fremont,* (c. h.,) Sandusky, Ohio	2,800
Fredonia, Ozaukee, Wis	75	Fremont, Chester, Pa	23
Fredric, Monroe, Iowa	120	Fremont, Waupaca, Wis	140
Freeborn, Freeborn, Minn	140	Fremont Centre, Lake, Ill	27
Freeburgh, St. Clair. Ill	790	Fremont Centre, Newaygo, Mich	67
Freeburgh, Houston, Minn	17	Fremont Centre, Sullivan, N. Y	74
Freeburgh, Stark, Ohio	30	French Bar, Lewis and Clarke, Mont.	12
Freeburgh, Snyder, Pa	150	French Corral, Nevada, Cal	12
Freedom, La Salle, Ill	120	French Creek, Allamakee, Iowa	16
Freedom, Owen, Ind	120	French Creek, Chautauqua, N. Y	21
Freedom, Lucas, Iowa	25	French Creek, Mercer, Pa	13
Freedom, Barren, Ky	10	French Creek, Upshur, W. Va	60
Freedom, Waldo, Me	140	French Creek Church, Bladen, N. C.	10
Freedom, Carroll, Md	24	French Grove, Peoria, Ill	21
Freedom, La Fayette, Mo	91	French Gulch, Shasta, Cal	68
Freedom, Carroll, N. H	84	French Gulch, Deer Lodge, Mont	12
Freedom, Portage, Ohio	89	French Hay, Hanover, Va	10
Freedom, Beaver, Pa	170	French Lake, Wright, Minn	8
Freedom, Washington, Tenn	170	French Lick, Orange, Ind	39
Freedom, Outagamie, Wis	14	French Mountain, Warren, N. Y	57
Freedom Centre, La Salle, Ill	18	Frenchton, Upshur, W. Va	11
Freedom Mills, Henry, Ohio	12	Frenchtown, Missoula, Mont	12
Freedom Plains, Dutchess, N. Y	31	Frenchtown,* Hunterdon, N. J	580
Freedom Station, Portage, Ohio	95	Frenchtown, Crawford, Pa	12
Freehold,* (c. h.,) Monmouth, N. J.	1,500	French Village, St. Clair, Ill	21
Freehold, Greene, N. Y	48	French Village, St. Francois, Mo	25
Freehold, Warren, Pa	68	Frenchville, Clearfield, Pa	35
Freeland, De Kalb, Ill	65	Frenchville, Trempealeau, Wis	71
Freeland, Baltimore, Md	85	Fresh Pond, Suffolk, N. Y	25
Freelandville, Knox, Ind	70	Frewsburgh, Chautauqua, N. Y	230
Freeman, Franklin, Me	7	Frey's Bush, Montgomery, N. Y	50
Freeman, Licking, Ohio	16	Friar's Point, (c. h.,) Coahoma, Miss.	230
Freeman, Crawford, Wis	11	Frick's Gap, Walker, Ga	
Freemansburgh, Northampton, Pa	230	Friedburgh, Forsyth, N. C	

* Money-order office.

FUL

Friedensbnrgh, Schuylkill, Pa	$23
Friedensville, Lehigh, Pa..........	340
Friend Grove, Wabash, Ill.........	12
Friendship, Ripley, Ind....	71
Friendship, Caldwell, Ky..........	12
Friendship, Knox, Me.............	72
Friendship, Anne Arundel, Md.....	140
Friendship, Allegany, N. Y.........	840
Friendship, Guilford, N. C........	21
Friendship, Scioto, Ohio..........	18
Friendship, Clarendon, S. C	12
Friendship, Dyer, Tenn...........	12
Friendship, (c. h.,) Adams, Wis.....	140
Friendshipville, King George, Va..	24
Friendsville, Wabash, Ill..........	110
Friendsville, Medina, Ohio....	30
Friendsville, Susquehanna, Pa.....	140
Friendsville, Blount, Tenn........	53
Friendswood, Hendricks, Ind	12
Fritztown, Berks, Pa..............	19
Frizellburgh, Carroll, Md.........	39
Frog Level, Newberry, S. C.......	88
Frohna, Perry, Mo......	12
Frontenac, Goodhue, Minn..........	150
Frontier, Hillsdale, Mich.........	21
Frontier, Clinton, N. Y...........	59
Front Royal, (c. h.,) Warren, Va....	370
Frost, Pocahontas, W. Va.........	5
Frostburgh,* Alleghany, Md.......	890
Frostburgh, Jefferson, Pa.........	27
Frost's Station, Fayette, Pa.......	12
Fruitland, Burlington, N. J.......	87
Fruitport, Muskegon, Mich........	74
Frumet, Jefferson, Mo............	12
Fryburgh, Auglaize, Ohio........ ..	63
Fryburgh, Clarion, Pa.............	59
Fryeburgh, Wright, Iowa....	20
Fryeburgh, Oxford, Me............	290
Fryeburgh Centre, Oxford, Me.....	50
Fudgy's Creek, Cabell, W. Va.... .	12
Fulda, Spencer, Ind..............	34
Fulkerson, Scott, Va..............	4
Fullen's, Greene, Tenn...........	78
Fullersburgh, Du Page, Ill....	68
Fuller's Point, Coles, Ill..........	12
Fullerville Iron Works, St. Lawrence, N. Y	85
Fullwood's Store, Mecklenburgh, N. C..........................	5
Fulmer Valley, Allegany, N. Y.....	12
Fulton, Sumter, Ala.............	12
Fulton, Hempstead, Ark	24
Fulton,* Whitesides, Ill	1,200
Fulton, Fulton, Ind..............	68
Fulton, Jackson, Iowa...........	43
Fulton, Kalamazoo, Mich	42
Fulton, Prentiss, Miss...........	44
Fulton, (c. h.,) Callaway, Mo	940
Fulton,* Oswego, N. Y......	2,200
Fulton, Davie, N. C..............	9
Fulton, Westmoreland, Pa.........	20
Fulton, Lauderdale, Tenn....	64
Fulton, Refugio, Tex.............	12
Fulton, Rock, Wis...............	75
Fultonham, Schoharie, N. Y......	35
Fultonham, Muskingum, Ohio	110

GAL

Fulton House, Lancaster, Pa	$22
Fulton Station, Fulton, Ky........	190
Fultonville, Montgomery, N. Y....	830
Funkhouser, Effingham, Ill........	12
Funkstown, Washington, Md......	130
Funny Louis, Catahoula, La........	11
Furnessville, Porter, Ind......	67
Fussville, Waukesha, Wis..........	64

G.

Gabilan, Monterey, Cal...........	12
Gadsden, (c. h.,) Etowah, Ala	460
Gadsden, Madison, Tenn..........	95
Gage's Lakes, Lake, Ill..........	18
Gagetown, Tuscola, Mich..........	12
Gahanna, Franklin, Ohio.........	65
Gaines, Orleans, N. Y.............	120
Gaines, Tioga, Pa................	46
Gainesborough, (c. h.,) Jackson, Tenn.	50
Gainesborough, Frederick, Va.....	21
Gaines' Cross Roads, Rappahannock, Va...........................	18
Gaines Farm, Henry, Mo.........	21
Gaines Station, Genesee, Mich....	200
Gainestown, Clarke, Ala....	20
Gainesville, Sumter, Ala.........	790
Gainesville, (c. h.,) Greene, Ark	140
*Gainesville,** (c. h.,) Alachua, Fla...	950
Gainesville, (c. h.,) Hall, Ga....	130
Gainesville, Kent, Mich..........	34
Gainesville, Hancock, Miss........	18
Gainesville, (c. h.,) Ozark, Mo.......	22
Gainesville, Wyoming, N. Y.......	140
Gainesville, Prince William, Va....	160
Gainesville Junction, Kemper, Miss.	12
Gainsville, Allen, Ky.............	12
Gainsville, (c. h.,) Cooke, Tex.....	170
Galbraith's Store, Henry, Mo......	39
*Galena,** (c. h.,) Jo Daviess, Ill.....	2,900
Galena, Floyd, Ind...............	28
Galena, Kent, Md................	290
Galena, (c. h.,) Stone, Mo	20
Galena, Dodge, Nebr.............	12
Galena, Humboldt, Nev......	12
Galena, Delaware, Ohio..........	200
Gales, Sullivan, N. Y.............	7
Galesburgh,* Knox, Ill.............	3,200
Galesburgh, Jasper, Iowa.........	60
Galesburgh,* Kalamazoo, Mich....	770
Galesburgh, Jasper, Mo......	12
Gale's Ferry, New London, Conn...	43
Gales Town, Dorchester, Md......	22
Galesville, Washington, N. Y......	130
Galesville, Douglas, Oreg.........	22
Galesville, (c. h.,) Trempealeau, Wis.	260
Galeville Mills, Ulster, N. Y.......	29
Galien, Berrien, Mich.............	230
Galigher, Guernsey, Ohio.........	6
Galilee, Wayne, Pa...............	3
Galion, Crawford, Ohio..........	1,400
Galivant's Ferry, Horry, S. C......	17
Gallant Green, Charles, Md.......	12
Gallatia, Saline, Ill	41
Gallatin, Copiah, Miss............	12
*Gallatin,** (c. h.,) Daviess, Mo.......	370

* Money-order office.

GAR

GEN

Gallatin, Gallatin, Mont	$110
Gallatin,* (c. h.,) Sumner, Tenn	830
Gallatinville, Columbia, N. Y	42
Gallaudet, Marion, Ind	12
Gallaway's Station, Osage, Mo	12
Galley Rock, Pope, Ark	12
Gallia Furnace, Gallia. Ohio	24
Gallipolis,* (c. h.,) Gallia, Ohio	2,000
Gallitzin, Cambria, Pa	160
Galloway, La Salle, Ill	23
Gallupville, Schoharie, N. Y	170
Galt, Sacramento, Cal	12
Galt, Whitesides, Ill	130
Galt's Mills, Amherst, Va	12
Galum, Perry, Ill	12
Galva,* Henry, Ill	2,200
Galveston, Cass, Ind	270
Galveston,* (c. h.,) Galveston, Tex	4,000
Galway, Saratoga, N. Y	220
Galway, Fayette, Tenn	81
Gamaliel, Monroe, Ky	12
Gambier,* Knox, Ohio	560
Gamble's, Allegheny, Pa	19
Gamble's Store, Blount, Tenn	46
Game Hill, Franklin, Ark	21
Ganges, Allegan, Mich	110
Ganges, Richland, Ohio	30
Gansevoort, Saratoga, N. Y	210
Gap, Lancaster, Pa	280
Gap Ciril, (c. h.,) Alleghany, N. C.	13
Gap Creek, Ashe, N. C	23
Gap Creek, Knox, Tenn	12
Gap Grove, Lee, Ill	60
Gap Mills, Monroe, W. Va	19
Gap Run, Carter, Tenn	6
Gapsville, Fulton, Pa	12
Garber's Mills, Washington, Tenn	9
Garden, Delta, Mich	17
Garden, Athens, Ohio	17
Garden City, Blue Earth, Minn	330
Garden Cottage, Pulaski, Ky	3
Garden Grove, Decatur, Iowa	200
Garden Grove, Ralls, Mo	12
Garden Prairie, Boone, Ill	310
Garden Prairie, Blue Earth, Minn	10
Garden Valley, Smith, Tex	12
Gardenville, Erie, N. Y	99
Gardenville, Bucks, Pa	48
Gardiner,* Kennebec, Me	2,200
Gardiner, Douglas, Oreg	43
Gardner, Grundy, Ill	570
Gardner, Johnson, Kans	110
Gardner, Worcester, Mass	900
Gardner, Noble, Ohio	12
Gardner's Corner, Beaufort, S. C	12
Gardner's Ford, Cleveland, N. C	13
Gardner's Station, Weakley, Tenn	39
Gardnersville, Pendleton, Ky	12
Gard's Point, Wabash, Ill	7
Garfield, La Salle, Ill	12
Garfield, Mahoning, Ohio	12
Garibaldi, Saguache, Colo	12
Garibaldi, Keokuk, Iowa	33
Garibaldi, Tillamook, Oreg	12
Garland, Butler, Ala	47
Garland, Penobscot, Me	140

Garland, Warren, Pa	$180
Garlandville, Jasper, Miss	37
Garman's Mills, Cambria, Pa	13
Garnavillo,* Clayton, Iowa	200
Garner, Cass, Ill	12
Garner's Station, Yalabusha, Miss	24
Garnett,* (c. h.,) Anderson, Kans	1,000
Garnettsville, Meade, Ky	180
Garoga, Fulton, N. Y	40
Garrattsville, Otsego. N. Y	130
Garretson's Landing, Jefferson, Ark	32
Garrett, Meade, Ky	23
Garrettsburgh, Christian, Ky	48
Garrettsville,* Portage, Ohio	1,500
Garrison Point, Walker, Ala	5
Garrison's, Putnam, N. Y	360
Garrisonville, Stafford, Va	40
Garrote, Tuolumne, Cal	20
Garry Owen, Jackson, Iowa	34
Gartsides, St. Clair, Ill	78
Gary's Store, Buckingham, Va	39
Garysville, Prince George, Va	12
Gasconade City, Gasconade, Mo	42
Gasconade Ferry, Gasconade, Mo	23
Gas Jet, Humboldt, Cal	12
Gaskill's Corners, Tioga, N. Y	10
Gasport, Niagara, N. Y	180
Gassett's Station, Windsor, Vt	70
Gaston, Sumter, Ala	28
Gaston, Lewis, W. Va	5
Gatchellville, York, Pa	16
Gates, Newton, Mo	13
Gates, Monroe, N. Y	12
Gates' Mills, Cuyahoga, Ohio	20
Gatesville, Clay, Ga	12
Gatesville, Clay, Kans	14
Gatesville, (c. h.,) Gates, N. C	39
Gatesville, (c. h.,) Coryell, Tex	30
Gatewood, Ripley, Mo	4
Gatlinburgh, Sevier, Tenn	9
Gauley Bridge, Fayette, W. Va	62
Gavers, Columbiana, Ohio	25
Gayhead, Greene, N. Y	12
Gaylesville, Cherokee, Ala	42
Gaylordsville, Litchfield, Conn	180
Gayoso, (c. h.,) Pemiscot, Mo	24
Gaysville, Windsor, Vt	280
Gazelle, Siskiyou, Cal	12
Geary, Doniphan, Kans	37
Geary, Clinton, Mich	12
Geary, Westmoreland, Pa	12
Gebhart's, Somerset, Pa	63
Geddes, Onondaga, N. Y	390
Geetingsville, Clinton, Ind	30
Geiger's Mills, Berks, Pa	48
Gem, Clayton, Iowa	35
General Wayne, Montgomery, Pa	12
Genesee, Waukesha, Wis	80
Genesee Depot, Waukesha, Wis	93
Genesee Fork, Potter, Pa	28
Genesee Village, Genesee, Mich	23
Genesee,* Henry, Ill	1,900
Geneseo, Cerro Gordo, Iowa	12
Geneseo,* (c. h.,) Livingston, N. Y.	1,600
Geneva, (c. h.,) Geneva, Ala	22
Geneva, Talbot, Ga	200

* Money-order office.

GER

Geneva,* (c. h.,) Kane, Ill	$860
Geneva, Franklin, Iowa	8
Geneva, Allen, Kans	88
Geneva, Lenawee, Mich	32
Geneva, Freeborn, Minn	61
Geneva,* Ontario, N. Y	3,000
Geneva, Ashtabula, Ohio	950
Geneva, Walworth, Wis	830
Genevia, Henderson, Ky	12
Genito, Powhatan, Va	140
Genoa, De Kalb, Ill	93
Genoa, Wayne, Iowa	73
Genoa, Livingston, Mich	39
Genoa, Platte, Nebr	53
Genoa, (c. h.,) Douglas, Nev	270
Genoa, Cayuga, N. Y	140
Genoa, Ottawa, Ohio	170
Genoa, Vernon, Wis	33
Genoa Bluff, Iowa, Iowa	49
Gentryville, Spencer, Ind	53
Gentryville, Gentry, Mo	260
George Lake, Stearns, Minn	4
George's Creek, Pickens, S. C	10
George's Mills, Sullivan, N. H	38
George's Store, Lincoln, Tenn	7
Georgesville, Franklin, Ohio	15
Georgetown, Pope, Ark	13
Georgetown,* El Dorado, Cal	350
Georgetown,* Clear Creek, Colo	2,000
Georgetown, Fairfield, Conn	200
Georgetown, (c. h.,) Sussex, Del	540
Georgetown,* Washington, D. C	2,500
Georgetown, Putnam, Fla	12
Georgetown, (c. h.,) Quitman, Ga	81
Georgetown, Vermilion, Ill	250
Georgetown, Floyd, Ind	23
Georgetown, Monroe, Iowa	48
Georgetown,* (c. h.,) Scott, Ky	1,100
Georgetown, Sagadahoc, Me	12
Georgetown, Essex, Mass	590
Georgetown, Ottawa, Mich	11
Georgetown, Clay, Minn	21
Georgetown, Pettis, Mo	99
Georgetown, Lewis and Clarke, Mont	12
Georgetown, Jefferson, Nebr	12
Georgetown, Burlington, N. J	53
Georgetown, Madison, N. Y	140
Georgetown, (c. h.,) Brown, Ohio	470
Georgetown, Beaver, Pa	68
Georgetown, (c. h.,) Georgetown, S. C	1,100
Georgetown, Hamilton, Tenn	18
Georgetown, (c. h.,) Williamson, Tex	200
Georgetown, Lewis, W. Va	12
Georgetown, Grant, Wis	80
Georgeville, Monongalia, Minn	40
Georgeville, Ray, Mo	10
Georgia, Lawrence, Ind	19
Georgia, Franklin, Vt	85
Georgia City, Jasper, Mo	12
Georgiana, Butler, Ala	40
Georgia Plain, Franklin, Vt	36
Georgiaville, Providence, R. I	240
German, Chenango, N. Y	16
German, Darke, Ohio	50
German Gulch, Deer Lodge, Mont	12

GIL

Germania, Potter, Pa	$83
Germania, Marquette, Wis	250
Germano, Harrison, Ohio	120
German Settlement, Preston, W. Va	60
Germanton, Stokes, N. C	50
Germantown, Clinton, Ill	120
Germantown, Mason, Ky	140
Germantown, Montgomery, Md	23
Germantown,* Henry, Mo	360
Germantown, Columbia, N. Y	200
Germantown, Montgomery, Ohio	500
Germantown, Shelby, Tenn	150
Germantown, Juneau, Wis	34
German Valley, Morris, N. J	84
Germanville, Jefferson, Iowa	32
Germany, Warren, Pa	6
Gerrardstown, Berkeley, W. Va	77
Gery's, Bucks, Pa	33
Gethsemane, Nelson, Ky	39
Gettysburgh, Darke, Ohio	180
Gettysburgh,* (c. h.,) Adams, Pa	1,700
Getzville, Erie, N. Y	19
Ghent, Carroll, Ky	220
Ghent, Columbia, N. Y	140
Ghent, Summit, Ohio	32
Gholson, Noxubee, Miss	200
Gholsonville, Brunswick, Va	12
Giard, Clayton, Iowa	71
Gibb's Cross Roads, Cumberland, N. C	12
Gibb's Cross Roads, Macon, Tenn	12
Gibbsville, Sheboygan, Wis	88
Gibesonville, Hocking, Ohio	29
Gibraltar, Lyons, Iowa	12
Gibraltar, Wayne, Mich	6
Gibson, (c. h.,) Glascock, Ga	10
Gibson, Steuben, N. Y	40
Gibson, Pike, Ohio	11
Gibson, Susquehanna, Pa	160
Gibsonburgh, Luzerne, Pa	12
Gibson's Station, Lake, Ind	41
Gibson's Station, Guernsey, Ohio	64
Gibsonville,* Sierra, Cal	100
Gibsonville, Guilford, N. C	39
Gibsonville, Russell, Va	12
Gilbert, Scott, Iowa	35
Gilbert, Monroe, Pa	19
Gilbert Hollow, Lexington, S. C	12
Gilbert's, Kane, Ill	12
Gilbertsborough, Limestone, Ala	8
Gilbert's Creek Station, Lincoln, Ky	12
Gilbert's Mills, Oswego, N. Y	43
Gilbertsville, Montgomery, Pa	60
Gilbertville, Black Hawk, Iowa	27
Gilbertville, Worcester, Mass	170
Gilbirdsport, Brown, Ill	12
Gilboa, Schoharie, N. Y	180
Gilboa, Putnam, Ohio	88
Gilchrist, Pope, Minn	61
Gilchrist's Bridge, Marion, S. C	10
Gilead, Tolland, Conn	59
Gilead, Calhoun, Ill	20
Gilead, Miami, Ind	49
Gilead, Oxford, Me	36
Gilead, Branch, Mich	52
Gilead, Lewis, Mo	31

* Money-order office.

Gilford, Tuscola, Mich	$12	Glasgow,* Howard, Mo	$830
Gilford Village, Belknap, N. H	15	Glasgow, Columbiana, Ohio	35
Gilgal, Pike, Ill	9	Glasgow Junction, Barren, Ky	80
Gill, Franklin, Mass	130	Glassborough, Gloucester, N. J	280
Gillem's Station, Dickson, Tenn	44	Glass River, Shiawassee, Mich	19
Gillen's Landing, Phillips, Ark	18	Glass Village, Pope, Ark	6
Gillespie, Macoupin, Ill	300	Glastenbury, Hartford, Conn	310
Gillespieville, Ross, Ohio	87	Glaze City, Camden, Mo	11
Gillespieville, Kanawha, W. Va	12	Gleeson Station, Weakley, Tenn	12
Gillett's Grove, Clay, Iowa	12	Gleu, Montgomery, N. Y	96
Gill Hall, Allegheny, Pa	12	Glen Allen, Henrico, Va	20
Gillisonville, Beaufort, S. C	50	Glenaloon, Moore, N. C	4
Gill's Mills, Rowan, Ky	12	Glen Alta, Marion, Ga	12
Gillsville, Hall, Ga	33	Glen Arbor, Leelenaw, Mich	61
Gilman, Iroquois, Ill	950	Glen Aubrey, Broome, N. Y	19
Gilman, Hamilton, N. Y	5	Glenbeulah, Sheboygan, Wis	200
Gilmanton, Belknap, N. H	250	Glenburn, Penobscot, Me	26
Gilmanton Iron Works, Belknap,		Glen Carbon, Schuylkill, Pa	12
N. H	160	Glen Castle, Broome, N. Y	61
Gilmantown, Buffalo, Wis	75	Glencoe, Cook, Ill	21
Gilmer, Lake, Ill	23	Glencoe, Gallatin, Ky	12
Gilmer,* (c. h.,) Upshur, Tex	120	Glencoe,* (c. h.,) McLeod, Minn	160
Gilmer, Uintah, Wyo	300	Glencoe, St. Louis, Mo	20
Gilmer's, Lowndes, Ala	12	Glencoe, Belmont, Ohio	72
Gilmer's Store, Guilford, N. C	4	Glencoe, Buffalo, Wis	45
Gilmore, Sarpy, Nebr	12	Glencoe Mills, Columbia, N. Y	17
Gilmore, Tuscarawas, Ohio	54	Glen Cove, Queens, N. Y	450
Gilmore's Mills, Rockbridge, Va	12	Glendale, Pope, Ill	24
Gilpin, Indiana, Pa	8	Glen Dale, Daviess, Ind	10
Gilroy,* Santa Clara, Cal	800	Glendale, Jefferson, Iowa	97
Gilson, Knox, Ill	10	Glendale, Bourbon, Kans	10
Gilsum, Cheshire, N. H	130	Glendale, Hardin, Ky	150
Ginger Hill, Washington, Pa	60	Glendale, Berkshire, Mass	100
Ginghamsburgh, Miami, Ohio	8	Glendale, Van Buren, Mich	22
Girard, Macoupin, Ill	720	Glendale, McLeod, Minn	12
Girard,* (c. h.,) Crawford, Kans	240	Glendale, Cass, Nebr	17
Girard, Branch, Mich	120	Glendale, Hamilton, Ohio	420
Girard, Trumbull, Ohio	310	Glendale, Cambria, Pa	100
Girard,* Erie, Pa	720	Glendale, Monroe, Wis	20
Girard Manor, Schuylkill, Pa	51	Glendower, Albemarle, Va	12
Girardsville, Schuylkill, Pa	440	Glen Easton, Marshall, W. Va	94
Girdletree Hill, Worcester, Md	12	Glen Elder, Mitchell, Kans	12
Gird's Creek, Missoula, Mont	12	Glenelg, Howard, Md	14
Gishe's Mills, Roanoke, Va	59	Glengary, Berkeley, W. Va	8
Givin, Mahaska, Iowa	19	Glen Grove, Douglas, Colo	12
Glade, Somerset, Pa	12	Glen Hall, Tippecanoe, Ind	40
Glade Creek, Ashe, N. C	8	Glenham, Dutchess, N. Y	360
Glade Farms, Preston, W. Va	7	Glen Haven, Leelenaw, Mich	12
Glade Hill, Franklin, Va	9	Glen Haven, Cortland, N. Y	38
Glade Mills, Butler, Pa	160	Glen Haven, Grant, Wis	62
Gladen's Run, Bedford, Pa	12	Glen Hope, Clearfield, Pa	140
Glades, Morgan, Tenn	4	Glenloch, Chester, Pa	180
Gladesborough, Randolph, N. C	3	Glen Mills, Delaware, Pa	45
Gladesborough, Carroll, Va	3	Glenmore, Ware, Ga	20
Glade Spring, Washington, Va	83	Glenmore, Oneida, N. Y	16
Gladesville, Preston, W. Va	5	Glenmore, Buckingham, Va	20
Gladeville, Wilson, Tenn	24	Glenn, Johnson, Kans	12
Glad Tidings, Clackamas, Oreg	9	Glenn, McKean, Pa	4
Glasco, Cloud, Kans	12	Glenn's, Gloucester, Va	12
Glasco, Ulster, N. Y	84	Glenn Springs, Spartanburgh, S. C.	36
Glasford, Peoria, Ill	110	Glenn's Valley, Marion, Ind	40
Glasgow, New Castle, Del	36	Glennville, Barbour, Ala	190
Glasgow, Scott, Ill	53	Glenora, Yates, N. Y	58
Glasgow, Jefferson, Iowa	89	Glen Park, Wyandotte, Kans	12
Glasgow,* (c. h.,) Barren, Ky	680	Glen Riddle, Delaware, Pa	180
Glasgow, Wabashaw, Minn	6	Glen Rock, Nemaha, Nebr	28

*Money-order office.

GOL

Glen Rock, York, Pa	$360
Glen Roy, Howard, Iowa	300
Glen Roy, Chester, Pa	19
Glensdale, Lewis, N. Y	100
Glen's Falls,* Warren, N. Y	2,200
Glen's Fork, Adair, Ky	8
Glen Union, Clinton, Pa	51
Glenville, Fairfield, Conn	24
Glenville, Harford, Md	64
Glenville, Schenectady, N. Y	76
Glenville, Cuyahoga, Ohio	70
Glenville, (c. h.,) Gilmer, W. Va	150
Glen Wild, Sullivan, N. Y	22
Glenwood,* (c. h.,) Mills, Iowa	1,200
Glenwood, Leavenworth, Kans	20
Glenwood, Aroostook, Me	33
Glenwood, (c. h.,) Pope, Minn	120
Glenwood, Schuyler, Mo	310
Glenwood, Sussex, N. J	40
Glenwood, Erie, N. Y	52
Glenwood, Susquehanna, Pa	120
Glidden, Carroll, Iowa	120
Globe, Caldwell, N. C	18
Globe Creek, Marshall, Tenn	10
Globe Village, Worcester, Mass	480
Gloucester,* Essex, Mass	2,700
Gloucester C. H., Gloucester, Va	170
Gloucester City, Camden, N. J	320
Glover, Orleans, Vt	210
Glover's Creek, Metcalfe, Ky	2
Glover's Gap, Marion, W. Va	34
Gloversville, Fulton, N. Y	1,600
Glymont, Charles, Md	56
Glyndon, Crawford, Pa	25
Gnadenhutten, Tuscarawas, Ohio	84
Godfrey, Madison, Ill	410
Godwinville, Bergen, N. J	140
Goff's, Ritchie, W. Va	9
Goff's Falls, Hillsborough, N. H	47
Goff's Mills, Steuben, N. Y	18
Goffstown, Hillsborough, N. H	210
Goffstown Centre, Hillsborough, N.H	83
Gogginsville, Franklin, Va	32
Goheenville, Armstrong, Pa	30
Golconda, (c. h.,) Pope, Ill	520
Golconda, Humboldt, Nev	12
Golden City, (c. h.,) Jefferson, Colo	600
Golden City, Barton, Mo	12
Golden Corners, Wayne, Ohio	28
Golden Gate, Brown, Minn	87
Golden Hill, Dorchester, Md	16
Golden Hill, Wyoming, Pa	16
Golden Lake, Waukesha, Wis	31
Golden Pond, Trigg, Ky	14
Golden Prairie, Delaware, Iowa	12
Golden Ridge, Aroostook, Me	6
Golden's Bridge, Westchester, N. Y.	160
Golden Springs, Anderson, S. C	12
Golden Valley, Rutherford, N. C	5
Goldfield, Wright, Iowa	66
Gold Hill, Storey, Nev	1,700
Gold Hill, Rowan, N. C	59
Gold Hill, Buckingham, Va	29
Golding, Oceana, Mich	37
Gold Mine, Marion, Ala	12
Gold Run, Placer, Cal	200

GOS

Goldsborough, Caroline, Md	$12
Goldsborough,* (c. h.,) Wayne, N. C.	1,100
Goldville, Tallapoosa, Ala	7
Goliad, (c. h.,) Goliad, Tex	260
Golindo, Falls, Tex	47
Gomber, Guernsey, Ohio	63
Gomer, Allen, Ohio	88
Gomeria, Republic, Kans	12
Gomer's Mills, Douglas, Colo	12
Gonic, Strafford, N. H	100
Gonzales,* (c. h.,) Gonzales, Tex	1,000
Goochland, Rock Castle, Ky	12
Goochland C. H., Goochland, Va	5
Gooch's Mill, Cooper, Mo	36
Goodale's Corner, Penobscot, Me	49
Goodall's, Hanover, Va	23
Goodfield, Meigs, Tenn	3
Goodgion's Factory, Laurens, S. C	12
Good Ground, Suffolk, N. Y	76
Good Harbor, Leelenaw, Mich	34
Good Hope, McDonough, Ill	200
Good Hope, Leake, Miss	16
Good Hope, Fayette, Ohio	62
Good Hope, Cumberland, Pa	23
Good Hope, Milwaukee, Wis	20
Goodhue Centre, Goodhue, Minn	59
Gooding's Grove, Will, Ill	51
Good Intent, Washington, Pa	12
Goodland, Newton, Ind	290
Goodland, Lapeer, Mich	68
Goodland, Knox, Mo	22
Goodlettsville, Davidson, Tenn	100
Goodman, Holmes, Miss	320
Goodrich, Genesee, Mich	200
Good Spring, Giles, Tenn	2
Good View, Bedford, Va	5
Goodville, Lancaster, Pa	28
Goodwin's Mills, York, Me	49
Goodwynsville, Dinwiddie, Va	21
Goodyear's Bar, Sierra, Cal	16
Goole, Vernon, Wis	13
Goose Creek, Ritchie, W. Va	2
Goose Island, Alexander, Ill	16
Gopher Prairie, Wabashaw, Minn	7
Gordon, Henry, Ala	99
Gordon, Wilkinson, Ga	100
Gordon, Darke, Ohio	54
Gordon, Schuylkill, Pa	21
Gordonsville, Logan, Ky	37
Gordonsville, Freeborn, Minn	6
Gordonsville, Lancaster, Pa	69
Gordonsville, Smith, Tenn	16
Gordonsville,* Orange, Va	680
Gore, Hocking, Ohio	13
Goresville, Loudoun, Va	67
Goresville, Johnson, Ill	10
Gorham,* Cumberland, Me	660
Gorham,* Coos, N. H	700
Gorham, Ontario, N. Y	140
Gorham, Fulton, Ohio	120
Gorman's Depot, Cocke, Tenn	12
Gorsuch's Mills, Baltimore, Md	20
Goshen, Litchfield, Conn	180
Goshen, Lincoln, Ga	10
Goshen, (c. h.,) Elkhart, Ind	2,200
Goshen, Oldham, Ky	71

GRA   GRA

Goshen, Montgomery, Md	$20	Granby, Essex, Vt	$26
Goshen, Hampshire, Mass	160	Granby Centre, Oswego, N. Y	88
Goshen, Mercer, Mo	37	Grand Blanc, Genesee, Mich	190
Goshen, Sullivan, N. H	23	Grand Bluff, Panola, Tex	16
Goshen, Cape May, N. J	80	Grand Cane, De Soto, La	10
Goshen,* (c. h.,) Orange, N. Y	1,500	Grand Chenier, Vermillion, La	15
Goshen, Clermont, Ohio	200	Grand Coteau, St. Landry, La	120
Goshen, Lancaster, Pa	52	Grand Detour, Ogle, Ill	200
Goshen, Lincoln, Tenn	12	Grand Forks, Pembina, Dak	12
Goshen Bridge, Rockbridge, Va	250	Grand Glade, Crawford, Ill	12
Goshen Hill, Union, S. C	10	Grand Glaze, Jackson, Ark	12
Goshen Springs, Rankin, Miss	8	Grand Gulf, Claiborne, Miss	74
Goshenville, Chester, Pa	22	Grand Haven,* (c. h.,) Ottawa, Mich.	1,700
Gosport, Clarke, Ala	4	Grand Island, Colusa, Cal	50
Gosport, Owen, Ind	490	Grand Island Station,* (c. h.,) Hall,	
Gosport, Marion, Iowa	47	Nebr	330
Gonge's, Grant, Ky	16	Grand Isle, Grand Isle, Vt	110
Gouglersville, Berks, Pa	4	Grand Junction, Greene, Iowa	61
Gouldsborough, Hancock, Me	100	Grand Junction, Hardeman, Tenn	150
Gouldsborough, Luzerne, Pa	83	Grand Lake, Chicot, Ark	130
Gouldsville, Washington, Vt	130	Grand Lodge, Eaton, Mich	380
Gourley's Bridge, Greene, Tenn	12	Grand Marsh, Adams, Wis	27
Gouverneur,* St. Lawrence, N. Y	1,300	Grand Meadow, Mower, Minn	97
Govanstown, Baltimore, Md	120	Grand Mound, Clinton, Iowa	140
Gowanda, Cattaraugus, N. Y	640	Grand Mound, Thurston, Wash	16
Gowdeysville, Union, S. C	25	Grand Portage, Lake, Minn	12
Gowensville, Greenville, S. C	19	Grand Prairie, Brown, Kans	12
Gower, Du Page, Ill	12	Grand Prairie, Lewis, Wash	18
Gower's Ferry, Cedar, Iowa	12	Grand Prairie, Green Lake, Wis	21
Graafschap, Allegan, Mich	75	Grand Rapids,* (c. h.,) Kent, Mich.	4,000
Graceham, Frederick, Md	45	Grand Rapids,* Wood, Ohio	310
Gradyville, Adair, Ky	16	Grand Rapids,* (c. h.,) Wood, Wis	670
Graefenberg, Shelby, Ky	45	Grand River, Buffalo, Dak	12
Graefenburg, Herkimer, N. Y	15	Grand River, Wayne, Iowa	84
Graefenburgh, Adams, Pa	23	Grand Ronde, Polk, Oreg	8
Grafton, Yolo, Cal	170	Grand Tower, Jackson, Ill	16
Grafton, Jersey, Ill	220	Grand Valley, Hamilton, Ohio	12
Grafton, Oxford, Me	10	Grand View, Edgar, Ill	150
Grafton, Worcester, Mass	710	Grand View, Spencer, Ind	230
Grafton, Monroe, Mich	17	Grand View, Louisa, Iowa	170
Grafton, Grafton, N. H	140	Grand View, Hardin, Ky	12
Grafton, Rensselaer, N. Y	54	Grand View, Washington, Ohio	72
Grafton, Lorain, Ohio	78	Grandville, Kent, Mich	230
Grafton, Windham, Vt	270	Granger, Fillmore, Minn	84
Grafton,* Taylor, W. Va	640	Granger, Allegany, N. Y	17
Grafton, Ozaukee, Wis	140	Granger, Medina, Ohio	75
Grafton Centre, Grafton, N. H	70	Granite, (c. h.,) Lake, Colo	12
Graham, Jefferson, Ind	13	Granite Falls, Chippewa, Minn	10
Graham, Nodaway, Mo	190	Granite Hall, Adams, Pa	37
Graham, (c. h.,) Alamance, N. C	250	Graniteville, Nevada, Cal	12
Graham Lake, Noble, Minn	5	Graniteville, Middlesex, Mass	130
Graham's Forge, Wythe, Va	12	Graniteville, Edgefield, S. C	260
Graham Station, Mason, W. Va	5	Grant, Pima, Ariz	12
Graham's Turn Out, Barnwell, S. C	140	Grant, Park, Colo	12
Grahamsville, Sullivan, N. Y	60	Grant, Vermilion, Ill	12
Grahamsville, Jackson, Ohio	12	Grant, Montgomery, Iowa	46
Grahamton, Clearfield, Pa	42	Grant, Wabaunsee, Kans	12
Grahamville, York, Pa	21	Grant, Boone, Ky	12
Grahamville, Beaufort, S. C	97	Grant, Kent, Mich	10
Grampian Hills, Clearfield, Pa	58	Grant, Faribault, Minn	3
Granada, Nemaha, Kans	35	Grant, Holt, Mo	12
Granbury, (c. h.,) Hood, Tex	12	Grant, Nemaha, Nebr	26
Granby, Hartford, Conn	240	Grant, Herkimer, N. Y	43
Granby, Hampshire, Mass	150	Grant, Hardin, Ohio	12
Granby, Nicollet, Minn	20	Grant, Grant, Oreg	12
Granby,* Newton, Mo	430	Grant, Indiana, Pa	180

* Money-order office.

GRA

Grant, Portage, Wis	$4
Grant C. H., Grant, W. Va	59
Grant Centre, Monona, Iowa	12
Grant City, Sac, Iowa	64
Grant City, (c. h.,) Worth, Mo	260
Grantfork, Madison, Ill	12
Grantham, Sullivan, N. H	64
Grant Isle, Aroostook, Me	12
Grantsborough, Craven, N. C	12
Grantsburgh, Johnson, Ill	13
Grantsburgh, Crawford, Ind	17
Grantsburgh, (c. h.,) Burnett, Wis	48
Grant's Hill, Worth, Mo	90
Grant's Lick, Campbell, Ky	16
Grant's Mills, Delaware, N. Y	1
Grant's Pass, Jackson, Oreg	19
Grantsville, Alleghany, Md	180
Grantsville, Linn, Mo	46
Grantsville, Tooele, Utah	95
Grantsville, (c. h.,) Calhoun, W. Va.	15
Grantville, Coweta, Ga	150
Grantville, Jefferson, Kans	93
Grantville, Norfolk, Mass	200
Grantville, Dauphin, Pa	30
Granville, Putnam, Ill	200
Granville, Delaware, Ind	99
Granville, Mahaska, Iowa	54
Granville, Monroe, Mo	74
Granville, Washington, N. Y	610
Granville,* Licking, Ohio	950
Granville, Mifflin, Pa	43
Granville, Jackson, Tenn	21
Granville, Addison, Vt	47
Granville, Monongalia, W. Va	10
Granville, Milwaukee, Wis	66
Granville Centre, Bradford, Pa	53
Granville Corners, Hampden, Mass.	150
Granville, Summit, Bradford, Pa	60
Grape Island, Pleasants, W. Va	15
Grapeland, Faribault, Minn	52
Grapeville, Greene, N. Y	12
Grapeville, Westmoreland, Pa	12
Grason, Andrew, Mo	16
Grasshopper Falls,*Jefferson, Kans.	370
Grass Lake,* Jackson, Mich	830
Grassland, Harrison, W. Va	3
Grass Lick, Jackson, W. Va	10
Grass Valley,* Nevada, Cal	3,260
Grassy Creek, Livingston, Mo	23
Grassy Creek, Yancey, N. C	3
Grassy Pond, Spartanburgh, S. C.	5
Grater's Ford, Montgomery, Pa	37
Gratiot, Licking, Ohio	71
Gratiot, La Fayette, Wis	170
Gratis, Preble, Ohio	140
Grattan, Kent, Mich	96
Gratz, Owen, Ky	16
Gratz, Dauphin, Pa	68
Gravel Hill, Buckingham, Va	63
Gravella, Conecuh, Ala	12
Gravelly Spring, Lauderdale, Ala.	29
Gravel Ridge, Bradley, Ark	14
Gravel Run, Washtenaw, Mich	10
Gravel Spring, Frederick, Va	14
Gravelton, Wayne, Mo	17
Grave Run Mills, Baltimore, Md.	14

GRE

Gravesend, Kings, N. Y	$70
Graves' Mill, Madison, Va	9
Graveston, Knox, Tenn	8
Gravesville, Herkimer, N. Y	44
Gravesville, Calumet, Wis	100
Gravity, Taylor, Iowa	11
Gravois Mills, Morgan, Mo	14
Gray, Cumberland, Me	200
Gray, Herkimer, N. Y	61
Gray Eagle, Buncombe, N. C	12
Gray Hawk, Jackson, Ky	3
Gray Rock, Titus, Tex	20
Graysburgh, Greene, Tenn	3
Gray's Chapel, Jackson, Ala	12
Gray's Creek, Cumberland, N. C	12
Gray's Flat, Marion, W. Va	4
Gray's Hill, Roane, Tenn	8
Gray's Landing, Greene, Pa	43
Grayson, Crittenden, Ark	5
Grayson, (c. h.,) Carter, Ky	82
Grayson Springs, Grayson, Ky	66
Graysonville, Stanislaus, Cal	12
Gray's Point, Lawrence, Mo	11
Graysport, Grenada, Miss	17
Gray's Summit, Franklin, Mo	140
Gray's Valley, Tioga, Pa	16
Graysville, Catoosa, Ga	40
Graysville, Sullivan, Ind	39
Graysville, Monroe, Ohio	53
Graysville, Huntingdon, Pa	120
Graytown, Bexar, Tex	8
Grayville,* White, Ill	360
Gray Willow, Kane, Ill	30
Greason, Cumberland, Pa	48
Greasy, Macoupin, Ill	4
Greasy Creek, Floyd, Va	22
Greasy Ridge, Lawrence, Ohio	34
Great Barrington,* Berkshire, Mass.	1,500
Great Bend, Jefferson, N. Y	90
Great Bend, Meigs, Ohio	22
Great Bend, Susquehanna, Pa	810
Great Bend Village, Susquehanna, Pa	260
Great Bridge, Norfolk, Va	10
Great Crossings, Scott, Ky	21
Great Falls,* Strafford, N. H	2,300
Great Mills, St. Mary's, Md	120
Great Neck, Queens, N. Y	94
Great Oak, Palo Alto, Iowa	16
Great Pond, Hancock, Me	8
Great Valley, Cattaraugus, N. Y	51
Great Works, Penobscot, Me	93
Greble, Lebanon, Pa	15
Greece, Monroe, N. Y	28
Greeley, Weld, Colo	12
Greeley, Delaware, Iowa	90
Greeley, Anderson, Kans	100
Green, Licking, Ohio	10
Greenback, Jefferson, Ark	20
Green Bank, Burlington, N. J	23
Green Bank, Lancaster, Pa	8
Green Bank, Pocahontas, W. Va	32
Green Bay, Clarke, Iowa	61
Green Bay, Prince Edward, Va	39
Green Bay, (c. h.,) Brown, Wis	2,500
Green Bottom, Cabell, W. Va	10

* Money-order office.

GRE

Greenbrier, Limestone, Ala........	$12
Greenbrier, Conway, Ark..........	9
Green Brier, Orange, Ind..........	5
Green Brier, Monroe, Ohio........	7
Greenbrier, Northumberland, Pa...	21
Green Brier, Robertson, Tenn......	22
Greenbush, Walker, Ga............	11
Greenbush, Warren, Ill............	77
Greenbush, Penobscot, Me........	15
Green.Bush, Alcona, Mich.........	12
Greenbush, Sheboygan, Wis.......	110
Green Camp, Marion, Ohio........	44
Greencastle,* (c. h.,) Putnam, Ind...	2,400
Greencastle, Jasper, Iowa.........	110
Green Castle, Warren, Ky.........	16
Green Castle, Sullivan, Mo........	96
Green Castle, Fairfield, Ohio......	32
Greencastle,* Franklin, Pa	780
Green Centre, Noble, Ind........	12
Green Cove Springs, Clay, Fla.....	96
Green Creek, Cape May, N. J......	68
Greendale, Armstrong, Pa........	12
Greene, Jay, Ind.................	25
Greene, Androscoggin, Me........	84
Greene, Chenango, N. Y	860
Greene, Lancaster, Pa............	77
Greene, Kent, R. I	130
Greene Corner, Androscoggin, Me..	28
Greeneville,* (c. h.,) Greene, Tenn...	690
Greenfield, Colquitt, Ga..........	12
Greenfield, Greene, Ill...........	330
Greenfield,* (c. h.,) Hancock, Ind...	540
Greenfield, Adair, Iowa	51
Greenfield, Penobscot, Me	10
Greenfield,* (c. h.,) Franklin, Mass..	2,800
Greenfield, Wayne, Mich.........	49
Greenfield,* (c. h.,) Dade, Mo	370
Greenfield, Hillsborough, N. H.....	170
Greenfield, Ulster, N. Y..........	22
Greenfield,* Highland, Ohio.......	1,100
Greenfield, Erie, Pa..............	12
Greenfield, Nelson, Va	24
Greenfield, Milwaukee, Wis.......	24
Greenfield Centre, Saratoga, N. Y..	77
Greenfield Hill, Fairfield, Conn....	98
Greenfield Mills, Frederick, Md....	64
Greenford, Mahoning, Ohio.......	130
Green Forest, Carroll, Ark	12
Green Garden, Will, Ill	38
Green Garden, Beaver, Pa........	10
Green Grove, Madison, Ala.......	12
Green Grove, Luzerne, Pa........	22
Green Hall, Jackson, Ky	6
Green Haven, Dutchess, N. Y......	51
Green Hill, Lauderdale, Ala.......	9
Green Hill, Stewart, Ga..........	40
Green Hill, Warren, Ky..........	12
Green Hill, Wicomico, Md........	13
Green Hill, Rutherford, N. C	6
Green Hill, Columbiana, Ohio	14
Green Hill, Wilson, Tenn.........	73
Green Hill, Campbell, Va.........	12
Greenhorn, Huerfano, Colo.......	12
Green Island, Albany, N. Y........	250
Green Isle, Sibley, Minn..........	7
Green Lake, Monongalia, Minn....	47

GRE

Green Lake, Green Lake, Wis......	$41
Greenland, Fayette, Ill............	40
Greenland, Outonagon, Mich	210
Greenland, Boone, Mo............	36
Greenland, Rockingham, N. H.....	190
Greenland, Ross, Ohio............	23
Greenland, Lancaster, Pa.........	10
Greenland, Barnwell, S. C........	12
Greenland, Grant, W. Va........	54
Greenland Depot, Rockingham, N. H.	41
Greenleaf, Meeker, Minn	240
Green Level, Wake, N. C	5
Green Mount, Drew, Ark........	22
Green Mount, Adams, Pa.........	24
Greenmount, Rockingham, Va.....	13
Green Oak, Fulton, Ind	24
Green Oak, Livingston, Mich.....	23
Green Park, Perry, Pa...........	56
Green Plain, Southampton, Va	12
Green Point,* Kings, N. Y........	2,000
Greenpoint, Bedford, Pa..........	12
Green Pond, Pike, Ill...........	12
Green Pond, Colleton, S. C	12
Greenport,* Suffolk, N. Y	990
Green Prairie, Morrison, Minn.....	6
Green Ridge, Pettis, Mo..........	69
Green Ridge, Adams, Pa..........	16
Green River, Henry, Ill	280
Green River, Columbia, N. Y	36
Green River, Henderson, N. C.....	12
Green River, Windham, Vt.......	49
Green River City, Sweetwater, Wyo	12
Greensborough,* (c. h.,) Hale, Ala...	940
Greensborough, Craighead, Ark....	57
Greensborough, (c. h.,) Greene, Ga ..	660
Greensborough, Henry, Ind........	120
Greensborough,* Caroline, Md.....	320
Greensborough, (c. h.,) Choctaw, Miss.	70
Greensborough,* (c. h.,) Guilford, N. C.	1,400
Greensborough, Greene, Pa.......	130
Greensborough, Orleans, Vt	170
Greensburgh, Clay, Ill	11
Greensburgh,* (c. h.,) Decatur, Ind..	1,600
Greensburgh,* (c. h.,) Greene, Ky ...	500
Greensburgh, (c. h.,) St. Helena, La..	160
Greensburgh, Knox, Mo..........	46
Greensburgh, Mercer, N. J.......	46
Greensburgh, Trumbull, Ohio......	110
Greensburgh,* (c. h.,) Westmoreland, Pa	1,400
Greensburgh × Roads, Sandusky, Ohio	29
Green Sea, Horry, S. C...........	12
Green's Fork, Wayne, Ind........	150
Greenside, Webster, Iowa	12
Green's Landing, Hancock, Me	51
Greensport, St. Clair, Ala.........	16
Green Spring, Seneca, Ohio.......	330
Green Spring Furnace, Washington, Md	22
Green Spring Run, Hampshire, W. Va.	13
Green Sulphur Springs, Greenbrier, W. Va.	8

* Money-order office.

GRE

Greenton, La Fayette, Mo.........	$73
Green Top, Schuyler, Mo..........	150
Greentown, Howard, Ind..........	47
Greentown, Stark, Ohio...........	53
Green Tree, Allegheny, Pa	53
Green Tree, White, Tenn..........	2
Greenup, Cumberland, Ill	190
Greenup, (c. h.,) Greenup, Ky	350
Greenvale, Jo Daviess, Ill........	23
Greenvale, Dallas, Iowa..........	14
Green Vale, Franklin, Me	10
Greenvale, Queens, N. Y	22
Green Valley, El Dorado, Cal	57
Green Valley, Tazewell, Ill	20
Green Valley, Decatur, Iowa.......	12
Green Valley, Bath, Va...........	6
Greenview, Menard, Ill...........	220
Green Village, Morris, N. J	46
Green Village, Franklin, Pa.......	58
Greenville, (c. h.,) Butler, Ala......	1,200
Greenville, Washington, Ark	5
Greenville, Plumas, Cal	12
Greenville, New London, Conn.....	760
Greenville, (c. h.,) Meriwether, Ga..	150
Greenville, (c. h.,) Bond, Ill	780
Greenville, Floyd, Ind...........	84
Greenville, (c. h.,) Muhlenburgh, Ky.....................	420
Greenville, Piscataquis, Me.......	250
Greenville, Montcalm, Mich	1,100
Greenville, (c. h.,) Washington, Miss.	800
Greenville, (c. h.,) Wayne, Mo	10
Greenville, Hudson, N. J	130
Greenville, Greene, N. Y	220
Greenville, (c. h.,) Pitt, N. C	270
Greenville, (c. h.,) Darke, Ohio	1,200
Greenville, Mercer, Pa..........	1,600
Greenville, Providence, R. I	170
Greenville, (c. h.,) Hunt, Tex......	770
Greenville, Augusta, Va	77
Greenville, Outagamie, Wis.......	13
Greenville C. H., Greenville, S. C ..	1,500
Greenway, Nelson, Va...........	12
Greenwich, Fairfield, Conn.......	710
Greenwich, Hampshire, Mass......	120
Greenwich, Cumberland, N. J	270
Greenwich, Washington, N. Y	920
Greenwich Station, Huron, Ohio ..	200
Greenwich Village, Hampshire, Mass.....................	110
Greenwood, Etowah, Ala.........	7
Greenwood, (c. h.,) Sebastian, Ark ..	31
Greenwood, El Dorado, Cal.......	22
Greenwood, (c. h.,) Charles Mix, Dak.	20
Greenwood, Sussex, Del..........	110
Greenwood, Jackson, Fla.........	92
Greenwood, McHenry, Ill.........	48
Greenwood, Johnson, Ind........	250
Greenwood, Polk, Iowa	27
Greenwood, Franklin, Kans	10
Greenwood, Caddo, La	8
Greenwood, Oxford, Me	16
Greenwood, Baltimore, Md	25
Greenwood, Middlesex, Mass	56
Greenwood, Hennepin, Minn	20
Greenwood, Carroll, Miss.........	450

GRO

Greenwood, Jackson, Mo	$270
Greenwood, Deer Lodge, Mont	12
Greenwood, Cass, Nebr...........	12
Green Wood, Bergen, N. J.........	12
Greenwood, Steuben, N. Y.........	90
Greenwood, Columbia, Pa.........	20
Greenwood, Abbeville, S. C........	390
Greenwood, Shelby, Tenn.........	83
Greenwood, Doddridge, W. Va......	59
Greenwood Centre, Kossuth, Iowa..	12
Greenwood Depot, Albemarle, Va ..	91
Greenwood Furnace, Marquette, Mich.....................	20
Greenwood Furnace, Huntingdon, Pa.....................	57
Greenwood Iron Works, Orange, N. Y......................	160
Greersville, Knox, Ohio	37
Greggsville, Ohio, W. Va	16
Gregory Landing, Clarke, Mo	12
Greig, Lewis, N. Y..............	50
Greigsville, Livingston, N. Y	52
Grenada, (c. h.,) Grenada, Miss....	1,100
Greshville, Berks, Pa	16
Gretna, Jefferson, La............	12
Greystone, Wilson, Kans	10
Grider, Cumberland, Ky.........	29
Gridley, McLean, Ill....	330
Grier's Point, Perry, Pa.........	8
Griesemersville, Berks, Pa	12
Griffin, (c. h.,) Spalding, Ga	1,700
Griffin's Corners, Delaware, N. Y...	140
Griffin's Mills, Erie, N. Y	60
Griffinsville, Appanoose, Iowa	4
Griffithsville, Lincoln, W. Va......	6
Grigg's Corners, Ashtabula, Ohio ..	12
Griggstown, Somerset, N. J........	76
Griggsville, Pike, Ill...........	720
Grim's Store, Upshur, W. Va.......	5
Grimville, Berks, Pa............	31
Grinnell, Grundy, Mo...........	12
Grinnell, Poweshiek, Iowa	1,500
Grinnell, Wallace, Kans....	12
Grinstead's Mills, Hart, Ky........	12
Grinton, Will, Ill..............	8
Grissom's Landing, Daviess, Ky ...	12
Grist's Station, Columbus, N. C	22
Griswold, New London, Conn......	73
Griswold, Hamilton, Ill...........	8
Griswold's Mills, Washington, N. Y.	15
Griswoldville, Jones, Ga.........	52
Griswoldville, Franklin, Mass	120
Grizzly Bear House, Placer, Cal ...	20
Grizzly Flat, El Dorado, Cal	56
Groesbeck, Hamilton, Ohio.......	69
Groff's Store, Lancaster, Pa.......	26
Groom's Corners, Saratoga, N. Y ...	22
Groomsville, Tipton, Ind.........	12
Grooverville, Brooks, Ga	25
Grosvenor Dale, Windham, Conn ..	200
Groton, New London, Conn	380
Groton, Middlesex, Mass..........	610
Groton, Grafton, N. H...........	77
Groton, Tompkins, N. Y..........	440
Groton, Caledonia, Vt...........	76
Groton City, Tompkins, N. Y	34

* Money-order office.

GUM   HAI

Groton Junction,* Middlesex, Mass.	$770
Grouse, Kane, Ill	29
Grove, Geauga, Ohio	22
Grove, Chatham, N. C	10
Grove, Walworth, Wis	9
Grove City, Christian, Ill	210
Grove City, Cass, Iowa	45
Grove City, Jefferson, Kans	12
Grove City, Franklin, Ohio	63
Grove Cottage, Perry, Ala	12
Grove Creek, Jones, Iowa	12
Grove Hill, (c. h.,) Clarke, Ala	55
Grove Hill, Crawford, Ohio	10
Grove Hill, Page, Va	11
Groveland, Tazewell, Ill	92
Groveland, Putnam, Ind	22
Groveland, Essex, Mass	210
Groveland, Oakland, Mich	10
Groveland, Livingston, N. Y	43
Grevenor's Corners, Schoharie, N. Y	39
Groveport, Franklin, Ohio	220
Grover, Ottawa, Kans	12
Grover Town, Stark, Ind	47
Groves, Fayette, Ind	35
Grove Station, Greenville, S. C	19
Groveton, Coos, N. H	220
Grubbtown, Grundy, Mo	12
Grubville, Franklin, Mo	27
Grundy, (c. h.,) Buchanan, Va	12
Grundy Centre, (c. h.,) Grundy, Iowa	300
Guahonga, San Diego, Cal	12
Gualala, Mendocino, Cal	85
Gubser's Mills, Campbell, Ky	12
Guenoc, Lake, Cal	20
Guerneville, Sonoma, Cal	12
Guest's Station, Wise, Va	12
Guilderland, Albany, N. Y	120
Guilderland Centre, Albany, N. Y	82
Guilderland Station, Albany, N. Y	20
Guildford, Freeborn, Minn	8
Guildhall, (c. h.,) Essex, Vt	100
Guilford,* New Haven, Conn	920
Guilford, Jo Daviess, Ill	12
Guilford, Dearborn, Ind	82
Guilford, Wilson, Kans	12
Guilford, Piscataquis, Me	190
Guilford, Nodaway, Mo	83
Guilford, Chenango, N. Y	240
Guilford, Medina, Ohio	330
Guilford, Windham, Vt	98
Guilford, Accomack, Va	17
Guilford Centre, Chenango, N. Y	44
Guilford Centre, Windham, Vt	88
Guilford Station, Loudoun, Va	45
Guiney's, Caroline, Va	200
Guionsville, Dearborn, Ind	9
Guittard Station, Marshall, Kans	15
Gulf Mills, Montgomery, Pa	44
Gulf Summit, Broome, N. Y	32
Gull Lake, Barry, Mich	33
Gully Branch, Coffee, Ga	6
Gumborough, Sussex, Del	39
Gum Branch, Onslow, N. C	10
Gum Spring, Louisa, Va	24
Gum Sulphur, Rock Castle, Ky	12
Gum Tree, Chester, Pa	67

Gundrum, Pulaski, Ind	$12
Gun Marsh, Allegan, Mich	19
Gunnison, San Pete, Utah	51
Guntersville, (c. h.,) Marshall, Ala	210
Guntown, Lee, Miss	210
Gurleysville, Madison, Ala	14
Gurleyville, Tolland, Conn	56
Gussettville, Live Oak, Tex	27
Gustavus, Trumbull, Ohio	200
Guthrie, Lawrence, Ind	1
Guthrie, Guthrie, Iowa	240
Guthrie, Todd, Ky	110
Guthrie Centre, Guthrie, Iowa	120
Guthriesville, Chester, Pa	61
Guthriesville, York, S. C	31
Guttenberg,* Clayton, Iowa	280
Guyandotte, Cabell, W. Va	200
Guymard, Orange, N. Y	83
Guy's Mills, Crawford, Pa	57
Guysville, Athens, Ohio	29
Guyton, Effingham, Ga	65
Gwynedd, Montgomery, Pa	76
Gypsum, Ontario, N. Y	45
Gypsum Creek, McPherson, Kans	9

H

Hackberry, Floyd, Iowa	12
Hackberry, Lavaca, Tex	45
Hackensack, (c. h.,) Bergen, N. J	870
Hacker's Creek, Lewis, W. Va	8
Hacker's Valley, Webster, W. Va	4
Hackettstown,* Warren, N. J	1,100
Haddam, (c. h.,) Middlesex, Conn	150
Haddam, Washington, Kans	12
Haddam Neck, Middlesex, Conn	78
Haddonfield, Camden, N. J	410
Haden's, Madison, Ala	12
Hadensville, Todd, Ky	20
Hadensville, Goochland, Va	16
Hader, Goodhue, Minn	81
Hadley, Will, Ill	58
Hadley, Warren, Ky	22
Hadley, Hampshire, Mass	420
Hadley, Lapeer, Mich	170
Hadley, Saratoga, N. Y	150
Hadley, Mercer, Pa	29
Hadley's Mills, Chatham, N. C	10
Hadley Station, Lawrence, Ill	47
Hadlock, Northampton, Va	23
Hadlyme, New London, Conn	85
Hagaman's Mills, Montgomery, N. Y	90
Hagarstown, Fayette, Ill	12
Hagedorn's Mills, Saratoga, N. Y	34
Hager's Grove, Shelby, Mo	10
Hagerstown,* Wayne, Ind	410
Hagerstown, (c. h.,) Washington, Md	2,200
Hagersville, Bucks, Pa	52
Hagley, Cass, Ill	30
Hague, Warren, N. Y	46
Hague, Westmoreland, Va	69
Hailesborough, St. Lawrence, N. Y	17
Hailsville, Montgomery, Ala	12
Hainesburgh, Warren, N. J	70
Hainesport, Burlington, N. J	18
Hainesville, Lake, Ill	72

* Money-order office.

HAM   HAM

Hainesville, Clinton, Mo	$140	Hamburgh, Calhoun, Ill	$99
Hainesville, Sussex, N. J	42	Hamburgh, Franklin, Ind	15
Hainesville, Berkeley, W. Va	34	Hamburgh, Fremont, Iowa	730
Hair's Valley, Huntingdon, Pa	12	Hamburgh, Livingston, Mich	67
Halcott Centre, Greene, N. Y	8	Hamburgh, Franklin, Miss	12
Halcottsville, Delaware, N. Y	37	Hamburgh, St. Charles, Mo	21
Halcyon Dale, Scriven, Ga	15	Hamburgh, Sussex, N. J	110
Haldane, Ogle, Ill	45	Hamburgh, Erie, N. Y	20
Hale, Ogle, Ill	86	Hamburgh, Fairfield, Ohio	5
Hale, Trempealeau, Wis	12	Hamburgh, Berks, Pa	570
Hale's Corners, Milwaukee, Wis	56	Hamburgh, Edgefield, S. C	41
Hale's Creek, Scioto, Ohio	46	Hamburgh, Hardin, Tenn	42
Hale's Eddy, Delaware, N. Y	110	Hamburgh, Shenandoah, Va	12
Hale's Ford, Franklin, Va	26	Hamden, New Haven, Conn	250
Hale's Mills, Fentress, Tenn	10	Hamden, Delaware, N. Y	170
Hale's Point, Lauderdale, Tenn	8	Hamer, Paulding, Ohio	11
Haley's, Marion, Ala	5	Hamersville, Brown, Ohio	91
Haley's Station, Bedford, Tenn	22	Hamilton, Park, Colo	55
Half Day, Lake, Ill	98	*Hamilton,* (c. h.,) Harris, Ga	180
Half Moon, Saratoga, N. Y	74	Hamilton,* Hancock. Ill	490
Half Moon, Centre, Pa	68	Hamilton, Steuben, Ind	80
Halfmoon Bay, San Mateo, Cal	200	Hamilton, Marion, Iowa	65
Half Rock, Mercer, Mo	8	Hamilton, Crawford, Kans	12
Half Way, Polk, Mo	35	Hamilton, Boone, Ky	13
Half Way, Onondaga, N. Y	12	Hamilton, Essex, Mass	110
Half Way, Montgomery, Pa	12	Hamilton, Allegan, Mich	62
Half Way Creek, La Crosse, Wis	100	Hamilton, Fillmore, Minn	110
Half Way House, Vermilion, Ill	12	Hamilton, Monroe, Miss	6
Half Way Prairie, Monroe, Iowa	12	Hamilton, Caldwell, Mo	1,100
Halifax, Plymouth, Mass	160	Hamilton, Gallatin, Mont	90
Halifax, (c. h.,) Halifax, N. C	410	*Hamilton,* (c. h.,) White Pine, Nev.	1,200
Halifax, Dauphin, Pa	180	Hamilton,* Madison, N. Y	1,400
Halifax, Windham, Vt	50	Hamilton, Martin, N. C	98
Halifax C. H., Halifax, Va	340	*Hamilton,* (c. h.,) Butler, Ohio	3,000
Hall, Morgan, Ind	44	Hamilton, Jefferson, Pa	59
Hall, York, Pa	9	Hamilton, Shelby, Tex	12
Hall Centre, Wayne, N. Y	12	Hamilton, Loudoun, Va	190
Halleck, Buchanan, Mo	64	Hamilton Square, Mercer, N. J	81
Hallettsville, (c. h.,) Lavaca, Tex	370	Hamilton Station, Scott, Minn	54
Hallock, Peoria, Ill	33	Hamlet, Mercer, Ill	97
Hallock's Mills, Westchester, N. Y	50	Hamlet, Stark, Ind	38
Hallowell, Kennebec, Me	1,300	Hamlet, Chautauqua, N. Y	98
Hallsa's Ferry, Nodaway, Mo	23	Hamlin, McLean, Ill	16
Hallsborough, Chesterfield, Va	18	Hamlin, Brown, Kans	15
Hall's Corners, Allen, Ind	20	Hamlin, Monroe, Mich	16
Hall's Corners, Ontario, N. Y	78	Hamlin, Monroe, N. Y	110
Hall's Gap Station, Lincoln, Ky	12	Hamlin, Lebanon, Pa	18
Hall's Hill, Rutherford, Tenn	12	*Hamlin,* (c. h.,) Lincoln, W. Va	36
Hall's Mill, Bartow, Ga	38	Hamlin, Trempealeau, Wis	13
Hallsport, Allegany, N. Y	19	Hamlin Grove, Audubon, Iowa	24
Hall's Valley, Morgan, Ohio	7	Hamlinton, Wayne, Pa	120
Hallsville, Pike, Ala	12	Hammersley's Fork, Clinton, Pa	50
Hallsville, De Witt, Ill	24	Hammond, Tangipahoa, La	92
Hallsville, Boone, Mo	120	Hammond, Kent. Mich	12
Hallsville, Montgomery, N. Y	29	Hammond, St. Lawrence, N. Y	150
Hallsville, Duplin, N. C	14	Hammond, Barnwell, S. C	7
Hallsville, Ross, Ohio	57	Hammond, Robertson, Tex	12
Hallsville, Harrison, Tex	20	Hammond, St. Croix, Wis	95
Halltown, Saline, Ill	12	Hammondsburgh, Warren, Iowa	18
Halltown, Jefferson, W. Va	120	Hammond's Creek, Tioga, Pa	17
Halsellville, Chester, S. C	8	Hammondsport, Steuben, N. Y	540
Halsey Valley, Tioga, N. Y	39	Hammondsville, Jefferson, Ohio	288
Hambaugh's, Warren, Va	12	Hammonton,* Atlantic, N. J	700
Hamburgh, Perry, Ala	15	Hammonville, Hart, Ky	31
Hamburgh, (c. h.,) Ashley, Ark	250	Hamorton, Chester, Pa	100
Hamburgh, New London, Conn	130	Hampden, Penobscot, Me	180

* Money-order office.

HAN　　　　　　　　HAR

Hampden, Geauga, Ohio	$66	Hanover, Jefferson, Mo	$59
Hampden Corner, Penobscot, Me	230	Hanover,* Grafton, N. H	1,800
Hampden Sidney College, Prince Edward, Va	370	Hanover, Morris, N. J	68
		Hanover, Licking, Ohio	82
Hampshire, Kane, Ill	92	Hanover,* York, Pa	1,000
Hampshire, Maury, Tenn	33	Hanover, Rock, Wis	95
Hampstead, Carroll, Md	61	Hanover C. H., Hanover, Va	100
Hampstead, Rockingham, N. H	130	Hanover Centre, Grafton, N. H	46
Hampstead, King George, Va	35	Hanover Junction, York, Pa	160
Hampton, (c. h.,) Calhoun, Ark	48	Hanoverton, Columbiana, Ohio	110
Hampton, Windham, Conn	400	Hanoverville, Northampton, Pa	46
Hampton, Rock Island, Ill	200	Hansel's, Dearborn, Ind	12
Hampton,* (c. h.,) Franklin, Iowa	120	Hansen, Oceana, Mich	14
Hampton, Dakota, Minn	49	Hanson, Hopkins, Ky	12
Hampton, Platte, Mo	16	Hanson, Plymouth, Mass	93
Hampton, Rockingham, N. H	380	Hansonville, Frederick, Md	12
Hampton, Washington, N. Y	100	Hansonville, Russell, Va	40
Hampton, Adams, Pa	58	Happy Camp, Del Norte, Cal	26
Hampton, Carter, Tenn	12	Happy Hollow, Wapello, Iowa	12
Hampton, (c. h.,) Elizabeth City, Va	690	Happy Home, Burke, N. C	12
Hampton Falls, Rockingham, N. H	110	Happy Valley, Harrison, Mo	11
Hamptonville, Yadkin, N. C	20	Happy Valley, Carter, Tenn	10
Hamrick's Station, Putnam, Ind	12	Harbeson, Sussex, Del	12
Ham's Prairie, Callaway, Mo	24	Harbour Creek, Erie, Pa	120
Hanby's Mills, Walker, Ala	12	Harbour's Mills, Putnam, W. Va	12
Hancock, Harrison, Ind	9	Hardeeville, Beaufort, S. C	12
Hancock, Hancock, Me	88	Hardenburgh, Ulster, N. Y	6
Hancock,* Washington, Md	440	Hardin, (c. h.,) Calhoun, Ill	93
Hancock, Berkshire, Mass	120	Hardin, Clayton, Iowa	74
Hancock, Houghton, Mich	1,500	Hardin, Ray, Mo	27
Hancock, Pulaski, Mo	12	Hardin, Shelby, Ohio	62
Hancock, Hillsborough, N. H	220	Hardin, (c. h.,) Hardin, Tex	21
Hancock,* Delaware, N. Y	510	Hardin City, Hardin, Iowa	21
Hancock, Addison, Vt	93	Hardinsburgh, Washington, Ind	54
Hancock, Waushara, Wis	73	Hardinsburgh, (c. h.,) Breckinridge, Ky	200
Hancock's Bridge, Salem, N. J	38	Hardinsville, Crawford, Ill	21
Handsborough, Harrison, Miss	50	Hardison's Mills, Maury, Tenn	12
Handy, Fayette, Ala	12	Hardwick, Worcester, Mass	170
Handy, Fulton, Ohio	14	Hardwick, Warren, N. J	8
Hanerville, Dane, Wis	28	Hardwick, Caledonia, Vt	200
Hanesville, Kent, Md	72	Hardwicksville, Nelson, Va	22
Haneyville, Lycoming, Pa	8	Hardy, Dallas, Ala	12
Hanford's Landing, Monroe, N. Y	35	Hardy Station, Grenada, Miss	12
Hanging Rock, Lawrence, Ohio	150	Hardyville, Mohave, Ariz	180
Hanging Rock, Hampshire, W. Va	12	Hardyville, Hart, Ky	25
Hankins, Sullivan, N. Y	130	Hare's Corner, New Castle, Del	24
Hanley, Ottawa, Mich	12	Harewood, Baltimore, Md	12
Hanlin Station, Washington, Pa	10	Harford, Cortland, N. Y	72
Hanly, Jessamine, Ky	37	Harford, Susquehanna, Pa	300
Hannahatchee, Stewart, Ga	10	Harford Furnace, Harford, Md	73
Hannahsville, Tucker, W. Va	13	Harford Mills, Cortland, N. Y	54
Hanna Station, La Porte, Ind	110	Hark, Shelby, Ill	8
Hannersville, Davidson, N. C	4	Harker's Corners, Peoria, Ill	16
Hannibal,* Marion, Mo	3,400	Harlan, Allen, Ind	95
Hannibal, Oswego, N. Y	340	Harlan, (c. h.,) Shelby, Iowa	68
Hannibal, Monroe, Ohio	150	Harlan, (c. h.,) Harlan, Ky	16
Hannibal Centre, Oswego, N. Y	51	Harlem, Winnebago, Ill	31
Hanover, Coosa, Ala	4	Harlem, Clay, Mo	190
Hanover, New London, Conn	62	Harlem, Delaware, Ohio	31
Hanover, Jo Daviess, Ill	190	Harlem Spring, Carroll, Ohio	89
Hanover, Jefferson, Ind	400	Harlemville, Columbia, N. Y	35
Hanover, Washington, Kans	12	Harlensburgh, Lawrence, Pa	84
Hanover, Oxford, Me	64	Harleysville, Montgomery, Pa	57
Hanover, Howard, Md	23	Harlingen, Somerset, N. J	74
Hanover, Plymouth, Mass	290	Harmar, Washington, Ohio	590
Hanover, Jackson, Mich	47		

* Money-order office.

HAR   HAR

Harmarville, Allegheny, Pa	$71	Harris Lot, Charles, Md	$12
Harmon, Bracken, Ky	12	Harrison, (c. h.,) Boone, Ark	33
Harmonsburgh, Crawford, Pa	84	Harrison, Winnebago, Ill	56
Harmony, McHenry, Ill	30	Harrison, Delaware, Ind	12
Harmony, Clay, Ind	300	Harrison, Cumberland, Me	230
Harmony, Taylor, Iowa	11	Harrison, Dorchester, Md	24
Harmony, Owen, Ky	11	Harrison, Monongalia, Minn	96
Harmony, Somerset, Me	120	Harrison, Madison, Mont	12
Harmony, Fillmore, Minn	12	Harrison, Westchester, N. Y	60
Harmony, Washington, Mo	27	Harrison,* Hamilton, Ohio	650
Harmony, Warren, N. J	20	Harrison, (c. h.,) Hamilton, Tenn	81
Harmony, Chautauqua, N. Y	170	Harrisonburgh,(c. h.,) Catahoula, La.	170
Harmony, Clark, Ohio	20	Harrisonburgh,* (c. h.,) Rockingham,	
Harmony, Butler, Pa	130	Va	1,900
Harmony, Providence, R. I	21	Harrison City, Westmoreland, Pa	49
Harmony, York, S. C	3	Harrison Mills, Scioto, Ohio	8
Harmony, Halifax, Va	21	Harrison's Creek, Bladen, N. C	12
Harmony, Mason, W. Va	12	Harrison's Mills, Crawford, Mo	10
Harmony, Vernon, Wis	21	Harrison Square, Norfolk, Mass	650
Harmony Centre, Susquehanna, Pa.	50	Harrison's Store, Shelby, Tenn	12
Harmony Grove, Jackson, Ga	67	Harrison Station, Tallahatchie, Miss	160
Harmony Hill, Rusk, Tex	77	Harrison Valley, Potter, Pa	37
Harmony Village, Middlesex, Va	12	Harrisonville, Monroe, Ill	32
Harmsburgh, Armstrong, Pa	12	Harrisonville, Shelby, Ky	16
Harnedsville, Somerset, Pa	23	Harrisonville, Baltimore. Md	16
Harnett C. H., Harnett, N. C	14	Harrisonville,* (c. h.,) Cass, Mo	1,000
Harney, Carroll, Md	27	Harrisonville, Gloucester, N. J	93
Harold, Montgomery, Ark	12	Harrisonville, Meigs, Ohio	83
Harp, De Witt, Ill	12	Harrisonville, Fulton, Pa	55
Harper, Logan, Ohio	38	Harris Station, Limestone, Ala	12
Harper's Ferry, Allamakee, Iowa	43	Harris Station, Obion, Tenn	12
Harper's Ferry, Henry, Ky	12	Harristown, Macon, Ill	230
Harper's Ferry,* Jefferson, W. Va	760	Harristown, Washington, Ind	53
Harpersfield, Delaware, N. Y	100	Harrisville, Randolph, Ind	15
Harpersfield, Ashtabula, Ohio	62	Harrisville, (c. h.,) Alcona, Mich	270
Harper's Mills, Pendleton, W. Va	8	Harrisville, Cheshire, N. H	210
Harpersville, Broome, N. Y	350	Harrisville, Lewis, N.Y	110
Harpswell Centre, Cumberland, Me.	37	Harrisville, Harrison, Ohio	150
Harreldsville, Butler, Ky	10	Harrisville, Butler, Pa	170
Harrell, Decatur, Ga	12	Harrisville, Bell, Tex	45
Harrell's Store, New Hanover, N. C.	15	Harrisville, (c. h.,) Ritchie, W. Va	120
Harrellsville, Hertford, N. C	78	Harrisville, Marquette, Wis	57
Harriettsville, Noble, Ohio	43	Harrmann's Station, Dearborn, Ind.	12
Harrington, Kent, Del	140	Harrodsburgh, Monroe, Ind	130
Harrington, Washington, Me	200	Harrodsburgh,* (c. h.,) Mercer, Ky	300
Harrington, Harnett, N. C	10	Harshasville, Adams, Ohio	38
Harris, Louisa, Va	18	Harshaville, Beaver, Pa	14
Harrisburgh, (c. h.,) Poinsett, Ark	86	Harshmansville, Montgomery, Ohio	45
Harrisburgh, Alameda, Cal	13	Hart,* (c. h.,) Oceana, Mich	360
Harrisburgh,* (c. h.,) Saline, Ill	270	Hartfield, Chautauqua, N. Y	50
Harrisburgh, Fayette, Ind	25	HARTFORD,* (c. h.,) Hartford, Conn.	4,000
Harrisburgh, Lyon, Kans	13	Hartford, Saline, Ill	3
Harrisburgh, Deer Lodge, Mont	12	Hartford, Ohio, Ind	13
Harrisburgh, Lewis, N. Y	16	Hartford, Warren, Iowa	79
Harrisburgh, Franklin, Ohio	69	Hartford, Lyon, Kans	76
Harrisburgh, Linn, Oreg	150	Hartford,* (c. h.,) Ohio, Ky	320
HARRISBURGH,* (c. h.,) Dauphin, Pa	3,600	Hartford, Oxford, Me	49
Harrisburgh, Harris, Tex	170	Hartford, Van Buren, Mich	210
Harrisburgh, Washington, Utah	28	Hartford, Todd, Minn	12
Harris Creek, Kent, Mich	26	Hartford, Putnam, Mo	17
Harris Creek, Amherst, Va	12	Hartford, Burlington, N. J	37
Harris Depot, Cabarrus, N. C	40	Hartford, Washington, N. Y	190
Harris' Ferry, Wood, W. Va	24	Hartford, Trumbull, Ohio	98
Harris Grove, Jefferson, Ill	16	Hartford, Windsor, Vt	490
Harris Grove, Harrison, Iowa	24	Hartford, Washington, Wis	500
Harris Hill, Erie, N. Y	20	Hartford City,* (c.h.,) Blackford, Ind	440

* Money-order office.

HAS   HAY

Hartford City, Mason, W. Va......	$100
Harthegig, Mercer, Pa......	40
Hartland, Hartford, Conn	72
Hartland, Worth, Iowa.............	21
Hartland, Somerset, Me....	320
Hartland, Livingston, Mich........	230
Hartland, Freeborn, Minn	15
Hartland, Niagara, N.Y......	95
Hartland, Huron, Ohio.............	12
Hartland, Windsor, Vt....	250
Hartland, Waukesha, Wis..........	260
Hartland Four Corners, Windsor,Vt	70
Hartleton, Union, Pa...............	120
Hartley, York, Pa.................	12
Hartleyville, Athens, Ohio	16
Hart Lot, Onondaga, N.Y.........	140
Hartmonsville, Mineral, W. Va	10
Hart's Corners, Westchester, N.Y..	87
Hart's Falls, Rensselaer, N.Y.....	520
Hart's Grove, Ashtabula, Ohio.....	75
Hartshorn, Alamance, N. C.........	3
Hartstown, Crawford, Pa..........	170
Hartsville, Bartholomew, Ind......	190
Hartsville, Berkshire, Mass........	120
Hartsville, Bucks, Pa.............	89
Hartsville, Darlington, S.C.......	24
Hartsville, Sumner, Tenn.........	250
Hartville, (c. h.,) Wright, Mo	60
Hartville, Stark, Ohio.............	29
Hartwell, (c. h.,) Hart, Ga........	71
Hartwell, Hamilton, Ohio	12
Hartwellville, Shiawassee, Mich...	64
Hartwick, Otsego, N.Y............	86
Hartwick Seminary, Otsego, N.Y..	79
Hartwood, Stafford, Va............	23
Harvard,* McHenry, Ill............	910
Harvard, Worcester, Mass.........	310
Harvard, Delaware, N.Y.........	60
Harvey, Marquette, Mich..........	29
Harvey, Dane, Wis...............	70
Harvey's, Greene, Pa.............	58
Harveysburgh, Fountain, Ind......	37
Harveysburgh, Warren, Ohio.....	260
Harvey's Mills, Jefferson, Iowa....	15
Harvey's Store, Charlotte, Va.....	23
Harveyville, Wabaunsee, Kans	12
Harveyville, Luzerne, Pa..........	64
Harwich, Barnstable, Mass........	370
Harwich Port, Barnstable, Mass. ..	240
Harwinton, Litchfield, Conn.......	180
Harwood, Muskegon, Mich........	30
Hasbrouck, Sullivan, N.Y........	13
Haskell, La Porte, Ind	18
Haskell Flats, Cattaraugus, N.Y...	21
Haskins, Wood, Ohio.............	160
Haskinsville, Greene, Ky........	17
Haskinville, Steuben, N.Y	36
Hasler, Lapeer, Mich.............	25
Hassan, Hennepin, Minn....	6
Hassan, Hancock, Ohio...........	67
Hastings, (c. h.,) Barry, Mich......	1,200
Hastings, (c. h.,) Dakota, Minn....	2,000
Hastings, Oswego, N.Y..........	82
Hastings, Richland, Ohio..........	16
Hastings Centre, Oswego, N.Y....	35
Hastings Landing, Calhoun, *Ill.*...	12

Hastings-upon-Hudson, Westchester, N.Y..........	$400
Hatborough, Montgomery, Pa....	160
Hatchechubbee, Russell, Ala.......	31
Hatcher's Station, Quitman, Ga....	21
Hatch Hollow, Erie, Pa...........	16
Hatchsophka, Elmore, Ala.........	12
Hatchville, Barnstable, Mass	55
Hat Creek, Campbell, Va.........	8
Hatfield, Hampshire, Mass.........	290
Hatfield, Montgomery, Pa	99
Haubstadt, Gibson, Ind.......:....	97
Haught's Store, Dallas, Tex	8
Hauppauge, Suffolk, N.Y.........	49
Hausertown, Owen, Ind...........	48
Havana, (c. h.,) Mason, Ill........	1,100
Havana, Gentry, Mo....	19
Havana,* Schuyler, N.Y........	800
Havana, Huron, Ohio	170
Havanna, Hale, Ala...............	12
Havanna, Steele, Minn...........	12
Havelock, Cook, Ill	65
Havelock, Washington, Pa.•...... ..	83
Haverford, Delaware, Pa	38
Haverhill,* Essex, Mass...........	3,100
Haverhill, (c. h.,) Grafton, N.H...	520
Haverhill, Scioto, Ohio...........	43
Haverstraw, Rockland, N.Y.......	1,000
Havilah, (c. h.,) Kern, Cal........	230
Haviland Hollow, Putnam, N.Y...	21
Havilandsville, Harrison, Ky......	27
Havre de Grace,* Harford, Md.....	730
Haw Branch, Onslow, N.C....	5
Haw Creek, Benton, Mo..........	12
Hawes' Cross Roads, Washington, Tenn.....................	14
Hawesville, (c. h.,) Hancock, Ky	160
Hawk Creek, Chippewa, Minn.....	26
Hawk Eye, Fayette, Iowa.........	12
Hawkinstown, Shenandoah, Va....	12
Hawkinsville, (c. h.,) Pulaski, Ga....	560
Hawkinsville, Oneida, N.Y.......	120
Hawkinsville, Sussex, Va.........	12
Hawk Point, Lincoln, Mo.........	17
Hawk's Nest, Fayette, W.Va......	12
Hawley, Franklin, Mass...........	50
Hawley, Wayne, Pa..............	660
Hawley's Store, Sampson, N.C....	8
Hawleysville, Page, Iowa......	85
Hawleyton, Broome, N.Y.......	22
Hawleyville, Fairfield, Conn......	120
Haw Ridge, Dale, Ala...........	37
Haw River, Alamance, N.C.......	83
Haw's Ford, Floyd, Ky...........	12
Hawthorne, Passaic, N.J........	8
Hayden Row, Middlesex, Mass....	62
Haydenville, Hampshire, Mass....	520
Haydenville, Hocking, Ohio......	12
Hayes' Store, Madison, Ala.......	8
Hayes' Store, Gloucester, Va.....	12
Hayesville, Keokuk, Iowa........	190
Hayesville,* Ashland, Ohio.......	340
Hayesville, (c. h.,) Clay, N.C....	12
Hayesville, Chester, Pa..........	71
Hayesville, Greene, Tenn.........	12
Hayfield, Crawford, Pa...........	68

Hayfield, Frederick, Va	$11	Hebron, McHenry, Ill	$130
Hay Market, Prince William, Va..	85	Hebron, Porter, Ind	220
Hay Meadow, Wilkes, N. C	10	Hebron, Adair, Iowa	25
Haymond, Franklin, Ind	25	Hebron, Boone, Ky	17
Haynerville, Rensselaer, N. Y	6	Hebron, Oxford, Me	58
Haynes, Union, Tenn	12	Hebron, Nicollet, Minn	15
Haynesville, Claiborne, La	12	Hebron, Jefferson, Nebr	12
Haynesville, Aroostook, Me	10	Hebron, Grafton, N. H	88
Hayneville, (c. h.,) Lowndes, Ala	220	Hebron, Washington, N. Y	15
Haynie, Mills, Iowa	20	Hebron, Licking, Ohio	110
Hays City, (c. h.,) Ellis, Kans	1,300	Hebron, Potter, Pa	19
Hays' Store, Wake, N. C	6	Hebron, Spartanburgh, S. C	3
Haystack, Surry, N. C	10	Hebron, Pleasants, W. Va	31
Haysville, Dubois, Ind	41	Hebron, Jefferson, Wis	93
Hayward, Freeborn, Minn	10	Hebronville, Bristol, Mass	110
Haywood, Alameda, Cal	80	Hecker, Monroe, Ill	87
Haywood, Chatham, N. C	33	Hecktown, Northampton, Pa	31
Hazard, Cherokee, Iowa	12	Hecla, Whitley, Ind	31
Hazard, (c. h.,) Perry, Ky	5	Hecla Works, Oneida, N. Y	28
Hazardville, Hartford, Conn	180	Hector, Jay, Ind	4
Hazelettville, Woodson, Kans	12	Hector, Schuyler, N. Y	41
Hazel Green, Madison, Tenn	12	Hedgesville, Steuben, N. Y	17
Hazel Green, Grant, Wis	310	Hedgesville, Berkeley, W. Va	160
Hazelton, Buchanan, Iowa	18	Hedwig's Hill, Mason, Tex	12
Hazelton, Shiawassee, Mich	12	Heffren, Washington, Ind	16
Hazelwood, Rice, Minn	15	Hegarty's X Roads, Clearfield, Pa.	18
Hazen, Cass, Mo	12	Hegins, Schuylkill, Pa	20
Hazle Barrens, Barry, Mo	12	Heidlersburgh, Adams, Pa	29
Hazle Dell, Cumberland, Ill	63	Heistersburgh, Fayette, Pa	12
Hazle Green, Delaware, Iowa	30	*Helena,* (c. h.,) Phillips, Ark	1,700
Hazle Green, Wolfe, Ky	6	Helena, Lake, Colo	17
Hazle Green, Shiawassee, Mich	12	Helena, Tama, Iowa	18
Hazle Green, Laclede, Mo	22	Helena, Mason, Ky	45
Hazlehurst, Appling, Ga	12	Helena, Scott, Minn	20
Hazlehurst,* Copiah, Miss	170	HELENA,* (c. h.,) Lewis & Clarke,	
Hazle Patch, Laurel, Ky	9	Mont	4,000
Hazleton, Gibson, Ind	260	Helena, Johnson, Nebr	21
Hazleton,* Luzerne, Pa	1,600	Helena, St. Lawrence, N. Y	63
Hazlettville, Kent, Del	18	*Helena, (c. h.,) Karnes, Tex*	230
Hazlewood, Ballard, Ky	12	Helena Station, Iowa, Wis	62
Hazlewood, Webster, Mo	12	Helen Furnace, Clarion, Pa	20
Hazlewood, Chester, S. C	12	Helenville, Jefferson, Wis	40
Hazlitt, Rock Island, Ill	17	Helham, Overton, Tenn	12
Headland, Saunders, Nebr	11	Hellam, York, Pa	33
Head of Barren, Claiborne, Tenn..	6	Hellen, Elk, Pa	33
Head of Elm, Montague, Tex	12	Heller's Corners, Allen, Ind	16
Head Quarters, Nicholas, Ky	20	Hellertown, Northampton, Pa	280
Headsville, Mineral, W. Va	12	Helmick, Coshocton, Ohio	11
Head Waters, Highland, Va	5	Helton, Ashe, N. C	6
Healdsburgh,* Sonoma, Cal	560	Heltonville, Lawrence, Ind	27
Healdville, Rutland, Vt	88	Helvetia, Waupaca, Wis	12
Healing Springs, Bath, Va	30	Hematite, Jefferson, Mo	99
Hearne, Robertson, Tex	12	Hemlock, Cambria, Pa	63
Heart Prairie, Walworth, Wis	35	Hemlock City, Saginaw, Mich	18
Heartwellville, Bennington, Vt	90	Hemlock Grove, Meigs, Ohio	8
Heaslyville, Marshall, Kans	12	Hemlock Hollow, Wayne, Pa	12
Heath, Franklin, Mass	76	Hemlock Lake, Livingston, N. Y..	200
Heathsville, Halifax, N. C	6	Hempfield, Lancaster, Pa	78
Heathsville, (c. h.,) Northumberland,		*Hemphill, (c. h.,) Sabine, Tex*	12
Va	76	Hemp's Creek, Catahoula, La	5
Hebbardsville, Henderson, Ky	45	Hempstead, Calloway, Mo	6
Hebbardsville, Athens, Ohio	52	Hempstead,* Queens, N. Y	690
Hebbertsburgh, Cumberland, Tenn.	8	Hempstead, Austin, Tex	680
Heber, (c. h.,) Wasatch, Utah	19	Henderson, Pike, Ala	·12
Hebron, Tolland, Conn	180	Henderson, Knox, Ill	150
Hebron, Washington, Ga	12	Henderson, Lucas, Iowa	50

* Money-order office.

HER

HIC

Henderson, (c. h.,) Henderson, Ky.	$1,600
Henderson, Caroline, Md	24
Henderson, (c. h.,) Sibley, Minn	560
Henderson, Webster, Mo	10
Henderson, Jefferson, N. Y	210
Henderson, Granville, N. C	620
Henderson, Mercer, Pa	41
Henderson, (c. h.,) Rusk, Tex	430
Henderson's Mills, Marshall, Ky	20
Henderson's Springs, Sevier, Tenn	12
Henderson Station, Madison, Tenn	180
Hendersonville, (c. h.,) Henderson, N. C	160
Hendersonville, Sumner, Tenn	71
Hendricks, Otoe, Nebr	16
Hendricksburgh, Luzerne, Pa	430
Hendrick's Store, Bedford, Va	10
Hendrysburgh, Belmont, Ohio	110
Henley, Siskiyou, Cal	57
Hennepin, (c. h.,) Putnam, Ill	500
Henniker, Merrimack, N. H	310
Henning's Mills, Clermont, Ohio	34
Henrietta, Jackson, Mich	32
Henrietta, Monroe, N. Y	110
Henrietta, Lorain, Ohio	31
Henrietta, Richland, Wis	2
Henry,* Marshall, Ill	1,400
Henry, Ray, Mo	12
Henry, Sussex, Va	20
Henry Clay Factory, New Castle, Del	250
Henry's × Roads, Sevier, Tenn	23
Henry's Fork, Roane, W. Va	12
Henry Station, Henry, Tenn	110
Henrysville, Marshall, Ala	7
Henrysville, Logan, Ky	36
Henrysville, Monroe, Pa	39
Henryville, Clarke, Ind	150
Henryville, Lawrence, Tenn	9
Hensonville, Greene, N, Y	23
Hepler, Schuylkill, Pa	7
Hepton, Kosciusko, Ind	12
Herbert, Kemper, Miss	5
Hereford, Baltimore, Md	53
Hereford, Berks, Pa	64
Herkimer, (c. h.,) Herkimer, N. Y.	1,000
Hermaan, Ripley, Ind	13
Herman, Dodge, Wis	22
Hermann, (c. h.,) Gasconade, Mo	750
Hermansville, Coos, Oreg	12
Hermitage, Mendocino, Cal	4
Hermitage, Point Coupee, La	96
Hermitage, (c. h.,) Hickory, Mo	150
Hermitage, Wyoming, N. Y	83
Hermitage, Mercer, Pa	320
Hermitage, Augusta, Va	20
Hermon, Knox, Ill	71
Hermon, Penobscot, Me	40
Hermon,* St. Lawrence, N. Y	410
Hermon Pond, Penobscot, Me	83
Hermosilla, Pueblo, Colo	12
Hernando, (c. h.,) De Soto, Miss	520
Herndon, Greene, Ark	12
Herndon, Burke, Ga	50
Herndon, Montgomery, Ill	20
Herndon, Northumberland, Pa	65

Herndon, Fairfax, Va	$110
Herrick, Bradford, Pa	37
Herrick Centre, Susquehanna, Pa	77
Herrickville, Bradford, Pa	57
Herriman, Salt Lake, Utah	10
Herring, Allen, Ohio	150
Herrington's Corners, Chemung, N. Y	5
Herrin's Prairie, Williamson, Ill	21
Herriottsville, Washington, Pa	19
Hersey, (c. h.,) Osceola, Mich	270
Herseyville, Monroe, Wis	18
Hersman's, Brown, Ill	58
Hertford, (c. h.,) Perquimons, N. C	190
Herzhorn, Renville, Minn	10
Heshbou, Indiana, Pa	17
Hesper, Winneshiek, Iowa	210
Hesper, Douglas, Kans	12
Hesperia, Oceana, Mich	56
Hesperian, Webster, Iowa	46
Hess Road, Niagara, N. Y	39
Hessville, Harrison, W. Va	6
Hester, Marion, Mo	16
Hester Mills, Meigs, Tenn	23
Hester's Store, Person, N. C	12
Hetricks, York, Pa	25
Hetslersville, Darke, Ohio	12
Heuvelton, St. Lawrence, N. Y	210
Hewlett's, Hanover, Va	88
Heyworth, McLean, Ill	400
Hiawassee, (c. h.,) Towns, Ga	12
Hiawatha, (c. h.,) Brown, Kans	470
Hibbetts, Carroll, Ohio	14
Hibbsville, Appanoose, Iowa	18
Hibernia, Duval, Fla	38
Hibernia, Morris, N. J	340
Hibernia, Dutchess, N. Y	22
Hickman, (c. h.,) Fulton, Ky	860
Hickman Mills, Jackson, Mo	97
Hickman's, Tuscaloosa, Ala	9
Hickory, Benton, Ark	18
Hickory, Lake, Ill	10
Hickory, Van Buren, Iowa	160
Hickory, Newton, Miss	210
Hickory, Lucas, Ohio	8
Hickory, Washington, Pa	110
Hickory Barren, Greene, Mo	23
Hickory Branch, Posey, Ind	24
Hickory Corners, Barry, Mich	160
Hickory Corners, Niagara, N. Y	9
Hickory Corners, Northumberland, Pa	25
Hickory Creek, Fayette, Ill	15
Hickory Creek, Audrian, Mo	9
Hickory Flat, Chambers, Ala	13
Hickory Flat, Tippah, Miss	24
Hickory Fork, Gloucester, Va	83
Hickory Grove, Crawford, Ga	14
Hickory Grove, Massac, Ill	1
Hickory Grove, Graves, Ky	22
Hickory Grove, York, S. C	11
Hickory Hill, Marion, Ill	4
Hickory Hill, Cole, Mo	44
Hickory Hill, Chester, Pa	30
Hickory Hill, Davis, Tex	31
Hickory Plains, Prairie, Ark	52

* Money-order office.

HIG   HIL

Hickory Ridge, Hancock, Ill	$39	Highland Mills, Orange, N. Y	$85
Hickory Run, Carbon, Pa	77	Highland Park, Lake, Ill	220
Hickory Springs, Texas, Mo	12	Highland Station, Galveston, Tex	12
Hickory Tavern, Harford, Md	67	Highland Town, Grundy, Ill	8
Hickory Tavern, Catawba, N. C	160	Highlandville, Winneshiek, Iowa	76
Hickory Town, Montgomery, Pa	14	High Point, Walker, Ga	12
Hickory Valley, Hardeman, Tenn	26	High Point, Mercer, Ill	20
Hickaford, (c. h.,) Greenville, Va	260	High Point, Decatur, Iowa	20
Hicks' Mills, De Kalb, Ill	23	High Point, Moniteau, Mo	110
Hicks Station, Prairie, Ark	62	High Point, Guilford, N. C	420
Hicksville, Sacramento, Cal	68	High Ridge, Fairfield, Conn	53
Hicksville, Queens, N. Y	150	High Ridge, Jefferson, Mo	17
Hicksville, Defiance, Ohio	130	High Shoals, Gaston, N. C	23
Hick's Wharf, Matthews, Va	12	High Spire, Dauphin, Pa	88
Hico, Benton, Ark	12	Hightown, Highland, Va	33
Hico, Callaway, Ky	7	Hightstown,* Mercer, N. J	920
Hidalgo, Jasper, Ill	11	High View, Frederick, Va	13
Hiester's Mill, Berks, Pa	20	Higaville, Lancaster, Pa	41
Higganum, Middlesex, Conn	84	Hika, Manitowoc, Wis	100
Higginsport, Jackson, Iowa	4	*Hiko, (c. h.,) Lincoln, Nev*	130
Higginsport, Brown, Ohio	170	Hill, Grafton, N. H	230
Higginsville, Vermilion, Ill	90	Hill, Mercer, Pa	86
Higginsville, La Fayette, Mo	12	Hillabee, Clay, Ala	11
Higginsville, Oneida, N. Y	160	Hill Church, Berks, Pa	12
High Blue, Cass, Mo	18	Hillegass, Montgomery, Pa	12
High Bluff, Dale, Ala	12	Hill Grove, Meade, Ky	14
High Bridge, Hunterdon, N. J	130	Hill Grove, Darke, Ohio	69
High Creek, Fremont, Iowa	12	Hill Grove, Pittsylvania, Va	45
High Falls, Geneva, Ala	12	Hillham, Dubois, Ind	16
High Falls, Ulster, N. Y	120	Hillhouse, Lake, Ohio	18
High Forest, Olmsted, Minn	180	Hillians' Store, Marshall, Ala	12
Highgate, Franklin, Vt	160	Hilliard's, Allegan, Mich	12
Highgate Centre, Franklin, Vt	110	Hilliards, Franklin, Ohio	150
Highgate Springs, Franklin, Vt	92	Hilliardston, Nash, N. C	12
High Grove, Nelson, Ky	38	Hills, Owen, Ky	4
High Grove, Maries, Mo	8	Hills, Washington, Ohio	11
High Health, Johnson, Tenn	6	Hillsborough, Shelby, Ala	31
High Hill, Leake, Miss	8	Hillsborough, Union, Ark	81
High Hill, Montgomery, Mo	240	*Hillsborough,* (c. h.,) Montgomery, Ill	1,100
High Hill, Muskingum, Ohio	42	Hillsborough, Fountain, Ind	70
High Hill, Fayette, Tex	160	Hillsborough, Henry, Iowa	100
High Lake, Emmett, Iowa	12	Hillsborough, Fleming, Ky	100
High Lake, Wayne, Pa	22	Hillsborough, Caroline, Md	140
Highland,* Madison, Ill	900	*Hillsborough, (c. h.,) Scott, Miss*	81
Highland, Clayton, Iowa	38	*Hillsborough, (c. h.,) Jefferson, Mo*	290
Highland, Doniphan, Kans	300	Hillsborough, Hillsborough, N. H	360
Highland, Lincoln, Ky	12	*Hillsborough,* (c. h.,) Orange, N. C	670
Highland, Somerset, Me	8	*Hillsborough,* (c. h.,) Highland, Ohio	1,300
Highland, Oakland, Mich	54	*Hillsborough, (c. h.,) Washington,* Oreg	82
Highland, Fillmore, Minn	100	Hillsborough, Coffee, Tenn	12
Highland, Tishemingo, Miss	11	*Hillsborough, (c. h.,) Hill, Tex*	170
Highland, Moniteau, Mo	12	Hillsborough, Loudoun, Va	96
Highland, Richardson, Nebr	12	Hillsborough,* Vernon, Wis	96
Highland, Ulster, N. Y	380	Hillsborough Bridge, Hillsborough, N. H	510
Highland, Highland, Ohio	170	Hillsborough Centre, Hillsborough, N. H	61
Highland, Clackamas, Oreg	12	Hillsdale, Mills, Iowa	12
Highland, Bradford, Pa	43	Hillsdale, Miami, Kans	160
Highland, Jackson, Tenn	12	*Hillsdale,* (c. h.,) Hillsdale, Mich	2,400
Highland, Collin, Tex	44	Hillsdale, Nemaha, Nebr	12
Highland, Ritchie, W. Va	6	Hillsdale, Bergen, N. J	12
Highland, Iowa, Wis	170	Hillsdale, Columbia, N. Y	360
Highland Centre, Wapello, Iowa	12	Hillsdale, Guilford, N. C	13
Highland Falls, Orange, N. Y	460		
Highland Grove, Jones, Iowa	18		
Highland Grove, Greenville, S. C	5		
Highland Home, Laurens, S. C	6		

* Money-order office.

HOD

Hillsdale, Indiana, Pa	$41
Hill's Ferry, Stanislaus, Cal	12
Hill's Fork, Adams, Ohio	19
Hill's Grove, Sullivan, Pa	26
Hillside, Westmoreland, Pa	58
Hill's Point, Dorchester, Md	19
Hill Spring, Morris, Kans	4
Hill Spring, Henry, Ky	60
Hill's Station, Rock Island, Ill	12
Hill's Store, Randolph, N. C	7
Hill's View, Westmoreland, Pa	6
Hillsville, Lawrence, Pa	47
Hillsville, (c. h.,) Carroll, Va	190
Hilltown, Bucks, Pa	33
Hill Valley, Huntingdon, Pa	36
Hilton, Tazewell, Ill	42
Hilton, Monroe, Ky	8
Himrod's, Yates, N. Y	120
Hinckley, Pine, Minn	12
Hinckley, Medina, Ohio	53
Hindsburgh, Orleans, N. Y	22
Hindsville, Madison, Ark	12
Hiner's Run, Clinton, Pa	110
Hinesberg, Fond du Lac, Wis	64
Hinesburgh, Chittenden, Vt	210
Hine's Mills, Ohio, Ky	12
Hinesville, (c. h.,) Liberty, Ga	9
Hingham, Plymouth, Mass	700
Hingham, Sheboygan, Wis	97
Hingham Centre, Plymouth, Mass	230
Hinkleton, Lancaster, Pa	49
Hinkleville, Ballard, Ky	12
Hinmansville, Oswego, N. Y	60
Hinnaut's Mills, Johnston, N. C	12
Hinsdale, Du Page, Ill	92
Hinsdale, Berkshire, Mass	570
Hinsdale,* Cheshire, N. Y	1,700
Hinsdale, Cattaraugus, N. Y	330
Hinton, Plymouth, Iowa	12
Hiram, Oxford, Me	100
Hiram, Portage, Ohio	330
Hiramsburgh, Noble, Ohio	25
Hiseville, Barren, Ky	47
Hitchcock's Station, Washington, Ind	36
Hitesville, Union, Ky	16
Hitt, Scotland, Mo	12
Hixton, Jackson, Wis	19
Hoag's Corner, Rensselaer, N. Y	29
Hobart, Lake, Ind	180
Hobart, Delaware, N, Y	280
Hobart's Mills, Sheboygan, Wis	12
Hobbie, Luzerne, Pa	16
Hobbieville, Greene, Ind	22
Hobbs' Ferry, Giles, Va	12
Hobbs' Station, Jefferson, Ky	240
Hobbysville, Spartanburg, S. C	2
Hoboken,* Hudson, N. J	2,300
Hochheim, De Witt, Tex	12
Hockanum, Hartford, Conn	78
Hockessin, New Castle, Del	49
Hocking, Athens, Ohio	12
Hockingport, Athens, Ohio	66
Hockley, Harris, Tex	170
Hockley, Vernon, Wis	8
Hodgdon, Aroostook, *Me*	64

HOL

Hodgdon's Mills, Lincoln, Me	$150
Hodgensville, (c. h.,) La Rue, Ky	150
Hodges, Abbeville, S. C	130
Hodge's Mill, Kendall, Tex	6
Hodge's Prairie, Sebastian, Ark	12
Hoffman's Ferry, Schenectady, N. Y.	39
Hogansburgh, Franklin, N. Y	120
Hogansville, Troup, Ga	330
Hogarth's Landing, St. John's, Fla	7
Hog Branch, St. Helena, La	5
Hog Creek, Allen, Ohio	8
Hoge, Leavenworth, Kans	43
Hogestown, Cumberland, Pa	78
Hog Island, Surry, Va	12
Hog Mountain, Hall, Ga	10
Hohokus, Bergen, N. J	200
Hokah, Houston, Minn	190
Hokendauqua, Lehigh, Pa	280
Holaday's, Adair, Iowa	15
Holbrook, Suffolk, N. Y	78
Holbrook, Greene, Pa	12
Holbrook, Ritchie, W. Va	5
Holcombe, Burke, Ga	52
Holcomb's Rock, Bedford, Va	21
Holden, Penobscot, Me	37
Holden, Worcester, Mass	330
Holden, Goodhue, Minn	120
Holden,* Johnson, Mo	1,300
Holden, Millard, Utah	22
Holiday's Cove, Hancock, W. Va	140
Holland, Shelby, Ill	6
Holland, Dubois, Ind	51
Holland, Hampden, Mass	21
Holland,* Ottawa, Mich	790
Holland, Hunterdon, N. J	20
Holland, Erie, N. Y	370
Holland, Lucas, Ohio	90
Holland, Bucks, Pa	12
Holland, Orleans, Vt	25
Holland, Brown, Wis	16
Holland Patent, Oneida, N. Y	250
Holland's Store, Anderson, S. C	12
Hollandville, Kent, Del	18
Holley, Orleans, N. Y	520
Holliday, Macoupin, Ill	1
Hollidaysburgh, (c. h.,) Blair, Pa	1,800
Holling, Douglass, Kans	12
Hollingsworth, Banks, Ga	11
Hollis, York, Me	33
Hollis, Hillsborough, N. H	230
Hollis Centre, York, Me	45
Hollister, Monterey, Cal	12
Hollisterville, Wayne, Pa	120
Holliston,* Middlesex, Mass	1,000
Holloway's Store, Walker, Tex	12
Hollowayville, Bureau, Ill	37
Hollow Rock, Carroll, Tenn	10
Hollow Square, Hale, Ala	43
Hollowtown, Highland, Ohio	13
Hollowville, Columbia, N. Y	61
Holly,* Oakland, Mich	710
Holly Grove, Walker, Ala	10
Holly Grove, Madison, N. C	9
Holly Hill, Charleston, S. C	27
Holly Meadows, Tucker, W. Va	4
Holly River, Braxton, W. Va	3

* Money-order office.

HON

Holly Springs, Dallas, Ark	$53
Holly Springs, (c. h.,) Marshall, Miss	1,600
Hollyville, Sussex, Del	5
Hollywood, Clark, Ark	12
Hollywood, St. Mary's, Md	12
Holman, Dearborn, Ind	15
Holman Station, Scott, Ind	12
Holmdel, Monmouth, N. J	110
Holmes, Boone, Ind	12
Holmes City, Douglas, Minn	12
Holmes' Hole, Dukes, Mass	690
Holmes' Mills, Jefferson, Ohio	42
Holmesville, (c. h.,) Appling, Ga	39
Holmesville, Avoyelles, La	20
Holmesville, Holmes, Ohio	90
Holstein, Warren, Mo	26
Holston, Washington, Va	1
Holston Furnace, Sullivan, Tenn	8
Holston Valley, Sullivan, Tenn	12
Holt, Taylor, Iowa	16
Holt, Ingham, Mich	80
Holt, Clay, Mo	12
Holt, Wood, Ohio	16
Holt, Beaver, Pa	8
Holton, Ripley, Ind	120
Holton, (c. h.,) Jackson, Kans	410
Holt's Mills, Penobscot, Me	12
Holt's Summit, Callaway, Mo	12
Holtsville, Suffolk, N. Y	63
Holy Cross, Clay, Minn	12
Holy Cross, Ozaukee, Wis	6
Holyoke,* Hampden, Mass	2,300
Home, Wayne, Ill	12
Home, Jefferson, Ind	13
Home, Van Buren, Iowa	3
Home, Newaygo, Mich	9
Home, Brown, Minn	13
Home, Indiana, Pa	60
Home, Greene, Tenn	91
Home, Trempealeau, Wis	9
Homer, (c. h.,) Banks, Ga	22
Homer,* Champaign, Ill	690
Homer, Rush, Ind	50
Homer, Hamilton, Iowa	120
Homer, (c. h.,) Claiborne, La	120
Homer, Calhoun, Mich	410
Homer, Winona, Minn	43
Homer,* Cortland, N. Y	1,300
Homer, Licking, Ohio	88
Homer, Potter, Pa	5
Homer, (c. h.,) Angelina, Tex	23
Homer Creek, Greenwood, Kans	4
Homerville, (c. h.,) Clinch, Ga	120
Homerville, Medina, Ohio	66
Homestead,* Iowa, Iowa	370
Homestead, Benzie, Mich	40
Homestead, Burt, Nebr	14
Homet's Ferry, Bradford, Pa	12
Homewood, Cook, Ill	130
Homewood, Scott, Miss	16
Homewood, Beaver, Pa	220
Homeworth, Columbiana, Ohio	190
Hominy Creek, Buncombe, N. C	59
Homowack, Ulster, N. Y	140
Houaker's Ferry, Warren, Ky	6

HOP

Honcut, Yuba, Cal	$12
Honea Path, Anderson, S. C	75
Honek, Saline, Kans	96
Honeoye, Ontario, N. Y	260
Honeoye Falls, Monroe, N. Y	470
Honesdale, (c. h.,) Wayne, Pa	2,200
Honey Brook, Chester, Pa	240
Honey Creek, Henry, Ind	34
Honey Creek, Pottawattomie, Iowa	27
Honey Creek, McDonald, Mo	37
Honey Creek, Walworth, Wis	78
Honey Grove, Juniata, Pa	21
Honey Grove, Fannin, Tex	150
Honorville, Crenshaw, Ala	8
Hood River, Wasco, Oreg	7
Hood's Fork, Johnson, Ky	5
Hood's Mills, Carroll, Md	76
Hoodsville, Monongalia, W. Va	5
Hooker, Shelby, Ill	160
Hooker, Van Buren, Mich	35
Hooker, Gage, Nebr	17
Hooker, Butler, Pa	28
Hooker, Trempealeau, Wis	6
Hooker's Station, Fairfield, Ohio	12
Hookersville, Nicholas, W. Va	3
Hookerton, Greene, N. C	56
Hookset, Merrimack, N. H	180
Hook's Point, Hamilton, Iowa	84
Hookstown, Baltimore, Md	29
Hookstown, Beaver, Pa	150
Hooktown, Nicholas, Ky	21
Hoopa Valley, Klamath, Cal	43
Hooper, Broome, N. Y	75
Hooper, Weber, Utah	12
Hooper's Valley, Tioga, N. Y	39
Hoopersville, Dorchester, Md	2
Hooppole, Ross, Ohio	6
Hoosac Tunnel, Berkshire, Mass	240
Hoosick, Rensselaer, N. Y	200
Hoosick Falls,* Rensselaer, N. Y	1,000
Hoover Hill, Randolph, N. C	7
Hooversville, Anne Arundel, Md	130
Hop Bottom, Susquehanna, Pa	180
Hope, Vermilion, Ill	12
Hope, Bartholomew, Ind	290
Hope, Knox, Me	57
Hope, Somerset, Md	6
Hope, Warren, N. J	240
Hope, Franklin, Ohio	92
Hope, Providence, R. I	55
Hope, Lavaca, Tex	12
Hope Centre, Hamilton, N. Y	7
Hope Church, Allegheny, Pa	35
Hopedale, Tazewell, Ill	120
Hopedale, Worcester, Mass	280
Hopedale, Harrison, Ohio	230
Hope Falls, Hamilton, N. Y	16
Hope Farm, Moniteau, Mo	12
Hopefield, Crawford, Kans	12
Hope Furnace, Vinton, Ohio	81
Hope Mills, Page, Va	26
Hope Ridge, Monroe, Ohio	15
Hope Station, Lexington, S. C	14
Hopeton, Merced, Cal	170
Hope Valley, Washington, R. I	170
Hopeville, Clarke, Iowa	150

* Money-order office.

Hopeville, Grant, W. Va	$3	Horsham, Montgomery, Pa	$95
Hopewell, Mahaska, Iowa	40	Horton, Bremer, Iowa	110
Hopewell, Somerset, Md	12	Horton's, Indiana, Pa	30
Hopewell, Calhoun, Miss	7	Hortonville, Red River, Tex	12
Hopewell, Mercer, N. J	120	Hortonville, Rutland, Vt	48
Hopewell, Ontario, N. Y	59	Hortonville, Outagamie, Wis	110
Hopewell, Mecklenburgh, N. C	6	Hosensack, Lehigh, Pa	25
Hopewell, Muskingum, Ohio	89	Hoskinsville, Noble, Ohio	10
Hopewell, Bedford, Pa	210	Host, Berks, Pa	20
Hopewell, York, S. C	6	Hotchkissville, Litchfield, Conn	180
Hopewell Academy, Warren, Mo	53	Hot Creek, Nye, Nev	85
Hopewell Centre, Ontario, N. Y	56	Hotel, Bertie, N. C	57
Hopewell Centre, York, Pa	51	Hot House, Fannin, Ga	3
Hopewell Cotton Works, Chester, Pa	33	Hot Springs,* Hot Spring, Ark	830
		Hot Springs, Bath, Va	25
Hopewell × Roads, Harford, Md	100	Houcksville, Carroll, Md	17
Hopewell Furnace, Washington, Mo	48	Houcktown, Hancock, Ohio	19
Hopewell Junction, Dutchess, N. Y	12	Houghton, Jo Daviess, Ill	25
Hopewell Springs, Monroe, Tenn	12	Houghton,* (c. h.,) Houghton, Mich	1,900
Hopkins, Allegan, Mich	75	Houghton Creek, Allegany, N. Y	10
Hopkins' Mill, Greene, Pa	16	Houghtonville, Windham, Vt	14
Hopkins' Station, Allegan, Mich	12	Houlka, Chickasaw, Miss	12
Hopkins' Turnout, Richland, S. C	24	Houlton,* (c. h.,) Aroostook, Me	1,100
Hopkinsville,* (c. h.,) Christian, Ky	1,700	Houma,* (c. h.,) Terre Bonne, La	540
Hopkinsville, Warren, Ohio	25	Housatonic, Berkshire, Mass	320
Hopkinsville, Gonzales, Tex	22	House Creek, Wilcox, Ga	14
Hopkinton,* Delaware, Iowa	370	Houserville, Centre, Pa	12
Hopkinton,* Middlesex, Mass	600	House's Springs, Jefferson, Mo	6
Hopkinton, Merrimack, N. H	310	House's Store, Clay, Ky	10
Hopkinton, St. Lawrence, N. Y	170	Houseville, Lewis, N. Y	62
Hopkinton, Washington, R. I	64	Houston, (c. h.,) Winston, Ala	10
Hoppenville, Montgomery, Pa	21	Houston, (c. h.,) Suwannee, Fla	120
Hopper's Mills, Henderson, Ill	80	Houston, Heard, Ga	20
Hoquiam, Chehalis, Wash	10	Houston, Jackson, Ind	21
Hord, Clay, Ill	15	Houston, Bourbon, Ky	22
Horicon, Martin, Minn	11	Houston, Houston, Minn	350
Horicon, Warren, N. Y	36	Houston, (c. h.,) Chickasaw, Miss	200
Horicon,* Dodge, Wis	580	Houston, (c. h.,) Texas, Mo	170
Horine Station, Jefferson, Mo	20	Houston, Shelby, Ohio	98
Horn, Jasper, Iowa	9	Houston,* (c. h.,) Harris, Tex	4,000
Hornbrook, Bradford, Pa	18	Houston Station, Kent, Del	20
Hornby, Steuben, N. Y	16	Houtzdale, Clearfield, Pa	12
Hornellsville,* Steuben, N. Y	2,000	Howard, Conway, Ark	12
Hornerstown, Ocean, N. J	48	Howard, Taylor, Ga	42
Hornitas, Mariposa, Cal	270	Howard, Parke, Ind	20
Horn Lake, De Soto, Miss	70	Howard, Howard, Kans	12
Hornsby, Macoupin, Ill	50	Howard, Piscataway, Me	12
Horn's Mills, Carroll, N. H	25	Howard, Muskegon, Mich	46
Horntown, Accomack, Va	78	Howard, Wright, Minn	47
Horr's, Champaign, Ohio	12	Howard, Nemeha, Nebr	12
Horr's Ranch, Stanislaus, Cal	12	Howard, Warren, N. J	8
Horse Cove, Macon, N. C	12	Howard, Steuben, N. Y	120
Horse Creek, Barton, Mo	20	Howard, Centre, Pa	190
Horse Creek, Ashe, N. C	5	Howard, Bell, Tex	16
Horse Creek, Greene, Tenn	24	Howard Centre, Howard, Iowa	59
Horse Head, Prince George's, Md	60	Howard City, Montcalm, Mich	12
Horseheads, Chemung, N. Y	820	Howard's Grove, Sheboygan, Wis	110
Horseley's Landing, Nelson, Va	16	Howard's Lick, Hardy, W. Va	5
Horse Pasture, Henry, Va	22	Howard's Mills, Montgomery, Ky	6
Horse Plains, Missoula, Mont	12	Howard's Mills, St. Clair, Mo	12
Horse Prairie, Beaver Head, Mont	12	Howard Springs, Cumberland, Tenn	12
Horse Shoe Bend, Boise, Idaho	12	Howardsville, Jo Daviess, Ill	15
Horse Shoe Bend, Scott, Tenn	12	Howardsville, St. Joseph, Mich	8
Horse Shoe Bottom, Russell, Ky	12	Howardsville, Albemarle, Va	120
Horse Shoe Run, Preston, W. Va	18	Howardville, Floyd, Iowa	9
Horsetown, Shasta, Cal	17	Howell, (c. h.,) Livingston, Mich	970

* Money-order office.

Howell's Depot, Orange, N. Y	$170	Humboldt Basin, Baker, Oreg	$64
Howellville, Delaware, Pa	64	Humburd, Clark, Wis	12
Howel's Cross Roads, Cherokee, Ala.	22	Hume, Allegany, N. Y	150
Howe's Cave, Schoharie, N. Y	10	Hummell's Wharf, Snyder, Pa	12
Howe's Corners, Waushara, Wis	7	Hummel's Store, Berks, Pa	8
Howe's Mill, Dent, Mo	22	Hummelstown, Dauphin, Pa	330
Howe's Valley, Hardin, Ky	16	Humphrey, Cattaraugus, N. Y	85
Howesville, Clay, Ind	12	Humphreysville, Columbia, N. Y	21
Howland, Penobscot, Me	28	Humphreysville, Luzerne, Pa	28
Howland, Trumbull, Ohio	18	Humphreyville, Holmes, Ohio	12
Howlet Hill, Onondaga, N. Y	18	Hunlock Creek, Luzerne, Pa	22
Howlett, Sangamon, Ill	100	Hunnewell, Shelby, Mo	290
Hoyleton, Washington, Ill	89	Hunsucker's Store, Montgomery,	
Hubbard,* Trumbull, Ohio	510	N. C	12
Hubbardston, Worcester, Mass	390	Hunter, Boone, Ill	17
Hubbardston, Ionia, Mich	410	Hunter, Greene, N. Y	180
Hubbardstown, Wayne, W. Va	12	Hunter, Belmont, Ohio	41
Hubbardsville, Madison, N. Y	210	Hunter's Bridge, Beaufort, N. C	6
Hubbardton, Rutland, Vt	21	Hunter's Cave, Greene, Pa	14
Hubbleton, Jefferson, Wis	44	Hunter's Creek, Lapeer, Mich	32
Hubelsville, Huntingdon, Pa	13	Hunter's Depot, Nelson, Ky	14
Hubertville, Robertson, Tenn	12	Hunter's Land, Schoharie, N. Y	42
Hublersburgh, Centre, Pa	68	Hunter's Lodge, Fluvanna, Va	14
Huckleberry, Echols, Ga	12	Hunter's Mills, Pickens, S. C	10
Huddleston, Pike, Ark	8	Hunter's Mills, Fairfax, Va	16
Hudson, McLean, Ill	200	Hunterstown, Adams, Pa	47
Hudson, Black Hawk, Iowa	18	Huntersville, Hardin, Ohio	36
Hudson, Penobscot, Me	64	Huntersville, Lycoming, Pa	15
Hudson, Middlesex, Mass	910	Huntersville, Greenville, S. C	4
Hudson,* Lenawee, Mich	2,100	Huntersville, Rutherford, Tenn	12
Hudson, Bates, Mo	23	Huntersville, (c. h.,) Pocahontas, W.	
Hudson, Hillsborough, N. H	130	Va	120
Hudson, Hudson, N. J	1,800	Huntertown, Allen, Ind	75
Hudson,* (c. h.,) Columbia, N. Y	3,000	Huntingburgh, Dubois, Ind	170
Hudson,* Summit, Ohio	1,000	Huntingdale, Henry, Mo	10
Hudson, Jefferson, Pa	19	Huntingdon,* (c.h.,) Huntingdon, Pa.	2,100
Huason,* (c. h.,) St. Croix, Wis	1,200	Huntingdon, (c. h.,) Carroll, Tenn	300
Hudson City, Worth, Mo	18	Huntingdon Valley, Montgomery,	
Hudsondale, Carbon, Pa	12	Pa	89
Hudsonville, Breckinridge, Ky	20	Huntington, Fairfield, Conn	45
Hudsonville, Marshall, Miss	46	Huntington,* (c. h.,) Huntington, Ind.	1,600
Huerfano, Pueblo, Colo	12	Huntington, Hampshire, Mass	530
Huff's Creek, Hancock, Ky	6	Huntington,* Suffolk, N. Y	990
Hugginsville, Gentry, Mo	20	Huntington, Lorain, Ohio	100
Hughes, Schuylkill, Pa	36	Huntington, Chittenden, Vt	74
Hughesburgh, Habersham, Ga	12	Huntington Centre, Chittenden, Vt.	63
Hughesville, Charles, Md	68	Huntingtown, Calvert, Md	58
Hughesville, Saginaw, Mich	12	Huntley Grove,* McHenry, Ill	290
Hughesville, Lycoming, Pa	290	Huntsburgh, Geauga, Ohio	96
Hughesville, Loudoun, Va	17	Hunt's Corners, Cortland, N. Y	19
Hughsonville, Dutchess, N. Y	160	Hunt's Hollow, Livingston, N. Y	67
Huguenot, Orange, N. Y	35	Hunt's Mills, Sussex, N. J	32
Hulburton, Orleans, N. Y	92	Hunt's Station, Knox, Ohio	65
Hull, Plymouth, Mass	24	Hunt's Station, Franklin, Tenn	190
Hull Prairie, Wood, Ohio	12	Huntsville,* (c. h.,) Madison, Ala	2,000
Hull's, Athens, Ohio	23	Huntsville, (c. h.,) Madison, Ark	12
Hull's Mills, Dutchess, N. Y	5	Huntsville, Douglas, Colo	12
Hulmesville, Bucks, Pa	110	Huntsville, Litchfield, Conn	59
Hulton, Allegheny, Pa	150	Huntsville, Schuyler, Ill	84
Humansville, Polk, Mo	88	Huntsville, Madison, Ind	35
Humboldt, Humboldt, Iowa	10	Huntsville, Choctaw, Miss	21
Humboldt,* Allen, Kans	800	Huntsville,* (c. h.,) Randolph, Mo	480
Humboldt, Marquette, Mich	12	Huntsville, Sussex, N. J	12
Humboldt, Pulaski, Mo	280	Huntsville, Yadkin, N. C	62
Humboldt, Richardson, Nebr	64	Huntsville, Logan, Ohio	270
Humboldt,* Gibson, Tenn	1,600	Huntsville, Luzerne, Pa	18

* Money-order office.

IBE — IND

Huntsville, (*c. h.,*) Scott, Tenn	$56	Iceland, Blue Earth, Minn	$8
*Huntsville,** (*c. h.,*) Walker, Tex	640	Ichatucknee, Columbia, Fla	11
Huntsville, Weber, Utah	26	Ickesburgh, Perry, Pa	110
Huntsville, Jackson, W. Va	76	Iconium, Appanoose, Iowa	65
Hurd, Clearfield, Pa	23	*Ida,* (*c. h.,*) Ida, Iowa	85
Hurdle's Mills, Person, N. C	6	Ida, Monroe, Mich	110
Hurdtown, Morris, N. J	88	*Idaho,* (*c. h.,*) Clear Creek, Colo	250
Hurffville, Camden, N. J	50	Idaho, Pike, Ohio	12
Hurlbut's Corners, Crawford, Wis	13	*Idaho City,** (*c. h.,*) Boise, Idaho	1,400
Hurley, Ulster, N. Y	61	Idaville, White, Ind	120
Hurlock, Dorchester, Md	12	Idaville, Adams, Pa	33
Huron, Lawrence, Ind	120	Idell, Crawford, Kans	12
Huron, Des Moines, Iowa	30	Iderbide, Wythe, Va	12
Huron, Atchison, Kans	420	Ijamsville, Frederick, Md	78
Huron, Wayne, N. Y	47	Ilchester Mills, Howard, Md	61
Huron, Erie, Ohio	200	Ilion,** Herkimer, N. Y	1,800
Huron City, Huron, Mich	91	Illawara, Carroll, La	20
Huron Station, Wayne, Mich	130	Illinois City, Rock Island, Ill	45
Hurricane, Montgomery, Ill	38	Illinois Grove, Marshall, Iowa	22
Hurricane, Crittenden, Ky	30	Illiopolis, Sangamon, Ill	280
Hurricane, Warren, Miss	30	Illyria, Fayette, Iowa	35
Hurricane, Carroll, Mo	12	Imlay, Lapeer, Mich	14
Hurricane Bridge, Putnam, W. Va	29	Imlaystown, Monmouth, N. J	88
Hurricane Grove, Grant, Wis	20	Imlertown, Bedford, Pa	12
Hurricane Switch, Maury, Tenn	12	Increase, Warren, Tenn	26
Hurt's Cross Roads, Maury, Tenn	12	Independence, Autauga, Ala	1
Hurtville, Russell, Ala	150	*Independence,* (*c. h.,*) Inyo, Cal	180
Hustisford, Dodge, Wis	220	Independence, Warren, Ind	55
Hustontown, Fulton, Pa	20	*Independence,** (*c. h.,*) Buchanan, Iowa	2,200
Hustonville, Lincoln, Ky	120	Independence, Montgomery, Kans	12
Hutchinson, McLeod, Minn	270	Independence, Kenton, Ky	83
Hutchison's, Bourbon, Ky	54	Independence, Tangipahoa, La	71
Huth, Franklin, Ind	12	*Independence,** (*c. h.,*) Jackson, Mo	1,900
Hutsonville, Crawford, Ill	140	Independence, Allegany, N. Y	49
Hutton, Coles, Ill	14	Independence, Caswell, N. C	10
Hutton's Switch, Alleghany, Md	43	Independence, Cuyahoga, Ohio	71
Huttonsville, Randolph, W. Va	84	Independence, Polk, Oreg	51
Hyannis, Barnstable, Mass	790	Independence, Washington, Pa	81
Hyattstown, Montgomery, Md	64	Independence, Washington Tex	220
Hyattsville, Garrard, Ky	12	*Independence,* (*c. h.,*) Grayson, Va	170
Hyattsville, Prince George's, Md	73	Independent Hill, Prince William, Va	21
Hyco, McPherson, Kans	12	*Indiana,** (*c. h.,*) Indiana, Pa	1,500
Hyco, Halifax, Va	21	INDIANAPOLIS,** (*c. h.,*) Marion, Ind	4,000
Hyde Park, Cook, Ill	220	Indianapolis, Mahaska, Iowa	87
Hyde Park, Norfolk, Mass	530	Indian Bay, Monroe, Ark	120
Hyde Park, Wabashaw, Minn	16	Indian Bottom, Letcher, Ky	1
Hyde Park, Dutchess, N. Y	590	Indian Camp, Guernsey, Ohio	12
Hyde Park, Luzerne, Pa	1,400	Indian Creek, Kent, Mich	33
Hyde Park, Cache, Utah	24	Indian Creek, Monroe, Mo	24
Hyde Park, (*c. h.,*) Lamoille, Vt	320	Indian Creek, Fayette, Pa	14
Hydesburgh, Ralls, Mo	22	Indian Creek, Washington, Tenn	1
Hyde's Mills, Iowa, Wis	48	Indian Creek, Monroe, W. Va	66
Hydesville, Humboldt, Cal	77	Indian Falls, Genesee, N. Y	40
Hydeville, Rutland, Vt	360	Indian Field, Knox, Ohio	12
Hynddale, Morgan, Ind	12	Indian Fields, Albany, N. Y	37
Hyndville, Schoharie, N. Y	83	Indian Ford, Stoddard, Mo	11
Hyremansville, Lehigh, Pa	6	Indian Ford, Rock, Wis	15
Hyrum, Cache, Utah	42	Indian Gulch, Mariposa, Cal	10
		Indian Lake, Hamilton, N. Y	34
I.		Indian Mound, Stewart, Tenn	42
		Indianola, Vermilion, Ill	170
Iamton, Montgomery, Ohio	12	*Indianola,** (*c. h.,*) Warren, Iowa	1,100
Iatan, Platte, Mo	32	*Indianola,** (*c. h.,*) Calhoun, Tex	1,500
Iba, De Kalb, Ind	94	Indian Orchard, Hampden, Mass	290
Iberia, Brown, Minn	12		
Iberia, Morrow, Ohio	180		

* Money-order office.

Indian Ridge, Currituck, N.C	$12	Ireland, Hampden, Mass	$39
Indian River, Washington, Me	80	Ireland, Lewis, W. Va	9
Indian River, Lewis, N. Y	4	Ireland Corners, Albany, N. Y	5
Indian Run, Mercer, Pa	36	Ireland Hill, Marion, Ala	4
Indian Springs, Nevada, Cal	12	Irene, Sioux, Iowa	12
Indian Springs, Butts, Ga	36	Irisburgh, Henry, Va	15
Indian Springs, Campbell, Ky	4	Irish Grove, Atchison, Mo	61
Indian Springs, Washington, Md	24	Irishtown, Mercer, Pa	18
Indian Town, Mason, Mich	17	Irona, Talladega, Ala	12
Indian Valley, Floyd, Va	4	Irona, Clinton, N. Y	48
Indian Village, Noble, Ind	17	Iron, Iron, Utah	12
Industry, McDonough, Ill	170	Iron Clad, Limestone, Tex	10
Industry, Franklin, Me	36	Iron Creek, Austin, Tex	16
Industry, Beaver, Pa	150	Irondale,* Washington, Mo	210
Industry, Austin, Tex	120	Irondale, Jefferson, Ohio	370
Ingall's Crossing, Oswego, N. Y	12	Iron Furnace, Scioto, Ohio	120
Ingart Grove, Ringgold, Iowa	12	Iron Hill, Northampton, Pa	12
Ingham, Franklin, Iowa	10	Iron Hills, Jackson, Iowa	24
Ingham's Mills, Herkimer, N. Y	52	Iron Mountain, St. Francois, Mo	260
Inglefield, Vanderburgh, Ind	24	Iron Mountain, Rusk, Tex	12
Ingleside, Hardin, Tenn	14	Iron Ridge, Dodge, Wis	150
Ingomar, Issaquena, Miss	16	Iron Rod, Madison, Mont	12
Ingraham, Clay, Ill	57	Iron Station, Lincoln, N. C	12
Ingraham, Clinton, N. Y	26	*Ironton,* (c. h.,) Iron, Mo	690
Inkermann, Hardy, W. Va	3	*Ironton,* (c. h.,) Lawrence, Ohio	2,000
Inkster, Wayne, Mich	56	Ironton, Lehigh, Pa	71
Inland, Cedar, Iowa	60	Ironton, Sauk, Wis	210
Inland, Benzie, Mich	39	Ironville, Perry, Ala	12
Inland, Summit, Ohio	69	Ironwood, Liberty, Tex	13
Inskip, Butte, Cal	5	Iroquois, Iroquois, Ill	99
Intercourse, Sumter, Ala	12	*Irvine,* (c. h.,) Estill, Ky	270
Intercourse, Lancaster, Pa	79	Irvine, Warren, Pa	250
Inverness, Cumberland, N. C	12	Irving, Montgomery, Ill	260
Inverness, Columbiana, Ohio	12	Irving,* Marshall, Kans	400
Inwood, Marshall, Ind	160	Irving, Barry, Mich	61
Ioka, Keokuk, Iowa	73	Irving, Monongalia, Minn	13
Iola, Calhoun, Fla	12	Irving, Chautauqua, N. Y	120
Iola, Marion, Iowa	13	Irving, Jackson, Wis	85
Iola, (c. h.,) Allen, Kans	590	Irving College, Warren, Tenn	11
Iola, Columbia, Pa	18	Irvington, Washington, Ill	170
Iola, Waupaca, Wis	75	Irvington, Kossuth, Iowa	70
Ion, Allamakee, Iowa	14	Irvington, Essex, N. J	230
Iona, Cape Girardeau, Mo	12	Irvington, Westchester, N. Y	430
Iona, Fairfax, Va	12	Irwin, Union, Ohio	63
Iona Island, Rockland, N. Y	450	Irwin's Station, Westmoreland, Pa	720
Ione City, Nye, Nev	65	*Irwinton,* (c. h.,) Wilkinson, Ga	190
Ione Valley,* Amador, Cal	230	*Irwinville,* (c. h.,) Irwin, Ga	10
Ionia, Warren, Ill	57	Isaac's Camp, Doddridge, W. Va	12
Ionia, Chickasaw, Iowa	12	*Isabella,* (c. h.,) Worth, Ga	20
Ionia, (c. h.,) Ionia, Mich	2,200	Isabella, Ozark, Mo	12
Ionia, Dixon, Nebr	29	Isabella City, Isabella, Mich	12
Ionia City, Pettis, Mo	54	Isadora, Worth, Mo	38
Iowa Centre,* Story, Iowa	120	Isanti, Isanti, Minn	160
Iowa City, Placer, Cal	150	Ischua, Cattaraugus, N. Y	53
Iowa City, (c. h.,) Johnson, Iowa	2,700	Ishpeming, Marquette, Mich	1,200
Iowa City, Crawford, Kans	12	Island, Clinton, Pa	19
Iowa Falls,* Hardin, Iowa	1,100	Island City, Owsley, Ky	3
Iowa Point, Doniphan, Kans	77	Island City, Gentry, Mo	24
Iowaville, Van Buren, Iowa	59	Island Creek, Jasper, Ill	7
Ipava, Fulton, Ill	230	Island Creek, Jefferson, Ohio	13
Ipswich, Essex, Mass	1,000	Island Falls, Aroostook, Me	36
Ira, Cayuga, N. Y	100	Island Pond,* Essex, Vt	830
Ira, Rutland, Vt	19	Isle La Motte, Grand Isle, Vt	69
Irasburgh, (c. h.,) Orleans, Vt	270	Islesborough, Hocking, Ohio	20
Irbyville, Fulton, Ga	5	Islip, Suffolk, N. Y	290
Ireland, Dubois, Ind	43	Issequena, Goochland, Va	10

* Money-order office.

JAC		JAR	
Itasca, Anoka, Minn	$51	Jacksonville,* (c. h.,) Duval, Fla	$3,200
Italy Hill, Yates, N. Y	61	Jacksonville, (c. h.,) Telfair, Ga	28
Italy Hollow, Yates, N. Y	16	Jacksonville,* (c. h.,) Morgan, Ill	2,800
Ithaca,* (c. h.,) Gratiot, Mich	410	Jacksonville. Chickasaw, Iowa	63
Ithaca, Saunders, Nebr	12	Jacksonville, Neosho, Kans	210
Ithaca,* (c. h.,) Tompkins, N. Y	2,900	Jacksonville, Shelby, Ky	12
Ithaca, Darke, Ohio	47	Jacksonville, Randolph, Mo	170
Ithaca, Richland, Wis	13	Jacksonville, Burlington, N. J	15
Iuka, Marion, Ill	170	Jacksonville, Tompkins, N. Y	210
Iuka, (c. h.,) Tishemingo, Miss	1,500	Jacksonville,* (c. h.,) Jackson, Oreg.	640
Ivesdale, Champaign, Ill	98	Jacksonville, Lehigh, Pa	39
Ives' Grove, Racine, Wis	39	Jacksonville, Cherokee, Tex	52
Ivor, Southampton, Va	75	Jacksonville, Windham, Vt	170
Ivy Depot, Albemarle, Va	86	Jacksonville, Lewis, W. Va	20
Ivy Log, Union, Ga	4	Jack's Reef, Onondaga, N. Y	40
Ivy Mills, Delaware, Pa	50	Jacksville, Butler, Pa	15
Ixonia Centre, Jefferson, Wis	97	Jacobsburgh, Belmont, Ohio	28
		Jacob's Church, Shenandoah, Va	17
J.		Jacob's Creek, Westmoreland, Pa	42
		Jacob's Fork, Catawba, N. C	15
Jacinto, Colusa, Cal	12	Jacobstown, Burlington, N. J	100
Jacinto, Alcorn, Miss	39	Jadden, Grant, Ind	8
Jacksborough, (c. h.,) Campbell, Tenn	78	Jaffrey, Cheshire, N. H	100
Jacksborough, (c. h.,) Jack, Tex	260	Jake's Prairie, Gasconade, Mo	32
Jack's Fork, Texas, Mo	12	Jake's Run, Monongalia, W. Va	12
Jackson,* (c. h.,) Amador, Cal	700	Jalapa, Grant, Ind	39
Jackson, (c. h.,) Butts, Ga	20	Jalapa, Newberry, S. C	12
Jackson, Adair, Iowa	12	Jalapa, Monroe, Tenn	10
Jackson, Linn, Kans	10	Jamaica,* (c. h.,) Queens, N. Y	1,000
Jackson, (c. h.,) Breathitt, Ky	12	Jamaica, Windham, Vt	280
Jackson, East Feliciana, La	310	Jamaica, Middlesex, Va	15
Jackson, Waldo, Me	37	Jamaica Plain, Norfolk, Mass	1,000
Jackson,* (c. h.,) Jackson, Mich	3,000	James' Bayou, Mississippi, Mo	31
Jackson, (c. h.,) Jackson, Minn	240	Jamesburgh, Middlesex, N. J	260
JACKSON,* (c. h.,) Hinds, Miss	2,700	James' Creek, Huntingdon, Pa	140
Jackson, (c. h.,) Cape Girardeau, Mo	370	James' Crossing, Jackson, Kans	13
Jackson, Dakota, Nebr	64	James' Fork, Sebastian, Ark	10
Jackson, Carroll, N. H	72	Jamesport, Daviess, Mo	120
Jackson, (c. h.,) Northampton, N. C	420	Jamesport, Suffolk, N. Y	190
Jackson,* (c. h.,) Jackson, Ohio	840	James' Switch, Marion, Ind	26
Jackson, Susquehanna, Pa	70	Jamestown, Conecuh, Ala	6
Jackson,* (c. h.,) Madison, Tenn	2,000	Jamestown, Tuolumne, Cal	170
Jackson, Louisa, Va	12	Jamestown, Boulder, Colo	23
Jackson, Washington, Wis	12	Jamestown, Chattahoochee, Ga	23
Jackson C. H., Jackson, W. Va	140	Jamestown, Clinton, Ill	53
Jacksonborough, Butler, Ohio	31	Jamestown, Boone, Ind	170
Jacksonborough, Colleton, S. C	12	Jamestown, (c. h.,) Russell, Ky	55
Jackson Brook, Washington, Me	12	Jamestown, Ottawa, Mich	58
Jacksonburgh, Wayne, Ind	32	Jamestown, Moniteau, Mo	93
Jackson Centre, Shelby, Ohio	35	Jamestown,* Chautauqua, N. Y	3,000
Jackson Corners, Dutchess, N. Y	21	Jamestown, Guilford, N. C	140
Jackson Corners, Monroe, Pa	8	Jamestown, Greene, Ohio	260
Jackson Hall, Franklin, Pa	38	Jamestown, Mercer, Pa	420
Jacksonham, Lancaster, S. C	12	Jamestown, Newport, R. I	61
Jacksonport,* (c. h.) Jackson, Ark	740	Jamestown, (c. h.,) Fentress, Tenn	74
Jacksonport, Door, Wis	22	Jamestown, Grant, Wis	82
Jackson's Corners, Sullivan, Mo	19	Jamesville, Onondaga, N. Y	330
Jackson's Creek, Randolph, N. C	6	Jamesville, Martin, N. C	190
Jackson's Mills, Ocean, N. J	13	Janelew, Lewis, W. Va	76
Jackson Springs, Jackson, N. C	12	Janesville, Lassen, Cal	30
Jackson Station, Tipton, Ind	35	Janesville, Greenwood, Kans	31
Jackson Station, Seneca, Ohio	10	Janesville, Waseca, Minn	220
Jackson Store, Conecuh, Ala	12	Janesville,* (c. h.,) Rock, Wis	3,300
Jacksontown, Licking, Ohio	84	Janney's, Richland, Wis	12
Jackson Valley, Susquehanna, Pa	9	Jarratt's, Sussex, Va	110
Jacksonville, (c. h.,) Calhoun, Ala	500	Jarrettown, Montgomery, Pa	24

* Money-order office.

JEF   JES

Jarrett's Ford, Kanawha, W. Va...	$4	Jeffersonton, Culpeper, Va........	$68
Jarrettsville, Harford, Md........	89	Jeffersontown, Jefferson, Ky......	130
Jarrold's Valley, Raleigh, W. Va..	12	Jefferson Valley, Westchester, N.Y.	69
Jasonville, Greene, Ind...........	25	Jeffersonville, (c. h.,) Twiggs, Ga....	56
Jasper, (c. h.,) Walker, Ala........	71	Jeffersonville, Wayne, Ill........	170
Jasper, (c. h.,) Newton, Ark........	43	Jeffersonville*, Clarke, Ind........	2,100
Jasper, (c. h.,) Hamilton, Fla.......	20	Jeffersonville, Lee, Iowa........	20
Jasper, (c. h.,) Pickens, Ga........	50	Jeffersonville, Cowley, Kans.......	12
Jasper, (c. h.,) Dubois, Ind........	170	Jeffersonville, Montgomery, Ky....	16
Jasper, Jasper, Mo...............	21	Jeffersonville, Cass, Mich.......	30
Jasper, Steuben, N.Y.............	160	Jeffersonville, Sullivan, N.Y......	290
Jasper, Pike, Ohio..............	39	Jeffersonville, Fayette, Ohio.......	120
Jasper, (c. h.,) Marion, Tenn.......	200	Jeffersonville, Montgomery, Pa.....	45
Jasper, (c. h.,) Jasper, Tex.........	100	Jeffersonville, Lamoille, Vt.......	290
Jasper City, Jasper, Iowa........	380	Jeffress' Store, Nottaway, Va.....	12
Jasper Mills, Fayette, Ohio........	67	Jeffrey's Creek, Marion, S.C......	2
Jatt, Grant, La.................	10	Jeffries, Clearfield, Pa..........	30
Java, Wyoming, N.Y.............	47	Jeffriesburgh, Franklin, Mo.......	12
Java, Lucas, Ohio..............	12	Jelloway, Knox, Ohio.............	77
Java Village, Wyoming, N.Y.....	67	Jena, Tuscaloosa, Ala.............	3
Jay, Franklin, Me...............	140	Jena, Falls, Tex................	8
Jay, Saginaw, Mich.............	92	Jenkins' Bridge, Accomack, Va....	37
Jay, Harrison, Mo...............	5	Jenkins' Creek, Jasper, Mo.......	5
Jay, Essex, N.Y................	83	Jenkins' Mills, Jefferson, Nebr.....	71
Jay, Orleans, Vt................	44	Jenkintown, Montgomery, Pa.....	310
Jayne's Store, Randolph, Ark......	7	Jenksville, Tioga, N.Y..........	36
Jaynesville,* Bremer, Iowa........	310	Jenner's Cross Roads, Somerset, Pa.	120
Jaynesville, Covington, Miss......	8	Jennerstown, Somerset, Pa........	20
Jaysville, Darke, Ohio...........	32	Jennersville, Chester, Pa........	110
Jayville, Conecuh, Ala...........	12	Jennieton, Iowa, Wis.............	21
Jeanerett, Iberia, La.............	180	Jennings, Hamilton, Fla..........	15
Jeansville, Luzerne, Pa...........	280	Jennings' Fork, Smith, Tenn......	19
Jeddo, Allen, Kans..............	8	Jennings' Ordinary, Nottaway, Va.	12
Jeddo, St. Clair, Mich...........	74	Jenningsville, Wyoming, Pa.......	18
Jeddo, Orleans, N.Y.............	140	Jenny, Marathon, Wis............	39
Jeddo, Jefferson, Ohio..........	31	Jenny Lind, Sebastian, Ark.......	54
Jeddo, Luzerne, Pa..............	390	Jenny Lind, Calaveras, Cal.......	80
Jeddo, Marquette, Wis...........	17	Jericho, Perry, Ala.............	12
Jefferson, (c. h.,) Jackson, Ga......	170	Jericho, Kane, Ill..............	27
Jefferson, Cook, Ill.............	170	Jericho, Henry, Ky.............	68
Jefferson, Clinton, Ind..........	74	Jericho, Queens, N.Y...........	70
Jefferson,* (c. h.,) Greene, Iowa....	990	Jericho, Chittenden, Vt..........	190
Jefferson, Douglas, Kans.........	320	Jericho Centre, Chittenden, Vt....	94
Jefferson, Jefferson, La..........	24	Jerome, Howard, Ind............	66
Jefferson, Lincoln, Me..........	130	Jerome, Appanoose, Iowa........	10
Jefferson, Frederick, Md.........	100	Jerome, Phelps, Mo.............	12
Jefferson, Hillsdale, Mich........	13	Jerome, Westchester, N.Y........	130
Jefferson, Winona, Minn.........	7	Jerome, Union, Ohio.............	44
Jefferson, Coos, N.H...........	51	Jeromesville, Ashland, Ohio......	65
Jefferson, Schoharie, N.Y........	190	Jersey, Oakland, Mich...........	10
Jefferson, (c. h.,) Ashe, N.C........	59	Jersey, Licking, Ohio...........	78
Jefferson,* (c. h.,) Ashtabula, Ohio.	830	Jersey City,* (c. h.,) Hudson, N.J..	3,100
Jefferson, Marion, Oreg..........	79	Jersey Mills, Lycoming, Pa.......	32
Jefferson, Greene, Pa...........	140	Jersey Shore,* Lycoming, Pa......	880
Jefferson, Chesterfield, S.C.......	10	Jerseytown, Columbia, Pa........	17
Jefferson,* (c. h.,) Marion, Texas....	1,800	Jerseyville,* (c. h.,) Jersey, Ill...	1,300
Jefferson, Powhatan, Va.........	25	Jerseyville, Monmouth, N.J......	12
Jefferson,* (c. h.,) Jefferson, Wis....	1,100	Jerusalem, Albany, N.Y.........	24
Jefferson Barracks,* St. Louis, Mo.	480	Jerusalem, Davie, N.C..........	73
JEFFERSON CITY,* (c. h.,) Cole, Mo.	2,400	Jerusalem, Monroe, Ohio........	69
Jefferson City, Jefferson, Mont...	290	*Jerusalem*, (c. h.,) Southampton, Va.	70
Jefferson Corners, Whitesides, Ill..	8	Jerusalem Mills, Harford, Md......	41
Jefferson Furnace, Clarion, Pa....	37	Jessamine, Jessamine, Ky........	12
Jefferson Lake, Le Sueur, Minn...	10	Jesse's Mills, Russell, Va.......	12
Jefferson Line, Clearfield, Pa......	22	Jesse's Store, Shelby, Ky.......	4
Jefferson Station, York, Pa........	16	Jessup,* Buchanan, Iowa..........	440

* Money-order office.

Jessup's Station, Parke, Ind......	$9
Jesuit's Bend, Plaquemine, La....	15
Jetersville, Amelia, Va............	140
Jewell, Jewell, Kans..............	12
Jewett, Greene, N. Y..............	51
Jewett, Harrison, Ohio...........	110
Jewett Centre, Greene, N. Y.......	15
Jewett City, New London, Conn...	510
Jewett Mills, St. Croix, Wis.......	47
Jimes, Jackson, Ohio..............	18
Joanna Furnace, Berks, Pa........	16
Jobe, Oregon, Mo.................	15
Jobe, Monongalia, W. Va..........	8
Jobstown, Burlington, N. J........	62
Joe's Lick, Madison, Ky...........	12
Joetta, Hancock, Ill..............	12
Johanesburgh, Washington, Ill....	12
John Day City, Grant, Oreg.......	12
John Day's Creek, Idaho, Idaho...	12
John's Branch, Audrian, Mo......	10
Johnsburgh, McHenry, Ill.........	24
Johnsburgh, Warren, N. Y........	79
Johnsburgh, Somerset, Pa.........	12
Johnson, Jones, Iowa.............	25
Johnson, Macon, Mo..............	12
Johnson, Barnwell, S. C...........	16
Johnson,* Lemoille, Vt............	370
Johnsonburgh, Warren, N. J......	66
Johnson City, Washington, Tenn..	280
Johnson's, Orange, N. Y..........	12
Johnsonsburgh, Wyoming, N. Y....	62
Johnson's Corners, Summit, Ohio...	34
Johnson's Creek, Carroll, Ill......	10
Johnson's Creek, Niagara, N. Y....	180
Johnson's Creek, Jefferson, Wis....	160
Johnson's Cross Roads, Monroe, W. Va.....................	10
Johnson's Fork, Magoffin, Ky.....	6
Johnson's Grove, Haywood, Tenn..	12
Johnson's Mills, Marion, Ala......	12
Johnson's Mills, Pitt, N. C	9
Johnson's Springs, Goochland, Va..	12
Johnson's Station, Tarrant, Tex....	33
Johnson's Store, Anne Arundel, Md.	27
Johnsontown, Northampton, Va ...	48
Johnsonville, Wayne, Ill..........	140
Johnsonville, Rensselaer, N. Y.....	210
Johnsonville, Trumbull, Ohio.....	110
Johnsonville, Northampton, Pa....	25
Johnsonville, Williamsburgh, S. C.	6
Johnsonville, Humphreys, Tenn...	210
Johnsonville, Sheboygan, Wis.....	12
Johnston's Depot, Edgefield, S. C..	12
Johnston's Institute, Hays, Tex....	12
Johnstown, Cumberland, Ill.......	31
Johnstown, Alleghany, Md........	12
Johnstown, Barry, Mich...........	30
Johnstown, Bates, Mo............	76
Johnstown,* (c. h.,) Fulton, N. Y	1,400
Johnstown, Licking, Ohio	100
Johnstown,* Cambria, Pa.........	2,500
Johnstown, Harrison, W. Va......	11
Johnstown, Rock, Wis............	83
Johnstown Centre, Rock, Wis.....	84
Johnsville, Bradley, Ark.........	24
Johnsville, Frederick, Md.........	68

Johnsville, Dutchess, N. Y.........	$52
Johnsville, Montgomery, Ohio	33
Joliet,* (c. h.,) Will, Ill.............	2,900
Joliett, Schuylkill, Pa.............	12
Jolly, Monroe, Ohio...............	59
Jollytown, Greene, Pa	24
Jollyville, Lee, Iowa..............	35
Jonas Ridge, Burke, N. C.........	12
Jonathan's Creek, Haywood, N. C..	2
Jones' Bluff, Sumter, Ala.........	44
Jonesborough, Jefferson, Ala	34
Jonesborough, (c. h.,) Craighead, Ark.	92
Jonesborough, (c. h.,) Clayton, Ga...	330
Jonesborough, (c. h.,) Union, Ill.....	460
Jonesborough, Grant, Ind........	370
Jonesborough, Washington, Me....	42
Jonesborough, Tippah, Miss.......	30
Jonesborough, Moore, N. C........	300
Jonesborough,* (c. h.,) Washington, Tenn...................	570
Jonesborough, Brunswick, Va	17
Jonesburg, Montgomery, Mo	260
Jones' Chapel, Winston, Ala......	12
Jones' Corners, Holmes, Ohio	12
Jones' Creek, Newton, Mo........	12
Jones' Cross Roads, Tallapoosa, Ala.	34
Jones' Mills, Meriwether, Ga......	5
Jones' Mills, Westmoreland, Pa....	61
Jonesport, Washington, Me.......	140
Jones' Springs, Berkeley, W. Va....	12
Jones' Station, Dearborn, Ind.....	53
Jones' Station, Butler, Ohio	66
Jones' Station, Haywood, Tenn....	12
Jones' Tan Yard, Callaway, Mo....	20
Jonestown,* Lebanon, Pa..........	270
Jonesville, Bartholomew, Ind	140
Jonesville,* Hillsdale, Mich	1,200
Jonesville, Cass, Mo	18
Jonesville, Saratoga, N. Y........	140
Jonesville, Yadkin, N. C	32
Jonesville, Union, S. C...........	27
Jonesville, Chittenden, Vt.........	84
Jonesville, (c. h.,) Lee, Va.........	130
Joppa Village, Plymouth, Mass....	220
Jordan, Vermilion, Ill............	48
Jordan, Jay, Ind.................	33
Jordan, Onondaga, N. Y..........	820
Jordan, Green, Wis	20
Jordan's Chapel, Mercer, W. Va....	12
Jordan's Grove, Randolph, Ill......	50
Jordan's Saline, Van Zandt, Tex ...	10
Jordan Spring, Montgomery, Tenn.	19
Jordan Station, Fulton, Ky........	99
Jordan Store, Williamson, Tenn ...	29
Jordan's Valley, Rutherford, Tenn.	82
Jordan Valley, Baker, Oreg.......	12
Jordan Village, Owen, Ind	10
Jordanville, Herkimer, N. Y.......	110
Jo's Branch, Wyoming, W. Va	5
Josco, Livingston, Mich	10
Joseph's Mills, Tyler, W. Va.......	18
Joslyn, Rock Island, Ill...........	12
Joy, Wayne, N. Y.................	62
Joy Creek, Washington, Kans......	12
Joyfield, Benzie, Mich............	35
Joyner's Depot, Wilson, N. C	140

* Money-order office.

KAO | KEL

Juda, Green, Wis	$220	Kaolin, Chester, Pa	$16
Judesville, Surry, N. C	7	Kappa, Woodford, Ill	91
Judson, White, Ark	12	Karrsville, Warren, N. J	19
Judson, Kankakee, Ill	17	Karthaus, Clearfield, Pa	30
Judson, Blue Earth, Minn	61	Kasey's, Bedford, Va	6
Judson, Sullivan, Mo	15	Kaseyville, Macon, Mo	17
Julesburgh, Weld, Colo	50	Kaskaskia, Randolph, Ill	82
Julian, San Diego, Cal	12	Kasoag, Oswego, N. Y	66
Julian Furnace, Centre, Pa	140	Kasota, La Sueur, Minn	60
Julietta, Marion, Ind	23	Kasson, Vanderburgh, Ind	8
Juliustown, Burlington, N. J	24	Kasson, Madison, Iowa	18
Jumping Branch, Mercer, W. Va	13	Kasson,* Dodge, Minn	360
Junction, Pulaski, Ill	26	Kasson, McKean, Pa	14
Junction, Madison, Mont	12	Kasson, Barbour, W. Va	13
Junction, Hunterdon, N. J	210	Kasson, Manitowoc, Wis	18
Junction, Rensselaer, N. Y	54	Katahdin Iron Works, Piscataquis,	
Junction, Paulding, Ohio	66	Me	23
Junction, Lancaster, Pa	27	Katonah, Westchester, N. Y	480
Junction, Hanover, Va	12	Kattelville, Broome, N. Y	31
Junction, Dane, Wis	35	Kaufman, (c. h.) Kaufman, Tex	220
Junction City, Trinity, Cal	13	Kaukauna, Outagamie, Wis	74
Junction City, Mills, Iowa	12	Kawkawlin, Bay, Mich	80
Junction City,* (c. h.,) Davis, Kans	2,200	Kaysville, Davis, Utah	70
Junction House, Lassen, Cal	12	Kearney, Clay, Mo	170
Juneau,* (c. h.,) Dodge, Wis	310	Kearney City, (c. h.) Kearney, Nebr	50
Juniata, Pueblo, Colo	12	Keatchie, De Soto, La	100
Juniata, Perry, Pa	43	Keating, McKean, Pa	12
Junius, Seneca, N. Y	81	Keck's Centre, Fulton, N. Y	13
Juno, Henderson, Tenn	18	Keck's Church, Martin, Ind	23
Jupiter, Madison, Ark	5	Kedron, Fillmore, Minn	6
		Keedysville, Washington, Md	110
K.		Keefer's Corners, Albany, N. Y	3
		Keefer's Store, Franklin, Pa	6
Kabletown, Jefferson, W. Va	60	Keeler's Bay, Grand Isle, Vt	12
Kahle's, Clarion, Pa	14	Keelersburgh, Wyoming, Pa	22
Kalama, Cowlitz, Wash	1	Keelersville, Van Buren, Mich	140
Kalamazoo,* (c. h.,) Kalamazoo,		Keelville, Cherokee, Kans	12
Mich	3,500	Keene, Jessamine, Ky	91
Kalamo, Eaton, Mich	72	Keene, Ionia, Mich	12
Kalida, (c. h.,) Putnam, Ohio	83	Keene,* (c. h.,) Cheshire, N. H	2,300
Kamas, Summit, Utah	12	Keene, Essex, N. Y	58
Kanarraville, Iron, Utah	34	Keene, Coshocton, Ohio	91
Kanawha C. H.,* Kanawha, W. Va	1,500	Keene, Portage, Wis	12
Kanawha Saline, Kanawha, W. Va	120	Keene Flats, Essex, N. Y	5
Kanawha Station, Wood, W. Va	36	Keeney's Settlement, Cortland, N.Y	35
Kandiyohi, Kandiyohi, Minn	120	Keeneyville, Tioga, Pa	63
Kandiyohi Station, (c. h.,) Kandiyohi,		Keenville, Wayne, Ill	17
Minn	12	Keep Tryst, Washington, Md	12
Kane, Greene, Ill	270	Keepville, Erie, Pa	12
Kane, Campbell, Ky	24	Keeseville,* Essex, N. Y	1,200
Kane, McKean, Pa	380	Keezletown, Rockingham, Va	25
Kane City, Venango, Pa	12	Keith's, Noble, Ohio	27
Kaneville, Kane, Ill	120	Keithsburgh,* Mercer, Ill	540
Kankakee,* (c. h.,) Kankakee, Ill	2,800	Kekoskee, Dodge, Wis	130
Kankakee, Starke, Ind	12	Kellersville, Monroe, Pa	14
Kanona, Steuben, N. Y	97	Kellerville, Dubois, Ind	12
Kanosh, Millard, Utah	32	Kelley, Mifflin, Pa	24
Kansas, Walker, Ala	2	Kelley's Island, Erie, Ohio	280
Kansas, Edgar, Ill	330	Kelley's Mills, Lawrence, Ohio	12
Kansas, Graves, Ky	22	Kellis' Store, Kemper, Miss	140
Kansas, Seneca, Ohio	100	Kellogg's, Douglas, Oreg	5
Kansas, Jefferson, Tenn	3	Kelloggsville, Kent, Mich	27
Kansas City,* Jackson, Mo	4,000	Kelloggsville, Cayuga, N. Y	120
Kansasville, Racine, Wis	270	Kelloggsville, Ashtabula, Ohio	130
Kantz, Snyder, Pa	14	Kellyburgh, Lycoming, Pa	10
Kaolin, Iron, Mo	12	Kelly Point, Union, Pa	12

KEN   KIL

Kelly's Corners, Lenawee, Mich...	$8	Kentontown, Robertson, Ky.......	$16
Kelly's Creek, St. Clair, Ala....	12	Kent's Hill, Kennebec, Me....	370
Kelly's Station, Armstrong, Pa....	78	Kentucky, Vermilion, Ill..........	4
Kellysville, Delaware, Pa........ ..	110	Kentucky Town, Grayson, Tex....	190
Kelsey, El Dorado, Cal....	23	Kenyon, Jackson, Ark..........	34
Kelso, Dearborn, Ind.............	16	Kenyon, Goodhue, Minn.........	100
Kelso, Sibley, Minn...............	4	Kenyonville, Orleans, N. Y......	35
Kelso, Lincoln, Tenn........	12	Keokuk,* Lee, Iowa.:...........	3,700
Kelton, Box Elder, Utah........	12	Keokuk Junction, Adams, Ill......	200
Kemblesville, Chester, Pa.........	130	*Keosauqua,* (c. h.,) Van Buren, Iowa	490
Kemp, Kaufman, Tex......	12	Keowee, Oconee, S. C.............	12
Kemper City, Victoria, Tex......	20	*Kerby,* (c. h.,) Josephine, Oreg.....	35
Kemp's Creek, Cleburne, Ala......	12	Kerhonkson, Ulster, N. Y....	120
Kemptown, Frederick, Md....	13	Kernersville, Forsyth, N. C.......	36
Kenansville, (c. h.,) Duplin, N. C..	240	Kerneysville, Jefferson, W. Va.....	150
Kendaia, Seneca, N. Y......... ...	72	Kernville, Kern, Cal.............	74
Kendall, Kendall, Ill....	46	Kerr's Station, Washington, Pa....	13
Kendall, Van Buren, Mich........	12	Kerr's Store, Clarion, Pa....	57
Kendall, Orleans, N. Y..........	80	Kerrsville, Cumberland, Pa......	50
Kendall, Anson, N. C....	12	*Kerrville,* (c. h.,) Kerr, Tex....	50
Kendall, Beaver, Pa.............	17	Kersey's, Elk, Pa	76
Kendall Creek, McKean, Pa......	22	Kershena, Shawanaw, Wis	27
Kendall Mills, Orleans, N. Y.......	12	Kesler's Cross Lanes, Nicholas,W.Va	9
Kendall's Mills, Somerset, Me.....	820	Kessler's, Northampton, Pa	6
Kendallville,* Noble, Ind.......	1,500	Keswick Depot, Albemarle, Va	270
Kendrick's Creek, Sullivan, Tenn..	12	Ketcham, Luzerne, Pa	8
Kenduskeag, Penobscot, Me.......	200	Ketchum's Corners, Saratoga, N. Y.	43
Kenesaw, Cobb, Ga.............	33	Ketchumville, Tioga, N. Y.........	20
Kennamer Cove, Marshall, Ala....	12	Kettle Creek, Potter, Pa........ ..	110
Kennard, Champaign, Ohio.......	58	Kewanee,* Henry, Ill	1,700
Kennard, Mercer, Pa.............	68	Kewanee, Lauderdale, Miss........	15
Kennebunk, York, Me.....	640	Kewanna, Fulton, Ind............	90
Kennebunk Depot, York, Me.....	490	Kewaskum, Washington, Wis	110
Kennebunk Landing, York, Me....	10	*Kewaunee,* (c. h.,) Kewaunee, Wis .	200
Kennebunkport, York, Me..... ..	440	Keyesport, Clinton, Ill	41
Kennedale, Tuscaloosa, Ala.... ..	12	Key Port,* Monmouth, N. J	740
Kennedy, Chautauqua, N. Y.......	210	Keysburgh, Logan, Ky	12
Kennedy's, Brunswick, Va........	25	Keystone, Douglas, Colo.........	12
Kennedyville, Kent, Md....	210	Keystone, Jackson, Ohio	37
Kennekuk, Atchison, Kans........	150	Keystone, Perry, Pa..............	7
Kenner, Jefferson, La.............	35	Keysville, Charlotte, Va..........	160
Kennerdell, Venango, Pa..........	22	*Keytesville,* (c. h.,) Chariton, Mo ...	340
Kennett, (c. h.,) Dunklin, Mo.......	61	*Key West,* (c. h.,) Monroe, Fla ...	1,400
Kennett's Square, Chester, Pa.....	780	Kezar Falls, York, Me............	110
Kennon, Belmont, Ohio..........	19	Kiantone, Chautauqua, N. Y.......	51
Kennonsburgh, Noble, Ohio......	22	Kickapoo, Peoria, Ill	110
Kenockee, St. Clair, Mich........	15	Kickapoo, Anderson, Tex..........	20
Kenosha, (c. h.,) Kenosha, Wis....	2,500	Kickapoo, Vernon, Wis...........	12
Kensico, Westchester, N. Y........	60	Kickapoo City, Leavenworth, Kans	81
Kensington, Hartford, Conn......	230	Kidder, Caldwell, Mo	310
Kensington, Oakland, Mich.......	53	Kidder's Ferry, Seneca, N. Y......	25
Kensington, Rockingham, N. H...	67	Kiddville, Clark, Ky	24
Kent, Litchfield, Conn...........	550	Kiddville, Ionia, Mich	11
Kent, Stephenson, Ill............	43	Kiddville, Sullivan, Mo	21
Kent, Jefferson, Ind............	53	Kidron, Coweta, Ga..............	15
Kent, Newton, Mo.............	9	Kidwell, Tyler, W. Va	9
Kent, Putnam, N. Y.............	5	Kiel, Manitowoc, Wis	110
Kent,* Portage, Ohio.............	1,200	Kier, Buchanan, Iowa............	15
Kent, Indiana, Pa...............	110	Kilbourn, Van Buren, Iowa	20
Kentland, (c. h.,) Newton, Ind....	650	Kilbourn City,* Columbia, Wis....	1,200
Kenton, Kent, Del..............	50	Kildare, Juneau, Wis	120
Kenton, Kenton, Ky............	25	Kilgore, Carroll, Ohio	60
Kenton, Christian, Mo.........	43	Kilgore, Venango, Pa	8
Kenton, (c. h.,) Hardin, Ohio.....	1,100	Kilkenny, Le Sueur, Minn........	36
Kenton, Obion, Tenn....	90	Killawog, Broome, N. Y	95
Kenton Furnace, Greenup, Ky....	14	Killbourne, Delaware, Ohio ......\	61

* Money-order office.

KIN

Killbuck, Ogle, Ill	$22
Kill Buck, Cattaraugus, N. Y	170
Killbuck, Holmes, Ohio	37
Killian's Mills, Lincoln, N. C	10
Killinger, Dauphin, Pa	32
Killingly, Windham, Conn	340
Killingworth, Middlesex, Conn	100
Kill Mills, Warren, N. J	4
Kilmarnock, Lancaster, Va	34
Kimberton, Chester, Pa	67
Kimbolton, Guernsey, Ohio	55
Kimmel, Indiana, Pa	10
Kimmer's Stand, Cumberland, Tenn	5
Kimmswick, Jefferson, Mo	140
Kimulga, Talladega, Ala	59
Kinard's Turnout, Newberry, S. C.	44
Kincheloe, Harrison, W. Va	8
Kinderhook, Van Buren, Ark	22
Kinderhook, Pike, Ill	120
Kinderhook, Branch, Mich	64
Kinderhook,* Columbia, N. Y	770
Kinderhook, Pickaway, Ohio	50
Kinderkamack, Bergen, N. J	12
King, Chattahoochee, Ga	5
King, Dubuque, Iowa	18
King City, Gentry, Mo	44
Kingfield, Franklin, Me	110
King George C. H., King George, Va.	12
King of Prussia, Montgomery, Pa..	71
King's, Barbour, Ala	5
King's, Athens, Ohio	31
Kingsboro, Edgecombe, N. C	7
Kingsborough, Fulton, N. Y	230
King's Bridge, Manitowoc, Wis	12
Kingsbridgeville, Westchester, N. Y	12
Kingsbury, Whitesides, Ill	38
Kingsbury, La Porte, Ind	57
Kingsbury, Piscataquis, Me	21
Kingsbury, Washington, N. Y	39
King's Cave, Harrison, Ind	12
King's Ferry, Nassau, Fla	18
King's Ferry, Cayuga, N. Y	240
King's Mountain, Gaston, N. C	10
King's Point, Dade, Mo	14
Kingsport, Sullivan, Tenn.	75
King's River, Fresno, Cal.	12
King's Settlement, Chenango, N. Y.	10
King's Station, Gibson, Ind	44
Kingston, Autauga, Ala	16
Kingston, Fresno, Cal	67
Kingston, Bartow, Ga	420
Kingston, De Kalb, Ill	30
Kingston, Decatur, Ind	41
Kingston, Des Moines, Iowa	41
Kingston, Madison, Ky	71
Kingston, Somerset, Md	100
Kingston, Plymouth, Mass	470
Kingston, Meeker, Minn	130
Kingston, (c. h.,) Caldwell, Mo	300
Kingston, Rockingham, N. H	160
Kingston, Somerset, N. J	170
Kingston,* (c. h.,) Ulster, N. Y	2,400
Kingston, Ross, Ohio	140
Kingston, Luzerne, Pa	840
Kingston, (c. h.,) Washington, R. I..	240
Kingston, (c. h.,) Roane, Tenn	390

KLI

Kingston, Green Lake, Wis	$170
Kingston Centre, Delaware, Ohio..	83
Kingston Furnace, Washington, Mo	38
Kingston Mines, Peoria, Ill	83
Kingstree, (c. h.,) Williamsburgh, S. C	240
Kingsville, Ashtabula, Ohio	480
Kingsville, Clarion, Pa	17
Kingsville, Richland, S. C	78
King William C. H., King William, Va	53
Kingwood, Hunterdon, N. J	20
Kingwood, Somerset, Pa	20
Kingwood, (c. h.,) Preston, W. Va	340
Kinlock, Lawrence, Ala	6
Kinmundy, Marion, Ill	620
Kinney's Four Corners, Oswego, N. Y	17
Kinnick Kinnick, St. Croix, Wis ..	10
Kinsale, Westmoreland, Va	60
Kinsman's,* Trumbull, Ohio	340
Kinston, (c. h.,) Lenoir, N. C	630
Kintnersville, Bucks, Pa	56
Kinzer's, Lancaster, Pa	150
Kinzua, Warren, Pa	50
Kiowa, Douglas, Colo	12
Kiowa, Jefferson, Nebr	12
Kipp's Corners, Genesee, Mich	8
Kipton, Lorain, Ohio	110
Kirby, Wyandot, Ohio	60
Kirby, Greene, Pa	23
Kirbyville, Berks, Pa	3
Kirchhayn, Washington, Wis	40
Kirkersville, Licking, Ohio	100
Kirkland, Oneida, N. Y	66
Kirkmansville, Todd, Ky	33
Kirk's Cross Roads, Clinton, Ind.	83
Kirk's Grove, Cherokee, Ala	5
Kirk's Mills, Lancaster, Pa	45
Kirksville, Madison, Ky	45
Kirksville,* (c. h.,) Adair, Mo	1,000
Kirkville, Wapello, Iowa	180
Kirkville, Onondaga, N. Y	85
Kirkwood, New Castle, Del	60
Kirkwood, St. Louis, Mo	270
Kirkwood, Camden, N. J	95
Kirkwood, Broome, N. Y	110
Kirkwood, Shelby, Ohio	58
Kirkwood, Lancaster, Pa	21
Kirkwood Centre, Broome, N. Y	13
Kirtland, Lake, Ohio	120
Kishacoquillas, Mifflin, Pa	62
Kishwaukee, Winnebago, Ill	45
Kiskiminitas, Armstrong, Pa	19
Kit Carson, (c. h.,) Greenwood, Colo.	12
Kittaning,* (c. h.,) Armstrong, Pa...	1,200
Kittery, York, Me	520
Kittery Depot, York, Me	120
Kittery Point, York, Me	240
Kittrell, Granville, N. C	240
Klamath, Siskiyou, Cal	12
Klecknersville, Northampton, Pa ..	22
Kleinfeltersville, Lebanon, Pa	12
Klikitat, Klikitat, Wash	12·
Kline's Grove, Northumberland, Pa	1
Klinesville, Hunterdon, N. J	6
Klinesville, Berks, Pa	11
Klingelhoeffer Landing, Perry, Ark.	14

* Money-order office.

KOS LAF

Klingerstown, Schuylkill, Pa	$4	Kossuth Centre, Kossuth, Iowa	$3
Knap of Reeds, Granville, N. C	11	Koszta, Iowa, Iowa	75
Knapp's Creek, Crawford, Wis	12	Kout's Station, Porter, Ind	78
Knauer's, Berks, Pa	9	Krakow, Franklin, Mo	12
Kniffin, Wayne, Iowa	16	Kratzerville, Snyder, Pa	34
Knight's Ferry, (c. h.,) Stanislaus,		Kreamer, Snyder, Pa	28
Cal	200	Kreidersville, Northampton, Pa	34
Knight's Mill, Berrien, Ga	12	Kresgeville, Monroe, Pa	85
Knight's Prairie, Hamilton, Ill	12	Krick's Mill, Berks, Pa	2
Knightstown, Henry, Ind	940	Kroghville, Jefferson, Wis	53
Knightsville, Clay, Ind	12	Kuckville, Orleans, N. Y	39
Knob, Beaver, Pa	6	Kulpsville, Montgomery, Pa	80
Knob, Tazewell, Va	23	Kunckle, Luzerne, Pa	11
Knob Creek, Cleveland, N. C	5	Kunkletown, Monroe, Pa	14
Knob Fork, Wetzel, W. Va	6	Kutztown, Berks, Pa	340
Knob Lick, Metcalfe, Ky	26	Kyger, Gallia, Ohio	20
Knob Lick, St. Francois, Mo	12	Kylertown, Clearfield, Pa	93
Knobnoster, Johnson, Mo	770	Kyserike, Ulster, N. Y	83
Knobsville, Fulton, Pa	25	Kyte River, Ogle, Ill	16
Knobview, Crawford, Mo	41		
Knott's Mills, Preston, W. Va	12	**L.**	
Knottsville, Daviess, Ky	37		
Knottsville, Tyler, W. Va	13	Labaddie, Franklin, Mo	57
Knowersville, Albany, N. Y	82	Labadieville, Assumption, La	13
Knowlesville, Orleans, N. Y	270	La Bajada, Santa Aña, N. Mex	12
Knowlton, Warren, N. J	24	La Belle, Lewis, Mo	87
Knowlton, Marathon, Wis	39	Labette, Labette, Kans	26
Knowlton's Landing, Desha, Ark	41	Lacelle, Clark, Iowa	12
Knox, (c. h.,) Stark, Ind	150	Lacey, Drew, Ark	12
Knox, Waldo, Me	80	Lacey, De Kalb, Ill	12
Knox, Albany, N. Y	90	Lacey, Muscatine, Iowa	10
Knox, Knox, Ohio	12	Lacey Spring, Rockingham, Va	36
Knox, Clarion, Pa	16	Lacey's Spring, Morgan, Ala	6
Knoxborough, Oneida, N. Y	160	Laceyville, Harrison, Ohio	26
Knox Dale, Jefferson, Pa	20	Laceyville, Wyoming, Pa	200
Knox Hill, Walton, Fla	14	Lackawack, Ulster, N. Y	31
Knoxville, Greene, Ala	27	Lackawanna, Luzerne, Pa	240
Knoxville, Lake, Cal	89	Lackawaxen, Pike, Pa	42
Knoxville, (c. h.,) Crawford, Ga	150	La Clair, De Kalb, Ill	41
*Knoxville,** (c. h.,) Knox, Ill	1,200	La Clede, Fayette, Ill	130
*Knoxville,** (c. h.,) Marion, Iowa	820	Laclede, Linn, Mo	430
Knoxville, Pendleton, Ky	6	*Lacon,** (c. h.,) Marshall, Ill	1,700
Knoxville, Claiborne, La	8	Lacon, Maries, Mo	9
Knoxville, Frederick, Md	240	Lacona, Warren, Iowa	12
Knoxville, Franklin, Miss	18	Lacona, Jefferson, Ky	27
Knoxville, Ray, Mo	77	Laconia, Harrison, Ind	54
Knoxville, Jefferson, Ohio	39	*Laconia,** (c. h.,) Belknap, N. H	1,400
Knoxville, Tioga, Pa	340	La Conner, Whatcom, Wash	10
*Knoxville,** (c. h.,) Knox, Tenn	3,400	La Crescent, Houston, Minn	130
Knoxville, Cherokee, Tex	22	La Crosse, Izard, Ark	120
Koch's, Wayne, Ohio	15	La Crosse, Hancock, Ill	12
Kodiak, ——, Alaska	68	La Crosse, La Porte, Ind	34
Koeltztown, Osage, Mo	23	*La Crosse,** (c. h.,) La Crosse, Wis	2,400
Kohlsville, Washington, Wis	12	La Cueva, Mora, N. Mex	12
*Kokomo,** (c. h.,) Howard, Ind	1,600	La Cygne, Linn, Kans	12
Koniska, McLeod, Minn	5	Laddsburgh, Bradford, Pa	14
Koro, Winnebago, Wis	21	Ladiesburgh, Frederick, Md	24
Koronis, Meeker, Minn	6	Ladiga, Calhoun, Ala	55
Kortright, Delaware, N. Y	30	*Ladoga,** Montgomery, Ind	460
Kosciusko, (c. h.,) Attala, Miss	620	Ladoga, Fond du Lac, Wis	79
Koskonong, Rock, Wis	32	Ladonia, Fannin, Tex	86
Kossuth, Washington, Ind	16	Ladora, Iowa, Iowa	81
Kossuth, Des Moines, Iowa	120	Ladore, Neosho, Kans	12
Kossuth, Alcorn, Miss	86	Laenna, Logan, Ill	28
Kossuth, Auglaize, Ohio	41	La Farge, Vernon, Wis	10
Kossuth, Clarion, Pa	30	La Fargeville, Jefferson, N. Y	280

* Money-order office.

LAK   LAK

La Fayette, Contra Costa, Cal	$20	Lake City, Siskiyou, Cal	$170
La Fayette, (c. h.,) Walker, Ga	120	Lake City, (c. h.,) Columbia, Fla....	750
La Fayette, Stark, Ill	170	Lake City, Stark, Ind.............	3
La Fayette,* (c. h.,) Tippecanoe, Ind.	3,800	Lake City, (c. h.,) Calhoun, Iowa....	91
La Fayette, Linn, Iowa	45	Lake City,* Wabashaw, Minn.....	1,600
La Fayette, Doniphan, Kans.......	21	Lake Comfort, Hyde, N. C........	5
La Fayette, Christian, Ky.........	180	Lake Como, Wayne, Pa	55
La Fayette, Gratiot, Mich	65	Lake Creek, Williamson, Ill.......	16
La Fayette, Sussex, N. J..........	150	Lake Creek, Benton, Mo	24
La Fayette, Onondaga, N. Y	78	Lake Creswell, Panola, Miss......	12
La Fayette, Madison, Ohio	42	Lake Crystal, Blue Earth, Minn....	7
La Fayette,* (c. h.,) Yam Hill, Oreg.	210	Lake Drummond, Norfolk, Va	42
La Fayette, McKean, Pa	12	Lake Five, Washington, Wis	12
La Fayette, Washington, R. I......	55	Lake Forest, Lake, Ill	420
La Fayette, (c. h.,) Macon, Tenn	110	Lake Fork, Ashland, Ohio........	17
La Fayette, Upshur, Tex	27	Lake Fremont, Sherburne, Minn...	8
La Fayette, Montgomery, Va	29	Lake Grove, Suffolk, N. Y........	48
La Fayette, Chippewa, Wis.......	8	Lake Harold, Meeker, Minn......	80
La Fayette Springs, La Fayette, Miss	23	Lake Hill, Ulster, N. Y...........	24
La Fayetteville, Dutchess, N. Y....	39	Lake Johanna, Pope, Minn.......	12
La Fontaine, Wabash, Ind.........	90	Lakeland, Washington, Minn.....	140
La Fontaine, Josh Bell, Ky.......	4	Lake Landing, Hyde, N. C	19
Laforme's Store, Braxton, W. Va...	12	Lake Lillian, Kandiyohi, Minn	10
La Fox, Kane, Ill	96	Lake Linden, Houghton, Mich.....	72
La Grande,* (c. h.,) Union, Oreg ...	320	Lake Maria, Green Lake, Wis......	19
La Grange, Phillips, Ark	31	Lake Mill, Van Buren, Mich......	58
La Grange, Stanislaus, Cal........	34	Lake Mills, Winnebago, Iowa.....	36
La Grange, (c. h.,) Troup, Ga.......	1,000	Lake Mills,* Jefferson, Wis........	360
La Grange,* (c. h.,) La Grange, Ind.	640	Lakenan, Shelby, Mo	46
La Grange, Lucas, Iowa..........	57	Lake Pleasant, Erie, Pa.........	20
La Grange, Morris, Kans..........	12	Lakeport, Lake, Cal............	82
La Grange, (c. h.,) Oldham, Ky....	350	Lakeport, Yankton, Dak	12
La Grange, Penobscot, Me........	100	Lake Port, St. Clair, Mich.......	110
La Grange, Cass, Mich	70	Lakeport, Madison, N. Y........	37
La Grange,* Lewis, Mo..........	500	Lake Providence, Carroll, La......	100
La Grange, Wyoming, N. Y........	62	Lake Ridge, Lenawee, Mich......	21
La Grange, Lenoir, N. C.........	120	Lake Ridge, Tompkins, N. Y......	44
La Grange, Lorain, Ohio	190	Lake Road, Niagara, N. Y........	16
La Grange, Wyoming, Pa........	14	Lake Shetik, Murray, Minn......	12
La Grange,* Fayette, Tenn......	450	Lake Sibley, Cloud, Kans........	100
La Grange, (c. h.,) Fayette, Tex....	850	Lake Side, Wayne, N. Y.........	130
La Grange, Grand Isle, Vt........	15	Lake Spring, Dent, Mo.........	24
La Grange, Walworth, Wis.......	38	Lake Station, Greenwood, Colo....	12
La Grange Bluff, Brown, Ill	12	Lake Station, Lake, Ind........	130
La Grangeville, Dutchess, N. Y....	37	Lakesville, Dorchester, Md.......	23
La Gro, Wabash, Ind	380	Laketon, Wabash, Ind..........	40
Laguardo, Wilson, Tenn	22	Laketon, Berrien, Mich.........	69
La Harpe, Hancock, Ill	430	Laketown, Carver, Minn........	8
Lahaska, Bucks, Pa............	180	Lake Traverse, Stone, Minn......	13
Laing's, Monroe, Ohio..........	29	Lake View, Cook, Ill...........	12
Laingsburgh, Shiawassee, Mich ...	340	Lakeview, Montcalm, Mich.......	52
Lairdsville, Oneida, N. Y.......	22	Lakeview, Cuming, Nebr.........	12
Lairdsville, Lycoming, Pa........	60	Lake View, Erie, N. Y..........	44
Lair's Station, Harrison, Ky......	31	Lake Village, (c. h.,) Chicot, Ark....	98
La Junta, Mora, N. Mex..........	12	Lake Village, McPherson, Kans....	12
Lake, Spencer, Ind.............	26	Lake Village, Belknap, N. H.......	910
Lake, Newaygo, Mich	12	Lakeville, Sonoma, Cal.........	69
Lake, Scott, Miss.............	130	Lakeville, Litchfield, Conn......	350
Lake, Washington, N. Y........	43	Lakeville, St. Joseph, Ind.......	70
Lake, Stark, Ohio.............	84	Lakeville, Plymouth, Mass.......	120
Lake, Luzerne, Pa.............	10	Lakeville, Oakland, Mich.......	20
Lake Addie, McLeod, Minn......	9	Lakeville, Dakota, Minn.......	59
Lake Arthur, Calcasieu, La.....	12	Lakeville, Stoddard, Mo.......	17
Lake Butler, (c. h.,) Bradford, Fla ..	12	Lakeville, Livingston, N. Y......	82
Lake Charles, (c. h.,) Calcasieu, La..	20	Lake Washington, LeSueur, Minn.	10
		Lake Zurich, Lake, Ill..........	85

* Money-order office.

Lakin's Grove, Hamilton, Iowa....	$11	Lane, Montgomery, Ind...........	$12
Lamar, Randolph, Ala............	12	Lane, Franklin, Kans............	60
Lamar, Marshall, Miss...........	150	Lanesborough, Berkshire, Mass....	240
Lamar, (c. h.,) Barton, Mo.......	240	Lanesborough, Fillmore, Minn.....	500
Lamar, Clinton, Pa..............	100	Lanesborough, Anson, N. C.......	10
Lamar, Refugio, Tex............	12	Lanesborough, Susquehanna, Pa...	210
Lamar Mills, Clinton, Pa........	12	Lanesfield, Johnson, Kans.......	86
Lamar's Station, Nodaway, Mo....	38	Lane's Prairie, Maries, Mo.......	32
Lamartine, Columbia, Ark.......	13	Lanesville, Litchfield, Conn.....	91
Lamartine, Carroll, Ohio........	84	Lanesville, Harrison, Ind........	130
Lamartine, Clarion, Pa..........	46	Lanesville, Floyd, Ky...........	18
Lamartine, Fond du Lac, Wis.....	63	Lanesville, Essex, Mass.........	210
Lamberton, Racine, Wis	54	Lanesville, King William, Va.....	52
Lambertville, Monroe, Mich.....	44	Laney, Shawanaw, Wis..........	12
Lambertville,* Hunterdon, N.J....	1,300	Langdon, Peoria, Ill............	9
Lamb's, Venango, Pa............	87	Langdon, Sullivan, N. H........	34
Lambsburgh, Carroll, Va........	6	Langford, Erie, N. Y...........	24
Lamb's Corners, Broome, N. Y....	40	Langley, Fairfax, Va...........	17
Lamb's Creek, Tioga, Pa........	41	Langola, Benton, Minn.........	20
La Mine, Cooper, Mo...........	39	Langston, Montcalm, Mich......	12
Lamira, Belmont, Ohio..........	54	Langsville, Meigs, Ohio........	16
Lamoille, Bureau, Ill...........	430	L'Anguille, St. Francis, Ark.....	12
Lamoille, Marshall, Iowa........	12	Langworth, Stanislaus, Cal......	46
Lamoille, Winona, Minn.........	2	Langworthy, Jones, Iowa........	74
Lamoine, Hancock, Me..........	36	Lannon Springs, Waukesha, Wis...	12
Lamont, Ottawa, Mich..........	190	Lannsdale, Monroe, Miss........	12
Lamonte, Pettis, Mo...........	200	Lansing, Cook, Ill............	64
La Motte, Jackson, Iowa........	100	Lansing,* Allamakee, Iowa.......	1,200
Lampasas, (c. h.,) Lampasas, Tex...	160	LANSING,* Ingham, Mich.........	2,600
Lampeter, Lancaster, Pa........	50	Lansing, Mower, Minn.........	170
Lamson's, Onondaga, N. Y......	55	Lansing, Tioga, Pa............	12
Lanark, Bradley, Ark..........	19	Lansingburgh,* Rensselaer, N. Y...	1,500
Lanark, Carroll, Ill...........	1,100	Lansingville, Tompkins, N. Y....	38
Lanark, Lehigh, Pa............	12	Lantz Mills, Shenandoah, Va.....	14
Lancaster, Cass, Ill...........	29	Laona, Winnebago, Ill.........	73
Lancaster, Jefferson, Ind.......	77	Laona, Gage, Nebr............	24
Lancaster, Keokuk, Iowa.......	51	Laona, Chautauqua, N. Y......	120
Lancaster, Atchison, Kans......	21	*La Paz,* (c. h.,) Yuma, Ariz.....	340
Lancaster, (c. h.,) Garrard, Ky.....	730	*Lapeer,* (c. h.,) Lapeer, Mich......	1,100
Lancaster, Worcester, Mass.....	620	Lapeer, Cortland, N. Y........	8
Lancaster, (c. h.,) Schuyler, Mo...	310	Lapidum, Harford, Md.........	66
Lancaster, (c. h.,) Coos, N. H.....	1,000	La Place, St. Martins, La.......	22
Lancaster, Erie, N. Y.........	430	La Plata, Macon, Mo..........	340
Lancaster, (c. h.,) Fairfield, Ohio...	2,200	*La Pointe,* (c. h.,) Ashland, Wis....	14
Lancaster, Lane, Oreg.........	20	La Porte,* Plumas, Cal........	340
Lancaster, (c. h.,) Lancaster, Pa...	2,800	*La Porte,* (c. h.,) Larimer, Colo....	12
Lancaster, Dallas, Tex........	180	*La Porte,* (c. h.,) La Porte, Ind....	2,900
Lancaster, (c. h.,) Grant, Wis.....	790	La Porte, Lorain, Ohio........	86
Lancaster C. H., Lancaster, S. C....	65	*Laporte,* (c. h.,) Sullivan, Pa......	340
Lancaster C. H., Lancaster, Va.....	31	Laporte City, Black Hawk, Iowa..	260
L'Ance, Houghton, Mich.......	26	La Prairie, Adams, Ill........	150
Lancha Plana, Amador, Cal.....	25	La Prairie Centre, Marshall, Ill....	36
Landaff, Grafton, N. H........	37	Lapwai, Nez Perces, Idaho......	100
Laudenburgh, Chester, Pa......	44	*Laramie City,* (c. h.,) Albany, Wyo..	1,800
Lander, Frederick, Md.........	24	*Laredo,* (c. h.,) Webb, Tex.....	150
Lander, Warren, Pa...........	97	Larimer Mills, Sarpy, Nebr.....	39
Landersdale, Morgan, Ind.......	12	Larimer's Station, Westmoreland,	
Landersville, Lawrence, Ala.....	19	Pa......................	98
Landingville, Schuylkill, Pa.....	93	Larissa, Winston, Ala.........	12
Landisburgh, Perry, Pa........	160	Larissa, Cherokee, Tex.........	59
Landis' Store, Berks, Pa.......	9	Larkinsburgh, Clay, Ill........	22
Landis Valley, Lancaster, Pa....	10	Larkin's Fork, Jackson, Ala.....	10
Landisville, Lancaster, Pa......	56	Larkinsville, Jackson, Ala......	130
Land Mark, Howard, Mo.......	12	Larone, Somerset, Me.........	32
Land of Promise, Princess Anne, Va	12	Larrabee, Manitowoc, Wis......	24
Landsdale, Montgomery, Pa......	250	Larrabee's Point, Addison, Vt.....	12

* Money-order office.

LAU   LEA

Larry's Creek, Lycoming, Pa	$24	Lavalle, Sauk, Wis	$45
La Rue, Benton, Ark	12	Lavansville, Somerset, Pa	47
Larue,* Marion, Ohio	230	La Vega, Des Moines, Iowa	18
Larwill, Whitley, Ind	290	La Vergne, Rutherford, Tenn	120
La Salle,* La Salle, Ill	2,600	Lavernia, Wilson, Tex	14
La Salle, Monroe, Mich	63	Lawler, Chickasaw, Iowa	300
La Salle, Niagara, N. Y	88	Lawndale, Logan, Ill	52
Las Cruces, Santa Barbara, Cal	12	Lawn Ridge, Marshall, Ill	190
Las Cruces, Doña Ana, N. Mex	100	Lawrence, McHenry, Ill	43
Lasellsville, Fulton, N. Y	53	Lawrence, Marion, Ind	85
Lassen, Tehama, Cal	12	Lawrence,* (c. h.,) Douglas, Kans	3,500
Lassiter's Mills, Randolph, N. C	11	Lawrence,* Essex, Mass	4,000
Last Chance, Lucas, Iowa	22\	Lawrence,* Van Buren, Mich	380
Las Vegas, (c. h.,) San Miguel, N. Mex	270	Lawrence, Newton, Miss	43
		Lawrence, Schuyler, N. Y	15
Latham, Pike, Ohio	15	Lawrence, Washington, Ohio	20
Lathrop, Clinton, Mo	490	Lawrence, Marquette, Wis	12
Lathrop, Susquehanna, Pa	8	Lawrenceburgh,* (c. h.,) Dearborn, Ind	1,400
Latimore, Adams, Pa	12		
Latonia Springs, Kenton, Ky	16	Lawrenceburgh, Warren, Iowa	11
Latrobe, El Dorado, Cal	85	Lawrenceburgh, Cloud, Kans	12
Latrobe, Johnson, Nebr	10	Lawrenceburgh, (c. h.,) Anderson, Ky	330
Latrobe, Westmoreland, Pa	780	Lawrenceburgh, Armstrong, Pa	890
Lattas, Ross, Ohio	22	Lawrenceburgh, (c. h.,) Lawrence, Tenn	190
Lattasburgh, Wayne, Ohio	47		
Lattner's, Dubuque, Iowa	15	Lawrenceville, Henry, Ala	34
Latty, Des Moines, Iowa	12	Lawrenceville, (c. h.,) Gwinnett, Ga	170
Laubach, Northampton, Pa	220	Lawrenceville, (c. h.,) Lawrence, Ill	290
Laud, Whitley, Ind	22	Lawrenceville, Dearborn, Ind	25
Lauderdale Station, Lauderdale, Miss	350	Lawrenceville, Mercer, N. J	270
		Lawrenceville, St. Lawrence, N. Y	240
Laughlintown, Westmoreland, Pa	59	Lawrenceville, Tioga, Pa	370
Laura, Miami, Ohio	38	Lawrenceville, (c. h.,) Brunswick, Va	280
Lauraville, Baltimore, Md	22	Lawson, Washington, Mo	12
Laurel, Sussex, Del	510	Lawson Station, Ray, Mo	12
Laurel, Franklin, Ind	290	Lawsonville, Rockingham, N. C	3
Laurel, Marshall, Iowa	12	Lawsville Centre, Susquehanna, Pa	72
Laurel, Clermont, Ohio	41		
Laurel Bluff, Muhlenburgh, Ky	25	Lawton, Clinch, Ga	21
Laurel Bridge, Laurel, Ky	12	Lawton,* Van Buren, Mich	620
Laurel Creek, Clay, Ky	3	Lawtonville, Burke, Ga	84
Laurel Creek, Lincoln, W. Va	12	Lawtonville, Beaufort, S. C	20
Laurel Factory,* Prince George's, Md	380	Lawyersville, Schoharie, N. Y	13
		Layman, Washington, Ohio	16
Laurel Fork, Carroll, Va	12	Layton, Sussex, N. J	42
Laurel Gap, Greene, Tenn	8	Laytonia, Venango, Pa	420
Laurel Grove, Pittsylvania, Va	21	Layton's Station, Fayette, Pa	59
Laurel Hill, Neshoba, Miss	12	Laytonville, Montgomery, Md	46
Laurel Hill, Perry, Mo	16	Lazaretto Station, Delaware, Pa	29
Laurel Hill, Richmond, N. C	7	Leacock, Lancaster, Pa	66
Laurel Hill, De Kalb, Tenn	12	Lead Hill, Marion, Ark	37
Laurel Iron Works, Mongalia, W. Va	12	Lead Mine, Tucker, W. Va	4
		Leadsville, Randolph, W. Va	31
Laurel Junction, Wood, W. Va	130	Leadvale, Jefferson, Tenn	96
Laurel Mills, Rappahannock, Va	19	Leaksville, Rockingham, N. C	94
Laurel Point, Monongalia, W. Va	16	Leaksville, Page, Va	10
Laurel Ridge, Kanawha, W. Va	12	Leaman Place, Lancaster, Pa	110
Laurel Run, Luzerne, Pa	210	Leamon Corner, Hancock, Ind	12
Laurel Springs, Ashe, N. C	6	Leanah, Estill, Ky	12
Laurelton, Union, Pa	94	Leasburgh, Crawford, Mo	59
Laurelville, Westmoreland, Pa	22	Leasburgh, Doña Ana, N. Mex	20
Laurens, Otsego, N. Y	200	Leasburgh, Caswell, N. C	97
Laurens C. H.,* Laurens, S. C	450	Lea's Chapel, Person, N. C	12
Laurens Hill, Laurens, Ga	15	Leasuresville, Butler, Pa	30
Laurinburgh, Richmond, N. C	9	Leathersville, Lincoln, Ga	9
Laury's Station, Lehigh, Pa	60	Leatherwood, Guernsey, Ohio	90

* Money-order office.

LEE

Leatherwood, Clarion, Pa	$40
Leavenworth,* (c. h.,) Crawford, Ind.	370
Leavenworth, Brown, Minn	29
Leavenworth City,* (c. h.,) Leavenworth, Kans	4,000
Leavitt, Carroll, Ohio	37
Leavittsburgh, Trumbull, Ohio	200
Lebanon, (c. h.,) De Kalb, Ala	120
Lebanon, New London, Conn	180
Lebanon, Kent, Del	81
Lebanon,* St. Clair, Ill	1,000
Lebanon,* (c. h.) Boone, Ind	760
Lebanon, Van Buren, Iowa	52
Lebanon,* (c. h.,) Marion, Ky	1,200
Lebanon, York, Me	47
Lebanon, (c. h.,) Laclede, Mo	370
Lebanon,* Grafton, N. H	1,300
Lebanon, Hunterdon, N. J	170
Lebanon, Madison, N. Y	91
Lebanon,* (c. h.,) Warren, Ohio	1,700
Lebanon, Linn, Oreg	88
Lebanon,* (c. h.,) Lebanon, Pa	1,600
Lebanon,* (c. h.,) Wilson, Tenn	1,300
Lebanon, (c. h.,) Russell, Va	140
Lebanon Church, Allegheny, Pa	16
Lebanon Church, Shenandoah, Va	22
Lebanon Junction, Bullitt, Ky	98
Lebœuf, Erie, Pa	51
Le Claire,* Scott, Iowa	460
Lecompton, Douglas, Kans	110
Lecompton, Monroe, Ohio	16
Leconte's Mills, Clearfield, Pa	44
Lederachsville, Montgomery, Pa	14
Ledge Dale, Wayne, Pa	51
Ledger, Mitchell, N. C	3
Ledyard, New London, Conn	42
Ledyard, Cayuga, N. Y	83
Lee, Warrick, Ind	4
Lee, Penobscot, Me	120
Lee,* Berkshire, Mass	1,500
Lee, Strafford, N. H	51
Lee, Oneida, N. Y	27
Lee,* Athens, Ohio	230
Lee Centre, Lee, Ill	300
Lee Centre, Oneida, N. Y	180
Leechburgh, Johnston, N. C	5
Leechburgh, Armstrong, Pa	560
Leech Lake, Cass, Minn	10
Leech's Corners, Mercer, Pa	33
Leechville, Beaufort, N. C	16
Leeds, Androscoggin, Me	65
Leeds, Hampshire, Mass	220
Leeds, Greene, N. Y	320
Leeds, Washington, Utah	12
Leeds, Columbia, Wis	100
Leeds Centre, Columbia, Wis	50
Leeds Junction, Adroscoggin, Me	61
Leeds Point, Atlantic, N. J	73
Leedston, Stearns, Minn	10
Leedsville, Monmouth, N. J	25
Leedsville, Dutchess, N. Y	27
Leesburgh, Cherokee, Ala	26
Leesburgh, Lemhi, Idaho	12
Leesburgh, Kosciusko, Ind	210
Leesburgh, Harrison, Ky	63
Leesburgh, Cumberland, N. J	44

LEN

Leesburgh, Highland, Ohio	$240
Leesburgh, Mercer, Pa	46
Leesburgh, Washington, Tenn	34
Leesburgh,* (c. h.,) Loudoun, Va	900
Lee's Creek, Crawford, Ark	20
Lee's Creek, Clinton, Ohio	10
Lee's Cross Roads, Cumberland, Pa.	76
Leesport, Bucks, Pa	320
Lee's Summit, Jackson, Mo	790
Leesville, Middlesex, Conn	25
Leesville, Boone, Ill	6
Leesville, Lawrence, Ind	51
Leesville, Henry, Mo	61
Leesville, Schoharie, N. Y	26
Leesville, Robeson, N. C	12
Leesville, Carroll, Ohio	110
Leesville, Lexington, S. C	25
Leesville, Campbell, Va	31
Leesville Cross Roads, Crawford, Ohio	47
Leetonia, Columbiana, Ohio	460
Leetown, Jefferson, W. Va	100
Leetsdale, Allegheny, Pa	18
Lee Valley, Hawkins, Tenn	7
Le Fever Falls, Ulster, N. Y	12
Leghorn, Pottawatomie, Kans	12
Le Grand, Marshall, Iowa	300
Lehi, Jefferson, Ark	12
Lehi City, Utah, Utah	73
Lehigh Gap, Carbon, Pa	95
Lehigh Tannery, Carbon, Pa	12
Lehighton, Carbon, Pa	410
Lehigh Valley, Lehigh, Pa	33
Lehman, Luzerne, Pa	40
Leicester, Worcester, Mass	650
Leicester, Buncombe, N. C	16
Leicester, Addison, Vt	37
Leicester, Dane, Wis	81
Leidy, Clinton, Pa	18
Leighton, Franklin, Ala	20
Leighton, Mahaska, Iowa	83
Leighton, Hennepin, Minn	5
Leighton's Corners, Carroll, N. H	30
Leinbach's, Berks, Pa	22
Leipersville, Delaware, Pa	65
Leipsic, Kent, Del	100
Leipsic, Orange, Ind	36
Leipsic, Putnam, Ohio	170
Leistville, Pickaway, Ohio	35
Leitersburgh, Washington, Md	110
Leithsville, Northampton, Pa	17
Leland, La Salle, Ill	690
Leland, Leelenaw, Mich	94
Leland, Josephine, Oreg	26
Lemars, Plymouth, Iowa	12
Lemington, Essex, Vt	5
Lemon, Wyoming, Pa	21
Lemond, Steele, Minn	8
Lemont,* Cook, Ill	910
Lemont, Centre, Pa	12
Lemonweir, Juneau, Wis	49
Lempster, Sullivan, N. H	83
Lena,* Stephenson, Ill	870
Lenape, Leavenworth, Kans	12
Lenape, Chester, Pa	12
Lenexa, Johnson, Kans	20

*Money-order office.

LET   LEX

Lenhartsville, Berks, Pa	$32	Letcher, Bath, Va.................	$5
Lenni Mills, Delaware, Pa	100	Letohatchee, Lowndes, Ala	20
Lenoir, (c. h.,) Caldwell, N. C	290	Letsinger, Roane, Tenn	12
Lenoir's, Roane, Tenn	32	Letter Gap, Gilmer, W. Va....	5
Lenora, Fillmore, Minn	120	Letts, Louisa, Iowa.............	260
Lenox, Kane, Ill..............	12	Lettsville, Daviess, Ind......	12
Lenox, (c. h.,) Berkshire, Mass	900	Levan, Juab, Utah.................	12
Lenox, Madison, N. Y	44	Levanna, Cayuga, N. Y.............	42
Lenox, Ashtabula, Ohio....	84	Levanna, Brown, Ohio.............	34
Lenox Castle, Rockingham, N. C ..	23	Levant, Penobscot, Me.............	58
Lenox Furnace, Berkshire, Mass ...	160	Levee, Montgomery, Ky............	24
Lenoxville, Susquehanna, Pa	56	Level, Warren, Ohio...............	33
Lenz, Hennepin, Minn	28	Level Land, Abbeville, S. C	5
Lenzburgh, St. Clair, Ill...	66	Leverett, Franklin, Mass..........	250
Leo, White, Ga....	12	Levering, Knox, Ohio.............	59
Leo, Allen, Ind	78	Levingood, Pendleton, Ky..........	26
Leo, Stanly, N. C	5	Lewes,* Sussex, Del............. ...	460
Leominster, Worcester, Mass	1,500	Lewinsville, Fairfax, Va....	9
Leon, Crenshaw, Ala	6	Lewis, Kendall, Ill..................	8
Leon, Whitesides, Ill	16	Lewis, Vigo, Ind.................	52
*Leon,** (c. h.,) Decatur, Iowa	520	*Lewis,** (c. h.,) Cass, Iowa...........	480
Leon, Cattaraugus, N. Y....	110	Lewis, Essex, N. Y.................	92
Leon, Ashtabula, Ohio	16	Lewisberry, York, Pa..............	120
Leon, Madison, Va..............	13	Lewisborough, Westchester, N. Y ..	37
Leon, Monroe, Wis.....	82	Lewisburgh, Conway, Ark	140
Leona, Bradford, Pa......	58	Lewisburgh, Wayne, Iowa.........	32
Leona, Leon, Tex......	67	Lewisburgh, Preble, Ohio	120
Leonardsburgh, Delaware, Ohio ...	58	*Lewisburgh,** (c. h.,) Union, Pa	2,100
Leonardsville, Madison, N. Y	260	*Lewisburgh,* (c. h.,) Marshall, Tenn..	170
*Leonardtown,** (c. h.,) St. Mary's, Md.	310	*Lewisburgh,** (c. h.,) Greenbrier, W.	
Leonardville, Monmouth, N. J	43	Va.................	570
Leoni, Jackson, Mich	130	Lewis Centre, Delaware, Ohio	180
Leonia, Bergen, N. J	43	Lewis Creek, Shelby, Ind..........	23
Leonidas, St. Joseph, Mich........	180	Lewisport, Hancock, Ky......	130
Leon Springs, Bexar, Tex	19	Lewis' Station, Escambia, Ala	7
Leopard, Chester, Pa.............	35	Lewis' Store, Spottsylvania, Va....	8
Leopold, Perry, Ind......	37	Lewiston, Trinity, Cal	37
Leota Landing, Washington, Miss..	10	*Lewiston,** (c. h.,) Nez Perces, Idaho.	230
Leoti, Pike, Ind....................	8	Lewiston, Cherokee, Kans	12
L'Erable, Iroquois, Ill..............	16	Lewiston,* Androscoggin, Me	2,700
Le Raysville, Jefferson, N. Y	19	Lewiston, Dakota, Minn	54
Le Raysville, Bradford, Pa	260	Lewiston, Niagara, N. Y....	450
Le Roy, Union, Dak............	12	Lewiston, Columbia, Wis	19
Leroy, McLean, Ill......	390	Lewiston Station, Columbia, Wis ..	12
Le Roy, Lake, Ind......	12	*Lewistown,** (c. h.,) Fulton, Ill.......	1,000
Leroy, Bremer, Iowa..............	20	Lewistown, Frederick, Md	44
Le Roy,* Coffey, Kans..............	310	Lewistown, Logan, Ohio	27
Le Roy,* Mower, Minn.............	520	*Lewistown,** (c. h.,) Mifflin, Pa......	1,800
Le Roy, Barton, Mo..............	21	*Lewistown,* (c. h.,) La Fayette, Ark..	80
Le Roy,* Genesee, N. Y......	2,200	Lewisville, Henry, Ind.............	240
Le Roy, Medina, Ohio.............	340	Lewisville, Forsyth, N. C...........	9
Le Roy, Bradford, Pa.............	68	Lewisville, Monroe, Ohio..........	43
Le Roy, Jackson, W. Va............	29	Lewisville, Polk, Oreg......	12
Leroy, Dodge, Wis...............	33	Lewisville, Chester, Pa....	96
Le Roy Station, Monroe, Wis......	28	Lewisville, Denton, Tex...........	88
Leslie, Ingham, Mich......	500	Lexington, Santa Clara, Cal.......	56
Leslie, Van Wert, Ohio.............	20	*Lexington,** (c. h.,) Oglethorpe, Ga..	270
Lesser Cross Roads, Somerset, N. J.	67	Lexington, McLean, Ill............	660
Lester, Marion, Ill...............	22	*Lexington*, (c. h.,) Scott, Ind.........	260
Lester, Black Hawk, Iowa....	21	Lexington, Washington, Iowa	12
Lester's, Giles, Tenn.............	25	*Lexington,** (c. h.,) Fayette, Ky......	3,800
Lester's District, Burke, Ga........	120	Lexington, Somerset, Me	20
Lesterville, Reynolds, Mo....	9	Lexington, Middlesex, Mass.......	480
*Le Sueur,** (c. h.,) Le Sueur, Minn...	540	*Lexington,** (c. h.,) Sanilac, Mich .. .	620
Letart, Mason, W. Va............	51	Lexington, Le Sueur, Minn........	54
Letart Falls, Meigs, Ohio....	64	*Lexington*, (c. h.,) Holmes, Miss.....	640

* Money-order office.

LIC . LIN

Lexington,* (c. h.,) La Fayette, Mo ..	$1,900	Licksville, Frederick, Md.........	$12
Lexington, Greene, N. Y	77	Liddesdale, Columbia, Ark	15
Lexington, (c. h.,) Davidson, N. C...	330	Light Street, Columbia, Pa........	100
Lexington, Richland, Ohio........	280	Ligonier,* Noble, Ind	1,100
Lexington, (c. h.,) Henderson, Tenn.	110	Ligonier, Vernon, Mo	12
Lexington, Burleson, Tex	160	Ligonier, Westmoreland, Pa........	180
Lexington,* (c. h.,) Rockbridge, Va..	2,200	Likens, Crawford, Ohio	20
Lexington C. H., Lexington, S. C	100	Lilesville, Anson, N. C...........	54
Leyden, Cook, Ill	69	Lillard's Mills, Marshall, Tenn.....	20
Leyden, Franklin, Mass	39	Lillington, New Hanover, N. C....	16
Leyden, Lewis, N. Y...............	200	Lilly, Scioto, Ohio	23
Leyden, Rock, Wis	14	Lilly Dale, Perry, Ind............	10
Leyden Centre, Cook, Ill	12	Lilly Pond, Wright, Minn	12
Liberty, Ouachita, Ark............	10	Lima, Adams, Ill..................	96
Liberty, San Joaquin, Cal	93	Lima, La Grange, Ind.............	480
Liberty, Union, Dak	34	Lima, Fayette, Iowa	12
Liberty, Adams, Ill	140	Lima, Clay, Kans	13
Liberty,* (c. h.,) Union, Ind........	440	Lima, Washtenaw, Mich :........	48
Liberty, Clarke, Iowa............	47	Lima, Livingston, N. Y..........	1,600
Liberty, Montgomery, Kans	12	Lima,* (c. h.,) Allen, Ohio........	1,800
Liberty, (c. h.,) Casey, Ky	45	Lima, Delaware, Pa..............	55
Liberty, Waldo, Me	140	Lima, Greenville, S. C	11
Liberty, Jackson, Mich...........	81	Lima Centre, Rock, Wis	130
Liberty, (c. h.,) Amite, Miss	250	Limaville, Stark, Ohio	160
Liberty,* (c. h.,) Clay, Mo	890	Limber Lost, Adams, Ind.........	15
Liberty, Pawnee, Nebr	20	Lime Creek, Cerro Gordo, Iowa....	9
Liberty, Sullivan, N. Y	200	Lime Hill, Bradford, Pa	26
Liberty, Montgomery, Ohio........	58	Limekiln, Berks, Pa.............	12
Liberty, Tioga, Pa	240	Limeport, Lehigh, Pa	15
Liberty, De Kalb, Tenn	57	Limerick, Bureau, Ill	47
Liberty, (c. h.,) Liberty, Tex	150	Limerick, York, Me..............	300
Liberty, Rich, Utah..............	4	Limerick, Jefferson, N. Y	61
Liberty,* (c. h.,) Bedford, Va........	810	Limerick, Montgomery, Pa	82
Liberty, Vernon, Wis	76	Limerick Station, Montgomery, Pa.	200
Liberty Centre, Warren, Iowa.....	15	Lime Ridge, Columbia, Pa	55
Liberty Centre, Henry, Ohio......	160	Lime Ridge, Sauk, Wis..........	41
Liberty Corner, Somerset, N. J.....	84	Lime Rock, Litchfield, Conn.......	200
Liberty Corners, Crawford, Ohio...	32	Lime Rock, Outagamie, Wis.......	36
Liberty Corners, Bradford, Pa.....	18	Lime Spring, Howard, Iowa	84
Liberty Falls, Sullivan, N. Y.......	59	Limestone, Kankakee, Ill..........	23
Liberty Hall, Newberry, S. C	6	Limestone, Washington, Kans	13
Liberty Hill, Dallas, Ala	26	Limestone, Aroostook, Me	12
Liberty Hill, New London, Conn...	120	Limestone, Cattaraugus, N. Y.....	170
Liberty Hill, Pike, Ga.............	20	Limestone, Clarion, Pa..........	82
Liberty Hill, Williamson, Tex	16	Limestone, Marshall, W. Va	3
Liberty Mills, Wabash, Ind........	150	Limestone Cove, Carter, Tenn	12
Liberty Mills, Orange, Va	110	Limestone Springs, Spartanburgh,	
Liberty Pole, Vernon, Wis	76	S. C...........................	37
Liberty Prairie, Madison, Ill.......	12	Limestone Springs, Greene, Tenn ..	24
Liberty Ridge, Grant, Wis.........	12	Limestoneville, Montour, Pa......	80
Liberty Springs, Van Buren, Ark ..	12	Limington, York, Me.............	160
Liberty Square, Lancaster, Pa	43	Limitar, Socorro, N. Mex	18
Libertytown, Frederick, Md	170	Lincklaen, Chenango, N. Y	55
Libertyville, Lake, Ill............	160	Lincoln, Talladega, Ala	12
Libertyville, Jefferson, Iowa......	92	Lincoln,* Placer, Cal.............	210
Libertyville, St. Francois, Mo......	71	Lincoln, Clay, Dak	46
Libertyville, Sussex, N. J.........	21	Lincoln, Sussex, Del	290
Libertyville, Ulster, N. Y.........	8	Lincoln,* (c. h.,) Logan, Ill	2,000
Library, Allegheny, Pa...........	71	Lincoln, Cass, Ind	42
Lick, Fannin, Tex...............	12	Lincoln, Polk, Iowa.............	18
Lick Creek, Union, Ill...........	13	Lincoln, Penobscot, Me...........	340
Lick Creek, Hickman, Tenn	8	Lincoln, Middlesex, Mass..........	160
Licking, Texas, Mo	94	Lincoln, (c. h.,) Mason, Mich........	110
Licking Valley, Muskingum, Ohio..	69	Lincoln, Wabashaw, Minn.........	43
Lickingville, Clarion, Pa	21	Lincoln, Benton, Mo	84
Lick Run, Hamilton, Ohio........	26	Lincoln, Deer Lodge, Mont	100

* Money-order office.

LIN   LIT

Lincoln,* (c. h.,) Lancaster, Nebr..	$1,700	Lineville, Clay, Ala	$35
Lincoln, Sussex, N. J	12	Lineville, Venango, Pa	16
Lincoln, Wayne, N. Y	43	Lineville Station, Crawford, Pa....	230
Lincoln, Gallia, Ohio	16	Linganore, Frederick, Md	26
Lincoln, Polk, Oreg	7	Linglestown, Dauphin, Pa	71
Lincoln, Lancaster, Pa	70	Linkinson, Franklin, N. Y	39
Lincoln, Addison, Vt	9	Linkwood, Dorchester, Md	45
Lincoln, Loudoun, Va	92	Linlithgo, Columbia, N. Y	53
Lincoln, Kewaunee, Wis	12	Linn, (c. h.,) Osage, Mo	150
Lincoln Centre, Grundy, Iowa	12	Linn Creek, (c. h.,) Camden, Mo.....	170
Lincoln Centre, Lincoln, Kans	12	Linneus, Aroostook, Me	80
Lincoln Centre, Penobscot, Me	160	Linneus,* (c. h.,) Linn, Mo	510
Lincoln Centre, Polk, Wis	32	Linn Flat, Nacogdoches, Tex	12
Lincoln City, Summit, Colo	20	Linn Grove, Adams, Ind	61
Lincoln Falls, Sullivan, Pa	7	Linn's Valley, Kern, Cal	49
Lincoln Green, Johnson, Ill	9	Linnville, Licking, Ohio	59
Lincolnton, (c. h.,) Lincoln, Ga	35	Linnwood, Osage, Mo	30
Lincolnton, (c. h.,) Lincoln, N. C	360	Linton, Greene, Ind	77
Lincoln University, Chester, Pa....	190	Linton, Des Moines, Iowa	17
Lincolnville, Wabash, Ind	12	Linton, Trigg, Ky	18
Lincolnville, Marion, Kans	8	Linton, Jefferson, Ohio	60
Lincolnville, Pulaski, Ky	4	Linton Mills, Coshocton, Ohio	12
Lincolnville, Waldo, Me	170	Linville, Rockingham, Va	12
Lincolnville, Crawford, Pa	38	Linwood, Pike, Ala	12
Lind, Waupaca, Wis	37	Linwood, Carroll, Md	53
Lindale, Osage, Kans	12	Linwood, Anoka, Minn	9
Lindale, Clermont, Ohio	42	Linwood, Butler, Nebr	20
Linden, Marengo, Ala	87	Linwood, Davidson, N. C	12
Linden, San Joaquin, Cal	23	Linwood, Hamilton, Ohio	57
Linden, Montgomery, Ind	90	Linwood, Bradley, Tenn	12
Linden, Dallas, Iowa	21	Linwood, Cherokee, Tex	7
Linden, Genesee, Mich	240	Linwood Station, Delaware, Pa....	210
Linden, Brown, Minn	16	Lionville, Chester, Pa	130
Linden, Copiah, Miss	20	Lisbon, Union, Ark	32
Linden, Atchison, Mo	29	Lisbon, New London, Conn	160
Linden, Union, N. J	24	Lisbon, Kendall, Ill	310
Linden, Genesee, N. Y	110	Lisbon, Noble, Ind	54
Linden, Lycoming, Pa	66	Lisbon,* Linn, Iowa	440
Linden, (c. h.,) Perry, Tenn	42	Lisbon, Claiborne, La	20
Linden, (c. h.,) Davis, Tex	24	Lisbon, Androscoggin, Me	260
Linden, Warren, Va	97	Lisbon, Howard, Md	61
Linden, Iowa, Wis	140	Lisbon, Ottawa, Mich	160
Linden Hall, Centre, Pa	47	Lisbon, Sarpy, Nebr	12
Lindenville, Ashtabula, Ohio	130	Lisbon, Grafton, N. H	500
Lindenwood, Ogle, Ill	97	Lisbon, St. Lawrence, N. Y	23
Linder, Jasper, Ill	6	Lisbon, Dallas, Tex	12
Lindersville, Adair, Mo	10	Lisbon, Bedford, Va	12
Lind Grove, Morehouse, La	12	Lisbon Centre, St. Lawrence, N. Y.	150
Lindley, Grundy, Mo	130	Lisbon Falls, Androscoggin, Me....	530
Lindleytown, Steuben, N. Y	130	Lisburn, Cumberland, Pa	70
Lindly's Mills, Washington, Pa ...	31	Liscomb, Marshall, Iowa	100
Lindsborg, McPherson, Kans	12	Lisha's Kill, Albany, N. Y	22
Lindsey, (c. h.,) Ottawa, Kans	100	Lisle, Broome, N. Y	310
Lindsey, Sandusky, Ohio	140	Lisle Station, Du Page, Ill	89
Lindsey's Mill, Trigg, Ky	12	Litchfield,* (c. h.,) Litchfield, Conn.	1,200
Lindseyville, Worcester, Md	16	Litchfield,* Montgomery, Ill	2,000
Lindside, Monroe, W. Va	16	Litchfield, Taylor, Iowa	14
Line, Lyon, Kans	12	Litchfield, (c. h.,) Grayson, Ky	210
Line, Morehouse, La	12	Litchfield, Kennebec, Me	52
Line Creek, Bullock, Ala	12	Litchfield,* Hillsdale, Mich	390
Line Creek, Pulaski, Ky	3	Litchfield, (c. h.,) Meeker, Minn.....	240
Line Creek, Laurens, S. C	12	Litchfield, Herkimer, N. Y	18
Line Lexington, Montgomery, Pa..	170	Litchfield, Medina, Ohio	180
Line Mountain, Northumberland,		Litchfield, Bradford, Pa	37
Pa	10	Litchfield Corners, Kennebec, Me..	150
Line's Hollow, Crawford, Pa	69	Liter, Morgan, Ill	12

* Money-order office.

LIT | LIZ

Lithgow, Dutchess, N. Y	$78	Little Sturgeon, Door, Wis	$24
Lithonia, De Kalb, Ga	35	Little Suamico, Oconto, Wis	87
Lithopolis, Fairfield, Ohio	130	Little Sugar Loaf, Bladen, N. C	12
Lititz,* Lancaster, Pa	510	Littlesville, Winston, Ala	12
Little Black, Ripley, Mo	18	Little Toby, Clearfield, Pa	57
Little Britain, Lancaster, Pa	24	Littleton, Arapahoe, Colo	12
Little Canada, Ramsey, Minn	16	Littleton, Schuyler, Ill	87
Little Cedar, Mitchell, Iowa	12	Littleton, Aroostook, Me	61
Little Chucky, Greene, Tenn	10	Littleton, Middlesex, Mass	320
Little Chute, Outagamie, Wis	78	Littleton,* Grafton, N. H	1,100
Little Compton, Carroll, Mo	19	Littleton, Morris, N. J	12
Little Compton, Newport, R. I	240	Littleton, Halifax, N. C	220
Little Cooley, Crawford, Pa	55	Littleton, Sussex, Va	37
Little Creek, Pike, Ky	12	*Little Traverse*, (c. h.,) Emmett, Mich.	29
Little Creek Landing, Kent, Del	50	Little Turkey, Chickasaw, Iowa	27
Little Detroit, Tazewell, Ill	11	Little Utica, Onondaga, N. Y	45
Little Doe, Johnson, Tenn	8	Little Valley, Olmsted, Minn	31
Little Eagle, Scott, Ky	43	Little Valley, Cattaraugus, N. Y	410
Little Elk, Benton, Oreg	12	Little Warrior, Blount, Ala	12
Little Falls, (c. h.,) Morrison, Minn	130	Little Wind River, Sweetwater,	
Little Falls, Passaic, N. J	150	Wyo	12
Little Falls,* Herkimer, N. Y	2,400	Little Wolf, Waupaca, Wis	17
Little Flat, Bath, Ky	8	Little Yadkin, Stokes, N. C	17
Little Gap, Carbon, Pa	11	Little York, Nevada, Cal	17
Little Genesee, Allegany, N. Y	110	Little York, Warren, Ill	140
Little Georgetown, Berkeley, W. Va	38	Little York, Washington, Ind	25
Little Grant, Grant, Wis	20	Little York, Meade, Ky	11
Little Gunpowder, Baltimore, Md	63	Little York, Greene, Mo	49
Little Hickman, Jessamine, Ky	14	Little York, Hunterdon, N. J	35
Little Hockhocking, Washington,		Little York, Cortland, N. Y	49
Ohio	52	Little York, Montgomery, Ohio	43
Little Indian, Cass, Ill	12	Littsville, Nodaway, Mo	18
Little Lake, Mendocino, Cal	56	Litwalton, Lancaster, Va	12
Little Lake, Adams, Wis	12	Litzenberg, Lehigh, Pa	12
Little Lot, Hickman, Tenn	10	Lively Grove, Washington, Ill	32
Little Marsh, Tioga, Pa	21	Lively Oaks, Lancaster, Va	12
Little Meadows, Susquehanna, Pa	59	Live Oak, San Joaquin, Cal	12
Little Mount, Spencer, Ky	14	Live Oak, Suwannee, Fla	330
Little Mountain, Newberry, S. C	12	Live Oak Store, Livingston, La	12
Little Neck, Queens, N. Y	84	Livermore, Alameda, Cal	12
Little Oak, Crenshaw, Ala	12	Livermore, McLean, Ky	63
Little Osage, Vernon, Mo	97	Livermore, Androscoggin, Me	130
Little Otter, Braxton, W. Va	9	Livermore, Westmoreland, Pa	240
Little Plymouth, King and Queen,		Livermore Centre, Androscoggin, Me	47
Va	36	Livermore Falls, Androscoggin, Me.	340
Little Port, Clayton, Iowa	21	Liverpool, Fulton, Ill	24
Little Prairie, Walworth, Wis	23	Liverpool, Onondaga, N. Y	340
Little Prairie Ronde, Cass, Mich	51	Liverpool, Medina, Ohio	140
Little Rest, Dutchess, N. Y	33	Liverpool, Perry, Pa	320
Little River, Cherokee, Ala	12	*Livingston*, (c. h.,) Sumter, Ala	490
Little River, Mendocino, Cal	60	Livingston, Floyd, Ga	9
Little River, Allen, Ind	11	Livingston, Clark, Ill	48
Little River, Horry, S. C	89	Livingston, Appanoose, Iowa	44
Little River, Floyd, Va	5	Livingston, Essex, N. J	24
LITTLE ROCK,* (c. h.,) Pulaski, Ark	3,400	Livingston, Columbia, N. Y	74
Little Rock, Kendall, Ill	88	*Livingston*, (c. h.,) Overton, Tenn	95
Little Rock, Marion, S. C	120	*Livingston*, (c. h.,) Polk, Tex	200
Little Sandusky Wyandot, Ohio	63	Livingstonville, Schoharie, N. Y	34
Little Sandy, Jefferson, Nebr	12	Livonia, Washington, Ind	77
Little Sewall Mountain, Greenbrier,		Livonia, Point Coupee, La	12
W. Va	12	Livonia, Sherburne, Minn	9
Little Sioux, Harrison, Iowa	190	Livonia, Putnam, Mo	5
Little's Mills, Richmond, N. C	3	Livonia, Livingston, N. Y	140
Little's Mills, Tyler, W. Va	9	Livonia Station, Livingston, N. Y	550
Little Spring, Madison, Ark	20	Lizemore's, Clay, W. Va	12
Littlestown, Adams, Pa	350	Lizzard, Pocahontas, Iowa	12

* Money-order office.

8 P O

LOC

Llano, (c. h.,) Llano, Tex	$40
Llewellyn, Schuylkill, Pa	69
Lloyd, Tioga, Pa	12
Lloyds, Essex, Va	21
Loachapoka, Lee, Ala	350
Loag, Chester, Pa	51
Loami, Sangamon, Ill	110
Lobachsville, Berks,Pa	12
Lobelville, Perry, Tenn	13
Lochleven, Lunenburgh, Va	20
Loch Lomond, Goochland, Va	9
Loch Sheldrake, Sullivan, N. Y	38
Lock, La Salle, Ill	12
Lock, Knox, Ohio	42
Lock Berlin, Wayne, N. Y	54
Lockbourne, Franklin, Ohio	82
Locke, Elkhart, Ind	68
Locke, Ingham, Mich	16
Locke, Cayuga, N. Y	100
Lockeford, San Joaquin, Cal	95
Locke's Mills, Oxford, Me	130
Lockhart, Lauderdale, Miss	8
Lockhart, (c. h.,) Caldwell, Tex	310
Lockhart's, Jackson, W. Va	12
Lockhart's Run, Wood, W. Va	4
Lockhaven, (c. h.,) Clinton, Pa	2,600
Lockington, Shelby, Ohio	51
Lockland Station, Hamilton, Ohio	280
Lock No. 4, Washington, Pa	16
Lockport,* Will, Ill	1,200
Lockport, Carroll, Ind	19
Lockport, Henry, Ky	16
Lockport, (c. h.,) Niagara, N. Y	4,000
Lockport, Williams, Ohio	23
Lockport Station,Westmoreland, Pa	42
Lockridge, Jefferson, Iowa	80
Locksburgh, (c. h.,) Sevier, Ark	12
Lock Seventeen, Tuscarawas, Ohio	78
Lock's Village, Franklin, Mass	51
Locktown, Hunterdon, N. J	19
Lockville, Chatham, N. C	12
Lockville, Fairfield. Ohio	20
Locust Bottom, Botetourt, Va	56
Locust Corner, Clermont, Ohio	30
Locust Creek, Louisa, Va	12
Locust Gap, Northumberland, Pa	12
Locust Grove, Williamson, Ill	10
Locust Grove, Atchison, Kans	13
Locust Grove, Callaway, Ky	6
Locust Grove, Kent, Md	71
Locust Grove, Clarke, Mo	6
Locust Grove, Lewis, N. Y	74
Locust Grove, Adams, Ohio	63
Locust Grove, Fulton, Pa	12
Locust Grove, Orange, Va	6
Locust Hill, Knox, Mo	28
Locust Hill, Caswell, N. C	23
Locust Hill, Washington, Pa	38
Locust Hill, Middlesex, Va	17
Locust Lane, Winneshiek, Iowa	50
Locust Lane, Indiana, Pa	36
Locust Level, Stanly, N. C	12
Locust Level, Halifax, Va	12
Locust Mills, Bracken, Ky	6
Locust Mound, Miller, Mo	62
Locust Mount, Washington, Tenn	4

LON

Locust Mount, Accomack, Va	$43
Locust Point, Ottawa, Ohio	18
Locust Ridge, Brown, Ohio	15
Locust Spring, Greene, Tenn	12
Locust Valley, Queens, N. Y	90
Locust Valley, Lehigh, Pa	24
Locustville, Accomack, Va	41
Lodi, Clay, Dak	12
Lodi, Coweta, Ga	5
Lodi, Wabash, Ind	11
Lodi, Choctaw, Miss	24
Lodi, Newton, Mo	12
Lodi, Dakota, Nebr	12
Lodi, Bergen, N. J	230
Lodi, Seneca, N. Y	380
Lodi, Medina, Ohio	190
Lodi, (c. h.,) Wilson, Tex	12
Lodi, Washington, Va	5
Lodi,* Columbia, Wis	640
Lodi Centre, Seneca, N. Y	36
Lodi Station, Kane, Ill	200
Lodore, Amelia, Va	12
Logan, Edgar, Ill	19
Logan, Dearborn, Ind	14
Logan, Harrison, Iowa	150
Logan, Dodge, Nebr	50
Logan, Schuyler, N. Y	16
Logan, (c. h.,) Hocking, Ohio	550
Logan, (c. h.,) Cache, Utah	290
Logan C. H., Logan, W. Va	16
Logan Mills, Clinton, Pa	25
Logan's Creek, Reynolds, Mo	22
Logansport, Hamilton, Ill	9
Logansport, (c. h.,) Cass, Ind	2,800
Logansport, Butler, Ky	16
Logansport, De Soto, La	10
Logan's Store, Rutherford, N. C	3
Loganville, Logan, Ohio	12
Loganville, York, Pa	20
Loganville, Sauk, Wis	190
Log Cabin, Morgan, Ohio	21
Loggy Bayou, Natchitoches, La	12
Log Town, Ouachita, La	6
Lohmansville, Washington, Minn	12
Loma, Conejos, Colo	12
Lomax, Henderson, Ill	12
Lombard, Du Page, Ill	120
Lombardville, Stark, Ill	12
Lombardville, Scioto, Ohio	12
Lombardy, Columbia, Ga	12
Lombardy Grove, Mecklenburgh, Va	21
Lomira, Dodge, Wis	55
Lonaconing,* Alleghany, Md	560
London, Shelby, Ind	80
London, (c. h.,) Laurel, Ky	120
London, Monroe, Mich	38
London, Nemaha, Nebr	21
London, (c. h.,) Madison, Ohio	1,100
London, Mercer, Pa	31
London, Rusk, Tex	26
London Bridge, Princess Anne, Va	12
Londonderry, Rockingham, N. H	47
Londonderry, Guernsey, Ohio	55
Londonderry, Chester, Pa	10
Londonderry, Windham, Vt	150

* Money-order office.

London Grove, Chester, Pa	$97	Long's Mills, Stone, Mo	$12
Lone Cedar, Martin, Minn	9	Long's Mills, Randolph, N. C	11
Lone Cedar, Crawford, Mo	12	Long's Stand, Crawford, Pa	12
Lone Cedar, Jackson, W. Va	12	Long Street, De Soto, La	29
Lone Elm, Cooper, Mo	12	Long Swamp, Berks, Pa	80
Lone Elm, Henderson, Tenn	7	Long Tom, Lane, Oreg	9
Lone Jack, Jackson, Mo	130	Longton, Howard, Kans	12
Lone Oak, Bates, Mo	12	Longtown, Panola, Miss	16
Lone Oak, Hunt, Tex	12	Long Valley, Lassen, Cal	12
Lone Pine, Inyo, Cal	12	Long View, Ashley, Ark	12
Lone Pine, Washington, Pa	28	Long View, Christian, Ky	16
Lone Pine, Bedford, Va	12	Longville, Plumas, Cal	16
Lone Pine, Portage, Wis	23	Longwood, Pettis, Mo	120
Lone Rock, Richland, Wis	370	Longwood, Rockbridge, Va	9
Lone Star, Titus, Tex	40	Lonsdale, Providence, R. I	820
Lone Tree, Bureau, Ill	10	Loogootee,* Martin, Ind	290
Lone Tree, Cowley, Kans	12	Lookout, Laramie, Wyo	12
Lone Tree, (c. h.,) Merrick, Nebr	98	Lookout Mountain, Hamilton, Tenn	210
Lone Tree, Greene, Pa	12	Looney's Creek, Marion, Tenn	6
Lone Tree, Collin, Tex	12	Looneyville, Erie, N. Y	33
Lone Tree, Tyler, W. Va	12	Looniesville, McDonald, Mo	7
Lonetree Lake, Brown, Minn	12	Loose Creek, Osage, Mo	40
Lone Valley, Saunders, Nebr	12	Looxahoma, De Soto, Miss	12
Lone Well, Union, La	8	Loramies, Shelby, Ohio	110
Long, Vermilion, Ill	12	Loran, Stephenson, Ill	31
Long Bottom, Meigs, Ohio	53	Lordstown, Trumbull, Ohio	34
Long Branch, Tatnall, Ga	11	Lord's Valley, Pike, Pa	13
Long Branch, Monroe, Mo	35	Lordville, Delaware, N. Y	96
Long Branch, Richardson, Nebr	10	Lorentz Store, Upshur, W. Va	17
Long Branch,* Monmouth, N. J	1,400	Lorettee, Houston, Minn	10
Long Branch, Franklin, Va	4	Loretto, Marion, Ky	120
Long Creek, Decatur, Iowa	12	Loretto, Cambria, Pa	270
Long Creek Depot, Panola, Miss	12	Loretto, Essex, Va	79
Long Eddy, Sullivan, N. Y	260	Lorraine, Jefferson, N. Y	90
Long Falls Creek, McLean, Ky	32	Los Alisos, Santa Barbara, Cal.	12
Long Glade, Augusta, Va	43	Los Angeles,* (c. h.,) Los Angeles,	
Long Green Academy, Baltimore, Md	42	Cal	2,100
		Losantville, Randolph, Ind	40
Long Grove, Lake, Ill	34	Los Gatos, Santa Clara, Cal	12
Long Hill, Stearns, Minn	10	Los Luceros, Rio Arriba, N. Mex	18
Long Hill, Morris, N. J	55	Los Lunas, Valencia, N. Mex	130
Long Island, Jackson, Ala	10	Los Nietos, Los Angeles, Cal	20
Long Island City, Queens, N. Y	690	Lostant,* La Salle, Ill	350
Long Lake, Madison, Ill	12	Lost Branch, Lincoln, Mo	26
Long Lake, Hennepin, Minn	120	Lost Creek, Breathitt, Ky	8
Long Lake, Hamilton, N. Y	67	Lost Creek, Union, Tenn	10
Long Lane, Dallas, Mo	16	Lost Creek, Harrison, W. Va	31
Long Marsh, Queen Anne, Md	44	Lostine, Cherokee, Kans	74
Long Meadow, Hampden, Mass	210	Lost Mountain, Cobb, Ga	6
Longmire, Washington, Tenn	8	Lost Mountain, Greene, Tenn	4
Longmire's Store, Edgefield, S. C	23	Lost River, Hardy, W. Va	13
Long Pine, Anson, N. C	12	Lost Run, Breckinridge, Ky	7
Long Plain, Bristol, Mass	80	Lot, Whitley, Ky	12
Long Point, Livingston, Ill	150	Lottridge, Athens, Ohio	31
Long Pond, Caldwell, Ky	10	Lottsburgh, Northumberland, Va	12
Long Prairie, Wayne, Ill	38	Lott's Creek, Humboldt, Iowa	46
Long Prairie, (c. h.,) Todd, Minn	12	Lottsville, Warren, Pa	94
Long Prairie, Fayette, Tex	14	Lotus, Union, Ind	96
Long Reach, Tyler, W. Va	50	Lotville, Fulton, N. Y	13
Long Ridge, Fairfield, Conn	52	Louden City, Fayette, Ill	20
Long Ridge, Washington, N. C	2	Loudon, Merrimack, N. H	120
Long Run, Jefferson, Ky	60	Loudon, Franklin, Pa	140
Long Run, Licking, Ohio	6	Loudon, Roane, Tenn	350
Long Run, Armstrong, Pa	56	Loudon Centre, Merrimack, N. H	17
Long Run Station, Doddridge, W. Va	41	Loudon Ridge, Merrimack, N. H	51
		Loudonville,* Ashland, Ohio	470

* Money-order office.

LOW
LUD

Loudsville, White, Ga.	$12	Lower Bartlett, Carroll, N. H.	$34
Louina, Randolph, Ala	68	Lower Bern, Berks, Pa	28
Louisa, (c. h.,) Lawrence, Ky	100	Lower Boise, Ada, Idaho	12
Louisa C. H., Louisa, Va	470	Lower Gilmanton, Belknap, N. H	20
Louisburgh, Dallas, Mo	50	Lower Heidelberg, Berks, Pa	8
Louisburgh,* (c. h.,) Franklin, N. C	380	*Lower Lake*, (c. h.,) Lake, Cal	170
Louisiana,* Pike, Mo	1,500	Lower Lynxville, Crawford, Wis	34
Louisville, Barbour, Ala	24	Lower Mahantango, Schuylkill, Pa.	13
Louisville, (c. h.,) Jefferson, Ga	170	Lower Marlborough, Calvert, Md	12
Louisville, (c. h.,) Clay, Ill	280	Lower Merion, Montgomery, Pa	43
Louisville, (c. h.,) Pottawatomie, Kans	160	Lower Newport, Washington, Ohio	12
		Lower Peach Tree, Wilcox, Ala	24
Louisville,* (c. h.,) Jefferson, Ky	4,000	Lower Providence, Montgomery,Pa	120
Louisville, Franklin, La	12	Lower Salem, Washington, Ohio	84
Louisville, Carroll, Md	22	Lower Saucon, Northampton, Pa	7
Louisville, (c. h.,) Winston, Miss	240	Lower Sioux Agency, Redwood, Minn	12
Louisville, Lincoln, Mo	73		
Louisville, Missoula, Mont	12	Lower Squankum, Monmouth, N. J.	48
Louisville, Cass, Nebr	12	Lower Valley, Hunterdon, N. J	25
Louisville, St. Lawrence, N. Y	66	Lower Waterford, Caledonia, Vt	73
Louisville, Stark, Ohio	250	Lowe's Cross Roads, Sussex, Del	22
Louisville, Blount, Tenn	40	Lowe's Station, Bourbon, Ky	24
Louisville, Dunn, Wis	18	Low Hampton, Washington, N. Y	25
Louisville Landing, St. Lawrence, N. Y	36	Lowhill, Lehigh, Pa	16
		Lowland, St. Clair, Ill	18
Loutre, Audrian, Mo	230	Lowman, Chemung, N. Y	11
Loutre Island, Montgomery, Mo	38	Lowmansville, Lawrence, Ky	12
Lovejoy, Bureau, Ill	20	Low Moor, Clinton, Iowa	180
Lovejoy's Station, Clayton, Ga	28	Lowndes, Wayne, Mo	12
Lovelaceville, Ballard, Ky	62	Lowndesborough, Lowndes, Ala	87
Lovelady, Caldwell, N. C	5	Lowndesville, Abbeville, S. C	32
Loveland, Pottawattomie, Iowa	23	Low Point, Woodford, Ill	47
Loveland, Bladen, N. C	12	Lowry, Bedford, Va	72
Loveland,* Clermont, Ohio	260	*Lowville*, (c. h.,) Lewis, N. Y	1,200
Lovell, Oxford, Me	130	Lowville, Erie, Pa	12
Lovell's Station, Erie, Pa	24	Lowville, Columbia, Wis	31
Lovelton, Wyoming, Pa	21	Loxa, Coles, Ill	57
Lovely Dale, Knox, Ind	16	Loyal, Carroll, Ga	12
Lovely Mount, Montgomery, Va	49	Loyal, Clark, Wis	12
Love's Mills, Washington, Va	13	Loyal Hill, Greene, Ark	12
Lovett, Jennings, Ind	12	Loyal Oak, Summit, Ohio	12
Lovett's, Adams, Ohio	22	Loyalsock, Lycoming, Pa	21
Lovettsville, Loudoun, Va	130	Loyalton, Sierra, Cal	61
Loveville, New Castle, Del	22	Loyalty, Hamilton, Tenn	2
Loveville, Centre, Pa	16	Loyal Valley, Mason, Tex	30
Lovilia, Monroe, Iowa	40	Loyd, Ulster, N. Y	61
Lovilla, Hamilton, Ill	27	Loyd, Richland, Wis	12
Loving Creek, Bedford, Va	10	Loydsville, Belmont, Ohio	90
Lovingston, (c. h.,) Nelson, Va	100	Loy's Cross Roads, Union, Tenn	6
Lovington, Moultrie, Ill	150	Loysville, Perry, Pa	120
Lowden,* Cedar, Iowa	380	Luana, Clayton, Iowa	130
Lowell, La Salle, Ill	43	Lubec, Washington, Me	260
Lowell, Lake, Ind	170	Lubeck, Wood, W. Va	53
Lowell, Henry, Iowa	53	Lucas, Lucas, Iowa	17
Lowell, Cherokee, Kans	12	Lucas, Henry, Mo	86
Lowell, Garrard, Ky	86	Lucas, Richland, Ohio	190
Lowell, Penobscot, Me	63	Lucas, Dunn, Wis	12
Lowell,* Middlesex, Mass	4,000	Lucasville, Scioto, Ohio	78
Lowell, Kent, Mich	1,400	Lucerne, Knox, Ohio	11
Lowell, Oneida, N. Y	80	Lucesco, Westmoreland, Pa	66
Lowell, Washington, Ohio	160	Lucinda Furnace, Clarien, Pa	21
Lowell, Orleans, Vt	110	Luck, Polk, Wis	12
Lowell, Dodge, Wis	140	Luda, Ouachita, Ark	11
Lowell Mills, Bartholomew, Ind	22	Luda, Ogle, Ill	27
Lowellville, Mahoning, Ohio	260	Luddenville, Iroquois, Ill	12
Lower Bank, Burlington, N. J	54	Ludington,* Mason, Mich	400

LYN   MCC

Ludingtonville, Putnam, N. Y	$21	Lynd, Lyon, Minn	$18
Ludlow, Champaign, Ill	160	Lyndeborough, Hillsborough, N. H.	28
Ludlow, Dubois, Ind	9	Lyndon, Whitesides, Ill	170
Ludlow, Allamakee, Iowa	70	Lyndon, Osage, Kans	12
Ludlow, Kenton, Ky	6	Lyudon, Aroostook, Me	20
Ludlow, Hampden, Mass	120	Lyndon, Caledonia, Vt	420
Ludlow,* Windsor, Vt	810	Lyndon Centre, Caledonia, Vt	300
Ludlow Grove, Hamilton, Ohio	12	Lyndon Station, Ross, Ohio	110
Ludlowville, Tompkins, N. Y	210	Lyndonville, Orleans, N. Y	180
Ludville, Pickens, Ga	12	Lyndonville, Caledonia, Vt	370
Lumber City, Telfair, Ga	12	Lynn, Randolph, Ind	73
Lumber City, Clearfield, Pa	28	Lynn, Warren, Iowa	40
Lumberland, Sullivan, N. Y	32	Lynn, Greenup, Ky	22
Lumberman, Clark, Wis	12	Lynn,* Essex, Mass	2,600
Lumberport, Harrison, W. Va	42	Lynn, St. Clair, Mich	31
Lumberton, Burlington, N. J	110	Lynn, Susquehanna, Pa	72
Lumberton, (c. h.,) Robeson, N. C	290	Lynn, Clark, Wis	4
Lumberton, Clinton, Ohio	28	Lynn Camp, Knox, Ky	12
Lumberville, Delaware, N. Y	31	Lynn Camp, Marshall, W. Va	3
Lumberville, Bucks, Pa	130	Lynne, Weber, Utah	27
Lumberville, Iowa, Wis	12	Lynnfield, Essex, Mass	32
Lummisville, Wayne, N. Y	12	Lynnfield Centre, Essex, Mass	100
Lumpkin, (c. h.,) Stewart, Ga	280	Lynnport, Lehigh, Pa	12
Luna Landing, Chicot, Ark	60	Lynnville, Henry, Ala	12
Lundy's Lane, Erie, Pa	150	Lynnville, Morgan, Ill	100
Lunenburgh, Izard, Ark	12	Lynnville, Warrick, Ind	57
Lunenburgh, Worcester, Mass	240	Lynnville, Jasper, Iowa	150
Lunenburgh, Essex, Vt	230	Lynnville, Graves, Ky	70
Luney's Creek, Grant, W. Va	88	Lynnville, Lehigh, Pa	16
Luni, Wright, Iowa	20	Lynnville, Giles, Tenn	140
Luray, Henry, Ind	20	Lyon, Wabashaw, Minn	8
Luray, (c. h.,) Page, Va	340	Lyon, Laclede, Mo	28
Lusby's Mill, Owen, Ky	14	Lyona, Dickinson, Kans	8
Lusk, Pope, Ill	9	Lyons, Cook, Ill	100
Lusk's Springs, Parke, Ind	6	Lyons, Greene, Ind	12
Luthersburgh, Clearfield, Pa	180	Lyons,* Clinton, Iowa	2,200
Luther's Mills, Bradford, Pa	21	Lyons,* Ionia, Mich	390
Luthersville, Meriwether, Ga	20	Lyons, Burt, Nebr	12
Lutherville, Baltimore, Md	140	*Lyons,* (c. h.,) Wayne, N. Y	2,100
Lutzton, Nodaway, Mo	20	Lyons, Fulton, Ohio	140
Luverne, Rock, Minn	8	Lyons, Fayette, Tex	17
Luxemburgh, Stearns, Minn	20	Lyons, Walworth, Wis	140
Luzerne, Benton, Iowa	190	Lyonsdale, Lewis, N. Y	85
Luzerne, Warren, N. Y	220	Lyon's Falls, Lewis, N. Y	120
Luzerne, Luzerne, Pa	79	Lyon's Mill, Clinton, Mich	29
Lycippus, Westmoreland, Pa	32	Lyon's Station, Fayette, Ind	30
Lycurgus, Allamakee, Iowa	6	Lyon's Station, Berks, Pa	110
Lydia, Scott, Minn	11	Lyonsville, Cook, Ill	24
Lydia, Darlington, S. C	17	Lyon Valley, Lehigh, Pa	38
Lykens, Dauphin, Pa	590	Lyra, Scioto, Ohio	17
Lyles, Lancaster, Pa	53	Lysander, Onondaga, N. Y	170
Lylesford, Fairfield, S. C	12	Lytle City, Iowa, Iowa	56
Lyman, Pope, Ark	24		
Lyman, York, Me	8		
Lyman, Grafton, N. H	39		
Lyme, New London, Conn	500	**M.**	
Lyme, Grafton, N. H	400	McAfee, Mercer, Ky	120
Lynchburgh, Jefferson, Ill	44	McAfee Valley, Sussex, N. J	27
Lynchburgh, Nodaway, Mo	7	McAlevy's Fort, Huntingdon, Pa	98
Lynchburgh, Highland, Ohio	230	McAllister's X Roads, Montgomery	
Lynchburgh, Sumter, S. C	99	Tenn	10
Lynchburgh, Lincoln, Tenn	83	McAllisterville, Juniata, Pa	200
Lynchburgh, Campbell, Va	3,100	*McArthur,* (c. h.,) Vinton, Ohio	550
Lynch's Creek, Marion, S. C	14	McBean Depot, Richmond, Ga	68
Lynch's Lake, Williamsburgh, S. C.	33	McBride's Mill, Watauga, N. C	4
Lynchwood, Kershaw, S. C	3	McCainsville, Morris, N. J	12
		McCall, Hancock, Ill	28

* Money-order office.

MCK   MAC

McCall's Ferry, York, Pa	$10	McKenzie, Carroll, Tenn	$170
McCameron, Martin, Ind	12	McKinley, Marengo, Ala	58
McCandless, Butler, Pa	20	McKinley's Landing, Henderson, Ky	12
McCauleyville, Wilkin, Minn	14	*McKinney,* (c. h.,) Collin, Tex	400
McCleary, Noble, Ohio	28	McKinstry's Mills, Carroll, Md	18
McCleary, Beaver, Pa	6	McKnightstown, Adams, Pa	12
McClelland, Franklin, N. Y	23	McKune's Depot, Wyoming, Pa	12
McClellandsville, New Castle, Del	37	McLane, Erie, Pa	45
McClellandtown, Fayette, Pa	49	McLaughlin's Store, Westmoreland,	
McClellan Gulch, Deer Lodge, Mont	12	Pa	22
McCluney, Perry, Ohio	27	McLean, McLean, Ill	410
McClure, Buchanan, Va	12	McLean, Tompkins, N. Y	280
McClure Settlement, Broome, N. Y.	12	*McLeansborough,* (c. h.,) Hamilton,	
McComb, Hancock, Ohio	120	Ill	260
McConnellsburgh, (c. h.,) Fulton, Pa.	350	McLean's Corners, Crawford, Pa	8
McConnell's Grove, Stephenson, Ill	44	McLean's Station, Cherokee N.,	
McConnellstown, Huntingdon, Pa.	97	Ind. T	12
McConnellsville, Oneida, N. Y	73	McLeansville, Guilford, N. C	25
McConnellsville, (c. h.,) Morgan,		McLellan's Corners, Erie, Pa	12
Ohio	1,300	McLemoresville, Carroll, Tenn	59
McCordsville, Hancock, Ind	70	McLeod's Station, Logan, Ky	10
McCoy's Station, Decatur, Ind	22	McMath, Tuscaloosa, Ala	12
McCoy's Station, Jefferson, Ohio	110	McMillan, Knox, Tenn	67
McCoysville, Juniata, Pa	43	McMinnville, Yam Hill, Oreg	160
McCray's Store, Alamance, N. C	7	*McMinnville,* (c. h.,) Warren, Tenn	930
McCulloch's Mills, Juniata, Pa	26	McNairy Station, McNairy, Tenn	16
McCutchanville, Vanderburgh, Ind	13	*McNutt,* (c. h.,) Sunflower, Miss	11
McCutchenville, Wyandot, Ohio	66	McPherson, Coles, Ill	22
McDaniel's, Gallia, Ohio	20	McSherrystown, Adams, Pa	110
McDonald, Hardin, Ohio	12	McSherrysville, York, Pa	90
McDonald's Mill, Montgomery, Va	11	Mc'sVille, Shelby, Tenn	12
McDonaldsville, Stark, Ohio	13	McVeytown, Mifflin, Pa	460
McDonough, New Castle, Del	87	McVill, Armstrong, Pa	24
McDonough (c. h.,) Henry, Ga	140	McVille, Telfair, Ga	12
McDonough, Chenango, N. Y	140	McWilliamstown, Chester, Pa	25
McDowell, Yavapai, Ariz	12	McZena, Ashland, Ohio	19
McDowell, Highland, Va	61	Mabbettsville, Dutchess, N. Y	85
McElhattan, Clinton, Pa	66	Mabee's, Jackson, Ohio	8
McElroy, Doddridge, W. Va	4	Mace, Montgomery, Ind	28
McEwen's Station, Humphreys,		Macedon, Wayne, N. Y	460
Tenn	64	Macedon, Mercer, Ohio	50
McEwensville, Northumberland, Pa	120	Macedon Centre, Wayne, N. Y	120
McFadden, York, Nebr	20	Macedonia, Hamilton, Ill	25
McFarland's, Lunenburgh, Va	12	Macedonia, Pottawattomie, Iowa	16
McGaheysville, Rockingham, Va	100	Macedonia, Bradford, Pa	17
McGarvey's, Clearfield, Pa	6	Macedonia Depot, Summit, Ohio	120
McGill, Paulding, Ohio	8	Macfarland, Dane, Wis	130
McGonigle's Station, Butler, Ohio	24	*Machias,* (c. h.,) Washington, Me	840
McGrawsville, Miami, Ind	31	Machias, Cattaraugus, N. Y	130
McGrawville, Cortland, N. Y	310	Machias Port, Washington, Me	190
McGregor,* Clayton. Iowa	2,100	Machirville, Mason, W. Va	21
McHenry, McHenry, Ill	250	Mackerel Corner, Carroll, N. H	81
McIndoe's Falls,* Caledonia, Vt	280	Mackey's Grove, Boone, Iowa	12
McIntire, Wilkinson, Ga	12	Mackinaw, Tazewell, Ill	210
McIntosh, (c. h.,) La Fayette, Fla	12	*Mackinaw,* (c. h.,) Mackinac, Mich.	300
McIntosh, Liberty, Ga	160	Mack's, Carroll, Iowa	4
McKay, Ashland, Ohio	36	Macksville, Harrison, Tex	12
McKean, Erie, Pa	130	Macksville, Pendleton, W. Va	12
McKeansburgh, Schuylkill, Pa	12	Mackville, Washington, Ky	78
McKean's Old Stand, Westmoreland,		Mackville, Outagamie, Wis	19
Pa	61	*Macomb,* (c. h.,) McDonough, Ill	1,500
McKee, (c. h.,) Jackson, Ky	10	Macomb, Macomb, Mich	39
McKeen, Clark, Ill	12	Macomb, St. Lawrence, N. Y	92
McKee's Half Falls, Snyder, Pa	78	Macomb, Grayson, Tex	15
McKeesport,* Allegheny, Pa	1,000	*Macon,* (c. h.,) Bibb, Ga	4,000
McKenny's Mill, Rockbridge, Va	12	Macon,* Macon, Ill	710

* Money-order office.

MAG | MAN

Macon, Lenawee, Mich	$71	Magnolia, Harford, Md	$120
Macon, (c. h.,) Noxubee, Miss	1,000	Magnolia, Pike, Miss	48
Macon, Fayette, Tenn	110	Magnolia, Moniteau, Mo	12
Macon City,* (c. h.,) Macon, Mo	2,400	Magnolia, Duplin, N. C	230
Macon Depot, Warren, N. C	74	Magnolia, Stark, Ohio	57
Macon Station, Hale, Ala	55	Magnolia, Rock, Wis	50
Macoupin Station, Macoupin, Ill	12	Magnolia Centre, Lawrence, Mo	12
Macungie, Lehigh, Pa	240	Magnolia Springs, Jasper, Tex	16
Madalin, Dutchess, N. Y	170	Maguire's Store, Washington, Ark	41
Madawaska, Aroostook, Me	12	Mahalasville, Morgan, Ind	19
Maddensville, Huntingdon, Pa	16	Mahanoy, Northumberland, Pa	28
Madeira, Hamilton, Ohio	59	Mahanoy City,* Schuylkill, Pa	1,800
Madelia, (c. h.,) Watonwan, Minn	190	Mahanoy Plane, Schuylkill, Pa	430
Madely, Portage, Wis	12	Mahomet, Champaign, Ill	230
Madera, Clearfield, Pa	23	Mahomet, Burnet, Tex	16
Madison, (c. h.,) St. Francis, Ark	260	Mahoning, Indiana, Pa	67
Madison, New Haven, Conn	380	Mahopac, Oakland, Mich	10
Madison, (c. h.,) Madison, Fla	170	Mahopac, Putnam, N. Y	290
Madison,* (c. h.,) Morgan, Ga	1,000	Mahopac Falls, Putnam, N. Y	12
Madison, Richland, Ill	4	Mahwah, Bergen, N. J	12
Madison,* (c. h.,) Jefferson, Ind	2,800	Maiden Creek, Berks, Pa	45
Madison, Jones, Iowa	30	Maiden Rock, Pierce, Wis	120
Madison, Greenwood, Kans	43	Maidsville, Monongalia, W. Va	22
Madison, Somerset, Me	90	Maine, Waseca, Minn	13
Madison, Livingston, Mich	27	Maine, Broome, N. Y	190
Madison, Mower, Minn	16	Maine Prairie, Solano, Cal	40
Madison, Monroe, Mo	72	Maine Prairie, Stearns, Minn	50
Madison, Madison, Nebr	12	Mainesburgh, Tioga, Pa	92
Madison, Carroll, N. H	82	Mainville, Cook, Ill	11
Madison, Morris, N. J	1,000	Mainville, Warren, Ohio	130
Madison, Madison, N. Y	270	Mainville, Columbia, Pa	23
Madison, Rockingham, N. C	140	Majenica, Huntingdon, Ind	26
Madison,* Lake, Ohio	490	Majority Point, (c. h.,) Cumberland,	
Madison, Westmoreland, Pa	81	Ill	140
Madison, Davidson, Tenn	140	Malade City, (c. h.,) Oneida, Idaho	130
MADISON,* (c. h.,) Dane, Wis	3,800	Makanda, Jackson, Ill	390
Madison C. H., Madison, Va	240	Malaga, Gloucester, N. J	130
Madisonburgh, Wayne, Ohio	30	Malaga, Monroe, Ohio	40
Madisonburgh, Centre, Pa	38	Malakoff, Henderson, Tex	5
Madison Centre, Somerset, Me	34	Malcom,* Poweshiek, Iowa	520
Madison Mills, Fayette, Ohio	10	Malden, Bureau, Ill	280
Madison Mills, Madison, Va	18	Malden, Middlesex, Mass	1,400
Madison Run Station, Orange, Va	12	Malden, Ulster, N. Y	180
Madison Station, Madison, Ala	180	Malden Bridge, Columbia, N. Y	81
Madisonville,* (c. h.,) Hopkins, Ky	350	Mallet Creek, Medina, Ohio	110
Madisonville, St. Tammany, La	20	Mallory, Oswego, N. Y	36
Madisonville, Ralls, Mo	69	Malma, De Kalb, Ill	19
Madisonville, Hamilton, Ohio	130	Malone, Clinton, Iowa	42
Madisonville, Luzerne, Pa	37	Malone,* (c. h.,) Franklin, N. Y	2,200
Madisonville, (c. h.,) Monroe, Tenn	270	Malta, De Kalb, Ill	470
Madisonville, (c. h.,) Madison, Tex	74	Malta, Saratoga, N. Y	40
Madonaville, Monroe, Ill	18	Malta, Morgan, Ohio	290
Madrid, Franklin, Me	42	Malta Bend, Saline, Mo	220
Madrid,* St. Lawrence, N. Y	380	Maltaville, Saratoga, N. Y	18
Madrid Springs, St. Lawrence, N. Y	180	Malugin Grove, Lee, Ill	100
Madura, Clay, Kans	23	Malvern, Carroll, Ohio	160
Maeystown, Monroe, Ill	30	Mamaroneck, Westchester, N. Y	510
Magalia, Butte, Cal	74	Manack, Lowndes, Ala	12
Magazine, Scott, Ark	16	Manada Hill, Dauphin, Pa	19
Magee's Corners, Seneca, N. Y	22	Manahawkin, Ocean, N. J	93
Magnolia, (c. h.,) Columbia, Ark	190	Manalapan, Monmouth, N. J	87
Magnolia, Kent, Del	74	Manamuskin, Cumberland, N. J	30
Magnolia, Putnam, Ill	250	Manannah, Meeker, Minn	44
Magnolia, Crawford, Ind	1	Manassas,* Prince William, Va	270
Magnolia,* (c. h.,) Harrison, Iowa	500	Manatawny, Berks, Pa	19
Magnolia, La Rue, Ky	16	Manatee, Manatee, Fla	61

* Money-order office.

MAN

MAP

Manchaug, Worcester, Mass	$170	Mansfield, Parke, Ind	$47
Manchester, Hartford, Conn	140	Mansfield, Linn, Kans	45
Manchester, Scott, Ill	240	Mansfield, (c. h.,) De Soto, La	490
Manchester, Dearborn, Ind	43	Mansfield, Bristol, Mass	410
Manchester,* Delaware, Iowa	1,700	Mansfield, Dutchess, N. Y	6
Manchester, (c. h.,) Clay, Ky	83	Mansfield,* (c. h.,) Richland, Ohio	2,800
Manchester, Kennebec, Me	110	Mansfield, Tioga, Pa	620
Manchester, Carroll, Md	200	Mansfield, Tarrant, Tex	20
Manchester, Essex, Mass	560	Mansfield Centre, Tolland, Conn	220
Manchester, Washtenaw, Mich	650	Mansfield Depot, Tolland, Conn	87
Manchester, St. Louis, Mo	77	Mansfield Valley, Allegheny, Pa	320
Manchester,* Hillsborough, N. H	2,600	Manson, Warren, N. C	100
Manchester, Ocean, N. J	230	Mansura, Avoyelles, La	34
Manchester, Ontario, N. Y	180	Manteno,* Kankakee, Ill	630
Manchester, Adams, Ohio	280	Manteno, Shelby, Iowa	27
Manchester, York, Pa	82	Manteo, (c. h.,) Dare, N. C	12
Manchester, Sumter, S. C	110	Manti, Fremont, Iowa	37
Manchester, (c. h.,) Coffee, Tenn	290	Manti, (c. h.,) San Pete, Utah	100
Manchester,* (c. h.,) Bennington, Vt	600	Manton, Maries, Mo	14
Manchester, Chesterfield, Va	200	Manton, Providence, R. I	49
Manchester, Green Lake, Wis	72	Mantorville,* (c. h.,) Dodge, Minn	510
Manchester Bridge, Dutchess, N Y	12	Mantua, Gloucester, N. J	130
Manchester Centre, Ontario, N. Y	23	Mantua, Portage, Ohio	97
Mandana, Onondaga, N. Y	18	Mantua, Collin, Tex	12
Mandarin, Duval, Fla	59	Mantua Station, Portage, Ohio	250
Mandeville, St. Tammany, La	20	Manville, Mobile, Ala	12
Mandeville, Carroll, Mo	59	Manville, Jefferson, Ind	26
Mangohick, King William, Va	16	Manville, Providence, R. I	99
Mangum, Richmond, N. C	18	Maple, Ionia, Mich	38
Manhasset, Queens, N. Y	140	Maple, Brown, Ohio	13
Manhattan, Putnam, Ind	53	Maple Creek, Dodge, Nebr	12
Manhattan, Keokuk, Iowa	5	Maple Creek, Carroll, Tenn	12
Manhattan,* (c. h.,) Riley, Kans	1,200	Maple Glen, Scott, Minn	41
Manheim, Lancaster, Pa	360	Maple Grove, Edwards, Ill	19
Manilla, Rush, Ind	84	Maple Grove, Aroostook, Me	20
Manistee,* (c. h.,) Manistee, Mich	1,400	Maple Grove, Barry, Mich	34
Manito, Mason, Ill	320	Maple Grove, Hennepin, Minn	5
Manitowoc,* (c. h.,) Manitowoc, Wis	2,200	Maple Grove, Otsego, N. Y	4
Manitowoc Rapids, Manitowoc, Wis	13	Maple Hill, Montcalm, Mich	12
Mankato,* (c. h.,) Blue Earth, Minn	1,800	Maple Hill, Oswego, N. Y	120
Manlius, Allegan, Mich	46	Maple Hill, Lycoming, Pa	12
Manlius, Onondaga, N. Y	500	Maple Lake, Wright, Minn	8
Manlius Centre, Onondaga, N. Y	64	Maple Landing, Monona, Iowa	12
Manlius Station, Onondaga, N. Y	110	Maple Lawn, Monroe, W. Va	10
Manlyville, Henry, Tenn	41	Maple Plain, Hennepin, Minn	96
Mannborough, Amelia, Va	22	Maple Rapids, Clinton, Mich	220
Manning, (c. h.,) Clarendon, S. C	110	Maple Ridge, Isanti, Minn	12
Manningham, Butler, Ala	12	Maple Ridge, Tioga, Pa	10
Mannington, Marion, W. Va	250	Maple River, Blue Earth, Minn	13
Mann's Choice, Bedford, Pa	20	Maples, Allen, Ind	48
Mannsville, Taylor, Ky	22	Maple's Mill, Fulton, Ill	17
Mannsville, Jefferson, N. Y	420	Maple Springs, La Fayette, Miss	12
Mannsville, Perry, Ky	14	Maple Springs, Wilkes, N. C	6
Mannville, Sumter, S. C	12	Maple Springs, Red River, Tex	10
Manny, (c. h.,) Sabine, La	48	Maple Springs, Dunn, Wis	20
Manomin, Anoka, Minn	14	Maple Street, Niagara, N. Y	19
Manor, Lancaster, Pa	46	Maplesville, Baker, Ala	12
Manor Dale, Westmoreland, Pa	19	Mapleton, Monona, Iowa	10
Manor Hill, Huntingdon, Pa	32	Mapleton, Bourbon, Kans	120
Manor Kill, Schoharie, N. Y	39	Mapleton, Grand Traverse, Mich	16
Manor Station, Westmoreland, Pa	110	Mapleton, Blue Earth, Minn	47
Manorsville, Armstrong, Pa	87	Mapleton, Stark, Ohio	68
Manorville, Suffolk, N. Y	160	Mapleton, Waukesha, Wis	40
Manquin, King William, Va	12	Mapleton Depot, Huntingdon, Pa	190
Mansfield, Tolland, Conn	84	Mapletown, Greene, Pa	17
Mansfield, Piatt, Ill	12	Mapleville, Providence, R. I	140

* Money-order office.

MAR   MAR

Maplewood, Middlesex, Mass	$100	Marine City, * St. Clair, Mich	$430
Maple Works, Clark, Wis	8	Marine Mills, Washington, Minn	310
Maquoketa,* Jackson, Iowa	900	Mariner's Harbor, Richmond, N. Y	97
Maquon, Knox, Ill	260	Marinette, Oconto, Wis	370
Marak, Brown, Kans	12	Marion,* (c. h.,) Perry, Ala	1,100
Maramec, Phelps, Mo	75	Marion, (c. h.,) Crittenden, Ark	84
Marathon, Lapeer, Mich	14	Marion, Hartford, Conn	180
Marathon, Cortland, N. Y	660	Marion,* (c. h.,) Williamson, Ill	230
Marathon, Clermont, Ohio	100	Marion,* (c. h.,) Grant, Ind	1,300
Marathon City, Marathon, Wis	12	Marion,* (c. h.,) Linn, Iowa	870
Marble, Madison, Ark	12	Marion, Douglas, Kans	12
Marble, Brown, Ind	4	Marion, (c. h.,) Crittenden, Ky	170
Marble, Waupaca, Wis	6	Marion, Union, La	12
Marble Creek, Iron, Mo	20	Marion, Washington, Me	11
Marble Dale, Litchfield, Conn	57	Marion, Plymouth, Mass	350
Marblehead,* Essex, Mass	1,900	Marion, Livingston, Mich	7
Marblehead, Ottawa, Ohio	46	Marion, Olmsted, Minn	80
Marble Hill, (c. h.,) Bollinger, Mo	120	Marion, Cole, Mo	22
Marble Ridge, Sauk, Wis	130	Marion, Wayne, N. Y	460
Marble Rock, Floyd, Iowa	96	Marion, (c. h.,) McDowell, N. C	78
Marble Salt Works, Cherokee N., Ind. T	12	Marion,* (c. h.,) Marion, Ohio	1,300
Marbletown, Ulster, N. Y	20	Marion, Franklin, Pa	62
Marble Valley, Coosa, Ala	6	Marion, Angelina, Tex	10
Marbut's, Giles, Tenn	20	Marion,* (c. h.,) Smyth, Va	590
Marcella Falls, Lawrence, Tenn	25	Marion C. H., Marion, S. C	580
Marcelline, Adams, Ill	60	Marion Centre, (c. h.,) Marion, Kans.	50
Marcellon, Columbia, Wis	50	Marion Station, Lauderdale, Miss	150
Marcellus, Cass, Mich	62	Marionville, Lawrence, Mo	91
Marcellus, Onondaga, N. Y	340	Marionville, Forest, Pa	20
Marcellus Falls, Onondaga, N. Y	110	Mariposa,* (c. h.,) Mariposa, Cal	230
Marchand, Indiana, Pa	61	Marissa, St. Clair, Ill	110
Marco, Greene, Ind	37	Marits, Morrow, Ohio	17
Marcy, La Grange, Ind	2	Mark, Defiance, Ohio	4
Marcy, Oneida, N. Y	12	Markelsville, Perry, Pa	44
Marcy, Fairfield, Ohio	24	Markesan,* Green Lake, Wis	150
Marcy, Waukesha, Wis	35	Market Lake, Oneida, Idaho	8
Mardisville, Talladega, Ala	12	Markham Station, Fauquier, Va	160
Marengo,* McHenry, Ill	1,000	Markle, Huntington, Ind	27
Marengo, Crawford, Ind	32	Markleeville,* Alpine, Cal	46
Marengo,* (c. h.,) Iowa, Iowa	1,100	Markleville, Madison, Ind	24
Marongo, Calhoun, Mich	120	Markleysburgh, Fayette, Pa	13
Marengo, Wayne, N. Y	57	Marksborough, Warren, N. J	81
Marengo, Morrow, Ohio	57	Marksville, (c. h.,) Avoyelles, La	170
Margaretta Furnace, York, Pa	35	Marksville, Page, Va	49
Margarettsville, Northampton, N. C.	38	Mark West, Sonoma, Cal	27
Margaretville, Delaware, N. Y	250	Marlborough, Hartford, Conn	58
Mariah Hill, Spencer, Ind	26	Marlborough,* Middlesex, Mass	1,600
Marianna, Phillips, Ark	13	Marlborough, Cheshire, N. H	330
Marianna, (c. h.,) Jackson, Fla	280	Marlborough, Monmouth, N. J	100
Maria Stein, Mercer, Ohio	24	Marlborough, Ulster, N. Y	320
Mariaville, Schenectady, N. Y	56	Marlborough, Pitt, N. C	10
Maricopa Wells, Pima, Ariz	220	Marlborough, Stark, Ohio	130
Marietta,* (c. h.,) Cobb, Ga	1,200	Marlborough, Chester, Pa	12
Marietta, Fulton, Ill	38	Marlborough, Carroll, Tenn	13
Marietta, Shelby, Ind	30	Marlborough, Windham, Vt	43
Marietta, Marshall, Iowa	95	Marlborough Depot, Cheshire, N. H.	120
Marietta, Onondaga, N. Y	22	Marlette, Sanilac, Mich	34
Marietta,* (c. h.,) Washington, Ohio.	2,400	Marlin, (c. h..) Falls, Tex	360
Marietta,* Lancaster, Pa	860	Marlow, Cheshire, N. H	210
Marietta, Greenville, S. C	13	Marlsville, Bladen, N. C	12
Marietta, Crawford, Wis	8	Marlton, Burlington, N. J	180
Marilla, Erie, N. Y	110	Marmiton, Bourbon, Kans	37
Marindal, Yankton, Dak	12	Marmont, Marshall, Ind	22
Marine, Madison, Ill	290	Maroa, *Macon, Ill	660
Marine, Lewis, Ky	12	Marple, Delaware, Pa	84
		Marquand, Madison, Mo	12

* Money-order office.

MAR

MAS

Marquette,* (c. h.,) Marquette, Mich.	$2,600
Marquette, Green Lake, Wis.	120
Marriottsville, Howard, Md	77
Marron, Clearfield, Pa	10
Marrowbone, Moultrie, Ill	80
Marrowbone, Cumberland, Ky	28
Mars, Bibb, Ala	8
Mars Bluff, Marion, S. C	140
Marseilles,* La Salle, Ill	820
Marseilles, Wyandot, Ohio	91
Marsh, Chester, Pa	42
Marsh, (c. h.,) Searcy, Ark	39
Marshall,* (e. h.,) Clark, Ill	630
Marshall, Henry, Iowa	130
Marshall, Bath, Ky	13
Marshall,* (c. h.,) Calhoun, Mich	3,000
Marshall, (c. h.,) Saline, Mo	680
Marshall, Oneida, N. Y	40
Marshall, (c. h.,) Madison, N. C	64
Marshall, Highland, Ohio	20
Marshall, (c. h.,) Harrison, Tex	2,000
Marshall, Dane, Wis	155
Marshall College, Cabell, W. Va	11
Marshall Hall, Charles, Md	12
Marshall Prairie, Newton, Ark	13
Marshall's Creek, Monroe, Pa	42
Marshall's Ferry, Grainger, Tenn	10
Marshallsville, Macon, Ga	270
Marshallsville, Wayne, Ohio	170
Marshallton, Chester, Pa	170
Marshalltown,* (c. h.,) Marshall, Iowa	2,800
Marsh Creek, Whitley, Ky	9
Marshfield, Warren, Ind	100
Marshfield, Plymouth, Mass	220
Marshfield,* (c. h.,) Webster, Mo	630
Marshfield, Erie, N. Y	23
Marshfield, Athens, Ohio	190
Marshfield, Tioga, Pa	16
Marshfield, Washington, Vt	140
Mars Hill, Aroostook, Me	25
Marshland, Richmond, N. Y	48
Marshville, Oceana, Mich	12
Marshville, Montgomery, N. Y	18
Marston's Mills, Barnstable, Mass	67
Martell, Pierce, Wis	87
Martha Furnace, Centre, Pa	100
Marthasville, Warren, Mo	62
Marthaville, Natchitoches, La	8
Martickville, Lancaster, Pa	20
Martin, Allegan, Mich	160
Martin, Green, Wis	12
Martindale, Mecklenburgh, N. C	2
Martindale Depot, Columbia, N. Y.	47
Martinez,* (c. h.,) Contra Costa, Cal.	250
Martin's Bluff, Clark, Wash	12
Martinsburgh, Butte, Cal	12
Martinsburgh, Pike, Ill	20
Martinsburgh, Washington, Ind	57
Martinsburgh, Keokuk, Iowa	130
Martinsburgh, Monroe, Ky	12
Martinsburgh, Lewis, N. Y	270
Martinsburgh, Knox, Ohio	170
Martinsburgh, Blair, Pa	270
Martinsburgh,* (c. h.,) Berkeley, W. Va	1,600

Martin's Creek, Sharpe, Ark	$12
Martin's Creek, Northampton, Pa	41
Martin's Ferry, Klamath, Cal	5
Martin's Ferry, Belmont, Ohio	430
Martin's Lime Kilns, Stokes, N. C	7
Martinstown, Putnam, Mo	13
Martinsville, Clark, Ill	250
Martinsville,* (c. h.,) Morgan, Ind	850
Martinsville, Wayne, Mich	17
Martinsville, Copiah, Miss	12
Martinsville, Harrison, Mo	12
Martinsville, Adams, Nebr	12
Martinsville, Somerset, N. J	66
Martinsville, Niagara, N. Y	49
Martinsville, Clinton, Ohio	170
Martinsville, Lancaster, Pa	19
Martinsville, Nacogdoches, Tex	10
Martinsville, (c. h.,) Henry, Va	70
Martinville, Grant, Wis	33
Martville, Cayuga, N. Y	83
Martz, Clay, Ind	36
Marvel, Bates, Mo	76
Marvin, Henry, Mo	12
Marvin, Chautauqua, N. Y	21
Marydell, Caroline, Md	110
Maryland, Otsego, N. Y	95
Maryland Line, Baltimore, Md	55
Marysburgh, Le Sueur, Minn	49
Marysville,* (c. h.,) Yuba, Cal	3,200
Marysville, Vermilion, Ill	8
Marysville, Marion, Iowa	18
Marysville,* (c. h.,) Marshall, Kans	490
Marysville, St. Clair, Mich	68
Marysville,* (c. h.,) Union, Ohio	820
Marysville, Perry, Pa	210
Marysville, Campbell, Va	40
Marytown, Fond du Lac, Wis	12
Maryville,* (c. h.,) Nodaway, Mo	1,000
Maryville, (c. h.,) Blount, Tenn	300
Masardis, Aroostook, Me	29
Mascoutah,* St. Clair, Ill	480
Mashapaug, Tolland, Conn	24
Mason,* Effingham, Ill	1,100
Mason, Washington, Md	12
Mason,* (c. h.,) Ingham, Mich	880
Mason, Hillsborough, N. H	92
Mason, Warren, Ohio	220
Mason, Tipton, Tenn	220
Mason, (c. h.,) Mason, Tex	160
Mason, Mason, W. Va	420
Mason and Dixon, Franklin, Pa	83
Mason City, Mason, Ill	860
Mason City,* (c. h.,) Cerro Gordo, Iowa	700
Mason Creek, McLean, Ky	5
Mason's Depot, Amherst, Va	76
Masontown, Fayette, Pa	100
Masontown, Preston, W. Va	9
Mason Village, Hillsborough, N. H.	360
Masonville, Delaware, Iowa	200
Masonville, Daviess, Ky	33
Masonville, Burlington, N. J	7
Masonville, Delaware, N. Y	180
Maspeth, Queens, N. Y	19
Massac Creek, Massac, Ill	12
Massack, McCracken, Ky	9

* Money-order office.

MAY		MEC	
Massanatton, Page, Va	$17	Maynardsville, Calhoun, Ill	$8
Massena,* St. Lawrence, N. Y	520	*Maynardville, (c. h.,)* Union, Tenn	70
Massena Centre, St. Lawrence N. Y.	42	Mayo Forge, Patrick, Va	21
Massey's Cross Roads, Kent, Md	30	Mayport, Duval, Fla	12
Massie's Mills, Nelson, Va	50	Maysfield, Milam, Tex	60
Massillon, Cedar, Iowa	22	*May's Landing, (c. h.,)* Atlantic, N. J.	230
Massillon,* Stark, Ohio	2,600	May's Lick, Mason, Ky	160
Mastersonville, Lancaster, Pa	20	May Spring, Grainger, Tenn	9
Mastersville, McLennan, Tex	12	Maysville, Benton, Ark	40
Masterton, Monroe, Ohio	54	Maysville, Franklin, Iowa	130
Masthope, Pike, Pa	76	*Maysville,* (c. h.,) Mason, Ky	2,500
Mast Yard, Merrimack, N. H	55	*Maysville,* (c. h.,) De Kalb, Mo	410
Matagorda, (c. h.,) Matagorda, Tex.	200	Maysville, Columbiana, Ohio	110
Matamoras, Pike, Pa	37	Maysville, Mercer, Pa	24
Matanzas, St. John's, Fla	12	Maytown, Lancaster, Pa	130
Matawan, Monmouth, N. J	730	Mayview, La Fayette, Mo	86
Matfield Green, Chase, Kans	42	*Mayville,* (c. h.,) Chautauqua, N. Y.	700
Matherton, Ionia, Mich	150	Mayville,* Dodge, Wis	400
Mathews, Montgomery, Ala	12	Maywood, Cook, Ill	12
Matinicus, Knox, Me	23	Maywood, Benton, Minn	17
Matoax, Amelia, Va	25	Mazeppa, Wabashaw, Minn	110
Mattapan, Norfolk, Mass	140	Mazo Manie,* Dane, Wis	620
Mattapoisett, Plymouth, Mass	490	Mazon, Grundy, Ill	42
Mattawamkeag, Penobscot, Me	120	Mead Corners, Crawford, Pa	12
Mattawan, Van Buren, Mich	450	Meade, Macomb, Mich	20
Matteawan,* Dutchess, N. Y	720	Meadow, Millard, Utah	4
Matthews, (c. h.,) Matthews, Va	210	Meadow Bluff, Greenbrier, W. Va.	29
Matthews' Store, Howard, Md	77	Meadow Creek, Whitley, Ky	4
Mattison, Cook, Ill	160	Meadow Creek, Madison, Mont	15
Mattison, Branch, Mich	35	Meadow Dale, Highland, Va	10
Mattituck, Suffolk, N. Y	290	Meadow Gap, Huntingdon, Pa	15
Mattoon,* Coles, Ill	2,500	Meadows of Dan, Patrick, Va	6
Matville, Raleigh, W. Va	12	Meadow Valley, Plumas, Cal	38
Mauch Chunk, (c. h.,) Carbon, Pa.	2,200	Meadowville, Umatilla, Oreg	40
Mauckport, Harrison, Ind	87	Meadowville, Barbour, W. Va	21
Maumee City,* Lucas, Ohio	700	Mead's Basin, Passaic, N. J	60
Maumelle, Pulaski, Ark	6	Mead's Creek, Steuben, N. Y	10
Maune's Store, Franklin, Mo	12	Mead's Mills, Wayne, Mich	29
Maurertown, Shenandoah, Va	55	Meadville, Barry, Mich	12
Mauricetown, Cumberland, N. J	160	*Meadville, (c. h.,)* Franklin, Miss	14
Mauston, *Juneau, Wis	830	Meadville, Linn, Mo	230
Maxatawny, Berks, Pa	59	*Meadville,* (c. h.,) Crawford, Pa.	3,000
Maxey, Oglethorpe, Ga	110	Meadville, Halifax, Va	12
Maxfield, Penobscot, Me	9	Meagsville, Jackson, Tenn	12
Maxino, Stark, Ohio	66	Means, Harrison, Ohio	140
Maxinkuckee, Marshall, Ind	23	Mebanesville, Alamance, N. C	260
Max Meadows, Wythe, Va	40	Mecca, Trumbull, Ohio	110
Maxville, Perry, Ohio	53	Mechanicsburgh, Sangamon, Ill	130
Maxville, Dyer, Tenn	13	Mechanicsburgh, Henry, Ind	94
Maxville, Buffalo, Wis	57	Mechanicsburgh, Champaign, Ohio.	370
Maxwell, Delaware, Ohio	11	Mechanicsburgh,* Cumberland, Pa.	1,700
Maxwell's Creek, Mariposa, Cal	150	Mechanicsburgh, Bland, Va	15
May, Tuscola, Mich	72	Mechanic's Falls,*Androscoggin, Me.	600
May, Martin, Minn	7	Mechanic's Grove, Lancaster, Pa	43
May, Lancaster, Pa	15	Mechanicstown, Frederick, Md	190
Mayberry, Carroll, Md	12	Mechanicstown, Carroll, Ohio	52
Mayesville, Sumter, S. C	220	Mechanic's Valley, Cecil, Md	12
Mayfield, Santa Clara, Cal	240	Mechanicsville, Vanderburgh, Ind.	23
Mayfield, Hancock, Ga	58	Mechanicsville,* Cedar, Iowa	500
Mayfield, (c. h.,) Graves, Ky	470	Mechanicsville, Saratoga, N. Y	550
Mayfield, Grand Traverse, Mich	12	Mechanicsville, Ashtabula, Ohio	38
Mayfield, Fulton, N. Y	110	Mechanicsville, Bucks, Pa	62
Mayfield, Cuyahoga, Ohio	48	Mechanicsville, Sumter, S. C	20
Mayhew's Station, Sacramento,Cal.	12	Mechanicsville, Rutland, Vt	230
Mayhew's Station, Lowndes, Miss.	280	Mechum's River, Albemarle, Va	120
May Hill, Adams, Ohio	12	Mecklenburgh, Schuyler, N. Y	210

* Money-order office.

MEL | MER

Mecosta, Mecosta, Mich	$13	Melvin Village, Carroll, N. H	$88
Medarysville, Pulaski, Ind	160	Memory, Taylor, Iowa	41
Mederville, Clayton, Iowa	12	Memphis, Pickens, Ala	12
Medfield, Norfolk, Mass	400	Memphis, Clarke, Ind	79
Medford, Piscataquis, Me	21	Memphis,* Macomb, Mich	400
Medford, Middlesex, Mass	1,100	Memphis,* (c. h.,) Scotland, Mo	350
Medford, Steele, Minn	200	Memphis, Onondaga, N. Y	160
Medford, Burlington, N. J	360	Memphis, Clinton, Ohio	36
Medford Centre, Piscataquis, Me	15	Memphis,* (c. h.,) Shelby, Tenn	4,000
Media,* (c. h.,) Delaware, Pa	1,200	Memphis Junction, Warren, Ky	22
Medicine, Sullivan, Mo	12	Menallen, Adams, Pa	40
Medicine Bow, Carbon, Wyo	12	Menardville, (c. h.,) Menard, Tex	12
Medina, Jefferson, Kans	100	Menasha,* Winnebago, Wis	820
Medina, Lenawee, Mich	160	Menchville, Warwick, Va	12
Medina,* Orleans, N. Y	1,900	Mendham, Morris, N. J	330
Medina,* (c. h.,) Medina, Ohio	790	Mendocino,* Mendocino, Cal	380
Medina, Outagamie, Wis	100	Mendon, El Dorado, Cal	12
Medo, Blue Earth, Minn	22	Mendon, Adams, Ill	120
Medoc, Jasper, Mo	79	Mendon, Worcester, Mass	120
Medon, Madison, Tenn	120	Mendon, St. Joseph, Mich	310
Medora, Macoupin, Ill	60	Mendon, Monroe, N. Y	93
Medora, Jackson, Ind	220	Mendon, Mercer, Ohio	40
Medora, Warren, Iowa	13	Mendon, Westmoreland, Pa	45
Medora, Osage, Mo	140	Mendon, Cache, Utah	19
Medusa, Albany, N. Y	48	Mendon, Rutland, Vt	61
Medway, Penobscot, Me	24	Mendon Centre, Monroe, N. Y	56
Medway,* Norfolk, Mass	500	Mendota,* La Salle, Ill	2,700
Medway, Greene, N. Y	74	Mendota, Labette, Kans	12
Medway, Clark, Ohio	110	Mendota, Dakota, Minn	93
Medybemps, Washington, Me	17	Mendota, Putnam, Mo	25
Meeker, Washington, Wis	12	Menekaune, Oconto, Wis	250
Meeker's Grove, La Fayette, Wis	35	Menlo Park, San Mateo, Cal	12
Meeme, Manitowoc, Wis	50	Menno, Mifflin, Pa	47
Mehoopany, Wyoming, Pa	190	Menomonee,* (c. h.,) Menomonee,	
Meig's Creek, Morgan, Ohio	30	Mich	670
Meigsville, Morgan, Ohio	45	Menomonee,* (c. h.,) Dunn, Wis	950
Meinecke, San Joaquin, Cal	12	Menomonee Falls, Waukesha, Wis	120
Melburn, Williams, Ohio	37	Mentor, Bremer, Iowa	14
Melissa, Ozark, Mo	12	Mentor, Lake, Ohio	260
Melissadale, Butler, Pa	21	Menzie, Franklin, Iowa	12
Melita, Alameda, Cal	12	Mequon River, Ozaukee, Wis	140
Mellenbruch, Jackson, Ind	3	Merced Falls, Merced, Cal	23
Mellenville, Columbia, N. Y	95	Mercer, Somerset, Me	120
Melleray, Dubuque, Iowa	14	Mercer, Mercer, Mo	8
Mellington, Kendall, Ill	76	Mercer, Mercer, Ohio	20
Mellonville, Orange, Fla	200	Mercer,* (c. h.,) Mercer, Pa	1,100
Mellow Valley, Clay, Ala	8	Mercer's Bottom, Mason, W. Va	53
Mellwood, Prince George's, Md	12	Mercersburgh,* Franklin, Pa	610
Melmore, Seneca, Ohio	150	Mercerville, Gallia, Ohio	19
Meloy, Washington, Pa	12	Merchantville, Camden, N. J	20
Melpine, Muscatine, Iowa	27	Merchantville, Steuben, N. Y	71
Melrose, Clark, Ill	45	Mercury, Madison, Ind	44
Melrose, Middlesex, Mass	700	Mercyville, Macon, Mo	6
Melrose, Stearns, Minn	33	Meredith, Delaware, N. Y	120
Melrose, St. Louis, Mo	12	Meredith, Venango, Pa	180
Melrose, Robeson, N. C	12	Meredith Centre, Belknap, N. H	46
Melrose, Nacogdoches, Tex	12	Meredith's Tavern, Marion, W. Va	4
Melrose, Rockingham, Va	16	Meredith Village, Belknap, N. H	510
Melrose, Jackson, Wis	100	Meredosia, Morgan, Ill	270
Melton, Jefferson, Ark	2	Meriden, New Haven, Conn	1,500
Melton's Mill, Tallapoosa, Ala	12	Meriden, La Salle, Ill	150
Meltonsville, Marshall, Ala	11	Meriden, (c. h.,) Steele, Minn	53
Melvern, Osage, Kans	12	Meriden,* Sullivan, N. H	560
Melville, Chattooga, Ga	22	Meridian, Sutter, Cal	20
Melville, Leelenaw, Mich	39	Meridian,* (c. h.,) Lauderdale, Miss	1,900
Melvina, Monroe, Wis	22	Meridian, (c. h.,) Jefferson, Nebr	61

* Money-order office.

Meridian, Cayuga, N. Y	$390	Miccosukee, Leon, Fla	$16
Meridian, (c. h.,) Bosque, Tex	45	Michaelsville, Harford, Md	42
Meridianville, Madison, Ala	12	Micham, Leelenaw, Mich	4
Mermaid, New Castle, Del	12	Michigan Bar, Sacramento, Cal	88
Mermenton, St. Landry, La	23	Michigan Bluff, Placer, Cal	100
Meroa, Mitchell, Iowa	12	Michigan Centre, Jackson, Mich	35
Merom, Sullivan, Ind	240	Michigan City,* La Porte, Ind	1,400
Merriam, Noble, Ind	38	Michigantown, Clinton, Ind	80
Merrick, Queens, N. Y	27	Michigan Valley, Osage, Kans	12
Merrillsville, St. Clair, Mich	40	Middagh's, Northampton, Pa	32
Merrillsville, Franklin, N. Y	12	Middle Bass, Ottawa, Ohio	44
Merrilltown, Travis, Tex	7	Middleborough, Plymouth, Mass	1,100
Merrillville, Lake, Ind	52	Middlebourne, Guernsey, Ohio	120
Merrimac, Jefferson, Iowa	10	*Middlebourne*, (c. h.,) Tyler, W. Va	74
Merrimack, Hillsborough, N. H	12	Middle Branch, Stark, Ohio	11
Merrimack, Sauk, Wis	69	Middlebrook, Montgomery, Md	16
Merrimack Point, Monroe, Ill	57	Middlebrook, Iron, Mo	35
Merrimac Station, St. Louis, Mo	17	Middlebrook, Augusta, Va	93
Merritt, Scott, Ill	12	Middleburgh, Clay, Fla	23
Merritt's Bridge, Lexington, S. C	12	Middleburgh, Washington, Iowa	12
Merrittstown, Fayette, Pa	54	Middleburgh, Casey, Ky	37
Merrow Station, Tolland, Conn	80	Middleburgh, Carroll, Md	51
Merryall, Bradford, Pa	13	Middleburgh, Richardson, Nebr	29
Merry Oaks, Chatham, N. C	8	Middleburgh,* Schoharie, N. Y	540
Mershon's Cross Roads, Laurel, Ky	7	Middleburgh, Cuyahoga, Ohio	22
Merton, Steele, Minn	7	*Middleburgh*, (c. h.,) Snyder, Pa	130
Merton, Waukesha, Wis	110	Middleburgh, Hardeman, Tenn	12
Mertztown, Berks, Pa	72	Middleburgh, Loudoun, Va	410
Merwinsburgh, Monroe, Pa	18	Middlebury, New Haven, Conn	78
Mesback's Creek, Monroe, Ky	4	Middlebury, Elkhart, Ind	370
Meshannon, Centre, Pa	20	Middlebury, Grundy, Mo	80
Meshoppen, Wyoming, Pa	380	Middlebury, Summit, Ohio	490
Mesilla, (c. h.,) Doña Ana, N. Mex	120	*Middlebury*,* (c. h.,) Addison, Vt	1,400
Mesopotamia, Trumbull, Ohio	170	Middlebury, Iowa, Wis	30
Messengerville, Cortland, N. Y	50	Middlebury Centre, Tioga, Pa	9
Messongo, Accomack, Va	13	Middlebush, Somerset, N. J	94
Metamora,* (c. h.,) Woodford, Ill	580	Middle Creek, Hancock, Ill	18
Metamora, Franklin, Ind	170	Middle Creek, Chase, Kans	6
Metamora, Lapeer, Mich	60	Middle Creek, Gallatin, Mont	12
Metamora, Fulton, Ohio	49	Middle Creek, Noble, Ohio	30
Metea, Cass, Ind	15	Middle Creek, Snyder, Pa	18
Metedeconk, Ocean, N. J	34	Middle Fabius, Scotland, Mo	38
Methuen, Essex, Mass	820	Middlefield, Middlesex, Conn	320
Metomen, Fond du Lac, Wis	53	Middlefield, Buchanan, Iowa	9
Metropolis City,* (c. h.,) Massac, Ill	750	Middlefield, Hampshire, Mass	170
Metuchen, Middlesex, N. J	100	Middlefield, Otsego, N. Y	130
Metz, Steuben, Ind	93	Middlefield, Geauga, Ohio	69
Mexico, Miami, Ind	86	Middlefield Centre, Otsego, N. Y	66
Mexico, Oxford, Me	62	Middleford, Sussex, Del	17
Mexico,* (c. h.,) Audrian, Mo	1,100	Middle Fork, Clinton, Ind	68
Mexico, Oswego, N. Y	1,300	Middle Fork, Jackson, Ky	1
Mexico, Wyandot, Ohio	19	Middle Fork, Hocking, Ohio	11
Mexico, Juniata, Pa	110	Middle Fork, Randolph, W. Va	12
Meyer's Mills, Somerset, Pa	190	Middle Granville, Washington, N. Y	790
Meyerstown, Lebanon, Pa	500	Middle Grove, Fulton, Ill	18
Meyersville, De Witt, Tex	57	Middle Grove, Monroe, Mo	91
Miami, Miami, Ind	97	Middle Grove, Saratoga, N. Y	59
Miami, Saline, Mo	570	Middle Haddam, Middlesex, Conn	200
Miami, Hamilton, Ohio	59	Middle Hope, Orange, N. Y	26
Miamisburgh,* Montgomery, Ohio	620	Middle Island, Suffolk, N. Y	38
Miamiville, Clermont, Ohio	94	Middle Lancaster, Butler, Pa	39
Miami Village, Miami, Kans	6	Middle Point, Van Wert, Ohio	72
Mianus, Fairfield, Conn	200	*Middleport*, (c. h.,) Iroquois, Ill	330
Micanopy, Alachua, Fla	109	Middleport, Niagara, N. Y	556
Micklen, Jackson, Mo	48	Middleport, Meigs, Ohio	540
Micco, Creek N., Ind. T	15	Middleport, Schuylkill, Pa	94

* Money-order-office.

MIF

Middleport, Webster, W. Va	$5
Middle River, Banks, Ga	9
Middle River, Madison, Iowa	7
Middle Saluda, Greenville, S. C	12
Middlesex, Yates, N. Y	120
Middlesex, Washington, Vt	150
Middlesex Village, Middlesex, Mass	57
Middle Spring, Cumberland, Pa	37
Middle Sprite, Fulton, N. Y	13
Middlesworth, Shelby, Ill	12
Middleton, Ada, Idaho	47
Middleton, Essex, Mass	170
Middleton, Strafford, N. H	6
Middleton, Washington, Oreg	12
Middleton, Rutherford, Tenn	12
Middleton, Leon, Tex	3
Middleton, Dane, Wis	35
Middleton Station, Hardeman, Tenn	110
Middletown,* (c. h.,) Middlesex, Conn	3,400
Middletown,* New Castle, Del	1,100
Middletown, Logan, Ill	160
Middletown, Henry, Ind	280
Middletown, Des Moines, Iowa	71
Middletown, Jefferson, Ky	74
Middletown,* Frederick, Md	570
Middletown, Ingham, Mich	10
Middletown, Montgomery, Mo	300
Middletown, Monmouth, N. J	110
Middletown,* Orange, N. Y	2,200
Middletown,* Butler, Ohio	1,300
Middletown,* Dauphin, Pa	1,100
Middletown,* Rutland, Vt	540
Middletown, Frederick, Va	190
Middletown Centre, Susquehanna, Pa	13
Middle Valley, Morris, N. J	37
Middle Valley, Wayne, Pa	79
Middleville,* Barry, Mich	480
Middleville, Sussex, N. J	15
Middleville, Herkimer, N. Y	210
Middleway, Jefferson, W. Va	130
Midland,* (c h.,) Midland, Mich	700
Midland, Marquette, Wis	13
Midlothian, Chesterfield, Va	160
Mid Prairie, Louisa, Iowa	16
Midville, Burke, Ga	170
Midway, Bullock, Ala	150
Midway, Hot Spring, Ark	12
Midway, Alameda, Cal	12
Midway, Fulton, Ill	37
Midway, Spencer, Ind	33
Midway, Woodford, Ky	510
Midway, Hinds, Miss	12
Midway, Boone, Mo	12
Midway, Erie, N. Y	12
Midway, Davidson, N. C	8
Midway, Guernsey, Ohio	18
Midway, Washington, Pa	96
Midway, Barnwell, S. C	110
Midway, Greene, Tenn	76
Midway, Madison, Tex	12
Midway, Wasatch, Utah	15
Mier, Wabash, Ill	50
Mier, Grant, Ind	81
Mifflin, Crawford, Ind	11
Mifflin, Ashland, Ohio	17

MIL

Mifflin, Henderson, Tenn	$55
Mifflin, Iowa, Wis	70
Mifflinburgh, Union, Pa	440
Mifflintown,* (c. h.,) Juniata, Pa	600
Mifflinville, Franklin, Ohio	30
Mifflinville, Columbia, Pa	52
Milam, Sabine, Tex	280
Milan, Ripley, Ind	120
Milan, Lucas, Iowa	12
Milan, Washtenaw, Mich	64
Milan,* (c. h.,) Sullivan, Mo	250
Milan, Coos, N. H	89
Milan, Dutchess, N. Y	25
Milan, Erie, Ohio	680
Milan, Bradford, Pa	65
Milan Depot, Gibson, Tenn	120
Milanville, Wayne, Pa	27
Milburn, Ballard, Ky	16
Mile Creek, Muskegon, Mich	12
Mile Creek, Pickens, S. C	12
Milesburgh, Centre, Pa	300
Miles Grove, Erie, Pa	100
Miles Point, Carroll, Mo	65
Miles Pond, Essex, Vt	12
Miles Station, Macoupin, Ill	91
Milestown, St. Mary's, Md	21
Mile Strip, Madison, N. Y	13
Milford, Lassen, Cal	12
Milford,* New Haven, Conn	1,200
Milford,* Kent, Del	920
Milford, Iroquois, Ill	180
Milford, Kosciusko, Ind	160
Milford, Dickinson, Iowa	12
Milford, Riley, Kans	71
Milford, Bracken, Ky	24
Milford, Penobscot, Me	97
Milford,* Worcester, Mass	2,300
Milford,* Oakland, Mich	310
Milford, Brown, Minn	10
Milford, Barton, Mo	28
Milford, (c. h.,) Seward, Nebr	120
Milford,* Hillsborough, N. H	1,100
Milford, Hunterdon, N. J	310
Milford, Otsego, N. Y	390
Milford,* Clermont, Ohio	670
Milford,* (c. h.,) Pike, Pa	360
Milford, Ellis, Tex	110
Milford, Caroline, Va	33
Milford, Jefferson, Wis	89
Milford Centre, Union, Ohio	210
Milford Mills, Chester, Pa	24
Milford Square, Bucks, Pa	77
Milfordton, Knox, Ohio	30
Mill, Fayette, Iowa	15
Millard, Adair, Mo	12
Millard, Walworth, Wis	50
Millbach, Lebanon, Pa	17
Mill Bend, Hawkins, Tenn	12
Millborough Springs, Bath, Va	44
Millbrae, San Mateo, Cal	12
Millbridge, Washington, Me	280
Mill Brook, Litchfield, Conn	16
Millbrook, Kendall, Ill	21
Millbrook, Mecosta, Mich	92
Millbrook, Warren, N. J	19
Millbrook, Dutchess, N. Y	130

* Money-order office.

MIL   MIL

Mill Brook, Wayne, Ohio	$21	Millgrove, Blackford, Ind	$30
Mill Brook, Washington, Tenn	12	Mill Grove, Poweshiek, Iowa	8
Millbrook, Frederick, Va	12	Mill Grove, Erie, N. Y	49
Millburgh, Berrien, Mich	80	Mill Grove, Morgan, Ohio	11
Millburn, Lake, Ill	89	Mill Hall, Clinton, Pa	190
Millburn, Essex, N. J	330	Millheim, Centre, Pa	90
Millburnton, Green, Tenn	3	Millheim, Austin, Tex	20
Millbury, Worcester, Mass	1,100	Mill Hill, Cabarrus, N. C	12
Millbnry, Wood, Ohio	100	Mill Hollow, Luzerne, Pa	8
Mill City, Clear Creek, Colo	110	Millhousen, Decatur, Ind	100
Mill City, Humboldt, Nev	12	Millican, Brazos, Tex	300
Mill City, Wyoming, Pa	130	Milligan, Tuscarawas, Ohio	6
Mill Creek, Izard, Ark	7	Milliken's Bend, Madison, La	39
Mill Creek, Bourbon, Kans	10	Millin, Burke, Ga	16
Mill Creek, Calvert, Md	12	Millington, Middlesex, Conn	16
Mill Creek, Kent, Mich	16	Millington, Kent, Md	220
Mill Creek, Huntingdon, Pa	170	Millington, Franklin, Mass	58
Mill Creek, Salt Lake, Utah	12	Millington, Tuscola, Mich	20
Mill Creek, Berkeley, W. Va	71	Millington, Morris, N. J	44
Mill Creek, Richland, Wis	8	Millington, Albemarle, Va	25
Milldale, Warren, Va	10	Mill Plain, Fairfield, Conn	34
_Milledgeville,_* (c. h.,) Baldwin, Ga	1,200	Mill Point, Sullivan, Tenn	7
Milledgeville, Carroll, Ill	190	Mill Point, Pocahontas, W. Va	25
Milledgeville, Appanoose, Iowa	11	Millport, Sanford, Ala	12
Milledgeville, Lincoln, Ky	30	Millport, Washington, Ind	4
Milledgeville, Mercer, Pa	15	Millport, Knox, Mo	24
Milledgeville, McNairy, Tenn	12	Mill Port, Chemung, N. Y	360
Millen's Bay, Jefferson, N. Y	18	Millport, Columbiana, Ohio	68
Miller Grove, Hopkins, Tex	8	Millport, Potter, Pa	46
Miller's, Lawrence, Ohio	82	Mill River, Berkshire, Mass	140
Millersburgh, Mercer, Ill	120	Mill River, Henderson, N. C	19
Millersburgh, Elkhart, Ind	240	Mill Rock, Jackson, Iowa	64
Millersburgh, Iowa, Iowa	180	Mill Run, Fayette, Pa	200
Millersburgh, Bourbon, Ky	530	Millry, Washington, Ala	15
Millersburgh, Rice, Minn	15	Mills, Jackson, Wis	12
Millersburg, Callaway, Mo	100	Millsborough, Sussex, Del	79
_Millersburgh,_* (c. h.,) Holmes, Ohio	910	Millsborough, Washington, Pa	100
Millersburgh,* Dauphin, Pa	900	Mills Centre, Brown, Wis	55
Miller's Corners, Ontario, N. Y	86	Mills' Corners, Jay, Ind	12
Miller's Creek, Black Hawk, Iowa	12	Mills' Corners, Fulton, N. Y	9
Miller's Creek, Estill, Ky	19	Mill Shoals, White, Ill	12
Miller's Eddy, Armstrong, Pa	18	Mills' Mills, Allegany, N. Y	25
Miller's Falls, Franklin, Mass	130	Mills' Prairie, Edwards, Ill	14
Miller's Grove, Woodson, Kans	12	Mill Spring, St. Louis, Mo	100
Miller's Mill, Davidson, N. C	12	Mill Spring, Jefferson, Tenn	8
Miller's Place, Suffolk, N. Y	65	Mill Springs, Wayne, Ky	24
Millersport, Fairfield, Ohio	64	Millstadt, St. Clair, Ill	150
Miller's Station, Lake, Ind	36	Mill Station, Lapeer, Mich	10
Miller's Station, Harrison, Ohio	12	Millstone, Somerset, N. J	260
Miller's Station, Crawford, Pa	79	Millstone Point, Washington, Md	21
Miller's Tavern, Essex, Va	12	Milltown, Chambers, Ala	53
Millerstown, Champaign, Ohio	22	Mill Town, Berrien, Ga	62
Millerstown, Perry, Pa	320	Milltown, Crawford, Ind	23
Millerstown Station, Perry, Pa	25	Milltown, Adair, Ky	16
Millersville, Russell, Ky	4	Milltown, Washington, Me	390
Millersville, Anne Arundel, Md	100	Milltown, Chester, Pa	19
Millersville, Cape Girardeau, Mo	29	Millview, Sullivan, Pa	14
Millersville,* Lancaster, Pa	1,000	Mill Village, Sullivan, N. H	32
Millerton, (c. h.,) Fresno, Cal	170	Mill Village, Erie, Pa	170
Millerton, Dutchess, N. Y	520	Millville, Shasta, Cal	120
Millerville, Douglass, Minn	12	Millville, Henry, Ind	80
Mill Falls, Marion, W. Va	9	Millville, Clayton, Iowa	61
Millfield, Athens, Ohio	32	Millville, Worcester, Mass	350
Mill Ford, Cherokee, Ala	12	Millville, Wabashaw, Minn	8
Mill Gap, Highland, Va	10	Millville, Ray, Mo	80
Mill Green, Harford, Md	20	Millville,* Cumberland, N. J	1,200

* Money-order office.

MIL

MIN

Millville, Orleans, N. Y	$100	Milville, Rusk, Tex	$4
Millville, Butler, Ohio	93	Milwaukee, Clackamas, Oreg	66
Millville, Cumberland, Pa	90	Milwaukee, Luzerne, Pa	20
Millville, Spartanburgh, S. C	5	Milwaukee,* (c. h.,) Milwaukee, Wis.	4,000
Millville, Lincoln, Tenn	22	Mims, Barnwell, S. C	10
Millville, Cache, Utah	22	Mim's Store, Marion, Tex	12
Millville, Westmoreland, Va	24	Mina, Chautauqua, N. Y	47
Millville, Grant, Wis	36	Minaville, Montgomery, N. Y	110
Millville Depot, Pike, Pa	12	Minburn, Dallas, Iowa	60
Millway, Lancaster, Pa	49	Mincy, Taney, Mo	12
Millwood, Kosciusko, Ind	9	Minden, Claiborne, La	250
Millwood, Lincoln, Mo	62	Minden, Sanilac, Mich	58
Millwood, Knox, Ohio	70	Minden, Benton, Minn	12
Millwood, Westmoreland, Pa	68	Minden, Lawrence, Mo	21
Millwood, Washington, Tenn	60	Minden, Montgomery, N. Y	32
Millwood, Collin, Tex	12	Mindoro, La Crosse, Wis	140
Millwood, Clarke, Va	130	Mine Kill Falls, Schoharie, N. Y	12
Milnine, Piatt, Ill	80	Mine La Motte, Madison, Mo	20
Milner, Randolph, Ala	12	Mineola, Queens, N. Y	110
Milner, Pike, Ga	59	Miner, La Salle, Ill	12
Milner's Corners, Hancock, Ind	12	Mineral, Bureau, Ill	84
Milnersville, Guernsey, Ohio	85	Mineral City, White Pine, Nev	12
Milnesville, Augusta, Va	12	Mineral Mill, Elko, Nev	12
Milo, Pike, Ala	10	Mineral Point, Anderson, Kans	34
Milo, Bureau, Ill	44	Mineral Point, Washington, Mo	52
Milo, Delaware, Iowa	12	Mineral Point, Tuscarawas, Ohio	26
Milo, Piscataquis, Me	190	Mineral Point, Cambria, Pa	37
Milo, Barry, Mich	* 11	Mineral Point,* Iowa, Wis	1,700
Milo, Defiance, Ohio	8	Mineral Ridge, Boone, Iowa	210
Milo, Wetzel, W. Va	67	Mineral Ridge,* Mahoning, Ohio	260
Milo Centre, Yates, N. Y	87	Mineral Springs, Hampstead, Ark	13
Milor, Sebastian, Ark	5	Mineral Springs, Mower, Minn	8
Milpitas, Santa Clara, Cal	84	Mineral Springs, Schoharie, N. Y	40
Milquatay, San Diego, Cal	9	Mineral Springs, Adams, Minn	25
Milroy, Knox, Ill	16	Miner's Delight, Sweetwater, Wyo.	12
Milroy, Rush, Ind	160	Minersville, Henry, Ill	16
Milroy, Mifflin, Pa	290	Minersville, Christian, Mo	12
Milton, Litchfield, Conn	86	Minersville, Meigs, Ohio	100
Milton, Sussex, Del	260	Minersville,* Schuylkill, Pa	1,100
Milton, (c. h.,) Santa Rosa, Fla	170	Minersville, Beaver, Utah	38
Milton, Pike, Ill	140	Minerva, Marshall, Iowa	17
Milton, Wayne, Ind	350	Minerva, Mason, Ky	36
Milton, Van Buren, Iowa	30	Minerva, Essex, N. Y	20
Milton, Trimble, Ky	200	Minerva,* Stark, Ohio	500
Milton, Norfolk, Mass	870	Minetto, Oswego, N. Y	120
Milton, Macomb, Mich	33	Mineville, Essex, N. Y	250
Milton, Randolph, Mo	50	Mingo, Champaign, Ohio	88
Milton, Saunders, Nebr	12	Mingo Flat, Randolph, W. Va	20
Milton, Strafford, N. H	160	Minier, Tazewell, Ill	8
Milton, Morris, N. J	9	Mining, Morgan, Mo	16
Milton, Ulster, N. Y	370	Minisink, Orange, N. Y	21
Milton, Caswell, N. C	210	Minneapolis, Ottawa, Kans	41
Milton, Mahoning, Ohio	38	Minneapolis,* (c. h.,) Hennepin, Minn	4,000
Milton, Northumberland, Pa	1,400	Minneola, Goodhue, Minn	14
Milton, Rutherford, Tenn	12	Minnequa, Bradford, Pa	73
Milton, Chittenden, Vt	360	Minnereka, Mower, Minn	12
Milton,* Rock, Wis	560	Minneska, Wabashaw, Minn	120
Milton Centre, Saratoga, N. Y	27	Minnesota City, Winona, Minn	45
Milton Centre, Wood, Ohio	110	Minnesota Junction, Dodge, Wis	180
Milton Junction, Rock, Wis	320	Minnesota Lake, Faribault, Minn	110
Milton Mills, Strafford, N. H	220	Minnetonka, Hennepin, Minn	35
Milton Plantation, Oxford, Me	20	Minnetrista, Hennepin, Minn	8
Miltonsburgh, Monroe, Ohio	46	Minnora, Calhoun, W. Va	3
Milton Station, Coles, Ill	270	Minonk,* Woodford, Ill	1,200
Milton Station, Mills, Iowa	12	Minooka, Grundy, Ill	360
Milton Station, Wayne, Ohio	15	Minorsville, Scott, Ky	12

* Money-order office.

MOH | MON

Minot, Androscoggin, Me	$110	Mohawk Village, Coshocton, Ohio.	$80
Minster, Auglaize, Ohio	170	Mohegan, Providence, R. I	130
Minta, Indiana, Pa	55	Mohican, Ashland, Ohio	69
Mint Hill, Mecklenburgh, N. C	2	Mohn's Store, Berks, Pa	16
Mintonville, Casey, Ky	12	Mohontongo, Juniata, Pa.	20
Mint Spring, Augusta, Va	13	Mohrsville, Berks, Pa	69
Mirabile, Caldwell, Mo	120	Moingona,* Boone, Iowa	370
Miracle Run, Monongalia, W. Va	6	Moira, Franklin. N. Y	220
Miranda, Rowan, N. C	10	Mokelumne, San Joaquin, Cal	12
Miser's Station, Blount, Tenn	10	Mokelumne Hill,* (c. h.,) Calaveras,	
Mishawaka,* St. Joseph, Ind	1,600	Cal	530
Mishicot, Manitowoc, Wis	100	Mokena, Will, Ill	320
Mission Creek, Wabaunsee, Kans	15	Moksee, (c. h.,) Yakima, Wash	12
Mission San José, Alameda, Cal.	30	Molalla, Clackamas, Oreg	12
Mission Valley, Victoria, Tex	37	Mole Hill, Ritchie, W. Va	10
Mississippi City, (c. h.,) Harrison,		Moline, Rock Island, Ill	2,000
Miss	140	Moline, Allegan, Mich	34
Missoula, (c. h.,) Missoula, Mont	520	Molino, Escambia, Fla	110
Missouri City, Clay, Mo	260	Molino, Oswego, N. Y	14
Missouriton, St. Charles, Mo	15	Molino, Lincoln, Tenn	12
Missouri Valley,* Harrison, Iowa	670	Molltown, Berks, Pa	8
Mitchell,* Lawrence, Ind	730	Moluncus, Aroostook, Me	13
Mitchell,* (c. h.,) Mitchell, Iowa	280	Momence, Kankakee, Ill	470
Mitchell, Antrim, Mich	18	Mona, Mitchell, Iowa	12
Mitchellsburgh, Boyle, Ky	93	Mona, Juab, Utah	18
Mitchell's Creek, Tioga, Pa	37	Monagan, St. Clair, Mo	74
Mitchell's Mills, Indiana, Pa	37	Monches, Waukesha, Wis	32
Mitchell's Salt Works, Jefferson,		Monclova, Lucas, Ohio	85
Ohio	19	Monclova, Morgan, W. Va	9
Mitchell's Station, Culpeper, Va	110	Mondamin, Harrison, Iowa	130
Mitchellsville, Saline, Ill	16	Mondovi, Buffalo, Wis	100
Mitchellsville, Steuben, N. Y	12	Monee, Will, Ill	460
Mitchellsville, Sumner, Tenn	62	Money Creek, Houston, Minn	68
Mitchellville, Polk, Iowa	210	Mongaup, Sullivan, N. Y	29
Mitchellville, Prince George's, Md	67	Monganp Valley, Sullivan, N. Y	110
Mitchellville, Harrison, Mo	33	Mongoquinong, La Grange, Ind	74
Mitchie, Monroe, Ill	12	Monhegan Island, Lincoln, Me	10
Mittineague, Hampton, Mass	430	Monie, Somerset, Md	12
Mixersville, Franklin, Ind	24	Monitor, Alpine, Cal	160
Mixtown, Tioga, Pa	14	Monitor, Tippecanoe, Ind	34
Moberly, Randolph, Mo	630	Monitor, Marion, Oreg	12
Mobile,* (c. h.,) Mobile, Ala	4,000	Monk's Store, Sampson, N. C	1
Mobley Pond, Scriven, Ga	15	Monkton, Addison, Vt	160
Moccasin, Effingham, Ill	16	Monkton Mills, Baltimore, Md	120
Mockeson, Lawrence, Tenn	12	Monkton Ridge, Addison, Vt	32
Mock's Mill, Washington, Va	12	Monmouth,* (c. h.,) Warren, Ill	3,000
Mocksville, (c. h.,) Davie, N. C	160	Monmouth, Adams, Ind	29
Modale, Harrison, Iowa	33	Monmouth, Jackson, Iowa	79
Mode, Shelby, Ill	7	Monmouth, Crawford, Kans	120
Model City, Cass, Mich	59	Monmouth, Kennebec, Me	460
Modena, Stark, Ill	81	Monmouth, Polk, Oreg	96
Modena, Mercer, Mo	13	Monmouth, Rockbridge, Va.	4
Modena, Ulster, N. Y	38	Monmouth Junction, Middlesex,	
Modena, Buffalo, Wis	33	N. J	12
Modest Town, Accomack, Va	85	Monocacy, Montgomery, Md	12
Moe, Douglas, Minn	11	Monocacy, Berks, Pa	84
Moffatt's Creek, Augusta, Va	80	Monon, White, Ind	140
Moffettsville, Anderson, S. C	15	Monona, Clayton, Iowa	150
Moffitt's Grove, Guthrie, Iowa	1	Monongahela City,* Washington,	
Moffitt's Mills, Randolph, N. C	19	Pa	980
Moffitt's Store, Columbia, N. Y	57	Monroe, Fairfield, Conn	76
Mogadore, Summit, Ohio	84	Monroe, (c. h.,) Walton, Ga	150
Mohave City, (c. h.,) Mohave, Ariz.	80	Monroe,* Jasper, Iowa	710
Mohawk, Herkimer, N. Y.	800	Monroe, (c. h.,*) Ouachita, La	1,000
Mohawk Hill, Lewis, N. Y	20	Monroe, Waldo, Me	140
Mohawk Valley, Plumas, Cal	12	Monroe, Franklin, Mass	10

* Money-order office.

9 P O

MON   MON

Monroe, (*c. h.,*) Monroe, Mich.....	$2,100	Montesano, (*c. h.,*) Chehalis, Wash..	$15
Monroe, Perry, Miss................	8	Montevallo, Shelby, Ala.............	330
Monroe, Platte, Nebr....	25	Montevallo, Vernon, Mo	20
Monroe, Grafton, N. H	96	Monte Vista, Choctaw, Miss.	4
Monroe, Sussex, N. J	10	Montez, Cass, Ind	33
Monroe, Orange, N. Y	390	Montezuma, Tuolumne, Cal.........	20
Monroe, (*c. h.,*) Union, N. C.......	110	Montezuma, Macon, Ga.............	610
Monroe, Butler, Ohio	160	Montezuma, Pike, Ill...............	18
Monroe, Overton, Tenn	17	Montezuma, Parke, Ind............	170
*Monroe,** (*c. h.,*) Green, Wis........	1,500	*Montezuma,**(*c. h.,*) Poweshiek, Iowa	580
Monroe Centre, Ogle, Ill	15	Montezuma, Cayuga, N. Y....... ...	250
Monroe Centre, Waldo, Me	18	Montezuma, Mercer, Ohio..........	47
Monroe Centre, Grand Traverse,		Montezuma, McNairy, Tenn.... ...	12
Mich......	47	Montfort, Grant, Wis..............	150
Monroe Centre, Ashtabula, Ohio..	52	MONTGOMERY,*(*c. h.,*) Montgomery,	
Monroe City, Monroe, Ill	32	Ala...........................	4,000
Monroe City, Monroe, Mo.........	360	Montgomery, Kane, Ill.............	93
Monroe Draft, Greenbrier, W. Va..	12	Montgomery, Montgomery, Kans ..	12
Monroe Forge, Lebanon, Pa.......	13	Montgomery, Trigg, Ky....	17
Monroe Furnace, Jackson, Ohio.. .	40	Montgomery, Grant, La............	43
Monroe Mills, Knox, Ohio.........	30	Montgomery, Hampden, Mass......	42
Monroeton, Rockingham, N. C.....	8	Montgomery, Le Sueur, Minn......	25
Monroeton, Bradford, Pa..	180	Montgomery, Orange, N. Y	470
Monroeville, (*c. h.,*) Monroe, Ala	26	Montgomery, Montgomery, N. C.. .	6
Monroeville,* Allen, Ind..........	530	Montgomery, Hamilton, Ohio......	110
Monroeville, Salem, N. J	12	*Montgomery,* (*c. h.,*) Montgomery,	
Monroeville,* Huron, Ohio.......	820	Tex...........................	200
Monroeville, Allegheny, Pa.......	24	Montgomery, Franklin, Vt....	62
Monroe Works, Orange, N. Y......	52	Montgomery Centre, Franklin, Vt .	72
Monrovia, Morgan, Ind...........	160	Montgomery City, Park, Colo......	20
Monrovia, Atchison, Kans.........	65	Montgomery City,* Montgomery,	
Monrovia, Frederick, Md..........	120	Mo.........................	350
Monsey, Rockland, N. Y..........	120	Montgomery's Ferry, Perry, Pa	20
Morson, Piscataquis, Me......	160	Montgomery Springs, Montgomery,	
Monson, Hampden, Mass	840	Va............................	82
Montague, Franklin, Mass........	430	Montgomery Square, Montgomery,	
Montague,* Muskegon, Mich	190	Pa............................	71
Montague, Sussex, N. J...........	41	Montgomery's Station, Daviess, Ind	83
Montague, Lewis, N. Y...........	8	Montgomery Station, Lycoming, Pa	180
Montague, (*c. h.,*) Montague, Texas.	31	*Monticello,** (*c. h.,*) Drew, Ark	410
Montague, Essex, Va.............	19	Monticello, Napa, Cal.............	73
Montague City, Franklin, Mass	63	*Monticello,* (*c. h.,*) Jefferson, Fla....	610
Mont Alto, Franklin, Pa...........	59	*Monticello,* (*c. h.,*) Jasper, Ga..	140
Montana, Boone, Iowa...........	2100	*Monticello,** (*c. h.,*) Piatt, Ill......	720
Montana, Labette, Kans	270	*Monticello,** (*c. h.,*) White, Ind.... .	600
Montana, Beaver Head, Mont......	34	*Monticello,** Jones, Iowa..........	870
Montana, Warren, N. J...........	46	Monticello, Johnson, Kans........	60
Montandon, Northumberland, Pa ..	190	*Monticello,* (*c. h.,*) Wayne, Ky	120
Montauk, Dent, Mo....	12	Monticello, Aroostook, Me.........	63
Montaview, Montgomery, Ky......	4	Monticello,* Wright, Minn.........	400
Mont Clair, Essex, N. J...........	670	*Monticello,* (*c. h.,*) Lawrence, Miss..	48
Monte, Los Angeles, Cal......	77	*Monticello,* (*c. h.,*) Lewis, Mo.......	200
*Montello,** (*c. h.,*) Marquette, Wis ..	200	*Monticello,** (*c. h.,*) Sullivan, N. Y..	890
*Monterey,** (*c. h.,*) Monterey, Cal. ..	640	Monticello, Guilford, N. C....... ..	15
Monterey, Calhoun, Ill......	31	Monticello, Armstrong, Pa.........	61
Monterey, Pulaski, Ind.	12	Monticello, Fairfield, S. C.........	34
Monterey, Davis, Iowa...........	50	*Monticello,* (*c. h.,*) Cowlitz, Wash ..	58
Monterey, Owen, Ky......	58	Monticello, Green, Wis....	150
Monterey, Berkshire, Mass....... ..	140	Montmorency, Tippecanoe, Ind.. ..	54
Monterey, Allegan, Mich	54	Montpelier, Blackford, Ind....	100
Monterey, Richardson, Nebr.......	8	Montpelier, Adair, Ky.............	12
Monterey, Clermont, Ohio........	43	Montpelier, Chickasaw, Miss..	17
Monterey, Berks, Pa.............	20	Montpelier, Williams, Ohio........	41
Monterey, Abbeville, S. C........ ..	12	Montpelier, Rich, Utah...........	12
Monterey, (*c. h.;*) Highland, Va.....	280	MONTPELIER,* (*c. h.,*) Washington,	
Monterey, Waukesha, Wis.........	33	Vt......	2,400

* Money-order office.

MOO | MOR

Montpelier, Hanover, Va	$16	Mooringsport, Caddo, La	$12
Montpelier, Kewaunee, Wis.	24	Moorland, Wayne, Ohio	20
Montra, Shelby, Ohio	58	Moorman's River, Albemarle, Va..	7
Montreal, Nelson, Va	230	Moorton, Kent, Del	57
Montrose, Lee, Iowa	260	Moose Meadow, Tolland, Conn.. ..	32
Montrose, Montgomery, Md	18	Moose River, Somerset, Me	38
Montrose, Genesee, Mich	12	Mooshaunee, Moore, N. C	3
Montrose, Wright, Minn	20	Moosup, Windham, Conn	340
Montrose, Westchester, N. Y	10	*Mora, (c. h.,) Mora, N. Mex*	43
Montrose, Summit, Ohio	25	Moral, Shelby, Ind	11
Montrose, (c. h.,) Susquehanna, Pa.	1,500	Morales, Jackson, Tex.	8
Montrose Depot, Susquehanna, Pa .	44	Moravia, Appanoose, Iowa	230
Montross, (c. h.,) Westmoreland, Va.	43	Moravia, Cayuga, N. Y	470
Monturesville, Lycoming, Pa	270	Moravia, Lawrence, Pa	59
Montvale Springs, Blount, Tenn.. .	69	Mordansville, Columbia, Pa.	12
Montville, New London, Conn.	150	Moreau Station, Saratoga, N. Y	19
Montville, Waldo, Me	61	Moreauville, Avoyelles, La	64
Montville, Berkshire, Mass	65	*Morehead, (c. h.,)* Rowan, Ky	26
Montville, Geauga, Ohio	110	Morehead City, Carteret, N. C.	300
Monument, El Paso, Colo	12	Morehouseville, Hamilton, N. Y	59
Monument, Pike, Ill	36	Moreland, Pope, Ark	11
Monument, Barnstable, Mass	160	Moreland, Schuyler, N. Y	21
Monument House, Baltimore, Md..	12	Moreland, Lycoming, Pa	16
Moodna, Orange, N. Y	50	Morell's Mill, Sullivan, Tenn	5
Moodus, Middlesex, Conn	420	Morenci, Lenawee, Mich	590
Moodyville, Greene, Ky	12	Moresville, Delaware, N. Y	97
Mooers, Clinton, N. Y	390	Moretown, Washington, Vt	150
Mooers Forks, Clinton, N. Y	230	Morgan, Lake, Cal	7
Mooers' Prairie, Wright, Minn	210	*Morgan, (c. h.,)* Calhoun, Ga.	40
Moon, Allegheny, Pa	32	Morgan, Montgomery, Kans	12
Mooney, Jackson, Ind	61	Morgan, Pendletou, Ky	130
Moon Lake, Coahoma, Miss	12	Morgan, Marquette, Mich	130
Moons, Fayette, Ohio	18	Morgan,* Ashtabula, Ohio	370
Moon's Ranch, Tehama, Cal.	5	*Morgan, (c. h.,)* Morgan, Utah	150
Moorefield, Switzerland, Ind.	63	Morgan, Orleans, Vt	36
Moorefield, Nicholas, Ky	74	*Morganfield, (c. h.,)* Union, Ky	290
Moorefield, Harrison, Ohio	84	Morgan's Fork, Franklin, Miss	12
Moorefield, (c. h.,) Hardy, W. Va ..	320	Morgan's Glade, Preston, W. Va...	16
Moore's, Tyler, W. Va	3	Morgan's Mills, Union, N. C	5
Mooresborough, Cleveland, N. C..	13	Morgan Spring, Perry, Ala	12
Mooresburgh, Montour, Pa	25	Morgansville, Morgan, Ohio	12
Mooresburgh, Hawkins, Tenn	12	*Morganton, (c. h.,)* Fannin, Ga	72
Moore's Creek, New Haven, N. C..	12	*Morganton,* (c. h.,) Burke, N. C	350
Moore's Creek, Monroe, Wis.	12	Morgantown,* Morgan, Ind	250
Moore's Flat, Nevada, Cal	150	*Morgantown, (c. h.,)* Butler, Ky	87
Moore's Hill, Dearborn, Ind.	350	Morgantown, Berks, Pa	94
Moore's Mill, Dutchess, N. Y	12	Morgantown, Blount, Tenn	33
Moore's Ordinary, Prince Edward, Va	130	*Morgantown,* (c. h.,) Monongalia, W. Va	740
Moore's Prairie, Jefferson, Ill	54	Morgan Valley, Wyoming, W. Va..	1
Moore's Salt Works, Jefferson, Ohio	36	Morganville, Dade, Ga	40
Moore's Station, Butte, Cal	12	Morganville, Hillsdale, Mich	6
Moore's Store, Jackson, Tenn	12	Morganville, Monmouth, N. J	12
Moore's Store, Shenandoah, Va	20	Morganville, Genesee, N. Y	56
Moorestown,* Burlington, N. J	650	Morganville, Polk, Tex	12
Moorestown, Northampton, Pa	12	Morganza, St. Mary's, Md	20
Mooresville, Limestone, Ala.	140	Morganzia, Point Coupee, La	70
Mooresville,* Morgan, Ind	300	Moriah, Essex, N. Y	190
Mooresville, Livingston, Mo	170	Moriah Centre, Essex, N. Y	12
Mooresville, Monongalia, W. Va...	11	Morian, Schuyler, Nebr	12
Moore's Vineyard, Bartholomew, Ind	13	Moriches, Suffolk, N. Y	51
		Morley, Mecosta, Mich	12
Mooreville, Itawamba, Miss.	24	Morley, Scott, Mo	12
Moorhead, Allegheny, Pa	88	Morley, St. Lawrence, N. Y	210
Moorhead, Freestone, Tex	12	Mormon Island, Sacramento, Cal..	43
Moorheadville, Erie, Pa	100	Mormon Mills, Burnet, Tex	12

* Money-order office.

MOR

Morning Sun, Louisa, Iowa	$220
Morning Sun, Preble, Ohio	120
Mornington, Webster, Mo	9
Morning View, Kenton, Ky	53
Morning View, Belmont, Ohio	27
Moro, Monroe, Ark	10
Moro, Madison, Ill	170
Moro, Aroostook, Me	8
Moro Bay, Bradley, Ark	2
Morocco, Newton, Ind	66
Moroni, San Pete, Utah	92
Morrell, Huntingdon, Pa	12
Morrill, Jackson, Ky	13
Morrill, Waldo, Me	56
Morris, Litchfield, Conn	110
Morris,* (c. h.,) Grundy, Ill	2,500
Morris, Ripley, Ind	130
Morris, Otsego, N. Y	450
Morris, Tioga, Pa	21
Morris, Hanover, Va	5
Morrisania, Westchester, N. Y	1,200
Morris Corners, Crawford, Pa	12
Morris Cross Roads, Fayette, Pa	70
Morrisdale, Clearfield, Pa	41
Morris Hill, Alleghany, Va	10
Morrison,* (c. h.,) Whitesides, Ill	2,000
Morrison, Gasconade, Mo	67
Morrison, Luzerne, Pa	120
Morrison, Warren, Tenn	59
Morrison, Brown, Wis	28
Morrisonville, Clinton, N. Y	51
Morris Ridge, Harrison, Mo	12
Morris Run, Tioga, Pa	370
Morris Station, Quitman, Ga	10
Morristown, Henry, Ill	55
Morristown, Shelby, Ind	58
Morristown, Rice, Minn	100
Morristown, Cass, Mo	120
Morristown,* (c. h.,) Morris, N. J	2,500
Morristown, St. Lawrence, N. Y	230
Morris Town, Moore, N. C	12
Morristown,* Belmont, Ohio	220
Morristown,* Grainger, Tenn	590
Morristown,* Lamoille, Vt	57
Morrisville, Calhoun, Ala	18
Morrisville,* (c. h.,) Madison, N. Y	650
Morrisville, Wake, N. C	69
Morrisville, Clinton, Ohio	24
Morrisville, Bucks, Pa	310
Morrisville, Lamoille, Vt	390
Morrisville, Fauquier, Va	18
Morrow,* Warren, Ohio	520
Morrowville, Jefferson, Ala	5
Morse's, Graves, Ky	68
Morse's Mill, Jefferson, Mo	16
Morseville, Schoharie, N. Y	12
Morsston, Sullivan, N. Y	11
Morton, Tazewell, Ill	97
Morton, Putnam, Ind	40
Morton, Scott, Miss	160
Morton, Delaware, Pa	72
Morton's Corners, Erie, N. Y	18
Mortonsville, Clinton, Ind	12
Mortonsville, Woodford, Ky	110
Mortonville, Chester, Pa	67
Morven, Anson, N. C	6

MOU

Morven, Amelia, Va	$12
Moscow, Sanford, Ala	10
Moscow, Union, Ill	26
Moscow, Rush, Ind	50
Moscow, Muscatine, Iowa	110
Moscow, Hickman, Ky	130
Moscow, Hillsdale, Mich	150
Moscow, Freeborn, Minn	21
Moscow, Livingston, N. Y	170
Moscow, Clermont, Ohio	160
Moscow, Luzerne, Pa	150
Moscow, Fayette, Tenn	50
Moscow, Polk, Tex	62
Moscow, Iowa, Wis	41
Moscow Mills, Morgan, Ohio	13
Mosel, Sheboygan, Wis	23
Moselle, Franklin, Mo	120
Moselm, Berks, Pa	14
Mosherville, Hillsdale, Mich	110
Mosherville, Saratoga, N. Y	23
Mosiertown, Crawford, Pa	67
Mosinee, Marathon, Wis	100
Moss Bluff, Liberty, Tex	12
Mossing Ford, Charlotte, Va	130
Moss Point, Jackson, Miss	12
Moss Run, Washington, Ohio	22
Mossville, Peoria, Ill	98
Mossy Creek, Jefferson, Tenn	310
Mossy Creek, Augusta, Va	12
Motier, Pendleton, Ky	10
Motley, Lancaster, Pa	12
Mott Haven, Westchester, N. Y	400
Mottomosa, Atascosa, Tex	20
Mott's Corners, Tompkins, N. Y	88
Mottville, St. Joseph, Mich	120
Mottville, Onondaga, N. Y	270
Moulton, (c. h.,) Lawrence, Ala	150
Moulton, Shelby, Ill	67
Moulton, Appanoose, Iowa	200
Moulton, Auglaize, Ohio	27
Moulton, Lavaca, Tex	20
Moultonborough, Carroll, N. H	25
Moultonville, Madison, Ill	16
Moultonville, Carroll, N. H	12
Moultrie, (c. h.,) Colquitt, Ga	10
Moultrie, Columbiana, Ohio	69
Mound City, Crittenden, Ark	12
Mound City,* Pulaski, Ill	760
Mound City,* (c. h.,) Linn, Kans	650
Mounds, Vernon, Mo	12
Mound Springs, Jackson, Wis	62
Mound Station, Brown, Ill	140
Moundsville, (c. h.,) Marshall, W. Va	500
Mound Valley, Labette, Kans	12
Moundville, Marquette, Wis	17
Mount Adams, Arkansas, Ark	16
Mount Aerial, Allen, Ky	8
Mount Ætna, Berks, Pa	20
Mountain, Berks, Pa	12
Mountain, Morgan, Utah	10
Mountain, Monroe, Wis	15
Mountain City, Elko, Nev	12
Mountain City, Hays, Tex	200
Mountain Cove, Fayette, W. Va	24
Mountain Creek, Catawba, N. C	10

* Money-order office.

MOU | | MOU

Mountain Creek, Cumberland, Pa..	$20	Mount Enterprise, Cedar, Mo......	$12
Mountain Creek, Warren, Tenn....	12	Mount Enterprise, Rusk, Tex......	89
Mountain Eagle, Centre, Pa......	36	Mount Eolia, Towns, Ga..........	10
Mountain Falls, Frederick, Va.....	12	Mount Ephraim, Camden, N. J.....	31
Mountain Grove, Bath, Va.........	8	Mount Ephraim, Noble, Ohio......	63
Mountain Hill, Harris, Ga........	7	Mount Erie, Wayne, Ill...........	80
Mountain Home, Lawrence, Ala...	6	Mount Etna, Huntington, Ind.....	100
Mountain Home, Bell, Tex	12	Mount Etna, Adams, Iowa	12
Mountain Home, Hardy, W. Va....	2	Mount Florence, Jefferson, Kans...	44
Mountain House, Yam Hill, Oreg ..	15	Mount Freedom, Pendleton, W. Va.	21
Mountain Lake, Bradford, Pa.....	18	Mount Gallagher, Laurens, S. C ...	5
Mountain Ranch, Calaveras, Cal...	24	Mount Gilead, Mason, Ky	12
Mountain Road, Halifax, Va.......	6	Mount Gilead, Montgomery, N. C..	12
Mountain Spring, Carroll, Ark.....	11	*Mount Gilead,* (c. h.,) Morrow, Ohio.	800
Mountain Spring, Martin, Ind.....	16	Mount Gilead, Loudoun, Va.......	17
Mountain Top, Luzerne, Pa	89	Mount Healthy, Bartholomew, Ind.	13
Mountain Valley, Luzerne, Pa.....	12	Mount Healthy, Hamilton, Ohio...	140
Mountain View, Santa Clara, Cal..	110	Mount Healthy, Somerset, Pa......	12
Mountainville, Hunterdon, N. J....	12	Mount Hebron, Greene, Ala	35
Mountainville, Lehigh, Pa	12	Mount Heron, Darke, Ohio	23
Mount Airy, Carroll, Md	180	Mount Hilliard, Bullock, Ala	16
Mount Airy, Randolph, Mo	12	*Mount Holly,* (c. h.,) Burlington,	
Mount Airy, Surry, N. C	110	N. J	1,800
Mount Airy, Hamilton, Ohio......	24	Mount Holly, Clermont, Ohio......	37
Mount Airy, Washington, Pa......	41	Mount Holly, Rutland, Vt........	76
Mount Airy, Bledsoe, Tenn	12	Mount Holly Springs, Cumberland,	
Mount Airy, Pittsylvania, Va......	10	Pa.........................	310
Mount Algor, Jackson, Iowa.......	57	Mount Hope, Lawrence, Ala	68
Mount Alvis, Blount, Ala.........	5	Mount Hope, Tolland, Conn.......	13
Mount Andrew, Barbour, Ala......	19	Mount Hope, De Kalb, Ind........	5
Mount Athos, Campbell, Va	12	Mount Hope, Delaware, Iowa......	10
Mount Auburn, Christian, Ill......	180	Mount Hope, Copiah, Miss	6
Mount Auburn, Shelby, Ind.......	33	Mount Hope, La Fayette, Mo......	50
Mount Auburn, Benton, Iowa......	23	Mount Hope, Morris, N. J	310
Mount Auburn, Middlesex, Mass...	320	Mount Hope, Orange, N. Y	59
Mount Ayr, (c. h.,) Ringgold, Iowa.	520	Mount Hope, Holmes, Ohio.......	55
Mount Bethel, Northampton, Pa...	130	Mount Hope, Lancaster, Pa.......	29
Mount Blanchard, Hancock, Ohio..	120	Mount Hope, Grant, Wis	71
Mount Blanco, Meigs, Ohio........	8	Mount Horeb, Dane, Wis..........	85
Mount Bullion, Mariposa, Cal......	38	*Mount Ida,* (c. h.,) Montgomery, Ark.	44
Mount Calm, Limestone, Tex......	16	Mount Ida, Grant, Wis..........	17
Mount Carmel, New Haven, Conn..	290	Mount Idaho, Nez Perces, Idaho ...	12
Mount Carmel, (c. h.,) Wabash, Ill.	500	Mount Jackson, Lawrence, Pa.....	140
Mount Carmel, Franklin, Ind......	79	Mount Jackson, Shenandoah, Va ..	240
Mount Carmel Fleming, Ky.......	72	Mount Jefferson, Lee, Ala........	51
Mount Carmel, Baltimore, Md.....	61	Mount Joy, Scott, Iowa..........	26
Mount Carmel, Covington, Miss....	55	*Mount Joy,* Lancaster, Pa........	750
Mount Carmel, Clermont, Ohio ...	73	Mount Joy, Union, S. C	12
Mount Carmel, Northumberland, Pa.	710	Mount Judea, Newton, Ark........	3
Mount Carmel, Wilson, Tenn......	12	Mount Kisco, Westchester, N. Y...	380
Mount Carmel, Halifax, Va.......	7	Mount Landing, Essex, Va........	12
Mount Carrick, Monroe, Ohio......	6	Mount Laurel, Burlington, N. J....	38
Mount Carroll, (c. h.,) Carroll, Ill..	1,600	Mount Laurel, Halifax, Va.......	18
Mount Chesnut, Butler, Pa	18	Mount Lebanon, Bienville, La.....	29
Mount Clemens, (c. h.,) Macomb,		Mount Lebanon, Columbia, N. Y...	220
Mich......................	820	Mount Lebanon, Allegheny, Pa....	41
Mount Clifton, Shenandoah, Va....	15	Mount Liberty, Brown, Ind	13
Mount Clinton, Rockingham, Va ..	10	Mount Liberty, Knox, Ohio.......	49
Mount Comfort, Hancock, Ind.....	17	Mount Meigs, Montgomery, Ala....	20
Mount Crawford, Rockingham, Va.	170	Mount Meridian, Putnam, Ind.....	38
Mount Croghan, Chesterfield, S. C.	12	Mount Meridian, Augusta, Va.....	45
Mount Desert, Hancock, Me......	120	Mount Moriah, Ouachita, Ark	12
Mount Eaton, Wayne, Ohio	110	Mount Moriah, Kent, Del.........	12
Mount Eden, Alameda, Cal.......	100	Mount Moriah, Brown, Ind.......	5
Mount Eden, Spencer, Ky.........	8	Mount Moriah, Harrison, Mo	14
Mount Elba, Bradley, Ark........	12	*Mount Morris,* Ogle, Ill	400

* Money-order office.

MOU   MOU

Mount Morris,* Livingston, N. Y...	$1,400	Mount Sinai, Suffolk, N. Y	$33
Mount Morris, Greene, Pa..........	60	Mount Solon, Augusta, Va	53
Mount Morris, Waushara, Wis.....	25	Mount Sterling, Choctaw, Ala	20
Mount Morris Station, Genesee, Mich	330	*Mount Sterling,* (c. h.,) Brown, Ill..	760
		Mount Sterling, Switzerland, Ind..	27
Mount Mourne, Iredell, N. C.......	11	Mount Sterling, Van Buren, Iowa..	60
Mount Murphy, Pocahontas, W. Va.	17	Mount Sterling, Bourbon, Kans....	18
Mount Nebo, Miami, Kans.........	12	*Mount Sterling,* (c. h.,) Montgomery,	
Mount Nebo, Yadkin, N. C.........	18	Ky.............................	1,200
Mount Nebo, Lancaster, Pa........	29	Mount Sterling, Madison, Ohio	130
Mount Niles, St. Clair, Ala	10	Mount Sterling, Crawford, Wis....	98
Mount Olive, Coosa, Ala	12	Mount Storm, Grant, W. Va........	10
Mount Olive, (c. h.,) Izard, Ark....	13	Mount Summit, Henry, Ind........	12
Mount Olive, Macoupin, Ill	27	Mount Sumner, Jo Daviess, Ill.....	9
Mount Olive, Wayne, N. C	140	Mount Sylvan, Smith, Tex	12
Mount Olive, Clermont, Ohio......	13	Mount Tabor, Forsyth, N. C........	2
Mount Olive, Shenandoah, Va.....	19	Mount Tabor, Vernon, Wis........	14
Mount Olivet, (c. h.,) Robertson, Ky.	69	Mount Tirzah, Person, N. C........	11
Mount Orab, Brown, Ohio.........	30	Mount Top, York, Pa	16
Mount Palatine, Putnam, Ill	120	Mount Ulla, Rowan, N. C..........	15
Mount Parnel, Franklin, Pa......	11	Mount Union, Stark, Ohio........	420
Mount Parthenon, Newton, Ark....	12	Mount Union, Huntingdon, Pa.....	370
Mount Perry, Perry, Ohio........	8	Mount Upton, Chenango, N. Y.....	250
Mount Pinson, Jefferson, Ala	7	Mount Vernon, Mobile, Ala.......	78
Mount Pisgah, La Grange, Ind	26	Mount Vernon, Jefferson, Colo.....	12
Mount Pisgah, Clermont, Ohio....	60	*Mount Vernon,* (c. h.,) Montgomery,	
Mount Pisgah, Overton, Tenn	7	Ga.............................	13
Mount Pisgah, Monroe, Wis	38	*Mount Vernon,** (c. h.,) Jefferson,	
Mount Pleasant, Monroe, Ala......	12	Ill..............................	980
Mount Pleasant, Carroll, Ark......	60	*Mount Vernon,** (c. h.,) Posey, Ind..	800
Mount Pleasant, New Castle, Del..	86	Mount Vernon,* Linn, Iowa.......	1,000
Mount Pleasant, Union, Ill	17	*Mount Vernon,* (c. h.,) Rock Castle,	
Mount Pleasant, Perry, Ind.......	12	Ky.............................	240
*Mount Pleasant,** (c.h.,) Henry, Iowa.	2,600	Mount Vernon, Kennebec, Me......	250
Mount Pleasant, Atchison, Kans...	81	Mount Vernon, Macomb, Mich.....	16
Mount Pleasant, Frederick, Md....	34	*Mount Vernon,* (c. h.,) Lawrence, Mo.	390
Mount Pleasant, (c. h.,) Isabella, Mich	490	Mount Vernon, Hillsborough, N. H.	220
		Mount Vernon, Westchester, N. Y..	680
Mount Pleasant, Gentry, Mo.......	22	*Mount Vernon,** (c. h.,) Knox, Ohio.	2,300
Mount Pleasant, Cass, Nebr	22	Mount Vernon, Chester, Pa........	14
Mount Pleasant, Hunterdon, N. J..	80	Mount Vernon, Providence, R. I...	22
Mount Pleasant, Cabarrus, N.C....	63	Mount Vernon, Monroe, Tenn.....	9
Mount Pleasant, Jefferson, Ohio ...	370	Mount Vernon, Dane, Wis.........	92
Mount Pleasant, Westmoreland, Pa.	520	Mount Vernon Forge, Rockingham, Va..............................	12
Mount Pleasant, Laurens, S. C	10		
Mount Pleasant, Maury, Tenn.....	110	Mount Vernon Tannery, Frederick, Va..............................	11
Mount Pleasant, (c. h.,) Titus, Tex..	200		
Mount Pleasant, San Pete, Utah...	250	Mount Victory, Hardin, Ohio	190
Mount Pleasant, Spottsylvania, Va.	6	Mount View, Benton, Mo..........	18
Mount Pleasant Mills, Snyder, Pa..	52	Mountville, Troup, Ga............	12
Mount Polk, Calhoun, Ala........	12	Mountville, Effingham, Ill........	37
Mount Prospect, Crawford, Ind....	8	Mountville, Lancaster, Pa.........	100
Mount Pulaski, Logan, Ill.........	450	Mountville, Loudoun, Va..........	12
Mount Read, Monroe, N. Y	27	Mount Vinco, Buckingham, Va....	7
Mount Repose, Clermont, Ohio	16	Mount Vision, Otsego, N. Y.......	120
Mount Riga, Dutchess, N. Y	29	Mount Vitio, Bullitt, Ky..........	42
Mount Rock, Cumberland, Pa......	23	Mount Washington, Bullitt, Ky....	120
Mount Roszell, Limestone, Ala	12	Mount Washington, Baltimore, Md.	150
Mount Royal, York, Pa............	12	Mount Washington, Hamilton, Ohio............................	150
Mount Salem, Sussex, N. J	12		
Mount Salem, Putnam, W. Va.....	12	Mount Washington, Allegheny, Pa.	66
Mount Savage, Carter, Ky	5	Mount Wolf, York, Pa............	37
Mount Savage, Alleghany, Md....	390	Mount Zion, Hancock, Ga.........	12
Mount Shasta, Siskiyou, Cal......	12	Mount Zion, Macon, Ill..........	120
*Mount Sherman, La Rue, Ky......	18	Mount Zion, Van Buren, Iowa.....	140
*Mount Sidney, Augusta, Va.......	96	Mount Zion, Grant, Ky...........	12

* Money-order office.

MUN.   NAC

Mount Zion, Simpson, Miss	$15	Munfordsville, (c. h.,) Hart, Ky	$380
Mount Zion, Lebanon, Pa	16	Mungen, Wood, Ohio	12
Mount Zion, Tipton, Tenn	12	Munger's Mill, Reynolds, Mo	5
Mount Zion, Campbell, Va	25	Mungerville, Shiawassee, Mich	57
Mount Zion, Juneau, Wis	11	Munising, Schoolcraft, Mich	82
Mouse Creek, McMinn, Tenn	140	Munnsville, Coshocton, Ohio	11
Mouse's, Grant, W. Va	6	Munntown, Washington, Pa	55
Mouth of Indian, Monroe, W. Va	12	Munsonville, Cheshire, N. H	73
Mouth of Laurel, Lewis, Ky	7	Munster, Cambria, Pa	24
Mouth of Pond, Pike, Ky	4	Munsville, Madison, N. Y	140
Mouth of Scary, Putnam, W. Va	25	Munterville, Wapello, Iowa	12
Mouth of Seneca, Pendleton, W. Va	20	Murdock, Warren, Ohio	70
Mouth of Wilson, Grayson, Va	44	Murdocksville, Washington, Pa	18
Mouth of Wolf, Overton, Tenn	12	Murfreesborough,* (c. h.,) Pike, Ark	37
Mouth Short Creek, Boone, W. Va	20	Murfreesboróugh, Hertford, N. C	270
Moweaqua, Shelby, Ill	410	Murfreesborough,* (c. h.,) Ruther-	
Mower City, Mower, Minn	65	ford, Tenn	1,700
Mowersville, Franklin, Pa	49	Murphey, (c. h.,) Cherokee, N. C	93
Mowry's Mills, Bedford, Pa	12	Murphey's Creek, Lewis, W. Va	12
Mowrystown, Highland, Ohio	23	Murphree's Valley, Blount, Ala	5
Moyer's Store, Bucks, Pa	17	Murphy's, Calaveras, Cal	230
Muchinippe, Logan, Ohio	6	Murphysborough,* (c. h.,) Jackson,	
Mud Bridge, Cabell, W. Va	16	Ill	650
Mud Creek, St. Clair, Ill	120	Murphy's Mill, Wood, W. Va	14
Mud Creek, Eaton, Mich	17	Murphysville, Mason, Ky	18
Muddy Creek, Lancaster, Pa	30	Murray, Wells, Ind	49
Muddy Creek, Preston, W. Va	7	Murray, Clark, Iowa	43
Muddy Creek Forks, York, Pa	6	Murray*, (c. h.,) Callaway, Ky	170
Muddy Fork, Clark, Ind	12	Murray, Orleans, N. Y	61
Muddy Fork, Cleveland, N. C	5	Murraysville, Jackson, W. Va	31
Muddy Lake, Livingston, Mo	8	Murrayville, Morgan, Ill	140
Mud Lick, Jefferson, Ind	6	Murrinsville, Butler, Pa	22
Mad Lick, Monroe, Ky	22	Murrysville, Westmoreland, Pa	81
Mud Lick, Chatham, N. C	22	Muscatine,* (c. h.,) Muscatine, Iowa	2,600
Muhlenburgh, Luzerne, Pa	20	Muscle Fork, Chariton, Mo	12
Muir, Ionia, Mich	670	Muscoda, Grant, Wis	300
Muirkirk, Prince George's, Md	160	Musconetcong, Warren, N. J	130
Mukilteo, Snohomish, Wash	20	Muscotah, Atchison, Kans	250
Mukwonago, Waukesha, Wis	160	Muse's Bottom, Jackson, W. Va	16
Mulberry, Clinton, Ind	54	Mush Creek, Greenville, S. C	4
Mulberry, Wilkes, N. C	5	Muskego Centre, Waukesha, Wis	43
Mulberry, Clermont, Ohio	50	Muskegon,* (c. h.,) Muskegon, Mich	2,500
Mulberry, York, Pa	9	Muskootink, Chisago, Minn	5
Mulberry, Lincoln, Tenn	80	Musson, Iberville, La	12
Mulberry Corners, Geauga, Ohio	51	Mutual, Champaign, Ohio	81
Mulberry Gap, Hancock, Tenn	20	Myers, Howard, Mo	25
Mulberry Grove, Harris, Ga	9	Myersburgh, Bradford, Pa	34
Mulberry Grove, Bond, Ill	140	Myers Valley, Pottawatomie, Kans	12
Mulberry Grove, Crawford, Kans	12	Myersville, Vermilion, Ill	91
Mule Creek, Cumberland, Ill	11	Myersville, Frederick, Md	95
Mulford, Cook, Ill	12	Myersville, Williamsburgh, S. C	23
Mulkeyton, Franklin, Ill	13	Myra, Washington, Wis	9
Mull Grove, Catawba, N. C	5	Myrickville, Bristol, Mass	78
Mullica Hill, Gloucester, N. J	210	Myron, Allamakee, Iowa	33
Mullin's, Baker, Ala	5	Myrtle, Knox, Mo	88
Mullin's Depot, Marion, S. C	54	Myrtle Creek, Douglas, Oreg	20
Mulloy's, Robertson, Tenn	8	Mystic, New London, Conn	310
Mumford, Monroe, N. Y	250	Mystic Bridge,* New London, Conn	1,200
Mummasburgh, Adams, Pa	24	Mystic River, New London, Conn	630
Muncie,* (c. h.,) Delaware, Ind	1,400		
Muncie, Vernon, Wis	12	**N.**	
Muncy,* Lycoming, Pa	1,200		
Muncy Bottom, Sullivan, Pa	9	Naches, Houston, Tex	19
Muncy Station, Lycoming, Pa	230	Nachusa, Lee, Ill	110
Mundy, Genesee, Mich	20	Nacogdoches, (c. h.,) Nacogdoches,	
Munford, Talladega, Ala	94	Tex	400

*Money-order office.

NAT　　　　　　NEI

Nacoochee, White, Ga	$24
Naff's, Franklin, Va	8
Nahant, Essex, Mass	370
Nahma, Delta, Mich	15
Nahunta, Wayne, N. C	12
Nail's Creek, Banks, Ga	12
Nairn, Scioto, Ohio	19
Namaqua, Larimer, Colo	41
Nanaupa, Fond du Lac, Wis.	6
Nancy, Pottawatomie, Kans	12
Nanjemoy, Charles, Md	34
Nankin, Wayne, Mich	100
Nankin, Ashland, Ohio	54
Nannie, Floyd, Ga	12
Nanticoke, Wicomico, Md	12
Nanticoke, Luzerne, Pa	140
Nantucket, (*c. h.,*) Nantucket, Mass.	2,100
Nanuet, Rockland, N. Y	240
Naomi, Walker, Ga	12
Napa City, (*c. h.,*) Napa, Cal	1,300
Napanock, Ulster, N. Y	350
Naperville, (*c. h.,*) Du Page, Ill	1,100
Naples, Scott, Ill	310
Naples, Cumberland, Me	130
Naples, Ontario, N. Y	520
Napoleon, (*c. h.,*) Desha, Ark	180
Napoleon, Ripley, Ind	150
Napoleon, Gallatin, Ky	20
Napoleon, Jackson, Mich	220
Napoleon, La Fayette, Mo	94
Napoleon, (*c. h.,*) Henry, Ohio	1,200
Napoli, Cattaraugus, N. Y	290
Narragansett, Washington, R. I	19
Narragansett Pier, Washington, R. I	290
Narraguagus, Washington, Me	500
Narrows Bridge, Daviess, Ky	8
Narrowsburgh, Sullivan, N. Y	230
Narrows Creek, Macon, Mo	12
Nash Depot, Vanderburgh, Ind	12
Nashotah Mission, Waukesha, Wis	310
Nashport Muskingum, Ohio	110
Nashua, Chickasaw, Iowa	670
Nashua, Hillsborough, N. H	3,200
Nashville, El Dorado, Cal	12
Nashville, (*c. h.,*) Berrien, Ga	26
Nashville, (*c. h.,*) Washington, Ill	650
Nashville, (*c. h.,*) Brown, Ind	140
Nashville, Barry, Mich	320
Nashville, Barton, Mo	12
Nashville, Chautauqua, N. Y	33
Nashville, (*c. h.,*) Nash, N. C	47
Nashville, Holmes, Ohio	130
NASHVILLE,* (*c. h.,*) Davidson, Tenn	4,000
Nashville Centre, Martin, Minn	21
Nason's Mills, York, Me	12
Nasonville, Wood, Wis	14
Nassau, Nassau, Fla	12
Nassau, Rensselaer, N. Y	290
Natchez, Martin, Ind	6
Natchez, (*c. h.,*) Adams, Miss	3,300
Natchitoches, (*c. h.,*) Natchitoches, La	630
Natick,* Middlesex, Mass	1,500
Natick, Kent, R. I	250
National, Clayton, Iowa	81
National City, San Diego, Cal	12

National Military Asylum,* Kennebec, Me	$330
National Military Asylum,* Montgomery, Ohio	620
National Military Asylum, Milwaukee, Wis	12
Natividad, Monterey, Cal	87
Natrona, Mason, Ill	12
Natrona, Allegheny, Pa	270
Natural Bridge, Jefferson, N. Y	58
Natural Bridge, Rockbridge, Va	57
Naubuc, Hartford, Conn	52
Naugart, Marathon, Wis	38
Naugatuck,* New Haven, Conn	1,400
Naughrightville, Morris, N. J	29
Naumburgh, Lewis, N. Y	17
Nautrille, Black Hawk, Iowa	15
Nauvoo, Hancock, Ill	340
Nauvoo, Tioga, Pa	10
Navarino, Onondaga, N. Y	42
Navarre, Stark, Ohio	300
Navarro Ridge, Mendocino, Cal	12
Navasink, Monmouth, N. J	280
Navasota, Grimes, Tex	1,000
Navau, Winneshiek, Iowa	12
Navidad, Jackson, Tex	12
Nayatt Point, Bristol, R. I	120
Naylor, Lowndes, Ga	12
Nazareth,* Northampton, Pa	490
Neabsco Mills, Prince William, Va.	18
Nealey's Corner, Penobscot, Me	58
Nealsville, McDowell, N. C	12
Nearman, Wyandotte, Kans	18
Neatsville, Adair, Ky	17
Neblett's Landing, Bolivar, Miss	12
Nebo, Hopkins, Ky	20
Nebo, Laclede, Mo	10
Nebraska, Scott, Ark	12
Nebraska, Jennings, Ind	98
Nebraska, Pickaway, Ohio	48
Nebraska, Forest, Pa	12
Nebraska, Jefferson, Tenn	12
Nebraska, Appomattox, Va	13
Nebraska City, (*c. h.,*) Otoe, Nebr	3,200
Nocedah,* Juneau, Wis	320
Needham,* Norfolk, Mass	320
Needham's Station, Johnson, Ind	12
Needy, Clackamas, Oreg	44
Neely's Landing, Cape Girardeau, Mo	20
Neelysville, Morgan, Ohio	20
Neelyville, Morgan, Ill	81
Neenah, Winnebago, Wis	1,800
Neersville, Loudoun, Va	6
Neese's Store, Fayette, Tex	55
Neff, Randolph, Ind	15
Neffs, Lehigh, Pa	17
Neffs' Mills, Huntingdon, Pa	52
Neffsville, Lancaster, Pa	34
Negaunee, Marquette, Mich	1,500
Negro Foot, Hanover, Va	13
Negro Hill, White, Ark	12
Nehalem, Clatsop, Oreg	12
Neil's Creek, Jefferson, Ind	12
Neil's Creek, Steuben, N. Y	29
Neilsville, (*c. h.,*) Clark, Wis	460

* Money-order office.

Nekama, Winnebago, Wis	$37	Nevada Mills, Steuben, Ind	$12
Nekoma, Henry, Ill	12	Neversink, Sullivan, N. Y	50
Nellie, Ashley, Ark	12	Neville, Winona, Minn	12
Nelly's Ford, Nelson, Va	49	Neville, Clermont, Ohio	97
Nelson, Lee, Ill	63	Nevin, Highland, Ohio	43
Nelson, Vigo, Ind	12	Nevinville, Adams, Iowa	53
Nelson, Kent, Mich	12	New Alba, Winneshiek, Iowa	24
Nelson, Cheshire, N. H	58	New Albany,* (c. h.,) Floyd, Ind	4,000
Nelson, Madison, N. Y	80	New Albany, Wilson, Kans	120
Nelson, Portage, Ohio	56	New Albany, Pontotoc, Miss	78
Nelson, Tioga, Pa	130	New Albany, Mahoning, Ohio	25
Nelson, Hardin, Tenn	22	New Albany, Bradford, Pa	81
Nelson, Buffalo, Wis	40	New Albion, Cattaraugus, N. Y	50
Nelson Furnace, Nelson, Ky	28	New Alexander, Columbiana, Ohio.	20
Nelson Point, Plumas, Cal	12	New Alexandria, Jefferson, Ohio	85
Nelsonville, Franklin, Ala	14	New Alexandria, Westmoreland, Pa	140
Nelsonville, Charlevoix, Mich	10	New Alsace, Dearborn, Ind	40
Nelsonville, Marion, Mo	38	New Alstead, Cheshire, N. H	61
Nelsonville, * Athens, Ohio	330	New Amsterdam, Harrison, Ind	47
Nelta Boc, Sevier, Ark	13	New Amsterdam, La Crosse, Wis	51
Nemaha City, Nemaha, Nebr	91	New Aphalt, Burleson, Tex	12
Nenno, Washington, Wis	33	New Antioch, Clinton, Ohio	83
Neodesha, Wilson, Kans	12	Newark,* New Castle, Del	660
Neoga, Cumberland, Ill	450	Newark, Kendall, Ill	340
Neola, Pottawattomie, Iowa	12	Newark, Greene, Ind	46
Neosho, * (c. h.,) Newton, Mo	620	Newark, Worcester, Md	10
Neosho, Dodge, Wis	100	Newark, Gratiot, Mich	6
Neosho Falls,* (c. h.,) Woodson,		Newark, Knox, Mo	180
Kans	240	Newark,* (c. h.,) Essex, N. J	3,700
Neosho Rapids, Lyon, Kans	78	Newark,* Wayne, N. Y	1,300
Nepaug, Litchfield, Conn	100	Newark,* (c. h.,) Licking, Ohio	2,500
Neperan, Westchester, N. Y	140	Newark, White, Tenn	13
Nepeuskun, Winnebago, Wis	51	Newark, Caledonia, Vt	30
Neponset,* Bureau, Ill	550	Newark, Wirt, W. Va	59
Neponset Village, Norfolk, Mass	670	Newark Valley, Tioga, N. Y	310
Neptune, Mercer, Ohio	47	New Ashford, Berkshire, Mass	14
Neptune, Richland, Wis	10	New Athens, St. Clair, Ill	240
Nero, Manitowoc, Wis	37	New Athens, Harrison, Ohio	120
Nesbit's Station, De Soto, Miss	12	New Auburn, Sibley, Minn	110
Nescopeck, Luzerne, Pa	20	Newaygo,* (c. h.,) Newaygo, Mich	500
Neshaminy, Bucks, Pa	28	New Baden, Clinton, Ill	35
Neshanic, Somerset, N. J	69	New Baltimore, Wayne, Ill	2
Neshannock Falls, Lawrence, Pa	22	New Baltimore, Macomb, Mich	300
Neshkoro, Marquette, Wis	28	New Baltimore, Greene, N. Y	240
Nesquehoning, Carbon, Pa	140	New Baltimore, Stark, Ohio	49
Nestocton, Tillamook, Oreg	8	New Baltimore, Somerset, Pa	14
Nestorville, Barbour, W. Va	6	New Baltimore, Fauquier, Va	19
Netarts, Tillamook, Oreg	12	New Barden, Tippah, Miss	12
Netawaka, Jackson, Kans	160	New Bavaria, Henry, Ohio	43
Netherland, Overton, Tenn	26	New Bedford, Bureau, Ill	90
Nettle Carrier, Overton, Tenn	26	New Bedford,* Bristol, Mass	3,600
Nettle Lake, Williams, Ohio	29	New Bedford, Monmouth, N. J	67
Nettle Ridge, Patrick, Va	12	New Bedford, Coshocton, Ohio	42
Nettleton, Marion, Mo	12	New Bedford, Lawrence, Pa	74
Nettletonville, Caldwell, Mo	12	New Bellsville, Brown, Ind	20
Neuchatel, Nemaha, Kans	44	Newberg, Yam Hill, Oreg	12
Neutral City, Cherokee, Kans	61	New Berlin, Sangamon, Ill	200
Nevada, Livingston, Ill	12	New Berlin, Chenango, N. Y	690
Nevada, Tipton, Ind	54	New Berlin, Stark, Ohio	75
Nevada,* (c. h.,) Story, Iowa	810	New Berlin, Union, Pa	270
Nevada, Mercer, Ky	16	New Berlin, Waukesha, Wis	19
Nevada, Mower, Minn	24	New Berlin Centre, Chenango, N. Y.	23
Nevada,* (c. h.,) Vernon, Mo	680	Newbern, Hale, Ala	65
Nevada,* Wyandot, Ohio	390	Newbern, Jersey, Ill	32
Nevada City,* (c. h.,) Nevada, Cal	2,400	Newbern, Bartholomew, Ind	22
Nevada City, Madison, Mont	100	Newbern, Marion, Iowa	71

* Money-order office.

NEW   NEW

Newbern, Dyer, Tenn	$120	Newburyport,* Essex, Mass	$3,000
Newbern, (c. h.,) Pulaski, Va	190	New California, Union, Ohio	25
New Berne, (c. h.,)* Craven, N. C	2,600	New California, Grant, Wis	21
Newberry, Greene, Ind	75	New Cambria, Macon, Mo	370
Newberry, Lycoming, Pa	210	New Canaan, Fairfield, Conn	900
Newberry C. H., Newberry, S. C	1,500	New Canton, Hawkins, Tenn	15
Newberrytown, York, Pa	37	New Canton, Buckingham, Va	150
New Bethlehem, Clarion, Pa	130	New Carlisle,* St. Joseph, Ind	350
New Bloomfield, Callaway, Mo	100	New Carlisle, Clark, Ohio	420
New Bloomfield, (c. h.,) Perry, Pa	640	New Casco, Cumberland, Me	38
New Bloomington, Marion, Ohio	120	New Casco, Allegan, Mich	54
New Boston, Windham, Conn	72	New Cassel, Fond du Lac, Wis	96
New Boston, Mercer, Ill	590	Newcastle, Placer, Cal	200
New Boston, Lee, Iowa	15	*New Castle,* (c. h.,)* New Castle, Del.	860
New Boston, Berkshire, Mass	160	*Newcastle,* (c. h.,)* Henry, Ind	940
New Boston, Wayne, Mich	37	*Newcastle, (c. h.,)* Henry, Ky	370
New Boston, Winona, Minn	50	New Castle, Lincoln, Me	910
New Boston, Macon, Mo	18	New Castle, Gentry, Mo	41
New Boston, Hillsborough, N. H	290	Newcastle, Dixon, Nebr	26
New Boston, Henry, Tenn	12	New Castle, Rockingham, N. H	110
New Braintree, Worcester, Mass	180	New Castle, Westchester, N. Y	220
New Branch, Monmouth, N. J	12	New Castle, Coshocton, Ohio	30
New Braunfels, (c. h.,)* Comal, Tex.	660	*Newcastle,* (c. h.,)* Lawrence, Pa	2,700
New Bremen, Cook, Ill	110	New Castle, Hardeman, Tenn	30
New Bremen, Lewis, N. Y	110	*Newcastle, (c. h.,)* Craig, Va	51
New Bremen,* Auglaize, Ohio	220	New Centreville, Oswego, N. Y	69
New Bridge, Lumpkin, Ga	10	New Centreville, Chester, Pa	57
New Bridge, Bergen, N. J	56	New Centreville, St. Croix, Wis	33
New Bridge, Franklin, Pa	12	New Chambersburgh, Columbiana,	
New Bridgeport, Bedford, Pa	12	Ohio	20
New Bridgeville, York, Pa	24	New Chester, Adams, Pa	28
New Brighton, Richmond, N. Y	550	New Chester, Adams, Wis	22
New Brighton,* Beaver, Pa	1,200	New Chicago, Neosho, Kans	12
New Brighton, Fauquier, Va	25	New Church, Accomack, Va	30
New Britain,* Hartford, Conn	2,500	New Clifton, Monroe, Wis	4
New Britain, Bucks, Pa	72	New Coeln, Milwaukee, Wis	9
New Britton, Hamilton, Ind	60	New Columbia, Massac, Ill	20
New Brunswick, (c. h.,)* Middlesex,		New Columbia, Union, Pa	88
N. J	2,900	New Columbus, Owen, Ky	12
New Buda, Decatur, Iowa	25	New Columbus, Luzerne, Pa	65
New Buena Vista, Bedford, Pa	12	Newcomb, Champaign, Ill	24
New Buffalo,* Berrien, Mich	370	Newcomb, Essex, N. Y	21
New Buffalo, Perry, Pa	100	New Comerstown, Tuscarawas,	
Newburgh, Franklin, Ala	14	Ohio	450
Newburgh, Izard, Ark	23	New Concord, Columbia, N. Y	45
Newburgh, Macon, Ill	12	New Concord, Muskingum, Ohio	330
Newburgh,* Warrick, Ind	360	New Corner, Delaware, Ind	16
Newburgh, Mitchell, Iowa	73	New Corwin, Highland, Ohio	16
Newburgh, Jefferson, Ky	10	New Corydon, Jay, Ind	120
Newburgh, Penobscot, Me	45	*New Creek, (c. h.,)* Mineral, W. Va.	310
Newburgh, Charles, Md	58	New Cumberland, Grant, Ind	72
Newburgh, Cass, Mich	27	New Cumberland, Tuscarawas,	
Newburgh, Fillmore, Minn	110	Ohio	66
Newburgh, Macon, Mo	12	New Cumberland, Cumberland, Pa.	230
Newburgh, (c. h.,)* Orange, N. Y	3,500	New Cumberland, Hancock, W. Va.	130
Newburgh, Cuyahoga, Ohio	980	New Dale, Wetzel, W. Va.	9
Newburgh, Cumberland, Pa	180	New Danville, Lancaster, Pa	12
Newburgh, Preston, W. Va	240	New Danville, Rusk, Tex	81
Newburgh, Washington, Mich	110	New Derry, Westmoreland, Pa	98
Newburgh Centre, Penobscot, Me	19	New Diggings, La Fayette, Wis	76
New Burlington, Delaware, Ind	26	New Douglas, Madison, Ill	51
New Burlington, Clinton, Ohio	89	New Dorp, Richmond, N. Y	100
Newbury, Wabaunsee, Kans	12	New Dover, Union, Ohio	52
Newbury, Tuscola, Mich	39	New Dublin, Scott, Minn	23
Newbury, Merrimack, N. H	30	*New Dungeness, (c. h.,)* Clallam, Wash	14
Newbury, Orange, Vt	500	New Durham, Hudson, N. J	38

* Money-order office.

NEW   NEW

New Eagle Mills, Grant, Ky	$12	New Harmony, Pike, Mo	$42
New Egypt, Ocean, N. J	260	New Harmony, Brown, Ohio	16
New Elizabeth, Hendricks, Ind	47	New Harmony, Washington, Utah	13
Newell, Anderson, S. C	1	New Harrisburgh, Carroll, Ohio	28
Newell's Run, Washington, Ohio	23	New Hartford, Litchfield, Conn	610
Newellsville, Marion, Oreg	16	New Hartford, Pike, Ill	46
New England, Athens, Ohio	110	New Hartford, Butler, Iowa	220
New England Village, Worcester, Mass	340	New Hartford, Winona, Minn	5
		New Hartford, Oneida, N.Y	400
New Enterprise, Bedford, Pa	110	Newharts, Northampton, Pa	11
New Era, De Kalb, Ind	16	NEW HAVEN,* (c. h.,) New Haven, Conn	4,000
New Era, Bradford, Pa	8		
New Eureka, Jackson, Kans	96	New Haven, Gallatin, Ill	87
New Fairfield, Fairfield, Conn	32	New Haven, Allen, Ind	340
Newfane, Niagara, N.Y	110	New Haven, Nelson, Ky	150
Newfane, Fond du Lac, Wis	18	New Haven, Macomb, Mich	180
Newfield, York, Me	56	New Haven, Franklin, Mo	290
Newfield, Gloucester, N. J	130	New Haven, Oswego, N. Y	240
Newfield, Tompkins, N. Y	210	New Haven, Huron, Ohio	160
New Florence, Montgomery, Mo	340	New Haven, Addison, Vt	230
New Florence, Westmoreland, Pa	220	New Haven, Mason, W. Va	91
New Forestville, Anson, N. C	12	New Haven, Adams, Wis	11
Newfoundland, Elliott, Ky	12	New Haven Centre, Gratiot, Mich	14
Newfoundland, Morris, N. J	83	New Haven Mills, Addison, Vt	16
Newfoundland, Wayne, Pa	78	New Hebron, Crawford, Ill	14
New Fountain, Medina, Tex	16	New Hill, Wake, N. C	9
New Franken, Brown, Wis	12	New Holland, Wabash, Ind	79
New Frankfort, Saline, Mo	100	New Holland, Pickaway, Ohio	100
New Franklin, Wayne, Ill	16	New Holland, Lancaster, Pa	240
New Franklin, Stark, Ohio	47	New Holstein, Calumet, Wis	140
New Freedom, York, Pa	160	New Home, Montcalm, Mich	8
New Freeport, Greene, Pa	14	New Hope, Madison, Ala	6
New Galilee, Beaver, Pa	250	New Hope, Wabash, Ill	12
New Garden, Wayne, Ind	110	New Hope, Nelson, Ky	16
New Garden, Ray, Mo	23	New Hope, Caroline, Md	49
New Garden, Guilford, N.C	74	New Hope, Lincoln, Mo	170
New Garden, Columbiana, Ohio	110	New Hope, Cayuga, N. Y	47
New Garden, Chester, Pa	20	New Hope, Iredell, N. C	4
New Garden, Russell, Va	14	New Hope, Brown, Ohio	36
New Gascony, Jefferson, Ark	20	New Hope, Bucks, Pa	410
New Genesee, Whitesides, Ill	23	New Hope, Augusta, Va	82
New Geneva, Fayette, Pa	94	New Hope, Portage, Wis	50
New Geneva, Jackson, W. Va	2	New Hope Academy, Randolph, N. C	3
New Germantown, Hunterdon, N. J	160		
New Germantown, Perry, Pa	74	New Hope Mills, Granville, N. C	12
New Glarus, Green, Wis	97	New House, York, S. C	6
New Gloucester, Cumberland, Me	190	New Hudson, Oakland, Mich	110
New Goshen, Vigo, Ind	53	New Hudson, Allegany, N. Y	12
New Grenada, Fulton, Pa	35	New Hurley, Ulster, N. Y	23
New Gretna, Burlington, N. J	85	New Iberia,* (c. h.,) Iberia, La	1,200
New Guilford, Coshocton, Ohio	36	New Idria, Fresno, Cal	88
New Hackensack, Dutchess, N. Y	56	Newington, Hartford, Conn	51
New Hagerstown, Carroll, Ohio	67	Newington, Rockingham, N. H	43
New Hamburgh, Scott, Iowa	7	Newington Junction, Hartford, Conn	150
New Hamburgh, Dutchess, N. Y	400		
New Hamburgh, Mercer, Pa	120	New Interest, Randolph, W. Va	44
New Hampden, Highland, Va	25	New Ipswich,* Hillsborough, N. H	590
New Hampshire, Auglaize, Ohio	49	New Jasper, Greene, Ohio	20
New Hampton, Madison, Ill	35	New Jerusalem, Berks, Pa	13
New Hampton, Chickasaw, Iowa	390	New Kent C. H., New Kent, Va	80
New Hampton, Belknap, N. H	570	New Kingston, Delaware, N. Y	29
New Hampton, Hunterdon, N. J	56	New Kingstown, Cumberland, Pa	140
New Hampton, Orange, N. Y	190	New Knoxville, Auglaize, Ohio	30
New Hanover, Montgomery, Pa	96	New Lancaster, Tipton, Ind	17
New Harmony, Sangamon, Ill	8	New Lancaster, Miami, Kans	56
New Harmony,* Posey, Ind	420	New Lebanon, De Kalb, Ill	17

* Money-order office.

NEW   NEW

New Lebanon, Sullivan, Ind......	$53
New Lebanon, Columbia, N. Y....	560
New Lebanon, Montgomery, Ohio.	53
New Lebanon, Mercer, Pa.........	110
New Lebanon Centre, Columbia, N. Y.............................	73
New Lebanon Springs, Columbia, N. Y.............................	270
New Lenox, Will, Ill.............	110
New Lenox, Berkshire, Mass......	54
New Lexington, Tuscaloosa, Ala...	12
New Lexington, (c. h.,) Perry, Ohio.	690
New Lexington, Somerset, Pa.....	48
New Liberty, Pope, Ill...........	91
New Liberty, Scott, Iowa.........	18
New Liberty, Owen, Ky...........	210
New Light, Wake, N. C...........	4
New Limerick, Aroostook, Me.....	10
New Lisbon, Henry, Ind..........	77
New Lisbon, Burlington, N. J.....	13
New Lisbon, Otsego, N. Y.........	61
New Lisbon, (c. h.,) Columbiana, Ohio............................	1,000
New Lisbon, (c. h.,) Juneau, Wis..	780
New London, (c. h.,) New London, Conn...........................	2,900
New London, Howard, Ind........	95
New London,* Henry, Iowa.......	350
New London, Frederick, Md......	54
New London, (c. h.,) Monongalia, Minn............................	110
New London, (c. h.,) Ralls, Mo......	160
New London,* Merrimack, N. H...	320
New London, Oneida, N. Y........	200
New London,* Huron, Ohio.......	540
New London, Chester, Pa.........	170
New London, Campbell, Va.......	43
New London, Waupaca, Wis......	510
New Lyme, Ashtabula, Ohio......	130
New Madison, Wabash, Ind......	12
New Madison, Darke, Ohio........	170
New Madrid, (c. h.,) New Madrid, Mo.............................	330
New Mahoning, Carbon, Pa.......	19
Newman, Douglas, Ill.............	89
Newman, Jefferson, Kans.........	12
Newman, Sanilac, Mich..........	25
Newmansville, Clarion, Pa........	26
New Marion, Ripley, Ind.........	26
New Market, Madison, Ala........	68
New Market, Sebastian, Ark......	12
New Market, Monroe, Ga.........	9
New Market, Gallatin, Ill.........	18
New Market, Marion, Ky.........	28
New Market, Frederick, Md.......	120
New Market, Scott, Minn.........	11
New Market, Platte, Mo..........	110
New Market, Rockingham, N. H...	730
New Market, Middlesex, N. J.....	250
New Market, Randolph, N. C......	23
New Market, Highland, Ohio.....	54
New Market, Abbeville, S. C......	12
New Market, Jefferson, Tenn.....	240
New Market, Shenandoah, Va.....	350
New Marlborough, Berkshire, Mass.	180
New Martinsburgh, Fayette, Ohio.	29

New Martinsville, (c. h.,) Wetzel, W. Va.............................	$140
New Maysville, Putnam, Ind......	46
New Melle, St. Charles, Mo........	63
New Memphis, Clinton, Ill........	28
New Metamora, Washington, Ohio.	170
New Michigan, Livingston, Ill....	75
New Middleton, Smith, Tenn.....	94
New Middletown, Harrison, Ind...	12
New Middletown, Mahoning, Ohio.	94
New Milford,* Litchfield, Conn....	1,100
New Milford, Winnebago, Ill......	100
New Milford, Orange, N. Y........	53
New Milford, Portage, Ohio......	72
New Milford, Susquehanna, Pa....	360
New Millport, Clearfield, Pa......	25
New Milton, Doddridge, W. Va....	7
New Minden, Washington, Ill.....	12
New Mollis, Outagamie, Wis......	12
New Monmouth, Monmouth, N. J..	86
New Moorefield, Clark, Ohio......	40
New Moscow, Coshocton, Ohio....	13
New Mount Pleasant, Jay, Ind....	46
New Mount Pleasant, Monroe, Pa..	85
New Munich, Stearns, Minn......	160
Newnan, (c. h.,) Coweta, Ga.......	1,100
Newnanville, Alachua, Fla........	110
New Offenburgh, St. Genevieve, Mo.............................	33
New Ohio, Broome, N. Y..........	29
New Oregon, (c. h.,) Howard, Iowa.	34
New Oregon, Erie, N. Y...........	15
NEW ORLEANS,* (c. h.,) Orleans, La.	4,000
New Oxford, Adams, Pa...........	270
New Palestine, Cooper, Mo........	12
New Palestine, Clermont, Ohio....	26
New Paltz, Ulster, N. Y...........	430
New Paris, Elkhart, Ind..........	92
New Paris,* Preble, Ohio..........	280
New Paris, Bedford, Pa...........	46
New Petersburgh, Highland, Ohio.	47
New Petersburgh, Jefferson, Pa...	12
New Philadelphia, McDonough, Ill.	65
New Philadelphia, Washington, Ind.............................	150
New Philadelphia, (c. h.,) Tuscarawas, Ohio.......................	1,300
New Pittsburgh, St. Clair, Ill.....	12
New Pittsburgh, Randolph, Ind...	25
New Pittsburgh, Wayne, Ohio....	79
New Pleasant Grove, Huntingdon, Pa.............................	32
New Plymouth,* Vinton, Ohio....	53
New Point, Decatur, Ind..........	12
Newport, New Castle, Del.........	220
Newport, Lake, Ill...............	8
Newport, (c. h.) Vermillion, Ind...	220
Newport, Johnson, Iowa..........	12
Newport, Neosho, Kans...........	12
Newport, (c. h.,) Campbell, Ky.....	2,400
Newport, Winn, La..............	12
Newport, Penobscot, Me..........	450
Newport, Charles, Md............	34
Newport, Monroe, Mich..........	82
Newport, Washington, Minn......	65
Newport, (c. h.,) Sullivan, N. H....	870

* Money-order office.

Newport, Cumberland, N. J.......	$92	New Scottsville, Beaver, Pa......	$5
Newport, Herkimer, N. Y.........	240	News Ferry, Halifax, Va...........	190
Newport, Carteret, N. C..........	57	New Sharon, Mahaska, Iowa......	170
Newport, Washington, Ohio.......	130	New Sharon, Franklin, Me........	330
Newport, Benton, Oreg............	26	New Sharon, Monmouth, N. J.....	10
Newport,* Perry, Pa..............	680	New Sheffield, Beaver, Pa........	42
NEWPORT,* (c. h.,) Newport, R. I..	2,800	New Shoreham, Newport, R. I.....	160
Newport, (c. h.,) Cocke, Tenn......	200	New Site, Tallapoosa, Ala.........	11
Newport, Walker, Tex............	18	New Smyrna, Volusia, Fla........	12
Newport,* Orleans, Vt............	690	New Somerset, Jefferson, Ohio.....	12
Newport, Giles, Va..............	20	Newson's Depot, Southampton, Va.	89
New Portage, Summit, Ohio.......	63	New Springfield, Mahoning, Ohio..	40
Newport Centre, Orleans, Vt......	73	New Springville, Richmond, N. Y..	50
New Portland, Somerset, Me	120	New Stanton, Westmoreland, Pa...	28
Newport News, Warwick, Va.....	12	Newstead, Christian, Ky..........	24
Newportville, Bucks, Pa..........	100	New Stirling, Iredell, N. C........	5
New Preston, Litchfield, Conn....	230	New Store, Buckingham, Va......	74
New Prospect, Winston, Miss......	51	New Texas, Allegheny, Pa	63
New Prospect, Spartanburgh, S. C.	11	*Newton*, (c. h.,) Dale, Ala........	65
New Prospect, Fond du Lac, Wis..	7	*Newton*, (c. h.,) Baker, Ga..........	300
New Providence, Pike, Ala.......	16	*Newton*, (c. h.,) Jasper, Ill..........	250
New Providence, Clarke, Ind......	80	*Newton*,* (c. h.,) Jasper, Iowa.....	2,400
New Providence, Hardin, Iowa....	130	Newton,* Middlesex, Mass........	1,200
New Providence, Osage, Mo.......	12	Newton, Calhoun, Mich...........	6
New Providence, Union, N. J.....	170	Newton, Newton, Miss...........	86
New Providence, Lancaster, Pa...	52	Newton, Rockingham, N. H.......	87
New Providence, Montgomery, Tenn......................	140	*Newton*,* (c. h.,) Sussex, N. J.....	2,100
		Newton, (c. h.,) Catawba, N. C.....	200
New Republic, Monterey, Cal......	12	Newton, Benton, Oreg	12
New Richland, Waseca, Minn.....	12	*Newton*, (c. h.,) Newton, Tex.......	6
New Richland, Logan, Ohio.......	21	Newton, Cache, Utah.............	12
New Richmond, Montgomery, Ind.	27	Newton, Roane, W. Va...........	13
New Richmond,* Clermont, Ohio..	770	Newton, Vernon, Wis.............	22
New Richmond, Crawford, Pa.....	40	Newton Academy, Monroe, Ala....	12
New Richmond, St. Croix, Wis....	140	Newtonburgh, Manitowoc, Wis....	39
New Ringgold, Schuylkill, Pa.....	150	Newton Centre, Middlesex, Mass..	610
New River, Fayette, Ala..........	12	Newton Depot, Rockingham, N. H.	51
New River, Ascension, La........	66	Newton Factory, Newton, Ga.....	20
New River, Huron, Mich..........	43	Newton Falls, Trumbull, Ohio....	360
New River, Alleghany, N. C......	12	Newton Grove, Sampson, N. C.....	14
New River Depot, Pulaski, Va....	12	Newton Hamilton, Mifflin, Pa.....	260
New Rochelle, Westchester, N. Y..	1,100	Newtonia, Newton, Mo...........	300
New Rochester, Wood, Ohio.......	20	Newton Lower Falls, Middlesex, Mass......................	330
New Rome, Adams, Wis..........	16		
New Ross, Montgomery, Ind......	49	Newton's Retreat, Tippecanoe, Ind.	14
New Rumley, Harrison, Ohio.....	44	Newton Stewart, Orange, Ind.....	20
New Russia, Essex, N. Y.........	36	Newtonsville, Clermont, Ohio.....	22
New Rutland, La Salle, Ill........	480	Newton Upper Falls, Middlesex, Mass......................	330
Newry, Oxford, Me...............	28		
Newry, Blair, Pa	130	Newtonville, Spencer, Ind.........	31
Newry, Vernon, Wis..............	28	Newtonville, Buchanan, Iowa.....	12
News, Calhoun, Ill................	60	Newtonville, Middlesex, Mass.....	610
New Salem, Pike, Ill.............	120	Newtonville, Albany, N. Y........	51
New Salem, Rush, Ind...........	60	New Topia, Barbour, Ala.........	6
New Salem, Franklin, Mass.......	76	Newtown, El Dorado, Cal.........	33
New Salem, Allegan, Mich	29	Newtown, Fairfield, Conn........	470
New Salem, Albany, N. Y........	41	Newtown, Fountain, Ind..........	120
New Salem, Randolph, N. C......	34	Newtown, Scott, Ky.............	35
New Salem, Fairfield, Ohio.......	84	Newtown, Worcester, Md.........	310
New Salem, Fayette, Pa..........	80	Newtown, Putnam, Mo...........	20
New Salem, Rusk, Tex...........	56	Newtown, Queens, N. Y..........	300
New Salem, Harrison, W. Va.....	72	Newtown, Hamilton, Ohio.........	120
New Salisbury, Harrison, Ind.....	18	Newtown, Bucks, Pa.............	520
New Santa Fé, Jackson, Mo.......	86	Newtown, King and Queen, Va....	20
New Scandinavia, Republic, Kans.	12	New Town Landing, Warren, Miss.	12
New Scotland, Albany, N. Y.......	30	Newtown Mills, Forest, Pa	40

* Money-order office.

Newtown Square, Delaware, Pa....	$80	Niles, Manitowoc, Wis.............	$24
Newtown Stephensburgh, Frede-		Niles Centre, Cook, Ill.............	24
rick, Va.......................	210	Niles Valley, Tioga, Pa............	50
New Trenton, Franklin, Ind.......	92	Nilwood, Macoupin, Ill............	170
New Trier, Dakota, Minn..........	100	Nimisila, Summit, Ohio...........	100
New Tripoli, Lehigh, Pa...........	16	Nine Mile, Allen, Ind.............	18
New Troy, Berrien, Mich..........	59	Nine Points, Lancaster, Pa........	22
New Ulm,* (c. h.,) Brown, Minn	590	Nine Times, Pickens, S. C.........	12
New Ulm, Austin, Tex.............	46	Ninety Six, Abbeville, S. C........	140
New Upton, Gloucester, Va........'.	12	Nineveh, Johnson, Ind............	96
New Utrecht, Kings, N. Y.........	130	Nineveh, Adair, Mo	15
New Vernon, Morris, N. J..........	71	Nineveh, Broome, N. Y	240
New Vernon, Mercer, Pa...........	40	Nineveh, Warren, Va.............	16
New Vienna, Dubuque, Iowa	110	Nininger, Dakota, Minn...........	26
New Vienna, Clinton, Ohio	360	Niobrara, (c. h.,) L'Eau qui Court,	
New Village, Warren, N. J.........	46	Nebr.......................	28
Newville, Colusa, Cal	53	Nippenose, Lycoming, Pa..........	57
Newville, De Kalb, Ind...........	130	Nisbet, Lycoming, Pa	12
Newville, Herkimer, N. Y.........	22	Niskayuna, Schenectady, N. Y	40
Newville, Richland, Ohio.........	54	Nittany, Centre, Pa	70
Newville, Cumberland, Pa........	930	Niven, Susquehanna, Pa..........	19
Newville, Vernon, Wis	14	Niverville, Columbia, N. Y........	180
New Vineyard, Franklin, Me	62	Nixon, De Witt, Ill..............	15
New Virginia, Warren, Iowa.......	33	Noah, Shelby, Ind...............	18
New Washington, Clarke, Ind	110	Noank, New London, Conn	290
New Washington, Crawford, Ohio..	140	Noble, Richland, Ill	370
New Washington, Clearfield, Pa ...	89	Noble, Noble, Ind	150
New Waterford, Columbiana, Ohio.	120	Noble Centre, Branch, Mich.......	38
New Waverly, Cass, Ind..........	68	Noblesborough, Lincoln, Me	61
Newway, Licking, Ohio	26	Noblestown, Allegheny, Pa........	150
New Wells, Cape Girardeau, Mo....	54	Noblesville,* (c. h.,) Hamilton, Ind ..	740
New Westville, Preble, Ohio.......	47	Nobleville, Noble, Ohio...........	8
New Wilmington, Lawrence, Pa ...	580	Nobob, Barren, Ky	13
New Winchester, Hendricks, Ind...	43	Nochway, Randolph, Ga..........	61
New Windsor, Mercer, Ill..........	440	Nockenut, Guadalupe, Tex........	5
New Windsor, Carroll, Md.........	290	Nodaway, Andrew, Mo	12
New Woodstock, Madison, N. Y	220	Nodaway Mills, Page, Iowa........	12
New York, Wayne, Iowa	83	Nohart, Richardson, Nebr.........	18
New York,* (c. h.,) New York, N. Y..	6,000	Nokesville, Prince William, Va	17
New York Mills, Oneida, N. Y	480	Nokomis,* Montgomery, Ill........	800
New Zion, Clarendon, S. C........	12	Nolensville, Williamson, Tenn.....	100
Ney, De Kalb, Ill................	32	Nolin, Hardin, Ky...............	64
Ney, Defiance, Ohio	16	Nolo, Indiana, Pa	33
Niagara Falls,* Niagara, N. Y......	2,100	Nominy Grove, Westmoreland, Va.	24
Niantic, New London, Conn	290	Non Intervention, Lunenburgh, Va.	12
Niantic, Macon, Ill................	150	Nonpariel, Knox, Ohio...........	38
Nicholas C. H., Nicholas, W. Va	45	Nooseneck Hill, Kent, R. I........	19
Nicholasville,* (c. h.,) Jessamine, Ky.	760	Nora, Jo Daviess, Ill	190
Nichols, Montgomery, Md	12	Nora, Berks, Pa.................	20
Nichols, Tioga, N. Y..............	220	Nora, Dane, Wis	10
Nichols, Marion, S. C	12	Nora Springs, Floyd, Iowa........	22
Nicholson, Wyoming, Pa	450	Norbeck, Montgomery, Md	36
Nicholsonville, Cleveland, N. C	2	Norborne, Carroll, Mo...........	200
Nicholsville, Clermont, Ohio.......	31	Nordyk, Dallas, Iowa	12
Nicholville, St. Lawrence, N. Y.....	240	Norfolk, Litchfield, Conn..........	280
Nickleville, Venango, Pa	12	Norfolk, Norfolk, Mass	150
Nicojack, Marion, Tenn...........	84	Norfolk, (c. h.,) Madison, Nebr......	74
Nicolaus, Sutter, Cal	36	Norfolk, St. Lawrence, N. Y.......	260
Nicollet, Nicollet, Minn...........	30	Norfolk,* (c. h.,) Norfolk, Va........	4,000
Niconza, Miami, Ind	40	Normal, McLean, Ill	1,500
Nile, Allegany, N. Y	99	Normanda, Tipton, Ind...........	12
Niles, Cook, Ill..................	57	Normandy, St. Louis, Mo	16
Niles, Van Buren, Iowa...........	5	Normandy, Bedford, Tenn	78
Niles,* Berrien, Mich.............	2,600	Norman's Kill, Albany, N. Y	20
Niles, Cayuga, N. Y..............	45	Normanville, Doniphan, Kans......	33
Niles,* Trumbull, Ohio	910	Norridgewock, (c. h.,) Somerset, Me..	350

* Money-order office.

Office	$
Norris, Fulton, Ill	$91
Norris Fork, Henry, Mo	12
Norristown, Pope, Ark	12
Norristown, Carroll, Ohio	12
Norristown, (c. h.,) Montgomery, Pa	2,400
Norrisville, Harford, Md	12
Norrisville, Crawford, Pa	12
Norrisville, Caledonia, Vt	100
Norritonville, Montgomery, Pa	18
Norseland, Nicollet, Minn	100
North Abington, Plymouth, Mass	320
North Acton, York, Me	22
North Adams,* Berkshire, Mass	2,700
North Adams, Hillsdale, Mich	120
North Alfred, York, Me	27
North Amherst, Hampshire, Mass	300
North Amity, Aroostook, Me	12
Northampton, (c. h.,) Hampshire, Mass	2,400
Northampton, Fulton, N. Y	210
North Andover, Essex, Mass	310
North Andover Depot, Essex, Mass	670
North Anson, Somerset, Me	590
North Appleton, Knox, Me	42
North Argyle, Washington, N. Y	82
North Ashford, Windham, Conn	30
North Attleborough, Bristol, Mass	910
North Auburn, Androscoggin, Me	95
North Aurelius, Ingham, Mich	10
North Aurora, Kane, Ill	22
North Baldwin, Cumberland, Me	12
North Bangor, Penobscot, Me	23
North Bangor, Franklin, N. Y	170
North Barnstead, Belknap, N. H	33
North Barrier, Cabarrus, N. C	12
North Barrington, Strafford, N. H	3
North Barton, Tioga, N. Y	20
North Bass Island, Ottawa, Ohio	48
North Bay, Oneida, N. Y	130
North Bay, Door, Wis	12
North Belgrade, Kennebec, Me	35
North Bellingham, Norfolk, Mass	73
North Bend, Stark, Ind	4
North Bend, Dodge, Nebr	180
North Bend, Jackson, Wis	52
North Bennington, Bennington, Vt	680
North Benson, Shelby, Ky	44
North Benton, Mahoning, Ohio	64
North Bergen, Genesee, N. Y	56
North Berne, Fairfield, Ohio	47
North Berwick, York, Me	460
North Bethel, Oxford, Me	27
North Beverly, Essex, Mass	60
North Billerica, Middlesex, Mass	170
North Blanford, Hampden, Mass	150
North Blenheim, Schoharie, N. Y	81
North Bloomfield, Nevada, Cal	42
North Bloomfield, Ontario, N. Y	32
North Bloomfield, Trumbull, Ohio	240
North Blue Hill, Hancock, Me	34
North Boothbay, Lincoln, Me	180
Northborough, Worcester, Mass	540
North Boscawen, Merrimack, N. H	24
North Boston, Erie, N. Y	34
North Bradford, Penobscot, Me	86
North Branch, Baltimore, Md	35
North Branch, Lapeer, Mich	$120
North Branch, Isanti, Minn	17
North Branch, Hillsborough, N. H	68
North Branch, Somerset, N. J	110
North Branch, Sullivan, N. Y	50
North Branch, Jackson, Wis	12
North Branch Depot, Somerset, N. J	74
North Branford, New Haven, Conn	75
Northbridge, Worcester, Mass	190
Northbridge Centre, Worcester, Mass	130
North Bridgeton, Cumberland, Me	160
North Bridgewater,* Plymouth, Mass	1,700
North Bridgewater, Oneida, N. Y	38
North Bristol, Trumbull, Ohio	12
North Broadalbin, Fulton, N. Y	41
North Brook, Lincoln, N. C	17
North Brookfield,* Worcester, Mass	1,100
North Brookfield, Madison, N. Y	160
North Brooklin, Hancock, Me	23
North Brooksville, Hancock, Me	12
North Buckfield, Oxford, Me	18
North Bucksport, Hancock, Me	40
North Buffalo, Armstrong, Pa	12
North Byron, Kent, Mich	13
North Cambridge, Middlesex, Mass	940
North Cambridge, Lamoille, Vt	23
North Camden, Lorain, Ohio	20
North Cameron, Steuben, N. Y	8
North Canton, Hartford, Conn	19
North Canyonville, Douglas, Oreg	100
North Cape, Racine, Wis	120
North Carmel, Penobscot, Me	11
North Carver, Plymouth, Mass	42
North Castine, Hancock, Me	76
North Castle, Westchester, N. Y	20
North Cedar, Jackson, Kans	10
North Charlestown, Sullivan, N. H	140
North Chatham, Barnstable, Mass	63
North Chatham, Columbia, N. Y	86
North Chelmsford, Middlesex, Mass	240
North Chelsea, Suffolk, Mass	100
North Chemung, Chemung, N. Y	34
North Chester, Hampden, Mass	24
North Chester, Windsor, Vt	150
North Chesterville, Franklin, Me	100
North Chichester, Merrimack, N. H	64
North Chili, Monroe, N. Y	140
North Clarendon, Rutland, Vt	62
North Clarkson, Monroe, N. Y	45
North Clayton, Miami, Ohio	9
North Clayton, Crawford, Wis	12
North Clove, Dutchess, N. Y	34
North Clymer, Chautauqua, N. Y	51
North Cohasset, Norfolk, Mass	90
North Cohocton, Steuben, N. Y	200
North Colebrook, Litchfield, Conn	28
North Colesville, Broome, N. Y	14
North Columbia, Nevada, Cal	60
North Columbus, Franklin, Ohio	30
North Copake, Columbia, N. Y	130
North Conway, Carroll, N. H	700
North Cornville, Somerset, Me	33
North Cornwall, Litchfield, Conn	64

* Money-order office.

Post Office	Amount
North Cove, McDowell, N. C	$5
North Coventry, Chester, Pa	12
North Craftsbury, Orleans, Vt..	180
North Creek, Phillips, Ark	16
North Creek, Warren, N. Y	44
North Cutler, Washington, Me	22
Northcutt, Linn, Mo	45
North Dana, Worcester, Mass	95
North Danville, Caledonia, Vt	63
North Dartmouth, Bristol, Mass	85
North Deer Isle, Hancock, Me	39
North Derby, Orleans, Vt	83
North Dighton, Bristol, Mass	260
North Dixmont, Penobscot, Me	78
North Dorchester, Grafton, N. H	27
North Dorset, Bennington, Vt	. 81
North Dover, Cuyahoga, Ohio	11
North Dunbarton, Merrimack, N. H	18
North Duxbury, Washington, Vt.	39
North Eagle, Clinton, Mich	130
Northeast,* Cecil, Md	370
North East,* Erie, Pa	930
North East Centre, Dutchess, N. Y.	31
North Eastham, Barnstable, Mass.	59
Northeast Harbor, Hancock, Me	53
North Easton, Bristol, Mass	900
North Easton, Washington, N. Y.	86
North Eaton, Lorain, Ohio	44
North Edgecomb, Lincoln, Me	82
North Egremont, Berkshire, Mass	140
Northeim, Manitowoc, Wis	36
North Elba, Essex, N. Y	20
North Elk Grove, La Fayette, Wis.	24
North Ellsworth, Hancock, Me	12
North English, Iowa, Iowa	64
North Enosburgh, Franklin, Vt	17
Northern Depot, Boone, Ind	16
North Evans, Erie, N. Y	79
North Fairfax, Franklin, Vt	39
North Fairfield, Somerset, Me	25
North Fairfield, Huron, Ohio	350
North Falmouth, Barnstable, Mass.	82
North Farmington, Franklin, Me.	12
North Farmington, Oakland, Mich	20
North Fayette, Kennebec, Me	80
North Fayston, Washington, Vt	12
North Fenton, Broome, N. Y	63
North Ferrisburgh, Addison, Vt.	160
Northfield, Litchfield, Conn	140
Northfield, Boone, Ind	25
Northfield, Des Moines, Iowa	67
Northfield, Washington, Me	12
Northfield, Franklin, Mass	480
Northfield,* Rice, Minn	1,300
Northfield, Summit, Ohio	130
Northfield,* Washington, Vt	1,200
Northfield Farms, Franklin, Mass.	73
Northford, New Haven, Conn	100
North Fork, Mason, Ky	100
North Fork, Stearns, Minn	12
North Fork, Ashe, N. C	7
North Fork, Henry, Tenn	12
North Franklin, Delaware, N. Y	20
North Fryeburgh, Oxford, Me	74
North Gage, Oneida, N. Y	39
North Galway, Saratoga, N. Y	25

Post Office	Amount
North Garden, Albemarle, Va	$15
North Georgetown, Columbiana, Ohio	94
North Granby, Hartford, Conn	70
North Grantham, Sullivan, N. H	27
North Granville, Washington, N. Y.	430
North Gray, Cumberland, Me	96
North Greece, Monroe, N. Y	65
North Greenfield, Saratoga, N. Y	41
North Greenfield, Logan, Ohio	12
North Greensborough, Orleans, Vt.	17
North Greenwich, Washington, N. Y	55
North Grosvenor Dale, Windham, Conn	84
North Grafton, Grafton, N. H	54
North Grove, Miami, Ind	160
North Guilford, New Haven, Conn	42
North Hadley, Hampshire, Mass.	190
North Hamden, Delaware, N. Y	20
North Hamlin, Monroe, N. Y	12
North Hammond, St. Lawrence, N. Y	38
North Hampton, Peoria, Ill	18
North Hampton, Rockingham, N. H	260
North Hampton, Clark, Ohio	48
North Hancock, Hancock, Me	16
North Hannibal, Oswego, N. Y	79
North Harpersfield, Delaware, N. Y.	28
North Harpswell, Cumberland, Me	45
North Hartland, Niagara, N. Y	41
North Hartland, Windsor, Vt	82
North Harwich, Barnstable, Mass	52
North Hatfield, Hampshire, Mass	110
North Haven, New Haven, Conn.	260
North Haven, Knox, Me	120
North Haverhill, Grafton, N. H	220
North Hebron, Washington, N. Y.	17
North Hector, Schuyler, N. Y	150
North Heidelberg, Berks, Pa	9
North Hermon, Penobscot, Me	15
North Hero, (c. h.,) Grand Isle, Vt.	60
North Hogan, Ripley, Ind	12
North Hoosick, Rensselaer, N. Y	140
North Hope, Butler, Pa	100
North Hudson, Essex, N. Y	38
North Huron, Wayne, N. Y	59
North Hyde Park, Lemoille, Vt.	60
North Industry, Stark, Ohio	21
North Irving, Barry, Mich	31
North Isleborough, Waldo, Me	110
North Jackson, Mahoning, Ohio	90
North Jackson, Susquehanna, Pa	22
North Jasper, Steuben, N. Y	8
North Java, Wyoming, N. Y	110
North Jay, Franklin, Me	88
North Judson, Stark, Ind	110
North Kennebunk Port, York, Me.	2
North Kingston, De Kalb, Ill	90
North Kingsville, Ashtabula, Ohio	190
North Kortright, Delaware, N. Y	60
North La Crosse, La Crosse, Wis.	130
North Lake, Waukesha, Wis	30
North Landgrove, Bennington, Vt	69
North Lansing, Tompkins, N. Y	57
North Lawrence, St. Lawrence, N. Y	260

* Money order office.

North Lawrence, Stark, Ohio	$91
North Lebanon, York, Me	22
North Leeds, Androscoggin, Me....	29
North Leeds, Columbia, Wis	61
North Leominster, Worcester, Mass.	300
North Leverett, Franklin, Mass....	76
North Lewisburgh, Champaign, Ohio.......	290
North Liberty, St. Joseph, Ind.....	110
North Liberty, Johnson, Iowa	58
North Liberty, Knox, Ohio	51
North Liberty, Mercer, Pa	50
North Lima, Mahoning, Ohio	60
North Limington, York, Me	29
North Lincklaen, Chenango, N. Y ..	12
North Linneus, Aroostook, Me	21
North Lisbon, Grafton, N. H	16
North Litchfield, Herkimer, N. Y ..	50
North Littleton, Grafton, N. H.....	19
North Livermore, Androscoggin, Me..............	89
North Londonderry, Rockingham, N. H.............................	51
North Lovell, Oxford, Me...........	35
North Lubec, Washington, Me.....	12
North Lyme, New London, Conn...	66
North Lyndeborough, Hillsborough, N. H.............................	35
North McGregor, Clayton, Iowa....	370
North Madison, New Haven, Conn.	34
North Madison, Jefferson, Ind......	290
North Madison, Somerset, Me......	12
North Madison, Lake, Ohio	120
North Manchester, Hartford, Conn.	360
North Manchester,* Wabash, Ind ..	270
North Manlius, Onondaga, N. Y	82
North Mariaville, Hancock, Me	35
North Marshfield, Plymouth, Mass..	45
North Middleborough, Plymouth, Mass.............................	180
North Middletown, Bourbon, Ky...	200
North Milford, Penobscot, Me......	39
North Monmouth, Kennebec, Me...	110
North Monroe, Waldo, Me	12
North Monroe, Grafton, N. H	32
North Montpelier, Washington, Vt.	49
North Mountain, Berkeley, W. Va..	73
North Mount Pleasant, Marshall, Miss	64
North Nassau, Rensselaer, N. Y....	22
North Newberg, Shiawassee, Mich..	77
North Newburgh, Penobscot, Me...	20
North Newbury, Geauga, Ohio	19
North New Castle, Lincoln, Me	48
North Newfield, York, Me	23
North Newport, Penobscot, Me.....	19
North New Portland, Somerset, Me.	140
North Newry, Oxford, Me..........	79
North New Salem, Franklin, Mass..	49
North Norfolk, Litchfield, Conn....	22
North Norway, Oxford, Me	42
North Norwich, Chenango, N. Y....	130
North Oakfield, Genesee, N. Y.....	10
North Oakland, Butler, Pa	25
North Ogden, Weber, Utah	34
North Orange, Franklin, Mass	88

North Orwell, Bradford, Pa.........	$40
North Oxford, Worcester, Mass	170
North Palermo, Waldo, Me	32
North Paris, Oxford, Me	150
North Parma, Monroe, N. Y	130
North Parsonfield, York, Me	54
North Pembroke, Plymouth, Mass..	42
North Pembroke, Genesee, N. Y	46
North Penn, Schuylkill, Pa	14
North Penobscot, Hancock, Me.....	34
North Perry, Washington, Me	37
North Petersburg, Rensselaer, N. Y.	36
North Pharsalia, Chenango, N. Y...	12
North Pine Grove, Clarion, Pa	8
North Pitcher, Chenango, N. Y.....	20
North Pittston, Kennebec, Me......	28
North Plains, Ionia, Mich..........	20
North Plato, Kane, Ill	14
North Platte, (c. h.,) Lincoln, Nebr..	400
North Plympton, Plymouth, Mass..	23
North Point, Pulaski, Ark	3
North Point, Holt, Mo.............	50
North Pomfret, Windsor, Vt	98
Northport, Tuscaloosa, Ala	65
Northport, Waldo, Me	100
Northport,* (c. h.,) Leelenaw, Mich..	190
Northport, Suffolk, N. Y ....,	310
Northport, Waupaca, Wis	62
North Powder, Union, Oreg........	12
North Pownal, Cumberland, Me....	54
North Pownal, Bennington, Vt	130
North Prairie, Knox, Ill	21
North Prairie, Morrison, Minn	10
North Prairie Station, Waukesha, Wis	160
North Prescott, Hampshire, Mass ..	100
North Raisinville, Monroe, Mich ...	19
North Randolph, Orange, Vt.......	61
North Raymond, Cumberland, Me..	42
North Reading, Middlesex, Mass ...	160
North Reading, Schuyler, N. Y.....	14
North Rehoboth, Bristol, Mass	30
North Richmond, Cheshire, N. H ..	28
North Richmond, Ashtabula, Ohio..	12
North Ridge, Niagara, N. Y	49
North Ridgeville, Lorain, Ohio.....	76
North Ridgeway, Orleans, N. Y.....	31
North River, Tuscaloosa, Ala	12
North River, Marion, Mo	12
North River, Warren, N. Y..........	55
North River Mills, Hampshire, W. Va	16
North Robinson, Crawford, Ohio...	53
North Rome, Bradford, Pa.........	11
North Rose, Wayne, N. Y	22
North Royalton, Cuyahoga, Ohio...	100
North Rumford, Oxford, Me	17
North Rush, Monroe, N. Y	35
North Russel, St. Lawrence, N. Y...	8
North Rutland, Worcester, Mass ...	52
North Salem, Hendricks, Ind	96
North Salem, Linn, Mo	39
North Salem, Rockingham, N. H ..	30
North Salem, Westchester, N. Y	91
North Salem, Guernsey, Ohio......	12
North Sanbornton, Belknap, N. H..	91

North San Diego, (c. h.,) San Diego, Cal	$150
North Sandwich, Barnstable, Mass.	55
North Sandwich, Carroll, N. H	120
North Sandy, Mercer, Pa	5
North Sanford, Broome, N. Y	9
North San Juan, Nevada, Cal	390
North Santee, Georgetown, S. C	12
North Scituate, Plymouth, Mass	130
North Scituate, Providence, R. I	250
North Scriba, Oswego, N. Y	52
North Searsmont, Waldo, Me	40
North Searsport, Waldo, Me	36
North Sedgwick, Hancock, Me	47
North Sewickly, Beaver, Pa	54
North Shapleigh, York, Me	44
North Sheffield, Ashtabula, Ohio	15
North Sheldon, Franklin, Vt	26
North Shenango, Crawford, Pa	89
Northside, Goochland, Va	12
North Sidney, Kennebec, Me	30
North's Landing, Switzerland, Ind.	24
North's Mills, Mercer, Pa	43
North Smithfield, Bradford, Pa	9
North Solon, Cuyahoga, Ohio	39
North Somerville, Middlesex, Mass.	260
North Sparta, Livingston, N. Y	22
North Spencer, Worcester, Mass	18
North Springfield, Greene, Mo	12
North Springfield, Erie, Pa	120
North Springfield, Windsor, Vt	150
North Springs, Jackson, Tenn	2
North Stamford, Fairfield, Conn	40
North Star, Gratiot, Mich	26
North Star, Atchison, Mo	58
North Star, Darke, Ohio	20
North Star, Allegheny, Pa	29
North Star, Crawford, Wis	6
North Stephentown, Rensselaer, N.Y	23
North Sterling, Cayuga, N. Y	12
North Stockholm, St. Lawrence, N. Y	160
North Stonington, New London, Conn	130
North Stoughton, Norfolk, Mass	·92
North Strafford, Strafford, N. H	10
North Sudbury, Middlesex, Mass	13
North Sutton, Merrimack, N. H	90
North Swansea, Bristol, Mass	45
North Taycheedah, Fond du Lac, Wis	19
North Thetford, Orange, Vt	130
North Tisbury, Dukes, Mass	12
North Towanda, Bradford, Pa	13
North Troy, Orleans, Vt	370
North Truro, Barnstable, Mass	95
North Tunbridge, Orange, Vt	35
North Turner, Androscoggin, Me	98
North Turner Bridge, Androscoggin, Me	47
Northumberland, Coos, N. H	99
Northumberland, Saratoga, N. Y	72
Northumberland,* Northumberland, Pa	940
North Underhill, Chittenden, Vt	21
North Union, Knox, Me	54

North Uniontown, Highland, Ohio.	$8
North Unity, Leelanaw, Mich	24
Northup, Gallia, Ohio	6
North Urbana, Steuben, N. Y	19
North Uxbridge, Worcester, Mass	140
North Vassalborough, Kennebec, Me	480
North Vernon, Jennings, Ind	710
North Vernon, Shiawassee, Mich	2
North Victory, Cayuga, N. Y	43
North Vienna, Kennebec, Me	38
Northville, Litchfield, Conn	51
Northville, La Salle, Ill	85
Northville, Greene, Iowa	22
Northville, Wayne, Mich	390
Northville, Fulton, N. Y	320
Northville, Erie, Pa	100
North Vineland, Cumberland, N. J.	110
North Volney, Oswego, N. Y	20
North Wakefield, Carroll, N. H	59
North Waldoborough, Lincoln, Me.	44
North Wales, Montgomery, Pa	160
North Walton, Delaware, N. Y	49
North Warren, Winona, Minn	8
North Washington, Chickasaw, Iowa	25
North Washington, Knox, Me	19
North Washington, Hardin, Ohio	42
North Washington, Westmoreland, Pa	45
North Waterborough, York, Me	27
North Waterford, Oxford, Me	110
North Wayne, Kennebec, Me	75
North Weare, Hillsborough, N. H	140
North West, Williams, Ohio	21
North West Bridgewater, Plymouth, Mass	13
North Western, Oneida, N. Y	130
North Wethersfield, Wyoming, N. Y	28
North Weymouth, Norfolk, Mass	250
North Wharton, Potter, Pa	12
North Whitefield, Lincoln, Me	47
North Whitehall, Lehigh, Pa	43
North Williston, Chittenden, Vt	92
North Wilmington, Middlesex, Mass	66
North Wilna, Jefferson, N. Y	34
North Wilton, Fairfield, Conn	70
North Windham, Windham, Conn	74
North Windham, Cumberland, Me	42
North Windham, Windham, Vt	79
North Windsor, Dane, Wis	54
North Winfield, Herkimer, N. Y	39
North Winterport, Waldo, Me	31
North Woburn, Middlesex, Mass	190
North Wolcott, Lamoille, Vt	52
North Wolfborough, Carroll, N. H.	46
Northwood, (c. h.,) Worth, Iowa	53
Northwood, Logan, Ohio	65
Northwood Centre, Rockingham, N. H	120
Northwood Narrows, Rockingham, N. H	74
North Woodstock, Windham, Conn.	160
North Woodstock, Oxford, Me	35
North Woodstock, Grafton, N. H	10
North Woodville, Penobscot, Me	8
North Yam Hill, Yam Hill, Oreg	45

* Money-order office.

NUR

OAK

North Yarmouth, Cumberland, Me.	$76	Nursery Hill, Otoe, Nebr	$80
Norton, Kankakee, Ill	27	Nuzums, Marion, W. Va	53
Norton, Bristol, Mass	410	Nyack,* Rockland, N. Y	1,300
Norton, Delaware, Ohio	49	Nyack Turnpike, Rockland, N. Y	68
Norton Centre, Summit, Ohio	18	Nyce's, Pike, Pa	31
Norton Hill, Greene, N. Y	71		
Norton Mills, Essex, Vt	160	**O.**	
Norton's Bluff, McCracken, Ky	12		
Nortonville, Clarke, Iowa	12	Oak, Pope, Ill	12
Norval, Harnett, N. C	2	Oak, Pulaski, Ind	23
Norvell, Jackson, Mich	150	Oak, Wayne, Mich	21
Norwalk,* Fairfield, Conn	2,400	Oakalla, Iroquois. Ill	820
Norwalk, Warren, Iowa	36	Oak Bower, Hart, Ga	5
Norwalk, Manistee, Mich	32	Oak Creek, Milwaukee, Wis	140
Norwalk, (c. h.,) Huron, Ohio	2,700	Oakdale, Livingston, Ill	12
Norway, La Salle, Ill	120	Oakdale, Jennings, Ind	10
Norway,* Oxford, Me	760	Oakdale, Worcester, Mass	230
Norway, Goodhue, Minn	180	Oak Dale, Washington, Minn	17
Norway, Herkimer, N. Y	130	Oak Dale, Hunterdon, N. J	20
Norway, Racine, Wis	31	Oakdale, Delaware, Pa	160
Norway Lake, Monongalia, Minn	120	Oakdale, Rockbridge, Va	3
Norwegian, Watonwan, Minn	10	Oakdale Station, Suffolk, N. Y	52
Norwich, (c. h.,) New London, Conn	3,900	Oakdale Station, Allegheny, Pa	12
Norwich, Hampshire, Mass	30	Oakdain, Vanderburgh, Ind	4
Norwich, (c. h.,) Chenango, N. Y	2,200	Oak Farm, Brown, Ind	13
Norwich, Muskingum, Ohio	110	Oakfield, Audubon, Iowa	56
Norwich, McKean, Pa	8	Oakfield, Kent, Mich	44
Norwich, Windsor, Vt	400	Oakfield, Franklin, Mo	30
Norwich Town, New London, Conn	290	Oakfield, Genesee, N. Y	330
Norwood, Mercer, Ill	190	Oakfield, Perry, Ohio	26
Norwood, Lucas, Iowa	12	Oakfield, Fond du Lac, Wis	190
Norwood, Franklin, Kans	12	Oakfield Centre, Fond du Lac, Wis	110
Norwood, Charlevoix, Mich	35	Oak Flat, Pendleton, W. Va	16
Norwood, Carter, Mo	12	Oakford, Howard, Ind	92
Norwood, Bergen, N, J	10	Oakford, Daviess, Ky	17
Norwood, Stanly, N. C	24	Oakford, Bucks, Pa	16
Norwood, Hamilton, Ohio	12	Oak Forest, Franklin, Ind	15
Norwood, Chester, Pa	12	Oak Forest, Iredell, N. C	1
Norwood, Nelson, Va	340	Oak Forest, Greene, Pa	14
Norwood Park, Cook, Ill	12	Oak Forest, Cumberland, Va	33
Nossville, Huntingdon, Pa	33	Oakfuskee, Cleburne, Ala	10
Notasulga, Macon, Ala	170	Oak Glen, Steele, Minn	64
Notre Dame,* St. Joseph, Ind	1,000	Oak Grove, Sussex, Del	12
Nottingham, Wells, Ind	32	Oak Grove, McLean, Ill	41
Nottingham, Prince George's, Md	41	Oak Grove, Christian, Ky	46
Nottingham, Rockingham, N. H	77	Oak Grove, Prince George's, Md	35
Nottingham, Cuyahoga, Ohio	79	Oak Grove, Livingston, Mich	74
Nottingham, Chester, Pa	65	Oak Grove, Anoka, Minn	9
Nottoway C. H., Nottoway, Va	220	Oak Grove, Jackson, Mo	12
Nova, Ashland, Ohio	22	Oak Grove, Hunterdon, N. J	2
Novelty, Knox, Mo	69	Oak Grove, Union, N. C	9
Novi, Oakland, Mich	74	Oak Grove, Marion, S. C	10
Nuckollsville, Grayson, Va	55	Oak Grove, Jefferson, Tenn	4
Nueces, Nueces, Tex	16	Oak Grove, Westmoreland, Va	100
Nugent's Grove, Linn, Iowa	55	Oak Grove, Dodge, Wis	100
Nulhegan, Essex, Vt	44	Oak Grove Furnace, Westmoreland,	
Null's Mills, Fayette, Ind	13	Pa	14
Numa, Parke, Ind	11	Oak Groves, Seward, Nebr	10
Numa, Appanoose, Iowa	26	Oakham, Worcester, Mass	150
Numidia, Columbia, Pa	59	Oak Harbor, Ottawa, Ohio	160
Nunda, McHenry, Ill	240	Oak Hill, Cumberland, Me	180
Nunda, Freeborn, Minn	23	Oak Hill, Oakland, Mich	16
Nunda,* Livingston, N. Y	1,100	Oak Hill, Gasconade, Mo	6
Nunda Station, Livingston, N. Y	320	Oak Hill, Greene, N. Y	120
Nunica, Ottawa, Mich	150	Oak Hill, Granville, N. C	15
Nursery Hill, Dent, Mo	12	Oak Hill, Jackson, Ohio	330

* Money-order office.

OAK   ODE

Oak Hill, Lancaster, Pa	$65
Oak Hill, Overton, Tenn	16
Oak Hill, Travis, Tex	12
Oak Hill, Fayette, W. Va	6
Oak Hill, Jefferson, Wis	27
Oakhurst, Miller, Mo	49
Oakington, Harford, Md	12
Oakland,* Alameda, Cal	2,100
Oakland, Coles, Ill	220
Oakland, Spencer, Ind	35
Oakland, Marshall, Ky	16
Oakland, Alleghany, Md	560
Oakland, Oakland, Mich	10
Oakland, Yalabusha, Miss	70
Oakland, Laclede, Mo	16
Oakland, Burt, Nebr	33
Oakland, Livingston, N. Y	89
Oakland, Clinton, Ohio	41
Oakland, Douglas, Oreg	170
Oakland, Armstrong, Pa	82
Oakland, Fayette, Tenn	72
Oakland, Colorado, Tex	40
Oakland, (c. h.,) Mason, Wash	12
Oakland, Jefferson, Wis	25
Oakland City, Gibson, Ind	52
Oakland Cross Roads, Westmoreland, Pa	36
Oakland Mills, Henry, Iowa	30
Oakland Mills, Nicholas, Ky	27
Oakland Mills, Howard, Md	10
Oakland Mills, Guernsey, Ohio	12
Oakland Mills, Juniata, Pa	70
Oaklandon, Marion, Ind	38
Oakland Station, Warren, Ky	82
Oakland Valley, Franklin, Iowa	21
Oak Lawn, Shelby, Tenn	12
Oak Level, Cleburne, Ala	12
Oak Level, Henry, Va	12
Oakley, Macon, Ill	100
Oakley, Franklin, La	10
Oakley, Saginaw, Mich	57
Oakley, New Hanover, N. C	12
Oakley, Hamilton, Ohio	32
Oakley, Susquehanna, Pa	23
Oakley, Mecklenburg, Va	38
Oakley, Green, Wis	13
Oakley Depot, Charleston, S. C	89
Oak Mills, Atchison, Kans	18
Oak Orchard, Frederick, Md	14
Oak Orchard, Orleans, N. Y	17
Oak Park, Cook, Ill	220
Oak Park, Madison, Va	15
Oak Point, Clark, Ill	14
Oak Point, Van Buren, Iowa	15
Oak Point, Wilson, Tenn	8
Oak Point, Cowlitz, Wash	67
Oak Ridge, Jefferson, Ala	12
Oak Ridge, Menard, Ill	13
Oak Ridge, Winona, Minn	17
Oak Ridge, Cape Girardeau, Mo	46
Oak Ridge, Hancock, Ohio	16
Oaks, Orange, N. C	26
Oaks, Sauk, Wis	16
Oak's Corners, Ontario, N. Y	130
Oak Shade, Lancaster, Pa	13
Oak Spring, Davis, Iowa	5
Oak Spring, Rutherford, N. C	$5
Oak Springs, Anoka, Minn	10
Oak Springs, Dodge, Nebr	12
Oaksville, Otsego, N. Y	45
Oaktown, Knox, Ind	160
Oakville, Lawrence, Ala	6
Oakville, Jefferson, Ark	12
Oakville, Napa, Cal	41
Oakville, New Haven, Conn	92
Oakville, Hickman, Ky	12
Oakville, St. Mary's, Md	16
Oakville, Monroe, Mich	22
Oakville, Cumberland, Pa	110
Oakville, (c. h.,) Live Oak, Tex	16
Oakville, Appomattox, Va	16
Oakway, Oconee, S. C	6
Oak Well, Hawkins, Tenn	12
Oakwood, Vermilion, Ill	12
Oakwood, Linn, Kans	7
Oakwood, Oakland, Mich	74
Oakwood, Paulding, Ohio	10
Oakwood, Montgomery, Tenn	17
Oak Woods, Fleming, Ky	33
Oaky Streak, Butler, Ala	10
Oasis, Johnson, Iowa	15
Oasis, Waushara, Wis	22
Oatlands, Loudoun, Va	12
Oatmeal, Burnet, Tex	10
O'Bannon, Jefferson, Ky	120
Oberle's Corners, Carver, Minn	9
Oberlin,* Lorain, Ohio	2,400
Oblong, Crawford, Ill	60
Oblong, Dutchess, N. Y	44
O'Brien, (c. h.,) O'Brien, Iowa	5
Ocala, (c. h.,) Marion, Fla	270
Ocate, Mora, N. Mex	12
Occoquan, Prince William, Va	81
Ocean, Alleghany, Md	45
Oceana, (c. h.,) Wyoming, W. Va	60
Ocean Port, Monmouth, N. J	88
Ocean Springs, Jackson, Miss	92
Ocean View, Sonoma, Cal	12
Ocean View, Sussex, Del	25
Oceola, St. Joseph, Ind	30
Oceola,* (c. h.,) Clarke, Iowa	900
Oceola, Greene, Ky	16
Oceola, Crawford, Ohio	29
Oceola, Fond du Lac, Wis	14
Oceola Centre, Livingston, Mich	35
Ocheltree, Johnson, Kans	12
Ochesee, Calhoun, Fla	12
Ochlochnee, Thomas, Ga	12
Ocona Lufty, Jackson, N. C	5
Oconee, Washington, Ga	50
Oconee Station, Shelby, Ill	159
Oconomowoc,* Waukesha, Wis	1,100
Oconto,* (c. h.,) Oconto, Wis	1,000
Ocoya, Livingston, Ill	56
Ocracocke, Hyde, N. C	10
Octagon, Tippecanoe, Ind	12
Octavia, Early, Ga	12
Octoraro, Lancaster, Pa	43
Oddville, Harrison, Ky	26
Odell, Livingston, Ill	880
Odessa, New Castle, Del	370
Odessa, Schuyler, N. Y	82

* Money-order office.

OLD

OMA

Odin,* Marion, Ill...................	$720
Odin, Vernon, Wis..................	5
Ofahoma, Leake, Miss.............	12
O'Fallon, St. Charles, Mo.........	140
O'Fallon Depot, St. Clair, Ill.......	210
Offutt's Cross Roads, Montgomery, Md................................	12
Ogden, Champaign, Ill............	12
Ogden, Henry, Ind................	83
Ogden, Dubuque, Iowa............	5
Ogden, Riley, Kans..............	210
Ogden, Monroe, N. Y.............	61
Ogden, Clinton, Ohio..............	69
Ogden Centre, Lenawee, Mich.....	12
Ogden City, (c. h.,) Weber, Utah....	190
Ogdensburgh, Sussex, N. J........	61
Ogdensburgh,* St. Lawrence, N. Y.	2,600
Ogdensburgh, Tioga, Pa..........	37
Ogdensburgh, Waupaca, Wis......	52
Ogden's Landing, Ballard, Ky	12
Ogee, Blount, Ala.................	12
Ogeechee, Scriven, Ga..........	25
Ogemaw, Iosco, Mich	12
Ogle, Butler, Pa..................	23
Oglesby, La Salle, Ill.............	210
Oglethorpe, (c. h.,) Macon, Ga.......	320
Ogunquit, York, Me.............	80
Ohio, Bureau, Ill.................	54
Ohio, Madison, Iowa.............	18
Ohio, Herkimer, N. Y.............	35
Ohio Mill, Ottawa, Mich.........	12
Ohioville, Ulster, N. Y............	64
Ohioville, Beaver, Pa............	42
Ohl's Town, Trumbull, Ohio	28
Oil City,* Venango, Pa............	2,600
Oil Creek, Perry, Ind............	16
Oil Creek, Crawford, Pa..........	170
Oil Diggins, Trumbull, Ohio.......	12
Oil Mill Village, Hillsborough, N. H.	60
Oil Rock, Wirt, W. Va	100
Oil Springs, Johnson, Ky..........	2
Oil Trough, Independence, Ark	12
Okaman, Waseca, Minn	48
Okaw, Washington, Ill............	84
Okeana, Butler, Ohio..............	50
Okee, Columbia, Wis..............	38
Okemos, Ingham, Mich............	130
Okmulkee, Creek Nation, Ind. T. ..	12
Okolona,* Chickasaw, Miss........	1,000
Okolona, Henry, Ohio	47
Okolona, Carter, Tenn	12
Okonoko, Hampshire, W. Va.......	12
Ola, Lucas, Iowa.................	9
Olamon, Penobscot, Me...........	85
Olathe,* (c. h.,) Johnson, Kans	1,300
Olcott, Niagara, N. Y............	110
Old Alexandria, Lincoln, Mo.......	22
Old Bridge, Middlesex, N. J........	68
Old Church, Hanover, Va..........	58
Old Creek, San Luis Obispo, Cal. ..	12
Oldenburgh, Franklin, Ind....	180
Old Forge, Luzerne, Pa.......	150
Old Fort, McDowell, N. C..........	250
Old Furnace, Gaston, N. C........	3
Oldham's Cross Roads, Westmoreland, Va....	15

Old Hickory, Conway, Ark	$16
Old Hickory, Wayne, Ohio....	40
Old Hickory, Botetourt, Va........	18
Old Line, Lancaster, Pa	10
Old Mines, Washington, Mo	19
Old Mission, Winneshiek, Iowa	8
Old Mission, Grand Traverse, Mich.	52
Old Monroe, Lincoln, Mo..........	39
Old Point Comfort,* Elizabeth City, Va......................	1,200
Old Richmond, Forsyth, N. C	4
Old Ripley, Bond, Ill.............	22
Old Store, Chesterfield, S. C........	12
Old Town, Phillips, Ark...........	12
Old Town, Penobscot, Me..........	720
Old Town, Alleghany, Md.........	12
Old Town, Forsyth, N. C..........	8
Oldtown, Claiborne, Tenn.........	8
Old Westbury, Queens, N. Y	170
Olean, Ripley, Ind...............	90
Olean,* Cattaraugus, N. Y.........	1,400
Olema, Marin, Cal...............	86
Olena, Henderson, Ill	100
Olena, Huron, Ohio	81
Oleopolis, Venango, Pa...........	110
Oley, Berks, Pa.................	75
Olin, Iredell, N. C...............	22
Olin, Adams, Wis................	16
Olio, Scott, Ark.................	4
Olive, Lawrence, Ill.............	12
Olive, Marshall, Ky.............	12
Olive, Clinton, Mich	12
Olive, Ulster, N. Y..............	50
Olive Branch, De Soto, Miss	83
Olive Branch, Lancaster, Nebr	10
Olive Branch, Union, N. C	12
Olive Branch, Clermont, Ohio	41
Olive Bridge, Ulster, N. Y........	30
Oliveburgh, Jefferson, Pa..........	12
Olive Green, Noble, Ohio..........	12
Olive Hill, Wayne, Ind...........	26
Olive Hill, Carter, Ky...........	22
Olive Hill, Hardin, Tenn	12
Oliver's, Anderson, Tenn	8
Oliver's Landing, Phillips, Ark	12
Olivesburgh, Richland, Ohio.......	97
Olivet, Osage, Kans..............	12
Olivet,* Eaton, Mich.............	540
Olivet, Armstrong, Pa............	28
Olivet, Pierce, Wis..............	12
Olivia, Blair, Pa.................	55
Olmstead, Logan, Ky....	130
Olmsted, Cuyahoga, Ohio....	240
Olmstedville, Essex, N. Y.........	92
Olney,* (c. h.,) Richland, Ill.........	2,100
Olney, Montgomery, Md..........	120
Olneyville, Providence, R. I	1,100
Olustee, Baker, Fla..............	4
Olustee Creek, Pike, Ala..........	31
OLYMPIA,* (c. h.,) Thurston, Wash.	1,300
Olympian Springs, Bath, Ky......	12
Olympus, Overton, Tenn....	11
Olyphant, Luzerne, Pa............	270
Omadi, Dakota, Nebr.............	12
Omaha, Putnam, Mo	12
Omaha Agency, Blackbird, Nebr ...	30

*Money-order office.

OQU

Omaha Barracks, Douglas. Nebr ...	$12
Omaha City, (c. h.,) Douglas, Nebr.	4, 000
Omar, Jefferson, N. Y	19
Omega, Nevada, Cal	24
Omega, Marion, Ill	20
Omega, Hamilton, Ind	12
Omega, Hart, Ky	16
Omega, Pike, Ohio	95
Omega, Upshur, Tex	8
Omega, Halifax, Va	18
Omena, Leelenaw, Mich	23
Omph Gheut, Madison, Ill	14
Omro,* Winnebago, Wis	940
Onalaska, La Crosse, Wis	150
Onancock, Accomack, Va	130
Onarga,* Iroquois, Ill	1, 100
Onawa City, (c. h.,) Monona, Iowa	450
Onberg, Indiana, Pa	12
O'Neal's Mills, Troup, Ga	8
Oneco, Windham, Conn	100
Oneco, Stephenson, Ill	29
Oneida,* Knox, Ill	790
Oneida, Kosciusko, Ind	9
Oneida,* Madison, N. Y	2, 200
Oneida, Brown, Wis	11
Oneida Castle, Oneida, N. Y	200
Oneida Lake, Madison, N. Y	25
Oneida Mills, Carroll, Ohio	97
Oneida Valley, Madison, N. Y	59
Oneonta, Otsego, N. Y	840
Oneota, St. Louis, Minn	65
Onion Creek, Travis, Tex	25
Onion River, Sheboygan, Wis	23
Onisbo, Sacramento, Cal	27
Ono, Lebanon, Pa	56
Ono, Pierce, Wis	12
Onondaga, Ingham, Mich	50
Onondaga, Onondaga, N. Y	94
Onondaga Castle, Onondaga, N. Y.	18
Onondaga Valley, Onondaga, N. Y.	140
Onota, Schoolcraft, Mich	12
Onoville, Cattaraugus, N. Y	22
Onslow C. H., Onslow, N. C	3
Ontario, Knox, Ill	60
Ontario, La Grange, Ind	150
Ontario, Story, Iowa	69
Ontario, Jackson, Kans	6
Ontario, Wayne, N. Y	160
Ontario, Richland, Ohio	150
Ontario, Vernon, Wis	100
Ontario Centre, Wayne, N. Y	12
Ontonagon (c. h.,) Ontonagon, Mich.	310
Onward, Cass, Ind	25
Onyx, Yell, Ark	12
Ooltewah, Hamilton, Tenn	100
Oostburgh, Sheboygan, Wis	12
Opelika, (c. h.,) Lee, Ala	920
Opelousas, (c. h.,) St. Landry, La.	730
Opequan, Lancaster, Nebr	12
Ophir Cherokee, Ga	19
Ophir, Washoe, Nev	40
O'Plain, Lake, Ill	19
Oporto, St. Joseph, Mich	20
Oppelo, Perry, Ark	14
Oppenheim, Fulton, N. Y	52
Oquawka, (c. h.,) Henderson, Ill ...	410

ORE

Ora, Jackson, Ill	$12
Oral, Scott, Minn	63
Ora Labor, Huron, Mich	28
Oral Oaks, Lunenburgh, Va	12
Oramel, Allegany, N. Y	170
Oran, Fayette, Iowa	10
Oran, Onondaga, N. Y	45
Orange, New Haven, Conn	35
Orange, Cherokee, Ga	12
Orange, Fayette, Ind	71
Orange, Clinton, Iowa	9
Orange, Franklin, Mass	690
Orange, Ionia, Mich	12
Orange, Essex, N. J	2, 500
Orange, Schuyler, N. Y	120
Orange, Mahoning, Ohio	93
Orange, Luzerne, Pa	32
Orange, (c. h.,) Orange, Tex	85
Orange, Orange, Vt	35
Orange, Juneau, Wis	35
Orange C. H., Orange, Va	600
Orangeburgh, Mason, Ky	47
Orangeburgh C.H., Orangeburgh,S.C.	1, 100
Orange Factory, Orange, N. C	15
Orange Grove, Dallas, Ala	12
Orange Lake, Orange, N. Y	12
Orange Mills, St. John's, Fla	53
Orangeport, Niagara, N. Y	70
Orange Springs, Marion, Fla	12
Orange Station, Delaware, Ohio	37
Orange Valley, Essex, N. J.,	12
Orangeville, Stephenson, Ill	120
Orangeville, Orange, Ind	37
Orangeville, Baltimore, Md	12
Orangeville, Branch, Mich	31
Orangeville, Wyoming, N. Y	41
Orangeville, Trumbull, Ohio	390
Orangeville, Columbia, Pa	100
Orangeville, Fannin, Tex	15
Orangeville Mills, Barry, Mich	80
Ora Oak, Grant, Wis	12
Orbisonia, Huntingdon, Pa	130
Orchard, Mitchell, Iowa	12
Orchard Grove, Lake, Ind	38
Orcutt Creek, Bradford, Pa	31
Orcuttville, Neosho, Kans	12
Ordino, Marquette, Wis	8
Oreana, Humboldt, Nev	44
Ore Banks, Buckingham, Va	12
Orefield, Lehigh, Pa	46
Oregon, Jefferson, Ala	5
Oregon, (c. h.,) Ogle, Ill	540
Oregon, Clarke, Ind	33
Oregon, (c. h.,) Holt, Mo	650
Oregon, Chautauqua, N. Y	57
Oregon, Warren, Ohio	85
Oregon, Lancaster, Pa	36
Oregon, Lincoln, Tenn	11
Oregon, Dane, Wis	360
Oregon City, (c. h.,) Clackamas, Oreg	820
Oregon Hill, Lycoming, Pa	12
Oregon House, Yuba, Cal	52
Oregonia, Tuscaloosa, Ala	7
Ore Hill, Litchfield, Conn	33
Orell, Jefferson, Ky	32

* Money-order office.

ORW		OSW	
Oreville, Dutchess, N. Y.	$12	Orwin, Schuylkill, Pa.	$12
Orford, Tama, Iowa.	330	Osaga, Bourbon, Kans.	12
Orford, Grafton, N. H.	310	Osage, Carroll, Ark	12
Orfordville, Grafton, N. H.	75	Osage, Franklin, Ill.	4
Orfordville, Rock, Wis.	270	Osage, Mitchell, Iowa	720
Organ Spring, Washington, Ind.	11	Osage, Crawford, Mo.	18
Orient, Adair, Iowa	21	Osage Bluff, Cole, Mo.	4
Orient, Aroostook, Me.	24	Osage City, Osage, Kans.	160
Orient, Suffolk, N. Y.	270	Osage City, Cole, Mo	79
Orihula, Winnebago, Wis.	21	Osage Mills, Benton, Ark	12
Orion, Pike, Ala.	30	Osage Mission,* Neosho, Kans.	620
Orion, Henry, Ill.	200	Osakis, Douglas, Minn.	140
Orion, Kosciusko, Ind.	9	Osanippa, Chambers, Ala.	10
Orion, Oakland, Mich	230	Osawatomie,* Miami, Kans.	360
Orion, Henry, Mo.	12	Osborn, Rock Island, Ill.	12
Orion, Richland, Wis.	50	Osborn, Neosho, Kans.	24
Oriskany, Oneida, N. Y.	300	Osborn, De Kalb, Mo.	80
Oriskany Falls, Oneida, N. Y.	390	Osborn,* Greene, Ohio.	380
Orizaba, Tippah, Miss.	33	Osborne Hollow, Broome, N. Y.	48
Orkney Springs, Shenandoah, Va.	18	Osborne's Mills, Kanawha, W. Va.	3
Orland, Cook, Ill.	27	Osborn's Bridge, Fulton, N. Y.	30
Orland,* Steuben, Ind.	360	Osborn's Ford, Scott, Va.	12
Orland, Hancock, Me.	320	Osborn's Store, Issaquena, Miss.	12
Orlando, (c. h.,) Orange, Fla.	64	Oscar, Armstrong, Pa.	17
Orlando, Sherburne, Minn.	6	Osceola, (c. h.,) Mississippi, Ark	83
Orlean, Fauquier, Va.	12	Osceola, Stark, Ill.	52
Orleans, (c. h.,) Klamath, Cal.	20	Osceola,* (c. h.,) St. Clair, Mo.	440
Orleans, Morgan, Ill.	35	Osceola, Lewis, N. Y.	62
Orleans,* Orange, Ind.	400	Osceola, Tioga, Pa.	210
Orleans, Appanoose, Iowa.	27	Osceola Mills, Clearfield, Pa.	780
Orleans,* Barnstable, Mass.	370	Osceola Mills, (c. h.,) Polk, Wis.	160
Orleans, Ionia, Mich	43	Oseuma, Cherokee Nation, Ind. T.	53
Orleans, Polk, Mo.	23	Osgood,* Ripley, Ind.	240
Orleans, Ontario, N. Y.	84	Oshaukuta, Columbia, Wis.	41
Orleans Cross Roads, Morgan, W. Va.	58	Oshawa, Osage, Mo.	12
Orleans Four Corners, Jefferson, N. Y.	22	Oshkosh,* (c. h.,) Winnebago, Wis.	4,000
Ormanville, Wapello, Iowa.	12	Oshtemo, Kalamazoo, Mich.	160
Orme's Store, Bledsoe, Tenn.	20	Oskaloosa, Clay, Ill.	52
Ormsby, Allegheny, Pa.	380	Oskaloosa,* (c. h.,) Mahaska, Iowa.	2,200
Orneville, Piscataquis, Me.	13	Oskaloosa,* (c. h.,) Jefferson, Kans.	340
Oro, Chesterfield, S. C.	26	Oslo, Manitowoc, Wis.	18
Oro City, Placer, Cal.	12	Osman's, Adams, Ohio.	24
Oro City, Lake, Colo.	210	Osnaburgh, Stark, Ohio.	120
Orodell, Union, Oreg.	63	Oso, Fayette, Tex.	20
Oro Fino, Siskiyou, Cal.	35	Osprey, Monroe, Iowa.	12
Orono, Penobscot, Me.	510	Osseo, Hillsdale, Mich.	170
Orono, (c. h.,) Sherburne, Minn.	77	Osseo, Hennepin, Minn.	84
Oronoco, Olmsted, Minn.	97	Osseo, Trempealeau, Wis.	93
Oronoco, Amherst, Va.	12	Ossian, Wells, Ind.	180
Oroville,* (c. h.,) Butte, Cal	1,000	Ossian,* Winneshiek, Iowa.	550
Orrington, Penobscot, Me.	110	Ossian, Livingston, N. Y.	24
Orr's Island, Cumberland, Me.	42	Ossineke, Alpena, Mich.	68
Orrstown, Franklin, Pa.	85	Ossipee, (c. h.,) Carroll, N. H.	170
Orrsville, Armstrong, Pa.	130	Ossipee Mills, York, Me.	12
Orrville, Dallas, Ala.	42	Ostend, McHenry, Ill.	12
Orrville,* Wayne, Ohio.	590	Ostend, Clearfield, Pa.	12
Orth, Montgomery, Ind.	16	Osterville, Barnstable, Mass.	160
Ortonville, Oakland, Mich.	110	Osterville, Caldwell, Mo.	5
Orville, Pope, Ill.	7	Ostrander, Delaware, Ohio.	100
Orwell, Oswego, N. Y.	130	Oswaldville, Lehigh, Pa.	12
Orwell,* Ashtabula, Ohio.	240	Oswayo, Potter, Pa.	89
Orwell, Bradford, Pa.	59	Oswego,* Kendall, Ill	500
Orwell, Addison, Vt.	280	Oswego, Koscinsko, Ind.	22
Orwigsburgh, Schuylkill, Pa.	170	Oswego,* (c. h.,) Labette, Kans.	200
		Oswego,* (c. h.,) Oswego, N. Y.	3,800
		Oswego, Clackamas, Oreg.	12

* Money-order office.

OUT   OYS

Oswego Centre, Oswego, N. Y	$12	Outville, Licking, Ohio	$46
Oswego Falls, Oswego, N.Y	180	Overbrook, Montgomery, Pa	160
Osyka, Pike, Miss	360	Overisel, Allegan, Mich	60
Otay, San Diego, Cal	12	Overfield, Barbour, W. Va	19
Otego, Otsego, N.Y	520	Overpeck's Station, Butler, Ohio	35
Othello, Olmsted, Minn	30	Overton, Pah Ute, Ariz	12
Otho, Webster, Iowa	60	Overton, Cooper, Mo	58
Otis, Hancock, Me	12	Overton, Bradford, Pa	43
Otis, Berkshire, Mass	150	Ovid, Madison, Ind	17
Otisco, Clarke, Ind	12	Ovid, Taylor, Iowa	12
Otisco, Ionia, Mich	130	Ovid,* Clinton, Mich	690
Otisco, Waseca, Minn	12	Ovid, (c. h.,) Seneca, N. Y	730
Otisco, Onondaga, N. Y	100	Ovid, Franklin, Ohio	10
Otisco Valley, Onandaga, N. Y	14	Ovid, Rich, Utah	12
Otisfield, Cumberland, Me	75	Owaneco, Christian, Ill	20
Otisville, Franklin, Iowa	110	Owasco, Sullivan, Mo	40
Otisville, Genesee, Mich	150	Owasco, Cayuga, N. Y	160
Otisville, Orange, N. Y	350	Owasco Lake, Cayuga, N.Y	11
Otley, Marion, Iowa	150	Owatonna,* (c. h.,) Steele, Minn	1,600
Oto, Woodbury, Iowa	3	Owego,* (c. h.,) Tioga, N.Y	2,800
Otoe Agency, Gage, Nebr	21	Owego, Shawanaw, Wis	12
Otranto, Mitchell, Iowa	60	Owensborough,* (c. h.,) Daviess, Ky	1,900
Otsdawa, Otsego, N. Y	12	Owensburgh, Greene, Ind	48
Otsego, Fayette, Iowa	80	Owen's Cross Roads, Madison, Ala	10
Otsego, Allegan, Mich	570	Owen's Grove, Cerro Gordo, Iowa	10
Otsego, Wright, Minn	16	Owensville, Saline, Ark	5
Otsego, Ray, Mo	5	Owensville, Gibson, Ind	220
Otsego, Muskingum, Ohio	46	Owensville, Gasconade, Mo	19
Otsego, Columbia, Wis	93	Owensville, Clermont, Ohio	120
Otselic, Chenango, N.Y	52	Owensville, (c. h.,) Robertson, Tex	270
Ottawa,* (c. h.,) La Salle, Ill	3,400	Owenton, (c. h.) Owen, Ky	120
Ottawa, Clarke, Iowa	70	Owing's Mills, Baltimore, Md	130
Ottawa,* (c. h.,) Franklin, Kans	1,700	Owingsville,* (c. h.,) Bath, Ky	120
Ottawa, Le Sueur, Minn	95	Owl Hill, Cumberland, Tenn	10
Ottawa,* Putnam, Ohio	650	Owl Prairie, Daviess, Ind	21
Ottawa, Waukesha, Wis	20	Owl Run, Fauquier, Va	46
Ottawa Lake, Monroe, Mich	52	Owosso,* Shiawassee, Mich	1,300
Otter Creek, Jersey, Ill	110	Oxbow, Jefferson, N. Y	160
Otter Creek, Jackson, Iowa	26	Oxen Hill, Prince George's, Md	12
Otter Creek, Clay, Kans	12	Oxford, Calhoun, Ala	370
Otter Creek, Jackson, Mich	18	Oxford, New Haven, Conn	120
Otter Creek, Wayne, Mo	6	Oxford, Newton, Ga	450
Otter Creek, Rutherford, N.C	14	Oxford, Henry, Ill	88
Otter Creek, Eau Claire, Wis	15	Oxford,* (c. h.,) Benton, Ind	270
Otter Lake, Pottawatomie, Kans	12	Oxford, Johnson, Iowa	80
Otter River, Worcester, Mass	220	Oxford, Scott, Ky	15
Otter Tail City, Otter Tail, Minn	18	Oxford, Oxford, Me	290
Otterville, Buchanan, Iowa	15	Oxford, Talbot, Md	79
Otterville, Cooper, Mo	400	Oxford, Worcester, Mass	680
Otto, Fulton, Ill	20	Oxford, Oakland, Mich	280
Otto, Clarke, Ind	45	Oxford, (c. h.,) Isanti, Minn	33
Otto, Pope, Minn	14	Oxford,* (c. h.,) La Fayette, Miss	2,200
Otto, Cattaraugus, N. Y	280	Oxford, Worth, Mo	44
Ottobine, Rockingham, Va	10	Oxford, Warren, N. J	470
Ottokee, (c. h.,) Fulton, Ohio	120	Oxford, Chenango, N.Y	1,200
Ottsville, Bureau, Ill	17	Oxford, (c. h.,) Granville, N. C	270
Ottsville, Bucks, Pa	37	Oxford,* Butler, Ohio	1,500
Ottumwa,* (c. h.,) Wapello, Iowa	2,100	Oxford,* Chester, Pa	1,000
Ottumwa, Coffey, Kans	140	Oxford, Cache, Utah	12
Otway, Scioto, Ohio	12	Oxford, Doddridge, W. Va	14
Otwell, Pike, Ind	43	Oxford, Marquette, Wis	96
Ouaquaga, Broome, N.Y	100	Oxford Depot, Orange, N. Y	120
Ouleout, Delaware, N. Y	24	Oxford Mills, Jones, Iowa	67
Our Town, Sheboygan, Wis	21	Oxford Valley, Bucks, Pa	45
Ouslie's Gap, Cabell, W. Va	12	Oyster, Lewis, Mo	16
Outlaw's Bridge, Duplin, N. C	12	Oyster Bay, Queens, N. Y	430

* Money-order office.

PAL   PAN

Oysterville, (*c. h.,*) Pacific, Wash....	$54	Palestine, Johnson, Iowa	$35
Ozark, Dale, Ala....................	12	Palestine, Pickaway, Ohio.........	20
Ozark, (*c. h.,*) Franklin, Ark.......	300	Palestine, Lewis, Tenn.............	10
Ozark, Jackson, Iowa....	14	*Palestine,* (*c. h.,*) Anderson, Tex....	600
Ozark, Allen, Kans	12	Palestine, Greenbrier, W. Va.......	18
Ozark, (*c. h.,*) Christian, Mo........	130	Palisade, Lander, Nev.............	12
Ozark, Monroe, Ohio.....	22	Palisades, Rockland, N. Y	89
Ozaukee,* (*c. h.,*) Ozaukee, Wis.....	810	Pallas, Green, Mo.................	3
Ozawkie, Jefferson, Kans...........	75	Pallas, Snyder, Pa......	12
		Palm, Montgomery, Pa.............	17
P.		Palma, Marshall, Ky......	27
		Palmer, Christian, Ill.............	12
Paces, Metcalfe, Ky...............	20	Palmer,* Hampden, Mass...........	990
Pacheco, Contra Costa, Cal	320	Palmer's Springs, Mecklenburgh,	
Pacific, Franklin, Mo..............	290	Va..............................	6
Pacific, Franklin, N. C......	54	Palmersville, Allegheny, Pa.......	62
Pacific, Columbia, Wis......	18	Palmetto, Pickens, Ala	7
Pacific City, Mills, Iowa...........	42	Palmetto, Campbell, Ga.........	260
Packard, Vinton, Ohio......	12	Palmetto, Bedford, Tenn....... ...	32
Packer, Jefferson, Pa.............	19	Palmyra, Macoupin, Ill..........	160
Pack's Ferry, Monroe, W. Va........	11	Palmyra, Harrison, Ind	54
Pack's Mills, Sanilac, Mich........	9	Palmyra, Warren, Iowa......	120
Packsville, Clarendon, S. C........	25	Palmyra, Somerset, Me............	51
Packwaukee, Marquette, Wis.......	58	Palmyra, Lenawee, Mich	150
Pacolett Depot, Spartanburgh, S. C.	34	*Palmyra,** (*c. h.,*) Marion, Mo.......	1,500
Pactolus, Pitt, N. C......	12	Palmyra, Otoe, Nebr..............	26
Paddock's Grove, Madison, Ill......	25	Palmyra, Burlington, N. J	77
Paddy's Run, Butler, Ohio........	60	Palmyra,* Wayne, N. Y	2,200
Padonia, Brown, Kans......	61	Palmyra, Portage, Ohio..........	120
Padoria, Crawford, Ind............	4	Palmyra, Lebanon, Pa.............	240
Padua, McLean, Ill...... ...., ...	51	*Palmyra,* (*c. h.,*) Fluvanna, Va.....	100
Paducah,* (*c. h.,*) McCracken, Ky...	2,800	Palmyra,* Jefferson, Wis...........	460
Page City, Page, Iowa....	18	Palo, Marion, Ala.................	12
Pagetown, Morrow, Ohio.........	59	Palo, Linn, Iowa..................	94
Pahaquarry, Warren, N. J........	1	Palo, Ionia, Mich.................	120
Paincourtville, Assumption, La....	24	Palo Alto, Louisa, Iowa	12
Paine's Hollow, Herkimer, N. Y....	41	Palo Alto, Neosho, Kans..........	12
Paine's Point, Ogle, Ill...........	58	Palo Alto, Chickasaw, Miss........	45
Painesville,* (*c. h.,*) Lake, Ohio.....	2,800	Palo Alto, Seneca, Ohio	16
Paineville, Amelia, Va......	40	Palo Alto, Schuylkill, Pa.........	12
Paint, Highland, Ohio............	25	Palo Alto, Lawrence, Tenn........	20
Paint Creek, Washtenaw, Mich....	16	Palo Alto, Highland, Va...........	3
Paint Creek, Kanawha, W. Va.....	12	Paloma, Adams, Ill................	42
Painted Post, Steuben, N. Y........	590	*Palo Pinto,* (*c. h.,*) Palo Pinto, Tex.	20
Painter Creek, Darke, Ohio........	21	Palos, Cook, Ill....	25
Painterhood, Howard, Kans.......	12	Pamelia Four Corners, Jefferson,	
Paintersville, Greene, Ohio.......	12	N. Y............................	69
Paint Lick, Garrard, Ky...........	72	Pamlico, Craven, N. C.............	12
Paint Rock, Jackson, Ala..........	41	Pamplin's Depot, Appomattox, Va.	200
Paintsville, (*c. h.,*) Johnson, Ky.....	59	Pana,* Christian, Ill.............	1,600
Paint Valley, Holmes, Ohio........	12	Panaca, Washington, Utah	59
Paisley, Otoe, Nebr...............	12	Panama, Lancaster, Nebr..........	12
Palatine, Cook, Ill...............	300	Panama, Chautauqua, N. Y........	230
Palatine, Salem, N. J.............	49	Panamore Hill, Scriven, Ga........	16
Palatine, Marion, W. Va...........	120	Pancoastburgh, Fayette, Ohio	41
Palatine] Bridge, Montgomery, N. Y.	170	Pandora, Johnson, Tenn...........	5
Palenvile, Greene, N. Y...........	140	Pan Handle, Brooke, W. Va	38
Palermo, Edgar, Ill......	18	Panoche, Fresno, Cal.............	12
Palermo, Doniphan, Kans	79	*Panola,* (*c. h.,*) Panola, Miss........	230
Palermo, Waldo, Me	120	Panola Station, Woodford, Ill......	120
Palermo, Oswego, N. Y......	87	*Panora,** (*c. h.,*) Guthrie, Iowa	170
Palermo, Carroll, Ohio......	12	Pantego, Beaufort, N. C	44
Palermo Centre, Waldo, Me........	38	Panther Creek, Daviess, Ky	3
Palestine, Columbia, Ark..........	18	Panther Creek, Yadkin, N. C.......	12
Palestine,* Crawford, Ill..........	210	Panther Rock, Forest, Pa.........	12
Palestine, Kosciusko, Ind..........	57	Panther Springs, Jefferson, Tenn...	30

PAR   PAT

Panton, Addison, Vt	$24
Paola,* (c. h.,) Miami, Kans	1,900
Paoli, (c. h.,) Orange, Ind	360
Paoli, Chester, Pa	50
Paoli, Dane, Wis	58
Papakating, Sussex, N. J	100
Papalote, Bee, Tex	12
Pa Pa Me, Oceana, Mich	6
Paper Mills, Baltimore, Md	32
Papillion, Sarpy, Nebr	12
Papinsville, Bates, Mo	270
Paraclifta, Sevier, Ark	150
Paradise, Stanislaus, Cal	200
Paradise, Coles, Ill	18
Paradise, Muhlenburgh, Ky	10
Paradise, Clay, Mo	10
Paradise, Lancaster, Pa	130
Paradise, Cache, Utah	17
Paradise Valley, Monroe, Pa	13
Paragon, Morgan, Ind	12
Paragonah, Iron, Utah	39
Paraje, Socorro, N. Mex	40
Parallel, Riley, Kans	23
Pardee, Atchison, Kans	93
Pardeeville, Columbia, Wis	160
Parham's Store, Sussex, Va	12
Paris,* (c. h.,) Edgar, Ill	1,800
Paris, Jennings, Ind	130
Paris, Linn, Iowa	23
Paris,* (c. h.,) Bourbon, Ky	2,000
Paris,* (c. h.,) Oxford, Me	420
Paris, Mecosta, Mich	91
Paris,* (c. h.,) Monroe, Mo	720
Paris, Oneida, N. Y	120
Paris, Stark, Ohio	81
Paris, Washington, Pa	84
Paris,* (c. h.,) Henry, Tenn	800
Paris,* (c. h.,) Lamar, Tex	400
Paris, Rich, Utah	24
Paris, Fauquier, Va	50
Paris, Kenosha, Wis	38
Parish, Oswego, N. Y	130
Parishville, St. Lawrence, N. Y	260
Parishville Centre, St. Lawrence, N. Y	22
Paris Landing, Henry, Tenn	76
Parisville, Portage, Ohio	46
Park, Greene, Ind	10
Park, Barren, Ky	19
Park, St. Joseph, Mich	10
Parker, Randolph, Ind	72
Parker, Montgomery, Kans	170
Parker's Bluff, Anderson, Tex	12
Parkersburgh, Richland, Ill	92
Parkersburgh, Montgomery, Ind	42
Parkersburgh, Butler, Iowa	460
Parkersburgh,* (c. h.,) Wood, W. Va.	2,200
Parker's Head, Sagadahoc, Me	110
Parker's Settlement, Posey, Ind	18
Parker's Store, Hart, Ga	12
Parker's Store, Giles, Tenn	5
Parkersville, Morris, Kans	12
Parkersville, Bates, Mo	38
Parkersville, Chester, Pa	57
Parkesburgh, Chester, Pa	640
Parkinson's Landing, Hardin, Ill	34

Park Lane, Litchfield, Conn	$24
Parkman, Piscataquis, Me	91
Parkman, Geauga, Ohio	440
Park Ridge, Bergen, N. J	12
Parks, Scott, Ark	12
Parks, Edgefield, S. C	6
Park's Corners, Boone, Ill	120
Park's Creek, Bradford, Pa	12
Park's Grove, St. Clair, Mo	30
Park's Mills, Franklin, Ohio	6
Park's Store, Jackson, Ala	12
Parksville, Boyle, Ky	82
Parksville, Sullivan, N. Y	100
Parksville, Polk, Tenn	21
Parkton, Baltimore, Md	120
Parkville, Parke, Ind	16
Parkville, St. Joseph, Mich	140
Parkville, Platte, Mo	230
Parkville, Kings, N. Y	47
Parkwood, Indiana, Pa	12
Parma,* Jackson, Mich	800
Parma, Monroe, N. Y	120
Parma, Cuyahoga, Ohio	57
Parma Centre, Monroe, N. Y	78
Parmleysville, Wayne, Ky	14
Parnassus, Westmoreland, Pa	65
Parnassus, Marlborough, S. C	10
Parnassus, Augusta, Va	35
Parowan, (c. h.,) Iron, Utah	130
Parrish, Franklin, Ill	10
Parrish, Des Moines, Iowa	22
Parrottsville, Cocke, Tenn	46
Parryville, Carbon, Pa	210
Parshallville, Livingston, Mich	52
Parsippany, Morris, N. J	94
Parsonfield, York, Me	39
Parson's Seminary, Travis, Tex	12
Partello, Calhoun, Mich	33
Partlow's, Spottsylvania, Va	23
Partridge, Letcher, Ky	4
Partridge Island, Delaware, N. Y	12
Pascagoula, Jackson, Miss	200
Pascoag, Providence, R. I	320
Paskack, Bergen, N. J	70
Paso Robles, San Luis Obispo, Cal.	12
Passadumkeag, Penobscot, Me	85
Passaic, Passaic, N. J	1,000
Passaic Valley, Morris, N. J	47
Pass Christian, Harrison, Miss	560
Passe de Terre, Stevens, Minn	12
Passumpsic, Caledonia, Vt	190
Pastoria, Jefferson, Ark	18
Pataskala, Licking, Ohio	220
Patch Grove, Grant, Wis	160
Patchin, Erie, N. Y	29
Patchinsville, Clearfield, Pa	25
Patchogue,* Suffolk, N. Y	530
Paterson,* (c. h.,) Passaic, N. J	3,000
Patesville, Hancock, Ky	7
Patmos, Mahoning, Ohio	21
Patoka, Marion, Ill	180
Patoka, Gibson, Ind	320
Patrick C. H., Patrick, Va.	40
Patricksburgh, Owen, Ind	64
Patrick Springs, Patrick, Va	5
Patriot, Switzerland, Ind	200

* Money-order office.

PAY

Patriot, Decatur, Iowa	$12
Patriot, Gallia, Ohio	33
Patriot, Wayne, Tenn	12
Patroon, Shelby, Tex	12
Pattagumpus, Penobscot, Me	9
Patten, Penobscot, Me	350
Pattenburgh, Hunterdon, N. J	32
Patten's Mill, Washington, Ohio	17
Patten's Mills, Washington, N. Y	24
Patterson, Nevada, Cal	33
Patterson, Wayne, Mo	110
Patterson, Putnam, N. Y	290
Patterson, Caldwell, N. C	33
Patterson, Hardin, Ohio	180
Patterson, Juniata, Pa	300
Patterson's Bluff, Johnson, Ark	12
Patterson's Depot, Mineral, W. Va	20
Patterson's Mills, Ionia, Mich	56
Patterson's Mills, Washington, Pa	69
Patterson's Store, Alamance, N. C	7
Pattersonville, St. Mary's, La	140
Patton, Bollinger, Mo	24
Pattonsburgh, Daviess, Mo	80
Patton's Home, Rutherford, N. C	4
Pattonsville, Scott, Va	8
Pattonville, Bedford, Pa	74
Patty's Mill, Lyon, Kans	12
Patuxent, Anne Arundel, Md	80
Paul, Benton, Iowa	12
Paulding, (c h.,) Jasper, Miss	96
*Paulding,** (c h.,)* Paulding, Ohio	200
Paulina, Warren, N. J	31
Paulinville, Yuba, Cal	40
Paulsborough, Gloucester, N. J	130
Paul's Cross Roads, Essex, Va	15
Paulton, Westmoreland, Pa	12
Paulville, Adair, Mo	73
Paupac, Pike, Pa	14
Pavia, Bedford, Pa	12
Pavilion, Kendall, Ill	22
Pavilion, Kalamazoo, Mich	51
Pavilion, Genesee, N. Y	91
Pavilion Centre, Genesee, N. Y	42
Pawlet, Rutland, Vt	330
Pawling, Dutchess, N. Y	400
Pawling, Chester, Pa	71
Pawnee, Sangamon, Ill	75
Pawnee, Bourbon, Kans	16
*Pawnee City,** (c. h.,)* Pawnee, Nebr.	500
Paw Paw, Miami, Ind	12
*Paw Paw,** (c. h.,)* Van Buren, Mich	1,400
Paw Paw, Morgan, W. Va	90
Paw Paw Ford, Roane, Tenn	14
Paw Paw Grove, Lee, Ill	130
Pawselin, Wabashaw, Minn	12
Pawtucket,** Providence, R. I	3,000
Pawtuxet, Providence, R. I	100
Pawtuxett, Wakulla, Fla	6
Paxinos, Northumberland, Pa	54
*Paxton,** (c. h.,)* Ford, Ill	1,500
Paxton, Harrison, Ky	4
Paxton, Worcester, Mass	180
Paxton, Dauphin, Pa	29
Paxton's, Sullivan, Ind	35
Paxton's Store, Pike, Mo	12
Pay Down, Maries, Mo	5

PEL

Payetteville, Ada, Idaho	$12
Payne, Paulding, Ohio	5
Payne's Corners, Trumbull, Ohio	10
Payne's Depot, Scott, Ky	21
Paynesville, Stearns, Minn	110
Paynesville, Pike, Mo	92
Paynesville, Milwaukee, Wis	25
Payneville, Meade, Ky	12
Payson, Adams, Ill	230
Payson, Utah, Utah	120
Peabody, Essex, Mass	1,700
Peace Creek, (c. h.,) Polk, Fla	32
Peace Dale, Washington, R. I	290
Peacham,** Caledonia, Vt	330
Peach Bottom, York, Pa	66
Peacher's Mills, Montgomery, Tenn	36
Peachland, Osage, Mo	12
Peachville, Butler, Pa	12
Peacock's Store, Columbus, N. C	34
Peakesville, Clarke, Mo	37
Peak's Hill, Calhoun, Ala	17
Peaksville, Henry, Ga	12
Peapack, Somerset, N. J	99
Pea Ridge, Caswell, N. C	12
Pearisburgh, (c. h.,) Giles, Va	260
Pearl, Pike, Ill	12
Pearl City, Madison, Miss	24
Pearl Creek, Wyoming, N. Y	37
Pearlington, Hancock, Miss	23
Pearson's Corner, Kent, Del	12
Peart's Eddy, Armstrong, Pa	41
Peasleeville, Clinton, N. Y	17
Pebble Creek, Dodge, Nebr	32
Pecan Point, Mississippi, Ark	50
Pecatonica,** Winnebago, Ill	770
Peck, Sanilac, Mich	84
Pecksburgh, Hendricks, Ind	26
Peck's Run, Upshur, W. Va	15
Peckville, Luzerne, Pa	64
Peconic, Suffolk, N. Y	180
Peculiar, Cass, Mo	92
Pedee, Cedar, Iowa	37
Pedee, Green, Wis	7
Peden, Kemper, Miss	12
Pedricktown, Salem, N. J	54
Pee Dee, Marion, S. C	12
Peekskill,** Westchester, N. Y	2,400
Peeled Oak, Bath, Ky	12
Peel Tree, Barbour, W. Va	49
Pee Pee, Pike, Ohio	12
Peerysville, (c. h.,) McDowell, W. Va.	5
*Pekin,** (c. h.,)* Tazewell, Ill	2,300
Pekin, Washington, Ind	12
Pekin, Jessamine, Ky	100
Pekin, Niagara, N. Y	180
Pekin, Montgomery, N. C	13
Pekin, Putnam, Tenn	12
Pekin, Clark, Wash	8
Pelahatchee Depot, Rankin, Miss	12
Peletier's Mills, Carteret, N. C	6
Pelham, Hampshire, Mass	11
Pelham, Hillsborough, N. H	52
Pelham, Westchester, N. Y	350
Pelham, Caswell, N. C	10
Pelham, Grundy, Tenn	12
Pella, Dearborn, Ind	12

* Money-order office.

PEN

Pella,* Marion, Iowa...	$1,200
Pella, Shawanaw, Wis	8
Pellonia, Massac, Ill	15
Pellville, Hancock, Ky	27
Pemaquid, Lincoln, Me	130
Pemberton, Burlington, N. J	280
Pemberton, Shelby, Ohio	73
Pemberton, Goochland, Va	45
Pemberville, Wood, Ohio	16
Pembina, (c. h.,) Pembina, Dak	750
Pembroke, Christian, Ky	210
Pembroke*, Washington, Me	390
Pembroke, Plymouth, Mass	59
Pembroke, Merrimack, N. H	82
Pembroke, Genesee, N. Y	130
Pembroke, Giles, Va	13
Pence's Mills, Warren, Ohio	18
Pendarvis, Wayne, Ga	12
Pendleton, Arkansas, Ark	12
Pendleton,* Madison, Ind	480
Pendleton, Henry, Ky	31
Pendleton, Warren, Mo	110
Pendleton, Niagara, N. Y	40
Pendleton, Putnam, Ohio	37
Pendleton, (c. h.,) Umatilla, Oreg	12
Pendleton, Anderson, S. C	380
Pendleton Centre, Niagara, N. Y	14
Pendleton Hill, Windham, Conn	30
Penfield, Greene, Ga	240
Penfield, Monroe, N. Y	220
Penfield, Lorain, Ohio	83
Penfield, Clearfield, Pa	99
Penhook, Franklin, Va	12
Penick, Marion, Ky	24
Peninsula, Summit, Ohio	140
Penllyn, Montgomery, Pa	110
Penn, Lancaster, Pa	13
Pennellville, Oswego, N. Y	28
Penn Hall, Centre, Pa	72
Penn Haven, Carbon, Pa	310
Penninger, Union, Ill	12
Pennington, Mercer, N. J	500
Pennington, Houston, Tex	20
Pennington Point, McDonough, Ill.	21
Pennington's Mills, Pulaski, Ark	9
Penningtonville, Chester, Pa	340
Penn Line, Crawford, Pa	70
Penn Line, Keweenaw, Mich	74
Penn Run, Indiana, Pa	85
Pennsborough, Ritchie, W. Va	170
Pennsburgh, Montgomery, Pa	140
Penn's Creek, Snyder, Pa	42
Penn's Grove, Salem, N. J	130
Penn's Park, Bucks, Pa	48
Penn's Square, Montgomery, Pa	19
Penn's Station, Westmoreland, Pa	200
Penn's Store, Patrick, Va	17
Pennsville, Salem, N. J	12
Pennsville, Morgan, Ohio	110
Pennsville, Fayette, Pa	55
Pennville, Jay, Ind	230
Pennville, Sullivan, Mo	12
Penn Yan, (c. h.,) Yates, N. Y	2,500
Penobscot, Hancock, Me	45
Penola, Caroline, Va	12
Pensacola, (c. h.,) Escambia, Fla	1,600

PER

Pensaukie, Oconto, Wis	$160
Pent Water,* Oceana, Mich	960
Pentz, Butte, Cal	34
Peoa, Summit, Utah	12
Peola Mills, Madison, Va	12
Peoli, Tuscarawas, Ohio	30
Peoria, (c. h.,) Peoria, Ill	4,000
Peoria, Mahaska, Iowa	39
Peoria, Franklin, Kans	91
Peoria, Wyoming, N. Y	64
Peoria, Linn, Oreg	66
Peoria, Hill, Tex	14
Peoria City, Polk, Iowa	85
Peosta, Dubuque, Iowa	110
Peotone, Will, Ill	310
Pepacton, Delaware, N. Y	17
Pepin, Pepin, Wis	100
Pepperell, Middlesex, Mass	310
Peppertown, Franklin, Ind	28
Pepperville, Butler, Nebr	12
Pequabuck, Litchfield, Conn	85
Pequea, Lancaster, Pa	55
Peralta, Valencia, N. Mex	18
Perch Lake, Blue Earth, Minn	10
Perch River, Jefferson, N. Y	46
Percival, Fremont, Iowa	20
Percy, Carbon, Wyo	12
Perdenales, Travis, Tex	11
Perin's Mills, Clermont, Ohio	44
Perkins' Mills, Braxton, W. Va	1
Perkinsville, Madison, Ind	47
Perkinsville, Steuben, N. Y	56
Perkinsville, Burke, N. C	3
Perkinsville,* Windsor, Vt	200
Perkinsville, Goochland, Va	15
Perkiomenville, Montgomery, Pa	20
Perote, Bullock, Ala	41
Perrine, Mercer, Pa	39
Perrineville, Monmouth, N. J	91
Perrinsville, Wayne, Mich	64
Perry, (c. h.,) Houston, Ga	420
Perry, Pike, Ill	470
Perry, Dallas, Iowa	250
Perry, Jefferson, Kans	230
Perry, Washington, Me	84
Perry, Shiawassee, Mich	56
Perry, Ralls, Mo	120
Perry, Wyoming, N. Y	780
Perry, Lake, Ohio	250
Perry, Forest, Pa	41
Perry, Dane, Wis	100
Perry Centre, Wyoming, N. Y	140
Perry City, Schuyler, N. Y	58
Perrydale, Polk, Oreg	12
Perrymansville, Harford, Md	200
Perryopolis, Fayette, Pa	110
Perry's Bridge, Vermillion, La	10
Perrysburgh, Miami, Ind	43
Perrysburgh, Cattaraugus, N. Y	200
Perrysburgh, (c. h.,) Wood, Ohio	880
Perry's Mills, Clinton, N. Y	94
Perry Springs, Pike, Ill	7
Perrysville, Vermillion, Ind	350
Perrysville, Allegheny, Pa	81
Perrysville, Washington, R. I	14
Perryton, Licking, Ohio	36

* Money-order office.

PET   PIC

Perryville, **Perry**, Ala	$12	Pettis, Crawford, Pa	$9
Perryville, (*c. h.,*) Perry, Ark	110	Pettisville, Fulton, Ohio	140
Perryville, Boyle, Ky	210	Pettit, Tippecanoe, Ind	50
Perryville, Cecil, Md	96	Pettysville, Livingston, Mich	12
Perryville, (*c. h.,*) Perry, Mo	260	Pevely, Jefferson, Mo	150
Perryville, Hunterdon, N. J	24	Pewamo, Ionia, Mich	300
Perryville, Madison, N. Y	74	Pewaukee, Waukesha, Wis	250
Perryville, Ashland, Ohio	280	Pewee Valley, Oldham, Ky	130
Perryville, Decatur, Tenn	12	Peytona, Boone, W. Va	23
Persia, Cattaraugus, N. Y	16	Peyton's, Adams, Ill	4
Persia, Hawkins, Tenn	12	Peytonsburgh, Pittsylvania, Va	10
Personville, Venango, Pa	12	Peytonsville, Little River, Ark	12
Personville, Limestone, Tex	8	Peytonsville, Williamson, Tenn	49
Perth, Jefferson, Miss	12	Pharisburgh, Union, Ohio	16
Perth, Fulton, N. Y	42	Pharsalia, Chenango, N. Y	42
Perth Amboy,* Middlesex, N. J	930	Pheasant Branch, Dane, Wis	29
Peru,* (*c. h.,*) La Salle, Ill	1,500	Phelps, Lawrence, Mo	12
Peru,* (*c. h.,*) Miami, Ind	2,000	Phelps, Ontario, N. Y	1,100
Peru, Madison, Iowa	22	Phelps City,* Atchison, Mo	280
Peru, Howard, Kans	12	Phelps Mills, Clinton, Pa	19
Peru, Oldham, Ky	26	Phenix, Ashtabula, Ohio	8
Peru, Oxford, Me	43	Phenix, Kent, R. I	450
Peru, Berkshire, Mass	61	Philadelphia, Hancock, Ind	71
Peru, Nemaha, Nebr	200	*Philadelphia*, (*c. h.,*) Neshoba, Miss.	54
Peru, Clinton, N. Y	280	Philadelphia, Marion, Mo	58
Peru, Huron, Ohio	88	Philadelphia, Jefferson, N. Y	240
Peru, Bennington, Vt	49	*Philadelphia*,* (*c. h.,*) Philadelphia,	
Peru, Hardy, W. Va	5	Pa	4,000
Peru, Dunn, Wis	32	Philadelphia, Monroe, Tenn	170
Peru Mills, Juniata, Pa	31	Philander, Gentry, Mo	18
Peruville, Tompkins, N. Y	14	Philanthropy, Butler, Ohio	24
Pescadero, San Mateo, Cal	160	*Philippi*, (*c. h.,*) Barbour, W. Va	130
Peshtigo,* Oconto, Wis	380	Philipsburgh, Deer Lodge, Mont	43
Pesotum, Champaign, Ill	150	Philipsburgh, Jefferson, Ohio	96
Petaluma,* Sonoma, Cal	1,500	Philipsburgh, Centre, Pa	1,100
Peterborough,* Hillsborough, N.H.	1,000	Philip's Mills, Indiana, Pa	84
Peterborough, Madison, N. Y	310	Philipston, Clarion, Pa	58
Petersburgh, Klamath, Cal	12	Phillips,* Franklin, Me	420
Petersburgh,* Menard, Ill	1,000	Phillip's Bayou, Phillips, Ark	12
Petersburgh,* (*c. h.,*) Pike, Ind	350	Phillipsburgh,* Warren, N. J	1,400
Petersburgh, Leavenworth, Kans	18	Phillip's Creek, Allegany, N. Y	18
Petersburgh, Boone, Ky	96	Phillipsport, Sullivan, N. Y	220
Petersburgh, Monroe, Mich	230	Phillipston, Worcester, Mass	100
Petersburgh, Jackson, Minn	6	Phillipstown, White, Ill	62
Petersburgh, Cape May, N. J	80	Philmont, Columbia, N. Y	220
Petersburgh, Rensselaer, N. Y	75	Philo, Champaign, Ill	250
Petersburgh, Mahoning, Ohio	140	Philo, Muskingum, Ohio	48
Petersburgh, Butler, Pa	20	Philomath, Benton, Oreg	12
Petersburgh, Lincoln, Tenn	47	Philomont, Loudoun, Va	40
Petersburgh, Lavaca, Tex	22	Philopolis, Baltimore, Md	280
Petersburgh, Millard, Utah	12	*Phil Sheridan*, (*c. h.,*) Wallace, Kans.	220
Petersburgh,* Dinwiddie, Va	3,900	Phippsburgh, Sagadahoc, Me	86
Peter's Creek, Stokes, N. C	12	Phœnicia, Ulster, N. Y	97
Peter's Creek, Lancaster, Pa	30	Phœnix, Yavapai, Ariz	12
Petersham, Worcester, Mass	396	Phœnix, Douglas, Ill	12
Peter's Landing, Perry, Tenn	12	Phœnix, Baltimore, Md	81
Peterson, (*c. h.,*) Clay, Iowa	130	Phœnix, Keweenaw, Mich	160
Peterstown, Monroe, W. Va	63	Phœnix, Oswego, N. Y	550
Petersville, Frederick, Md	77	Phœnix, Jackson, Oreg	35
Petersville, Northampton, Pa	47	Phœnix, Armstrong, Pa	28
Petit Jean, Yell, Ark	10	Phœnix Mills, Otsego, N. Y	12
Petra, Saline, Mo	70	Phœnixville, Windham, Conn	49
Petroleum Centre,* Venango, Pa	2,600	Phœnixville,* Chester, Pa	1,700
Petrolia, Humboldt, Cal	62	Piasa, Macoupin, Ill	74
Petroliopolis, Los Angeles, Cal	93	Picacho, Monterey, Cal	12
Petrolium, Vernon, Wis	4	Pickard's Mill, Clinton, Ind	16

* Money-order office.

PIK   PIN

Pickens C. H., Pickens, S. C	$88	Pikeville, Wayne, N. C	$22
Pickens Station, Holmes, Miss	34	Pikeville, Darke, Ohio	19
Pickensville, Pickens, Ala	320	Pikeville, (c. h.,) Bledsoe, Tenn	100
Pickensville, Pickens, S. C	13	Piland's Store, Ozark, Mo	12
Pickerel, Greene, Mo	12	Pilatka,* (c. h.,) Putnam, Fla	530
Pickereltown, Logan, Ohio	60	Pilcher, Belmont, Ohio	24
Pickering, Chester, Pa	77	Pile Falls, Fayette, Pa	24
Pickerington, Fairfield, Ohio	36	Pilgrim's Rest, Fayette, Ala	12
Pickwick, Winona, Minn	58	Pillar Point, Jefferson, N. Y	130
Picture Rocks, Lycoming, Pa	90	Pillow, Dauphin, Pa	67
Piedmont,* Mineral, W. Va	700	Pilot, Vermilion, Ill	63
Piedmont, Uintah, Wyo	12	Pilot, Montgomery, Va	12
Piedmont Springs, Burke, N. C	12	Pilot Centre, Kankakee, Ill	12
Piedmont Station, Fauquier, Va	210	Pilot Grove, Newton, Ind	37
Piedra Blanca, San Luis Obispo, Cal	12	Pilot Grove, Lee, Iowa	68
Pierce, Will, Ill	13	Pilot Grove, Faribault, Minn	11
Pierce, Callaway, Mo	12	Pilot Grove, Cooper, Mo	60
Pierce, Stark, Ohio	38	Pilot Grove, Grayson, Tex	140
Pierce, Armstrong, Pa	26	Pilot Hill, (c. h.,) Fulton, Ark	37
Pierce, Kewaunee, Wis	12	Pilot Hill, El Dorado, Cal	49
Pierce City, (c. h.,) Shoshone, Idaho	38	Pilot Hill, Washington, Tenn	14
Pierce City, Lawrence, Mo	12	Pilot Knob, Crawford, Ind	19
Pierce's, Goochland, Va	11	Pilot Knob, Todd, Ky	7
Pierce Station, Weakley, Tenn	68	Pilot Knob,* Iron, Mo	280
Pierceton,* Kosciusko, Ind	740	Pilot Knob, Greene, Tenn	4
Piercetown, Anderson, S. C	12	Pilot Knob, Adams, Wis	14
Piercerille, (c. h.,) Hernando, Fla	80	Pilot Mound, Boone, Iowa	21
Pierceville, De Kalb, Ill	17	Pilot Mound, Fillmore, Minn	61
Pierceville, Ripley, Ind	70	Pilot Mountain, Stokes, N. C	8
Pierceville, Van Buren, Iowa	24	Pilot Point, Denton, Tex	100
Pierceville, Wyoming, Pa	24	Pilot Rock, Cherokee, Iowa	32
Piermont, Grafton, N. H	120	Pilot Rock, Umatilla, Oreg	12
Piermont, Rockland, N. Y	420	Pima Village, Yavapai, Ariz	10
Pierpont, Ashtabula, Ohio	160	Pimento, Vigo, Ind	76
Pierrepont, St. Lawrence, N. Y	70	Pinckney, Livingston, Mich	350
Pierrepont Manor, Jefferson, N. Y	160	Pinckney, Warren, Mo	11
Pierron, Madison, Ill	12	Pinckney, Lewis, N. Y	28
Pierson, Montcalm, Mich	72	Pinckneyville, Clay, Ala	20
Piffard, Livingston, N. Y	39	Pinckneyville, (c. h.,) Perry, Ill	230
Pigeon Cove, Essex, Mass	220	Pine, Linn, Oreg	6
Pigeon Creek, Butler, Pa	12	Pine Bend, Dakota, Minn	26
Pigeon Creek Centre, Jackson, Wis	12	Pine Bluff,* (c. h.,) Jefferson, Ark	1,900
Pigeon Forge, Sevier, Tenn	8	Pine Bluff, Callaway, Ky	10
Pigeon Hill, Union, Ark	35	Pine Bluff, Chickasaw, Miss	12
Pigeon River, Lake, Minn	12	Pine Bluff, Pulaski, Mo	10
Pigeon River, Haywood, N. C	21	Pine Bluff, Warren, Tenn	8
Pigeon Run, Campbell, Va	22	Pine Bluff, Dane, Wis	38
Pigeon Roost, Choctaw, Miss	12	Pine Bluff, Laramie, Wyo	12
Pig River, Franklin, Va	14	Pine Brook, Morris, N. J	32
Pike, Muscatine, Iowa	9	Pine Bush, Orange, N. Y	120
Pike,* Wyoming, N. Y	500	Pine City, Pine, Minn	12
Pike, Bradford, Pa	13	Pine Creek, Butte, Cal	12
Pike Mills, Potter, Pa	18	Pine Creek, Calhoun, Mich	27
Pike Pond, Sullivan, N. Y	74	Pine Creek, Laclede, Mo	12
Pike Rapids, Morrison, Minn	2	Pine Creek, Schuyler, N. Y	18
Pike Run, Washington, Pa	41	Pine Creek, Tioga, Pa	8
Pike's Peak, Brown, Ind	8	Pine Flats, Indiana, Pa	32
Pike's Peak, Deer Lodge, Mont	12	Pine Glen, Centre, Pa	33
Pike Station, Wayne, Ohio	130	Pine Grove, Amador, Cal	53
Pikesville, Baltimore, Md	210	Pine Grove, Clarke, Ky	45
Piketon, (c. h.,) Pike, Ky	81	Pine Grove, Tuscola, Mich	50
Piketon, Stoddard, Mo	43	Pine Grove, Esmeralda, Nev	12
Piketon, (c. h.,) Pike, Ohio	170	Pine Grove, Schuyler, N. Y	16
Pike Township, Berks, Pa	14	Pine Grove, Montgomery, N. C	12
Pikeville, (c. h.,) Marion, Ala	39	Pine Grove, Gallia, Ohio	69
Pikeville, Pike, Ind	10	Pine Grove, Schuylkill, Pa	470

* Money-order office.

PIN

Pine Grove, Henderson, Tex	$5
Pine Grove, Wetzel, W. Va	13
Pine Grove, Brown, Wis	4
Pine Grove Mills, Van Buren, Mich.	20
Pine Grove Mills, Centre, Pa	160
Pine Hill, Wilcox, Ala	12
Pine Hill, Ashley, Ark	12
Pine Hill, Sanilac, Mich	18
Pine Hill, Shannon, Mo	12
Pine Hill, Ulster, N. Y	56
Pine Hill, York, Pa	11
Pine Hill, Washington, R. I	6
Pine Hill, Rusk, Tex	50
Pine Hill, Jackson, Wis	21
Pine House Depot, Edgefield, S. C.	12
Pine Island, Goodhue, Minn	170
Pine Island, Orange, N. Y	12
Pine Knob, Iowa, Wis	7
Pine Lake, Fulton, N. Y	12
Pine Land, Meigs, Tenn	12
Pine Level, Montgomery, Ala ●	33
Pine Level, Johnston, N. C	24
Pine Log, Bartow, Ga	29
Pine Meadow, Litchfield, Conn	230
Pine Mills, Muscatine, Iowa	12
Pine Mountain, Campbell, Tenn	8
Pine Plains, Dutchess, N. Y	420
Pine Ridge, Winn, La	6
Pine Ridge, Lexington, S. C	12
Pine River, Lake, Mich	12
Pine River, Washara, Wis	110
Pine Run, Genesee, Mich	140
Pine's Bridge, Westchester, N. Y	35
Pine Springs, Rowan, Ky	12
Pine Station, Clinton, Pa	34
Pine Summit, Columbia, Pa	12
Pinetown, Cherokee, Tex	10
Pine Township, Armstrong, Pa	9
Pine Tree, Chesterfield, S. C	5
Pine Tree, Upshur, Tex	12
Pine Tucky, Perry, Ala	9
Pine Valley, Yalabusha, Miss	12
Pine Valley, Chemung, N. Y	97
Pine Valley, Washington, Utah	17
Pine Village, Warren, Ind	62
Pine View, Fauquier, Va	21
Pineville, Izard, Ark	44
Pineville, Pike, Ill	12
Pineville, (c. h.,) Josh Bell, Ky	12
Pineville, (c. h.,) McDonald, Mo	92
Pineville, Mecklenburgh, N. C.	54
Pineville, Bucks, Pa	50
Pine Wood, Hickman, Tenn	64
Pine Woods, Madison, N. Y	54
Piney Creek, Carroll, Md	8
Pine Creek, Alleghany, N. C	12
Piney Flats, Sullivan, Tenn	6
Piney Grove, Prince George, Va.	10
Piney Point, Saint Mary's, Md	12
Pingree Grove, Kane, Ill	15
Pink Hill, Jackson, Mo	74
Pink Hill, Lenoir, N. C	10
Pinkleyville, Oregon, Mo	12
Pink Prairie, Henry, Ill	25
Pinnebog, Huron, Mich	12
Pinnellville, Jones, Miss	2

PIT

Pino, Placer, Cal	$55
Pin Oak, Wayne, Ill	26
Pin Oak, Dubuque, Iowa	20
Pin Oak, Warren, Mo.	8
Pin Oak, Fayette, Tex	22
Pinos Altos, (c. h.,) Grant, N. Mex.	37
Pinson, Madison, Tenn	88
Pinto, Iron, Utah	17
Piny, Clarion, Pa	10
Pioche, Lincoln, Nev	12
Pioneer, Greene, Ill	21
Pioneer, Deer Lodge, Mont	12
Pioneer, Williams, Ohio	190
Pioneer, Venango, Pa	660
Pioneer Mills, Cabarrus, N. C	33
Pioneerville, Boise, Idaho	12
Piper City, Ford, Ill	480
Piper's Gap, Carroll, Va	5
Pipersville, Bucks, Pa	22
Pipersville, Jefferson, Wis	38
Pipestone, Berrien, Mich	36
Piqua,* Miami, Ohio	2,500
Pireway Ferry, Columbus, N. C	12
Piscataway, Prince George's, Md.	50
Pisgah, Charles, Md	9
Pisgah, Cooper, Mo	61
Pisgah, Butler, Ohio	60
Pisgah, Giles, Tenn	8
Pishon's Ferry, Kennebec, Me	62
Pitcairn, St. Lawrence, N. Y	12
Pitcher, Chenango, N. Y	150
Pitcher Springs, Chenango, N. Y	11
Pitcherville, Jo Daviess, Ill	20
Pit Hole City,* Venango, Pa	880
Pitman, Randolph, Ark	12
Pitts, Warren, Mo	10
Pittsborough, Hendricks, Ind	110
Pittsborough, (c. h.,) Calhoun, Miss.	130
Pittsborough,* (c. h.,) Chatham, N. C.	320
Pittsburgh, Johnson, Ark	12
Pittsburgh, Carroll, Ind	180
Pittsburgh, Van Buren, Iowa	45
Pittsburgh, Shiawassee, Mich	62
Pittsburgh, Hickory, Mo	10
Pittsburgh, Coos, N. H	16
Pittsburgh,* (c. h.,) Allegheny, Pa	4,000
Pittsburgh, Upshur, Tex	52
P'·t's Cross Roads, Bledsoe, Tenn	5
Pittsfield,* (c. h.,) Pike, Ill	1,200
Pittsfield, Somerset, Me	400
Pittsfield,* Berkshire, Mass	3,300
Pittsfield, Merrimack, N. H	470
Pittsfield, Otsego, N. Y	20
Pittsfield, Lorain, Ohio	56
Pittsfield, Warren, Pa	160
Pittsfield, Rutland, Vt	110
Pittsford, Hillsdale, Mich	140
Pittsford, Monroe, N. Y	520
Pittsford, Rutland, Vt	330
Pitt's Grove, Salem, N. J	100
Pitt's Point, Bullitt, Ky	54
Pittston, Kennebec, Me	410
Pittston, Luzerne, Pa	2,600
Pittstown, Hunterdon, N. J	81
Pittstown, Rensselaer, N. Y	230
Pittsville, Wicomico, Md	12

* Money-order office.

PLA

Pittsville, Johnson, Mo	$36
Pittsville, Venango, Pa	35
Pittsville, Fort Bend, Tex	12
Pittsylvania C. H., Pittsylvania, Va.	310
Placerville, (*c. h.*,) El Dorado, Cal.	1,200
Placerville, Boise, Idaho	210
Plain, Wayne, Ohio	31
Plain, Greenville, S. C	6
Plain, Sauk, Wis	19
Plain City, Weber, Utah	40
Plainfield, Windham, Conn	270
Plainfield, Will, Ill	650
Plainfield,* Hendricks, Ind	480
Plainfield, Bremer, Iowa	130
Plainfield, Hampshire, Mass	93
Plainfield, Livingston, Mich	24
Plainfield, Sullivan, N. H	120
Plainfield,* Union, N. J	2,600
Plainfield, Coshocton, Ohio	62
Plainfield, Cumberland, Pa	370
Plainfield, Washington, Vt	150
Plainfield, Waushara, Wis	170
Plain Grove, Lawrence, Pa	56
Plainsberg, Merced, Cal	12
Plainsborough, Middlesex, N. J	16
Plains of Dura, Sumter, Ga	48
Plainsville, Luzerne, Pa	100
Plain View, Macoupin, Ill	96
Plain View,* Wabashaw, Minn	600
Plain View, King and Queen, Va	12
Plainville, Hartford, Conn	650
Plainville, Daviess, Ind	27
Plainville, Norfolk, Mass	32
Plainville, Onondaga, N. Y	85
Plainville, Hamilton, Ohio	100
Plainville, Adams, Wis	22
Plainwell, Allegan, Mich	710
Plaistow, Rockingham, N. H	270
Plane No. Four, Frederick, Md	12
Plank Road, Wayne, Mich	16
Plank Road, Onondaga, N. Y	140
Plank Road, Belmont, Ohio	42
Plank Road, York, Pa	12
Plano, Kendall, Ill	810
Plano, Collin, Tex	20
Plantation No. Fourteen, Washington, Me	3
Planter's, Phillips, Ark	12
Planter's Hall, Breckinridge, Ky	10
Plantersville, Dallas, Ala	18
Plantersville, Grimes, Tex	50
Plantersville, Lunenburgh, Va	3
Plants, Meigs, Ohio	19
Plantsville, Hartford, Conn	780
Plantsville, Morgan, Ohio	20
Plaquemine, (*c. h.*,) Iberville, La	180
Plaquemine Brulee, St. Landry, La.	12
Platea, Erie, Pa	86
Plato, Iroquois, Ill	14
Plato, Pulaski, Ky	10
Plato, McLeod, Minn	10
Plato, Texas, Mo	12
Plato, Lorain, Ohio	440
Platt, Taylor, Iowa	9
Platte, Benzie, Mich	12
Platte City, (*c. h.*,) Platte, Mo	480

PLE

Plattekill, Ulster, N. Y	$27
Platte River, Buchanan, Mo	8
Platteville, Taylor, Iowa	98
Platteville, Saunders, Nebr	12
Platteville,* Grant, Wis	1,300
Plattford, Sarpy, Nebr	14
Plattsburgh, (*c. h.*,) Clinton, Mo	600
*Plattsburgh,** (*c. h.*,) Clinton, N. Y	2,500
Plattsburgh, Clark, Ohio	69
*Plattsmouth,** (*c. h.*,) Cass, Nebr	1,400
Plattsville, Fairfield, Conn	12
Plattsville, Shelby, Ohio	12
Plattville, Kendall, Ill	120
Plattville, Cambria, Pa	16
Pleasant, Switzerland, Ind	56
Pleasant, Kent, Mich	27
Pleasant, Claiborne, Tenn	10
Pleasant Brook, Otsego, N. Y	61
Pleasant Corners, Franklin, Ohio	16
Pleasant Corners, Carbon, Pa	16
Pleasant Creek, Barbour, W. Va	23
Pleasant Dale, Hampshire, W. Va	29
Pleasant Farm, Miller, Mo	11
Pleasant Gap, Cherokee, Ala	29
Pleasant Gap, Bates, Mo	55
Pleasant Gap, Centre, Pa	43
Pleasant Gap, Pittsylvania, Va	5
Pleasant Green, Stark, Ill	23
Pleasant Green, Cooper, Mo	12
Pleasant Grove, Pickens, Ala	18
Pleasant Grove, Wayne, Ill	51
Pleasant Grove, Jasper, Ind	6
Pleasant Grove, Des Moines, Iowa	72
Pleasant Grove, Olmsted, Minn	92
Pleasant Grove, Morris, N. J	12
Pleasant Grove, Almance, N. C	12
Pleasant Grove, Lancaster, Pa	47
Pleasant Grove, Bedford, Tenn	12
Pleasant Grove, Utah, Utah	78
Pleasant Grove, Lunenburgh, Va	8
Pleasant Grove Creek, Sutter, Cal	12
Pleasant Hall, Franklin, Pa	18
Pleasant Hill, Dallas, Ala	50
Pleasant Hill, Franklin, Ark	12
Pleasant Hill, New Castle, Del	13
Pleasant Hill, Talbot, Ga	14
Pleasant Hill, Pike, Ill	62
Pleasant Hill, Montgomery, Ind	69
Pleasant Hill, Cedar, Iowa	26
Pleasant Hill, Mercer, Ky	20
Pleasant Hill,* Cass, Mo	1,500
Pleasant Hill, Saline, Nebr	35
Pleasant Hill, Northampton, N. C	72
Pleasant Hill, Miami, Ohio	150
Pleasant Hill, Lane, Oreg	22
Pleasant Hill, Lancaster, S. C	20
Pleasant Hill, Cumberland, Tenn	12
Pleasant Hill, Preston, W. Va	12
Pleasant Home, Owen, Ky	120
Pleasant Home, Putnam, Mo	9
Pleasant Hope, Polk, Mo	24
Pleasant Lake, Steuben, Ind	72
Pleasant Mills, Adams, Ind	35
Pleasant Mills, Atlantic, N. J	35
Pleasant Mound, Bond, Ill	61
Pleasant Mound, Montgomery, Tenn	3

* Money-order office.

PLE   POE

Pleasant Mounds, Blue Earth, Minn	$21	Pleasantville, Harford, Md	$61
Pleasant Mount, Panola, Miss	20	Pleasantville, Westchester, N. Y	190
Pleasant Mount, Miller, Mo	70	Pleasantville, Fairfield, Ohio	98
Pleasant Mount, Wayne, Pa	200	Pleasantville,* Venango, Pa	2,800
Pleasant Oaks, Brunswick, Va	12	Pleasureville, Henry, Ky	91
Pleasanton, Alameda, Cal	94	Plenitude, Anderson, Tex	12
Pleasanton, Decatur, Iowa	210	Plesis, Jefferson, N. Y	120
Pleasanton,* Linn, Kans	460	Plimpton, Holmes, Ohio	97
Pleasanton, Manistee, Mich	46	Pliny, Saline, Kans	12
Pleasanton, Prentiss, Miss	5	Pliny, Greenville, S. C	12
Pleasanton, Athens, Ohio	23	Plover, (c. h.,) Portage, Wis	280
Pleasanton, (c. h.,) Atascosa, Tex	14	Plowden's Mills, Sumter, S. C	5
Pleasant Park, Carroll, Mo	24	Pluckemin, Somerset, N. J	130
Pleasant Plain, Jefferson, Iowa	81	Plum, Venango, Pa	24
Pleasant Plain, Warren, Ohio	93	Plum Bayou, Jefferson, Ark	20
Pleasant Plains, Sangamon, Ill	140	Plum City, Pierce, Wis	10
Pleasant Plains, Dutchess, N. Y	20	Plum Creek, Jefferson, Kans	12
Pleasant Plains, Sullivan, Tenn	7	Plum Creek, Caldwell, Tex	20
Pleasant Prairie, Bond, Ill	20	Plumer, Venango, Pa	210
Pleasant Prairie, Muscatine, Iowa	28	Plum Grove, Butler, Kans	12
Pleasant Prairie, Martin, Minn	7	Plum Hill, Washington, Ill	26
Pleasant Prairie, Kenosha, Wis	12	Plum Hollow, Fremont, Iowa	58
Pleasant Retreat, White, Ga	11	Plummer's Landing, Fleming, Ky	9
Pleasant Retreat, Scotland, Mo	20	Plummer's Mills, Fleming, Ky	12
Pleasant Retreat, McDowell, N. C	16	Plummersville, Robeson, N. C	12
Pleasant Ridge, Greene, Ala	110	Plum River, Jo Daviess, Ill	70
Pleasant Ridge, Rock Island, Ill	18	Plumsteadville, Bucks, Pa	110
Pleasant Ridge, Greene, Ind	12	Plum Valley, Sierra, Cal	12
Pleasant Ridge, Leavenworth, Kans	50	Plum Valley, Texas, Mo	9
Pleasant Ridge, Daviess, Ky	17	Plumville, Indiana, Pa	77
Pleasant Ridge, Harrison, Mo	18	Plunkett, Sullivan, Pa	12
Pleasant Ridge, Hamilton, Ohio	76	Plymouth, Litchfield, Conn	430
Pleasant Ridge, Princess Anne, Va	12	Plymouth, Hancock, Ill	340
Pleasant Ridge, Clark, Wis	3	Plymouth,* (c. h.,) Marshall, Ind	1,500
Pleasant Run, Pottawatomie, Kans	12	Plymouth, Cerro Gordo, Iowa	38
Pleasant Run, Stanton, Nebr	16	Plymouth, Lyon, Kans	53
Pleasant Run, Hunterdon, N. J	28	Plymouth, Penobscot, Me	120
Pleasant Run, Hamilton, Ohio	6	Plymouth,* (c. h.,) Plymouth, Mass.	2,600
Pleasant Site, Franklin, Ala	29	Plymouth, Wayne, Mich	450
Pleasant Unity, Westmoreland, Pa.	100	Plymouth,* (c. h.,) Grafton, N. H.	1,000
Pleasant Vale, Pike, Ill	38	Plymouth, Chenango, N. Y	92
Pleasant Valley, El Dorado, Cal	48	Plymouth,* (c. h.,) Washington,	
Pleasant Valley, Litchfield, Conn	110	N. C	720
Pleasant Valley, Jo Daviess, Ill	26	Plymouth,* Richland, Ohio	580
Pleasant Valley, Scott, Iowa	86	Plymouth,* Luzerne, Pa	1,300
Pleasant Valley, Berrien, Mich	12	Plymouth, Windsor, Vt	130
Pleasant Valley, Sherburne, Minn	14	Plymouth, Sheboygan, Wis	370
Pleasant Valley, Wright, Mo	10	Plymouth Centre, (c. h.,) Plymouth,	
Pleasant Valley, Sussex, N. J	16	Iowa	12
Pleasant Valley, Dutchess, N. Y	200	Plymouth Meeting, Montgomery,	
Pleasant Valley, Morgan, Ohio	14	Pa	79
Pleasant Valley, Bucks, Pa	49	Plymouth Rock, Winneshiek, Iowa	26
Pleasant Valley, Lancaster, S. C	12	Plympton, Plymouth, Mass	110
Pleasant Valley, Chittenden, Vt	33	Plympton Station, Plymouth, Mass.	54
Pleasant Valley, Fairfax, Va	21	Po, Allen, Ind	31
Pleasant Valley, Monongalia, W. Va	34	Poage's Mill, Roanoke, Va	10
Pleasant Valley, St. Croix, Wis	42	Poast Town, Butler, Ohio	45
Pleasant Valley Mills, Nicholas, Ky	12	Pocahontas, (c. h.,) Randolph, Ark.	260
Pleasant View, Schuyler, Ill	64	Pocahontas, Bond, Ill	130
Pleasant View, Madison, Iowa	12	Pocahontas, Cape Girardeau, Mo	31
Pleasant View, Cherokee, Kans	110	Pocahontas, Somerset, Pa	4
Pleasant View, Ray, Mo	16	Pocahontas, Hardeman, Tenn	140
Pleasant View, Juniata, Pa	24	Pocasset, Barnstable, Mass	120
Pleasant View, Cheatham, Tenn	12	Pocataligo, Kanawha, W. Va	6
Pleasantville, Sullivan, Ind	40	Poe, Medina, Ohio	12
Pleasantville, Marion, Iowa	250	Poe, Beaver, Pa	10

* Money-order office.

POM

POP

Poestenkill, Rensselaer, N. Y	$31
Pohocco, Saunders, Nebr	12
Poindexter's Store, Louisa, Va	5
Point à la Hache, (c. h.,) Placque-	
mines, La	92
Point Bluff, Adams, Wis	38
Point Cedar, Clark, Ark	4
Point Coupee, (c. h.,) Point Coupee,	
La	120
Point Douglass, Washington, Minn	54
Point Eastern, Caroline, Va	19
Point Hope, Grayson, Va	6
Point Isabel, Grant, Ind	13
Point Isabel, Clermont, Ohio	39
Point Isabel, Cameron, Tex	32
Point Jefferson, Morehouse, La	17
Point Lookout, St. Mary's, Md	12
Point of Rocks, Frederick, Md	230
Point of Rocks, Uintah, Wyo	80
Point of Timber, Contra Costa, Cal	12
Point Peninsula, Jefferson, N. Y	13
Point Peter, Searcy, Ark	5
Point Peter, Oglethorpe, Ga	30
Point Pleasant, Vermilion, Ill	25
Point Pleasant, Hardin, Iowa	43
Point Pleasant, Ohio, Ky	20
Point Pleasant, New Madrid, Mo	110
Point Pleasant, Ocean, N. J	39
Point Pleasant, Clermont, Ohio	39
Point Pleasant, Bucks, Pa	140
Point Pleasant, Upshur, Tex	12
Point Pleasant, (c. h.,) Mason, W.Va.	420
Point Truth, Scott, Va	16
Pointville, Burlington, N. J	45
Pojuaque, Santa Fé, N. Mex	12
Pokagon, Cass, Mich	220
Poland, Clay, Ind	38
Poland, Androscoggin, Me	64
Poland, Herkimer, N. Y	130
Poland, Mahoning, Ohio	360
Poland Centre, Chautauqua, N. Y	35
Pole Grove, Jackson, Wis	100
Polk, Ashland, Ohio	93
Polk, Venango, Pa	75
Polk Bayou, Independence, Ark	14
Polk City, Polk, Iowa	160
Polk Patch, Warrick, Ind	41
Polk Run, Clarke, Ind	12
Polksville, Hall, Ga	11
Polkville, Smith, Miss	14
Polkville, Warren, N. J	18
Polkville, Columbia, Pa	5
Pollard, (c. h.,) Escambia, Ala	240
Pollinger, Madison, Mont	12
Pollock, Clarion, Pa	110
Pollocksville, Jones, N. C	49
Polo,* Ogle, Ill	1,500
Polo, Caldwell. Mo	12
Polsgrove, Carroll, Ill	16
Polsgrove's Store, Franklin, Ky	12
Pomaria, Newberry, S. C	17
Pomeroy, Calhoun, Iowa	12
Pomeroy, Wyandotte, Kans	59
*Pomeroy,** (c. h.,) Meigs, Ohio	1,600
Pomeroy, Chester, Pa	120
Pomfret, Windham, Conn	420

Pomfret, Windsor, Vt	$67
Pomfret Landing, Windham, Conn	96
Pomme de Terre, Grant, Minn	12
Pomona, Franklin, Kans	12
Pomona, Cumberland, Tenn	33
Pomonkey, Charles, Md	45
Pompanoosuc, Windsor, Vt	68
Pompei, Gratiot, Mich	78
Pompey, Onondaga, N. Y	200
Pompey Centre, Onondaga, N. Y	38
Pompton, Passaic, N. J	200
Pompton Plains, Morris, N. J	54
Ponama, Newaygo, Mich	22
Ponca, (c. h.,) Dixon, Nebr	96
Ponce de Leon, Holmes, Fla	4
Ponchatoula, Tangipahoa, La	150
Pond, St. Louis, Mo	21
Pond Creek, Campbell, Ky	4
Pond Creek Mills, Knox, Ind	4
Pond Eddy, Sullivan, N. Y	81
Ponder's Mill, Montgomery, Ala	12
Pond Grove, Benton, Ind	35
Pond Run, Scioto, Ohio	12
Pond Spring, Walker, Ga	8
Pond Spring, Williamson, Tex	8
Pond's Shop, Southampton, Va	12
Pond Valley, Howard, Iowa	12
Poney Hollow, Tompkins, N. Y	15
Ponka Agency, Todd, Dak	24
*Pontiac,** (c. h.,) Livingston, Ill	1,500
*Pontiac,** (c. h.,) Oakland, Mich	2,700
Pontiac, Erie, N. Y	27
Pontiac, Huron, Ohio	21
Pontiac, Kent, R. I	12
Pontoosuc, Hancock, Ill	94
Pontotoc, (c. h.,) Pontotoc, Miss	340
Ponville, Wilson, Tenn	12
Pool, Lapeer, Mich	14
Poole's Mill, Webster, Ky	29
Poolesville, Montgomery, Md	120
Poolsville, Warren, Ind	59
Poolville, Madison, N. Y	110
Poor Fork, Harlan, Ky	2
Poor's Mills, Waldo, Me	15
Poor Valley, Hawkins, Tenn	12
Pope's Depot, Panola, Miss	140
Pope's Mills, St. Lawrence, N. Y	24
Pope Valley, Napa, Cal	12
Poplar, Crawford, Ohio	74
Poplar Bluff, Ashley, Ark	12
Poplar Bluff, (c. h.,) Butler, Mo	18
Poplar Branch, Currituck, N. C	5
Poplar Creek, Choctaw, Miss	20
Poplar Flat, Lewis, Ky	15
Poplar Grove, Boone, Ill	120
Poplar Grove, Howard, Ind	41
Poplar Grove, Owen, Ky	12
Poplar Hill, McDonald, Mo	12
Poplar Hill, Anson, N. C	12
Poplar Hill, Giles, Tenn	61
Poplar Mount, Greenville, Va	17
Poplar Plains, Fleming, Ky	130
Poplar Ridge, Cayuga, N. Y	150
Poplar Ridge, Darke, Ohio	7
Poplar Run, Blair, Pa	12
Poplar Spring, Henderson, Tenn	5

* **Money-order office.**

POR   POS

Poplar Springs, Hall, Ga	$12	Portland, Dallas, Ala		$12
Poplar Springs, Howard, Md	150	Portland, Middlesex, Conn		1,000
Poquetannck, New London, Conn	57	Portland, Whitesides, Ill		35
Poquonock, Hartford, Conn	110	*Portland,* (c. h.,) Jay, Ind		280
Poquonock Bridge, New London,		*Portland,* (c. h.,) Cumberland, Me		4,000
Conn	52	Portland, Ionia, Mich		600
Porche's Prairie, Chariton, Mo	25	Portland, Callaway, Mo		120
Portage, Kalamazoo, Mich	53	Portland, Chautauqua, N. Y		140
Portage, Wood, Ohio	150	Portland, Meigs, Ohio		73
Portage, Box Elder, Utah	13	*Portland,* (c. h.,) Multnomah, Oreg.		4,000
Portage Centre, Hancock, Ohio	5	Portland, Northampton, Pa		210
Portage City, (c. h.,) Columbia, Wis.	2,000	Portland, Preston, W. Va		230
Portage Lake, Aroostook, Me	13	Portland Mills, Parke, Ind		130
Portageville, Wyoming, N. Y	260	Portlandville, Otsego, N. Y		150
Port Allegheny, McKean, Pa	150	Port Lavaca, Calhoun, Tex		1,200
Port Allen, Louisa, Iowa	58	Port Leyden, Lewis, N. Y		380
Port Andrew, Richland, Wis	75	Port Louisa, Louisa, Iowa		33
Port Angeles, Clallam, Wash	76	Port Ludlow, Jefferson, Wash		69
Port Austin, (c. h.,) Huron, Mich	200	*Port Madison,* (c. h.,) Kitsap, Wash.		97
Port Blanchard, Luzerne, Pa	33	Port Matilda, Centre, Pa		81
Port Byron, Rock Island, Ill	570	Port Monmouth, Monmouth, N. J		110
Port Byron, Cayuga, N. Y	1,100	Port Murry, Warren, N. J		71
Port Carbon, Schuylkill, Pa	530	Port Ontario, Oswego, N. Y		37
Port Chester,* Westchester, N. Y	1,500	Port Oram, Morris, N. J		160
Port Clinton, (c. h.,) Ottawa, Ohio.	310	Port Orange, Volusia, Fla		18
Port Clinton, Schuylkill, Pa	120	Port Orchard, Kitsap, Wash		12
Port Colden, Warren, N. J	49	Port Orford, Curry, Oreg		30
Port Conway, Prince George, Va	12	Port Penn, New Castle, Del		160
Port Crane, Broome, N. Y	26	Port Perry, Allegheny, Pa		170
Port Crescent, Huron, Mich	53	Port Providence, Montgomery, Pa		33
Port Deposit,* Cecil, Md	1,300	Port Republic, Calvert, Md		20
Port Dickinson, Broome, N. Y	69	Port Republic, Atlantic, N. J		160
Port Discovery, Jefferson, Wash	16	Port Republic, Rockingham, Va		100
Port Edwards, Wood, Wis	37	Port Richmond, Wapello, Iowa		16
Port Elizabeth, Cumberland, N. J	180	Port Richmond, Richmond, N. Y		400
Porter, Oxford, Me	77	Port Royal, Henry, Ky		71
Porter, Midland, Mich	12	Port Royal, Juniata, Pa		400
Porter, Jefferson, Pa	7	Port Royal, Beaufort, S. C		37
Porterfield, Venango, Pa	14	Port Royal, Montgomery, Tenn		18
Porter's, Carroll, Md	14	Port Royal, Caroline, Va		140
Porter's Corners, Saratoga, N. Y	18	Port Sanilac, Sanilac, Mich		180
Porter's Cross Roads, Porter, Ind	18	Port Sheldon, Ottawa, Mich		20
Porter's Falls, Wetzel, W. Va	10	Portsmouth, Bay, Mich		400
Porter's Sideling, York, Pa	22	*Portsmouth,* (c. h.,) Rockingham,		
Porter Station, Porter, Ind	100	N. H		2,800
Porter Station, Henry, Tenn	12	Portsmouth, Carteret, N. C		34
Portersville, DeKalb, Ala	73	*Portsmouth,* (c. h.,) Scioto, Ohio		2,900
Portersville, Dubois, Ind	22	Portsmouth, Newport, R. I		170
Portersville, Perry, Ohio	20	Portsmouth,* Norfolk, Va		2,400
Portersville, Butler, Pa	97	Port Sullivan, Milam, Tex		72
Portersville, Tipton, Tenn	85	*Port Tobacco,* (c. h.,) Charles, Md		320
Port Ewen, Ulster, N. Y	88	*Port Townsend,* (c. h.,) Jefferson,		
Port Gibson, (c. h.,) Claiborne, Miss.	350	Wash		740
Port Gibson, Ontario, N. Y	74	Port Treverton, Snyder, Pa		140
Port Henry,* Essex, N. Y	880	Portuguee, Shasta, Cal		12
Port Homer, Jefferson, Ohio	33	Port Union, Butler, Ohio		15
Port Hope, Huron, Mich	160	Portville, Cattaraugus, N. Y		540
Port Hope, Columbia, Wis	25	Port Washington, Queens, N. Y		97
Port Hudson, East Feliciana, La	90	Port Washington, Tuscarawas,		
Port Hudson, Franklin, Mo	17	Ohio		260
Port Huron,* St. Clair, Mich	2,500	Port William, Clinton, Ohio		53
Port Jackson, Montgomery, N. Y	82	Port Wine, Sierra, Cal		12
Port Jefferson,* Suffolk, N. Y	510	Poseyville, Posey, Ind		99
Port Jervis,* Orange, N. Y	2,200	Post Creek, Chemung, N. Y		14
Port Kennedy, Montgomery, Pa	170	Post Mill Village, Orange, Vt		150
Port Kent, Essex, N. Y	77	Post Oak, Calhoun, Ark		12

* Money-order office.

POW   PRE

Post Oak, Yalabusha, Miss	$6	Pownal, Bennington, Vt	$190
Post Oak, Lincoln, Mo	30	Pownal Centre, Bennington, Vt	28
Post Oak Springs, Roane, Tenn	35	Poygan, Winnebago, Wis	47
Poston, Ripley, Ind	41	Poyuett, Columbia, Wis	200
Postville,* Allamakee, Iowa	470	Poy Sippi, Waushara, Wis	56
Potato Creek, Montgomery, Ind	14	Prag, Manitowoc, Wis	47
Potecasi, Northampton, N. C	6	Prairie, Yolo, Cal	57
Potosi, Livingston, Ill	69	Prairie, Mower, Minn	12
Potosi, Stevens, Minn	12	Prairie, Clinton, Mo	12
Potosi, (c. h.,) Washington, Mo	800	Prairie, Houston, Tex	20
Potosi, Grant, Wis	100	Prairie Bird, Adair, Mo	7
Potsdam,* St. Lawrence, N. Y	2,000	Prairie Bluff, Wilcox, Ala	18
Potsdam, Miami, Ohio	24	Prairieburgh, Linn, Iowa	95
Potsdam Junction, St. Lawrence, N. Y	510	Prairie Centre, Prairie, Ark	13
		Prairie Centre, La Salle, Ill	82
Pottamie, Ottawa, Mich	12	Prairie City, McDonough, Ill	720
Potter, Yates, N. Y	83	Prairie City,* Jasper, Iowa	590
Potter, Wood, Ohio	14	Prairie City, Douglas, Kans	96
Potter Hill, Rensselaer, N. Y	14	Prairie City, Bates, Mo	150
Potter Hill, Washington, R. I	58	Prairie City, Grant, Oreg	12
Pottersburgh, Union, Ohio	12	Prairie Creek, Vigo, Ind	68
Potter's Corners, Crawford, Pa	34	Prairie Creek, Martin, Minn	10
Potter's Hollow, Albany, N. Y	68	Prairie Depot, Wood, Ohio	78
Potter's Landing, Caroline, Md	69	Prairie du Chien, Neosho, Kans	12
Potter's Mills, Dale, Ala	12	*Prairie du Chien,* (c. h.,) Crawford, Wis	1,200
Potter's Mills, Centre, Pa	100	Prairie du Rocher, Randolph, Ill	95
Potter's Mills, Calumet, Wis	12	Prairie du Sac, Sauk, Wis	430
Pottersville, Cheshire, N. H	23	Prairie Edge, Montgomery, Ind	18
Pottersville, Hunterdon, N. J	47	Prairie Farm, Barron, Wis	92
Pottersville, Warren, N. Y	150	Prairie Grove, Washington, Ark	12
Potterville, Eaton, Mich	12	Prairie Grove, Clarke, Iowa	41
Potterville, Bradford, Pa	61	Prairie Hall, Macon, Ill	12
Pott's Grove, Northumberland, Pa	82	Prairie Hill, Boone, Iowa	19
Pottstown,* Montgomery, Pa	2,100	Prairie Hill, Chariton, Mo	12
Pottsville, (c. h.,) Schuylkill, Pa	3,000	Prairie Home, Shelby, Ill	28
Poughkeepsie, (c. h.,) Dutchess, N. Y	4,000	Prairie Home, Cooper, Mo	18
		Prairie Home, Montgomery, Tex	12
Poughquag, Dutchess, N. Y	130	Prairie Landing, Desha, Ark	11
Poultney, Rutland, Vt	960	Prairie Lea, Caldwell, Tex	84
Pound, Wise, Va	5	Prairie Mills, Muscatine, Iowa	76
Poundridge, Westchester, N. Y	56	Prairie Park, Nodaway, Mo	14
Powar's Store, Casey, Ky	12	Prairie Plains, Grimes, Tex	51
Poway, San Diego, Cal	12	Prairie Pond, De Kalb, Ill	30
Powder Spring Gap, Grainger, Tenn	7	Prairie Station, Monroe, Miss	12
Powder Springs, Cobb, Ga	25	Prairieton, Vigo, Ind	35
Powell, Delaware, Ohio	40	Prairie Town, Madison, Ill	46
Powell Grove, Bowie, Tex	12	Prairieville, Barry, Mich	150
Powell's Point, Currituck, N. C	12	Prairieville, Pike, Mo	39
Powell's Station, Knox, Tenn	31	Prairieville, Kaufman, Tex	24
Powellton, Harrison, Tex	15	Pratt, Whitesides, Ill	12
Powellton, Brunswick, Va	12	Pratt, Shelby, Ohio	140
Powellville, Wicomico, Md	17	Prattsburgh, Talbot, Ga	7
Powel's Creek, Dauphin, Pa	14	Prattsburgh,* Steuben, N. Y	590
Powelton, Richmond, N. C	12	Pratt's Corner, Franklin, Me	11
Powelton, Centre, Pa	130	Pratt's Fork, Athens, Ohio	12
Powers, Terrell, Ga	65	Pratt's Hollow, Madison, N. Y	95
Powers, Jay, Ind	16	Pratt's Junction, Worcester, Mass	41
Powersville, Houston, Ga	26	Prattsville, Saline, Ark	6
Powersville, Bracken, Ky	16	Prattsville, Greene, N. Y	270
Powhatan, Lawrence, Ark	67	*Prattville,* (c. h.,) Autauga, Ala	380
Powhatan, Baltimore, Md	25	Preble, Cortland, N. Y	210
Powhatan, Richmond, N. C	49	Pre-emption, Mercer, Ill	110
Powhatan C. H., Powhatan, Va	48	Prentice, Morgan, Ill	75
Powhatan Point, Belmont, Ohio	140	Prentiss, Penobscot, Me	10
Powl's Valley, Dauphin, Pa	36	Prentiss Vale, McKean, Pa	19
Pownal, Cumberland, Me	87		

PRI

Prescott,* (c. h.,) Yavapai, Ariz	$540
Prescott, Shelby, Ind	35
Prescott, Adams, Iowa	12
Prescott, Hampshire, Mass	42
Prescott,* Pierce, Wis	570
President, Venango, Pa	110
Presidio, Presidio, Tex	12
Presque Isle,* Aroostook, Me	350
Preston, New London, Conn	61
Preston, (c. h.,) Webster, Ga	100
Preston, Randolph, Ill	39
Preston, Caroline, Md	100
Preston,* (c. h.,) Fillmore, Minn	500
Preston, Jasper, Mo	12
Preston, Chenango, N. Y	37
Preston, Hamilton, Ohio	17
Preston, Wayne, Pa	23
Preston Bluff, Arkansas, Ark	12
Prestonburgh, (c. h.,) Floyd, Ky	56
Preston Hollow, Albany, N. Y	76
Prestonville, Cameron, Pa	20
Prestonville, Rhea, Tenn	7
Prewitt's Ferry, Desha, Ark	12
Priam, Blackford, Ind	13
Price, Mercer, Ohio	8
Price's Branch, Montgomery, Mo	41
Price's Creek, De Witt, Tex	16
Price's Landing, Scott, Mo	24
Price's Store, Rockingham, N. C	12
Pricetown, Highland, Ohio	11
Pricetown, Berks, Pa	8
Priceville, Wayne, Pa	2
Prickley Pear, Jefferson, Mont	69
Pride's Station, Colbert, Ala	12
Prillaman's, Franklin, Va	15
Primrose, Lee, Iowa	110
Primrose, Lewis, Mo	48
Primrose, Douglas, Nebr	23
Primrose, Williams, Ohio	11
Primrose, Dane, Wis	67
Prince Edward C. H., Prince Edward, Va	60
Prince Fredericktown, (c. h.,) Calvert, Md	120
Prince George C. H., Prince George, Va	42
Prince's Bay, Richmond, N. Y	52
Princess Anne,* (c. h.,) Somerset, Md	760
Princess Anne C. H., Princess Anne, Va	12
Princeton, Jackson, Ala	24
Princeton, (c. h.,) Dallas, Ark	120
Princeton, Colusa, Cal	64
Princeton,* (c. h.,) Bureau, Ill	2,400
Princeton,* (c. h.,) Gibson, Ind	1,000
Princeton, Scott, Iowa	280
Princeton, Franklin, Kans	20
Princeton,* (c. h.,) Caldwell, Ky	460
Princeton, Washington, Me	150
Princeton, Worcester, Mass	370
Princeton, (c. h.,) Mille Lacs, Minn	230
Princeton,* (c. h.,) Mercer, Mo	260
Princeton,* Mercer, N. J	2,000
Princeton, Butler, Ohio	11
Princeton, Lawrence, Pa	38
Princeton, (c. h.,) Mercer, W. Va	30

PRY

Princeton, Green Lake, Wis	$460
Princeville,* Peoria, Ill	370
Prince William, Carroll, Ind	42
Principio, Cecil, Md	48
Principio Furnace, Cecil, Md	64
Prior's Station, Polk, Ga	12
Privateer, Sumter, S. C	12
Proctor, (c. h.,) Lee, Ky	8
Proctor, Wetzel, W. Va	43
Proctor's Creek, Chesterfield, Va	12
Proctorsville, Windsor, Vt	630
Proctorville, Caldwell, Mo	12
Profile House, Grafton, N. H	17
Progress, Dauphin, Pa	17
Promise City, Wayne, Iowa	54
Prompton, Wayne, Pa	54
Prophetstown, Whitesides, Ill	250
Prospect, New Haven, Conn	150
Prospect, Madison, Ind	7
Prospect, Waldo, Me	99
Prospect, Harford, Md	42
Prospect, Oneida, N. Y	240
Prospect, Marion, Ohio	140
Prospect, Butler, Pa	130
Prospect, Burleson, Tex	10
Prospect, Prince Edward, Va	140
Prospect Ferry, Waldo, Me	170
Prospect Grove, Scotland, Mo	14
Prospect Hall, Bladen, N. C	12
Prospect Harbor, Hancock, Me	65
Prospect Hill, Linn, Iowa	20
Prospect Hill, Clay, Mo	35
Prospect Hill, Caswell, N. C	16
Prospect Hill, Fairfax, Va	8
Prospect Hill, Waukesha, Wis	59
Prospect Lake, Van Buren, Mich	18
Prospect Plains, Middlesex, N. J	66
Prospect Station, Chautauqua, N. Y	13
Prospect Station, Giles, Tenn	65
Prospect Valley, Harrison, W. Va	9
Prospectville, Montgomery, Pa	47
Prosper, Fillmore, Minn	20
Prosperity, Franklin, Ill	12
Prosperity, Madison, Ind	12
Prosperity, Lawrence, Ky	4
Prosperity, Moore, N. C	6
Prosperity, Washington, Pa	46
Protection, Erie, N. Y	62
Providence, Pickens, Ala	5
Providence, Searcy, Ark	2
Providence, Bureau, Ill	40
Providence, Webster, Ky	18
Providence, Boone, Mo	27
Providence, Saratoga, N. Y	33
Providence, Luzerne, Pa	940
PROVIDENCE,* (c. h.,) Providence, R. I	4,000
Providence, Cache, Utah	38
Providence Forge, New Kent, Va	36
Provincetown,* Barnstable, Mass	1,200
Proviso, Cook, Ill	30
Provo City, (c. h.,) Utah, Utah	300
Prunty's, Henry, Va	1
Pruntytown, (c. h.,) Taylor, W. Va	130
Pryorsburgh, Graves, Ky	9
Pryor's Creek, Choctaw N., Ind. T	12

* Money-order office.

QUE

Pryor's Store, Douglas, Mo	$10
Pueblo,* (c. h.,) Pueblo, Colo	800
Pugh, Belmont, Ohio	39
Pughtown, Chester, Pa	100
Pulaski, Hancock, Ill	28
Pulaski, Pulaski, Ind	22
Pulaski, Davis, Iowa	16
Pulaski, Jackson, Mich	58
Pulaski,* (c. h.,) Oswego, N. Y	1,100
Pulaski, Williams, Ohio	56
Pulaski, Lawrence, Pa	200
Pulaski,* (c. h.,) Giles, Tenn	1,100
Pulaskiville, Morrow, Ohio	30
Pulley's Mill, Williamson, Ill	14
Pultney, Steuben, N. Y	56
Pultneyville, Wayne, N. Y	230
Pulver's Corners, Dutchess, N. Y	63
Pumphrey's Landing, Lewis, Wash.	12
Pungoteague, Accomack, Va.	87
Punjaub, St. Genevieve, Mo	20
Punta Arenas, Mendocino, Cal	230
Punxatawney,* Jefferson, Pa	290
Purcell, Bedford, Pa	12
Purchase Line, Indiana, Pa	12
Purdy, (c. h.,) McNairy, Tenn	150
Purdy Creek, Steuben, N. Y	18
Purdy's Station, Westchester, N. Y.	280
Purgitsville, Hampshire, W. Va.	120
Purlear's Creek, Wilkes, N. C	6
Purley, Caswell, N. C	22
Pursley, Tyler, W. Va	10
Purvis, Sullivan, N. Y	11
Pushmataha, Choctaw, Ala	12
Put in Bay, Ottawa, Ohio	250
Putnam,* Windham, Conn	400
Putnam, Fayette, Iowa	8
Putnam, Washington, N. Y	81
Putnam, Muskingum, Ohio	470
Putnamville, Putnam, Ind	110
Putney, Windham, Vt	380
Putneyville, Armstrong, Pa	47
Pylesville, Harford, Md	24
Pyrmont, Carroll, Ind	19
Pyrmont, Montgomery, Ohio	38

Q.

Quacken Kill, Rensselaer, N. Y.	20
Quaker Bottom, Lawrence, Ohio	140
Quaker Hill, Vermillion, Ind	16
Quaker Hill, Dutchess, N. Y.	39
Quaker Springs, Saratoga, N. Y.	88
Quaker Street, Schenectady, N. Y.	170
Quakertown, Union, Ind	40
Quakertown, Hunterdon, N. J	50
Quakertown, Bucks, Pa	340
Quality Valley, Butler, Ky	7
Quallatown, Jackson, N. C	5
Quantico, Wicomico, Md	71
Quarry, Marshall, Iowa	12
Quarryville, Hawkins, Tenn	18
Quarryville, Tolland, Conn	42
Quarryville, Ulster, N. Y	22
Quarryville, Lancaster, Pa	65
Quasqueton, Buchanan, Iowa	310
Quechee, Windsor, Vt	360

RAI

Queen City, Schuyler, Mo	$13
Queens, Queens, N. Y	85
Queensbury, Warren, N. Y	36
Queenstown, Queen Anne, Md	230
Queensville, Jennings, Ind	94
Quenemo, Osage, Kans	14
Quercus Grove, Switzerland, Ind	40
Query's, Mecklenburgh, N. C	9
Quiet Dell, Harrison, W. Va	23
Quincy, (c. h.,) Plumas, Cal	140
Quincy, (c. h.,) Gadsden, Fla	600
Quincy,* (c. h.,) Adams, Ill	4,000
Quincy, Owen, Ind	52
Quincy,* (c. h.,) Adams, Iowa	260
Quincy, Greenwood, Kans	12
Quincy, Lewis, Ky	48
Quincy,* Norfolk, Mass	1,500
Quincy,* Branch, Mich	730
Quincy, Olmsted, Minn	18
Quincy, Hickory, Mo	50
Quincy, Logan, Ohio	240
Quincy, Franklin, Pa	91
Quincy, Gibson, Tenn	23
Quincy, Adams, Wis	35
Quincy Point, Norfolk, Mass	190
Quindaro, Wyandotte, Kans	50
Quinn, Macomb, Mich	12
Quinney, Calumet, Wis	21
Quinton, Salem, N. J	42
Quitman, Van Buren, Ark	43
Quitman, (c. h.,) Brooks, Ga	480
Quitman, Clark, Miss	140
Quitman, Nodaway, Mo	56
Quitman, (c. h.,) Wood, Tex	140
Quito, Butler, Kans	12
Quogue, Suffolk, N. Y	150
Quonochontaug, Washington, R. I.	19

R.

Rabbittsville, Logan, Ky	14
Raccoon, Laurel, Ky	6
Raccoon, Washington, Pa	45
Raccoon Ford, Culpeper, Va	33
Raccoon Valley, Union, Tenn	12
Raceland, La Fourche, La	12
Racine, Newton, Mo	12
Racine, Meigs, Ohio	190
Racine,* (c. h.,) Racine, Wis	3,000
Racoon, Marion, Ill	20
Racoon, Preston, W. Va	190
Radersburgh, (c. h.,) Jefferson, Mont.	12
Radford Furnace, Pulaski, Va	12
Radfordsville, Perry, Ala	20
Radical, Madison, Ga	12
Radical City, Montgomery, Kans.	12
Radnor, Delaware, Ohio	110
Radnor, Delaware, Pa	150
Raglesville, Daviess, Ind	37
Rahway,* Union, N. J	2,000
Raif Branch, Montgomery, Ala	12
Rail Road York, Pa	120
Rail Road Flat, Calaveras, Cal	69
Rainbow, Hartford, Conn	130
Rainey Creek, Camden, Mo	12
Rainey's Creek, Coryell, Tex	12

* Money-order office.

RAP   REA

Rainier, Columbia, Oreg	$24	Rapp's Mill, Rockbridge, Va	$7
Rainsborough, Highland, Ohio	50	Rarden, Scioto, Ohio	25
Rainsburgh, Bedford, Pa	78	Raritan, Henderson, Ill	170
Rainsville, Warren, Ind	120	Raritan, Somerset, N. J	350
Raisin Centre, Lenawee, Mich	35	Rathboneville, Steuben, N. Y	130
Raleigh, Saline, Ill	63	Rathbun, Sheboygan, Wis	22
Raleigh, Rush, Ind	22	Rattlesnake, Lane, Oreg	21
Raleigh, Union, Ky	9	Rauch's Gap, Clinton, Pa	30
Raleigh, (c. h.,) Smith, Miss	12	Raught's Mills, Forest, Pa	20
RALEIGH,* (c. h.,) Wake, N. C	2,500	Ravanna, Mercer, Mo	84
Raleigh, Shelby, Tenn	23	Ravena City, Los Angeles, Cal	12
Raleigh C. H., Raleigh, W. Va	50	Ravenna, Muskegon, Mich	71
Ralston, Lycoming, Pa	110	*Ravenna*,* (c. h.,) Portage, Ohio	1,800
Ralston's Station, Weakley, Tenn	61	Raven Rock, Hunterdon, N. J	27
Ramapo Works, Rockland, N. Y	160	Raven's Eye, Fayette, W. Va	23
Ramer, Montgomery, Ala	40	Raven's Nest, Washington, Va	5
Ramer, McNairy, Tenn	12	Raven Stream, Scott, Minn	14
Ramey, Johnson, Mo	150	Ravenswood, Cook, Ill	17
Ramsaytown, Yancey, N. C	5	Ravenswood, Queens, N. Y	22
Ramsey, Fayette, Ill	280	Ravenswood,* Jackson, W. Va	210
Ramsey's, Bergen, N. J	110	Rawley Springs, Rockingham, Va	12
Rancho, Gonzales, Tex	12	*Rawling's Springs*, (c. h.,) Carbon,	
Rancocas, Burlington, N. J	160	Wyo	950
Randall, Jefferson, Ark	12	Rawling's Station, Alleghany, Md	38
Randall, Allen, Ind	44	Rawlingsville, De Kalb, Ala	32
Randall, Hamilton, Iowa	13	Rawlinsville, Lancaster, Pa	28
Randall, Saginaw, Mich	12	Rawson, Aroostook, Me	4
Randall, Montgomery, N. Y	43	Rawson, Cattaraugus, N. Y	31
Randall, Cuyahoga, Ohio	12	Rawson, Hancock, Ohio	46
Randall, Smith, Tex	12	Rawsonville, Wayne, Mich	110
Randall, Monongalia, W. Va	12	Rawsonville, Lorain, Ohio	220
Randallstown, Baltimore, Md	35	Ray, Bedford, Tenn	12
Randallsville, Madison, N. Y	12	Ray Centre, Macomb, Mich	12
Randellsville, Christian, Ill	21	Raymertown, Rensselaer, N. Y	40
Randolph, Bibb, Ala	100	Raymilton, Venango, Pa	71
Randolph, La Fayette, Ark	12	Raymond, Champaign, Ill	12
Randolph, McLean, Ill	17	Raymond, Black Hawk, Iowa	130
Randolph, Randolph, Ind	140	Raymond, Cumberland, Me	50
Randolph, Riley, Kans	140	Raymond, Stearns, Minn	12
Randolph, Metcalfe, Ky	20	*Raymond*, (c. h.,) Hinds, Miss	470
Randolph, Norfolk, Mass	900	Raymond, Rockingham, N. H	290
Randolph, Randolph, Mo	220	Raymond, Racine, Wis	62
Randolph, Dakota, Nebr	12	Raymond City, Putnam, W. Va	59
Randolph, Coos, N. H	11	Raymonds, Union, Ohio	130
Randolph,* Cattaraugus, N. Y	650	Raymonds, Potter, Pa	18
Randolph, Portage, Ohio	210	Raymondville, St. Lawrence, N. Y	110
Randolph, Coos, Oreg	38	Raynham, Bristol, Mass	82
Randolph, Crawford, Pa	35	Raynold, Montcalm, Mich	12
Randolph, Tipton, Tenn	20	Rays, Jackson, Ohio	74
Randolph, Orange, Vt	310	Ray's Crossing, Shelby, Ind	12
Randolph Centre, Broome, N. Y	10	Ray's Hill, Bedford, Pa	67
Randolph Centre, Columbia, Wis	27	Raysville, Henry, Ind	160
Rangeley, Franklin, Me	14	*Rayville*, (c. h.,) Richland, La	12
Ranger, Perry, Ind	12	Rayville, Baltimore, Md	51
Rankin's Depot, Cocke, Tenn	12	Rayville, Ray, Mo	12
Ransom, Hillsdale, Mich	120	Raywick, Marion, Ky	41
Ransom, Luzerne, Pa	33	Read, Clayton, Iowa	40
Ransom's Bridge, Nash, N. C	10	Readfield, Kennebec, Me	340
Ransomville, Niagara, N. Y	100	Readfield, Waupaca, Wis	16
Rantoul,* Champaign, Ill	670	Readfield Depot, Kennebec, Me	140
Rantoul, Calumet, Wis	12	Reading, Livingston, Ill	49
Rapid Ann Station, Culpeper, Va	370	Reading, Lyon, Kans	12
Rapids, Niagara, N. Y	21	Reading, Middlesex, Mass	940
Rapids, Portage, Ohio	30	Reading, Hillsdale, Mich	500
Rapids City, Rock Island, Ill	44	Reading, Pike, Mo	12
Rappahannock Academy, Caroline,		Reading, Schuyler, N. Y	8
Va	12	Reading, Hamilton, Ohio	160

* Money-order office.

RED   REE

Reading, (c. h.,) Berks, Pa	$3,500	Red Mountain, Orange, N. C	$2
Reading, Windsor, Vt	49	Red Mountain City, Deer Lodge,	
Reading Centre, Schuyler, N. Y	65	Mont	12
Readington, Hunterdon, N. J	91	Red Oak, Fayette, Ga	6
Readsborough, Bennington, Vt	120	Red Oak, Choctaw N., Ind. T	12
Readstown, Vernon, Wis	36	Red Oak, Cedar, Iowa	61
Readsville, Callaway, Mo	38	Red Oak, Grayson, Ky	7
Readville Station, Norfolk, Mass	320	Red Oak, Brown, Ohio	55
Readyville, Rutherford, Tenn	64	Red Oak, Ellis, Tex	83
Ream's Chapel, Hart, Ky	12	Red Oak Grove, Charlotte, Va	43
Ream's Station, Dinwiddie, Va	93	*Red Oak Junction,* (c. h.,) Montgom-	
Reamstown, Lancaster, Pa	36	ery, Iowa	700
Reaville, Hunterdon, N. J	71	Red Plains, Yadkin, N. C	8
Rebecca, Lancaster, Nebr	38	Red River, Kewaunee, Wis	12
Rebersburgh, Centre, Pa	120	Red River Iron Works, Estill, Ky	23
Rebucks, Northumberland, Pa	8	Red River Landing, Point Coupee,	
Recklesstown, Burlington, N. J	53	La	24
Rectortown Station, Fauquier, Va	110	Red River Mills, Logan, Ky	12
Rectorville, Hamilton, Ill	11	Red Rock, Marion, Iowa	69
Red Apple, Marshall, Ala	12	Red Rock, Lincoln, Kans	10
Red Bank,* Monmouth, N. J	1,300	Red Rock, Columbia, N. Y	35
Red Bank, Halifax, Va	26	Red Rock, Luzerne, Pa	10
Red Bank Furnace, Armstrong, Pa	47	Red Rock, Bastrop, Tex	12
Red Banks, Marshall, Miss	12	Red Shoals, Stokes, N. C	12
Red Banks, Robeson, N. C	20	Red Stone, Cloud, Kans	12
Red Beach, Washington, Me	64	Red Stone, Nicollet, Minn	13
Red Bluff, Jefferson, Ark	12	Redstone, Fayette, Pa	45
Red Bluff, (c. h.,) Tehama, Cal	430	Red Sulphur Springs, Monroe, W.Va	43
Red Bluff, Coffee, Ga	7	*Red Wing,* (c. h.,) Goodhue, Minn	2,600
Red Brick, Sullivan, N. Y	10	Redwood, Jefferson, N. Y	290
Red Bridge, Ingham, Mich	18	*Redwood City,* (c. h.,) San Mateo, Cal	360
Red Bud,* Randolph, Ill	410	*Redwood Falls,* (c. h.,) Redwood, Minn	250
Red Clay, Whitfield, Ga	90	Reed, Oceana, Mich	14
Red Creek, Wayne, N. Y	290	Reed Creek, Randolph, N. C	7
Red Creek, Tucker, W. Va	1	Reeder's Mills, Harrison, Iowa	31
Redden, Sussex, Del	12	Reed Island, Wythe, Va	12
Redding, Fairfield, Conn	110	Reed Level, Covington, Ala	6
Redding, Ringgold, Iowa	17	Reedsburgh, Wayne, Ohio	55
Redding Ridge, Fairfield, Conn	90	Reedsburgh,* Sauk, Wis	530
Red Falls, Greene, N. Y	71	Reed's Corners, Ontario, N. Y	67
Redfield, Dallas, Iowa	250	Reed's Creek, Lawrence, Ark	40
Redfield, Carver, Minn	13	Reed's Ferry, Hillsborough, N. H	110
Redfield, Oswego, N. Y	140	Reed's Gap, Juniata, Pa	12
Redford, Wayne, Mich	94	Reed's Landing, Pulaski, Ark	12
Redford, Clinton, N. Y	120	Reed's Landing, Wabashaw, Minn	350
Red Fork, Desha, Ark	33	Reed's Mills, Vinton, Ohio	290
Red Haw, Ashland, Ohio	47	Reedsville, Meigs, Ohio	33
Red Hill, Marshall, Ala	16	Reedsville, Mifflin, Pa	220
Red Hill, Hardin, Ky	13	Reedsville, Preston, W. Va	40
Red Hill, Mitchell, N. C	2	Reedsville, Manitowoc, Wis	48
Red Hill, Montgomery, Pa	26	Reedtown, Seneca, Ohio	34
Red Hook, Dutchess, N. Y	410	Reedy, Jackson, W. Va	12
Red House, Morgan, Ind	12	Reedy Creek, Davidson, N. C	12
Red House, Cattaraugus, N. Y	67	Reedy Creek, Marion, S. C	11
Red House, Charlotte, Va	11	Reedy Ripple, Wirt, W. Va	12
Red House Shoals, Putnam, W. Va	35	Reedyville, Butler, Ky	9
Redington, Northampton, Pa	12	Reedyville, Roane, W. Va	12
Red Jacket, Erie, N. Y	12	Reelsville, Putnam, Ind	55
Redkey, Jay, Ind	64	Reem's Creek, Buncombe, N. C	13
Red Land, Pike, Ark	6	Reese Mill, Etowah, Ala	12
Redland, Montgomery, Md	16	Reese's Mill, Boone, Ind	39
Red Land, Pontotoc, Miss	32	Reeseville, Chester, Pa	100
Red Land, Adams, Pa	39	Reeseville, Dodge, Wis	80
Red Lion, New Castle, Del	56	Reeson, Chippewa, Minn	12
Red Lion, Warren, Ohio	95	Reesville, Clinton, Ohio	94
Red Mound, Henderson, Tenn	12	Reeves' Landing, Arkansas, Ark	12

* Money-order office.

REX   RIO

Reeves' Station, Gordon, Ga	$12	Reyburn, Hot Spring, Ark	$12
Reeves' Station, Butler, Mo	36	Reynale's Basin, Niagara, N. Y	40
Reevesville, Colleton, S. C	25	Reynolds, Taylor, Ga	120
Reform, Pickens, Ala	13	Reynolds,* White, Ind	230
Reform, Jefferson, Ark	12	Reynolds, Schuylkill, Pa	12
Reform, Callaway, Mo	13	Reynoldsburgh, Johnson, Ill	27
Refugio, (c. h.,) Refugio, Tex	20	Reynoldsburgh, Franklin, Ohio	240
Regnier's Mills, Washington, Ohio	70	Reynoldson, Gates, N. C	12
Rego, Orange, Ind	32	Reynoldsville, Schuyler, N. Y	41
Rehoboth, Wilcox, Ala	13	Reynoldsville, Jefferson, Pa	96
Rehoboth, Bristol, Mass	48	Rhea, Lawrence, Ark	12
Rehoboth, Perry, Ohio	15	Rhea's Mills, Washington, Ark	24
Rehoboth, Edgefield, S. C	9	Rheatown, Greene, Tenn	110
Rehoboth, Lunenburgh, Va	17	Rhine, Sheboygan, Wis	32
Rehrersburgh, Berks, Pa	71	Rhinebeck,* Dutchess, N. Y	1,200
Rei, Ripley, Ind	99	Rhinecliff, Dutchess, N. Y	180
Reidenbach's Store, Lancaster, Pa	33	Rhineland, Montgomery, Mo	28
Reid's, Paulding, Ohio	19	Rialto, Chatham, N. C	5
Reidsburgh, Clarion, Pa	120	Rice Depot, Prince Edward, Va	82
Reidsville, (c. h.,) Tatnall, Ga	20	Riceford, Houston, Minn	68
Reidsville, Albany, N. Y	27	Rice Lake, Dodge, Minn	32
Reidsville, Rockingham, N. C	200	Rice's Landing, Greene, Pa	62
Reidsville, Spartanburgh, S. C	60	Rice's Store, Westmoreland, Va	14
Reiffsburgh, Wells, Ind	13	Riceville, Mitchell, Iowa	83
Reiley, Butler, Ohio	82	Riceville, Crawford, Pa	140
Reinersville, Morgan, Ohio	33	Riceville, McMinn, Tenn	150
Reinhold's Station, Lancaster, Pa	53	Riceville, Pittsylvania, Va	17
Reinholdsville, Lancaster, Pa	33	Rich, Atchison, Mo	41
Reisterstown, Baltimore, Md	280	Richardson, St. Joseph, Ind	20
Relfe, Phelps, Mo	16	Richardson, Osage, Kans	12
Relf's Bluff, Drew, Ark	49	Richardson's, Montgomery, Tenn	12
Remington, Jasper, Ind	190	Richardson's Landing, Meade, Ky	12
Remington, Allegheny, Pa	20	Richardsonville, Chariton, Mo	12
Remsen, Oneida, N. Y	250	Richardsonville, Edgefield, S. C	8
Remson's Corners, Medina, Ohio	73	Richardsville, Jefferson, Pa	32
Renault, Monroe, Ill	47	Richardsville, Culpeper, Va	20
Reno, Leavenworth, Kans	72	Richborough, Bucks, Pa	140
Reno, Pope, Minn	10	Richburgh, Allegany, N. Y	140
Reno, Washoe, Nev	550	Rich Creek, Logan, W. Va	4
Reno, Venango, Pa	190	Richfield, Adams, Ill	40
Renovo,* Clinton, Pa	960	Richfield, Fayette, Iowa	17
Renrock, Noble, Ohio	33	Richfield, Genesee, Mich	52
Rensselaer,* (c. h.,) Jasper, Ind	460	Richfield, Hennepin, Minn	59
Rensselaer Falls, St. Lawrence, N. Y	160	Richfield, Otsego, N. Y	44
Rensselaerville,* Albany, N. Y	250	Richfield, Summit, Ohio	210
Renwick, Lee, Ga	170	Richfield, Juniata, Pa	80
Repose, Haralson, Ga	12	Richfield, Washington, Wis	460
Republic, Seneca, Ohio	270	Richfield Springs, Otsego, N. Y	1,100
Republic, Yadkin, N. C	9	Richford, Tioga, N. Y	170
Republican, Choctaw, Miss	12	Richford, Franklin, Vt	300
Republican, Darke, Ohio	44	Richford, Waushara, Wis	23
Republican City, Clay, Kans	12	Rich Fountain, Osage, Mo	24
Republican Grove, Halifax, Va	20	Rich Hill, Knox, Ohio	12
Resaca, Gordon, Ga	78	Richland, Sacramento, Cal	35
Resaca, Duplin, N. C	12	Richland, Union, Dak	100
Reserve, Miami, Ind	22	Richland, Sangamon, Ill	23
Reserve, Erie, N. Y	22	Richland, Rush, Ind	53
Rest, Iowa, Iowa	12	Richland,* Keokuk, Iowa	270
Retreat, Jackson, Ind	36	Richland, Shawnee, Kans	12
Retreat, Franklin, Va	13	Richland, Kalamazoo, Mich	240
Retreat, Vernon, Wis	31	Richland, Pulaski, Mo	12
Reveille, Nye, Nev	5	Richland, Oswego, N. Y	65
Reville, Scott, Ark	21	Richland, Tazewell, Va	7
Rexford Flats, Saratoga, N. Y	110	Richland Centre, Bucks, Pa	320
Rexville, Ripley, Ind	12	Richland Centre,* (c. h.,) Richland,	
Rexville, Steuben, N. Y	56	Wis	680

*Money-order office.

RID   RIM

Richland City, Richland, Wis	$46
Richland Crossing, Navarro, Tex	6
Richland Grove, Mercer, Ill	20
Richland Mill, Stafford, Va	12
Richland's, Onslow, N. C	21
Richland Station, Lebanon, Pa	98
Richland Station, Sumner, Tenn	50
Richlandtown, Bucks, Pa	48
Richland Valley, Haywood, N. C	23
Richman Falls, Raleigh, W. Va	6
Richmond, Dallas, Ala	41
Richmond, Little River, Ark	12
Richmond,* McHenry, Ill	450
Richmond,* Wayne, Ind	2,800
Richmond, Washington, Iowa	240
Richmond, Franklin, Kans	12
Richmond, (c. h.,) Madison, Ky	1,100
Richmond, Madison, La	50
Richmond,* Sagadahoc, Me	830
Richmond, Berkshire, Mass	150
Richmond, Macomb, Mich	240
Richmond, Winona, Minn	15
Richmond, (c. h.,) Ray, Mo	840
Richmond, Cheshire, N. H	89
Richmond, (c. h.,) Richmond, N. Y	180
Richmond, Jefferson, Ohio	260
Richmond, Northampton, Pa	40
Richmond, Bedford, Tenn	12
Richmond, (c. h.,) Fort Bend, Tex	360
Richmond, Cache, Utah	29
Richmond, Chittenden, Vt	350
RICHMOND,* (c. h.,) Henrico, Va	4,000
Richmond, Walworth, Wis	64
Richmond Centre, Ashtabula, Ohio	50
Richmond Corner, Sagadahoc, Me	40
Richmond Dale, Ross, Ohio	82
Richmond Hill, Yadkin, N. C	8
Richmond Hill, Susquehanna, Pa	6
Richmond Mills, Ontario, N. Y	6
Richmond Switch, Washington, R. I	12
Richmondville, Sanilac, Mich	47
Richmondville, Schoharie, N. Y	670
Rich Patch, Alleghany, Va	6
Rich Pond Grove, Warren, Ky	48
Rich Square, Northampton, N. C	69
Rich Valley, Wabash, Ind	48
Rich Valley, Montgomery, Ky	12
Rich Valley, Dakota, Minn	24
Richview,* Washington, Ill	450
Richville, Tuscola, Mich	10
Richville, Douglas, Mo	12
Richville, St. Lawrence, N. Y	220
Richville, Addison, Vt	250
Richwood, Union, Ohio	400
Richwood, Dodge, Wis	90
Richwoods, Delaware, Ind	13
Richwoods, Washington, Mo	60
Rickardsville, Dubuque, Iowa	47
Rickoe's Bluff, Gadsden, Fla	12
Rickreall, Polk, Oreg	23
Riddicksville, Hertford, N. C	18
Riddlesburgh, Bedford, Pa	120
Riddle's Cross Roads, Butler, Pa	8
Riddlesville, Washington, Ga	12
Rider's Mills, Columbia, N. Y	70

Rider's Mills Station, Columbia, N. Y	$12
Ridge, St. Mary's, Md	26
Ridge, Carroll, Mo	12
Ridge, Livingston, N. Y	38
Ridge, Noble, Ohio	4
Ridge, Edgefield, S. C	5
Ridge, Colorado, Tex	17
Ridgebury, Fairfield, Conn	21
Ridgebury, Orange, N. Y	15
Ridgebury, Bradford, Pa	25
Ridgedale, Polk, Iowa	110
Ridge Farm, Vermilion, Ill	150
Ridgefield, Fairfield, Conn	460
Ridgefield, McHenry, Ill	150
Ridgefield Station, Fairfield, Conn.	82
Ridgeland, Henry, Ohio	8
Ridgely, Caroline, Md	75
Ridge Mills, Oneida, N. Y	45
Ridge Prairie, St. Clair, Ill	110
Ridge Prairie, Saline, Mo	57
Ridge Road, Niagara, N. Y	130
Ridge Spring, Pitt, N. C	6
Ridgeview, Westmoreland, Pa	12
Ridgeville, Randolph, Ind	210
Ridgeville, Warren, Ohio	57
Ridgeville, Colleton, S. C	38
Ridgeville, Mineral, W. Va	42
Ridgeville, Monroe, Wis	33
Ridgeville Corners, Henry, Ohio	46
Ridgeway, Winneshiek, Iowa	210
Ridgeway, Osage, Kans	58
Ridgeway, Lenawee, Mich	100
Ridgeway, Winona, Minn	20
Ridgeway, Orleans, N. Y	170
Ridgeway, Warren, N. Y	250
Ridgeway, Hardin, Ohio	110
Ridgeway, Fairfield, S. C	170
Ridgeway, Henry, Va	12
Ridgeway, Iowa, Wis	16
Ridgewood, Bergen, N. J	280
Ridgewood, Queens, N. Y	12
Ridgeley, Platte, Mo	68
Ridgway, (c. h.,) Elk, Pa	790
Ridott, Stephenson, Ill	280
Riegelsville, Bucks, Pa	210
Rienza, Mecosta, Mich	12
Rienzi, Alcorn, Miss	290
Rifton Glen, Ulster, N. Y	66
Riga, Lenawee, Mich	120
Riga, Monroe, N. Y	60
Rigdon, Madison, Ind	62
Riggsbee's Store, Chatham, N. C	2
Rigg's Cross Roads, Williamson, Tenn	40
Riggsville, Izard, Ark	51
Riker's Hollow, Steuben, N. Y	18
Riley, McHenry, Ill	22
Riley, Vigo, Ind	17
Riley, Clinton, Mich	22
Riley Centre, Riley, Kans	12
Riley Centre, St. Clair, Mich	16
Riley's Station, Marion, Ky	26
Rileyville, Wayne, Pa	16
Rimer, Armstrong, Pa	23
Rimersburgh, Clarion, Pa	230

* Money-order office.

RIV   ROB

Rinard's Mills, Monroe, Ohio	$12	Riverhead,* (c. h.,) Suffolk, N. Y	$1,000
Rindge, Cheshire, N. H	210	River Point, Steele, Minn	8
Rinehart, Anglaize, Ohio	10	River Point, Kent, R. I	390
Ring, Winnebago, Wis	12	River Raisin, Washtenaw, Mich	44
Ringgold, Cherokee, Ala	6	River Side, New Haven, Conn	34
Ringgold,* (c. h.,) Catoosa, Ga	390	Riverside, Clay, Dak	12
Ringgold, La Grange, Ind	18	Riverside, Kane, Ill	12
Ringgold, Ringgold, Iowa	12	Riverside, Kennebec, Me	130
Ringgold, Bienville, La	42	Riverside, Burt, Nebr	6
Ringgold, Washington, Md	51	Riverside, Burlington, N. J	300
Ringgold, Morgan, Ohio	24	Riverside, Broome, N. Y	12
Ringgold, Jefferson, Pa	25	Riverside, Buncombe, N. C	7
Ringgold, Montgomery, Tenn	23	Riverside, Northumberland, Pa	12
Ringgold, Pittsylvania, Va	59	River Side, Cocke, Tenn	12
Ringoes, Hunterdon, N. J	140	River Styx, Medina, Ohio	73
Ringo's Point, Adair, Mo	11	Riversville, Amherst, Va	12
Ringtown, Schuylkill, Pa	92	Riverton, Litchfield, Conn	230
Ringville, Hampshire, Mass	75	Riverton, Wicomico, Md	13
Ringwood, McHenry, Ill	75	Riverton, Mason, Mich	11
Ringwood, Halifax, N. C	20	Riverton, Warren, Va	13
Ringwood Furnace, Passaic, N. J	12	River Vale, Lawrence, Ind	30
Rinosa, Kankakee, Ill	2	River View, Jefferson, Ky	27
Rio, Hart, Ky	16	Rives, Richland, Ohio	55
Rio, Kemper, Miss	5	Rives Junction, Jackson, Mich	57
Rio, Columbia, Wis	430	Rivesville, Marion, W. Va	38
Rio Grande, Cape May, N. J	42	Rixeyville, Culpeper, Va	12
Rio Grande, Gallia, Ohio	18	Rix's Mills, Muskingum, Ohio	78
Rio Grande City, (c. h.,) Starr, Tex	170	Roachton, Wood, Ohio	17
Rio Mimbres, Grant, N. Mex	46	Road House Station, Greene, Ill	73
Rio Seco, Butte, Cal	12	Roadstown, Cumberland, N. J	100
Rio Vista, Solano, Cal	95	Roadville, Charleston, S. C	14
Ripley, Brown, Ill	120	Roan Mountain, Carter, Tenn	14
Ripley, Somerset, Me	20	Roann, Wabash, Ind	6
Ripley, (c. h.,) Tippah, Miss	230	Roanoke, Randolph, Ala	87
Ripley, Chautauqua, N. Y	330	Roanoke, Huntingdon, Ind	440
Ripley,* Brown, Ohio	1,000	Roanoke, Howard, Mo	300
Ripley, (c. h.,) Lauderdale, Tenn	200	Roanoke, Martin, N. C	12
Ripley Landing, Jackson, W. Va	35	Roanoke, Putnam, Ohio	160
Ripley's, Tyler, W. Va	63	Roan's Prairie, Grimes, Tex	12
Ripley's Mills, Craig, Va	21	Roaring Branch, Lycoming, Pa	100
Ripleyville, Huron, Ohio	33	Roaring Creek, Columbia, Pa	43
Ripon, Labette, Kans	12	Roaring Creek, Randolph, W. Va	12
Ripon,* Fond du Lac, Wis	2,000	Roaring Creek, Jackson, Wis	20
Rippey, Greene, Iowa	34	Roaring Gap, Wilkes, N. C	7
Rippon, Jefferson, W. Va	140	Roaring Run, Botetourt, Va	47
Rippon's Hall, York, Va	12	Roaring Spring, Trigg, Ky	71
Ripton, Addison, Vt	78	Roaring Spring, Blair, Pa	100
Rippyville, Anderson, Ky	29	Robard's Station, Henderson, Ky	12
Risdon, St. Clair, Ill	12	Robbinston, Washington, Me	120
Rish's Store, Lexington, S. C	9	Robbinsville, Mercer, N. J	27
Rising Fawn, Dade, Ga	14	Robbinsville, Red River, Tex	8
Rising Sun, (c. h.,) Ohio, Ind	680	Rob Camp, Claiborne, Tenn	12
Rising Sun, Polk, Iowa	34	Robella, Allegheny, Pa	23
Rising Sun,* Cecil, Md	320	Roberson's Cross Roads, Bledsoe,	
Rising Sun, Crawford, Wis	86	Tenn	18
Risingville, Steuben, N. Y	12	Roberts' Landing, St. Clair, Mich	29
Ritchieville, Dinwiddie, Va	14	Robertson's, Anderson, Tenn	12
Rittersville, Lehigh, Pa	18	Robertson's Mill, Stone, Mo	5
River, Dane, Wis	48	Robertson's Station, Harrison, Ky	32
River aux Vases, St. Genevieve, Mo	12	Robertsonville, Hardin, Ky	97
Riverdale, Clay, Kans	12	Robertsonville, Calhoun, Miss	12
Riverdale, Westchester, N. Y	240	Robertsonville, Sullivan, N. Y	20
Riverdale, Hamilton, Ohio	66	Robertsville, Litchfield, Conn	68
Riverdale, Weber, Utah	40	Robertsville, Stark, Ohio	32
River Edge, Bergen, N. J	12	Robertsville, Anderson, Tenn	15
River Falls,* Pierce, Wis	600	Robeson, Brunswick, N. C	16

* Money-order office.

ROO   ROO

Robeson, Berks, Pa	$12	Rock Creek, Lyon, Kans	$12
Robesonia Furnaces, Berks, Pa	140	Rock Creek, Alamance, N. C	6
Robeystewn, Prince George's, Md	47	Rock Dale, Dubuque, Iowa	80
Robin, Benton, Iowa	21	Rock Dale, Owen, Ky	12
Robin's Nest, Peoria, Ill	58	Rockdale, Chenango, N. Y	96
Robinson, (c. h.,) Crawford, Ill	230	Rock Dale Mills, Berkshire, Mass	12
Robinson, Brown, Kans	93	Rockdale Mills, Jefferson, Pa	69
Robinson, Ottawa, Mich	24	Rock Dam, Falls, Tex	16
Robinson, Brown, Wis	16	Rock Dell, Olmsted, Minn	52
Robinson Creek, Pike, Ky	5	Rock Elm, Pierce, Wis	24
Robinson's Mills, Menard, Ill	24	Rock Elm Centre, Pierce, Wis	58
Robisonville, Bedford, Pa	10	Rock Falls, Whitesides, Ill	570
Rob Roy, Jefferson, Ark	12	Rock Falls, Huron, Mich	85
Rob Roy, Fountain, Ind	44	Rock Falls, Dunn, Wis	77
Robtown, Pickaway, Ohio	8	Rock Farm, Russell, Va	17
Roby's Corner, Merrimack, N. H	46	Rockfield, Carroll, Ind	120
Roche-a-Cri, Adams, Wis	13	Rockfield, Warren, Ky	43
Rochdale, Worcester, Mass	300	Rock Fish, Duplin, N. C	3
Rochelle,* Ogle, Ill	1,100	Rockfish Depot, Nelson, Va	88
Rochelle, Madison, Va	45	*Rockford*, (c. h.,) Coosa, Ala	38
Rocheport, Boone, Mo	380	*Rockford*,* (c. h.,) Winnebago, Ill	3,600
Rochester, Sangamon, Ill	450	Rockford, Jackson, Ind	53
Rochester,* (c. h.,) Fulton, Ind	500	Rockford, Floyd, Iowa	210
Rochester, Cedar, Iowa	80	Rockford, Bourbon, Kan	10
Rochester, Neosho, Kans	12	Rockford,* Kent, Mich	400
Rochester, Butler, Ky	66	Rockford, Wright, Minn	140
Rochester, Plymouth, Mass	120	Rock Ford, Lincoln, Mo	12
Rochester, Oakland, Mich	330	Rockford, Surry, N. C	20
Rochester,* (c. h.,) Olmsted, Minn	2,800	Rockford, Blount, Tenn	40
Rochester, Andrew, Mo	110	Rockford, Harrison, W. Va	22
Rochester, Madison, Mont	12	Rock Grove, Stephenson, Ill	72
Rochester, Strafford, N. H	690	Rock Grove City, Floyd, Iowa	54
Rochester,* (c. h.,) Monroe, N. Y	4,000	Rock Hall, Kent, Md	65
Rochester, Beaver, Pa	920	Rock Haven, Meade, Ky	37
Rochester, Windsor, Vt	360	Rock Hill, St. Louis, Mo	28
Rochester,* Racine, Wis	210	Rock Hill, York, S. C	370
Rochester Depot, Lorain, Ohio	170	Rockhold's, Whitley, Ky	4
Rochester Mills, Wabash, Ill	27	*Rockhouse*, (c. h.,) Menifee, Ky	7
Rock, Pope, Ill	3	Rock House, Hocking, Ohio	12
Rock, Cerro Gordo, Iowa	10	Rock House Prairie, Buchanan, Mo	46
Rock, Cowley, Kans	12	*Rockingham*, (c. h.,) Richmond, N. C	300
Rock, Plymouth, Mass	77	Rockingham, Windham, Vt	80
Rock, Schuylkill, Pa	12	*Rock Island*,* (c. h.,) Rock Island, Ill	2,800
Rockabema, Aroostook, Me	4	Rock Island, Perry, Ind	12
Rockaway, Morris, N. J	570	Rock Island, White, Tenn	12
Rockaway, Queens, N. Y	54	Rock Lake, Wayne, Pa	11
Rock Bluff, Liberty, Fla	5	Rockland, New Haven, Conn	8
Rock Bluff, Cass, Nebr	110	Rockland, Lake, Ill	38
Rock Bottom, Middlesex, Mass	110	*Rockland*,* (c. h.,) Knox, Me	2,800
Rockbridge, Greene, Ill	68	Rockland, Ontonagon, Mich	500
Rock Bridge, Monroe, Ky	12	Rockland, Sullivan, N. Y	69
Rockbridge, Ozark, Mo	12	Rockland, Venango, Pa	81
Rockbridge, Hocking, Ohio	24	Rockland, Providence, R. I	76
Rockbridge, Richland, Wis	30	Rockland Lake, Rockland, N. Y	81
Rockbridge Baths, Rockbridge, Va	37	Rockland Mills, Metcalfe, Ky	20
Rock Butte, Douglas, Colo	9	Rock Lick, Breckinridge, Ky	12
Rock Camp, Lawrence, Ohio	10	Rock Lick, Marshall, W. Va	29
Rock Castle, Patrick, Va	12	Rocklin, Placer, Cal	150
Rock Castle, Mason, W. Va	4	Rock Mills, Randolph, Ala	46
Rock Cave, Upshur, W. Va	37	Rock Mills, Anderson, S. C	8
Rock City, Dutchess, N. Y	64	Rock Mills, Rappahannock, Va	12
Rock City Falls, Saratoga, N. Y	150	Rock Oak, Athens, Ohio	12
Rock Creek, Clark, Ark	12	Rock Point, Jackson, Oreg	51
Rock Creek, Butte, Cal	44	Rock Point, Beaver, Pa	140
Rock Creek, Carroll, Ill	23	*Rockport*, (c. h.,) Hot Spring, Ark	59
Rock Creek, Mitchell, Iowa	18	Rockport, Pike, Ill	72

* Money-order office.

ROC — RON

Rockport,* (c. h.,) Spencer, Ind	$800	Rocky Mount, Miller, Mo		$15
Rockport, Ohio, Ky	14	Rocky Mount, Edgecombe, N. C		410
Rockport, Knox, Me	420	Rocky Mount, (c. h.,) Franklin, Va		150
Rockport, Essex, Mass	740	Rocky Point, New Hanover, N. C		12
Rockport, Copiah, Miss	10	Rocky River, Warren, Tenn		12
Rockport,* (c. h.,) Atchison, Mo	360	Rocky Run, McLeod, Minn		9
Rockport, Cuyahoga, Ohio	160	Rocky Run, Columbia, Wis		30
Rockport, Carbon, Pa	44	Rocky Springs, Claiborne, Miss		12
Rockport, Refugio, Tex	210	Rocky Station, Lee, Va		10
Rockport, Wood, W. Va	18	Rodman, Jefferson, N. Y		220
Rock Prairie, Dade, Mo	12	Rodney, Jefferson, Miss		520
Rock Prairie, Rock, Wis	25	Rodney, Gallia, Ohio		29
Rock Rift, Delaware, N. Y	54	Ro Ellen, Dyer, Tenn		12
Rock River, Rock, Wis	12	Roesburgh, Grant, Ind		10
Rock Run, Stephenson, Ill	120	Roesville, Queen Anne, Md		86
Rocksburgh, Warren, N. J	16	Rogers, Ritchie, W. Va		140
Rock Spring, Chickasaw N., Ind. T.	12	Rogersville, Lauderdale, Ala		40
Rock Spring, Walker, Ga	12	Rogersville, Henry, Ind		25
Rock Spring, Washington, Mo	8	Rogersville, Tuscarawas, Ohio		73
Rock Spring, Orange, N. C	12	Rogersville, Greene, Pa		14
Rock Spring, Centre, Pa	89	Rogersville,* (c. h.,) Hawkins, Tenn		360
Rock Spring, Patrick, Va	5	Rohrersville, Washington, Md		52
Rock Springs, Cecil, Md	61	Rohrsburgh, Columbia, Pa		67
Rock Stream, Yates, N. Y	60	Rokeby, Morgan, Ohio		40
Rockton, Winnebago, Ill	380	Roland, White, Ill		39
Rockton, Clearfield, Pa	62	Roland, Story, Iowa		12
Rockton, Vernon, Wis	12	Roland, Centre, Pa		30
Rock Valley, Redwood, Minn	12	Rolesville, Wake, N. C		21
Rock View, Wyoming, W. Va	5	Rolfe, (c. h.,) Pocahontas, Iowa		83
Rockville, Jefferson, Ala	40	Rolla,* (c. h.,) Phelps, Mo		1,100
Rockville,* Tolland, Conn	2,000	Rollersville, Sandusky, Ohio		67
Rockville, Kankakee, Ill	24	Rollin, Lenawee, Mich		62
Rockville,* (c. h.,) Parke, Ind	800	Rolling Fork, Pope, Minn		12
Rockville, Miami, Kans	39	Rolling Hill, Charlotte, Va		8
Rockville, Knox, Me	40	Rolling Home, Randolph, Mo		5
Rockville,* (c. h.,) Montgomery, Md.	380	Rolling Prairie, Marion, Ark		64
Rockville, Norfolk, Mass	100	Rolling Prairie, La Porte, Ind		220
Rockville, Stearns, Minn	4	Rolling Prairie, Dodge, Wis		140
Rockville, Chester, Pa	51	Rolling Stone, Winona, Minn		24
Rockville, Washington, R. I	42	Rollinsburgh, Monroe, W. Va		16
Rockville, Kane, Utah	20	Rollo, Iosco, Mich		5
Rockville, Hanover, Va	12	Roma, Starr, Tex		20
Rockville, Grant, Wis	47	Romance, Vernon, Wis		4
Rockville Centre, Queens, N. Y	110	Rome,* (c. h.,) Floyd, Ga		3,200
Rockwall, Kaufman, Tex	140	Rome, Peoria, Ill		67
Rockwood, Randolph, Ill	130	Rome, Perry, Ind		110
Rockwood, Fulton, N. Y	100	Rome, Henry, Iowa		76
Rockwood, Roane, Tenn	95	Rome, Kennebec, Me		51
Rocky Bar, (c. h.,) Alturas, Idaho	150	Rome, Lenawee, Mich		99
Rocky Brook, Washington, R. I	66	Rome, Winston, Miss		12
Rocky Comfort, (c. h.,) Little River, Ark	50	Rome,* (c. h.,) Oneida, N. Y		2,800
Rocky Comfort, Newton, Mo	50	Rome, Ashtabula, Ohio		61
Rocky Ford, Scriven, Ga	12	Rome, Bradford, Pa		180
Rocky Ford, Pontotoc, Miss	12	Rome, Smith, Tenn		37
Rocky Fork, Licking, Ohio	12	Rome, Jefferson, Wis		65
Rocky Gap, Bland, Va	14	Rome City, Noble, Ind		190
Rocky Glade, Iron, Mo	12	Romeo,* Macomb, Mich		1,100
Rocky Head, Dale, Ala	12	Romeo, Greene, Tenn		8
Rocky Hill, Hartford, Conn	140	Romine's Mills, Harrison, W. Va		31
Rocky Hill, Somerset, N. J	240	Romney, Tippecanoe, Ind		89
Rocky Hill, Jackson, Ohio	28	Romney, (c. h.,) Hampshire, W. Va		330
Rocky Hill, Fayette, W. Va	6	Romulus, Tuscaloosa, Ala		6
Rocky Hill Station, Edmonson, Ky	92	Romulus, Wayne, Mich		28
Rocky Mount, Meriwether, Ga	19	Romulus, Seneca, N. Y		200
Rocky Mount, Bossier, La	12	Romulus Centre, Seneca, N. Y		12
		Rondo, La Fayette, Ark		72

* Money-order office.

ROS   ROU

Rondo, Polk, Mo	$41
Rondout,* Ulster, N. Y	2,600
Roney, Hickory, Mo	7
Ronkonkoma, Suffolk, N. Y	100
Rono, Perry, Ind	18
Rook's Creek, Livingston, Ill	14
Root, Allen, Ind	41
Root, Montgomery, N. Y	83
Root Creek, Milwaukee, Wis	23
Root River, Mower, Minn	9
Rootstown, Portage, Ohio	110
Rootville, Antrim, Mich	19
Roperville, Gage, Nebr	12
Rosalia, Butler, Kans	12
Rosaryville, Prince George's, Md	12
Rosby's Rock, Marshall, W. Va	38
Roscoe,* Winnebago, Ill	300
Roscoe, Goodhue, Minn	17
Roscoe, St. Clair, Mo	190
Roscoe, Coshocton, Ohio	290
Roscoe Centre, Goodhue, Minn	20
Roscommon, Monroe, Pa	6
Rose, Woodson, Kans	12
Rose, Oakland, Mich	24
Rose, Wayne, N. Y	240
Roseberry, Knox, Tenn	10
Roseboom, Otsego, N. Y	50
Rose Bud, White, Ark	10
Rose Bud, Pope. Ill	12
Roseburgh,* (c. h.,) Douglas, Oreg	420
Roseburgh, Perry, Pa	11
Rosecrans, Lake, Ill	28
Rosecrans, Clinton, Pa	12
Rosecrans, Manitowoc, Wis	23
Rose Creek, Mower, Minn	12
Rose Creek, Jefferson, Nebr	22
Rosedale, Parke, Ind	77
Rosedale, Iberville, La	30
Rosedale, Pasquotank, N. C	12
Rosedale, Madison, Ohio	12
Rosedale, Greene, Pa	18
Rosedale, Russell, Va	23
Rosefield, Peoria, Ill	160
Rose Grove, Hamilton, Iowa	12
Rose Head, (c. h.,) Taylor, Fla	12
Rose Hill, Covington, Ala	6
Rose Hill, Ouachita, Ark	12
Rose Hill, Jasper, Ill	13
Rose Hill, Kosciusko, Ind	6
Rose Hill, Mercer, Ky	12
Rose Hill, Neosho, Kans	12
Rose Hill, Johnson, Mo	12
Rose Hill, Seneca, N. Y	43
Rose Hill, Darke, Ohio	27
Rose Hill, Harris, Tex	16
Rose Hill, Lee, Va	12
Rose Lake, Martin, Minn	9
Roselle, Union, N. J	12
Rosemond, Christian, Ill	300
Rose Mount, Warren, Iowa	15
Rosemount, Dakota, Minn	100
Rosendale, Andrew, Mo	12
Rosendale, Ulster, N. Y	140
Rosendale, Fond du Lac, Wis	200
Rosenhayn, Cumberland, N. J	12
Rose Point, Lawrence, Pa	46

Rose's Valley, Lycoming, Pa	$15
Rose Vale, Clay, Kans	12
Roseville, Franklin, Ark	24
Roseville, Placer, Cal	61
Roseville, Warren, Ill	270
Roseville, Parke, Ind	36
Roseville, Barren, Ky	5
Roseville, Macomb, Mich	82
Roseville, Monongalia, Minn	24
Roseville, Muskingum, Ohio	170
Rosewood, Cleburne, Ala	12
Rosewood, Harrison, Ind	12
Rosiclare, Hardin, Ill	26
Rosindale, Bladen, N. C	53
Roslin, Cumberland, N. C	12
Roslindale, Norfolk, Mass.	12
Roslyn, Queens, N. Y	310
Ross, Lake, Ind	28
Ross, Butler, Ohio	150
Ross, Anderson, Tenn	27
Ross' Corners, York, Me	22
Rosseau, Morgan, Ohio	12
Ross Fork, Oneida, Idaho	12
Ross Grove, De Kalb, Ill	17
Rossie, St. Lawrence, N. Y	130
Rossland, Monroe, Pa	2
Rosston, Armstrong, Pa	16
Rossville, Vermilion, Ill	150
Rossville, Clinton, Ind	160
Rossville, Allamakee, Iowa	88
Rossville, Shawnee, Kans	77
Rossville, Baltimore, Md	120
Rossville, Richmond, N. Y	200
Rossville, Darke, Ohio	12
Rossville, York, Pa	36
Rossville, Chester, S. C	6
Rossville, Fayette, Tenn	140
Rossville, Fayette, Tex	11
Rostraver, Westmoreland, Pa	27
Roswell, Cobb, Ga	200
Rothrock's Mills, Harrison, Ind	4
Rothsville, Lancaster, Pa	20
Rothville, Chariton, Mo	12
Roubidoux, Texas, Mo	9
Rough and Ready, Nevada, Cal	180
Rough and Ready, Anderson, Ky	54
Rough and Ready, Schuylkill, Pa	4
Rough and Ready Furnace, Stewart, Tenn	12
Rough Creek, Laurel, Ky	12
Roulette, Potter, Pa	27
Round Bottom, Monroe, Ohio	24
Round Bottom, Wayne, W. Va	12
Round Grove, Whitesides, Ill	72
Round Grove, Scott, Iowa	40
Round Head, Hardin, Ohio	54
Round Hill, Fairfield, Conn	78
Round Hill, Orange, N. C	2
Round Hill, Adams, Pa	36
Round Hill, Loudoun, Va	34
Round Island, Clinton, Pa	88
Round Knob, Putnam, W. Va	21
Round Lake, Branch, Mich	2
Round Lake, Gonzales, Tex	12
Round Mountain, Blanco, Tex	23
Round Pond, Lincoln, Me	230

* Money-order office.

Round Prairie, Todd, Minn	$10	Ruddel's Mills, Bourbon, Ky	$34
Round Prairie, Vernon, Mo	17	Rudd's Mills, Monroe, Wis	12
Round Rock, Williamson, Tex	100	Rudolph, Le Sueur, Minn	20
Round Top, Wilson, Tenn	8	Rudyville, Hidalgo, Tex	12
Round Top, Fayette, Tex	180	Ruff Creek, Greene, Pa	17
Round Valley, Plumas, Cal	16	Ruffin, Rockingham, N. C	85
Rouse's Point,* Clinton, N. Y	1,000	Ruggles, Ashland, Ohio	51
Rouseville,* Venango, Pa	1,900	Rulo,* Richardson, Nebr	240
Rousseau, Brown, Wis	5	Ruma, Randolph, Ill	50
Rover, Yell, Ark	12	Rumford, Oxford, Me	54
Rowan Mills, Rowan, N. C	1	Rumford Centre, Oxford, Me	93
Rowayton, Fairfield, Conn	140	Rumford Point, Oxford, Me	58
Rowe, Franklin, Mass	56	Rummerfield Creek, Bradford, Pa	61
Rowes, Crawford, Wis	4	Rumney, Grafton, N. H	330
Rowe's Pump, Orangeburgh, S. C	6	Rumsey, McLean, Ky	42
Rowland, Isabella, Mich	6	Rundell's, Crawford, Pa	22
Rowland, Pike, Pa	62	Running Creek, Douglas, Colo	12
Rowland Mills, Hunterdon, N. J	11	Rupert, Columbia, Pa	150
Rowlandsville, Cecil, Md	110	Rupert, Bennington, Vt	590
Rowlesburgh, Preston, W. Va	180	Rural, Rock Island, Ill	24
Rowletta, Pettis, Mo	130	Rural, Linn, Iowa	5
Rowlett's Depot, Hart, Ky	24	Rural, Waupaca, Wis	110
Rowley, Essex, Mass	180	Rural Dale, Grundy, Mo	31
Rows, Ashland, Ohio	90	Rural Dale, Muskingum, Ohio	80
Roxabell, Ross, Ohio	110	Rural Dale, Upshur, W. Va	12
Roxalana, Roane, W. Va	9	Rural Hill, Jefferson, N. Y	65
Roxana, Sussex, Del	32	Rural Hill, Wilson, Tenn	9
Roxana, Eaton, Mich	12	Rural Retreat, Coles, Ill	12
Roxanna, Paulding, Ga	12	Rural Retreat, Wythe, Va	170
Roxborough, (c. h.,) Person, N. C	94	Rural Ridge, Allegheny, Pa	12
Roxbury, Litchfield, Conn	130	Rural Shade, Navarro, Tex	20
Roxbury, Oxford, Me	10	Rural Vale, Lapeer, Mich	10
Roxbury, Delaware, N. Y	210	Rural Valley, Armstrong, Pa	75
Roxbury, Morgan, Ohio	19	Rush, Jo Daviess, Ill	20
Roxbury, Franklin, Pa	52	Rush, Monroe, N. Y	99
Roxbury, Washington, Vt	210	Rush, Tuscarawas, Ohio	16
Roxbury, Dane, Wis	15	Rush, Susquehanna, Pa	78
Roxbury Mills, Howard, Md	18	Rushbottom, Holt, Mo	8
Roxobel, Bertie, N. C	51	Rush City, Chisago, Minn	12
Roxton, Lamar, Tex	8	Rush Creek, Union, Ohio	20
Royal Centre, Cass, Ind	150	Rush Creek, Navarro, Tex	32
Royal Oak, Talbot, Md	110	Rushford,* Fillmore, Minn	800
Royal Oak, Oakland, Mich	150	Rushford, Allegany, N. Y	440
Royal Oak, Paulding, Ohio	37	Rush Four Corners, Susquehanna,	
Royalston, Worcester, Mass	160	Pa	10
Royalton, Boone, Ind	32	Rush Lake, Palo Alto, Iowa	12
Royalton, Russell, Ky	2	Rush Lake, Otter Tail, Minn	12
Royalton, Niagara, N. Y	56	Rush River, Sibley, Minn	10
Royalton, Fairfield, Ohio	46	Rush Run, Jefferson, Ohio	86
Royalton, Crawford, Pa	24	Rush Run, Ritchie, W. Va	12
Royalton, Windsor, Vt	320	Rushsylvania, Logan, Ohio	240
Royalton, Waupaca, Wis	52	Rushtown, Northumberland, Pa	3
Royer's Ford, Montgomery, Pa	260	*Rushville*,* (c. h.,) Schuyler, Ill	870
Royerton, Delaware, Ind	23	*Rushville*,* (c. h.,) Rush, Ind	960
Roysfield, Somerset, N. J	22	Rushville, Buchanan, Mo	99
Royston, Pike, Ark	10	Rushville, Yates, N. Y	400
Rozetta, Henderson, Ill	59	Rushville, Fairfield, Ohio	110
Rubicon, Dodge, Wis	130	Rushville, Susquehanna, Pa	63
Ruby, St. Clair, Mich	50	Rusk, Surry, N. C	3
Ruby Valley, Elko, Nev	68	*Rusk*, (c. h.,) Cherokee, Tex	250
Ruckersville, Elbert, Ga	23	Russell, Lucas, Iowa	130
Ruckersville, Tippah, Miss	8	Russell, Hampden, Mass	170
Ruckersville, Green, Va	40	Russell, St. Lawrence, N. Y	220
Ruckerville, Clark, Ky	9	Russell, Geauga, Ohio	20
Rucksville, Lehigh, Pa	27	Russell, Sheboygan, Wis	20
Rudd, Floyd, Iowa	12	Russell Hill, Wyoming, Pa	21

* Money-order office.

SAC | SAI

Russellsburgh, Warren, Pa	$91	Sac City, (c. h.,) Sac, Iowa	$110
Russell's Hill, Shannon, Mo	5	Sacket's Harbor,* Jefferson, N. Y	750
Russell's Mills, Parke, Ind	16	Saco,* York, Me	2, 100
Russell's Place, Lawrence, Ohio	21	Sacramento. White, Ill	37
Russell's Station, Highland, Ohio	64	Sacramento, McLean, Ky	60
Russellville, (c. h.,) Franklin, Ala	72	Sacramento, Wright, Mo	12
Russellville, Pope, Ark	150	Sacramento, Schuylkill, Pa	14
Russellville, Monroe, Ga	20	SACRAMENTO CITY,* (c. h.,) Sacramento, Cal	4, 000
Russellville, Lawrence, Ill	59	Sacred Heart, Renville, Minn	8
Russellville, Putnam, Ind	84	Sadawga, Windham, Vt	71
Russellville,* (c. h.,) Logan, Ky	1, 100	Saddle River, Bergen, N. J	44
Russellville, Cole, Mo	28	Saddler's Creek, Anderson, S. C	14
Russellville, Brown, Ohio	100	Sadowa, Randolph, Ill	12
Russellville, Chester, Pa	72	Sadsburyville, Chester, Pa	44
Russellville, Jefferson, Tenn	230	Saegerstown, Crawford, Pa	190
Russellville, Fayette, W. Va	12	Saegersville, Lehigh, Pa	26
Russia, Herkimer, N. Y	64	Safe Harbor, Lancaster, Pa	82
Russia, Shelby, Ohio	23	Sagetown, Henderson, Ill	180
Russiaville, Howard, Ind	82	Sagerille, (c. h.,) Hamilton, N. Y	28
Rutersville, Fayette, Tex	110	Sag Harbor,* Suffolk, N. Y	1, 200
Ruth, Texas, Mo	12	Saginaw,* (c. h.,) Saginaw, Mich	2, 800
Rutherford Depot, Gibson, Tenn	310	Sago, Muskingum, Ohio	110
Rutherford Park, Bergen, N. J	280	Sago, Upshur, W. Va	6
Rutherfordton, (c. h.,) Rutherford, N. C	370	Sagone, Du Page, Ill	22
Ruther Glen, Caroline, Va	94	Saguache, (c. h.,) Saguache, Colo	31
Rutland, Humboldt, Iowa	16	Saidora, Mason, Ill	12
Rutland, Harrison, Ky	4	Saint Albans, Hancock, Ill	6
Rutland, Anne Arundel, Md	41	Saint Albans, Somerset, Me	230
Rutland, Worcester, Mass	160	Saint Albans,* (c. h.,) Franklin, Vt	2, 400
Rutland, Martin, Minn	10	Saint Albans Bay, Franklin, Vt	82
Rutland, Jefferson, N. Y	79	Saint Andrew's, Orange, N. Y	62
Rutland, Meigs, Ohio	110	Saint Anna, Calumet, Wis	55
Rutland, Tioga, Pa	63	Saint Anne, Kaukakee, Ill	100
Rutland,* (c. h.,) Rutland, Vt	2, 400	Saint Annie, Pulaski, Mo	26
Rutland, Dane, Wis	58	Saint Ansgar, Mitchell, Iowa	220
Rutledge, (c. h.,) Crenshaw, Ala	21	Saint Anthony's Falls,* Hennepin, Minn	1, 700
Rutledge, Morgan, Ga	97	Saint Aubert's, Callaway, Mo	18
Rutledge, (c. h.,) Grainger, Tenn	80	Saint Augusta, Stearns, Minn	22
Ryan, Kewaunee, Wis	12	Saint Augustine,* (c. h.,) St. John's, Fla	950
Ryan Creek, Winston, Ala	19	Saint Augustine, Knox, Ill	99
Ryan's Well, Prentiss, Miss	12	Saint Augustine, Cecil, Md	42
Rye, Rockingham, N. H	69	Saint Augustine, Cambria, Pa	90
Rye, Westchester, N. Y	740	Saint Benedict, Doniphan, Kans	12
Ryegate, Caledonia, Vt	69	Saint Bernard, (c. h.,) St. Bernard, La.	6
Ryerson's Station, Greene, Pa	38	Saint Bernice, Vermillion, Ind	14
Rye Valley, Baker, Oreg	12	Saint Bethlehem, Montgomery, Tenn	12
Rye Valley, Smyth, Va	8	Saint Bonifacius, Hennepin, Minn	30
Ryland's Depot, Greenville, Va	6	Saint Bonifacius, Cambria, Pa	12
Rynex's Corners, Schenectady, N. Y.	10	Saint Bridget, Marshall, Kans	5
		Saint Catharine, Linn, Mo	280
S.		Saint Charles, Arkansas, Ark	69
		Saint Charles, Pueblo, Colo	12
Sabattus, Androscoggin, Me	210	Saint Charles,* Kane, Ill	900
Sabbath Rest, Blair, Pa	52	Saint Charles, Madison, Iowa	130
Sabbot Island, Goochland, Va	12	Saint Charles, (c. h.,) St. Charles, La.	13
Sabetha, Nemaha, Kans	34	Saint Charles, Saginaw, Mich	390
Sabillisville, Frederick, Md	41	Saint Charles,* Winona, Minn	890
Sabina, Clinton, Ohio	130	Saint Charles,* (c. h.,) St. Charles, Mo.	1, 700
Sabinal, Socorro, N. Mex	12	Saint Charles, Cuming, Nebr	56
Sabinal, Uvalde, Tex	12	Saint Charles, Butler, Ohio	10
Sabine Pass, Jefferson, Tex	63	Saint Charles, (c. h.,) Rich, Utah	15
Sabinetown, Sabine, Tex	16	Saint Clair, Monona, Iowa	8
Sabinsville, Tioga, Pa	26		
Sabula,* Jackson, Iowa	660		
Saccarappa, Cumberland, Me	470		

* Money-order office.

SAI   SAI

Saint Clair,* (c. h.,) St. Clair, Mich.	$1,000	Saint Johnsbury Centre, Caledonia,	
Saint Clair, Franklin, Mo	250	Vt	$210
Saint Clair, Columbiana, Ohio	13	Saint JohnsburyEast, Caledonia,Vt.	160
Saint Clair,* Schuylkill, Pa	890	Saint Johnsville, Montgomery,N.Y.	720
Saint Clairsville,* (c. h.,) Belmont,		Saint Joseph, Pah Ute, Ariz	44
Ohio	630	Saint Joseph, Pembina, Dak	10
Saint Clairsville, Bedford, Pa	120	Saint Joseph,Vanderburgh,Ind	8
Saint Clement's Bay, St. Mary's, Md.	29	Saint Joseph,* Berrien, Mich	1,400
Saint Cloud, Heard, Ga	10	Saint Joseph, Stearns, Minn	180
Saint Cloud,* (c. h.,) Stearns, Minn..	1,700	Saint Joseph,* (c. h.,) Buchanan, Mo.	4,000
Saint Cloud, Scott, Mo	12	Saint Joseph, Susquehanna, Pa	22
Saint Croix Falls, Polk, Wis	270	Saint Joseph's, Champaign, Ill	62
Saint David, Fulton, Ill	37	Saint Joseph's, (c. h.,) Tensas, La	40
Saint Denis, Baltimore, Md	120	Saint Joseph's College, Perry, Ohio.	36
Saint Deroin, Nemaha, Nebr	88	Saint Joseph's Hill, Clarke, Ind	11
Saint Donatus, Jackson, Iowa	87	Saint Lawrence, Scott, Minn	39
Saint Elmo, Fayette, Ill	74	Saint Lawrence, Jefferson, N. Y	97
Saint Elmo, Christian, Ky	10	Saint Lawrence, Chatham, N. C	28
Saint Elmo, Allegheny, Pa	10	Saint Lawrence, Cambria, Pa	12
Saint Francis, Anoka, Minn	68	Saint Lawrence, Washington, Wis.	160
Saint Francis Station, Milwaukee,		Saint Leger, Ozark, Mo	7
Wis	330	Saint Leon, Dearborn, Ind	25
Saint Francisville, Lawrence, Ill	46	Saint Leonard's, Calvert, Md	16
Saint Francisville,* (c. h.,) W. Feli-		Saint Louis, Sierra, Cal	59
ciana, La	670	Saint Louis, Miami, Kans	15
Saint Francisville, Clarke, Mo	97	Saint Louis, Gratiot, Mich	240
Saint Frederick, Nemaha, Nebr	13	Saint Louis,* (c. h.,) St. Louis, Mo ..	4,000
Saint Gabriel, Iberville, La	72	Saint Louis, Jefferson, Mont	12
Saint Genevieve, (c. h.,) St. Genevieve,		Saint Louis, Marion, Oreg	30
Mo	330	Saint Louis Crossing, Bartholomew,	
Saint George, Kankakee, Ill	8	Ind	65
Saint George, Pottawatomie, Kans.	120	Saint Louisville, Licking, Ohio	91
Saint George, Knox, Me	59	Saint Lucie, (c. h.,) Brevard, Fla	12
Saint George, McLeod, Minn	12	Saint Margaret's, Anne Arundel, Md.	25
Saint George, (c. h.,) Washington,		Saint Marie, Jasper, Ill	77
Utah	440	Saint Mark's, Wakulla, Fla	83
Saint George, Chittenden, Vt	150	Saint Mark's, Randolph, Ill	12
Saint George,* (c. h.,) Tucker, W. Va.	47	Saint Martin's, Worcester, Md	17
Saint George's, New Castle, Del	350	Saint Martin's, Morgan, Mo	54
Saint George's, Colleton, S. C	73	Saint Martin's, Brown, Ohio	140
Saint Helen, (c. h.,) Columbia, Oreg.	150	Saint Martin's, Milwaukee, Wis	55
Saint Helena, Napa, Cal	290	Saint Martinville, (c. h.,) St. Martin's,	
Saint Helena, (c. h.,) Cedar, Nebr	62	La	120
Saint Henry, Le Sueur, Minn	12	Saint Mary's, Huerfano, Colo	12
Saint Henry's, Mercer, Ohio	38	Saint Mary's, Camden, Ga	190
Saint Hubertus, Le Sueur, Minn	21	Saint Mary's, Vigo, Ind	150
Saint Inigoes, St. Mary's, Md	54	Saint Mary's, Marion, Ky	120
Saint Jacob, Madison, Ill	87	Saint Mary's, St. Genevieve, Mo	100
Saint James, (c. h.,) Manitou, Mich.	12	Saint Mary's,* Auglaize, Ohio	720
Saint James, Phelps, Mo	190	Saint Mary's, Elk, Pa	850
Saint James, Cedar, Nebr	54	Saint Mary's, Refugio, Tex	85
Saint James, Suffolk, N. Y	98	Saint Mary's, (c.h.,) Pleasants,W.Va.	8
Saint John, Bradley, Ark	14	Saint Mary's, Monroe, Wis	34
Saint John, Colusa, Cal	18	Saint Mary's Mission, Pottawato-	
Saint John, Perry, Ill	120	mie, Kans	160
Saint John, Lake, Ind	38	Saint Matthew's, Jefferson, Ky	24
Saint John, Harrison, Iowa	32	Saint Matthew's, Orangeburgh, S. C.	100
Saint John, Putnam, Mo	42	Saint Maurice, Decatur, Ind	19
Saint John, Hertford, N. C	6	Saint Maurice, Winn, La	8
Saint John's,* (c. h.,) Clinton, Mich.	1,700	Saint Meinrad, Spencer, Ind	54
Saint John's, Auglaize, Ohio	53	Saint Michael's, Talbot, Md	230
Saint John's, Stewart, Tenn	12	Saint Michael's, Wright, Minn	25
Saint Johnsburgh, Niagara, N. Y	20	Saint Morgan, Madison, Ill	25
Saint Johnsbury,* (c. h.,) Caledonia,		Saint Nazians, Manitowoc, Wis	12
Vt	2,100	Saint Nicholas, Atchison, Kans	12
		Saint Nicholas, Schuylkill, Pa	520

* Money-order office.

12 P O

SAL

Saint Omer, Coles, Ill	$14
Saint Omer, Decatur, Ind	60
Saint Paris, Champaign, Ohio	310
Saint Paul, Madison, Ark	13
Saint Paul, Decatur, Ind	260
Saint Paul, Lee, Iowa	44
Saint Paul, Montgomery, Kans	12
SAINT PAUL,* (c. h.,) Ramsey, Minn.	4,000
Saint Paul's, Robeson, N. C	12
Saint Paul's, Pickaway, Ohio	33
Saint Peter,* (c. h.,) Nicollet, Minn.	1,200
Saint Peter's, Franklin, Ind	24
Saint Peter's, St. Landry, La	12
Saint Peter's, St. Charles, Mo	61
Saint Peter's, Chester, Pa	39
Saint Petersburgh, Clarion, Pa	13
Saint Rose, Grant, Wis	31
Saint Sebald, Clayton, Iowa	64
Saint Stephen's Church, King and Queen, Va	50
Saint Stephen's Depot, Charleston, S. C	100
Saint Tammany's, Mecklenburgh, Va	24
Saint Thomas, (c. h.,) Pah Ute, Ariz.	39
Saint Thomas, Cole, Mo	44
Saint Thomas, Franklin, Pa	120
Saint Vrain, Weld, Colo	10
Saint Wendell's, Posey, Ind	36
Sakeville, Randolph, Ill	17
Salado, Bell, Tex	190
Salamanca, Cattaraugus, N. Y	560
Salamonia, Jay, Ind	48
Sale Creek, Hamilton, Tenn	16
Salem, Lee, Ala	240
Salem, New London, Conn	170
Salem, Walker, Ga	12
Salem,* (c. h.,) Marion, Ill	1,400
Salem,* (c. h.,) Washington, Ind	750
Salem,* Henry, Iowa	490
Salem, Livingston, Ky	63
Salem, Franklin, Me	38
Salem, Dorchester, Md	17
Salem,* (c. h.,) Essex, Mass	3,200
Salem, Washtenaw, Mich	24
Salem, Olmsted, Minn	37
Salem, (c. h.,) Dent, Mo	240
Salem, Richardson, Nebr	190
Salem, Rockingham, N. H	210
Salem,* (c. h.,) Salem, N. J	1,600
Salem, (c. h.,) Washington, N. Y	1,000
Salem,* Forsyth, N. C	920
Salem,* Columbiana, Ohio	2,400
SALEM,* (c. h.,) Marion, Oreg	2,000
Salem, Snyder, Pa	12
Salem, Newton, Tex	10
Salem,* (c. h.,) Roanoke, Va	950
Salem, Kenosha, Wis	190
Salem Centre, Steuben, Ind	42
Salem Centre, Westchester, N. Y.	43
Salem Centre, Meigs, Ohio	18
Salem Chapel, Forsyth, N. C	3
Salem Church, Randolph, N. C	4
Salem Cross Roads, Westmoreland, Pa	270
Salem Depot, Rockingham, N. H.	130

SAL

Salem Fauquier, Fauquier, Va	$210
Salesville, Guernsey, Ohio	49
Salfordville, Montgomery, Pa	49
Salina, Kankakee, Ill	12
Salina, Harrison, Ind	12
Salina, Jefferson, Iowa	110
Salina,* (c. h.,) Saline, Kans	1,100
Salina, Onondaga, N. Y	780
Salina, Athens, Ohio	120
Salina, Westmoreland, Pa	37
Salinas, Monterey, Cal	150
Saline, Bienville, La	6
Saline, Washtenaw, Mich	480
Saline, Mercer, Mo	14
Saline City, Saline, Mo	12
Saline Mines, Gallatin, Ill	21
Saline Valley, Saline, Kans	12
Salineville,* Columbiana, Ohio	480
Salisbury, Litchfield, Conn	240
Salisbury, Sangamon, Ill	42
Salisbury,* (c. h.,) Wicomico, Md	800
Salisbury, Essex, Mass	190
Salisbury, Chariton, Mo	530
Salisbury, Merrimack, N. H	170
Salisbury, Herkimer, N. Y	110
Salisbury,* (c. h.,) Rowan, N. C	1,200
Salisbury, Lancaster, Pa	21
Salisbury, Addison, Vt	120
Salisbury Centre, Herkimer, N. Y.	150
Salisbury Cove, Hancock, Me	68
Salisbury Mills, Orange, N. Y	110
Salladyburgh, Lycoming, Pa	65
Salmon Brook, Aroostook, Me	19
Salmon City, (c. h.,) Lemhi, Idaho	12
Salmon Falls, El Dorado, Cal	24
Salmon Falls, Strafford, N. H	500
Salmon River, Oswego, N. Y	56
Saloma, Taylor, Ky	16
Salona, Clinton, Pa	140
Sal Soda, Crenshaw, Ala	6
Salt Creek, Porter, Ind	12
Salt Creek, Perry, Ky	2
Salt Creek, Chariton, Mo	87
Salt Creek, Holmes, Ohio	24
Salt Creek, Polk, Oreg	13
Salt Creek, (c. h.,) Juab, Utah	200
Salt Creek, Amherst, Va	45
Saltersville, Hudson, N. J	48
Saltillo, Lee, Miss	120
Saltillo, Lancaster, Nebr	15
Saltillo, Holmes, Ohio	10
Saltillo, Huntingdon, Pa	12
Saltillo, Hardin, Tenn	41
Saltillo, Hopkins, Tex	9
Saltilloville, Washington, Ind	79
SALT LAKE CITY,* (c. h.,) Salt Lake, Utah	3,600
Salt Lick, Clearfield, Pa	17
Salt Lick Ridge, Braxton, W. Va.	11
Salt Marsh, (c. h.,) Republic, Kans.	34
Saltpetre Cave, Botetourt, Va	16
Salt Point, Dutchess, N. Y	76
Salt River, Isabella, Mich	130
Saltsburgh, Indiana, Pa	450
Salt Springs, Howard, Kans	14
Salt Sulphur Springs, Monroe, W. Va.	77

* Money-order office.

SAN   SAN

Saltville, Washington, Va	$200	Sandstone, Jackson, Mich	$75
Salubria, Ada, Idaho	12	Sand Stone, Vernon, Mo	12
Saluda, Jefferson, Ind	24	Sandt's Eddy, Northampton, Pa	12
Saluda, (c. h.,) Middlesex, Va	48	Sandusky, Lee, Iowa	370
Saluda Oldtown, Newberry, S. C	15	Sandusky, Cattaraugus, N. Y	140
Salunga, Lancaster, Pa	50	*Sandusky,** (c. h.,) Erie, Ohio	3,200
Saluria, Calhoun, Tex	50	Sandusky, Sauk, Wis	81
Salvisa, Mercer, Ky	150	Sandwich,* DeKalb, Ill	1,200
Salyersville, (c. h.,) Magoffin, Ky	37	Sandwich,* Barnstable, Mass	960
Salzburgh, Bay, Mich	51	Sandwich, Carroll, N. H	87
Samantha, Highland, Ohio	12	Sandy, Columbiana, Ohio	190
Samaria, Johnson, Ind	36	Sandy, Jackson, W. Va	23
Sammonsville, Fulton, N. Y	27	Sandy Beach, Cumberland, Me	3
Sampson Creek, Harrison, Mo	12	Sandy Bottom, Middlesex, Va	27
Sam's Creek, Carroll, Md	35	Sandy Creek, Oswego, N. Y	430
Samsonville, Ulster, N. Y	26	Sandy Creek, Randolph, N. C	19
Samsonville, Jackson, Ohio	100	Sandy Creek, Crawford, Pa	10
Samsville, Edwards, Ill	30	Sandy Cross, Oglethorpe, Ga	12
Samuel's Depot, Nelson, Ky	53	Sandy Flat, Greenville, S. C	4
San Anders, Milam, Tex	9	Sandy Ford, Madison, Fla	20
San Andreas, Calaveras, Cal	370	Sandy Grove, Chatham, N. C	9
San Antonio, Monterey, Cal	150	Sandy Hill, Worcester, Md	47
San Antonio, Socorro, N. Mex	12	*Sandy Hill,** (c. h.,) Washington,	
San Antonio,* (c. h.,) Bexar, Tex	3,600	N. Y	1,100
San Augustine, (c.h.,)San Augustine,		Sandy Hill, Perry, Pa	21
Tex	190	Sandy Hill, Henry, Tenn	13
San Benito, Monterey, Cal	12	Sandy Hook, Fairfield, Conn	390
San Bernadino,* (c.h.,) San Bernard-		*Sandy Hook,* (c. h.,) Elliott, Ky	12
ino, Cal	460	Sandy Hook, Harford, Md	12
Sanborn, Niagara, N. Y	130	Sandy Hook, Rappahannock, Va	12
Sanbornton, Belknap, N. H	120	Sandy Lake, Mercer, Pa	230
San Buenaventura, Santa Barbara,		Sandy Level, Pittsylvania, Va	12
Cal	160	Sandy Mush, Buncombe, N. C	6
Sanburn, Johnson, Ill	12	Sandy Point, Waldo, Me	78
Sand Bank, Oswego, N. Y	280	Sandy Point, Brazoria, Tex	12
Sand Beach, Huron, Mich	100	Sandy Spring,* Montgomery, Md	370
Sandborn, Knox, Ind	12	Sandy Springs, Grant, Ark	12
Sand Brook, Hunterdon, N. J	14	Sandyville, Warren, Iowa	120
Sand Creek,* Scott, Minn	280	Sandyville, Tuscarawas, Ohio	35
Sand Cut, Wayne, Pa	220	Sanel, Mendocino, Cal	12
Sandefer's Store, Carroll, Ky	8	San Elizario, El Paso, Tex	20
Sander's Hill, Montgomery, N. C	6	San Felipe, Santa Clara, Cal	12
Sanderson, (c. h.,) Baker, Fla	12	San Felipe, Austin, Tex	60
Sanders' Store, Carteret, N. C	12	Sanford, York, Me	160
Sandersville, (c.h.,) Washington, Ga.	390	Sanford, Broome, N. Y	49
Sand Fly, Bastrop, Tex	14	Sanford's Corners, Jefferson, N. Y	50
Sandford, Vigo, Ind	84	Sanfordville, Cherokee, Kans	12
Sand Fork, Gallia, Ohio	8	*San Francisco,** (c.h.,) San Francisco,	
Sand Fork, Gilmer, W. Va	12	Cal	4,000
Sandgate, Bennington, Vt	44	San Gabriel, Los Angeles, Cal	19
Sand Hill, Lewis, Ky	18	San Gabriel, Milam, Tex	11
Sand Hill, Scotland, Mo	36	Sangamon Station, Macon, Ill	41
Sand Hollow, Morgan, Ohio	5	Sangerfield, Oneida, N. Y	100
San Diego, Nueces, Tex	12	Sangerville, Piscataquis, Me	100
Sandisfield, Berkshire, Mass	28	Sangerville, Augusta, Va	28
Sand Lake, Lake, Ill	16	San Jacinto, San Diego, Cal	12
Sand Lake, Kent, Mich	12	San Jacinto, Jennings, Ind	11
Sand Lake, Monongalia, Minn	15	San Jacinto, Houston, Minn	10
Sand Lake, Rensselaer, N. Y	210	*San José,** (c.h.,) Santa Clara, Cal	3,400
Sandoval, Marion, Ill	460	San José, Mason, Ill	220
Sandown, Rockingham, N. H	24	San José, San Miguel, N. Mex	12
Sand Patch, Somerset, Pa	130	San Juan, Monterey, Cal	350
Sand Point, Volusia, Fla	12	San Juan, Rio Arriba, N. Mex	12
Sand Rock, Cherokee, Ala	12	*San Leandro,* (c. h.,) Alameda, Cal	380
Sand Spring, Delaware, Iowa	350	San Lorenzo, Alameda, Cal	140
Sand Springs, Webster, Mo	19	*San Luis,* (c. h.,) Costilla, Colo	33

* Money-order office.

SEN   SHA

*Searcy,** (c. h.,) White, Ark	$410
Searight's, Fayette, Pa	40
Searsburgh, Schuyler, N. Y	120
Searsburgh, Bennington, Vt	58
Searsmout, Waldo, Me	150
Searsport,* Waldo, Me	620
Searsville, San Mateo, Cal	53
Searsville, Orange, N. Y	28
Seaton, Fayette, Iowa	13
Seattle, (c. h.,) King, Wash	330
Sea View, Northampton, Va	18
Seaville, Cape May, N. J	120
Sebago, Cumberland, Me	54
Sebago, Linn, Mo	5
Sebastopol, Sonoma, Cal	82
Sebec, Piscataquis, Me	83
Sebewa, Ionia, Mich	29
Sebewaing, Huron, Mich	100
Sebree, Webster, Ky	12
Sechlersville, Jackson, Wis	56
Secillia, Calhoun, Mich	10
Second Creek, Greenbrier, W. Va	47
Secor, Woodford, Ill	420
*Sedalia,** (c. h.,) Pettis, Mo	2,500
Sedge's Garden, Forsyth, N. C	6
Sedgewick, Decatur, Iowa	12
Sedgwick, Sedgwick, Kans	12
Sedgwick, Hancock, Me	210
Seekonk, Bristol, Mass	12
Seely Creek, Chemung, N. Y	49
Seelyville, Vigo, Ind	36
Sego, Perry, Ohio	30
Seguin, (c. h.,) Guadalupe, Tex	420
Seiad Valley, Siskiyou, Cal	9
Seiberlingville, Lehigh, Pa	10
Seidersville, Northampton, Pa	23
Seigfried's Bridge, Northampton, Pa	150
Seisholtzville, Berks, Pa	24
Selbysport, Alleghany, Md	20
Selbyville, Sussex, Del	45
Selden, Suffolk, N. Y	45
Selin's Grove,* Snyder, Pa	890
Selkirk, Marion, S. C	12
Sellersburgh, Clarke, Ind	96
Seller's Landing, Hardin, Ill	36
Sellersville, Bucks, Pa	310
Sell's Station, Adams, Pa	39
*Selma,** (c. h.,) Dallas, Ala	3,000
Selma, Drew, Ark	52
Selma, McLean, Ill	72
Selma, Delaware, Ind	150
Selma, Wayne, Iowa	59
Selma, Johnston, N. C	140
Selma, Clark, Ohio	120
Selma, Bexar, Tex	29
Selma, Alleghany, Va	41
Seminary, Ouachita, Ark	12
Sempronius, Cayuga, N. Y	32
Sempronius, Austin, Tex	12
Senatobia, De Soto, Miss	320
Seneca, La Salle, Ill	580
Seneca, Kossuth, Iowa	5
*Seneca,** (c. h.,) Nemaha, Kans	480
Seneca, Montgomery, Md	12
seneca, Lenawee, Mich	16
seneca, Newton, Mo	12
Seneca, Schuyler, N. Y	$8
Seneca, Venango, Pa	80
Seneca, Crawford, Wis	44
Seneca Castle, Ontario, N. Y	100
Seneca Falls,* Seneca, N. Y	2,800
Senecaville, Guernsey, Ohio	140
Senex, McLean, Ill	89
Sennet, Cayuga, N. Y	96
Senoia, Coweta, Ga	32
Sentinel, Juneau, Wis	18
Sentinel Prairie, Polk, Mo	22
Serbin, Bastrop, Tex	24
Serena, La Salle, Ill	10
Serena, Stafford, Va	12
Sereno, Columbia, Pa	12
Sergeant Bluffs, Woodbury, Iowa	120
Sergeantsville, Hunterdon, N. J	45
Service, Beaver, Pa	13
Setauket, Suffolk, N. Y	130
Setzler's Store, Chester, Pa	85
Sevastopol, Kosciusko, Ind	65
Seven Fountains, Shenandoah, Va	49
Seven Islands, Fluvanna, Va	25
Seven Mile, Butler, Ohio	150
Seven Mile Ford, Smyth, Va	80
Seven Mile House, Erie, Ohio	51
Seven Stars, Adams, Pa	13
Seventy-Eight, Johnson, Iowa	4
Seventy-Six, Clinton, Ky	5
Seventy-Six, Beaver, Pa	14
Seventy-Six Center, Washington, Iowa	12
Seven Valleys, York, Pa	83
Severance, Doniphan, Kans	12
Sevierville, (c. h.,) Sevier, Tenn	70
Seville, Fulton, Ill	29
Seville, Madison, Va	8
Sewanee, Franklin, Tenn	300
Seward, Seward, Nebr	59
Seward, Schoharie, N. Y	30
Sewee, Meigs, Tenn	21
Sewellsville, Belmont, Ohio	48
Sewicklyville, Allegheny, Pa	300
Sexton's Creek, Clay, Ky	2
Sextonville, Richland, Wis	120
Seymour, New Haven, Conn	1,000
Seymour,* Jackson, Ind	1,200
Seymour, Hart, Ky	10
Seymour, Allegany, N. Y	51
Seymour, Outagamie, Wis	12
Seymoursville, Grant, W. Va	26
Shabbonas Grove, De Kalb, Ill	160
Shabonier, Fayette, Ill	82
Shackelford, Henderson, Tex	12
Shade, Athens, Ohio	20
Shade Furnace, Somerset, Pa	9
Shade Gap, Huntingdon, Pa	150
Shade Mills, Alleghany, Md	12
Shade Valley, Juniata, Pa	12
Shadeville, Franklin, Ohio	90
Shadwell, Albemarle, Va	47
Shady, Johnson, Tenn	2
Shady Grove, Taylor, Fla	12
Shady Grove, Crittenden, Ky	12
Shady Grove, Washington, La	12
Shady Grove, Franklin, Pa	59

* Money-order office.

SHA | SHE

Shady Grove, Franklin, Va	$21	Sharpsville, Washington, Ky	$11
Shady Hill, Henderson, Tenn	8	Sharpsville Furnace, Mercer, Pa	600
Shady Plain, Armstrong, Pa	27	Sharptown, Wicomico, Md	52
Shady Spring, Raleigh, W. Va	5	Sharptown, Salem, N. J	85
Shaefferstown, Lebanon, Pa	160	Shartlesville, Berks, Pa	58
Shaft's Bridge, Somerset, Pa	38	*Shasta,* (*c. h.,*) Shasta, Cal	540
Shaftsbury, Bennington, Vt	79	Shattuckville, Franklin, Mass	12
Shaker Village, Merrimack, N. H	71	Shauck's, Morrow, Ohio	81
Shakleford's, King and Queen, Va	48	Shaumburgh, Cook, Ill	25
Shakopee, (*c. h.,*) Scott, Minn	710	Shave Head, Cass, Mich	12
Shaler's Mills, Knox, Ohio	81	Shaver's Creek, Huntingdon, Pa	260
Shalersville, Portage, Ohio	91	Shavertown, Delaware, N. Y	20
Shambling's Mills, Roane, W. Va	3	*Shawanaw,* (*c. h.,*) Shawanaw, Wis	120
Shamburgh,* Venango, Pa	1,700	Shawangunk, Ulster, N. Y	83
Shamokin,* Northumberland, Pa	1,300	Shawhan, Bourbon, Ky	70
Shamokin Dam, Snyder, Pa	37	Shaw Hill, Crawford, Wis	12
Shamong, Burlington, N. J	40	Shawnee, Johnson, Kans	260
Shamrock, Callaway, Mo	18	Shawnee, Niagara, N. Y	22
Shanandoah, Richland, Ohio	36	Shawnee, Monroe, Pa	54
Shandaken, Ulster, N. Y	160	Shawnee Mission, Johnson, Kans	12
Shaudsville, Pope, Ill	12	Shawnee Mound, Tippecanoe, Ind	49
Shane, Baltimore, Md	12	Shawnee Mound, Henry, Mo	74
Shane's Crossings, Mercer, Ohio	68	*Shawneetown,* (*c. h.,*) Gallatin, Ill	790
Shanesville, Tuscarawas, Ohio	180	Shawnee Village, Mississippi, Ark	12
Shanesville, Berks, Pa	19	Shawn's Cross Roads, Johnson, Ten	6
Shanghai, Howard, Ind	12	Shaw's Flat, Tuolumne, Cal	83
Shanghai, Berkeley, W. Va	11	Shaw's Landing, Crawford, Pa	21
Shanksville, Somerset, Pa	35	Shaw's Mills, Guilford, N. C	13
Shannock Mills, Washington, R. I	130	Shaw's Point, Macoupin, Ill	16
Shannon,* Carroll, Ill	650	Shawsville, Clearfield, Pa	12
Shannon, Lee, Miss	160	Shawsville, Montgomery, Va	12
Shannondale, Montgomery, Ind	7	Sheakleyville, Mercer, Pa	210
Shannondale, Clarion, Pa	53	Shearer's Cross Roads, Westmore-	
Shannon Hill, Goochland, Va	27	land, Pa	22
Shannonville, Montgomery, Pa	57	*Sheboygan,* (*c. h.,*) Sheboygan, Wis	1,700
Shapleigh, York, Me	64	Sheboygan Falls, Sheboygan, Wis	720
Shark River, Monmouth, N. J	55	Shed's Corners, Madison, N. Y	34
Sharlow, Bourbon, Kans	5	Sheenwater, Erie, N. Y	15
Sharon, Litchfield, Conn	420	Sheepscott Bridge, Lincoln, Me	97
Sharon, Taliaferro, Ga	12	Sheffield, Fayette, Ala	12
Sharon, Henry, Ill	23	Sheffield, Bureau, Ill	490
Sharon, Delaware, Ind	16	Sheffield, Dubuque, Iowa	12
Sharon, Warren, Iowa	18	Sheffield, Berkshire, Mass	590
Sharon, Norfolk, Mass	300	Sheffield, Lorain, Ohio	20
Sharon, Schoharie, N. Y	51	Sheffield, Warren, Pa	86
Sharon, Noble, Ohio	82	Sheffield, Caledonia, Vt	110
Sharon,* Mercer, Pa	2,400	Sheffield Depot, Warren, Pa	260
Sharon, Windsor, Vt	180	Sheffield Lake, Lorain, Ohio	27
Sharon, Bland, Va	25	Shelbina,* Shelby, Mo	990
Sharon, Chehalis, Wash	12	Shelburn, Sullivan, Ind	100
Sharon, Walworth, Wis	330	Shelburne, Franklin, Mass	82
Sharon Centre, Schoharie, N. Y	54	Shelburne, Coos, N. H	78
Sharon Centre, Medina, Ohio	130	Shelburne, Chittenden, Vt	270
Sharon Centre, Potter, Pa	15	Shelburne Falls,* Franklin, Mass	1,400
Sharon Grove, Todd, Ky	12	Shelby, Shelby, Iowa	12
Sharon Springs, Schoharie, N. Y	760	Shelby, Oceana, Mich	82
Sharon Station, Dutchess, N. Y	78	Shelby, Orleans, N. Y	97
Sharonville, Hamilton, Ohio	120	*Shelby,* (*c. h.,*) Cleveland, N. C	180
Sharpsburgh, Bath, Ky	270	Shelby,* Richland, Ohio	1,100
Sharpsburgh,* Washington, Md	260	Shelby, Austin, Tex	110
Sharpsburgh, Allegheny, Pa	290	Shelby, La Crosse, Wis	8
Sharp's Chapel, Union, Tenn	9	Shelby Basin, Orleans, N. Y	20
Sharp's Cross Roads, Independence,		Shelby City, Boyle, Ky	160
Ark	11	Shelby Iron Works, Shelby, Ala	12
Sharp's Mills, Harrison, Ind	11	Shelby Springs, Shelby, Ala	82
Sharpsville, Tipton, Ind	190	*Shelbyville,* (*c. h.,*) Shelby, Ill	1,700

SHE   SHI

*Shelbyville,** (c. h.,) Shelby, Ind....	$1,300	Sherman, Grant, Ky................	$12
*Shelbyville,** (c. h.,) Shelby, Ky....	1,600	Sherman, Aroostook, Me..........	77
Shelbyville, Blue Earth, Minn....	100	*Sherman, (c. h.,) Wexford, Mich....	8
*Shelbyville, (c. h.,) Shelby, Mo......	370	Sherman, Blue Earth, Minn.......	10
*Shelbyville,** (c. h.,) Bedford, Tenn..	1,200	Sherman, St. Louis, Mo..........	36
*Shelbyville, (c. h.,) Shelby, Tex....	31	Sherman, Nemaha, Nebr...........	7
Sheldon, Sacramento, Cal....	12	Sherman, Chautauqua, N. Y........	660
Sheldon, Iroquois, Ill....	250	Sherman, Summit, Ohio..........	130
Sheldon, Allen, Ind....	12	*Sherman, (c. h.,) Grayson, Tex......	560
Sheldon, Houston, Minn..........	35	Sherman, Marathon, Wis..........	77
Sheldon, Wyoming, N. Y....:....	42	Sherman, Albany, Wyo............	190
Sheldon,* Franklin, Vt...........	590	Sherman City, Cherokee, Kans.....	30
Sheldon, Monroe, Wis.......	7	Sherman Mills, Aroostook, Me	67
Sheldon's Grove, Schuyler, Ill....	30	Sherman's Dale, Perry, Pa........	68
Sheldonville, Norfolk, Mass........	100	Shermantown, White Pine, Nev....	12
Sheldrake, Seneca, N. Y......	82	Sherman Wells, Venango, Pa......	130
Shell Mound, Sunflower, Miss....	24	Sherodsville, Carroll, Ohio........	14
Shell Rock, Butler, Iowa..........	180	Sherrard, Marshall, W. Va........	21
Shell Rock, Freeborn, Minn......	28	Sherrett, Armstrong, Pa..........	8
Shell Rock Falls, Cerro Gordo, Iowa..................	56	Sherrill's Ford, Catawba, N. C.....	11
		Sherrill's Mount, Dubuque, Iowa...	81
Shellsburgh,* Benton, Iowa......	470	Sherwood, Branch, Mich..........	55
Shelocta, Indiana, Pa....	68	Sherwood, Jasper, Mo............	32
Shelter Island, Suffolk, N. Y......	160	Sherwood, Cayuga, N. Y..........	110
Shelton, Fairfield, S. C...........	12	Sherwood, Calumet, Wis..........	59
Sheltonville, Forsyth, Ga	17	Sherwood's Mills, Mason, Wash....	12
Shenandoah, Schuylkill, Pa......	670	Sherwood Valley, Mendocino, Cal..	17
Shenandoah Iron Works, Page, Va.	110	Sheshequin, Bradford, Pa.........	76
Shepardsville, Clinton, Mich......	170	Shibley's Point, Adair, Mo........	14
Shepherd's Store, Anne Arundel, Md..................	12	Shickshinny, Luzerne, Pa..........	180
		Shields, Jackson, Ind............	38
Shepherdstown, Belmont, Ohio....	14	Shields, Belmont, Ohio..........	40
Shepherdstown, Cumberland, Pa..	78	*Shieldsborough, (c. h.,) Hancock, Miss.	340
Shepherdstown, (c. h.,) Jefferson, W. Va....	580	Shieldsville, Rice, Minn..........	94
		Shielville, Hamilton, Ind...⌐.....	130
*Shepherdsville, (c. h.,) Bullitt, Ky....	210	Shiloh, Marengo, Ala............	20
Sheppardville, Wicomico, Md....	16	Shiloh, St. Clair, Ill............	78
Sherando, Augusta, Va......... ...	10	Shiloh, Callaway, Ky	15
Sherborn, Middlesex, Mass........	200	Shiloh, Cumberland, N. J........	170
Sherburne,* Chenango, N. Y......	920	Shiloh, Richland, Ohio..........	210
Sherburne, Rutland, Vt......	63	Shiloh, Camden, N. C............	4
Sherburne Four Corners, Chenango, N. Y..................	12	Shiloh, Sumter, S. C............	4
		Shiloh, Montgomery, Tenn	12
Sherburne Mills, Fleming, Ky... ..	72	Shiloh, Hunt, Tex..............	16
Sherburneville, Kankakee, Ill....	95	Shiloh, King George, Va..........	12
*Sheridan, (c. h.,) Grant, Ark........	12	Shiloh Academy, Lamar, Tex	12
Sheridan, Placer, Cal...........	21	Shiloh Hill, Randolph, Ill........	26
Sheridan, La Salle, Ill...........	27	Shimerville, Lehigh, Pa	51
Sheridan, Van Buren, Iowa........	34	Shinbone, Fayette, Pa...........	12
Sheridan, Montcalm, Mich........	73	Shin Creek, Sullivan, N. Y........	19
Sheridan, Macon, Mo............	12	Shingle Creek, St. Lawrence, N. Y..	140
Sheridan, Madison, Mont	170	Shinglehouse, Potter, Pa	22
Sheridan, Nemaha, Nebr..........	12	Shingle Springs, El Dorado, Cal ...	150
Sheridan, Douglas, Nev	44	Shinn's Point, Johnson, Ill	14
Sheridan, Chautauqua, N. Y	83	Shinnston, Harrison, W. Va........	62
Sheridan, Putnam, Ohio..........	15	Shiocton, Outagamie, Wis	43
Sheridan, Yam Hill, Oreg..........	12	Shipman, Macoupin, Ill	300
Sheridan, Lebanon, Pa...........	160	*Shippensburgh,* Cumberland, Pa.⌐	1,200
Sheridan, Waupaca, Wis..........	14	Shippensville, Clarion, Pa........	100
Sheridan Coal Works, Lawrence, Ohio..................	8	Shippingport, Beaver, Pa.........	12
		Shiremantown, Cumberland, Pa ...	190
*Sherman, (c. h.,) Marion, Ark.......	12	Shirland, Winnebago, Ill	94
Sherman, Fairfield, Conn........	82	Shirland, Allegheny, Pa..........	56
Sherman, Sangamon, Ill......	61	Shirley, Covington, Ala	12
Sherman, Jennings, Ind	23	Shirley, McLean, Ill..............	72
*Sherman, Poweshiek, Iowa........	32	Shirley, Cloud, Kans	29

* Money-order office.

SIA   SIL

Shirley, Piscataquis, Me	$32	Sibley, Sibley, Minn	$7
Shirley, Middlesex, Mass	72	Sibley, Jackson, Mo	56
Shirley, Erie, N. Y	23	Sicily, Highland, Ohio	16
Shirley, Tyler, W. Va	6	Sideling Hall, Fulton, Pa	12
Shirley Mills, Piscataquis, Me	14	Side View, Montgomery, Ky	24
Shirleysburgh, Huntingdon, Pa	230	Sidney, Champaign, Ill	260
Shirley Village, Middlesex, Mass	320	Sidney,* (c. h.,) Fremont, Iowa	720
Shivelton, Platte, Mo	40	Sidney, Coffey, Kans	61
Shoal Creek, Johnson, Ark	12	Sidney, Kennebec, Me	12
Shoal Creek, Livingston, Mo	12	Sidney, Montcalm, Mich	12
Shoal Creek Station, Clinton, Ill	200	Sidney, Ralls, Mo	26
Shoals, Martin, Ind	310	Sidney, Cheyenne, Nebr	240
Shoalsburgh, Newton, Mo	27	Sidney, Hunterdon, N. J	26
Shobe's Grove, Franklin, Iowa	12	Sidney, Delaware, N. Y	18
Shockeysville, Frederick, Va	12	Sidney,* (c. h.,) Shelby, Ohio	2,200
Shoe Heel, Robeson, N. C	280	Sidney, Venango, Pa	30
Shoemakers, Monroe, Pa	19	Sidney Centre, Delaware, N. Y	76
Shoemakersville, Berks, Pa	130	Sidney Plains,* Delaware, N. Y	340
Shoemakertown, Montgomery, Pa	190	Sidonsburgh, York, Pa	43
Shoenersville, Lehigh, Pa	27	Siegle's Store, Lincoln, N. C	8
Shohola, Pike, Pa	120	Sierra, Vernon, Wis	6
Shokan, Ulster, N. Y	160	Sierra City, Sierra, Cal	85
Shokokon, Henderson, Ill	59	Sierra Valley, Sierra, Cal	71
Shoneytown, Putnam, Mo	12	Sigel, Clayton, Iowa	10
Shongo, Allegany, N. Y	70	Sigel, Douglas, Kans	37
Shootman, Carroll, Mo	12	Sigel, Pettis, Mo	41
Shop Creek, Montgomery, Ill	14	Sigel, Jefferson, Pa	41
Shopiere, Rock, Wis	160	Sigourney,* (c. h.,) Keokuk, Iowa	690
Shop Spring, Wilson, Tenn	43	Sikeston, Scott, Mo	16
Shopville, Pulaski, Ky	4	Siloam, Greene, Ga	12
Shoreham, Addison, Vt	220	Siloam, Oktibbeha, Miss	12
Short Bend, Dent, Mo	11	Siloam, Madison, N. Y	20
Short Creek, Marshall, Ala	12	Silver Bow, Deer Lodge, Mont	12
Short Creek, Grayson, Ky	33	Silver Brook, Schuylkill, Pa	57
Short Creek, Harrison, Ohio	110	Silver City,* (c. h.,) Owyhee, Idaho	300
Short Creek, Brooke, W. Va	31	Silver City, Lewis and Clarke, Mont	12
Shorter's Depot, Macon, Ala	15	Silver City, Lyon, Nev	400
Short Falls, Merrimack, N. H	12	Silver Creek, Stephenson, Ill	51
Short Mountain, Dauphin, Pa	11	Silver Creek, Chase, Kans	8
Short Mountain, Cannon, Tenn	12	Silver Creek, Madison, Ky	62
Shortsville,* Ontario, N. Y	310	Silver Creek, Allegan, Mich	53
Short Tract, Allegany, N. Y	97	Silver Creek, Wright, Minn	14
Shoshone, Alturas, Idaho	12	Silver Creek, Lawrence, Miss	12
Shotwell, Franklin, Mo	32	Silver Creek, Cedar, Mo	3
Shoustown, Allegheny, Pa	44	Silver Creek, Burt, Nebr	26
Shovel Mount, Burnet, Tex	12	Silver Creek, Chautauqua, N. Y	630
Shreve, Wayne, Ohio	380	Silver Creek, Hardin, Ohio	24
Shreveport,* (c. h.,) Caddo, La	2,800	Silver Creek, Schuylkill, Pa	65
Shrewsbury, Worcester, Mass	290	Silver Glen, Merrick, Nebr	38
Shrewsbury, Monmouth, N. J	130	Silver Hill, Prince George's, Md	130
Shrewsbury, York, Pa	370	Silver Hill, Wetzel, W. Va	7
Shrewsbury, Rutland, Vt	62	Silver Lake, Koscinsko, Ind	130
Shrewsbury, Kanawha, W. Va	34	Silver Lake, Worth, Iowa	34
Shrub Oak, Westchester, N. Y	55	Silver Lake, Shawnee, Kans	12
Shubuta, Clark, Miss	550	Silver Lake, McLeod, Minn	57
Shuey's Mills, Green, Wis	17	Silver Lake, Perry, Mo	26
Shueyville, Johnson, Iowa	39	Silver Lake, Clinton, N. Y	4
Shufordville, Henderson, N. C	50	Silver Lake, Susquehanna, Pa	24
Shullsburgh, La Fayette, Wis	460	Silver Mountain, (c. h.,) Alpine, Cal	130
Shunk, Sullivan, Pa	27	Silver Peak, Esmeralda, Nev	12
Shunpike, Columbia, N. Y	12	Silver Run, Talladega, Ala	43
Shuqualak, Noxubee, Miss	270	Silver Run, Carroll, Md	24
Shushan, Washington, N. Y	190	Silver Run, Meigs, Ohio	8
Shutesbury, Franklin, Mass	87	Silver Spring, Lancaster, Pa	87
Shutter's Corners, Schoharie, N. Y	21	Silver Spring, Wilson, Tenn	51
Siam. Taylor, Iowa	41	Silver Springs, Alcorn, Miss	18

* **Money-order office.**

SKI   SMI

Silver Star, Madison, Mont	$12	Skinner's Eddy, Wyoming, Pa	$88
Silver Street, Newberry, S. C	20	Skinquarter, Chesterfield, Va	39
Silverton, Ocean, N. J	6	Skipanon, Clatsop, Oreg	12
Silverton, Marion, Oreg	77	Skippack, Montgomery, Pa	100
Silverville, Lawrence, Ind	13	Skipperville, Dale, Ala	12
Silveyville, Solano, Cal	40	Skipton, Talbot, Md	23
Simmou's Bluff, Wilson, Tenn	7	Skipwith's Landing, Issaquena,Miss	200
Simmonsville, Craig, Va	14	Skokomish, Mason, Wash	18
Simonsville, Windsor, Vt	65	Skookumchuck, Lewis, Wash	10
Simpson, Adams, Iowa	24	Skowhegan,* Somerset, Me	1,800
Simpson's, Floyd, Va	12	Skull Valley, Yavapai, Ariz	12
Simpson's Corner, Penobscot, Me	33	Slabtown, Boone, Ind	12
Simpson's Creek, Taylor, W. Va	48	Slack, Mason, Ky	13
Simpson's Mills, Laurens, S. C	5	Slack Water, Lancaster, Pa	17
Simpson's Store, Washington, Pa	12	Sladesburgh, Crawford, Wis	6
Simpsonville, Shelby, Ky	140	Sladesville, Hyde, N. C	25
Simpsonville, Howard, Md	32	Slanesville, Hampshire, W. Va	22
Simpsonville, Upshur, Tex	4	Slash, Grant, Ind	15
Simsbury, Hartford, Conn	250	Slate, Jennings, Ind	12
Sinclairville, Chautauqua, N. Y	450	Slate Creek, Josephine, Oreg	19
Sineath's, Charleston, S. C	12	Slate Cut, Clarke, Ind	11
Singer's Glen, Rockingham, Va	200	Slateford, Northampton, Pa	90
Sing Sing,* Westchester, N. Y	2,500	Slate Hill, Orange, N. Y	10
Sinkin, Shannon, Mo	12	Slate Hill, York, Pa	85
Sinking Creek, Craig, Va	2	Slate Lick, Armstrong, Pa	75
Sinking Fork, Christian, Ky	12	Slate Mills, Rappahannock, Va	14
Sinking Spring, Highland, Ohio	38	Slatersville, Weber, Utah	12
Sinking Spring, Berks, Pa	86	Slaterville, Tompkins, N. Y	110
Sinking Valley, Blair, Pa	100	Slaterville, Providence, R. I	440
Sink's Grove, Monroe, W. Va	26	Slatington, Lehigh, Pa	930
Sinnamahoning, Cameron, Pa	170	Slaughter, Kent, Del	12
Sinnett's Mills, Ritchie, W. Va	3	Slaughter, King, Wash	12
Sinsinawa Mound, Grant, Wis	99	Slaughtersville, Webster, Ky	40
Sioux City,* (c. h.,) Woodbury, Iowa.	2,600	Sleepy Creek Bridge, Morgan,W.Va.	34
Sioux Falls, Minnehaha, Dak	55	Slick Rock, Barren, Ky	23
Sioux Rapids, Buena Vista, Iowa	12	Slifer, Union, Pa	90
Sioux Valley, Union, Dak	36	Sligo, Montgomery, Md	30
Sipes' Mill, Fulton, Pa	12	Sligo, Clarion, Pa	88
Sipestown, Lehigh, Pa	6	Slippery Ford, El Dorado, Cal	20
Sipesville, Somerset, Pa	26	Slippery Rock, Butler, Pa	190
Sipsey Turnpike, Tuscaloosa, Ala	12	Sloan, Woodbury, Iowa	77
Sipsy Mills, Pickens, Ala	17	Sloan's Point, Adair, Mo	10
Sir John's Run, Morgan, W. Va	73	Sloan's Station, Jefferson, Ohio	120
Sissonville, Kanawha, W. Va	7	Sloansville, Schoharie, N. Y	130
Sisterdale, Kendall, Tex	15	Sloatsburgh, Rockland, N. Y	110
Sistersville, Tyler, W. Va	200	Slocum's Grove, Muskegon, Mich	15
Sitka, (c. h.,) ——, Alaska	240	Slocumville, Washington, R. I	48
Sitka, Martin, Ind	12	Small Point, Sagadahoc, Me	36
Sitka, Newaygo, Mich	12	Smartt's Station, Warren, Tenn	12
Siuslaw, Lane, Oreg	10	Smartville, Yuba, Cal	300
Siverly, Vinton, Ohio	34	Smicksburgh, Indiana, Pa	84
Six Corners, Ottawa, Mich	30	Smiley, Susquehanna, Pa	22
Six Mile, Jennings, Ind	140	Smileytown, Spencer, Ky	29
Six Mile Falls, Penobscot, Me	20	Smith, Dade, Ga	12
Six Mile Run, Somerset, N. J	82	Smith City, Pettis, Mo	220
Six Mile Run, Bedford, Pa	190	Smithdale, Livingston, Ill	12
Six Oaks, Olmsted, Minn	23	Smithdale, Amite, Miss	19
Six Points, Butler, Pa	12	Smithfield, Fulton, Ill	12
Six Roads, Bedford, Pa	15	Smithfield, Henry, Ky	130
Sixteen Mile Stand, Hamilton, Ohio.	36	Smithfield, Somerset, Me	84
Skaneateles,* Onondaga, N. Y	1,400	Smithfield, Wabashaw, Minn	43
Skeel's Cross Roads, Mercer, Ohio	31	Smithfield, (c. h.,) Johnston, N. C	260
Skiddy, Morris, Kans	12	Smithfield, Jefferson, Ohio	310
Skinner, Campbell, Ga	2	Smithfield, Fayette, Pa	220
Skinner, Bay, Mich	12	Smithfield, Providence, R. I	31
Skinner, Green, Wis	20	Smithfield, Polk, Tex	12

* Money-order office.

SMY   SOM

Smithfield, Cache, Utah	$43	Smyrna, Chenango, N. Y	$260
Smithfield,* (c. h.,) Isle of Wight, Va.	460	Smyrna, Harrison, Ohio.	63
Smithfield Summit, Bradford, Pa...	14	Smyrna, Lancaster, Pa	37
Smith Grove, Davie, N. C	7	Smyrna, Rutherford, Tenn	110
Smithland, Shelby, Ind	26	Smyrna Mills, Aroostook, Me	10
Smithland, Woodbury, Iowa	110	Snachwine, Putnam, Ill	160
Smithland, Jackson, Kans	11	Snake Root, McDowell, Va	12
Smithland,* (c. h.,) Livingston, Ky..	320	Snapping Shoals, Newton, Ga	49
Smithport, (c. h.,) McKean, Pa	270	Snead's Ferry, Onslow, N. C	12
Smith River, Del Norte, Cal	12	Snedekerville, Bradford, Pa	27
Smith Road, Medina, Ohio	20	Sneedsville, (c. h.,) Hancock, Tenn...	43
Smith's Basin, Washington, N. Y...	100	Snelling's Ranch, (c. h.,) Merced, Cal.	200
Smithsborough, Tioga, N. Y	79	Snibar, La Fayette, Mo	14
Smithsburgh, Washington, Md	130	Snicarte, Mason, Ill	26
Smith's Corners, Oceana, Mich	10	Snickersville, Loudoun, Va	88
Smith's Creek, St. Clair, Mich	140	Snidersville, Outagamie, Wis,	23
Smith's Creek, Washington, Va	55	Snipe's Store, Chatham, N. C	4
Smith's Cross Roads, Rhea, Tenn...	36	Snoddy's Mills, Fountain, Ind	10
Smith's Ferry, Beaver, Pa	280	Snohomish, (c. h.,) Snohomish Wash.	27
Smith's Ford, Cabarrus, N. C	12	Snoqualmie, King, Wash	12
Smith's Ford, Union, S. C	8	Snow Camp, Alamance, N. C	36
Smith's Gap, Hampshire, W. Va	16	Snow Creek, Iredell, N. C	12
Smith's Grove, Warren, Ky	170	Snow Creek, Smith, Tenn	12
Smith's Landing, Atlantic, N. J	74	Snow Creek, Franklin, Va	5
Smith's Landing, Clermont, Ohio..	15	Snowdoun, Montgomery, Ala	6
Smith's Mills, Henderson, Ky	40	Snow Falls, Oxford, Me.	45
Smith's Mills, Passaic, N. J	8	Snow Hill, Randolph, Ind	18
Smith's Mills, Chautauqua, N. Y..	140	Snow Hill,* (c. h.,) Worcester, Md...	390
Smith's Mills, Clearfield, Pa	99	Snow Hill, St. Charles, Mo	130
Smithson's Valley, Comal, Tex	5	Snow Hill, (c. h.,) Greene, N. C	50
Smith's Ranch, Sonoma, Cal	80	Snow Hill, Titus, Tex	24
Smith's Ridge, Fairfield, Conn	10	Snow Hill, Nicholas, W. Va	5
Smith's Station, Lee, Ala	66	Snow Shoe, Centre, Pa	170
Smith's Station, York, Pa	21	Snowville, Pulaski, Va	45
Smith's Turn Out, York, S. C	28	Snyder, Dallas, Iowa	15
Smith's Valley, Johnson, Ind	12	Snydersville, Monroe, Pa	23
Smithton, St. Clair, Ill	25	Snydertown, Northumberland, Pa.	46
Smithton, Worth, Mo	12	Social Circle, Walton, Ga	310
Smithton, Doddridge, W. Va	58	Society Hill, Macon, Ala	21
Smithtown, Suffolk, N. Y	180	Society Hill, Darlington, S. C	250
Smithtown Branch, Suffolk, N. Y..	290	Socorro, (c. h.,) Socorro, N. Mex....	43
Smith Valley, Schuyler, N. Y	36	Soda Bar, Palo Alto, Iowa	46
Smithville, Lawrence, Ark	120	Soda Springs, Linn, Oreg	12
Smithville, Peoria, Ill	50	Soddy, Hamilton, Tenn	16
Smithville, Monroe, Ind	93	Sodorus, Champaign, Ill	230
Smithville, Caroline, Md	15	Sodus, Berrien, Mich	61
Smithville, Worcester, Mass	53	Sodus, Wayne, N. Y	340
Smithville, Wayne, Mich	11	Sodus Centre, Wayne, N. Y	49
Smithville, Monroe, Miss	38	Sodus Point, Wayne, N. Y	110
Smithville, Clay, Mo	91	Soldiers' Grove, Crawford, Wis	21
Smithville, Burlington, N. J	160	Soledad, Monterey, Cal	12
Smithville, Jefferson, N. Y	120	Solomon City, Saline, Kans	210
Smithville, (c. h.,) Brunswick, N. C.	170	Solomon Rapids, Mitchell, Kans	12
Smithville, Wayne, Ohio	370	Solomon's Island, Calvert, Md	12
Smithville, Lancaster, Pa	20	Solon, Johnson, Iowa	180
Smithville, (c. h.,) De Kalb, Tenn	81	Solon, Somerset, Me.	290
Smithville Flats, Chenango, N. Y.	120	Solon, Leelenaw, Mich	12
Smithville South, Queens, N. Y	20	Solon, Otoe, Nebr	12
Smitten, Indiana, Pa	10	Solon, Cortland, N. Y	73
Smoky Ordinary, Brunswick, Va...	12	Solon, Cuyahoga, Ohio	270
Smootsdell, Hendricks, Ind	34	Solon, White, Tenn	12
Smyrna,* Kent, Del	1,100	Solon Mills, McHenry, Ill	29
Smyrna, Cobb, Ga	12	Solsberry, Greene, Ind	63
Smyrna, Clarke, Iowa	53	Solsville, Madison, N. Y	130
Smyrna, Aroostook, Me	15	Somerfield, Somerset, Pa	110
Smyrna, Ionia, Mich	160	Somers, Tolland, Conn	180

* Money-order office.

SOU · SOU

Somers, Westchester, N. Y	$180	South Arkansas, Lake, Colo	$12
Somers, Kenosha, Wis.	12	South Arlington, Montgomery, Ohio	13
Somerset' Saline, Ill.	4	South Ashfield, Franklin, Mass	74
Somerset, Wabash, Ind.	110	South Atkinson, Piscataquis, Me	39
Somerset, (c. h.,) Pulaski, Ky	350	South Attleborough, Bristol, Mass.	110
Somerset, Bristol, Mass	380	South Auburn, Androscoggin, Me.	58
Somerset, Hillsdale, Mich	45	South Auburn, Susquehanna, Pa	15
Somerset, Monroe, Mo	12	South Avon, Livingston, N. Y	21
Somerset, Niagara, N. Y	170	South Ballston, Saratoga, N.Y.	73
Somerset, Perry, Ohio	400	South Bangor, Buckingham, Va.	12
Somerset, (c. h.,) Somerset, Pa	690	South Barnstead, Belknap, N. H	10
Somerset, Atascosa, Tex	12	South Barre, Orleans, N. Y	27
Somerset, Windham, Vt	27	South Barre, Washington, Vt	46
Somerset, St. Croix, Wis	47	South Barton, Orleans, Vt.	68
Somerset Furnace, Somerset, Pa	20	South Beddington, Washington, Me	12
Somerset Mills, Somerset, Me	140	South Belmont, Waldo, Me	12
Somers' Point, Atlantic, N. J.	190	South Bend, Arkansas, Ark	18
Somersville, Contra Costa, Cal.	110	*South Bend,* (c. h.,) St. Joseph, Ind.	3,000
Somerton, Belmont, Ohio	110	South Bend, Blue Earth, Minn	350
Somerville, (c. h.,) Morgan, Ala.	89	South Bend, Cass, Nebr	10
Somerville, Tolland, Conn	75	South Bend, Armstrong, Pa	44
Somerville, Gibson, Ind	24	South Bend, Trempealeau, Wis	60
Somerville, Lincoln, Me.	41	South Berlin, Rensselaer, N. Y.	32
Somerville, Middlesex, Mass	920	South Berne, Albany, N. Y.	12
Somerville, (c. h.,) Somerset, N. J	1,000	South Berwick,* York, Me	750
Somerville, St. Lawrence, N. Y	56	South Berwick Junction, York, Me.	44
Somerville, Butler, Ohio	210	South Bethany, Bartholomew, Ind.	32
Somerville, (c. h.,) Fayette, Tenn	720	South Bethlehem,* Northampton, Pa	610
Somerville, Fauquier, Va.	13	South Bloomfield, Pickaway, Ohio.	140
Somonauk, De Kalb, Ill.	550	South Bloomingville, Hocking, Ohio	40
Sonestown, Sullivan, Pa.	31	South Bolivar, Allegany, N. Y.	14
Sonman, Cambria, Pa	47	South Bombay, Franklin, N. Y.	14
Sonoma, Sonoma, Cal	260	Southborough, Worcester, Mass	360
Sonora, (c. h.,) Tuolumne, Cal	1,000	South Boston, Ionia, Mich.	25
Sonora, Hancock, Ill	110	South Boston Depot, Halifax, Va.	160
Sonora, Hardin, Ky.	180	South Bradford, Steuben, N. Y.	24
Sonora, Chickasaw, Miss	12	South Braintree, Norfolk, Mass	280
Sonora, Steuben, N. Y	43	South Branch, Somerset, N. J.	97
Sonora, Muskingum, Ohio.	56	South Branch, Bradford, Pa.	15
Sopchoppy, Wakulla, Fla	12	South Branch Depot, Hampshire,	
Soquel, Santa Cruz, Cal	73	W. Va	46
Sorghotown, Daviess, Ky	12	South Brewster, Barnstable, Mass	72
Sorrel Horse, Montgomery, Pa.	35	Southbridge,* Worcester, Mass	900
Soudersburgh, Lancaster, Pa	39	South Bridgeton, Cumberland, Me.	70
Souder's Station, Montgomery, Pa.	120	South Bristol, Lincoln, Me.	46
Sour Spring, Caldwell, Tex	22	South Bristol, Ontario, N. Y.	10
South Abington, Plymouth, Mass	660	South Britain, New Haven, Conn.	210
South Acton, York, Me	13	South Brookfield, Madison, N. Y.	51
South Acton, Middlesex, Mass.	210	South Brooks, Waldo, Me	22
South Acworth, Sullivan, N. H	130	South Brooksville, Hancock, Me.	13
South Addison, Steuben, N. Y.	53	Southbury, New Haven, Conn.	200
South Alabama, Genesee, N. Y.	72	South Butler, Butler, Ala	21
South Albany, Orleans, Vt.	50	South Butler, Branch, Mich	8
South Albion, Kennebec, Me.	51	South Butler, Wayne, N. Y.	210
South Albion, Oswego, N. Y.	24	South Byron, Genesee, N. Y.	200
South Amboy,* Middlesex, N. J.	540	South Cabot, Washington, Vt	12
South Amenia, Dutchess, N. Y	74	South Cairo, Greene, N. Y.	32
South America, Saline, Ill	23	South Camden, Hillsdale, Mich.	12
South Amesbury, Essex, Mass	150	South Cameron, Steuben, N. Y	11
South Amherst, Hampshire, Mass	83	South Canaan, Litchfield, Conn	10
Southampton, Peoria, Ill	47	South Carrollton, Muhlenburgh,	
Southampton, Hampshire, Mass.	190	Ky	120
Southampton, Suffolk, N. Y.	330	South Carthage, Franklin, Me.	16
Southampton Mills, Somerset, Pa	12	South Carver, Plymouth, Mass	120
South Andover, Oxford, Me.	110	South Casco, Cumberland, Me.	25
South Argyle, Washington, N. Y.	52	South Cass, Ionia, Mich.	55

* Money-order office.

SPA   SPR

South Warren, Bradford, Pa	$14	Sparta,* (c. h.,) Monroe, Wis	$1,800
South Warsaw, Allen, Ohio	20	Sparta Centre, Kent, Mich	110
South Washington, New Hanover,		Spartanburgh, Randolph, Ind	54
N. C	12	Spartanburgh C. H., Spartanburgh,	
South Waterford, Oxford, Me	140	S. C	970
South Weare, Hillsborough, N. H.	91	Spartansburgh, Crawford, Pa	400
South Wellfleet, Barnstable, Mass	70	Sparta Station, Gallatin, Ky	12
South West, Warren, Pa	130	Spavinaw, Benton, Ark	7
South Westerlo, Albany, N. Y	67	Speakeville, Lavaca, Tex	19
South West Harbor, Hancock, Me.	260	Spears, Jessamine, Ky	33
South West, Aroostook, Me	76	Spearsville, Brown, Ind	15
South West Oswego, Oswego, N. Y.	80	Speedsville, Tompkins, N. Y	120
South Westport, Bristol, Mass	20	Speedwell, Madison, Ky	8
South Weymouth, Norfolk, Mass	390	Speedwell, Claiborne, Tenn	16
South Whitehall, Lehigh, Pa	17	Speedwell, Wythe, Va	12
South Whitley, Whitley, Ind	110	Speight's Bridge, Greene, N. C	13
Southwick, Hampden, Mass	120	Spencer, Will, Ill	55
South Wilbraham, Hampden, Mass.	220	Spencer,* (c. h.,) Owen, Ind	580
South Williamstown, Berkshire,		Spencer, Clay, Iowa	45
Mass	260	Spencer, Worcester, Mass	980
South Willow Creek, Lee, Ill	11	Spencer, Lawrence, Mo	12
South Wilson, Niagara, N. Y	27	Spencer, Tioga, N. Y	460
South Wilton, Saratoga, N. Y	10	Spencer, Davidson, N. C	6
South Windham, Windham, Conn.	160	Spencer, Medina, Ohio	91
South Windham, Cumberland, Me.	160	Spencer, (c. h.,) Van Buren, Tenn.	36
South Windham, Windham, Vt	37	Spencer, (c. h.,) Roane, W. Va	130
South Windsor, Hartford, Conn	120	Spencer Brook, Isanti, Minn	27
South Windsor, Kennebec, Me	46	Spencerburgh, Pike, Mo	56
South Winn, Penobscot, Me	11	Spencer Creek, Antrim, Mich	12
South Wolfborough, Carroll, N. H.	69	Spencer Grove, Benton, Iowa	8
South Woodbury, Washington, Vt.	77	Spencerport, Monroe, N. Y	340
South Woodstock, Windham, Conn.	36	Spencer's Mill, Kent, Mich	12
South Woodstock, Windsor, Vt	160	Spencer Springs, Tioga, N. Y	59
South Worcester, Otsego, N. Y	120	Spencer's Shop, Crawford, Ark	12
South Worthington, Hampshire,		Spencer's Station, Guernsey, Ohio	88
Mass	36	Spencer's Store, Henry, Va	12
South Wright, Hillsdale, Mich	38	Spencertown, Columbia, N. Y	130
South Yarmouth, Barnstable, Mass.	300	Spencerville, De Kalb, Ind	120
Spade's Depot, Ripley, Ind	52	Spencerville, Montgomery, Md	17
Spadra, Los Angeles, Cal	26	Spencerville, Allen, Ohio	120
Spafford, Onondaga, N. Y	36	Speonk, Suffolk, N. Y	36
Spafford, La Fayette, Wis	44	Sperry, Des Moines, Iowa	12
Spaldingville, Knox, Ind	1	Sperryville, Rappahannock, Va	79
Spangville, Berks, Pa	9	Spiceland, Henry, Ind	180
Spanish Bar, Clear Creek, Colo	94	Spillville, Winneshiek, Iowa	140
Spanishburgh, Mercer, W. Va	11	Spinnerstown, Bucks, Pa	51
Spanish Flat, El Dorado, Cal	25	Spirit Lake, (c. h.,) Dickinson, Iowa.	63
Spanish Fork, Utah, Utah	77	Spokan Bridge, Stevens, Wash	34
Spanish Hollow, Wasco, Oreg	12	Spooner's Corners, Otsego, N. Y	16
Spanish Ranch, Plumas, Cal	52	Sporting Hill, Lancaster, Pa	18
Spark's Hill, Hardin, Ill	10	Spotswood, Middlesex, N. J	200
Sparksville, Jackson, Ind	18	Spottsylvania C. H., Spottsylvania,	
Sparland,* Marshall, Ill	460	Va	58
Sparrow Bush, Orange, N. Y	160	Spout Spring, Appomattox, Va	140
Sparta, Conecuh, Ala	25	Spout Springs, Harnett, N. C	12
Sparta, (c. h.,) Hancock, Ga	590	Spragg's, Greene, Pa	9
Sparta,* Randolph, Ill	830	Spragueville, Jackson, Iowa	69
Sparta, Dearborn, Ind	26	Spraker's Basin, Montgomery, N. Y.	96
Sparta, (c. h.,) Bienville, La	40	Sprankle's Mills, Jefferson, Pa	23
Sparta, Chickasaw, Miss	61	Spread Eagle, Chester, Pa	110
Sparta, Sussex, N. J	120	Spring, Crawford, Pa	270
Sparta, Edgecombe, N. C	33	Spring Arbor, Jackson, Mich	41
Sparta, Morrow, Ohio	130	Spring Bay, Woodford, Ill	70
Sparta, Washington, Pa	36	Spring Bluff, Choctaw N., Ind. T	12
Sparta, (c. h.,) White, Tenn	260	Spring Bluff, Adams, Wis	32
Sparta, Caroline, Va	16	Springborough, Warren, Ohio	240

* Money-order office.

SPR   SPR

Spring Branch, Comal, Tex........	$8
Spring Brook, Jackson, Iowa......	20
Spring Brook, Gratiot, Mich.......	25
Spring Brook, Erie, N. Y.........	55
Spring Brook, Luzerne, Pa........	12
Spring Church, Armstrong, Pa	30
Spring City, San Pete, Utah	130
Spring Creek, Pike, Ill..............	12
Spring Creek, Tama, Iowa ....--	12
Spring Creek, Oceana, Mich.......	1
Spring Creek, Goodhue, Minn	23
Spring Creek, Phelps, Mo..........	12
Spring Creek, Johnson, Nebr......	12
Spring Creek, Madison, N. C	4
Spring Creek, Warren, Pa........	94
Spring Creek, Madison, Tenn......	74
Spring Creek, Rockingham, Va....	12
Spring Creek, Adams, Wis	28
Spring Dale, Cedar, Iowa..........	140
Springdale, Leavenworth, Kans....	82
Springdale, Mason, Ky..........	8
Spring Dale, La Fayette, Miss	43
Spring Dale, Hamilton, Ohio	77
Spring Dale, Allegheny, Pa.......	61
Springdale, Claiborne, Tenn	12
Springdale, Kane, Utah	10
Spring Dale, Dane, Wis	15
Springerton, White, Ill	12
Springfield, (c. h.,) Conway, Ark....	54
Springfield, Bonhomme, Dak	12
Springfield, (c. h.,) Effingham, Ga ...	27
SPRINGFIELD,* (c.h.,) Sangamon, Ill	4,000
Springfield, Franklin, Ind	10
Springfield, Keokuk, Iowa	110
Springfield, Linn, Kans.............	12
Springfield, (c. h.,) Washington, Ky.	440
Springfield, (c. h.,) Livingston, La..	14
Springfield, Penobscot, Me	330
Springfield,* (c. h.,) Hampden, Mass.	4,000
Springfield, Oakland, Mich	21
Springfield,* (c. h.,) Greene, Mo.....	2,700
Springfield, Sullivan, N. H....	23
Springfield, Union, N. J.............	140
Springfield, Otsego, N. Y........	69
Springfield,* (c. h.,) Clark, Ohio....	3,000
Springfield, Lane, Oreg..........	26
Springfield, Bradford, Pa..........	130
Springfield, (c. h.,) Robertson, Tenn.	390
Springfield, (c. h.,) Limestone, Tex..	190
Springfield,* Windsor, Vt........	1,200
Springfield, Hampshire, W. Va	90
Springfield, Walworth, Wis	130
Springfield Centre, Otsego, N. Y..	180
Springfield Furnace, Blair, Pa	36
Springfield Store, Queens, N. Y	20
Spring Forge, York, Pa.............	22
Spring Garden, Cherokee, Ala.....	12
Spring Garden, Jefferson, Ill.......	87
Spring Garden, Lancaster, Pa......	59
Spring Garden, Pittsylvania, Va ...	5
Spring Green, Sauk, Wis	380
Spring Grove, Warren, Ill	43
Spring Grove, Linn, Iowa	11
Spring Grove, Houston, Minn......	260
Spring Grove, Dallas, Mo..........	3
Spring Grove, Rowan, N. C......	65

Spring Grove, Lancaster, Pa........	$12
Spring Grove, Surry, Va......	12
Spring Hill, Hempstead, Ark	12
Spring Hill, Whitesides, Ill.........	100
Spring Hill, Decatur, Ind	26
Spring Hill, Johnson, Kans	200
Spring Hill, Barnstable, Mass......	140
Spring Hill, Stearns, Minn	8
Spring Hill, Livingston, Mo	99
Spring Hill, Bradford, Pa..........	21
Spring Hill, Maury, Tenn	260
Spring Hill, Navarro, Tex...... ...	20
Spring Hill, Mecklenburgh, Va	9
Spring Hill Academy, Henry, Tenn.	12
Spring Hill Depot, Henry, Ky	12
Springhill Furnace, Fayette, Pa....	32
Spring Hills, Champaign, Ohio	70
Spring Hope, Bedford, Pa	12
Spring House, Montgomery, Pa	51
Spring House, Grainger, Tenn......	6
Spring Lake, Bremer, Iowa	23
Spring Lake, Ottawa, Mich........	630
Spring Lake, Williams, Ohio	28
Spring Lake, Waushara, Wis	96
Spring Meadow, Bedford, Pa	21
Spring Mills, Oakland, Mich	51
Spring Mills, Allegany, N. Y	78
Spring Mills, Richland, Ohio......	22
Spring Mills, Centre, Pa......	67
Spring Mills, Appomattox, Va.....	2
Spring Mountain, Coshocton, Ohio.	48
Spring Place, (c. h.,) Murray, Ga....	120
Spring Place, Marshall, Tenn	12
Springport, Henry, Ind	12
Springport, Henry, Ky	30
Springport, Jackson, Mich	81
Spring Prairie, Walworth, Wis	200
Spring Ridge, Caddo, La	◄ 12
Spring River Falls, Cherokee, Kans.	12
Spring Run, Franklin, Pa..........	41
Springs, Suffolk, N. Y......	32
Spring Side, Pottawatomie, Kans...	12
Spring's Station, Brown, Ill	12
Spring Station, Woodford, Ky......	77
Springtown, Warren, N. J	44
Springtown, Bucks, Pa.............	40
Springvale, Humboldt, Iowa	180
Springvale,* York, Me	350
Spring Vale, Fairfax, Va	30
Spring Valley, Colusa, Cal	21
Spring Valley, Douglas, Colo	40
Spring Valley, Marion, Ind .... -	12
Spring Valley, Decatur, Iowa	38
Spring Valley,* Fillmore, Minn	230
Spring Valley, Adair, Mo........ ...	3
Spring Valley, Bergen, N. J	66
Spring Valley, Rockland, N. Y	430
Spring Valley, Greene, Ohio.......	190
Spring Valley, Grayson, Va...... ...	7
Spring Valley, Pierce, Wis	12
Springville, St. Clair, Ala....	49
Springville, Coles, Ill	15
Springville, Lawrence, Ind	44
Springville, Linn, Iowa	260
Springville, Lenawee, Mich........	46
Springville, Jefferson, Mont.......	28

* Money-order office.

STA — STA

Post Office	Amount	Post Office	Amount
Springville, Erie, N. Y	$610	Stanton, New Castle, Del	$140
Springville, Wayne, Ohio	12	Stanton, Montgomery, Iowa	12
Springville, Multnomah, Oreg	22	Stanton, Miami, Kans	58
Springville, Susquehanna, Pa	130	Stanton, (c. h.,) Powell, Ky	8
Springville, Henry, Tenn	12	Stanton, (c. h.,) Montcalm, Mich	330
Springville, Utah, Utah	120	Stanton, Goodhue, Minn	25
Springville, Tazewell, Va	5	Stanton, Hunterdon, N. J	44
Springville, Vernon, Wis	100	Stanton, Jefferson, Pa	45
Springwater, Winneshiek, Iowa	10	Stanton Depot, Haywood, Tenn	170
Springwater, Livingston, N. Y	230	Stanton Copper Mines, Franklin, Mo	10
Spring Water, Waushara, Wis	10	Stantonsburgh, Wilson, N. C	12
Sprout Brook, Montgomery, N. Y	130	Stantonville, McNairy, Tenn	12
Sprout Creek, Dutchess, N. Y	30	Stanwich, Fairfield, Conn	34
Spruce, Indiana, Pa	12	Stanwix, Oneida, N. Y	44
Spruce Creek, Huntingdon, Pa	230	Stanwood, Cedar, Iowa	180
Spruce Hill, Juniata, Pa	20	Stanwood, Leavenworth, Kans	12
Spruce Hill, Highland, Va	3	Stapleton, Chickasaw, Iowa	9
Spruce Pine, Franklin, Ala	12	Stapleton, Meade, Ky	13
Sprys Landing, Kent, Md	55	Stapleton,* Richmond, N. Y	1,100
Spurgeon, Pike, Ind	12	Stapleton, Morgan, Tenn	12
Spurlockville, Lincoln, W. Va	12	Stapleton Mills, Amherst, Va	12
Spuyten Duyvil, Westchester, N. Y	230	Star, Rush, Ind	20
Squak, King, Wash	12	Star, Marion, Iowa	12
Squam Village, Monmouth, N. J	200	Star, Warren, Pa	12
Square Corner, Adams, Pa	23	Star, Lavaca, Tex	12
Square Pond, Tolland, Conn	12	Star, Vernon, Wis	44
Squaw Creek, Boise, Idaho	12	Star City, Pulaski, Ind	140
Squaw Grove, De Kalb, Ill	66	Stark, Butts, Ga	26
Staatsburgh, Dutchess, N. Y	110	Stark, Somerset, Me	75
Staatsville, Washington, Wis	54	Stark, Chisago, Minn	43
Stablersville, Baltimore, Md	8	Stark, Coos, N. H	58
Staceyville, Mitchell, Iowa	170	Starke, Bradford, Fla	170
Stafford, Tolland, Conn	150	Starkesville, Lamar, Tex	4
Stafford, Genesee, N. Y	130	Starkey, Yates, N. Y	91
Stafford, Monroe, Ohio	47	Starksborough, Addison, Vt	110
Stafford, Fort Bend, Tex	12	Starkville, (c. h.,) Lee, Ga	46
Stafford C. H., Stafford, Va	15	Starkville, (c. h.,) Oktibbeha, Miss	220
Stafford Springs,* Tolland, Conn	890	Starkville, Herkimer, N. Y	120
Stafford Store, Stafford, Va	21	Star of the West, Pike, Ark	12
Staffordville, Tolland, Conn	210	Star Prairie, St. Croix, Wis	78
Staffordville, Clark, Wis	80	Starr's Point, Benton, Oreg	63
Stagville, Orange, N. C	12	Starrville, Smith, Tex	56
Stahlstown, Westmoreland, Pa	24	Starucca, Wayne, Pa	50
Stairfield, Clinton, Mo	12	State Bridge, Oneida, N. Y	97
Stamford,* Fairfield, Conn	2,500	Stateburgh, Sumter, S. C	80
Stamford, Delaware, N. Y	170	State Centre, Marshall, Iowa	620
Stamford, Bennington, Vt	140	Stateley's Run, Grant, Ky	8
Stamper's Creek, Orange, Ind	4	State Line, Columbia, Ark	12
Stamping Ground, Scott, Ky	55	State Line, Heard, Ga	12
Stanard's Corners, Allegany, N. Y	13	State Line,* Warren, Ind	250
Stanardsville, (c. h.,) Greene, Va	160	State Line, Berkshire, Mass	150
Stanchfield, Isanti, Minn	12	State Line, Freeborn, Minn	34
Standing Pine, Leake, Miss	2	State Line, Franklin, Pa	55
Standing Stone, Bradford, Pa	52	State Line Mills, McKean, Pa	12
Standish, Cumberland, Me	230	Statenville, Echols, Ga	93
Stanford, McLean, Ill	12	State Road, Chemung, N. Y	6
Stanford, Monroe, Ind	52	State Road, Surry, N. C	12
Stanford, Marshall, Iowa	12	Statesville,* (c. h.,) Iredell, N. C	450
Stanford, (c. h.,) Lincoln, Ky	600	Statesville, Wilson, Tenn	10
Stanfordville, Dutchess, N. Y	100	Station Creek, Covington, Miss	12
Stanhope, Sussex, N. J	340	Station Creek, Coryell, Tex	12
Stanhope, Nash, N. C	7	Station Fifteen, Harrison, Ohio	33
Stanley, Morris, N. J	10	Statler's Run, Monongalia, W. Va	4
Stanley, Putnam, Ohio	11	Staunton, Macoupin, Ill	330
Stanley Corners, Ontario, N. Y	110	Staunton, Clay, Ind	210
Stanley's Creek, Gaston, N. C	12		

* Money-order office.

Staunton, Fayette, Ohio	$32	Stevens, Lancaster, Pa	$40
Staunton,* (c. h.,) Augusta, Va	2,400	Stevensburgh, Culpeper, Va	39
Staunton's Mills, Somerset, Pa	39	Stevenson, Jackson, Ala	210
Steamboat Rock, Hardin, Iowa	110	Stevenson's Mills, Wayne, Mo	12
Steamburgh, Cattaraugus, N. Y	110	Stevenson's Mills, Wayne, Pa	64
Steamburgh, Ashtabula, Ohio	16	Stevenson Station, Baltimore, Md	37
Steamburgh, Crawford, Pa	19	Stevens' Plains, Cumberland, Me	260
Steam Corner, Fountain, Ind	19	Stevens Point,* Portage, Wis	540
Steam Corners, Morrow, Ohio	12	Stevenstown, Crawford, Kans	12
Steam Mill, Warren, Pa	50	Stevenstown, La Crosse, Wis	66
Stebbinsville, Oceana, Mich	12	Stevensville, Missoula, Mont	12
Stedman, Chautauqua, N. Y	25	Stevensville, Sullivan, N. Y	67
Steedman's, Lexington, S. C	2	Stevensville, Bradford, Pa	110
Steele Centre, Steele, Minn	6	Stevensville, King and Queen, Va	54
Steele's, Rush, Ind	71	Stewart, Erie, Pa	16
Steele's Grove, Tyler, Tex	12	Stewart, Stewart, Tenn	21
Steele's Mills, Randolph, Ill	100	Stewart, Green, Wis	64
Steele's Tavern, Augusta, Va	85	Stewart's Run, Venango, Pa	36
Steeleville, Chester, Pa	30	Stewartstown, Coos, N. H	25
Steelville, (c. h.,) Crawford, Mo	160	Stewartstown, York, Pa	110
Steen's Prairie, Maries, Mo	8	Stewartstown, Monongalia, W. Va	12
Steep Falls, Cumberland, Me	57	Stewartsville, Posey, Ind	56
Steer Creek, Gilmer, W. Va	14	Stewartsville, Grant, Ky	8
Stegall's Depot, Bartow, Ga	12	Stewartsville,* De Kalb, Mo	370
Steilacoom City,*(c. h.,) Pierce,Wash.	370	Stewartsville, Warren, N. J	110
Steinsburgh, Bucks, Pa	9	Stewartsville, Westmorland, Pa	40
Stelapolis, Iowa, Iowa	78	Stewartville, Olmsted, Minn	63
Stella, Gratiot, Mich	15	Stice's Shoal, Cleveland, N. C	37
Stelvidio, Darke, Ohio	22	Sticklerville, Sullivan, Mo	42
Stembersville, Carbon, Pa	15	Stickleyville, Lee, Va	25
Stephens, Oglethorpe, Ga	60	Stiflesville, Crawford, Ill	34
Stephens, Boone, Mo	12	Stiles, Davis, Iowa	83
Stephensburgh, Hardin, Ky	45	Stiles, Oconto, Wis	70
Stephensburgh, Morris, N. J	43	Stilesborough, Bartow, Ga	69
Stephens' Chapel, Bledsoe, Tenn	2	Stilesville, Hendricks, Ind	140
Stephens' Mills, Steuben, N. Y	57	Still Pond, Kent, Md	120
Stephenson's Depot, Frederick, Va.	200	Still River, Worcester, Mass	98
Stephensport, Breckinridge, Ky	51	Still Valley, Warren, N. J	16
Stephen's Store, Callaway, Mo	44	Stillwater, Shasta, Cal	12
Stephensville, Wilkinson, Ga	12	Stillwater,* (c. h.,) Washington, Minn	2,000
Stephensville, (c. h.,) Erath, Tex	110	Stillwater, Sussex, N. J	60
Stephensville, Outagamie, Wis	71	Stillwater, Saratoga, N. Y	430
Stephentown, Rensselaer, N. Y	120	Stillwater, Columbia, Pa	11
Stepney, Fairfield, Conn	39	Stillwell, La Porte, Ind	12
Stepney Depot, Fairfield, Conn	140	Stinesville, Monroe, Ind	60
Sterling, Windham, Conn	29	Stinesville, Lehigh, Pa	21
Sterling,* Whitesides, Ill	2,500	Stinson, Outagamie, Wis	12
Sterling, Jackson, Iowa	62	Stip's Hill, Franklin, Ind	6
Sterling, Worcester, Mass	300	Stirling, Montgomery, Ga	6
Sterling, Madison, Mont	76	Stirrup Grove, Macoupin, Ill	14
Sterling, Johnson, Nebr	16	Stissing, Dutchess, N. Y	12
Sterling, Cayuga, N. Y	160	Stittville, Oneida, N. Y	90
Sterling, Wayne, Ga	67	Stockbridge, Henry, Ga	12
Sterling Bush, Lewis, N. Y	11	Stockbridge, Berkshire. Mass	990
Sterling Centre, Blue Earth, Minn	12	Stockbridge, Ingham, Mich	100
Sterling Hill, Windham, Conn	21	Stockbridge, Madison, N. Y	110
Sterling Run, Cameron, Pa	160	Stockbridge, Windsor, Vt	98
Sterling Valley, Cayuga, N. Y	56	Stockbridge, Calumet, Wis	120
Sterlingville, Jefferson, N. Y	63	Stock Creek, Scott, Va	10
Sterrettania, Erie, Pa	22	Stockdale, Miami, Ind	82
Sterrett's Gap, Perry, Pa	29	Stockertown, Northampton, Pa	36
Stetson, Penobscot, Me	250	Stockholm, Sussex, N. J	39
Stettin, Marathon, Wis	20	Stockholm, St. Lawrence, N. Y	110
Steuben, Washington, Me	130	Stockholm, Pepin, Wis	150
Steuben, Oneida, N. Y	59	Stockholm Depot, St. Lawrence,	
Steuben, Huron, Ohio	100	N. Y	210
Steubenville,* (c. h.,) Jefferson, Ohio.	2,600	Stockland, Montgomery, Mo	13

* Money-order office.

STO   STR

Stockport, Columbia, N. Y	$120	Stony Fork, Watauga, N. C	$7
Stockport, Morgan, Ohio	52	Stony Fork, Tioga, Pa	42
Stockport Station, Delaware, N. Y.	43	Stony Man, Page, Va	48
Stocksville, Buncombe, N. C.	9	Stony Point, White, Ark.	49
Stockton, Baldwin, Ala.	12	Stony Point, Sonoma, Cal.	34
Stockton,* (c. h.,) San Joaquin, Cal..	3,600	Stony Point, Jefferson, Ind	8
Stockton, Clinch, Ga	97	Stony Point, East Baton Rouge, La.	20
Stockton, Jo Daviess, Ill	11	Stony Point, Jackson, Mo	24
Stockton, Owen, Ind	11	Stony Point, Rockland, N. Y	170
Stockton, Waldo, Me	440	Stony Point, Alexander, N. C.	12
Stockton, Winona, Minn	100	Stony Point, Crawford, Pa.	29
Stockton,* (c. h.,) Cedar, Mo	450	Stony Point, Anderson, S. C	12
Stockton, Hunterdon, N. J	280	Stony Point, Hawkins, Tenn	69
Stockton, Chautaqua, N. Y	210	Stony Point, Albemarle, Va	12
Stockton, Luzerne, Pa.	260	Stony Point Mills, Cumberland, Va.	16
Stockton, Roane, Tenn	13	Stony Ridge, Wood, Ohio	16
Stockton, Tooele, Utah	25	Stony Run, Oakland, Mich.	26
Stockton, Portage, Wis	20	Stony Run, Berks, Pa.	21
Stockwell,* Tippecanoe, Ind	370	Storeville, Anderson, S. C	13
Stoddard, Cheshire, N. H	110	Storm Lake, Buena Vista, Iowa	12
Stoddard, Vernon, Wis	9	Stormville, Dutchess, N. Y	71
Stoddartsville, Luzerne, Pa.	55	Stormville, Monroe, Pa	31
Stoker, Davis, Utah	100	Storrs, Hamilton, Ohio	140
Stokes, Oneida, N. Y	54	Story City, Story, Iowa	99
Stokes' Bridge, Darlington, S. C.	12	Stottville, Columbia, N. Y	75
Stokes' Mound, Carroll, Mo	12	Stouchsburgh, Berks, Pa.	130
Stone Arabia, Montgomery, N. Y.	15	Stoughstown, Cumberland, Pa.	19
Stone Bank, Waukesha, Wis.	50	Stoughton, Norfolk, Mass	600
Stone Bluffs, Fountain, Ind	18	Stoughton,* Dane, Wis	710
Stoneborough, Mercer, Pa.	150	Stoutland, Camden, Mo.	12
Stone Church, Genesee, N. Y	32	Stout's, Adams, Ohio	97
Stone Church, Northampton, Pa.	52	Stout's, Northampton, Pa.	18
Stone Creek, Tuscarawas, Ohio	65	Stoutsville, Fairfield, Ohio	65
Stone Fort, Saline, Ill	14	Stover, Dallas, Ark	9
Stoneham, Middlesex, Mass	1,200	Stow, Oxford, Me.	37
Stoneham, Warren, Pa	12	Stow, Middlesex, Mass	120
Stone House, Lawrence, Ky	8	Stowe,* Lamoille, Vt	610
Stone House, Morgan, Mo.	12	Stowell's Corners, Jefferson, N. Y.	11
Stone House Hotel, Prince William, Va.	6	Stoyestown, Somerset, Pa.	160
		Strabane, Washington, Pa.	12
Stone Lick, Clermont, Ohio	12	Strafford, Greene, Mo.	12
Stone Mills, Jefferson, N. Y	81	Strafford, Strafford, N. H	82
Stone Mountain, De Kalb, Ga.	190	Strafford, Orange, Vt	150
Stone Mountain, Carroll, Va.	3	Strafford Blue Hills, Strafford, N. H.	46
Stoner, Clarke, Ky	49	Strafford Corner, Strafford, N. H.	32
Stone Ridge, Ulster, N. Y.	170	Straight Fork, Scott, Ky	12
Stoner's Prairie, Dane, Wis	16	Strait Creek, Highland, Va.	8
Stonersville, Carroll, Md.	12	Strait's Corners, Tioga, N. Y.	28
Stonersville, Berks, Pa.	34	Strait's Lake, Oakland, Mich.	6
Stone's Bay, Onslow, N. C.	12	Straitsville, Perry, Ohio.	20
Stone's Prairie, Adams, Ill.	72	Stranger, Leavenworth, Kans.	12
Stoneville, Rockingham, N. C.	12	Stranger's Home, Lawrence, Ark.	12
Stonewall, Scott, Ky	33	Strasburgh, Tuscarawas, Ohio.	20
Stoney Brook, Suffolk, N. Y.	240	Strasburgh, Lancaster, Pa.	400
Stoney Hill, Gasconade, Mo	13	Strasburgh, Shenandoah, Va.	200
Stoney Point, Bourbon, Ky	21	Strata, Montgomery, Ala.	12
Stonington, New London, Conn	1,200	Stratford, Fairfield, Conn.	990
Stonington, Christian, Ill	57	Stratford, Coos, N. H.	97
Stono, St. Francois, Mo	24	Stratford, Fulton, N. Y.	93
Stony Bluff, Jefferson, Tenn	12	Stratham, Rockingham, N. H.	87
Stony Brook, Morris, N. J.	12	Stratton, Windham, Vt	19
Stony Creek, New Haven, Conn	100	Stratton's Falls, Delaware, N. Y.	17
Stony Creek, Washtenaw, Mich.	50	Strattonville, Clarion, Pa.	170
Stony Creek, Somerset, Pa.	41	Straughn's Station, Henry, Ind.	36
Stony Creek, Carter, Tenn.	12	Strausstown, Berks, Pa.	42
Stony Creek Warehouse, Sussex, Va.	98	Strawberry Plains, Jefferson, Tenn.	190

* Money-order office.

Office	Amount
Strawberry Point,* Clayton, Iowa.	$410
Strawberry Valley, Yuba, Cal....	55
Strawbridge, York, Pa	25
Strawtown, Hamilton, Ind........	17
Streator,* La Salle, Ill	740
Street Road, Chester, Pa	340
Streetsborough, Portage, Ohio.....	58
Stribling Springs, Augusta, Va....	51
Strickersville, Chester, Pa.........	97
Strickland, Isabella, Mich........	12
Strickland's Ferry, Androscoggin, Me	50
Strinestown, York, Pa	12
Stringtown, Richland, Ill	10
Stringtown, Cole, Mo	13
String Town, Pickaway, Ohio.....	18
Stringtown, Wilson, Tenn........	23
Stroderville, Cape Girardeau, Mo..	12
Strode's Mills, Mifflin, Pa........	58
Stronach, Manistee, Mich..........	36
Strong, Franklin, Me	210
Strong's Prairie, Adams, Wis.....	49
Strongstown, Indiana, Pa.........	15
Strongsville, Cuyahoga, Ohio......	60
Strother, Fairfield, S.C	31
Stroudsburgh,* (c. h.,) Monroe, Pa..	1,100
Struther's Station, Mahoning, Ohio.	110
Stryker, Williams, Ohio...........	440
Strykersville, Wyoming, N. Y......	100
Stuart, Adair, Iowa	140
Stuart's Draft, Augusta, Va........	12
Stuart's Mill, Christian, Ky........	16
Stuckeysville, Bedford, Pa........	6
Stump Knob, Johnson, Tenn.......	12
Sturbridge, Worcester, Mass......	200
Sturgeon, Fulton, Ind............	12
Sturgeon,* Boone, Mo	400
Sturgeon Bay,* (c. h.,) Door, Wis....	380
Sturgeonville, Brunswick, Va......	12
Sturgis,* St. Joseph, Mich.........	1,500
Stuyvesant, Columbia, N. Y......	170
Stuyvesant Falls, Columbia, N. Y..	150
Suamico, Brown, Wis.............	70
Sublett, Adair, Mo...............	4
Sublette, Lee, Ill	490
Sublett's Tavern, Powhatan, Va...	52
Sublimity, Pulaski, Ky............	5
Sublimity, Marion, Oreg..........	28
Sub Rosa, Franklin, Ark........	10
Sucarnoochee, Kemper, Miss......	12
Success, Suffolk, N. Y...........	22
Suckasunny, Morris, N. J.........	250
Sudbury, Middlesex, Mass........	120
Sudbury, Rutland, Vt............	130
Sudlersville, Queen Anne, Md.....	50
Sudley, Anne Arundel, Md........	12
Sue City, Macon, Mo.............	16
Suez, Mercer, Ill	77
Suffern, Rockland, N. Y..........	180
Suffield, Hartford, Conn..........	800
Suffield, Portage, Ohio..........	40
Suffolk, Suffolk, N. Y............	100
Suffolk,* (c. h.,) Nansemond, Va ...	640
Sugar Branch, Switzerland, Ind...	79
Sugar Bush, Outagamie, Wis	15
Sugar Creek, Benton, Ark.........	12
Sugar Creek, Vermilion, Ill ... ..|	12

Office	Amount
Sugar Creek, Hancock, Ind........	$79
Sugar Creek, Jasper, Iowa........	25
Sugar Creek, Gallatin, Ky........	36
Sugar Creek, Claiborne, La.......	12
Sugar Creek, Walworth, Wis......	30
Sugar Grove, Kane, Ill...........	33
Sugar Grove, Tippecanoe, Ind.....	63
Sugar Grove, Butler, Ky..........	43
Sugar Grove, Watauga, N. C......	7
Sugar Grove, Fairfield, Ohio.	83
Sugar Grove, Warren, Pa.........	260
Sugar Grove, Pendleton, W. Va....	12
Sugar Grove, Vernon, Wis........	8
Sugar Hill, Hall, Ga.............	12
Sugar Hill, Grafton, N. H........	62
Sugar Hill, Schuyler, N. Y........	12
Sugar Hill, McDowell, N. C.......	12
Sugar Hill, Panola, Tex..........	2
Sugar Lake, Crawford, Pa........	11
Sugar Land, Fort Bend, Tex... ...	30
Sugar Loaf, Sebastian, Ark.......	7
Sugar Loaf, Boulder, Colo.........	8
Sugar Loaf, Ford, Ill............	12
Sugar Loaf, Orange, N. Y.........	83
Sugar Notch, Luzerne, Pa........	200
Sugar Pine, Tuolumne, Cal.......	12
Sugar Run, Bradford, Pa.........	31
Sugartown, Chester, Pa..........	26
Sugartree, Guernsey, Ohio........	15
Sugar Tree Ridge, Highland, Ohio.	60
Sugar Valley, Gordon, Ga........	15
Sugar Valley, Clinton, Pa........	180
Suggsville, Clarke, Ala...........	53
Suisun City,* (c. h.,) Solano, Cal. ..	320
Suitsville, Prince George's, Md....	25
Sullivan,* (c. h.,) Moultrie, Ill......	460
Sullivan,* (c. h.,) Sullivan, Ind.....	760
Sullivan, Hancock, Me...........	100
Sullivan, Franklin, Mo...........	180
Sullivan, Cheshire, N. H.........	22
Sullivan, Ashland, Ohio..........	110
Sullivan, Tioga, Pa..............	20
Sullivan, Jefferson, Wis..........	12
Sullivan Centre, Livingston, Ill....	12
Sullivanville, Chemung, N. Y......	38
Sulphur Bluff, Hopkins, Tex......	21
Sulphur Fork, Henry, Ky.........	12
Sulphur Hill, Shelby, Ind........	12
Sulphur Lick, Monroe, Ky........	10
Sulphur Rock, Independence, Ark..	24
Sulphur Spring, Crawford, Ohio...	120
Sulphur Springs, Williamson, Ill...	12
Sulphur Springs, Henry, Ind......	200
Sulphur Springs, Montgomery, N.C.	11
Sulphur Springs, Rhea, Tenn.....	82
Sulphur Springs Landing, Jefferson, Mo.............	73
Sulphur Well, Shelby, Tenn.......	65
Sumac, Bollinger, Mo............	12
Summerfield, Dallas, Ala.........	180
Summerfield, St. Clair, Ill........	300
Summerfield, Noble, Ohio........	140
Summerford, Madison, Ohio......	31
Summer Hill, Pike, Ill...........	75
Summer Hill, Cayuga, N. Y.......	32
Summer Hill, Cambria, Pa........	94

* Money-order office.

Summers, Rockbridge, Va	$5	Sunderland, Bennington, Vt	$130
Summerset, Warren, Iowa	54	Sunderlandville, Calvert, Md	56
Summerton, Gratiot, Mich	12	Sunderlinville, Potter, Pa	16
Summerville, Calhoun, Ark	12	Sunfield, Eaton, Mich	20
Summerville, (c. h.,) Chattooga, Ga	55	Sun Hill, Wyoming, W. Va	5
Summerville, Peoria, Ill	33	Sunman, Ripley, Ind	160
Summerville, Cass, Mich	59	Sunny Dale, Pickens, S. C	12
Summerville, (c. h.,) Harnett, N. C	9	Sunny Side, Chicot, Ark	50
Summerville, Union, Oreg	43	Sunny Side, Marion, Ind	12
Summerville, Jefferson, Pa	73	Sunny Side, Buchanan, Iowa	44
Summerville, Charleston, S. C	180	Sunny Side, Wright, Mo	12
Summit, Blount, Ala	51	Sunny Side, Washington, N. C	12
Summit, Plumas, Cal	49	Sunny Side, Allegheny, Pa	46
Summit, Cook, Ill	18	Sunny Side, Cumberland, Va	15
Summit, Muscatine, Iowa	19	Sun Prairie,* Dane, Wis	620
Summit, Jefferson, Ky	12	Sun Rise, Bath, Va	10
Summit, Washtenaw, Mich	7	Sunrise City, Chisago, Minn	81
Summit, Jackson, Minn	3	Sun River, Lewis and Clarke, Mont	12
Summit, Pike, Miss	650	Sunville, Venango, Pa	46
Summit, Madison, Mont	24	Superior, (c. h.,) Douglas, Wis	510
Summit, Union, N. J	340	Surgeon's Hall, Allegheny, Pa	24
Summit, Schoharie, N. Y	250	Surgoinsville, Hawkins, Tenn	12
Summit, Summit, Ohio	24	Surrency, Appling, Ga	12
Summit, Benton, Oreg	12	Surrey, Portage, Wis	14
Summit, Cambria, Pa	82	Surry, Hancock, Me	92
Summit, Kent, R. I	78	Surry, Cheshire, N. H	50
Summit, Iron, Utah	40	Surry C. H., Surry, Va	90
Summit, Waukesha, Wis	61	Susanville,* (c. h.,) Lassen, Cal	530
Summit Bridge, New Castle, Del	81	Suspension, Bullock, Ala	55
Summit Hill, Carbon, Pa	600	Suspension Bridge,* Niagara, N. Y	1,800
Summit Mills, Somerset, Pa	25	Susquehanna, Dauphin, Pa	52
Summit Point, Jefferson, W. Va	230	Susquehanna Depot,* Susquehanna,	
Summit Station, Onondaga, N. Y	84	Pa	1,100
Summit Station, Licking, Ohio	11	Sussex, Waukesha, Wis	110
Summit Station, Schuylkill, Pa	22	Sussex C. H., Sussex, Va	32
Summitville, Madison, Ind	20	Sutersville, Westmoreland, Pa	53
Summitville, Lee, Iowa	48	Sutherland, Dinwiddie, Va	19
Summitville, Columbiana, Ohio	92	Sutherland Falls, Rutland, Vt	210
Summitville, Coffee, Tenn	13	Sutherland Springs, Wilson, Tex	82
Summum, Fulton, Ill	52	Sutter Creek, Amador, Cal	440
Sumner, Lawrence, Ill	410	Sutton, Worcester, Mass	210
Sumner, Rush, Ind	25	Sutton, Merrimack, N. H	110
Sumner, Bremer, Iowa	30	Sutton, Caledonia, Vt	120
Sumner, Oxford, Me	25	Sutton's Bay, Leelenaw, Mich	19
Sumner, Gratiot, Mich	12	Sutton's Corners, Crawford, Pa	92
Sumner, Freeborn, Minn	8	Sutton's Station, Robertson, Tex	130
Sumnerville, Ottawa, Kans	12	Suwanee, Gwinnett, Ga	12
Sumneytown, Montgomery, Pa	71	Suwannee Shoals, Columbia, Fla	16
Sumpter, (c. h.,) Trinity, Tex	46	Swain, Allegany, N. Y	66
Sumption Prairie, St. Joseph, Ind	12	Swainsborough, (c. h.,) Emanuel, Ga	12
Sumter, Moultrie, Ill	12	Swale, Steuben, N. Y	8
Sumter, McLeod, Minn	12	Swampscott, Essex, Mass	630
Sumter C. H.,* Sumter, S. C	1,300	Swan, Noble, Ind	75
Sumterville, Sumter, Ala	24	Swan, Vinton, Ohio	67
Sumterville, (c. h.,) Sumter, Fla	51	Swan City, (c. h.,) Saline, Nebr	29
Sun, St. Tammany, La	6	Swan Creek, Warren, Ill	57
Sunapee, Sullivan, N. H	140	Swan Creek, Saginaw, Mich	12
Sunbeam, Mercer, Ill	170	Swan Creek, Gallia, Ohio	41
Sunbury, Livingston, Ill	10	Swander's Crossing, Shelby, Ohio	12
Sunbury, Gates, N. C	18	Swangstown, Cleveland, N. C	12
Sunbury, Delaware, Ohio	180	Swan Lake, Arkansas, Ark	25
Sunbury, (c. h.,) Northumberland,		Swan Lake, Lincoln, Dak	12
Pa	1,600	Swannano, Buncombe, N. C	9
Suncliff, Indiana, Pa	14	Swann's Station, Moore, N. C	10
Suncook,* Merrimack, N. H	750	Swan Pond, Knox, Ky	4
Sunderland, Franklin, Mass	290	Swan Quarter, (c. h.,) Hyde, N. C	10

* Money-order office.

Swan River, Morrison, Minn	$11
Swansborough, Onslow, N. C	20
Swansea, Bristol, Mass	150
Swansea, Lincoln, Minn	12
Swan's Island, Hancock, Me.	85
Swansonville, Pittsylvania, Va	8
Swan Station, Erie, Pa	52
Swanton, Butler, Iowa	22
Swanton, Alleghany, Md	60
Swanton, Fulton, Ohio	160
Swanton,* Franklin, Vt	490
Swanton Centre, Franklin, Vt	21
Swanton Junction, Franklin, Vt	20
Swanville, Jefferson, Ind	24
Swanville, Waldo, Me	55
Swanzey, Cheshire, N. H	64
Swartswood, Sussex, N. J	12
Swartwout, Polk, Tex	8
Swartz Creek, Genesee, Mich	6
Swartzville, Lancaster, Pa	12
Swatara, Schuylkill, Pa	76
Swatara Station, Dauphin, Pa	96
Sweadel, (c. h.,) McPherson, Kans	12
Swede Grove, Meeker, Minn	38
Sweden, Oxford, Me	44
Sweden, Monroe, N. Y	32
Sweden, Potter, Pa	3
Sweden Valley, Potter, Pa	5
Swedesborough, Gloucester, N. J	270
Swedesburgh, Henry, Iowa	12
Swede's Forest, Redwood, Minn	12
Swedona, Mercer, Ill	220
Sweede Point, Boone, Iowa	160
Sweedlin Hill, Pendleton, W. Va	5
Sweet Air, Baltimore, Md	34
Sweet Chalybeate, Alleghany, Va	150
Sweet Home, Nodaway, Mo	21
Sweet Home, Iredell, N. C	6
Sweet Home, Lavaca, Tex	66
Sweetland, Nevada, Cal	28
Sweetland Centre, Muscatine, Iowa.	16
Sweetser's, Grant, Ind	12
Sweet Springs, Monroe, W. Va	110
Sweet Valley, Luzerne, Pa	12
Sweet Water, Gwinnett, Ga	12
Sweet Water, Menard, Ill	120
Sweetwater, Esmeralda, Nev	12
Sweet Water, Monroe, Tenn	360
Sweet Wine, Hamilton, Ohio	6
Swift Creek Bridge, Craven, N. C	10
Swift Island, Montgomery, N. C	5
Swift Lake, Meeker, Minn	10
Swingleville, Washington, Tenn	10
Swit's City, Greene, Ind	12
Switzler, Monroe, Mo	12
Swoope's Depot, Augusta, Va	83
Sybertsville, Luzerne, Pa	54
Sycamore,* (c. h.,) De Kalb, Ill	1,500
Sycamore, Wyandot, Ohio	49
Sycamore, Cheatham, Tenn	19
Sycamore, Calhoun, W. Va	4
Sycamore Dale, Harrison, W. Va	18
Sycamore Grove, Putnam, W. Va	12
Sycamore Springs, Butler, Kans	7
Sydnorsville, Franklin, Va	10
Syene, Dane, Wis	28

Sykes' Mills, Elmore, Ala	$12
Sykesville, Carroll, Md	200
Sykesville, Burlington, N. J	16
Sylacauga, Talladega, Ala	12
Sylamore, Izard, Ark	7
Sylarsville, Monroe, Ark	12
Sylliman, Schuylkill, Pa	14
Sylvan, Washtenaw, Mich	59
Sylvan, Franklin, Pa	9
Sylvan, Richland, Wis	28
Sylvan Dale, Hancock, Ill	12
Sylvan Hill, Meeker, Minn	12
Sylvania, Parke, Ind	24
Sylvania, Dade, Mo	12
Sylvania, Lucas, Ohio	330
Sylvania, Bradford, Pa	86
Sylvania, Racine, Wis	27
Sylvan Lodge, Newton, Mo	12
Sylvarena, Smith, Miss	12
Sylvester, Green, Wis	39
Symco, Waupaca, Wis	29
Symmes, Hamilton, Ohio	10
Symmes' Corners, Butler, Ohio	41
Syosset, Queens, N. Y	66
Syracuse, Kosciusko, Ind	64
Syracuse,* Morgan, Mo	230
Syracuse,* (c. h.,) Onondaga, N. Y	4,000
Syracuse, Meigs, Ohio	120

T.

Taberg, Oneida, N. Y	260
Tabernacle, Tipton, Tenn	12
Taberville, St. Clair, Mo	42
Table Bluff, Humboldt, Cal	12
Table Grove, Fulton, Ill	77
Table Mountain, Pickens, S. C	5
Table Rock, Izard, Ark	12
Table Rock, Sierra, Cal	140
Table Rock, Pawnee, Nebr	53
Table Rock, Adams, Pa	14
Table Rock, Raleigh, W. Va	8
Tabo, La Fayette, Mo	89
Tabor,* Fremont, Iowa	400
Tabor, Roane, Tenn	5
Tacoma, Pierce, Wash	12
Tadmer, Montgomery, Ohio	77
Taffe, Wayne, Nebr	12
Tafton, Pike, Pa	7
Taftsville, Windsor, Vt	120
Taghkanick, Columbia, N. Y	5
Tahlequah, (c. h.,) Cherokee N., Ind. T	46
Taho, El Dorado, Cal	15
Talbotton, (c. h.,) Talbot, Ga	420
Talbott's Mills, Jefferson, Tenn	51
Talbotville, Chester, Pa	16
Talcott, Charlotte, Va	229
Talcottville, Tolland, Conn	96
Talking Rock, Pickens, Ga	28
Talladega,* (c. h.,) Talladega, Ala	1,000
TALLAHASSEE,* (c. h.,) Leon, Fla	2,100
Tallahoma, Lucas, Iowa	36
Tallapoosa, Haralson, Ga	12
Talleyrand, Keokuk, Iowa	140
Tallmadge, Ottawa, Mich	16

* Money-order office.

Tallmadge, Summit, Ohio	$220
Tallman, Rockland, N. Y	27
Tallmansville, Upshur, W. Va	2
Tallula, Menard, Ill	260
Tallulah, Habersham, Ga	14
Tallulah, (c. h.,) Issoquena, Miss	24
Talley Cavey, Allegheny, Pa	37
Talley Ho, Granville, N. C	10
Talmage, Baldwin, Ga	30
Tama City, Tama, Iowa	1,200
Tamaqua,* Schuylkill, Pa	1,400
Tamarac, Crawford, Pa	30
Tamarack, Montcalm, Mich	12
Tamaroa, Perry, Ill	410
Tamola Station, Kemper, Miss	12
Tamorack, Will, Ill	60
Tampa, (c. h.,) Hillsborough, Fla	280
Tampico, Whitesides, Ill	12
Tampico, Jackson, Ind	24
Tampico, Darke, Ohio	14
Tampico, Grainger, Tenn	21
Tamworth, Carroll, N. H	180
Tamworth Iron Works, Carroll, N. H.	110
Taneytown, Carroll, Md	230
Tangapaho, St. Helena, La	200
Tanktown, Delaware, Ohio	28
Tanners, Gilmer, W. Va	6
Tanner's Falls, Wayne, Pa	21
Tannersville, Greene, N. Y	21
Tannersville, Monroe, Pa	55
Tannery, Indiana, Pa	56
Taos, Cole, Mo	25
Tappahannock, (c. h.,) Essex, Va	190
Tappan, Harrison, Ohio	26
Tappantown, Rockland, N. Y	93
Tarborough, (c. h.,) Edgecombe, N. C	1,200
Tardyville, Pontotoc, Miss	26
Tarentum, Allegheny, Pa	290
Tariffville, Hartford, Conn	190
Tarkio, Page, Iowa	32
Tarlton, Pickaway, Ohio	150
Tarrant, (c. h.,) Hopkins, Tex	12
Tarr Farm,* Venango, Pa	860
Tarrytown,* Westchester, N. Y	1,900
Tassinong, Porter, Ind	20
Tate Creek, Braxton, W. Va	9
Tate's Station, Montgomery, Tenn	17
Tatesville, Bedford, Pa	12
Taunton, (c. h.,) Bristol, Mass	3,300
Taverner's Woods, Talbot, Md	33
Tawas City, (c. h.,) Iosco, Mich	320
Tawawa, Shelby, Ohio	20
Taxahau, Lancaster, S. C	12
Taycheedah, Fond du Lac, Wis	62
Taylor, Ogle, Ill	47
Taylor, Harford, Md	40
Taylor, Cortland, N. Y	83
Taylor Centre, Wayne, Mich	10
Taylor Hill, Franklin, Ill	7
Taylor's, Sumpter, S. C	5
Taylor's Creek, St. Francis, Ark	24
Taylor's Creek, Liberty, Ga	32
Taylor's Creek, Hamilton, Ohio	26
Taylor's Depot, La Fayette, Miss	37
Taylor's Fall's, Chisago, Minn	470
Taylor's Island, Dorchester, Md	$83
Taylor's Mills, Randolph, W. Va	12
Taylor's Stand, Crawford, Pa	12
Taylor's Station, Franklin, Ohio	12
Taylor's Store, Franklin, Va	27
Taylorstown, Washington, Pa	50
Taylorstown, Loudoun, Va	56
Taylorsville, Plumas, Cal	150
Taylorsville, Bartholomew, Ind	170
Taylorsville, Fayette, Iowa	94
Taylorsville, (c. h.,) Spencer, Ky	190
Taylorsville, Montgomery, Ohio	20
Taylorsville, Bucks, Pa	94
Taylorsville, (c. h.,) Johnson, Tenn	75
Taylorsville, Hanover, Va	64
Taylorville, (c. h.) Christian, Ill	750
Taylorville, (c. h.,) Alexander, N. C	65
Taymouth, Saginaw, Mich	17
Tazewell, (c. h.,) Claiborne, Tenn	130
Tazewell C. H., Tazewell, Va	230
T. B., Prince George's, Md	96
Teachey's, Duplin, N. C	17
Teague's Mills, Hardeman, Tenn	12
Tebeanville, Ware, Ga	240
Tecolote, San Miguel, N. Mex	42
Tecumseh, Shawnee, Kans	60
Tecumseh, Warren, Ky	12
Tecumseh, Lenawee, Mich	1 600
Tecumseh, (c. h.,) Johnson, Nebr	280
Tedrow, Fulton, Ohio	89
Teekalet, Kitsap, Wash	140
Tehama, Tehama, Cal	120
Tehichipa, Kern, Cal	12
Tehuacana, Limestone, Tex	12
Tekamah, (c. h.,) Burt, Nebr	100
Tekonsha, Calhoun, Mich	260
Telegraph City, Calaveras, Cal	61
Telford, Bucks, Pa	12
Tell City,* Perry, Ind	410
Teller's Corners, Crawford, Wis	8
Tellico Plains, Monroe, Tenn	16
Teloga Springs, Chattooga, Ga	10
Temecula, San Diego, Cal	12
Temperance, Telfair, Ga	15
Temperance Hall, De Kalb, Tenn	10
Temperance Hill, Monroe, Miss	4
Temperance Hill, Marion, S. C	12
Temperance Mount, Simpson, Ky	11
Temperanceville, Belmont, Ohio	27
Temperanceville, Allegheny, Pa	400
Temperanceville, Accomack, Va	22
Temple, Hillsborough, N. H	110
Temple, Berks, Pa	62
Temple Hill, Barren, Ky	5
Templeman's Cross Roads, Westmoreland, Va	12
Temple Mills, Franklin, Me	56
Temple of Health, Abbeville, S. C	5
Templeton, Worcester, Mass	430
Templeton, Prince George, Va	12
Templeville, Queen Anne, Md	32
Tenafly, Bergen, N. J	100
Tenallytown, Washington, D. C	31
Tenant's Harbor, Knox, Me	140
Tenhassen, Martin, Minn	38
Ten Mile, Campbell, Ky	12

* Money-order office.

THO · THR

Ten Mile, Macon, Mo	$12
Ten Mile, Douglas, Oreg	12
Ten Mile, Washington, Pa	58
Ten Mile, Lincoln, W. Va	4
Ten Mile Bottom, Venango, Pa	12
Ten Mile House, Clinton, Iowa	12
Ten Mile House, Milwaukee, Wis	38
Ten Mile Stand, Meigs, Tenn	56
Tennessee, McDonough, Ill	130
Tennessee Colony, Anderson, Tex	12
Tennessee Ridge, Stewart, Tenn	20
Tennessee River Station, Stewart, Tenn	12
Tennille, Washington, Ga	140
Tensaw, Baldwin, Ala	37
Tenth Legion, Rockingham, Va	20
Terre Bonne, Terre Bonne, La	52
Terre Coupee, St. Joseph, Ind	19
Terre Haute, Henderson, Ill	160
Terre Haute, (c. h.,) Vigo, Ind	4,000
Terre Haute, Decatur, Iowa	8
Terre Haute, Putnam, Mo	28
Terre Haute, Champaign, Ohio	29
Terre Hill, Lancaster, Pa	110
Terry, Hinds, Miss	370
Terry, Carroll, Tenn	9
Terrysville, Litchfield, Conn	370
Terrytown, Bradford, Pa	47
Terryville, De Witt, Tex	12
Tess Corners, Waukesha, Wis	21
Tetersburgh, Tipton, Ind	57
Teutopolis, Effingham, Ill	200
Tewksbury, Middlesex, Mass	170
Texana, (c. h.,) Jackson, Tex	94
Texas, Washington, Ky	12
Texas, Oswego, N. Y	41
Texas, Henry, Ohio	89
Texas, Lycoming, Pa	16
Texas, Tucker, W. Va	2
Texas City, Saline, Ill	12
Texas Valley, Cortland, N. Y	14
Thacker's Creek, Blount, Ala	12
Thaxton's, Bedford, Va	86
Thayer, Union, Iowa	49
Thebes, Alexander, Ill	35
The Corner, Ulster, N. Y	33
The Dalles, (c. h.,) Wasco, Oreg	760
The Forks, Somerset, Me	93
The Glen, Warren, N. Y	13
The Grove, Cook, Ill	59
The Grove, Caroline, Va	12
The Narrows, Crawford, Ark	3
Theological Seminary, Fairfax, Va	180
The Plains, Fauquier, Va	220
Theresa, Jefferson, N. Y	470
Theresa, Dodge, Wis	130
The Rock, Upson, Ga	22
The Rock, Mercer, W. Va	12
The Square, Cayuga, N. Y	22
Thetford, Orange, Vt	150
Thetford Centre, Genesee, Mich	3
Thetford Centre, Orange, Vt	110
Thibodeaux, (c. h.,) La Fourche, La	820
Thivener, Gallia, Ohio	15
Thomas, Oceana, Mich	20
Thomas, Harrison, Mo	12

Thomasborough, Champaign, Ill	$24
Thomas' Run, Harford, Md	33
Thomas Station, Bullock, Ala	17
Thomaston,* Litchfield, Conn	1,000
Thomaston, (c. h.,) Upson, Ga	170
Thomaston, Knox, Me	1,200
Thomastown, Leake, Miss	12
Thomasville, (c. h.,) Thomas, Ga	700
Thomasville, Oregon, Mo	97
Thomasville, Davidson, N. C	330
Thomasville, York, Pa	12
Thomasville, Cheatham, Tenn	12
Thompson, Windham, Conn	330
Thompson, Columbia, Ga	270
Thompson, Geauga, Ohio	100
Thompson, Susquehanna, Pa	130
Thompson, Washington, Wis	3
Thompson's Cross Roads, Louisa, Va	18
Thompson's River, Missoula, Mont	12
Thompson's Station, Williamson, Tenn	33
Thompsontown, Juniata, Pa	230
Thompsonville, Carroll, Ark	12
Thompsonville,* Hartford, Conn	970
Thompsonville, Pulaski, Ky	3
Thompsonville, Sullivan, N. Y	31
Thompsonville, Rockingham, N. C	4
Thompsonville, Washington, Pa	43
Thompsonville, Gonzales, Tex	12
Thompsonville, Racine, Wis	63
Thomson, Carroll, Ill	520
Thoms' Run, Greene, Pa	11
Thornburgh, Spottsylvania, Va	28
Thornbury, Chester, Pa	26
Thorndale Iron Works, Chester, Pa	120
Thorndike, Waldo, Me	12
Thorndike, Hampden, Mass	230
Thorndike, Cabell, W. Va	13
Thorn Grove, Knox, Tenn	28
Thorn Hill, Marion, Ala	10
Thorn Hill, Onondaga, N. Y	21
Thorn Hill, Grainger, Tenn	17
Thornhill, Orange, Va	20
Thornton, Cook, Ill	59
Thornton, St. Clair, Mich	36
Thornton, Grafton, N. H	20
Thornton, Delaware, Pa	16
Thornton, Taylor, W. Va	96
Thornton's Bluff, Etowah, Ala	12
Thornton's Depot, Fairfax, Va	10
Thornton's Ferry, Hillsborough, N. H	140
Thorntown,* Boone, Ind	1,000
Thornville, Lapeer, Mich	46
Thornville, Perry, Ohio	110
Three Bridges, Hunterdon, N. J	45
Three Grove, Cass, Nebr	31
Three Locusts, Marion, Ohio	24
Three Mile Bay, Jefferson, N Y	250
Three Oaks,* Berrien, Mich	340
Three Rivers, Hampden, Mass	110
Three Rivers,* St. Joseph, Mich	1,700
Three Runs, Clearfield, Pa	17
Three Springs, Hart, Ky	20
Three Springs, Huntingdon, Pa	94
Three Tons, Montgomery, Pa	50

* Money-order office.

TIT   TOQ

Throopville, Cayuga, N. Y	$73	Tiverton, Newport, R. I	$80
Thurlow, Delaware, Pa	77	Tiverton Four Corners, Newport,	
Thurman, Warren, N. Y	25	R. I	110
Thurman, Gallia, Ohio	180	Tivoli, Dubuque, Iowa	25
Thurston, Steuben, N. Y	12	Tivoli, Blue Earth, Minn	38
Tibbatt's Cross Roads, Campbell, Ky	6	Tivoli, Dutchess, N. Y	320
Tibby Station, Lowndes, Miss	97	Tivoli, Lycoming, Pa	38
Ticonderoga, Essex, N. Y	680	Tobacco Stick, Dorchester, Md	33
Ticonic, Monona, Iowa	15	Toboso, Licking, Ohio	43
Tidioute,* Warren, Pa	3,200	Tobyhanna Mills, Monroe, Pa	200
Tiffany, Rock, Wis	54	Toccopola, Pontotoc, Miss	58
Tiffin, Johnson, Iowa	12	Todd, Huntingdon, Pa	5
Tiffin, (c. h.,) Seneca, Ohio	2,400	Todd's, Morgan, Ohio	30
Tigerville, Terre Bonne, La	22	Todd's, Shelby, Tex	12
Tilden, Hancock, Me	27	Todd's Point, Shelby, Ill	64
Tillamook, (c. h.,) Tillamook, Oreg	12	Todd's Point, Shelby, Ky	18
Tillatoba, Yalabusha, Miss	12	Todd's Valley, Placer, Cal	35
Tiller's Ferry, Kershaw, S. C	2·	Toddsville, Otsego, N. Y	95
Tilton, Whitfield, Ga	83	Token Creek, Dane, Wis	130
Tilton, Fleming, Ky	81	Toland's Prairie, Washington, Wis	30
Tilton,* Belknap, N. H	760	*Toledo,* (c. h.,) Tama, Iowa	1,100
Timber Cove, Sonoma, Cal	99	Toledo, Chase, Kans	19
Timber Creek, Marshall, Iowa	23	*Toledo,* (c. h.,) Lucas, Ohio	3,700
Timber Creek, Riley, Kans	12	Toledo, Benton, Oreg	24
Timber Creek, Hunt, Tex	7	Tolersville, Louisa, Va	150
Timber Hill, Labette, Kans	12	Tolesborough, Lewis, Ky	23
Timber Ridge, Union, S. C	6	Toleston, Lake, Ind	51
Timber Ridge, Greene, Tenn	12	*Tolland,* (c. h.,) Tolland, Conn	360
Timber Ridge, Rockbridge, Va	11	Tolland, Hampden, Mass	45
Timberville, Dodge, Nebr	75	Tolona, Champaign, Ill	620
Timberville, Paulding, Ohio	12	Tomah,* Monroe, Wis	690
Timberville, Rockingham, Va	81	Tomahawk Springs, Berkeley,	
Timbuctoo, Yuba, Cal	63	W.Va	18
Time, Pike, Ill	79	Tomales, Marin, Cal	80
Timmonsville, Darlington, S. C	240	Tomb's Run, Lycoming, Pa	7
Tindell, Grundy, Mo	12	Tomhannock, Rensselaer, N. Y	48
Tingley, Union, Iowa	23	Tomkin's Cove, Rockland, N. Y	88
Tinker Run, Westmoreland, Pa	40	Tompkins, Jackson, Mich	22
Tinmouth, Rutland, Vt	20	Tompkins' Corners, Chemung, N. Y	12
Tinney's Grove, Ray, Mo	49	*Tompkinsville,* (c. h.,) Monroe, Ky	110
Tinton Falls, Monmouth, N. J	45	Tompkinsville, Richmond, N. Y	480
Tioga, Neosho, Kans	160	Tompkinsville, Luzerne, Pa	22
Tioga, Tioga, Pa	540	Tompson's Station, Andrian, Mo	36
Tioga Centre, Tioga, N. Y	77	Tom's Creek, Surry, N. C	21
Tioga Valley, Bradford, Pa	3	Tom's River,* Ocean, N. J	540
Tionesta, (c. h.,) Forest, Pa	310	Tonawanda,* Erie, N. Y	890
Tippecanoe, Harrison, Ohio	25	Tongaloo, Madison, Miss	12
Tippecanoe, Fayette, Pa	35	Tonganoxie, Leavenworth, Kans	290
Tippecanoe City,* Miami, Ohio	710	Tonica,* La Salle, Ill	630
Tippecanoetown, Marshall, Ind	22	Tontogany, Wood, Ohio	310
Tip's Branch, Pawnee, Nebr	12	Tontzville, Miami, Kans	17
Tipton, (c. h.,) Tipton, Ind	580	*Tooele,* (c. h.,) Tooele, Utah	55
Tipton, (c. h.,) Cedar, Iowa	980	Toolsborough, Louisa, Iowa	38
Tipton, Lenawee, Mich	26	Toomsborough, Wilkinson, Ga	89
Tipton,* Moniteau, Mo	630	Toomsuba, Lauderdale, Miss	38
Tipton, Lancaster, Nebr	12	Tooner's Station, Hardeman, Tenn	10
Tipton, Blair, Pa	110	Topeka, Mason, Ill	146
Tipton Grove, Hardin, Iowa	5	TOPEKA,* (c. h.,) Shawnee, Kans	3,600
Tiptonville, Obion, Tenn	130	Topin's Grove, Jackson, W. Va	10
Tirade, Walworth, Wis	8	Topsail Sound, New Hanover, N. C	12
Tiro, Crawford, Ohio	20	Topsfield, Washington, Me	80
Tisheminge, Chickasaw N., Ind. T	12	Topsfield, Essex, Mass	180
Tiskilwa, Bureau, Ill	670	Topsham, Sagadahoc, Me	420
Titusville, Ripley, Ind	14	Topsham, Orange, Vt	110
Titusville, Mercer, N. J	160	Topton, Berks, Pa	35
Titusville,* Crawford, Pa	3,400	*Toquerville,* (c. h.,) Kane, Utah	74

* **Money-order office.**

TRA

TRI

Torah, Stearns, Minn	$91	Transitville, Tippecanoe, Ind	$88
Torch, Athens, Ohio	28	Trap Hill, Wilkes, N.C	13
Torch Lake, Antrim, Mich	30	Trappe, Talbot, Md	180
Toronto, Vermillion, Ind	44	Trappe, Montgomery, Pa	210
Toronto, Clinton, Iowa	45	Trask, Grant, Ind	23
Toronto, Woodson, Kans	12	Traveller's Repose, Pocahontas,	
Toronto, Miller, Mo	12	W. Va	13
Torrance, Grenada, Miss	85	Traveller's Rest, Coosa, Ala	4
Torringford, Litchfield, Conn	25	Traveller's Rest, Owsley, Ky	8
Torrington, Litchfield, Conn	97	Traveller's Rest, Greenville, S.C	12
Toto, Stark, Ind	16	Travers des Sioux, Nicollet, Minn	70
Tottonville, Richmond, N. Y	260	Traverse City,* (c. h.,) Grand Tra-	
Touchet, Walla-Walla, Wash	12	verse, Mich	810
Tough Kenamon, Chester, Pa	180	Travis, Austin, Tex	32
Toulon,* (c. h.,) Stark, Ill	570	Travisville, Fentress, Tenn	5
Towanda, McLean, Ill	230	Traylorsville, Henry, Va	22
Towanda, Butler, Kans	59	Treasure City, White Pine, Nev	1, 100
Towanda,* (c. h.,) Bradford, Pa	2, 400	Tremont, Tazewell, Ill	230
Towash, Hill, Tex	12	Tremont, Hancock, Me	110
Tower City, Schuylkill, Pa	43	Tremont, Westchester, N. Y	450
Tower Hill, Shelby, Ill	200	Tremont, Clark, Ohio	61
Tower Hill, Delaware, Iowa	16	Tremont, Schuylkill, Pa	610
Tower Hill, Appomattox, Va	25	Trempealeau,* Trempealeau, Wis	600
Towerville, Crawford, Pa	32	Trent, Muskegon, Mich	48
Towlesville, Steuben, N. Y	10	Trenton, Jackson, Ala	5
Town Bluff, Tyler, Tex	12	Trenton, Phillips, Ark	20
Town Creek, Lawrence, Ala	12	Trenton, (c. h.,) Dade, Ga	87
Towner's, Putnam, N. Y	130	Trenton,* Clinton, Ill	390
Townesville, Granville, N. C	80	Trenton, Randolph, Ind	63
Town Hill, Luzerne, Pa	54	Trenton, Henry, Mo	100
Town Line, Erie, N. Y	45	Trenton, Todd, Ky	140
Town Line, Luzerne, Pa	39	Trenton, Ouachita, La	26
Townsbury, Warren, N. J	18	Trenton, Baltimore, Md	7
Townsend, New Castle, Del	310	Trenton, Wayne, Mich	250
Townsend, Middlesex, Mass	440	Trenton, Freeborn, Minn	6
Townsend, Schuyler, N. Y	38	Trenton, Smith, Miss	12
Townsend, Sandusky, Ohio	110	Trenton, (c. h.,) Grundy, Mo	600
Townsend Harbor, Middlesex, Mass.	120	TRENTON,* (c. h.,) Mercer, N. J	3, 500
Townsend Inlet, Cape May, N. J	96	Trenton, Oneida, N. Y	250
Townsend's Mills, Gilmer, W. Va	6	Trenton, (c. h.,) Jones, N. C	25
Townsend Station, Huron, Ohio	110	Trenton, Butler, Ohio	170
Townsendville, Seneca, N. Y	39	Trenton,* (c. h.,) Gibson, Tenn	850
Townshend, Windham, Vt	320	Trenton, Pierce, Wis	12
Townsville, Butler, Ky	12	Trenton Falls, Oneida, N. Y	130
Townville, Crawford, Pa	130	Tresckow, Carbon, Pa	120
Townville, Anderson, S. C	17	Trevilian's Depot, Louisa, Va	250
Towsontown, (c. h.,) Baltimore, Md	450	Trevorton, Northumberland, Pa	290
Tracy, Barren, Ky	12	Trexlertown, Lehigh, Pa	92
Tracy City, Marion, Tenn	12	Trezevant, Carroll, Tenn	140
Tracy Creek, Broome, N. Y	15	Triadelphia, Montgomery, Md	6
Tracy's Landing, Anne Arundel, Md.	56	Triadelphia, Morgan, Ohio	15
Trade, Johnson, Tenn	6	Triadelphia, Ohio, W. Va	91
Trader's Hill, (c. h.,) Charlton, Ga.	23	Triana, Madison, Ala	22
Trader's Point, Marion, Ind	25	Triangle, Broome, N. Y	96
Tradersville, Madison, Ohio	10	Tribe's Hill, Montgomery, N. Y	96
Trafalgar, Johnson, Ind	77	Trim Belle, Pierce, Wis	32
Trail Ridge, Clay, Fla	12	Trimble, Athens, Ohio	34
Trail Run, Monroe, Ohio	6	Trinidad, Klamath, Cal	17
Trammel, Sumner, Tenn	10	Trinidad,* (c. h.,) Los Animas, Colo.	460
Tranquility, Appanoose, Iowa	12	Trinity, Trinity, Cal	19
Tranquility, Sussex, N. J	12	Trinity, Catahoula, La	71
Tranquility, Adams, Ohio	53	Trinity Centre, Trinity, Cal	19
Tranquilla, Washington, Ark	12	Trinity College,* Randolph, N. C	260
Transfer, Mercer, Pa	77	Trinity Springs, Martin, Ind	75
Transit, Sibley, Minn	9	Trinity Station, Morgan, Ala	60
Transit, Hamilton, Ohio	20	Trion, Tuscaloosa, Ala	43

* Money-order office.

TRY

TUR

Trion, Jefferson, Tenn.	$7
Trion Factory, Chattooga, Ga.	59
Tripoli, Bremer, Iowa.	55
Triumph, La Salle, Ill.	37
Triune, Williamson, Tenn.	89
Trivoli, Peoria, Ill.	150
Trostville, Saginaw, Mich.	23
Trotwood, Montgomery, Ohio.	390
Troublesome, Rockingham, N. C.	7
Troup, Smith, Tex.	58
Troupsburgh, Steuben, N. Y.	60
Trout Creek, Meagher, Mont.	50
Trout Creek, Delaware, N. Y.	50
Trout River, Franklin, N. Y.	90
Trout Run, Lycoming, Pa.	100
Trout Run, Hardy, W. Va.	7
Troutsville, Botetourt, Va.	12
Troutville, Clearfield, Pa.	40
Troxelville, Snyder, Pa.	14
Troy,* (c. h.,) Pike, Ala.	230
Troy,* Madison, Ill.	290
Troy, Perry, Ind.	180
Troy, Davis, Iowa.	150
Troy,* (c. h.,) Doniphan, Kans.	400
Troy, Woodford, Ky.	12
Troy, Waldo, Me.	77
Troy, Oakland, Mich.	66
Troy, Winona, Minn.	81
Troy, (c. h.,) Lincoln, Mo.	360
Troy, Cheshire, N. H.	260
Troy,* (c. h.,) Rensselaer, N. Y.	4,000
Troy, (c. h.,) Montgomery, N. C.	30
Troy,* (c. h.,) Miami, Ohio.	1,900
Troy,* Bradford, Pa.	1,200
Troy, Kershaw, S. C.	12
Troy, (c. h.,) Obion, Tenn.	130
Troy, Orleans, Vt.	160
Troy, Gilmer, W. Va.	20
Troy, Walworth, Wis.	70
Troy Centre, Waldo, Me.	24
Troy Centre, Walworth, Wis.	22
Troy Grove, La Salle, Ill.	120
Troy Mills, Linn, Iowa.	22
Troy Mills, Adair, Mo.	7
Troy Station, Obion, Tenn.	20
Troy's Store, Randolph, N. C.	16
Truckee, Nevada, Cal.	400
Truckee Meadows, Washoe, Nev.	140
Trucksville, Luzerne, Pa.	46
Trumansburgh, Tompkins, N. Y.	910
Trumansburgh Landing, Seneca, N.Y	19
Trumbaursville, Bucks, Pa.	40
Trumbull, Fairfield, Conn.	31
Trumbull, Ashtabula, Ohio.	80
Trumbull Corners, Tompkins, N. Y.	20
Trumbull Long Hill, Fairfield, Conn.	36
Trundle's Cross Roads, Sevier, Tenn.	22
Trunkeyville, Forest, Pa.	12
Truro, Knox, Ill.	22
Truro, Barnstable, Mass.	180
Trust, Osage, Kans.	12
Truxton, Bureau, Ill.	9
Truxton, Lincoln, Mo.	60
Truxton,* Cortland, N. Y.	220
Tryon, Polk, N. C.	4
Tryonville, Crawford, Pa.	100

Tualitin, Washington, Oreg.	$12
Tubac, Pima, Ariz.	10
Tuckahoe, Cape May, N. J.	220
Tuckahoe, Westchester, N. Y.	210
Tuckaleechee Cove, Blount, Tenn.	6
Tucker's Cross Roads, Wilson, Tenn	30
Tucker's Mills, Limestone, Tex.	12
Tuckerton, Burlington, N. J.	280
Tuckerton, Berks, Pa.	38
TUCSON, (c. h.,) Pima, Ariz.	620
Tuftonborough, Carroll, N. H.	39
Tugalo, Oconee, S. C.	12
Tug River, McDowell, W. Va.	7
Tukannon, Walla-Walla, Wash.	12
Tulalip, Snohomish, Wash.	14
Tule, Tulare, Cal.	220
Tulin, Cabarrus, N. C.	12
Tulip, Dallas, Ark.	97
Tullahoma,* Coffee, Tenn.	500
Tullamore, Tazewell, Ill.	9
Tullvania, Macon, Mo.	19
Tully,* Onondaga, N. Y.	350
Tully, Van Wert, Ohio.	93
Tullytown, Bucks, Pa.	88
Tully Valley, Onondaga, N. Y.	8
Tulpehocken, Berks, Pa.	25
Tumble, Hunterdon, N. J.	5
Tumbling Shoals, Laurens, S. C.	13
Tumwater, Thurston, Wash.	100
Tunbridge, Orange, Vt.	70
Tunkhannock, (c. h.,) Wyoming, Pa.	840
Tunnel, Washington, Ohio.	30
Tunnel City, Monroe, Wis.	130
Tunnel Hill, Whitfield, Ga.	200
Tunnel Hill, Oconee, S. C.	10
Tunnelton, Lawrence, Ind.	64
Tunnelton, Indiana, Pa.	58
Tunnelton, Preston, W. Va.	110
Tunstalls, New Kent, Va.	79
Tuolumne City, Stanislaus, Cal.	220
Tupelo, (c. h.,) Lee, Miss.	440
Tupper's Plains, Meigs, Ohio.	51
Tuque, Warren, Mo.	10
Turbotville, Northumberland, Pa.	270
Turin, Saline, Ark.	6
Turin, Coweta, Ga.	9
Turin,* Lewis, N. Y.	410
Turkey, Monmouth, N. J.	96
Turkey Cove, Lee, Va.	2
Turkey Creek, Dooly, Ga.	12
Turkey Creek, Steuben, Ind.	41
Turkey Creek, Bourbon, Kans.	110
Turkey Foot, Somerset, Pa.	25
Turman's Creek, Sullivan, Ind.	53
Turnback, Dade, Mo.	9
Turner, Du Page, Ill.	250
Turner, Androscoggin, Me.	280
Turner's, Clay, Ind.	12
Turner's, Orange, N. Y.	190
Turnersburgh, Iredell, N. C.	15
Turner's Point, Kaufman, Tex.	18
Turnersport, Manistee, Mich.	51
Turner's Store, Somerset, Pa.	36
Turnersville, Camden, N. J.	15
Turnersville, Crawford, Pa.	12
Turnersville, Robertson, Tenn.	18

* Money-order office.

Turnerville, Tolland, Conn	$60
Turnerville, Jasper, Miss	19
Turney's Station, Clinton, Mo	22
Turnpike, Buncombe, N. C	15
Turnwood, Ulster, N. Y	47
Turtle Creek, Allegheny, Pa	150
Turtle Point, McKean, Pa	12
Tuscaloosa,* (c. h.,) Tuscaloosa, Ala.	1,200
Tuscarawas, Tuscarawas, Ohio	130
Tuscarora, Livingston, N. Y	65
Tuscarora, Schuylkill, Pa	87
Tuscola,* (c. h.,) Douglas, Ill	1,500
Tuscumbia,* (c. h.,) Colbert, Ala	740
Tuscumbia, (c. h.,) Miller, Mo	130
Tuskegee,* (c. h.,) Macon, Ala.	650
Tusquitee, Clay, N. C	5
Tustenuggee, Columbia, Fla	12
Tustin, Waushara, Wis	14
Tuthill, Ulster, N. Y	45
Tuttle's Cross Roads, Caldwell, N. C	12
Twelve Mile, Cass, Ind	30
Twenty Mile Stand, Warren, Ohio.	41
Twenty-six Mile House, Stanislaus, Cal	12
Twiggs, Pleasants, W. Va	6
Twiggsville, Twiggs, Ga	12
Twin Bridges, Madison, Mont	12
Twin Corners, Cass, Ind	12
Twin Falls, Greenwood, Kans	12
Twin Grove, Green, Wis	44
Twin Lakes, Calhoun, Iowa	16
Twin Lakes, Carlton, Minn	6
Twin Mound, Douglas, Kans	50
Twin Mountain, Coos, N. H	12
Twin River, Nye, Nev	110
Twinsburgh, Summit, Ohio	220
Twin Sisters, Blanco, Tex	10
Twin Spring, Winneshiek, Iowa	12
Twin Springs, Linn, Kans	150
Twinville, Knox, Tenn	6
Two Bayous, Ouachita, Ark	12
Two Mile Branch, Smyth, Va	12
Two Rivers, Morrison, Minn	18
Two Rivers, Manitowoc, Wis	240
Two Rocks, Sonoma, Cal	12
Two Taverns, Adams, Pa	29
Twyman's Store, Spottsylvania, Va.	16
Tyaskin, Wicomico, Md	42
Tye River Depot, Nelson, Va	89
Tyler, Winnebago, Ill	24
Tyler,* (c. h.,) Smith, Tex	860
Tyler Mountain, Kanawha, W. Va	12
Tyler's, Brown, Kans	4
Tyler's, Clearfield, Pa	18
Tylersburgh, Clarion, Pa	74
Tyler's Port, Montgomery, Pa	74
Tylersville, Clinton, Pa	28
Tylersville, Laurens, S. C	12
Tymochtee, Wyandot, Ohio	21
Tyner, Hamilton, Tenn	27
Tyner City, Marshall, Ind	120
Tyngsborough, Middlesex, Mass	110
Tyre, Sanilac, Mich	48
Tyre, Seneca, N. Y	42
Tyringham, Berkshire, Mass	69
Tyro, Poweshiek, Iowa	3

Tyro, Marshall, Miss	$96
Tyrone, Monroe, Iowa	37
Tyrone, Livingston, Mich	29
Tyrone, Schuyler, N. Y	120
Tyrone, Coshocton, Ohio	12
Tyrone,* Blair, Pa	1,500
Tyson Furnace, Windsor, Vt	88
Tyson's Mills, Webster, Iowa	12

U.

Uchee, Russell, Ala	12
Uchee Anna, (c. h.,) Walton, Fla	11
Udina, Kane, Ill	53
Uhlersville, Northampton, Pa	24
Uhricksville,* Tuscarawas, Ohio	860
Uintah, Weber, Utah	12
Ukiah, (c. h.,) Mendocino, Cal	50
Ulah, Henry, Ill	32
Ullin, Pulaski, Ill	160
Ulman's Ridge, Miller, Mo	16
Ulster, Floyd, Iowa	18
Ulster, Bradford, Pa	140
Ulster Park, Ulster, N. Y	32
Ulsterville, Ulster, N. Y	47
Ulysses, Butler, Nebr	12
Ulysses, Potter, Pa	110
Umatilla,* Umatilla, Oreg	420
Unadilla, Livingston, Mich	160
Unadilla, Otsego, N. Y	830
Unadilla Centre, Otsego, N. Y	13
Unadilla Forks, Otsego, N. Y	200
Uncasville, New London, Conn	150
Uncle Sam, Lake, Cal	77
Underhill, Chittenden, Vt	190
Underhill Centre, Chittenden, Vt	120
Underwood, Hopkins, Ky	12
Unger's Store, Morgan, W. Va	14
Union, Greene, Ala	20
Union, Merced, Cal	64
Union, Tolland, Conn	16
Union, McHenry, Ill	180
Union, Pike, Ind	24
Union, Hardin, Iowa	62
Union, Chase, Kans	11
Union, Boone, Ky	100
Union, Knox, Me	290
Union, Cass, Mich	70
Union, Houston, Minn	16
Union, Newton, Miss	18
Union, (c. h.,) Franklin, Mo	290
Union, Cass, Nebr	43
Union, Carroll, N. H	220
Union, Union, N. J	45
Union, Broome, N. Y	480
Union, Montgomery, Ohio	85
Union, Union, Oreg	130
Union, York, Pa	24
Union, Salt Lake, Utah	44
Union,* (c. h.,) Monroe, W. Va	280
Union, Rock, Wis	60
Union Bridge, Carroll, Md	140
Unionburgh, Harrison, Iowa	19
Union Centre, Cumberland, Ill	12
Union Centre, Jackson, Iowa	20
Union Centre, Le Sueur, Minn	4

* Money-order office.

Post Office	Amount	Post Office	Amount
Union Centre, Broome, N. Y	$65	Union Valley, Cortland, N. Y	$41
Union Church, Jefferson, Miss	55	Union Village, Orange, Vt	120
Union Church, Albany, N. Y	16	Unionville, Hartford, Conn	650
Union Church, Racine, Wis	23	Unionville, Monroe, Ga	10
Union City, Perry, Ark	12	Unionville, Monroe, Ind	12
Union City,* Randolph, Ind	1,200	Unionville, Appanoose, Iowa	120
Union City, Union, Iowa	28	Unionville, Frederick, Md	74
Union City, Branch, Mich	410	Unionville, Tuscola, Mich	80
Union City,* Obion, Tenn	720	Unionville,* (c. h.,) Putnam, Mo	290
Union Corner, Northumberland, Pa.	10	Unionville,Lewis and Clarke, Mont.	12
Union Corners, Livingston, N. Y	23	Unionville, (c. h.,) Humboldt, Nev	230
Union Cross Roads, Union, La	38	Unionville, Gloucester, N. J	43
Union Dale, Susquehanna, Pa	58	Unionville, Orange, N. Y	260
Union Deposit, Dauphin, Pa	100	Unionville, Lake, Ohio	170
Union Depot, Sullivan, Tenn	110	Unionville, Chester, Pa	160
Union Falls, Clinton, N. Y	6	Unionville,* (c. h.,) Union, S. C	710
Union Forge, Lebanon, Pa	20	Unionville, Bedford, Tenn	60
Union Grove, Whitesides, Ill	8	Unionville, Orange, Va	9
Union Grove, Page, Iowa	20	Unionville, Lake, Ohio	80
Union Grove, Gentry, Mo	8	Uniopolis, Auglaize, Ohio	5
Union Grove, Delaware, N. Y	12	Unison, Loudoun, Va	50
Union Grove, Iredell, N. C	5	Unitia, Blount, Tenn	30
Union Grove,* Racine, Wis	310	Unity, Alexander, Ill	9
Union Hall, Franklin, Va	5	Unity,* Waldo, Me	230
Union Hill, Kankakee, Ill	21	Unity, Montgomery, Md	44
Union Hill, Ringgold, Iowa	6	Unity, Sullivan, N. H	50
Union Lakes, Rice, Minn	15	Unity, Columbiana, Ohio	32
Union Meeting House, Baltimore, Md	55	Unity, Pacific, Wash	16
Union Mills, La Porte, Ind	36	Unityville, Lycoming, Pa	18
Union Mills, Mahaska, Iowa	49	University of Virginia, Albemarle, Va	1,400
Union Mills, Carroll, Md	59	Ununda, Brown, Kans	10
Union Mills, Tippah, Miss	12	Upatoie, Muscogee, Ga	14
Union Mills, Platte, Mo	17	Updegraft's, Jefferson, Ohio	14
Union Mills, Fulton, N. Y	19	Upland, Grant, Ind	12
Union Mills,* Erie, Pa	880	Upland, Mason, W. Va	6
Union Mills, Fluvanna, Va	26	Uplands, Delaware, Pa	12
Union Mills, Pleasants, W. Va	12	Upper Alton, Madison, Ill	850
Union Mills, Iowa, Wis	16	Upper Aquebogue, Suffolk, N. Y	100
Union Pier, Berrien, Mich	12	Upper Bern, Berks, Pa	17
Union Plains, Brown, Ohio	12	Upper Black Eddy, Bucks, Pa	96
Union Point, Greene, Ga	65	Upper Blue Licks, Fleming, Ky	8
Union Point, Union, Ill	6	Upper Clear Lake, Lake, Cal	47
Unionport, Jefferson, Ohio	62	Upperco, Baltimore, Md	38
Union Prairie, Allamakee, Iowa	16	Upper Cross Roads, Harford, Md	53
Union Ridge, Brown, Ill	8	Upper Darby, Delaware, Pa	44
Union Ridge, Butler, Iowa	30	Upper Dublin, Montgomery, Pa	89
Union Ridge, Sullivan, Mo	7	Upper Falls, Baltimore, Md	77
Union Ridge, Clark, Wash	17	Upper Falls, Windsor, Vt	78
Union Society, Greene, N. Y	12	Upper Falls of Coal, Kanawha, W. Va	14
Union Spring, Dodge, Minn	16	Upper Gloucester, Cumberland, Me.	120
Union Springs, (c. h.,) Bullock, Ala.	600	Upper Grove, Hancock, Iowa	81
Union Springs,* Cayuga, N. Y	1,300	Upper Jay, Essex, N. Y	37
Union Square, Oswego, N. Y	65	Upper Lehigh, Luzerne, Pa	150
Union Square, Montgomery, Pa	1	Upper Lisle, Broome, N. Y	85
Union Star, Breckinridge, Ky	34	Upper Madawaska, Aroostook, Me.	12
Union Star, De Kalb, Mo	89	Upper Mahantango, Schuylkill, Pa.	20
Union Station, Licking, Ohio	12	Upper Marlborough, (c. h.,) Prince George's, Md	560
Union Station, Lancaster, Pa	50	Upper Middletown, Fayette, Pa	25
Uniontown, Perry, Ala	650	Upper Providence, Delaware, Pa	10
Uniontown, Delaware, Iowa	14	Upper Red Hook, Dutchess, N. Y	80
Uniontown,* Union, Ky	360	Upper St. Clair, Allegheny, Pa	39
Uniontown, Carroll, Md	230	Upper Sandusky,* (c. h.,) Wyandot, Ohio	1,200
Uniontown, Perry, Mo	23		
Uniontown, Belmont, Ohio	73		
Uniontown,* (c. h.,) Fayette, Pa	1,300		

* Money-order office.

VAL

Upper Stillwater, Penobscot, Me..	$160
Upper Strasburgh, Franklin, Pa...	85
Upper Tract, Pendleton, W. Va....	47
Upper Trappe, Somerset, Md	28
Upper Tygart, Carter, Ky........	4
Upperville, Fauquier, Va..........	310
Upshur, Preble, Ohio.............	34
Upsonville, Susquehanna, Pa	17
Upton, Van Buren, Iowa	37
Upton, Oxford, Me	48
Upton, Worcester, Mass	360
Upton, Franklin, Pa	140
Uptonville, Hardin, Ky...........	120
Urban, Butler, Nebr..............	12
Urban, Northumberland, Pa	8
Urbana, (c. h.,) Champaign, Ill.....	1,200
Urbana, Wabash, Ind	18
Urbana, Neosho, Kans............	12
Urbana, Frederick, Md	63
Urbana, Dallas, Mo..............	45
Urbana, (c. h.,) Champaign, Ohio..	2,400
Urbana, Middlesex, Va...........	90
Urbanna, Benton, Iowa	85
Urbanna City, Monroe, Iowa.....	12
Urieville, Kent, Md	12
Urmeyville, Johnson, Ind	30
Ursa, Adams, Ill	24
Ursina, Somerset, Pa	12
Usquepaugh, Washington, R. I	90
Utah, Warren, Ill	18
Utah, Indiana, Pa.................	28
Utahville, Clearfield, Pa	41
Ute Creek, Colfax, N. Mex........	12
Utica, La Salle, Ill	450
Utica, Clarke, Ind	110
Utica, Van Buren, Iowa	37
Utica,* Macomb, Mich	350
Utica, Winona, Minn.............	100
Utica, Hinds, Miss	86
Utica,* Livingston, Mo...........	290
Utica, (c. h.,) Oneida, N. Y	4,000
Utica, Licking, Ohio	400
Utica, Venango, Pa	150
Utica, Dane, Wis	96
Utica Mills, Frederick, Md	23
Utsaladdy, Island, Wash	38
Uvalde, (c. h.,) Uvalde, Tex	110
Uwchland, Chester, Pa...........	38
Uxbridge,* Worcester, Mass......	650

V.

Vaca, Solano, Cal	12
Vacaville,* Solano, Cal	210
Vacherie Roads, St. James, La	12
Vaiden, Carroll, Miss	290
Vail's Cross Roads, Morrow, Ohio..	38
Vail's Gate, Orange, N. Y	56
Vail's Mills, Fulton, N. Y	54
Valatie,* Columbia, N. Y..........	610
Valcour, Clinton, N. Y	12
Valdosta, (c. h.,) Lowndes, Ga......	620
Valeene, Orange, Ind	21
Vale Mills, Giles, Tenn..........	22
Valentine, La Grange, Ind	8
Valhalla, Westchester, N. Y	58

VAN

Valhermoso Springs, Morgan, Ala..	$8
Vallejo,* Solano, Cal.............	1,800
Valley, Washington, Iowa	29
Valley, Douglas, Nebr	12
Valley, Columbiana, Ohio........	12
Valley, Clarion, Pa	12
Valley, Guadalupe, Tex...........	12
Valley, Vernon, Wis	12
Valley Bend, Randolph, W. Va	5
Valley Brook, Osage, Kans........	12
Valley City, Harrison, Ind	22
Valley City, Neosho, Kans	12
Valley Creek, Chester, Pa........	12
Valley Crucis, Watauga, N. C	4
Valley Falls, Rensselaer, N. Y	210
Valley Falls, Providence, R. I	620
Valley Falls, Spartanburgh, S. C ..	4
Valley Falls, Marion, W. Va	14
Valley Farm, Linn, Iowa..........	24
Valley Ford, Meigs, Ohio	11
Valley Forge, Chester, Pa.........	53
Valley Furnace, Barbour, W. Va ..	5
Valley Grove, Ohio, W. Va........	74
Valley Head, De Kalb, Ala........	73
Valley Head, Randolph, W. Va	12
Valley Junction, Hamilton, Ohio ..	24
Valley Mills, Marion, Ind	46
Valley Mills, Madison, N. Y	12
Valley Mills, Bosque, Tex.........	67
Valley Mills, Wood, W. Va	12
Valley Oak, Pulaski, Ky	15
Valley Point, Preston, W. Va	11
Valley Stream, Queens, N. Y	12
Valley Town, Cherokee, N. C......	30
Vallicita, Calaveras, Cal	65
Vallonia, Jackson, Ind...........	65
Vallonia Springs, Broome, N. Y....	22
Valmont, Boulder, Colo	78
Valparaiso, (c. h.,) Porter, Ind.....	1,600
Valparaiso, Sullivan, Mo	34
Valton, Sauk, Wis................	13
Vanatta, Licking, Ohio	35
Van Buren, (c. h.,) Crawford, Ark..	580
Van Buren, De Kalb, Ill	16
Van Buren, Jackson, Iowa	70
Van Buren, Aroostook, Me	30
Van Buren, (c. h.,) Carter, Mo......	5
Van Buren, Onondaga, N. Y	19
Van Buren, Hancock, Ohio.......	89
Van Buren, Washington, Pa.......	38
Van Buren Furnace, Shenandoah, Va.....................	15
Van Camp, Columbia, Pa	18
Van Camp, Wetzel, W. Va	20
Vanceburgh, (c. h.,) Lewis, Ky	200
Vancefort, Allegheny, Pa.........	23
Vance's Ferry, Orangeburgh, S. C..	28
Vanceville, Washington, Pa.......	18
Vancil's Point, Macoupin, Ill.....	12
Vancleave's, Jackson, Miss........	12
Van Clevesville, Berkeley, W. Va..	49
Vancouver, (c. h.,) Clark, Wash....	560
Vandalia, (c. h.,) Fayette, Ill	1,200
Vandalia, Owen, Ind.............	42
Vandalia, Jasper, Iowa	120
Vandalia, Cass, Mich.............	96

VER   VIC

Vandalia, Cattaraugus, N. Y	$23	Vermillion, Erie, Ohio	$410
Vandalia, Montgomery, Ohio	94	Vermillion Lake, St. Louis, Minn	12
Vanderbilt, Lander, Nev	12	Vermillionville, La Salle, Ill	51
Vanderburgh, Webster, Ky	21	Vermillionville, (c. h.,) La Fayette,	
Vandergriff's, Knox, Tenn	2	La	260
Van Deusenville, Berkshire. Mass	76	Vermont, Fulton, Ill	610
Van Dyke's Mill, Spencer, Ky	24	Vermont, Cooper, Mo	36
Van Dyne, Fond du Lac, Wis	25	Vermont, Chautauqua, N. Y	52
Van Etten, Chemung, N. Y	8	Vermontville, Eaton, Mich	430
Van Ettenville, Chemung, N. Y	98	Vernon, Sanford, Ala	29
Van Hill, Hawkins, Tenn	12	Vernon, Tolland, Conn	120
Van Hiseville, Ocean, N. J	24	Vernon, Kent, Del	13
Van Hook's Store, Person, N. C	10	Vernon, (c. h.,) Washington, Fla	16
Van Horn, Carroll, Mo	12	Vernon, Troup, Ga	10
Van Hornesville, Herkimer, N. Y	110	Vernon,* (c. h.,) Jennings, Ind	550
Vanlue, Hancock, Ohio	90	Vernon, Van Buren, Iowa,	220
Van Metre, Dallas, Iowa	110	Vernon, (c. h.,) Jackson, La	24
Vannatterville, Lincoln, W. Va	12	Vernon, Shiawassee, Mich	390
Vannoy's Mill, Pike, Mo	6	Vernon, Dodge, Minn	30
Van's Valley, Delaware, Ohio	17	Vernon,* Sussex, N. J	580
Van Vechten, Schenectady, N. Y	65	Vernon, Oneida, N. Y	440
Vanville, Chippewa, Wis	75	Vernon, Trumbull, Ohio	48
Van Wert, Polk, Ga	66	Vernon, Marion, Oreg	10
Van Wert,* (c. h.,) Van Wert, Ohio	1,390	Vernon, Wyoming, Pa	5
Van Wert, Juniata, Pa	12	Vernon, Hickman, Tenn	13
Varick, Seneca, N. Y	38	Vernon, Windham, Vt	200
Variety Mills, Nelson, Va	21	Vernon, Waukesha, Wis	56
Varna, Tompkins, N. Y	58	Vernon Centre, Blue Earth, Minn	140
Varnell's Station, Whitfield, Ga	87	Vernon Centre, Oneida, N. Y	150
Varysburgh, Wyoming, N. Y	100	Vernon Depot, Tolland, Conn	130
Vasa, Goodhue, Minn	60	Vernon Hill, Halifax, Va	19
Vassalborough, Kennebec, Me	270	Verona, Boone, Ky	18
Vassar,* (c. h.,) Tuscola, Mich	430	Verona, Lee, Miss	310
Vaughnsville, Putnam, Ohio	34	Verona, Lawrence, Mo	83
Veazie, Penobscot, Me	99	Verona, Essex, N. J	58
Vedder, Calhoun, Ill	43	Verona, Oneida, N. Y	300
Velasco, Brazoria, Tex	25	Verona, Westmoreland, Pa	9
Velp, Brown, Wis	15	Verona, Marshall, Tenn	12
Venango, Crawford, Pa	200	Verona, Dane, Wis	34
Venedocia, Van Wert, Ohio	15	Verona Mills, Huron, Mich	35
Venedy, Washington, Ill	120	Verplank, Westchester, N. Y	120
Veni, Effingham, Ill	4	Versailles, Brown, Ill	290
Venice, Madison, Ill	120	Versailles,* (c. h.,) Ripley, Ind	220
Venice, Cayuga, N. Y	46	Versailles, (c. h.,) Woodford, Ky	900
Venice, Erie, Ohio	18	Versailles,* (c. h.,) Morgan, Mo	310
Venice, Washington, Pa	75	Versailles, Cattaraugus, N. Y	140
Venice Centre, Cayuga, N. Y	36	Versailles, Darke, Ohio	230
Ventura, Ottawa, Mich	25	Versailles, Rutherford, Tenn	15
Venus, Madison, Iowa	7	Vershire, Orange, Vt	140
Vera, Fayette, Ill	86	Vervilla, Warren, Tenn	44
Vera Cruz, Wells, Ind	96	Vesper, Onondaga, N. Y	40
Vera Cruz, Douglas, Mo	22	Vesta, Johnson, Nebr	40
Vera Cruz, Lehigh, Pa	23	Vestal, Broome, N. Y	30
Verbank, Dutchess, N. Y	47	Vestal Centre, Broome, N. Y	23
Verdi,* Wilson, Kans	140	Veto, Washington, Ohio	18
Verdi, Washoe, Nev	63	Vevay,* (c. h.,) Switzerland, Ind	680
Verdierville, Orange, Va	39	Vicar, Russell, Va	12
Verdigris Falls, Greenwood, Kans	18	Vickery's Creek, Forsyth, Ga	58
Verdon, Hanover, Va	58	Vickeryville, Montcalm, Mich	24
Vergennes, Jackson, Ill	12	Vicksburgh, Jewell, Kans	12
Vergennes, Kent, Mich	14	Vicksburgh,* (c. h.,) Warren, Miss	4,000
Vergennes,* Addison, Vt	1,200	Vicksburgh, Union, Pa	31
Vermillion, (c. h.,) Clay, Dak	360	Vicksville, Southampton, Va	13
Vermillion, Edgar, Ill	260	Victor,* Iowa, Iowa	330
Vermillion, Nemaha, Kans	12	Victor, Clinton, Mich	37
Vermillion, Oswego, N. Y	61	Victor,* Ontario, N. Y	540

* Money-order office.

VIN   WAD

Victor Centre, De Kalb, Ill	$19	Vinton, Gallia, Ohio	$84
Victoria, Coffee, Ala	12	Vinton Station, Vinton, Ohio	110
Victoria, Jefferson, Ark	12	Viola, Mercer, Ill	140
Victoria, Knox, Ill	290	Viola, Linn, Iowa	98
Victoria, (c. h.,) Victoria, Tex	670	Viola, Warren, Tenn	12
Victoria Station, Jefferson, Mo	40	Viola, Richland, Wis	51
Victory, Mason, Mich	33	Viola Station, Graves, Ky	47
Victory, Cayuga, N. Y	120	Viona, Humboldt, Iowa	5
Victory, Essex, Vt	19	Virden,* Macoupin, Ill	1,300
Victory, Vernon, Wis	30	Virgil, Greenwood, Kans	19
Victory Mills, Saratoga, N. Y	200	Virgil, Cortland, N. Y	99
Vidalia, (c. h.,) Concordia, La	12	Virgil City, Cedar, Mo	240
Vienna, (c. h.,) Dooly, Ga	87	Virgin City, Kane, Utah	37
Vienna,* (c. h.,) Johnson, Ill	240	Virginia, Douglas, Colo	12
Vienna, Scott, Ind	140	Virginia, Union, Dak	12
Vienna, Marshall, Iowa	5	Virginia, Cass, Ill	660
Vienna, Pottawatomie, Kans	40	*Virginia City,** (c. h.,) Madison, Mont	2,000
Vienna, Clarke, Ky	10	*Virginia City,** (c. h.,) Storey, Nev.	4,000
Vienna, Jackson, La	70	Virginia Grove, Louisa, Iowa	20
Vienna, Kennebec, Me	6?	Virginville, Berks, Pa	23
Vienna, Dorchester, Md	77	*Viroqua,** (c. h.,) Vernon, Wis	320
Vienna, (c. h.,) Maries, Mo	59	*Visalia,** (c. h.,) Tulare, Cal	690
Vienna, Warren, N. J	100	Visalia, Kenton, Ky	44
Vienna, Oneida, N. Y	110	Vischer's Ferry, Saratoga, N. Y	92
Vienna, Forsyth, N. C	7	Vista, Westchester, N. Y	22
Vienna, Trumbull, Ohio	94	Vista Ridge, Carroll, La	12
Vienna, Fairfax, Va	50	Vistula, Elkhart, Ind	43
Vienna, Walworth, Wis	20	Vivian, Waseca, Minn	20
Vienna Cross Roads, Clark, Ohio	54	Voak, Yates, N. Y	16
Vigo, Ross, Ohio	55	Vogansville, Lancaster, Pa	24
Village Creek, Allamakee, Iowa	81	Volant, Lawrence, Pa	8
Village Green, Delaware, Pa	75	Volga, Jefferson, Ind	19
Village Springs, Blount, Ala	19	Volga City, Clayton, Iowa	89
Villanova, Chautauqua, N. Y	30	Volcano, Amador, Cal	130
Villanow, Walker, Ga	25	Volcano,* Wood, W. Va	240
Villa Rica, Carroll, Ga	57	Volinia, Cass, Mich	36
Villa Ridge, Pulaski, Ill	290	Volney, Allamakee, Iowa	29
Villa Platte, St. Landry, La	21	Volney, Oswego, N. Y	44
Villisca, Montgomery, Iowa	160	Volo, Lake, Ill	60
Villula, Russell, Ala	54	Volo, Bell, Tex	12
Vincennes,* (c. h.,) Knox, Ind	2,500	Voluntown, Windham, Conn	130
Vincennes, Lee, Iowa	80	Volusia, Volusia, Fla	22
Vincent, St. Clair, Mich	4	Volusia, Chautauqua, N. Y	37
Vincent, Washington, Ohio	100	Voorheesville, Albany, N. Y	25
Vincent, Chester, Pa	47	Vosburgh, Wyoming, Pa	12
Vincentown, Burlington, N. J	270	Vriesland, Ottawa, Mich	62
Vine Grove, Hardin, Ky	24		
Vine Grove, Washington, Tex	28	**W.**	
Vineland, Jefferson, Mo	120		
Vineland,* Cumberland, N. J	2,300	Wabash, Wayne, Ill	12
Vinemount, Bollinger, Mo	12	*Wabash,** (c. h.,) Wabash, Ind	1,800
Vine's Mills, Worth, Ga	12	*Wabashaw,** (c. h.,) Wabashaw,	
Vine's Springs, Ripley, Ind	25	Minn	870
Vine Valley, Yates, N. Y	4	Wabaunsee, Wabaunsee, Kans	150
Vineyard, Bradley, Ark	12	Wachusett Village, Worcester, Mass	49
Vineyard, Tama, Iowa	12	Waco, Franklin, Ala	8
Vineyard Grove, Dukes, Mass	12	Waco, Madison, Ky	100
Vineyard Hill, Adams, Ohio	12	*Waco,** (c. h.,) McLennan, Tex	1,800
Vineyard Hill, Kanawha, W. Va	12	Waconda, Marion, Oreg	48
Vineyard Mills, Huntingdon, Pa	12	Waconia, Carver, Minn	37
Viney Grove, Washington, Ark	12	Wacousta, Humboldt, Iowa	12
Vining Station, Cobb, Ga	12	Wacousta, Clinton, Mich	76
Vinland, Douglas, Kans	12	Wadaloup, Grundy, Iowa	12
Vinland, Winnebago, Wis	23	Waddam's Centre, Stephenson, Ill.	12
Vinton,* (o. h.,) Benton, Iowa	1,700	Waddington, St. Lawrence, N. Y	380
Vinton, Riley, Kans	12	Wade, Washington, Ohio	74

* Money-order office.

WAL   WAL

Office	$	Office	$
Wade's, Bedford, Va	$27	Wales, St. Clair, Mich	$48
Wadesborough, Callaway, Ky	34	Wales, Erie, N. Y	62
Wadesborough, (c. h.,) Anson, N. C..	220	Wales, Gallia, Ohio	28
Wadesburgh, Cass, Mo	100	Wales, San Pete, Utah	12
Wadestown, Monongalia, W. Va...	28	Wales Centre, Erie, N. Y	75
Wadesville, Posey, Ind	23	Wales Station, Giles, Tenn	51
Wadesville, Clarke, Va	85	Walesville, Oneida, N. Y	67
Wadesville, Wood, W. Va	12	Walhain, Kewaunee, Wis	14
Wadhams' Mills, Essex, N. Y	89	Walhalla, (c. h.,) Oconee, S. C.	250
Wading River, Burlington, N. J	32	Walhonding, Coshocton, Ohio	36
Wading River, Suffolk, N. Y	56	Walker, Centre, Pa	84
Wadley's Falls, Strafford, N. H.	59	Walker, Wood, W. Va	97
Wadsworth, Washoe, Nev	470	Walker's, Columbia, Ark	12
Wadsworth,* Medina, Ohio	760	Walker's Church, Appomattox, Va.	18
Waggoner's Ripple, Adams, Ohio ..	17	Walker's Ford, Amherst, Va	12
Wagner, Clayton, Iowa	17	Walker's Mills, Allegheny, Pa	26
Wagon Landing, Polk, Wis	24	Walkerstown, Forsyth, N. C	1
Wagontown, Chester, Pa	90	Walkersville, Frederick, Md	73
Wagram, Licking, Ohio	16	Walkersville, Union, N. C	8
Wahaghbonsy, Mills, Iowa	7	Walkersville, Lewis, W. Va	20
Wahalak Station, Hempler, Miss ..	27	Walkerton, St. Joseph, Ind	250
Wahjamega, Tuscola, Mich	59	Walkerton, King and Queen, Va...	45
Wahoo, Saunders, Nebr	12	Walker Valley, Ulster, N. Y	40
Wah Wah, Butler, Kans	12	Walkerville, Greene, Ill	17
Wah Wah Suk, Shawnee, Kans.	12	Wallace, Fountain, Ind	24
Wailesborough, Bartholomew, Ind.	46	Wallace, Steuben, N. Y	92
Waite, Washington, Me	19	Wallace, Duplin, N. C	47
Waitesville, Jefferson, Wis	28	Wallace, Chester, Pa	25
Waitsfield,* Washington, Vt	280	Wallace's Cross Roads, Anderson,	
Wait's River, Orange, Vt	77	Tenn	15
Wakarusa, Elkhart, Ind	94	Wallaceton, Clearfield, Pa	12
Wakarusa, Shawnee, Kans	20	Wallaceville, Wayne, Mich	20
Wakatomica, Coshocton, Ohio	28	Wallaceville, Venango, Pa	27
Wakefield, Richland, Ill	19	Walla Walla,* (c. h.,) Walla Walla,	
Wakefield, Clay, Kans	12	Wash	1,200
Wakefield, Carroll, Md	23	Walled Lake, Oakland, Mich	100
Wakefield, Middlesex, Mass	1,300	Waller, Ross, Ohio	67
Wakefield, Carroll, N. H	160	Wallingford, New Haven, Conn ...	1,400
Wakefield, Wake, N. C	1	Wallingford, Will, Ill	25
Wakefield, Lancaster, Pa	54	Wallingford, Rutland, Vt	420
Wakefield,* Washington, R. I.	380	Walling's Ferry, Rusk, Tex	16
Wakefield, Outagamie, Wis	20	Wallin's Creek, Harlan, Ky	3
Wakefield Station, Sussex, Va	90	Wallis Run, Lycoming, Pa	4
Wakeman, Huron, Ohio	340	Wallisville, (c. h.,) Chambers, Tex..	12
Wakeshma, Kalamazoo, Mich	13	Wallpack Centre, Sussex, N. J	8
Walbridge, Pulaski, Ill	160	Wall Rose, Beaver, Pa	29
Walcott, Green, Ark	12	Wallsville, Luzerne, Pa	23
Walden, Orange, N. Y	460	Wallula, Walla Walla, Wash	50
Walden, Caledonia, Vt	32	Walnford, Monmouth, N. J	15
Waldenburgh, Macomb, Mich	24	Walnut, Bureau, Ill	100
Walden's, Rappahannock, Va	12	Walnut, Marshall, Ind	45
Walden's Creek, Sevier, Tenn	1	Walnut, Butler, Kans	12
Waldingfield, Kanawha, W. Va.	12	Walnut, Juniata, Pa	20
Waldo, Alachua, Fla	42	Walnut Bottom, Cumberland, Pa..	62
Waldo, Waldo, Me	59	Walnut City, Appanoose, Iowa....	39
Waldo, Webster, Mo	12	Walnut Cove, Stokes, N. C	70
Waldo, Marion, Ohio	57	Walnut Creek, Contra Costa, Cal..	71
Waldo, Josephine, Oreg	28	Walnut Creek, Fremont, Iowa	12
Waldoborough, Lincoln, Me	850	Walnut Creek, Crawford, Kans....	58
Waldron, (c. h.,) Scott, Ark	140	Walnut Creek, Buncombe, N.C....	10
Waldron, Platte, Mo	12	Walnut Creek, Holmes, Ohio	22
Waldrop's Mill, Jefferson, Ala	2	Walnut Creek Station, Pottawatto-	
Wales, Ogle, Ill	80	mie, Iowa	12
Wales, Worth, Iowa	12	Walnut Fork, Jones, Iowa	63
Wales, Androscoggin, Me	11	Walnut Grove, Blount, Ala	10
Wales, Hampden, Mass	170	Walnut Grove, Sacramento, Cal ...	20

* Money-order office.

WAR

Walnut Grove, Walton, Ga........	$4	Ward's Corners, Buchanan, Iowa ..	$10
Walnut Grove, Scott, Iowa........	34	Ward's Iron Works, Johnson, Tenn.	15
Walnut Grove, Caldwell, Ky	28	Wardville, Chowan, N. C..........	12
Walnut Grove, Martin, Minn......	18	Ware,* Hampshire, Mass	1, 400
Walnut Grove, Greene, Mo	96	War Eagle, Madison, Ark..........	12
Walnut Grove, Morris, N. J	62	Wareham, Plymouth, Mass	580
Walnut Hill, Tallapoosa, Ala.....	5	Warehouse Point, Hartford, Conn..	380
Walnut Hill, La Fayette, Ark.....	27	Warfield, Lawrence, Ky	12
Walnut Hill, Marion, Ill	20	Warfieldburgh, Carroll, Md........	21
Walnut Hill, Marshall, Ind.......	9	Warfordsburgh, Fulton, Pa........	38
Walnut Hill, Bourbon, Kans	6	War Gap, Hawkins, Tenn	12
Walnut Hill, Buchanan, Mo.......	35	Warm Fork, Oregon, Mo	12
Walnut Hill, Ashe, N. C..........	12	Warminster, Bucks, Pa............	31
Walnut Hill, Sequatchie, Tenn	10	Warminster, Nelson, Va...........	51
Walnut Hill, Panola, Tex	4	Warm Springs, Meriwether, Ga	6
Walnut Hill, Lee, Va	14	Warm Springs, Madison, N. C......	12
Walnut Hills, Hamilton, Ohio....	550	Warner, Merrimack, N. H	450
Walnut Lake, Faribault, Minn	12	Warner's, Onondaga, N. Y	94
Walnut Lick, Gallatin, Ky	19	Warner's Landing, Vernon, Wis ...	10
Walnut Ridge, Lawrence, Ark.....	12	Warner's Ranch, San Diego, Cal ...	12
Walnut Run, Madison, Ohio.......	17	Warnerville, Meriwether, Ga	24
Walnut Shade, Taney, Mo.........	20	Warnerville, Schoharie, N. Y......	50
Walnut Tree, Yell, Ark	7	Warnock, Belmont, Ohio	40
Walnut Valley, Warren, N. J	30	Warpole, Wyandot, Ohio	12
Walnut Valley, Sequatchie, Tenn..	4	Warren, (c. h.,) Bradley, Ark......	180
Walpole, Norfolk, Mass	410	Warren, Litchfield, Conn.........	95
Walpole, Cheshire, N. H	670	Warren,* Jo Daviess, Ill	1, 200
Walshville, Montgomery, Ill......	120	Warren, Huntington, Ind.........	190
Walterborough, (c. h.,) Colleton, S. C.	270	Warren, Lee, Iowa	25
Walter Hill, Rutherford, Tenn.....	12	Warren, Knox, Me	300
Waltham, Tama, Iowa............	73	Warren, Baltimore, Md...........	59
Waltham, Hancock, Me...........	14	Warren, Worcester, Mass..........	960
Waltham,* Middlesex, Mass.......	2, 600	Warren, Macomb, Mich...........	35
Waltham, Mower, Minn..........	10	Warren, Marion, Mo	18
Walthourville, Liberty, Ga........	150	Warren, Grafton, N. H	290
Walton, Cass, Ind	130	Warren, Herkimer, N. Y..........	23
Walton, Boone, Ky	190	Warren,* (c. h.,) Trumbull, Ohio	2, 400
Walton, Delaware, N. Y..........	650	Warren,* (c. h.,) Warren, Pa	2, 000
Walton, Roane, W. Va...........	21	Warren,* Bristol, R. I...........	820
Walton Mills, Washington, Mo	12	Warren, Fannin, Tex.............	17
Walton's Ford, Habersham, Ga....	12	Warren, Washington, Vt..........	38
Walts Mills, Westmoreland, Pa ...	10	Warren, Albemarle, Va...........	45
Walworth, Wayne, N. Y..........	270	Warren, Wood, W. Va...........	2
Walworth, Walworth, Wis	180	Warren, St. Croix, Wis	23
Wamego,* Pottawatomie, Kans....	400	Warren Centre, Bradford, Pa	47
Wampsville, Madison, N. Y	100	Warren Grove, Jasper, Iowa.......	12
Wampum, Lawrence, Pa..........	110	Warrenham, Bradford, Pa........	21
Wamsley's, Adams, Ohio	15	Warren Plains, Warren, N. C	33
Wanaminga, Goodhue, Minn.......	190	Warrensburgh,* (c. h.,) Johnson, Mo.	2, 100
Wanatah, Laporte, Ind..........	200	Warrensburgh,* Warren, N. Y	490
Waneka, Dunn, Wis	43	Warrensburgh, Greene, Tenn	25
Wanship, Summit, Utah..........	65	Warren's Corners, Niagara, N. Y ...	37
Wapakoneta,* (c. h.,) Auglaize, Ohio.	850	Warrensville, Du Page, Ill	130
Wapella, DeWitt, Ill.............	270	Warrensville, Cuyahoga, Ohio	49
Wapello,* (c. h.,) Louisa, Iowa	460	Warrensville, Lycoming, Pa	44
Wapping, Hartford, Conn	50	Warren Tavern, Chester, Pa.......	130
Wappinger's Falls, Dutchess, N. Y .	550	Warrenton, Marshall, Ala	44
Wapwallopen, Luzerne, Pa	9	Warrenton, (c. h.,) Warren, Ga......	640
Waquoit, Barnstable, Mass	95	Warrenton, Warren, Miss	31
Waranancoke, King William, Va...	12	Warrenton,* (c. h.,) Warren, Mo	790
Warburgh, Callaway, Ky..........	4	Warrenton,* (c. h.,) Warren, N. C....	820
War Creek, Hancock, Tenn.......	5	Warrenton, Jefferson, Ohio.......	120
Ward District, Boulder, Colo	27	Warrenton,* (c. h.,) Fauquier, Va....	1, 200
Wardena, Fayette, Iowa...........	22	Warrenville, Somerset, N. J	19
Wardensville, Hardy, W. Va.......	63	War Ridge, Hancock, Tenn........	12
Wardsborough, Windham, Vt	150	Warrington,* Escambia, Fla	450

* Money-order office.

WAS   WAT

Warrington, Hancock, Ind	$21	Washington, Washington, Utah ...	$180
Warrington, Bucks, Pa	29	Washington, Orange, Vt	130
Warrior Creek, Wilkes, N. C	6	*Washington, (c. h.,)* Rappahannock,	
Warrior's Mark, Huntingdon, Pa ..	· 80	Va	230
Warsaw, Milton, Ga	12	*Washington C. H.,** Fayette, Ohio ..	1,200
Warsaw,* Hancock, Ill	1,400	Washington Centre, Whitley, Ind..	4
Warsaw,* *(c. h.,)* Kosciusko, Ind ...	1,800	Washington Corners, Alameda, Cal.	12
Warsaw, Wayne, Iowa	54	Washington Gulch, Deer Lodge,	
Warsaw, (c. h.,) Gallatin, Ky	240	Mont	12
Warsaw, Franklin, La	28	Washington Harbor, Door, Wis	54
Warsaw, Rice, Minn	44	Washington Heights, Cook, Ill	12
Warsaw,* *(c. h.,)* Benton, Mo	490	Washington Hollow, Dutchess, N. Y	310
Warsaw,* *(c. h.,)* Wyoming, N. Y ...	1,400	Washington Mills, Oneida, N. Y	160
Warsaw, Duplin, N. C	44	Washingtonville, Mahoning, Ohio .	200
Warsaw, Coshocton, Ohio	35	Washingtonville, Montour, Pa	94
Warsaw, Jefferson, Pa	32	*Washoe City, (c. h.,)* Washoe, Nev...	440
Warsaw, (c. h.,) Richmond, Va	100	Washta, Cherokee, Iowa	14
Warthen's Store, Washington, Ga .	12	Wasioga, Dodge, Minn	200
Wartrace Depot, Bedford, Tenn ...	240	Waskoy's Mills, Botetourt, Va	36
Warwick, Worth, Ga	12	Wassaic, Dutchess, N. Y	140
Warwick, Cecil, Md	130	Wassonville, Washington, Iowa ...	54
Warwick, Franklin, Mass	200	Wastedo, Goodhue, Minn	120
Warwick, Orange, N. Y	820	Watab, Benton, Minn	33
Warwick, Chester, Pa	19	Wataga, Knox, Ill	470
Warwick, Kent, R. I	330	Watauga Falls, Watauga, N. C	2
Warwick C. H., Warwick, Va	11	Watauwon, Blue Earth, Minn	290
Warwick Neck, Kent, R. I	45	Watchemoket, Providence, R. I	110
Warwick's Cross Roads, Union,		Waterborough, York, Me	110
Tenn	85	Waterborough Centre, York, Me...	18
War Woman, Rabun, Ga	12	Waterburgh, Tompkins, N. Y	37
Wasatch, Summit, Utah	340	Waterbury,* New Haven, Conn ..	3,300
Wasco, Wasco, Oreg	12	Waterbury, Anne Arundel, Md	51
Waseca,* Waseca, Minn	680	Waterbury,* Washington, Vt	1,000
Washburn, Woodford, Ill	220	Waterbury Centre, Washington, Vt	170
Washburn, Franklin, Iowa	12	Water Cure, Beaver, Pa	160
Washburn, Barry, Mo	92	Waterford, New London, Conn	90
Washburn, Grant, Wis	51	Waterford, Spencer, Ky	13
Washington, (c. h.,) Hempstead, Ark.	460	Waterford, Oxford, Me	140
Washington, Nevada, Cal	86	Waterford, Oakland, Mich	180
Washington, Litchfield, Conn	320	Waterford, Dakota, Minn	23
WASHINGTON,* *(c. h.,)* Washington,		Waterford, Marshall, Miss	77
D. C	4,000	Waterford, Saratoga, N. Y	1,200
Washington, (c. h.,) Wilkes, Ga	680	Waterford, Washington, Ohio	68
Washington, (c. h.,) Idaho, Idaho	12	Waterford, Erie, Pa	770
Washington,* Tazewell, Ill	810	Waterford, Caledonia, Vt	96
Washington,* *(c. h.,)* Daviess, Ind ..	1,300	Waterford, Loudoun, Va	220
Washington,* *(c. h.,)* Washington,		Waterford, Racine, Wis	200
Iowa	1,500	Waterford Mills, Elkhart, Ind	49
Washington, (c. h.,) Washington,		Waterford Works, Camden, N. J...	88
Kans	250	Water Lick, Warren, Va	12
Washington, Mason, Ky	150	Waterloo, Lauderdale, Ala	22
Washington, St. Landry, La	1,000	Waterloo, San Joaquin, Cal	17
Washington, Knox, Me	93	*Waterloo,** *(c. h.,)* Monroe, Ill	460
Washington, Berkshire, Mass	58	Waterloo,* De Kalb, Ind	730
Washington, Macomb, Mich	100	*Waterloo,***(c. h.,)* Black Hawk, Iowa.	2,700
Washington, Fillmore, Minn	41	Waterloo, Lyon, Kans	29
Washington,* Franklin, Mo	820	Waterloo, Pulaski, Ky	22
Washington, Nye, Nev	12	Waterloo, Point Coupee, La	24
Washington, Sullivan, N. H	120	Waterloo, Jackson, Mich	25
Washington,* Warren, N. J	1,000	*Waterloo, (c. h.,)* Clarke, Mo	110
Washington, Dutchess, N. Y	90	Waterloo, Sussex, N. J	100
Washington,* *(c. h.,)* Beaufort, N. C.	1,200	*Waterloo, (c. h.,)* Seneca, N. Y	2,000
Washington, Guernsey, Ohio	340	Waterloo, Lawrence, Ohio	26
Washington,* *(c. h.,)* Washington, Pa	1,800	Waterloo, Juniata, Pa	54
Washington, (c. h.,) Rhea, Tenn	57	Waterloo, Laurens, S. C	5
Washington, Washington, Tex	140	Waterloo,* Jefferson, Wis	480

* **Money-order office.**

WAU — WAY

Waterloo Mills, Orange, N. Y	$11
Waterman, Parke, Ind	13
Waterman's Mills, Stephenson, Ill.	12
Water Mill, Suffolk, N. Y	66
Waterport, Orleans, N. Y	83
Water Proof, Tensas, La	160
Waterside, Bedford, Pa	51
Water Street, Huntingdon, Pa	61
Watersville, Carroll, Md	31
Watertown, Litchfield, Conn	440
Watertown, Rock Island, Ill	28
Watertown, Floyd, Iowa	19
Watertown,* Middlesex, Mass	1,300
Watertown, Tuscola, Mich	27
Watertown, Carver, Minn	210
Watertown,* (c. h.,) Jefferson, N. Y.	3,200
Watertown, Washington, Ohio	94
Watertown, Wilson, Tenn	52
Watertown,* Jefferson, Wis	2,500
Watervale, Onondaga, N. Y	22
Water Valley, Yalabusha, Miss	1,000
Water Valley, Erie, N. Y	79
Water Village, Carroll, N. H	16
Waterville, New Haven, Conn	120
Waterville, Allamakee, Iowa	73
Waterville,* Marshall, Kans.	510
Waterville,* Kennebec, Me	1,500
Waterville, Le Sueur, Minn	130
Waterville, Oneida, N. Y	890
Waterville, Lucas, Ohio	100
Waterville, Lycoming, Pa	20
Waterville, Lamoille, Vt	120
Waterville, Waukesha, Wis	27
Watervliet, Berrien, Mich	170
Watervliet Centre, Albany, N. Y.	47
Wathena,* Doniphan, Kans	840
Watkins, (c. h.,) Schuyler, N. Y.	2,000
Watkins, Union, Ohio	16
Watkinsville, (c. h.,) Clarke, Ga.	84
Watopa, Wabashaw, Minn	4
Watrousville, Tuscola, Mich	160
Watseka,* Iroquois, Ill	1,100
Watson, Effingham, Ill	100
Watson, Prince George's, Md	12
Watson, Allegan, Mich	12
Watson, Atchison, Mo	93
Watson, Beaver Head, Mont	12
Watson, Lewis, N. Y	31
Watson Creek, Fillmore, Minn	800
Watson's Station, Seneca, Ohio	22
Watsontown,* Northumberland, Pa	430
Watsonville,* Santa Cruz, Cal	900
Watt, Indiana, Pa	12
Watterson's Ferry, Clarion, Pa	110
Wattsborough, Lunenburgh, Va	10
Wattsburgh, Erie, Pa	240
Watt's Flats, Chautauqua, N. Y	71
Wattsville, Carroll, Ohio	20
Waubeck, Linn, Iowa	65
Waubeck, Pepin, Wis	17
Waucoma, Fayette, Iowa	63
Wauconda, Lake, Ill	170
Waucousta, Fond du Lac, Wis	32
Wauhatchie, Hamilton, Tenn	12
Waukau, Winnebago, Wis	150
Waukecheon, Shawanaw, Wis	12

Waukeenah, Jefferson, Fla	$30
Waukee Station, Dallas, Iowa	12
Waukegan,* (c. h.,) Lake, Ill	2,400
Waukesha,* (c. h.,) Waukesha, Wis.	1,900
Waukokee, Fillmore, Minn	12
Waukon,* (c. h.,) Allamakee, Iowa	500
Waumandee, Buffalo, Wis	47
Waupaca,* (c. h.,) Waupaca, Wis.	760
Waupecong, Miami, Ind	8
Waupun,* Fond du Lac, Wis	1,900
Wauregan, Windham, Conn	230
Wausau,* (c. h.,) Marathon, Wis	620
Wauseon,* Fulton, Ohio	960
Waushara, Lyon, Kans	36
Wautiska, Saunders, Nebr	12
Wautoma,* (c. h.,) Waushara, Wis.	330
Wauwatosa, Milwaukee, Wis	190
Wauzeka, Crawford, Wis	55
Waveland, Montgomery, Ind	240
Waveland, Pottawattomie, Iowa	12
Waveland, Shawnee, Kans	60
Waverlie, Rockingham, Va	31
Waverly, Morgan, Ill	490
Waverly, Morgan, Ind	51
Waverly,* (c. h.,) Bremer, Iowa	1,500
Waverly, Caldwell, La	12
Waverly, Baltimore, Md	190
Waverly, Middlesex, Mass	85
Waverly, Van Buren, Mich	17
Waverly, Martin, Minn	11
Waverly,* La Fayette, Mo	370
Waverly,* Tioga, N. Y	1,600
Waverly, Pike, Ohio	490
Waverly, Luzerne, Pa	230
Waverly, (c. h.,) Humphreys, Tenn.	190
Waverly, Walker, Tex	24
Waverly Hall, Harris, Ga	25
Waverly Heights, Montgomery, Pa.	64
Waverly Mills, Wright, Minn	28
Waverly Station, Sussex, Va	93
Wawaka, Noble, Ind	190
Wawarsing, Ulster, N. Y	72
Wawayanda, Sussex, N. J	12
Waxahachie, (c. h.,) Ellis, Tex	400
Wayland, Schuyler, Ill	17
Wayland, Middlesex, Mass	190
Wayland,* Allegan, Mich	360
Wayland Depot, Steuben, N. Y	320
Waylandsburgh, Culpeper, Va	5
Wayland Springs, Lawrence, Tenn	10
Waymansville, Bartholomew, Ind.	12
Waymart, Wayne, Pa	240
Wayne, Du Page, Ill	180
Wayne, Henry, Iowa	27
Wayne, Kennebec, Me	180
Wayne, Wayne, Mich	360
Wayne, Steuben, N. Y	150
Wayne, Wayne, Ohio	12
Wayne, Erie, Pa	47
Wayne, Washington, Wis	33
Wayne C. H., Wayne, W. Va	12
Wayne Centre, Wayne, N. Y	20
Wayne Centre, Crawford, Pa	4
Wayne Four Corners, Steuben, N.Y.	6
Waynesborough, (c. h.,) Burke, Ga.	400
Waynesborough, (c. h.,) Wayne, Miss.	24

* Money-order office.

WEB | WEL

Waynesborough,* Franklin, Pa....	$790	Webster Groves, St. Louis, Mo.....	$220
Waynesborough, (c. h.,) Wayne, Tenn	98	Webster Place, Elbert, Ga.........	12
Waynesborough, Augusta, Va......	390	Webster's Crossing, Livingston,	
Waynesburgh, Decatur, Ind......	78	N. Y	12
Waynesburgh, Lincoln, Ky........	21	Webster's Mills, Fulton, Pa.......	21
Waynesburgh, Stark, Ohio......	300	*Wedowee,* (c. h.,) Randolph, Ala.....	66
Waynesburgh, * (c. h.,) Greene, Pa...	1,000	Weedsport, Cayuga, N. Y	930
Waynesfield, Auglaize, Ohio.......	42	Weehawken, Hudson, N. J	420
Waynesville, (c. h.,) Wayne, Ga.....	12	Week's Mills, Kennebec, Me......	75
Waynesville, De Witt, Ill..........	130	Weeksville, Southampton, Va	12
Waynesville, Bartholomew, Ind...	24	Weelaunee, Jefferson, Fla	12
Waynesville, * (c. h.,) Pulaski, Mo...	88	Weelaunee, Winnebago, Wis.......	44
Waynesville, (c. h.,) Haywood, N. C.	80	Weeping Water, Cass, Nebr........	140
Waynesville,* Warren, Ohio.......	610	Weesatch, Goliad, Tex	12
Waynetown, Montgomery, Ind	130	Weesaw, Berrien, Mich...........	19
Waynewood, Marion, Ind	12	Weewokaville, Talladega, Ala......	6
Waynmanville, Upson, Ga........	25	Wegatchie, St. Lawrence, N. Y.....	31
Wayside, Mecklenburgh, Va......	12	Wegee, Belmont, Ohio............	20
Wayside, Brown, Wis.............	13	Wehoga, Calhoun, Ala	5
Way's Station, Bryan, Ga..........	12	Weidasville, Lehigh, Pa...........	5
Wayzata, Hennepin, Minn	24	Weir's Bridge, Belknap, N. H	29
Weare, Oceana, Mich.............	12	Weisburgh, Dearborn, Ind.......	65
Weare, Hillsborough, N. H	97	Weisenburgh, Lehigh, Pa	8
Wear's Valley, Sevier, Tenn......	12	Weisesburgh, Baltimore, Md......	11
Weatherford, (c. h.,) Parker, Tex ...	530	Weishample, Schuylkill, Pa.......	12
Weatherly, Carbon, Pa.............	250	Weissport, Carbon, Pa...........	190
Weathersfield, Windsor, Vt :......	59	Weister, Vernon, Wis.............	14
Weathersfield Centre, Windsor, Vt.	12	Welaka, Putnam, Fla.............	51
Weatogue, Hartford, Conn........	69	Welch Glade, Webster, W. Va.....	4
Weaver's Old Stand, Westmore-		Welch's Creek, Butler, Ky.......	3
land, Pa	57	Welchville, Oxford, Me.........	150
Weaver's Station, Darke, Ohio....	45	Weld, Weld, Colo.................	12
Weaversville, Northampton, Pa....	45	Weld, Franklin, Me.............	210
Weaversville, Fauquier, Va.......	18	Weldon, Redwood, Minn	12
Weaverton, Wayne, Ky............	18	Weldon,* Halifax, N. C	880
Weaverville, * (c. h.,) Trinity, Cal ...	390	Weldon, Houston, Tex	8
Webber's Falls, Cherokee Nation,		Well, Faribault, Minn..........	14
Ind. T	12	Wellborn, Suwannee, Fla..........	53
Webberville, Ingham, Mich	26	Weller, Monroe, Iowa...........	7
Webberville, Travis, Tex..........	110	Wellersburgh, Somerset, Pa.......	65
Webbs, Greene, Ky...............	6	Wellerville, Crawford, Ohio.......	18
Webb's Ford, Rutherford, N. C.....	13	Wellesley, Norfolk, Mass........	300
Webb's Mills, Cumberland, Me	36	Wellfleet,* Barnstable, Mass.......	550
Webb's Mills, Chemung, N. Y...:.	140	Wellington, Piscataquis, Me.......	22
Webb's Mills, Ritchie, W. Va.....	7	Wellington, La Fayette, Mo.......	170
Webb's Prairie, Franklin, Ill......	11	Wellington, Esmeralda, Nev.......	12
Webbville, Lawrence, Ky..........	4	Wellington,* Lorain, Ohio.......	1,300
Webertown, Highland, Ohio	11	Wells, York, Me	250
Webster, Hancock, Ill	52	Wells, Attala, Miss............	12
Webster, Wayne, Ind.............	13	Wells, Elko, Nev.............	12
Webster, Keokuk, Iowa........	48	Wells, Hamilton, N. Y	68
Webster, Breckinridge, Ky........	14	Wells, Bradford, Pa............	50
Webster, Androscoggin, Me......	20	Wells, Rutland, Vt............	120
Webster,* Worcester, Mass........	1,700	*Wellsborough,* * (c. h.,) Tioga, Pa....	1,100
Webster, Washtenaw, Mich.......	19	Wells' Bridge, Otsego, N. Y.......	73
Webster, Winston, Miss	39	Wellsburgh, Page, Iowa..........	12
Webster, Oregon, Mo........	23	Wellsburgh, St. Charles, Mo.......	72
Webster, Merrimack, N. H	120	Wellsburgh, Chemung, N. Y.......	210
Webster, Monroe, N. Y.............	200	*Wellsburgh,* * (c. h.,) Brooke, W. Va.	560
Webster, (c. h.,) Jackson, N. C.....	63	Wells Corner, Orange, N. Y.......	13
Webster, Darke, Ohio...........	66	Wells Depot, York, Me.........	150
Webster, Westmoreland, Pa	130	Wells' Mills, Appanoose, Iowa.....	25
Webster, Roane, Tenn............	12	Wells' Mills, Richardson, Nebr.....	13
Webster, Taylor, W. Va..........	120	Well Spring, Campbell, Tenn......	14
Webster C. H., Webster W. Va......	19	Wells River, Orange, Vt..........	620
Webster City, * (c. h.,) Hamilton, Iowa.	600	Wells Tannery, Fulton, Pa........	32

WES | WES

Wellsville, Lenawee, Mich	$16
Wellsville, Montgomery, Mo	220
Wellsville,* Allegany, N. Y	1,400
Wellsville,* Columbiana, Ohio	1,200
Wellsville, York, Pa	96
Wellsville, Cache, Utah	360
Wellville, Nottaway, Va	62
Well Water, Buckingham, Va	5
Wellwood, Haywood, Tenn	21
Welshfield, Geauga, Ohio	89
Welsh Run, Franklin, Pa	50
Welton, Clinton, Iowa	42
Weltonville, Tioga, N. Y	19
Wendell, Franklin, Mass	50
Wendell Depot, Franklin, Mass	*76
Wenham, Essex, Mass	210
Wenks, Adams, Pa	12
Wennersville, Lehigh, Pa	9
Wenona, Bay, Mich	490
Wenona Station,* Marshall, Ill	1,100
Wentworth, Mitchell, Iowa	12
Wentworth, Grafton, N. H	340
Wentworth, (c. h.,) Rockingham, N.C.	100
Wentworth's Location, Coos, N. H.	9
Wentzville, St. Charles, Mo	360
Weogufka, Coosa, Ala	4
Wequiock, Brown, Wis	25
Werner, Juneau, Wis	64
Wernersville, Berks, Pa	22
Wertsville, Hunterdon, N. J	63
Wescosville, Lehigh, Pa	40
Wesley, Montgomery, Ind	16
Wesley, Hickman, Ky	17
Wesley, Washington, Me	31
Wesley, Washington, Ohio	7
Wesley, Venango, Pa	22
Wesley, Austin, Tex	49
Wesleyville, Erie, Pa	130
Wesson, Copiah, Miss	140
West, Wetzel, W. Va	5
West Acton, Middlesex, Mass	260
West Addison, Steuben, N. Y	29
West Addison, Addison, Vt	23
West Albany, Wabashaw, Minn	19
West Albany, Albany, N. Y	36
West Alexander, Washington, Pa	190
West Alexandria, Preble, Ohio	210
West Almond, Allegany, N. Y	40
West Alton, Belknap, N. H	21
West Amboy, Oswego, N. Y	36
West Amesbury, Essex, Mass	430
West Andover, Merrimack, N. H	87
West Andover, Ashtabula, Ohio	120
West Appleton, Knox, Me	20
West Arlington, Bennington, Vt	51
West Ashford, Windham, Conn	59
West Athens, Somerset, Me	12
West Auburn, Androscoggin, Me	150
West Auburn, Susquehanna, Pa	20
West Avon, Hartford, Conn	27
West Baden, Orange, Ind	66
West Baldwin, Cumberland, Me	81
West Baltimore, Montgomery, Ohio.	51
West Bangor, Franklin, N. Y	94
West Bangor, York, Pa	220
West Barnet, Caledonia, Vt	85

West Barnstable, Barnstable, Mass.	$130
West Barre, Orleans, N. Y	33
West Barre, Fulton, Ohio	7
West Batavia, Genesee, N. Y	41
West Beaver, Columbiana, Ohio	11
West Becket, Berkshire, Mass	28
West Bedford, Coshocton, Ohio	64
West Bend, Palo Alto, Iowa	25
West Bend, Powell, Ky	12
West Bend,* (c. h.,) Washington, Wis.	480
West Bergen, Genesee, N. Y	27
West Berkshire, Franklin, Vt	140
West Berlin, Worcester, Mass	35
West Berne, Albany, N. Y	34
West Bethany, Genesee, N. Y	24
West Bethel, Oxford, Me	110
West Bingham, Potter, Pa	12
West Bloomfield, Ontario, N. Y	240
West Blue Mound, Iowa, Wis	79
West Bolton, Chittenden, Vt	33
Westborough,* Worcester, Mass	1,500
Westborough, Clinton, Ohio	130
West Bowdoin, Sagadahoc, Me	40
West Boxford, Essex, Mass	65
West Boylston, Worcester, Mass	330
West Braintree, Orange, Vt	39
West Branch, Cedar, Iowa	320
West Branch, Oneida, N. Y	66
West Branch, Richland, Wis	34
West Brattleborough, Windham, Vt.	300
West Brewster, Barnstable, Mass	60
West Bridgeton, Cumberland, Me	8
West Bridgewater, Plymouth, Mass.	310
West Bridgewater, Windsor, Vt	15
West Brighton, Monroe, N. Y	44
West Brook, Middlesex, Conn	250
West Brook, Delaware, N. Y	14
West Brook, Bladen, N. C	5
Westbrook, Blanco, Tex	6
West Brookfield, Worcester, Mass	510
West Brookfield, Stark, Ohio	310
West Brooklyn, Poweshiek, Iowa	12
West Brooksville, Hancock, Me	74
West Brookville, Sullivan, N. Y	46
West Brownsville, Washington, Pa.	76
West Brunswick, Cumberland, Me.	15
West Buena Vista, Gibson, Ind	11
West Buffalo, Williams, Ohio	44
West Burke, Caledonia, Vt	210
West Burlington, Otsego, N. Y	50
West Burlington, Bradford, Pa	59
Westbury, Cayuga, N. Y	86
West Butler, Wayne, N. Y	33
West Butte, Sutter, Cal	20
West Buxton, York, Me	230
West Cairo, Allen, Ohio	86
West Camden, Knox, Me	74
West Camden, Oneida, N. Y	83
West Camp, Ulster, N. Y	31
West Campbell, Ionia, Mich	27
West Campton, Grafton, N. H	110
West Canaan, Grafton, N. H	80
West Canaan, Madison, Ohio	21
West Candor, Tioga, N. Y	22
West Carlisle, Coshocton, Ohio	63
West Carrollton, Montgomery, Ohio	12

* Money-order office.

West Casco, Allegan, Mich	$20	West Elkton, Preble, Ohio	$94
West Castleton, Rutland, Vt	100	West Ellsworth, Hancock, Me	10
West Charleston, Penobscot, Me	32	West Ely, Marion, Mo	26
West Charleston, Miami, Ohio	31	West Embden, Somerset, Me	6
West Charleston, Orleans, Vt	250	West End, Bedford, Pa	34
West Charlotte, Chittenden, Vt	95	West Enfield, Penobscot, Me	8
West Charlton, Saratoga, N. Y	70	West Enfield, Concord, N. H	12
West Chatham, Barnstable, Mass	49	West Enosburgh, Franklin, Vt	67
West Chazy, Clinton, N. Y	210	West Epping, Rockingham, N. H	54
West Chehalem, Yam Hill, Oreg	12	Westerlo, Albany, N. Y	88
West Chelmsford, Middlesex, Mass	140	Westerly,* Washington, R. I	2,700
West Cheshire, New Haven, Conn.	250	Western College, Linn, Iowa	190
Westchester, New London, Conn	52	Western Port, Alleghany, Md	260
Westchester, Jay, Ind	38	Western Saratoga, Union, Ill	8
West Chester, Wabashaw, Minn	16	Western Star, Summit, Ohio	47
West Chester, Westchester, N. Y	670	Westernville, Oneida, N. Y	220
West Chester, Butler, Ohio	110	Westerville, Decatur, Iowa	46
West Chester,* Chester, Pa	2,500	Westerville, Franklin, Ohio	440
West Chesterfield, Hampshire, Mass	70	West Exeter, Otsego, N. Y	70
West Chesterfield, Cheshire, N. H.	41	West Fairfield, Westmoreland, Pa	73
West Claremont, Sullivan, N. H	48	West Fairlee, Orange, Vt	480
West Clarksville, Allegany, N. Y	79	West Fairview, Cumberland, Pa	200
West Colesville, Broome, N. Y	12	West Falls, Erie, N. Y	61
West Columbia, Mason, W. Va	96	West Falmouth, Cumberland, Me	72
West Concord, Merrimack, N. H	190	West Falmouth, Barnstable, Mass	110
West Concord,* Essex, Vt	240	West Farmingdale, Kennebec, Me	30
West Conesville, Schoharie, N. Y	23	West Farmington, Ontario, N. Y	35
West Constable, Franklin, N. Y	54	West Farmington,* Trumbull, Ohio	290
West Copake, Columbia, N. Y	12	West Farms, Westchester, N. Y	430
West Corinna, Penobscot, Me	2	West Fayette, Seneca, N. Y	28
West Corinth, Orange, Vt	45	Westfield, Clark, Ill	340
West Cornville, Somerset, Me	23	Westfield, Hamilton, Ind	210
West Cornwall, Litchfield, Conn	340	Westfield, Worth, Iowa	12
West Cornwall, Addison, Vt	120	Westfield, Aroostook, Me	11
West Covington, Tioga, Pa	24	Westfield,* Hampden, Mass	2,700
West Creek, Lake, Ind	40	Westfield, Pope, Minn	12
West Creek, Ocean, N. J	96	Westfield, Union, N. J	300
West Cumberland, Cumberland, Me	62	Westfield,* Chautauqua, N. Y	1,400
West Damascus, Wayne, Pa	12	Westfield, Stokes, N. C	12
West Danby, Tompkins, N. Y	40	Westfield, Morrow, Ohio	60
West Danvers, Essex, Mass	38	Westfield, Tioga, Pa	210
West Danville, Caledonia, Vt	77	Westfield, Orleans, Vt	67
West Davenport, Delaware, N. Y	49	Westfield,* Marquette, Wis	120
West Day, Saratoga, N. Y	75	West Finley, Washington, Pa	23
West Dayton, Webster, Iowa	200	West Fitchburgh, Worcester, Mass	440
West Decatur, Clearfield, Pa	33	West Florence, Preble, Ohio	38
West Dedham, Norfolk, Mass	120	Westford, Windham, Conn	160
West Deering, Hillsborough, N. H.	12	Westford, Middlesex, Mass	210
West Deer Isle, Hancock, Me	12	Westford, Otsego, N. Y	140
West Dennis, Barnstable, Mass	280	Westford, Chittenden, Vt	140
West Derby, Orleans, Vt	69	Westford, Dodge, Wis	410
West Dover, Piscataquis, Me	11	West Fork, Washington, Ark	9
West Dover, Windham, Vt	75	West Fork, Monona, Iowa	13
West Dresden, Lincoln, Me	12	West Fork, Overton, Tenn	10
West Dryden, Tompkins, N. Y	32	West Fork Furnace, Floyd, Va	13
West Dublin, Fulton, Pa	11	West Fort Ann, Washington, N. Y.	45
West Dudley, Worcester, Mass	58	West Foxborough, Norfolk, Mass	38
West Dummerston, Windham, Vt	80	West Franklin, Bradford, Pa	20
West Durham, Androscoggin, Me	41	West Freedom, Clarion, Pa	42
West Duxbury, Plymouth, Mass	67	West Freehold, Monmouth, N. J	60
West Earl, Lancaster, Pa	62	West Freeman, Franklin, Me	5
West Eaton, Madison, N. Y	260	West Friendship, Howard, Md	16
West Eau Claire,* Eau Claire, Wis.	1,100	West Fulton, Schoharie, N. Y	44
West Eden, Hancock, Me	35	West Galway, Fulton, N. Y	140
West Edmeston, Otsego, N. Y	88	West Gardiner, Kennebec, Me	46
West Elizabeth, Allegheny, Pa	100	West Garland, Penobscot, Me	2A

* Money-order office.

WES

West Geneva, Van Buren, Mich....	$22
West Georgia, Franklin, Vt........	18
West Gloucester, Cumberland, Me..	31
West Gloucester, Essex, Mass......	92
West Gloucester, Providence, R. I..	20
West Glover, Orleans, Vt	47
West Gorham, Cumberland, Me....	66
West Goshen, Litchfield, Conn....	170
West Gouldsborough, Hancock, Me.	100
West Granby, Hartford, Conn......	63
West Granville, Hampden, Mass....	86
West Granville, Milwaukee, Wis...	53
West Granville Corners, Washington, N. Y............	67
West Great Works, Penobscot, Me..	81
West Greece, Monroe, N. Y.........	67
West Greene, Erie, Pa............	36
West Greenfield, Saratoga, N. Y....	12
West Green Lake, Green Lake, Wis.	10
West Greenwich Centre, Kent, R. I.	9
West Greenwood, Crawford, Pa....	14
West Groton, Middlesex, Mass....	81
West Groton, Tompkins, N. Y......	36
West Grove, Davis, Iowa..........	8
West Grove Station, Chester, Pa ...	350
West Halifax, Windham, Vt.......	55
West Hallock, Peoria, Ill.........	76
West Hamburgh, Erie, N. Y.......	13
Westham Locks, Henrico, Va......	9
West Hampden, Penobscot, Me....	48
West Hampstead, Rockingham, N. H.....	62
West Hampton, Hampshire, Mass...	89
West Hampton, Suffolk, N. Y......	58
West Hanover, Plymouth, Mass ...	80
West Hanover, Dauphin, Pa........	35
West Harpswell, Cumberland, Me.	73
West Hartford, Hartford, Conn....	240
West Hartford, Ralls, Mo.	12
West Hartford, Windsor, Vt	170
West Hartland, Hartford, Conn....	43
West Harwich, Barnstable, Mass ...	150
West Haven, New Haven, Conn....	360
West Haven, Shiawassee, Mich....	12
West Haven, Rutland, Vt	32
West Haverford, Delaware, Pa	400
West Hawley, Franklin, Mass.....	20
West Hebron, Washington, N. Y ..	130
West Henniker, Merrimack, N. H..	65
West Henrietta, Monroe, N. Y.....	100
West Hickory, Forest, Pa.........	16
West Hoboken, Hudson, N. J......	280
West Hoosick, Rensselaer, N. Y ...	30
West Hope, Henry, Ohio	12
West Hopkinton, Merrimack, N. H.	15
West Hurley, Ulster, N. Y.........	130
West Independence, Hancock, Ohio.	32
West Irving, Tama, Iowa....	76
West Jasper, Steuben, N. Y.......	5
West Jefferson,* Madison, Ohio....	330
West Jersey, Stark, Ill..........	110
West Jordan, Salt Lake, Utah.....	10
West Junius, Seneca, N. Y....	14
West Kendall, Orleans, N. Y.... ..	62
West Kill, Greene, N. Y...........	59
West Killingly,* Windham, Conn..	1,500

WES

West Kinderhook, Tipton, Ind.....	$8
West Kortright, Delaware, N. Y...	24
West La Fayette, Coshocton, Ohio.	66
West Lancaster, Fayette, Ohio	28
Westland, Hancock, Ind	14
West Laurens, Otsego, N. Y........	46
West Lebanon,* Warren, Ind......	290
West Lebanon, York, Me..........	100
West Lebanon,* Grafton, N. H....	540
West Lebanon, Wayne, Ohio	57
West Lebanon, Indiana, Pa.......	87
West Leeds, Androscoggin, Me	26
West Lenox, Susquehanna, Pa	14
West Leroy, Calhoun, Mich........	16
West Levant, Penobscot, Me	31
West Leyden, Lewis, N. Y....	82
West Liberty, Howard, Ind........	12
West Liberty,* Muscatine, Iowa...	770
*West Liberty, (c. h.,) Morgan, Ky....	36
West Liberty, Putnam, Mo........	8
West Liberty,* Logan, Ohio.......	830
West Liberty, Butler, Pa..........	28
West Liberty, Ohio, W. Va........	110
West Lima, Richland, Wis........	23
West Lodi, Seneca, Ohio......	70
West Louisville, Daviess, Ky......	12
West Lowville, Lewis, N. Y	16
West Lubec, Washington, Me	89
West Lyons, Cook, Ill	67
West Macedon,* Wayne, N. Y.....	620
West Magnolia, Rock, Wis....	12
West Manchester, Preble, Ohio	67
West Mansfield, Bristol, Mass......	72
West Mansfield, Logan, Ohio......	28
West Marlborough, Windham, Vt..	8
West Martinsburgh, Lewis, N. Y...	59
West Medford, Middlesex, Mass....	100
West Medway, Norfolk, Mass......	380
West Meredith, Delaware, N. Y....	12
West Meriden,* New Haven, Conn.	3,300
West Middleburgh, Logan, Ohio ..	88
West Middlesex, Mercer, Pa	500
West Middleton, Dane, Wis	20
West Middletown, Washington, Pa.	250
West Milan, Monroe, Mich........	12
West Milan, Coos, N. H..........	85
West Milford, Passaic, N. J........	55
West Milford, Harrison, W. Va....	44
West Millbury, Worcester, Mass...	260
West Mill Grove, Wood, Ohio.....	83
West Milton, Strafford, N. H	59
West Milton, Saratoga, N. Y.......	97
West Milton, Miami, Ohio........	210
West Milton, Union, Pa	53
West Milton, Chittenden, Vt	40
West Minot, Androscoggin, Me....	120
Westminster, Windham, Conn	48
Westminster, (c. h.,) Carroll, Md...	930
Westminster, Worcester, Mass.....	419
Westminster, Guilford, N. C........	20
Westminster, Allen, Ohio...... ..	46
Westminster, Windham, Vt.......	85
Westminster Depot, Worcester, Mass.........................	50
Westminster West, Windham, Vt..	96
West Mitchell, Mitchell, Iowa.....	400

* Money-order office.

WHI   WHI

Wheatland Furnace, Mercer, Pa....	$310	White Hall, Madison, Ky..........	$70
Wheatland Mills, Lancaster, Pa....	20	White Hall, Baltimore, Md	40
Wheaton,* Du Page, Ill	760	Whitehall, Muskegon, Mich........	710
Wheaton, Montgomery, Md........	41	Whitehall, Jefferson, Mont........	14
Wheatonville, Warrick, Ind	8	Whitehall,* Washington, N. Y	1,900
Wheat Ridge, Adams, Ohio	15	White Hall, Bladen, N. C	12
Wheatville, Miami, Ind............	7	White Hall, Montour, Pa	41
Wheatville, Genesee, N. Y	46	White Hall, Davis, Tex............	12
Wheatville, Titus, Tex	12	White Hall, Frederick, Va.........	39
Wheatville, Crawford, Wis	6	Whitehallville, Bucks, Pa	94
Wheeler, Porter, Ind	83	Whitehaven, Wicomico, Md	18
Wheeler, Gratiot, Mich	12	White Haven, Erie, N. Y..........	12
Wheeler, Steuben, N. Y...........	43	White Haven, Luzerne, Pa	1,100
Wheelersburgh, Scioto, Ohio.......	150	Whitehead's Store, Pittsylvania, Va	12
Wheeler's Grove, Pottawattomie,		White Horn, Hawkins, Tenn.......	12
Iowa.........................	10	White Horse, Chester, Pa..........	12
Wheeler Station, Lawrence, Ala....	12	White Horse, Greenville, S. C......	12
Wheelersville, Northampton, N. C..	12	White House, Hunterdon, N. J.....	100
Wheeling, Cook, Ill	87	White House, Randolph, N. C......	10
Wheeling, Delaware, Ind..........	47	White House, Lucas, Ohio..........	190
Wheeling, Marion, Iowa...........	31	White House, Cumberland, Pa......	53
Wheeling, Winn, La	14	White House, Mecklenburgh, Va...	12
Wheeling, Rice, Minn	23	White House Station, Hunterdon,	
Wheeling, Livingston, Mo	170	N. J	75
WHEELING,* (c. h.,) Ohio, W. Va...	3,800	White Lake, Oakland, Mich	67
Wheelock, Choctaw N., Ind. T	11	White Lake, Sullivan, N. Y........	160
Wheelock, Robertson, Tex........	37	Whiteland, Johnson, Ind..........	40
Wheelock, Caledonia, Vt	81	Whiteley, Greene, Pa.............	20
Whetham, Clinton, Pa............	23	Whiteleysburgh, Caroline, Md.....	8
Whetstone, Morrow, Ohio.........	17	White Lick, Boone, Ind	24
Whetstone Agency, ——, Dak....	12	White Lily, Laurel, Ky............	7
Whig Valley, Holt, Mo	12	White Marsh, Montgomery, Pa.....	190
Whigville, Noble, Ohio	17	White Mills, Hardin, Ky..........	35
Whilden's Factory, Greenville, S.C.	10	White Mills, Wayne, Pa	91
Whippany, Morris, N. J	89	White Mound, Sauk, Wis..........	31
Whippoorwill, Laurel, Ky	5	White Mountain House, Coos, N. H.	10
Whistler, Mobile, Ala	110	White Oak, Montgomery, Ill.......	10
Whitaker's, Edgecombe, N. C	12	White Oak, Mahaska, Iowa........	38
Whitcomb, Franklin, Ind..........	24	White Oak, Ingham, Mich.........	20
White Ash, Allegheny, Pa.........	160	White Oak, Lancaster, Pa	8
White Bear Centre, Pope, Minn....	12	White Oak, Hopkins, Tex	12
White Bear Lake, Ramsey, Minn...	29	White Oak, Ritchie, W. Va	22
White Bird, Idaho, Idaho..........	12	White Oak Gap, Pulaski, Ky.......	9
White Bluff, Dallas, Ala..........	12	White Oak Grove, Greene, Mo......	6
White Bluffs, Dickson, Tenn.......	95	White Oak Springs, Barbour, Ala..	14
White Breast, Lucas, Iowa	4	White Oak Springs, Brown, Ill.....	8
White Church, Wyandotte, Kans...	12	White Oak Springs, Lee, Va.......	12
White Cloud, Mills, Iowa..........	120	White Oak Springs, La Fayette, Wis	47
White Cloud,* Doniphan, Kans....	320	White Pigeon, Keokuk, Iowa	7
White Cloud, Nodaway, Mo	26	White Pigeon, St. Joseph, Mich	940
White Cottage, Muskingum, Ohio..	50	White Pine, Lycoming, Pa.........	45
White Cottage, Greene, Pa	16	White Plains, Calhoun, Ala........	26
White Creek, Jackson, Ind	23	White Plains, Greene, Ga..........	16
White Creek, Washington, N. Y....	83	White Plains,* (c. h.,) Westchester,	
White Creek, Adams, Wis	35	N. Y	1,500
White Day, Monongalia, W. Va....	44	White Plains, Cleveland, N. C......	5
White Deer Mills, Union, Pa.......	34	White Plains, Chesterfield, S. C....	12
White Eyes Plains, Coshocton, Ohio	34	White Plains, Putnam, Tenn	12
Whitefield, Lincoln, Me	73	White Plains, Brunswick, Va.......	12
Whitefield, Oktibbeha, Miss	16	White Pond, Barbour, Ala.........	12
Whitefield, Coos, N. H............	350	White Post, Clarke, Va...........	57
Whiteford Centre, Monroe, Mich...	23	White River, Desha, Ark	30
White Gate, Giles, Va............	12	White River, Muskegon, Mich	61
Whitehall, Yankton, Dak..........	12	White River, King, Wash	12
White Hall, Greene, Ill...........	750	White River Junction,* Windsor, Vt	790
White Hall, Owen, Ind............	44	White Road, Forsyth, N. C	6

* Money-order office.

WHI | WIL

White Rock, Ogle, Ill	$69	Whitlock, Halifax, Va	$120
White Rock, Republic, Kans	12	Whitman, Lowndes, Ala	12
White Rock, Cumberland, Me	100	Whitman, Walla Walla, Wash	12
White Rock, Huron, Mich	92	Whitmell, Pittsylvania, Va	28
White Rock, Hunt, Tex	48	Whitmire's, Newberry, S. C	19
White Rock Prairie, McDonald, Mo	12	Whitmore Lake, Washtenaw, Mich.	69
White Sand, Lawrence, Miss	9	Whitney, Boulder, Colo	35
Whitesborough, Harrison, Iowa	19	Whitney's Crossings, Allegany, N. Y	7
Whitesborough, Grayson, Tex	12	Whitney's Point,* Broome, N. Y	420
Whitesburgh, Madison, Ala	12	Whitneyville, Cass, Iowa	10
Whitesburgh, (c. h.,) Letchor, Ky	12	Whitneyville, Washington, Me	86
Whitesburgh, Genesee, Mich	27	Whittington, Hot Spring, Ark	15
Whitesburgh, Armstrong, Pa	32	Whittle, Washington, Ga	12
Whitesburgh, Jefferson, Tenn	110	Whittlesey, Medina, Ohio	68
White's Corner, Waldo, Me	20	Whittle's Mills, Mecklenburgh, Va.	12
White's Corners, Erie, N. Y	310	Wichita, (c. h.,) Sedgwick, Kans	12
White's Corners, Potter, Pa	20	Wick, Tyler, W. Va	10
White's Creek, Wayne, W. Va	14	Wickenburgh, Yavapai, Ariz	100
Whiteside, Marion, Tenn	190	Wickford,* Washington, R. I	490
White Shoals, Lee, Va	12	Wickle's Store, Macon, N. C	12
White's Mills, Logan, W. Va	12	Wickliffe, Crawford, Ind	6
White Springs, Hamilton, Fla	64	Wickliffe, Jackson, Iowa	27
White's Station, Shelby, Tenn	48	Wickliffe, Lake, Ohio	39
White's Store, Chenango, N. Y	25	Wicomico Church, Northumber-	
White's Store, Anson, N. C	12	land, Va	17
White's Tannery, Monroe, Pa	78	Wiconisco. Dauphin, Pa	160
Whitestone, Queens, N. Y	410	Wiess Bluff, Jasper, Tex	54
Whitestown, Boone, Ind	220	Wilbar, Wilkes, N. C	7
Whitestown, Oneida, N. Y	670	Wilborn, Madison, Ill	16
Whitestown, Butler, Pa	45	Wilbraham, Hampden, Mass	660
White Sulphur, Scott, Ky	6	Wilbur, Ulster, N. Y	160
White Sulphur, Delaware, Ohio	39	Wilbur, Douglas, Oreg	12
White Sulphur Springs, Jefferson, Ark	12	Wilcox, Elk, Pa	490
		Wilcox Wharf, Charles City, Va	74
White Sulphur Springs, Meriwether, Ga	20	Wildbrier, Chester, Pa	56
		Wild Cat, Carroll, Ind	40
White Sulphur Springs, Catahoula, La	25	Wild Cat, Riley, Kans	12
		Wild Cat, Lancaster, S. C	5
White Sulphur Springs,* Green-brier, W. Va	170	Wilderness, Spottsylvania, Va	45
		Wiley, Greene, Pa	18
Whitesville, Harris, Ga	43	Wiley's Cove, Searcy, Ark	6
Whitesville, Montgomery, Ind	58	Wiley Station, Darke, Ohio	20
Whitesville, Daviess, Ky	53	Wileysville, Steuben, N. Y	3
Whitesville, Andrew, Mo	100	Wilkesbarre,* (c. h.,) Luzerne, Pa.	2,900
Whitesville, Allegany, N. Y	95	Wilkesborough, (c. h.,) Wilkes, N. C.	120
Whitesville, (c. h.,) Columbus, N. C.	180	Wilkesville, Vinton, Ohio	100
Whitesville, Halifax, Va	8	Wilkins, Allegheny, Pa.*	560
White Swan, Charles Mix, Dak	12	Wilkinsburgh,* Allegheny, Pa	260
Whiteville, Marion, Ark	92	Wilkinson's Shop, Amelia, Va	12
Whiteville, Hardeman, Tenn	23	Wilkinsonville, Worcester, Mass	220
White Water, Pike, Ala	12	Wilkins' Run, Licking, Ohio	8
White Water, Fayette, Ga	5	Willamette Forks, Lane, Oreg	7
White Water, Wayne, Ind	62	Willard, Greene, Mo	38
Whitewater,* Walworth, Wis	2,000	Willard, Box Elder, Utah	70
White Water Falls, Winona, Minn.	16	Willard's Landing, Union, Ill	12
White Willow, Kendall, Ill	17	Willet, Cortland, N. Y	81
Whiting, Jackson, Kans	12	Willet, Indiana, Pa	30
Whiting, Washington, Me	46	Willet, Green, Wis	21
Whiting, Ocean, N. J	25	Willey, Preston, W. Va	20
Whiting, Addison, Vt	100	William Penn, Montgomery, Pa	12
Whitingham, Windham, Vt	39	Williams, Hamilton, Iowa	12
Whiting Station, Addison, Vt	110	Williams, Christian, Ky	25
Whitinsville, Worcester, Mass	840	Williams, Bay, Mich	12
Whitley C. H., Whitley, Ky	49	Williamsburgh, Jefferson, Fla	12
Whitley's Point, Moultrie, Ill	76	Williamsburgh, Wayne, Ind	240
Whitleyville, Jackson, Tenn	8	Williamsburgh, Wapello, Iowa	12

* Money-order office.

Williamsburgh, Franklin, Kans....	$68	Willow, Jo Daviess, Ill.............	$12
Williamsburgh, Piscataquis, Me ...	20	Willow Branch, Hancock, Ind.....	20
Williamsburgh, Dorchester, Md....	36	Willow Creek, Lee, Ill	55
Williamsburgh,* Hampshire, Mass.	480	Willow Creek, Blue Earth, Minn ..	8
Williamsburgh, Grand Traverse, Mich..........................	12	Willow Creek, Gallatin, Mont......	12
		Willow Dale, Ida, Iowa	12
Williamsburgh, (c. h.,) Covington, Miss	24	Willowdale, Chester, Pa...........	38
		Willow Grove, Kent, Del	65
Williamsburgh, Callaway, Mo	97	Willow Grove, Cumberland, N. J...	12
Williamsburgh,* Kings, N. Y	2,600	Willow Grove, Montgomery, Pa....	95
Williamsburgh, Iredell, N. C......	11	Willow Hill, Jasper, Ill............	66
Williamsburgh, Clermont, Ohio....	200	Willow Hole, Madison, Tex	12
Williamsburgh, Blair, Pa..........	380	Willow Island, Pleasants, W. Va...	58
Williamsburgh, (c. h.,) James City, Va..............................	400	Willow Shade, Metcalfe, Ky	16
		Willow Spring, Cook, Ill	58
Williamsburgh, Trempealeau, Wis.	12	Willow Spring, Russell, Va........	4
Williams Centre, Williams, Ohio...	91	Willow Springs, Douglas, Kans	12
Williamsfield, Ashtabula, Ohio.....	97	Willow Springs, Howell, Mo.......	12
Williams' Grove, Clearfield, Pa	12	Willow Springs, Jackson, Oreg	24
Williams' Mill, Roane, Tenn	3	Willow Springs, Columbia, Pa.....	26
Williamson, Wayne, N. Y..........	370	Willow Street, Lancaster, Pa......	68
Williamsport, (c. h.,) Warren, Ind..	380	Willow Tree, Greene, Pa	10
Williamsport,* Washington, Md ...	330	Willow Tree, Mason, W. Va.......	12
Williamsport, Pickaway, Ohio.....	100	Willow Wood, Lawrence, Ohio	8
Williamsport, (c. h.,) Lycoming, Pa.	3,800	Willsborough, Essex, N. Y	230
Williamsport, Maury, Tenn........	15	Will's Creek, Coshocton, Ohio.....	10
Williamsport, Grant, W. Va........	24	Willseyville, Tioga, N. Y..........	97
Williams' Store, Casey, Ky........	32	Willshire, Van Wert, Ohio	110
Williamston, (c. h.,) Martin, N. C ...	380	Will's Ridge, Floyd, Va...........	12
Williamston, Anderson, S. C	110	Wilmarth, Elk, Pa.................	18
Williamstown, Chickasaw, Iowa...	26	Wilmette, Cook, Ill	12
Williamstown, Jefferson, Kans.....	43	Wilmington, Walker, Ala	12
Williamstown, (c. h.,) Grant, Ky	250	Wilmington, Union, Ark	12
Williamstown,* Berkshire, Mass...	1,000	Wilmington,* Los Angeles, Cal	830
Williamstown, Ingham, Mich......	270	Wilmington,* New Castle, Del.....	2,500
Williamstown, Lewis, Mo	100	Wilmington,* Will, Ill	1,800
Williamstown, Camden N. J.......	130	Wilmington, Dearborn, Ind	54
Williamstown, Oswego, N. Y	420	Wilmington, Osage, Kans.........	24
Williamstown, Hancock, Ohio	52	Wilmington, Middlesex, Mass	64
Williamstown, Dauphin, Pa	110	Wilmington, Houston, Minn.......	62
Williamstown, Orange, Vt	290	Wilmington, Essex, N. Y·.........	46
Williamstown, Wood, W. Va.......	50	*Wilmington,* (c. h.,) New Hanover, N. C	3,200
Williamsville, Sangamon, Ill	250		
Williamsville, Cass, Mich..........	54	*Wilmington,* (c. h.,) Clinton, Ohio..	1,200
Williamsville, Richardson, Nebr ...	12	Wilmington, Windham, Vt........	420
Williamsville, Erie, N. Y	320	Wilmington, Fluvanna, Va........	25
Williamsville, Elk, Pa	5	Wilmore, Cambria, Pa	190
Williamsville, Windham, Vt.......	190	Wilmot, Noble, Ind	6
Williamsville, Bath, Va	6	Wilmot, Merrimack, N. H	65
Willimansett, Hampden, Mass	200	Wilmot, Stark, Ohio..............	170
Willimantic,* Windham, Conn	1,800	Wilmot, Bradford, Pa.............	4
Willington, Tolland, Conn.........	80	Wilmot, Kenosha, Wis............	98
Willington, Abbeville, S. C	14	Wilmot Flat, Merrimack, N. H.....	110
Willink, Erie, N. Y...............	180	Wilna, Harford, Md...............	21
Willisburgh, Washington, Ky......	24	Wilna, Jefferson, N. Y............	12
Willis Station, Fayette, Tenn......	12	Wilseyville, Defiance, Ohio.......	20
Williston, Erie, N. Y	25	Wilson, Montgomery, Iowa........	12
Williston, Potter, Pa	12	Wilson, Adair, Mo	24
Williston, Barnwell, S. C	130	Wilson, Otoe, Nebr	5
Williston, Chittenden, Vt	340	Wilson, Niagara, N. Y	190
Willistown Inn, Chester, Pa	22	*Wilson,* (c. h.,) Wilson, N. C	1,100
Willmar, Kandiyohi, Minn	12	Wilson, Adams, Ohio.............	12
Willmathsville, Adair, Mo	30	Wilsonburgh, Richland, Ill........	14
Willoughby, Butler, Iowa	21	Wilsonburgh, Harrison, W. Va	96
Willoughby, Lake, Ohio...........	780	Wilson Creek, Tioga, N. Y........	5
Willoughby Lake, Orleans, Vt.....	36	Wilson Grove, Fayette, Iowa	20

* Money-order office.

WIN   WIN

Wilson's, Anderson, Tenn	$12
Wilson's, Crossing, Rockingham, N. H	54
Wilson's Cross Roads, Hempstead, Ark............................	12
Wilson's Depot, Dinwiddie, Va....	62
Wilson's Landing, Charles City, Va	92
Wilson's Mills, Oxford, Me	·7
Wilson's Mills, Johnston, N. C.....	12
Wilson's Mills, Cuyahoga, Ohio....	22
Wilson's Mills, Venango, Pa.......	6
Wilson's Store, Stokes, N. C.......	9
Wilsonville, Shelby, Ala	120
Wilsonville, Windham, Conn......	65
Wilsonville, Spencer, Ky..........	34
Wilsonville, Highland, Va	5
Wilton, Pike, Ark	23
Wilton, Fairfield, Conn	250
Wilton, Franklin, Me	430
Wilton,* (c. h.,) Waseca, Minn	220
Wilton,* Hillsborough, N. H.......	670
Wilton, Saratoga, N. Y...........	62
Wilton, Granville, N. C	6
Wilton, Ellis, Tex	24
Wilton, Monroe, Wis..............	54
Wilton Junction,* Muscatine, Iowa	910
Winamac,* (c. h.,) Pulaski, Ind....	460
Winameg, Fulton, Ohio...........	25
Winchendon,* Worcester, Mass	2,000
Winchester,* (c. h.,) Scott, Ill......	770
Winchester,* (c. h.,) Randolph, Ind..	710
Winchester, Van Buren, Iowa	96
Winchester,* (c. h.,) Clarke, Ky.....	840
Winchester, Jefferson, Kans	40
Winchester, Middlesex, Mass	790
Winchester, Wayne, Miss	12
Winchester, Clarke, Mo...........	100
Winchester, Cheshire, N. H	610
Winchester, Union, N. C	6
Winchester, Guernsey, Ohio.......	72
Winchester,* (c. h.,) Franklin, Tenn.	630
Winchester, Fayette, Tex	130
Winchester,* (c. h.,) Frederick, Va..	2,600
Winchester, Winnebago, Wis.....	110
Winchester Centre, Litchfield, Conn	110
Windermere, Tolland, Conn	170
Windfall, Tipton, Ind	190
Wind Gap, Northampton, Pa	75
Windham, Windham, Conn........	230
Windham, Johnson, Iowa	49
Windham, Cumberland, Me	120
Windham, Rockingham, N. H......	68
Windham, Portage, Ohio........	290
Windham, Bradford, Pa........	57
Windham, Windham, Vt	82
Windham Centre, Greene, N. Y ...	330
Windham Centre, Bradford, Pa	28
Windham Depot, Rockingham, N. H	100
Windham Station, Portage, Ohio..	81
Windham Summit, Bradford, Pa...	4
Wind Ridge, Greene, Pa...........	80
Windsor, Sonoma, Cal.............	140
Windsor, Hartford, Conn..........	380
Windsor, Shelby, Ill..............	410
Windsor, Randolph, Ind...........	6
Windsor, Ottawa, Kans ....|	12

Windsor, Kennebec, Me	$61
Windsor, Berkshire, Mass..........	50
Windsor, Eaton, Mich.............	36
Windsor, Henry, Mo	260
Windsor, Mercer, N. J.............	64
Windsor, Broome, N. Y......	230
Windsor, (c. h.,) Bertie, N. C	270
Windsor, Ashtabula, Ohio	120
Windsor, York, Pa.................	18
Windsor, Barnwell, S. C	47
Windsor,* Windsor, Vt.............	1,400
Windsor, Dane, Wis...............	35
Windsor Castle, Berks, Pa	13
Windsor Locks,* Hartford, Conn...	900
Windsor Station, Isle of Wight, Va.	67
Windsorville, Hartford, Conn.....	74
Winesburgh, Holmes, Ohio	100
Winfield, Columbia, Ga	6
Winfield, Du Page, Ill.............	32
Winfield, Luke, Ind....	26
Winfield, Henry, Iowa.............	92
Winfield, (c. h.,) Cowley, Kans......	12
Winfield, (c. h.,) Winn, La..........	21
Winfield, Carroll, Md.............	28
Winfield, Ingham, Mich..........	27
Winfield, Herkimer, N. Y	65
Winfield, Tuscarawas, Ohio........	45
Winfield, Union, Pa.........	96
Winfield, Scott, Tenn.............	3
Winfield, (c. h.,) Putnam, W. Va	98
Wingos Station, Graves, Ky........	28
Wing's Station, Dutchess, N. Y....	180
Winhall, Bennington, Vt	12
Winn, Penobscot, Me.............	160
Winn, Isabella, Mich.............	6
Winnebago, Dakota, Nebr	12
Winnebago Agency, Blue Earth, Minn...........................	55
Winnebago City,* Faribault, Minn.	400
Winnebago Depot, Winnebago, Ill.	370
Winnebago Valley, Houston, Minn.	28
Winneconne, Winnebago, Wis.....	370
Winnegance, Sagadahoc, Me.......	62
Winnemucca, Humboldt, Nev......	300
Winnetka, Cook, Ill	60
Winnipauk, Fairfield, Conn.......	250
Winnsborough, (c. h.,) Franklin, La.	25
Winnsborough, (c. h.,) Fairfield, S. C.	850
Winnton, Gonzales, Tex	12
Winona, Henry, Iowa......	12
Winona, Trimble, Ky	16
Winona,* (c. h.,) Winona, Minn	2,800
Winona, Carroll, Miss.............	580
Winona, Pitt, N. C	26
Winona, Columbiana, Ohio........	120
Winooski, Sheboygan, Wis	180
Winooski Falls, Chittenden, Vt	850
Winslow, Stephenson, Ill	130
Winslow, Pike, Ind......	56
Winslow, Kennebec, Me	97
Winslow, De Kalb, Mo...........	12
Winslow, Camden, N. J	170
Winspear, Erie, N. Y.............	17
Winsted,* Litchfield, Conn........	970
Winsted Lake, McLeod, Minn.....	10
Winter Harbor, Hancock, Me ......|	41

* Money-order office.

WOL   WOO

Winterpock, Chesterfield, Va	$56	Wolf Hill, Albany, N. Y	$12
Winterport,* Waldo, Me	800	Wolf Island, Mississippi, Mo	16
Winterroud, Shelby, Ind	31	Wolf Lake, Noble, Ind	60
Winterrowd, Effingham, Ill	12	Wolf Run, Lycoming, Pa	19
Winterset,* (c. h.,) Madison, Iowa	1,300	Wolf's Store, Centre, Pa	28
Winter's Station, Sandusky, Ohio	52	Wolf Summit, Harrison, W. Va	20
Wintersville, Decatur, Ind	27	Wolfsville, Frederick, Md	34
Wintersville, Sullivan, Mo	59	Wolfsville, Union, N. C	5
Wintersville, Jefferson, Ohio	63	Wolf Trap, Halifax, Va	17
Wintersville, Berks, Pa	18	Womelsdorf,* Berks, Pa	390
Winterville, Oglethorpe, Ga	32	Wonewoc, Juneau, Wis	110
Winthrop, Middlesex, Conn	12	Wood, Orange, N. Y	12
Winthrop, Buchanan, Iowa	420	Wood, Wood, Wis	14
Winthrop, Kennebec, Me	800	Woodbank, Marion, Ind	12
Winthrop, Suffolk, Mass	49	Woodberry, Baltimore, Md	210
Winthrop, Buchanan, Mo	62	Woodbine, Harrison, Iowa	200
Winton, (c. h.,) Hertford, N. C	320	Woodbine, Carroll, Md	51
Winton Place, Hamilton, Ohio	12	Woodbourne, Sullivan, N. Y	83
Wiota, Isabella, Mich	18	Woodbridge, San Joaquin, Cal	120
Wiota, La Fayette, Wis	78	Woodbridge, Middlesex, N. J	440
Wiretown, Ocean, N. J	59	Woodburn, Macoupin, Ill	120
Wirt, Jefferson, Ind	42	Woodburn, Allen, Ind	31
Wirt C. H., Wirt, W. Va	150	Woodburn, Warren, Ky	130
Wirt Centre, Allegany, N. Y	31	Woodbury, Litchfield, Conn	490
Wirtonia, Cherokee, Kans	100	Woodbury, Meriwether, Ga	25
Wiscasset,* (c. h.,) Lincoln, Me	840	Woodbury, Cumberland, Ill	86
Wiscoy, Winona, Minn	11	Woodbury, Hancock, Ind	16
Wiscoy, Allegany, N. Y	110	Woodbury, Butler, Ky	46
Wisdom's Store, Harris, Ga	8	Woodbury, Washington, Minn	12
Wise C. H., Wise, Va	12	Woodbury, (c. h.,) Gloucester, N. J	640
Wiseville, Accomack, Va	25	Woodbury, Queens, N. Y	15
Wistar, Clinton, Pa	43	Woodbury, Wood, Ohio	51
Withamsville, Clermont, Ohio	65	Woodbury, Bedford, Pa	150
Witherup's, Venango, Pa	180	Woodbury, (c. h.,) Cannon, Tenn	140
Witoka, Winona, Minn	40	Woodbury, Washington, Vt	28
Witt, Montgomery, Ill	12	Woodcock, Crawford, Pa	170
Wittenberg, Alexander, N. C	1	Woodensburgh, Baltimore, Md	49
Wittenberg, Somerset, Pa	28	Woodford, Bennington, Vt	28
Wittenburgh, Perry, Mo	99	Woodford, Barbour, W. Va	12
Witten's, Monroe, Ohio	12	Woodford's, Alpine, Cal	35
Wittman, Talbot, Md	12	Woodford's, Cumberland, Me	12
Wittsburgh, (c. h.,) Cross, Ark	83	Wood Grove, Morgan, Ohio	19
Witt's Foundry, Jefferson, Tenn	12	Woodhaven, Queens, N. Y	120
Woburn, Bond, Ill	20	Woodhull, Henry, Ill	620
Woburn,* Middlesex, Mass	1,600	Woodhull, Steuben, N. Y	280
Wolcott, New Haven, Conn	13	Woodhull, Fond du Lac, Wis	14
Wolcott, White, Ind	85	Woodington, Darke, Ohio	57
Wolcott, Scott, Iowa	250	Wood Lake, Montcalm, Mich	31
Wolcott,* Wayne, N. Y	580	Woodland,* Yolo, Cal	630
Wolcott, Lamoille, Vt	170	Woodland, St. Joseph, Ind	6
Wolcottsville, Niagara, N. Y	60	Woodland, East Feliciana, La	12
Wolcottville,* Litchfield, Conn	920	Woodland, Barry, Mich	31
Wolcottville, La Grange, Ind	150	Woodland, Wabashaw, Minn	15
Wolfborough, Carroll, N. H	700	Woodland, Ulster, N. Y	54
Wolfborough Centre, Carroll, N. H.	12	Woodland, Northampton, N. C	12
Wolf Branch, Coffee, Ala	12	Woodland, Union, Ohio	21
Wolf Creek, Pike, Ark	12	Woodland, Clearfield, Pa	46
Wolf Creek, Tama, Iowa	25	Woodland, Robertson, Tex	6
Wolf Creek, Meade, Ky	56	Woodland, Dodge, Wis	84
Wolf Creek, Wright, Mo	4	Woodland Mills, Obion, Tenn	12
Wolf Creek, Cherokee, N. C	11	Woodlands, Marshall, W. Va	44
Wolf Creek, Mercer, Pa	62	Woodlawn, Ouachita, Ark	12
Wolf Creek, Scott, Tenn	12	Woodlawn, Cecil, Md	50
Wolf Creek, Monroe, W. Va	5	Woodlawn, Monroe, Mo	52
Wolfdale, Woodbury, Iowa	45	Wood Lawn, Westchester, N. Y	62
Wolf Glade, Carroll, Va	20	Woodlawn, Gaston, N. C	10

Woodlawn, Montgomery, Tenn	$15	Woodward's Hollow, Erie, N. Y	$17
Wood Lawn. Carroll. Va	12	Woodworth, Kenosha, Wis	69
Woodman, Grant, Wis	210	Woodyards, Athens, Ohio	27
Woodmansie, Burlington, N. J	8	Wool, Pope, Ill	24
Wood River, Hall, Nebr	22	Wooldridge's Store, Christian, Ky	8
Wood River, Burnett, Wis	19	Woolfolk, Orange, Va	21
Woodrow, Washington, Pa	4	Woollam, Gasconade, Mo	22
Woodruff's, Spartanburgh, S. C	22	Woolstock, Wright, Iowa	9
Woods, Panola, Tex	27	Woolwich, Sagadahoc, Me	160
Woodsborough, Frederick, Md	110	Woonsocket Falls,* Providence,	
Wood's Corners, Ionia, Mich	57	R. I	2,800
Wood's Cross Roads, Gloucester, Va.	12	Wooster, Kosciusko, Ind	42
Woodsdale, Person, N. C	23	Wooster, Jefferson, Iowa	47
Wood's Falls, Clinton, N. Y	56	Wooster,* (c. h.,) Wayne, Ohio	2,400
Woodsfield,* (c. h.,) Monroe, Ohio	360	Wooster Summit, Wayne, Ohio	38
Wood's Hill, Roane, Tenn	12	Woostertown, Scott, Ind	54
Wood's Hole, Barnstable, Mass	250	Woosung, Ogle, Ill	99
Woodside, San Mateo, Cal	67	Wootten, Lee, Ga	130
Woodside, Kent, Del	12	Worcester,* (c. h.,) Worcester, Mass.	4,000
Woodside, Sangamon, Ill	25	Worcester, Otsego, N. Y	260
Woodside, Queens, N. Y	43	Worcester, Montgomery, Pa	30
Woodside, St. Croix, Wis	84	Worcester, Washington, Vt	110
Wood's Mills, St. Francois, Mo	12	Worley Furnace, Dickson, Tenn	12
Woodson, Morgan, Ill	57	Worth, Boone, Iowa	22
Woodsonville, Hart, Ky	240	Worth, Tuscola, Mich	160
Wood's Run, Allegheny, Pa	320	Worth, Winona, Minn	16
Wood's Station, Butler, Ohio	35	Worth, Mercer, Pa	150
Woodstock, Tuscaloosa, Ala	6	Worth Centre, Jefferson, N. Y	12
Woodstock, Windham, Conn	150	Worthington, Greene, Ind	400
Woodstock, Cherokee, Ga	55	Worthington, Dubuque, Iowa	170
Woodstock,* (c. h.,) McHenry, Ill	1,300	Worthington, Jefferson, Ky	12
Woodstock, Oxford, Me	16	Worthington, Hampshire, Mass	190
Woodstock, Howard, Md	120	Worthington, Franklin, Ohio	230
Woodstock, Lenawee, Mich	10	Worthington, Armstrong, Pa	130
Woodstock, Grafton, N. H	57	Worthington, Marion, W. Va	25
Woodstock, Ulster, N. Y	79	Worthville, Butts, Ga	10
Woodstock, Champaign, Ohio	160	Worthville, Carroll, Ky	16
Woodstock,* (c. h.,) Windsor, Vt	1,300	Worthville, Jefferson, N. Y	44
Woodstock,* (c. h.,) Shenandoah, Va.	430	Worthville, Jefferson, Pa	29
Woodstock, Richland, Wis	26	Wrentham, Norfolk, Mass	400
Woodstock Valley, Windham, Conn.	59	Wright, Greene, Ind	18
Woodstown, Salem, N. J	520	Wright City, Warren, Mo	200
Woodsville, Grafton, N. H	190	Wright's Bluff, Clarendon, S. C	62
Woodsville, Mercer, N. J	16	Wrightsborough, Gonzales, Tex	12
Woodview, Morrow, Ohio	34	Wright's Corners, Dearborn, Ind	30
Woodville, Jackson, Ala	12	Wright's Corners, Niagara, N. Y	43
Woodville, Litchfield, Conn	33	Wright's Dale, Lancaster, Pa	18
Woodville, Greene, Ga	15	Wright's Ferry, Crawford, Wis	6
Woodville, Adams, Ill	36	Wrightstown, Burlington, N. J	88
Woodville, Winneshiek, Iowa	79	Wrightstown, Bucks, Pa	100
Woodville, McCracken, Ky	94	Wrightstown, Brown, Wis	210
Woodville, Jackson, La	24	Wrightsville, (c. h.,) Johnson, Ga	23
Woodville, Frederick, Md	24	Wrightsville, York, Pa	370
Woodville, Penobscot, Me	10	Wrightsville, Jackson, Wis	12
Woodville, Middlesex, Mass	77	Wurtemburgh, Lawrence, Pa	35
Woodville,* (c. h.,) Wilkinson, Miss	600	Wurtsborough, Sullivan, N. Y	190
Woodville, Macon, Mo	23	Wyaconda, Scotland, Mo	14
Woodville, Jefferson, N. Y	180	Wyalusing, Bradford, Pa	150
Woodville, Perquimons, N. C	30	Wyalusing, Grant, Wis	26
Woodville, Sandusky, Ohio	140	Wyandot, Wyandot, Ohio	36
Woodville, Allegheny, Pa	40	Wyandotte, Tippecanoe, Ind	12
Woodville, Washington, R. I	120	Wyandotte,* (c. h.,) Wyandotte,	
Woodville, Haywood, Tenn	37	Kans	2,300
Woodville, (c. h.,) Tyler, Tex	38	Wyandotte, Wayne, Mich	480
Woodville, Rappahanock, Va	83	Wyanet, Bureau, Ill	560
Woodward, Centre, Pa	64	Wyatt's Store, Mariposa, Cal	3

* Money-order office.

YAT   YOR

Office	$
Wyattville, Winona, Minn	$7
Wyckoff, Bergen, N. J	12
Wye Mills, Talbot, Md	54
Wykertown, Sussex, N. J	3
Wylliesburgh, Charlotte, Va	47
Wynant, Shelby, Ohio	98
Wyantskill, Rensselaer, N. Y	46
Wynn, Franklin, Ind	19
Wyocena, Columbia, Wis	180
Wyoming, Kent, Del	230
Wyoming,* Stark, Ill	240
Wyoming,* Jones, Iowa	310
Wyoming, Marshall, Kans	10
Wyoming, Bath, Ky	20
Wyoming, Chisago, Minn	120
Wyoming, Otoe, Nebr	46
Wyoming, Wyoming, N. Y	300
Wyoming, Luzerne, Pa	350
Wyoming, Washington, R. I	200
Wyoming, Iowa, Wis	42
Wyoming, Albany, Wyo	12
Wysox, Bradford, Pa	68
Wythe Depot, Shelby, Tenn	12
Wytheville, (c. h.,) Wythe, Va	1,000

X.

Office	$
Xenia, Clay, Ill	500
Xenia, Miami, Ind	110
Xenia, Dallas, Iowa	50
Xenia, Bourbon, Kans	120
Xenia, Nodaway, Mo	23
Xenia, Sarpy, Nebr	12
*Xenia,** (c. h.,) Greene, Ohio	2,800
Xenia, York, Pa	12

Y.

Office	$
Yadkin College, Davidson, N. C	25
Yadkinville, (c. h.,) Yadkin, N. C	38
Yakima, Yakima, Wash	120
Yale, Jasper, Ill	27
Yalesville, New Haven, Conn	160
Yancy, Phelps, Mo	12
Yanceyville, (c. h.,) Caswell, N. C	100
Yankee Hill, Butte, Cal	20
Yankee Hollow, Jo Daviess, Ill	14
Yankee Jim's, Placer, Cal	38
Yankee Ridge, Coshocton, Ohio	1,600
Yankee Settlement, Clayton, Iowa	60
Yankee Spring, Barry, Mich	21
Yankeetown, Warrick, Ind	12
Yankeetown, Crawford, Wis	17
YANKTON,* (c. h.,) Yankton, Dak	1,200
Yantic, New London, Conn	180
Yaphank, Suffolk, N. Y	170
Yarborough, Floyd, Ga	14
Yardleyville, Bucks, Pa	240
Yardville, Mercer, N. J	88
Yarmouth,* Cumberland, Me	620
Yarmouth, Barnstable, Mass	120
Yarmouth Port,* Barnstable, Mass	560
Yates, Orleans, N. Y	120
Yates City, Knox, Ill	400
Yatesville, Morgan, Ill	12
Yatesville, Calhoun, Iowa	20

Office	$
Yatesville, Schuylkill, Pa	$82
Yatesville, Lunenburgh, Va	15
Yatton, Washington, Iowa	36
Yazoo, Harrison, Iowa	16
*Yazoo City,** (c. h.,) Yazoo, Miss	1,000
Yeater's Mills, Doddridge, W. Va	7
Yellow Bluff, Duval, Fla	3
Yellow Branch, Campbell, Va	14
Yellow Bud, Ross, Ohio	27
Yellow Creek, Stephenson, Ill	22
Yellow Creek, Josh Bell, Ky	12
Yellow Creek, Bedford, Pa	32
Yellow Creek, Dickson, Tenn	12
Yellow House, Berks, Pa	21
Yellow Medicine, Redwood, Minn	24
Yellow River, Gwinnett, Ga	36
Yellow Spring, Blair, Pa	100
Yellow Spring, Hampshire, W.Va	6
Yellow Springs,* Greene, Ohio	1,000
Yellow Stone, La Fayette, Wis	9
Yellow Store, Hawkins, Tenn	12
Yellville, (c. h.,) Marion, Ark	140
Yelm, Thurston, Wash	7
Yelverton, Hardin, Ohio	47
Yelvington, Daviess, Ky	12
Yemassee, Beaufort, S. C	12
Yew, Wayne, Mich	23
Yocony, Itawamba, Miss	6
Yocumtown, York, Pa	41
Yocumville, Klamath, Cal	12
Yohoghany, Westmoreland, Pa	180
Yokum Station, Lee, Va	4
Yolo, (c. h.,) Yolo, Cal	130
Yoncalla, Douglas, Oreg	16
Yongesborough, Lee, Ala	12
Yonguesville, Fairfield, S. C	78
Yonkers,* Westchester, N. Y	2,800
York, Walker, Ala	6
York, Clark, Ill	64
York, Delaware, Iowa	63
York, York, Me	270
York, Washtenaw, Mich	89
York, (c. h.,) York, Nebr	12
York, Livingston, N. Y	200
York, Union, Ohio	24
*York,** (c. h.,) York, Pa	2,600
York, Dane, Wis	18
York Centre, Iowa, Iowa	5
York Centre, Steuben, Ind	24
York Collegiate Institute, Alexander, N. C	7
York Furnace, York, Pa	33
York Neck, Adams, Ill	18
York Prairie, Cedar, Iowa	12
Yorkshire, Cattaraugus, N. Y	100
Yorkshire Centre, Cattaraugus, N.Y	110
York Station, Sumter, Ala	12
York Sulphur Springs, Adams, Pa	360
Yorktown, Bureau, Ill	77
Yorktown, Delaware, Ind	110
Yorktown, Salem, N. J	57
Yorktown, Westchester, N. Y	46
Yorktown, De Witt, Tex	140
Yorktown, (c. h.,) York, Va	220
Yorkville, Mendocino, Cal	12
Yorkville, (c. h.,) Kendall, Ill	400

* Money-order office.

15 P O

YUC   ZWI

Yorkville, Dearborn, Ind	$32	**Z.**	
Yorkville, Kalamazoo, Mich	22		
Yorkville, Bladen, N. C	2	Zackville, Wirt, W. Va	$7
Yorkville, Jefferson, Ohio	68	Zaleski, Vinton, Ohio	290
Yorkville, (c. h.,) York, S. C	800	Zanesfield, Logan, Ohio	210
Yorkville, Gibson, Tenn	65	Zanesville, Montgomery, Ill	71
Yorkville, Racine, Wis	43	Zanesville, Wells, Ind	69
Yortysville, Washington, Pa	10	*Zanesville,* (c. h.,) Muskingum, Ohio	3,200
Yosemite, Mariposa, Cal	12	Zanzenburgh, Kerr, Tex	12
You Bet, Nevada, Cal	64	*Zebulon, (c. h.,) Pike, Ga*	82
Yough, Boone, Iowa	11	Zeeland, Ottawa, Mich	79
Young America,* Warren, Ill	570	Zeiglersville, Montgomery, Pa	62
Young America, Carver, Minn	110	Zelienople, Butler, Pa	150
Young America, Washington, Wis	69	Zem Zem, Lake, Cal	12
Young Hickory, Steuben, N. Y	8	Zena, Polk, Oreg	12
Young Hickory, Muskingum, Ohio	21	Zenas, Jennings, Ind	36
Young Hickory, Washington, Wis	32	Zeno, Muskingum, Ohio	28
Young's Creek, Orange, Ind	8	Zeno, York, S. C	7
Young's Creek, Whitley, Ky	12	Zif, Wayne, Ill	20
Young's Creek, Audrian, Mo	29	Zig, Adair, Mo	12
Young's Cross Roads, Granville, N. C.	12	Zilwaukee, Saginaw, Mich	150
Young's Mills, Guilford, N. C	12	Zimmerman, Greene, Ohio	90
Young's Mills, Monroe, Ohio	12	Zinsburgh, Madison, Ind	6
Young's Settlement, Bastrop, Tex	16	Zion, Henderson, Ky	4
Young's Store, Franklin, Va	2	Zion, Cecil, Md	98
Youngstown, Vigo, Ind	34	Zion, Yadkin, N. C	6
Youngstown, Niagara, N. Y	390	Zion, Centre, Pa	61
Youngstown,* Mahoning, Ohio	2,400	Zion's, Stearns, Minn	9
Youngstown, Westmoreland, Pa	130	Zion's Grove, Schuylkill, Pa	12
Youngsville, Sullivan, N. Y	87	Zion's Mills, Lee, Va	6
Youngsville, Adams, Ohio	34	Zionsville, Boone, Ind	370
Youngsville, Warren, Pa	290	Zoar, Cedar, Iowa	19
Young Womanstown, Clinton, Pa	110	Zoar, Franklin, Mass	'120
Yountville, Napa, Cal	37	Zoar, Tuscarawas, Ohio	59
Ypsilanti, (c. h.,) Washtenaw, Mich.	2,700	Zoar Station, Tuscarawas, Ohio	27
Yreka, (c. h.,) Siskiyou, Cal	820	Zollarsville, Washington, Pa	63
Yuba, Grand Traverse, Mich	28	Zumbro Falls, Wabashaw, Minn	12
Yuba, Richland, Wis	16	Zumbrota, Goodhue, Minn	290
Yuba City, (c. h.,) Sutter, Cal	280	Zuni Station, Isle of Wight, Va	93
Yucatan, Houston, Minn	16	Zwingle, Dubuque, Iowa	28

* Money-order office.

POST OFFICES IN THE UNITED STATES.

SEPTEMBER 1, 1870.

ARRANGED BY STATES AND COUNTIES.

ALABAMA.

AUTAUGA COUNTY.

Autaugaville,   Kingston,
Independence,   *Prattville*, (c. h.)

BAKER COUNTY.

Chesnut Creek, (c. h.,)   Mullins.
Maplesville,

BALDWIN COUNTY.

Bay Minette,   Tensaw.
Stockton,

BARBOUR COUNTY.

Clayton, (c. h.,)   Kings,
Clio,   Louisville,
Cowikee,   Mount Andrew,
Eufaula,*   Newtopia,
Fort Browder,   White Oak Springs,
Glennville,   White Pond.

BIBB COUNTY.

Brierfield,   Randolph,
Centreville, (c. h.,)   Scottsville.
Mars,

BLOUNT COUNTY.

Balm,   Murphree's Valley,
Blount Springs,   Ogee,
Blountsville, (c. h.,)   Summit,
Brooksville,   Thacker's Creek,
Chepultepec,   Village Springs,
Little Warrior,   Walnut Grove.
Mount Alvis,

BULLOCK COUNTY.

Aberfoil,   Midway,
Arbor Vitæ,   Mount Hilliard,
Bruceville,   Perote,
Enon,   Suspension,
Fitzpatrick's,   Thomas Station,
Line Creek,   *Union Springs*, (c. h.)

BUTLER COUNTY.

Butler Springs,   Manningham,
Emma,   Oaky Streak,
Garland,   Pigeon Creek,
Georgiana,   South Butler.
Greenville,* (c. h.;)

CALHOUN COUNTY.

Blue Mountain,   Mount Polk,
Corn Grove,   Oxford,
Cross Plains,   Peak's Hill,
Jacksonville, (c. h.,)   Wehoga,
Ladiga,   White Plains.
Morrisville,

CHAMBERS COUNTY.

Chambers C. H.,*   Hickory Flat,
Cusseta,   Milltown,
Fredonia.   Osanippa.

CHEROKEE COUNTY.

Blue Pond,   Kirk's Grove,
Broomtown,   Leesburgh,
Cedar Bluff,   Little River,
Cedar Springs,   Mill Ford,
Centre, (c. h.,)   Pleasant Gap,
Coloma,   Ringgold,
Gaylesville,   Sand Rock,
Howel's ✕ Roads,   Spring Garden.

CHOCTAW COUNTY.

Bladen Springs,   Mount Sterling,
Butler, (c. h.,)   Pushmataha.
Desotoville,

CLARKE COUNTY.

Choctaw Bluff,   Gosport,
Choctaw Corner,   *Grove Hill*, (c. h.,)
Gainestown,   Suggsville.

* Money-order office.

CLAY COUNTY.

Ashland, (*c. h.*,)
Bluff Spring,
Coleta,
Copper Mines,
Hillabee,
Lineville,
Mellow Valley,
Pinckneyville.

CLEBURNE COUNTY.

Chulafinnee,
Edwardsville, (*c. h.*,)
Kemp's Creek,
Oakfuskee,
Oak Level,
Rosewood.

COFFEE COUNTY.

Elba, (*c. h.*,)
Victoria,
Wolf Branch.

COLBERT COUNTY.

Barton,
Cherokee,
Dickson,
Pride's Station,
Tuscumbia,* (*c. h.*)

CONECUH COUNTY.

Belleville,
Brooklyn,
Castleberry,
Evergreen, (*c. h.*,)
Gravella,
Jackson Store,
Jamestown,
Jayville,
Sparta.

COOSA COUNTY.

Central Institute,
Equality,
Fig Grove,
Hanover,
Marble Valley,
Mount Olive,
Rockford, (*c. h.*,)
Traveller's Rest,
Weogufka.

COVINGTON COUNTY.

Cottle's Mills,
Reed Level,
Rose Hill,
Shirley.

CRENSHAW COUNTY.

Argus,
Bullock,
Honorville,
Leon,
Little Oak,
New Providence,
Rutledge, (*c. h.*,)
Sal Soda.

DALE COUNTY.

Barnes' × Roads,
Beaver Creek,
Clopton,
Daleville,
Haw Ridge,
High Bluff,
Newton, (*c. h.*,)
Ozark,
Potter's Mills,
Rocky Head,
Skipperville,
Westville.

DALLAS COUNTY.

Bellevue,
Burnsville,
Cahaba,
Cambridge,
Elm Bluff,
Forts,
Hardy,
Liberty Hill,

DALLAS COUNTY—Continued.

Orange Grove,
Orrville,
Plantersville,
Pleasant Hill,
Portland,
Richmond,
Selma,* (*c. h.*,)
Summerfield,
White Bluff.

DE KALB COUNTY.

Brandon,
Camp Station,
Crossville,
Fort Payne,
Lebanon, (*c. h.*,)
Portersville,
Rawlingsville,
Valley Head.

ELMORE COUNTY.

Channahatchie,
Hatchsophka,
Syke's Mills,
Wetumpka,* (*c. h.*)

ESCAMBIA COUNTY.

Brewton,
Canoe Station,
Lewis' Station,
Pollard, (*c. h.*)

ETOWAH COUNTY.

Atalla,*
Aurora,
Ball Play,
Bennettsville,
Collinsville,
Cove Creek,
Gadsden, (*c. h.*,)
Greenwood,
Rees Mill,
Thornton's Bluff.

FAYETTE COUNTY.

Dublin,
Eagle Mills,
Fayette C. H.,
Handy,
New River,
Newtonville,
Pilgrim's Rest,
Sheffield.

FRANKLIN COUNTY.

Blue Lick,
Burleson,
Chickasaw,
Frankfort,
Leighton,
Nelsonville,
Newburgh,
Pleasant Site,
Russellville, (*c. h.*,)
South Florence,
Spruce Pine,
Waco.

GENEVA COUNTY.

Big Creek,
Geneva, (*c. h.*,)
High Falls,

GREENE COUNTY.

Clinton,
*Eutaw** (*c. h.*)
Knoxville,
Mount Hebron.
Pleasant Ridge,
Union.

HALE COUNTY.

Five Mile,
Greensborough,*(*c.h.*,)
Havanna,
Hollow Square,
Macon Station,
Newbern.

* Money-order office.

HENRY COUNTY.

Abbeville, (c. h.,)
Columbia,
Franklin,
Gordon,
Lawrenceville,
Lynnville.

JACKSON COUNTY.

Bass Station,
Bellefonte,
Big Coon,
Boyd's Switch,
Bridgeport,
Dodsonville,
Dry Cove,
Estill's Fork,
Fackler,
Gray's Chapel,
Larkin's Fork,
Larkinsville,
Long Island,
Paint Rock,
Park's Store,
Princeton,
Scottsborough, (c. h.,)
Stevenson,
Trenton,
Woodville.

JEFFERSON COUNTY.

Argo,
Cedar Grove,
Chester,
Elyton, (c. h.,)
Jonesborough,
Morrowville,
Mount Pinson,
Oak Ridge,
Oregon,
Rockville,
Waldrop's Mill.

LAUDERDALE COUNTY.

Centre Star,
Florence, (c. h.,)
Gravelly Spring,
Green Hill,
Rogersville,
Waterloo.

LAWRENCE COUNTY.

Avoca,
Concord,
Courtland,
Dry Creek,
Kinlock,
Landersville,
Moulton, (c. h.,)
Mountain Home,
Mount Hope,
Oakville,
Town Creek,
Wheeler Station.

LEE COUNTY.

Auburn,*
Loachapoka,
Mount Jefferson,
Opelika, (c. h.,)
Salem,
Smith's Station,
Yongesborough.

LIMESTONE COUNTY.

Athens, (c. h.,)*
Fort Hampton,
Gilbertsborough,
Greenbrier,
Harris Station,
Mooresville,
Mount Roszell.

LOWNDES COUNTY.

Benton,
Bragg's,
Calhoun,
Farmersville,
Fort Deposit,
Gilmer's,
Hayneville, (c. h.,)
Letohatchee,
Lowndesborough,
Manack,
Whitman.

MACON COUNTY.

Cowles' Station,
Notasulga,
Shorter's Depot,
Society Hill,
Tuskegee, (c. h.,)*

MADISON COUNTY.

Bell Factory,
Berkley,
Brownsborough,
Flint Factory,
Green Grove,
Gurleysville,
Haden's,
Hayes' Store,
Huntsville, (c. h.,)*
Madison Station,
Meridianville,
New Hope,
New Market,
Owen's × Roads,
Triana,
Whitesburgh.

MARENGO COUNTY.

Clay Hill,
Dayton,
Demopolis, (o. h.,)
Faunsdale,
Linden,
McKinley,
Shiloh.

MARION COUNTY.

Allen's Factory,
Chalk Bluff,
Gold Mine,
Haley's,
Ireland Hill,
Johnson's Mills,
Palo,
Pikeville, (c. h.,)
Thorn Hill.

MARSHALL COUNTY.

Claysville,
Cottonville,
Guntersville, (c. h.,)
Henrysville,
Hillian's Store,
Kennamer Cove,
Meltonsville,
Red Apple,
Red Hill,
Short Creek,
Southern,
Warrenton.

MOBILE COUNTY.

Chickasabogue,
Citronelle,
Manville,
Mobile, (c. h.,)*
Mount Vernon,
Whistler.

MONROE COUNTY.

Bell's Landing,
Burnt Corn,
Claiborne,
Dennard's Bluff,
Monroeville, (c. h.,)
Mount Pleasant,
Newton Academy.

MONTGOMERY COUNTY.

Dreyspring,
Hailsville,
Mathews,
MONTGOMERY,*(c.h.,)
Mount Meigs,
Pine Level,
Ponder's Mill,
Raif Branch,
Rainer,
Snowdoun,
Strata.

MORGAN COUNTY.

Apple Grove,
Basham's Gap,
Cedar Plains,
Danville,

* Money-order office.

MORGAN COUNTY—Continued.

Decatur,*	Somerville,* (c. h.,)
Flint River,	Trinity Station,
Folkville,	Valhermoso Springs.
Lacey's Spring,	

PERRY COUNTY.

Brush Creek,	Morgan Spring,
Grove Cottage,	Perryville,
Hamburgh,	Pine Tucky,
Ironville,	Radfordsville,
Jericho,	Uniontown.
Marion, (c. h.,)	

PICKENS COUNTY.

Andersonville,	Pickensville,
Antioch,	Pleasant Grove,
Bridgeville,	Providence,
Carrollton, (c. h.,)	Reform,
Memphis,	Sipsy Mills.
Palmetto,	

PIKE COUNTY.

China Grove,	New Providence,
Hallsville,	Olustee Creek,
Henderson,	Orion,
Linwood,	Troy,* (c. h.,)
Milo,	White Water.

RANDOLPH COUNTY.

Almond,	Louina,
Blake's Ferry,	Milner,
Carter's Store,	Roanoke,
Delta,	Rock Mills,
Fair Play,	Wedowee, (c. h.)
Lamar,	

RUSSELL COUNTY.

Crawford,	Seale's Station, (c. h.,)
Fort Mitchell,	Uchee,
Hatchechubbee,	Villula.
Hurtville,	

SAINT CLAIR COUNTY.

Ashville, (c. h.,)	Ferryville,
Beaver Valley,	Greensport,
Branchville,	Kelly's Creek,
Broken Arrow,	Mount Niles,
Cropwell,	Springville.

SANFORD COUNTY.

Andalusia,	Millport,
Beaverton,	Moscow,
Big Pond,	Vernon.
Detroit,	

SHELBY COUNTY.

Calera,	Columbiana, (c. h.,)

SHELBY COUNTY—Continued.

Hillsborough,	Shelby Springs,
Montevallo,	Wilsonville.
Shelby Iron Works,	

SUMTER COUNTY.

Bennett's Station,	Intercourse,
Coatopa,	Jones' Bluff,
Cuba Station,	Livingston, (c. h.,)
Fulton,	Sumterville,
Gainesville,	York Station.
Gaston,	

TALLADEGA COUNTY.

Alpine,	Mardisville,
Childersburgh,	Munford,
Easta Boga,	Silver Run,
Flat Rock,	Sylacauga,
Irona,	Talladega,* (c. h.,)
Kimulga,	Wewokaville.
Lincoln,	

TALLAPOOSA COUNTY.

Dadeville, (c. h.,)	Jones' X Roads,
Emuckfaw,	Meiton's Mill,
Fish Pond,	New Site,
Goldville,	Walnut Hill

TUSCALOOSA COUNTY.

Carthage,	North Port,
Cushing,	North River,
Fosters',	Oregonia,
Hickman's,	Romulus,
Jena,	Sipsey Turnpike,
Kennedale,	Trion,
McMath,	Tuscaloosa, (c. h.,)
New Lexington,	Woodstock.

WALKER COUNTY.

Arkadelphia,	Holly Grove,
Democrat,	Jasper, (c. h.,)
Eldridge,	Kansas,
Fairview,	Wilmington,
Garrison Point,	York.
Hanby's Mills,	

WASHINGTON COUNTY.

Deer Park,	Millry.
Escatawpa,	

WILCOX COUNTY.

Allenton,	Lower Peach Tree,
Burford's Landing,	Pine Hill,
Camden, (c. h.,)	Prairie Bluff,
Clifton,	Rehoboth.
Fatama,	

* Money-order office.

WINSTON COUNTY.

Clear Creek Falls, Jones' Chapel,
Houston, (c. h.,)

WINSTON COUNTY—Continued.

Larissa, Ryan Creek.
Littlesville,

ALASKA TERRITORY.

Fort Tongass, Fort Wrangel, Kodiak, *Sitka,* (c. h.,)

ARIZONA TERRITORY.

MOHAVE COUNTY.

Hardyville, *Mohave City,* (c. h.)

PAH UTE COUNTY.

Overton, *Saint Thomas,* (c. h.)
Saint Joseph,

PIMA COUNTY.

Apache Pass, Grant,
Florence, Maricopa Wells,

PIMA COUNTY—Continued.

Sasabi Flat, TUCSON, (c. h.)
Tubac,

YAVAPAI COUNTY.

McDowell, *Prescott,** (c. h.,)
Phœnix, Skull Valley,
Pima Village, Wickenburgh.

YUMA COUNTY.

Arizona City,* *La Paz,* (c. h.)
Ehrenberg,

ARKANSAS.

ARKANSAS COUNTY.

Arkansas Post, Pendleton,
Auburn, Preston Bluff,
Casscoe, Reeves' Landing,
Crockett's Bluff, Saint Charles,
De Witt, (c. h.,) South Bend,
Mount Adams, Swan Lake.

ASHLEY COUNTY.

Beech Creek, Nellie,
Fountain Hill, Pine Hill,
*Hamburgh,** (c. h.,) Poplar Bluff.
Long View,

BENTON COUNTY.

Bentonville, (c. h.,) La Rue,
Bloomington, Maysville,
Cross Hollow, Osage Mills,
Double Springs, Pea Ridge,
Hickory, Spavinaw,
Hico, Sugar Creek.

BOONE COUNTY.

Boone, *Harrison,* (c. h.)

BRADLEY COUNTY.

Adamsville, Moro Bay,
Bradley, Mount Elba,
Eagle Creek, Saint John,
Gravel Ridge, Vineyard,
Johnsville, *Warren,* (c. h.)
Lanark,

CALHOUN COUNTY.

Chambersville, Post Oak,
Hampton, (c. h.,) Summerville.

CARROLL COUNTY.

Berryville, Mountain Spring,
Carrollton, (c. h.,) Mount Pleasant,
Elm Wood, Osage,
Green Forest, Thompsonville.

CHICOT COUNTY.

Chicora, *Lake Village,* (c. h.,)
Eunice, Luna Landing,
Grand Lake, Sunny Side.

* Money-order office.

CLARK COUNTY.

Alpine,	Clear Spring,
Amity,	De Roche,
Antoine,	Point Cedar,
Arkadelphia, (c. h.,)	Rock Creek.

COLUMBIA COUNTY.

Atlanta,	Liddesdale,
Bell's Store,	*Magnolia,* (c. h.,)
Calhoun,	Palestine,
Dorcheat,	State Line,
Falcon,	Walker's.
Lamartine,	

CONWAY COUNTY.

Cadron,	Howard,
Cane Creek,	Lewisburgh,
El Paso,	Old Hickory,
Greenbrier,	*Springfield,* (c. h.)

CRAIGHEAD COUNTY.

Greensborough,	*Jonesborough* (c., h.)

CRAWFORD COUNTY.

Belmont,	The Narrows,
Lee's Creek,	*Van Buren,* (c. h.)
Spencer's Shop,	

CRITTENDEN COUNTY.

Blackfish,	Grayson,
Bledsoe,	*Marion,* (c. h.,)
Council Bend,	Mound City.
Crawfordsville,	

CROSS COUNTY.

Cold Water,	*Wittsburgh,* (c. h.)

DALLAS COUNTY.

Fairview,	Stover,
Holly Springs,	Tulip.
Princeton, (c. h.,)	

DESHA COUNTY.

Chester,	Prairie Landing,
Cypress Creek,	Prewitt's Ferry,
Knowlton's Landing,	Red Fork,
Napoleon, (c. h.,)	White River.

DREW COUNTY.

Bartholomew,	Lacey,
Branchville,	*Monticello,* (c. h.,)
Cut Off,	Relf's Bluff,
Florence,	Selma.
Green Mount,	

FRANKLIN COUNTY.

Cass,	Pleasant Hill,
Charleston,	Roseville,
Game Hill,	Sub Rosa.
Ozark, (c. h.,)	

FULTON COUNTY.

Bennett's Bayou,	Franklin,
Bennett's River,	*Pilot Hill,* (c. h.)

GRANT COUNTY.

Sandy Springs,	*Sheridan,* (c. h.)

GREENE COUNTY.

Big Creek,	Herndon,
Crowley,	Loyal Hill,
Gainesville, (c. h.,)	Walcott.

HEMPSTEAD COUNTY.

Clayton,	Spring Hill,
Columbus,	*Washington,* (c. h.,)
Fulton,	Wilson's × Roads.
Mineral Springs,	

HOT SPRING COUNTY.

Hot Springs,*	*Rockport,* (c. h.,)
Midway,	Whittington.
Reyburn,	

INDEPENDENCE COUNTY.

Batesville, (c. h.,)	Polk Bayou,
Buck Horn,	Sharp's Cross Roads,
Oil Trough,	Sulphur Rock.

IZARD COUNTY.

Blue Mountain,	Newburgh,
La Crosse,	Pineville,
Lunenburgh,	Riggsville,
Mill Creek,	Sylamore,
Mount Olive, (c. h.,)	Table Rock.

JACKSON COUNTY.

Elgin,	*Jacksonport,* (c .h.,)
Grand Glaze,	Kenyon.

JEFFERSON COUNTY.

Adamsburgh,	*Pine Bluff,* (c. h.,)
Byrd's Springs,	Plum Bayou,
Carson,	Randall,
Darysaw,	Red Bluff,
Garretson's Landing,	Reform,
Greenback,	Rob Roy,
Melton,	Victoria,
New Gascony,	White Sulphur
Oakville,	Springs.
Pastoria,	

* Money-order office.

JOHNSON COUNTY.

Calico,
Clarksville,* (c. h.,)
Ellsworth,

Patterson's Bluff,
Pittsburgh,
Shoal Creek.

LAFAYETTE COUNTY.

Lewisville, (c. h.,)
Randolph,

Rondo,
Walnut Hill.

LAWRENCE COUNTY.

Ash Flat,
Canton,
Clover Bend, (c. h.,)
Powhatan,
Reed's Creek,

Rhea,
Smithville,
Stranger's Home,
Walnut Ridge.

LITTLE RIVER COUNTY.

Peytonsville,
Richmond,

Rocky Comfort, (c. h.)

MADISON COUNTY.

Clifty,
Drake's Creek,
Hindsville,
Huntsville, (c. h.,)
Jupiter,

Little Spring,
Marble,
Saint Paul,
War Eagle.

MARION COUNTY.

Clear Creek,
Lead Hill,
Rolling Prairie,

Sherman, (c. h.,)
Whiteville,
Yellville.

MISSISSIPPI COUNTY.

Barfield,
Osceola, (c. h.,)

Pecan Point,
Shawnee Village.

MONROE COUNTY.

Brinkley,
Clarendon (c. h.,)
Cypress,
Duncan,

Indian Bay,
Moro,
Sylarsville.

MONTGOMERY COUNTY.

Black Springs,
Centreville,
Crystal Hill,

Harold,
Mount Ida, (c. h.)

NEWTON COUNTY.

Beech Woods,
Cave Creek,
Jasper, (c. h.,)

Marshall Prairie,
Mount Judea,
Mount Parthenon.

OUACHITA COUNTY.

Camden,* (c. h.,)
Caney,
Freco,

Liberty,
Luda,
Mount Moriah,

OUACHITA COUNTY—Continued.

Rose Hill,
Seminary,

Two Bayous,
Woodlawn.

PERRY COUNTY.

Casa,
Klingelhoeffer
Landing,

Oppello,
Perryville, (c. h.,)
Union City.

PHILLIPS COUNTY.

Askew,
Gillen's Landing,
Helena,* (c. h.,)
La Grange,
Marianna,
North Creek,

Old Town,
Oliver's Landing,
Phillips Bayou,
Planters,
Trenton.

PIKE COUNTY.

Brocktown,
Dora,
Huddleston,
Murfreesboro', (c. h.,)
Red Land,

Royston,
Star of the West,
Wilton,
Wolf Creek.

POINSETT COUNTY.

Harrisburgh, (c. h.)

POLK COUNTY.

Big Bend,
Big Fork,

Cove,
Dallas, (c. h.)

POPE COUNTY.

Dover, (c. h.,)
Galley Rock,
Georgetown,
Glass Village,

Lyman,
Moreland,
Norristown,
Russellville.

PRAIRIE COUNTY.

Austin,
Des Arc,
Devall's Bluff,* (c.h.,)

Hickory Plains,
Hicks' Station,
Prairie Centre.

PULASKI COUNTY.

Ashley Mills,
Eagle Landing,
LITTLE ROCK,*(c.h.,)
Maumelle,

North Point,
Pennington's Mills,
Reed's Landing.

RANDOLPH COUNTY.

Downey's Spring,
Elm Store,
Jayne's Store.

Pitman,
Pocahontas, (c. h.)

ST. FRANCIS COUNTY.

Calvert's,
Forest City,
L'Anguille,

Madison, (c. h.,)
Taylor's Creek.

* Money-order office.

SALINE COUNTY.

Benton, (c. h.,)
Cherry Grove,
Collegeville,
Owensville,
Prattsville,
Turin.

SCOTT COUNTY.

Black Jack,
Boles,
Booneville,
Chismville,
Magazine,
Nebraska,
Olio,
Parks,
Revilee,
Waldron, (c. h.)

SEARCY COUNTY.

Calf Creek,
Marshall, (c. h.,)
Point Peter.
Providence,
Wiley's Cove.

SEBASTIAN COUNTY.

Bloomer,
Chocoville,
Fort Smith,*
Greenwood, (c. h.,)
Hodge's Prairie,
James' Fork,
Jenny Lind,
Milor,
New Market,
Sugar Loaf.

SEVIER COUNTY.

Ben Lomond,
Centre Point,
Farribaville,
Locksburgh, (c. h.,)
Nelta Boc,
Paraclifta.

SHARP COUNTY.

Evening Shades,(c.h.,) Martin's Creek.

UNION COUNTY.

Champagnolle,   El Dorado, (c. h.,)

UNION COUNTY—Continued.

Hillsborough,
Lisbon,
Pigeon Hill,
Wilmington.

VAN BUREN COUNTY.

Bee Branch,
Clinton, (c. h.,)
Eglantine,
Kinderhook,
Liberty Springs,
Quitman.

WASHINGTON COUNTY.

Billingsly,
Boonsborough,
Cincinnati,
Elm Springs,
Evansville,
Ever Green.
Farmington,
Fayetteville,* (c. h.,)
Greenville,
Maguire's Store,
Prairie Grove,
Rhea's Mills,
Tranquilla,
Viney Grove,
West Fork.

WHITE COUNTY.

Centre Hill,
Cold Well,
Judson,
Negro Hill,
Rose Bud.
Searcy,* (c. h.,)
Stony Point,
West Point.

WOODRUFF COUNTY.

Augusta, (c. h.,)
Britton,
Cotton Plant,
De View.

YELL COUNTY.

Bluffton,
Chikalah,
Danville, (c. h.,)
Dardanelle,*
Delaware,
Dutche's Creek,
Onyx,
Petit Jean,
Rover,
Walnut Tree.

CALIFORNIA.

ALAMEDA COUNTY.

Alameda,
Alvarado,
Brooklyn,
Centreville,
Dougherty's Stat'n,
Harrisburgh,
Haywood,
Livermore,
Melita,
Midway,
Mission San José,
Mount Eden,
Oakland, *
Pleasanton,
San Leandro, (c. h.,)
San Lorenzo,
Washington Corners.

ALPINE COUNTY.

Bulliona,
Carey's Mills,
Markleeville, *
Monitor,
Silver Mountain, (c.h.,)
Woodford's.

AMADOR COUNTY.

Amador City,   Buena Vista,

AMADOR COUNTY—Continued.

Drytown,
Fiddletown,
Forest Home,
Ione Valley, *
Jackson,* (c. h.,)
Lancha Plana,
Pine Grove,
Sutter Creek,
Volcano.

BUTTE COUNTY.

Bangor,
Bidwell's Bar,
Brush Creek,
Butte Valley,
Central House,
Cherokee,
Chico, *
Clipper Mills,
Forbestown,
Inskip,
Magalia,
Martinsburgh,
Mooro's Station,
Oroville,* (c. h.,)
Pentz,
Pine Creek,
Rio Seco,
Rock Creek,
Yankee Hill.

* Money-order office.

CALAVERAS COUNTY.

Angel's Camp,
Big Trees,
Camanche,
Campo Seco,
Copperopolis,
Fourth Crossing,
Jenny Lind,
Mokelumne Hill,* (c. h.,)

Mountain Ranch,
Murphy's,
Railroad Flat,
San Andreas,
Telegraph City,
Vallicita,
West Point.

COLUSA COUNTY.

Coast Range,
Colusa,* (c. h.,)
Grand Island,
Jacinto,

Newville,
Princeton,
Saint John,
Spring Valley.

CONTRA COSTA COUNTY.

Alamo,
Antioch,*
Black Diamond,
Clayton,
Danville,
La Fayette,

Martinez,* (c. h.,)
Pacheco,
Point of Timber,
San Pablo,
Somersville,
Walnut Creek.

DEL NORTE COUNTY.

Crescent City, (c. h.,) Smith River.
Happy Camp,

EL DORADO COUNTY.

Clarksville,
Cold Spring,
Coloma,
Diamond Spring,
El Dorado,
Fair Play,
Georgetown,*
Green Valley,
Greenwood,
Grizzly Flats,
Indian Diggings,
Kelsey,

Latrobe,
Mendon,
Nashville,
Newton,
Pilot Hill,
Placerville,* (c. h.,)
Pleasant Valley,
Salmon Falls,
Shingle Springs,
Slippery Ford,
Spanish Flat,
Taho.

FRESNO COUNTY.

Big Dry Creek,
Firebaugh,
King's River,
Kingston,

Millerton, (c. h.,)
New Idria,
Panoche.

HUMBOLDT COUNTY.

Arcata,
Camp Grant,
Eel River,
Eureka,* (c. h.,)
Ferndale,

Gas Jet,
Hydesville,
Petrolia,
Table Bluff.

INYO COUNTY.

Big Pine,
Cerro Gordo,
Fish Springs,

Independence, (c. h.,)
Lone Pine.

KERN COUNTY.

Bakersfield,
Havilah, (c. h.,)
Kernville,

Linn's Valley,
Tehichipa.

KLAMATH COUNTY.

Bed Rock,
Black Bear,
Cottage Grove,
Forks of Salmon,
Hoopa Valley,
Martin's Ferry,

Orleans, (c. h.,)
Petersburgh,
Sawyer's Bar,
Trinidad,
Yocumville.

LAKE COUNTY.

Guenoc,
Knoxville,
Lakeport,
Lower Lake, (c. h.,)

Morgan,
Uncle Sam,
Upper Clear Lake,
Zem Zem.

LASSEN COUNTY.

Copper Vale,
Janesville,
Junction House,

Long Valley,
Milford,
Susanville,* (c. h.)

LOS ANGELES COUNTY.

Anaheim,
Capistrano,
Compton,
Los Angeles,* (c. h.,)
Los Nietos,
Monte,

Petroliopolis,
Ravena City,
San Gabriel,
Santa Ana,
Spadra,
Wilmington.*

MARIN COUNTY.

Black Point,
Bolinas,
Olema,

San Quentin,
San Rafael,* (c. h.,)
Tomales.

MARIPOSA COUNTY.

Bear Valley,
Hornitas,
Indian Gulch,
Mariposa,* (c. h.,)

Maxwell's Creek,
Mount Bullion,
Wyatt's Store.
Yo Semite.

MENDOCINO COUNTY.

Albion,
Anderson,
Cahto,
Calpella,
Conway's Landing,
Covelo,
Cuffey's Cove,
Gualala,
Hermitage,

Little Lake,
Little River,
Mendocino,*
Navarro Ridge,
Punta Arenas,
Sanel,
Sherwood Valley,
Ukiah, (c. h.,)
Yorkville.

MERCED COUNTY.

Alexandria,
Brickville,
Dover,
Hopeton,

Merced Falls,
Plainsberg,
Snelling's Ranch,(c.h.,)
Union.

* Money-order office.

MONO COUNTY.

Benton,	*Bridgeport,* (c. h.,)
Bishop Creek,	Coleville.

MONTEREY COUNTY.

Castroville,	Picacho,
Gabilon,	Salinas,
Hollister,	San Antonio,
Monterey, (c. h.,)	San Benito,
Natividad,	San Juan,
New Republic,	Soledad.

NAPA COUNTY.

Adelante,	Oakville,
Calistoga,	Pope Valley,
Monticello,	Saint Helena,
Napa City, (c. h.,)	Yountville.

NEVADA COUNTY.

Anthony House,	North Columbia,
French Corral,	North San Juan,
Graniteville,	Omega,
Grass Valley,*	Patterson,
Indian Springs,	Rough and Ready,
Little York,	Sweetland,
Moore's Flat,	Truckee,
Nevada City, (c. h.,)	Washington,
North Bloomfield,	You Bet.

PLACER COUNTY.

Auburn, (c. h.,)	Iowa City,
Bath,	Lincoln,*
Blue Canyon,	Michigan Bluff,
Cisco,	Newcastle,
Clipper Gap,	Oro City,
Colfax,*	Pino,
Dutch Flat,*	Rocklin,
Emigrant Gap,	Roseville,
Forest Hill,*	Sheridan,
Gold Run,	Todd's Valley,
Grizzly Bear House,	Yankee Jim's.

PLUMAS COUNTY.

Beckwith,	Mohawk Valley,
Big Meadows,	Nelson Point,
Buck's Ranch,	*Quincy,* (c. h.,)
Crescent Mills,	Round Valley,
Greenville,	Sawpit,
La Porte,*	Spanish Ranch,
Longville,	Summit,
Meadow Valley,	Taylorsville.

SACRAMENTO COUNTY.

Brighton,	Galt,
Cosumne,	Hicksville,
Elk Grove,	Mayhew's Station,
Florin,	Michigan Bar,
Folsom City,*	Mormon Island,
Franklin,	Onisbo,
Freeport,	Richland,

SACRAMENTO COUNTY—Continued.

SACRAMENTO CITY,*	Sheldon,
(c. h.)	Walnut Grove.

SAN BERNARDINO COUNTY.

Cucamonga,	*San Bernardino,* *(c.h.)

SAN DIEGO COUNTY.

Ballena,	Poway,
Branson,	*San Diego,* (c. h.,)
Guahonga,	San Jacinto,
Julian,	San Luis Rey,
Milquatay,	South San Diego,*
National City,	Temecula,
Otay,	Warner's Ranch.

SAN FRANCISCO COUNTY.

San Francisco, * (c. h.)

SAN JOAQUIN COUNTY.

Atlanta,	Linden,
Banta,	Live Oak,
Bellota,	Lockeford,
Burwood,	Meinecke,
Collegeville,	Mokelumne,
Elliott,	*Stockton,* * (c. h.,)
Ellis,	Waterloo,
Farmington,	Woodbridge.
Liberty,	

SAN LUIS OBISPO COUNTY

Arroyo Grande,	Piedra Blanca,
Berros Creek,	*San Luis Obispo,*(c.h.,)
Cambria,	San Marcos,
Old Creek,	Santa Margarita.
Paso Robles,	

SAN MATEO COUNTY.

Belmont,	*Redwood City,* (c. h.,)
Fair Oaks,	San Mateo,
Halfmoon Bay,	School-house Station,
Menlo Park,	Searsville,
Millbrae,	Woodside.
Pescadero,	

SANTA BARBARA COUNTY.

Carpenteria,	*Santa Barbara,* *(c.h.,)
Las Cruces,	San Buenaventura,
Los Alisos,	Santa Maria.

SANTA CLARA COUNTY.

Alviso,	Mountain View,
Burnett,	San Felipe,
Gilroy,*	*San José,* * (c. h.,)
Lexington,	Santa Clara,
Los Gatos,	San Ysidro,
Mayfield,	Saratoga.
Milpitas,	

* Money-order office.

SANTA CRUZ COUNTY.

Aptos,	Soquel,
*Santa Cruz,** (c. h.,)	Watsonville.*

SHASTA COUNTY.

American Ranch,	Portuguee,
French Gulch,	*Shasta,** (c. h.)
Horsetown,	Stillwater.
Millville,	

SIERRA COUNTY.

Alleghany,	Plum Valley,
*Downieville,** (c. h.,)	Port Wine,
Fir Cap,	Saint Louis,
Forest City,	Sierra City,
Gibsonville,*	Sierra Valley,
Goodyear's. Bar,	Table Rock.
Loyalton,	

SISKIYOU COUNTY.

Berryvale,	Henley,
Callahan's Ranch,	Klamath,
Cedarville,	Lake City,
Eagleville,	Mount Shasta,
Edgwood,	Oro Fino,
Etna Mills,	Scott River,
Fort Bidwell,	Seiad Valley,
Fort Jones,	*Yreka,* (c. h.)
Gazelle,	

SOLANO COUNTY.

Batavia,	Rio Vista,
Benicia,*	Silveyville,
Binghamton,	South Vallejo,
Cordelia,	*Suisun City,** (c. h.,)
Denverton,	Vaca,
Dixon,	Vacaville,*
Maine Prairie,	Vallejo.*

SONOMA COUNTY.

Bloomfield,	Ocean View,
Clairville,	Petaluma,*
Cloverdale,	*Santa Rosa,** (c. h.,)
Duncan's Mills,	Sebastopol,
Fisherman's Bay,	Smith's Ranch,
Freestone,	Sonoma,
Guerneville,	Stony Point,
Healdsburgh,*	Timber Cove,
Lakeville,	Two Rocks,
Mark West,	Windsor.

STANISLAUS COUNTY.

Crow's Landing,	Langworth,
Graysonville,	Paradise,
Hill's Ferry,	Tuolumne City,
Horr's Ranch,	Twenty-six-Mile
Knight's Ferry, (c. h.,)	House.
La Grange,	

SUTTER COUNTY.

Colegrove's Point,	Pleasant Grove Cr'k.
Meridian,	West Butte,
Nicolaus,	*Yuba City,* (c. h.)

TEHAMA COUNTY.

Battle Creek,	Moon's Ranch,
Cottonwood,	*Red Bluff,** (c. h.,)
Lassen,	Tehama.

TRINITY COUNTY.

Big Bar,	Lewiston,
Burnt Ranch,	Trinity,
Douglas City,	Trinity Centre,
Junction City,	*Weaverville,** (c. h.)

TULARE COUNTY.

Farmersville,	*Visalia,** (c. h.)
Tule,	

TUOLUMNE COUNTY.

Big Oak Flat,	Montezuma,
Chinese Camp,	Shaw's Flat,
Columbia,*	*Sonora,** (c. h.,)
Garrote,	Sugar Pine.
Jamestown,	

YOLO COUNTY.

Antelope,	Davisville,
Buck Eye,	Grafton,
Cache Creek,	Prarie,
Capay,	Woodland,
Charleston,	*Yolo,** (c. h.)

YUBA COUNTY.

Brown's Valley,	Oregon House,
Brownsville,	Paulinville,
Bullard's Bar,	Smartville,
Camptonville,*	Strawberry Valley,
Honcut,	Timbuctoo,
*Marysville,** (c. h.,)	Wheatland.

COLORADO TERRITORY.

ARAPAHOE COUNTY.

Cherry Creek,	Littleton.
DENVER,* (c. h.,)	

BENT COUNTY.

Bent's Fort,	South Side.
Fort Lyon, (c. h.,)	

*Money-order office.

BOULDER COUNTY.

Boulder, (c. h.,) Sugar **Loaf,**
Burlington,* Valmont,
Coal Creek, Ward District,
Jamestown, * Whitney.

CLEAR CREEK COUNTY

Empire City, Mill City,
Georgetown,* Spanish Bar.
Idaho, (c. h.,)

CONEJOS COUNTY.

Conejos, (c. h.,) Loma.

COSTILLA COUNTY.

Costilla, *San Luis,* (c. h.)
Fort Garland,

DOUGLAS COUNTY.

Bear Canyon, Kiowa,
Franktown, (c. h.,) Rock Butte,
Glen Grove, Running Creek,
Gomer's Mills, Spring Valley,
Huntsville, Virginia.
Keystone,

EL PASO COUNTY.

Bassett's Mill, El Paso,
Bijou Basin, Fountain,
Colorado City, (c. h.,) Monument,
Edgerton, Wheatland.

FREMONT COUNTY.

Canyon City, (c. h.,) Currant Creek.
Colfax,

GILPIN COUNTY.

Bald Mountain, *Central City,** (c. h.)
Black Hawk Point,

GREENWOOD COUNTY.

Kit Carson, (c. h.,) Lake Station.

HUERFANO COUNTY.

Badito, (c. h.,) Butte **Valley,**

HUERFANO COUNTY—Continued.

Carson, Saint Mary's.
Greenhorn,

JEFFERSON COUNTY.

Golden City, (c. h.,) Mount Vernon.

LAKE COUNTY.

Cash Creek, Helena,
Centreville, Oro City,
Granite, (c. h.,) South Arkansas.

LARIMER COUNTY.

Big Thompson, *La Porte,* (c. h.,)
Fort Collins, Namaqua.

LAS ANIMAS COUNTY.

*Trinidad,** (c. h.)

PARK COUNTY.

Buckskin, Grant,
Deer Valley, Hamilton,
Fair Play, (c. h.,) Montgomery City.

PUEBLO COUNTY.

Beaver Creek, Huerfano,
Booneville, Juniata,
Excelsior, *Pueblo,** (c. h.,)
Hermosilla, Saint Charles.

SAGUACHE COUNTY.

Carnero, *Saguache,* (c. h.)
Garibaldi,

SUMMIT COUNTY.

Breckinridge, (c. h.,) Lincoln City.
Delaware City,

WELD COUNTY.

Evans, (c. h.,) Julesburgh,
Flemming's Ranch, Saint Vrain,
Fort Lupton, Weld.
Greeley,

CONNECTICUT.

FAIRFIELD COUNTY.

Ball's Pond, Brookfield Centre,
Banksville, Cannon's Station,
Bethel, Cold Spring,
Black Rock, *Danbury,** (c. h.,)
Bridgeport,* Darien,
Brookfield, Darien Depot,

FAIRFIELD COUNTY—Continued.

Easton, Hawleyville,
Fairfield, (c. h.,) High Ridge,
Georgetown, Huntington,
Glenville, Long Ridge,
Greenfield Hill, Mianus,
Greenwich, Mill Plain,

* Money-order office.

FAIRFIELD COUNTY—Continued.

Monroe,
New Canaan,
New Fairfield,
Newtown,
North Stamford,
North Wilton,
Norwalk,*
Plattsville,
Redding,
Redding Ridge,
Ridgebury,
Ridgefield,
Ridgefield Station,
Round Hill,
Rowayton,
Sandy Hook,
Saugatuck,

Sherman,
Smith's Ridge,
South Norwalk,
Southport,
Stamford,*
Stanwich,
Stepney,
Stepney Depot,
Stratford,
Trumbull,
Trumbull L'g Hill,
West Norwalk,
Weston,
Westport,
West Redding,
Wilton,
Winnipauk.

HARTFORD COUNTY.

Avon,
Berlin,
Bloomfield,
Bristol,*
Broad Brook,
Buckingham,
Buckland,
Burlington,
Burnside,
Canton,
Canton Centre,
Centre Hill,
Collinsville,*
East Berlin,
East Glastenbury,
East Granby,
East Hartford,
East Windsor,
East Windsor Hill,
Enfield,
Farmington,
Farm's Village,
Forestville,
Glastenbury,
Granby,
HARTFORD,* (c. h.,)
Hartland,
Hazardville,
Hockanum,
Kensington,
Manchester,
Marion,
Marlborough,
Naubuc,

New Britain,*
Newington,
Newington Junct'n,
North Canton,
North Granby,
North Manchester,
Plainville,
Plantsville,
Poquonock,
Rainbow,
Rocky Hill,
Scitico,
Simsbury,
South Glastenbury,
Southington,*
South Manchester,
South Windsor,
Suffield,
Tariffville,
Thompsonville,*
Unionville,
Wapping,
Warehouse Point,
Weatogue,
West Avon,
West Granby,
West Hartford,
West Hartland,
West Suffield,
Wethersfield,
Windsor,
Windsor Locks,*
Windsorville.

LITCHFIELD COUNTY.

Bakersville,
Bantam Falls,
Barkhamsted,
Bethlehem,
Bridgewater,
Burrville,
Campville,
Canaan,

Canaan Valley,
Chalybes,
Colebrook,
Colebrook River,
Cornwall,
Cornwall Bridge,
Cornwall Hollow,
East Canaan,

LITCHFIELD COUNTY—Continued.

East Cornwall,
East Kent,
East Litchfield,
Ellsworth,
Falls Village,*
Gaylordsville,
Goshen,
Harwinton,
Hotchkissville,
Huntsville,
Kent,
Lakeville,
Lanesville,
Lime Rock,
Litchfield, (c. h.,)
Marble Dale,
Mill Brook,
Milton,
Morris,
Nepaug,
New Hartford,
New Milford,*
New Preston,
Norfolk,
North Colebrook,
North Cornwall,
Northfield,
North Norfolk,
Northville,
Ore Hill,

Park Lane,
Pequabuck,
Pine Meadow,
Pleasant Valley,
Plymouth,
Riverton,
Robertsville,
Roxbury,
Salisbury,
Sharon,
South Canaan,
South Norfolk,
Southville,
Terrysville,
Thomaston,*
Torringford,
Torrington,
Warren,
Washington,
Watertown,
West Cornwall,
West Goshen,
West Norfolk,
West Winsted,*
Winchester Centre,
Winsted,*
Wolcottville,*
Woodbury,
Woodville.

MIDDLESEX COUNTY.

Centre Brook,
Chester,
Clinton,
Cobalt,
Cromwell,
Deep River,
Durham,
Durham Centre,
East Haddam,
East Hampton,
Essex,*
Haddam, (c. h.,)
Haddam Neck,

Higganum,
Killingworth,
Leesville,
Middlefield,
Middle Haddam,
Middletown,* (c. h.,)
Millington,
Moodus,
Portland,
Saybrook,
Westbrook, ₵
Winthrop.

NEW HAVEN COUNTY.

Ansonia,
Beacon Falls,
Bethany,
Branford,
Brook's Vale,
Cheshire,*
Derby,*
East Haven,
East River,
Fair Haven,
Guilford,*
Hamden,
Madison,
Meriden,
Middlebury,
Milford,*

Mount Carmel,
Naugatuck,*
NEW HAVEN,*(c.h.,)
North Branford,
Northford,
North Guilford,
North Haven,
North Madison,
Oakville,
Orange,
Oxford,
Prospect,
River Side,
Rockland,
Seymour,
South Britain,

* Money-order office.

NEW HAVEN COUNTY—Continued.

Southbury,	Waterville,
Southford,	West Cheshire,
South Haven,	West Haven,
South Meriden,	West Meriden,*
Stony Creek,	Westville,
Wallingford,	Wolcott,
Waterbury,*	Yalesville.

NEW LONDON COUNTY.

Baltic,	Montville,
Bozrah,	Mystic,
Bozrahville,	Mystic Bridge,*
Centre Groton,	Mystic River,
Chesterfield,	New London,* (c. h.,)
Clark's Falls,	Niantic,
Colchester,*	Noank,
East Lyme,	North Lyme,
Franklin,	North Stonington,
Gale's Ferry,	Norwich,* (c. h.,)
Greenville,	Norwich Town,
Griswold,	Poquetanuck,
Groton,	Poquonock Bridge,
Hadlyme,	Preston,
Hamburgh,	Salem,
Hanover,	South Lyme,
Jewett City,	Stonington,
Lebanon,	Uncasville,
Ledyard,	Waterford,
Liberty Hill,	Westchester,
Lisbon,	Yantic.
Lyme,	

TOLLAND COUNTY.

Andover,	Ellington,
Bolton,	Gilead,
Columbia,	Gurleyville,
Coventry,	Hebron,
Coventry Depot,	Mansfield,
Eagleville,	Mansfield Centre,

TOLLAND COUNTY—Continued.

Mansfield Depot,	Stafford Springs,*
Mashapaug,	Staffordville,
Merrow Station,	Talcottville,
Moose Meadow,	Tolland, (c. h.,)
Mount Hope,	Turnerville,
Quarryville,	Union,
Rockville,*	Vernon,
Somers,	Vernon Depot,
Somerville,	West Stafford,
South Coventry,	West Willington,
Square Pond,	Willington,
Stafford,	Windermere.

WINDHAM COUNTY.

Abington,	Phœnixville,
Ashford,	Plainfield,
Brooklyn, (c. h.,)	Pomfret,
Campbell's Mills,	Pomfret Landing,
Canterbury,	Putnam,*
Central Village,	Scotland,
Chaplin,	South Killingly,
Eastford,	South Windham,
East Killingly,	South Woodstock,
East Putnam,	Sterling,
East Thompson,	Sterling Hill,
East Woodstock,	Thompson,
Ekonk,	Voluntown,
Grosvenor Dale,	Wauregan,
Hampton,	West Ashford,
Killingly,	Westford,
Moosup,	West Killingly,*
New Boston,	Westminster,
North Ashford,	West Thompson,
North Grosvenor	West Woodstock,
Dale,	Willimantic,*
North Windham,	Wilsonville,
North Woodstock,	Windham,
Oneco,	Woodstock,
Pendleton Hill,	Woodstock Valley.

DAKOTA TERRITORY.

BONHOMME COUNTY.

Bonhomme, (c. h.,)	Emanuel,
Chouteau Creek,	Springfield.

BUFFALO COUNTY.

Fort Sully,	Grand River.

CHARLES MIX COUNTY.

Antelope,	White Swan.
Greenwood, (c. h.,)	

CLAY COUNTY.

Lincoln,	Saybrook,
Riverside,	Vermillion, (c. h.,)

DEUEL COUNTY.

Fort Wadsworth.

LINCOLN COUNTY.

Canton, (c. h.,)	Fairview,
Eden,	Swan Lake.

MINNEHAHA COUNTY.

Sioux Falls.

PEMBINA COUNTY.

Grand Forks,	Saint Joseph.
Pembina, (c. h.,)	

* Money-order office.

SHYENNE COUNTY.

Fort Abercrombie.

TODD COUNTY.

Fort Randall, (c. h.,) Ponka Agency.

UNION COUNTY.

Adelescat, *Elk Point,* (c. h.,)
Big Sioux, Liberty,

UNION COUNTY—Continued.

Richland, Virginia.
Sioux Valley,

YANKTON COUNTY.

Lakeport, Whitehall,
Marindal, YANKTON,* (c. h.)

COUNTIES UNKNOWN.

Crow Creek, Whetstone Agency.
Fort Totten,

DELAWARE.

KENT COUNTY.

Adamsville. Lebanon,
Brenford, Leipsic,
Camden, Little Creek Landing,
Canterbury, Magnolia,
Clayton, Milford, *
DOVER,* (c. h.,) Moorton,
Farmington, Mount Moriah,
Felton Station, Pearson's Corner,
Frederica, Slaughter,
Harrington, Smyrna,*
Hazlettville, Vernon,
Hollandville, Willow Grove,
Houston Station, Woodside,
Kenton, Wyoming.

NEW CASTLE COUNTY.

Beaver Valley, Deakyneville,
Black Bird, Delaware City,*
Centreville, Fieldsborough,
Chambersville, Glasgow,
Chippewa, Hare's Corner,
Christiana, Henry Clay Factory,
Claymont, Hockessin,
Cooch's Bridge, Kirkwood,

NEW CASTLE COUNTY—Continued.

Loveville, Odessa,
McClellandsville, Pleasant Hill,
McDonough, Port Penn,
Mermaid, Red Lion,
Middletown, * Saint George's,
Mount Pleasant, Stanton,
Newark, * Summit Bridge,
New Castle, (c. h.,) Townsend,
Newport, Wilmington, *

SUSSEX COUNTY.

Angola, Laurel,
Black Water, Lewes, *
Bridgeville, Lincoln,
Concord, Lowe's Cross Roads,
Dagsborough, Middleford,
Delmar, Millsborough,
Draw Bridge, Milton,
Ellendale, Ocean View,
Frankford, Redden,
Georgetown, (c. h.,) Roxana,
Greenwood, Seaford, *
Gumborough, Selbyville,
Harbeson, Tunnell's Store.
Hollyville,

DISTRICT OF COLUMBIA.

WASHINGTON COUNTY.

Anacostia, Brightwood, Georgetown,* Tenallytown,
WASHINGTON* (c. h.)

FLORIDA.

ALACHUA COUNTY.

Archer, Newnanville,
Gainesville, (c. h.,) Waldo.
Micanopy,

BAKER COUNTY.

Olustee, *Sanderson,* (c. h.)

BRADFORD COUNTY.

Lake Butler (c. h.) Starke.

* Money-order office.

16 P O

BREVARD COUNTY.

Saint Lucie, (c. h.)

CALHOUN COUNTY.

Iola,   Ochesee.

CLAY COUNTY.

Green Cove Springs, Trail Ridge.
Middleburgh.

COLUMBIA COUNTY.

Benton,   *Lake City, (c. h.,)*
Blount's Ferry,   Suwannee Shoals,
Ellisville,   Tustenuggee.
Ichatucknee,

DADE COUNTY.

Biscayne, (c. h.)

DUVAL COUNTY.

Fort George,   Mandarin,
Hibernia,   Mayport,
Jacksonville, (c. h.,) Yellow Bluff.

ESCAMBIA COUNTY.

Bluff Springs,   *Pensacola,* (c. h.,)
Molino,   Warrington.*

FRANKLIN COUNTY.

Apalachicola, (c. h.)

GADSDEN COUNTY.

Chattahoochee,   *Quincy, (c. h.,)*
Concord,   Rickoe's Bluff.

HAMILTON COUNTY.

Bellville,   Jennings,
Jasper, (c. h.,)   White Springs.

HERNANDO COUNTY.

Bay Port,   Fort Taylor,
Cedar Tree,   *Pierceville, (c. h.)*
Fort Dade,

HILLSBOROUGH COUNTY.

Alafia,   Cork,
Clear Water Harbor, *Tampa,* (c. h.,)

HOLMES COUNTY.

Cerro Gordo, (c. h.,) Ponce de Leon.

JACKSON COUNTY.

Campbellton,   *Marianna, (c. h.)*
Greenwood,

JEFFERSON COUNTY.

Monticello, (c. h.,) Weelannee,
Waukeenah,   Williamsburgh.

LA FAYETTE COUNTY.

McIntosh, (c. h.)

LEON COUNTY.

Bailey's Mill,   TALLAHASSEE,* (c. h.)
Miccosukee,

LEVY COUNTY.

Bronson,   Cedar Keys.

LIBERTY COUNTY.

Blue Creek,   Rock Bluff.
Bristol, (c. h.,)

MADISON COUNTY.

Columbus,   Sandy Ford.
Madison, (c. h.,)

MANATEE COUNTY.

Manatee.

MARION COUNTY.

Camp Izard,   *Ocala, (c. h.,)*
Cotton Plant,   Orange Springs.
Flemington,

MONROE COUNTY.

Cayo Largo,   *Key West,* (c. h.)

NASSAU COUNTY.

Callahan,   King's Ferry,
Fernandina, (c. h.,) Nassau.

ORANGE COUNTY.

Apopka,   *Orlando, (c. h.)*
Mellonville,

POLK COUNTY.

Peace Creek, (c. h.)

PUTNAM COUNTY.

Buffalo Bluff,   *Pilatka, (c. h.,)*
Federal Point,   Welaka.
Georgetown,

ST. JOHN'S COUNTY.

Esparanza,   Orange Mills,
Hogarth's Landing, *St. Augustine,* (c. h.)
Matanzas,

* Money-order office.

SANTA ROSA COUNTY.

Chalk Spring,	*Milton*, (c. h.)

SUMTER COUNTY.

Sumterville, (c. h.)

SUWANNEE COUNTY.

Houston, (c. h.,)	Suwannee,
Live Oak,	Wellborn.

TAYLOR COUNTY.

Rose Head, (c. h.)

VOLUSIA COUNTY.

Blue Springs,	Port Orange,
Enterprize, (c. h.,)	Sand Point,
New Smyrna,	Volusia.
Palmetto,	

WAKULLA COUNTY.

Crawfordville, (c. h.,)	Saint Marks,
Pautuxett,	Sopchoppy.

WALTON COUNTY.

Knox Hill,	*Uchee Anna*, (c. h.)

WASHINGTON COUNTY.

Vernon, (c. h.)

GEORGIA.

APPLING COUNTY.

Hazlehurst,	Screven,
Holmesville, (c. h.,)	Surrency.

BAKER COUNTY.

Newton, (c. h.)

BALDWIN COUNTY.

Milledgeville,* (c. h.,) Talmage.

BANKS COUNTY.

Allandale,	*Homer*, (c. h.,)
Banksville,	Middle River,
Erastus,	Nail's Creek.
Hollingsworth,	

BARTOW COUNTY.

Adairsville,	Hall's Mill,
Allatoona,	Kingston,
Cartersville,* (c. h.,)	Pine Log,
Cass Station,	Stegall's Depot,
Cassville,	Stilesborough.
Euharlee,	

BERRIEN COUNTY.

Knight's Mill,	*Nashville*, (c. h.)
Milltown,	

BIBB COUNTY.

Macon,* (c. h.)

BROOKS COUNTY.

Grooverville,	*Quitman*, (c. h.)

BRYAN COUNTY.

Way's Station.

BURKE COUNTY.

Brinsonville,	Lester's District,
Herndon,	Midville,
Holcombe,	Millin,
Lawtonville,	*Waynesborough*, (c. h.)

BUTTS COUNTY.

Indian Springs,	Stark,
Jackson, (c. h.,)	Worthville.

CALHOUN COUNTY.

Morgan, (c. h.)

CAMDEN COUNTY.

Berne,	Satilla Mills.
Saint Mary's,	

CAMPBELL COUNTY.

Campbellton, (c. h.,)	Fairburn,
Chapel Hill,	Palmetto,
County Line,	Skinner.
Dark Corner,	

CARROLL COUNTY.

Bowdon,	Loyal, .
Bowenville,	Villa Rica.
Carrollton, (c. h.,)	

CATOOSA COUNTY.

Graysville,	*Ringgold*,* (c. h.)

CHARLTON COUNTY.

Centre Village,	*Trader's Hill*, (c. h.)

CHATHAM COUNTY.

Savannah,* (c. h.)

* Money-order office.

CHATTAHOOCHEE COUNTY.

Cottage Mills,   Jamestown,
Cusseta, (c. h.,)   King.

CHATTOOGA COUNTY.

Alpine,   *Summerville, (c. h.,)*
Chattoogaville,   Teloga Springs,
Dirt Town,   Trion Factory.
Melville,

CHEROKEE COUNTY.

Canton, (c. h.,)   Ophir,
Cherokee Mills,   Orange,
Fort Buffington,   Woodstock.
Freemansville,

CLARKE COUNTY.

Athens,*   *Watkinsville, (c. h.)*

CLAY COUNTY.

Fort Gaines, (c. h.,)   Gatesville.

CLAYTON COUNTY.

Forest Station,   Lovejoy's Station.
Jonesborough, (c. h.,)

CLINCH COUNTY.

Homerville, (c. h.,)   Stockton.
Lawton,

COBB COUNTY.

Acworth,   *Marietta,* (c. h.,)*
Big Shanty,   Powder Springs,
Boltonville,   Roswell,
Kenesaw,   Smyrna,
Lost Mountain,   Vining Station.

COFFEE COUNTY.

Douglas,   Red Bluff.
Gully Branch,

COLQUITT COUNTY.

Greenfield,   *Moultrie, (c. h.)*

COLUMBIA COUNTY.

Appling, (c. h.,)   Saw Dust,
Berzelia,   Thompson,
Lombardy,   Winfield.

COWETA COUNTY.

Campton,   *Newnan, (c. h.,)*
Grantville,   Senoia,
Kidron,   Turin.
Lodi,

CRAWFORD COUNTY.

Hickory Grove,   *Knoxville, (c. h.)*

DADE COUNTY.

Cloverdale,   Smith,
Morganville,   *Trenton, (c. h.)*
Rising Fawn,

DAWSON COUNTY.

Barrittsville,   *Dawsonville, (c. h.,)*
Big Savanna,   Dixon.

DECATUR COUNTY.

Bainbridge, (c. h.,)*   Harrell.
Calvary,

DE KALB COUNTY.

Cross Keys,   Lithonia,
Decatur, (c. h.,)   Stone Mountain.

DOOLY COUNTY.

Byromville,   *Vienna, (c. h.)*
Turkey Creek,

DOUGHERTY COUNTY.

Albany, (c. h.)*

EARLY COUNTY.

Blakely, (c. h.,)   Octavia.

ECHOLS COUNTY.

Huckleberry,   *Statenville, (c. h.)*

EFFINGHAM COUNTY.

Eden,   Guyton,
Egypt,   *Springfield, (c. h.)*

ELBERT COUNTY.

Dove's Creek,   Ruckersville,
Elberton, (c. h.,)   Webster Place.

EMANUEL COUNTY.

Canoochee,   *Swainsborough, (c. h.)*

FANNIN COUNTY.

Hot House,   *Morganton, (c. h.)*

FAYETTE COUNTY.

Fayetteville, (c. h.,)   White Water.
Red Oak,

FLOYD COUNTY.

Armuchee,   Livingston,
Cave Spring,   Nannie,
Coosa,   *Rome,* (c. h.)*
Cunningham's St'n,   Yarborough.

* Money-order office.

FORSYTH COUNTY.

Big Creek,	Sheltonville,
Cumming, (c. h.,)	Vickery's Creek.

FRANKLIN COUNTY.

Aquilla,	*Carnesville*, (c. h.,)
Bold Spring,	Franklin Springs.

FULTON COUNTY.

ATLANTA,* (c. h.,)	Irbyville.
East Point,	

GILMER COUNTY.

Ellijay, (c. h.)

GLASCOCK COUNTY.

Gibson, (c. h.)

GLYNN COUNTY.

Brunswick,* (c. h.,)   Frederica.

GORDON COUNTY.

Blue Spring,	Reeves' Station,
Calhoun, (c. h.,)	Resaca,
Fairmount,	Sugar Valley.

GREENE COUNTY.

Greenesborough,(c.h.,)	Union Point,
Penfield,	White Plains,
Siloam,	Woodville.

GWINNETT COUNTY.

Auburn,	Suwanee,
Cain's,	Sweet Water,
Lawrenceville, (c. h.,)	Yellow River.

HABERSHAM COUNTY.

Clarkesville, (c. h.,)	Tallulah,
Currohee,	Walton's Ford.
Hughesburgh,	

HALL COUNTY.

Gainesville, (c. h.,)	Polksville,
Gillsville,	Poplar Springs,
Hog Mountain,	Sugar Hill.

HANCOCK COUNTY.

Culverton,	Mount Zion,
Mayfield,	*Sparta*, (c. h.)

HARALSON COUNTY.

Buchanan, (c. h.,)	Tallapoosa.
Repose,	

HART COUNTY.

Air Line,	Ford's Store,
Amandaville,	*Hartwell*, (c. h.,)
Bowersville,	Oak Bower,
Eagle Grove,	Parker's Store.

HARRIS COUNTY.

Cataula,	Mulberry Grove,
Ellerslie,	Waverly Hall,
Hamilton, (c.h.,)	Whitesville,
Mountain Hill,	Wisdom's Store.

HEARD COUNTY.

Franklin, (c. h.,)	Saint Cloud,
Houston,	State Line.

HENRY COUNTY.

Bear Creek,	Peaksville,
Crumley's,	Stockbridge.
McDonough, (c. h.)	

HOUSTON COUNTY.

Byron,	*Perry*, (c. h.,)
Fort Valley,	Powersville.

IRWIN COUNTY.

Irwinville, (c. h.)

JACKSON COUNTY.

Harmony Grove,   *Jefferson*, (c. h.)

JASPER COUNTY.

Monticello, (c. h.)

JEFFERSON COUNTY.

Bartow,	Fenn's Bridge,
Bethany,	*Louisville*, (c. h.)
Bostick,	

JOHNSON COUNTY.

Wrightsville, (c. h.)

JONES COUNTY.

Clinton, (c. h.,)   Griswoldville.

LAURENS COUNTY.

Dublin, (c. h.,)   Laurens Hill.

LEE COUNTY.

Renwick,	Wootten.
Starkville, (c. h.)	

LIBERTY COUNTY.

Fleming,	Taylor's Creek,
Hinesville, (c. h.,)	Walthourville.
McIntosh,	

* Money-order office.

LINCOLN COUNTY.

Clay Hill,
Goshen,
Leathersville,
Lincolnton, (c. h.)

LOWNDES COUNTY.

Cat Creek,
Naylor,
Valdosta, (c. h.)

LUMPKIN COUNTY.

Auraria,
Dahlonega, (c. h.,)
New Bridge.

MAC INTOSH COUNTY.

Darien, (c. h.)

MACON COUNTY.

Marshallsville,
Montezuma,
Oglethorpe, (c. h.)

MADISON COUNTY.

Danielsville, (c. h.,)
Fort Lamar,
Radical.

MARION COUNTY.

Buena Vista, (c. h.,)   Glen Alta.

MERIWETHER COUNTY.

Chalybeate Springs,
Erin,
Flat Shoals,
Greenville, (c. h.,)
Jones' Mills,
Luthersville,
Rocky Mount,
Warm Springs,
Warnerville,
White Sulphur
Springs,
Woodbury.

MILLER COUNTY.

Colquit, (c. h.)

MILTON COUNTY.

Alpharetta, (c. h.,)   Warsaw.

MITCHELL COUNTY.

Camilla, (c. h.)

MONROE COUNTY.

Colaparchee,
Culloden,
Forsyth, (c. h.,)
New Market,
Russellville,
Unionville.

MONTGOMERY COUNTY.

Mount Vernon, (c. h.,) Stirling.

MORGAN COUNTY.

Buck Head,
Madison,* (c. h.)
Rutledge.

MURRAY COUNTY.

Spring Place, (c. h.)

MUSCOGEE COUNTY.

Columbus,* (c. h.,)   Upatoie.

NEWTON COUNTY.

Conyers,
Covington, (c. h.,)
Newton Factory,
Oxford,
Snapping Shoals.

OGLETHORPE COUNTY.

Bairdstown,
Crawford,
Lexington,* (c. h.,)
Maxey,
Point Peter,
Sandy Cross,
Stephens,
Winterville.

PAULDING COUNTY.

Branch,
Brownsville,
Dallas, (c. h.,)
Ludville,
Roxanna.

PICKENS COUNTY.

Jasper, (c. h.,)   Talking Rock.

PIERCE COUNTY.

Blackshear, (c. h.)

PIKE COUNTY.

Barnesville,
Concord,
Liberty Hill,
Milner,
Zebulon, (c. h.)

POLK COUNTY.

Cedartown, (c. h.,)   Van Wert.
Prior's Station,

PULASKI COUNTY.

Bishop's Store,
Cochran,
Dubois,
Eartmon.
Hawkinsville, (c. h.)

PUTNAM COUNTY.

Eactonton, (c. h.)

QUITMAN COUNTY.

Georgetown, (c. h.,)   Morris Station.
Hatcher's Station,

RABUN COUNTY.

Clayton, (c. h.,)   War Woman.

RANDOLPH COUNTY.

Coleman's Depot,
Cuthbert,* (c. h.,)
Nochway.

* Money-order office.

RICHMOND COUNTY.

Allen's,   Belair,
Augusta, (c. h.,)   McBean Depot.

SCHLEY COUNTY.

Ellaville, (c. h.)

SCRIVEN COUNTY.

Cameron,   Panamore Hill,
Halcyon Dale,   Rocky Ford,
Mobley Pond,   Scarborough.
Ogeechee,

SPALDING COUNTY.

Griffin,* (c. h.)

STEWART COUNTY.

Florence,   Hannahatchee,
Green Hill,   *Lumpkin,* (c. h.)

SUMTER COUNTY.

*Americus,** (c. h.,)   Plains of Dura.
Andersonville,

TALBOT COUNTY.

Bluff Spring,   Pleasant Hill,
Box Spring,   Prattsburgh,
Geneva,   *Talbotton,* (c. h.)

TALIAFERRO COUNTY.

Crawfordville, (c. h.,)   Sharon.

TATNALL COUNTY.

Long Branch,   *Reidsville,* (c. h.)

TAYLOR COUNTY.

Butler, (c. h.,)   Reynolds.
Howard,

TELFAIR COUNTY.

Copeland,   McVille,
Jacksonville, (c. h.,)   Temperance.
Lumber City,

TERRELL COUNTY.

Dawson, (c. h.,)   Powers.

THOMAS COUNTY.

Boston,   Ochlochnee,
Cairo,   *Thomasville,* (c. h.)

TOWNS COUNTY.

Hiawassee, (c. h.)   Mount Eolia.

TROUP COUNTY.

Antioch,   O'Neal's Mills,
Hogansville,   Vernon,
La Grange, (c. h.,)   West Point.
Mountville,

TWIGGS COUNTY.

Bullard's,   Pace's Station,
Jeffersonville, (c. h.,)   Twiggsville.

UNION COUNTY.

Blairsville, (c. h.,)   Ivy Log.

UPSON COUNTY.

The Rock,   Waynmanville.
Thomaston, (c. h.,)

WALKER COUNTY.

Cane Creek,   *La Fayette,* (c. h.,)
Cassandra,   Naomi,
Cedar Grove,   Pond Spring,
Duck Creek,   Rock Spring,
Frick's Gap,   Salem,
Greenbush,   Villanow.
High Point,

WALTON COUNTY.

Monroe, (c. h.,)   Walnut Grove.
Social Circle,

WARE COUNTY.

Glenmore,   Tebeanville.

WARREN COUNTY.

Camac,   *Warrenton,* (c. h.,)
Double Wells,

WASHINGTON COUNTY.

Davisborough,   *Sandersville,* (c. h.,)
Hebron,   Tennille,
Oconee,   Warthen's Store,
Riddlesville,   Whittle.

WAYNE COUNTY.

Doctor Town,   Pendarvis,
Drady's,   *Waynesville,* (c. h.)

WEBSTER COUNTY.

Preston, (c. h.)

WHITE COUNTY.

Cleveland, (c. h.,)   Nacoochee,
Leo,   Pleasant Retreat.
Loudsville,

* Money-order office.

WHITFIELD COUNTY.

Cove City,
Dalton, (c. h.,)
Red Clay,

Tilton,
Tunnel Hill,
Varnell's Station.

WILCOX COUNTY.

Abbeville, (c. h.,)
Adams,

House Creek.

WILKES COUNTY.

Danburgh,

Washington, (c. h.)

WILKINSON COUNTY.

Gordon,
Irwinton, (c. h.,)
McIntire,

Stephensville,
Toomsborough.

WORTH COUNTY.

Isabella, (c. h.,)
Vine's Mills,

Warwick.

IDAHO TERRITORY.

ADA COUNTY.

BOISE CITY,* (c. h.,)
Lower Boise,

Middleton,
Payetteville.

ALTURAS COUNTY.

Atlanta,
Rocky Bar, (c. h.,)

Shoshone.

BOISE COUNTY.

Centreville,
Idaho City, (c. h.,)

Pioneerville,
Placerville.

IDAHO COUNTY.

Florence City, (c. h.,)
John Day's Creek.

White Bird.

LEMHI COUNTY.

Fort Lemhi,
Leesburgh,

Salmon City, (c. h.)

NEZ PERCES COUNTY.

Lapwai,

Lewiston, (c. h.)

ONEIDA COUNTY.

Eagle Rock,
Malade City, (c. h.,)

Market Lake,
Ross Fork.

OWYHEE COUNTY.

Silver City, (c. h.)

SHOSHONE COUNTY.

Pierce City, (c. h.)

ILLINOIS.

ADAMS COUNTY.

Adams,
Beverly,
Big Neck,
Burton,
Camp Point,*
Chattan,
Clayton,*
Cliola,
Coatsburgh,
Columbus,
Elm Grove,
Fair Weather,
Fowler,
Keokuk Junction,

La Prairie,
Liberty,
Lima,
Marcelline,
Mendon,
Paloma,
Payson,
Peyton's,
Quincy, (c. h.;)
Richfield,
Stones' Prairie,
Ursa,
Woodville,
York Neck.

ALEXANDER COUNTY.

Cairo,* (c. h.,)
Clear Creek Landing,
Boose Island,

Santa Fé,
Thebes,
Unity.

BOND COUNTY.

Baden Baden,
Beaver Creek,
Cottonwood Grove,
Dudleyville,
Elm Point,
Greenville, (c. h.,)

Mulberry Grove,
Old Ripley,
Pleasant Mound,
Pleasant Prairie,
Pocahontas,
Woburn.

BOONE COUNTY.

Belvidere, (c. h.,)
Bonus,
Caledonia Station,
Capron,
Garden Prairie,

Hunter,
Leesville,
Park's Corners,
Poplar Grove.

BROWN COUNTY.

Buck Horn,
Cooperstown,
Gilbirdsport,
Hersman's,
La Grange Bluff,
Mound Station,

Mount Sterling, (c.h.,)
Ripley,
Spring's Station,
Union Ridge,
Versailles,
White Oak Springs.

* Money-order office.

BUREAU COUNTY.

Arlington,*
Buda,
Bureau Junction,
De Pue,
Dover,
Hollowayville,
Lamoille,
Limerick,
Lone Tree,
Lovejoy,
Malden,
Milo,
Mineral,
Neponset,*
New Bedford,
Ohio,
Ottsville,
Princeton,* (c. h.,)
Providence,
Sheffield,
Tiskilwa,
Truxton,
Walnut,
Wyanet,
Yorktown.

CALHOUN COUNTY.

Belleview,
Deer Plain,
Gilead,
Hamburgh,
Hardin, (c. h.,)
Hastings Landing,
Maynardsville,
Monterey,
News,
Vedder.

CARROLL COUNTY.

Argo,
Elk Horn Grove,
Fair Haven,
Johnson's Creek,
Lanark,
Milledgeville,
Mount Carroll,*(c.k.,)
Polsgrove,
Rock Creek,
Savanna,
Shannon,*
Thomson.

CASS COUNTY.

Arenzville,
Ashland,
Beardstown,* (c. h.,)
Berryton,
Chandlerville,
Hagley.
Lancaster,
Little Indian,
Virginia.

CHAMPAIGN COUNTY.

Champaign,*
Homer,*
Ivesdale,
Ludlow,
Mahomet,
Newcomb,
Ogden,
Pesotum,
Philo,
Rantoul,*
Raymond,
Saint Joseph's,
Savoy,
Sidney,
Sodorus,
Thomasborough,
Tolona,
Urbana, (c. h.)

CHRISTIAN COUNTY.

Assumption,
Edinburgh,
Grove City,
Mount Auburn,
Owaneco,
Palmer,
Pana,*
Randellsville,
Rosemond,
Stonington,
Taylorville, (c. h.)

CLARK COUNTY.

Casey,
Clark Centre,
Dalson,
Darwin,
Livingston,
McKeen,
Marshall,* (c. h.,)
Martinsville,
Melrose,
Oak Point,
Westfield,
York.

CLAY COUNTY.

Bible Grove,
Clay City,
Flora,
Greensburgh,
Hord,
Ingraham,
Larkinsburgh,
Louisville, (c. h.,)
Oskaloosa,
Xenia.

CLINTON COUNTY.

Aviston,
Buxton,
Carlyle,* (c. h.,)
Clement,
Damiansville,
Germantown,
Jamestown,
Keyesport,
New Baden,
New Memphis,
Shoal Creek Station,
Trenton.*

COLES COUNTY.

Ashmore,
Campbell,
Charleston,* (c. h.,)
Diona,
Etna,
Fuller's Point,
Hutton,
Loxa,
McPherson,
Mattoon,*
Milton Station,
Oakland,
Paradise,
Rural Retreat,
Saint Omer,
Springville.

COOK COUNTY.

Ainsworth Station,
Austin,
Barrington Station,
Bloom,
Blue Island,
Brickton,
Calumet,
Chicago,* (c. h.)
Des Plaines,
Dolten's Station,
Dunton,
East Northfield,
Elk Grove,
Englewood,
Evanston,*
Glencoe,
Havelock,
Homewood,
Hyde Park,
Jefferson,
Lake View,
Lansing,
Lemont,
Leyden,
Leyden Centre,
Lyons,
Lyonsville,
Mainville,
Mattison,
Maywood,
Mulford,
New Bremen,
Niles,
Niles Centre,
Norwood Park,
Oak Park,
Orland,
Palatine,
Palos,
Proviso,
Ravenswood,
Shaumburgh,
South Holland,
South Northfield,
Summit,
The Grove,
Thornton,
Washington Heights,
West Lyons,
West Northfield,
Wheeling,
Willow Spring,
Wilmette,
Winnetka.

CRAWFORD COUNTY.

Annapolis,
Bell Air,
Eaton,
Elkton,
Flat Rock,
Grand Glade,
Hardinsville,
Hutsonville,
New Hebron,
Oblong,
Palestine,*
Robinson, (c. h.,)
Stiflesville.

* Money-order office.

CUMBERLAND COUNTY.

Greenup,	Mule Creek,
Hazle Dell,	Neoga,
Johnstown,	Union Centre,
Majority Point, (*c.h.*,)	Woodbury.

DE KALB COUNTY.

Courtland Station,	New Lebanon,
Deerfield Prairie,	Ney,
De Kalb Centre,*	North Kingston,
Dorset,	Pierceville,
Dustin,	Prairie Pond,
East Paw Paw,	Ross Grove,
Freeland,	Sandwich,*
Genoa,	Shabbonas Grove,
Hick's Mills,	Somonauk,
Kingston,	South Grove,
Lacey,	Squaw Grove,
La Clair,	*Sycamore,* (*c. h.,*)
Malma,	Van Buren,
Malta,	Victor Centre.

DE WITT COUNTY.

Clinton, (*c. h.,*)	Harp,
De Witt,	Nixon,
Farmer City,	Wapella,
Hallsville,	Waynesville,

DOUGLAS COUNTY.

Arcola,*	Cottage Grove,
Bono,	Newman,
Brushy Fork,	*Tuscola,* (*c. h.*)
Camargo,	

DU PAGE COUNTY.

Addison,	Lisle Station,
Bloomingdale,	Lombard,
Cass,	*Naperville,* (*c. h.,*)
Danby,	Sagone,
Downer's Grove,	Turner,
Elmhurst,	Warrensville,
Fullersburgh,	Wayne,
Gower,	Wheaton,*
Hinsdale,	Winfield.

EDGAR COUNTY.

Baldwinsville,	Elbridge,
Bloomfield,	Grand View,
Bonwell,	Kansas,
Catfish,	Logan,
Cherry Point City,	Palermo,
Conlogue,	*Paris,* (*c. h.,*)
Dudley,	Vermillion.

EDWARDS COUNTY.

Albion, (*c. h.,*)	Mills Prairie,
Bennington,	Samsville,
Bone Gap,	West Salem.
Maple Grove,	

EFFINGHAM COUNTY.

Edgewood,	Moccasin,
Effingham, (*c. h.,*)	Mountville,
Elliottstown,	Teutopolis,
Freemanton,	Veni,
Funkhouser,	Watson,
Mason,*	

FAYETTE COUNTY.

Bowling Green,	Louden City,
Brownstown,	Ramsey,
Farina,	Saint Elmo,
Greenland,	Shabonier,
Hickory Creek,	*Vandalia,* (*c. h.,*)
La Clede,	Vera.

FORD COUNTY.

East Bend,	Piper City,
Eldredgeville,	Sugar Loaf.
Paxton, (*c. h.,*)	

FRANKLIN COUNTY.

Akin,	Frankfort,
Benton, (*c. h.,*)	Mulkeyton,
Big Muddy,	Osage,
Cave,	Parrish,
Crittenden,	Prosperity,
Eastern,	Taylor Hill,
Ewing,	Webb's Prairie.
Fitt's Hill,	

FULTON COUNTY.

Astoria,	Liverpool,
Avon,	Maple's Mill,
Bernadotte,	Marietta,
Bryant,	Middle Grove,
Canton,*	Midway,
Civer,	Norris,
Cuba,	Otto,
Duncan's Mills,	Saint David,
Ellisville,	Seville,
Fairview,	Smithfield,
Farmington,*	Summum,
Fiatt,	Table Grove,
Ipava,	Vermont.
Lewistown, (*c. h.,*)	

GALLATIN COUNTY.

Cottonwood,	New Market,
Crawford,	Saline Mines,
Elba,	*Shawneetown,* (*c. h.,*)
Equality,	South Hampton.
New Haven,	

GREENE COUNTY.

Athensville,	Kane,
Berdan,	Negro Lick,
Bluff Dale,	Pioneer,
Breese,	Road House Station,
Carrollton, (*c. h.,*)	Rockbridge,
Fayette,	Walkerville,
Greenfield,	White Hall.

* Money-order office.

GRUNDY COUNTY.

Braceville,
Gardner,
Highland Town,
Mazon,
Minooka,
Morris,* (c. h.)

HAMILTON COUNTY.

Belle Prairie,
Knight's Prairie,
Griswold,
Logansport,
Lovilla,
Macedonia,
McLeaneboro',* (c. h.,)
Rectorville.

HANCOCK COUNTY.

Adrian,
Appanoose,
Augusta,
Basco,
Bently,
Bowensburgh,
Burnside,
Carthage,* (c. h.,)
Chili,
Dallas City,*
Denver,
Durham,
Elvaston,
Ferris,
Fountain Green,
Hamilton,*
Hickory Ridge,
Joetta,
La Crosse,
La Harpe,*
McCall,
Middle Creek,
Nauvoo,
Plymouth,
Pontoosuc,
Pulaski,
Saint Albans,
Sonora,
Sylvan Dale,
Warsaw.*
Webster,
West Point.

HARDIN COUNTY.

Cave in Rock,
Elizabethtown, (c. h.,)
Parkinson's Land'g,
Rosiclare,
Seller's Landing,
Spark's Hill.

HENDERSON COUNTY.

Biggsville,
Hopper's Mills,
Lomax,
Olena,
Oquawka,* (c. h.,)
Raritan,
Rozetta,
Sagetown,
Shokokon,
South Prairie,
Terre Haute.

HENRY COUNTY.

Andover,
Annawan,
Atkinson,
Bishop Hill,
Burns,
Cambridge,* (c. h.,)
Cleveland,
Colona Station,
Galva,*
Geneseo,*
Green River,
Kewanee,*
Minersville,
Morristown,
Nekoma,
Orion,
Oxford,
Pink Prairie,
Saxon,
Sharon,
Ulah,
Wethersfield,
Woodhull.

IROQUOIS COUNTY.

Ash Grove,
Ashkum,
Beaverville,
Buckley,
Chebanse,
Clifton,

IROQUOIS COUNTY—Continued.

Crescent City,
Danforth Station,
Del Rey,
Eden,
Gilman,
Iroquois,
L'Erable,
Luddenville,
Middleport, (c. h.,)
Milford,
Oakalla,
Onarga,*
Plato,
Sheldon,
Watseka.

JACKSON COUNTY.

Ava,
Bradley,
Carbondale,*
De Soto,
Elkville,
Fountain Bluff,
Grand Tower,
Hat Island,
Makauda,
Murphysboro',* (c. h.,)
Ora,
Vergennes,
Worthington.

JASPER COUNTY.

Hidalgo,
Island Creek,
Linder,
Newton* (c. h.,)
Rose Hill,
Saint Marie,
Willow Hill,
Yale.

JEFFERSON COUNTY.

Cub Prairie,
Dix,
Lynchburgh,
Harris Grove,
Moore's Prairie,
Mount Vernon,* (c.h.,)
Spring Garden.

JERSEY COUNTY.

Delhi,
Elsah,
Fidelity,
Fieldon,
Grafton,
Jerseyville,* (c. h.,)
Newbern,
Otter Creek.

JO DAVIESS COUNTY.

Apple River,
Avery,
Council Hill,
Council Hill Station,
Derinda,
Dunleith,
Elizabeth,
Excelsior Mills,
Galena,* (c. h.,)
Greenvale,
Guilford,
Hanover,
Houghton,
Howardsville,
Mount Sumner,
Nora,
Pitcherville,
Pleasant Valley,
Plum River,
Rush,
Scales Mound,
Stockton,
Warren,*
Willow,
Yankee Hollow.

JOHNSON COUNTY.

Cedar Bluff,
Cypress Creek,
Elvira,
Goreville,
Grantsburgh,
Lincoln Green,
Reynoldsburgh,
Sanburn,
Shinn's Point,
Vienna,* (c. h.,)

* Money-order office.

KANE COUNTY.

Aurora,*
Batavia,*
Big Rock,
Blackberry,
Blackberry Station,
Burlington,
Campton,
Carpentersville,
Clintonville,
Dundee,
East Burlington,
Elgin,*
Geneva*, (c. h.,)
Gilbert's,
Gray Willow,
Grouse,
Hampshire,
Jericho,
Kaneville,
Lafox,
Lodi Station,
Montgomery,
North Aurora,
North Plato,
Pingree Grove,
Saint Charles,*
Sugar Grove,
Udina.

KANKAKEE COUNTY.

Aroma,
Bourbonnais Grove,
Caberay,
Deselm,
Judson,
Kankakee,* (c. h.,)
Limestone,
Manteno,*
Momence,
Norton,
Rinosa,
Rockville,
Saint Anne,
Saint George,
Salina,
Sherburneville,
Union Hill.

KENDALL COUNTY.

Bristol,
Bristol Station,
Kendall,
Lewis,
Lisbon,
Little Rock,
Mellington,
Millbrook,
Newark,
Oswego,*
Pavilion,
Plano,
Plattville,
White Willow,
Yorkville, (c. h.)

KNOX COUNTY.

Abingdon,*
Altona,*
Centre Point,
Douglas,
Eugene,
Galesburgh,*
Gilson,
Henderson,
Hermon,
Knoxville,* (c. h.,)
Maquon,
Milroy,
North Prairie,
Oneida,*
Ontario,
Saint Augustine,
Truro,
Victoria,
Wataga,
Yates City.

LAKE COUNTY.

Antioch,
Dean's Corners,
Deerfield,
Diamond Lake,
Ela,
Emmett,
Fort Hill,
Fox Lake,
Fremont Centre,
Gage's Lakes,
Gilmer,
Hainesville,
Half Day,
Hickory,
Highland Park,
Lake Forrest,
Lake Zurich,
Libertyville,
Long Grove,
Millburn,
Newport,
O'Plain,
Rockland,
Rosecrans,
Sand Lake,
Volo,
Wauconda,
Waukegan,* (c. h.)

LA SALLE COUNTY.

Asbury,
Bruceville,
Cornville,
Dayton,
Deer Park,
Earlville,*
Farm Ridge,
Freedom,
Freedom Centre,
Galloway,
Garfield,
La Salle,*
Leland,
Lock,
Lostant,*
Lowell,
Marseilles,*
Mendota,*
Meriden,
Miner,
New Rutland,
Northville,
Norway,
Oglesby,
Ottawa,* (c. h.,)
Peru,*
Prairie Centre,
Seneca,
Serena,
Sheridan,
Streator,*
Tonica,*
Triumph,
Troy Grove,
Utica,
Vermillionville.

LAWRENCE COUNTY.

Bridgeport,
Hadley Statton,
Lawrenceville, (c. h.,)
Olive,
Russellville,
Saint Francisville,
Sumner.

LEE COUNTY.

Amboy,*
Ashton,
Dixon,* (c. h.,)
Eldena,
Franklin Grove,*
Gap Grove,
Lee Centre,
Malugin Grove,
Nachusa,
Nelson,
Paw Paw Grove,
South Willow Creek,
Sublette,
Willow Creek.

LIVINGSTON COUNTY.

Amity,
Ancona,
Blackstone,
Cayuga,
Chatsworth,*
Coalville,
Dwight,*
Fairbury,*
Forest,
Long Point,
Nevada,
New Michigan,
Oakdale,
Ocoya,
Odell,
Pontiac,* (c. h.,)
Potosi,
Reading,
Rook's Creek,
Sannemin,
Smithdale,
Sullivan Centre,
Sunbury.

LOGAN COUNTY.

Atlanta,*
Broadwell,
Elkhart City,*
Eminence,
Laenna,
Lawndale,
Lincoln,* (c. h.,)
Middletown,
Mount Pulaski.

MCDONOUGH COUNTY.

Adair,
Bardolph,
Blandinsville,*
Bushnell,*
Colchester,
Colmar,
Good Hope,
Industry,
Macomb,* (c. h.,)
New Philadelphia,
Pennington Point,
Prairie City,
Sciota,
Tennessee.

* Money-order office.

RICHLAND COUNTY.

Boot,
Calhoun,
Claremont,
Dundas,
Fransonia,
Madison,
Noble,
Olney,* (c. h.,)
Parkersburgh,
Stringtown,
Wakefield,
Wilsonburgh.

ROCK ISLAND COUNTY.

Andalusia,
Buffalo Prairie,
Camden Mills,
Carbon Cliff,
Coal Valley,
Copper Creek,
Cordova,
Drury,
Edington,
Franklin Crossing,
Hampton,
Hazlitt,
Hill's Station,
Illinois City,
Joslyn,
Moline,
Osborn,
Pleasant Ridge,
Port Byron,
Rapids City,
Rock Island* (c. h.)
Rural,
Watertown.

ST. CLAIR COUNTY.

Belleville,* (c. h.,)
Caseyville,
Centreville Station,
Creswell,
Darnstadt,
Dutch Hill,
East St. Louis,*
Fayetteville,
Floraville,
Freeburgh,
French Village,
Gartsides,
Lebanon,*
Lenzburgh,
Lowland,
Marissa,
Mascoutah,*
Millstadt,
Mud Creek,
New Athens,
New Pittsburgh,
O'Fallon Depot,
Ridge Prairie,
Risdon,
Shiloh,
Smithton,
Summerfield.

SALINE COUNTY.

Bankston,
El Dorado,
Gallatia,
Halltown,
Harrisburgh,* (c. h.,)
Hartford,
Mitchellsville,
Raleigh,
Somerset,
South America,
Stone Fort,
Texas City.

SANGAMON COUNTY.

Auburn,
Bates,
Berlin,
Berry,
Buffalo,
Chatham,
Chinkapin Hill,
Cotton Hill,
Curran,
Dawson,
Howlett,
Illiopolis,
Loami,
Mechanicsburgh,
New Berlin,
New Harmony,
Pawnee,
Pleasant Plains,
Richland,
Rochester,
Salisbury,
Sherman,
SPRINGFIELD,*(c.h.,)
Wheatfield,
Williamsville,
Woodside.

SCHUYLER COUNTY.

Birmingham,
Brooklyn,
Browning,
Camden,
Centre,
Doddsville,
Fredericksville,
Huntsville,
Littleton,
Pleasant View,
Rushville,* (c. h.,)
Sheldon's Grove,
Wayland.

SCOTT COUNTY.

Exeter,
Glasgow,
Manchester,
Merritt,
Naples,
Winchester,* (c. h.,)

SHELBY COUNTY.

Beck's Creek,
Big Spring,
Cold Spring,
Hark,
Holland,
Hooker,
Middlesworth,
Mode,
Moulton,
Moweaqua,
Oconee Station,
Prairie Home,
Shelbyville, (c. h.,)
Todd's Point,
Tower Hill,
Windsor.

STARK COUNTY.

Bradford,
Camp Grove,
Castleton,
Duncan,
Elmira,
La Fayette,
Lombardville,
Modena,
Osceola,
Pleasant Green,
Toulon,* (c. h.,)
West Jersey,
Wyoming.*

STEPHENSON COUNTY.

Buena Vista,
Cedarville,
Dakota,
Damascus,
Davis,*
Duncanon,
Eleroy,
Florence Station,
Freeport,* (c. h.,)
Kent,
Lena,*
Loran,
McConnell's Grove,
Oneco,
Orangeville,
Ridott,
Rock Grove,
Rock Run,
Silver Creek,
Waddam's Centre,
Waterman's Mills,
Winslow,
Yellow Creek.

TAZEWELL COUNTY.

Armington,
Boynton,
Circleville,
Deer Creek,
Delavan,*
Dillon,
Green Valley,
Groveland,
Hilton,
Hopedale,
Little Detroit,
Mackinaw,
Minier,
Morton,
Pekin,* (c. h.,)
Tremont,
Tullamore,
Washington.*

UNION COUNTY.

Anna,*
Dongola,
Jonesborough, (c. h.,)
Lick Creek,

* Money-order office.

UNION COUNTY—Continued.

Moscow,
Mount Pleasant,
Penninger,
South Pass,*
Union Point,
Western Saratoga,
Willard's Landing.

VERMILION COUNTY.

Blue Grass,
Catlin,
Circle,
Danville,* (c. h.,)
Fairmount,
Fithian,
Georgetown,
Grant,
Half-Way House,
Higginsville,
Hope,
Indianola,
Jordan,
Kentucky,
Long,
Marysville,
Myersville,
Oakwood,
Pilot,
Point Pleasant,
Ridge Farm,
Rossville,
Sugar Creek.

WABASH COUNTY.

Armstrong,
Corrieville,
Friend Grove,
Friendsville,
Gard's Point,
Mier,
Mount Carmel,*(c. h.,)
New Hope,
Rochester Mills.

WARREN COUNTY.

Berwick,
Cameron,
Colfax,
Denny,
Duck Creek,
Ellison,
Greenbush,
Ionia,
Little York,
Monmouth,* (c. h.,)
Roseville,
Spring Grove,
Swan Creek,
Utah,
Young America.*

WASHINGTON COUNTY.

Ashley,*
Ayer's Point,
Dubois,
Elkhorn,
Hoyleton,
Irvington,
Johanesburgh,
Lively Grove,
Nashville,* (c. h.,)
New Minden,
Okaw,
Plum Hill,
Richview,*
Venedy.

WAYNE COUNTY.

Enterprise,
Fairfield,* (c. h.,)
Home,
Jeffersonville,
Johnsonville,
Keenville,
Long Prairie,
Mount Erie,
New Baltimore,
New Franklin,
Pin Oak,
Pleasant Grove,
Wabash,
Zif.

WHITE COUNTY.

Burnt Prairie,
Carmi,* (c. h.,)
Emma,
Enfield,
Grayville,*
Mill Shoals,
Phillipstown,
Roland,

WHITE COUNTY—Continued.

Sacramento,
School,
Springerton.

WHITESIDES COUNTY.

Albany,
Coleta,
Como,
Erie,
Fenton,
Fulton,*
Galt,
Jefferson Corners,
Kingsbury,
Leon,
Lyndon,
Morrison,* (c. h.,)
New Genesee,
Portland,
Pratt,
Prophetstown,
Rock Falls,
Round Grove
South Hume,
Spring Hill,
Sterling,*
Union Grove.

WILL COUNTY.

Beecher,
Bird's Bridge,
Braidwood,
Channahon,
Crete,
Dupage,
Eagle Lake,
East Wheatland,
Elwood,
Endor,
Frankfort Station,
Gooding's Grove,
Green Garden,
Grinton,
Hadley,
Joliet,* (c. h.,)
Lockport,*
Mokena,
Monee,
New Lenox,
Peotone,
Pierce,
Plainfield,
Spencer,
Tamorack,
Wallingford,
Wilmington.*

WILLIAMSON COUNTY.

Attila,
Bainbridge,
Blairsville,
Coriuth,
Crab Orchard,
Fredonia,
Herrin's Prairie,
Lake Creek,
Locust Grove,
Marion,* (c. h.,)
Pulley's Mill,
Sarahsville,
Sulphur Springs.

WINNEBAGO COUNTY

Argyle,
Burritt,
Cherry Valley,*
Durand Station,*
Elida,
Fountaindale,
Harlem,
Harrison,
Kishwaukee,
Laona,
New Milford,
Pecatonica,*
Rockford,* (c. h.,)
Rockton,
Roscoe,*
Shirland,
Tyler,
Winnebago Depot.

WOODFORD COUNTY.

Cruger,
El Paso,*
Eureka,
Farmsville,
Kappa,
Low Point,
Metamora,* (c. h.,)
Minonk,*
Panola Station,
Secor,
Spring Bay,
Washburn.

---

* Money-order office.

INDIANA.

ADAMS COUNTY.

Canoper,
Decatur, (c. h.,)
Limber Lost,
Linn Grove,
Monmouth,
Pleasant Mills.

ALLEN COUNTY.

Aboite,
Arcola,
Cedarville,
Chamberlain,
Eel River,
Fort Wayne, (c. h.,)
Hall's Corners,
Harlan,
Heller's Corners,
Huntertown,
Leo,
Little River,
Maples,
Monroeville,*
New Haven,
Nine Mile,
Po,
Randall,
Root,
Sheldon,
Woodburn.

BARTHOLOMEW COUNTY.

Azalia,
Bray's Mills,
Burnsville,
Clifford,
Columbus, (o. h.,)
Elizabethtown,
Hartsville,
Hope,
Jonesville,
Lowell Mills,
Moore's Vineyard,
Mount Healthy,
Newbern,
St. Louis Crossing,
South Bethany,
Taylorsville,
Wailesborough,
Waymansville,
Waynesville.

BENTON COUNTY.

Aydelott,
Oxford, (c. h.,)
Pond Grove.

BLACKFORD COUNTY.

Hartford City, (c. h.,)
Millgrove,
Montpelier,
Priam.

BOONE COUNTY.

Dover,
Elizaville,
Holmes,
Jamestown,
Lebanon, (c. h.,)
Northern Depot,
Northfield,
Reese's Mill,
Royalton,
Slabtown,
Thorntown,*
White Lick,
Whitestown,
Zionsville.

BROWN COUNTY.

Bean Blossom,
Beck's Grove,
Cleona,
Elkinsville,
Marble,
Mount Liberty,
Mount Moriah,
Nashville, (c. h.,)
New Bellsville,
Oak Farm,
Pike's Peak,
Spearsville.

CARROLL COUNTY.

Burlington,
Burrows,
Camden,
Carroll,
Deer Creek,
Delphi, (c. h.,)
Lockport,
Pittsburgh,
Prince William.
Pyrmont,
Rockfield,
Wild Cat.

CASS COUNTY.

Amsterdam,
Anoka,
Big Indian,
Crittenden,
Curveton,
Dow,
Galveston,
Lincoln,
Logansport, (c. h.,)
Metea,
Montez,
New Waverly,
Onward,
Royal Centre,
Twelve Mile,
Twin Corners,
Walton.

CLARKE COUNTY.

Bennettsville,
Bethlehem,
Blue Lick,
Cementville,
Charlestown, (c. h.,)
Henryville,
Jeffersonville,*
Memphis,
Muddy Fork,
New Providence,
New Washington,
Oregon,
Otisco,
Otto,
Polk Run,
St. Joseph's Hill,
Sellersburgh,
Slate Cut,
Utica.

CLAY COUNTY.

Ashborough,
Bowling Green, (c.h.,)
Brazil,*
Centre Point,
Christy's Prairie,
Cloverland,
Coffee,
Eaglesfield,
Harmony,
Howesville,
Knightsville,
Martz,
Poland,
Staunton,
Turner's.

CLINTON COUNTY.

Berlin,
Burget's Corner,
Burnside,
Colfax,
Frankfort, (c. h.,)
Geetingsville,
Jefferson,
Kirk's Cross Roads,
Michigantown,
Middle Fork,
Mortousville,
Mulberry,
Pickard's Mill,
Rossville.

CRAWFORD COUNTY.

Alton,
Down Hill,
English,
Fredonia,
Grantsburgh,
Leavenworth, (c. h.,)
Magnolia,
*Marengo,
Mifflin,
Milltown,
Mount Prospect,
Padoria,
Pilot Knob,
Wickliffe.

* **Money-order office.**

17 P O

DAVIESS COUNTY.

Alfordsville,
Black Oak Ridge,
Clark's Prairie,
Epsom,
Glen Dale,
Lettsville,

Montgomery's Sta'n,
Owl Prairie,
Plainville,
Raglesville,*
Washington, (c. h.)

DEARBORN COUNTY.

Aurora, *
Bright,
Dillsborough,
Farmer's Retreat,
Guilford,
Guionsville,
Hansel's,
Harrmann's Station,
Holman,
Jones' Station,
Kelso,
Lawrenceburgh,
(c. h.,)

Lawrenceville,
Logan,
Manchester,
Moore's Hill,
New Alsace,
Pella,
Saint Leon,
Sparta,
Weisburgh,
Wilmington,
Wright's Corners,
Yorkville.

DECATUR COUNTY.

Adams,
Alert,
Clarksburgh,
Clifty,
Forest Hill,
Greensburgh, (c. h.f)
Kingston,
McCoy's Station,
Millhousen,

New Point,
Saint Maurice,
Saint Omer,
Saint Paul,
Sardinia,
Spring Hill,
Waynesburgh,
Westport,
Wintersville.

DE KALB COUNTY.

Auburn, (c. h.,)
Butler,
Coburn's Corners,
Coles' Corners,
Corunna,
Fairfield Centre,

Iba,
Mount Hope,
New Era,
Newville,
Spencerville,
Waterloo.*

DELAWARE COUNTY.

Albany,
Anthony,
Cowan,
Daleville,
Eaton,
Granville,
Harrison,
Muncie, (c. h.,)

New Burlington,
New Corner,
Richwoods,
Royerton,
Selma,
Sharon,
Wheeling,
Yorktown.

DUBOIS COUNTY.

Birdseye,
Bretzville,
Celestine,
Ditney Hill,
Duff,
Ferdinand,
Haysville,
Hillham,

Holland,
Huntingburgh,
Ireland,
Jasper, (c. h.,)
Kellerville,
Ludlow,
Portersville,
Schnellville.

ELKHART COUNTY.

Benton,
Bristol,
Elkhart,*
Fish Lake,
Goshen, (c. h.,)
Locke,

Middlebury.
Millersburgh,
New Paris,
Vistula,
Wakarusa,
Waterford Mills.

FAYETTE COUNTY.

Alpine,
Alquina,
Bentonville,
Columbia,
Connersville, (c. h.,)
Everton,

Groves,
Harrisburgh,
Lyon's Station,
Null's Mills,
Orange.

FLOYD COUNTY

Edwardsville,
Floyd's Knobs,
Galena,
Georgetown,

Greenville,
New Albany, (c. h.,)
Scottsville.

FOUNTAIN COUNTY.

Attica,*
Cole Creek,
Covington, (c. h.,)
Fountain,
Harveysburgh,
Hillsborough,

Newtown,
Rob Roy,
Snoddy's Mills,
Steam Corner,
Stone Bluffs,
Wallace,

FRANKLIN COUNTY.

Andersonville,
Blooming Grove,
Blue Creek,
Brookville, (c. h.,)
Cedar Grove,
Drewersburgh,
Enochsburgh,
Fairfield,
Hamburgh,
Haymond,
Huth,
Laurel,
Metamora,

Mixersville,
Mount Carmel,
New-Trenton,
Oak Forest,
Oldenburgh,
Peppertown,
Saint Peters,
South Gate,
Springfield,
Stip's Hill,
Whitcomb,
Wynn.

FULTON COUNTY.

Akron,
Bloomingsburgh,
Blue Grass,
Bruce's Lake,
Fulton,

Green Oak,
Kewanna,
Rochester, (c. h.,)
Sturgeon.

GIBSON COUNTY.

Bovine,
Buckskin,
Fort Branch,*
Francisco,
Haubstadt,
Hazleton,
King's Station,

Oakland City,
Owensville,
Patoka,
Princeton, (c. h.,)
Somerville,
West Buena Vista.

* Money-order office.

GRANT COUNTY.

Arcana,	New Cumberland,
Fairmount,	Point Isabel,
Jadden,	Roesburgh,
Jalapa,	Slash,
Jonesborough,	Sweetser's,
Marion,* (c. h.,)	Trask,
Mier,	Upland.

GREENE COUNTY.

Bloomfield,* (c. h.,)	Owensburgh,
Hobbieville,	Park,
Jasonville,	Pleasant Ridge,
Linton,	Scotland,
Lyons,	Solsberry,
Marco,	Swit's City,
Newark,	Worthington,
Newberry,	Wright.

HAMILTON COUNTY.

Arcadia,	New Britton,
Boxley,	Noblesville,* (c. h.,)
Carmel,	Omega,
Cicero,	Shielville,
Clarksville,	Strawtown,
Deming,	Westfield.
Eagletown,	

HANCOCK COUNTY.

Carrollton,	Milner's Corners,
Charlottesville,	Mount Comfort,
Cleveland,	Philadelphia,
Eden,	Sugar Creek,
Fortville,	Warrington,
Greenfield,* (c. h.,)	Westland,
Leaman Corner,	Willow Branch,
McCordsville,	Woodbury.

HARRISON COUNTY.

Barren,	Mauckport,
Bradford,	New Amsterdam,
Byrneville,	New Middletown,
Corydon,* (c. h.,)	New Salisbury,
Crisp's Cross Roads,	Palmyra,
Elizabeth,	Rosewood,
Evans' Landing,	Rothrock's Mills,
Hancock,	Salina,
King's Cave,	Sharp's Mills,
Laconia,	Valley City.
Lanesville,	

HENDRICKS COUNTY.

Amo,	New Elizabeth,
Belleville,	New Winchester,
Brownsburgh,	North Salem,
Cartersburgh,	Pecksburgh,
Centre Valley,	Pittsborough,
Clayton,	Plainfield,*
Coatesville,	Smootsdell,
Danville,* (c. h.,)	Stilesville.
Friendswood,	

HENRY COUNTY.

Ashland,	Millville,
Blountsville,	Mount Summit,
Cadiz,	New Castle,* (c. h.,)
Dunreith,	New Lisbon,
Greensborough,	Ogden,
Honey Creek,	Raysville,
Knightstown,	Rogersville,
Lewisville,	Spiceland,
Luray,	Springport,
Mechanicsburgh,	Straughn's Station,
Middletown,	Sulphur Springs.

HOWARD COUNTY.

Alto,	New London,
Cassville,	Oakford,
Centre,	Poplar Grove,
Ervin,	Russiaville,
Greentown,	Shanghai,
Jerome,	West Liberty.
Kokomo,* (c. h.,)	

HUNTINGTON COUNTY.

Antioch,	Markle,
Bracken,	Mount Etna,
Brown's Corner,	Roanoke,
Huntington,* (c. h.,)	Warren.
Majenica,	

JACKSON COUNTY.

Brownstown,* (c. h.,)	Mellenbruch,
Conlogue,	Mooney,
Cortland,	Retreat,
Crothersville,	Rockford,
Dudleytown,	Seymour,*
Ewing,	Shields,
Findley's Mills,	Sparksville,
Freetown,	Tampico,
Houston,	Vallonia,
Medora,	White Creek.

JASPER COUNTY.

Pleasant Grove,	Rensselaer,* (c. h.,)
Remington,	

JAY COUNTY.

Balbec,	Mills' Corners,
Bear Creek,	New Corydon,
Bluff Point,	New Mt. Pleasant,
Boundary,	Pennville,
College Corner,	Portland,* (c. h.,)
Dunkirk,	Powers,
Greene,	Redkey,
Hector,	Salamonia,
Jordan,	Westchester.

JEFFERSON COUNTY.

Barbersville,	Creswell,
Bryantsburgh,	Deputy,
Canaan,	Dupont,

* Money-order office.

JEFFERSON COUNTY—Continued.

Eagle Springs,
Graham,
Hanover,
Home,
Kent,
Lancaster,
Madison, (c. h.,)
Manville,

Mud Lick,
Neil's Creek,
North Madison,
Saluda,
Stony Point,
Swanville,
Volga,
Wirt.

JENNINGS COUNTY.

Benville,
Brewersville,
Butlerville,
Cana,
Commiskey,
Lovett,
Nebraska,
North Vernon,
Oakdale,

Paris,
Queensville,
San Jacinto,
Scipio,
Sherman,
Six Mile,
Slate,
Vernon, (c. h.,)
Zenas.

JOHNSON COUNTY.

Amity,
Bargersville,
Bluff Creek,
Edinburgh,*
Franklin, (c. h.,)
Greenwood,
Needham's Station,

Nineveh,
Samaria,
Smith's Valley,
Trafalgar,
Urmeyville,
Whiteland.

KNOX COUNTY.

Bicknell,
Bruceville,
Busseron,
Decker's Station,
Edwardsport,
Emison Station,
Freelandville,

Lovely Dale,
Oaktown,
Pond Creek Mills,
Sandborn,
Spaldingville,
Vincennes, (c. h.,)
Wheatland.

KOSCIUSKO COUNTY.

Atwood,
Beaver Dam,
Boydston's Mills,
Etna Green,
Hepton,
Leesburgh,
Milford,
Millwood,
Oneida,
Orion,

Oswego,
Palestine,
Pierceton,*
Rose Hill,
Sevastopol,
Silver Lake,
Syracuse,
Warsaw, (c. h.,)
Wooster.

LA GRANGE COUNTY.

Brighton,
Brushy Prairie,
Eden Mills,
La Grange, (c. h.,)
Lima,
Marcy,
Mongoquinong,

Mount Pisgah,
Ontario,
Ringgold,
Scott,
South Milford,
Valentine,
Wolcottville.

LAKE COUNTY.

Brunswick,
Cassella,
Cedar Lake,
Clarke Station,
Crown Point, (c. h.,)
Deep River,
Dyer,
Gibson's Station,
Hobart,
Lake Station,
Le Roy,

Lowell,
Merrillville,
Miller's Station,
Orchard Grove,
Ross,
Saint John,
Schererville,
Toleston,
West Creek,
Winfield.

LA PORTE COUNTY.

Callao,
Corymbo,
Crossing,
Door Village,
Hanna Station,
Haskell,
Kingsbury,
La Crosse,

La Porte, (c. h.,)
Michigan City,*
Rolling Prairie,
Stillwell,
Union Mills,
Wanatah,
Westville.*

LAWRENCE COUNTY.

Avoca,
Bedford, (c. h.,)
Bono,
Bryantsville,
Erie,
Fayetteville,
Fort Ritner,
Georgia,
Guthrie,

Heltonville,
Huron,
Leesville,
Mitchell,*
River Vale,
Silverville,
Springville,
Tunnelton.

MADISON COUNTY.

Alexandria,
Alfonte,
Anderson, (c. h.,)
Chesterfield,
Elwood,
Fishersburgh,
Florida,
Forestville,
Frankton,
Huntsville,

Markleville,
Mercury,
Ovid,
Pendleton,*
Perkinsville,
Prospect,
Prosperity,
Rigdon,
Summitville,
Zinsburgh.

MARION COUNTY.

Acton,
Augusta Station,
Bridgeport,
Broad Ripple,
Castleton,
Clermont,
Cumberland,
Fall Creek,
Gallaudet,
Glenn's Valley,
INDIANAPOLIS,*
(c. h.,)

James Switch,
Julietta,
Lawrence,
Oaklandon,
Southport,
Spring Valley,
Sunny Side,
Trader's Point,
Valley Mills,
Waynewood,
West Newton,
Woodbank.

* Money-order office.

MARSHALL COUNTY.

Argos,	Plymouth,* (c. h.,)
Bourbon,	Tippecanoetown,
Bremen,	Tyner City,
Inwood,	Walnut,
Marmont,	Walnut Hill.
Maxinkuckee,	

MARTIN COUNTY.

Dover Hill,* (c. h.,)	Natchez,
Dye,	Shoals,
Keck's Church,	Sitka,
Loogootee,*	South Martin,
McCameron,	Trinity Springs.
Mountain Spring,	

MIAMI COUNTY.

Allen,	Mexico,
Amboy,	Miami,
Bennett's Switch,	Niconza,
Birmingham,	North Grove,
Bunker Hill,	Paw Paw,
Busaco,	Perrysburgh,
Chili,	Peru,* (c. h.,)
Courter,	Reserve,
Deedsville,	Santa Fé,
Denver,	Stockdale,
Five Corners,	Wawpecong,
Gilead,	Wheatville,
McGrawsville,	Xenia.

MONROE COUNTY.

Bloomington,* (c. h.,)	Smithville,
Bryant's Creek,	Stanford,
Clear Creek,	Stinesville,
Ellittsville,	Unionville.
Harrodsburgh,	

MONTGOMERY COUNTY.

Alamo,	New Ross,
Ashby's Mills,	Orth,
Boston Store,	Parkersburgh,
Brown's Valley,	Pleasant Hill,
Clouser's Mills,	Potato Creek,
Crawfordsville,* (c.h.,)	Prairie Edge,
Darlington,	Shannondale,
Ladoga,*	Waveland,
Lane,	Waynetown,
Linden,	Wesley,
Mace,	Whitesville.
New Richmond,	

MORGAN COUNTY.

Alaska,	Martinsville,* (c. h.,)
Brooklyn,	Monrovia,
Centreton,	Mooresville,
Eminence,	Morgantown,*
Hall,	Paragon,
Hyndsdale,	Red House,
Landersdale,	Waverly.
Mahalasville,	

NEWTON COUNTY.

Beaver City,	Kentland,* (c. h.,)
Brook,	Morocco,
Goodland,	Pilot Grove.

NOBLE COUNTY.

Albion, (c. h.,)	Lisbon,
Avilla,	Merriam,
Brimfield,	Noble,
Cromwell,	Rome City,
Green Centre,	Swan,
Indian Village,	Wawaka,
Kendallville,*	Wilmot,
Ligonier,*	Wolf Lake.

OHIO COUNTY.

Aberdeen,	Hartford,
Bear Branch,	Rising Sun, (c. h.)

ORANGE COUNTY.

Chambersburgh,	Paoli,* (c. h.,)
French Lick,	Rego,
Greenbrier,	Stamper's Creek,
Leipsic,	Valeene,
Newton Stewart,	West Baden,
Orangeville,	Young's Creek.
Orleans,*	

OWEN COUNTY.

Arney,	Hausertown,
Atkinsonville,	Jordan Village,
Cataract,	Patricksburgh,
Cuba,	Quincy,
Deem,	Spencer,* (c. h.,)
Farmer's Station,	Stockton,
Freedom,	Vandalia,
Gosport,	White Hall.

PARKE COUNTY.

Annapolis,	Lusk's Springs,
Armiesburgh,	Mansfield,
Bellmore,	Montezuma,
Bethany,	Numa,
Bloomingdale,	Parkville,
Bridgeton,	Portland Mills,
Bruin's Cross Roads,	Rockville,* (c. h.,)
Catlin,	Rosedale,
Clinton Rock,	Roseville,
Coloma,	Russell's Mills,
Delta,	Sylvania,
Howard,	Waterman.
Jessup's Station,	

PERRY COUNTY.

Adyeville,	Lilly Dale,
Cannelton,* (c. h.,)	Mount Pleasant,
Celina,	Oil Creek,
Derby,	Ranger,
Dexter,	Rock Island,
Don Juan,	Rome,
Doolittle's Mills,	Rono,
Foster's Ridge,	Tell City,*
Leopold,	Troy.

* Money-order office.

PIKE COUNTY.

Leoti,	Spurgeon,
Otwell,	Union,
Petersburgh, (c. h.,)	Winslow.
Pikeville,	

PORTER COUNTY.

Boon Grove,	Porter Station,
Chesterton,	Salt Creek,
Furnessville,	Tassinong,
Hebron,	*Valparaiso*, (c. h.,)
Kout's Station,	Wheeler.
Porter's Cross Roads,	

POSEY COUNTY.

Black Hawk Mills,	New Harmony,*
Blairsville,	Parker's Settlem'nt,
Cynthiana,	Poseyville,
Farmersville,	Saint Wendells,
Hickory Branch,	Stewartsville,
Mount Vernon,(c.h.,)	Wadesville.

PULASKI COUNTY.

Francesville,	Oak,
Gundrum,	Pulaski,
Medarysville,	Star City,
Monterey,	*Winamac,* (c. h.,)

PUTNAM COUNTY.

Bainbridge,	Hamrick's Station,
Belle Union,	Manhattan,
Cairo,	Morton,
Carpentersville,	Mount Meridian,
Cloverdale,	New Maysville,
Fillmore,	Putnamville,
Greencastle, (c. h.,)	Reelsville,
Groveland,	Russellville.

RANDOLPH COUNTY.

Arba,	Neff,
Balaka,	New Pittsburgh,
Bartonia,	Parker,
Bloomingport,	Randolph,
Castle,	Ridgeville,
Cerro Gordo,	Saratoga,
Deerfield,	Snow Hill,
Fairview,	Spartanburgh,
Farmland,	Trenton,
Harrisville,	Union City,*
Losantville,	*Winchester,* (c. h.,)
Lynn,	Windsor.

RIPLEY COUNTY.

Ballstown,	Hermann,
Batesville,	Holton,
Benham's Store,	Milan,
Cross Plains,	Morris,
Delaware,	Napoleon,
Elrod,	New Marion,
Friendship,	North Hogan,

RIPLEY COUNTY—Continued.

Olean,	Spade's Depot,
Osgood,*	Sunman,
Pierceville,	Titusville,
Poston,	*Versailles,* (c. h.,)
Rei,	Vine's Springs.
Rexville,	

RUSH COUNTY.

Beech Grove,	New Salem,
Carthage,	Raleigh,
Falmouth,	Richland,
Homer,	*Rushville,* (c. h.,)
Manilla,	Star,
Milroy,	Steele's,
Moscow,	Sumner.

ST. JOSEPH COUNTY.

Lakeville,	Richardson,
Mishawaka,*	*South Bend,* (c. h.,)
New Carlisle,*	Sumption Prairie,
North Liberty,	Terre Coupee,
Notre Dame,*	Walkerton,
Oceola,	Woodland.

SCOTT COUNTY.

Afton,	*Lexington,* (c. h.,)
Alpha,	Vienna,
Austin,	Woostertown.
Holman Station,	

SHELBY COUNTY.

Blue Ridge,	Marietta,
Boggstown,	Moral,
Brookfield,	Morristown,
Conn's Creek,	Mount Auburn,
Fairland,	Noah,
Fenn's	Prescott,
Flat Rock,	Ray's Crossing,
Fountaintown,	*Shelbyville,* (c. h.,)
Freeport,	Smithland,
Lewis Creek,	Sulphur Hill,
London,	Winterroud.

SPENCER COUNTY.

Buffaloville,	Mariah Hill,
Dale,	Midway,
Enterprise,	Newtonville,
Fulda,	Oakland,
Gentryville,	*Rockport,* (c. h.,)
Grand View,	Saint Meinrad,
Lake,	Santa Claus.

STARKE COUNTY.

Brandtwood,	Lake City,
English Lake,	North Bend,
Grover Town,	North Judson,
Hamlet,	San Pierre,
Kankakee,	Toto.
Knox, (c. h.,)	

* Money-order office.

STEUBEN COUNTY.

Alvarado,	Metz,
Angola,* (c. h.,)	Nevada Mills,
Clear Lake,	Orland,*
Crooked Creek,	Pleasant Lake,
Fish Creek,	Salem Centre,
Flint,	Turkey Creek,
Fremont,	York Centre.
Hamilton,	

SULLIVAN COUNTY.

Ascension,	Paxton's,
Bateham,	Pleasantville,
Carlisle,*	Shelburn,
Graysville,	Sullivan,* (c. h.,)
Merom,	Turman's Creek.
New Lebanon,	

SWITZERLAND COUNTY.

Bennington,	North's Landing,
Centre Square,	Patriot,
Craig,	Pleasant,
East Enterprise,	Quercus Grove,
Florence,	Sugar Branch,
Moorefield,	Vevay,* (c. h.)
Mount Sterling,	

TIPPECANOE COUNTY.

Americus,	Monitor,
Ash Grove,	Montmorency,
Battle Ground,	Newton's Retreat,
Chauncey,	Octagon,
Clark's Hill,	Pettit,
Colburn,	Romney,
County Line,	Shawnee Mound,
Culver's Station,	Stockwell,*
Dayton,	Sugar Grove,
Farmer's Institute,	Transitville,
Glen Hall,	West Point,
La Fayette,* (c. h.,)	Wyandotte.

TIPTON COUNTY.

Curtisville,	Sharpsville,
Groomsville,	Tetersburgh,
Jackson Station,	Tipton,* (c. h.,)
Nevada,	West Kinderhook,
New Lancaster,	Windfall.
Normanda,	

UNION COUNTY.

Beechy Mire,	Dunlapsville,
Billingsville,	Liberty,* (c. h.,)
Brownsville,	Lotus,
Clifton,	Quakertown.
Cottage Grove,	

VANDERBURGH COUNTY.

Armstrong,	Kasson,
Evansville,* (c. h.,)	McCutchanville,
Inglefield,	Mechanicsville,

VANDERBURGH COUNTY—Continued.

Nash Depot,	St. Joseph.
Oakdam,	

VERMILLION COUNTY.

Clinton,	Quaker Hill,
Eugene,	Saint Bernice,
Newport,* (c. h.,)	Toronto.
Perrysville,	

VIGO COUNTY.

Burnett,	Prairieton,
Cookerly,	Riley,
Ellsworth,	Saint Mary's,
Lewis,	Sandford,
Nelson,	Seelyville,
New Goshen,	Terre Haute,* (c. h.,)
Pimento,	Youngstown.
Prairie Creek,	

WABASH COUNTY.

America,	New Holland,
Belden,	New Madison,
Dora,	North Manchester,*
La Fontaine,	Rich Valley,
La Gro,	Roann,
Laketon,	Somerset,
Liberty Mills,	Urbana,
Lincolnville,	Wabash, (c. h.*)
Lodi,	

WARREN COUNTY.

Independence.	Rainsville,
Marshfield,	State Line, *
Pine Village,	West Lebanon,*
Poolsville,	Williamsport,* (c. h.)

WARRICK COUNTY.

Boonville,* (c. h.,)	Lee,
Canal,	Lynnville,
Crowville,	Newburgh,*
Elberfeld,	Polk Patch,
Ely,	Wheatonville,
Folsomville,	Yankeetown.

WASHINGTON COUNTY.

Beck's Mills,	Kossuth,
Campbellsburgh,	Little York,
Canton,	Livonia,
Chesnut Hill,	Martinsburgh,
Claysville,	Millport,
Farabee's Station,	New Philadelphia
Fredericksburgh.	Organ Spring,
Hardinsburgh,	Pekin,
Harristown,	Salem,* (c. h.,)
Heffren,	Saltilloville.
Hitchcock's Station,	

* Money-order office.

WAYNE COUNTY.

Abington,	Green's Fork,
Bethel,	Hagerstown, *
Boston,	Jacksonburgh,
Cambridge City,*	Milton,
Centreville, (c. h.,)	New Garden,
Chester,	Olive Hill,
Cox's Mills,	Richmond,*
Dalton,*	Webster,
Dublin,*	White Water,
East Germantown,	Williamsburgh.
Economy,	

WELLS COUNTY.

Barber's Mills,	Murray,
Bluffton, (c. h.,)	Nottingham,
Fox,	Ossian,

WELLS COUNTY—Continued.

Reiffsburgh,	Zanesville.
Vera Cruz,	

WHITE COUNTY.

Brookston,	Monon,
Burnett's Creek,	*Monticello,* * (c. h.,)
Chalmers,	Reynolds,*
Flowerville,	Seafield,
Idaville,	Wolcott.

WHITLEY COUNTY.

Alma,	Larwill,
Churubusco,	Laud,
Coesse,	Saturn,
Collamer,	South Cleveland,
Columbia City,(c. h.,)	South Whitley,
Hecla,	Washington Centre.

INDIAN TERRITORY.

CHEROKEE NATION.

Coodey's Bluff,	Marble Salt Works,
Flint,	Oseuma,
Fort Gibson,	*Tahlequah,* (c. h.,)
McLean's Station,	Webber's Falls.

CHICKASAW NATION.

Carriage Point,	Rock Spring,
Fort Arbuckle,	Tishemingo.
Fort Washita,	

CHOCTAW NATION.

Atoka,	Boggy Depot,

CHOCTAW NATION—Continued.

Brushey,	Pryor's Creek,
Buckluxy,	Red Oak,
Choctaw Agency.	Spring Bluff,
Doaksville,	Wheelock.
Fort Sill,	

CREEK NATION.

Creek Agency,	Okmulkee.
Micco.	

SEMINOLE NATION.

We-Wo-Ka.

IOWA.

ADAIR COUNTY.

Arbor Hill,	Holaday's,
Casey,	Jackson,
Fontanelle, * (c. h.,)	Orient,
Greenfield,	Stuart.
Hebron,	

ADAMS COUNTY.

Carl,	Nevinville,
Corning,	Prescott,
East Nodoway,	*Quincy,* * (c. h.,)
Mount Etna,	Simpson.

ALLAMAKEE COUNTY.

Allamakee,	Clear Creek,

ALLAMAKEE COUNTY—Continued.

Dalby,	Myron,
Dorchester,	Postville,*
Elon,	Rossville,
French Creek,	Union Prairie,
Harper's Ferry,	Village Creek,
Ion,	Volney,
Lansing,*	Waterville,
Ludlow,	*Waukon,* * (c. h.)
Lycurgus,	

APPANOOSE COUNTY.

Beetrace,	Dennis,
Caldwell,	Griffinsville,
Centerville, * (c. h.,)	Hibbsville,
Cincinnati,	Iconium,

* Money-order office.

APPANOOSE COUNTY—Continued.

Jerome,
Livingston,
Milledgeville,
Moravia,
Moulton,
Numa,

Orleans,
Tranquility,
Unionville,
Walnut City,
Wells' Mills.

AUDUBON COUNTY.

Exira, (c. h.,)
Hamlin Grove,

Oakfield.

BENTON COUNTY.

Belle Plaine,*
Benton Centre,
Blairstown,*
Burk,
Florence,
Luzerne,
Mount Auburn,

Paul,
Robin,
Shellsburgh,*
Spencer Grove,
Urbanna,
Vinton, (c. h.)

BLACK HAWK COUNTY.

Barclay,
Blakeville,
Cedar Falls,*
Cedar Valley,
Enterprise,
Gilbertville,
Hudson,

Laporte City,
Lester,
Miller's Creek,
Nautrille,
Raymond,
Waterloo, (c. h.)

BOONE COUNTY.

Boonesborough,(c.h.,)
Casady's Corner,
Mackey's Grove,
Mineral Ridge,
Moingona,*
Montana,

Pilot Mound,
Prairie Hill,
Sweede Point,
Worth,
Yough.

BREMER COUNTY.

Buck Creek,
Denver,
Eagle,
Frederica,
Horton,
Jaynesville,*
Leroy,

Mentor,
Plainfield,
Spring Lake,
Sumner,
Tripoli,
Waverly, (c. h.)

BUCHANAN COUNTY.

Atlanta,
Brandon,
Buffalo Grove,
Castleville,
Chatham,
Fairbank,
Hazelton,
Independence, (c. h.,)
Jessup,

Kier,
Middlefield,
Newtonville,
Otterville,
Quasqueton,
Sunny Side,
Ward's Corners,
Winthrop.

BUENA VISTA COUNTY.

Sargentsville,
Sioux Rapids,

Storm Lake.

BUTLER COUNTY.

Aplington,
Boylan's Grove,
Butler Centre, (c. h.,)
Clarksville,
Elm Springs,
New Hartford,

Parkersburgh,
Shell Rock,
Swanton,
Union Ridge,
Willoughby.

CALHOUN COUNTY.

Lake City, (c. h.,)
Pomeroy,

Twin Lakes,
Yatesville.

CARROLL COUNTY.

Browning,
Carroll City,
Carrollton, (c. h.,)

Coon Rapids,
Glidden,
Mack's.

CASS COUNTY.

Anita,
Atlantic,*
Edna,

Grove City,
Lewis, (c. h.,)
Whitneyville.

CEDAR COUNTY.

Cedar Bluff,
Cessford,
Clarence,*
Downey,
Durant,*
Gower's Ferry,
Inland,
Lowden,*
Massillon,
Mechanicsville,*

Pedee,
Pleasant Hill,
Red Oak,
Rochester,
Spring Dale,
Stanwood,
Tipton, (c. h.,)
West Branch,
York Prairie,
Zoar.

CERRO GORDO COUNTY.

Clear Lake,
Geneseo,
Lime Creek,
Mason City, (c. h.,)

Owen's Grove,
Plymouth,
Rock,
Shell Rock Falls

CHEROKEE COUNTY.

Aurelia,
Cherokee, (c. h.,)
Hazard,

Pilot Rock,
Washta.

CHICKASAW COUNTY.

Bradford,
Chickasaw, (c. h.,)
Deerfield,
Fredericksburgh,
Ionia,
Jacksonville,
Lawler,

Little Turkey,
Nashua,*
New Hampton,
North Washington,
Stapleton,
Williamstown.

CLARKE COUNTY.

Green Bay,
Hopeville,
Lacelle,
Liberty,
Murray,

Nortonville,
Oceola, (c. h.,)
Ottawa,
Prairie Grove,
Smyrna.

Money-order office

CLAY COUNTY.

Annieville.
Douglas Centre,
Gillett's Grove,
Peterson, (*c. h.,*)
Spencer.

CLAYTON COUNTY.

Ceres,
Clayton,
Communia,
Council Hill,
Cox's Creek,
Elkader,* (*c. h.,*)
Elkport,
Farmersburgh,
Garnavillo,*
Gem,
Giard,
Guttenberg,*
Hardin,
Highland,
Little Port,
Luana,
McGregor,*
Mederville,
Millville,
Monona,
National,
North McGregor,
Read,
Saint Sebald,
Sigel,
Strawberry Point,*
Volga City,
Wagner,
Yankee Settlement.

CLINTON COUNTY.

Boon Spring,
Brookfield,
Buena Vista,
Burgess,
Calmus,
Camanche,
Charlotte,
Clinton,*
De Witt,* (*c. h.,*)
Elk River,
Elvira,
Grand Mound,
Low Moor,
Lyons,*
Malone,
Orange,
Ten-mile House,
Toronto,
Welton,
Wheatland.*

CRAWFORD COUNTY.

Boyer River,
Crawford,
Denison, (*c. h.,*)
West Side.

DALLAS COUNTY.

Adel,* (*c. h.,*)
Boone,
Dallas Centre,
De Soto,*
Dexter,*
Greenvale,
Linden,
Minburn,
Nordyk,
Perry,
Redfield,
Snyder,
Van Metre,
Waukee Station,
Xenia.

DAVIS COUNTY.

Albany,
Bloomfield,* (*c. h.,*)
Brown's Mills,
Chequist,
Drakesville,
Floris,
Monterey,
Oak Spring,
Pulaski,
Savannah,
Stiles,
Troy,
West Grove.

DECATUR COUNTY.

Davis City,
Decatur,
Elk,
Franklin,

DACATUR COUNTY—Continued.

Garden Grove,
Green Valley,
High Point,
Leon,* (*c. h.,*)
Long Creek,
New Buda,
Patriot,
Pleasanton,
Sedgewick,
Spring Valley,
Terre Haute,
Westerville.

DELAWARE COUNTY.

Almoral,
Bartyville,
Campton,
Colesburgh,
Delaware,
Delhi, (*c. h.,*)
Earlville,
Forestville,
Golden Prairie,
Greeley,
Hazle Green,
Hopkinton,*
Manchester,*
Masonville,
Milo,
Mount Hope,
Sand Spring,
Tower Hill,
Uniontown,
York.

DES MOINES COUNTY.

Augusta,
Burlington,* (*c. h.,*)
Danville,
Dodgeville,
Franklin Mills,
Huron,
Kingston,
Kossuth,
Latty,
La Vega,
Linton,
Middletown,
Northfield,
Parrish,
Pleasant Grove,
South Flint,
Sperry.

DICKINSON COUNTY.

Milford,
Spirit Lake, (*c. h.*)

DUBUQUE COUNTY.

Allison,
Ballyclough,
Bankston,
Cascade,
Cottage Hill,
Dubuque,* (*c. h.,*)
Durango,
Dyersville,*
Epworth,
Farley,
Fillmore,
King,
Lattner's,
Melleray,
New Vienna,
Ogden,
Peosta,
Pin Oak,
Rickardsville,
Rock Dale,
Sheffield,
Sherrill's Mount,
Tivoli,
Worthington,
Zwingle.

EMMETT COUNTY.

Armstrong's Grove,
Emmett,
Estherville, (*c. h.,*)
High Lake.

FAYETTE COUNTY.

Bethel,
Brush Creek,
Clermont,*
Douglass,
Eden,
El Dorado,
Elgin,
Fayette,*
Hawk Eye,
Illyria,
Lima,
Mill,

* Money-order office.

FAYETTE COUNTY—Continued.

Oran,
Otsego,
Putnam,
Richfield,
Scott Centre,
Seaton,

Taylorsville,
Wardena,
Waucoma,
West Union,* (c. h.,)
Wilson Grove.

FLOYD COUNTY.

Charles City,* (c. h.,)
Floyd,
Hackberry,
Howardville,
Marble Rock,
Nora Springs,

Rockford,
Rock Grove City,
Rudd,
Ulster,
Watertown.

FRANKLIN COUNTY.

Chapin,
Coldwater,
Geneva,
Hampton,* (c. h.,)
Ingham,
Maysville,

Menzie,
Oakland Valley,
Otisville,
Shobe's Grove,
Washburn.

FREMONT COUNTY.

Bartlett,
Eastport,
Hamburgh,
High Creek,
Manti,

Percival,
Plum Hollow,
Sidney,* (c. h.,)
Tabor,*
Walnut Creek.

GREENE COUNTY.

Grand Junction,
Jefferson,* (c. h.,)
Northville,

Rippey,
Scranton Station.

GRUNDY COUNTY.

Grundy Centre, (c. h.,)
Lincoln Centre,

Wadiloup.

GUTHRIE COUNTY.

Bear Grove,
Dale City,
Dalmanutha,
Dodge,

Guthrie,
Guthrie Centre,
Moffitt's Grove,
Panora,* (c. h.)

HAMILTON COUNTY.

Blairsburgh,
Homer,
Hook's Point,
Lakin's Grove,

Randall,
Rose Grove,
Webster City,* (c. h.,)
Williams.

HANCOCK COUNTY.

Concord,
Crystal Lake,

Ellington, (c. h.,)
Upper Grove.

HARDIN COUNTY.

Ackley,*
Alden,
Berlin,
Cottage,
Delanti,
Eldora,* (c. h.,)
Hardin City,

Iowa Falls,*
New Providence,
Point Pleasant,
Steamboat Rock,
Tipton Grove,
Union.

HARRISON COUNTY.

Calhoun,
Dunlap,
Harris Grove,
Little Sioux,
Logan,
Magnolia,* (c. h.,)
Missouri Valley,*
Modale,

Mondamin,
Reeder's Mills,
Saint John,
Unionburgh,
Whitesborough,
Woodbine,
Yazoo.

HENRY COUNTY.

Boyleston,
Cotton Grove,
Hillsborough,
Lowell,
Marshall,
Mt. Pleasant,* (c. h.,)
New London,*
Oakland Mills,

Rome,
Salem,*
Swedesburgh,
Trenton,
Wayne,
Winfield,
Winona.

HOWARD COUNTY.

Busti,
Chester,
Cresco,*
Foreston,
Glen Roy,

Howard Centre,
Lime Spring,
New Oregon,* (c. h.,)
Pond Valley,
Saratoga.

HUMBOLDT COUNTY.

Addison,
Dakotah, (c. h.,)
Humboldt,
Lott's Creek,

Rutland,
Springvale,
Viona,
Wacousta.

IDA COUNTY.

Ida, (c. h.,)

Willow Dale.

IOWA COUNTY.

Boltonville,
Foote,
Genoa Bluff,
Homestead,*
Koszta,
Ladore,
Lytle City,

Marengo,* (c. h.,)
Millersburgh,
North English,
Rest,
Stelapolis,
Victor,*
York Centre.

JACKSON COUNTY.

Andrew, (c. h.,)
Bellevue,*
Bridgeport,
Canton,

Cottonville,
Farmer's Creek,
Fulton,
Garry Owen,

* Money-order office.

JACKSON COUNTY—Continued.

Higginsport,
Iron Hills,
La Motte,
Maquoketa,*
Mill Rock,
Monmouth,
Mount Algor,
Otter Creek,
Ozark,
Sabula,*
Saint Donatus,
Spragueville,
Spring Brook,
Sterling,
Union Centre,
Van Buren,
Wickliffe.

JASPER COUNTY.

Amboy,
Clyde,
Colfax,
Galesburgh,
Greencastle,
Horn,
Jasper City,
Lynnville,
Monroe,*
Newton, (c. h.,)
Prairie City,*
Sugar Creek,
Vandalia,
Warren Grove.

JEFFERSON COUNTY.

Abingdon,
Baker,
Botavia,
Brookville,
Fairfield, (c. h.,)
Germanville,
Glasgow,
Glendale,
Harvey's Mills,
Libertyville,
Lockridge,
Merrimac,
Pleasant Plain,
Salina,
Wooster.

JOHNSON COUNTY.

Amish,
Belle Air,
Bon Accord,
Chase,
Copi,
Coralville,
Danforth,
Frank Pierce,
Iowa City, (c. h.,)
Newport,
North Liberty,
Oasis,
Oxford,
Palestine,
Seventy-eight,
Shueyville,
Solon,
Tiffin,
Windham.

JONES COUNTY.

Anamosa, (c. h.,)
Bowen's Prairie,
Castle Grove,
Clayford,
Clay Mills,
Edinburgh,
Fairview,
Grove Creek,
Highland Grove,
Johnson,
Langworthy,
Madison,
Monticello,*
Oxford Mills,
Scotch Grove,
Walnut Fork,
Wyoming.*

KEOKUK COUNTY.

Aurora,
Baden,
Butler,
Chandaller,
Coal Creek,
Creswell,
Garibaldi,
Hayesville,
Ioka,
Lancaster,
Manhattan,
Martinsburgh,
Richland,*
Sigourney, (c. h.,)
South English,
Springfield,
Talleyrand,
Webster,
What Cheer,
White Pigeon.

KOSSUTH COUNTY.

Algona, (c. h.,)
Buffalo Fork,
Darien,
Greenwood Centre,
Irvington,
Kossuth Centre,
Seneca.

LEE COUNTY.

Belfast,
Big Mound,
Camackville,
Charleston,
Clay's Grove,
Croton,
Denmark,*
Dover,
Fort Madison, (c. h.,)
Franklin Centre,
Jeffersonville,
Jollyville,
Keokuk,*
Montrose,
New Boston,
Pilot Grove,
Primrose,
Saint Paul,
Sandusky,
Summitville,
Vincennes,
Warren,
West Point.

LINN COUNTY.

Bertram,
Cedar Rapids,*
Central City,
Centre Point,
Dry Creek,
Fairfax,
Flemingville,
La Fayette,
Lisbon,*
Marion, (c. h.,)
Mount Vernon,*
Nugent's Grove,
Palo,
Paris,
Prairieburgh,
Prospect Hill,
Rural,
Spring Grove,
Springville,
Troy Mills,
Valley Farm,
Viola,
Waubeck,
Western College,
West Prairie.

LOUISA COUNTY.

Cairo,
Clifton,
Columbus City,*
Fredonia,
Grand View,
Letts,
Mid Prairie,
Morning Sun,
Palo Alto,
Port Allen,
Port Louisa,
Toolsborough,
Virginia Grove,
Wapello, (c. h.)

LUCAS COUNTY.

Argo,
Belinda,
Chariton, (c. h.,)
Earle,
Freedom,
Henderson,
La Grange,
Last Chance,
Lucas,
Milan,
Norwood,
Ola,
Russell,
Tallahoma,
White Breast.

LYONS COUNTY.

Gibralter.

MADISON COUNTY.

Clanton,
Earlham,
Ellsworth,
Kasson,
Middle River,
Ohio,
Peru,
Pleasant View,
Saint Charles,
Venus,
Winterset, (c. h.)

*Money-order office.

MAHASKA COUNTY.

Agricola,
Auburn,
Beacon,
Belle Fountain,
Buck Horn,
Eveland Grove,
Farmersville,
Ferry,
Flint,
Fremont,
Givin,
Granville,
Hopewell,
Indianapolis,
Leighton,
New Sharon,
Oskaloosa,* (c. h.,)
Peoria,
Union Mills,
White Oak.

MARION COUNTY.

Attica,
Caloma,
Columbia,
Dallas,
English Settlement,
Gosport,
Hamilton,
Iola,
Knoxville,* (c. h.,)
Marysville,
Newbern,
Otley,
Pella,*
Pleasantville,
Red Rock,
Star,
Wheeling.

MARSHALL COUNTY.

Albion,
Bangor,
Biven's Grove,
Edenville,
Illinois Grove,
Lamoille,
Laurel,
Le Grand,
Liscomb,
Marietta,
Marshalltown,* (c. h.,)
Minerva,
Quarry,
Stanford,
State Centre,
Timber Creek,
Vienna.

MILLS COUNTY.

Benton,
Emerson,
Glenwood,* (c. h.,)
Haynie,
Hillsdale,
Junction City,
Milton Station,
Pacific City,
Wahaghboney,
White Cloud.

MITCHELL COUNTY.

Brownville,
Cardiff,
Doran,
Little Cedar,
Meroa,
Mitchell,* (c. h.,)
Mona,
Newburgh,
Orchard,
Osage,
Otranto,
Riceville,
Rock Creek,
Saint Ansgar,
Staceyville,
Wentworth,
West Mitchell.

MONONA COUNTY.

Arcola,
Belvidere,
Castana,
Grant Centre,
Maple Landing,
Mapleton,
Onawa City,* (c. h.,)
St. Clair,
Ticonic,
West Fork.

MONROE COUNTY.

Albia,* (c. h.,)
Coalton,
East Melrose,
Fredric,
Georgetown,
Half Way Prairie,
Lovilia,
Osprey,
Tyrone,
Urbanna City,
Weller.

MONTGOMERY COUNTY.

Frankfort,
Grant,
Red Oak Junction,* (c. h.,)
Sciola,
Stanton,
Villisca,
Wilson.

MUSCATINE COUNTY.

Atalissa,
Conesville,
Fairport,
Lacey,
Melpine,
Moscow,
Muscatine,* (c. h.,)
Pike,
Pine Mills,
Pleasant Prairie,
Prairie Mills,
Summit,
Sweetland Centre,
West Liberty,*
Wilton Junction.*

O'BRIEN COUNTY.

O'Brien, (c. h.)

PAGE COUNTY.

Braddyville,
Centre,
Clarinda,* (c. h.,)
College Springs,
Franklin Grove,
Hawleysville,
Nodaway Mills,
Page City,
Tarkio,
Union Grove,
Wellsburgh.

PALO ALTO COUNTY.

Black Walnut,
Ellenton,
Emmittsburgh, (c. h.,)
Fern Valley,
Great Oak,
Rush Lake,
Soda Bar,
West Bend.

PLYMOUTH COUNTY.

Hinton,
Lemars,
Plymouth Centre,(c. h.)

POCAHONTAS COUNTY.

Lizzard,
Rolfe, (c. h.)

POLK COUNTY.

Adelphi,
Altoona,
Avon,
Commerce Mills,
DES MOINES, (c. h.,)
Elkhart,
Greenwood,
Lincoln,
Mitchellville,
Peoria City,
Polk City,
Ridgedale,
Rising Sun,
Saylorville.

* Money-order office.

POTTAWATTAMIE COUNTY.

Avoca,	Macedonia,
Big Grove,	Neola,
Council Bluffs,* (c.h.,)	Walnut Creek Sta'n,
Crescent City,	Waveland,
Honey Creek,	Wheeler's Grove.
Loveland,	

POWESHIEK COUNTY.

Blue Point,	Mill Grove,
Brooklyn,*	Montezuma,* (c. h.,)
Deep River,	Sherman,
Forest Home,	Tyro,
Grinnell,*	West Brooklyn.
Malcom,*	

RINGGOLD COUNTY.

Caledonia,	Mount Ayr,* (c. h.,)
Cross,	Redding,
Estella,	Ringgold,
Eugene,	Union Hill.
Ingart Grove,	

SAC COUNTY.

Grant City,	Sac City, (c. h.)

SCOTT COUNTY.

Allen's Grove,	Mount Joy,
Amity,	New Hamburgh,
Big Rock,	New Liberty,
Blue Grass,	Pleasant Valley,
Buffalo,	Princeton,
Davenport,* (c. h.,)	Round Grove,
Dixon,	Walnut Grove,
Gilbert,	Wolcott.
Le Claire,*	

SHELBY COUNTY.

Altamont,	Harlan, (c. h.,)
Botany,	Manteno,
Elk Horn,	Shelby.

SIOUX COUNTY.

Calliope, (c. h.,)	Irene.

STORY COUNTY.

Ames,	Nevada,* (c. h.,)
Cambridge,	Ontario,
Colo,	Roland,
Iowa Centre,	Story City.

TAMA COUNTY.

Badger Hill,	Dryden,
Bovina,	Ettie,
Buckingham,*	Evergreen,
Butlerville,	Fifteen Mile Grove,
Chelsea,	Helena,
Crystal,	Orford,

TAMA COUNTY—Continued.

Spring Creek,	Waltham,
Tama City,	West Irving.
Toledo,* (c. h.,)	Wolf Creek.
Vineyard,	

TAYLOR COUNTY.

Bedford,* (c. h.,)	Ovid,
Gravity,	Platt,
Harmony,	Platteville,
Holt,	Siam.
Memory,	

UNION COUNTY.

Afton,* (c. h.,)	Thayer,
Creston,	Tingley,
Cromwell,	Union City.

VAN BUREN COUNTY.

Benton's Port,	Mount Sterling,
Birmingham, *	Mount Zion,
Bonaparte,*	Niles,
Doud Station,	Oak Point,
Farmington,*	Pierceville,
Hickory,	Pittsburgh,
Home,	Sheridan,
Iowaville,	Upton,
Keosauqua,* (c. h.,)	Utica,
Kilbourn,	Vernon,
Lebanon,	Winchester.
Milton,	

WAPELLO COUNTY.

Agency City,*	Dudley,
Alpine,	Eddyville, *
Ashland,	Happy Hollow,
Bladensburgh,	Highland Centre,
Blakesburgh,	Kirkville,
Chillicothe,	Munterville,
Christiansburgh,	Ormanville,
Competine,	Ottumwa,* (c. h.,)
Comstock,	Port Richmond,
Coopersville,	Williamsburgh.
Dahlonega,	

WARREN COUNTY.

Bellemont,	Lynn,
Carlisle,	Medora,
Fort Plain,	New Virginia,
Hammondsburgh,	Norwalk,
Hartford,	Palmyra,
Indianola,* (c. h.,)	Rose Mount,
Lacona,	Sandyville,
Lawrenceburgh,	Sharon,
Liberty Centre,	Summerset.

WASHINGTON COUNTY.

Ainsworth,	Crawfordsville,
Brighton,*	Dairy,
Clay,	Dutch Creek,

* Money-order office.

WASHINGTON COUNTY—Continued.

Lexington,
Middleburgh,
Richmond,
Seventy-six Center,

Valley,
Washington, (c. h.,)
Wassonville,
Yatton.

WAYNE COUNTY.

Bethlehem,
Cambria,
Clio,
Confidence,
Corydon, (c. h.,)
Genoa,
Grand River,

Kniffin,
Lewisburgh,
New York,
Promise City,
Selma,
Warsaw.

WEBSTER COUNTY.

Border Plains,
Carbon,
Duncombe,
Fort Dodge, (c. h.,)
Greenside,

Hesperian,
Otho,
Tyson's Mills,
West Dayton.

WINNEBAGO COUNTY.

Benson Grove,
Forest City, (c. h.,)

Lake Mills.

WINNESHIEK COUNTY.

Bluffton,
Burr Oak,

Calmar,*
Canoe,

WINNESHEIK COUNTY—Continued.

Castalia,
Counover,*
Decorah, (c. h.,)
Festina,
Fort Atkinson,
Frankville,
Freeport,
Hesper,
Locust Lane,
Navau,

New Alba,
Old Mission,
Ossian,*
Plymouth Rock,
Ridgeway,
Spillville,
Springwater,
Twin Spring,
Woodville.

WOODBURY COUNTY.

Correctionville,
Oto,
Sergeant Bluffs,
Sioux City, (c. h.,)

Sloan,
Smithland,
Wolfdale.

WORTH COUNTY.

Bristol,
Fertile,
Hartland,
Northwood, (c. h.,)

Silver Lake,
Wales,
Westfield.

WRIGHT COUNTY.

Bach Grove,
Belmond,
Clarion, (c. h.,)
Eagle Grove,
Empire,

Fryeburgh,
Goldfield,
Luni.
Woolstock.

KANSAS.

ALLEN COUNTY.

Carlyle,
Elsinore,
Geneva,
Humboldt,*

Iola, (c. h.,)
Jeddo,
Ozark.

ANDERSON COUNTY.

Central City,
Delmont,
Elizabethtown,
Emerald,

Garnett, (c. h.,)
Greeley,
Mineral Point,
Scipio.

ATCHISON COUNTY.

Arington,
Atchison, (c. h.,)
Eden,
Effingham,
Farmington,
Huron,
Kennekuk,
Lancaster,

Locust Grove,
Monrovia,
Mount Pleasant,
Muscotah,
Pardee,
Oak Mills,
Saint Nicholas.

BOURBON COUNTY.

Appleton,
Barnesville,
Dayton,
Fort Lincoln,
Fort Scott, (c. h.,)
Glendale,
Mapleton,
Marmiton,
Mill Creek,

Mount Sterling,
Osaga,
Pawnee,
Rockford,
Sharlow,
Turkey Creek,
Walnut Hill,
Xenia.

BROWN COUNTY.

Buncomb,
Carson,
Claytonville,
Fairview,
Grand Prairie,
Hamlin,

Hiawatha, (c. h.,)
Marak,
Padonia,
Robinson,
Tyler's,
Ununda.

BUTLER COUNTY.

Augusta,
Chelsea,
Douglass,
El Dorado, (c. h.,)

Four Mile,
Plum Grove,
Quito,
Rosalia,

* Money-order office.

BUTLER COUNTY—Continued.

Sycamore Springs,	Wah Wah,
Towanda,	Walnut.

CHASE COUNTY.

Bazaar,	Middle Creek,
Cedar Point,	Silver Creek,
Cottonwood Falls,*	Toledo,
(*c. h.*,)	Union.
Matfield Green,	

CHEROKEE COUNTY.

Baxter Springs,*	Lostine,
Checo,	Neutral City,
Cherokee Mound,	Pleasant View,
Columbus,* (*c. h.*,)	Sanfordville,
Fly Creek,	Sherman City,
Keelville,	Spring River Falls,
Lewiston,	Wirtonia.

CLAY COUNTY.

Clay Centre, (*c. h.*,)	Otter Creek,
Deep Creek,	Republican City,
Fayetteville,	Riverdale,
Gatesville,	Rosevale,
Lima,	Wakefield.
Madura,	

CLOUD COUNTY.

Arion,	Lake Sibley,
Clyde,	Lawrenceburgh,
Concordia, (*c. h.*,)	Red Stone,
Glasco,	Shirley.

COFFEY COUNTY.

Avon,	Le Roy,*
Burlington,* (*c. h.*,)	Ottumwa,
Corona,	Sidney.
Fredericktown,	

COWLEY COUNTY.

Arkansas City,	Lone Tree,
Dexter,	Rock,
Jeffersonville,	*Winfield*, (*c. h.*)

CRAWFORD COUNTY.

Arcadia,	Hopefield,
Base Line,	Idell,
Cato,	Iowa City,
Cherokee,	Monmouth,
Crawfordsville,	Mulberry Grove,
Farlington,	Stevenstown,
Girard,* (*c. h.*,)	Walnut Creek.
Hamilton,	

DAVIS COUNTY.

Alida,	*Junction City*,* (*c. h.*)
Fort Riley,	

DICKINSON COUNTY.

Abilene, (*c. h.*,)	Detroit,
Aroma,	Lyona.
Chapman's Creek,	

DONIPHAN COUNTY.

Doniphan,	Palermo,
Elwood,	Saint Benedict,
Geary,	Severance,
Highland,	*Troy*,* (*c. h.*,)
Iowa Point,	Wathena,*
La Fayette,	White Cloud.*
Normanville,	

DOUGLAS COUNTY.

Baldwin City,*	Kanwaka,
Belvoir,	*Lawrence*,* (*c. h.*,)
Big Springs,	Lecompton,
Black Jack,	Marion,
Clinton,	Prairie City,
Eudora,	Sigel,
Hesper,	Twin Mound,
Holling,	Vinland,
Jefferson,	Willow Springs.

ELLIS COUNTY.

Ellis,	*Hays City*, (*c. h.*)

ELLSWORTH COUNTY.

Ellsworth,* (*c. h.*,)	Fort Harker.

FRANKLIN COUNTY.

Appanoose,	*Ottawa*,* (*c. h.*,)
Berea,	Peoria,
Centropolis,	Ponoma,
Forest Home,	Princeton,
Greenwood,	Richmond,
Lane,	Williamsburgh.
Norwood,	

GREENWOOD COUNTY.

Belle Grove,	Madison,
Eureka,* (*c. h.*,)	Quincy,
Fame,	Twin Falls,
Homer Creek,	Verdigris Falls,
Janesville,	Virgil.

HOWARD COUNTY.

Caney,	Longton,
Cedar Vale,	Painterhood,
Elk Falls, (*c. h.*,)	Peru,
Howard,	Salt Springs.

JACKSON COUNTY.

Banner,	North Cedar,
Circleville,	Ontario,
Holton,* (*c. h.*,)	Smithland,
James' Crossing,	South Cedar,
Netawaka,	Whiting.
New Eureka,	

* Money-order office.

JEFFERSON COUNTY.

Chester,	Oskaloosa,* (c. h.,)
Cook's Ford,	Ozawkie,
Grantville,	Perry,
Grasshopper Falls,*	Plum Creek,
Grove City,	Scott Land,
Medina,	Williamstown,
Mount Florence,	Winchester.
Newman,	

JEWELL COUNTY.

Jewell,	Vicksburgh.

JOHNSON COUNTY.

Aubrey,	Monticello,
De Soto,	Ocheltree,
Gardner,	Olathe,* (c. h.,)
Glenn,	Shawnee,
Lanesfield,	Shawnee Mission,
Lenexa,	Spring Hill.

LABETTE COUNTY.

Big Hill,	Labette,
Chetopah,*	Mendota,
Clymore,	Montana,
Creswell,	Mound Valley,
Daytonville,	Oswego,* (c. h.,)
Dora,	Ripon,
Elston,	Timber Hill.

LEAVENWORTH COUNTY.

Delaware City,	Lenape,
Dimon,	Petersburgh,
Easton,	Pleasant Ridge,
Fairmount,	Reno,
Fort Leavenworth,	Springdale,
Glenwood,	Stanwood,
Hoge,	Stranger,
Kickapoo City,	Tonganoxie.
Leavenworth City,*(c.h.,)	

LINCOLN COUNTY.

Elkhorn,	Red Rock.
Lincoln Centre,	

LINN COUNTY.

Barnard,	La Cygne,
Blooming Grove,	Mansfield,
Blue Mounds,	Mound City,* (c. h.,)
Brooklyn,	Oakwood,
Centreville,	Pleasanton,*
Coal Centre,	Springfield,
Farlinville,	Twin Springs.
Jackson,	

LYON COUNTY.

Allen,	Cross,
Americus.	Eagle Creek,
Bunker Hill,	Elmendaro,

LYON COUNTY—Continued.

Emporia,* (c. h.,)	Patty's Mill,
Forest Hill,	Plymouth,
Fremont,	Reading,
Harrisburgh,	Rock Creek,
Hartford,	Waterloo,
Line,	Waushara.
Neosho Rapids,	

McPHERSON COUNTY.

Gypsum Creek,	Lindsborg,
Hyco,	Sweadel, (c. h.)
Lake Village,	

MARION COUNTY.

Antelope,	Lincolnville,
Bethel,	Marion Centre, (c. h.)
Doyle,	

MARSHALL COUNTY.

Barrett,	Irving,*
Blue Rapids,	Marysville,* (c. h.,)
Elisabeth,	Saint Bridget,
Frankfort,	Waterville,*
Guittard Station,	Wyoming.
Heaslyville,	

MIAMI COUNTY.

Fontania,	Paola,* (c. h.,)
Hillsdale,	Rockville,
Miami Village,	Saint Louis,
Mount Nebo,	Stanton,
New Lancaster,	Tontzville.
Osawatomie,*	

MITCHELL COUNTY.

Asherville,	Glen Elder,
Beloit,	Solomon Rapids.
Cawker City,	

MONTGOMERY COUNTY.

Cherryville,	Morgan,
Coffeyville,	Parker,
Elk City,	Radical City,
Independence,	Saint Paul,
Liberty,	Westralia.
Montgomery,	

MORRIS COUNTY.

Council Grove,* (c. h.,)	La Grange,
Diamond Springs,	Parkersville,
Hill Spring,	Skiddy.

NEMAHA COUNTY.

Albány,	Granada,
America City,	Neuchatel,
Capioma,	Sabetha,
Centralia,	Seneca,* (c. h.,)
Clear Creek,	Vermillion,
Corning,	Wetmore.

* Money-order office.

NEOSHO COUNTY.

Big Labette.
Canville,
Cremona,
Erie,* (c. h.,)
Flat Rock,
Jacksonville,
Ladore,
New Chicago,
Newport,
Orcuttville,

Osage Mission,*
Osborn,
Palo Alto,
Prairie du Chien,
Rochester,
Roger's Mills,
Rose Hill,
Tioga,
Urbana,
Valley City.

OSAGE COUNTY.

Arvonia,
Burlingame,* (c. h.,)
Carbondale,
Lindale,
Lyndon,
Melvern,
Michigan Valley,
Osage City,

Olivet,
Quenemo,
Richardson,
Ridgeway,
Trust,
Valley Brook,
Wilmington.

OTTAWA COUNTY.

Bennington,
Churchill,
Coal Creek,
Delphos,
Grover,

Lindsey, (c. h.,)
Minneapolis,
Sumnerville,
Windsor.

PAWNEE COUNTY.

Fort Larned.

POTTAWATOMIE COUNTY.

Adam's Peak,
Leghorn,
Louisville, (c. h.,)
Myers' Valley,
Nancy,
Otter Lake,
Pleasant Run,

Saint George,
Saint Mary's Miss'n,
Savannah,
Spring Side,
Vienna,
Wamego,*
Westmoreland.

REPUBLIC COUNTY.

Belleville,
Cuba,
Gomeria,

New Scandinavia,
Salt Marsh, (c. h.,)
White Rock.

RILEY COUNTY.

Big Timber,
Manhattan,* (c. h.,)
Milford,
Ogden,
Parallel,

Randolph,
Riley Centre,
Timber Creek,
Vinton,
Wild Cat.

SALINE COUNTY.

Brookville,
Falun,

Honek,
Pliny,

SALINE COUNTY—Continued.

Salina,* (c. h.,)
Saline Valley,

Solomon City.

SEDGWICK COUNTY.

Cosmosa,
Sedgwick,

Wichita, (c. h.)

SHAWNEE COUNTY.

Auburn,
Dover,
Eugene,
Richland,
Rossville,
Silver Lake,

Tecumseh,
TOPEKA,* (c. h.,)
Wah Wah Snk,
Wakarusa.
Waveland.

WABAUNSEE COUNTY.

Alma, (c. h.,)
Bismarck,
Eskridge,
Exonville,
Grant,

Harveyville,
Mission Creek,
Newbury,
Wabaunsee.

WALLACE COUNTY.

Fort Wallace,
Grinnell,

Phil Sheridan; (c. h.)

WASHINGTON COUNTY.

Ballard's Falls,
Butler,
Chepstow,
Clifton,
Donald,
Erin,

Haddam,
Hanover,
Joy Creek,
Limestone,
Washington, (c. h.)

WILSON COUNTY.

Altoona,
Buffalo,
Clarke,
Coyville,
Fredonia, (c. h.,)

Greystone,
Guilford,
Neodesha,
New Albany,
Verdi.*

WOODSON COUNTY.

Belmont,
Byron,
Chellis,
Cherry Creek,
Coloma.

Hazelettville,
Miller's Grove,
Neosho Falls,* (c. h.,)
Rose,
Toronto.

WYANDOTTE COUNTY

Conner's Station,
Edwardsville,
Glen Park,
Nearman,

Pomeroy,
Quindaro,
White Church,
Wyandotte,* (c. h.)

* Money-order office.

KENTUCKY.

ADAIR COUNTY.

Breeding's,
Cane Valley,
Casey Creek,
Columbia, (c. h.,)
Glen's Fork,
Gradyville,
Milltown,
Montpelier,
Neatsville.

ALLEN COUNTY.

Allen Springs,
Butlersville,
Gainsville,
Mount Aerial,
Scottsville, (c. h.)

ANDERSON COUNTY.

Coldwell's Store,
Lawrenceburgh, (c. h.,)
Ripyville,
Rough and Ready.

BALLARD COUNTY.

Blandville, (c. h.,)
Hazlewood,
Hinkleville,
Lovelaceville,
Milburn,
Ogden's Landing.

BARREN COUNTY.

Cave City,
Coral Hill,
Dry Fork,
Eighty-eight,
Elbow Spring,
Freedom
Glasgow,* (c. h.,)
Glasgow Junction,
Hiseville,
Nobob,
Park,
Roseville,
Slick Rock,
Temple Hill,
Tracy,

BATH COUNTY.

Bethel,
Costigon,
Little Flat,
Marshall,
Olympian Springs,
Owingsville, (c. h.,)
Peeled Oak,
Sharpsburgh,
Wyoming.

BOONE COUNTY.

Bullitsville,
Burlington, (c. h.,)
Constance,
Florence,
Grant,
Hamilton,
Hebron,
Petersburgh,
Union,
Verona,
Walton.

BOURBON COUNTY.

Centreville,
Clintonville,
Flat Rock,
Houston,
Hutchison's,
Lowe's Station,
Millersburgh,
North Middletown,
Paris,* (c. h.,)
Ruddel's Mills,
Shawhan,
Stoney Point.

BOYD COUNTY.

Ashton,
Bolt's Fork,
Cannonsburgh,
Catlettsburgh,* (c. h.,)
Coalton,

BOYLE COUNTY.

Aliceton,
Brumfield Station,
Danville,* (c. h.,)
Mitchellsburgh,
Parksville,
Perryville,
Shelby City.

BRACKEN COUNTY.

Augusta,
Berlin,
Bradford,
Brookville, (c. h.,)
Browningsville,
Foster,
Harmon,
Locust Mills,
Milford,
Powersville.

BREATHITT COUNTY.

Jackson, (c. h.,)
Lost Creek.

BRECKINRIDGE COUNTY.

Bewleyville,
Big Spring,
Clifton Mills,
Cloverport,
Hardinsburgh, (c. h.,)
Hudsonville,
Lost Run,
Planter's Hall,
Rock Lick,
Stephensport,
Union Star,
Webster.

BULLITT COUNTY.

Bardstown Junction,
Belmont,
Cane Spring Depot,
Lebanon Junction,
Mount Vitio,
Mount Washington,
Pitt's Point,
Shepherdsville, (c. h.)

BUTLER COUNTY.

Berry's Lick,
Brooklyn,
Harreldsville,
Logansport,
Morgantown, (c. h.,)
Quality Valley,
Reedyville,
Rochester,
Sugar Grove,
Townsville,
Welch's Creek,
Woodbury.

CALDWELL COUNTY.

Fredonia,
Friendship,
Long Pond,
Princeton,* (c. h.,)
Walnut Grove.

CALLAWAY COUNTY.

Coldwater,
Crossland,
Hico,
Locust Grove,
Murray,* (c. h.,)
Pine Bluff,
Shiloh,
Wadesborough,
Warburgh.

CAMPBELL COUNTY.

Alexandria,
California,
Carthage,
Cold Spring,
Dale;
Dayton,
Flagg Spring,
Grant's Lick,
Guber's Mills,
Indian Springs,
Kane,
Newport, (c. h.,)
Pond Creek,
Ten Mile,
Tibbatt's X Roads.

* Money-order office.

CARROLL COUNTY.

Carrollton,* (c. h.,)   Sandefer's Store,
Eagle Station,   Worthville.
Ghent,

CARTER COUNTY.

Boone Furnace,   Grayson, (c. h.,)
Bruin,   Mount Savage,
Deer Creek,   Olive Hill,
Estill Flats,   Upper Tygart.

CASEY COUNTY.

Liberty, (c. h.,)   Powar's Store,
Middleburgh,   Williams's Store,
Mintonville,

CHRISTIAN COUNTY,

Bainbridge,   Longview,
Bennettstown,   Newstead,
Beverly,   Oak Grove,
Casky's Station,   Pembroke,
Church Hill,   Saint Elmo,
Fairview,   Sinking Fork,
Garrettsburgh,   Stuart's Mill,
Hopkinsville,* (c. h.,)   Williams,
La Fayette,   Wooldridge's Store.

CLARKE COUNTY.

Kiddville,   Stoner,
Pine Grove,   Vienna,
Ruckerville,   Winchester,* (c. h.)

CLAY COUNTY.

House's Store,   Manchester, (c. h.,)
Laurel Creek,   Sexton's Creek.

CLINTON COUNTY.

Albany, (c. h.,)   Cumberland City,
Alpha,   Seventy-six.

CRITTENDEN COUNTY.

Crittenden Springs,   Marion, (c. h.,)
Dycusburgh,   Shady Grove,
Ford's Ferry,   Westonburgh.
Hurricane,

CUMBERLAND COUNTY.

Amandaville,   Grider,
Big Renox,   Marrowbone.
Burkesville, (c. h.,)

DAVIESS COUNTY.

Birk's City,   Owensborough,* (c. h.,)
Curdsville,   Panther Creek,
Grissom's Landing,   Pleasant Ridge,
Knottsville,   Sorghotown,
Masonville,   West Louisville,
Narrows Bridge,   Whitesville,
Oakford,   Yelvington.

EDMONSON COUNTY.

Bee Spring,   Brownsville, (c. h.,)
Big Reedy,   Rocky Hill Station.

ELLIOTT COUNTY.

Newfoundland,   Sandy Hook, (c. h.)

ESTILL COUNTY.

Irvine, (c. h.,)   Miller's Creek,
Leanah,   Red River Iron W'ks.

FAYETTE COUNTY.

Athens,   Cleveland,
Chilesburgh,   Lexington,* (c. h.)

FLEMING COUNTY.

Elizaville,   Plummer's Mills,
Flemingsburgh,*(c.h.,)   Poplar Plains,
Hillsborough,   Sherburne Mills,
Mount Carmel,   Tilton,
Oak Woods,   Upper Blue Licks.
Plummer's Landing,

FLOYD COUNTY.

Haw's Ford,   Prestonsburgh, (c. h.)
Lanesville,

FRANKLIN COUNTY.

Benson,   Forks of Elkhorn,
Bridgeport,   FRANKFORT,* (c. h.,)
Farmdale,   Polsgrove's Store.

FULTON COUNTY.

Cacey's Station,   Hickman,* (c. h.,)
Fulton Station,   Jordan Station.

GALLATIN COUNTY.

Bramlette,   Sugar Creek,
Glencoe,   Walnut Lick,
Napoleon,   Warsaw, (c. h.)
Sparta Station,

GARRARD COUNTY.

Bryantsville,   Lowell,
Buckeye,   Paint Lick,
Hyattsville,   Saunders' Ferry.
Lancaster, (c. h.,)

GRANT COUNTY.

Clark's Creek,   Gouge's,
Cordova,   Mount Zion,
Corinth,   New Eagle Mills,
Crittenden,   Sherman,
Downingsville,   Stateley's Run,
Dry Ridge,   Stewartsville,
Elliston,   Williamstown, (c. h.)

* Money-order office.

GRAVES COUNTY.

Boaz,
Boydsville,
Clear Spring,
Dublin,
Fancy Farm,
Farmington,
Hickory Grove,

Kansas,
Lynnville,
Mayfield, (c. h.,)
Morse's,
Pryorsburgh,
Viola Station,
Wingo's Station.

GRAYSON COUNTY.

Big Clifty,
Caneyville,
Falls of Rough,
Grayson Springs,

Litchfield, (c. h.,)
Red Oak,
Short Creek.

GREEN COUNTY.

Allendale,
Catalpa Grove,
*Greensburgh,** (c. h.,)

Haskinsville,
Oceola,
Webbs.

GREENUP COUNTY.

*Greenup,** (c. h.,)
Kenton Furnace,

Lynn.

HANCOCK COUNTY.

Hawesville, (c. h.,)
Huff's Creek,
Lewisport,

Patesville,
Pellville.

HARDIN COUNTY.

Dorret's Run,
*Elizabethtown,**(c. h.,)
Franklin's × Roads,
Glendale,
Grand View,
Howe's Valley,
Nolin,
Red Hill,

Robertsonville,
Sonora,
Stephensburgh,
Uptonville,
Vine Grove,
West Point,
White Mills.

HARLAN COUNTY.

Big Rock,
Harlan, (c.h.,)

Poor Fork,
Wallin's Creek.

HARRISON COUNTY.

Berry's Station,
Boyd's Station,
Broadwell,
Claysville,
Colemansville,
Connersville,
Curry's Run,
*Cynthiana,** (c. h.,)

Havilandsville,
Lair's Station,
Leesburgh,
Oddville,
Paxton,
Robertson's Station,
Rutland.

HART COUNTY.

Bacon Creek,
Caverna,
Grinstead's Mills,
Hammonville,
Hardyville,
Munfordsville, (c. h.,)
Omega,

Ream's Chapel,
Rio,
Rowlett's Depot,
Seymour,
Three Springs,
Woodsonville.

HENDERSON COUNTY.

Cairo,
Genevia,
Hebbardsville,
*Henderson,** (c. h.,)
McKinley's Landing,

Robard's Station,
Scuffletown,
Smith's Mills,
Zion.

HENRY COUNTY.

Bethlehem,
Campbellsburgh,
Eminence,
Franklinton,
Harper's Ferry,
Hill Spring,
Jericho,
Lockport,

New Castle, (c. h.,)
Pendleton,
Pleasureville,
Port Royal,
Smithfield,
Spring Hill Depot,
Springport,
Sulphur Fork.

HICKMAN COUNTY.

Clinton, (c. h.,)
Columbus,*
Moscow,

Oakville,
Wesley.

HOPKINS COUNTY.

Ashbysburgh,
Ellwood,
Hanson,

*Madisonville,** (c. h.,)
Nebo,
Underwood.

JACKSON COUNTY.

Birch Lick,
Chinkapin Roof,
Clover Bottom,
Gray Hawk,

Green Hall,
McKee, (c. h.,)
Middle Fork,
Morrill.

JEFFERSON COUNTY.

Deposit,
Edwards,
Fairmount,
Fern Creek,
Fisherville,
Hobb's Station,
Jeffersontown,
Lacona,
Long Run,

*Louisville,** (c. h.,)
Middletown,
Newburgh,
O'Bannon,
Orell,
River View,
Summit,
Saint Matthews,
Worthington.

JESSAMINE COUNTY.

Hanly,
Jessamine,
Keene,
Little Hickman,

Mount Freedom,
*Nicholasville,** (c. h.,)
Pekin,
Spear's.

JOHNSON COUNTY.

Hood's Fork,
Oil Springs,

Paintsville, (c. h.)

JOSH BELL COUNTY.

Callaway,
La Fontaine,

Pineville, (c. h.,)
Yellow Creek.

* Money-order office.

KENTON COUNTY.

Bank Lick,
Covington,* (c. h.,)
Independence,
Kenton,
Latonia Springs,
Ludlow,
Morning View,
Scott,
Visalia.

KNOX COUNTY.

Barboursville, (c. h.,)
Brafford's Store,
Flat Lick,
Lynn Camp,
Swan Pond.

LARUE COUNTY.

Buffa'.,
Hodgensville, (c. h.,)
Magnolia,
Mount Sherman.

LAUREL COUNTY.

Bush's Store,
Hazle Patch,
Laurel Bridge,
London, (c. h.,)
Mershon's × Roads,
Raccoon,
Rough Creek,
Whippoorwill,
White Lily.

LAWRENCE COUNTY.

Blaine,
Buchanan,
Cherokee,
Falls of Blaine,
Louisa, (c. h.,)
Lowmansville,
Prosperity,
Stone House,
Warfield,
Webbville,

LEE COUNTY.

Beattyville,
Proctor, (c. h.)

LETCHER COUNTY.

Indian Bottom,
Partridge,
Whitesburgh, (c. h.)

LEWIS COUNTY.

Cabin Creek,
Carr's,
Concord,
Marine,
Mouth of Laurel,
Poplar Flat,
Quincy,
Sand Hill,
Tolesborough,
Vanceburgh, (c. h.)

LINCOLN COUNTY.

Bee Lick,
Crab Orchard,
Gilbert's Creek Station,
Hall's Gap Station,
Highland,
Hustonville,
Milledgeville,
Stanford, (c. h.,)
Waynesburgh.

LIVINGSTON COUNTY.

Birdsville,
Carrsville,
Salem,
Smithland,* (c. h.)

LOGAN COUNTY.

Adairville,
Auburn,*
Baugh's Station,
Dallam's Creek,
Ferguson's Station,
Gordonsville,
Henrysville,
Keysburgh,
McLeod's Station,
Olmstead,
Rabbittsville,
Red River Mills,
Russellville,* (c. h.,)
South Union.

LYON COUNTY.

Cave Spring Station, *Eddyville,* (c. h.)

McCRACKEN COUNTY.

Florence Station,
Massack,
Norton's Bluff,
Paducah,* (c. h.,)
Woodville.

McLEAN COUNTY.

Calhoun, (c. h.,)
Livermore,
Long Falls Creek,
Mason Creek,
Rumsey,
Sacramento.

MADISON COUNTY.

Berea,
Big Hill,
Edenton,
Kingston,
Kirksville,
Richmond,* (c. h.,)
Silver Creek,
Speedwell,
Waco,
White Hall.

MAGOFFIN COUNTY.

Johnson's Fork,
Salyersville, (c. h.)

MARION COUNTY.

Bradfordsville,
Chicago,
Lebanon,* (c. h.,)
Loretto,
New Market,
Penick,
Raywick,
Riley's Station,
St. Mary's.

MARSHALL COUNTY.

Altona,
Aurora,
Benton, (c. h.,)
Birmingham,
Brewer's Mill,
Briensburgh,
Fair Dealing,
Henderson's Mill,
Oakland,
Olive,
Palma.

MASON COUNTY.

Dover,
Fern Leaf,
Germantown,
Helena,
May's Lick,
Maysville,* (c. h.,)
Minerva,
Mount Gilead,
Murphysville,
North Fork,
Orangeburgh,
Sardis,
Slack,
Springdale,
Washington.

* Money-or

MEADE COUNTY.

Brandenburgh, (c. h.,)	Payneville,
Flint Island,	Richardson's Landing,
Garnettsville,	
Garrett,	Rock Haven,
Hill Grove,	Stapleton,
Little York,	Wolf Creek.

MENIFEE COUNTY.

Rockhouse, (c. h.)

MERCER COUNTY.

Bohon,	McAfee,
Cornishville,	Nevada,
Dugansville,	Pleasant Hill,
Duncan,	Rose Hill,
Harrodsburgh,*(c.h.,)	Salvisa.

METCALFE COUNTY.

Centre,	Knob Lick,
Cross Plains,	Pace's,
East Fork,	Randolph,
Edmonton, (c. h.,)	Rockland Mills,
Glover's Creek,	Willow Shade.

MONROE COUNTY.

Centre Point,	Meshack's Creek,
Flippin,	Mud Lick,
Fountain Run,	Rock Bridge,
Gamaliel,	Sulphur Lick,
Hilton,	*Tompkinsville,* (c. h.)
Martinsburgh,	

MONTGOMERY COUNTY.

Aaron's Run,	Montaview,
Elm Hill,	*Mount Sterling,**(c.h.,)
Howard's Mills,	Rich Valley,
Jeffersonville,	Side View.
Levee,	

MORGAN COUNTY.

Bangor,	*West Liberty,* (c. h.)
Black Water,	

MUHLENBURGH COUNTY.

Bremen,	Laurel Bluff,
Earle's,	Paradise,
Greenville,* (c. h.,)	South Carrollton.

NELSON COUNTY.

Bardstown,* (c. h.,)	Gethsemane,
Bloomfield,	High Grove,
Boston,	Hunter's Depot,
Botland,	Nelson Furnace,
Chaplin,	New Haven,
Cox's Creek,	New Hope,
Deatsville,	Samuel's Depot.
Fairfield,	

NICHOLAS COUNTY.

Blue Lick Springs,	Moorefield,
Carlisle, (c. h.,)	Oakland Mills,
Head Quarters,	PleasantValley Mills,
Hooktown,	Weston.

OHIO COUNTY.

Beaver Dam,	Fordsville,
Buck Horn,	*Hartford,** (c. h.,)
Buford,	Hines' Mills,
Ceralvo,	Point Pleasant,
Cool Spring,	Rockport.
Cromwell,	

OLDHAM COUNTY.

Beard's Station,	*La Grange,* (c. h.,)
Brownsborough,	Peru,
Buckner's Station,	Pewee Valley,
Centrefield,	Westport.
Goshen,	

OWEN COUNTY.

Eagle Hill,	New Liberty,
Gratz,	*Owenton,* (c. h.,)
Harmony,	Rock Dale,
Hills,	Pleasant Home,
Lusby's Mill,	Poplar Grove,
Monterey,	West Union.
New Columbus,	

OWSLEY COUNTY.

Booneville, (c. h.,)	South Fork,
Island City,	Traveller's Rest.

PENDLETON COUNTY.

Batchelor's Rest,	*Falmouth,* (c. h.,)
Boston Station,	Flower Creek,
Butler,	Gardnersville,
Catawba,	Knoxville,
De Mossville,	Levingood,
Dividing Ridge,	Morgan,
Elizabethville,	Motier.

PERRY COUNTY.

Hazard, (c. h.,)	Salt Creek.

PIKE COUNTY.

Bent Branch,	Mouth of Pond,
Coal Run,	*Piketon,* (c. h.,)
Little Creek,	Robinson Creek.

POWELL COUNTY.

Stanton, (c. h.,)	West Bend.

PULASKI COUNTY.

Adams' Mills,	Clio,
Cain's Store,	Dallas,

* Money-order office.

PULASKI COUNTY—Continued.

Garden Cottage,
Lincolnville,
Line Creek, •
Plato,
Shopville,
Somerset, (c. h.,)
Sublimity,
Thompsonville,
Valley Oak,
Waterloo,
White Oak Gap.

ROBERTSON COUNTY.

Bratton's Mills,
Kentontown,
Mount Olivet, (c. h.)

ROCKCASTLE COUNTY.

Broadhead,
Goochland,
Gum Sulphur,
Mount Vernon, (c. h.)

ROWAN COUNTY.

Cassity's Mills,
Farmers,
Gill's Mills,
Morehead, (c. h.,)
Pine Springs.

RUSSELL COUNTY.

Creelsborough,
Horse Shoe Bottom,
Jamestown, (c. h.,)
Millersville,
Royalton.

SCOTT COUNTY.

Dry Run,
Georgetown, (c. h.,)
Great Crossings,
Little Eagle,
Minorsville,
Newtown,
Oxford,
Payne's Depot,
Stamping Ground,
Stonewall,
Straight Fork.
White Sulphur.

SHELBY COUNTY.

Bailey's Store,
Bagdad,
Chesnut Grove,
Christiansburgh,
Clay Village,
Cropper's Depot,
Graefenberg,
Harrisonville,
Jacksonville,
Jesse's Store,
North Benson,
Shelbyville, (c. h.,)
Simpsonville,
Todd's Point.

SIMPSON COUNTY.

Franklin, (c. h.,)
Temperance Mount.

SPENCER COUNTY.

Elk Creek,
Little Mount,
Mount Eden,
Smileytown,
Taylorsville, (c. h.,)
Van Dyke's Mill,
Waterford,
Wilsonville.

TAYLOR COUNTY.

Campbellsville, (c. h.,)
Mannsville,
Saloma.

TODD COUNTY.

Allensville,
Clifty,
Daysville,
Elkton, (c. h.,)
Guthrie,
Hadensville,
Kirkmansville,
Pilot Knob,
Sharon Grove,
Trenton.

TRIGG COUNTY.

Cadiz, * (c. h.,)
Canton,
Cerulean Springs,
Empire Iron Works,
Golden Pond,
Lindsey's Mill,
Linton,
Montgomery,
Roaring Spring.

TRIMBLE COUNTY.

Bedford, (c. h.,)
Milton,
Winona.

UNION COUNTY.

Bordley,
Boxville,
Caseyville,
Hitesville,
Lindle's Mills,
Morganfield, (c. h.,)
Raleigh,
Uniontown.*

WARREN COUNTY.

Bowling Green, *
(c. h.,)
Bristow Station,
Claypool,
Elk Spring,
Green Hill,
Green Castle,
Hadley,
Honaker's Ferry,
Memphis Junction,
Oakland Station,
Rich Pond Grove,
Rockfield,
Smith's Grove,
Woodburn.

WASHINGTON COUNTY.

Antioch,
Beech Fork,
Beechland,
Fredericktown,
Mackville,
Sharpsville,
Springfield, (c. h.,)
Texas,
Willisburgh.

WAYNE COUNTY.

Berryville,
Mill Springs,
Monticello, (c. h.,)
Parmleysville
Weaverton.

WEBSTER COUNTY.

Clay,
Dixon, (c. h.,)
Poole's Mill,
Providence,
Sebree,
Slaughterville,
Vanderburgh.

WHITLEY COUNTY.

Bark Camp Mills,
Lot,
Marsh Creek,
Meadow Creek,
Rockhold's,
Whitley C. H.,
Young's Creek.

WOLFE COUNTY.

Campton, (c. h.,)
Hazle Green.

WOODFORD COUNTY.

Ducker's,
Midway,
Mortonsville,
Spring Station,
Troy,
Versailles, (c. h.)

---

* Money-order office.

LOUISIANA.

ASCENSION PARISH.

Donaldsonville, (o. h.,) New River.

ASSUMPTION PARISH.

Albemarle,	Labadieville,
Assumption, (c. h.,)	Paincourtville.

AVOYELLES PARISH.

Big Bend,	Mansura,
Evergreen,	*Marksville*, (c. h.,)
Holmesville,	Moreauville.

BIENVILLE PARISH.

Arcadia,	Ringgold,
Buckhorn,	Saline,
Mount Lebanon,	*Sparta*, (c. h.)

BOSSIER PARISH.

Bellevue, (c. h.,)	Collinsburgh,
Benton,	Rocky Mount.
Coleville,	

CADDO PARISH.

Currie's Store,	*Shreveport*,* (c. h.,)
Greenwood,	Spring Ridge.
Mooringsport,	

CALCASIEU PARISH.

Lake Arthur, *Lake Charles*, (o. h.)

CALDWELL PARISH.

Columbia, (c. h.,)	Waverly.
Copenhagen,	

CARROLL PARISH.

Illawara,	Vista Ridge.
Lake Providence,	

CATAHOULA PARISH.

Ford's Creek,	Hemp's Creek,
Funny Louis,	Trinity,
Harrisonburgh, (c. h.,)	White Sulphur Sp'gs.

CLAIBORNE PARISH.

Arizonia,	Knoxville,
Cane Ridge,	Lisbon,
Haynesville,	Minden,
Homer, (c. h.,)	Sugar Creek.

CONCORDIA PARISH.

Fairview, *Vidalia*, (c. h.)

DE SOTO PARISH.

Grand Cane,	Longstreet,
Keatchie,	*Mansfield*, (c. h.)
Logansport,	

EAST BATON ROUGE PARISH.

Baton Rouge, (c. h.,)	Stony Point.
Burlington,	

EAST FELICIANA PARISH.

Clinton,* (c. h.,)	Port Hudson,
Jackson,	Woodland.

FRANKLIN PARISH.

Louisville,	Warsaw,
Oakley,	*Winnsborough*, (o. h.)

GRANT PARISH.

Colfax, (c. h.,)	Montgomery.
Jatt,	

IBERIA PARISH.

Jeanerette, *New Iberia*,* (c. h.)

IBERVILLE PARISH.

Bayou Goula,	Rosedale.
Musson,	St. Gabriel.
Plaquemine,* (c. h.,)	

JACKSON PARISH.

Bonner,	*Vernon*, (c. h.,)
Brookline,	Vienna,
Douglas,	Woodville.

JEFFERSON PARISH.

Carrollton, (c. h.,)	Jefferson,
Gretna,	Kenner.

LA FAYETTE PARISH.

Bertrandville,	*Vermillionville*, (c. h.)
Cote Gelee,	

LA FOURCHE PARISH.

Raceland, *Thibodeaux*,* (c. h.)

LIVINGSTON PARISH.

Bayou Barbary,	Live Oak Store,
Benton's Ferry,	*Springfield*, (c. h.)
Coelk,	

* Money-order office.

MADISON PARISH.

Delta, (c. h.,)   Milliken's Bend,
Duckport,   Richmond.

MOREHOUSE PARISH.

Bastrop, (c. h.,)   Line,
Lind Grove,   Point Jefferson.

NATCHITOCHES PARISH.

Campti,   Loggy Bayou,
Cloutierville,   Marthaville,
Conshatte Chute,   *Natchitoches,* (c. h.)
DeLoche's Landing,

ORLEANS PARISH.

Algiers,   NEW ORLEANS,* (c. h.)
Fort Pike,

OUACHITA PARISH.

Cuba,   *Monroe,* (c. h.,)
Forksville,   Trenton.
Log Town,

PLAQUEMINES PARISH.

Buras,   *Point á la Hache,* (c. h.)
Jesuit's Bend,

POINT COUPEE PARISH.

Hermitage,   *Point Coupee, (c. h.,)*
Livonia,   Red River Landing,
Morganzia,   Waterloo.

RAPIDES PARISH.

Alexandria, (c. h.,)   Cotile,
Cheneyville,   Cotile Landing.

RICHLAND PARISH.

Delhi,   *Rayville, (c. h.)*

SABINE PARISH.

Fort Jesup,   *Manny, (c. h.)*

SAINT BERNARD PARISH.

St. Bernard, (c. h.)

SAINT CHARLES PARISH.

Boutte,   *St. Charles, (c. h.)*

SAINT HELENA PARISH.

Arcola,   Hog Branch,
Darlington,   Tangapaho.
Greensburgh, (c. h.,)

SAINT JAMES PARISH.

Cantrelle,   Vacherie Roads.
Convent, (c. h.,)

SAINT JOHN BAPTIST PARISH.

Bonnet Carre,   *Edgard, (c. h.)*

SAINT LANDRY PARISH.

Arnaudville,   *Opelousas,* (c. h.,)
Bayou Bœuf,   Plaquemine Brulee,
Bayou Chicot,   Saint Peter's,
Big Cane,   Ville Platte,
Grand Coteau,   Washington.
Mermenton,

SAINT MARTIN'S PARISH.

Breaux Bridge,   *St. Martinville, (c. h.)*
La Place,

SAINT MARY'S PARISH.

Baldwin,   Cypre-mort,
Brashear,   *Franklin, (c. h.,)*
Centreville,   Pattersonville.

SAINT TAMMANY PARISH.

Covington, (c. h.,)   Mandeville,
Madisonville,   Sun.

TANGIPAHOA PARISH.

Amite City, (c. h.,)   Independence,
Hammond,   Ponchatoula.

TENSAS PARISH.

Ashwood,   Water Proof.
St. Joseph's, (c. h.,)

TERRE BONNE PARISH.

Houma, (c. h.,)   Tigerville.
Terre Bonne,

UNION PARISH.

Downsville,   Marion,
Farmersville, (c. h.,)   Union Cross Roads.
Lone Well,

VERMILLION PARISH.

Abbeville, (c. h.,)   Perry's Bridge.
Grand Chenier,

WASHINGTON PARISH.

Franklinton, (c. h.,)   Shady Grove.

WEST BATON ROUGE PARISH.

Belle Vale.

WEST FELICIANA PARISH.

Bayou Tunica,   *St. Francisville,* (c. h.)

WINN PARISH.

Atlanta,   Saint Maurice,
Newport,   Wheeling,
Pine Ridge,   *Winfield, (c. h.)*

---

* Money-order office.

MAINE.

ANDROSCOGGIN COUNTY.

Auburn,* (c. h.,)
Curtis' Corner,
Danville,
Durham,
East Auburn,
East Livermore,
East Poland,
East Turner,
East Wales,
Greene,
Greene Corner,
Leeds,
Leeds Junction,
Lewiston,*
Lisbon,
Lisbon Falls,
Livermore,
Livermore Centre,
Livermore Falls,
Mechanics Falls,*
Minot,
North Auburn,

North Leeds,
North Livermore,
North Turner,
N. Turner Bridge,
Poland,
Sabattus,
South Auburn,
South Durham,
South Leeds,
South Lewiston,
South Livermore,
South Poland,
Strickland's Ferry,
Turner,
Wales,
Webster,
West Auburn,
West Durham,
West Leeds,
West Minot,
West Poland.

AROOSTOOK COUNTY.

Alva,
Amity,
Ashland,
Bancroft,
Bridgewater,
Caribou,
Castle Hill,
Conway,
Dickeyville,
Dyer Brook,
Easton,
Fort Fairfield,*
Fort Kent,
Glenwood,
Golden Ridge,
Grant Isle,
Haynesville,
Hodgdon,
Houlton,* (c. h.,)
Island Falls,
Limestone,
Linneus,
Littleton,
Lyndon,
Madawaska,

Maple Grove,
Mars Hill,
Masardis,
Moluncus,
Monticello,
Moro,
New Limerick,
North Amity,
North Linneus,
Orient,
Portage Lake,
Presque Isle,*
Rawson,
Rockabema,
Salmon Brook,
Sherman,
Sherman Mills,
Smyrna,
Smyrna Mills,
South Moluncus,
South Weston,
Upper Madawaska,
Van Buren,
Westfield,
Weston.

CUMBERLAND COUNTY.

Bolster's Mills,
Bonny Eagle,
Bridgeton,
Brunswick,*
Cape Elizabeth Depot,
Casco,
Chebeauge Island,

Cumberland,
Cumberland Centre,
Dry Mills,
Duck Pond,
East Baldwin,
East Harpswell,
E. North Yarmouth,
East Otisfield,

CUMBERLAND COUNTY—Continued.

East Raymond,
East Windham,
Edes' Falls,
Falmouth,
Ferry Village,
Freeport,
Gorham,*
Gray,
Harpswell Centre,
Harrison,
Naples,
New Casco,
New Gloucester,
North Baldwin,
North Bridgeton,
North Gray,
North Harpswell,
North Pownal,
North Raymond,
North Windham,
North Yarmouth,
Oak Hill,
Orr's Island,
Otisfield,
Portland,* (c. h.,)
Pownal,
Raymond,

Saccarappa,
Sandy Beach,
Scarborough,
Sebago,
South Bridgeton,
South Casco,
South Freeport,
South Windham,
Standish,
Steep Falls,
Stevens' Plains,
Upper Gloucester,
Webb's Mills,
West Baldwin,
West Bridgeton,
West Brunswick,
West Cumberland,
West Falmouth,
West Gloucester,
West Gorham,
West Harpswell,
West Pownal,
White Rock,
Windham,
Woodford's,
Yarmouth.*

FRANKLIN COUNTY.

Avon,
Bean's Corners,
Berry's Mill,
Chesterville,
East New Sharon,
East New Vineyard,
East Wilton,
Eustis,
Farmington,* (c. h.,)
Farmington Falls,
Freeman,
Green Vale,
Industry,
Jay,
Kingfield,
Madrid,
New Sharon,

New Vineyard,
North Chesterville,
North Farmington,
North Jay,
Phillips,*
Pratt's Corner,
Rangeley,
Salem,
South Carthage,
South Chesterville,
Strong,
Temple Mills,
Weld,
West Freeman,
Wests' Mills,
Wilton.

HANCOCK COUNTY.

Amherst,
Aurora,
Blue Hill,
Blue Hill Falls,
Brooklin,
Brooksville,
Buck's Mills,
Bucksport,
Bucksport Centre,
Castine,
Cranberry Isles,

Dedham,
Deer Isle,
East Bucksport,
East Eden,
East Lamoine,
East Sullivan,
Eden,
Ellsworth,* (c. h.,)
Franklin,
Gouldsborough,
Great Pond,

* Money-order office.

HANCOCK COUNTY—Continued.

Green's Landing,	Sargentville,
Hancock,	Seal Cove,
Lamoine,	Sedgwick,
Mount Desert,	South Brooksville,
North Blue Hill,	South Hancock,
North Brooklin,	South Deer Isle,
North Brooksville,	South Penobscot,
North Bucksport,	South West Harbor,
North Castine,	Sullivan,
North Deer Isle,	Surry,
Northeast Harbor,	Swan's Island,
North Ellsworth,	Tilden,
North Hancock,	Tremont,
North Mariaville,	Waltham,
North Penobscot,	West Brooksville,
North Sedgwick,	West Deer Isle,
Orland,	West Eden,
Otis,	West Ellsworth,
Penobscot,	West Gouldsboro'h,
Prospect Harbor,	West Trenton,
Salisbury Cove,	Winter Harbor.

KENNEBEC COUNTY.

Albion,	North Sidney,
AUGUSTA,* (c. h.,)	North Vassalboro'h,
Belgrade,	North Vienna,
Belgrade Mills,	North Wayne,
Benton,	Pishon's Ferry,
Centre Sidney,	Pittston,
China,	Readfield,
Clinton,	Readfield Depot,
Cross Hill,	Riverside,
Dirigo,	Rome,
East Benton,	Sidney,
East Monmouth,	South Albion,
East Pittston,	South China,
East Readfield,	South Gardiner,
East Vassalborough,	South Litchfield,
East Winthrop,	South Monmouth,
Fayette,	South Vassalboro'h,
Fayette Ridge,	South Windsor,
Gardiner,*	Vassalborough,
Hallowell,	Vienna,
Kent's Hill,	Waterville,*
Litchfield,	Wayne,
Litchfield Corners,	Week's Mills,
Manchester,	West Farmingdale,
Monmouth,	West Gardiner,
Mount Vernon,	West Mount Vernon,
Nat'al Mil. Asylum,*	West Waterville,
North Belgrade,	Windsor,
North Fayette,	Winslow,
North Monmouth,	Winthrop.
North Pittston,	

KNOX COUNTY.

Appleton,	North Appleton,
Camden,*	North Haven,
Carver's Harbor,	North Union,
Cushing,	North Washington,
Friendship,	*Rockland,* (c. h.,)
Hope,	Rockport,
Matinicus,	Rockville,

KNOX COUNTY—Continued.

Saint George,	Union,
South Hope,	Warren,
South Saint George,	Washington,
South Thomaston,	West Appleton,
Tenant's Harbor,	West Camden,
Thomaston,	West Washington.

LINCOLN COUNTY.

Alna,	North New Castle,
Booth Bay,	North Waldoboro'h,
Bristol,	North Whitefield,
Cooper's Mills,	Pemaquid,
Damariscotta Mills,	Round Pond,
Dresden,	Sheepscott Bridge,
Dresden Mills,	Somerville,
Edgecomb,	South Bristol,
Hodgdon's Mills,	South Jefferson,
Jefferson,	Southport,
Monhegan Island,	Waldoborough,
New Castle,	West Dresden,
Noblesborough,	Westport,
North Boothbay,	Whitefield,
North Edgecomb,	*Wiscasset,* (c. h.)

OXFORD COUNTY.

Albany,	North Buckfield,
Andover,	North Fryeburgh,
Bethel,*	North Lovell,
Brownfield,	North Newry,
Bryant's Pond,	North Norway,
Buckfield,	North Paris,
Byron,	North Rumford,
Canton,	North Waterford,
Canton Point,	North Woodstock,
Centre Lovell,	Norway,*
Denmark,	Oxford,
Dixfield,	*Paris,* (c. h.,)
Dixfield Centre,	Peru,
East Dixfield,	Porter,
East Fryeburgh,	Roxbury,
East Hebron,	Rumford,
East Peru,	Rumford Centre,
East Rumford,	Rumford Point,
East Stoneham,	Snow Falls,
East Sumner,	South Andover,
Fryeburgh,	South Paris,
Fryeburgh Centre,	South Waterford,
Gilead,	Stow,
Grafton,	Sumner,
Greenwood,	Sweden,
Hanover,	Upton,
Hartford,	Waterford,
Hebron,	Welchville,
Hiram,	West Bethel,
Locke's Mills,	West Paris,
Lovell,	West Peru,
Mexico,	West Sumner,
Milton Plantation,	Wilson's Mills,
Newry,	Woodstock.
North Bethel,	

* Money-order office.

PENOBSCOT COUNTY.

Alton,
Argyle,
Bangor,* (c. h.,)
Bradford,
Brewer,
Brewer Village,
Burlington,
Carmel,
Carroll,
Charleston,
Chester,
Clifton,
Corinna,
Corinna Centre,
Corinth,
Dexter,*
Dixmont,
Dixmont Centre,
East Bangor,
East Bradford,
East Corinth,
East Dixmont,
East Eddington,
East Exeter,
East Hampden,
East Holden,
East Lincoln,
East Lowell,
East Newport,
East Orrington,
Eddington,
Enfield,
Etna,
Etna Centre,
Exeter,
Exeter Mills,
Garland,
Glenburn,
Goodale's Corner,
Great Works,
Greenbush,
Greenfield,
Hampden,
Hampden Corner,
Hermon,
Hermon Pond,
Holden,
Holt's Mills,
Howland,
Hudson,
Kenduskeag,
La Grange,
Lee,

Levant,
Lincoln,
Lincoln Centre,
Lowell,.
Mattawamkeag,
Maxfield,
Medway,
Milford,
Nealey's Corner,
Newburgh,
Newburgh Centre,
Newport,
North Bangor,
North Bradford,
North Carmel,
North Dixmont,
North Hermon,
North Milford,
North Newburgh,
North Newport,
North Woodville,
Olamon,
Old Town,
Orono,
Orrington,
Passadumkeag,
Pattagumpus,
Patten,
Plymouth,
Prentiss,
Simpson's Corner,
Six Mile Falls,
South Corinth,
South Exeter,
South Levant,
South Newburgh,
South Orrington,
South Winn,
Springfield,
Stetson,
Upper Stillwater,
Veazie,
West Charleston,
West Corinna,
West Enfield,
West Garland,
West Great Works,
West Hampden,
West Levant,
West Newburgh,
Winn,
Woodville.

PISCATAQUIS COUNTY.

Abbot,
Abbot Village,
Atkinson,
Barnard,
Blanchard,
Boyd Lake,
Brockway's Mills,
Brownsville,
Dover, (c. h.,)

Dover South Mills,
East Dover,
East Sangerville,
Foxcroft,*
Greenville,
Guilford,
Howard,
Katahdin Iron Works,
Kingsbury,

PISCATAQUIS COUNTY—Continued.

Medford,
Medford Centre,
Milo,
Monson,
Orneville,
Parkman,
Sangerville,
Sebec,
Shirley,

Shirley Mills,
South Atkinson,
South Dover,
South Sangerville,
South Sebec,
Wellington,
West Dover,
Williamsburgh.

SAGADAHOC COUNTY.

Bath,* (c. h.,)
Bowdoin,
Bowdoin Centre,
Bowdoinham,
East Bowdoinham,
Georgetown,
Parker's Head,
Phippsburgh,

Richmond,*
Richmond Corner,
Small Point,
Topsham,
West Bowdoin,
Winnegance,
Woolwich.

SOMERSET COUNTY.

Anson,
Athens,
Bingham,
Brighton,
Cambridge,
Canaan,
Canada Road,
Carritunk,
Concord,
Cornville,
Dead River,
Detroit,
East Madison,
East New Portland,
Embden,
Fairfield,
Fairfield Corners,
Flagstaff,
Harmony,
Hartland,
Highland,
Kendall's Mills,
Larone,
Lexington,
Madison,

Madison Centre,
Mercer,
Moose River,
New Portland,
Norridgewock, (c. h.,)
North Anson,
North Cornville,
North Fairfield,
North New Portland,
Palmyra,
Pittsfield,
Ripley,
Saint Albans,
Skowhegan,*
Smithfield,
Solon,
Somerset Mills,
South Norridgewock,
South Solon,
Stark,
The Forks,
West Athens,
West Cornville,
West Embden,
West Pittsfield.

WALDO COUNTY.

Belfast,* (c. h.,)
Belmont,
Brooks,
Burnham Village,
Centre Lincolnville,
Centre Montville,
East Knox,
East Montville,
East Northport,
East Palermo,
East Thorndike,
Ellingwood's Corner,
Frankfort,
Freedom,

Jackson,
Knox,
Liberty,
Lincolnville,
Monroe,
Monroe Centre,
Montville,
Morrill,
North Isleborough,
North Monroe,
North Palermo,
Northport,
North Searsmont,
North Searsport,

* Money-order office.

WALDO COUNTY—Continued.

North Winterport,
Palermo,
Palermo Centre,
Poor's Mills,
Prospect,
Prospect Ferry,
Sandy Point,
Searsmont,
Searsport,*
South Belmont,
South Brooks,
South Liberty,

South Montville,
Stockton,
Swanville,
Thorndike,
Troy,
Troy Centre,
Unity,*
Waldo,
West Troy,
West Winterport,
White's Corner,
Winterport.*

WASHINGTON COUNTY.

Addison Point,
Alexander,
Baileyville,
Baring,
Beddington,
Calais,*
Charlotte,
Columbia,
Cooper,
Crawford,
Cutler,
Deblois,
Dennysville,
East Machias,
Eastport,*
Harrington,
Indian River,
Jackson Brook,
Jonesborough,
Jonesport,
Lubec,
Machias,* (c. h.,)
Machias Port,·

Marion,
Medybemps,
Millbridge,
Milltown,
Narraguagus,
North Cutler,
Northfield,
North Lubec,
North Perry,
Pembroke,*
Perry,
Plantation No. 14,
Princeton,
Red Beach,
Robbinston,
South Beddington,
South Robbinston,
Steuben,
Topsfield,
Waite,
Wesley,
West Lubec,
West Pembroke,

WASHINGTON COUNTY—Continued.

Whiting,

Whitneyville.

YORK COUNTY.

Acton,
Alfred,* (c. h.,)
Bar Mills,
Berwick,
Biddeford,*
Biddeford Pool
Buxton,
Buxton Centre,
Cape Neddick,
Cape Porpoise,
Centre Lebanon,
Cornish,
Dayton,
East Limington,
East Parsonfield,
East Waterborough,
Elliot,
Elliot Depot,
Emery's Mills,
Goodwin's Mills,
Hollis,
Hollis Centre,
Kennebunk,
Kennebunk Depot,
Kennebunk Landing,
Kennebunk Port,
Kezar Falls,
Kittery,
Kittery Depot,
Kittery Point,
Lebanon,
Limerick,
Limington,
Lyman,
Nason's Mills,
Newfield,

North Acton,
North Alfred,
North Berwick,
North Kennebunk
Port,
North Lebanon,
North Limington,
North Newfield,
North Parsonfield,
North Shapleigh,
North Waterborough,
Ogunquit,
Ossipee Mills,
Parsonfield,
Ross' Corners,
Saco,*
Sanford,
Shapleigh,
South Acton,
South Berwick,*
South Berwick Junction,
South Limington,
South Parsonfield,
South Sanford,
Springvale,*
Waterborough,
Waterboro'h Centre,
Wells,
Wells Depot,
West Buxton,
West Lebanon,
West Newfield,
West Parsonfield,
York.

MARYLAND.

ALLEGHANY COUNTY.

Accident,
Altamont,
Barton,
Bloomington,
Brady's Mill,
Corriganville,
Cumberland,* (c. h.,)
Davis Mill,
Deer Park,
Ellerslie,
Flint Stone,
Frankville,
Frostburgh,*

Grantsville,
Hutton's Switch,
Johnstown,
Lonaconing,*
Mount Savage,
Oakland,
Ocean,
Old Town,
Rawling's Station,
Selbysport,
Shade Mills,
Swanton,
Western Port.

ANNE ARUNDEL COUNTY.

ANNAPOLIS,* (c. h.,) Annapolis Junction,

ANNE ARUNDEL COUNTY—Continued.

Arnold's Store,
Bristol,
Brooklyn,
Crownsville,
Davidsonville,
Friendship,
Hooversville,
Johnson's Store,
Millersville,
Patuxent,

Rutland,
Saint Margaret's,
Sappington,
Shepherd's Store,
South River,
Sudley,
Tracy's Landing,
Waterbury,
West River.

BALTIMORE COUNTY.

Baltimore,*
Beckleysville,
Belfast,
Bentley's Springs,

Black Rock,
Brooklandville,
Butler,
Calverton Mills,

* Money-order office.

BALTIMORE COUNTY—Continued.

Catonsville,
Carroll.
Cockeysville,*
Cub Hill,
Dulaney's Valley,
Ellengowan,
Fork Meet'g House,
Freeland,
Gorsuch's Mills,
Govanstown,
Grave Run Mills,
Greenwood,
Harewood,
Harrisonville,
Hereford,
Hookstown,
Lauraville,
Little Gunpowder,
Long Green Acad'y,
Lutherville,
Maryland Line,
Monkton Mills,
Monument House,
Mount Carmel,
Mount Washington,
North Branch,
Orangeville,
Owing's Mills,

Paper Mills,
Parkton,
Philopolis,
Phœnix,
Pikesville,
Powhatan,
Randallstown,
Rayville,
Reisterstown,
Rossville,
Saint Denis,
Shane,
Stablersville,
Stevenson Station,
Sweet Air,
Towsontown, (*c. h.,*)
Trenton,
Union Meet'g House,
Upperco,
Upper Falls,
Warren,
Waverly,
Weisesburgh,
Wetheredville,
White Hall,
Woodberry,
Woodensburgh.

CALVERT COUNTY.

Cove Point,
Dunkirk,
Huntingtown,
Lower Marlborough,
Mill Creek,
Port Republic,

Prince Fredericktown,
(*c. h.,*)
Saint Leonards,
Solomon's Island,
Sunderlandville.

CAROLINE COUNTY.

Bethlehem,
Bridgetown,
Burrsville,
*Denton,** (*c. h.,*)
Federalsburgh,
Fowling Creek,
Goldsborough,
Greensborough,*
Henderson,

Hillsborough,
Marydell,
New Hope,
Potter's Landing,
Preston,
Ridgely,
Smithville,
Whiteleysburgh.

CARROLL COUNTY.

Bachman's Mills,
Bird Hill,
Bruceville,
Carrollton,
Dennings,
Double Pipe Creek,
Dug Hill,
Finksburgh,
Franklinville,
Freedom,
Frizellburgh,
Hampstead,
Harney,

Hood's Mills,
Houcksville,
Linwood,
Louisville,
McKinstry's Mills,
Manchester,
Mayberry,
Middleburgh,
Mount Airy,
New Windsor,
Piney Creek,
Porters,
Sam's Creek,

CARROLL COUNTY—Continued.

Silver Run,
Stonersville,
Sykesville,
Taneytown,
Union Bridge,
Union Mills,
Uniontown,

Wakefield,
Warfieldburgh,
Watersville,
*Westminster,** (*c. h.,*)
Winfield,
Woodbine.

CECIL COUNTY.

Bay View,
Brick Meet'g House,
Cecilton,
Charlestown,
Cherry Hill,
Chesapeake City,*
Colora,
Conowingo,
*Elkton,** (*c. h.,*)
Fair Hill,
Farmington,
Mechanics' Valley,

Northeast,*
Perryville,
Port Deposit,*
Principio,
Principio Furnace,
Rising Sun,*
Rock Springs,
Rowlandsville,
Saint Augustine,
Warwick,
Woodlawn,
Zion.

CHARLES COUNTY.

Allen's Fresh,
Beantown,
Bryantown,
Cross Roads,
Doncaster,
Duffield,
Gallant Green,
Glymont,
Harris' Lot,

Hughesville,
Marshall Hall,
Nanjemoy,
Newburgh,
Newport,
Pisgah,
Pomonkey,
Port Tobacco, (*c. h.*)

DORCHESTER COUNTY.

Airey's,
Bishop's Head,
*Cambridge,** (*c. h.,*)
Cedar Creek,
Church Creek,
Cornersville,
Draw Bridge,
East New Market,
Fishing Creek,
Gales Town,
Golden Hill,

Harrison,
Hill's Point,
Hoopersville,
Hurlock,
Lakesville,
Linkwood,
Salem,
Taylor's Island,
Tobacco Stick,
Vienna,
Williamsburgh.

FREDERICK COUNTY.

Adamstown,
Barry,
Bolivar,
Bridgeport,*
Broad Run,
Buckeystown,
Burkettsville,
Catocton Furnace,
Creagerstown,
Emmittsburgh,*
Foxville,
*Frederick,** (*c. h.,*)
Graceham,
Greenfield Mills,

Hansonville,
Ijamsville,
Jefferson,
Johnsville,
Kemptown,
Knoxville,
Ladiesburgh,
Lander,
Lewistown,
Libertytown,
Licksville,
Linganore,
Mechanicstown,
Middletown,*

* Money-order office.

FREDERICK COUNTY—Continued.

Monrovia,
Mount Pleasant,
Myersville,
New London, ·
New Market,
Oak Orchard,
Petersville,
Plane No. Four,
Point of Rocks,

Sabillisville,
Unionville,
Urbana,
Utica Mills,
Walkersville,
Wolfsville,
Woodsborough,
Woodville.

HARFORD COUNTY.

Aberdeen,
Abingdon,
Bel Air, (c. h.,)
Black Horse,
Boothby Hill,
Chrome Hill,
Churchville,
Clayton,
Clermont Mills,
Darlington, ·
Dublin,
Edgewood,
Emmorton,
Fallston,
Federal Hill,
Forest Hill,
Fountain Green,
Glenville,
Harford Furnace,
Havre de Grace,*

Hickory Tavern,
Hopewell X Roads,
Jarrettsville,
Jerusalem Mills,
Lapidum,
Magnolia,
Michaelsville,
Mill Green,
Norrisville,
Oakington,
Perrymansville,
Pleasantville,
Prospect,
Pylesville,
Sandy Hook,
Taylor,
Thomas' Run,
Upper X Roads,
Wilna.

HOWARD COUNTY.

Alberton,
Clarksville,
Cooksville,.
Dayton,
Elk Ridge Landing,
Ellicott City,* (c. h.,)
Florence,
Glenelg,
Hanover,
Ilchester Mills,

Lisbon,
Marriottsville,
Matthew's Store,
Oakland Mills,
Poplar Springs,
Roxbury Mills,
Savage,
Simpsonville,
West Friendship,
Woodstock.

KENT COUNTY.

Chestertown, (c. h.,)
Chesterville,
Edesville,
Fairlee,
Galena,
Hanesville,
Kennedyville,
Locust Grove,

Massey's X Roads,
Millington,
Rock Hall,
Sassafras,
Spry's Landing,
Still Pond,
Urieville.

MONTGOMERY COUNTY.

Barnesville,
Beallsville,
Brighton,
Brookville,
Clarksburgh,
Colesville,

Damascus,
Darcey's Store,
Darnestown,
Dawsonville,
Forest Oak,
Germantown,

MONTGOMERY COUNTY—Continued.

Goshen,
Hyattstown,
Laytonville,
Middlebrook,
Monocacy,
Montrose,
Nichols,
Norbeck,
Offutt's X Roads,
Olney,

Poolesville,
Redland,
Rockville,* (c. h.)
Sandy Spring,*
Seneca,
Sligo,
Spencerville,
Triadelphia,
Unity,
Wheaton.

PRINCE GEORGE'S COUNTY.

Accokeek,
Agricultural College,
Aquasco,
Beltsville,
Bladensburgh,
Branchville,
Brandywine,
Buena Vista,
Collington,
Croom,
Forestville,
Fort Washington,
Horse Head,
Hyattsville,
Laurel Factory,*

Mellwood,
Mitchellville,
Muirkirk,
Nottingham,
Oak Grove,
Oxen Hill,
Piscataway,
Robeystown,
Rosaryville,
Silver Hill,
Suitsville,
T. B.,
Upper Marlboro, (c.h.,)
Watson.

QUEEN ANNE'S COUNTY.

Broad Creek,
Centreville,* (c. h.,)
Church Hill,
Crumpton,
Long Marsh,

Queenstown,
Roesville,
Sudlersville,
Templeville.

ST. MARY'S COUNTY.

Budd's Creek,
Chaptico,
Charlotte Hall,
Fairfield,
Great Mills,
Hollywood,
Leonardtown,* (c. h.,)
Milestown,

Morganza,
Oakville,
Piney Point,
Point Lookout,
Ridge,
St. Clement's Bay,
St. Inigoes.

SOMERSET COUNTY.

Burnettsville,
Crisfield,
Dames Quarter,
Deal's Island,
Fairmount,
Hope,

Hopewell,
Kingston,
Monie,
Princess Anne,* (c. h.,)
Upper Trappe,
Westover.

TALBOT COUNTY.

Bay Hundred,
Broad Creek Neck,
Cordova,
Easton,* (c. h.,)
Oxford,
Royal Oak,

Saint Michaels,
Skipton,
Taverner's Woods,
Trappe,
Wittman,
Wye Mills.

* Money-order office.

WASHINGTON COUNTY.

Bakersville,
Beaver Creek,
Benevola,
Boonsborough,
Breathedsville,
Brownsville,
Cavetown,
Chewsville,
Clear Spring,
Conococheague,
Downsville,
Eakle's Mills,
Fair Play,
Fairview,
Funkstown,
Green Spring Furnace,
Hagerstown,* (c. h.,)
Hancock,*
Indian Springs,
Keedysville,
Keep Tryst,
Leitersburgh,
Mason,
Millstone Point,
Ringgold,
Rohrersville,
Sharpsburgh,*
Smithsburgh,
Williamsport.*

WICOMICO COUNTY.

Barren Creek Spr'gs,
Forktown,
Green Hill,
Nanticoke,
Pittsville,
Powellville,
Quantico,
Riverton,
Salisbury,* (c. h.,)
Sharptown,
Sheppardsville,
Tyaskin,
Whitehaven.

WORCESTER COUNTY.

Berlin,*
Bishopville,
Girdletree Hill,
Lindseyville,
Newark,
Newtown,
Saint Martins,
Sandy Hill,
Snow Hill,* (c. h.,)
Whaleysville.

MASSACHUSETTS.

BARNSTABLE COUNTY.

Barnstable, (c. h.,)
Brewster,
Centreville,
Chatham,
Chatham Port,
Cotuit Port,
Dennis,
Dennis Port,
East Brewster,
East Dennis,
East Falmouth,
Eastham,
East Harwich,
East Orleans,
East Sandwich,
Falmouth,
Harwich,
Harwich Port,
Hatchville,
Hyannis,
Marston's Mills,
Monument,
North Chatham,
North Eastham,
North Falmouth,
North Harwich,
North Sandwich,
North Truro,
Orleans,*
Osterville,
Pocasset,
Provincetown,*
Sandwich,*
South Brewster,
South Chatham,
South Dennis,
South Harwich,
South Orleans,
South Sandwich,
South Wellfleet,
South Yarmouth,
Spring Hill,
Truro,
Waquoit,
Wellfleet,*
West Barnstable,
West Brewster,
West Chatham,
West Dennis,
West Falmouth,
West Harwich,
West Sandwich,
West Yarmouth,
Wood's Hole,
Yarmouth,
Yarmouth Port.*

BERKSHIRE COUNTY.

Adams,
Alford,
Ashley Falls,
Bancroft,
Becket,
Becket Centre,
Berkshire,
Blackinton,
Cheshire,
Cold Spring,
Curtisville,
Dalton,
East Lee,
East Otis,
East Sheffield,
East Windsor,
Florida,
Glendale,
Great Barrington,*
Hancock,

BERKSHIRE COUNTY—Continued

Hartsville,
Hinsdale,
Hoosac Tunnel,
Housatonic,
Lanesborough,
Lee,*
Lenox, (c. h.,)
Lenox Furnace,
Mill River,
Monterey,
Montville,
New Ashford,
New Boston,
New Lenox,
New Marlborough,
North Adams,*
North Egremont,
Otis,
Peru,
Pittsfield,*
Richmond,
Rock Dale Mills,
Sandisfield,
Savoy,
Sheffield,
South Egremont,
Southfield,
South Lee,
South Sandisfield,
South Williamstown,
State Line,
Stockbridge,
Tyringham,
Van Deusenville,
Washington,
West Becket,
West Otis,
West Pittsfield,
West Stockbridge,
West Stockbridge Centre,
Williamstown,
Windsor.*

BRISTOL COUNTY.

Acushnet,
Attleborough,
Berkley,
Central Village,
Dartmouth,
Dighton,
East Freetown,
Easton,
East Taunton,
Fairhaven,
Fall River,*
Freetown,
Hebronville,
Long Plain,
Mansfield,
Myrickville,
New Bedford,*
North Attleborough,
North Dartmouth,
North Dighton,
North Easton,
North Rehoboth,
North Swansea,
Norton,
Raynham,
Rehoboth,
Seekonk,
Somerset,
South Attleborough,
South Dartmouth,
South Easton,
South Seekonk,

* Money-order office.

BRISTOL COUNTY—Continued.

South Westport,
Swansea,
Taunton, (c. h.,)

West Mansfield,
Westport,
Westport Point.

DUKES COUNTY.

Chilmark,
Edgartown, (c. h.,)
Holmes' Hole,

North Tisbury,
Vineyard Grove,
West Tisbury.

ESSEX COUNTY.

Amesbury,
Andover,*
Annisquam,
Ayers' Village,
Ballard Vale,
Bay View,
Beverly,
Beverly Farms,
Boxford,
Bradford,
Byfield,
Clifton Dale,
Danvers,
Danvers Centre,
Danversport,
East Gloucester,
East Haverhill,
East Salisbury,
Essex,
Georgetown,
Gloucester,*
Groveland,
Hamilton,
Haverhill,*
Ipswich,
Lanesville,
Lawrence,*
Lynn,*
Lynnfield,

Lynnfield Centre,
Manchester,
Marblehead,*
Methuen,
Middleton,
Nahant,
Newburyport,*
North Andover,
North Andover Dep't,
North Beverly,
Peabody,
Pigeon Cove,
Rockport,
Rowley,
Salem, (c. h.,)
Salisbury,
Saugus,
Saugus Centre,
South Amesbury,
South Groveland,
Swampscott,
Topsfield,
Wenham,
West Amesbury,
West Boxford,
West Danvers,
West Gloucester,
West Newbury.

FRANKLIN COUNTY.

Adamsville,
Ashfield,
Bardwell's Ferry,
Bernardstown,
Buckland,
Charlemont,
Colerain,
Conway,
Deerfield,
East Charlemont,
East Shelburne,
East Whately,
Elm Grove,
Erving,
Factory Village,
Gill,
Greenfield, (c. h.,)
Griswoldville,
Hawley,
Heath,
Leverett,

Leyden,
Lock's Village,
Miller's Falls,
Millington,
Monroe,
Montague,
Montague City,
New Salem,
Northfield,
Northfield Farms,
North Leverett,
North New Salem,
North Orange,
Orange,
Rowe,
Shattuckville,
Shelburne,
Shelburne Falls,*
Shutesbury,
South Ashfield,
South Deerfield,

FRANKLIN COUNTY—Continued.

Sunderland,
Warwick,
Wendell,
Wendell Depot,

West Hawley,
West Northfield,
Whately,
Zoar.

HAMPDEN COUNTY.

Agawam,
Ashleyville,
Blanford,
Bond's Village,
Brimfield,
Chester,
Chester Centre,
Chicopee,*
Chicopee Falls,*
Collins' Depot,
East Brimfield,
East Granville,
East Long Meadow,
Feeding Hills,
Granville Corners,
Holland,
Holyoke,*
Indian Orchard,
Ireland,
Long Meadow,

Ludlow,
Mittineague,
Monson,
Montgomery,
North Blanford,
North Chester,
Palmer,*
Russell,
Southwick,
South Wilbraham,
Springfield, (c. h.,)
Thorndike,
Three Rivers,
Tolland,
Wales,
Westfield,*
West Granville,
West Springfield,
Wilbraham,
Willimansett.

HAMPSHIRE COUNTY.

Amherst,*
Babylon,
Belchertown,
Chesterfield,
Cummington,
Cummington West
  Village,
East Hampton,*
Enfield,
Florence,
Goshen,
Granby,
Greenwich,
Greenwich Village,
Hadley,
Hatfield,
Haydenville,
Huntington,
Leeds,
Middlefield,
North Amherst,

Northampton, (c. h.,)
North Hadley,
North Hatfield,
North Prescott,
Norwich,
Pelham,
Plainfield,
Prescott,
Ringville,
South Amherst,
Southampton,
South Hadley,
South Hadley Falls,
South Worthington,
Ware,*
West Chesterfield,
West Hampton,
West Worthington,
Williamsburgh,*
Worthington.

MIDDLESEX COUNTY.

Acton,
Allston,
Arlington,
Ashby,
Ashland,
Assabet,
Auburn Dale,
Bedford,
Belmont,
Billerica,
Boxborough,

Braggville,
Brighton,*
Burlington,
Cambridge,*
Cambridgeport,*
Carlisle,
Charlestown,*
Chelmsford,
Chesnut Hill,
Cochituate,
College Hill,

* Money-order office.

MIDDLESEX COUNTY—Continued.

Concord* (c. h.),
Dracut,
Dunstable,
East Cambridge,
East Holliston,
East Lexington,
East Pepperell,
East Somerville,
East Woburn,
Forge Village,
Framingham,
Graniteville,
Greenwood,
Groton,
Groton Junction,*
Hayden Row,
Holliston,*
Hopkinton,*
Hudson,
Lexington,
Lincoln,
Littleton,
Lowell,*
Malden,
Maplewood,
Marlborough,*
Medford,
Melrose,
Middlesex Village,
Mount Auburn,
Natick,*
Newton,*
Newton Centre,
Newton Lower Falls,
Newton Upper Falls,
Newtonville,
North Billerica,
North Cambridge,
North Chelmsford,
North Reading,
North Somerville,

North Sudbury,
North Wilmington,
North Woburn,
Pepperell,
Reading,
Rock Bottom,
Saxonville,
Sherborn,
Shirley,
Shirley Village,
Somerville,
South Acton,
South Chelmsford,
South Framingham,
South Malden,
South Natick,
South Sudbury,
Stoneham,
Stow,
Sudbury,
Tewkesbury,
Townsend,
Townsend Harbor,
Tyngsborough,
Wakefield,
Waltham,*
Watertown,*
Waverly,
Wayland,
West Acton,
West Chelmsford,
Westford,
West Groton,
West Medford,
West Newton,
Weston,
West Townsend,
Wilmington,
Winchester,
Woburn,*
Woodville.

NANTUCKET COUNTY.

Nantucket,* (c. h.)

NORFOLK COUNTY.

Bellingham,
Braintree,
Brookline,
Canton,
Caryville,
Charles Riv. Village,
Cohasset,
Dedham,* (c. h.,)
Dorchester,
Dover,
East Foxborough,
East Medway,
East Randolph,
East Sharon,
East Stoughton,
East Walpole,
East Weymouth.

Foxborough,*
Franklin,*
Franklin City,
Grantville,
Harrison Square,
Hyde Park,
Jamaica Plain,
Mattapan,
Medfield,
Medway,*
Milton,
Needham,
Neponset Village,
Norfolk,
North Bellingham,
North Cohasset,
North Stoughton,

NORFOLK COUNTY—Continued.

North Weymouth,
Plainville,
Quincy,*
Quincy Point,
Randolph,
Readville Station,
Rockville,
Roslindale,
Sharon,
Sheldonville,
South Braintree,
South Dedham,
South Franklin,

South Randolph,
South Walpole,
South Weymouth,
Stoughton,
Walpole,
Wellesley,
West Dedham,
West Foxborough,
West Medway,
West Roxbury,
West Wrentham,
Weymouth,
Wrentham.

PLYMOUTH COUNTY.

Abington,
Bridgewater,*
Campello,
Carver,
Chiltonville,
Cochesett,
Duxbury,
East Abington,
East Bridgewater,
East Marshfield,
East Middleborough,
East Pembroke,
East Wareham,
Halifax,
Hanover,
Hanson,
Hingham,
Hingham Centre,
Hull,
Joppa Village,
Kingston,
Lakeville,
Marion,
Marshfield,
Mattapoisett,
Middleborough,
North Abington,
North Bridgewater,*
North Carver,

North Marshfield,
No. Middleborough,
North Pembroke,
North Plympton,
North Scituate,
N. W. Bridgewater,
Pembroke,
Plymouth,* (c. h.,)
Plympton,
Plympton Station,
Rochester,
Rock,
Scituate,
Scotland,
South Abington,
South Carver,
South Duxbury,
South Hanover,
South Hanson,
South Hingham,
So. Middleborough,
South Plymouth,
South Scituate,
Wareham,
West Bridgewater,
West Duxbury,
West Hanover,
West Scituate,
West Wareham.

SUFFOLK COUNTY.

BOSTON,* (c. h.,)
Chelsea,*

North Chelsea,
Winthrop.

WORCESTER COUNTY.

Ashburnham,
Ashburnham Depot,
Athol,
Athol Depot,
Auburn,
Baldwinsville,
Barre,
Barre Plains,
Berlin,
Blackstone,
Bolton,
Boylston,

Boylston Centre,
Brookfield,
Burrageville,
Charlton,
Charlton City,
Charlton Depot,
Cherry Valley,
Clinton,*
Coldbrook Springs,
Cordaville,
Dana,
Douglass,

* Money-order office.

WORCESTER COUNTY—Continued.

Dudley,
East Blackstone,
East Brookfield,
Esat Douglass,
East Princeton,
East Templeton,
Farnumsville,
Fayville,
Fiskedale,
Fitchburgh,*
Gardner,
Gilbertville,
Globe Village,
Grafton,
Hardwick,
Harvard,
Holden,
Hopedale,
Hubbardston,
Lancaster,
Leicester,
Leominster,
Lunenburgh,

Manchaug,
Mendon,
Milford,*
Millbury,
Millville,
New Braintree,
New Engl'd Village,
Northborough,
Northbridge,
Northbridge Centre,
North Brookfield,*
North Dana,
North Leominster,
North Oxford,
North Rutland,
North Spencer,
North Uxbridge,
Oakdale,
Oakham,
Otter River,
Oxford,
Paxton,
Petersham,

WORCESTER COUNTY—Continued.

Phillipston,
Pratt's Junction,
Princeton,
Rochdale,
Royalston,
Rutland,
Saundersville,
Shrewsbury,
Smithville,
Southborough,
Southbridge,*
South Gardner,*
South Lancaster,
South Milford, .
South Royalston,
Spencer,
Sterling,
Still River,
Sturbridge,
Sutton,
Templeton,
Upton,

Uxbridge,*
Wachusett Village,
Warren,
Webster,*
West Berlin,
Westborough,*
West Boylston,
West Brookfield,
West Dudley,
West Fitchburgh,
West Millbury,
Westminster,
Westminster Depot,
West Rutland,
West Sterling,
West Sutton,
West Upton,
West Warren,
Whitinsville,
Wilkinsonville,
Winchendon,*
Worcester, (c. h.)

MICHIGAN.

ALCONA COUNTY.

Alcona,
Greenbush,

Harrisville, (c. h.)

ALLEGAN COUNTY.

*Allegan,** (c. h.,)
Bradley,
Burnip's Corners,
Cheshire,
Dorr,
Douglas,
Dunningville,
Fenn's Mills,
Ganges,
Graafschap,
Gun Marsh,
Hamilton,
Hilliard's,
Hopkins,
Hopkins Station,

Manlius,
Martin,
Moline,
Monterey,
New Casco,
New Salem,
Otsego,
Overisel,
Plainwell,
Saugatuck,*
Silver Creek,
Watson,
Wayland,*
West Casco.

ALPENA COUNTY.

*Alpena,** (c. h.,)

Ossineke.

ANTRIM COUNTY.

Antrim City,
Atwood,
Central Lake,
Clear Water,
Creswell,

Elk Rapids, (c. h.,)
Mitchell,
Rootville,
Spencer Creek,
Torch Lake.

BARRY COUNTY.

Assyria,
Baltimore,
Barryville, .
Blair,
Bowen's Mills,
Cedar Creek,
Fillmore,
Gull Lake,
*Hastings,** (c. h.,)
Hickory Corners,
Irving,

Johnstown,
Maple Grove,
Meadville,
Middleville,*
Milo,
Nashville,*
North Irving,
Orangeville Mills,
Prairieville,
Woodland,
Yankee Spring.

BAY COUNTY.

Arenac,
Au Gres,
*Bay City,** (c. h.,)
Kawkawlin,
Portsmouth,

Salzburgh,
Skinner,
Wenona,
Williams.

BENZIE COUNTY.

Almira,
Benzonia, (c. h.,)
Frankfort,
Homestead,

Inland,
Joyfield,
Platte.

BERRIEN COUNTY.

Avery,
Bainbridge,
Benton Harbor,*
Berrien Centre,*

Berrien Springs, (c. h.,)
Bertrand,
Buchanan,*
Chickaming,

* Money-order office.

BERRIEN COUNTY—Continued.

Coloma,	Pipestone,
Dayton,	Pleasant Valley,
Eau Claire,	Saint Joseph,*
Galien,	Sawyer,
Laketon,	Sodus,
Millburgh,	Three Oaks,*
New Buffalo,*	Union Pier,
New Troy,	Watervleit,
Niles,*	Weesaw.

BRANCH COUNTY.

Algansee,	Kinderhook,
Batavia,	Mattison,
Bethel,	Noble Centre,
Bronson's Prairie,	Orangeville,
Butler,	Quincy,*
California,	Round Lake,
Cold Water,* (c. h.,)	Sherwood,
East Gilead,	South Butler,
Gilead,	Union City.
Girard,	

CALHOUN COUNTY.

Abscota,	East Leroy,
Albion,*	Homer,
Athens,	Marengo,
Battle Creek,*	Marshall,* (c. h.,)
Bedford,	Newton,
Burlington,	Partello,
Ceresco,	Pine Creek,
Clarence,	Secillia,
Clarendon Centre,	Tekonsha,
Convis Centre,	West Leroy,

CASS COUNTY.

Adamsville,	Model City,
Brownsville,	Newburgh,
Calvin,	Pokagon,
Cassopolis,* (c. h.,)	Shave Head,
Dowagiac,*	Summerville,
Edwardsburgh,	Union,
Jeffersonville,	Vandalia,
La Grange,	Volinia,
Little Prairie Ronde,	Williamsville.
Marcellus,	

CHARLEVOIX COUNTY.

Barnard,	Nelsonville,
Boyne,	Norwood.
Charlevoix, (c. h.,)	

CHEBOYGAN COUNTY.

Cheboygan, (c. h.)

CHIPPEWA COUNTY.

Detour,	Sault de Ste. Marie, (c. h.)

CLINTON COUNTY.

Bath,	Maple Rapids,
Bengal,	North Eagle,
Dallas,	Olive,
De Witt,	Ovid,*
Du Plain,	Riley,
Eagle,	Saint John's,* (c. h.,)
Elsie,	Shepardsville,
Essex,	South Riley,
Eureka,	Victor,
Geary,	Wacousta,
Lyon's Mill,	Westphalia.

DELTA COUNTY.

Esconawba,* (c. h.,)	Nahma.
Garden,	

EATON COUNTY.

Allen's,	Grand Ledge,
Bellevue,*	Kalamo,
Brookfield,	Mud Creek,
Carlisle,	Olivet,*
Centre,	Pottersville,
Charlotte,* (c. h.,)	Roxana,
Chester,	Sunfield,
County Line,	Vermontville,
Delta,	West Windsor,
Eaton Rapids,	Windsor.
Elmira,	

EMMETT COUNTY.

Bear River,	Little Traverse, (c. h.)

GENESEE COUNTY.

Argentine,	Kipp's Corners,
Atlas,	Linden,
Clio,	Montrose,
Davison,	Mt. Morris Station,
Elgin,	Mundy,
Fentonville,*	Otisville,
Flint,* (c. h.,)	Pine Run,
Flushing,	Richfield,
Gaines' Station,	Swartz Creek,
Genesee Village,	Thetford Centre,
Goodrich,	Whitesburgh.
Grand Blanc,	

GRAND TRAVERSE COUNTY.

Acme,	Monroe Centre,
Betsey Lake,	Old Mission,
Cedar Run,	Traverse City,* (c. h.,)
East Traverse Bay,	Williamsburgh,
Mapleton,	Yuba.
Mayfield,	

GRATIOT COUNTY.

Alma,	North Star,
Beaver Creek,	Pompei.
Bridgeville,	Saint Louis,
Elm Hall,	Spring Brook,
Forest Hill,	Stella,
Ithaca,* (c. h.,)	Summerton,
La Fayette,	Sumner,
Newark,	Wheeler.
New Haven Centre,	

* Money-order office.

HILLSDALE COUNTY.

Allen,
Amboy,
Cambria Mills,
Camden,
Cass,
Church's Corners,
Edinburgh,
Frontier,
Hillsdale,* (c. h.,)
Jefferson,
Jonesville,*
Litchfield,*
Morganville,
Moscow,
Mosherville,
North Adams,
Osseo,
Pittsford,
Ransom,
Reading,
Somerset,
South Camden,
South Wright,
Wheatland Centre.

HOUGHTON COUNTY.

Baraga,
Calumet,
Hancock,
Houghton,* (c. h.,)
Lake Linden,
L'Ance.

HURON COUNTY.

Can,
Caseville,
Cracow,
Forest Bay,
Huron City,
New River,
Ora Labor,
Pinnebog,
Port Austin, (c. h.,)
Port Crescent,
Port Hope,
Rock Falls,
Sand Beach,
Sebewaing,
Verona Mills,
White Rock.

INGHAM COUNTY.

Alverson,
Aurelius,
Bunker Hill,
Dansville,
Eden,
Felt's,
Fitchburgh,
Holt,
LANSING,*
Leslie,
Locke,
Mason,* (c. h.,)
Middletown,
North Aurelius,
Okemos,
Onondaga,
Red Bridge,
Stockbridge,
Webberville,
White Oak,
Williamstown,
Winfield.

IONIA COUNTY.

Algodon,
Campbell,
Danby,
Easton,
Hubbardston,
Ionia,* (c. h.,)
Keene,
Kiddville,
Lyons,*
Maple,
Matherton,
Muir,
North Plains,
Orange,
Orleans,
Otisco,
Palo,
Patterson's Mills,
Pewamo,
Portland,
Saranac,
Sebewa,
Smyrna,
South Boston,
South Cass,
West Campbell,
Wood's Corners.

IOSCO COUNTY.

Alabaster,
Au Sable,
East Tawas,
Ogemaw,
Rollo,
Tawas City,* (c. h.)

ISABELLA COUNTY.

Crawford,
Isabella City,
Mt. Pleasant, (c. h.,)
Rowland,
Salt River,
Strickland,
Winn,
Wiota.

JACKSON COUNTY.

Arland,
Baldwin's Mills,
Brooklyn,*
Columbia,
Concord,
Franciscoville,
Grass Lake,*
Hanover,
Henrietta,
Jackson,* (c. h.,)
Leoni,
Liberty,
Michigan Centre,
Napoleon,
Norvell,
Otter Creek,
Parma,*
Pulaski,
Rives Junction,
Sandstone,
South Jackson,
Spring Arbor,
Springport,
Tompkins,
Waterloo.

KALAMAZOO COUNTY.

Alamo,
Augusta,
Brady,
Climax Prairie,
Comstock,
Cooper,
Fulton,
Galesburgh,*
Kalamazoo,* (c. h.,)
Oshtemo,
Pavilion,
Portage,
Richland,
Schoolcraft,
South Climax,
Wakeshma,
Yorkville.

KENT COUNTY.

Ada,
Alaska,
Alpine,
Alto,
Alton,
Ashley,
Austerlitz,
Belmont,
Bostwick Lake,
Bowne,
Burch's,
Byron Centre,
Caledonia,
Caledonia Station,
Cannonsburgh,
Cascade,
Casnovia,
Cedar Springs,
Cody's Mills,
Cortland Centre,
Edgerton,
Englishville,
Fallassburgh,
Gainesville,
Grand Rapids,* (c. h.,)
Grandville,
Grant,
Grattan,
Hammond,
Harris' Creek,
Indian Creek,
Kelloggsville,
Lowell,
Mill Creek,
Nelson,
North Byron,
Oakfield,
Pleasant,
Rockford,*
Sand Lake,
Sparta Centre,
Spencer's Mill,
Vergennes.

KEWEENAW COUNTY.

Copper Falls Mine,
Copper Harbor,
Eagle Harbor,
Eagle River, (c. h.,)
Penn Mine,
Phœnix.

* Money-order office.

LAKE COUNTY.

Pine River.

LAPEER COUNTY.

Almont,	Hunter's Creek,
Burnside,	Imlay,
Clifford,	*Lapeer,* (*c. h.,*)
Columbiaville,	Marathon,
Dryden,	Metamora,
Farmer's Creek,	Mill Station,
Five Lakes,	North Branch,
Goodland,	Pool,
Hadley,	Rural Vale,
Hasler,	Thornville.

LEELENAW COUNTY.

Burdickville,	Micham,
Empire,	*Northport,** (*c. h.,*)
Glen Arbor,	North Unity,
Glen Haven,	Omena,
Good Harbor,	Solon,
Leland,	Sutton's Bay.
Melville,	

LENAWEE COUNTY.

Addison,	Ogden Centre,
*Adrian,** (*c. h.,*)	Palmyra,
Blissfield,	Raisin Centre,
Cambridge,	Ridgeway,
Canandaigua,	Riga,
Clayton,	Rollin,
Clinton,	Rome,
Deerfield,	Seneca,
Fairfield,	Springville,
Geneva,	Tecumseh,*
Hudson,*	Tipton,
Kelly's Corners,	Wellsville,
Lake Ridge,	West Ogden,
Macon,	Weston,
Medina,	Woodstock.
Morenci,	

LIVINGSTON COUNTY.

Brighton,	Josco,
Cohoctah,	Madison,
Conway,	Marion,
Deer Creek,	Oak Grove,
Fleming,	Oceola Centre,
Fowlerville,	Parshallville,
Genoa,	Pettysville,
Green Oak,	Pinckney,
Hamburgh,	Plainfield,
Hartland,	Tyrone,
Howell, (*c. h.,*)	Unadilla.

MACKINAC COUNTY.

Mackinaw, (*c. h.*)

MACOMB COUNTY.

Armada,	New Haven,
Cady,	Quinn,
Disco,	Ray Centre,
Fraser.	Richmond,
Macomb,	Romeo,*
Meade,	Roseville,
Memphis,	Utica,*
Milton,	Waldenburgh,
*Mt. Clemens,** (*c. h.,*)	Warren,
Mount Vernon,	Washington.
New Baltimore,	

MANISTEE COUNTY.

Bear Lake,	Pleasanton,
Filer City,	Stronach,
*Manistee,** (*c. h.,*)	Turnersport.
Norwalk,	

MANITOU COUNTY.

St. James, (*c. h.*)

MARQUETTE COUNTY.

Clarksburgh,	Ishpeming,
Greenwood Furnace,	*Marquette,** (*c. h.,*)
Harvey,	Morgan,
Humboldt,	Negaunee.

MASON COUNTY.

Amber,	*Lincoln,* (*c. h.,*)
Colfax,	Ludington,*
Fairview,	Riverton,
Indian Town,	Victory.

MECOSTA COUNTY.

Big Creek,	Millbrook,
*Big Rapids,** (*c. h.,*)	Morley,
Chippewa Lake,	Paris,
Fork,	Rienza,
Mecosta,	Satterlee's Mills.

MENOMONEE COUNTY.

Cedar Fork,	*Menomonee,** (*c. h.*)

MIDLAND COUNTY.

Averill's Station,	*Midland,** (*c. h.,*)
Edenville,	Porter.

MONROE COUNTY.

Athlone,	London,
Dundee,	*Monroe,** (*c. h.,*)
East Milan,	Newport,
Erie,	North Raisinville,
Exeter,	Oakville,
Grafton,	Ottawa Lake,
Hamlin,	Petersburgh,
Ida,	West Milan,
Lambertville,	Whiteford Centre.
La Salle,	

* Money-order office.

MONTCALM COUNTY.

Amsden,
Bloomer Centre,
Bushnell Centre,
Carson City,
Cato,
Coral,
Crystal,
Ferris,
Greenville,*
Howard City,
Lakeview,
Langston,
Maple Hill,
New Home,
Pierson,
Raynold,
Sheridan,
Sidney,
Stanton, (c. h.,)
Tamarack,
Vickeryville,
Wood Lake.

MUSKEGON COUNTY.

Black Lake,
Blue Lake,
Bluffton,
Brown's Mills,
Carleton,
Forest City,
Fruitport,
Harwood,
Howard,
Mile Creek,
Montague,*
Muskegon, (c. h.,)
Ravenna,
Slocum's Grove,
Trent,
Whitehall,
White River.

NEWAYGO COUNTY.

Ætna,
Ashland,
Barton,
Big Prairie,
Bridgeton,
Cook's Station,
Croton, *
Denver,
Ensley,
Fremont Centre,
Home,
Lake,
Martinsburgh,
Newago, (c. h.,)
Ponama,
Sitka.

OAKLAND COUNTY.

Austin,
Big Beaver,
Birmingham,
Brandon,
Clarkston,
Commerce,
Davisburgh,
Drayton Plains,
Farmington,
Four Towns,
Franklin,
Groveland,
Highland,
Holly, *
Jersey,
Kensington,
Lakeville,
Mahopac,
Milford, *
New Hudson,
North Farmington,
Novi,
Oak Hill,
Oakland,
Oakwood,
Orion,
Ortonville,
Oxford,
Pontiac, (c. h.,)
Rochester,
Rose,
Royal Oak,
Southfield,
South Lyon,
Springfield,
Spring Mills,
Stony Run,
Strait's Lake,
Troy,
Walled Lake,
Waterford,
West Novi,
White Lake.

OCEANA COUNTY.

Alice,
Benona,
Blackberry Ridge,
Clay Bank,
Cob Moo Sa,
Flower Creek,
Golding,
Hansen,
Hart, (c. h.,)
Hesperia,

OCEANA COUNTY—Continued.

Marshville,
Pa Pa Me,
Pentwater, *
Reed,
Shelby,
Spring Creek,
Smith's Corners,
Stebbinsville,
Thomas,
Weare.

ONTONAGON COUNTY.

Greenland,
Ontonagon, (c. h.,)
Rockland.

OSCEOLA COUNTY.

Bates,
Brookside,
Crapo,
Evarts,
Hersey, (c. h.)

OTTAWA COUNTY.

Allendale,
Berlin,
Big Spring,
Blendon,
Coopersville,
Dennison,
Eastmansville,
Ferrysburgh,
Georgetown,
Grand Haven, (c. h.,)
Hanley,
Holland*
Jamestown,
Lamont,
Lisbon,
Nunica,
Ohio Mill,
Port Sheldon,
Pottamie,
Robinson,
Six Corners,
South Georgetown,
Spring Lake,
Tallmadge,
Ventura,
Vriesland,
Zeeland.

SAGINAW COUNTY.

Birch Run,
Blumfield,
Blumfield Junction,
Bridgeport Centre,
Buena Vista,
Carrollton,
Cass Bridge,
Chesaning,
East Saginaw, *
Elk,
Frankenlust,
Frankenmuth,
Hemlock City
Hughesville,
Jay,
Oakley,
Randall,
Saginaw, (c. h.,)
Saint Charles,
South Saginaw,
Swan Creek,
Taymouth,
Trostville,
Zilwaukee.

SAINT CLAIR COUNTY.

Algonac,
Belle River,
Berville,
Brockway,
Brockway Centre,
Capac,
Casco,
China,
Clyde Mills,
Columbus,
Emmett,
Fair Haven,
Fort Gratiot,
Jeddo,
Kenockee,
Lake Port,
Lynn,
Marine City,*
Marysville,
Merrillsville,
Port Huron,*
Riley Centre,
Robert's Landing,
Ruby,
Saint Clair, (c. h.,)
Smith's Creek,
Thornton,
Vincent,
Wales.

* Money-order office.

SAINT JOSEPH COUNTY.

Burr Oak, *	Mendon,
Centreville, (*c. h.,*)	Mottville,
Colon,	Oporto,
Constantine,	Park,
Fawn River,	Parkville,
Florence,	Sturgis, *
Flowerfield,	Three Rivers, *
Howardsville,	White Pigeon.
Leonidas,	

SANILAC COUNTY.

Amadore,	Marlette,
Buel,	Minden,
Cedar Dale,	Newman,
Davisville,	Pack's Mills,
Deckerville,	Peck,
Farmer's,	Pine Hill,
Forestville,	Port Sanilac,
Forrester,	Richmondville,
Lexington, * (*c. h.,*)	Tyre.

SCHOOLCRAFT COUNTY.

Munising,	Onota.

SHIAWASSEE COUNTY.

Bennington,	Laingsburgh,
Burns,	Mungerville,
Byron,	North Newberg,
Corunna, * (*c. h.,*)	North Vernon,
Fremont,	Owosso, *
Glass River,	Perry,
Hartwellville,	Pittsburgh,
Hazelton,	Vernon,
Hazel Green,	West Haven.

TUSCOLA COUNTY.

Akron,	Milfington,
Caro, * (*c. h.,*)	Newbury,
Cass City,	Pine Grove,
Denmark,	Richville,
East Dayton,	Unionville,
Elkland,	*Vassar,* * (*c. h.,*)
Ellington,	Wahjamega,
Fair Grove,	Watertown,
Gagetown,	Watrousville,
Gilford,	Worth.
May,	

VAN BUREN COUNTY.

Almena,	Kendall,
Arlington,	Lake Mill,
Bangor,	Lawrence, *
Bear Lake Mills,	Lawton, *
Bloomingdale,	Mattawan,
Breedsville,	*Paw Paw,* * (*c. h.,*)
Covert,	Pine Grove Mills,
Decatur,	Prospect Lake,
Glendale,	South Haven,
Hartford,	Waverly,
Hooker,	West Geneva.
Keelersville,	

WASHTENAW COUNTY.

Ann Arbor, * (*c. h.,*)	River Raisin,
Base Lake,	Salem,
Benton,	Saline,
Chelsea,	Scio,
Dexter,	Stony Creek,
Fredonia,	Summit,
Gravel Run,	Sylvan,
Lima.	Webster,
Manchester,	Whitmore Lake,
Milan,	York,
Paint Creek,	Ypsilanti. *

WAYNE COUNTY.

Belleville,	Nankin,
Brownstown,	Northville,
Canton,	Oak,
Conner's Creek,	Perrinsville,
Dalton's Corners,	Plank Road,
Dearbornville,	Plymouth,
Delroy,	Rawsonville,
Denton,	Redford,
Detroit, * (*c. h.,*)	Romulus,
Ecorse,	Smithville,
Elm,	Taylor Centre,
Gibraltar,	Trenton,
Greenfield,	Wallaceville,
Huron Station,	Wayne,
Inkster,	Wyandotte,
Martinsville,	Yew.
Mead's Mills,	

WEXFORD COUNTY.

Clay Hill,	Wexford.
Sherman, (*c. h.,*)	

·MINNESOTA.

ANOKA COUNTY.

Anoka, * (*c. h.,*)	Linwood,
Bethel,	Manomin,
Centreville,	Oak Grove,
Coon Creek,	Oak Springs,
Itaska,	Saint Francis.

BENTON COUNTY.

Duelin,	Minden,
Langola,	*Sauk Rapids,* (*c. h.,*)
Maywood,	Watab.

* Money-order office.

BLUE EARTH COUNTY.

Beauford,
Butternut Valley,
Castle Garden,
Decoria,
Garden City,
Garden Prairie,
Iceland,
Judson,
Lake Crystal,
Mankato, (c. h.,)
Maple River,
Mapleton,
Medo,
Perch Lake,
Pleasant Mounds,
Shelbyville,
Sherman,
South Bend,
Sterling Centre,
Tivoli,
Vernon Centre,
Watauwon,
Willow Creek,
Winnebago Agency.

BROWN COUNTY.

Backville,
Cottonwood,
Golden Lake,
Home,
Iberia,
Leavenworth,
Linden,
Lone Tree Lake,
Milford,
New Ulm, (c. h.)

CARVER COUNTY.

Benton,
Carver,*
Chaska, (c. h.,)
Laketown,
Oberle's Corners,
Redfield,
Waconia,
Watertown,
Young America.

CASS COUNTY.

Leech Lake.

CHIPPEWA COUNTY.

Benson,
Chippewa City, (c. h.,)
Granite Falls,
Hawk Creek,
Reeson.

CHISAGO COUNTY.

Chisago City, (c. h.,)
Chisago Lake,
Franconia,
Muskootink,
Rush City,
Stark,
Sunrise City,
Taylor's Falls,
Wyoming.

CLAY COUNTY.

Georgetown,
Holy Cross.

CROW WING COUNTY.

Crow Wing, (c. h.)

DAKOTA COUNTY.

Castle Rock,
Christiana,
East Castle Rock,
Empire City,
Farmington,*
Hampton,
Hastings, (c. h.,)
Lakeville,
Lewiston,
Mendota,
New Trier,
Nininger,
Pine Bend,
Rich Valley,
Rosemount,
Waterford,
West Saint Paul.

DODGE COUNTY.

Ashland,
Berne,
Claremont,
Concord,
Dodge Centre,
Ellington,
Kasson,*
Mantorville, (c. h.,)
Rice Lake,
Union Spring,
Vernon,
Wasioga.

DOUGLAS COUNTY.

Alexandria, (c. h.,)
Brandon,
Evansville,
Holmes City,
Millenville,
Moe,
Osakis.

FARIBAULT COUNTY.

Banks,
Barber,
Bass Lake,
Blue Earth City,
(c. h.,)
Clayton,
Eden,
Elmore,
Ewald,
Grant,
Grapeland,
Minnesota Lake,
Pilot Grove,
Walnut Lake,
Well,
Winnebago City.*

FILLMORE COUNTY.

Alba,
Amherst,
Arendahl,
Belleville,
Big Spring,
Bratsberg,
Canfield,
Carimona,
Carrollton,
Chatfield,*
Cherry Grove,
Elliota,
Etna,
Fairview,
Farmer's Grove,
Fillmore,
Forestville,
Free Soil,
Granger,
Hamilton,
Harmony,
Highland,
Kedron,
Lanesborough,
Lenora,
Newburgh,
Pilot Mound,
Preston, (c. h.,)
Prosper,
Rushford,*
Spring Valley,*
Washington,
Watson Creek,
Waukokee,
Whalan.

FREEBORN COUNTY.

Albert Lea, (c. h.,)
Alden,
Bancroft,
Clark's Grove,
Freeborn,
Fremont,
Geneva,
Gordonsville,
Guildford,
Hartland,
Hayward,
Moscow,
Nunda,
Shell Rock,
State Line,
Sumner,
Trenton.

GOODHUE COUNTY.

Ayr,
Belle Creek,
Cannon River Falls,
Fair Point,
Frontenac,
Goodhue Centre,
Hader,
Holden,
Kenyon,
Minneola,

* Money-order office.

GOODHUE COUNTY—Continued.

Norway,	Stanton,
Pine Island,	Vasa,
*Red Wing,** (c. h.,)	Wanaminga,
Roscoe,	Wastedo,
Roscoe Centre,	Zumbrota.
Spring Creek,	

GRANT COUNTY.

Pomme de Terre.

HENNEPIN COUNTY.

Bloomington,	Lenz,
Bloomington Ferry,	Long Lake,
Brooklyn,	Maple Grove,
Champlin,	Maple Plain,
Corcoran,	*Minneapolis,** (c. h.,)
Dayton,	Minnetonka,
Eden Prairie,	Minnetrista,
Excelsior,	Osseo,
Fort Snelling,	Richfield,
Greenwood,	St. Anthony's Falls,*
Hassan,	Saint Bonifacius,
Leighton,	Wayzata.

HOUSTON COUNTY.

Brownsville,	Riceford,
*Caledonia,** (c. h.,)	San Jacinto,
Eitzen,	Sheldon,
Freeburgh,	Spring Grove,
Hokah,	Union,
Houston,	Wilmington,
La Crescent,	Winnebago Valley,
Lorettee,	Yucatan.
Money Creek,	

ISANTI COUNTY.

Cambridge,	*Oxford,* (c. h.,)
Isanti,	Spencer Brook,
Maple Ridge,	Stanchfield.
North Branch,	

JACKSON COUNTY.

Jackson, (c. h.,)	Summit.
Petersburgh,	

KANABEC COUNTY.

Brunswick, (c. h.)

KANDIYOHI COUNTY.

Atwater,	Lake Lillian,
Kandiyohi,	Willmar.
Kandiyohi St'n, (c. h.,)	

LAKE COUNTY.

Beaver Bay, (c. h.,)	Pigeon River.
Grand Portage,	

LE SUEUR COUNTY.

Anawauk,	Lexington,
Cleveland,	Marysburgh,
Cordova,	Montgomery,
Dresselville,	Ottawa,
Elysian,	Rudolph,
Jefferson Lake,	Saint Henry,
Kasota,	Saint Hubertus,
Kilkenny,	Union Centre,
Lake Washington,	Waterville.
*Le Sueur,** (c. h.,)	

LINCOLN COUNTY.

Swansea.

LYON COUNTY.

Ceresco,	Lynd.

McLEOD COUNTY.

Bergen,	Lake Addie,
Brush Prairie,	Plato,
E. Hutchinson,	Rocky Run,
*Glencoe,** (c. h.,)	Saint George,
Glendale,	Silver Lake,
Hutchinson,	Sumter,
Koniska,	Winsted Lake,

MARTIN COUNTY.

Amber,	May,
Andrew Johnson,	Nashville Centre,
Cedarville,	Pleasant Prairie,
Centre Creek,	Prairie Creek,
Chain Lake Centre,	Rose Lake,
East Chain Lakes,	Rutland,
Fairmont, (c. h.,)	Tenhassen,
Horicon,	Walnut Grove,
Lone Cedar,	Waverly.

MEEKER COUNTY.

Collinwood,	Koronis,
Crow River,	Lake Harold,
Darwin,	*Litchfield,* (c. h.,)
Dassel,	Mananah,
Forest City,*	Swede Grove,
Greenleaf,	Swift Lake,
Kingston,	Sylvan Hill.

MILLE LACS COUNTY.

Princeton, (c. h.)

MONONGALIA COUNTY.

Burbank,	*New London,* (c. h.,)
Georgeville,	Norway Lake,
Green Lake,	Roseville,
Harrison,	Sand Lake.
Irving,	

* Money-order office.

MORRISON COUNTY.

Belle Prairie,	North Prairie,
Culdrum,	Pike Rapids,
Fort Ripley,	Swan River,
Green Prairie,	Two Rivers.
Little Falls, (c. h.,)	

MOWER COUNTY.

Adams,	Minnereka,
Austin,* (c. h.)	Mower City,
Frankford,	Nevada,
Grand Meadow,	Prairie,
Lansing,	Root River,
Leroy,*	Rose Creek,
Madison,	Waltham.
Mineral Springs,	

MURRAY COUNTY.

Lake Shetek.

NICOLLET COUNTY.

Courtland,	Norseland,
Fort Ridgely,*	Redstone,
Granby,	*Saint Peter*,* (c. h.,)
Hebron,	Travers des Sioux,
Nicollet,	West Newton.

NOBLE COUNTY.

Graham Lake.

OLMSTED COUNTY.

Byron,	Oronoco,
Cascade,	Othello,
Chester,	Pleasant Grove,
Dover Centre,	Quincy,
Eyota,	*Rochester*,* (c. h.,)
Farm Hill,	Rock Dell,
High Forest,	Salem,
Little Valley,	Six Oaks,
Marion,	Stewartville.

OTTER TAIL COUNTY.

Balmoral,	*Otter Tail City*,(c. h.,)
Clitheral,	Rush Lake.
Fergus Falls,	

PINE COUNTY.

Hinckley,	Pine City.
Chengwatana,(c. h.,)	

POPE COUNTY.

Anderson,	Reno,
Gilchrist,	Rolling Fork,
Glenwood, (c. h.,)	Westfield,
Lake Johanna,	White Bear Centre.
Otto,	

RAMSEY COUNTY.

Little Canada,	White Bear Lake.
SAINT PAUL,* (c. h.)	

REDWOOD COUNTY.

Lower Sioux Agency,	Swedes Forest,
Redwood Falls, (c. h.,)	Weldon,
Rock Valley,	Yellow Medicine.

RENVILLE COUNTY.

Beaver Falls, (c. h.,)	Franklin,
Birch Cooley,	Herzhorn,
Cedar Mills,	Sacred Heart.
Cosmos,	

RICE COUNTY.

Cannon City,	Morristown,
Dundas,	Northfield,*
East Prairieville,	Shieldsville,
Faribault,* (c. h.,)	Union Lakes,
Fowlersville,	Warsaw,
Hazelwood,	Wheatland,
Millersburgh,	Wheeling.

ROCK COUNTY.

Luverne.

ST. LOUIS COUNTY.

Du Luth, (c. h.,)	Oneoto,
Fond du Lac,	Vermillion Lake.

SCOTT COUNTY.

Belle Plaine,*	New Dublin,
Blakeley,	New Market,
Cedar Lake,	Oral,
Hamilton Station,	Raven Stream,
Helena,	St. Lawrence,
Lydia,	Sand Creek,*
Maple Glen,	*Shakopee*,* (c. h.)

SHERBURNE COUNTY.

Big Lake,	Livonia,
Brantford,	Orlando,
Clear Lake,	*Orono*, (c. h.,)
Elk River Station,	Pleasant Valley,
Lake Fremont,	Santiago.

SIBLEY COUNTY.

Arlington,	*Henderson*,* (c. h.,)
Cornish,	Kelso,
Dryden,	New Auburn,
Eagle City,	Rush River,
Faxon,	Sibley,
Green Isle,	Transit.

STEARNS COUNTY.

Brockway,	Long Hill,
Cold Spring City,	Luxemburgh,
Fair Haven,	Maine Prairie,
George Lake,	Melrose,
Kennebec,	New Munich,
Leedston,	North Fork,

* Money-order office.

STEARNS COUNTY—Continued.

Paynesville,
Raymond,
Rockville,
Saint Augusta,
Saint Cloud, (c. h.,)
Saint Joseph,
Sauk Centre,*
Spring Hill,
Torah,
Zions.

STEELE COUNTY.

Aurora,
Berlin,
Blooming Prairie,
Clinton Falls,
Cooleysville,
Deerfield,
Dodge City,
East Meriden,
Elwood,
Havanna,
Lemond,
Medford,
Meriden, (c. h.,)
Merton,
Oak Glen,
Owatonna,*
River Point,
Steele Centre,

STEVENS COUNTY.

Passe de Terre,
Potosi,
Scandia.

STONE COUNTY.

Lake Traverse.

TODD COUNTY.

Burnhamsville,
Hartford,
Long Prairie, (c. h.,)
Round Prairie.

WABASHAW COUNTY.

Bear Valley,
Cook's Valley,
Elgin,
Forest Mound,
Glasgow,
Gopher Prairie,
Hyde Park,
Lake City,*
Lincoln,
Lyon,
Mazeppa,
Millville,
Minneska,
Pawselin,
Plainview,*
Reed's Landing,
Smithfield,
South Troy,
Wabashaw, (c. h.,)
Watopa,
West Albany,
West Chester,
Woodland,
Zumbro Falls.

WASECA COUNTY.

Alma City,
Blooming Grove,
Cobb River,
Janesville,
Maine,
New Richland,
Okaman,
Otisco,

WASECA COUNTY—Continued.

Vivian,
Waseca,*
Wilton, (c. h.,)

WASHINGTON COUNTY.

Afton,
Cottage Grove,
Forest Lake,
Lakeland,
Lohmansville,
Marine Mills,
Newport,
Oak Dale,
Point Douglas,
Stillwater, (c. h.,)
Woodbury.

WATONWAN COUNTY.

Antrim,
Ashippen,
Madelia, (c. h.,)
Norwegian.

WILKIN COUNTY.

McCauleyville.

WINONA COUNTY.

Argo,
Beaver,
Dresbach,
Elba,
Enterprise,
Frank Hill,
Homer,
Jefferson,
Lamoille,
Minnesota City,
Nevill,
New Boston,
New Hartford,
North Warren,
Oak Ridge,
Pickwick,
Richmond,
Ridgeway,
Rolling Stone,
Saint Charles,*
Saratoga,
Stockton,
Troy,
Utica,
White Water Falls,
Winona, (c. h.,)
Wiscoy,
Witoka,
Worth,
Wyattville.

WRIGHT COUNTY.

Albion,
Big Woods,
Buffalo, (c. h.,)
Cassel,
Chatham,
Clear Water,
Corrinna,
Dean Lake,
Delano,
French Lake,
Howard,
Lilly Pond,
Maple Lake,
Monticello*,
Montrose,
Mooer's Prairie,
Otsego,
Rockford,
Saint Michael's,
Silver Creek,
Waverly Mills.

MISSISSIPPI.

ADAMS COUNTY.
Natchez, (c. h.)

ALCORN COUNTY.
Anderson,
Antioch,

ALCORN COUNTY—Continued.

Corinth, (c. h.,)
Danville,
Jacinto,
Kossuth,
Rienzi,
Silver Springs.

* Money-order office

AMITE COUNTY.

Centreville, Smithdale.
Liberty, (c. h.,)

ATTALA COUNTY.

Kosciusko, (c. h.,) Wells.

BOLIVAR COUNTY.

Australia, Carson's Landing,
Beulah, (c. h.,) Neblett's Landing.
Bolivar,

CALHOUN COUNTY.

Banner, Hopewell,
Benela, Pittsborough, (c. h.,)
Concord, Robertsonville,
Erin, Sarepta.

CARROLL COUNTY.

Black Hawk, Greenwood,
Carrollton, (c. h.,) Vaiden,
Duck Hill, Winona.

CHICKASAW COUNTY.

Big Springs, Okolona,*
Buena Vista, Palo Alto,
Egypt, Pine Bluff,
Houlka, Sonora,
Houston, (c. h.,) Sparta.
Montpelier,

CHOCTAW COUNTY.

Ada, Greensborough, (c. h.,)
Bankston, Huntsville,
Bellefontaine, Lodi,
Black's Wells, Monte Vista,
Cadaretta, Pigeon Roost,
Cumberland, Poplar Creek,
Dido, Republican.

CLAIBORNE COUNTY.

Grand Gulf, Rocky Springs.
Port Gibson, (c. h.,)

CLARK COUNTY.

De Soto, Quitman,
Enterprise, (c. h.,) Shubuta.

COAHOMA COUNTY.

Dowd's Landing, Moon Lake.
Friar's Point, (c. h.,)

COPIAH COUNTY.

Bahala, Martinsville,
Crystal Springs,* Mount Hope,
Gallatin, Pine Ridge,
Hazlehurst,* Rockport,
Linden, Wesson.

COVINGTON COUNTY.

Janesville, Station Creek,
Mount Carmel, Williamsburgh, (c. h.)

DE SOTO COUNTY.

Arkabutla, Looxahoma,
Coldwater, Nesbit's Station,
De Soto Front, Olive Branch,
Hernando, (c. h.,) Senatobia.
Horn Lake,

FRANKLIN COUNTY.

Hamburgh, Meadville, (c. h.,)
Knoxville, Morgan's Fork.

GRENADA COUNTY.

Bowen, Grenada,* (c. h.,)
Elliott, Hardy Station,
Graysport, Torrance.

HANCOCK COUNTY.

Gainesville, Shieldsborough, (c. h.)
Pearlington,

HARRISON COUNTY.

Biloxi, Mississippi City,(c. h.,)
Handsborough, Pass Christian.

HINDS COUNTY.

Bear Creek, JACKSON,* (c. h.,)
Bolton's Depot, Midway,
Byram, Raymond,
Clinton, Terry,
Dry Grove, Utica.
Edward's Depot,

HOLMES COUNTY.

Durant, Pickens' Station,
Goodman, West's Station.
Lexington, (c. h.,)

ISSAQUENA COUNTY.

Ingomar, Skipwith's Landing,
Osborn's Store, Tallulah, (c. h.)

ITAWAMBA COUNTY.

Mooreville, Yocony.

JACKSON COUNTY.

Americus, (c. h.,) Pascagoula,
Moss Point, Vancleave's.
Ocean Springs,

JASPER COUNTY.

Claiborne, Paulding, (c. h.,)
Garlandville, Turnerville.

* Money-order office.

JEFFERSON COUNTY.

Church Hill,	Rodney,
Fayette, (c. h.,)	Union Church.
Perth,	

JONES COUNTY.

Ellisville, (c. h.,)	Pinnellville.
Erata,	

KEMPER COUNTY.

De Kalb, (c. h.,)	Rio,
Fort Stephens,	Scooba,
Gainesville Junction,	Sucarnoochee,
Herbert,	Tamola Station,
Kellis' Store,	Wahalak Station.
Peden,	

LA FAYETTE COUNTY.

Abbeville,	*Oxford,* (c. h.,)
Caswell,	Spring Dale,
La Fayette Springs,	Taylor's Depot.
Maple Springs,	

LAUDERDALE COUNTY.

Daleville,	Marion Station,
Kewanee,	*Meridian,* (c. h.,)
Lauderdale Station,	Toomsuba.
Lockhart,	

LAWRENCE COUNTY.

Monticello, (c. h.,)	White Sand.
Silver Creek,	

LEAKE COUNTY.

Carthage, (c. h.,)	High Hill,
Conway,	Ofahoma,
Edinburgh,	Standing Pine,
Good Hope,	Thomastown.

LEE COUNTY.

Baldwyn,	Saltillo,
Coonewar,	Shannon,
Ellistown,	*Tupelo,* (c. h.,)
Guntown,	Verona.

LINCOLN COUNTY.

Bogue Chitto,	*Brookhaven,* (c. h.)

LOWNDES COUNTY.

Artesia,	Mayhew's Station,
Caledonia,	Tibby Station,
Columbus, (c. h.,)	West Point.
Crawfordville,	

MADISON COUNTY.

Breckville,	*Canton,* (c. h.,)
Calhoun,	Pearl City,
Camden,	Tongaloo.

MARION COUNTY.

Columbia, (c. h.,)	Fordsville.

MARSHALL COUNTY.

Byhalia,	Lamar,
Chulahoma,	North Mt. Pleasant,
Early Grove,	Red Banks,
Holly Springs, (c. h.,)	Tyro,
Hudsonville,	Waterford.

MONROE COUNTY.

Aberdeen, (c. h.,)	Lunnsdale,
Aberdeen Junction,	Prairie Station,
Athens,	Smithville,
Cotton Gin Port,	Temperance Hill.
Hamilton,	

NESHOBA COUNTY.

Coffadeliah,	*Philadelphia,* (c h.)
Laurel Hill,	

NEWTON COUNTY.

Chunkey's Station,	Lawrence,
Decatur,	Newton,
Hickory,	Union.

NOXUBEE COUNTY.

Brookville,	*Macon,* (c. h.,)
Gholson,	Shuqualak.

OKTIBBEHA COUNTY.

Ash Creek,	Siloam,
Choctaw Agency,	*Starkville,* (c. h.,)
Double Springs,	Whitefield

PANOLA COUNTY.

Batesville,	Longtown,
Como Depot,	*Panola,* (c. h.,)
Elliott's Mill,	Pleasant Mount,
Lake Creswell,	Pope's Depot,
Long Creek Depot,	Sardis.

PERRY COUNTY.

Augusta, (c. h.,)	Monroe.
Enon,	

PIKE COUNTY.

Chatawa,	Magnolia,
China Grove,	Osyka,
Conerly's,	Summit.

PONTOTOC COUNTY.

Cherry Creek,	Red Land,
Chesterville,	Rocky Ford,
New Albany,	Tardyville,
Pontotoc, (c. h.,)	Toccopola.

* Money-order office.

PRENTISS COUNTY.

Allen's Store,   Fulton,
Bay Springs,   Pleasonton,
Booneville, (c. h.,)   Ryan's Well.
Dry Run,

RANKIN COUNTY.

Brandon,* (c. h.,)   Goshen Springs,
Cato,   Pelahatchee Depot.
Fannin,

SCOTT COUNTY.

Damascus,   Homewood,
Forest,   Lake,
Hillsborough, (c. h.,)   Morton.

SIMPSON COUNTY.

Mount Zion,   *Westville*, (c. h.)
Saunders' Creek,

SMITH COUNTY.

Polkville,   Sylvarena,
Raleigh, (c. h.,)   Trenton.

SUN FLOWER COUNTY.

McNutt, (c. h.,)   Shell Mound.

TALLAHATCHEE COUNTY.

Charleston, (c. h.,)   Harrison Station.

TIPPAH COUNTY.

Cotton Plant,   Orizaba,
Dumas,   *Ripley*, (c. h.,)
Hickory Flat,   Ruckersville,
Jonesborough,   Union Mills.
New Barden,

TISHEMINGO COUNTY.

Barnes' Store,   Eastport,
Burnsville,   Highland,
Cartersville,   *Iuka*, (c. h.)

TUNICA COUNTY.

Austin, (c. h.,)   Commerce.
Bennett's Landing,

WARREN COUNTY.

Bovina,   *Vicksburgh*,* (c. h.,)
Hurricane,   Warrenton.
New Town Landing,

WASHINGTON COUNTY.

Egg's Point,   Leeta Landing.
Greenville, (c. h.,)

WAYNE COUNTY.

Bucatunna,   Winchester.
Waynesborough, (c. h.,)

WILKINSON COUNTY.

Fort Adams,   *Woodville*,* (c. h.)

WINSTON COUNTY.

Buckhorn,   New Prospect,
Fearn's Springs,   Rome,
Louisville, (c. h.,)   Webster.

YALABUSHA COUNTY.

Air Mount,   Pine Valley,
Coffeeville, (c. h.,)   Post Oak,
Garner's Station,   Tillatoba,
Oakland,   Water Valley.

YAZOO COUNTY.

Benton,   *Yazoo City*,* (c. h.)
Satartia,

MISSOURI.

ADAIR COUNTY.

Floyd's Creek,   Shibley's Point,
Kirksville,* (c. h.,)   Sloan's Point,
Lindersville,   Spring Valley,
Millard,   Sublett,
Nineveh,   Troy Mills,
Paulville,   Willmathsville,
Prairie Bird,   Wilson,
Ringo's Point,   Zig.

ANDREW COUNTY.

Amazonia,   Bolckow,

ANDREW COUNTY—Continued.

Castle,   Nodaway,
Empire Prairie,   Rochester,
Fillmore,   Rosendale,
Flag Springs,   *Savannah*,* (c. h.,)
Grason,   Whitesville.

ATCHISON COUNTY.

Irish Grove,   Rich,
Linden,   *Rockport*,* (c. h.,)
North Star.*   Watson.
Phelps City,*

* Money-order office.

AUDRIAN COUNTY.

Benton City,   *Mexico,* (c. h.,)
Hickory Creek,   Tompson's Station,
John's Branch,   Young's Creek.
Loutre,

BARRY COUNTY.

Cassville, (c. h.,)   Flat Creek,
Corsicana,   Hazle Barrens,
Eva,   Washburn.

BARTON COUNTY.

Baker's Grove,   Horse Creek,
Barton.   *Lamar,* (c. h.,)
Coon Creek,   Le Roy,
Doylesport,   Milford,
Golden City,   Nashville.

BATES COUNTY.

Altona,   Marvel,
Burdett,   Papinsville,
Butler, (c. h.,)   Parkersville,
Crescent Hill,   Pleasant Gap,
Hudson,   Prairie City,
Johnstown,   West Point.
Lone Oak,

BENTON COUNTY.

Cloverdale,   Haw Creek,
Cole Camp,   Lake Creek,
Dell Delight,   Lincoln,
Duroc,   Mount View,
Fairfield,   *Warsaw,* (c. h.)
Fort Lyon,

BOLLINGER COUNTY.

Buchanan,   Patton,
Castor,   Sumac,
Marble Hill, (c. h.,)   Vinemount.

BOONE COUNTY.

Ashland,   Hallsville,
Burlington,   Midway,
Centralia,   Providence,
Claysville,   Rocheport,
Columbia, (c. h.,)   Stephens,
Greenland,   Sturgeon.*

BUCHANAN COUNTY.

Arnoldsville,   Rock House Prairie,
De Kalb,   Rushville,
Easton,   *Saint Joseph,* (c. h.,)
Eveline,   Walnut Hill,
Halleck,   Winthrop.
Platte River,

BUTLER COUNTY.

Cane Creek,   *Poplar Bluff,* (c. h.,)
Fredie,   Reeve's Station.

CALDWELL COUNTY.

Black Oak,   Mirabile,
Breckinridge,   Nettletonville,
Hamilton,   Osterville,
Kidder,   Polo,
Kingston, (c. h.,)   Proctorville.

CALLAWAY COUNTY.

Cedar City,   New Bloomfield,
Concord,   Pierce,
Cote Sans Dessein,   Portland,
Fulton, (c. h.,)   Readsville,
Ham's Prairie,   Reform,
Hempstead,   Saint Aubert's,
Holt's Summit,   Shamrock,
Jones' Tan Yard,   Stephens' Store,
Millersburgh,   Williamsburgh.

CAMDEN COUNTY.

Barnumton,   *Linn Creek,* (c. h.,)
Cave Pump,   Rainey Creek,
Decaturville,   Stoutland,
Glaze City,   Wet Glaze.

CAPE GIRARDEAU COUNTY.

Allenville,   *Jackson,* (c. h.,)
Appleton,   Millersville,
Burfordville,   Neely's Landing,
Cape Girardeau,*   New Wells,
Dutchtown,   Oak Ridge,
Egypt Mills,   Pocahontas,
Iona,   Stroderville.

CARROLL COUNTY.

Bower's City,   Mandeville,
Bridge Creek,   Miles' Point,
Carrollton, (c. h.,)   Norborne,
Coloma,   Pleasant Park,
De Witt,   Ridge,
Eugene City,   Shootman,
Hurricane,   Stokes Mound,
Little Compton,   Van Horn.

CARTER COUNTY.

Norwood,   *Van Buren,* (c. h.)

CASS COUNTY.

Austin,   High Blue,
Brosley,   Jonesville,
Crawford's Fork,   Morristown,
Dayton,   Peculiar,
Everett,   Pleasant Hill,*
Harrisonville, (c. h.,)   Schuyler,
Hazen,   Wadesburgh.

CEDAR COUNTY.

Alice,   Clintonville,
Bear Creek,   Mount Enterprise,
Cane Hill,   Silver Creek,
Caplinger's Mills,   *Stockton,* (c. h.,)
Claire Springs,   Virgil City.

* Money-order office

CHARITON COUNTY.

Brunswick,*
Bynumville,
Dalton,
Keytesville,* (c. h.,)
Muscle Fork,
Porche's Prairie,

Prairie Hill,
Richardsonville,
Rothville,
Salisbury,
Salt Creek.

CHRISTIAN COUNTY.

Bull's Mills,
Kenton,

Minersville,
Ozark, (c. h.)

CLARKE COUNTY.

Acasto,
Alexandria,
Ashton,
Athens,
Cahoka,
Chambersburgh,
Clarke City,
Clay,

El Dorado,
Fairmont,
Gregory Landing,
Locust Grove,
Peakesville,
Saint Francisville,
Waterloo, (c. h.,)
Winchester.

CLAY COUNTY.

Barry,
Blue Eagle,
Harlem,
Holt,
Kearney,

Liberty,* (c. h.,)
Missouri City,
Paradise,
Prospect Hill,
Smithville.

CLINTON COUNTY.

Anderson,
Bainbridge,
Barnesville,
Cameron,*
Carpenter's Store,
Hainesville,

Lathrop,
Plattsburgh, (c. h.,)
Prairie,
Stairfield,
Turney's Station.

COLE COUNTY.

Brazito,
Centre Town,
Elston Station,
Hickory Hill,
JEFFERSON CITY,*
(c. h.,)
Marion.

Osage Bluff,
Osage City,
Russellville,
St. Thomas,
Stringtown,
Taos.

COOPER COUNTY.

Bell Air,
Boonville,* (c. h.,)
Bunceton,
Clark's Fork,
Cold Neck,
Conner's Mills,
Gooch's Mill,
La Mine,
Lone Elm,

New Palestine,
Otterville,
Overton,
Pilot Grove,
Pisgah,
Pleasant Green,
Prairie Home,
Vermont.

CRAWFORD COUNTY.

Argo,
Bourbon,
Cherryville
Cuba,
Dry Creek,
Harrison's Mills,

Knob View,
Leasburgh,
Lone Cedar,
Osage
Steelville, (c. h.)

DADE COUNTY.

Cedarville,
Dadeville,
Engleman's Mills,
Greenfield,* (c. h.,)

King's Point,
Rock Prairie,
Sylvania,
Turnback.

DALLAS COUNTY.

Boyd,
Buffalo, (c. h.,)
Long Lane,

Louisburgh,
Spring Grove,
Urbana.

DAVIESS COUNTY.

Alta Vista,
Bancroft,
Civil Bend,
Coffeysburgh,
Crittenden,

Gallatin,* (c. h.,)
Jamesport,
Pattonsburgh,
Santa Rosa.

DE KALB COUNTY.

Arica,
Boxford,
Dayton City,
Fair Port,
Maysville,* (c. h.,)

Osborn,
Stewartsville,*
Union Star,
Winslow.

DENT COUNTY.

Deep Ford,
Howe's Mill,
Lake Spring,
Montauk,

Nursery Hill,
Salem, (c. h.,)
Short Bend.

DOUGLAS COUNTY.

Arno, (c. h.,)
Beaver,
Cow Skin,
Falling Springs,

Pryor's Store,
Richville,
Vera Cruz.

DUNKLIN COUNTY.

Clarkton,
Four Mile,

Kennett, (c. h.,)
West Prairie.

FRANKLIN COUNTY.

Beaufort,
Berger,
Bœuf Creek,
Boles,
Calvy,
Campbellton,
Catawissa,
Clover Bottom,
Dry Branch.
Dundee,
Etlah,
Gray's Summit,
Grubville,
Jeffriesburgh,
Krakow,

Labaddie,
Maune's Store,
Moselle,
New Haven,
Oakfield,
Pacific,
Port Hudson,
St. Clair,
Shotwell,
South Point,
Stanton Cop. Mines,
Sullivan,
Union, (c. h.,)
Washington.*

* Money-order office.

GASCONADE COUNTY.

Bay,
Burbois,
Canaan,
Drake,
Gasconade City,
Gasconade Ferry,
Hermann,* (c. h.,)

Jake's Prairie,
Morrison,
Oak Hill,
Owensville,
Stoney Hill,
Woollam.

GENTRY COUNTY.

Alanthus Grove,
Albany,* (c. h.,)
Buhlsville,
Douglas,
Ellenorah,
Ettieville,
Gentryville,
Havana,

Hugginsville,
Island City,
King City,
Mount Pleasant,
New Castle,
Philander,
Union Grove.

GREENE COUNTY.

Ash Grove,
Bois D'Arc,
Ebenezer,
Fair Grove,
Hickory Barren,
Little York,
North Springfield,

Pallas,
Pickerel,
Springfield,* (c. h.,)
Strafford,
Walnut Grove,
White Oak Grove,
Willard.

GRUNDY COUNTY.

Alpha,
Buttsville,
Edinburgh,
Grinell,
Grubtown,

Lindley,
Middlebury,
Rural Dale,
Tindell,
Trenton, (c. h.)

HARRISON COUNTY.

Akron,
Bethany,* (c. h.,)
Blue Ridge,
Bolton,
Brooklyn,
Burr Oak,
Cainesville,
Eagle,
Happy Valley,

Jay,
Martinsville,
Mitchellville,
Morris Ridge,
Mount Moriah,
Pleasant Ridge,
Sampson Creek,
Thomas.

HENRY COUNTY.

Calhoun,
Clinton,* (c. h.,)
Consville,
Gaines' Farm,
Galbraith's Store,
Germantown,*
Huntingdale,

Leesville,
Lucas,
Marvin,
Norris Fork,
Orion,
Shawnee Mound,
Windsor.

HICKORY COUNTY.

Black Oak Point,
Cross Timbers,
Elkton,
Hermitage, (c. h.,)

Pittsburgh,
Quincy,
Roney,
Wheatland.

HOLT COUNTY.

Bigelow,
Corning,
Craig,
Elm Grove,
Forest City,*

Grant,
North Point,
Oregon,* (c. h.,)
Rushbottom,
Whig Valley.

HOWARD COUNTY.

Fayette,* (c. h.,)
Franklin,
Glasgow,*

Land Mark,
Myers,
Roanoke.

HOWELL COUNTY.

Chapel,
Frankville,

West Plains, (c. h.,)
Willow Springs.

IRON COUNTY.

Belleview,
Ironton,* (c. h.,)
Kaolin,
Marble Creek,

Middle Brook,
Pilot Knob,*
Rocky Glade.

JACKSON COUNTY.

Blue Mill,
Blue Springs,
Fire Prairie,
Greenwood,
Hickman Mills,
Independence,* (c. h.,)
Kansas City,*
Lee's Summit,

Lone Jack,
Micklen,
New Santa Fé,
Oak Grove,
Pink Hill,
Sibley,
Stony Point,
Westport.

JASPER COUNTY.

Alba,
Avilla,
Blytheville,
Buck Branch,
Carthage,* (c. h.,)
Centre Creek,
Diamond Grove,
Fidelity,

Galesburgh,
Georgia City,
Jasper,
Jenkins' Creek,
Medoc,
Preston,
Sarcoxie,
Sherwood.

JEFFERSON COUNTY.

Avoca,
Belew's Creek,
Bushberg,
Cedar Hill,
De Soto,
Dittmer's Store,
Frumet,
Hanover,
Hematite,
High Ridge,

Hillsborough, (c. h.,)
Horine Station,
House's Springs,
Kimmswick,
Morse's Mill,
Pevely,
Sulphur Sp'gs L'd'g,
Victoria Station,
Vineland.

JOHNSON COUNTY.

Carbon Hill,
Centre View,
Chalybeate,
Chilhowie,
Columbus,
Cornelia,
Fayetteville,

Holden,*
Knobnoster,
Pittsville,
Ramey,
Rose Hill,
Warrensburgh, (c. h.)

* Money-order office.

KNOX COUNTY.

Boe Ridge,	Locust Hill,
Colony,	Millport,
Edina, (c. h.,)	Myrtle,
Goodland,	Newark,
Greensburgh,	Novelty.

LACLEDE COUNTY.

Brush Creek,	Lyon,
Case,	Nebo,
Competition,	Oakland,
Hazle Green,	Pine Creek.
Lebanon, (c. h.,)	

LA FAYETTE COUNTY.

Chapel Hill,	Mayview,
Concordia,	Mount Hope,
Dover,	Napoleon,
Freedom,	Snibar,
Greenton,	Tabo,
Higginsville,	Waverly,*
Lexington, (c. h.,)	Wellington.

LAWRENCE COUNTY.

Bower's Mills,	Minden,
Chesapeake,	*Mount Vernon,* (c. h.,)
Dunkle's Store,	Phelps,
Elk Horn,	Pierce City,
Gray's Point,	Spencer,
Magnolia Centre,	Verona
Marionville,	

LEWIS COUNTY.

Benjamin,	La Grange,*
Canton,*	*Monticello,* (c. h.,)
Deer Ridge,	Oyster,
Durgen's Creek,	Primrose,
Gilead,	Williamstown
La Belle,	

LINCOLN COUNTY.

Auburn,	Millwood,
Cap au Gris,	New Hope,
Chain of Rocks,	Old Alexandria,
Chantilly,	Old Monroe,
Cuivre,	Post Oak,
Hawk Point,	Rock Ford,
Lost Branch,	*Troy,* (c. h.,)
Louisville,	Truxton.

LINN COUNTY.

Brookfield,*	Meadville,
Bucklin,*	Northcutt,
Elm,	North Salem,
Grantsville,	Saint Catherine,
Laclede,	Sebago.
Linneus, (c. h.,)	

LIVINGSTON COUNTY.

Asper,	Grassy Creek,
Bedford,	Mooresville,
Blue Mound,	Muddy Lake,
Bluff City,	Shoal Creek,
Chillicothe, (c. h.,)	Spring Hill,
Cream Ridge,	Utica,*
Dawn,	Wheeling.
Farmersville,	

McDONALD COUNTY.

Bethpage,	Looniesville,
Elk Mills,	*Pineville,* (c. h.,)
Enterprise,	Poplar Hill,
Erie,	White Rock Prairie.
Honey Creek,	

MACON COUNTY.

Atlanta,	*Macon City,* (c. h.,)
Beverly,	Mercyville,
Bevier,	Narrows Creek,
Bloomington,	New Boston,
Callao,	Newburgh,
College Mound,	New Cambria,
Economy,	Sheridan,
Excello,	Sue City,
Johnson,	Ten Mile,
Kaseyville,	Tullvania,
La Plata,	Woodville.

MADISON COUNTY.

Cornwall,	Marquand,
Fredericktown, (c. h.,)	Mine La Motte.

MARIES COUNTY.

Clifty Dale,	Manton,
High Grove,	Pay Down,
Lacon,	Steen's Prairie,
Lane's Prairie,	*Vienna,* (c. h.)

MARION COUNTY.

Benbow,	*Palmyra,* (c. h.,)
Emerson,	Philadelphia,
Hannibal,*	Sharpsburgh,
Hester,	Warren,
Nelsonville,	West Ely,
Nettleton,	West Quincy.
North River,	

MERCER COUNTY.

Cleopatra,	Modena,
Goshen,	*Princeton,* (c. h.,)
Half Rock,	Ravanna,
Mercer,	Saline.

MILLER COUNTY.

Bliss,	Pleasant Mount,
Brumley,	Rocky Mount,
Locust Mound,	Toronto,
Oakhurst,	*Tuscumbia,* (c. h.,)
Pleasant Farm,	Ulman's Ridge.

* Money-order office.

MISSISSIPPI COUNTY.

Belmont,	James' Bayou.
Charleston, (c. h.,)	Wolf Island.

MONITEAU COUNTY.

California,* (c. h.,)	Hope Farm,
Clarksburgh,	Jamestown,
Highland,	Magnolia,
High Point,	Tipton.*

MONROE COUNTY.

Elliottsville,	Monroe City,
Florida,	*Paris,** (c. h.,)
Granville,	Santa Fé,
Indian Creek,	Somerset,
Long Branch,	Switzler,
Madison,	Woodlawn.
Middle Grove,	

MONTGOMERY COUNTY.

Americus,	Middletown,
Big Spring,	Montgomery City,*
Bluffton,	New Florence,
Danville, (c. h.,)	Price's Branch,
High Hill,	Rhineland,
Jonesburgh,	Stockland,
Loutre Island,	Wellsville.

MORGAN COUNTY.

Boyler's Mill,	Saint Martin's,
Excelsior,	Stone House,
Florence,	Syracuse,*
Gravois Mills,	*Versailles,** (c. h.)
Mining,	

NEW MADRID COUNTY.

*New Madrid,** (c. h.,) Point Pleasant.

NEWTON COUNTY.

Almeda,	*Neosho,** (c. h.,)
Capp's Creek,	Newtonia,
Gates,	Racine,
Granby,*	Rocky Comfort,
Jones' Creek,	Seneca,
Kent,	Shoalsburgh,
Lodi,	Sylvan Lodge.

NODAWAY COUNTY.

Conception,	Lynchburgh,
Graham,	*Maryville,** (c. h.,)
Guilford,	Prairie Park,
Hallsa's Ferry,	Quitman,
Lamar's Station,	Sweet Home,
Littsville,	White Cloud,
Lutzton,	Xenia.

OREGON COUNTY.

Alton, (c. h.,)	Thomasville,
Jobe,	Warm Fork,
Pinkleyville,	Webster.

OSAGE COUNTY.

Bailey's Creek,	*Linn,* (c. h.,)
Byron,	Linnwood,
Castle Rock,	Loose Creek,
Chamois,	Medora,
Cooper's Hill,	New Providence,
Dauphine,	Oshawa.
Fredericksburgh,	Peachland.
Gallaway's Station,	Rich Fountain,
Koeltztown,	Westphalia.

OZARK COUNTY.

Caney,	Piland's Store,
Gainesville, (c. h.,)	Rockbridge,
Isabella,	Saint Leger.
Melissa,	

PEMISCOT COUNTY.

Caruthersville,	*Gayoso,* (c. h.)
Cottonwood Point,	

PERRY COUNTY.

Abernathy,	Laurel Hill,
Altenburgh,	*Perryville,* (c. h.,)
Biehle,	Silver Lake,
Bois Brule,	Uniontown,
Frohna,	Wittenburgh.

PETTIS COUNTY.

Buncombe,	Longwood,
Dresden,	Rowletts,
Georgetown,	*Sedalia,** (c. h.,)
Green Ridge,	Sigel,
Ionia City,	Smith City.
Lamonte,	

PHELPS COUNTY.

Arlington,	Relfe,
Blooming Rose,	*Rolla,** (c. h.,)
Dillon,	St. James,
Edgar Springs,	Sarvis Spring,
Jerome,	Spring Creek,
Maramec,	Yancey.

PIKE COUNTY.

Ashburn,	New Harmony,
Ashley,	Paxton's Store,
Bowling Green, (c. h.,)	Paynesville,
Clarksville,	Prairieville,
Curryville,	Reading,
Frankford,	Spencerburgh,
Louisiana,*	Vannoy's Mill.

PLATTE COUNTY.

Beverly Station,	Parkville,
Camden Point,	*Platte City,* (c. h.,)
City Point,	Ridgley,
Farley,	Shivelton,
Hampton,	Union Mills,
Iatan,	Waldron,
New Market.	Weston.*

* Money-order office.

POLK COUNTY.

Bolivar,* (c. h.,)
Brighton,
Fair Play,
Half Way,
Humansville,
Orleans,
Pleasant Hope,
Rondo,
Sentinel Prairie.

PULASKI COUNTY.

Brittain's,
Dixon,
Dundas,
Hancock,
Humboldt,
Pine Bluff,
Richland,
St. Annie,
Waynesville,* (c. h.)

PUTNAM COUNTY.

Ayorsville,
Central City,
Hartford,
Livonia,
Martinstown,
Mendota,
Newtown,
Omaha,
Pleasant Home,
St. John,
Shoneytown,
Terre Haute,
Unionville,* (c. h.,)
West Liberty.

RALLS COUNTY.

Crigler's Mills,
Garden Grove,
Hydesburgh,
Madisonville,
New London, (c. h.,)
Perry,
Saverton,
Sidney,
West Hartford,

RANDOLPH COUNTY.

Cairo,
Clifton Hill,
Darksville,
Fort Henry,
Huntsville,* (c. h.,)
Jacksonville,
Milton,
Moberly,
Mount Airy,
Randolph,
Rolling Home.

RAY COUNTY.

Ada,
Camden,
Crab Orchard,
Fox,
Georgeville,
Hardin,
Henry,
Knoxville,
Lawson Station.
Millville,
New Garden,
Otsego,
Pleasant View,
Rayville.
Richmond,* (c. h.,)
Tinney's Grove.

REYNOLDS COUNTY.

Centreville, (c. h.,)
Edge Hill,
Lesterville,
Logan's Creek,
Munger's Hill.

RIPLEY COUNTY.

Doniphan, (c. h.,)
Gatewood,
Little Black.

SAINT CHARLES COUNTY.

Augusta,
Cappelu,
Cottleville,
Dalhoff,
Femme Osage,
Flint Hill,
Hamburgh,
Missouriton,
New Melle,
O'Fallon,
St. Charles,* (c. h.,)
Saint Peter's,
Schleursburgh,
Schumacker's Store,
Snow Hill,
Wellsburgh,
Wentzville.

SAINT CLAIR COUNTY.

Baker,
Chalk Level,
Howard's Mills,
Monagan,
Osceola,* (c. h.,)
Park's Grove,
Roscoe,
Taberville.

SAINT FRANCOIS COUNTY.

Big River Mills,
Bismarck,
Blackwell's Station,
Bontear,
De Lassus,
Farmington, (c. h.,)
Flat River,
French Village,
Iron Mountain,
Knob Lick,
Libertyville,
Stono,
Wood's Mills.

SAINT GENEVIEVE COUNTY.

Avon,
Bloomsdale,
Bowling Brook,
Chesnut Ridge,
New Offenburgh,
Punjaub,
River Aux Vases,
St. Genevieve, (c. h.,)
Saint Mary's.

SAINT LOUIS COUNTY.

Allenton,
Baden,
Ballwin,
Barret's Station,
Bellefontaine,
Bonfil's Station,
Bonhomme,
Bridgeton,
Brotherton,
Carondelet,
Central,
Cheltenham,
Colman,
Creve Cœur,
Des Peres,
Elleard,
Ellisville,
Eureka,
Fairview,
Fenton,
Ferguson,
Florissant,
Fox Creek,
Glencoe,
Jefferson Barracks,*
Kirkwood,
Manchester,
Melrose,
Merrimac Station,
Mill Spring,
Normandy,
Pond,
Rock Hill,
Saint Louis,* (c. h.,)
Sappington,
Sherman,
Webster Groves.

SALINE COUNTY.

Arrow Rock,
Brownsville,
Cambridge,
Elm Wood,
Fairview,
Finney's Creek,
Malta Bend,
Marshall, (c. h.,)
Miami,
New Frankfort,
Petra,
Ridge Prairie,
Saline City.

* Money-order office.

SCHUYLER COUNTY.

Cherry Grove,
Clifton,
Coatsville,
Glenwood,

Green Top,
Lancaster,* (c. h.,)
Queen City.

SCOTLAND COUNTY.

Arbela,
Bible Grove,
Etna,
Hitt,
Memphis,* (c. h.,)

Middle Fabius,
Pleasant Retreat,
Prospect Grove,
Sand Hill,
Wyaconda.

SCOTT COUNTY.

Benton,
Blodgett,
Commerce, (c. h.,)
Diehlstadt,

Morley,
Price's Landing,
Saint Cloud,
Sikeston.

SHANNON COUNTY.

Birch Tree,
Carpenterville,
Eminence, (c. h.,)

Pine Hill,
Russell's Hill,
Sinkin.

SHELBY COUNTY.

Bethel,
Cherry Box,
Clarence,
Hager's Grove,

Hunnewell,
Lakenan,
Shelbina,*
Shelbyville, (c. h.)

STODDARD COUNTY.

Altha,
Bloomfield, (c. h.,)
Indian Ford,

Lakeville,
Piketon.

STONE COUNTY.

Blue Eye,
Galena, (c. h.,)

Long's Mills,
Robertson's Mill.

SULLIVAN COUNTY.

Bairdstown,
Colfax,
Green Castle,
Jackson's Corners,
Judson,
Kiddville,
Medicine,
Milan,* (c. h.,)

Owasco,
Pennville,
Scottsville,
Sticklerville,
Union Ridge,
Valparaiso,
Wintersville.

TANEY COUNTY.

Bald Knob,
Bradleyville,
Forsyth, (c. h.,)

Mincy,
Walnut Shade.

TEXAS COUNTY.

Big Creek,

Centre,

TEXAS COUNTY—Continued.

Elk Creek,
Jack's Fork,
Hickory Springs,
Houston, (c. h.,)
Licking,

Plato,
Plum Valley,
Roubidoux,
Ruth.

VERNON COUNTY.

Avola,
Belvoir,
Deerfield,
Dry Wood,
Duncan Creek,
Ligonier,
Little Osage,

Montevallo,
Mounds,
Nevada,* (c. h.,)
Pleasant Run,
Round Prairie,
Sand Stone.

WARREN COUNTY.

Bridgeport,
Dutzow,
Holstein,
Hopewell Academy,
Marthasville,
Pendleton,

Pinckney,
Pin Oak,
Pitts,
Tuque,
Warrenton,* (c. h.,)
Wright City.

WASHINGTON COUNTY.

Belgrade,
Cadet,
Caledonia,
Fourche à Renault,
Harmony,
Hopewell Furnace,
Irondale,*
Kingston Furnace,

Lawson,
Mineral Point,
Old Mines,
Potosi, (c. h.,)
Richwoods,
Rock Spring,
Walton Mills.

WAYNE COUNTY.

Brunot,
Cold Water,
Gravelton,
Greenville, (c. h.,)

Lowndes,
Otter Creek,
Patterson,
Stevenson's Mills

WEBSTER COUNTY.

Dallas,
Elkland,
Forkner's Hill,
Hazlewood,
Henderson,

Marshfield,* (c. h.,)
Mornington,
Sand Springs,
Sarvis Point,
Waldo.

WORTH COUNTY.

Allendale,
Grant City, (c. h.,)
Grant's Hill,
Hudson City,

Isadora,
Oxford,
Smithton.

WRIGHT COUNTY.

Astoria,
Aurora,
Hartville, (c. h.,)
Pleasant Valley,

Sacramento,
Sunny Side,
Wolf Creek.

---

* Money-order office.

MONTANA TERRITORY.

BEAVER HEAD COUNTY.

Bannack City, (c. h.,) Montana,
Horse Prairie, Watson.

CHOUTEAU COUNTY.

Fort Benton, (c. h.)

DEER LODGE COUNTY.

Beartown, Harrisburgh,
Blackfoot City, Lincoln,
Butte City, McClellan Gulch,
Deer Lodge City, Philipsburgh,
(c. h.,) Pike's Peak,
Emmettsburgh, Pioneer,
French Gulch, Red Mountain City,
German Gulch, Silver Bow,
Greenwood, Washington Gulch.

GALLATIN COUNTY.

Bozeman, (c. h.,) Hamilton,
East Gallatin, Middle Creek.
Gallatin,

JEFFERSON COUNTY.

Boulder Valley, *Radersburgh,* (c. h.,)
Fish Creek, Saint Louis,
Jefferson City, Springville,
Prickly Pear, Whitehall.

LEWIS AND CLARKE COUNTY.

Fort Shaw, Silver City,
French Bar, Sun River,
Georgetown, Unionville.
Helena, (c. h.,)

MADISON COUNTY.

Beaver Head Rock, Sheridan,
Cicero, Silver Star,
Harrison, Sterling,
Iron Rod, Summit,
Junction, Twin Bridges,
Meadow Creek, VIRGINIA CITY,*
Nevada City, (c. h.,)
Pollinger, Willow Creek.
Rochester,

MEAGHER COUNTY.

Canyon Ferry, Trout Creek.
Diamond City, (c. h.,)

MISSOULA COUNTY.

Cedar Junction, Louisville,
Frenchtown, *Missoula,* (c. h.,)
Gird's Creek, Stevensville,
Horse Plains, Thompson's River.

NEBRASKA.

ADAMS COUNTY.

Martinsville.

BLACK BIRD COUNTY.

Omaha Agency.

BURT COUNTY.

Arizona, Oakland,
Decatur,* Riverside,
Homestead, Silver Creek,
Lyons, *Tekamah,* (c. h.)

BUTLER COUNTY.

Linwood, Ulysses,
Pepperville, Urban.
Savannah, (c. h.,)

CASS COUNTY.

Avoca, Elmwood,
Centre Valley, Factoryville,
Eagle, Glendale,
Eight Mile Grove, Greenwood,

CASS COUNTY—Continued.

Louisville, South Bend,
Mount Pleasant, Three Grove,
Plattsmouth, (c. h.,) Union,
Rock Bluff, Weeping Water.

CEDAR COUNTY.

Saint Helena, (c. h.,) Saint James.

CHEYENNE COUNTY.

Sidney.

COLFAX COUNTY.

El Dorado, *Schuyler,* (c. h.)
Morian,

CUMING COUNTY.

Bismarck, Saint Charles,
De Witt, *West Point,* (c. h.)
Lakeview,

* Money-order office.

DAKOTA COUNTY.

Covington,
Dakota,* (c. h.,)
Jackson,
Lodi,
Omadi,
Randolph,
Winnebago.

DIXON COUNTY.

Ionia,
Newcastle,
'Ponca, (c. h.)

DODGE COUNTY.

Fremont,* (c. h.,)
Galena,
Jalapa,
Logan,
Maple Creek,
North Bend,
Oak Springs,
Pebble Creek,
Timberville.

DOUGLAS COUNTY.

Chicago,
Elkhorn City,
Florence,
Omaha Barracks,
Omaha City,* (c. h.,)
Primrose,
Valley.

GAGE COUNTY.

Baden,
Beatrice,* (c. h.,)
Blue Springs,
Cropsey,
Hooker,
Laona,
Otoe Agency,
Roperville.

HALL COUNTY.

Grand Island Sta- Wood River.
tion,* (c. h.,)

HAMILTON COUNTY.

Farmers' Valley.

JEFFERSON COUNTY.

Antelope,
Bowerville,
Caroline,
Cub Creek,
Dryden,
Elm Grove,
Fairbury, (c. h.,)
Georgetown,
Hebron,
Jenkins' Mills,
Kiowa,
Little Sandy,
Meridian, (c. h.,)
Rose Creek.

JOHNSON COUNTY.

Butler,
Crab Orchard,
Helena,
Latrobe,
Spring Creek,
Sterling,
Tecumseh,* (c. h.,)
Vesta.

KEARNEY COUNTY.

Fort Kearney,*
Kearney City, (c. h.)

L'EAU QUI COURT COUNTY.

Frankfort,
Niobrara, (c. h.,)
Santee Agency.

LANCASTER COUNTY.

Camp Creek,
Centreville,
LINCOLN,* (c. h.,)
Olive Branch,
Opequan,
Panama,
Rebecca,
Saltillo,
South Pass,
Tipton.

LINCOLN COUNTY.

Cottonwood Spr'gs,* North Platte.

MADISON COUNTY.

Battle Creek,
Madison,
Norfolk, (c. h.)

MERRICK COUNTY.

Chapman,
Clarksville,
Lone Tree, (c. h.,)
Silver Glen.

NEMAHA COUNTY.

Aspinwall,
Bratton,
Brownville,* (c. h.,)
Clifton,
Glen Rock,
Grant,
Hillsdale,
Howard,
London,
Nemaha City,
Peru,
Saint Deroin,
Saint Frederick,
Sheridan,
Sherman.

OTOE COUNTY.

Burr Oak,
Emerson,
Hendricks,
Nebraska City,*(c. h.,)
Nursery Hill,
Paisley,
Palmyra,
Solon,
Wilson,
Wyoming.

PAWNEE COUNTY.

Calla,
Cincinnati,
Liberty,
Pawnee City,* (c. h.,)
Table Rock,
Tip's Branch.

PLATTE COUNTY.

Cherry Grove,
Columbus,* (c. h.,)
Genoa,
Monroe.

RICHARDSON COUNTY.

Arago,*
Athens,
Dawson's Mill,
Elmore,
Falls City,* (c. h.,)
Highland,
Humboldt,
Long Branch,
Middleburgh,
Monterey,
Nohart,
Rulo,*
Salem,
Well's Mills,
Williamsville.

SALINE COUNTY.

Blue Island,
Crete,
Equality,
Pleasant Hill,
Swan City, (c. h.)

* Money-order office.

SARPY COUNTY.

Bellevue, (c. h.,) Lisbon,
Forest City, Papillion,
Gilmore, Plattford,
Larimer Mills, Xenia.

SAUNDERS COUNTY.

Ashland, (c. h.,) Ithaca,
Attica, Lone Valley,
Benton, Milton,
Cedar Bluffs, Platteville,
Ceresco, Pohocco,
Eldred, Wahoo,
Esteina, Wautisca.
Headland,

SEWARD COUNTY.

Beaver Crossing, Oak Groves,
Camden, Seward,
Milford, (c. h.,) West's Mill.

STANTON COUNTY.

Canton, Pleasant Run.
Clinton, (c. h.,)

WASHINGTON COUNTY.

Belle Creek, De Soto,
Blair, (c. h.,) Fontanelle,
Bono, Fort Calhoun.
Cuming City,

WAYNE COUNTY.

Taffe.

YORK COUNTY.

Blue Valley, York, (c. h.)
McFadden,

NEVADA.

DOUGLAS COUNTY.

Genoa, (c. h.,) Sheridan.

ELKO COUNTY.

Camp Halleck, Mountain City,
Coral Hill, Ruby Valley,
Elko, (c. h.,) Wells.
Mineral Hill,

ESMERALDA COUNTY.

Aurora,* (c. h.,) Silver Peak,
Columbus, Sweetwater,
Pine Grove, Wellington.

HUMBOLDT COUNTY.

Battle Mountain, Mill City,
Camp McDermitt, Oreana,
Dun Glen, Unionville, (c. h.,)
Galena, Winnemucca.
Golconda,

LANDER COUNTY.

Argenta, Egan Canyon,
Austin,* (c. h.,) Eureka,
Beowawe, Palisade,
Carlin, Vanderbilt.

LINCOLN COUNTY.

Hiko, (c. h.,) Pioche.

LYON COUNTY.

Dayton, (c. h.,) Silver City.

NYE COUNTY.

Belmont, (c. h.,) Reveille,
Ellsworth, Twin River,
Hot Creek, Washington.
Ione City.

ORMSBY COUNTY.

Carson City,*(c. h.,) Empire City.

STOREY COUNTY.

Gold Hill, Virginia City,* (c. h.)

WASHOE COUNTY.

Franktown, Verdi,
Ophir, Wadsworth,
Reno, Washoe City, (c. h.)
Truckee Meadows,

WHITE PINE COUNTY.

Diamond Mountain, Shermantown,
Hamilton,* (c. h.,) Treasure City.
Mineral City,

* Money-order office.

NEW HAMPSHIRE.

BELKNAP COUNTY.

Alton,
Alton Bay,
Barnstead,
Belmont,
Centre Barnstead,
Centre Harbor,
East Alton,
East Tilton,
Gilford Village,
Gilmanton,
Gilmanton Iron
  Works,
Laconia, (c. h.,)

Lake Village,
Lower Gilmanton,
Meredith Centre,
Meredith Village,
New Hampton,
North Barnstead,
North Sanbornton,
Sanbornton,
South Barnstead,
Tilton,*
Weir's Bridge,
West Alton.

CARROLL COUNTY.

Bartlett,
Brookfield,
Centre Conway,
Centre Effingham,
Centre Ossipee,
Centre Sandwich,
Conway,
Cram's Corner,
East Madison,
East Moultonboro',
East Wakefield,
Eaton Centre,
Effingham,
Effingham Falls,
Freedom,
Horn's Mills,
Jackson,
Leighton's Corners,
Lower Bartlett,
Mackerel Corner,
Madison,

Melvin Village,
Moultonborough,
Moultonville,
North Conway,
North Sandwich,
North Wakefield,
North Wolfborough.
Ossipee, (c. h.,)
Sandwich,
South Tamworth,
South Wolfborough,
Tamworth,
Tamworth Iron
  Works,
Tuftonborough,
Union,
Wakefield,
Water Village,
West Ossipee,
Wolfborough,
Wolrborough Centre.

CHESHIRE COUNTY.

Alstead,
Alstead Centre,
Ashuelot.
Blakeville,
Chesterfield,
Chesterfield Factory,
Drewsville,
Dublin,
East Jaffrey,
East Sullivan,
East Westmoreland,
Fitzwilliam,
Fitzwilliam Depot,
Gilsum,
Harrisville,
Hinsdale,*
Jaffrey,
Keene, (c. h.,)
Marlborough,
Marlborough Depot,
Marlow,

Munsonville,
Nelson,
New Alstead,
North Richmond,
Pottersville,
Richmond,
Rindge,
South Stoddard,
Stoddard,
Sullivan,
Surry,
Swanzey,
Troy,
Walpole,
West Chesterfield,
Westmoreland,
Westmorel'nd Depot,
Westport,
West Swanzey,
Winchester.

COOS COUNTY.

Berlin Falls,
Carroll,
Clarksville,
Colebrook, ¡
Columbia,
Connecticut Lake,
Coos,
Crawford House,
Dalton,
Errol,
Gorham,*
Groveton,
Jefferson,
Lancaster, (c. h.,)
Milan,
Northumberland,

Pittsburgh,
Randolph,
Shelburne,
South Columbia,
Stark,
Stewartstown,
Stratford,
Twin Mountain,
Wentworth's Loca-
  tion,
West Milan,
West Stewartstown,
Whitefield,
White Mountain
  House.

GRAFTON COUNTY.

Alexandria,
Ashland,
Bath,
Benton,
Bethlehem,
Bridgewater,
Bristol,*
Campton,
Campton Village,
Canaan,
Danbury,
Dorchester,
East Canaan,
East Haverhill,
East Landaff,
East Lebanon,
Ellsworth,
Enfield,
Enfield Centre,
Franconia,
Grafton,
Grafton Centre,
Groton,
Hanover,*
Hanover Centre,
Haverhill, (c. h.,)
Hebron,
Hill,
Landaff,
Lebanon,*
Lisbon,

Littleton,*
Lyman,
Lyme,
Monroe,
North Dorchester,
North Groton,
North Haverhill,
North Lisbon,
North Littleton,
North Monroe,
North Woodstock,
Orford,
Orfordville,
Piermont,
Plymouth, (c. h.,)
Profile House,
Rumney,
South Danbury,
Sugar Hill,
Thornton,
Warren,
Wentworth,
West Campton,
West Canaan,
West Enfield,
West Lebanon,*
West Plymouth,
West Rumney,
West Thornton,
Woodstock,
Woodsville.

HILLSBOROUGH COUNTY.

Amherst, (c. h.,)
Amoskeag,
Antrim,
Bedford,
Bennington,
Brookline,
Deering,
East Deering,

East Weare,
Francistown,
Goff's Falls,
Goffstown,
Goffstown Centre,
Greenfield,
Hancock,
Hillsborough,

* Money-order office.

HILLSBOROUGH COUNTY—Continued.

Hillsborough Bridge, North Weare,
Hillsboro'h Centre, Oil Mill Village,
Hollis, Pelham,
Hudson, Peterborough,*
Lyndeborough, Reed's Ferry,
Manchester,* South Lyndeboro'h,
Mason, South Merrimack,
Mason Village, South Weare,
Merrimack, Temple,
Milford,* Thornton's Ferry,
Mount Vernon, Weare,
Nashua,* West Deering,
New Boston, West Peterborough,
New Ipswich,* West Wilton,
North Branch, Wilton.*
North Lyndeboro'h,

MERRIMACK COUNTY.

Allenstown, North Boscawen,
Andover, North Chichester,
Boscawen, North Dunbarton,
Bow, North Sutton,
Bradford, Pembroke,
Canterbury, Pittsfield,
Chichester, Roby's Corner,
CONCORD,* (c. h.,) Salisbury,
Contoocook Village, Scytheville,
Dunbarton, Shaker Village,
East Andover, Short Falls,
East Concord, South Newbury,
East Pembroke, South Sutton,
Epsom, Suncook,*
Fishersville,* Sutton,
Franklin,* Warner,
Henniker, Webster,
Hookset, West Andover,
Hopkinton, West Concord,
Loudon, West Henniker,
Loudon Centre, West Hopkinton,
Loudon Ridge, West Salisbury,
Mast Yard, Wilmot,
Newbury, Wilmot Flat.
New London,*

ROCKINGHAM COUNTY.

Atkinson, Deerfield,
Atkinson Depot, Deerfield Centre,
Auburn, Derry,
Boar's Head, Derry Depot,
Brentwood, East Derry,
Candia, East Hampstead,
Candia Village, East Kingston,
Chester, East Northwood,
Danville, Epping,

ROCKINGHAM COUNTY—Continued.

Exeter,* (c. h.,) Plaistow,
Fremont, Portsmouth,* (c. h.,)
Greenland, Raymond,
Greenland Depot, Rye,
Hampstead, Salem,
Hampton, Salem Depot,
Hampton Falls, Sandown,
Kensington, Seabrook,
Kingston, South Deerfield,
Londonderry, South Hampton,
New Castle, South Kingston,
Newington, South New Market,
New Market, Stratham,
Newton, West Epping,
Newton Depot, West Hampstead,
North Hampton, West Nottingham,
North Londonderry, West Windham,
North Salem, Wilson's Crossing,
Northwood Centre, Windham,
N'thwood Narrows, Windham Depot.
Nottingham,

STRAFFORD COUNTY.

Barrington, Milton Mills,
Centre Strafford, North Barrington,
Dover,* (c. h.,) North Strafford.
Downing's Mills, Rochester,
Durham, Salmon Falls,
East Rochester, South Milton,
Farmington, Strafford,
Gonic, Strafford Blue Hills,
Great Falls,* Strafford Corner,
Lee, Wadley's Falls,
Middleton, West Milton.
Milton,

SULLIVAN COUNTY.

Acworth, Lempster,
Charlestown,* Meriden,*
Claremont,* Mill Village,
Cornish Flat, Newport,* (c. h.,)
Croydon, North Charlestown,
Croydon Flat, North Grantham,
East Acworth, Plainfield,
East Lempster, South Acworth,
East Plainfield, South Charlestown,
East Springfield, South Sunapee,
East Unity, Springfield,
East Washington, Sunapee,
George's Mills, Unity,
Goshen, Washington,
Grantham, West Claremont,
Langdon, West Springfield.

---

* Money-order office.

NEW JERSEY.

ATLANTIC COUNTY.

Absecom,*
Atlantic City,*
Bargaintown,
Cedar Lake,
Decosta,
Egg Harbor City,*
Elwood,
English's Creek,
Estelville.

Hammonton,*
Leeds Point,
May's Landing, (c. h.,)
Pleasant Mills,
Port Republic,
Smith's Landing,
Somers' Point,
Weymouth.

BERGEN COUNTY.

Allendale,
Arcola,
Carlstadt,
Closter,
Cresskill,
Englewood,
Fairview,
Fort Lee,
Godwinville,
Green Wood,
Hackensack, (c. h.,)
Hillsdale,
Hohokus,
Kinderkamack,
Leonia,
Lodi,

Mahwah,
New Bridge,
Norwood,
Park Ridge,
Paskack,
Ramsey's,
Ridgewood,
River Edge,
Rutherford Park,
Saddle River,
Schraalenburgh,
Spring Valley,
Tenafly,
Westwood,
Wyckoff.

BURLINGTON COUNTY.

Arneytown,
Beverly,
Birmingham,
Bordentown,*
Bridgeborough,
Brown's Mills,
Budd Town,
Burlington,*
Cinnaminson,
Columbus,
Cookstown,
Crosswicks,
Delanco,
Fellowship,
Florence,
Fruitland,
Georgetown,
Green Bank,
Hainesport,
Hartford,
Jacksonville,
Jacobstown,
Jobstown,
Juliustown,

Lower Bank,
Lumberton,
Marlton,
Masonville,
Medford,
Moorestown,*
Mount Holly,* (c. h.,)
Mount Laurel,
New Gretna,
New Lisbon,
Palmyra,
Pemberton,
Pointville,
Rancocas,
Recklesstown,
Riverside,
Shamong,
Smithville,
Sykesville,
Tuckerton,
Vincentown,
Wading River,
Woodmansie,
Wrightstown.

CAMDEN COUNTY.

Ancora,
Atco,
Berlin,

Blackwoodtown
Camden,* (c. h.,)
Chew's Landing,

CAMDEN COUNTY—Continued.

Cross Keys,
Gloucester City,
Haddonfield,
Hurffville,
Kirkwood,
Merchantville,

Mount Ephraim,
Turnersville,
Waterford Works,
Williamstown,
Winslow.

CAPE MAY COUNTY.

Beesley's Point,
Cape May,*
Cape May C. H.,
Cold Spring,
Dennisville,
Dias Creek,
East Creek,
Fishing Creek,

Goshen,
Green Creek,
Petersburgh,
Rio Grande,
Seaville,
South Seaville,
Townsend Inlet,
Tuckahoe.

CUMBERLAND COUNTY.

Belle Plain,
Bridgeton,* (c. h.,)
Cedarville,
Cohansey,
Deerfield Street,
Dividing Creek,
Ewing's Neck,
Fairton,
Finley Station,
Greenwich,
Leesburgh,
Manamuskin,

Mauricetown,
Millville,*
Newport,
North Vineland,
Port Elizabeth,
Roadstown,
Rosenhayn,
Shiloh,
South Vineland,
Vineland,*
Willow Grove.

ESSEX COUNTY.

Belleville,
Bloomfield,*
Caldwell,
Franklin,
East Orange,
Irvington,
Livingston,

Millburn,
Mont Clair,
Newark,* (c. h.,)
Orange,
Orange Valley,
South Orange,
Verona.

GLOUCESTER COUNTY.

Barnsborough,
Bridgeport,
Clarksborough,
Clayton,
Ewan's Mills,
Five Points,
Forest Grove,
Franklinville,
Glassborough.
Harrisonville,

Malaga,
Mantua,
Mullica Hill,
Newfield,
Paulsborough,
Swedesborough,
Unionville,
Westville,
Woodbury, (c. h.)

HUDSON COUNTY.

Bayonne,
Bergen.
Bergen Point,
Greenville,
Hoboken,*
Hudson,

Jersey City,* (c. h.,)
New Durham,
Saltersville,
Weehawken,
West Hoboken.

* Money-order office.

HUNTERDON COUNTY.

Anthony,
Baptistown,
Bethlehem,
Bloomsbury,
Centreville,
Cherryville,
Clarksville,
Clinton,
Clinton Station,
Clover Hill,
Copper Hill,
Croton,
Everittstown,
Fair Mount,
Flemington,* (c. h.,)
Frenchtown,*
High Bridge
Holland,
Junction,
Kingwood,
Klinesville,
Lambertville,*
Lebanon,
Little York,
Locktown,
Lower Valley,
Milford,
Mountainville,

Mount Pleasant,
New Germantown,
New Hampton,
Oak Dale,
Oak Grove,
Pattenburgh,
Perryville,
Pittstown,
Pleasant Run,
Potterstown,
Pottersville,
Quakertown,
Raven Rock,
Readington,
Reaville,
Ringoes,
Rowland Mills,
Sand Brook,
Sergeantsville,
Sidney,
Stanton,
Stockton,
Three Bridges,
Tumble,
Wertsville,
White House,
White House Station.

MERCER COUNTY.

Baker's Basin,
Dutch Neck,
Edinburgh,
Ewingville,
Greensburgh,
Hamilton Square,
Hightstown,*
Hopewell,
Lawrenceville,

Pennington,
Princeton,*
Robbinsville,
Titusville,
TRENTON,* (c. h.,)
Windsor,
Woodsville,
Yardville.

MIDDLESEX COUNTY.

Clay Bank,
Cranbury,
Dayton,
Dun Ellen,
Jamesburgh,
Metuchen,
Monmouth Junction,
New Brunswick,*(c.h.,)
New Market,

Old Bridge,
Perth Amboy,*
Plainsborough,
Prospect Plains,
South Amboy,*
South River,
Spotswood,
Woodbridge.

MONMOUTH COUNTY.

Allentown,
Black's Mills,
Branch Shore,
Chapel Hill.
Clarksburgh,
Coburgh,
Colt's Neck,
Deal,
Eatontown,
Englishtown.

Farmingdale,
Fillmore,
Freehold,* (c. h.,)
Holmdel,
Imlaystown,
Jerseyville,
Key Port,*
Leedsville,
Leonardville,
Long Branch,*

MONMOUTH COUNTY—Continued.

Lower Squankum,
Manalapan,
Marlborough,
Mattawan,
Middletown,
Morganville,
Navasink,
New Bedford,
New Branch,
New Monmouth,
New Sharon,

Ocean Port,
Perrineville,
Port Monmouth,
Red Bank,*
Shark River,
Shrewsbury,
Squam Village,
Tinton Falls,
Turkey,
Walnford,
West Freehold.

MORRIS COUNTY.

Boonton,*
Brookside,
Budd's Lake,
Chatham,
Chester,
Denville,
Dover,*
Drakestown,
Drakesville,
Flanders,
German Valley,
Green Village,
Hanover,
Hibernia,
Hurdtown,
Littleton,
Long Hill,
McCainsville,
Madison,
Mendham,
Middle Valley,

Millington,
Milton,
Morristown,* (c. h.,)
Mount Hope,
Naughrightville,
Newfoundland,
New Vernon,
Parsippany,
Passaic Valley,
Pine Brook,
Pleasant Grove,
Pompton Plains,
Port Oram,
Rockaway,
Schooley's Mountain,
Stephensburgh,
Stanley,
Stony Brook,
Suckasunny,
Walnut Grove,
Whippany.

OCEAN COUNTY.

Barnegat,
Bayville,
Bennett's Mills,
Bricksburgh,
Cassville,
Cedar Creek,
Collier's Mill,
Ellisdale,
Forked River,
Hornerstown,
Jackson's Mills,

Manahawkin,
Manchester,
Metedeconk,
New Egypt,
Point Pleasant,
Silverton,
Tom's River,* (c. h.,)
Vanhiseville,
West Creek,
Whiting,
Wiretown.

PASSAIC COUNTY.

Bloomingdale,
Charlotteburgh,
Clifton,
Hawthorne,
Little Falls,
Mead's Basin,

Passaic,
Paterson,* (c. h.,)
Pompton,
Ringwood Furnace.
Smith's Mills.
West Milford.

SALEM COUNTY.

Allowaystown,
Auburn,
Canton,
Centreton.

Daretown.
Elmer,
Hancock's Bridge
Monroeville,

* Money-order office.

SALEM COUNTY—Continued.

Palatine,
Pedricktown,
Penn's Grove,
Pennsville,
Pitt's Grove,

Quinton,
*Salem,** (c. h.,)
Sharptown,
Woodstown,
Yorktown.

SOMERSET COUNTY.

Basking Ridge.
Blawenburgh,
Boundbrook,
Flaggtown,
Griggstown,
Harlingen,
Kingston,
Lesser Cross Roads,
Liberty Corner,
Martinsville,
Middlebush,
Millstone,
Neshanic,

North Branch,
North Branch Depot,
Peapack,
Pluckemin,
Raritan,
Rocky Hill,
Roysfield,
Six Mile Run,
*Somerville,** (c. h.,)
South Branch,
Warrenville,
Weston.

SUSSEX COUNTY.

Andover,
Beaver Run,
Beemerville,
Bevans,
Branchville,
Clove,
Colesville,
Deckertown,
Flatbrookville,
Franklin Furnace,
Fredon,
Glenwood,
Hainesville,
Hamburgh,
Hunt's Mills,
Huntsville,

La Fayette,
Layton,
Libertyville,
Lincoln,
McAfee Valley,
Middleville,
Monroe,
Montague,
Mount Salem,
*Newton,** (c. h.,)
Ogdensburgh,
Papakating,
Pleasant Valley,
Sparta,
Stanhope,
Stillwater,

SUSSEX COUNTY—Continued.

Stockholm,
Swartswood,
Tranquillity,
Vernon,*

Wallpack Centre,
Waterloo,
Wawayanda,
Wykertown.

UNION COUNTY.

Cranford,
*Elizabeth,** (c. h.,)
Elizabeth Port,
Linden,
New Providence,
Plainfield,*
Rahway,*

Roselle,
Scotch Plains,
Springfield,
Summit,
Union,
Westfield.

WARREN COUNTY.

Allamuchy,
Asbury,
Beatyestown,
*Belvidere,** (c. h.,)
Blairstown,
Brainards,
Bridgeville,
Broadway,
Brotzmanville,
Calno,
Carpentersville,
Changewater,
Columbia,
Danville,
Delaware Station,
Hackettstown,*
Hainesburgh,
Hardwick,
Harmony,
Hope,
Howard,
Johnsonburgh.
Karrsville,

Kill Mills,
Knowlton,
Marksborough,
Millbrook,
Montana,
Mount Bethel,
Musconetcong,
New Village,
Oxford,
Pahaquarry,
Paulina,
Phillipsburgh,*
Polkville,
Port Colden,
Port Murry,
Rocksburgh,
Springtown,
Stewartsville,
Still Valley,
Townsbury,
Vienna,
Walnut Valley,
Washington.*

NEW MEXICO TERRITORY.

BERNALILLO COUNTY.

Albuquerque, (c. h.,) Bernalillo.

COLFAX COUNTY.

Clifton,
Elizabethtown, (c. h.,)

Ute Creek.

DOÑA AÑA COUNTY.

Doña Aña,
Fort Selden,
Las Cruces,

Leasburgh,
Mesilla, (c. h.)

GRANT COUNTY.

Central City,
Fort Cummings,

Pinos Altos, (c. h.,)
Rio Mimbres.

MORA COUNTY.

Cimarron,
Fort Union,
La Cueva,

La Junta,
Mora, (c. h.,)
Ocate.

RIO ARRIBA COUNTY.

Abiqui,
Los Luceros,

San Juan.

SANTA AÑA COUNTY.

Algodones,

La Bajada,

SAN MIGUEL COUNTY.

Las Vegas, (c. h.,)
San José,

Tecolote

* Money-order office.

SANTA FÉ COUNTY.

Juana Lopez, SANTA FÉ, (c. h.)
Pajuaque,

SOCORRO COUNTY.

Aleman, Limitar,
Fort Craig, Paraje,
Fort Stanton, Sabinal,

SOCORRO COUNTY—Continued.

San Antonio, Socorro, (c. h.)
San Marcial,

TAOS COUNTY.

Fernandez de Taos, (c. h.)

VALENCIA COUNTY.

Los Lunas, Peralta.

NEW YORK.

ALBANY COUNTY.

Adams' Station, Knox,
ALBANY,* (c. h.,) Lisha's Kill,
Berne, Medusa,
Bethlehem Centre, New Salem,
Callanan's Corners, New Scotland,
Cedar Hill, Newtonville,
Clarksville, Norman's Kill,
Coeymans, Potter's Hollow,
Coeymans Hollow, Preston Hollow,
Cohoes,* Reidsville,
Cooksburgh, Rensselaerville,*
Dormansville, South Berne,
Dunnsville, South Westerlo,
East Berne, Union Church,
Green Island, Voorheesville,
Guilderland, Watervliet Centre,
Guilderland Centre, West Albany,
Guilderland Station, West Berne,
Indian Fields, Westerlo,
Ireland Corners, West Township,
Jerusalem, West Troy,
Keefer's Corners, Wolf Hill.
Knowersville,

ALLEGANY COUNTY.

Alfred, Fillmore,
Alfred Centre,* Friendship,
Allen, Fulmer Valley
Allen Centre, Granger,
Alma, Hallsport,
Almond, Houghton Creek,
Andover,* Hume,
Angelica, (c. h.,) Independence,
Belfast, Little Genesee,
Belmont, (c. h.,) Mills' Mills,
Belvidere, New Hudson,
Birdsall, Nile,
Black Creek, Oramel,
Bolivar, Phillips' Creek,
Burns, Richburgh,
Canaseraga, Rushford,
Caneadea, Scio,
Centreville, Seymour,
Ceres, Shongo,
Cuba,* Short Tract,
East Granger, South Bolivar,
East Rushford, Spring Mills,

ALLEGANY COUNTY—Continued.

Stanard's Corners, Whitesville,
Swain, Whitney's Crossings,
Wellsville,* Wirt Centre,
West Almond, Wiscoy.
West Clarksville,

BROOME COUNTY.

Belden, McClure Settlement,
Binghamton,* (c. h.,) Maine,
Cascade Valley, New Ohio,
Castle Creek, Nineveh,
Centre Lisle, North Colesville,
Centre Village, North Fenton,
Chenango Forks, North Sanford,
Choconut Centre, Osborne Hollow,
Colesville, Ouaquaga,
Conklin Centre, Port Crane,
Conklin Station, Port Dickinson,
Corbettsville, Randolph Centre,
Deposit,* Riverside,
Doraville, Sanford,
East Maine, Tracy Creek,
Glen Aubrey, Triangle,
Glen Castle, Union,
Gulf Summit. Union Centre,
Harpersville, Upper Lisle,
Hawleyton, Vallonia Springs,
Hoopor, Vestal,
Kattelville, Vestal Centre,
Killawog, West Colesville,
Kirkwood, West Windsor,
Kirkwood Centre, Whitney's Point,*
Lamb's Corners, Windsor.
Lisle,

CATTARAUGUS COUNTY.

Allegany, East Otto,
Ashford, East Randolph,
Cadiz, East Salamanca,
Carrollton, Eddyville,
Cattaraugus, Elgin,
Conewango, Ellicottsville,* (c. h.,)
Cottage, Elton,
Dayton, Fairview,
East Ashford, Farmersville,
East Leon, Franklinville,

CATTARAUGUS COUNTY—Continued.

Gowanda,
Great Valley,
Haskell Flats,
Hinsdale,
Humphrey,
Ischua,
Kill Buck,
Leon,
Limestone,
Little Valley,
Machias,
Napoli,
New Albion,
Olean,*
Onoville,
Otto,

Perrysburgh,
Persia,
Portville,
Randolph,*
Rawson,
Red House,
Salamanca,
Sandusky,
South Dayton,
Steamburgh,
Vandalia,
Versailles,
West Valley,
West Yorkshire,
Yorkshire,
Yorkshire Centre.

CAYUGA COUNTY.

Auburn,* (c. h.,)
Aurelius,
Aurora,
Bethel Corners,
Cato,
Cayuga,
Conquest,
Dresserville,
East Genoa,
East Venice,
Fair Haven,
Five Corners,
Fleming,
Fosterville,
Genoa,
Ira,
Kelloggsville,
King's Ferry,
Ledyard,
Levanna,
Locke,
Martville,
Meridian,
Montezuma,
Moravia,

New Hope,
Niles,
North Sterling,
North Victory,
Owasco,
Owasco Lake,
Poplar Ridge,
Port Byron,
Scipio,
Scipioville,
Sempronius,
Sennet,
Sherwood's,
Sterling,
Sterling Valley,
Summer Hill,
The Square,
Throopsville,
Union Springs,*
Venice,
Venice Centre,
Victory,
Weedsport,
Westbury.

CHAUTAUQUA COUNTY.

Arkwright Summit,
Bemus Point,
Blockville,
Brocton,
Broken Straw,
Busti,
Cassadaga,
Charlotte Centre,
Cherry Creek,
Clear Creek,
Clymer,
De Wittville,
Dunkirk,*
Ellery,
Ellington,
Elm Flat,
Fentonville,
Findley's Lake,

Fluvanna,
Forestville,
Fredonia,*
French Creek,
Frewsburgh,
Hamlet,
Harmony,
Hartfield,
Irving,
Jamestown,*
Kennedy,
Kiantone,
Laona,
Marvin,
Mayville,* (c. h.,)
Mina,
Nashville,
North Clymer,

CHAUTAUQUA COUNTY—Continued.

Oregon,
Panama,
Poland Centre,
Portland,
Prospect Station,
Ripley,
Sheridan,
Sherman,
Silver Creek,

Sinclairville,
Smith's Mills,
Stedman,
Stockton,
Vermont.
Villanova,
Volusia,
Watt's Flats,
Westfield. *

CHEMUNG COUNTY.

Big Flats,
Breesport,
Chemung,
Chemung Centre,
East Grove,
Elmira,* (c. h.,)
Erin,
Herrington's Corners,
Horseheads,
Lowman,
Mill Port,
North Chemung,

Pine Valley,
Post Creek,
Seely Creek,
Southport,
State Road,
Sullivanville,
Tompkins' Corners,
Van Etten,
Van Ettenville,
Webb's Mills,
Wellsburgh.

CHENANGO COUNTY.

Afton,
Bainbridge,
Bennettsville,
Columbus,
Coventry,
Coventryville,
East German,
East Greene,
East Guilford,
East McDonough,
East Pharsalia,
German,
Greene,
Guilford,
Guilford Centre,
King's Settlement,
Lincklaen,
McDonough,
Mount Upton,
New Berlin,
New Berlin Centre,
North Lincklaen,

North Norwich,
North Pharsalia,
North Pitcher,
Norwich,* (c. h.,)
Otselic,
Oxford
Pharsalia,
Pitcher,
Pitcher Springs,
Plymouth,
Preston,
Rockdale,
Sherburne,*
Sherburne Four Corners,
Smithville Flats,
Smyrna,
South New Berlin,
South Otselic,
South Oxford,
South Plymouth,
White's Store.

CLINTON COUNTY.

Altona,
Beekmantown,
Black Brook,
Cadyville,
Champlain,
Chazy,
Churubusco,
Clayburgh,
Clinton Mills,
Clintonville,
Coopersville,
Dannemora,
East Beekmantown,

Ellenburgh,
Ellenburgh Centre,
Ellenburgh Depot,
Ferrona,
Forest,
Frontier,
Ingraham,
Irona,
Mooers.
Mooers Forks,
Morrisonville,
Peasleeville,
Perry's Mills,

*Money-order office.

21 P O

CLINTON COUNTY—Continued.

Peru,
Plattsburgh,* (c. h.,)
Redford,
Rouse's Point,*
Saranac,
Schuyler's Falls,
Sciota,
Silver Lake,
South Plattsburgh,
Union Falls,
Valcour,
West Chazy,
West Plattsburgh,
Wood's Falls.

COLUMBIA COUNTY.

Ancram,
Ancram Centre,
Ancram Lead Mines,
Austerlitz,
Boston Corner,
Canaan,
Canaan Centre,
Canaan Four Corn's,
Cattskill Station,
Chatham,
Chatham Centre,
Chatham Village,
Churchtown,
Claverack,
Clermont,
Copake,
Copake Iron Works,
East Chatham,
Elizaville,
Flatbrook,
Gallatinville,
Germantown,
Ghent,
Glencoe Mills,
Green River,
Harlemville,
Hillsdale.
Hollowville.
Hudson,* (c. h.,)
Humphreysville,
Kinderhook,*
Linlithgo,
Livingston,
Malden Bridge,
Martindale Depot,
Mellenville,
Moffett's Store,
Mount Lebanon,
New Concord,
New Lebanon,
New Leb'on Centre,
New Lebanon Sp'gs,
Niverville,
North Chatham,
North Copake,
Philmont,
Red Rock,
Rider's Mills,
Rider's Mills Station,
Shunpike,
Spencertown,
Stockport,
Stottville,
Stuyvesant,
Stuyvesant Falls,
Taghkanick,
Valatie,*
West Copake,
West Taghkanick.

CORTLAND COUNTY.

Blodget Mills,
Cincinnatus,
Cortland Village,*
  (c. h.,)
Cresswell,
Cuyler,
East Homer,
East Scott,
East Virgil,
Freetown Corners,
Glen Haven,
Harford,
Harford Mills,
Homer,*
Hunt's Corners,
Keeney's Settlement,
Lapeer,
Little York,
McGrawville,
Marathon,
Messengerville,
Preble,
Scott,
Solon,
South Cortland,
Taylor,
Texas Valley,
Truxton,*
Union Valley,
Virgil,
Willet.

DELAWARE COUNTY.

Andes,
Barbourville,
Bloomville,
Bovina,
Bovina Valley,
Brushland,

DELAWARE COUNTY—Continued.

Cabin Hill,
Cadosia Valley,
Cannonsville,
Carpenter's Eddy,
Clark's Factory,
Clovesville,
Colchester,
Croton,
Davenport,
Davenport Centre,
Delhi,* (c. h.,)
Downsville,
East Branch,
East Masonville,
East Meredith,
Fergusonville,
Franklin,
Grant's Mills,
Griffin's Corners,
Halcottsville,
Hale's Eddy,
Hamden,
Hancock,*
Harpersfield,
Harvard,
Hobart,
Kortright,
Lordville,
Lumberville,
Margarettville,
Masonville,
Meredith,
Moresville,
New Kingston,
North Franklin,
North Hamden,
North Harpersfield,
North Kortright,
North Walton,
Ouleout,
Partridge Island,
Pepacton,
Rock Rift,
Roxbury,
Shavertown,
Sidney,
Sidney Centre,
Sidney Plains,*
South Kortright,
Stamford,
Stockport Station,
Stratton's Falls,
Trout Creek,
Union Grove,
Walton,
West Brook,
West Davenport,
West Kortright,
West Meredith.

DUTCHESS COUNTY.

Adriance,
Amenia,
Amenia Union,
Anandale,
Arthursburgh,
Attlebury,
Bangall,
Barrytown,
Beekman,
Billings,
Bull's Head,
Carthage Landing,
Chesnut Ridge,
City,
Clinton Corners,
Clinton Hollow,
Clinton Point,
Clove,
Clove Branch Junc.,
Coffin's Summit,
Crouse's Store,
Crum Elbow,
Dover,
Dover Furnace,
East Fishkill,
Fishkill,
Fishkill on the Hud-
  son,
Fishkill Plains,
Freedom Plains,
Glenham,
Green Haven,
Hibernia,
Hopewell Junction,
Hughsonville,
Hull's Mills,
Hyde Park,
Jackson Corners,
Johnsville,
La Fayetteville,
La Grangeville,
Leedsville,
Lithgow,
Little Rest,
Mabbettsville,
Madalin,
Manchester Bridge,
Mansfield,
Matteawan,*
Milan,
Millbrook,
Millerton,
Moore's Mill,
Mount Riga,
New Hackensack,
New Hamburgh,
North Clove,
Northeast Centre,
Oblong,
Oreville,
Pawling,
Pine Plains,
Pleasant Plains,
Pleasant Valley,

* Money-order office.

DUTCHESS COUNTY—Continued.

Poughkeepsie,*(c. h.,)
Poughquag,
Pulver's Corners,
Quaker Hill,
Red Hook,
Rhinebeck,*
Rhinecliff,
Rock City,
Salt Point,
Schultzville,
Sharon Station,
South Amenia,
South Dover,

Sprout Creek,
Staatsburgh,
Stanfordville,
Stissing,
Stormville,
Tivoli,
Upper Red Hook,
Verbank,
Wappinger's Falls,
Washington,
Washington Hollow,
Wassaic,
Wing's Station.

ERIE COUNTY.

Akron,
Alden,
Alden Centre,
Angola.
Big Tree Corners,
Boston,
Bowmansville,
Brant,
Buffalo,* (c. h.,)
Buffalo Plains,
Cheektowaga,
Clarence,
Clarence Centre,
Clarksburgh,
Colden,
Collins,
Collins Centre,
Crittenden,
East Amherst,
East Aurora,
East Clarence,
East Concord,
East Eden,
East Elma,
East Evans,
East Hamburgh,
Ebenezer,
Eden,
Eden Valley,
Eggertsville,
Ellicott,
Elma,
Evans,
Farnham,
Gardenville,
Getzville,
Glenwood,
Griffin's Mills,
Hamburgh,
Harris Hill,
Holland,

Lake View,
Lancaster,
Langford,
Looneyville,
Marilla,
Marshfield,
Midway,
Mill Grove,
Morton's Corners,
New Oregon,
North Boston,
North Evans,
Patchin,
Pontiac,
Protection,
Red Jacket,
Reserve,
Sardinia,
Sheenwater,
Shirley,
South Newstead,
South Wales,
Spring Brook,
Springville,
Tonawanda,*
Town Line,
Wales,
Wales Centre,
Water Valley,
West Falls,
West Hamburgh,
West Seneca,
West Seneca Centre,
West Wood,
White Haven,
White's Corners,
Williamsville,
Willink,
Williston,
Winspear,
Woodward's Hollow.

ESSEX COUNTY.

Aiden Lair,
Au Sable Forks,
Bloomingdale,
Crown Point,
Crown Point Centre,

Elizabethtown,* (c. h.,)
Essex,*
Jay,
Keene,
Keene Flats,

ESSEX COUNTY—Continued.

Keeseville,*
Lewis,
Minerva,
Mineville,
Moriah,
Moriah Centre,
Newcomb,
New Russia,
North Elba,
North Hudson,
Olmstedville,
Port Henry,*

Port Kent,
Schroon Lake,
Schroon River,
South Schroon,
Ticonderoga,
Upper Jay,
Wadham's Mills,
Westport,
Whallonsburgh,
Willsborough,
Wilmington.

FRANKLIN COUNTY.

Alder Brook,
Andrusville,
Bangor,
Bombay,
Brush's Mills,
Burke,
Chateaugay,
Chateaugay Lake,
Cook's Corners,
Dickinson,
Dickinson Centre,
Duane,
East Constable,
East Dickinson,
Fort Covington,

Ft.Covington Centre,
Franklin Falls,
Hogansburgh,
Linkinson,
McClelland,
Malone,* (c. h.,)
Merrillsville,
Moira,
North Bangor,
Saranac Lake,
South Bombay,
Trout River,
West Bangor,
West Constable,
Westville Centre.

FULTON COUNTY.

Bleecker,
Broadalbin,
Brockett's Bridge,
Cranberry Creek,
Crum Creek,
Ephratah,
Garoga,
Gloversville,
Johnstown,* (c. h.,)
Keck's Centre,
Kingsborough,
Lasellsville,
Lotville,
Mayfield,
Middle Sprite,

Mill's Corners,
Northampton,
North Broadalbin,
Northville,
Oppenheim,
Osborn's Bridge,
Perth,
Pine Lake,
Rockwood,
Sammonsville,
Stratford,
Union Mills,
Vail's Mills,
West Galway,
West Perth.

GENESEE COUNTY.

Alabama,
Alexander,
Batavia,* (c. h.,)
Bergen,*
Bethany,
Byron,
Corfu,*
Darien,
Darien Centre,
East Bethany,
East Elba,
East Pembroke,
Elba,
Indian Falls,
Le Roy,*
Linden,

Morganville,
North Bergen,
North Oakfield,
North Pembroke,
Oakfield,
Pavilion,
Pavilion Centre,
Pembroke,
South Alabama,
South Byron,
Stafford,
Stone Church,
West Batavia,
West Bergen,
West Bethany,
Wheatville.

* Money-order office.

GREENE COUNTY.

Acra,
Ashland,
Athens,
Big Hollow,
Bushnellsville,
Cairo,
Catskill,* (c. h.,)
Cornwallville,
Coxsackie,
Durham,
East Durham,
East Jewett,
East Windham,
Freehold,
Gayhead,
Grapeville,
Greenville,
Halcott Centre,
Hensonville,
Hunter,
Jewett,
Jewett Centre,
Leeds,
Lexington,
Medway,
New Baltimore,
Norton Hill,
Oak Hill,
Palenville,
Prattsville,
Red Falls,
South Cairo,
South Durham,
Tannersville,
Union Society,
West Kill,
Windham Centre.

HAMILTON COUNTY.

Benson,
Benson Centre,
Gilman,
Hope Centre,
Hope Falls,
Indian Lake,
Long Lake,
Morehouseville,
Sageville, (c. h.,)
Wells.

HERKIMER COUNTY.

Cedar Lake,
Cedarville,
Cold Brook,
Columbia,
Cullen,
Danube,
Denison,
East Creek,
East Schuyler,
Eatonville,
Emmonsburgh,
Fairfield,
Frankfort,
Frankfort Hill,
Graefenberg,
Grant,
Gravesville,
Gray,
Herkimer,* (c. h.,)
Ilion,*
Ingham's Mills,
Jordanville,
Litchfield,
Little Falls,*
Middleville,
Mohawk,
Newport,
Newville,
North Litchfield,
North Winfield,
Norway,
Ohio,
Paine's Hollow,
Poland,
Russia,
Salisbury,
Salisbury Centre,
South Columbia,
Starkville,
Van Hornesville,
Warren,
West Schuyler,
West Winfield,
Winfield.

JEFFERSON COUNTY.

Adams,
Adams Centre,
Alexandria,
Antwerp,
Belleville,
Bishop Street,
Black River,
Brownville,
Burr's Mills,
Cape Vincent,*
Carthage,*
Champion,
Chaumont,
Clayton,
Clayton Centre,
Depauville,
Dexter,
East Houndsfield,
East Rodman,
East Watertown,

JEFFERSON COUNTY—Continued.

Ellisburgh,
Evans' Mills,
Felt's Mills,
Great Bend,
Henderson,
La Fargeville,
Le Raysville,
Limerick,
Lorraine,
Mannsville,
Millen's Bay,
Natural Bridge,
North Wilna,
Omar,
Orleans Four Corners,
Oxbow,
Pamelia Four Corners,
Perch River,
Philadelphia,
Pierrepont Manor,
Pillar Point,
Plessis,
Point Peninsula,
Redwood,
Rodman,
Rural Hill,
Rutland,
Sacket's Harbor,*
Saint Lawrence,
Sanford's Corners,
Smithville,
South Champion,
South Rutland,
Sterlingville,
Stone Mills,
Stowell's Corners,
Theresa,
Three Mile Bay,
Watertown,* (c. h.,)
Wilna,
Woodville,
Worth Centre,
Worthville.

KINGS COUNTY.

Bay Ridge,
Brooklyn,* (c. h.,)
Canarsie,
East New York,
Flatbush,
Flatlands,
Fort Hamilton,*
Gravesend,
Green Point,*
New Utrecht,
Parkville,
Williamsburgh.*

LEWIS COUNTY.

Barnes' Corners,
Beaver Falls,
Brantingham,
Collinsville,
Constableville,
Copenhagen,
Croghan,
Deer River,
Denmark,
Diana,
Glensdale,
Greig,
Harrisburgh,
Harrisville,
Houseville,
Indian River,
Leyden,
Locust Grove,
Lowville, (c. h.,)
Lyonsdale,
Lyons' Falls,
Martinsburgh,
Mohawk Hill,
Montague,
Naumburgh,
New Bremen,
Osceola,
Pinckney,
Port Leyden,
Sterling Bush,
Turin,*
Watson,
West Leyden,
West Lowville,
West Martinsburgh.

LIVINGSTON COUNTY.

Avon,
Brooks' Grove,
Byersville,
Caledonia,
Conesus,
Conesus Centre,
Cuylerville,
Dansville,*
East Avon,
East Groveland,
Fowlerville,
Geneseo,* (c. h.,)
Greigsville,
Groveland,
Hemlock Lake,
Hunt's Hollow,
Lakeville,
Lima,

* Money-order office.

LIVINGSTON COUNTY—Continued.

Livonia,
Livonia Station,
Moscow,
Mount Morris,*
North Sparta,
Nunda,*
Nunda Station,
Oakland,
Ossian,
Piffard,

Ridge,
Scottsburgh,
South Avon,
South Lima,
South Livonia,
Springwater,
Tuscarora,
Union Corners,
Webster's Crossing,
York.

MADISON COUNTY.

Bennet's Corners,
Bouckville,
Bridgeport,
Brookfield,
Canastota,
Cazenovia,*
Chittenango,
Chittenango Falls,
Chittenango Station,
Clockville,
De Ruyter,
Earlville,
East Boston,
East Hamilton,
Eaton,
Erieville,
Fenner,
Georgetown,
Hamilton,*
Hubbardsville,
Lakeport,
Lebanon,
Lenox,
Leonardsville,
Madison,

Mile Strip,
Morrisville, (c. h.,)
Munsville,
Nelson,
New Woodstock,
North Brookfield,
Oneida,*
Oneida Lake,
Oneida Valley,
Perryville,
Peterborough,
Pine Woods,
Poolville,
Pratt's Hollow,
Randallsville,
Shed's Corners,
Siloam,
Solsville,
South Brookfield,
South Hamilton,
Stockbridge,
Valley Mills,
Wampsville,
West Eaton.

MONROE COUNTY.

Adams' Basin,
Brighton,
Brockport,*
Bushnell's Basin,
Charlotte,
Chili,
Churchville,
Clarkson,
Clifton,
Cold Water,
East Clarkson,
East Penfield,
Egypt,
Fairport,
Gates,
Greece,
Hamlin,
Hanford's Landing,
Henrietta,
Honeoye Falls,
Mendon,
Mendon Centre,
Mount Read,
Mumford,

North Chili,
North Clarkson,
North Greece,
North Hamlin,
North Parma,
North Rush,
Ogden,
Parma,
Parma Centre,
Penfield,
Pittsford,
Riga,
Rochester, (c. h.,)*
Rush,
Scottsville,
South Greece,
Spencerport,
Sweden,
Webster,
West Brighton,
West Greece,
West Henrietta,
West Rush,
West Webster.

MONTGOMERY COUNTY.

Ames,
Amsterdam,*
Auriesville,
Buel,
Burtonsville,
Canajoharie,
Charleston,
Charleston Four
  Corners,
Cranesville,
Flat Creek,
Fonda, (c. h.,)*
Fort Hunter
Fort Plain,*
Frey's Bush,
Fultonville,

Glen,
Hagaman's Mills,
Hallsville,
Marshville,
Minaville,
Minden,
Palatine Bridge,
Port Jackson,
Randall,
Root,
Saint Johnsville,
Scotch Bush,
Spraker's Basin,
Sprout Brook,
Stone Arabia,
Tribes Hill.

NEW YORK COUNTY.

New York, (c. h.)*

NIAGARA COUNTY.

Beach Ridge,
Bergholtz,
Cambria,
Coomer,
County Line,
Dickersonville,
East Porter,
East Wilson,
Gasport,
Hartland,
Hess Road,
Hickory Corners,
Johnson's Creek,
Lake Road,
La Salle,
Lewiston,
Lockport, (c. h.,)*
Maple Street,
Martinsville,
Middleport,
Newfane,
Niagara Falls,*
North Hartland,

North Ridge,
Olcott,
Orangeport,
Pekin,
Pendleton,
Pendleton Centre,
Ransomville,
Rapids,
Reynale's Basin,
Ridge Road,
Royalton,
Saint Johnsburgh,
Sanborn,
Shawnee,
Somerset,
South Wilson,
Suspension Bridge,*
Warren's Corners,
West Somerset,
Wilson,
Wolcottsville,
Wright's Corners,
Youngstown.

ONEIDA COUNTY.

Alder Creek,
Augusta,
Ava,
Babcock Hill,
Big Brook,
Blossvale,
Boonville,*
Bridgewater,
Camden,
Cassville,
Chadwick's Mills,
Clark's Mills,
Clayville,
Clinton,
Deansville,
Deerfield,

Delta,
Durhamville,
East Florence,
Fish Creek,
Florence,
Floyd,
Forest Port,
Franklin Iron Works,
Glenmore,
Hawkinsville,
Hecla Works,
Higginsville,
Holland Patent,
Kirkland,
Knoxborough,
Lairdsville,

* Money-order office.

ONEIDA COUNTY—Continued.

Lee,
Lee Centre,
Lowell,
McConnellsville,
Marcy,
Marshall,
New Hartford,
New London,
New York Mills,
North Bay,
North Bridgewater,
North Gage,
North Western,
Oneida Castle,
Oriskany,
Oriskany Falls,
Paris,
Prospect,
Remsen,
Ridge Mills,
Rome, (c. h.,)
Sangerfield,
Sauquoit,

South Trenton,
Stanwix,
State Bridge,
Steuben,
Stittville,
Stokes,
Taberg,
Trenton,
Trenton Falls,
Utica, (c. h.,)
Vernon,
Vernon Centre,
Verona,
Vienna,
Walesville,
Washington Mills,
Waterville,
West Branch,
West Camden,
Westernville,
Westmoreland,
West Vienna,
Whitestown.

ONONDAGA COUNTY.

Amber,
Apulia,
Baldwinsville,
Belle Isle,
Borodino,
Brewerton,
Camillus,
Cardiff,
Cicero,
Clay,
Collamer,
Collingwood,
Delphi,
De Witt,
Elbridge,
Euclid,
Fabius,
Fair Mount,
Fayetteville,
Geddes,
Half Way,
Hart Lot,
Howlet Hill,
Jack's Reef,
Jamesville.
Jordan,
Kirkville,
La Fayette,
Lamson's,
Little Utica,
Liverpool,
Lysander,
Mandana,

Manlius,
Manlius Centre,
Manlius Station,
Marcellus,
Marcellus Falls,
Marietta,
Memphis,
Mottville,
Navarino,
North Manlius,
Onondaga,
Onondaga Castle,
Onondaga Valley,
Oran,
Otisco,
Otisco Valley,
Plainville,
Plank Road,
Pompey,
Pompey Centre,
Salina,
Skaneateles,*
South Onondaga,
Spafford,
Summit Station,
Syracuse, (c. h.,)
Thorn Hill,
Tully,*
Tully Valley,
Van Buren,
Vesper,
Warner's,
Watervale.

ONTARIO COUNTY.

Academy,
Allen's Hill.
Bristol,

Bristol Centre,
Canadice,
Canandaigua, (c. h.,)

ONTARIO COUNTY—Continued.

Chapinville,
Cheshire,
Clifton Springs,*
East Bloomfield,
Farmington,
Fishers,
Flint Creek,
Geneva,*
Gorham,
Gypsum,
Hall's Corners,
Honeoye,
Hopewell,
Hopewell Centre,
Manchester,
Manchester Centre,

Miller's Corners,
Naples,
North Bloomfield,
Oak's Corners,
Orleans,
Phelps,
Port Gibson,
Reed's Corners,
Richmond Mills,
Seneca Castle,
Shortsville,*
South Bristol,
Stanley Corners,
Victor,*
West Bloomfield,
West Farmington.

ORANGE COUNTY.

Allard's Corners,
Amity,
Bellvale,
Blooming Grove,
Bullville,
Burnside,
Campbell Hall,
Chester,
Circleville,
Coldenham,
Cornwall,
Cornwall Landing,
Craigsville,
Cuddebackville,
Edenville,
Florida,
Fort Montgomery,
Goshen, (c. h.,)
Greenwood Iron
    Works,
Guymard,
Highland Falls,
Highland Mills,
Howell's Depot,
Huguenot,
Johnson's,
Middle Hope,
Middletown,*
Minisink,
Monroe,
Monroe Works,

Montgomery,
Moodna,
Mount Hope,
Newburgh, (c. h.,)
New Hampton,
New Milford,
Orange Lake,
Otisville,
Oxford Depot,
Pine Bush,
Pine Island,
Port Jervis,*
Ridgebury,
Saint Andrew's,
Salisbury Mills,
Savill,
Scotchtown,
Searsville,
Slate Hill,
Sparrow Bush,
Sugar Loaf,
Turner's,
Unionville,
Vail's Gate,
Walden,
Warwick,
Waterloo Mills,
Wells' Corner,
West Point,*
West Town,
Wood.

ORLEANS COUNTY.

Albion, (c. h.,)
Barre Centre,
Carlton,
Clarendon,
Eagle Harbor,
East Carlton,
East Gaines,
East Kendall,
East Shelby,
Gaines,
Hindsburgh,
Holley,

Hulburton,
Jeddo,
Kendall,
Kendall Mills,
Kenyonville,
Knowlesville,
Kuckville,
Lyndonville,
Medina,*.
Millville,
Murray,
North Ridgeway,

* Money-order office.

ORLEANS COUNTY—Continued.

Oak Orchard,
Ridgeway,
Shelby,
Shelby Basin,
South Barre,

Waterport,
West Barre,
West Kendall,
West Shelby,
Yates.

OSWEGO COUNTY.

Amboy Centre,
Bernhard's Bay,
Bowen's Corners,
Boylston Centre,
Butterfly,
Caughdenoy,
Central Square,
Cleaveland,
Colosse,
Constantia,
Constantia Centre,
Daysville,
Dugway,
East Boylston,
East Palermo,
East Sandy Creek,*
Fair Dale,
Fulton,*
Gilbert's Mills,
Granby Centre,
Hannibal,
Hannibal Centre,
Hastings,
Hastings Centre,
Hinmansville,
Ingalls' Crossing,
Kasoag,
Kinney's Four C'rs,
Mallory,
Maple Hill,
Mexico,
Minetto,
Molino,
New Centreville,

New Haven,
North Hannibal,
North Scriba,
North Volney,
Orwell,
Oswego,* (c. h.,)
Oswego Centre,
Oswego Falls,
Palermo,
Parish,
Pennellville,
Phœnix,
Port Ontario,
Pulaski,* (c. h.,)
Redfield,
Richland,
Salmon River,
Sand Bank,
Sandy Creek,
Scriba,
South Albion,
South Granby,
South Hannibal,
South Richland,
South Scriba,
South West Oswego,
Texas,
Union Square,
Vermillion,
Volney,
West Amboy,
West Monroe,
Williamstown.

OTSEGO COUNTY.

Burlington,
Burlington Flats,
Butternuts,
Centre Valley,
Chaseville,
Cherry Valley,
Colliersville,
Cooperstown,* (c. h.,)
Decatur,
East Springfield,
East Worcester,
Edmeston,
Elk Creek,
Exeter,
Fly Creek,
Garrattsville,
Hartwick,
Hartwick Seminary,
Laurens,
Maple Grove,

Maryland,
Middlefield,
Middlefield Centre,
Milford,
Morris,
Mount Vision,
New Lisbon,
Oaksville,
Onconta,
Otego,
Otsdawa,
Phœnix Mills,
Pittsfield,
Pleasant Brook,
Portlandville,
Richfield,
Richfield Springs,
Roseboom,
Schenevus,
Schuyler's Lake,

OTSEGO COUNTY—Continued.

South Edmeston,
South Hartwick,
South Valley,
South Worcester,
Spooner's Corners,
Springfield,
Springfield Centre,
Toddsville,
Unadilla,
Unadilla Centre,

Unadilla Forks,
Wells' Bridge,
West Burlington,
West Edmeston,
West Exeter,
Westford,
West Laurens,
West Oneonta,
Westville,
Worcester.

PUTNAM COUNTY.

Boyd's Corner,
Brewster's Station,
Carmel,* (c. h.,)
Cold Spring,*
Dykeman's,
Farmer's Mills,
Garrison's,

Haviland Hollow,
Kent,
Ludingtonville,
Mahopac,
Mahopac Falls,
Patterson,
Towner's.

QUEENS COUNTY.

Astoria,
Bay Side,
Central Park,
Clarenceville,
College Point,
East Norwich,
East Rockaway,
Farmingdale,
Flushing,*
Freeport,
Glen Cove,
Great Neck,
Greenvale,
Hempstead,*
Hicksville,
Jamaica,* (c. h.,)
Jericho,
Little Neck,
Locust Valley,
Long Island City,
Manhasset,
Maspeth,

Merrick,
Mineola,
Newtown,
Old Westbury,
Oyster Bay,
Port Washington,
Queens,
Ravenswood,
Ridgewood,
Rockaway,
Rockville Centre,
Roslyn,
Seaford,
Smithville South,
Springfield Store,
Syosset,
Valley Stream,
Whitestone,
Woodbury,
Woodhaven,
Woodside.

RENSSELAER COUNTY.

Alps,
Berlin,
Brainerd,
Castleton,
Centre Berlin,
Centre Brunswick,
Cropseyville,
Defreestville,
Eagle Bridge,
Eagle Mills,
East Greenbush,
East Nassau,
East Poestenkill,
East Schodack,
Grafton,
Harts Falls,
Haynerville,

Hoag's Corner,
Hoosick,
Hoosick Falls,*
Johnsonville,
Junction,
Lansingburgh,*
Nassau,
North Hoosick,
North Nassau,
North Petersburgh,
North Stephentown,
Petersburgh,
Pittstown,
Poestenkill,
Potter Hill,
Quacken Kill,
Raymertown,

RENSSELAER COUNTY—Continued.

Sand Lake,
Schodack Centre,
Schodack Depot,
Schodack Landing,
South Berlin,
South Sand Lake,
South Schodack,
Stephentown,

Tomhannock,
Troy, (c. h.,)
Valley Falls,
West Hoosick,
West Sand Lake,
West Stephentown,
Wynantskill.

RICHMOND COUNTY.

Mariner's Harbor,
Marshland,
New Brighton,
New Dorp,
New Springville,
Port Richmond,
Prince's Bay,

Richmond, (c. h.,)
Rossville,
South Side,
Stapleton,*
Tompkinsville,
Tottenville,
West New Brighton.

ROCKLAND COUNTY.

Blanveltville,
Clarkstown, (c. h.,)
Haverstraw,
Iona Island,
Monsey,
Nannet,
Nyack,*
Nyack Turnpike,
Palisades,
Piermont,

Ramapo Works,
Rockland Lake,
Sloatsburgh,
Spring Valley,
Stony Point,
Suffern,
Tallman,
Tappantown,
Tomkin's Cove.

ST. LAWRENCE COUNTY.

Brasher Falls,
Brasher Iron Works,
Brier Hill,
Canton, (c. h.,)
Chase's Mills,
Clarksborough,
Colton,
Crary's Mills,
DeKalb,
De Kalb Junction,
De Peyster,
East De Kalb,
East Pitcairn,
Edenton,
Edwards,
Edwardsville,
Ellsworth,
Fine,
Flackville,
Fowler,
Fullerville   Iron
Works.
Gouverneur,*
Hailesborough,
Hammond,
Helena,
Hermon,*
Heuvelton,
Hopkinton,
Lawrenceville,
Lisbon,

Lisbon Centre,
Louisville,
Louisville Landing,
Macomb,
Madrid,*
Madrid Springs,
Massena,*
Massena Centre,
Morley,
Morristown,
Nicholville,
Norfolk,
North Hammond,
North Lawrence,
North Russell,
North Stockholm,
Ogdensburgh,*
Parishville,
Parishville Centre,
Pierrepont,
Pitcairn,
Pope's Mills,
Potsdam,*
Potsdam Junction,
Raymondville,
Rensselaer Falls,
Richville,
Rossie,
Russell,
Shingle Creek,
Somerville,

ST. LAWRENCE COUNTY—Continued.

South Colton,
South Edwards,
Southville,
Stockholm,
Stockholm Depot,

Waddington,
Wegatchie,
West Potsdam,
West Stockholm.

SARATOGA COUNTY.

Bacon Hill,
Ballston, (c. h.,)
Ballston Centre,
Barkersville,
Batchellerville,
Bemus' Heights,
Burnt Hills,
Charlton,
Clifton Park,
Conklingville,
Corinth,
Coveville,
Crescent,
Day,
Deans' Corners,
East Galway,
East Line,
Edinburgh,
Fortsville,
Galway,
Gansevoort,
Greenfield Centre,
Groom's Corners,
Hadley,
Hagedorn's Mills,
Half Moon,
Jonesville,
Ketchum's Corners,
Malta.
Maltaville,

Mechanicsville,
Middle Grove,
Milton Centre,
Moreau Station,
Mosherville,
North Galway,
North Greenfield,
Northumberland,
Porter's Corners,
Providence,
Quaker Springs,
Rexford Flats,
Rock City Falls,
Saratoga Springs,*
Schuylersville,
South Ballston,
South Corinth,
South Galway,
South Glens Falls,
South Wilton,
Stillwater,
Victory Mills,
Vischer's Ferry,
Waterford,
West Charlton,
West Day,
West Greenfield,
West Milton,
West Providence,
Wilton.

SCHENECTADY COUNTY.

Braman's Corners,
Duanesburgh,
East Glenville,
Glenville,
Hoffman's Ferry,
Mariaville,

Niskayuna,
Quaker Street,
Rynex's Corners,
Schenectady, (c. h.,)
Scotia,
Van Vechten.

SCHOHARIE COUNTY.

Argusville,
Barnerville,
Breakabeen,
Broome Centre,
Carlisle,
Central Bridge,
Charlotteville,
Cobleskill,
Conesville,
East Cobleskill,
Eminence,
Esperance,
Franklinton,
Fultonham,
Gallupville,

Gilboa,
Grovenor's Corners
Howe's Cave,
Hunter's Land,
Hyndsville,
Jefferson,
Lawyersville,
Leesville,
Livingstonville,
Manor Kill,
Middleburgh,*
Mine Kill Falls,
Mineral Springs,
Morseville,
North Blenheim,

* Money-order office.

SCHOHARIE COUNTY—Continued.

Richmondville,
Schoharie,* (c. h.,)
Seward,
Sharon,
Sharon Centre,
Sharon Springs,
Shutter's Corners,
Sloansville,

South Gilboa,
South Jefferson,
Summit,
Warnerville,
West Conesville,
West Fulton,
West Richmondville.

SCHUYLER COUNTY.

Alpine,
Altay,
Beaver Dams,
Bennettsburgh,
Burdett,
Catharine,
Cayuta,
Cayutaville,
East Orange,
Havana,*
Hector,
Lawrence,
Logan,
Mecklenburgh,
Moreland,
North Hector,
North Reading,

Odessa,
Orange,
Perry City,
Pine Creek,
Pine Grove,
Reading,
Reading Centre,
Reynoldsville,
Searsburgh,
Seneca,
Smith Valley,
Sugar Hill,
Townsend,
Tyrone,
Watkins, (c. h.,)
Weston.

SENECA COUNTY.

Canoga,
Covert,
Cruso,
East Varick,
Farmer Village,
Fayette,
Junius,
Kendaia,
Kidder's Ferry,
Lodi,
Lodi Centre,
Magee's Corners,

Ovid, (c. h.,)
Romulus,
Romulus Centre,
Rose Hill,
Seneca Falls,*
Sheldrake,
Trumansburgh L'd'g,
Tyre,
Varick,
Waterloo, (c. h.,)
West Fayette,
West Junius.

STEUBEN COUNTY.

Addison,
Addison Hill,
Adrian,
Allen's Station,
Arkport,
Avoca,
Bath,* (c. h.,)
Bennett's Creek,
Big Creek,
Bradford,
Buena Vista,
Cameron,
Cameron Mills,
Campbelltown,
Canisteo,
Caton,
Centre Canisteo,
Cohocton,
Cooper's Plains,

Corning,*
Doty's Corner,
East Troupsburgh,
East Woodhull,
Erwin Centre,
Gibson,
Goff's Mills,
Greenwood,
Hammondsport,
Haskinville,
Hedgesville,
Hornby,
Hornellsville,*
Howard,
Jasper,
Kanona,
Lindleytown,
Mead's Creek,
Merchantville,

STEUBEN COUNTY—Continued.

Mitchellsville,
Neil's Creek,
North Cameron,
North Cohocton,
North Jasper,
North Urbana,
Painted Post,
Perkinsville,*
Prattsburgh,*
Pultney,
Purdy Creek,
Rathboneville,
Rexville,
Riker's Hollow,
Risingville,
Savona,
Sonora,
South Addison,
South Bradford,
South Cameron,
South Dansville,

South Howard,
South Pultney,
South Troupsburgh,
Stephens' Mills,
Swale,
Thurston,
Towlesville,
Troupsburgh,
Wallace,
Wayland Depot,
Wayne,
Wayne Four Corners,
West Addison,
West Jasper,
West Troupsburgh,
West Union,
Wheeler,
Wileysville,
Woodhull,
Young Hickory.

SUFFOLK COUNTY.

Amagansett,
Amityville,
Atlanticville,
Babylon,
Baiting Hollow,
Bay Shore,
Bellport,
Blue Point,
Brentwood,
Bridgehampton,
Calverton,
Centre Moriches,
Centreport,
Cold Spring Harbor,
Commack,
Coram,
Cutchogue,
Deer Park,
Dix Hills,
East Hampton,
East Marion,
East Moriches,
East Setauket,
Elwood,
Fire Island,
Fireplace,
Flanders,
Fresh Pond,
Good Ground,
Greenport,*
Hauppange,
Holbrook,
Holtsville,
Huntington,*
Islip,
Jamesport,
Lake Grove,

Manorville,
Mattituck,
Middle Island,
Miller's Place,
Moriches,
Mount Sinai,
Northport,
Oakdale Station,
Orient,
Patchogue,*
Peconic,
Port Jefferson,*
Quogue,
Riverhead,* (c. h.,)
Ronkonkoma,
Sag Harbor,*
Saint James,
Sayville,
Selden,
Setauket,
Shelter Island,
Smithtown,
Smithtown Branch,
Southampton,
South Haven,
Southold,
Speonk,
Springs,
Stoney Brook,
Success,
Suffolk,
Upper Aquebogue,
Wading River,
Water Mill,
West Hampton,
Yaphank.

SULLIVAN COUNTY.

Barryville,
Beaver Brook,

Beaver Kill,
Beech Wood,

* Money-order office.

SULLIVAN COUNTY—Continued.

Bethel,
Bloomingburgh,
Bridgeville,
Briscoe,
Burlingham,
Bushville,
Callicoon,
Callicoon Depot,
Claryville,
Cochecton,
Cochecton Centre,
De Bruce,
Eureka,
Fallsburgh,
Fall's Mill,
Forestburgh,
Fosterdale,
Fremont Centre,
Gales,
Glen Wild,
Grahamsville,
Hankins,
Hasbrouck,
Jeffersonville,
Liberty,
Liberty Falls,

Loch Sheldrake,
Long Eddy,
Lumberland,
Mongaup,
Mongaup Valley,
Monticello,* (c. h.,)
Morsston,
Narrowsburgh,
Neversink,
North Branch,
Parksville,
Phillipsport,
Pike Pond,
Pond Eddy,
Purvis,
Red Brick,
Robertsonville,
Rockland,
Shin Creek,
Stevensville,
Thompsonville,
West Brookville,
White Lake,
Woodbourne,
Wurtsborough,
Youngsville.

TIOGA COUNTY.

Apalachin,
Barton,
Berkshire,
Bingham's Mills,
Campville,
Candor,
Catatonk,
East Berkshire,
East Nichols,
Factoryville,
Flemingsville,
Gaskill's Corners,
Halsey Valley,
Hooper's Valley,
Jenksville,
Ketchumville,
Newark Valley,

Nichols,
North Barton,
Owego,* (c. h.,)
Richford,
Smithsborough,
South Owego,
Spencer,
Spencer Springs,
Strait's Corners,
Tioga Centre,
Waverly,*
Weltonville,
West Candor,
West Newark,
Willseyville,
Wilson Creek.

TOMPKINS COUNTY.

Caroline,
Caroline Centre,
Caroline Depot,
Danby,
Dryden,
East Lansing,
Enfield,
Enfield Centre,
Etna,
Freeville,
Groton,
Groton City,
Ithaca,* (c. h.,)
Jacksonville,
Lake Ridge,
Lansingville,
Ludlowville,

McLean,
Mott's Corners,
Newfield,
North Lansing,
Peruville,
Poney Hollow,
Slaterville,
South Danby,
South Lansing,
Speedsville,
Trumansburgh,
Trumbull Corners,
Varna,
Waterburgh,
West Danby,
West Dryden,
West Groton.

ULSTER COUNTY.

Accord,
Bearsville,
Bruynswick,
Clintondale,
Creek Locks,
Dairyland,
Denning,
Dry Brook,
Dwaar's Kill,
Ellenville,*
Esopus,
Fly Mountain,
Galeville Mills,
Glasco,
Greenfield,
Hardenburgh,
High Falls,
Highland,
Homowack,
Hurley,
Kerhonkson,
Kingston,* (c. h.,)
Kyserike,
Lackawack,
Lake Hill,
Le Fever Falls,
Libertyville,
Loyd,
Malden,
Marbletown,
Marlborough,
Milton,
Modena,

Napanock,
New Hurley,
New Paltz,
Ohioville,
Olive,
Olive Bridge,
Phœnicia,
Pine Hill,
Plattekill,
Port Ewen,
Quarryville,
Rifton Glen,
Rondout,*
Rosendale,
Samsonville,
Saugerties,
Shandaken,
Shawangunk,
Shokan,
Stone Ridge,
The Corner,
Turnwood,
Tuthill,
Ulster Park,
Ulsterville,
Walker Valley,
Wawarsing,
West Camp,
West Hurley,
Wilbur,
Woodland,
Woodstock.

WARREN COUNTY.

Athol,
Bolton,
Caldwell, (c. h.,)
Chestertown,
Creek Centre,
French Mountain,
Glens Falls,*
Hague,
Horicon,
Johnsburgh,

Luzerne,
North Creek,
North River,
Pottersville,
Queensbury,
The Glen,
Thurman,
Warrensburgh,*
Wevertown.

WASHINGTON COUNTY.

Adamsville,
Argyle,
Battenville,
Belcher,
Buskirk's Bridge,
Cambridge,*
Centre Cambridge,
Centre White Creek,
Coila,
Comstock's Landing,
Crandell's Corners,
East Greenwich,
Easton,
East Salem,
Fort Ann,
Fort Edward,*

Fort Miller,
Galesville,
Granville,
Greenwich,
Griswold's Mills,
Hampton,
Hartford,
Hebron,
Kingsbury,
Lake,
Low Hampton,
Middle Granville,
North Argyle,
North Easton,
North Granville,
North Greenwich,

* Money-order office.

WASHINGTON COUNTY—Continued.

North Hebron,
Patten's Mills,
Putnam,
Salem, (c. h.,)
Sandy Hill,* (c. h.,)
Shushan,
Smith's Basin,
South Argyle,
South Easton,
South Granville,
South Hartford,
West Fort Ann,
West Granville Corners,
West Hebron,
White Creek,
Whitehall.*

WAYNE COUNTY.

Alton,
Arcadia,
Clyde,
East Palmyra,
Fairville,
Hall Centre,
Huron,
Joy,
Lake Side,
Lincoln,
Lock Berlin,
Lummisville,
Lyons,* (c. h.,)
Macedon,
Macedon Centre,
Marengo,
Marion,
Newark,*
North Huron,
North Rose,
Ontario,
Ontario Centre,
Palmyra,
Pultneyville,
Red Creek,
Rose,
Savannah,
Sodus,
Sodus Centre,
Sodus Point,
South Butler,
South Sodus,
Walworth,
Wayne Centre,
West Butler,
West Macedon,*
West Walworth,
Williamson,
Wolcott.*

WESTCHESTER COUNTY.

Armonk,
Bedford, (c. h.,)
Bedford Station,
Boscobel,
Boutonville,
Bronxville,
Chappaqua,
City Island,
Cross' River,
Croton Falls,
Croton Landing,
Dobb's Ferry,
East Chester,
Elmsford,
Fordham,
Golden's Bridge,
Hallock's Mills,
Harrison,
Hart's Corners,
Hastings upon Hudson,
Irvington,
Jefferson Valley,
Jerome,
Katonah,
Kensico,
Kingsbridgeville,
Lewisborough,
Mamaroneck,
Montrose,
Morrisania,
Mott Haven,
Mount Kisco,
Mount Vernon,
Neperan,
New Castle,

WESTCHESTER COUNTY—Continued.

New Rochelle,
North Castle,
North Salem,
Peekskill, *
Pelham,
Pine's Bridge,
Pleasantville,
Port Chester, *
Poundridge,
Purdy's Station,
Riverdale,
Rye,
Salem Centre,
Scarborough,
Scarsdale,
Shrub Oak,
Sing Sing,*
Somers,
South Salem,
Spuyten Duyvil,
Tarrytown,*
Tremont,
Tuckahoe,
Valhalla,
Verplank,
Vista,
West Chester,
West Farms,
West Somers,
White Plains,* (c. h.,)
Wood Lawn,
Yonkers,*
Yorktown.

WYOMING COUNTY.

Arcade,*
Attica,
Bennington,
Castile,
Covington,
Cowlesville,
Dale,
Eagle,
Eagle Village,
East Arcade,
East Gainesville,
East Java,
East Orangeville,
East Pike,
Folsomdale,
Gainesville,
Hermitage,
Java,
Java Village,
Johnsonsburgh,
La Grange,
North Java,
North Sheldon,
North Wethersfield,
Orangeville,
Pearl Creek,
Peoria,
Perry,
Perry Centre,
Pike,*
Portageville,
Sheldon,
Strykersville,
Varysburgh,
Warsaw,* (c. h.,)
Wethersfield,
Wethersfield Spr'gs,
Wyoming.

YATES COUNTY.

Barrington,
Bellona,
Benton Centre,
Bluff Point,
Branchport,
Crystal Spring,
Dresden,
Dundee,
Eddytown,
Ferguson's Corners,
Glenora,
Himrod's,
Italy Hill,
Italy Hollow,
Middlesex,
Milo Centre,
Penn Yan,* (c. h.,)
Potter,
Rock Stream,
Rushville,
Starkey,
Vine Valley,
Voak.

NORTH CAROLINA.

ALAMANCE COUNTY.

Big Falls,
Clover Orchard,
Company's Shops,
Curtis' Mills,
McCray's Store,
Mebanesville,
Patterson's Store,
Pleasant Grove,

ALAMANCE COUNTY—Continued.

Graham, (c. h.,)
Hartshorn,
Haw River,
Rock Creek,
Saxapahaw,
Snow Camp.

* Money-order office.

ALEXANDER COUNTY.

Stony Point,   York Collegiate In-
Taylorville, (c. h.,)   stitute.
Wittenberg,

ALLEGHANY COUNTY.

Cherry Lane,   New River,
Gap Civil, (c. h.,)   Piney Creek.

ANSON COUNTY.

Ansonville,   Lanesborough,
Candle Mills,   Lilesville,
Cedar Hill,   Long Pine,
Deep Creek,   Morven,
Diamond Hill,   New Forestville,
Dumas Ferry,   Poplar Hill,
Flat Fork,   *Wadesborough*, (c. h.,)
Kendall,   White's Store.

ASHE COUNTY.

Elk Cross Roads,   *Jefferson*, (c. h.,)
Gap Creek,   Laurel Springs,
Glade Creek,   North Fork,
Helton,   Scottville,
Horse Creek,   Walnut Hill.

BEAUFORT COUNTY.

Bath,   Pantego,
Hunter's Bridge,   South Creek,
Leechville,   *Washington,** (c. h.)

BERTIE COUNTY.

Colerain,   Roxobel,
Hotel,   *Windsor*, (c. h.)

BLADEN COUNTY.

Abbottsburgh,   Loveland,
Bladenborough,   Martsville,
Dalton,   Prospect Hall,
Daniel's Landing,   Rosindale,
Elizabethtown, (c. h.,) West Brook,
French Creek Church, Whitehall,
Harrison's Creek,   Yorkville.
Little Sugar Loaf,

BRUNSWICK COUNTY.

Bernard,   Robeson,
Bolton,   *Smithville*, (c. h.)

BUNCOMBE COUNTY.

*Asheville,** (c. h.,)   Reem's Creek,
Avery's Creek,   Riverside,
Democrat,   Sandy Mush,
Fairview,   Stocksville,
Gray Eagle,   Swannano,
Hominy Creek,   Turnpike,
Leicester,   Walnut Creek.

BURKE COUNTY.

Bridgewater,   Jonas Ridge,
Brindletown,   *Morganton,** (c. h.,)
Fonta Flora,   Perkinsville,
Happy Home,   Piedmont Springs.

CABARRUS COUNTY.

Coddle Creek,   North Barrier,
*Concord,** (c. h.,)   Pioneer Mills,
Harris Depot,   Smith's Ford,
Mill Hill,   Tulin.
Mount Pleasant,

CALDWELL COUNTY.

Collettsville,   Lovelady,
Copenhagen,   Patterson,
Globe,   Tuttle's X Roads.
Lenoir, (c. h.,)

CAMDEN COUNTY.

Camden C. H.,   South Mills.
Shiloh,

CARTERET COUNTY.

Beaufort, (c. h.,)   Peletier's Mills,
Morehead City,   Portsmouth,
Newport,   Sanders' Store.

CASWELL COUNTY.

Anderson's Store,   Pea Ridge,
Independence,   Pelham,
Leasburgh,   Prospect Hill,
Locust Hill,   Purley,
Milton,   *Yanceyville*, (c. h.)

CATAWBA COUNTY.

Catawba Station,   Mountain Creek,
Chronicle,   Mull Grove,
Dry Ponds,   *Newton*, (c. h.,)
Hickory Tavern,   Sherrill's Ford.
Jacob's Fork,

CHATHAM COUNTY.

Bellevoir,   Mud Lick,
Cane Creek,   *Pittsborough,** (c. h.,)
Egypt Depot,   Rialto,
Grove,   Riggsbee's Store,
Hadley's Mills,   Saint Lawrence,
Haywood,   Sandy Grove,
Lockville,   Snipe's Store.
Merry Oaks,

CHEROKEE COUNTY.

Murphey, (c. h.,)   Wolf Creek.
Valley Town,

CHOWAN COUNTY.

*Edenton,** (c. h.,)   Wardville.

* **Money-order office.**

CLAY COUNTY.

Hayesville, (c. h.,)   Tusquitee.

CLEVELAND COUNTY.

Buffalo Paper Mill,   Muddy Fork,
Camp Call,   Nicholsonville,
Double Shoal,   *Shelby,* (c. h.,)
Erwinsville,   Stice's Shoal,
Gardner's Ford,   Swangstown,
Knob Creek,   White Plains.
Mooresborough,

COLUMBUS COUNTY.

Bogue,   Grist's Station,
Cerro Gordo,   Peacock's Store,
Fair Bluff,   Pireway Ferry,
Flemington,   *Whitesville,* (c. h.)

CRAVEN COUNTY.

Bay River,   *New Berne,** (c. h.,)
Dover,   Pamlico,
Grantsborough,   Swift Creek Bridge.

CUMBERLAND COUNTY.

Cedar Creek,   Gray's Creek,
*Fayetteville,** (c. h.,) Inverness,
Gibbs' Cross Roads,   Roslin.

CURRITUCK COUNTY.

Coinjock,   Poplar Branch,
Currituck C. H.,   Powell's Point.
Indian Ridge,

DARE COUNTY.

Manteo, (c. h.)

DAVIDSON COUNTY.

Abbott's Creek,   Midway,
Arcadia,   Miller's Mill,
Cedar Bush,   Reedy Creek,
Fair Grove,   Spencer,
Hannersville,   Thomasville,
Lexington, (c. h.,) Yadkin College.
Linwood,

DAVIE COUNTY.

Calahaln,   Fulton,
County Line,   Jerusalem,
Elbaville,   *Mocksville,* (c. h.,)
Farmington,   Smith Grove.

DUPLIN COUNTY.

Alberton's,   Outlaw's Bridge,
Branch's Store,   Resaca,
Buena Vista,   Rock Fish,
Faison's Depot,   Teachey's,
Hallsville,   Wallace,
*Kenansville,** (c. h.,) Warsaw.
Magnolia,

EDGECOMBE COUNTY.

Battleborough,   Sparta,
Kingsborough,   *Tarborough,** (c. h.,)
Rocky Mount,   Whitaker's.

FORSYTH COUNTY.

Belew Creek Mills,   Old Town,
Bethania,   Salem,**
Flat Branches,   Salem Chapel,
Friedburgh,   Sedges Garden,
Kernersville,   Vienna,
Lewisville,   Walkerstown
Mount Tabor,   White Road.
Old Richmond,

FRANKLIN COUNTY.

Cedar Rock,   *Louisburgh,** (c. h.,)
Franklinton,   Pacific.

GASTON COUNTY.

Cherryville,   King's Mountain,
Craigsville,   Old Furnace,
Crowder's Mountain,   South Point,
Dallas, (c. h.,)   Stanley's Creek,
High Shoals,   Woodlawn.

GATES COUNTY.

Buckland,   Reynoldson,
Crossville,   Sunbury.
Gatesville, (c. h.,)

GRANVILLE COUNTY.

Blue Wing,   New Hope Mills,
Brookville,   Oak Hill,
Brownsville,   *Oxford,* (c. h.,)
Buchanan,   Sassafras Fork,
Dutchville,   Tally Ho,
Fairport,   Townesville,
Henderson,   Wilton,
Kittrell,   Young's × Roads.
Knap of Reeds,

GREENE COUNTY.

Carolina Seminary,   *Snow Hill,* (c. h.,)
Cotton Valley,   Speight's Bridge.
Hookerton,

GUILFORD COUNTY.

Allemance,   High Point,
Brick Church,   Hillsdale,
Centre,   Jamestown,
Colfax,   McLeansville,
Deep River,   Monticello,
Fentriss,   New Garden,
Friendship,   Shaw's Mills,
Gibsonville,   Westminster,
Gilmer's Store,   Young's Mills.
*Greensborough,**(c. h.,)

* Money-order office.

HALIFAX COUNTY.

Brinkleyville,　　　Ringwood,
Enfield,　　　　　　Scotland Neck,
Halifax, (c. h.,)　South Gaston,
Heathsville,　　　　Weldon.*
Littleton,

HARNETT COUNTY.

Averysborough,　　Norval,
Chalk Level,　　　Spout Springs,
Harnett C. H.,　　Summerville,
Harrington,

HAYWOOD COUNTY

Crab Tree,　　　　Pigeon River,
Forks of Pigeon,　Richland Valley,
Jonathan's Creek,　*Waynesville*, (c. h.)

HENDERSON COUNTY.

Bear Wallow,　　　Flat Rock,
Blue Ridge,　　　　Green River,
Boilston,　　　　　*Hendersonville*, (c. h.,)
Boman's Bluff,　　Mill River,
Edneyville,　　　　Shufordville.

HERTFORD COUNTY.

Harrellsville,　　　Saint John,
Murfreesborough,　*Winton*, (c. h.)
Riddicksville,

HYDE COUNTY.

Fairfield,　　　　　Ocracoke,
Lake Comfort,　　　Sladesville,
Lake Landing,　　　*Swan Quarter*, (c. h.)

IREDELL COUNTY.

Amity Hill,　　　　Oak Forest,
Cool Spring,　　　Olin,
Eagle Mills,　　　Snow Creek,
Elk Shoals,　　　 *Statesville*,* (c. h.,)
Enola,　　　　　　Sweet Home,
Fancy Hill,　　　　Turnersburgh,
Mount Mourne,　　Union Grove,
New Hope,　　　　Williamsburgh.
New Stirling,

JACKSON COUNTY.

Big Spring,　　　　Jackson Springs,
Caler's Hill,　　　Ocona Lufty,
Casher's Valley,　Quallatown,
East Laport,　　　*Webster*, (c. h.)

JOHNSTON COUNTY.

Beulah,　　　　　　Leechburgh,
Boon Hill,　　　　Pine Level,
Clayton,　　　　　Selma,
Earpsborough,　　*Smithfield*, (c. h.,)
Hinnant's Mills,　Wilson's Mills.

JONES COUNTY.

Pollocksville,　　　*Trenton*, (c. h.)

LENOIR COUNTY.

Falling Creek,　　　La Grange,
Kinston, (c. h.,)　Pink Hill.

LINCOLN COUNTY.

Beattie's Ford,　　Killian's Mills,
Castania Grove,　　*Lincolnton*, (c. h.,)
Cottage Home,　　North Brook,
Iron Station,　　　Siegle's Store.

McDOWELL COUNTY.

Dysortville,　　　　Old Fort,
Marion, (c. h.,)　Pleasant Retreat,
Nealsville,　　　　Sugar Hill.
North Cove,

MACON COUNTY.

Aquone,　　　　　Horse Cove,
Franklin, (c. h.,)　Wickle's Store.

MADISON COUNTY.

Bone Camp,　　　　Spring Creek,
Holly Grove,　　　Warm Springs.
Marshall, (c. h.,)

MARTIN COUNTY.

Hamilton,　　　　　Roanoke,
Jamesville,　　　　*Williamston*, (c. h.)

MECKLENBURGH COUNTY.

Charlotte,* (c. h.,)　Hopewell,
Clear Creek,　　　Martindale,
Cowan's Ford,　　Mint Hill,
Craighead,　　　　Pineville,
Davidson College,　Query's.
Fullwood's Store,

MITCHELL COUNTY.

Bakersville, (c. h.,)　Fork Mountain,
Childsville,　　　Ledger,
Cranberry Forge,　Red Hill.

MONTGOMERY COUNTY.

Auman's Hill,　　　Pine Grove,
Edinborough,　　　Sanders' Hill,
Hunsucker's Store,　Sulphur Springs,
Montgomery,　　　Swift Island,
Mount Gilead,　　*Troy*, (c. h.)
Pekin,

MOORE COUNTY.

Carter's Mills,　　Jonesborough,
Carthage, (c. h.,)　Mooshannee,
Clark's Mills,　　Morris Town,
Crain's Creek,　　Prosperity,
Curriersville,　　Swann's Station.
Glenaloon,

* Money-order office.

NASH COUNTY.

Castalia,
Hilliardston,
Nashville, (c. h.,)
Ransom's Bridge,
Stanhope.

NEW HANOVER COUNTY.

Black River Chapel,
Burgaw Depot,
Cameron,
Castle Hayne,
Harrell's Store,
Lillington,
Moore's Creek,
Oakley,
Rocky Point,
South Washington,
Topsail Sound,
Wilmington,[*] (c. h.)

NORTHAMPTON COUNTY.

Jackson, (c. h.,)
Margarettsville,
Pleasant Hill,
Potecasi,
Rich Square,
Seaboard,
Wheelersville,
Woodland.

ONSLOW COUNTY.

Catharine Lake,
Gum Branch,
Haw Branch,
Onslow C. H.,
Richlands,
Snead's Ferry,
Stone's Bay,
Swansborough.

ORANGE COUNTY.

Caldwell,
Cedar Grove,
Chapel Hill,[*]
Durham's,
Flat River,
Oaks.
Orange Factory,
Red Mountain,
Rock Spring,
Round Hill,
South Lowell,
Stagville.
Hillsborough,[*] (c. h.,)

PASQUOTANK COUNTY.

Elizabeth City,[*] (c. h.,) Rosedale.

PERQUIMONS COUNTY.

Belvidere,
Durant's Neck,
Hertford, (c. h.,)
Woodville.

PERSON COUNTY.

Allensville,
Bushy Fork,
Centre Grove,
Cunningham's Store,
Hester's Store,
Hurdles Mills,
Lea's Chapel,
Mount Tirzah,
Roxborough, (c. h.,)
Van Hook's Store,
Woodsdale.

PITT COUNTY.

Falkland,
Farmville,
Greenville, (c. h.,)
Johnson's Mills,
Marlborough,
Pactolus,
Ridge Spring,
Winona.

POLK COUNTY.

Columbus, (c. h.,) Tryon.

RANDOLPH COUNTY.

Ashborough, (c. h.,)
Brower's Mills,
Buffalo Ford,
Burney's Mills,
Bush Hill,
Eden,
Foust's Mills,
Franklinville,
Gladesborough,
Hill's Store,
Hoover Hill,
Jackson's Creek,
Lassiter's Mills,
Long's Mills,
Moffit's Mills,
New Hope Academy
New Market,
New Salem,
Reed Creek,
Salem Church,
Sandy Creek,
Sawyersville,
Science Hill,
Trinity College,[*]
Troy's Store,
White House.

RICHMOND COUNTY.

Bear Branch,
Bostick's Mills,
Capell's Mills,
Covington,
Laurel Hill,
Laurinburgh,
Little's Mills,
Mangum,
Powelton,
Powhatan,
Rockingham, (c. h.)

ROBESON COUNTY.

Antioch,
Dundarrach,
Leesville,
Lumberton, (c. h.,)
Melrose,
Plummerville,
Red Banks,
Saint Paul's,
Shoe Heel.

ROCKINGHAM COUNTY.

Aspin Grove,
Benaja,
Berry Hill,
Douglas,
Lawsonville,
Leaksville,
Lenox Castle,
Madison,
Monroeton,
Price's Store,
Reidsville,
Ruffin,
Stoneville,
Thompsonville,
Troublesome,
Wentworth, (c. h.)

ROWAN COUNTY.

China Grove,
Gold Hill,
Miranda,
Mount Ulla,
Rowan Mills,
Salisbury, (c. h.,)
Spring Grove.

RUTHERFORD COUNTY.

Brittain,
Burnt Chimney,
Chimney Rock,
Cooper's Gap,
Cuba,
Duncan's Creek,
First Broad,
Golden Valley,
Green Hill,
Logan's Store,
Oak Spring,
Otter Creek,
Patton's Home,
Rutherfordton, (c. h.,)
Webb's Ford.

SAMPSON COUNTY.

Blackman's Mills,
Clinton, (c. h.,)
Dismal,
Hawley's Store,
Monk's Store,
Newton Grove,
Owenville.

[*] Money-order office.

STANLY COUNTY.

Albemarle, (c. h.,)	Leo,
Big Lick,	Locust Level,
Efird's Mills,	Norwood.

STOKES COUNTY.

Ayersville,	Martin's Lime Kilns,
Blakely,	Peter's Creek,
Colesville,	Pilot Mountain,
Crooked Creek,	Red Shoals,
Danbury, (c. h.,)	Walnut Cove,
Francisco,	Westfield,
Germanton,	Wilson's Store.
Little Yadkin,	

SURREY COUNTY.

Dobson, (c. h.,)	Mount Airy,
Elkin.	Rockford,
Flat Shoal,	Rusk,
Haystack,	State Road,
Judesville,	Tom's Creek.

TRANSYLVANIA COUNTY.

Brevard, (c. h.,)	Cherryfield,
Calhoun,	Claytonville,
Cathey's Creek,	Davidson's River,
Cedar Mountain,	Dunn's Rock.

TYRREL COUNTY.

Columbia, (c. h.)

UNION COUNTY.

Beaver Dam,	Olive Branch,
Coburn's Store,	Walkersville,
Monroe, (c. h.,)	Winchester,
Morgan's Mills,	Wolfsville.
Oak Grove,	

WAKE COUNTY.

Auburn,	Hays' Store,
Brassfield,	Morrisville,
Cary,	New Hill,
Dayton,	New Light,
Eagle Rock,	RALEIGH,* (c. h.,)
Fish Dam,	Rolesville,
Forestville,	Wakefield.
Green Level,	

WARREN COUNTY.

Macon Depot,	Warren Plains,
Manson,	*Warrenton,** (c. h.)
Ridgeway,	

WASHINGTON COUNTY.

Long Ridge,	Scuppernong.
*Plymouth,** (c. h.,)	

WATAUGA COUNTY.

Blowing Rock,	Sugar Grove,
Boone, (c. h.,)	Valley Crucis,
McBride's Mill,	Watauga Falls.
Stony Fork,	

WAYNE COUNTY.

Dudley,	Nahunta,
*Goldsborough,** (c. h.,)	Pikeville.
Mount Olive,	

WILKES COUNTY.

Elkville,	Roaring Gap,
Hay Meadow,	Trap Hill,
Maple Springs,	Warrior Creek,
Mulberry,	Wilbar,
Purlear's Creek,	*Wilkesborough,* (c. h.)

WILSON COUNTY.

Black Creek,	Stantonsburgh,
Joyner's Depot,	*Wilson,* (c. h.)

YADKIN COUNTY.

Booneville,	Mount Nebo,
Chesnut Ridge,	Panther Creek,
East Bend,	Red Plains,
Footville,	Republic,
Hamptonville,	Richmond Hill,
Huntsville,	*Yadkinville,* (c. h.,)
Jonesville,	Zion.

YANCEY COUNTY.

Bald Creek,	Flinty Branch,
Burnsville, (c. h.,)	Grassy Creek,
Day Book,	Ramsaytown.

OHIO.

ADAMS COUNTY.

Beasley's Fork,	Dunbarton,
Bentonville,	Dunkinsville,
Blue Creek,	Eckmansville,
Bradyville,	Emerald,
Cedar Mills,	Harshasville,
Cherry Fork,	Hill's Fork,

ADAMS COUNTY—Continued.

Locust Grove,	Scott,
Lovett's,	South Liberty,
Manchester,	Stouts,
May Hill,	Tranquility,
Mineral Springs,	Vineyard Hill,
Osman's,	Waggoner's Ripple,

* Money-order office.

ADAMS COUNTY—Continued.

Wamsley's,
West Union, (c. h.,)
Wheat Ridge,

Wilson,
Youngsville.

ALLEN COUNTY.

Beaver Dam,
Blue Lick,
Bluffton,*
Cranberry,
Elida,
Gomer,
Herring,

Hog Creek,
Lima,* (c. h.,)
South Warsaw,
Spencerville,
West Cairo,
Westminster,
West Newton.

ASHLAND COUNTY.

Albion,
Ashland,* (c. h.,)
Hayesville,*
Jeromesville,
Lake Fork,
Loudonville,*
McKay,
McZena,
Mifflin,
Mohican,

Nankin,
Nova,
Perryville,
Polk,
Red Haw,
Rows,
Ruggles,
Savannah,*
Sullivan.

ASHTABULA COUNTY.

Amboy,
Andover,
Ashtabula,*
Austinburgh,
Cherry Valley,
Clark's Corner,
Colebrook,
Conneaut,*
Cork,
Denmark,
Dorset,
Eagleville,
East Plymouth,
East Trumbull,
Geneva,
Grigg's Corners,
Harpersfield,
Hart's Grove,
Jefferson,* (c. h.,)
Kelloggsville,
Kingsville,
Lenox,

Leon,
Lindenville,
Mechanicsville,
Monroe Centre,
Morgan,*
New Lyme,
North Kingsville,
North Richmond,
North Sheffield,
Orwell,*
Phœnix,
Pierpont,
Richmond Centre,
Rome,
Saybrook,
South Ridge,
Steamburgh,
Trumbull,
West Andover,
West Williamsfield,
Williamsfield,
Windsor.

ATHENS COUNTY.

Amesville,
Athens,* (c. h.,)
Big Run,
Cannanville,
Chauncey,
Coolville,
Federalton,
Garden,
Guysville,
Hartleyville,
Hebbardsville,
Hocking,
Hockingport,
Hull's,
Kings,

Lee,*
Lottridge,
Marshfield,
Millfield,
Nelsonville,*
New England,
Pleasanton,
Pratt's Fork,
Rock Oak,
Salina,
Shade,
Torch,
Trimble,
Woodyards.

AUGLAIZE COUNTY.

Cridersville,
Deep Cut,
Fryburgh,
Kossuth,
Minster,
Moulton,
New Bremen,*
New Hampshire,

New Knoxville,
Rinehart,
Saint John's,
Saint Mary's,*
Uniopolis,
Wapakonetta,* (c. h.,)
Waynesfield.

BELMONT COUNTY.

Armstrong's Mills,
Atlas,
Bailey's Mills,
Barnesville,*
Bellaire,*
Belmont,
Bethesda,
Bridgeport,
Businessburgh,
Captina,
Colerain,
Demos,
Dille's Bottom,
East Richland,
Flushing,
Glencoe,
Hendrysburgh,
Hunter,
Jacobsburgh,

Kennon,
Lamira,
Loydsville,
Martin's Ferry,
Morning View,
Morristown,*
Pilcher,
Plank Road,
Powhatan Point,
Pugh,
St. Clairsville,* (c. h.,)
Sewellsville,
Shepherdstown,
Shields,
Somerton,
Temperanceville,
Uniontown,
Warnock,
Wegee.

BROWN COUNTY.

Aberdeen,
Arnheim,
Ash Ridge,
Decatur,
De La Palma,
Fayetteville,
Feesburgh,
Fincastle,
Five Mile,
Georgetown, (c. h.,)
Hamersville,
Higginsport,

Levanna,
Locust Ridge,
Maple,
Mount Orab,
New Harmony,
New Hope,
Red Oak,
Ripley,*
Russellville,
Saint Martin's,
Sardinia,
Union Plains.

BUTLER COUNTY.

Alert,
Bethany,
Blue Ball,
College Corner,
Collinsville,
Contreras,
Darrtown,
Hamilton,* (c. h.,)
Jacksonborough,
Jones' Station,
McGonigle's Station,
Middletown,*
Millville,
Monroe,
Okeana,
Overpeck's Station,

Oxford,*
Paddy's Run,
Philanthropy,
Pisgah,
Poast Town,
Port Union,
Princeton,
Reiley,
Ross,
Saint Charles,
Seven Mile,
Somerville.
Symmes' Corners.
Trenton,
West Chester,
Wood's Station.

* **Money-order office.**

CARROLL COUNTY.

Algonquin,	Malvern,
Augusta,	Mechanicstown,
Carrollton, (c. h.,)	New Hagerstown,
Eckley,	New Harrisburgh,
Harlem Springs,	Norristown,
Hibbett's,	Oneida Mills,
Kilgore,	Palermo,
Lamartine,	Scroggsfield,
Leavitt,	Sherodsville,
Leesville,	Wattsville.

CHAMPAIGN COUNTY.

Brinton,	Mutual,
Cable,	North Lewisburgh,
Carysville,	Saint Paris,
Christiansburgh,	Spring Hills,
Horr's,	Terre Haute,
Kennard,	*Urbana,* (c. h.,)
Mechanicsburgh,	Westville,
Millerstown,	Woodstock.
Mingo,	

CLARK COUNTY.

Bowlusville,	New Moorefield,
Catawba,	North Hampton,
Dialton,	Plattsburgh,
Donnelsville,	Selma,
Enon,	South Charleston,
Harmony,	*Springfield,* (c. h.,)
Medway,	Tremont,
New Carlisle,	Vienna Cross Roads.

CLERMONT COUNTY.

Afton,	Mount Carmel,
Amelia,	Mount Holly,
Angola,	Mount Olive,
Bantam,	Mount Pisgah,
Batavia, (c. h.,)	Mount Repose,
Belfast,	Mulberry,
Bethel,	Neville,
Cedron,	New Palestine,
Chilo,	New Richmond,*
Edenton,	Newtonsville,
Felicity,*	Nicholsville,
Goshen,	Olive Branch,
Henning's Mills,	Owensville,
Laurel,	Perins' Mills,
Lindale,	Point Isabel,
Locust Corner,	Point Pleasant,
Loveland,*	Smith's Landing,
Marathon,	Stone Lick,
Miamiville,	West Woodville,
Milford*,	Williamsburgh,
Monterey,	Withamsville.
Moscow,	

CLINTON COUNTY.

Blanchester,	Clinton Station
Bloomington,	Clinton Valley,
Clarksville,	Cuba,

CLINTON COUNTY—Continued.

Farmer's Station,	New Vienna,
Lee's Creek,	Oakland,
Lumberton,	Ogden,
Martinsville,	Port William,
Memphis,	Reesville,
Morrisville,	Sabina,
New Antioch,	Westborough,
New Burlington,	*Wilmington,* (c. h.)

COLUMBIANA COUNTY.

Bayard,	Leetonia,
Bucks,	Maysville,
Calcutta,	Millport,
Cannon's Mill,	Moultrie,
Clarkson,	New Alexander,
Columbiana,	New Chambersb'rgh,
Damascoville,	New Garden,
Dungannon,	*New Lisbon,* (c. h.,)
East Carmel,	New Waterford,
East Fairfield,	North Georgetown,
East Liverpool,*	Saint Clair,
East Palestine,	Salem,*
East Rochester,	Salineville,*
Elkton,	Sandy,
Franklin Square,	Summitville,
Gavers,	Unity,
Glasgow,	Valley,
Green Hill,	Wellsville,*
Hanoverton,	West Beaver,
Homeworth,	West Point,
Inverness,	Winona.

COSHOCTON COUNTY.

Bacon,	New Guilford,
Bakersville,	New Moscow,
Boyd's Mills,	Plainfield,
Canal Lewisville,	Roscoe,
Chili,	Spring Mountain,
Clark's,	Tyrone,
Coshocton, (c. h.,)	Wakatomika,
Evansburgh,	Walhonding,
Franklin Station,	Warsaw,
Helmick,	West Bedford,
Keene,	West Carlisle,
Linton Mills,	West La Fayette,
Mohawk Village,	White Eyes Plains,
Munnsville,	Will's Creek,
New Bedford,	Yankee Ridge.
New Castle,	

CRAWFORD COUNTY.

Broken Sword,	Liberty Corners,
Bucyrus, (c. h.,)	Likens,
Camp Run,	New Washington,
Chatfield,	North Robinson,
Crestline,*	Oceola,
De Kalb,	Poplar,
Galion,	Sulphur Spring,
Grove Hill,	Tiro,
Leesville × Roads,	Wellerville.

* Money-order office.

CUYAHOGA COUNTY.

Barry,	Mayfield,
Bedford,	Middleburgh,
Berea,*	Newburgh,
Bricksville,	North Dover,
Brooklyn,	North Royalton,
Brooklyn Village,	North Solon,
Chagrin Falls,*	Nottingham,
Cleveland,* (c. h.,)	Olmsted,
Coe Ridge,	Parma,
Collamer,	Randall,
Dover,	Rockport,
East Cleveland,	Solon,
East Rockport,	Strongsville,
Euclid,	Warrensville,
Gates' Mills,	West View,
Glenville,	Wilson's Mills.
Independence,	

DARKE COUNTY.

Ansonia,	Mount Heron,
Arcanum,	New Madison,
Beamsville,	North Star,
Brock,	Painter Creek,
Castine,	Pikeville,
Darke,	Poplar Ridge,
Dawn,	Republican,
De Lisle,	Rose Hill,
German,	Rossville,
Gettysburgh,	Stelvideo,
Gordon,	Tampico,
Greenville,* (c. h.,)	Versailles,
Hetslerville,	Weaver's Station,
Hill Grove,	Webster,
Ithaca,	Wiley Station,
Jaysville,	Woodington.

DEFIANCE COUNTY.

Adams Ridge,	Farmer,
Ayersville,	Hicksville,
Brunersburgh,	Mark,
Cicero,	Milo,
Defiance,* (c. h.,)	Ney,
Evansport,	Wilseyville.

DELAWARE COUNTY.

Alum Creek,	Leonardsburgh,
Ashley,	Lewis Centre,
Belle Point,	Maxwell,
Berkshire,	Norton,
Centre Village,	Orange Station,
Condit,	Ostrander,
Constantia,	Powell,
Delaware,* (c. h.,)	Radnor,
East Orange,	Sunbury,
Galena,	Tanktown,
Harlem,	Van's Valley,
Kilbourne,	White Sulphur.
Kingston Centre,	

ERIE COUNTY.

Berlin Heights,	Birmingham,
Berlin Station,	Bloomingville,
Berlinville,	Castalia,

ERIE COUNTY—Continued.

Florence,	Sandusky,* (c. h.,)
Huron,	Seven Mile House,
Kelley's Island,	Venice,
Milan,	Vermillion.

FAIRFIELD COUNTY.

Amanda,	Lithopolis,
Baltimore,	Lockville,
Basil,	Marcy,
Bremen,	Millersport,
Carroll,	New Salem,
Cedar Hill,	North Berne,
Clear Creek,	Pickerington,
Clear Port,	Pleasantville,
Colfax,	Royalton,
Dumontville,	Rushville,
Green Castle,	Stoutsville,
Hamburgh,	Sugar Grove,
Hooker's Station,	West Rushville.
Lancaster,* (c. h.,)	

FAYETTE COUNTY.

Bloomingburgh,	New Martinsburgh,
Good Hope,	Pancoastburgh,
Jasper Mills,	South Plymouth,
Jeffersonville,	Staunton,
Madison Mills,	Washington C. H.,*
Moons,	West Lancaster.

FRANKLIN COUNTY.

Alton,	Hilliards,
Black Lick,	Hope,
Canal Winchester,*	Lockbourne,
Central College,	Mifflinville,
Clintonville,	North Columbus,
COLUMBUS,* (c. h.,)	Ovid,
Dublin,	Park's Mills,
Flint,	Pleasant Corners,
Gahanna,	Reynoldsburgh,
Georgesville,	Shadeville,
Grove City,	Taylor's Station,
Groveport,	Westerville,
Harrisburgh,	Worthington.

FULTON COUNTY.

Ai,	Metamora,
Archbold,	Ottokee, (c. h.,)
Beta,	Pettisville,
Delta,*	Swanton,
Elmira,	Tedrow,
Emery,	Wauseon,*
Gorham,	West Barre,
Handy,	Winameg.
Lyons,	

GALLIA COUNTY.

Addison,	Eureka,
Cheshire,	Ewington,
Clipper Mills,	Gallia Furnace,
Crown City,	Gallipolis,* (c. h.,)

* Money-order office.

GALLIA COUNTY—Continued.

Kyger,
Lincoln,
McDaniel's,
Mercerville,
Northup,
Patriot,
Pine Grove,
Rio Grande,

Rodney,
Sand Fork,
South Newcastle,
Swan Creek,
Thivener,
Thurman,
Vinton,
Wales.

GEAUGA COUNTY.

Auburn,
Bissell's,
Bridge Creek,
Burton,
Chardon,* (c. h.,)
Chester Cross Roads,
Claridon,
East Claridon,
Ford,
Fowler's Mills,
Grove,
Hampden,

Huntsburgh,
Middlefield,
Montville,
Mulberry Corners,
North Newbury,
Parkman,
Russell,
South Newbury,
South Thompson,
Thompson,
Welshfield.

GREENE COUNTY.

Alpha,
Bellbrook,
Bowersville,
Byron,
Cedarville,
Clifton,
Fairfield,
Jamestown,

New Jasper,
Osborn,*
Paintersville,
Spring Valley,
Xenia,* (c. h.,)
Yellow Springs,*
Zimmerman.

GUERNSEY COUNTY.

Antrim,
Bird's Run,
Buffalo,
Cambridge,* (c. h.,)
Claysville,
Creighton,
Cumberland,
Dyson's,
Fairview,
Galigher,
Gibson's Station,
Gomber,
Indian Camp,
Kimbolton,

Leatherwood,
Londonderry,
Middlebourne,
Midway,
Milnersville,
North Salem,
Oakland Mills,
Salesville,
Senecaville,
Spencer's Station,
Sugartree,
Washington,
Winchester.

HAMILTON COUNTY.

Bevis' Tavern,
California,
Carthage,
Cherry Grove,
Cheviot,
Cincinnati,* (c. h.,)
Cleves,
College Hill,
Columbia,
Covedale,
Cumminsville,

Delhi,
Dent,
Dry Ridge,
Dunlap,
East Sycamore,
Glendale,
Groesbeck,
Grand Valley,
Harrison,*
Hartwell,
Lick Run,

HAMILTON COUNTY—Continued.

Linwood,
Lockland Station,
Ludlow Grove,
Madeira,
Madisonville,
Miami,
Montgomery,
Mount Airy,
Mount Healthy,
Mount Washington,
Newtown,
Norwood,
Oakley,
Plainville,
Pleasant Ridge,
Pleasant Run,

Preston,
Reading,
Riverdale,
Sharonville,
Sixteen Mile Stand,
South Pendleton,
Spring Dale.
Storrs,
Sweet Wine,
Symmes,
Taylor's Creek,
Transit,
Valley Junction,
Walnut Hills,
Winton Place.

HANCOCK COUNTY.

Arcadia,
Arlington,
Benton Ridge,
Cannonsburgh,
Ewing's Corner,
Findley,* (c. h.,)
Hassan,
Houcktown,
McComb,

Mount Blanchard,
Oak Ridge,
Portage Centre,
Rawson,
Van Buren,
Vanlue,
West Independence,
Williamstown.

HARDIN COUNTY.

Ada,*
Dunkirk,
Forest,*
Grant,
Huntersville,
Kenton,* (c. h.,)
McDonald,

Mount Victory,
North Washington,
Patterson,
Ridgeway,
Round Head,
Silver Creek,
Yelverton.

HARRISON COUNTY.

Archer,
Bowerston,
Cadiz,* (c. h.,)
Cassville,
Connotton,
Deersville,
Feed Spring,
Folk's Station,
Freeport,
Germano,
Harrisville,
Hopedale,
Jewett,

Laceyville,
Means,
Miller's Station,
Moorefield,
New Athens,
New Rumley,
Scio,
Short Creek,
Smyrna,
Station 15,
Tappan,
Tippecanoe.

HENRY COUNTY.

Colton,
Florida,
Freedom Mills,
Liberty Centre,
Napoleon,* (c. h.,)
New Bavaria,

Okolona,
Ridgeland,
Ridgeville Corners,
Texas,
West Hope.

* Money-order office.

HIGHLAND COUNTY.

Bell,
Berrysville,
Buckley,
Buford,
Carmel,
Centrefield,
Dallas,
Dodsonville,
East Monroe,
Fairfax,
Greenfield,*
Highland,
Hillsborough, (c. h.,)
Hollowtown,
Leesburgh,
Lynchburgh,

Marshall,
Mowrystown,
Nevin,
New Corwin,
New Market,
New Petersburgh,
North Uniontown,
Paint,
Pricetown,
Rainsborough,
Russell's Station,
Samantha,
Sicily,
Sinking Spring,
Sugar Tree Ridge,
Webertown.

HOCKING COUNTY.

Black Jack,
Enterprise,
Ewing,
Gibesonville,
Gore,
Haydenville,
Islesborough,

Logan, (c. h.,)
Middle Fork,
Rockbridge,
Rock House,
South Bloomingville,
South Perry.

HOLMES COUNTY.

Beck's Mills,
Benton,
Berlin,
Black Creek,
Holmesville,
Humphreyville,
Jones' Corners,
Killbuck,
Millersburgh, (c. h.,)

Mount Hope,
Nashville,
Paint Valley,
Plimpton,
Salt Creek,
Saltillo,
Walnut Creek,
Winesburgh.

HURON COUNTY.

Bellevue,*
Carson,
Centreton,
Clarksfield,
East Clarksfield,
East Norwalk,
East Townsend,
Fitchville,
Four Corners,
Greenwich Station,
Hartland,
Havana,

Monroeville,*
New Haven,
New London,*
North Fairfield,
Norwalk, (c. h.,)
Olena,
Peru,
Pontiac,
Ripleyville,
Steuben,
Townsend Station,
Wakeman.

JACKSON COUNTY.

Berlin Cross Roads,
Camba,
Clay,
Dawkin's Mills,
Grahamsville,
Jackson, (c. h.,)
Jimes,

Keystone,
Mabee's,
Monroe Furnace,
Oak Hill,
Ray's,
Rocky Hill,
Samsonville.

JEFFERSON COUNTY.

Adena,
Amsterdam,
Annapolis,
Bloomingdale,
Creswell,
Croxton,
East Springfield,
Fair Play,
Hammondsville,
Holmes' Mill,
Irondale,
Island Creek,
Jeddo,
Knoxville,
Linton,
McCoy's Station,
Mitchell's Salt Works,

Moore's Salt Works,
Mount Pleasant,
New Alexandria,
New Somerset,
Philipsburgh,
Port Homer,
Richmond,
Rush Run,
Sloan's Station,
Smithfield,
Steubenville, (c. h.,)
Unionport,
Updegraffs,
Warrenton,
Wintersville,
Yorkville.

KNOX COUNTY.

Bladensburgh,
Brandon,
Centreburgh,
Danville,
Democracy,
Fredericktown,*
Gambier, *
Greersville,
Hunt's Station,
Indian Field,
Jelloway,
Knox,
Levering,

Lock,
Lucerne,
Martinsburgh,
Milfordton,
Millwood,
Monroe Mills,
Mount Liberty,
Mount Vernon (c. h.,)
Nonpareil,
North Liberty,
Rich Hill,
Shaler's Mills.

LAKE COUNTY.

Concord,
Hillhouse,
Kirtland,
Madison,*
Mentor,
North Madison,

Painesville, (c. h.,)
Perry,
South Kirtland,
Unionville,
Wickliffe,
Willoughby.

LAWRENCE COUNTY.

Aid,
Arabia,
Athalia,
Bartramville,
Bradrickville,
Burlington,
Coal Grove,
Forest Dale,
Frampton,
Greasy Ridge,
Hanging Rock,

Ironton, (c. h.,)
Kelley's Mills,
Miller's,
Quaker Bottom,
Rock Camp,
Russell's Place,
Scott Town,
Sheridan Coal W'ks,
South Point,
Waterloo,
Willow Wood.

LICKING COUNTY.

Alexandria,
Appleton,
Beech,
Brownsville,
Chatham,
Clay Lick,

Columbia Centre,
Croton,
Etna,
Fallsburgh,
Fredonia,
Freeman,

* Money-order office.

LICKING COUNTY—Continued.

Granville,*
Gratiot,
Green,
Hanover,
Hebron,
Homer,
Jacksontown,
Jersey,
Johnstown,
Kirkersville,
Liunville,
Long Run,
Newark,* (c. h.,)
New-way,
Outville,
Pataskala,
Perryton,
Rocky Fork,
Saint Louisville,
Summit Station,
Toboso,
Union Station,
Utica,
Vanatta,
Wagram,
Wilkins' Run.

LOGAN COUNTY.

Belle Centre,
Bellefontaine,* (c. h.,)
Big Springs,
Bloom Centre,
De Graff,
East Liberty,
Harper,
Huntsville,
Lewistown,
Loganville,
Muchinippe,
New Richland,
North Greenfield,
Northwood,
Pickereltown,
Quincy,
Rushsylvania,
West Liberty,*
West Mansfield,
West Middleburgh,
Zanesfield.

LORAIN COUNTY.

Amherst,
Avon,
Avon Lake,
Black River,
Brighton,
Brownhelm,
Columbia Station,
Copopa,
Crandall,
Elyria,* (c. h.,)
Grafton,
Henrietta,
Huntington,
Kipton,
La Grange,
La Porte,
North Camden,
North Eaton,
North Ridgeville,
Oberlin,*
Penfield,
Pittsfield,
Plato,
Rawsonville,
Rochester Depot,
Sheffield,
Sheffield Lake,
Wellington.*

LUCAS COUNTY.

Berkey,
East Toledo,
Hickory,
Holland,
Java,
Maumee City,*
Monclova,
Sylvania,
Toledo,* (c. h.,)
Waterville,
White House.

MADISON COUNTY.

Big Plain,
Cross Roads,
Darby Creek,
La Fayette,
London,* (c. h.,)
Mount Sterling,
Rosedale,
South Solon,
Summerford,
Tradersville,
Walnut Run,
West Cannan,
West Jefferson.

MAHONING COUNTY.

Beloit,
Berlin Centre,
Boardman,
Boswell,
Canfield,* (c. h.,)
Coitsville,
East Lewistown,
Ellsworth,
Frederick,
Garfield,
Greenford,
Lowellville,
Milton,
Mineral Ridge,*
New Albany,
New Middletown,
New Springfield,
North Benton,
North Jackson,
North Lima,
Orange,
Patmos,
Petersburgh,
Poland,
Struther's Station,
Washingtonville,
Youngstown.*

MARION COUNTY.

Caledonia,
Cochranton,
Green Camp,
Larue,*
Marion,* (c. h.,)
New Bloomington,
Prospect,
Three Locusts,
Waldo.

MEDINA COUNTY.

Abbeyville,
Bennett's Corners,
Brunswick,
Chatham Centre,
Friendsville,
Granger,
Guilford,
Hinckley,
Homerville,
Le Roy,
Litchfield,
Liverpool,
Lodi,
Mallet Creek,
Medina,* (c. h.,)
Poe,
Remson's Corners,
River Styx,
Sharon Centre,
Smith Road,
Spencer,
Wadsworth,*
Weymouth,
Whittlesey.

MEIGS COUNTY.

Alfred,
Apple Grove,
Bashan,
Burlingham,
Chester,
Dexter,
Downington,
Great Bend,
Harrisonville,
Hemlock Grove,
Langsville,
Letart Falls,
Long Bottom,
Middleport,
Minersville,
Mount Blanco,
Plants,
Pomeroy,* (c. h.,)
Portland,
Racine,
Reedsville,
Rutland,
Salem Centre,
Saxon,
Silver Run,
Syracuse,
Tupper's Plains,
Valley Ford.

MERCER COUNTY.

Carthagena,
Celina,* (c. h.,)
Cold Water,
Cranberry Prairie,
Fort Recovery,
Macedon,
Maria Stein,
Mendon,
Mercer,
Montezuma,
Neptune,
Price,
Saint Henry's,
Shane's Crossing,
Skeels × Roads.

* Money-order office.

MIAMI COUNTY.

Alcony,	Laura,
Allen's,	North Clayton,
Bradford,	Piqua,
Brandt,	Pleasant Hill,
Casstown,	Potsdam,
Conover,	Tippecanoe City,*
Covington,	*Troy,* (c. h.,)
Fidelity,	West Charleston,
Fletcher,	West Milton.
Ginghamsburgh,	

MONROE COUNTY.

Antioch,	Lecompton,
Beallsville,	Lewisville,
Bingham,	Malaga,
Calais,	Masterton,
Cameron,	Miltonsburgh,
Centre View,	Mount Carrick,
Clarington,	Ozark,
Edwina,	Rinard's Mills,
Graysville,	Round Bottom,
Green Brier,	Sardis,
Hannibal,	Stafford,
Hope Ridge,	Trail Run,
Jerusalem,	Wittens,
Jolly,	*Woodsfield,* (c. h.,)
Laing's,	Young's Mills.

MONTGOMERY COUNTY.

Air Hill,	Liberty,
Bachman,	Little York,
Brookville,	Miamisburgh,*
Carrollton Station,	Nat'l Mil. Asylum,*
Centre,	New Lebanon,
Centreville,	Pyrmont,
Chambersburgh,	South Arlington,
Clayton,	Tadmer,
Davidson,	Taylorsville,
Dayton, (c. h.,)	Trotwood,
Farmersville,	Union,
Germantown,	Vandalia,
Harshmansville,	West Baltimore,
Iamton,	West Carrollton.
Johnsville,	

MORGAN COUNTY.

Bishopville,	Moscow Mills,
Bristol,	Neeleysville,
Calvary,	Pennsville,
Centre Bend,	Plantsville,
Chester Hill,*	Pleasant Valley,
Deavertown,	Reinersville,
Elliott's × Roads,	Ringgold,
Hall's Valley,	Rokeby,
Log Cabin,	Rosseau,
McConnellsville,	Roxbury,
(c. h.,)	Sand Hollow,
Malta,	Stockport,
Meigs' Creek,	Todd's,
Meigsville,	Triadelphia,
Mill Grove,	Wood Grove.
Morgansville,	

MORROW COUNTY.

Andrews,	Pagetown,
Bennington,	Pulaskiville,
Bloomfield,	Shauck's,
Cardington,*	Sparta,
Chesterville,	Steam Corners,
Corsica,	Vail's × Roads,
Iberia,	Westfield,
Marengo,	Whetstone,
Marit's,	Woodview.
Mount Gilead, (c. h.,)	

MUSKINGUM COUNTY.

Adams' Mills,	Nashport,
Adamsville,	New Concord,
Blue Rock,	Norwich,
Bridgeville,	Otsego,
Brush Creek,	Philo,
Chandlersville,	Putnam,
Confederate × Roads	Rix's Mills,
Cottage Hill,	Roseville,
Dresden,*	Rural Dale,
Duncan's Falls,	Sago,
East Greenwood,	Sonora,
Frazeysburgh,	West Zanesville,
Fultonham,	White Cottage,
High Hill,	Young Hickory,
Hopewell,	*Zanesville,* (c. h.,)
Licking Valley,	Zeno.

NOBLE COUNTY.

Ava,	McCleary,
Batesville,	Middle Creek,
Berne,	Mount Ephraim,
Caldwell, (c. h.,)	Nobleville,
Claytona,	Olive Green,
Crooked Tree,	Renrock,
Enoch,	Ridge,
Gardner,	Sarahsville,
Harriettsville,	Sharon,
Hiramsburgh,	South Olive,
Hoskinsville,	Summerfield,
Keith's,	Whigville.
Kennonsburgh,	

OTTAWA COUNTY.

Catawba Island,	Middle Bass,
Elmore,	North Bass Island,
Genoa,	Oak Harbor,
Locust Point,	*Port Clinton,* (c. h.,)
Marblehead,	Put-in Bay.

PAULDING COUNTY.

Antwerp,*	McGill,
Carryall,	Oakwood,
Cecil,	*Paulding,* (c. h.,)
Charloe,	Payne,
Emmett,	Reid's,
Hamer,	Royal Oak,
Junction,	Timberville.

* Money-order office.

PERRY COUNTY.

Buchanan,
Buckeye Cottage,
Chapel Hill,
Coal Dale,
Crooksville,
East Rush Creek,
McCluney,
Maxville,
Mount Perry,

New Lexington, *(c. h.,)
Oakfield,
Portersville,
Rehoboth,
St. Joseph's College,
Sego,
Somerset,
Straitsville,
Thornville.

PICKAWAY COUNTY.

Atlanta,
Beckett's Store,
Circleville, *(c. h.,)
Darbyville,
Deer Creek,
East Ringgold,
Five Points,
Kinderhook,
Leistville,

Nebraska,
New Holland,
Palestine,
Robtown,
Saint Paul's,
South Bloomfield,
String Town,
Tarlton,
Williamsport.

PIKE COUNTY.

Beaver,
Byington,
Cynthiana,
Flat,
Gibson,
Idaho,
Jasper,

Latham,
Omega,
Pee Pee,
Piketon, (c. h.,)
Waverly,
Wetmore.

PORTAGE COUNTY.

Atwater,
Atwater Centre,
Aurora,
Brimfield,
Charlestown,
Deerfield,
Earlville,
Edinburgh,
Freedom,
Freedom Station,
Garrettsville,*
Hiram,
Kent,*
Mantua,

Mantua Station,
Nelson,
New Milford,
Palmyra,
Parisville,
Randolph,
Rapids,
*Ravenna,** (c. h.,)
Rootstown,
Shalersville,
Streetsborough,
Suffield,
Windham,
Windham Station.

PREBLE COUNTY.

Brinley's Station,
Brown's Station,
Camden,
Campbellstown,
*Eaton,** (c. h.,)
Ebenezer,
El Dorado,
Euphemia,
Fair Haven,
Gratis,

Lewisburgh,
Morning Sun,
New Paris,*
New Westville,
Upshur,
West Alexandria,
West Elkton,
West Florence,
West Manchester,
West Sonora.

PUTNAM COUNTY.

Belmore,
Caskaid,
Columbus Grove,*

Dog Creek,
Dupont,
Fort Jennings,

PUTNAM COUNTY—Continued.

Gilboa,
Kalida, (c. h.,)
Leipsic,
Ottawa,*
Pendleton,

Roanoke,
Sheridan,
Stanley,
Vaughnsville.

RICHLAND COUNTY.

Adario,
Barnes,
Belleville,*
Butler,
Darlington,
Ganges,
Hastings,
Lexington,
Lucas,
*Mansfield,** (c. h.,)

Newville,
Olivesburgh,
Ontario,
Plymouth,*
Rives,
Shanandoah, ●
Shelby,*
Shiloh,
Spring Mills,
West Windsor.

ROSS COUNTY.

Adelphi,
Alma,
Anderson,
Bainbridge,*
Bourneville,
*Chillicothe,** (c. h.,)
Clarksburgh,
Frankfort,
Gillespieville,
Greenland,
Hallsville,

Hooppole,
Kingston,
Lattas,
Lyndon Station,
Richmond Dale,
Roxabell,
Schooley's Station,
South Salem,
Vigo, '
Waller,
Yellow Bud.

SANDUSKY COUNTY.

Black Swamp,
Clyde,*
*Fremont,** (c. h.,)
Greensburgh Cross
  Roads,

Lindsey,
Rollersville,
Townsend,
Winter's Station,
Woodville.

SCIOTO COUNTY.

Bloom Switch,
Franklin Furnace,
Freestone,
Friendship,
Hale's Creek,
Harrison Mills,
Haverhill,
Iron Furnace,
Lilly,
Lombardville,
Lucasville,

Lyra,
Nairn,
Otway,
Pond Run,
*Portsmouth,** (c. h.,)
Rarden,
Scioto,
Scioto Furnace,
Sciotoville,
Wheelersburgh.

SENECA COUNTY.

Adams,
Adrian,
Attica,*
Bascom,
Berwick,
Bettsville,
Bloomville,
Flat Rock,
Fort Seneca,
Fostoria,*
Frank,

Green Spring,
Jackson Station,
Kansas,
Melmore,
Palo Alto,
Reedtown,
Republic,
Saw Mill,
*Tiffin,** (c. h.,)
Watson Station,
West Lodi.

* Money-order office.

SHELBY COUNTY.

Anna,	Pemberton,
Dinsmore,	Plattsville,
Hardin,	Pratt,
Houston,	Russia,
Jackson Centre,	*Sidney,* (c. h.,)
Kirkwood,	Swander's Crossing,
Lockington,	Tawawa,
Loramie's,	Wynant.
Montra,	

STARK COUNTY.

Alliance,*	Maximo,
Barryville,	Middle Branch,
Cairo,	Minerva,*
Canal Fulton,	Mount Union,
Canton, (c. h.,)	Navarre,
East Greenville,	New Baltimore,
Freeburgh,	New Berlin,
Greentown,	New Franklin,
Hartville,	North Industry,
Lake,	North Lawrence,
Limaville,	Osnaburgh,
Louisville,	Paris,
McDonaldsville,	Pierce,
Magnolia,	Robertsville,
Mapleton,	Waynesburgh,
Marlborough,	West Brookfield,
Massillon,*	Wilmot.

SUMMIT COUNTY.

Akron, (c. h.,)	Montrose,
Bath,	New Portage,
Clinton,	Nimisila,
Copley,	Northfield,
Cuyahoga Falls,	Norton Centre,
Ghent,	Peninsula,
Hudson,*	Richfield,
Inland,	Sherman,
Johnson's Corners,	Summit,
Loyal Oak,	Tallmadge,
Macedonia Depot,	Twinsburgh,
Middlebury,	Western Star,
Mogadore,	West Richfield.

TRUMBULL COUNTY.

Bazetta,	Leavittsburgh,
Braceville,	Lordstown,
Bristolville,	Mecca,
Brookfield,	Mesopotamia,
Burgh Hill,	Newton Falls,
Church Hill,	Niles,*
Coalburgh,	North Bloomfield,
Farmington,	North Bristol,
Fowler,	Ohl's Town,
Girard,	Oil Diggins,
Greensburgh,	Orangeville,
Gustavus,	Payne's Corners,
Hartford,	Southington,
Howland,	Vernon,
Hubbard,*	Vienna,
Johnsonville,	*Warren,* (c. h.,)
Kinsman's,*	West Farmington.*

TUSCARAWAS COUNTY.

Albany,	*New Philadelphia,*
Bolivar,	(c. h.,)
Buena Vista,	Peoli,
Cadwallader,	Port Washington,
Canal Dover,	Rogersville,
Deardorff's Mills,	Rush,
Dennison,	Sandyville,
Dundee,	Shanesville,
Gilmore,	Stone Creek,
Gnadenhutten,	Strasburgh,
Lock Seventeen,	Tuscarawas,
Milligan,	Uhricksville,*
Mineral Point,	Winfield,
New Comerstown,	Zoar,
New Cumberland,	Zoar Station.

UNION COUNTY.

Boke's Creek,	Pharisburgh,
Broadway,	Pottersburgh,
Byhalia,	Raymond's,
Irwin,	Richwood,
Jerome,	Rush Creek,
Marysville, (c. h.,)	Unionville Centre,
Milford Centre,	Watkins,
New California,	Woodland,
New Dover,	York.

VAN WERT COUNTY.

Auglaize,	Middle Point,
Buena,	Tully,
Delphos,*	*Van Wert,* (c. h.,)
Dixon,	Venedocia.
Leslie,	Willshire.

VINTON COUNTY.

Agatha,	Packard,
Allensville,	Reed's Mills,
Dundas,	Siverly,
Eagle Mills,	Swan,
Hope Furnace,	Vinton Station,
McArthur, (c. h.,)	Wilkesville,
New Plymouth,*	Zaleski.

WARREN COUNTY.

Butlerville,	Mainville,
Carlisle Station,	Mason,
Dallasburgh,	Morrow,*
Deerfield Village,	Murdock,
Dunlevy,	Oregon,
Edwardsville,	Pence's Mills,
Fort Ancient,	Pleasant Plain,
Foster's Crossings,	Red Lion,
Franklin,*	Ridgeville,
Harveysburgh,	Springborough,
Hopkinsville,	Twenty Mile Stand.
Lebanon, (c. h.,)	Waynesville.*
Level,	

* Money-order office.

WASHINGTON COUNTY.

Barlow,
Bartlett,
Belpre,
Beverly,*
Bonn,
Brown's Mills,
Centre Belpre,
Coal Run,
Constitution,
Cow Run,
Cutler,
Decaturville,
Dunbar,
Dunham,
Fearing,
Fillmore,
Fleming,
Flint's Mills,
Grand View,
Harmar,
Hills,

Lawrence,
Layman,
Little Hockhocking,
Lowell,
Lower Newport,
Lower Salem,
Marietta,* (c. h.,)
Moss Run,
Newell's Run,
New Metamora,
Newport,
Patten's Mill,
Regnier's Mills,
Tunnel,
Veto,
Vincent,
Wade,
Waterford,
Watertown,
Wesley.

WAYNE COUNTY.

Apple Creek,
Baughman,
Big Prairie,
Blackleysville,
Burbank,
Canaan,
Cedar Valley,
Chippewa,
Congress,
Dalton,*
Easton,
East Union,
Fredericksburgh,
Golden Corners,
Koch's
Lattasburgh,

Madisonburgh,
Marshallville,
Mill Brook,
Milton Station,
Moorland,
Mount Eaton,
New Pittsburgh,
Old Hickory,
Orrville,*
Pike Station,
Plain,
Reedsburgh,
Shreve,
Smithville,
Springville,
Wayne,

WAYNE COUNTY—Continued.

West Lebanon,
West Salem,*

Wooster,* (c. h.,)
Wooster Summit.

WILLIAMS COUNTY.

Bridgewater,
Bryan,* (c. h.,)
Deer Lick,
Durbin's Corners,
Edgerton,*
Edon,
Lockport,
Melburn,
Montpelier,
Nettle Lake,

North West,
Pioneer,
Primrose,
Pulaski,
Spring Lake,
Stryker,
West Buffalo,
West Unity,*
Williams Centre.

WOOD COUNTY.

Bloom,
Bowling Green,*
Custar,
Fenton,
Grand Rapids,*
Haskins,
Holt,
Hull Prairie,
Millbury,
Milton Centre,
Mungen,
New Rochester,

Pemberville,
Perrysburgh,* (c. h.,)
Portage,.
Potter,
Prairie Depot.
Roachton,
Scotch Ridge,
Stony Ridge,
Tontogany,
West Mill Grove,
Weston,
Woodbury.

WYANDOT COUNTY.

Belle Vernon,
Carey,*
Kirby,
Little Sandusky,
McCutchenville,
Marseilles,
Mexico,
Nevada,*

Seal,
Sycamore,
Tymochtee,
Upper Sandusky,*
(c. h.,)
Warpole,
Whartonsburgh,
Wyandot.

OREGON.

BAKER COUNTY.

Auburn,
Baker City,* (c. h.,)
El Dorado,
Express Ranch,

Humboldt Basin,
Jordan Valley,
Rye Valley.

BENTON COUNTY.

Corvallis,* (c. h.,)
Liberty,
Little Elk,
Newport,
Newton,

Philomath,
Starr's Point,
Summit,
Toledo.

CLACKAMAS COUNTY.

Beaver,
Butte Creek,

Clear Creek,
Cuttingsville,

CLACKAMAS COUNTY—Continued.

Damascus,
Eagle Creek,
Glad Tidings,
Highland,
Milwaukee,

Molalla,
Needy,
Oregon City,* (c. h.,)
Oswego.

CLATSOP COUNTY.

Astoria,* (c. h.,)
Nehalem,

Skipanon,
Westport.

COLUMBIA COUNTY.

Rainier,
St. Helen, (c. h.,)

Sauvie's Island.

* Money-order office.

COOS COUNTY.

Coquille,
Empire City, (c. h.,)
Hermansville,
Randolph.

CURRY COUNTY.

Chetco,
Ellensberg, (c. h.,)
Port Orford.

DOUGLAS COUNTY.

Camas Valley,
Galesville,
Gardiner,
Kellogg's,
Myrtle Creek,
North Canyonville,
Oakland,
Roseburgh,* (c. h.,)
Scottsburgh,
Ten Mile,
Wilbur,
Yoncalla.

GRANT COUNTY.

Camp Watson,
Canyon City,* (c. h.,)
Dayville,
Grant,
John Day City,
Prairie City.

JACKSON COUNTY.

Applegate,
Ashland Mills,
Grant's Pass,
Jacksonville,* (c. h.,)
Phœnix,
Rock Point,
Willow Springs.

JOSEPHINE COUNTY.

Kerby, (c. h.,)
Leland,
Slate Creek,
Waldo.

LANE COUNTY.

Coast Fork,
Cottage Grove,
Eugene City,* (c. h.,)
Franklin,
Lancaster,
Long Tom,
Pleasant Hill,
Rattlesnake,
Siuslaw,
Springfield,
Willamette Forks.

LINN COUNTY.

Albany,* (c. h.,)
Boston Mills,
Brownsville,
Crawfordsville,
Harrisburgh,
Lebanon,
Peoria,
Pine,
Scio,
Soda Springs.

MARION COUNTY.

Aumsville,
Aurora Mills,
Belpassi,
Butteville,
Fairfield,
Jefferson,
Monitor,
Newellsville,

MARION COUNTY—Continued

Saint Louis,
SALEM,* (c. h.,)
Silverton,
Sublimity,
Vernon,
Waconda.

MULTNOMAH COUNTY.

East Portland,
Portland,* (c. h.,)
Springville.

POLK COUNTY.

Bethel,
Bridgeport,
Buena Vista,
Dallas,* (c. h.,)
Elk Horn,
Eola,
Grand Ronde,
Independence,
Lewisville,
Lincoln,
Monmouth,
Perrydale,
Rickreall,
Salt Creek,
Zena.

TILLAMOOK COUNTY.

Garibaldi,
Nestocton,
Netart's,
Tillamook, (c. h.)

UMATILLA COUNTY.

Cayuse,
Meadowville,
Pendleton, (c. h.,)
Pilot Rock,
Umatilla,*
Weston.

UNION COUNTY.

Cove,
La Grande,* (c. h.,)
North Powder,
Orodell,
Summerville,
Union.

WASCO COUNTY.

Bridge Creek,
Deschutes,
Hood River,
Scotts,
Spanish Hollow,
The Dalles,* (c. h.,)
Wasco.

WASHINGTON COUNTY.

Centreville,
Forest Grove,
Hillsborough, (c. h.,)
Middleton,
Tualitin.

YAM HILL COUNTY.

Amity,
Bellevue,
Dayton,
La Fayette,* (c. h.,)
McMinnville,
Mountain House,
Newberg,
North Yam Hill,
Sheridan,
West Chehalem,
Wheatland.

* Money-order office.

PENNSYLVANIA.

ADAMS COUNTY.

Abbottstown,
Arendtsville,
Bendersville,
Bermudian,
Bigler,
Cashtown,
East Berlin,
Fairfield,
Flora Dale,
Fountain Dale,
Gettysburgh,* (c. h.,)
Graefenburgh,
Granite Hill,
Green Mount,
Green Ridge,
Hampton,
Heidlersburgh,
Hunterstown,

Idaville,
Latimore,
Littlestown,
McKnightstown,
McSherrystown,
Menallen,
Mummasburgh,
New Chester,
New Oxford,
Red Land,
Round Hill,
Sell's Station,
Seven Stars,
Square Corner,
Table Rock,
Two Taverns,
Wenks,
York Sulphur Spr'gs.

ALLEGHENY COUNTY.

Allegheny,*
Bakerstown,
Beers,
Bennett,
Boston,
Braddock's Field,
Brinton,
Brodhead,
Buchanan,
Buena Vista,
Carrick,
Chartiers,
Claremont,
Clinton,
Coal Valley,
Dixmont,
Dorseyville,
Dravosburgh,
Duncan,
Eakin,
Elizabeth,
Etna,
Ewing's Mills,
Fayette,
Gamble's,
Gill Hall,
Green Tree,
Harmarville,
Hope Church,
Hulton,
Lebanon Church,
Leetsdale,
Library,
McKeesport,*
Mansfield Valley,
Monroeville,
Moon,
Moorhead,

Mount Lebanon,
Mount Washington,
Natrona,
New Texas.
Noblestown,
North Star,
Oakdale Station,
Ormsby,
Palmersville,
Perrysville,
Pittsburgh,* (c. h.,)
Port Perry,
Remington,
Robella,
Rural Ridge,
Saint Elmo,
Sewicklyville,
Sharpsburgh,
Shirland,
Shoustown,
Springdale,
Sunny Side,
Surgeon's Hall,
Talley Cavey,
Tarentum,
Temperanceville,
Turtle Creek,
Upper Saint Clair,
Vancefort,
Walker's Mills,
West Elizabeth,
West View,
Wexford,
White Ash,
Wilkins,
Wilkinsburgh,
Wood's Run,
Woodville.

ARMSTRONG COUNTY.

Adams,
Adrian,
Apollo,
Atwood,
Barnard's,
Belknap,
Blanket Hill,
Brady's Bend,
Cochran's Mills,
Cowansville,
Craigsville,
Dayton,
Echo,
Eddyville,
Elderton,
Foster's Mills,
Freeport,*
Goheenville,
Greendale,
Harmsburgh,
Kelly's Station,
Kiskiminitas,
Kittaning,* (c. h.,)
Lawrenceburgh,
Leechburgh,
Long Run,
McVill,

Manorsville,
Miller's Eddy,
Monticello,
North Buffalo,
Oakland,
Olivet,
Orrsville,
Oscar,
Peart's Eddy,
Phœnix,
Pierce,
Pine Township,
Putneyville,
Red Bank Furnace,
Rimer,
Rosston,
Rural Valley,
Schenley Station,
Shady Plain,
Sherrett,
Slate Lick,
South Bend,
Spring Church,
West Valley,
Whitesburgh,
Worthington.

BEAVER COUNTY.

Baden,
Beaver,* (c. h.,)
Beaver Falls,
Black Hawk,
Brush Creek,
Comettsburgh,
Darlington,
Economy,
Frankfort Springs,
Freedom,
Georgetown,
Green Garden,
Harshaville,
Holt,
Homewood,
Hookstown,
Industry,
Kendall,

Knob,
McCleary,
New Brighton,*
New Galilee,
New Scottsville,
New Sheffield,
North Sewickly,
Ohioville,
Poe,
Rochester,
Rock Point,
Service,
Seventy-Six,
Shippingport,
Smith's Ferry,
Wall Rose,
Water Cure.

BEDFORD COUNTY.

Alum Bank,
Bedford,* (c. h.,)
Bedford Springs,
Bloody Run,
Buffalo Mills,
Burns' Mills,
Chaneysville,
Charlesville,
Cherry Grove,
Clearville,

Cumberland Valley,
Dry Ridge,
Elbinsville,
Gladen's Run,
Green Point,
Hopewell,
Imlertown,
Mann's Choice,
Mowry's Mills,
New Bridgeport,

* Money-order office.

BEDFORD COUNTY—Continued.

New Buena Vista,
New Enterprise,
New Paris,
Pattonville,
Pavia,
Purcell,
Rainsburgh,
Ray's Hill,
Riddlesburgh,
Robisonville,
Saint Clairsville,
Saxton,
Schellsburgh,
Six Mile Run,
Six Roads,
Spring Hope,
Spring Meadow,
Stuckeysville,
Tatesville,
Waterside,
West End,
Woodbury,
Yellow Creek.

BERKS COUNTY.

Addams Tavern,
Albany,
Alsace,
Baumstown,
Bechtelsville,
Beckersville,
Bernville,
Bethel,
Birdsborough,
Blandon,
Bower's Station,
Boyerstown,
Brower,
Brumfieldville,
Centreport,
Clayton,
Colebrookdale,
Cross Kill Mills,
Cumru,
Dale,
Douglassville,
Dryville,
Eagle Point,
Earlville,
Exeter Station,
Fetherolffsville,
Fleetwood,
Fredericksville,
Fritztown,
Geiger's Mills,
Gouglersville,
Greshville,
Griesemersville,
Grimville,
Hamburgh,
Hereford,
Hiester's Mill,
Hill Church,
Host,
Hummel's Store,
Joanna Furnace,
Kirbyville,
Klinesville,
Knauer's,
Krick's Mill,
Kutztown,
Landis' Store,
Leesport,
Leinbach's,
Lenhartsville,
Limekiln,
Lobachsville,
Long Swamp,
Lower Bern,
Lower Heidelberg,
Lyon's Station,
Maiden Creek,
Manatawny,
Maxatawny,
Mertztown,
Mohn's Store,
Mohrsville,
Molltown,
Monocacy,
Monterey,
Morgantown,
Moselm,
Mount Ætna,
Mountain,
New Jerusalem,
Nora,
North Heidelberg,
Oley,
Pike Township,
Pricetown,
Reading, *(c. h.,)*
Rehrersburgh,
Robeson,
Robesonia Furnaces,
Scarlet's Mill,
Seisholtzville,
Shanesville,
Shartlesville,
Shoemakersville,
Sinking Spring,
South Evansville,
Spangville,
Stonersville,
Stouchsburgh,
Stony Run,
Strausstown,
Temple,
Topton,
Tuckerton,
Tulpehocken,
Upper Bern,
Virginville,
Wernersville,
Windsor Castle,
Wintersville,
Womelsdorf,*
Yellow House.

BLAIR COUNTY.

Altoona,*
Antestown,
Arch Spring,
Bennington Furnace,
Blue Knob,
Canoe Creek,
Clover Creek,
Duncansville,
East Freedom,
East Sharpsburgh,
El Dorado,
Fostoria,
Frankstown,
Hollidaysburgh, *(c. h.,)*
Martinsburgh,
Newry,
Olivia,
Poplar Run,
Roaring Spring,
Sabbath Rest,
Sarah,
Sinking Valley,
Springfield Furnace
Tipton,
Tyrone,*
Williamsburgh,
Yellow Spring.

BRADFORD COUNTY

Alba,
Allis Hollow,
Aspinwall,
Asylum,
Athens,
Austinville,
Barclay,
Bently Creek,
Big Pond,
Browntown,
Burlington,
Camptown,
Canton,
Cold Creek,
Columbia × Roads,
Durell,
East Canton,
East Smithfield,
East Springhill,
East Troy,
Edsallville,
Elwell,
Fassett,
Franklindale,
Granville Centre,
Granville Summit,
Herrick,
Herrickville,
Highland,
Hornet's Ferry,
Hornbrook,
Laddsburgh,
Leona,
Le Raysville,
Le Roy,
Liberty Corners,
Lime Hill,
Litchfield,
Luther's Mills,
Macedonia,
Merryall,
Milan,
Minnequa,
Monroeton,
Mountain Lake,
Myersburgh,
New Albany,
New Era,
North Orwell,
North Rome,
North Smithfield,
North Towanda,
Orcutt Creek,
Orwell,
Overton,
Park's Creek,
Pike,
Potterville,
Ridgebury,
Rome,
Rummerfield Creek,
Sheshequin,
Smithfield Summit,
Snedekerville,
South Branch,
South Creek,
South Hill,
South Litchfield,
South Warren,
Springfield,
Spring Hill,
Standing Stone,
Stevensville,
Sugar Run,
Sylvania,
Terrytown,
Tioga Valley,
Towanda, *(c. h.,)*
Troy,*
Ulster,
Warren Centre,
Warrenham,
Wells,
West Burlington,
West Franklin,
West Warren,
West Windham,
Wilmot,
Windham,
Windham Centre,
Windham Summit,
Wyalusing,
Wysox.

* * Money-order office.

BUCKS COUNTY.

Andalusia,
Applebachsville,
Attleborough,
Bedminster,
Bensalem,
Bridge Valley,
Bridgewater,
Bristol,*
Brownsburgh,
Buckingham,
Buckmanville,
Bucksville,
Bursonville,
Carversville,
Centre Bridge,
Danborough,
Davisville,
Dolington,
Doyleston,* (c. h.,)
Dublin,
Durham,
Eddington,
Edgwood,
Emilie,
Erwinna,
Fallsington,
Feasterville,
Gardenville,
Gery's,
Hagersville,
Hartsville,
Hilltown,
Holland,
Hulmesville,
Kintnersville,
Lahaska,
Lumberville,
Mechanicsville,

Milford Square,
Morrisville,
Moyer's Store,
Neshaming,
New Britain,
New Hope,
Newportville,
Newtown,
Oakford,
Ottsville,
Oxford Valley,
Penn's Park,
Pineville,
Pipersville,
Pleasant Valley,
Plumsteadville,
Point Pleasant,
Quakertown,
Richborough,
Richland Centre,
Richlandtown,
Riegelsville,
Schlichter,
Sellersville,
Spinnerstown,
Springtown,
Steinsburgh,
Taylorsville,
Telford,
Trumbaursville,
Tullytown,
Upper Black Eddy,
Warminster,
Warrington,
Whitehallville,
Wrightstown,
Yardleyville.

BUTLER COUNTY.

Anandale,
Anderson's Mills,
Baldwin,
Barnhart's Mills,
Bonnie Brook,
Breakneck,
Brownington,
Brownsdale,
Bruin,
Butler,* (c. h.,)
Coultersville,
Coyleville,
Eau Claire,
Glade Mills,
Harmony,
Harrisville,
Hooker,
Jacksville,
Leasuresville,
McCandless,

Melissadale,
Middle Lancaster,
Mount Chesnut,
Murrinsville,
North Hope,
North Oakland,
Ogle,
Peachville,
Petersburgh,
Portersville,
Prospect,
Riddle's × Roads,
Sarversville,
Saxenburgh,
Six Points,
Slippery Rock,
West Liberty,
Whitestown,
Zelienople.

CAMBRIA COUNTY.

Cambria,

Carrolltown,

CAMBRIA COUNTY—Continued.

Chest Springs,
Couemaugh,
Cooperdale,
Cresson,
Ebensburgh,* (c. h.,)
Fallen Timber,
Gallitzin,
Garman's Mills,
Glendale,
Hemlock,
Johnstown,*
Loretto,

Mineral Point,
Munster,
Plattville,
Saint Augustine,
Saint Bonifacius,
Saint Lawrence,
Scalp Level,
Sonman,
Summer Hill,
Summit,
Wilmore.

CAMERON COUNTY.

Beech Wood,
Cameron,
Driftwood,
Emporium,* (c. h.,)
First Fork,

Prestonville,
Second Fork,
Sinnamahoning,
Sterling Run.

CARBON COUNTY.

Albrightsville,
Aquashicola,
Audenried,
Beaver Meadows,
Buck Mountain,
Carbon,
East Mauch Chunk,
Hickory Run,
Hudsondale,
Lehigh Gap,
Lehigh Tannery,
Lehighton,
Little Gap,

Mauch Chunk,* (c. h.,)
Nesquehoning,
New Mahoning,
Parryville,
Penn Haven,
Pleasant Corners,
Rockport,
Stembersville,
Summit Hill,
Tresckow,
Weatherly,
Weissport.

CENTRE COUNTY.

Aaronsburgh,
Agricultural College,
Bellefonte,* (c. h.,)
Blanchard,
Boalsburgh,
Buddville,
Buffalo Run,
Centre Hall,
Centre Hill,
Centre Mills,
Fillmore,
Fleming,
Half Moon,
Houserville,
Howard,
Hublersburgh,
Julian Furnace,
Lemont,
Linden Hall,
Loveville,
Madisonburgh,
Martha Furnace,

Meshannon,
Milesburgh,
Millheim,
Mountain Eagle,
Nittany,
Penn Hall,
Philipsburgh,
Pine Glen,
Pine Grove Mills,
Pleasant Gap,
Port Matilda,
Potter's Mills,
Powelton,
Rebersburgh,
Rock Spring,
Roland,
Snow Shoe,
Spring Mills,
Walker,
Wolf's Store,
Woodward,
Zion.

* Money-order office.

CHESTER COUNTY.

Avondale,
Barneston,
Birch Run Ville,
Black Horse,
Blue Rock,
Brandywine Manor,
Caln,
Chatham,
Chester Springs,
Chester Valley,
Chesterville,
Chrome,
Coatesville,
Cochransville,
Collamer,
Cupola,
Dilworthtown,
Doe Run,
Dorlan's Mills,
Downingtown,
East Coventry,
East Vincent,
Elk Dale,
Elk Mills,
Elkview,
Embreeville,
Ercildoun,
Exton,
Fairville,
Frazer,
Frémont,
Glenloch,
Glen Roy,
Goshenville,
Gum Tree,
Guthriesville,
Hamorton,
Hayesville,
Hickory Hill,
Honey Brook,
Hopewell Cotton
 Works,
Jennersville,
Kaolin,
Kemblesville,
Kennett's Square,
Kimberton,
Landenburgh,
Lenape,
Leopard,
Lewisville,
Lincoln University,
Lionville,
Loag,
Loudonderry,
London Grove,
McWilliamstown,

Marlborough,
Marsh,
Marshallton,
Milford Mills,
Milltown,
Mortonville,
Mount Vernon,
New Centreville,
New Garden,
New London,
North Coventry,
Norwood,
Nottingham,
Oxford,*
Paoli,
Parkersville,
Parkesburgh,
Pawling,
Penningtonville,
Phœnixville,*
Pickering,
Pomeroy,
Pughtown,
Reeseville,
Rockville,
Russellville,
Sadsburyville,
Saint Peters,
Schuylkill,
Setzler's Store,
Spread Eagle,
Steelville,
Street Road,
Strickersville,
Sugartown,
Talbotville,
Thornbury,
Thorndale Iron
 Works,
Tough Kenamon,
Unionville,
Uwchland,
Valley Creek,
Valley Forge,
Vincent,
Wagontown,
Wallace,
Warren Tavern,
Warwick,
West Chester, (c. h.,)
West Grove Station,
West Vincent,
West Whiteland,
White Horse,
Wildbrier,
Willistown Inn,
Willowdale.

CLARION COUNTY.

Alum Rock,
Brinkerton,
Callensburgh,
Catfish,
Clarion, (c. h.,)
Cunningham,
Curllsville,
Fisher,
Foxburgh,
Fryburgh,

CLARION COUNTY—Continued.

Helen Furnace,
Jefferson Furnace,
Kahle's,
Kerr's Store,
Kingsville,
Knox,
Kossuth,
Lamartine,
Leatherwood,
Lickingville,
Limestone,
Lucinda Furnace,
New Bethlehem,
Newmansville,
North Pine Grove,
Philipston,

Piny,
Pollock,
Reidsburgh,
Rimersburgh,
Saint Petersburgh,
Scotch Hill,
Shannondale,
Shippensville,
Sligo,
Strattonville,
Tylersburgh,
Valley,
Watterson's Ferry,
West Freedom,
West Monterey,

CLEARFIELD COUNTY.

Alleman's,
Ansonville,
Bald Hill,
Bloomington,
Bower,
Burnside,
Chest,
Clearfield, (c. h.,)
Clearfield Bridge,
Curwinsville,
Cush,
East Ridge,
Forest,
Frenchville,
Glen Hope,
Grahamton,
Grampian Hills,
Hegarty's × Roads,
Houtzdale,
Hurd,
Jefferson Line,
Jeffries,
Karthaus,
Kylertown,
Leconte's Mills,
Little Toby,

Lumber City,
Luthersburgh,
McGarvey's,
Madera,
Marron,
Morrisdale,
New Millport,
New Washington,
Osceola Mills,
Ostend,
Patchinsville,
Penfield,
Rockton,
Salt Lick,
Shawsville,
Smith's Mills,
Three Runs,
Troutville,
Tylers,
Utahville,
Wallaceton,
West Decatur,
Westover's,
Williams Grove,
Woodland.

CLINTON COUNTY.

Beech Creek,
Booneville,
Carroll,
Cedar Springs,
Chatham Run,
Cross Fork,
Farrandsville,
Flemington,
Glen Union,
Hammersley's Fork,
Hiner's Run,
Island,
Lamar,
Lamar Mills,
Leidy,
Lockhaven, (c. h.,)

Logan Mills,
McElhattan,
Mill Hall,
Phelps Mills,
Pine Station,
Rauch's Gap,
Renovo,*
Rosecrans,
Round Island,
Salona,
Sugar Valley,
Tylersville,
Westport,
Whetham,
Wistar,
Young Womanstown.

* Money-order office.

COLUMBIA COUNTY.

Beaver Valley,
Benton,
Berwick,
Bloomsburgh, (c. h.,)
Brier Creek,
Buckhorn,
Catawissa,
Central,
Centralia,
Cole's Creek,
Espy,
Evansville,
Eyer's Grove,
Fishing Creek,
Forks,
Foundryville,
Fowlersville,
Greenwood,
Iola,

Jerseytown,
Light Street,
Lime Ridge,
Mainville,
Mifflinville,
Millville,
Mordansville,
Numidia,
Orangeville,
Pine Summit,
Polkville,
Roaring Creek,
Rohrsburgh,
Rupert,
Sereno,
Stillwater,
Van Camp,
Willow Springs.

CRAWFORD COUNTY.

Adamsville,
Beaver Centre,
Black Ash,
Bloomfield,
Blooming Valley,
Brown Hill,
Calvin's Corners,
Cambridgeborough,
Centre Road Station,
Centreville,
Chapinville,
Cochrantown,
Conneautville,*
Coon's Corners,
Crossingville,
Custard's,
Deckard,
Dicksonburgh,
Drake's Mills,
Dutch Hill,
Espyville,
Evansburgh,
Fallowfield,
Frenchtown,
Glyndon,
Guy's Mills,
Harmonsburgh,
Hartstown,
Hayfield,
Lincolnville,
Lines Hollow,
Lineville Station,
Little Cooley,
Long's Stand,
McLean's Corners,

Mead Corners,
Meadville, (c. h.,)
Miller's Station,
Morris Corners,
Mosiertown,
New Richmond,
Norrisville,
North Shenango,
Oil Creek,
Penn Line,
Pettis,
Potter's Corners,
Randolph,
Riceville,
Royalton,
Rundells,
Saegerstown,
Sandy Creek,
Shaw's Landing,
Spartansburgh,
Spring,
Steamburgh,
Stony Point,
Sugar Lake,
Sutton's Corners,
Tamarac,
Taylor's Stand,
Titusville,*
Townville,
Tryonville,
Turnersville,
Venango,
Wayne Centre,
West Greenwood,
Woodcock.

CUMBERLAND COUNTY.

Allen,
Big Spring,
Bloserville,
Boiling Springs,
Camp Hill,

Carlisle, (c. h.)
Carlisle Springs,
Dickinson,
Eberly's Mill,
Good Hope,

CUMBERLAND COUNTY—Continued.

Greason,
Hogestown,
Kerrsville,
Lee's Cross Roads,
Lisburn,
Mechanicsburgh,
Middle Spring,
Mountain Creek,
Mt. Holly Springs,
Mount Rock,
Newburgh,
New Cumberland,

New Kingstown,
Newville,
Oakville,
Plainfield,
Shepherdstown,*
Shippensburgh,
Shiremautown,
Stoughstown,
Walnut Bottom,
West Fairview,
White House.

DAUPHIN COUNTY.

Benvenue,
Berrysburgh,
Curtin,
Dauphin,
Derry Church,
Ellendale Forge,
Elizabethville,
Enders,
Enterline,
Fisherville,
Grantville,
Gratz,
Halifax,
HARRISBURGH,*
  (c.h.,)
High Spire,
Hummelstown,
Killinger,

Linglestown,
Lykens,
Manada Hill,
Middletown,*
Millersburgh,*
Paxton,
Pillow,
Powel's Creek,
Powl's Valley,
Progress,
Short Mountain,
Susquehanna,
Swatara Station,
Union Deposit,
West Hanover,
Wiconisco,
Williamstown.

DELAWARE COUNTY.

Booth Corner,
Brandywine Summit,
Broomall,
Chadd's Ford,
Chelsea,
Chester,*
Cheyney,
Concordville,
Darby,
Edgemont,
Elam,
Glen Mills,
Glen Riddle,
Haverford,
Howellville,
Ivy Mills,
Kellysville,
Lazaretto Station,

Leipersville,
Lenni Mills,
Lima,
Linwood Station,
Marple,
Media, (c. h.,)
Morton,
Newtown Square,
Oakdale,
Radnor,
Thornton,
Thurlow,
Uplands,
Upper Darby,
Upper Providence,
Village Green,
West Haverford.

ELK COUNTY.

Arroyo,
Benezett,
Brandy Camp,
Caledonia,
Dent's Run,
Earley,
Hellen,

Kerseys,
Ridgway, (c. h.,)
Saint Mary's,
Wilcox,
Williamsville,
Wilmarth.

* Money-order office.

ERIE COUNTY.

Albion,*
Avonia,
Belle Valley,
Carter Hill,
Cherry Hill,
Concord Station,
Corry,*
East Greene,
East Springfield,
Edenville,
Edinborough,
Elk Creek,
Erie,* (c. h.,)
Fairview,*
Franklin Corners,
Girard,*
Greenfield,
Harbour Creek,
Hatch Hollow,
Keepville,
Lake Pleasant,
Lebœuf,
Lovell's Station,

Lowville,
Lundy's Lane,
McKean,
McLane,
McLellan's Corners,
Miles' Grove,
Mill Village,
Moorheadville,
North East,*
North Springfield,
Northville,
Platea,
Sterrettania,
Stewart,
Swan Station,
Union Mills,*
Waterford,
Wattsburgh,
Wayne,
Wesleyville,
West Greene,
West Springfield.

FAYETTE COUNTY.

Belle Vernon,
Broad Ford,
Brownsville,*
Connellsville,
Davidson's Ferry,
Dawson's Station,
Dunbar,
East Liberty,
Elm,
Farmington,
Fayette City,
Fayette Springs,
Flatwoods,
Frost's Station,
Heistersburgh,
Indian Creek,
Layton's Station,
McClellandtown,

Markleysburgh,
Masontown,
Merrittstown,
Mill Run,
Morris Cross Roads,
New Geneva,
New Salem,
Pennsville,
Perryopolis,
Pile Falls,
Redstone,
Searight's,
Shinbone,
Smithfield,
Springhill Furnace,
Tippecanoe,
Uniontown,* (c. h.)
Upper Middletown.

FOREST COUNTY.

Clarington,
Cooksburgh,
East Hickory,
Marionville,
Nebraska,
Newtown Mills,

Panther Rock,
Perry,
Raught's Mills,
Tionesta,* (c. h.,)
Trunkeyville,
West Hickory.

FRANKLIN COUNTY.

Amberson's Valley,
Black's Gap,
Brown's Mills,
Chambersburgh,*
  (c. h.,)
Clay Lick,
Concord,
Doylesburgh,
Dry Run,
Fannettsburgh,
Fayetteville,
Greencastle,*

Green Village,
Jackson Hall,
Keefer's Store,
Loudon,
Mason and Dixon,
Marion,
Mercersburgh,*
Mont Alto,
Mount Parnel,
Mowersville,
New Bridge,
Orrstown,

FRANKLIN COUNTY—Continued.

Pleasant Hall,
Quincy,
Roxbury,
Saint Thomas,
Scotland,
Shady Grove,
Spring Run,

State Line,
Sylvan,
Upper Strasburgh,
Upton,
Waynesborough,*
Welsh Run.

FULTON COUNTY.

Akersville,
Big Cove Tannery,
Buck Valley,
Burnt Cabins,
Dublin Mills,
Emmaville,
Fort Littleton,
Gapsville,
Harrisonville,
Hustontown,
Knobsville,

Locust Grove,
McConnellsburgh,
  (c. h.,)
New Grenada,
Sideling Hill,
Sipe's Mill,
Warfordsburgh,
Webster's Mills,
Wells' Tannery,
West Dublin.

GREENE COUNTY.

Aleppo,
Big Tree,
Bristoria,
Carmichael's,
Ceylon,
Clarksville,
Crow's Mills,
Davistown,
Day's Store,
Delight,
Dent,
Dunkard,
Fordyce,
Gray's Landing,
Greensborough,
Harvey's,
Holbrook,
Hopkins' Mills,
Hunter's Cave,
Jefferson,

Jollytown,
Kirby,
Lone Tree,
Mapletown,
Mount Morris,
New Freeport,
Oak Forest,
Rice's Landing,
Rogersville,
Rosedale,
Ruff Creek,
Ryerson's Station,
Spragg's,
Thom's Run,
Waynesburgh,* (c. h.,
White Cottage,
Whiteley,
Wiley,
Willow Tree,
Wind Ridge.

HUNTINGDON COUNTY.

Airy Dale,
Alexandria,
Aughwick's Mills,
Barre Forge,
Birmingham,
Broad Top,
Calvin,
Cassville,
Coalmont,
Coffee Run,
Colerain Forge,
Colfax,
Cottage,
Cove Station,
Donation,
Dudley,
Eagle Foundry,
Ennisville,
Franklinville,
Graysville,
Greenwood Furnace,

Hair's Valley,
Hill Valley,
Hubelsville,
Huntingdon,* (c. h.,)
James Creek,
McAlevy's Fort,
McConnellstown,
Maddensville,
Manor Hill,
Mapleton Depot,
Meadow Gap,
Mill Creek,
Morrell,
Mount Union,
Neff's Mills,
New Pleasant Grove,
Nossville,
Orbisonia,
Saltillo,
Saulsburgh,
Shade Gap,

* Money-order office.

HUNTINGDON COUNTY—Continued.

Shaver's Creek,	Todd,
Shirleysburgh,	Vineyard Mills,
Spruce Creek,	Warrior's Mark,
Three Springs,	Water Street.

INDIANA COUNTY.

Advance,	Mahoning,
Armagh,	Marchand,
Ambrose,	Minta,
Black Lick Station,	Mitchell's Mills,
Blairsville,*	Nolo,
Brady,	Onberg,
Brush Valley,	Parkwood,
Chambersville,	Penn Run,
Clarksburgh,	Philip's Mills,
Covode,	Pine Flats,
Creekside,	Plumville,
Crete,	Purchase Line,
Decker's Point,	Saltsburgh,
Dixonville,	Shelocta,
Ebenezer,	Smicksburgh,
Elder's Ridge,	Smitten,
Gilpin,	Spruce,
Grant,	Strongstown,
Heshbon,	Suncliff,
Hillsdale,	Tannery,
Home,	Tunnelton,
Horton's,	Utah,
Indiana, (c. h.,)	Watt,
Kent,	West Lebanon,
Kimmel,	Willet.
Locust Lane,	

JEFFERSON COUNTY.

Bell's Mills,	Packer,
Big Run,	Porter,
Brockwayville,	Punxatawney,*
Brookville, (c. h.,)	Reynoldsville,
Canoe Ridge,	Richardsville,
Cool Spring,	Ringgold,
Corsica,	Rockdale Mills,
Dolingville,	Schoffner's Corners,
Frostburgh,	Sigel,
Hamilton,	Sprankle's Mills,
Hudson,	Stanton,
Knox Dale,	Summerville,
New Petersburgh,	Warsaw,
Oliveburgh,	Worthville.

JUNIATA COUNTY.

Academia,	Oakland Mills,
Cocolamus,	Patterson,
Doyle's Mills,	Peru Mills,
East Salem.	Pleasant View,
East Waterford.	Port Royal,
Evendale,	Reed's Gap,
Honey Grove,	Richfield,
McAllisterville.	Shade Valley,
McCoysville,	Spruce Hill,
McCulloch's Mills,	Thompsontown,
Mexico,	Van Wert,
Mifflintown, (c. h.,)	Walnut,
Mohontongo,	Waterloo.

LANCASTER COUNTY.

Adamstown,	Lyles,
Akron,	Manheim,
Bainbridge,	Manor,
Bareville,	Marietta,*
Bart,	Martickville,
Bartville,	Martinsville,
Beartown,	Mastersonville,
Bellemonte,	May,
Bethesda,	Maytown,
Binkley's Bridge,	Mechanic's Grove,
Blue Ball,	Millersville,*
Bowmansville,	Millway,
Brickerville,	Motley,
Brunnerville,	Mount Hope,
Buck,	Mount Joy,*
Buyerstown,	Mount Nebo,
Cain's,	Mountville,
Camargo,	Muddy Creek,
Cambridge,	Neffsville,
Chesnut Level,	New Danville,
Chickies,	New Holland,
Christiana,	New Providence,
Churchtown,	Nine Points,
Clonmell,	Oak Hill,
Cocalico,	Oak Shade,
Colemanville,	Octoraro,
Colerain,	Old Line,
Columbia,*	Oregon,
Conestoga,	Paradise,
Creswell,	Penn,
Durlach,	Pequea,
East Hempfield,	Peter's Creek,
Elizabethtown,	Pleasant Grove,
Enterprise,	Quarryville,
Ephratah,	Rawlinsville,
Falmouth,	Reamstown,
Farmersville,	Reidenbach's Store,
Fertility,	Reinhold's Station,
Fulton House,	Reinholdsville,
Gap,	Rothsville,
Goodville,	Safe Harbor,
Gordonsville,	Salisbury,
Goshen,	Salunga,
Green Bank,	Schoeneck,
Greene,	Silver Spring,
Greenland,	Slack Water,
Groff's Store,	Smithville,
Hempfield,	Smyrna,
Highville,	Soudersburgh,
Hinkleton,	South Hermitage,
Intercourse,	Sporting Hill,
Junction,	Spring Garden,
Kinzers,	Spring Grove,
Kirk's Mills,	Stevens,
Kirkwood,	Strasburgh,
Lampeter,	Swartzville,
Lancaster, (c. h.,)	Terre Hill,
Landis Valley,	Union Station,
Landisville,	Vogansville,
Leacock,	Wakefield,
Leaman Place.	West Earl,
Liberty Square,	Wheatland Mills,
Lincoln,	White Oak,
Litiz,*	Willow Street,
Little Britain,	Wright's Dale.

* Money-order office.

LAWRENCE COUNTY.

Chenango,	New Bedford,
Cross Cut,	*Newcastle,* (c. h.,)
East Brook,	New Wilmington,
Edinburgh,	Plain Grove,
Enon Valley,	Princeton,
Harlensburgh,	Pulaski,
Hillsville,	Rose Point,
Moravia,	Volant,
Mount Jackson,	Wampum,
Neshannock Falls,	Wurtemberg.

LEBANON COUNTY.

Annville,*	*Lebanon,* (c. h.,)
Avon,	Meyerstown,
Bellview,	Millbach,
Campbelltown,	Monroe Forge,
Colebrook,	Mount Zion,
Cornwall,	Ono,
East Hanover,	Palmyra,
Fredericksburgh,	Richland Station,
Greble,	Shaefferstown,
Hamlin,	Sheridan,
Jonestown,*	Union Forge.
Kleinfeltersville,	

LEHIGH COUNTY.

Alburtis.	Lyon Valley,
Allentown, (c. h.,)	Macungie,
Breinigsville,	Mountainville,
Catasauqua,	Neff's,
Centre Valley,	New Tripoli,
Claussville,	North Whitehall,
Coopersburgh,	Orefield,
Dillingersville,	Oswaldville,
Emaus,	Rittersville,
Fogelsville,	Rucksville,
Friedensville,	Saegersville,
Hokendauqua,	Schnecksville,
Hosensack,	Seiberlingville,
Hyremansville,	Shimerville,
Ironton,	Shoenersville,
Jacksonville,	Sipestown,
Lanark,	Slatington,
Laury's Station,	South Whitehall,
Lehigh Valley,	Stinesville,
Limeport,	Trexlertown,
Litzenberg,	Vera Cruz,
Locust Valley,	Weidasville,
Lowhill,	Weisenburgh,
Lynnport,	Wennersville,
Lynnville,	Wescosville.

LUZERNE COUNTY.

Archbald,	Cambra,
Bailey Hollow,	Carbondale,*
Bald Mount,	Carverton,
Beach Haven,	Charleston,
Bear Creek,	Clark's Green,
Belbend,	Clifton,
Black Creek,	Conyngham,
Bloomingdale,	Daleville,
Briggsville,	Dallas,

LUZERNE COUNTY—Continued.

Dorrance,	Muhlenburgh,
Drum's,	Nanticoke,
Dunmore,	Nescopeck,
Dunnings,	New Columbus,
East Benton,	Old Forge,
Eckley,	Olyphant,
Exeter,	Orange,
Fairmount Springs,	Peckville,
Fleetville,	Pittston,
Forty Fort,	Plainsville,
Gibsonburgh,	Plymouth,*
Gouldsborough,	Port Blanchard,
Green Grove,	Providence,
Harveyville,	Ransom,
Hazleton,*	Red Rock,
Hendricksburgh,	Schultzville,
Hobbie,	Scott,
Humphreysville,	Scranton,*
Hunlock Creek,	Shickshinny,
Huntsville,	Spring Brook,
Hyde Park,	Stockton,
Jeansville,	Stoddartsville,
Jeddo,	Sugar Notch,
Ketcham,	Sweet Valley,
Kingston,	Sybertsville,
Kunckle,	Tompkinsville,
Lackawanna,	Town Hill,
Lake,	Town Line,
Laurel Run,	Trucksville,
Lehman,	Upper Lehigh,
Luzerne,	Wallsville,
Madisonville,	Wapwallopen,
Mill Hollow,	Waverly,
Milwaukie,	West Nanticoke,
Morrison,	White Haven,
Moscow,	*Wilkesbarre,* (c. h.,)
Mountain Top,	Wyoming.
Mountain Valley,	

LYCOMING COUNTY.

Antes Fort,	Montgomery Station,
Barbour's Mills,	Monturesville,
Bastress,	Moreland,
Bodinesville,	Muncy,*
Carpenter,	Muncy Station,
Cedar Run,	Newberry,
Chesnut Grove,	Nippenose,
Clarkstown,	Nisbet,
Cogan House,	Oregon Hill,
Cogan Station,	Picture Rocks,
Collomsville,	Ralston,
Elimsport,	Roaring Branch,
English Centre,	Rose's Valley,
Fairfield Centre,	Salladyburgh,
Haneyville,	Texas,
Hughesville,	Tivoli,
Huntersville,	Tomb's Run,
Jersey Mills,	Trout Run,
Jersey Shore,*	Unityville,
Kellyburgh,	Wallis Run,
Lairdsville,	Warrensville,
Larry's Creek,	Waterville,
Linden,	White Pine,
Loyalsock,	*Williamsport,* (c. h.,)
Maple Hill,	Wolf Run.

* Money-order office.

McKEAN COUNTY.

Allegheny Bridge,
Alton,
Annin Creek,
Bradford,
Clermontville,
Colegrove,
De Golier,
Eden,
Farmer's Valley,
Glenn,
Kane,
Kasson,

Keating,
Kendall Creek,
La Fayette,
Norwich,
Port Allegheny,
Prentiss Vale,
Sargent,
Sartwell,
Smithport, (c. h.,)
State Line Mills,
Turtle Point.

MERCER COUNTY.

Balm,
Centretown,
Clark,
Delaware Grove,
Fredonia,
French Creek,
Greenville,*
Hadley,
Harthegig,
Henderson,
Hermitage,
Hill,
Indian Run,
Irishtown,
Jamestown,
Kennard,
Leech's Corners,
Leesburgh,
London,
Maysville,
Mercer, (c. h.,)

Milledgeville,
New Hamburgh,
New Lebanon,
New Vernon,
North Liberty,
North Sandy,
North's Mills,
Perrine,
Sandy Lake,
Satterfield,
Sharon,*
Sharpsville Furnace,
Sheakleyville,
Stoneborough,
Transfer,
West Middlesex,
West Salem,
Wheatland Furnace,
Wolf Creek,
Worth.

MIFFLIN COUNTY.

Allensville,
Atkinson's Mills,
Belleville,
Decatur,
Granville,
Kelley,
Kishacoquillas,

Lewistown, (c. h.,)
McVeytown,
Menno,
Milroy,
Newton Hamilton,
Reedsville,
Strode's Mills.

MONROE COUNTY.

Analomink,
Bartonsville,
Bossardsville,
Brodheadsville,
Canadensis,
Coolbaugh's,
Delaware   Water
    Gap,
East Stroudsburgh,
Effort,
Experiment Mills,
Gilbert,
Jackson Corners,
Henrysville,
Kellersville,
Kresgeville,
Kunkletown,

Marshall's Creek,
Merwinsburgh,
New Mt. Pleasant,
Paradise Valley,
Roscommon,
Rossland,
Saylorsburgh,
Sciota,
Shawnee,
Shoemaker's,
Snydersville,
Stormville,
Stroudsburgh, (c. h.,)
Tannersville,
Tobyhanna Mills,
White's Tannery.

MONTGOMERY COUNTY.

Abington,
Barren Hill,
Blue Bell,
Bridgeport,
Broad Axe,
Cabinet,
Centre Square,
Cheltenham,
Collegeville,
Conshohocken,
Crooked Hill,
Douglass,
Eagleville,
Fagleysville,
Fairview Village,
Fitzwatertown,
Flourtown,
Franconia,
Frederick,
General Wayne,
Gilbertsville,
Grater's Ford,
Gulf Mills,
Gwynedd,
Harleysville,
Half Way,
Hatborough,
Hatfield,
Hickory Town,
Hillegass,
Hoppenville,
Horsham,
Huntingdon Valley,
Jarrettown,
Jeffersonville,
Jenkintown,
King of Prussia,
Kulpsville,
Landsdale,
Lederachsville,
Limerick,
Limerick Station,

Line Lexington,
Lower Merion,
Lower Providence,
Montgomery Square,
New Hanover,
Norristown, (c. h.,)
Norritonville,
North Wales,
Overbrook,
Palm,
Penllyn,
Pennsburgh,
Penn's Square,
Perkiomenville,
Plymouth Meeting,
Port Kennedy,
Port Providence,
Pottstown,*
Prospectville,
Red Hill,
Royer's Ford,
Salfordville,
Schwenk's Store,
Shannonville,
Shoemakertown,
Skippack,
Sorrel Horse,
Souder's Station,
Spring House,
Sumneytown,
Three Tons,
Trappe,
Tyler's Port,
Union Square,
Upper Dublin,
Waverly Heights,
White Marsh,
William Penn,
Willow Grove,
Worcester,
Zeiglersville.

MONTOUR COUNTY.

Comly,
Danville, (c. h.,)
Exchange,
Limestoneville,

Mooresburgh,
Washingtonville,
White Hall.

NORTHAMPTON COUNTY.

Ackermanville,
Bangor,
Bath,
Belfast,
Berlinsville,
Bethlehem,*
Blue Mountain,
Bush Kiln Centre,
Butztown,
Chapman Quarries,
Cherryville,
Danielsville,
Delpsburgh,

Easton, (c. h.,)
Freemansburgh,
Hanoverville,
Hecktown,
Hellertown,
Iron Hill,
Johnsonville,
Kessler's,
Klecknersville,
Kreidersville,
Laubach,
Leithsville,
Lower Saucon,

* Money-order office.

NORTHAMPTON COUNTY—Continued.

Martin's Creek,	Seidersville,
Middagh's,	Seigfried's Bridge,
Moorestown,	Slateford,
Mount Bethel,	South Bethlehem,*
Nazareth,*	South Easton,
Newhart's,	Stockertown,
Petersville,	Stone Church,
Portland,	Stouts,
Redington,	Uhlersville,
Richmond,	Weaversville,
Sandt's Eddy,	Wind Gap.

NORTHUMBERLAND COUNTY.

Augusta,	Milton,
Bear Gap,	Montandon,
Chillisquaque,	Mount Carmel,
Chulasky,	Northumberland,*
Dalmatia,	Paxinos,
Dewart,	Pott's Grove,
Dornsife,	Rebuck's,
Elysburgh,	Riverside,
Excelsior,	Rushtown,
Fisher's Ferry,	Shamokin,*
Greenbrier,	Snydertown,
Herndon,	Sunbury, (c. h.,)
Hickory Corners,	Trevorton,
Kline's Grove,	Turbotville,
Line Mountain,	Union Corner,
Locust Gap,	Urban,
McEwensville,	Watsontown.*
Mahanoy,	

PERRY COUNTY.

Andersonburgh,	Mannsville,
Blain,	Markelsville,
Centre,	Marysville,
Dellville,	Millerstown,
Donally's Mills,	Millerstown Stat'n,
Duncannon,	Montgomery's Ferry,
Elliottsburgh,	New Bloomfield, (c. h.,)
Green Park,	New Buffalo,
Grier's Point,	New Germantown,
Ickesburgh,	Newport,*
Juniata,	Roseburgh,
Keystone,	Sandy Hill,
Landisburgh,	Sherman's Dale,
Liverpool,	Sterrett's Gap.
Loysville,	

PHILADELPHIA COUNTY.

Philadelphia,* (c. h.)

PIKE COUNTY.

Bushkill,	Matamoras,
Delaware,	Milford,* (c. h.,)
Dingman's Ferry,	Millville Depot,
Egypt Mills,	Nyces,
Field Bend,	Paupac,
Lackawaxen,	Rowland,
Lord's Valley,	Shohola,
Masthope,	Tafton.

POTTER COUNTY.

Ayer's Hill,	Homer,
Bingham Centre,	Kettle Creek,
Brookland,	Millport,
Burtville,	North Wharton,
Carter Camp,	Oswayo,
Clara,	Pike Mills,
Colesburgh,	Raymond's,
Coudersport,* (c. h.,)	Roulette,
East Hebron,	Sharon Centre,
East Homer,	Shinglehouse,
East Sharon,	Sunderlinville,
Eleven Mile,	Sweden,
Ellisburgh,	Sweden Valley,
Eulalia,	Ulysses,
Forest Home,	West Bingham,
Genesee Fork,	West Pike,
Germania,	Wharton,
Harrison Valley,	White's Corners,
Hebron,	Williston.

SCHUYLKILL COUNTY.

Ashland,*	Orwigsburgh,
Auburn,	Orwin,
Barnesville,	Palo Alto,
Barry,	Pine Grove,
Branch Dale,	Port Carbon,
Brandonville,	Port Clinton,
Broad Mountain,	Pottsville,* (c. h.,)
Cressona,	Reynolds,
Delano,	Ringtown,
Donaldson,	Rock,
Drehersville,	Rough and Ready,
Ellwood,	Sacramento,
Friedensburgh,	Saint Clair,*
Girard Manor,	Saint Nicholas,
Girardsville,	Schneider,
Glen Carbon,	Schuylkill Haven,
Gordon,	Shenandoah,
Hegins,	Silver Brook,
Hepler,	Silver Creek,
Hughes,	Summit Station,
Joliett,	Swatara,
Klingerstown,	Sylliman,
Landingville,	Tamaqua,*
Llewellyn,	Tower City,
Lower Mahantango,	Tremont,
McKeansburgh,	Tuscarora,
Mahanoy City,*	Upper Mahantango,
Mahanoy Plane,	Weishample,
Middleport,	West Penn,
Minersville,*	Yatesville,
New Ringgold,	Zion's Grove.
North Penn,	

SNYDER COUNTY.

Bannerville,	Middleburgh, (c. h.,)
Beaver Springs,	Middle Creek,
Beavertown,	Mt. Pleasant Mills,
Chapman,	Pallas,
Freeburgh,	Penn's Creek,
Hummell's Wharf,	Port Treverton,
Kantz,	Salem,
Kratzerville,	Selin's Grove,*
Kreamer,	Shamokin Dam,
McKee's Half Falls,	Troxelville.

* Money-order office.

SOMERSET COUNTY.

Addison,	New Lexington,
Bakersville,	Pocahontas,
Benford's Store,	Sand Patch,
Berkley's,	Shade Furnace,
Berlin,	Shaff's Bridge,
Buckstown,	Shanksville,
Casselman,	Sipesville,
Davidsville,	Somerfield,
Dividing Ridge,	*Somerset,* (c. h.,)
Elk Lick,	Somerset Furnace,
Gebhart's,	Southampton Mills,
Glade,	Staunton's Mills,
Harnedsville,	Stony Creek,
Jenner's X Roads,	Stoyestown,
Jennerstown,	Summit Mills,
Johnsburgh,	Turkey Foot,
Kingwood,	Turner's Store,
Lavansville,	Ursina,
Meyer's Mills,	Wellersburgh,
Mount Healthy,	Wittenberg.
New Baltimore,	

SULLIVAN COUNTY.

Campbellville,	*Laporte,* (c. h.,)
Colley,	Lincoln Falls,
Davidson,	Millview,
Dushore, *	Muncy Bottom,
Eagle's Mere,	Plunkett,
Eldredsville,	Shunk,
Forksville,	Sonestown.
Hill's Grove,	

SUSQUEHANNA COUNTY.

Ararat,	Lanesborough,
Auburn Centre,	Lathrop,
Auburn Four Corn's,	Lawsville Centre,
Birchardville,	Lenoxville,
Brackney,	Little Meadows,
Brookdale,	Lynn,
Brooklyn,	Middletown Centre,
Choconut,	*Montrose,* (c. h.,)
Clifford,	Montrose Depot,
Dimock,	New Milford,
Dundaff,	Niven,
East Bridgewater,	North Jackson,
East Dimock,	Oakley,
East Rush,	Richmond Hill,
Elk Lake,	Rush,
Fairdale,	Rush Four Corners,
Forest Lake,	Rushville,
Forest Lake Centre,	Saint Joseph,
Friendsville,	Silver Lake,
Gibson,	Smiley,
Glenwood,	South Auburn,
Great Bend,	South Gibson,
Great Bend Village,	Springville,
Harmony Centre,	Susquehanna Depot, *
Harford,	Thompson,
Herrick Centre,	Union Dale,
Hop Bottom,	Upsonville,
Jackson,	West Auburn,
Jackson Valley,	West Lenox.

TIOGA COUNTY.

Arnot,	Liberty,
Blossburgh, *	Little Marsh,
Brookfield,	Lloyd,
Canoe Camp,	Mainesburgh,
Charleston,	Mansfield,
Chase's Mills,	Maple Ridge,
Chatham Valley,	Marshfield,
Cherry Flats,	Middlebury Centre,
Covington,	Mitchell's Creek,
Cowanesque Valley,	Mixtown,
Crooked Creek,	Morris,
Daggett's Mills,	Morris Run,
East Charleston,	Nauvoo,
East Chatham,	Nelson,
Elkland,	Nile's Valley,
Elk Run,	Osceola,
Fall Brook,	Ogdensburgh,
Farmington Centre,	Pine Creek,
Farmington Hill,	Rutland,
Gaines,	Sabinsville,
Gray's Valley,	Stony Fork.
Hammond's Creek,	Sullivan,
Keeneyville,	Tioga,
Knoxville.	*Wellsborough,* (c. h.,)
Lamb's Creek,	West Covington,
Lansing,	Westfield.
Lawrenceville,	

UNION COUNTY.

Alvira,	Mifflinburgh,
Buffalo Cross Roads,	New Berlin,
Cowan,	New Columbia,
Forest Hill,	Slifer,
Hartleton,	Vicksburgh,
Kelly Point,	West Milton,
Laurelton,	White Deer Mills,
Lewisburgh, (c. h.,)	Winfield.

VENANGO COUNTY.

Agnew's Mills,	Meredith,
Barkeyville,	Nickleville,
Big Bend,	Oil City, *
Canal,	Oleopolis,
Cass,	Personville,
Cherry Tree,	Petroleum Centre, *
Clintonville,	Pioneer,
Coal City,	Pit Hole City, *
Columbia Farm,	Pittsville,
Cooperstown,	Pleasantville, *
Cranberry,	Plum,
Dempseytown,	Plumer,
Diamond,	Polk,
Eagle Rock,	Porterfield,
East Sandy,	President,
Emlenton,	Raymilton,
Fertigs,	Reno,
Franklin, (c. h.,)	Rockland,
Kane City,	Rouseville, *
Kennerdell,	Seneca,
Kilgore,	Shamburgh, *
Lamb's,	Sherman Wells,
Laytonia,	Sidney,
Lineville,	Stewart's Run,

* Money-order office.

VENANGO COUNTY—Continued.

Sunville,	Wallaceville,
Tarr Farm,*	Wesley,
Ten Mile Bottom,	Wilson's Mills,
Utica,	Witherup's.

WARREN COUNTY.

Bear Lake,	Pittsfield,
Chandler's Valley,	Russellsburgh,
Cobham,	Sheffield,
Columbus,	Sheffield Depot,
Cornplanter,	South West,
Corydon,	Spring Creek,
Eagle,	Star,
Freehold,	Steam Mill.
Garland,	Stoneham,
Germany,	Sugar Grove.
Irvine,	Tidioute,*
Kinzua,	*Warren,* (c. h.,)
Lander,	West Spring Creek,
Lottsville,	Youngsville.

WASHINGTON COUNTY.

Allenport,	Independence.
Amity,	Kerr's Station.
Atchison,	Lindly's Mills,
Bavington,	Lock No. 4,
Beallsville,	Locust Hill,
Beck's Mills,	Lone Pine,
Bentleyville,	Meloy,
Bower Hill,	Midway,
Brush Run,	Millsborough,
Buffalo,	Monongahela City,*
Bulger,	Mount Airy,
Burgettstown,	Munntown,
California,	Murdocksville,
Candor,	Paris,
Cannonsburgh,*	Patterson's Mills,
Cardville,	Pike Run,
Cherry Valley,	Prosperity,
Claysville,	Raccoon,
Clokey,	Scenery Hill,
Coal Bluff,	Simpson's Store,
Coon Island,	Sparta,
Cross Creek Village,	Strabane,
Dinsmore,	Taylorstown,
Donley,	Ten Mile,
Dunningsville,	Thompsonville,
Dunsfort,	Van Buren,
East Bethlehem,	Vancoville,
East Finley,	Venice,
Finleyville,	*Washington,* (c. h.,)
Florence,	West Alexander,
Fredericktown,	West Brownsville,
Ginger Hill,	West Finley,
Good Intent,	West Middletown,
Hanlin Station,	Woodrow,
Havelock,	Yortysville,
Herriottsville,	Zollarsville.
Hickory,	

WAYNE COUNTY.

Aldenville,	Ariel,

WAYNE COUNTY—Continued.

Arlington,	Lodge Dale,
Beach Pond,	Middle Valley,
Berlin Centre,	Milanville,
Bethany,	Newfoundland,
Canaan,	Pleasant Mount,
Cherry Ridge,	Preston,
Cold Spring,	Priceville,
Damascus,	Prompton,
Dyberry,	Rileyville,
Eldred,	Rock Lake,
Equinunk,	Sand Cut,
Galilee,	South Sterling,
Hamlinton,	Starucca,
Hawley,	Sterling,
Hemlock Hollow,	Stevenson's Mills,
High Lake,	Tanner's Falls,
Hollisterville,	Waymart,
Honesdale, (c. h.,)	West Damascus,
Lake Como,	White Mills.

WESTMORELAND COUNTY.

Adamsburgh,	Manor Station,
Beatty,*	Mendon,
Bolivar,	Millwood,
Bradenville,	Mount Pleasant,
Branch Junction,	Murrysville,
Burrell,	New Alexandria,
Cavettsville,	New Derry,
Congruity,	New Florence,
Crab Tree,	New Stanton,
Cribb's,	North Washington,
Derry Station,	Oak Grove Furnace,
Donegal,	Oakland × Roads,
Fitz Henry,	Parnassus,
Fulton,	Paulton,
Geary,	Penn's Station,
Grapeville,	Pleasant Unity,
Greensburgh, (c. h.,)	Ridgeview,
Harrison City,	Rostraver,
Hillside,	Salem Cross Roads,
Hill's View,	Salina,
Irwin's Station,	Sardis,
Jacob's Creek,	Shearer's × Roads,
Jones' Mills,	Stahlstown,
Larimer's Station,	Stewartsville,
Latrobe,	Sutersville,
Laughlintown,	Tinker Run,
Laurelville,	Verona,
Ligonier,	Walts' Mills,
Livermore,	Weaver's Old Stand
Lockport Station,	Webster,
Lucesco,	West Fairfield,
Lycippus,	West Newton,
McKean's Old Stand,	West Overton,
McLaughlin's Store,	Yohoghany,
Madison,	Youngstown.
Manor Dale,	

WYOMING COUNTY.

Bellasylva,	Centre Moreland,
Black Walnut,	Clinton Corners,
Bowman's Creek,	Dixon,
Carney,	Eaton,

* Money-order office.

WYOMING COUNTY—Continued.

Factoryville,
Falls,
Forkston,
Golden Hill,
Jenningsville,
Keelersburgh,
Laceyville,
La Grange,
Lemon,
Lovelton,
McKune's Depot,
Mehoopany,

Meshoppen,
Mill City,
Nicholson,
Pierceville,
Russell Hill,
Scottsville,
Skinner's Eddy,
South Eaton,
Tunkhannock, (c. h.,)
Vernon,
Vosburgh.

YORK COUNTY.

Alpine,
Apple Grove,
Bald Eagle,
Brodbeck's,
Bryansville,
Castle Fin,
Chanceford,
Clear Spring,
Codorus,
Constitution,

Cross Roads,
Dallastown,
Davidsburgh,
Delta,
Dillsburgh,
Dover,
Emigsville,
Etter's,
Fawn Grove,
Franklintown,

YORK COUNTY—Continued.

Gatchellville,
Glen Rock,
Grahamville,
Hall,
Hanover,*
Hanover Junction,
Hartley,
Hellam,
Hetricks,
Hopewell Centre,
Jefferson Station,
Lewisberry,
Loganville,
McCall's Ferry,
McSherrysville,
Manchester,
Margaretta Furnace,
Mount Royal,
Mount Top,
Mount Wolf,
Muddy Creek Forks,
Mulberry,
Newberrytown,
New Bridgeville,
New Freedom,

Peach Bottom,
Pine Hill,
Plank Road,
Porter's Sideling,
Rail Road,
Rossville,
Seven Valleys,
Shrewsbury,
Sidonsburgh,
Slate Hill,
Smith's Station,
Spring Forge,
Stewartstown,
Strawbridge,
Strinestown,
Thomasville,
Union,
Wellsville,
West Bangor,
Windsor,
Wrightsville,
Xenia,
Yocumtown,
York,* (c. h.,)
York Furnace.

RHODE ISLAND.

BRISTOL COUNTY.

Barrington,
Barrington Centre,
Bristol,* (c. h.,)

Nayatt Point,
Warren.*

KENT COUNTY.

Anthony,
Centreville,
Coventry,
Coventry Centre,
East Greenwich,(c.h.)
Escoheag,
Greene,
Natick,
Nooseneck Hill,

Phœnix,
Pontiac,
River Point,
Summit.
Warwick,
Warwick Neck,
West Greenwich Centre.

NEWPORT COUNTY.

Adamsville,
Jamestown,
Little Compton,
NEWPORT,* (c. h.,)
New Shoreham,

Portsmouth,
South Portsmouth,
Tiverton,
Tiverton Four Corners.

PROVIDENCE COUNTY.

Albion,
Ashton,
Burrillville,
Central Falls,
Centredale,
Chepachet,
Cranston Print W'ks,

Cumberland Hill,
Diamond Hill,
East Providence,
Fiskeville,
Foster,
Foster Centre,
Georgiaville,

PROVIDENCE COUNTY—Continued.

Greenville,
Harmony,
Hope,
Lonsdale,
Manton,
Manville,
Mapleville,
Mohegan,
Mount Vernon,
North Scituate,
Olneyville,
Pascoag,

Pawtucket,*
Pawtuxet,
PROVIDENCE,* (c. h.,)
Rockland,
Slaterville,
Smithfield,
South Foster,
South Scituate,
Valley Falls,
Watchemoket,
West Gloucester,
Woonsocket Falls.*

WASHINGTON COUNTY.

Allenton,
Arcadia,
Ashaway,
Carolina Mills,
Charlestown,
Davisville,
Dorrville,
Exeter,
Hope Valley,
Hopkinton,
Kingston, (c. h.,)
La Fayette,
Narragansett,
Narragansett Pier,
Peace Dale,

Perrysville,
Pine Hill,
Potter Hill,
Quonochontaug,
Richmond Switch,
Rockville,
Rocky Brook,
Shannock Mills,
Slocumville,
Usquepaugh,
Wakefield,*
Westerly,*
Wickford,*
Woodville,
Wyoming.

---

* Money-order office.

SOUTH CAROLINA.

ABBEVILLE COUNTY.

Abbeville C. H.,	Level Land,
Antreville,	Lowndesville,
Calhoun's Mills,	Monterey,
Cokesbury,	New Market,
Donnaldsville,	Ninety-six,
Due West,	Temple of Health,
Greenwood,	Willington.
Hodges,	

ANDERSON COUNTY.

*Anderson C. H.,**	Pendleton,
Belton,	Piercetown,
Brushy Creek,	Rock Mills,
Equality,	Saddler's Creek,
Golden Springs,	Stony Point,
Holland's Store,	Storeville,
Honea Path,	Townville,
Moffettsville,	Williamston.
Newell,	

BARNWELL COUNTY.

Aiken,	Greenland,
Allendale,	Hammond,
Bamberg,	Johnson,
Barnwell,	Midway,
Blackville, (c. h.,)	Mims,
Dunbarton,	Williston,
Graham's Turn Out,	Windsor.

BEAUFORT COUNTY.

*Beaufort,** (c. h.,)	Grahamville,
Bluffton,	Hardeeville,
Brighton,	Lawtonville,
Coosawhatchie,	Port Royal,
Gardner's Corner,	Robertsville,
Gillisonville,	Yemassee.

CHARLESTON COUNTY.

Bonneau's Depot,	Roadville,
*Charleston,** (c. h.,)	St. Stephen's Depot,
Enterprise Landing,	Sineath's,
Holly Hill,	Summerville.
Oakley Depot,	

CHESTER COUNTY.

Black Stocks,	Halsellville,
Chesnut Grove,	Hazlewood,
*Chester C. H.,**	Rossville.
Crosbyville,	

CHESTERFIELD COUNTY.

Cheraw,*	Old Store,
Chesterfield C. H.,	Oro,
Deep Creek,	Pine Tree,
Jefferson,	White Plains.
Mount Croghan,	

CLARENDON COUNTY.

Bethlehem,	New Zion,
Friendship,	Packsville,
Manning, (c. h.,)	Wright's Bluff.

COLLETON COUNTY.

Adam's Run,	Reevesville,
Ashepoo,	Ridgeville,
Edisto Island,	Saint George's,
Green Pond,	*Walterborough,* (c. h.)
Jacksonborough,	

DARLINGTON COUNTY.

*Darlington C. H.**	Lydia,
Dove's Depot,	Society Hill,
Florence,	Stokes' Bridge,
Hartsville,	Timmonsville.

EDGEFIELD COUNTY.

Bath,	Johnston's Depot,
Big Creek,	Longmire's Store,
Cold Springs,	Parks,
Dyson's Mills,	Pine House Depot,
Edgefield C. H.,	Rehoboth,
Graniteville,	Richardsonville,
Hamburgh,	Ridge.

FAIRFIELD COUNTY.

Buck Head,	Ridgeway,
Doko,	Shelton,
Feasterville,	Strother,
Lylesford,	*Winnsborough,* (c. h.,)
Monticello,	Yonguesville.

GEORGETOWN COUNTY.

Bull Creek,	North Santee.
Georgetown, (c. h.,)	

GREENVILLE COUNTY.

Buena Vista,	Marietta,
Chick's Springs,	Middle Saluda,
Fairview,	Mush Creek,
Fountain Inn,	Plain,
Gowensville,	Pliny,
*Greenville C. H.,**	Sandy Flat,
Grove Station,	Traveller's Rest,
Highland Grove,	Whilden's Factory,
Huntersville,	White Horse.
Lima,	

HORRY COUNTY.

Bayborough,	Galivant's Ferry,
Bucksville,	Green Sea,
Conwayborough, (c. h.,)	Little River.

* Money-order office.

KERSHAW COUNTY.

Camden,* (c. h.,)
Flat Rock,
Lynchwood,
Tiller's Ferry,
Troy.

LANCASTER COUNTY.

Belair,
Craigsville,
Flint Ridge,
Jacksonham,
Lancaster C. H.,
Pleasant Hill,
Pleasant Valley,
Taxahau,
Wild Cat.

LAURENS COUNTY.

Brewerton,
Clinton,
Eden,
Goodgiou's Factory,
Highland Home,
Laurens C. H.,*
Line Creek,
Mount Gallagher,
Mount Pleasant,
Simpson's Mills,
Tumbling Shoals,
Tylersville,
Waterloo.

LEXINGTON COUNTY.

Beaver Pond,
Countsville,
Gilbert Hollow,
Hope Station,
Leesville,
Lexington C. H.,
Merritt's Bridge,
Pine Ridge,
Rish's Store,
Sawyer's Mills,
Steedman's.

MARION COUNTY.

Aeriel,
Britton's Neck,
Campbell's Bridge,
Carolina,
Catfish,
Effingham Station,
Forestville,
Gilchrist's Bridge,
Jeffrey's Creek,
Little Rock,
Lynch's Creek,
Marion C. H.,
Mars Bluff,
Mullin's Depot,
Nichols,
Oak Grove,
Pee Dee,
Reedy Creek,
Selkirk,
Temperance Hill.

MARLBOROUGH COUNTY.

Bennettsville, (c. h.,)
Brownsville,
Clio,
Parnassus.

NEWBERRY COUNTY.

Chappell's Bridge,
Frog Level,
Jalapa,
Kinard's Turnout,
Liberty Hall,
Little Mountain,
Newberry C. H.,*
Pomaria,
Saluda Oldtown,
Silver Street,
Whitmire's.

OCONEE COUNTY.

Bachelor's Retreat,
Bounty Land,
Fair Play,
Keowee,
Oakway,
Tugalo,
Tunnel Hill,
Walhalla, (c. h.)

ORANGEBURGH COUNTY.

Branchville,
Fort Motte,
Orangeburgh C. H.,
Rowe's Pump,
Saint Matthews,
Vance's Ferry.

PICKENS COUNTY.

Anderson's Mills,
Arnold's Mills,
Dacusville,
Eastaloe,
Eighteen Mile,
Five Mile,
George's Creek,
Hunter's Mills,
Mile Creek,
Nine Times,
Pickens C. H.,
Pickensville,
Sunny Dale,
Table Mountain.

RICHLAND COUNTY.

COLUMBIA,* (c. h.,)
Hopkins Turn Out,
Kingsville.

SPARTANBURGH COUNTY.

Batesville,
Campobello,
Cross Anchor,
Earlesville,
Enoree,
Glenn Springs,
Grassy Pond,
Hebron,
Hobbysville,
Limestone Springs,
Millville,
New Prospect,
Pacolett Depot,
Reidsville,
Spartanburgh C. H.,
Valley Falls,
Woodruff's.

SUMTER COUNTY.

Bishopville,
Bradford Springs,
Lynchburgh,
Manchester,
Mannville,
Mayesville,
Mechanicsville,
Plowden's Mills,
Privateer,
Shiloh,
Stateburgh,
Sumter C. H.,*
Taylor's.

UNION COUNTY.

Cold Well,
Cross Keys,
Fish Dam,
Goshen Hill,
Gowdeysville,
Jonesville,
Mount Joy,
Santuck,
Smith's Ford,
Timber Ridge,
Unionville, (c. h.)

WILLIAMSBURGH COUNTY.

Black Mingo,
Camp Ridge,
China Grove,
Johnsonville,
Kingstree, (c. h.,)
Lynch's Lake,
Myersville.

YORK COUNTY.

Antioch,
Bethany,
Blairsville,
Bullock Creek,
Clark's Fork,
Fort Mill,
Guthriesville,
Harmony,
Hickory Grove,
Hopewell,
New House,
Rock Hill,
Smith's Turn Out,
Yorkville, (c. h.,)
Zeno.

*Money-order office.

TENNESSEE.

ANDERSON COUNTY.

Clinton, (c. h.,)	Ross,
Fairview,	Scarborough,
Oliver's,	Wallace's × Roads,
Robertson's,	Wilson's.
Robertsville,	

BEDFORD COUNTY.

Arnold's Store,	Palmetto,
Bedford, (c. h.,)	Pleasant Grove,
Bellbuckle,	Ray,
Fairfield,	Richmond,
Fall Creek,	Shelbyville,*
Flat Creek,	Unionville,
Haley's Station,	Wartrace Depot.
Normandy,	

BENTON COUNTY.

Big Sandy,	Danville.
Camden, (c. h.,)	

BLEDSOE COUNTY.

Bee Creek,	Orme's Store,
Braden's Knobs,	*Pikeville, (c. h.,)*
Cold Spring,	Pitt's × Roads,
Foster's × Roads.	Roberson's × Roads,
Mount Airy,	Stephen's Chapel.

BLOUNT COUNTY.

Brick Mill,	Louisville,
Cade's Cove,	*Maryville, (c. h.,)*
Chilhowee,	Miser's Station,
Clover Hill,	Montvale Springs,
Cloyd's Creek,	Morgantown,
Coytee,	Rockford,
Ellejoy,	Tuckaleechee Cove,
Friendsville,	Unitia.
Gamble's Store,	

BRADLEY COUNTY.

Charleston,	*Cleveland,* (c. h.,)
Chatata,	Linwood.

CAMPBELL COUNTY.

Archerville,	*Jacksborough, (c. h.,)*
Caryville,	Pine Mountain,
Coal Creek,	Well Spring.
Fincastle,	

CANNON COUNTY.

Auburn,	Short Mountain,
Bradyville.	*Woodbury, (c. h.)*

CARROLL COUNTY.

Buena Vista,	McLemoresville,
Clarksburgh,	Maple Creek,
Hollow Rock,	Marlborough,
Huntingdon, (c. h.,)	Terry,
McKenzie,	Trezevant.

CARTER COUNTY.

Carter's Depot,	Hampton,
Carter's Furnace,	Happy Valley,
Cave Spring,	Limestone Cove,
Dugger's Ferry.	Okolona,
Elizabethton, (c. h.,)	Roan Mountain,
Gap Run,	Stony Creek.

CHEATHAM COUNTY.

Ashland City, (c. h.,)	Sycamore,
Craggie Hope,	Thomasville.
Pleasant View,	

CLAIBORNE COUNTY.

Cumberland Gap,	Rob Camp,
Head of Barren,	Speedwell,
Oldtown,	Spring Dale,
Pleasant,	*Tazewell, (c. h.)*

COCKE COUNTY.

Big Creek,	Parrottsville,
Bridgeport,	Rankin's Depot,
Gorman's Depot,	River Side.
Newport, (c. h.,)	

COFFEE COUNTY.

Beech Grove,	Summitville,
Hillsborough,	Tullahoma.*
Manchester, (c. h.,)	

CUMBERLAND COUNTY.

Crossville, (c. h.,)	Owl Hill,
Hebbertsburgh,	Pleasant Hill,
Howard Springs,	Pomona.
Kimmer's Stand,	

DAVIDSON COUNTY.

Belleview,	Franklin College,
Couchville,	Goodlettsville,
Donelson,	Madison,
Edgefield Junction,	NASHVILLE,* (c. h.)

DECATUR COUNTY.

Brodie's Landing,	Fisher's Landing,
Brownsport Furnace,	Perryville.
Decaturville, (c. h.,)	

DE KALB COUNTY.

Alexandria,	*Smithville, (c. h.,)*
Laurel Hill,	Temperance Hall.
Liberty,	

DICKSON COUNTY.

Burns' Station,	Gillem's Station,
Charlotte, (c. h.,)	White Bluffs,
Cumberland Furn'ce,	Worley Furnace,
Danielsville,	Yellow Creek.
Dickson,	

DYER COUNTY.

Chesnut Bluffs,	Maxville,
Dyersburgh, (c. h.,)	Newbern.
Friendship,	

FAYETTE COUNTY.

Braden Station,	Oakland,
Galway,	Rossville,
La Grange,*	*Somerville,* (c. h.,)
Macon,	Willis Station.
Moscow,	

FENTRESS COUNTY.

Barren Springs,	*Jamestown, (c. h.,)*
Boatland,	Travisville.
Hale's Mills,	

FRANKLIN COUNTY.

Alto,	Hunt's Station,
Cowan,	Sewanee,
Decherd,	*Winchester,* (c. h.)
Estill Springs,	

GIBSON COUNTY.

Antioch,	Quincy,
Dyer's Station,	Rutherford Depot,
Humboldt,*	*Trenton,* (c. h.,)
Milan Depot,	Yorkville.

GILES COUNTY.

Aspen Hill,	Good Spring,
Bethel,	Lesters,
Bodenham,	Lynnville,
Bradshaw,	Marbut's,
Brick Church,	Parker's Store,
Buford's Station,	Pisgah,
Bunker Hill,	Prospect Station,
Campbellsville,	*Pulaski,* (c. h.,)
Cornersville,	Vale Mills,
Elkton,	Wales Station.

GRAINGER COUNTY.

Bean's Station,	Powder Spring Gap,
Blain's × Roads,	*Rutledge, (c. h.,)*
Clear Spring,	Spring House,
Marshall's Ferry,	Tampico.
May Spring,	Thorn Hill.
Morristown,*	

GREENE COUNTY.

Camp Creek,	Laurel Gap,
Caney Branch,	Limestone Springs,
Cedar Creek,	Little Chucky,
Cedar Lane,	Locust Spring,
Clear Creek,	Lost Mountain,
Cross Anchor,	Midway,
Fullen's,	Millburnton,
Gourley's Bridge,	Pilot Knob,
Graysburgh.	Rheatown,
Greeneville, (c. h.,)	Romeo,
Hayesville,	Timber Ridge,
Home,	Warrensburgh.
Horse Creek,	

GRUNDY COUNTY.

Altamont, (c. h.,)	Pelham.
Beersheba Springs,	

HAMILTON COUNTY.

Birchwood,	Lookout Mountain,
Chattanooga,	Loyalty,
Chickamauga,	Ooltewah,
Chickamauga Sta'n,	Sale Creek,
Dallas,	Soddy,
Georgetown,	Tyner,
Harrison, (c. h.,)	Wauhatchie.

HANCOCK COUNTY.

Alanthus Hill,	War Creek,
Mulberry Gap,	War Ridge.
Sneedsville, (c. h.,)	

HARDEMAN COUNTY.

Bolivar, (c. h.,)	New Castle,
Cedar Chapel,	Pocahontas,
Grand Junction,	Saulsbury,
Hickory Valley,	Teague's Mills,
Middleburgh,	Tooner's Station,
Middleton Station,	Whiteville.

HARDIN COUNTY.

Bell Air,	Ingleside,
Boyd's Landing,	Nelson,
Cerro Gordo,	Olive Hill,
Coffee Landing,	Saltillo,
Hamburgh,	*Savannah, (c. h.)*

HAWKINS COUNTY.

Austin's Mills,	Poor Valley,
Bull's Gap,	Quarrysville,
Burem's Store,	*Rogersville,* (c. h.,)
Lee Valley,	Stony Point,
Mill Bend,	Surgoinsville,
Mooresburgh,	Van Hill,
New Canton,	War Gap,
Oak Well,	White Horn,
Persia,	Yellow Store.

* Money-order office.

HAYWOOD COUNTY.

Bell's Depot,
Brownsville,* (c. h.,)
Cageville,
Dancyville,
Johnson's Grove,

Jones' Station,
Stanton Depot,
Wellwood,
Woodville.

HENDERSON COUNTY.

Farmville,
Juno,
Lexington, (c. h.,)
Lone Elm,
Mifflin,

Poplar Spring,
Red Mound,
Scott's Hill,
Shady Hill.

HENRY COUNTY.

Albany,
Como,
Conyersville,
Henry Station,
Manlyville,
New Boston,
North Fork,

Paris,* (c. h.)
Paris Landing,
Porter Station,
Sandy Hill,
Spring Hill Academy,
Springville.

HICKMAN COUNTY.

Bastinville,
Bluff Point,
Bon Aqua,
Centreville, (c. h.,)
Duck River,
Dunnington,

Ivy Bluff,
Lick Creek,
Little Lot,
Pine Wood,
Vernon.

HUMPHREYS COUNTY.

Buffalo,
Cuba Landing,
Fowler's Landing,

Johnsonville,
McEwen's Station,
Waverly, (c. h.)

JACKSON COUNTY.

Butler's Landing,
Celina,
Clementsville,
Flynn's Lick,
Gainesborough, (c. h.,)
Granville,

Highland,
Meagsville,
Moore's Store,
North Springs,
Whitleyville.

JEFFERSON COUNTY.

Beaver Creek,
Dandridge,* (c. h.,)
Flat Gap,
Kansas,
Leadvale,
Mill Spring,
Mossy Creek,
Nebraska,
New Market,

Oak Grove,
Panther Springs,
Russellville,
Stony Bluff,
Strawberry Plains,
Talbott's Mills,
Trion,
Whitesburgh,
Witts' Foundry.

JOHNSON COUNTY.

Baker's Gap,
Butler,
High Health,
Little Doe,
Pandora,
Shady,

Shawn's Cross Roads,
Stump Knob,
Taylorsville, (c. h.,)
Trade,
Ward's Iron Works.

KNOX COUNTY.

Ball Camp,
Beaver Ridge,
Bull Run,
Campbell's Station,
Church Grove,
Concord,
Gap Creek,
Graveston,

Knoxville,* (c. h.,)
McMillan,
Powell's Station,
Roseberry,
Thorn Grove,
Twinville,
Vandergriff's.

LAUDERDALE COUNTY.

Ashport,
Double Bridges,
Dry Hill,
Durhamville,

Fulton,
Hale's Point,
Ripley, (c. h.)

LAWRENCE COUNTY.

Appleton,
Henryville,
Lawrenceburgh,(c. h.,)
Marcella Falls,

Mockeson,
Palo Alto,
Wayland Springs,
West Point.

LEWIS COUNTY.

Flat Rock,

Palestine.

LINCOLN COUNTY.

Booneville,
Brighton Station,
County Line,
Cyruston,
Elora,
Fayetteville,* (c. h.,)
Flintville,
George's Store,

Goshen,
Kelso,
Lynchburgh,
Millville,
Molino,
Mulberry,
Oregon,
Petersburgh.

McMINN COUNTY.

Athens,* (c. h.,)
Cantrell's X Roads,
Cog Hill,

Mouse Creek,
Riceville.

McNAIRY COUNTY.

Adamsville,
Bethel Springs,
Chewalla,
McNairy Station,
Milledgeville,

Montezuma,
Purdy, (c. h.,)
Ramer,
Stantonville.

MACON COUNTY.

Echo,
Eulia,

Gibb's X Roads,
La Fayette, (c. h.)

MADISON COUNTY.

Andrew Chapel,
Carroll,
Clay Brook,
Denmark,
Gadsden,

Henderson Station,
Jackson,* (c. h.,)
Medon,
Pinson,
Spring Creek.

* Money-order office.

MARION COUNTY.

Battle Creek Mines, Nicojack,
Jasper, (*c. h.*,) Tracy City,
Looney's Creek, Whiteside.

MARSHALL COUNTY.

Berlin, Globe Creek,
Caney Spring, *Lewisburgh*, (*c. h.*,)
Catalpa Grove, Lillard's Mills,
Chapel Hill, Spring Place,
Farmington, Verona.

MAURY COUNTY.

Carter's Creek Sta- Hurricane Switch,
  tion, Hurt's Cross Roads,
Columbia,* (*c. h.*,) Mount Pleasant,
Culleoka, Santa Fé,
Fountain Creek, South Port,
Hampshire, Spring Hill,
Hardison's Mills, Williamsport.

MEIGS COUNTY.

Big Spring, Pine Land,
Decatur, (*c. h.*,) Sewee,
Goodfield, Ten Mile Stand.
Hester Mills,

MONROE COUNTY.

Ball Play, Jalapa,
Belltown, *Madisonville*, (*c. h.*,)
Citico, Mount Vernon,
Eve Mills, Philadelphia,
Four Mile Branch, Sweet Water,
Hopewell Springs, Tellico Plains.

MONTGOMERY COUNTY.

Clarksville,* (*c. h.*,) Port Royal,
Corbandale, Richardson's,
Jordan Springs, Ringgold,
McAllister's × Ro'ds, Saint Bethlehem,
New Providence, Shiloh,
Oakwood, Tate's Station,
Peacher's Mills, Woodlawn.
Pleasant Mound,

MORGAN COUNTY.

Crooked Fork, *Montgomery*, (*c. h.*,)
Glades, Stapleton.

OBION COUNTY.

Earlobion, *Troy*, (*c. h.*,)
Harris Station, Troy Station,
Kenton, Union City,*
Tiptonville, Woodland Mills.

OVERTON COUNTY.

Helham, Netherland,
Livingston, (*c. h.*,) Nettle Carrier,
Monroe, Oak Hill,
Mount Pisgah, Olympus,
Mouth of Wolf, West Fork.

PERRY COUNTY.

Beardstown, Cypress,
Britt's Landing, *Linden*, (*c. h.*,)
Cedar Creek Land- Lobelville,
  ing, Peter's Landing.

POLK COUNTY.

Benton, (*c. h.*,) Ducktown,*
Broad Shoals, Parksville.

PUTNAM COUNTY.

Buffalo Valley, ·Pekin,
Byrne, White Plains.
Cookville, (*c. h.*,)

RHEA COUNTY.

Prestonville, Sulphur Springs,
Smith's × Roads, *Washington*, (*c. h.*)

ROANE COUNTY.

Barnardsville, Paw Paw Ford,
Eagle Furnace, Post Oak Springs,
Erie, Rockwood,
Gray's Hill, Stockton,
Kingston, (*c. h.*,) Tabor,
Lenoir's, Webster,
Letsinger, Williams' Mill,
Loudon, Wood's Hill.

ROBERTSON COUNTY.

Adam's Station, Fort's Station,
Baggettsville, Green Brier,
Barren Plain, Hubertville,
Black Jack, Mulloy's,
Cedar Hill, *Springfield*, (*c. h.*,)
Coopertown, Turnersville.
Cross Plains,

RUTHERFORD COUNTY.

Eagleville, Middleton,
Florence Station, Milton,
Fosterville, *Murfreesboro'*,* (*c. h.*,)
Hall's Hill, Readyville,
Huntersville, Smyrna,
Jordan's Valley, Versailles,
La Vergne, Walter Hill.

SCOTT COUNTY.

Horse Shoe Bend, Winfield,
Huntsville, (*c. h.*,) Wolf Creek.

SEQUATCHIE COUNTY.

Dunlap, (*c. h.*,) Walnut Hill,
Fillmore, Walnut Valley.

SEVIER COUNTY.

Cannon's Store, Pigeon Forge,
Fair Garden, *Sevierville*, (*c. h.*,)
Gatlinburgh, Trundle's × Roads,
Henderson's Spr'gs, Walden's Creek,
Henry's × Roads, Wear's Valley.

* Money-order office.

SHELBY COUNTY.

Bartlett,	Mc's Ville,
Bond's Station,	*Memphis*,* (c. h.,)
Colliersville,	Oak Lawn,
Cuba,	*Raleigh*, (c. h.,)
Germantown,	Sulphur Well,
Greenwood,	White's Station,
Harrison's Store,	Wythe Depot.

SMITH COUNTY.

Bagdad,	Gordonsville,
Carthage, (c. h.,)	Jenning's Fork,
Chesnut Mound,	New Middleton,
Dificult,	Rome,
Dixon's Springs,	Snow Creek.

STEWART COUNTY.

Caleb's Valley,	Rough and Ready
Cumberland City,	Furnace,
Cumberland Iron	Saint John's,
Works,	Stewart,
Dover, (c. h.,)	Tennessee Ridge,
Erin,	Tennessee River
Indian Mound,	Station.

SULLIVAN COUNTY.

Arcadia,	Holston Valley,
Blountsville, (c. h.,)	Kendrick's Creek,
Bristol,*	Kingsport,
Eden's Ridge,	Mill Point,
Edgeworth,	Morell's Mill,
Fordtown,	Piney Flats,
Holston Furnace,	Union Depot.

SUMNER COUNTY.

Castalian Springs,	Hendersonville,
Enon College,	Mitchellsville,
Fountain Head,	Richland Station,
Gallatin,* (c. h.,)	Saundersville,
Hartsville,	Trammel.

TIPTON COUNTY.

Bloomington,	Portersville,
Covington,* (c. h.,)	Randolph,
Mason,	Tabernacle.
Mount Zion,	

UNION COUNTY.

Cedar Fork,	*Maynardville*, (c. h.,)
Haynes,	Raccoon Valley,
Lost Creek,	Sharp's Chapel,
Loy's Cross Roads,	Warwick's × Roads.

VAN BUREN COUNTY.

Boue Cave,	*Spencer*, (c. h.)

WARREN COUNTY.

Increase,	Pine Bluff,
Irving College,	Rocky River,
McMinnville,* (c. h.,)	Smartt's Station,
Morrison,	Vervilla,
Mountain Creek,	Viola.

WASHINGTON COUNTY.

Boon's Creek,	Hawes Cross Roads,
Brownsborough,	Indian Creek,
Buffalo Ridge,	Johnson City,
Carrville,	*Jonesborough*,* (c. h.,)
Cherry Grove,	Leesburgh,
Clear Branch,	Locust Mount,
Embryville,	Longmire,
Falls Branch,	Mill Brook,
Flag Pond,	Millwood,
Freedom,	Pilot Hill,
Garber's Mills,	Swingleville.

WAYNE COUNTY.

Clifton,	Patriot,
Eagle Tannery,	*Waynesboro'*, (c. h.)

WEAKLEY COUNTY.

Dresden, (c. h.,)	Gleeson Station,
Dukedom,	Pierce Station,
Elm Tree,	Ralston's Station.
Gardner's Station,	

WHITE COUNTY.

Cave,	Rock Island,
Green Tree,	Solon,
Newark,	*Sparta*, (c. h.)

WILLIAMSON COUNTY.

Basin Spring,	Jordan's Store,
Bethesda,	Nolensville,
Brentwood,	Peytonsville,
Christiana,	Rigg's × Roads,
College Grove,	Thompson's Station,
Franklin,* (c. h.,)	Triune.

WILSON COUNTY.

Austin,	Ponville,
Bellwood,	Round Top,
Cainsville,	Rural Hill,
Commerce,	Shop Spring,
Gladeville,	Silver Spring,
Green Hill,	Simmon's Bluff,
Laguardo,	Statesville,
Lebanon,* (c. h.,)	Stringtown,
Mount Carmel,	Tucker's × Roads,
Oak Point,	Watertown.

* Money-order office.

TEXAS.

ANDERSON COUNTY.

Barton,
Beaver,
Bethel,
Fosterville,
Kickapoo,

Parker's Bluff,
Palestine, (c. h.,)
Plenitude,
Tennessee Colony.

ANGELINA COUNTY.

Cheesland,
Homer, (c. h.,)

Marion.

ATASCOSA COUNTY.

Mottomosa,
Pleasanton, (c. h.,)

Somerset.

AUSTIN COUNTY.

Bellville, (c. h.,)
Cat Spring,
Hempstead,
Industry,
Iron Creek,
Millheim,

New Ulm,
San Felipe,
Sempronius,
Shelby,
Travis,
Wesley.

BANDERA COUNTY.

Bandera, (c. h.)

BASTROP COUNTY.

Alum Creek,
Bastrop, (c. h.,)
Cedar Creek,
Red Rock,

Sand Fly,
Serbin,
Young's Settlement.

BEE COUNTY.

Aransas,
Beeville, (c. h.,)

Papalote.

BELL COUNTY.

Aiken,
Belton, (c. h.,)
Harrisville,
Howard,

Mountain Home,
Salado,
Volo.

BEXAR COUNTY.

Camp Melvin,
Fort Concho,
Graytown,

Leon Springs,
*San Antonio,** (c. h.,)
Selma.

BLANCO COUNTY.

Blanco, (c. h.,)
Round Mountain,

Twin Sisters,
Westbrook.

BOSQUE COUNTY.

Clifton,
Meridian, (c. h.,)

Valley Mills.

BOWIE COUNTY.

Boston, (c. h.,)
De Kalb,

Powell Grove.

BRAZORIA COUNTY

Brazoria, (c. h.,)
Chenango,
Columbia,

Sandy Point,
Velasco.

BRAZOS COUNTY.

Bryan, (c. h.,)

Millican.

BROWN COUNTY.

Brownwood, (c. h.)

BURLESON COUNTY.

Caldwell, (c. h.,)
Lexington,

New Anhalt,
Prospect.

BURNET COUNTY.

Burnet, (c. h.,)
Double Horn,
Mahomet,

Mormon Mills,
Oatmeal,
Shovel Mount.

CALDWELL COUNTY.

Lockhart, (c. h.,)
Plum Creek,

Prairie Lea,
Sour Spring.

CALHOUN COUNTY.

*Indianola,** (c. h.,)
Port Lavaca,

Saluria.

CAMERON COUNTY.

Brazos Santiago,
*Brownsville,** (c. h.,)

Point Isabel.

CHAMBERS COUNTY.

Anahuac,

Wallisville, (c. h.)

CHEROKEE COUNTY.

Alto,
Atoy,
Jacksonville,
Knoxville,

Larissa,
Linwood,
Pinetown,
Rusk, (c. h.)

COLLIN COUNTY.

Farmersville,
Highland,
Lone Tree,
McKinney, (c. h.,)

Mantua,
Millwood,
Plano,
Weston.

* Money-order office.

COLORADO COUNTY.

Alleyton,	Frelsburgh,
Columbus, * (*c. h.,*)	Oakland,
Content,	Ridge.
Eagle Lake,	

COMAL COUNTY.

New Braunfels, *(*c.h.,*)	Smithson's Valley,
Sattler's,	Spring Branch.

COMANCHE COUNTY.

Comanche.

COOKE COUNTY.

Gainsville, (*c. h.*)

CORYELL COUNTY.

Eagle Springs,	Rainey's Creek,
Gatesville, (*c. h.,*)	Station Creek.

DALLAS COUNTY.

Cedar Hill,	Lancaster,
Dallas, * (*c. h.,*)	Lisbon,
Haught's Store,	Scyene.

DAVIS COUNTY.

Douglassville,	*Linden,* (*c. h.,*)
Hickory Hill,	White Hall.

DENTON COUNTY.

Denton, (*c. h.,*)	Pilot Point.
Lewisville,	

DE WITT COUNTY.

Clinton, (*c. h.,*)	Price's Creek,
Concrete,	Terryville,
Hochheim,	Yorktown.
Meyersville,	

ELLIS COUNTY.

Chambers' Creek,	Red Oak,
Cross Timbers,	*Waxahachie,* (*c. h.,*)
Cummins' Creek,	Wilton.
Milford,	

EL PASO COUNTY.

El Paso, (*c. h.,*)	San Elizario.
Fort Quitman,	

ERATH COUNTY.

Stephensville, (*c. h.*)

FALLS COUNTY.

Carolina,	*Marlin,* (*c. h.,*)
Golindo,	Rock Dam.
Jena,	

FANNIN COUNTY.

Bonham, (*c. h.,*)	Lick,
Honey Grove,	Orangeville,
Ladonia,	Warren.

FAYETTE COUNTY.

Black Jack Springs,	Lyons,
Bluff,	Neese's Store,
Cedar,	Oso,
Cistern,	Pin-Oak,
Fayetteville,	Rossville,
Flatonia,	Round Top,
High Hill,	Rutersville,
La Grange, (*c. h.,*)	Winchester.
Long Prairie,	

FORT BEND COUNTY.

Pittsville,	Stafford,
Richmond, (*c. h.,*)	Sugar Land.

FREESTONE COUNTY.

Butler,	*Fairfield,* (*c. h.,*)
Cotton Gin,	Moorhead.

GALVESTON COUNTY.

Galveston, * (*c. h.,*)	Highland Station.

GILLESPIE COUNTY.

Cherry Spring,	*Fredericksburgh,* (*c.h.*)

GOLIAD COUNTY.

Cummingsville,	Weesatch.
Goliad, (*c. h.,*)	

GONZALES COUNTY.

Belmont,	Round Lake,
Gonzales, * (*c. h.,*)	Thompsonville,
Hopkinsville,	Winnton,
Rancho,	Wrightsborough.

GRAYSON COUNTY.

Farmington,	Pilot Grove,
Kentucky Town,	*Sherman,* * (*c. h.,*)
Macomb,	Whitesborough.

GRIMES COUNTY.

Anderson, (*c. h.,*)	Plantersville,
Bedias,	Prairie Plains,
Courtney,	Roan's Prairie.
Navasota,	

GUADALUPE COUNTY.

Nockenut,	Valley.
Seguin, (*c. h.,*)	

* Money-order office.

HARDIN COUNTY.

Concord,   *Hardin, (c. h.)*

HARRIS COUNTY.

Cypress Top,   *Houston,* (c. h.,)
Harrisburgh,   Rose Hill.
Hockley,

HARRISON COUNTY.

Eight Mile Creek,   *Marshall, (c. h.,)*
Hallsville,   Powellton,
Macksville,   Scottsville.

HAYS COUNTY.

Johnston's Institute, *San Marcos, (c. h.)*
Mountain City,

HENDERSON COUNTY.

Athens, (c. h.,)   Malakoff,
Brownsborough,   Pine Grove,
Fincastle,   Shakelford.

HIDALGO COUNTY.

Edinburgh, (c. h.,)   Rudyville.
El Sauz,

HILL COUNTY.

Covington,   Peoria,
Hillsborough, (c. h.,)   Towash.

HOOD COUNTY.

Acton,   *Granbury, (c. h.)*

HOPKINS COUNTY.

Bacchus,   Miller Grove,
Black Jack Grove,   Saltillo,
Black Oak,   Sulphur Bluff,
Bright Star,   *Tarrant, (c. h.,)*
Charleston,   White Oak.

HOUSTON COUNTY.

Alabama,   Eliza,
Augusta,   Naches,
Coltharp's,   Pennington,
Creswell,   Prairie,
Crockett, (c. h.,)   Weldon.

HUNT COUNTY.

Greenville, (c. h.,)   Timber Creek,
Lone Oak,   White Rock.
Shiloh,

JACK COUNTY.

Jacksborough, (c. h.)

JACKSON COUNTY.

Morales,   *Texana, (c. h.)*
Navidad,

JASPER COUNTY.

Jasper, (c. h.,)   Wiess Bluff.
Magnolia Springs,

JEFFERSON COUNTY.

Beaumont, (c. h.,)   Sabine Pass.

JOHNSON COUNTY.

Alvarado,   *Cleburne, (c. h.)*
Caddo Grove,

KARNES COUNTY.

Daileyville,   *Helena, (c. h.)*
Ecleto,

KAUFMAN COUNTY.

Cedar Grove,   Prairieville,
Kaufman, (c. h.,)   Rockwall,
Kemp,   Turner's Point.

KENDALL COUNTY.

Boerne, (c. h.,)   Sisterdale.
Hodge's Mill,

KERR COUNTY.

Comfort,   Zanzenburgh.
Kerrville, (c. h.,)

KINNEY COUNTY.

Fort Clark, (c. h.)

LAMAR COUNTY.

Ben Franklin,   Roxton,
Blossom Prairie,   Shiloh Academy,
Cotton Plant,   Starkesville.
Paris, (c. h.,)

LAMPASAS COUNTY.

Lampasas, (c. h.)

LAVACA COUNTY.

Antioch,   Petersburgh,
Hackberry,   Speakeville,
Hallettsville, (c. h.,)   Star,
Hope,   Sweet Home.
Moulton,

LEON COUNTY.

Caldwell's Store,   Leona,
Centreville, (c. h.,)   Middleton.

* Money-order office.

LIBERTY COUNTY.

Ironwood, Moss Bluff.
Liberty, (c. h.,)

LIMESTONE COUNTY.

Eutaw, *Springfield*, (c. h.,)
Iron Clad, Tehuacana,
Mount Calm, Tucker's Mills.
Personville,

LIVE OAK COUNTY.

Echo, *Oakville*, (c. h.)
Gussettville,

LLANO COUNTY.

Llano, (c. h.)

McLENNAN COUNTY.

Acomb, Mastersville,
Bosqueville, *Waco,** (c. h.)

MADISON COUNTY.

Madisonville, (c. h.,) Willow Hole.
Midway,

MARION COUNTY.

*Jefferson,** (c. h.,) Mim's Store.

MASON COUNTY.

Hedwig's Hill, *Mason*, (c. h.)
Loyal Valley,

MATAGORDA COUNTY.

Caney, *Matagorda*, (c. h.)

MAVERICK COUNTY.

Eagle Pass, (c. h.)

MEDINA COUNTY.

Castroville, (c. h.,) New Fountain.
D'Hanis,

MENARD COUNTY.

Fort McKavett, *Menardville*, (c. h.)

MILAM COUNTY.

Cameron, (c. h.,) San Anders,
Maysfield, San Gabriel.
Port Sullivan,

MONTAGUE COUNTY.

Head of Elm, *Montague*, (c. h.)

MONTGOMERY COUNTY.

Danville, Prairie Home.
Montgomery, (c. h.,)

NACOGDOCHES COUNTY.

Cherino, Martinsville,
Douglass, Melrose,
Linn Flat, *Nacogdoches*, (c. h.)

NAVARRO COUNTY.

Birdston, Richland Crossing,
Chatfield, Rural Shade,
Corsicana, (c. h.,) Rush Creek,
Dresden, Spring Hill.

NEWTON COUNTY.

Bleakwood, *Newton*, (c. h.,)
Burkeville, Salem.

NUECES COUNTY.

Banquote, Nueces,
*Corpus Christi,**(c. h.,)San Diego.

ORANGE COUNTY.

Bunn's Bluff, *Orange*, (c. h.,)

PALO PINTO COUNTY.

Palo Pinto, (c. h.)

PANOLA COUNTY.

Beckville, Sugar Hill,
Carthage, (c. h.,) Walnut Hill,
Grand Bluff, Wood's.

PARKER COUNTY.

Cartersville, *Weatherford*, (c. h.)

POLK COUNTY.

Cold Spring, Moscow,
Livingston, (c. h.,) Smithfield,
Morganville, Swartwout.

PRESIDIO COUNTY.

Camp Stockton, Presidio.
Fort Davis,

RED RIVER COUNTY.

Clarksville, (c. h.,) Maple Springs
Cuthand, Robbinsville,
Hortonville, Savannah.

REFUGIO COUNTY.

Fulton, Rockport,
Lamar, Saint Mary's.
Refugio, (c. h.,)

* Money-order office.

ROBERTSON COUNTY.

Bremond,	*Owensville,* (c. h.,)
Calvert,*	Sutton's Station,
Hammond,	Wheelock,
Hearne,	Woodland.

RUSK COUNTY.

Alma,	Milville,
Belleview,	Mount Enterprise,
Caledonia,	New Danville,
Harmony Hill,	New Salem,
Henderson, (c. h.,)	Pine Hill,
Iron Mountain,	Walling's Ferry.
London,	

SABINE COUNTY.

Brookeland,	Milam,
Hemphill, (c. h.,)	Sabinetown.

SAN AUGUSTINE COUNTY.

San Augustine, (c. h.)

SAN PATRICIO COUNTY.

San Patricio, (c. h.)

SAN SABA COUNTY.

Cherokee,   *San Saba,* (c. h.)

SHACKELFORD COUNTY.

Fort Griffin.

SHELBY COUNTY.

Buena Vista,	Patroon,
Center,	*Shelbyville,* (c. h.,)
Hamilton,	Todd's.

SMITH COUNTY.

Aberdeen,	Randall,
Etna,	Starrville,
Garden Valley,	Troup,
Mount Sylvan,	*Tyler,* (c. h.)

STARR COUNTY.

Rio Grande City, (c.h.,) Roma.

TARRANT COUNTY.

Fort Worth, (c. h.,)   Mansfield.
Johnson's Station

TITUS COUNTY.

Clay Hill,	*Mount Pleasant,* (c. h.,)
Daingerfield,	Snow Hill,
Gray Rock,	Wheatville.
Lone Star,	

TRAVIS COUNTY.

AUSTIN,* (c. h.,)	Onion Creek,
Bee Caves,	Parsons' Seminary,
Merrilltown,	Perdenales,
Oak Hill,	Webberville.

TRINITY COUNTY.

Sumpter, (c. h.)

TYLER COUNTY.

Steele's Grove,   *Woodville,* (c. h.)
Town Bluff,

UPSHUR COUNTY.

Calloway,	Omega,
Carrollton,	Pine Tree,
Coffeeville,	Pittsburgh,
Gilmer, (c. h.,)	Point Pleasant,
La Fayette,	Simpsonville.

UVALDE COUNTY.

Sabinal,   *Uvalde,* (c. h.)

VAN ZANDT COUNTY.

Canton, (c. h.,)   Jordan's Saline.
Colfax,

VICTORIA COUNTY.

Kemper City,   *Victoria,* (c. h.)
Mission Valley,

WALKER COUNTY.

Holloway's Store,   Newport,
Huntsville, (c. h.,) Waverly.

WASHINGTON COUNTY.

Berlin,	Independence,
Brenham, (c. h.,)	Vine Grove,
Burton,	Washington.
Chapel Hill,	

WEBB COUNTY.

Laredo, (c. h.)

WHARTON COUNTY.

Bernard Station,   *Wharton,* (c. h.)
Egypt,

WILLIAMSON COUNTY.

Bagdad,	Liberty Hill,
Circleville,	Pond Spring,
Florence,	Round Rock.
Georgetown, (c. h.,)	

* Money-order office.

WILSON COUNTY.		WOOD COUNTY.
Fair View,	*Lodi, (c. h.,)*	*Quitman, (c. h.)*
Lavernia,	Sutherland Springs.	

WISE COUNTY.		ZAPATA COUNTY.
Boyd's Mill,	*Decatur, (c. h.)*	*Carrizo, (c. h.)*

UTAH TERRITORY.

BEAVER COUNTY.

Adamsville,   Minersville.
Beaver, (c. h.,)

BOX ELDER COUNTY.

Brigham City, (c. h.,)   Portage,
Corinne,   Willard.
Kelton,

CACHE COUNTY.

Clifton,	Oxford,
Franklin,	Paradise,
Hyde Park,	Providence,
Hyrum,	Richmond,
Logan, (c. h.,)	Smithfield,
Mendon,	Wellsville,
Millville,	Weston.
Newton,	

DAVIS COUNTY.

Centreville,	Kaysville,
Farmington, (c. h.,)	Stoker.

IRON COUNTY.

Cedar City,	*Parowan, (c. h.,)*
Iron City,	Pinto,
Kanarraville,	Summit.
Paragonah,	

JUAB COUNTY.

Chicken Creek,	Mona,
Levan,	*Salt Creek, (c. h.)*

KANE COUNTY.

Duncan's Retreat,	*Toquerville, (c. h.,)*
Rockville,	Virgin City.
Springdale,	

MILLARD COUNTY.

Deseret,	Meadow,
Fillmore City, (c. h.,)	Petersburgh,
Holden,	Scipio.
Kanosh,	

MORGAN COUNTY.

Croydon,	*Morgan, (c. h.,)*
Enterprise,	Mountain.

RICH COUNTY.

Bloomington,	Ovid,
Fish Haven,	Paris,
Liberty,	*Saint Charles, (c. h.)*
Montpelier,	

RIO VIRGEN COUNTY.

West Point.

SALT LAKE COUNTY.

Bingham Canyon,	SALT LAKE CITY,*
Draper,	*(c. h.,)*
Herriman,	South Cottonwood,
Mill Creek,	Union,
	West Jordan,

SAN PETE COUNTY.

Ephraim,	Moroni,
Fair View,	Mount Pleasant,
Fountain Green,	Spring City,
Gunnison,	Wales.
Manti, (c. h.,)	

SUMMIT COUNTY.

Coalville, (c. h.,)	Peoa,
Echo City,	Wanship,
Kamas,	Wasatch.

TOOELE COUNTY.

Grantsville,	*Tooele, (c. h.)*
Stockton,	

UTAH COUNTY.

Alpine City,	Pleasant Grove,
American Fork,	*Provo City, (c. h.,)*
Cedar Valley,	Santaquin,
Fairfield,	Spanish Fork,
Lehi City,	Springville.
Payson,	

WASATCH COUNTY.

Heber, (c. h.,)	Midway.

* Money-order office.

WASHINGTON COUNTY.

Bellevue,
Harrisburgh,
Leeds,
New Harmony,

Panaca,
Pine Valley,
Saint George, (c. h.,)
Washington.

WEBER COUNTY.

Alma,
Hooper,
Huntsville,
Lynne,
North Ogden,

Ogden City, (c. h.,)
Plain City,
Riverdale,
Slatersville,
Uintah.

VERMONT.

ADDISON COUNTY.

Addison,
Bridport,
Bristol,
Brooksville,
Chimney Point,
Chipman's Point,
Cornwall,
East Granville,
East Middlebury,
Ferrisburgh,
Granville,
Hancock,
Larrabee's Point,
Leicester,
Lincoln,
Middlebury,* (c. h.,)
Monkton,
Monkton Ridge,
New Haven,

New Haven Mills,
North Ferrisburgh,
Orwell,
Panton,
Richville,
Ripton,
Salisbury,
Shoreham,
South Starksbor'gh,
Starksborough,
Vergennes,*
West Addison,
West Cornwall,
West Salisbury,
Weybridge Lower Falls,
Whiting,
Whiting Station.

BENNINGTON COUNTY.

Arlington,
Bennington,* (c. h.,)
Bennington Centre,
Bondville,
Dorset,
East Arlington,
East Dorset,
East Rupert,
Factory Point,
Heartwellville,
Manchester,* (c. h.,)
North Bennington,
North Dorset,
North Landgrove,
North Pownal,
Peru,

Pownal,
Pownal Centre,
Readsborough,
Rupert,
Sandgate,
Searsburgh,
Shaftsbury,
South Dorset,
South Shaftsbury,
Stamford,
Sunderland,
West Arlington,
West Rupert,
Winhall,
Woodford.

CALEDONIA COUNTY.

Barnet,
Burke,
Danville,
East Burke,
East Hardwick,
Groton,
Hardwick,
Lower Waterford,
Lyndon,
Lyndon Centre,
Lyndonville,
McIndoe's Falls,*
Newark,

Norrisville,
North Danville,
Passumpsic,
Peacham,*
Ryegate,
St. Johnsbury,* (c. h.,)
St. Johnsbury Centre,
St. Johnsbury East,
Sheffield,
South Danville,
South Peacham,
South Ryegate,
South Walden,

CALEDONIA COUNTY—Continued.

Sutton,
Walden,
Waterford,
West Barnet,

West Burke,
West Danville,
West Waterford,
Wheelock,

CHITTENDEN COUNTY.

Bolton,
Burlington,* (c. h.,)
Charlotte,
Colchester,
Essex,
Essex Junction,
Hinesburgh,
Huntington,
Huntington Centre,
Jericho,
Jericho Centre,
Jonesville,
Milton,
North Underhill,

North Williston,
Pleasant Valley,
Richmond,
Saint George,
Shelburne,
South Hinesburgh,
Underhill,
Underhill Centre,
West Bolton,
West Charlotte,
Westford,
West Milton,
Williston,
Winooski Falls.

ESSEX COUNTY.

Bloomfield,
Brunswick,
Canaan,
Concord,
East Haven,
Granby,
Guildhall, (c. h.,)
Island Pond,*

Lemington,
Lunenburgh,
Miles Pond,
Norton Mills,
Nulhegan,
Victory,
West Concord.*

FRANKLIN COUNTY.

Bakersfield,
Berkshire,
Bordoville,
Buck Hollow,
East Berkshire,
East Fairfield,
East Franklin,
East Georgia,
East Highgate,
East Richford,
East Sheldon,
Enosburgh,
Enosburgh Falls,*
Fairfax,
Fairfield,
Fletcher,
Franklin,
Georgia,
Georgia Plain,

Highgate,
Highgate Centre,
Highgate Springs,
Montgomery,
Montgomery Centre,
North Enosburgh,
North Fairfax,
North Sheldon,
Richford,
Saint Albans,* (c. h.,)
Saint Albans Bay,
Sheldon,*
Swanton,*
Swanton Centre,
Swanton Junction,
West Berkshire,
West Enosburgh,
West Georgia.

-order office.

GRAND ISLE COUNTY.

Alburgh,	Isle La Motte,
Alburgh Centre,	Keeler's Bay,
Alburgh Springs,	La Grange,
East Alburgh,	*North Hero, (c. h.,)*
Grand Isle,	South Hero.

LAMOILLE COUNTY.

Belvidere,	Jeffersonville,
Belvidere Corners,	Johnson,*
Cady's Falls,	Morristown,
Cambridge,	Morrisville,
East Cambridge,	North Cambridge,
East Elmore,	North Hyde Park,
Eden,	North Wolcott,
Eden Mills,	Stowe,*
Elmore,	Waterville,
Hyde Park, (c. h.,)	Wolcott.

ORANGE COUNTY.

Boltonville,	Randolph,
Bradford,*	South Newbury,
Bradford Centre,	South Strafford,
Braintree,	Strafford,
Brookfield,	Thetford,
Chelsea, (c. h.,)	Thetford Centre,
Copperas Hill,	Topsham,
Corinth,	Tunbridge,
East Brookfield,	Union Village,
East Corinth,	Vershire,
East Orange,	Wait's River,
East Randolph,	Washington,
East Thetford,	Wells River,
Fairlee,	West Braintree,
Newbury,*	West Corinth,
North Randolph,	West Fairlee,
North Thetford,	West Randolph,*
North Tunbridge,	West Topsham,
Orange,	Williamstown.
Post Mill Village,	

ORLEANS COUNTY.

Albany,	Lowell,
Albany Centre,	Morgan,
Barton,*	Newport,*
Barton Landing,	Newport Centre,
Beebe Plain,	North Craftsbury,
Brownington,	North Derby,
Coventry,	N. Greensborough,
Craftsbury,	North Troy,
Derby,	South Albany,
Derby Line,*	South Barton,
East Albany,	South Glover,
East Charleston,	Troy,
East Coventry,	West Charleston,
East Craftsbury,	West Derby,
East Greensborough,	Westfield,
Glover,	West Glover,
Greensborough,	West Newport,
Holland,	Wetmore,
Irasburgh, (c. h.,)	Willoughby Lake.
Jay,	

RUTLAND COUNTY.

Benson,	Mechanicsville,
Benson Landing,	Mendon,
Brandon,*	Middletown,*
Castleton,*	Mount Holly,
Centre Rutland,	North Clarendon,
Chippenhook Spr'gs,	Pawlet,
Chittenden,	Pittsfield,
Clarendon,	Pittsford,
Clarendon Springs,	Poultney,
Cuttingsville,	*Rutland,* (c. h.,)
Danby,	Sherburne,
Danby Four Corners,	Shrewsbury,
East Clarendon,	South Wallingford,
East Hubbardton,	Sudbury,
East Poultney,	Sutherland Falls,
East Wallingford,	Tinmouth,
Fair Haven,*	Wallingford,
Forest Dale,	Wells,
Healdville,	West Castleton,
Hortonville,	West Haven,
Hubbardton,	West Pawlet,
Hydeville,	Rutland.
Ira,	

WASHINGTON COUNTY.

Barre,	North Fayston,
Berlin,	Northfield,*
Cabot,	North Montpelier,
Calais,	Plainfield,
East Cabot,	Roxbury,
East Calais,	South Barre,
East Montpelier,	South Cabot,
East Roxbury,	South Woodbury,
East Warren,	Waitsfield,*
Gouldsville,	Warren,
Marshfield,	Waterbury,*
Middlesex,	Waterbury Centre,
MONTPELIER,* (c. h.,)	Woodbury,
Moretown,	Worcester.
North Duxbury,	

WINDHAM COUNTY.

Athens,	Saxton's River,
Bartonsville,	Somerset,
Bellows Falls,*	South Halifax,
Brattleborough,*	South Londonderry,
Cambridgeport,	S'th Wardsborough,
Cornton,	South Windham,
Dover,	Stratton,
Dummerston,	Townshend,
East Dover,	Vernon,
Fayetteville, (c. h.,)	Wardsborough,
Grafton,	W. Brattleborough,
Green River,	West Dover,
Guilford,	West Dummerston,
Guilford Centre,	West Halifax,
Halifax,	West Marlborough,
Houghtonville,	Westminster,
Jacksonville,	Westminster West,
Jamaica,	West Townshend,
Londonderry,	W. Wardsborough,
Marlborough,	Whitingham,
North Windham,	Williamsville,
Putney,	Wilmington,
Rockingham,	Windham.
Sadawga,	

* Money-order office.

WINDSOR COUNTY.

Andover,
Ascutneyville,
Barnard,
Bethel,
Bridgewater,
Brownsville.
Cavendish,
Chester,*
East Barnard,
East Bethel,
Felchville,
Gassett's Station,
Gaysville,
Hartford,
Hartland,
Hartland Four Cor's,
Ludlow, *
North Chester,
North Hartland.
North Pomfret,
North Springfield,
Norwich,
Perkinsville,*
Plymouth,
Pomfret,
Pompanoosuc,

WINDSOR COUNTY—Continued.

Proctorsville,
Quechee,
Reading,
Rochester,
Royalton,
Sharon,
Simonsville,
South Pomfret,
South Reading,
South Royalton,
South Woodstock,
Springfield,*
Stockbridge,
Taftsville,
Tyson Furnace,
Upper Falls,
Weathersfield,
Weathersfield Centre,
West Bridgewater,
West Hartford,
Weston,
West Rochester,
White River Junc'n,*
Windsor,*
Woodstock, (c. h.)

VIRGINIA.

ACCOMACK COUNTY.

Accomack C. H.,
Belle Haven,
Chincoteague,
Chincoteague Isl'd,
Guilford,
Horntown,
Jenkins' Bridge,
Locust Mount,
Locustville,
Messongo,
Modest Town,
New Church,
Onancock,
Pungoteague,
Temperanceville,
Wiseville.

ALBEMARLE COUNTY.

Batesville,
Bentivoglio,
Brown's Cove,
Carter's Bridge,
Charlottesville,(c. h.,)
Cobham,
Earleysville,
Free Union,
Glendower,
Greenwood Depot,
Howardsville,
Ivy Depot,
Keswick Depot,
Mechum's River,
Millington,
Moorman's River,
North Garden,
Scottsville,*
Shadwell,
Stony Point,
University of Va.,
Warren.

ALEXANDRIA COUNTY.

Alexandria, (c. h.,)   Arlington.

ALLEGHANY COUNTY.

Alleghany Station,
Callaghan's,
Clifton Forge,
Covington, (c. h.,)
Cowpasture Bridge,
Morris Hill,
Rich Patch,
Selma,
Sweet Chalybeate.

AMELIA COUNTY.

Amelia C. H.,
Chula Depot,
Deatonsville,
Jetersville,
Lodore,
Mannborough,
Matoax,
Morven,
Paineville,
Wilkinson's Shop.

AMHERST COUNTY.

Allen's Creek,
Amherst C. H.,
Cool Well,
Galt's Mills,
Harris Creek,
Mason's Depot,
Oronoco,
Riversville,
Salt Creek,
Stapleton Mills,
Walker's Ford.

APPOMATTOX COUNTY.

Appomattox C. H.,
Bent Creek,
Evergreen,
Nebraska,
Oakville,
Pamplin's Depot,
Spout Spring,
Spring Mills,
Tower Hill,
Walker's Church.

AUGUSTA COUNTY.

Arbor Hill,
Burke's Mills,
Churchville,
Cline's Mills,
Craigsville,
Deerfield,
Elizabeth Furnace,
Fishersville,
Greenville,
Hermitage,
Long Glade,
Middlebrook,
Milnesville,
Mint Spring,
Moffatt Creek's,
Mossy Creek,
Mount Meridian,
Mount Sidney,
Mount Solon,
New Hope,
Parnassus,
Sangerville,
Sherando,
Staunton, (c. h.,)
Steele's Tavern,
Stuart's Draft,
Stribling Springs,
Swoope's Depot,
Waynesborough.

BATH COUNTY.

Bath Alum,
Bath C. H.,
Cady's Tunnel,
Cleek's Mills,
Green Valley,
Healing Springs,
Hot Springs,
Letcher,
Millborough Springs,
Mountain Grove,
Sun Rise,
Williamsville.

* Money-order office.

BEDFORD COUNTY.

Bellevue,
Big Island,
Body Camp,
Buford's,
Bunker Hill,
Chamblissburgh,
Charlemont,
Chesnut Fork,
Davis' Mills,
Emaus,
Fancy Grove,
Forest Depot,
Good View,
Hendrick's Store,
Holcomb's Rock,
Kasey's,
Liberty,* (c. h.,)
Lisbon,
Lone Pine,
Loving Creek,
Lowry,
Thaxton's,
Wade's.

BLAND COUNTY.

Bland C. H.,
Mechanicsburgh,
Rocky Gap,
Sharon.

BOTETOURT COUNTY.

Amsterdam,
Blue Ridge,
Buchanan,
Cloverdale,
Dagger's Springs,
Deisher's Mill,
Fincastle,* (c. h.,)
Flukes,
Locust Bottom
Old Hickory,
Roaring Run,
Saltpetre Cave,
Troutsville,
Waskey's Mills.

BRUNSWICK COUNTY.

Burntville,
Charlie Hope,
Gholsonville,
Jonesborough,
Kennedy's,
Lawrenceville, (c. h.,)
Pleasant Oaks,
Powellton,
Smoky Ordinary,
Sturgeonville,
White Plains.

BUCHANAN COUNTY.

Ava,
Grundy, (c. h.,)
McClure.

BUCKINGHAM COUNTY.

Bolling's Landing,
Buckingham C. H.,
Centenary,
Curdsville,
Diana Mills,
Gary's Store,
Glenmore,
Gold Hill,
Gravel Hill,
Mount Vinco,
New Canton,
New Store,
Ore Banks,
South Bangor,
Well Water.

CAMPBELL COUNTY.

Arnoldton,
Brook Neal,
Campbell C. H.,
Castle Craig,
Concord Depot,
Green Hill,
Hat Creek,
Leesville
Lynchburgh,*
Marysville,
Mount Athos,
Mount Zion,
New London,
Pigeon Run,
Yellow Branch.

CAROLINE COUNTY.

Applewood,
Bowling Green, (c. h.,)
Cedar Fork,
Central Point,
Chilesburgh,
Dunn's Store,
Flippo's,
Guiney's,
Milford,
Penola,
Point Eastern,
Port Royal,
Rappahannock
Academy,
Ruther Glen,
Sparta,
The Grove.

CARROLL COUNTY.

Chamber's Valley,
Cranberry Plains,
Dug Spur,
Fancy Gap.
Gladesborough,
Hillsville, (c. h.,)
Lambsburgh,
Laurel Fork,
Piper's Gap,
Stone Mountain,
Wolf Glade,
Wood Lawn.

CHARLES CITY COUNTY.

Apperson's,
Charles City C. H.,
Wilcox Wharf,
Wilson's Landing.

CHARLOTTE COUNTY.

Aspen Wall,
Barnesville,
Charlotte C. H.,
Cole's Ferry,
County Line Cross
Roads,
Drake's Branch,
Dupree's Old Store,
Harvey's Store,
Keysville,
Mossing Ford,
Red House,
Red Oak Grove,
Rolling Hill,
Talcott,
Wylliesburgh.

CHESTERFIELD COUNTY.

Chester,
Chesterfield C. H.,
Hallsborough,
Manchester,
Midlothian,
Proctor's Creek,
Skinquarter,
Winterpock.

CLARKE COUNTY.

Berryville, (c. h.,)
Castleman's Ferry,
Millwood,
Wadesville,
White Post.

CRAIG COUNTY.

New Castle, (c. h.,)
Ripley's Mills,
Simmonsville,
Sinking Creek.

CULPEPER COUNTY.

Boston,
Brandy Station,
Castleton,
Culpeper,* (c. h.,)
El Dorado,
Jeffersonton,
Mitchell's Station,
Racoon Ford,
Rapid Ann Station,
Richardsville,
Rixeyville,
Stevensburgh,
Waylandsburgh.

*Money-order office.

CUMBERLAND COUNTY.

Ca Ira,
Cartersville,
Cumberland C. H.,

Oak Forest,
Stony Point Mills,
Sunny Side.

DINWIDDIE COUNTY.

Burgess,
Dinwiddie C. H.,
Ford's Depot,
Goodwynsville,
Petersburgh,*

Ream's Station,
Ritchieville,
San Marino,
Sutherland,
Wilson's Depot.

ELIZABETH CITY COUNTY.

Hampton, (c. h.,)   Old Point Comfort.*

ESSEX COUNTY.

Centre Cross,
Dunnsville,
Lloyds,
Loretto,
Miller's Tavern,

Montague,
Mount Landing,
Paul's Cross Roads,
Tappahannock, (c. h.)

FAIRFAX COUNTY.

Accotink,
Burk's Station,
Centreville,
Chantilly,
Clifton Station,
Collingwood,
Dranesville,
Fairfax C. H.,
Falls Church,
Herndon,

Hunter's Mills,
Iona,
Langley,
Lewinsville,
Pleasant Valley,
Prospect Hill,
Spring Vale,
Theolog'l Seminary,
Thornton's Depot,
Vienna.

FAUQUIER COUNTY.

Bealeton,
Bowenville,
Bristersburgh,
Broad Run Station,
Casanova,
Catlett,
Elk Run,
Fauquier White Sul-
   phur Springs,
Markham Station,
Morrisville,
New Baltimore,
New Brighton,

Orlean,
Owl Run,
Paris,
Piedmont Station,
Pine View,
Rectortown Station,
Salem Fauquier,
Somerville,
The Plains,
Upperville,
Warrenton, (c. h.,)
Weaversville.

FLOYD COUNTY.

Connor's Mills,
Copper Hill,
Copper Valley,
Floyd C. H.,
Greasy Creek,

Indian Valley,
Little River,
Simpson's,
West Fork Furnace,
Wills' Ridge.

FLUVANNA COUNTY.

Boswell's,
Bremo Bluff,

Central Plains,
Chapel Hill,

FLUVANNA COUNTY—Continued.

Columbia,
Fork Union,
Hunter's Lodge,
Palmyra, (c. h.,)

Seven Islands,
Union Mills,
Wilmington.

FRANKLIN COUNTY.

Bonbrook,
Boone's Mill,
Cooper's,
Dickinson's,
Glade Hill,
Gogginsville,
Hale's Ford,
Long Branch,
Naff's,
Penhook,

Pig River,
Prillaman's,
Retreat,
Rocky Mount, (c. h.,)
Shady Grove,
Snow Creek,
Sydnorsville,
Taylor's Store,
Union Hall,
Young's Store.

FREDERICK COUNTY.

Acorn Hill,
Back Creek Valley,
Capper's Spring,
Cedar Creek,
Collinsville,
Gainesborough,
Gravel Spring,
Hayfield,
High View,
Middletown,

Millbrook,
Mountain Falls,
Mount Vernon Tan-
   nery,
Newtown Stephens-
   burgh,
Shockeysville,
Stephenson's Depot,
White Hall,
Winchester, (c. h.)

GILES COUNTY.

Eggleston's Springs,
Hobb's Ferry,
Newport,
Pearisburgh, (c. h.,)

Pembroke,
Poplar Hill,
White Gate.

GLOUCESTER COUNTY.

Glenn's,
Gloucester C. H.,
Hayes' Store,

Hickory Fork,
New Upton,
Wood's Cross Roads.

GOOCHLAND COUNTY.

Bula,
Dover Mines,
Elk Hill Mills,
Fite's,
Goochland C. H.,
Hadensville,
Issequena,
Johnson's Springs,

Loch Lomond,
North Side,
Pemberton,
Perkinsville,
Pierce's,
Sabbot Island,
Shannon Hill.

GRAYSON COUNTY.

Bridle Creek,
Elk Creek,
Independence, (c. h.,)
Mouth of Wilson,

Nuckollsville,
Point Hope,
Spring Valley.

GREENE COUNTY.

Dawsonville,
Ruckersville,

Stanardsville, (c. h.)

* **Money-order office.**

GREENVILLE COUNTY.

Hicksford, (*c. h.*,) Ryland's Depot.
Poplar Mount,

HALIFAX COUNTY.

Barkesdale, Mount Carmel,
Black Walnut, Mount Laurel,
Bloomsburgh, News Ferry,
Brooklyn, Omega,
Buck Shoal, Red Bank,
Clover Depot, Republican Grove,
Halifax C. H., Scottsburgh,
Harmony, South Boston Depot,
Hyco, Vernon Hill,
Locust Level, Whitesville,
Meadville, Whitlock,
Mountain Road, Wolf Trap.

HANOVER COUNTY.

Ashland, Montpelier,
Atlee's Station, Morris,
Beaver Dam Depot, Negro Foot,
French Hay, Old Church,
Goodall's, Rockville,
Hanover C. H., Taylorsville,
Hewlett's, Verdon.
Junction,

HENRICO COUNTY.

Curl's Wharf, RICHMOND,* (*c. h.*,)
Erin Shades, Westham Locks.
Glen Allen,

HENRY COUNTY.

Horse Pasture, Prunty's,
Irisburgh, Ridgeway,
Martinsville, (*c. h.*,) Spencer's Store,
Oak Level, Traylorsville.

HIGHLAND COUNTY.

Head Waters, New Hampden,
Hightown, Palo Alto,
McDowell, Spruce Hill,
Meadow Dale, Strait Creek,
Mill Gap, Wilsonville.
Monterey, (*c. h.*,)

ISLE OF WIGHT COUNTY.

Carrsville, Windsor Station,
Smithfield,* (*c. h.*,) Zuni Station.

JAMES CITY COUNTY.

Burnt Ordinary, *Williamsburgh*,* (*c. h.*)

KING AND QUEEN COUNTY.

Bruington, St. Stephen's Church,
Carlton's Store, Shakleford's,
Little Plymouth, Stevensville,
Nowtown, Walkerton.
Plainview,

KING GEORGE COUNTY.

Chatterton, Hampstead,
Comorn, *King George C. H.*,
Edge Hill, Port Conway,
Friendshipville, Shiloh.

KING WILLIAM COUNTY.

Aylett's, Lanesville,
Beulahville, Mangohick,
Cherry Lane, Manquin,
Enfield, Warauancoke,
Etna Mills, West Point.
King William C. H.,

LANCASTER COUNTY.

Kilmarnock, Litwalton,
Lancaster C. H., Lively Oaks.

LEE COUNTY.

Beech Spring, Turkey Cove,
Cany Hollow, Walnut Hill,
Jonesville, (*c. h.*,) White Oak Springs,
Rocky Station, White Shoals,
Rose Hill, Yokum Station,
Stickleyville, Zion's Mills.

LOUDOUN COUNTY.

Aldie, Lovettsville,
Arcola, Middleburgh,
Bloomfield, Mount Gilead,
Bolington, Mountville,
Circleville, Neersville,
Daysville, Oatlands,
Farmwell, Philomont,
Goresville, Round Hill,
Guilford Station, Snickersville,
Hamilton, Taylorstown,
Hillsborough, Unison,
Hughesville, Waterford,
Leesburgh,* (*c. h.*,) Wheatland.
Lincoln,

LOUISA COUNTY.

Apple Grove, Jackson,
Bell's X Roads, Locust Creek,
Buckner's Station, *Louisa C. H.*,
Bumpass, Poindexter's Store,
Cuckoo, Thompson's X Roads,
Fredericks Hall, Tolersville,
Gum Spring, Trevilian's Depot.
Harris,

LUNENBURGH COUNTY.

Brickland, Oral Oaks,
Columbian Grove, Plantersville,
Double Bridge, Pleasant Grove,
Lochleven, Rehoboth,
McFarland's, Wattsborough,
Non Intervention, Yatesville.

* Money-order office.

MADISON COUNTY.

Criglersville,
Decapolis,
Graves' Mill,
Leon,
Madison C. H.,

Madison Mills,
Oak Park,
Peola Mills,
Rochelle,
Seville.

MATTHEWS COUNTY.

Cobb's Creek,
Hicks' Wharf,

Matthews, (c. h.)

MECKLENBURGH COUNTY.

Abbyville,
Boydton, (c. h.,)
Christiansville,
Clarksville,
Drapersville,
Forksville,
Lombardy Grove,
Oakley,

Palmer's Springs,
Saint Tammany's,
South Hill,
Spring Hill,
Wayside,
White House,
Whittle's Mills.

MIDDLESEX COUNTY.

Church View,
Freeshade,
Harmony Village,
Jamaica,

Locust Hill,
Saluda, (c. h.,)
Sandy Bottom,
Urbana.

MONTGOMERY COUNTY.

Alleghany Spring,
Big Spring Depot,
Blacksburgh,
Center Mills,
Childress' Store,
Christiansburgh,(c.h.,)

La Fayette,
Lovely Mount,
McDonald's Mill,
Montgomery Springs,
Pilot,
Shawsville.

NANSEMOND COUNTY.

Chuckatuck,

Suffolk, (c. h.)

NELSON COUNTY.

Afton,
Arrington,
Elmington,
Faber's Mills,
Greenfield,
Greenway,
Hardwicksville,
Horseley's Landing,
Lovingston, (c. h.,)

Massie's Mills,
Montreal,
Nelly's Ford,
Norwood,
Rockfish Depot,
Tye River Depot,
Variety Mills,
Warminster.

NEW KENT COUNTY.

Barhamsville,
New Kent C. H.,

Providence Forge,
Tunstall's.

NORFOLK COUNTY.

Churchland,
Deep Creek,
Ferry Point,
Great Bridge,

Lake Drummond,
Norfolk, (c. h.,)
Portsmouth.*

NORTHAMPTON COUNTY.

Bay View,
Caperville,
Cherrystone,
Eastville, (c. h.,)

Franktown,
Hadlock,
Johnsontown,
Sea View.

NORTHUMBERLAND COUNTY.

Brown Store,
Heathsville, (c. h.,)

Lottsburgh,
Wicomico Church.

NOTTOWAY COUNTY.

Blacks and Whites,
Burkesville,
Forkland,
Jeffress' Store,

Jennings' Ordinary,
Nottoway C. H.,
Wellville.

ORANGE COUNTY.

Gordonsville,*
Liberty Mills,
Locust Grove,
Madison Run Station,
Orange C. H.,

Thornhill,
Unionville,
Verdicrville,
Woolfolk.

PAGE COUNTY.

Alma,
Cedar Point,
Grove Hill,
Hope Mills,
Leaksville,
Luray, (c. h.,)

Marksville,
Massanutton,
Shenandoah Iron
  Works,
Stony Man.

PATRICK COUNTY.

Ararat,
Carter's Mills,
Elamsville,
Mayo Forge,
Meadows of Dan,
Nettle Ridge,

Patrick C. H.,
Patrick Springs,
Penn's Store,
Rock Castle,
Rock Spring.

PITTSYLVANIA COUNTY.

Bachelor's Hall,
Berger's Store,
Callands,
Cartersburgh,
Cascade,
Chalk Level,
Danville,
Hill Grove,
Laurel Grove,
Mount Airy,

Peytonsburgh,
Pittsylvania C. H.,
Pleasant Gap,
Riceville,
Ringgold,
Sandy Level,
Spring Garden,
Swansonville,
Whitehead's Store,
Whitmell.

POWHATAN COUNTY.

Ballsville,
Fine Creek Mills,
Genito,

Jefferson,
Powhatan C. H.,
Sublett's Tavern.

* Money-order office.

PRINCE EDWARD COUNTY.

Darlington Heights, Moore's Ordinary,
Farmville, *Prince Edward C. H.,*
Green Bay, Prospect,
Hampden Sidney Rice Depot.
College,

PRINCE GEORGE COUNTY.

Brandon, Garysville,
Brandon Church, Piney Grove,
City Point, *Prince George C. H.,*
Disputanta, Templeton.

PRINCESS ANNE COUNTY.

Blossom Hill, Pleasant Ridge,
Land of Promise, *Princess Anne C. H.*
London Bridge,

PRINCE WILLIAM COUNTY.

Brentsville, (c. h.,) Independent Hill,
Bristoe Station, Manassas,*
Brook Vale, Neabsco Mills,
Buckland, Nokesville,
Dumfries, Occoquan,
Gainesville, Stone House Hotel.
Hay Market,

PULASKI COUNTY.

Dublin, Radford Furnace,
Newbern, (c. h.,) Snowville.
New River Depot,

RAPPAHANNOCK COUNTY.

Amissville, Slate Mills,
Flint Hill, Sperryville,
Gaines' × Roads, Walden's,
Laurel Mills, *Washington,* (c. h.,)
Rock Mills, Woodville.
Sandy Hook,

RICHMOND COUNTY.

Emmorton, Farnham Cross R'ds,
Farnham, *Warsaw,* (c. h.)

ROANOKE COUNTY.

Bent Mountain, Cave Spring,
Big Lick,* Gishe's Mills,
Bonsack's, Poage's Mill,
Botetourt Springs, *Salem,* (c. h.)
Catawba,

ROCKBRIDGE COUNTY.

Alum Springs, Cedar Grove Mills,
Balcony Falls, Collierstown,
Bell's Valley, Fairfield,
Brownsburgh, Fancy Hill,
Buffalo Forge, Gilmore's Mills,
Buffalo Mills, Goshen Bridge,

ROCKBRIDGE COUNTY—Continued.

*Lexington,** (c. h.,) Oakdale,
Longwood, Rapp's Mills,
McKenny's Mill, Rockbridge Baths,
Monmouth, Summers,
Natural Bridge, Timber Ridge.

ROCKINGHAM COUNTY.

Bowman's Mills, Linville,
Bridgewater, McGaheysville,
Broadway Depot, Melrose,
Cherry Grove, Mount Clinton,
Coote's Store, Mount Crawford,
Conrad's Store, Mount Vernon
Cross Keys, Forge,
Dayton, Ottobine,
Edom, Port Republic,
Fair Hill, Rawley Springs,
Greenmount, Singer's Glen,
*Harrisonburgh,** Spring Creek,
(c. h.,) Tenth Legion,
Keezletown, Timberville,
Lacey Spring, Waverlie.

RUSSELL COUNTY.

Alta Vista, *Lebanon,* (c. h.,)
Belfast Mills, New Garden,
Bickley's Mills, Rock Farm,
Dickensonville, Rosedale,
Gibsonville, Vicar,
Hansonville, Willow Spring.
Jesse's Mills,

SCOTT COUNTY.

Duncan's Mills, Osborn's Ford,
Estillville, (c. h.,) Pattonsville,
Fort Blackimore, Point Truth,
Fulkerson, Stock Creek.

SHENANDOAH COUNTY.

Alonzaville, Moore's Store,
Columbian Furnace, Mount Clifton,
Edenburgh, Mount Jackson,
Edith, Mount Olive,
Forestville, New Market,
Hamburgh, Orkney Springs,
Hawkinstown, Saumsville,
Jacob's Church, Seven Fountains,
Lantz Mills, Strasburgh,
Lebanon Church, Van Buren Furnace,
Maurertown, *Woodstock,** (c. h.)

SMYTH COUNTY.

Broadford, Rye Valley,
Chatham Hill, Seven Mile Ford,
*Marion,** (c. h.,) Two Mile Branch.

SOUTHAMPTON COUNTY.

Assamoosick, Boykin's Depot,
Berlin, Branchville,

* Money-order office.

SOUTHAMPTON COUNTY—Continued.

Drewryville,
Farmer's Grove,
Franklin Depot,
Green Plain,
Ivor,

Jerusalem, (c. h.,)
Newsom's Depot,
Pond's Shop,
Vicksville,
Weeksville.

SPOTTSYLVANIA COUNTY.

Andrews',
Brokenburgh,
Clover Green,
Fredericksburgh,*
Lewis' Store,
Mount Pleasant,

Partlow's,
Spottsylvania C. H.,
Thornburgh,
Twyman's Store,
Wilderness.

STAFFORD COUNTY.

Accokeek,
Belfair Mills,
Falmouth,
Garrisonville,
Hartwood,

Richland Mills,
Serena,
Stafford C. H.,
Stafford Store.

SURRY COUNTY.

Cabin Point,
Claremont Wharf,
Dallies,

Hog Island,
Spring Grove,
Surry C. H.

SUSSEX COUNTY.

Coman's Well,
Hawkinsville,
Henry,
Jarratts,
Littleton,
Parham's Store,

Stony Creek Ware-
house,
Sussex C. H.,
Wakefield Station,
Waverly Station.

TAZEWELL COUNTY.

Abb's Valley,
Baptist Valley,
Blue Stone,
Burke's Garden,
Cedar Bluff,
Cove Creek,

Croftsville,
Knob,
Richland,
Springville,
Tazewell C. H.

WARREN COUNTY.

Bentonville,
Buckton,
Front Royal, (c. h.,)
Hambaugh's,
Linden,

Milldale,
Nineveh,
Riverton,
Water Lick.

WARWICK COUNTY.

Menchville,
Newport News,

Warwick C. H.

WASHINGTON COUNTY.

*Abingdon,** (c. h.,)
Buffalo Pond,
Clear Branch,
Craig's Mills,
Emory,
Glade Spring,
Holston,

Lodi,
Love's Mills,
Mock's' Mills,
Raven's Nest,
Saltville,
Smith's Creek.

WESTMORELAND COUNTY.

Baynesville,
Eltham,
Hague,
Kinsale,
Millville,
Montross, (c. h.,)

Nominy Grove,
Oak Grove,
Oldham's × Roads,
Rice's Store.
Templeman's Cross
Roads.

WISE COUNTY.

Big Stone Gap,
Guest's Station,

Pound,
Wise C. H.

WYTHE COUNTY.

Browne Hill,
Eagle Iron Works,
Graham's Forge,
Iderbide,
Max Meadows,

Reed Island,
Rural Retreat,
Speedwell,
*Wytheville,** (c. h.)

YORK COUNTY.

Rippon's Hall,

Yorktown, (c. h.)

WASHINGTON TERRITORY.

CHEHALIS COUNTY.

Bruceport,
Cedarville,
Chehalis Point,
Elma,

Hoquiam,
Montesano, (c. h.,)
Satsop,
Sharon.

CLALLAM COUNTY.

New Dungeness, (c. h.,)Port Angeles.

CLARKE COUNTY.

Martin's Bluff,
Pekin,

Union Ridge,
*Vancouver,** (o. h.)

COWLITZ COUNTY.

Castle Rock,
Freeport,
Kalama,

Monticello, (c. h.,)
Oak Point.

* Money-order office.

ISLAND COUNTY.

| Coupville, | Utsaladdy. |
| *Coveland*, (c. h.,) | |

JEFFERSON COUNTY.

| Port Discovery, | *Port Townsend*,* (c. h.) |
| Port Ludlow, | |

KING COUNTY.

Black River,	Snoqualmie,
Seattle, (c. h.,)	Squak,
Slaughter,	White River.

KITSAP COUNTY.

Blakeley,	Seabeck,
Port Madison, (c. h.,)	Teekalet.
Port Orchard,	

KLIKITAT COUNTY.

Klikitat.

LEWIS COUNTY.

Boistfort,	Grand Prairie,
Claquato, (c. h.,)	Pumphrey's Landing,
Cowlitz,	Skookumchuck.

MASON COUNTY.

| Arkada, | Sherwood's Mills, |
| *Oakland*, (c. h.,) | Skokomish. |

PACIFIC COUNTY.

Bruceport,	*Oysterville*, (c. h.,)
Chinook,	Unity.
Fort Willopa,	

PIERCE COUNTY.

| Franklin, | Tacoma. |
| *Steilacoom City*, (c. h.,) | |

SKAMANIA COUNTY.

Cascades, (c. h.)

SNOHOMISH COUNTY.

| Mukilteo, | Tulalip. |
| *Snohomish*, (c. h.,) | |

STEVENS COUNTY.

Fort Colville, (c. h.,) Spokan Bridge.

THURSTON COUNTY.

Beaver,	OLYMPIA, (c. h.,)
Coal Bank,	Tumwater,
Grand Mound,	Yelm.

WAUKIAKUM COUNTY.

Cathlamet, (c. h.)

WALLA WALLA COUNTY.

Delta Mills,	*Walla Walla*,* (c. h.,)
Touchet,	Wallula,
Tukannon,	Whitman.

WHATCOM COUNTY.

La Conner, *Whatcom*, (c. h.)

YAKIMA COUNTY.

| Attanam, | *Moksce*, (c. h.,) |
| Fort Simcoe, | Yakima. |

WEST VIRGINIA.

BARBOUR COUNTY.

Belington,	Nestorville,
Burnersville,	Overfield,
Calhoun,	Peel Tree,
Coveton.	*Philippi*, (c. h.,)
Elk City,	Pleasant Creek,
Kasson,	Valley Furnace,
Meadowville,	Woodford.

BERKELEY COUNTY.

Darkesville,	Little Georgetown,
Falling Waters,	*Martinsburgh*,* (c. h.,)
Gerrardstown,	Mill Creek,
Glengary,	North Mountain,
Hainesville,	Shanghai,
Hedgesville,	Tomahawk Springs,
Jones' Springs,	Van Clevesville.

BOONE COUNTY.

Bald Knob,	Mouth Short Creek,
Ballardsville, (c. h.,)	Peytona.
Crook,	

BRAXTON COUNTY.

Braxton C. H.,	Little Otter,
Bulltown,	Perkins' Mills,
Flat Woods,	Salt Lick Ridge,
Holly River,	Tate Creek.
Laforme's Store,	

BROOKE COUNTY.

Bethany,*	Short Creek,
Fowler's,	*Wellsburgh*,* (c. h.)
Pan Handle,	

* Money-order office.

CABELL COUNTY.

Cabell C. H.,	Marshall College,
Fudgy's Creek,	Mud Bridge,
Green Bottom,	Ouslie's Gap,
Guyandotte,	Thorndike.

CALHOUN COUNTY.

Arnoldsburgh,	Minnora,
Big Bend,	Sycamore.
Grantsville, (c. h.,)	

CLAY COUNTY.

Big Sycamore,	Lizemore's.
Clay C. H.,	

DODDRIDGE COUNTY.

Central Station,	McElroy,
Clover Dale,	New Milton,
Cold Water,	Oxford,
Greenwood,	Smithton,
Isaac's Camp,	*West Union*,* (c. h.,)
Long Run Station,	Yeater's Mills.

FAYETTE COUNTY.

Clifty,	Mountain Cove,
Cotton Hill,	Oak Hill,
Fayetteville, (c. h.,)	Raven's Eye,
Gauley Bridge,	Rocky Hill,
Hawk's Nest,	Russellville.

GILMER COUNTY.

Batten's Mills,	Sand Fork.
Beall's Mills,	Steer Creek,
Cox's Mills,	Tanners,
Glenville, (c. h.,)	Townsend Mills,
Letter Gap,	Troy.

GRANT COUNTY.

Black Rock,	Mount Storm,
Grant C. H.,	Mouse's,
Greenland,	Seymoursville,
Hopeville,	Williamsport.
Luney's Creek,	

GREENBRIER COUNTY.

Alvon,	*Lewisburgh*,* (c. h.,)
Big Clear Creek,	Little Sewell M'tain,
Blue Sulphur Sp'gs,	Meadow Bluff,
Clintonville,	Monroe Draft,
Falling Spring,	Palestine,
Frankford,	Second Creek.
Green Sulphur Sp'gs,	White Sulph. Sp'gs.*

HAMPSHIRE COUNTY.

Barrettsville,	Cold Stream,
Bloomery,	Dillon's Run,
Capon Bridge,	Forks of Capon,
Capon Springs,	Green Spring Run,

HAMPSHIRE COUNTY—Continued.

Hanging Rock,	Slanesville,
North River Mills,	Smith's Gap,
Okonoko,	South Branch Depot,
Pleasant Dale,	Springfield,
Purgitsville,	Yellow Spring.
Romney, (c. h.,)	

HANCOCK COUNTY.

Blair,	Holiday's Cove,
Fairview, (c. h.,)	New Cumberland.
Freeman's Landing,	

HARDY COUNTY.

Baker's Run,	*Moorfield*,* (c. h.,)
Fabius,	Mountain Home,
Howard's Lick,	Peru,
Inkerman,	Trout Run,
Lost River,	Wardensville.

HARRISON COUNTY.

Adamsville,	New Salem,
Big Buffalo,	Prospect Valley,
Bridgeport,	Quiet Dell,
Brown's Creek,	Rockford,
Cherry Camp,	Romine's Mills,
Clarksburgh,* (c. h.,)	Sardis,
Grassland,	Shinnston,
Hessville,	Sycamore Dale,
Johnstown,	West Milford,
Kincheloe,	Wilsonburgh,
Lost Creek,	Wolf Summit.
Lumberport,	

JACKSON COUNTY.

Allen's Fork,	Lone Cedar,
Angerona,	Murraysville,
Cottageville,	Muse's Bottom,
Fisher's Point,	New Geneva,
Grass Lick,	Ravenswood,*
Jackson C. H.,	Reedy,
Huntsville,	Ripley Landing,
Le Roy,	Sandy,
Lockhart's,	Topin's Grove.

JEFFERSON COUNTY.

Charlestown,*	Leetown,
Duffield's,	Middleway,
Halltown,	Rippon,
Harper's Ferry,*	*Shepherdstown*,* (c. h.,
Kabletown,	Summit Point.
Kerneysville,	

KANAWHA COUNTY.

Cannelton,	Jarrett's Ford,
Carbonvale,	*Kanawha C. H.*,*
Clendenin,	Kanawha Saline,
Coalburgh,	Laurel Ridge,
Coalsmouth,	Osborne's Mills,
Gillespieville,	Paint Creek,

* Money-order office.

KANAWHA COUNTY—Continued.

Pocotaligo,
Shrewsbury,
Sissonville,
Tyler Mountain,

Upper Falls of Coal,
Vineyard Hill,
Waldingfield.

LEWIS COUNTY.

Alkire's Mills,
Big Skin Creek,
Fink's Creek,
Gaston,
Georgetown,
Hacker's Creek,

Ireland,
Jacksonville,
Janelew,
Murphey's Creek,
Walkersville,
Weston, (c. h.)

LINCOLN COUNTY.

Coalville,
Falls Mills,
Griffithsville,
Hamlin, (c. h.,)

Laurel Creek,
Spurlockville,
Ten Mile,
Vannatterville.

LOGAN COUNTY.

Chapmanville,
Logan C. H.,

Rich Creek,
White's Mills.

McDOWELL COUNTY.

Peerysville, (c. h.,)
Snake Root,

Tug River.

MARION COUNTY.

Barracksville,
Basnettsville,
Beaty's Mills,
Benton's Ferry,
Bingamon,
Boothsville,
Bunner's,
Canton,
Fairmont, (c. h.,)
Farmington,
Forksburgh,

Glover's Gap,
Gray's Flat,
Mannington,
Meredith's Tavern,
Mill Falls,
Nuzums,
Palatine,
Rivesville,
Valley Falls,
Worthington.

MARSHALL COUNTY.

Adaline,
Beeler's Station,
Bellton,
Benwood,
Cameron,
Dallas,
Fair Hill,
Glen Easton,

Limestone,
Lynn Camp,
Moundsville, (c. h.,)
Rock Lick,
Rosby's Rock,
Sherrard,
Woodlands.

MASON COUNTY.

Arbuckle,
Beech Hill,
Clifton,
Cologne.
Deer Lick,
Flat Rock,
Graham Station,

Harmony,
Hartford City,
Letart,
Machirville,
Mason,
Mercer's Bottom,
New Haven,

MASON COUNTY—Continued.

Point Pleasant, (c. h.,)
Rock Castle,
Upland,

West Columbia,
Willow Tree.

MERCER COUNTY.

Concord Church,
Flat Top,
Jordan's Chapel,
Jumping Branch,

Princeton, (c. h.,)
Spanishburgh,
The Rock.

MINERAL COUNTY.

Burlington,
Claysville,
Frankfort,
Hartmousville,
Headsville,

New Creek, (c. h.,)
Patterson's Depot,
Piedmont,
Ridgeville.

MONONGALIA COUNTY.

Andy,
Arnettsville,
Blacksville,
Cassville,
Center,
Clinton Furnace,
Easton,
Granville,
Hoodsville,
Jake's Run,
Jobe,
Laurel Iron Works,

Laurel Point,
Maidsville,
Miracle Run,
Mooresville,
Morgantown, (c. h.,)
Pleasant Valley,
Randall,
Statler's Run,
Stewartstown,
Wadestown,
White Day.

MONROE COUNTY.

Egypt,
Forest Hill,
Gap Mills,
Indian Creek,
Johnson's X Roads,
Lindside,
Maple Lawn,
Monclova,
Mouth of Indian,

Pack's Ferry,
Peterstown,
Red Sulphur Springs,
Rollinsburgh,
Salt Sulphur Springs,
Sinks Grove,
Sweet Springs,
Union, (c. h.,)
Wolf Creek.

MORGAN COUNTY.

Alpine Depot,
Berkeley Sp'gs, (c. h.,)
Cacapon Depot,
Cherry Run Depot,
Orleans X Roads,

Paw Paw,
Sir John's Run,
Sleepy Creek Bridge,
Unger's Store.

NICHOLAS COUNTY.

Birch River,
Fowler's Knob,
Hookersville,

Kesler's X Lanes,
Nicholas C. H.,
Snow Hill.

OHIO COUNTY.

Clinton,
Elm Grove,
Greggsville,
Triadelphia,

Valley Grove,
West Liberty,
WHEELING, (c. h.)

* Money-order office.

PENDLETON COUNTY.

Brushy Run,
Buck Horn,
Franklin, (c. h.,)
Harper's Mills,
Macksville,
Mount Freedom,

Mouth of Seneca,
Oak Flat,
Sugar Grove,
Sweedlin Hill,
Upper Tract,

PLEASANTS COUNTY.

Grape Island,
Hebron,
Saint Mary's, (c. h.,)

Twiggs,
Union Mills,
Willow Island.

POCAHONTAS COUNTY.

Academy,
Buckeye Cove,
Dunmore,
Edray,
Elk,
Frost,

Green Bank,
Huntersville, (c. h.,)
Mill Point,
Mount Murphy,
Traveller's Repose.

PRESTON COUNTY.

Allbright,
Austen,
Brandonville,
Bruceton Mills,
Cranesville,
Evansville,
Fellowsville,
German Settlement,
Glade Farms,
Gladesville,
Horse Shoe Run,
Kingwood, (c. h.,)
Knott's Mills,

Masontown,
Morgan's Glade,
Muddy Creek,
Newburgh,
Pleasant Hill,
Portland,
Racoon,
Reedsville,
Rowlesburgh,
Tunnelton,
Valley Point,
Willey.

PUTNAM COUNTY.

Buffalo,
Frazier's Bottom,
Harbour's Mills,
Hurricane Bridge,
Mount Salem,
Mouth of Scary,

Raymond City,
Red House Shoals,
Round Knob,
Sycamore Grove,
Winfield, (c. h.)

RALEIGH COUNTY.

Clear Creek,
Coal River Marshes,
Jarrold's Valley,
Matville,

Raleigh C. H.,
Richman Falls,
Shady Spring,
Table Rock.

RANDOLPH COUNTY.

Ash Lick,
Beverly, (c. h.,)
Camp Elkwater,
Cheat Mountain,
Fillmore,
Huttonsville,
Lendsville,

Middle Fork,
Mingo Flat,
New Interest,
Roaring Creek,
Taylor's Mills,
Valley Bend,
Valley Head.

RITCHIE COUNTY.

Bone Creek,
Cairo,
Cornwallis,
Cunningham's Mills,
Ellenborough,
Goffs,
Goose Creek,
Harrisville, (c. h.,)
Highland,

Holbrook,
Mole Hill,
Pennsborough,
Rogers,
Rush Run,
Sinnett's Mills,
Webb's Mills,
White Oak.

ROANE COUNTY.

Boggsville,
Flat Fork,
Henry's Fork,
Newton,
Reedyville,

Roxalana,
Shambling's Mills,
Spencer, (c. h.,)
Walton.

TAYLOR COUNTY.

Fetterman,
Flemington,
Grafton,*
Knottsville,

Pruntytown, (c. h.,)
Simpson's Creek,
Thornton,
Webster.

TUCKER COUNTY.

Black Fork,
Carrick's Ford,
Hannahsville,
Holly Meadows,

Lead Mine,
Red Creek,
Saint George, (c. h.,)
Texas.

TYLER COUNTY.

Ben's Run,
Booker's Mills,
Conaway,
Joseph's Mills,
Kidwell,
Little's Mills,
Lone Tree,
Long Reach,

Middlebourne, (c. h.,)
Moore's,
Pursley,
Ripley's,
Shirley,
Sistersville,
Wick.

UPSHUR COUNTY.

Buckhannon, (c. h.,)
French Creek,
Frenchton,
Grim's Store,
Lorentz Store,

Peck's Run,
Rock Cave,
Rural Dale,
Sago,
Tallmansville.

WAYNE COUNTY.

Adkin's Mills,
Buffalo Shoals,
Ceredo,
Cove Creek,
Dunleith,

Fort Gay,
Hubbardstown,
Round Bottom,
Wayne C. H.,
White's Creek.

WEBSTER COUNTY.

Hacker's Valley,
Middleport,

Webster C. H.,
Welch Glade.

* Money-order office.

WETZEL COUNTY.

Burton,	Pine Grove,
Fanlight,	Porter's Falls,
Knob Fork,	Proctor,
Milo,	Silver Hill,
New Dale,	Van Camp,
New Martinsville,	West.
(*c.h.,*)	

WIRT COUNTY.

Burning Springs,*	Reedy Ripple,
Newark,	*Wirt C. H.,*
Oil Rock,	Zackville.

WOOD COUNTY.

Belleville,	Briscoe Run,

WOOD COUNTY—Continued.

Bull Creek,	Murphy's Mill,
Davisville,	*Parkersburgh,** (*c. h.,*)
Deer Walk,	Rockport,
Fountain Spring,	Valley Mills,
Harris' Ferry,	Volcano,*
Kanawha Station,	Wadesville,
Laurel Junction,	Walker,
Lockhart's Run,	Warren,
Lubeck,	Williamstown.

WYOMING COUNTY.

Jo's Branch.	Rock View,
Morgan Valley,	Sun Hill.
Oceana, (*c. h.,*)	

WISCONSIN.

ADAMS COUNTY.

Adams Centre,	New Haven,
Arkdale,	New Rome,
Barnum,	Olin,
Big Flats,	Pilot Knob,
Big Spring,	Plainville,
Buckhorn,	Point Bluff,
Davis' Corners,	Quincy,
Dell Prairie,	Roche-a-Cri,
Easton,	Spring Bluff,
Friendship, (*c. h.,*)	Spring Creek,
Grand Marsh,	Strong's Prairie,
Little Lake,	White Creek.
New Chester,	

ASHLAND COUNTY.

La Pointe, (*c. h.*)

BARRON COUNTY.

Barron, (*c. h.*)

BAYFIELD COUNTY.

Bayfield, (*c. h.*)

BROWN COUNTY.

Askeaton,	New Franken,
Bay Settlement,	Oneida,
Denmark,	Pine Grove,
De Pere,*	Prairie Farm,
East Wrightstown,	Robinson,
Flintville,	Rousseau,
Fontenoy,	Schiller,
Fort Howard,	Suamico,
*Green Bay,** (*c. h.,*)	Velp,
Mills Centre,	Wequiock,
Morrison,	Wrightstown.

BUFFALO COUNTY.

Alma, (*c. h.,*)	Glencoe,
Anchorage,	Maxville,
Buffalo,	Modena,
Burnside,	Mondovi,
Fountain City,*	Nelson,
Gilmantown,	Waumandee.

BURNETT COUNTY.

Anderson,	*Grantsburgh,* (*c. h.,*)
Donersville,	Wood River.

CALUMET COUNTY.

Brant,	New Holstein,
Brillion,	Potter's Mills,
Brothertown,	Quinney,
Charlestown,	Rantoul,
*Chilton,** (*c. h.,*)	Saint Anna,
Dundas,	Sherwood,
Gravesville,	Stockbridge.

CHIPPEWA COUNTY.

Chippewa City,	La Fayette,
Chippewa Falls, (*c.h.,*)	Vanville.
Cook's Valley,	

CLARK COUNTY.

Frankville,	Maple Works,
Humburd,	*Neilsville,** (*c. h.,*)
Loyal,	Pleasant Ridge,
Lumberman,	Staffordville.
Lynn,	

COLUMBIA COUNTY.

Alloa,	Columbus,*
Bellefountain,	Dekorra,
Cambria, *	Doylestown,

* Money-order office.

COLUMBIA COUNTY—Continued.

Empire Junction,
Fall River,
Kilbourn City,*
Leeds,
Leeds Centre,
Lewiston,
Lewiston Station,
Lodi,*
Lowville,
Marcellon,
North Leeds,
Okee,

Oshaukuta,
Otsego,
Pacific,
Pardeeville,
Portage City,* (c. h.,)
Port Hope,
Poynett,
Randolph Centre,
Rio,
Rocky Run,
West Point,
Wyocena.

CRAWFORD COUNTY.

Bell Center,
Bridgeport,
Eastman,
Ferryville,
Freeman,
Hurlbut's Corners,
Knapp's Creek,
Lower Lynxville,
Marietta,
Mount Sterling,
North Clayton,
North Star,
Prairie du Chien,*
  (c. h.,)

Rising Sun,
Rowes',
Seneca,
Shaw Hill,
Sladesburgh,
Soldier's Grove,
Teller's Corners,
Towerville,
Wauzeka,
Wheatville,
Wright's Ferry,
Yankeetown.

DANE COUNTY.

Albion,
Aldeu's Corners,
Ashton,
Belleville,
Black Earth,
Blooming Grove,
Blue Mound,
Cambridge,
Christiana,
Cloutarf,
Cottage Grove,
Cross Plains,
Dane,
Deansville,
Deerfield,
Door Creek,
Dunkirk,
Fitchburgh,
Hanerville,
Harvey,
Junction,
Leicester,
Macfarland,
MADISON,* (c. h.,)
Marshall,
Mazo Manie,*

Middleton,
Mount Horeb,
Mount Vernon,
Nora,
North Windsor,
Oregon,
Paoli,
Perry,
Pheasant Branch,
Pine Bluff,
Primrose,
River,
Roxbury,
Rutland,
Spring Dale,
Stoner's Prairie,
Stoughton,*
Sun Prairie,*
Syene,
Token Creek,
Utica,
Verona,
West Middleton,
Westport,
Windsor,
York.

DODGE COUNTY.

Alderley,
Ashippun,
Beaver Dam,*
Burnett,

Burnett Station,
Chester Station,
Clyman,
Danville,

DODGE COUNTY—Continued.

Farmersville,
Fox Lake,*
Herman,
Horicon,*
Hustisford,
Iron Ridge,
Juneau,* (c. h.,)
ekoskee,
Leroy,
Lomira,
Lowell,

Mayville,*
Minnesota Junction,
Neosho,
Oak Grove,
Reeseville,
Richwood,
Rolling Prairie,
Rubicon,
Theresa,
Westford,
Woodland.

DOOR COUNTY.

Bailey's Harbor,
Brussels,
Clay Banks,
Duchateau,
Egg Harbor,
Ephraim,
Fish Creek,

Forestville,
Jacksonport,
Little Sturgeon,
North Bay,
Sturgeon Bay,* (c. h.,)
Washington Harbor.

DOUGLAS COUNTY.

Superior, (c. h.)

DUNN COUNTY.

Cedar Falls,
Colfax,
Downsville,
Dunnville,
Eau Galle,
Fall City,
Louisville,

Lucas,
Maple Springs,
Menomonee,* (c. h.,)
Peru,
Rock Falls,
Waneka.

EAU CLAIRE COUNTY.

Augusta,
Eau Claire,* (c. h.,)
Fairchild,

Otter Creek,
West Eau Claire.*

FOND DU LAC COUNTY.

Armstrong's Corn'rs,
Ashford,
Banner,
Brandon,
Byron,
Calumet Village,
Calvary,
Dotyville,
Dundee,
Eden,
El Dorado,
El Dorado Mills,
Elmore,
Empire,
Fair Water,
Fond du Lac,* (c. h.,)
Foster,
Hinesberg,
Ladoga,
Lamartine,

Marytown,
Metomen,
Nanaupa,
New Cassel,
Newfane,
New Prospect,
North Taycheedah,
Oakfield,
Oakfield Centre,
Osceola,
Ripon,*
Rosendale,
Saint Cloud,
Taycheedah,
Van Dyne,
Waucousta,
Waupun,*
West Rosendale,
Woodhull.

* Money-order office.

GRANT COUNTY.

Annaton,	Lancaster,* (c. h.,)
Beetown,	Liberty Ridge,
Big Patch,	Little Grant,
Bloomington,	Martinville,
Blue River,	Millville,
Boscobel,*	Montfort,
Bradtville,	Mount Hope,
British Hollow,	Mount Ida,
Bunker's Hill,	Muscoda,
Cassville,	New California,
Castle Rock,	Ora Oak,
Dickeysville,	Patch Grove,
Ellenborough,	Platteville,*
Fair Play,	Potosi,
Fairview,	Rockville,
Fennimore,	Saint Rose,
Georgetown,	Sinsinawa Mound,
Glen Haven,	Washburn,
Hazel Green,	Woodman,
Hurricane Grove,	Wyalusing.
Jamestown,	

GREEN COUNTY.

Albany,	Martin,
Attica,	Monroe,* (c. h.,)
Bem,	Monticello,
Brodhead,*	New Glarus,
Brooklyn,	Oakley,
Cadiz,	Pedee,
Clarno,	Shuey's Mills,
Dayton,	Skinner,
Exeter,	Stewart,
Farmer's Grove,	Sylvester,
Jordan,	Twin Grove,
Juda,	Willet.

GREEN LAKE COUNTY.

Berlin,*	Manchester,
Dartford, (c. h.,)	Markesan,*
Grand Prairie,	Marquette,
Green Lake,	Princeton,
Kingston,	West Green Lake.
Lake Maria,	

IOWA COUNTY.

Arena,	Lumberville,
Avoca,	Middlebury,
Cobb,	Mifflin,
Dodgeville,* (c. h.,)	Mineral Point,*
Dover,	Moscow,
Helena Station,	Pine Knob,
Highland,	Ridgeway,
Hyde's Mills,	Union Mills,
Jennieton,	West Blue Mound,
Linden,	Wyoming.

JACKSON COUNTY.

Athol,	Irving,
Black River Falls,*	Melrose,
(c. h.,)	Mills,
Hixton,	Mound Springs,

JACKSON COUNTY—Continued.

North Bend,	Pole Grove,
North Branch,	Roaring Creek,
Pigeon Creek Centre,	Sechlersville,
Pine Hill,	Wrightsville.

JEFFERSON COUNTY.

Aztalan,	Kroghville,
Busseyville,	Lake Mills,*
Cold Spring,	Milford,
Concord,	Oak Hill,
Erfurt,	Oakland,
Farmington,	Palmyra,*
Fort Atkinson,*	Pipersville,
Hebron,	Rome,
Helenville,	Sullivan,
Hubbleton,	Waitesville,
Ixonia Centre,	Waterloo,*
Jefferson,* (c. h.,)	Watertown.*
Johnson's Creek,	

JUNEAU COUNTY.

Armenia,	Mount Zion,
Elroy,	Necedah,*
Germantown,	New Lisbon,* (c. h.,)
Kildare,	Orange,
Lemonweir,	Sentinel,
Mauston,*	Werner,
Mill Haven, (c. h.,)	Wonewoc.

KENOSHA COUNTY.

Bassett's Station,	Pleasant Prairie,
Brighton,	Salem,
Bristol,	Somers,
Cypress,	Wheatland,
Fox River,	Wilmot,
Kenosha,* (c. h.,)	Woodworth.
Paris,	

KEWAUNEE COUNTY.

Alaska,	Lincoln,
Ahnapee,	Montpelier,
Carlton,	Pierce,
Casco,	Red River,
Dyckesville,	Ryan,
Ellisville,	Walhain.
Kewaunee,* (c. h.,)	

LA CROSSE COUNTY.

Bangor,	Mindoro,
Barre Mills,	New Amsterdam,
Bohemia,	North La Crosse,
Burns,	Onalaska,
Burr Oak,	Shelby,
Half Way Creek,	Stevenstown,
La Crosse,* (c. h.,)	West Salem.

LA FAYETTE COUNTY.

Argyle,	Benton,
Belmont,	Blanchardville,

* Money-order office.

LA FAYETTE COUNTY—Continued.

Calamine,
Cottage Inn,
Darlington, (c. h.,)
Elk Grove,
Etna,
Fayette,
Gratiot,
Meeker's Grove,

New Diggings,
North Elk Grove,
Shullsburgh,
Spafford,
White Oak Springs,
Wiota,
Yellow Stone.

MANITOWOC COUNTY.

Branch,
Clark's Mills,
Cooperstown,
East Gibson,
Eaton,
Elk,
Francis Creek,
Hika,
Kasson,
Kiel,
King's Bridge,
Larrabee,
Manitowoc, (c. h.,)
Manitowoc Rapids,

Meeme,
Mishicot,
Nero,
Newtonburgh,
Niles,
Northeim,
Oslo,
Prag,
Reedsville,
Rosecrans,
Saint Nazianz,
Two Rivers,
Wayside.

MARATHON COUNTY.

Jenny,
Knowlton,
Marathon City,
Mosinee,

Naugart,
Sherman,
Stettin,
Wausau, (c. h.)

MARQUETTE COUNTY.

Briggsville,
Douglas Centre,
Germania,
Harrisville,
Jeddo,
Lawrence,
Midland,

Montello, (c. h.,)
Moundville,
Neshkoro,
Ordino.
Oxford,
Packwaukee,
Westfield.*

MILWAUKEE COUNTY.

Bay View,
Butler,
Five Mile House,
Good Hope,
Granville,
Greenfield,
Hale's Corners,
Milwaukee, (c. h.,)
Nat'l Mil'y Asylum,

New Coeln,
Oak Creek,
Paynesville,
Root Creek,
St. Francis Station,
Saint Martins,
Ten Mile House,
Wauwatosa,
West Granville.

MONROE COUNTY.

Albanville,
Big Creek,
Cataract,
Clifton,
Dorset,
Emery,
Farmer's Valley,
Glendale,

Herseyville,
Leon,
Le Roy Station,
Melvina,
Moore's Creek,
Mountain,
Mount Pisgah,
New Clifton,

MONROE COUNTY—Continued.

Ridgeville,
Rudd's Mills,
Saint Marys,
Sheldon,

Sparta, (c. h.,)
Tomah,*
Tunnel City,
Wilton.

OCONTO COUNTY.

Little Suamico,
Marinette,
Menekaune,
Oconto, (c. h.,)

Pensaukie.
Peshtigo,*
Stiles,
West Pensaukie.

OUTAGAMIE COUNTY.

Appleton, (c. h.,)
Binghamton,
Freedom,
Greenville,
Holland,
Hortonville,
Kaukauna,
Lime Rock,
Little Chute,
Mackville,

Medina,
New Mollis,
Seymour,
Shiocton,
Snidersville,
South Osborn,
Stephensville,
Stinson,
Sugar Bush,
Wakefield.

OZAUKEE COUNTY.

Belgium,
Cedarburgh,
Fredonia,
Freistadt,
Grafton,

Holy Cross,
Mequon River,
Ozaukee, (c. h.,)
Saukville.

PEPIN COUNTY.

Arkansaw,
Durand, (c. h.,)
Ella,
Frankfort,

Pepin,
Stockholm,
Waubeck.

PIERCE COUNTY.

Bay City,
Beldenville,
Big River,
Clifton Mills,
Diamond Bluff,
Ellsworth, (c. h.,)
El Paso,
Maiden Rock,
Martell,
Olivet,

Ono,
Plum City,
Prescott,*
River Falls,*
Rock Elm,
Rock Elm Centre,
Spring Valley,
Trenton,
Trim Belle.

POLK COUNTY.

Alabama,
Alden,
Avondale,
Black Brook,
Cushing,
Farmington Centre,

Lincoln Centre,
Luck,
Osceola Mills, (c. h.,)
St. Croix Falls,
Wagon Landing.

* Money-order office.

PORTAGE COUNTY.

Almond,
Amherst,
Badger,
Buena Vista,
Eau Pleine,
Ellis,
Grant,
Keene,

Lone Pine,
Madely,
New Hope,
Plover, (*c. h.,*)
Stevens' Point,*
Stockton,
Surrey.

RACINE COUNTY.

Burlington,*
Caldwell Prairie,
Caledonia Centre,
Ives' Grove,
Kansasville,
Lamberton,
North Cape,
Norway,
*Racine,** (*c. h.,*)

Raymond,
Rochester,*
Sylvania,
Thompsonville,
Union Church,
Union Grove,*
Waterford,
Yorkville.

RICHLAND COUNTY.

Aken,
Bass Wood,
Bear,
Bear Valley,
Boaz,
Brady's,
Buck Creek,
Cazenovia,
Eagle Corners,
Excelsior,
Fancy Creek,
Forest,
Henrietta,
Ithaca,
Janney's,
Lone Rock,

Loyd,
Mill Creek,
Neptune,
Orion,
Port Andrew,
*Richland Centre,**(*c.h.*)
Richland City,
Rockbridge,
Sextonville,
Sylvan,
Viola,
West Branch,
West Lima,
Woodstock,
Yuba.

ROCK COUNTY.

Afton,
Avon Centre,
Beloit,*
Cainville,
Center,
Clinton,*
Cooksville,
Edgerton,
Emerald Grove,
Evansville,*
Fairfield,
Footville,
Fulton,
Hanover,
Indian Ford,
*Janesville,** (*o. h.,*)

Johnstown,
Johnstown Centre,
Koskonong,
Leyden,
Lima Centre,
Magnolia,
Milton,*
Milton Junction,
Oxfordville,
Rock Prairie,
Rock River,
Shopiere,
Tiffany,
Union,
West Magnolia.

ST. CROIX COUNTY.

Boardman,
Bouchea,
Brookville,
Cylon,

Erin,
Hammond,
*Hudson,** (*c. h.,*)
Jewett Mills,

ST. CROIX COUNTY—Continued.

Kinnick Kinnick,
New Centreville,
New Richmoud,
Pleasant Valley,

Somerset,
Star Prairie,
Warren,
Woodside.

SAUK COUNTY.

*Baraboo,** (*c. h.,*)
Black Hawk,
Cassell Prairie,
Dellona,
Delton,
Ironton,
Lavalle,
Lime Ridge,
Loganville,
Marble Ridge,

Merrimack,
Oaks,
Plain,
Prairie du Sac,
Reedsburgh,*
Sandusky,
Sauk City,*
Spring Green,
Valton,
White Mound.

SHAWANAW COUNTY.

Angelica,
Belle Plaine,
Bonduel,
Kershena,
Laney,

Pella,
Owego,
Shawanaw, (*c. h.,*)
Waukecheon.

SHEBOYGAN COUNTY.

Ada,
Adell,
Bamberg,
Beech Wood,
Cascade,
Cedar Grove,
Dacada,
Edwards,
Franklin,
Gibbsville,
Glenbuelah,
Greenbush,
Hingham,
Hobart's Mills,

Howard's Grove,
Johnsonville,
Mosel,
Onion River,
Oostburgh,
Our Town,
Plymouth,
Rathbun,
Rhine,
Russell,
Scott,
*Sheboygan,** (*c. h.,*)
Sheboygan Falls,
Winooski.

TREMPEALEAU COUNTY.

Alhambra,
Arcadia,
Coral City,
Elk Creek,
Ettrick,
Frenchville,
Galesville, (*c. h.,*)
Hale,

Hamlin,
Home,
Hooker,
Osseo,
Scotia,
South Bend,
Trempealeau,*
Williamsburgh.

VERNON COUNTY.

Avalanche,
Bloomingdale,
Breckinridge,
Burr,
Chaseburgh,
Chipmonk Cooley,
Coon Prairie,
Coon Valley,
Debello,

De Soto,
Enterprise,
Esofia,
Genoa,
Goole,
Harmony,
Hillsborough,*
Hockley,
Kickapoo,

* Money-order office.

VERNON COUNTY—Continued.

La Farge,	Rockton,
Liberty,	Romance,
Liberty Pole,	Sierra,
Mount Tabor,	Springville,
Muncie,	Star,
Newry,	Stoddard,
Newton,	Sugar Grove,
Newville,	Valley,
Odin,	Victory,
Ontario,	*Viroqua,** (c. h.,)
Petrolium,	Warner's Landing,
Readstown,	Weister,
Retreat,	West Prairie.

WALWORTH COUNTY.

Adams,	La Grange,
Allen's Grove,	Little Prairie,
Bay Hill,	Lyons,
Bloomfield,	Millard,
Darien,	Richmond,
Delavan,*	Sharon,
East Delavan,	Springfield,
East Troy,*	Spring Prairie,
East Troy Lake,	Sugar Creek,
Elk Horn,* (c. h.,)	Tirade,
Elton,	Troy,
Geneva,	Troy Centre,
Grove,	Vienna,
Heart Prairie,	Walworth,
Honey Creek,	White Water.*

WASHINGTON COUNTY.

Ackerville,	Myra,
Addison,	Nenno,
Aurora,	Newburgh,
Barton,	Richfield,
Boltonville,	Saint Lawrence,
Cedar Creek,	Schleisingerville,
Fillmore,	South Germantown,
Hartford,	Staatsville,
Jackson,	Thompson,
Kewaskum,	Toland's Prairie,
Kirchayn,	Wayne,
Kohlsville,	*West Bend,** (c. h.,)
Lake Five,	Young America,
Meeker,	Young Hickory.

WAUKESHA COUNTY.

Big Bend,	Eagle,
Brookfield Centre,	Elm Grove,
Delafield,	Fussville,
Dodge's Corners,	Genesee,
Dousman,	Genesee Depot,
Duplainville,	Golden Lake,
Durham Hill,	Hartland,

WAUKESHA COUNTY—Continued.

Lannon Springs,	North Prairie Stat'n,
Mapleton,	Oconomowoc,*
Marcy,	Ottawa,
Menomonee Falls,	Pewaukee,
Merton,	Prospect Hill,
Monches,	Stone Bank,
Monterey,	Summit,
Mukwonago,	Sussex,
Muskego Centre,	Tess Corners,
Nashotah Mission,	Vernon,
New Berlin,	Waterville,
North Lake,	*Waukesha,** (c. h.)

WAUPACA COUNTY.

Baldwin's Mills,	Marble,
Bear Creek,	New London,
Clintonville,	Northport,
Crystal Lake,	Ogdensburgh,
Dupont,	Readfield,
Embarrass,	Royalton,
Evanswood,	Rural,
Fremont,	Scandinavia,
Helvetia,	Sheridan,
Iola,	Symco,
Lind,	*Waupaca,* (s. h.,)
Little Wolf,	Weyauwega.

WAUSHARA COUNTY.

Aurorahville,	Pine River,
Brushville,	Plainfield,
Cedar Lake,	Poy Sippi,
Coloma,	Richford,
Dakota,	Saxeville,
East Oasis,	Spring Lake,
Hancock,	Spring Water,
Howe's Corners,	Tustin,
Mount Morris,	*Wautoma,** (c. h.)
Oasis,	

WINNEBAGO COUNTY.

Butte des Morts,	Omro,*
Clemansville,	Orihula,
Elo,	*Oshkosh,** (c. h.,)
Eureka,	Poygan,
Fisk's Corners,	Ring,
Koro,	Vinland,
Menasha,*	Waukau,
Neenah,	Weelaunee,
Nekama,	Winchester,
Nepeuskun,	Winneconne.

WOOD COUNTY.

Centralia,	Nasonville,
Dexterville,	Port Edwards,
Grand Rapids,* (c.h.,)	Wood.

* Money-order office.

WYOMING TERRITORY.

ALBANY COUNTY.

Laramie, (c. h.,)   Wyoming.
Sherman,

CARBON COUNTY.

Carbon,   Medicine Bow,
Fort Fred Steele,   Percy,
Fort Halleck,   Rawling'sSprings,(c.h)

LARAMIE COUNTY.

CHEYENNE C I T Y,* Lookout,
   (c. h.,)   Pine Bluff.
Fort Laramie,

SWEETWATER COUNTY.

Atlantic City,   Little Wind River,
Bitter Creek.   Miner's Delight,
Green River City,   South Pass City, (c. h.)

UINTAH COUNTY.

Bridger Station,   Fort Bridger, (c. h.,)
Bryan,   Gilmer,
Carter,   Piedmont,
Evanston,   Point of Rocks.